D0856971

The Cambridge History of American Poetry offers a comprehensive exploration of the development of American poetic traditions from their beginnings until the end of the twentieth century. Bringing together the insights of fifty distinguished scholars, this literary history emphasizes the complex roles that poetry has played in American cultural and intellectual life, detailing the variety of ways in which both public and private forms of poetry have met the needs of different communities at different times. *The Cambridge History of American Poetry* recognizes the existence of multiple traditions and a dramatically fluid canon, providing current perspectives on both major authors and a number of representative figures whose work embodies the diversity of America's democratic traditions.

ALFRED BENDIXEN teaches American literature at Princeton University and is the founder and Executive Director of the American Literature Association. His earlier scholarship emphasized the recovery of unjustly neglected literary texts and the exploration of neglected genres, but his current focus is on the role of genre in democratic culture. His most recent books include *A Companion to the American Novel* (2012); *A Companion to the American Short Story* (2010), co-edited with James Nagel; and *The Cambridge Companion to American Travel Writing* (2009), co-edited with Judith Hamera.

STEPHEN BURT is Professor of English at Harvard University. His books of literary criticism and scholarship include *The Art of the Sonnet* (2010), with David Mikics; *Close Calls with Nonsense* (2009), a finalist for the National Book Critics Circle Award; *The Forms of Youth: 20th-Century Poetry and Adolescence* (2007); and *Randall Jarrell and His Age* (2002), winner of the Warren-Brooks Award. He is also the author of three full-length books of poetry: *Belmont* (2013); *Parallel Play* (2006); and *Popular Music* (1999), winner of the Colorado Prize.

THE CAMBRIDGE
HISTORY OF
AMERICAN POETRY

*

Edited by
ALFRED BENDIXEN
Princeton University

STEPHEN BURT
Harvard University

CAMBRIDGE
UNIVERSITY PRESS

KALAMAZOO PUBLIC LIBRARY

CAMBRIDGE
UNIVERSITY PRESS

32 Avenue of the Americas, New York, NY 10013-2473, USA

Cambridge University Press is part of the University of Cambridge.

It furthers the University's mission by disseminating knowledge in the pursuit of education, learning, and research at the highest international levels of excellence.

www.cambridge.org
Information on this title: www.cambridge.org/9781107003361

© Cambridge University Press 2015

This publication is in copyright. Subject to statutory exception and to the provisions of relevant collective licensing agreements, no reproduction of any part may take place without the written permission of Cambridge University Press.

First published 2015

Printed in the United States of America

A catalog record for this publication is available from the British Library.

Library of Congress Cataloging in Publication data
The Cambridge History of American Poetry / [edited by] Alfred Bendixen, Princeton University; Stephen Burt, Harvard University.
pages   cm
Includes bibliographical references and index.
ISBN 978-1-107-00336-1 (hardback)
1. American poetry – History and criticism.   I. Bendixen, Alfred, editor.
II. Burt, Stephen, 1971– editor.
PS303.C29   2014
811.009–dc23   2014014830

ISBN 978-1-107-00336-1 Hardback

Cambridge University Press has no responsibility for the persistence or accuracy of URLs for external or third-party Internet Web sites referred to in this publication and does not guarantee that any content on such Web sites is, or will remain, accurate or appropriate.

KALAMAZOO PUBLIC LIBRARY

Contents

Contents

Contents

Contents

PART IV
BEYOND MODERNISM: AMERICAN POETRY,
1950–2000

viii

Contents

Notes on Contributors

CHARLES ALTIERI has taught modern poetry for more than forty years, the last twenty at the University of California at Berkeley, where he is now Rachel Stageberg Anderson Professor of English. He has written numerous essays and nine books of criticism on theoretical topics and on twentieth-century American poetry, including *Act and Quality* (1981), *Self and Sensibility in Contemporary American Poetry* (1984), *Painterly Abstraction in Modernist American Poetry* (1989), *Canons and Consequences* (1991), *The Particulars of Rapture: An Aesthetics of the Affects* (2003), *The Art of Modernist American Poetry* (2005), and the forthcoming *Wallace Stevens and the Challenges of Modernity: Towards a Phenomenology of Value.*

FAITH BARRETT is Associate Professor of English at Duquesne University. She is the author of *To Fight Aloud Is Very Brave: American Poetry and the Civil War* (2012) and of articles on the poetry of Emily Dickinson, Herman Melville, and Abraham Lincoln. With Cristanne Miller, she co-edited *Words for the Hour: A New Anthology of American Civil War Poetry* (2005).

ALFRED BENDIXEN teaches American literature at Princeton University. He is the founder of the American Literature Association, of which he currently serves as Executive Director. His books include *Haunted Women* (1985); an edition of the composite novel *The Whole Family* (1986); an edition of *"The Amber Gods" and Other Stories* by Harriet Prescott Spofford (1989); and *Edith Wharton: New Critical Essays* (1992). He is the associate editor of *The Continuum Encyclopedia of American Literature* (1999), the co-editor of *The Cambridge Companion to American Travel Writing* (2009) and *A Companion to the American Short Story* (2010), and editor of *A Companion to the American Novel* (2012).

DAVID BERGMAN, Professor of English at Towson University, is the author of *Gaiety Transfigured: Gay Self-Representation in American Literature* (1991) and *The Violet Hour: The Violet Quill and the Making of Gay Culture* (2004). He is also the author of two books of poetry: *Heroic Measures* (1998) and *Cracking the Code* (1985), winner of the George Elliston Poetry Prize. With Katia Sainson he has translated Jean Sénac's *Selected Poems* (2010).

EDWARD BRUNNER is Professor of American Literature at Southern Illinois University, Carbondale. His books include *Cold War Poetry: The Social Text in the Fifties Poem* (2004), *W. S. Merwin: The Labor and Privilege of Poetry* (1991), and *Splendid Failure: Hart Crane and the Making of "The Bridge"* (1985); his recent articles have appeared in *MELUS*, *American Periodicals*, *Iowa Journal of Cultural Studies*, and *International Journal of Comic Art.*

STEPHEN BURT is Professor of English at Harvard University. His books include *The Art of the Sonnet*, with David Mikics (2010); *Close Calls with Nonsense* (2009); and *The Forms of Youth: Twentieth-Century Poetry and Adolescence* (2007), as well as several collections of poems, most recently *Belmont* (2013). With Nick Halpern, he edited *Something Understood: Essays and Poetry for Helen Vendler* (2009).

SUSAN CASTILLO STREET is Harriet Beecher Stowe Emeritus Professor of American Literature at King's College London. Her books include *American Literature in Context to 1865* (2011), *American Travel Writing and Empire* (with David Seed, 2009), *Colonial Encounters in New World Writing 1500–1786: Performing America* (2005), and two books co-edited with Ivy Schweitzer, *A Companion to the Literatures of Colonial America* (2005) and *The Literatures of Colonial America* (2001). From 2005 to 2009 she edited the *Journal of American Studies*. She is also a published poet and literary translator.

MICHAEL C. COHEN is Assistant Professor of English at UCLA. He has written many essays on nineteenth-century poetry for journals such as *American Literature*, *Arizona Quarterly*, and *Victorian Poetry*, in addition to the entry "Poetry of the United States, Beginnings to 1900" for *The Princeton Encyclopedia of Poetry and Poetics* (2012). He is co-editor of *The Poetry of Charles Brockden Brown* (forthcoming) and is finishing a book, entitled *The Social Lives of Poems in Nineteenth-Century America*, that provides a material history of the ways people read, wrote, circulated, and otherwise used poems in early American culture.

ROBERT DALY, SUNY Distinguished Teaching Professor of English and Comparative Literature at the State University of New York at Buffalo, Leverhulme Fellow, and Guggenheim Fellow, has written *God's Altar: The World and the Flesh in Puritan Poetry* (1978), the introduction to the John Harvard Library edition of Cooper's *The Pioneers* (2011), and many articles and reviews published in *American Literature, Nineteenth-Century Fiction, American Literary History, Comparative Literature Studies,* and elsewhere.

BETTY BOOTH DONOHUE is an independent scholar and an enrolled member of the Cherokee Nation. She has written articles for the *American Indian Culture and Research Journal* and *Studies in American Indian Literature*. She contributed an essay on the Mvskogee poet Alexander Posey to the *Dictionary of Literary Biography* (1997) and a chapter entitled "Oktahutchee's Song" to *Teaching Nineteenth-Century American Poetry* (2007). Her latest work, *Bradford's Indian Book: Being the True Roote & Rise of American Letters as Revealed by the Native Text Embedded in Of Plimoth Plantation*, was published in 2011.

JIM EGAN is Professor of English at Brown University. He is the author of *Oriental Shadows: The Presence of the East in Early American Literature* (2011) and *Authorizing Experience: Refigurations of the Body Politic in Seventeenth-Century New England Writing* (1999). His other publications include essays on John Smith, eighteenth-century British-American mercantile poetry, Benjamin Franklin, and the wonder tale in early America. In addition to his scholarly publications, Professor Egan has published fiction.

RICHARD FLYNN, Professor of Literature at Georgia Southern University, is the author of *Randall Jarrell and the Lost World of Childhood* (1990). He has written essays on poets such as

Elizabeth Bishop, Robert Lowell, Muriel Rukeyser, Gwendolyn Brooks, and June Jordan, as well as a number of essays about children's poetry, including "The Fear of Poetry" in *The Cambridge Companion to Children's Literature* (2009) and "Randall Jarrell's *The Bat-Poet*: Poets, Children, and Readers in an Age of Prose" in *The Oxford Handbook of Children's Literature* (2011).

ED FOLSOM is the editor of the *Walt Whitman Quarterly Review*, co-director of the *Walt Whitman Archive* (www.whitmanarchive.org), and editor of the Whitman Series at the University of Iowa Press. The Roy J. Carver Professor of English at the University of Iowa, he is the author or editor of twelve books, including *Walt Whitman's Native Representations* (1994) and (with Kenneth M. Price) *Re-Scripting Walt Whitman* (2005), as well as numerous essays on Whitman and other American writers appearing in journals such as *American Literature*, *PMLA*, and the *Virginia Quarterly Review*. He was featured in an episode of the PBS documentary *American Experience* (2008), and he is now working on a biography of *Leaves of Grass*.

STEPHEN FREDMAN is Professor of English and Concurrent Professor of American Studies at the University of Notre Dame. He is the author of *Poet's Prose* (1983, 1990), *The Grounding of American Poetry* (1993), *A Menorah for Athena* (2001), and *Contextual Practice* (2010). He has edited *A Concise Companion to Twentieth-Century American Poetry* (2005) and, with Steve McCaffery, *Form, Power, and Person in Robert Creeley's Life and Work* (2010).

FRANK GADO is Professor Emeritus of English at Union College. The author of *First Person* (1974), a collection of interviews with Wescott, Dos Passos, Warren, Updike, Barth, and Coover; *The Passion of Ingmar Bergman* (1986); and *William Cullen Bryant: An American Voice* (2006), he has also edited, with introductory essays, selections of works by C. B. Brown, James Kirke Paulding, Stephen Crane, and Sherwood Anderson. He is currently writing an article about R. H. Dana and composing books on the death of the liberal arts college and on American literature's defining preoccupations.

ROGER GILBERT teaches in the English Department at Cornell University. He is the author of *Walks in the World: Representation and Experience in Modern American Poetry* (1991). His essays and reviews have appeared in *Southwest Review*, *Michigan Quarterly Review*, *Contemporary Literature*, *Parnassus*, and other journals. He is currently completing a critical biography of A. R. Ammons.

RIGOBERTO GONZÁLEZ is the author of thirteen books of poetry and prose and the editor of *Camino del Sol: Fifteen Years of Latina and Latino Writing* (2010). The recipient of Guggenheim and NEA fellowships, he is currently on the executive board of the National Book Critics Circle and is Associate Professor of English at Rutgers-Newark, the State University of New Jersey.

NICK HALPERN is Associate Professor of English at North Carolina State University. He is the author of *Everyday and Prophetic: The Poetry of Lowell, Ammons, Merrill and Rich* (2003) and the co-editor, with Jane Hedley and Willard Spiegelman, of *In the Frame: Women's*

Ekphrastic Poetry from Marianne Moore to Susan Wheeler (2009) and, with Stephen Burt, of *Something Understood: Essays and Poetry for Helen Vendler* (2009).

JEFFREY A. HAMMOND is Reeves Distinguished Professor in the Liberal Arts and Professor of English at St. Mary's College of Maryland. His scholarly books include *Edward Taylor: Fifty Years of Scholarship and Criticism* (1993); *Sinful Self, Saintly Self: The Puritan Experience of Poetry* (1993); and *The American Puritan Elegy: A Literary and Cultural Study* (2000). He is also a creative writer whose publications in literary nonfiction include *Ohio States: A Twentieth-Century Midwestern* (2002), *Small Comforts: Essays at Middle Age* (2008), and *Little Big World: Collecting Louis Marx and the American Fifties* (2010).

KEVIN J. HAYES, Professor of English at the University of Central Oklahoma, has written several books, including *A Journey through American Literature* (2012), *The Road to Monticello: The Life and Mind of Thomas Jefferson* (2008), and *The Mind of a Patriot: Patrick Henry and the World of Ideas* (2008). In addition, he is the editor of *The Oxford Handbook of Early American Literature* (2008). For *The Library of William Byrd of Westover* (1997), he received the Virginia Library History Award. He is also the recipient of a Distinguished Service Award presented by the Association for Documentary Editing.

MATTHEW HOFER is Associate Professor of English at the University of New Mexico. His books include *Oscar Wilde in America* (2009), *Sinclair Lewis Remembered* (2012), and a forthcoming expanded reprint of the 1966 photo-essay *The Shoshoneans* by poet Edward Dorn and photographer Leroy Lucas. He has contributed chapters on poets, poetry, and poetics to several volumes, and his essays have appeared in many journals, including *Modernism/Modernity, Paideuma, New German Critique*, and *Contemporary Literature*. He also edits, for the University of New Mexico Press, the series Recencies: Research and Recovery in Twentieth-Century American Poetics.

TYLER HOFFMAN is Professor of English at Rutgers University–Camden and Associate Dean of the Faculty of Arts and Sciences. He is the author of three books: *Robert Frost and the Politics of Poetry* (2001), *Teaching with* The Norton Anthology of Poetry: *A Guide for Instructors* (2005), and *American Poetry in Performance: From Walt Whitman to Hip Hop* (2011). He is currently working on a study of performance and celebrity in modernist American poetry, and he serves as editor of the electronic Whitman studies journal *The Mickle Street Review* and as associate editor of the *Robert Frost Review*.

CHRISTOPH IRMSCHER is Provost Professor of English at Indiana University–Bloomington. He is the author of *Louis Agassiz: Creator of American Science* (2013); *Public Poet, Private Man: Henry Wadsworth Longfellow at 200* (2009); *Longfellow Redux* (2006); and *The Poetics of Natural History* (1999), as well as the editor of the Library of America edition of John James Audubon's *Writings and Drawings* (1999) and co-editor, with Alan Braddock, of *A Keener Perception: Ecocritical Studies in American Art History* (2009).

VIRGINIA JACKSON is UC Irvine Chair of Rhetoric and Communication at the University of California–Irvine. She is the author of *Dickinson's Misery: A Theory of Lyric Reading* (2005) and co-editor (with Yopie Prins) of *The Lyric Theory Reader* (2013). Her next book, *Before*

Modernism: Nineteenth-Century American Poetry in Public, is forthcoming from Princeton University Press.

JOSEPH JONGHYUN JEON is Associate Professor of English and Asian American Studies at Pomona College. He is the author of *Racial Things, Racial Forms: Objecthood in Avant-Garde Asian American Poetry* (2012). He is currently writing a book about transnational Korean/ American film and globalization.

JOHN D. KERKERING is Associate Professor of English at Loyola University Chicago. He is the author of *The Poetics of National and Racial Identity in Nineteenth-Century American Literature* (2003). His articles have appeared in such journals as *American Literature*, *Studies in Romanticism*, and *Victorian Poetry* and such volumes as *The Cambridge Companion to Nineteenth-Century American Poetry* and volume six of *The Cambridge History of Literary Criticism*. He is currently at work on a study of aesthetics and racial identity in the twentieth-century United States called *Racial Rhapsody*.

GEORGE S. LENSING is Mann Family Distinguished Professor of English at the University of North Carolina at Chapel Hill. His many publications on Wallace Stevens and other modern poets include *Wallace Stevens and the Seasons* (2001) and *Wallace Stevens: A Poet's Growth* (1986).

MARY LOEFFELHOLZ is Professor of English and Vice Provost for Academic Affairs at Northeastern University. Her books include *Dickinson and the Boundaries of Feminist Theory* (1991); *Experimental Lives: Women and Literature, 1900–1945* (1992); and *From School to Salon: Reading Nineteenth-Century American Women's Poetry* (2004). She is the editor of *Volume D: 1914–1945* of *The Norton Anthology of American Literature*, and, with Martha Nell Smith, she co-edited *A Companion to Emily Dickinson*.

WENDY MARTIN is Professor of American Literature and American Studies at Claremont Graduate University, where she is also Vice Provost and Director of Transdisciplinary Studies and holds the George and Ronya Kozmetsky Endowed Chair of Transdisciplinary Studies. The author of numerous articles and reviews, she founded (in 1972) and continues to edit *Women's Studies: An Interdisciplinary Journal*. Her books include *The American Sisterhood: Feminist Writings from Colonial Times to the Present* (1972); *An American Triptych: The Lives and Work of Anne Bradstreet, Emily Dickinson, and Adrienne Rich* (1984); *Colonial American Travel Narratives* (1994); *The Beacon Book of Essays by Contemporary American Women* (1996); *The Cambridge Companion to Emily Dickinson* (2002); *Emily Dickinson* (2007); and *Best of Times, Worst of Times: Contemporary American Short Stories from the New Gilded Age* (2011). She also serves on the editorial board of the *Heath Anthology of American Literature*.

CRISTANNE MILLER is SUNY Distinguished Professor and Edward H. Butler Professor of Literature at the University at Buffalo SUNY. Her recent books include *Reading in Time: Emily Dickinson in the Nineteenth Century* (2012); *Cultures of Modernism: Marianne Moore, Mina Loy, and Else Lasker-Schüler*, a study of gender and literary community in New York and Berlin (2005); and *Marianne Moore: Questions of Authority* (1995), and she co-edited Moore's

Selected Letters (1997) and *Feminist Measures: Soundings in Poetry and Theory* (1994). She is currently preparing a new reader's edition of Emily Dickinson's complete poems.

DAVID CHIONI MOORE is Associate Professor of International Studies and English at Macalester College. He has published numerous articles on Langston Hughes and other African American as well as African writers, on postcolonial studies, and on globalization; he is the co-editor, with Martin Bernal, of *Black Athena Writes Back* (2001), and he is currently editing new editions of Hughes's *A Negro Looks at Soviet Central Asia* and Hughes's correspondence with black South African writers.

WALTON MUYUMBA is Associate Professor of American and African American literature at the University of North Texas. He is the author of *The Shadow and the Act: Black Intellectual Practice, Jazz Improvisation, and Philosophical Pragmatism* (2009); his essays have appeared in *College Literature, Oxford American,* and *The Los Angeles Review of Books.*

JOHN TIMBERMAN NEWCOMB is Professor of English at the University of Illinois at Urbana-Champaign. He has published three books on American poetry, *Wallace Stevens and Literary Canons* (1992), *Would Poetry Disappear? American Verse and the Crisis of Modernity* (2004), and *How Did Poetry Survive? The Making of Modern American Verse* (2012), along with a variety of essays on such topics as Edna St. Vincent Millay, Archibald MacLeish, Stephen Crane, W. B. Yeats, and skyscraper verse.

BOB PERELMAN is Professor of English at the University of Pennsylvania. His critical works include *The Marginalization of Poetry* (1996) and *The Trouble with Genius* (1994); his many books of poetry include *Iflife* (2006) and *Ten to One: Selected Poems* (1999).

SIOBHAN PHILLIPS is Assistant Professor of English at Dickinson College. She is the author of *The Poetics of the Everyday: Creative Repetition in Modern American Verse* (2009). Her poetry and essays have appeared in *PMLA, Modernism/Modernity, The Los Angeles Review of Books, Boston Review, Harvard Review, Yale Review,* and other publications. She is working on a book about poetry and letters in the period from 1950 to 2000.

BRIAN M. REED is Professor of English at the University of Washington, Seattle. He is the author of *Hart Crane: After His Lights* (2006), *Phenomenal Reading: Essays on Modern and Contemporary Poetics* (2012), and *Nobody's Business: Twenty-First Century Avant-Garde Poetics* (2013), as well as articles in such journals as the *African American Review, Boundary 2, Callaloo, Contemporary Literature, Modernism/Modernity,* and *Open Letter.*

ELIZABETH RENKER is Professor of English at The Ohio State University. Her books include *Strike Through the Mask: Herman Melville and the Scene of Writing* (1996) and *The Origins of American Literature Studies: An Institutional History* (2007). Her articles have appeared in journals including *American Literature, American Literary History, Early American Literature, ELH, Arizona Quarterly,* and *Leviathan.* Her book in progress is entitled *The Lost Era in American Poetry, 1866–1912.* She is the recipient of an array of distinguished teaching awards, at Ohio State and nationally.

ELIZA RICHARDS is an Associate Professor in the Department of English and Comparative Literature at the University of North Carolina at Chapel Hill. She is the author of *Gender and the Poetics of Reception in Poe's Circle* (2004) and the editor of *Emily Dickinson in Context* (2013). She is now completing a book on the relationship between poetry and journalism during the U.S. Civil War.

REENA SASTRI is Early Career Fellow in American Literature at the University of Oxford and the author of *James Merrill: Knowing Innocence* (2007). Her writing has appeared in journals including *Contemporary Literature*, *Twentieth-Century Literature*, and *PN Review*. She is at work on a book about the idea of lyric in contemporary American poetry.

ROBIN G. SCHULZE is Professor of English at the University of Delaware. She is the author of *The Web of Friendship: Marianne Moore and Wallace Stevens* (1995) and the editor of *Becoming Marianne Moore: The Early Poems, 1907–1924* (2002). *The Degenerate Muse: American Nature, Modernist Poetry, and the Problem of Cultural Hygiene* is forthcoming. She is the author of numerous articles in the fields of modernist American poetry, textual scholarship, and editorial theory.

MARK SCROGGINS is Professor of English at Florida Atlantic University. He is the author of *The Poem of a Life: A Biography of Louis Zukofsky* (2007) and *Louis Zukofsky and the Poetry of Knowledge* (1998) and the editor of *Upper Limit Music: The Writing of Louis Zukofsky* (1997); his books of poems include *Red Arcadia* (2012).

DAVID E. E. SLOANE is Professor of English and Education at the University of New Haven. His books include *Student Companion to Mark Twain* (2001); *New Directions in American Humor* (1998); *Sister Carrie: Theodore Dreiser's Sociological Tragedy* (1992); *Adventures of Huckleberry Finn: American Comic Vision* (1988); *American Humor Magazines and Comic Periodicals* (1987); *The Literary Humor of the Urban Northeast, 1830–1890* (1983); and *Mark Twain as a Literary Comedian* (1979). He is currently working on a biography of his grandmother titled *Edison's Daughter*; *American Humor Magazines and Comic Periodicals, Volume 2: 1985–2015*; and *Local Color and Dialect Poetry in America*.

ANGELA SORBY is Associate Professor of English at Marquette University. Her book *Schoolroom Poets: Childhood and the Place of American Poetry, 1865–1917*, appeared in 2005; she is also the author of two poetry collections, *Distance Learning* (1998) and *Bird Skin Coat* (2009), and co-editor, with Karen Kilcup, of a forthcoming anthology of nineteenth-century children's verse, *Over the River and Through the Woods*.

JULIANA SPAHR is Aurelia Henry Reinhardt Professor of English at Mills College. Her many books of poetry, criticism, and creative prose include *Well Then There Now* (2011), *The Transformation* (2007), *Fuck You-Aloha-I Love You* (2001), and *Everybody's Autonomy: Connective Reading and Collective Identity* (2001); she has edited several collections on poetry and poetics, among them, with Joan Retallack, *Poetry and Pedagogy: The Challenge of the Contemporary* (2006) and, with Claudia Rankine, *American Women Poets in the 21st Century* (2002).

WILLARD SPIEGELMAN, the Hughes Professor of English at Southern Methodist University and editor-in-chief of *Southwest Review*, is the author of *The Didactic Muse: Scenes of Instruction in Contemporary American Poetry* (1989) and *How Poets See the World: The Art of Description in Contemporary Poetry* (2005), as well as *Wordsworth's Heroes* (1985) and *Majestic Indolence: English Romantic Poetry and the Work of Art* (1995). He edited *Love, Amy: The Selected Letters of Amy Clampitt* (2005).

LISA M. STEINMAN is the Kenan Professor of English and Humanities at Reed College in Portland, Oregon. She is the author of nine books, including *Made in America: Science, Technology, and American Modernist Poets* (1989); *Masters of Repetition: Poetry, Culture, and Work* (1998); *Invitation to Poetry* (2008); and, most recently, *Absence & Presence* (2013).

ERNEST SUAREZ is Ordinary Professor and Chair of the Department of English at the Catholic University of America. He is the author of *James Dickey and the Politics of Canon* (1993) and of numerous essays on modern and contemporary poetry, and he is the editor of *Southbound: Interviews with Contemporary Southern Poets* (1999); his current work also includes studies of rock and blues.

JOSEPH T. THOMAS, JR., directs the National Center for the Study of Children's Literature at San Diego State University, where he serves as an Associate Professor of English. The inaugural Poetry Editor of *The Lion and the Unicorn*, Thomas writes on children's and adult poetry, the avant-garde, and comics. He is the author of two books, *Poetry's Playground* (2007), the first extended academic study of contemporary American children's poetry, and *Strong Measures* (2007), a collection of procedural poetry. His next book explores the life and work of Shel Silverstein.

LESLEY WHEELER is the Henry S. Fox Professor of English at Washington and Lee University. Her books include *Voicing American Poetry* (2008) and the poetry collections *Heterotopia* (2010) and *The Receptionist and Other Tales* (2012). She has held fellowships from Fulbright, the National Endowment for the Humanities, and other grantors, and she won an Outstanding Faculty Award in 2012 from the State Council of Higher Education in Virginia. Her blog is http://lesleywheeler.org.

DAVID WOJAHN is Professor of English and Director of the Program in Creative Writing at Virginia Commonwealth University. His many books of poems include *World Tree* (2011) and *Interrogation Palace: New and Selected Poems* (2006), a finalist for the Pulitzer Prize; many of his critical writings are collected in *Strange Good Fortune* (2001).

Acknowledgments

The editors want to thank Ray Ryan of Cambridge University Press for his continuous encouragement and excellent advice during the entire editorial process. We also want to express our appreciation to our copy editor, Laura Wilmot, for her meticulous attention to detail; to Diana Witt for preparing the index; and to Caitlin Gallagher, Louis Gulino, Nathalie Horner, and all the other people at Cambridge University Press who have helped to bring this book into being.

Our greatest obligation is to the forty-eight contributors who agreed to join us in this enterprise, produced splendid essays, offered insights that shaped the development of this literary history, and almost always responded to our requests for revisions with remarkable efficiency and cheerfulness. We value the expertise, advice, and commitment to this project that each of our contributors has demonstrated during the process of development and revision. We also want to thank the numerous friends and colleagues who have shared their knowledge about various aspects of American poetry. In particular, we want to express our gratitude to those who have organized sessions and symposia on American poets at the various meetings of the American Literature Association, where we have benefited from both formal presentations and informal conversation.

Alfred Bendixen also wants to thank Rene H. Treviño of Texas A&M University for his skillful editorial assistance during several phases of the production of the manuscript. He is most grateful for the continuous support of his wife and partner, Judith Hamera, brilliant scholar and inspiring teacher, who always reminds him of the best possibilities that life has to offer.

Stephen Burt thanks colleagues and staff in Harvard's Department of English for their attention and tolerance during the process of creating this book: James Engell, James Simpson, and Nicholas Watson, who served as chairs and acting chairs, and undergrad program administrator Lauren Bimmler have been especially helpful. Stephen thanks, additionally, Sandra and Jeffrey Burt, and Stephen is grateful first and last for the support, the patience, and the on-target advice of Jessica Bennett, and for the attention and patience of our not-so-little ones, Nathan and Cooper.

Introduction

ALFRED BENDIXEN AND STEPHEN BURT

The Cambridge History of American Poetry explores the development of poetry in the United States of America from its beginnings to the end of the twentieth century. As a literary history, it aims to provide an informative and reliable narrative of the crucial events, movements, authors, and works that mark the creation of poetic expression over several centuries. Its focus is on both historical context and artistic achievement: thus, the discussions of poetry here illuminate the ways in which verse mattered to different groups at various times as well as the ways in which individual poems exemplify particular values, achieve specific effects, and sometimes form artifacts of enduring power. The narrative thus assesses the aesthetic achievements of numerous works, paying appropriate attention to the artistic details that transform the arrangement of sounds and visual shapes into poetic forms that possess the capacity to move us emotionally, inspire us intellectually, or provoke us into action. Poetry can be pleasurable and it can be powerful. It can entertain and it can educate. At the foundation of this literary history is an inquiry into the many roles that poetry has played in the development of American democracy in the course of several centuries and in the private and public life of the American people. The essays here discuss poems that served political purposes, expressed religious convictions, explored philosophical ideas, detailed uniquely American experiences, celebrated triumphs, mourned personal tragedies, and expressed the entire range of human experience from love to loss.

In our time, literary history is a matter of multiple contexts, and we are committed to recognizing the complexity of historical forces and the multiplicity of audiences who found meaning in different kinds of poetic forms and experiences. This means a commitment to the popular as well as the elite, and to forms and writers excluded from previous discourse. There have been surprisingly few attempts to provide a literary history of poetry in the United States, and those have tended to focus on a relatively small number of major voices and movements. Typical treatments might give attention to a couple of Puritan poets and then leap over to the nineteenth century with a nod to Poe and the Transcendentalists and a dismissive shake of the head for the old Fireside Poets and a declaration that the two poets from this century who mattered – Walt Whitman and Emily Dickinson – achieved greatness by writing poetry in ways that poetry had not been written before. Even very perceptive critics such as Hyatt Waggoner and Donald Stauffer offered surveys of American poetry that treated the last half of the nineteenth century largely by providing lists of poets who were once popular and deemed important but could now safely be declared not worth reading. The twentieth century received a bit more generous treatment, but the focus was again on major authors and movements – especially the giants of high modernism. Although it has clearly been impossible for us to cover every poet who published verse during the past four hundred years, *The Cambridge History of American Poetry* has been designed to provide the most comprehensive study of the practice of poetry in the United States.

Recent challenges to literary canons, and to even the idea of a literary canon, have raised questions about figures who once seemed unassailable. Literary history is now marked by an increased recognition of the achievements of women writers and a greater attention to minority voices, especially African American ones. Moreover, there is also a deeper suspicion of the artificial wall that has separated popular from academic verse and a greater willingness to examine the roles that poetry has played in various aspects of American life. *The Cambridge History of American Poetry* seeks to capture many of the insights into the place of poetry in American culture that have developed in the past two decades. While avoiding the idea of a grand narrative into which all poetic works must either fit or be labeled idiosyncratic, we attempt to offer a literary history that is both coherent and capable of recognizing the multiplicity and diversity of roles that poetry has played and continues to play in the United States.

The editors have consulted with each other throughout the process, but Alfred Bendixen has assumed primary responsibility for the chapters focused on work from before the twentieth century, and Stephen Burt, for chapters on twentieth-century poetry. Instead of attempting to define a narrow tradition that can be traced back to Emerson or Whitman or some other single voice, *The Cambridge History of American Poetry* joins current scholarship in attempting to define and explore multiple traditions and multiple trajectories. For instance, the current process of canon revision is developing a fuller and richer sense of what nineteenth-century American poetry meant and what it achieved. Paul Laurence Dunbar, Emma Lazarus, Frances Harper, and others have found a place in college classrooms and textbooks and in this history. Whitman and Dickinson are in conversation with a variety of other voices, voices that represent the wide variety of verse forms that shaped our literary past, and some voices that speak as passionately and persuasively to us as they did to their own time.

The treatment of a drastically changing literary canon must be both sophisticated and sensitive. Although it recognizes that the criteria by which we distinguish important poetry from mere verse have changed (and will likely continue changing), this literary history does not shun the task of distinguishing major works from minor ones, while also respecting selected popular forms, such as poetry for children (which, it turns out, cannot be disentangled from the history of poetry for adults). In the process, we engage some of the most important questions about the ways in which poetry works and the ways in which poets matter. Definitions of poetry – like definitions of literature, of verse (or "mere verse"), and of art – change over time and vary at any one time, and we have tried to attend to that variation, without making the volume impossibly ambitious, or unmanageably long.

Selected bibliographies for each chapter, all at the end of the present volume, give recommended critical works (and, especially where such works are scarce, anthologies) for readers who want far more depth than we can provide here. Although our focus on poetry in the United States requires specific attention to the development of distinctively American literary traditions, including the role poetry played in the work of nation building and in shaping the social and political life of the United States, we also recognize that poetry crosses borders and boundaries, and that American verse has always existed in the context of the transatlantic, the transnational, and the international.

The Cambridge History of American Poetry emphasizes the complex roles that poetry has played in American cultural and intellectual life, detailing the variety of ways in which both public and private forms of poetry have met the needs of different communities at different times. The volume thus begins with a chapter – "Remembering Muskrat: Native Poetics and the American Indian Oral Tradition" – that is neither a survey of ancient nor of contemporary texts but instead a guide to the distinctive values that poetry possesses in Native communities. The second chapter moves on to a treatment of poetry's role in the age of exploration and conquest with attention to the major non-English traditions. The rest of this history focuses on poetry in English, but the inclusion of this chapter recognizes both the interest that present-day scholars take in the early non-English traditions and the basic fact that the land that is now occupied by the United States of America began as a multilingual and multicultural site of contest. The Puritan tradition receives emphasis in Chapter 3, which focuses on the major poets, and Chapter 4, which examines the development of the Puritan elegy. Early poets of what is now the American South receive attention in Chapter 5, which defines a colonial tradition quite different from its New England counterpart. The next two chapters survey the roles poetry played during the American Revolution and the early national period, with appropriate emphasis on the development of poetic forms, particularly the epic, directly related to the work of democratic nation building.

The complex process by which the principles of Romanticism emerged and were fashioned into a variety of poetic forms is the focus of Chapter 8, which also serves as an introduction to the chapters that follow on Emerson and his contemporaries, on Poe, and on Longfellow. Longfellow and the Fireside or Schoolroom Poets dominated the field of American poetry for decades, and no literary history can pretend to do justice to the nineteenth century without examining the appeal they once held. The implications of a process of canon formation that distinguishes between major and minor voices receives attention in Chapter 13, "Other Voices, Other Verses: Cultures of American Poetry at Midcentury." In addition to chapters on Emily Dickinson and Walt Whitman, we provide informative chapters on the poetry of the Civil War, postbellum Southern poetry, the genteel tradition, children's poetry, comic traditions, and the political poetry of the late nineteenth century. Our hope is that this volume will provide the foundation for further exploration of our poetic traditions.

As our volume shifts into the twentieth century, we again confront the need to recognize a canon in flux. "When the history of American poetry in our time comes to be written," F. O. Matthiessen decided in 1950, introducing the *Oxford Book of American Verse*, "its central figures will probably be Frost and Eliot."[1] Richard Ellman, revising the *Oxford Book* in 1976, proposed an all-male modernist quintet (Frost, Stevens, Williams, Pound, and Eliot), adding that "the labels which many recent poets have adopted, such as Black Mountain, projectivist, New York, beat, are not likely to survive."[2] (We think he was wrong.) Hugh Kenner declared his century the Pound Era; Marjorie Perloff followed up with "Pound-Stevens: Whose Era?" Readers in 1965 were told that they lived in the Age of Lowell, while a more recent scholar calls the postwar decades the Age of Auden; other readers have made it possible to believe that the early twentieth century shaped the late twentieth principally through the delayed influence of Gertrude Stein.[3] Harold Bloom, on the other hand, has announced that we live in the Age of Ashbery, and indeed John Ashbery's hard-to-interpret works have become lodestars, or touchstones, for writers who agree on little else.

All these accounts have some power; none can be allowed to control a literary history that aims to respond at once to many strands of argument about American poetry, to many accounts of its past, and (inevitably) to its contributors' sometimes divergent senses of what matters now.

Our account of the twentieth century begins, as the century did, just before the advent of the "New Poetry," the preferred term in the 1910s for a verse self-consciously modern (and, often, urban) in subject or style: we move from the belated articulations of Santayana and Moody through the austerities of Edwin Arlington Robinson and the vigor of Carl Sandburg. Robert Frost's New England people and places, his tragic sense, and his mastery of received forms made his poetry modern and American and classical all at once; we look at his career, and at some of his heirs. Later accounts of modernism as such often started with the early poetry and the later dictates of T. S. Eliot: we focus here on his earlier work, which is more influential and more informed by his American youth.

Despite the neglect that he felt early on, William Carlos Williams has turned out to be the most broadly influential of modernists, the one whose work built the greatest number of paths for later generations; we consider him as linguistic innovator, as craftsman, and as physician, along with that other innovator, Stein. Mina Loy and H.D. became unquestionably modern poets who led contrasting transatlantic lives; Marianne Moore's work allows us to look at paratexts and publishers, applying book history to modern poetry, while also considering how she invented her forms.

Other poets, among them the popular, sometimes scandalous Edna St. Vincent Millay and the exacting yet passionate Louise Bogan, adapted already extant forms. Wallace Stevens brought the philosophical problems of the Romantics and the emotive dilemmas of his own troubled, quiet life into his own compositions, at first apparently bountiful, later austere. While these poets transformed nineteenth-century legacies, Pound and Williams and their inheritors were making lines, forms, and modes that could sound wholly new; we discuss those inheritors, among them the charismatic Charles Olson and his colleagues at Black Mountain College. The 1920s saw a flood of new literary production by African Americans, some of it also traditional in form, some of it drawn from Black music and speech; preeminent was Langston Hughes, whose international, as well as national, accomplishments we highlight.

The writers of the 1930s were the first to ask what came after modernism: some wrote clear poems meant to alter public opinion, while others, such as Louis Zukofsky and his sometime allies, built a leftist politics into their work in more demanding ways. After the Second World War, poets who emphasized technique and tradition, who had learned from Stevens and Auden and Eliot, dominated tastes at many universities and centers of publishing (especially on the East Coast); some of those poets rejected their early styles for more obviously personal voices. Robert Lowell led that journey, and we look at him beside his contemporaries. Lowell's close friends Randall Jarrell and Elizabeth Bishop looked back to the Romantics, and at each other's work, to find paths of their own. These writers learned their craft among older, self-consciously Southern poet-critics such as John Crowe Ransom, Robert Penn Warren, and Allen Tate, whose regional tradition remains productive – and divided – to this day. Those poets represented – however uneasily – a postwar establishment, with roots not only in modernist attitudes but also in the British past. Their ways of writing and reading would face challenges from poets linked with youth culture, with the West Coast, with visual artists and musicians, and with a European avant-garde.

Especially as it approaches the present day, our history makes room not just for several so-called canons, several tastes and senses of what poets matter most, but also for several ways to write literary history. Some chapters organize themselves around single authors we see as major; others stay focused on authors in self-conscious groups, such as the Beats and the San Francisco Renaissance. Still other chapters organize themselves around a theme or an idea. We consider the so-called New York School, postwar poets who learned from the Continent and from painters; we then look at the political and cultural changes of the 1960s, seeing how some poets turned away from society, toward "authenticity," and others made their practice more public (in part to oppose the conflict in Vietnam). We look at deflections, riddles, and playful evasions throughout the work of James Merrill, a poet both epic and lyric, who set his elaborations against the raw fact of the age; we then look at facts and ideas from science and technology as poets have used them, focusing on A. R. Ammons. We look at the social fact and the social cohesion imagined – or denied – by poets who made their style, and their fame, in the 1970s, using (sometimes by antithesis) the model of that West Coast moralist, Yvor Winters; and we look at the strands of U.S. Latino/a poetics, including but hardly limited to the Puerto Rican poets and the Chicano *movimiento* in Texas and on the West Coast.

We then survey the poetry of Asian Americans, which began about a century ago and flourishes now. Midcentury poets were labeled "confessional" when they revealed private shames, but a better label for the most thoughtful among them is "psychoanalytic"; we look at the legacy of psychoanalysis and autobiography from Sylvia Plath to the end of the century. Two poets who gained fame in the 1980s, Charles Bernstein and Thylias Moss, show how stories about careers and institutions can at once shape and misshape our views about poems. African American poetry belongs at once to the broader history of American writing and to a history of its own: since 1960, that history incorporates the Black Arts Movement along with dissenters from it and the synthesis found in poets of recent vintage. Though the late century could seem hostile to inherited high culture, some poets continued to embrace it; we look at them, and then at modern authors who wrote for the least sophisticated, perhaps most demanding audience: children. American writing has always used more than one language, just as it has (in the words of Marianne Moore) "never been confined to one locality": we look at poets from Connecticut to Hawai'i who are creating new polyglot, hybrid work.

For periods when we can count all the books that got published, it is easy to say which ones were influential, but the modern writers we view as significant influences are likely to be the ones most important to the contemporaries whom we already like. Pick another set of contemporaries, and you will have another account of the moderns; and such accounts have proliferated since about 1960, in tandem with the exponential growth in publishing. We have tried to do justice to several such accounts, and to several ways of telling a story, without mistaking variety for indecision. Our history endorses a kind of pluralism without attempting to be all things to all people; it must embody judgments of value, because it allocates a limited space. The rise of self-skeptical and self-conscious pluralism – the once controversial, now unavoidable notion that no one story can encompass everything significant – is a story in itself. We conclude with poets who consider that story, among them Jorie Graham, Rae Armantrout, and C. D. Wright, along with the challenges to all historical thinking posed by Stein and by that other late modernist, Hart Crane.

"There is singularly nothing that makes a difference a difference in beginning and in the middle and in ending," Stein declared, "except that each generation has something different at which they are all looking.... The only thing that is different from one time to another is what is seen and what is seen depends upon how everybody is doing everything."[4] Everything might have been done another way; as T. S. Eliot also explained, each generation of literary creators rearranges the story of its predecessors in order to create the contexts it calls its own. This plural approach, in method as well as in canon, has made for exclusions and emphases that could easily have gone other ways. We might, for example, have organized entire chapters around Frank O'Hara, or around Stein, whose teasing, provocative, repetitive prose about imaginative writing captures the difficulty if not the necessity of doing literary history in the first place.

Other currently available stories make clear other directions we could have chosen, especially as we approach the present day; some have been chosen, and covered very effectively, by critics whose work we note. We might have devoted another chapter to antimodernist poet-critics such as Robert Hillyer, and another to the poetics of disability, with Larry Eigner at its center.[5] We might have had another chapter on religion and spirituality, connecting the later T. S. Eliot to Gary Snyder, Fanny Howe, and Donald Revell; a chapter on wilderness and farm in modern verse, on pastoral and antipastoral, linking Snyder to Robinson Jeffers, and to Wendell Berry; a chapter on visual form, from Cummings to Ronald Johnson; or a chapter on modern Americans abroad, with accents on Bishop, August Kleinzahler, and Claude McKay, himself both Jamaican and American.[6] We might have devoted an entire chapter to the post-1970 poetry and poetics of Native Americans, which we address instead diachronically in the first chapter and synchronically in the next-to-last. Earlier histories of modern poetry have often put all the Black poets they discuss into one or two chapters in which they rarely interact with non-Black ones; we present African American writers in conversation with one another, but also in chapters connecting them to non-Black work.

We might also have had whole chapters on poetic reactions to the First World War, to the Second World War, or to other military action abroad.[7] We might have examined the narrative impulse – and the resistance to it – among modern long poems, from Stephen Vincent Benét's once-popular *John Brown's Body* through Ed Dorn's *Gunslinger* and Anne Carson's *Autobiography of Red* (although Carson, influential in the United States, considers herself Canadian). We might have pursued the modern poetry best seller from the Benéts through Billy Collins and Maya Angelou.[8] Gender and its consequences, which some literary histories segregate into chapters on women or feminism, appear and reappear throughout our book. So do questions about the fate of premodernist forms, about meter and rhyme and stanza shape, in a postmodernist world. We might have given the Imagists or the Black Arts Movement or the language writers or the Iowa Writers' Workshop chapters of their very own. Instead, they are discussed – as are almost all the poets and topics named above – under other rubrics, with other connections, inevitably subsets of those that an infinitely long volume could have made.

As our collection approaches the third century of these United States, as it addresses the ever-increasing diversity of models and influences within

American poetry, we move away from some questions that gave structure to earlier literary histories; these questions loom large in our own coverage only when they loomed large for the poets involved. We do not always ask (because our poets have not always asked) what makes American poetry first and last American, nor do we attempt to construct (as previous literary historians have constructed) a unitary national tradition. Asked what makes American poems American, Randall Jarrell said that "when we read it, we are at home"; but some American poets have not felt at home, and we listen to their inventions too.[9] Nor do we take the poetry's ambition to be self-consciously American (as opposed to international, or local, or Californian, or Latino, or innovative, or musical) as an index of its value. We look instead at what poets and groups of poets have tried to do. "Some books are undeservedly forgotten," Auden remarked; "none are undeservedly remembered."[10] Some left out here will be remembered later elsewhere.

We end our history not at the moment of writing – we go to press in 2014 – but instead at the year 2000; poems written afterward appear here only sparingly, in order to illuminate what came before. The events of September 11, 2001, may or may not constitute a sharp break in American culture, but they certainly generated voluminous response; so did such later developments as Hurricane Katrina, the election of President Obama, the omnipresence of digital social media, and the rise of the awareness, among nonscientists, of the grave threat posed by global climate change. All these topics should merit sustained attention in the next generation of literary histories; for us, however, they are still current events.

We leave, as well, for the next generation to chronicle two more developments that most readers who encountered American poetry in books and paper magazines would not have noticed during the 1990s. The first is the rise of poetry in American Sign Language, in live performance and through video recordings; the second is the rise of poetic texts that depend on new digital and computational media. Both of these important phenomena began before the year 2000, but a responsible history of either would require its own chapter, with a *terminus ad quem* closer to the present day.[11]

Much older than – but integrally related to – these developments are other ways to see, hear, and create poetry not dependent on conventionally printed words, nor on verse lines. Questions about visuality and poetry, about material texts and of shapes that words make on a page, come up in several chapters. So do questions – thousands of years old – about poetic recitation, performance, and the status of the spoken word. We do not discuss song lyrics, conceived and reproduced as such, because they have their own history, inextricable from the history of American music, on record and in performance. Nor, for the same reason, do we give rap and hip-hop compositions much attention on their own, although we do consider their interplay with other poetic traditions. To include American music history from the sheet music era to the MP3 would have strained our remit beyond bearing. We do, however, discuss work for oral performance where it pre-dates, and where it has proven inseparable from, a written tradition, as in the case of Native American poetries, and of the Nuyorican Poets Café. We also omit the poetic prose of works that are usually discussed as prose fiction, or as rhetoric, even when they have had an inarguable effect on American poetry: we do not examine (although another history might) *Walden, The Making of Americans, On the Road,* or the Gettysburg Address. We do con-sider, more generally, the status of recitation, of printed or memorized poems read aloud: American poems, in the seventeenth and in the twentieth century, emerge from pages, but need not remain there, and address both the eye and the ear.

This volume, like all such volumes, is responsible to its era, to the expec-tations of its likely readers, and to our own sense of what matters and why. The unsettledness of such questions, the difficulty of deciding what matters, has toward the end of the twentieth century become one of the topics that American poetry characteristically takes up. To take part in – to edit, to write for, and indeed to read with attention – such a volume as this one is to con-sider a set of readers "back then," in the poets' own day, in 1666 or in 1999; to consider another set of readers, with settled opinions and expectations, today; and, not least, to consider an individual reader, with her overdeter-mined, unpredictable, even unique response to a poem heard aloud, memo-rized, rewritten, examined silently on a screen, or contemplated quietly on a page. We have tried to do justice to that experience too.

Notes

1. F. O. Matthiessen (ed.), *The Oxford Book of American Verse* (New York: Oxford University Press, 1950), p. xxx.
2. Richard Ellman (ed.), *The New Oxford Book of American Verse* (New York: Oxford University Press, 1976), pp. xxv, xxix.
3. Irvin Ehrenpreis, "The Age of Lowell," in Michael London and Robert Boyers (eds.), *Robert Lowell: A Portrait of the Artist in His Time* (New York: David Lewis, 1970), p. 155; Aidan Wasley, *The Age of Auden: Postwar Poetry and the American Scene* (Princeton, N.J.: Princeton University Press, 2011); Douglas Messerli (ed.), *The Gertrude Stein Awards in Innovative Poetry* (Los Angeles: Sun & Moon, 1994).

4. Gertrude Stein, *Selected Writings*, ed. Carl van Vechten (New York: Vintage, 1990), p. 513.
5. On Hillyer and midcentury antimodernism, see Alan Filreis, *Counter-Revolution of the Word* (Chapel Hill: University of North Carolina Press, 2007); on disability, start with Michael Davidson, "Disability Poetics," in Cary Nelson (ed.), *The Oxford Handbook of Modern and Contemporary American Poetry* (New York: Oxford University Press, 2012), pp. 581–601, and Jennifer Barlett, Sheila Black, and Michael Nothen (eds.), *Beauty Is a Verb: The New Poetry of Disability* (El Paso: Cinco Puntos, 2011).
6. On travel, see Jeffrey Gray, *Mastery's End: Travel and Postwar American Poetry* (Athens: University of Georgia Press, 2005); on pastoral, antipastoral, wilderness, and farm, starting points include Joshua Corey and G. C. Waldrep (eds.), *The Arcadia Project: North American Postmodern Pastoral* (Boise, Idaho: Ahsahta, 2012); Lawrence Buell, *Writing for an Endangered Planet* (Cambridge, Mass.: Harvard University Press, 2001); John Elder, *Imagining the Earth: Poetry and the Vision of Nature*, 2nd ed. (Athens: University of Georgia Press, 1996); and Guy Rotella, *Reading and Writing Nature: The Poetry of Robert Frost, Wallace Stevens, Marianne Moore and Elizabeth Bishop* (Boston: Northeastern University Press, 1990).
7. On U.S. poets' reactions to the First World War, see Mark Van Wienen, *Partisans and Poets: The Political Work of American Poetry in the Great War* (Cambridge: Cambridge University Press, 1997); on the Second World War, Diederik Oostdijk, *Among the Nightmare Fighters: American Poets of World War II* (Columbia, S.C.: University of South Carolina Press, 2011); Harvey Shapiro (ed.), *Poets of World War II* (New York: Library of America, 2003); and Paul Fussell, *Wartime* (New York: Oxford University Press, 1989); on Vietnam, Subarno Chattarji, *Memories of a Lost War: American Poetic Responses to the Vietnam War* (Oxford: Oxford University Press, 2001); and on twentieth-century U.S. war poetry in general, Philip Metres, "'With Ambush and Stratagem': American Poetry in the Age of Pure War," in Nelson (ed.), *The Oxford Handbook of Modern and Contemporary American Poetry*, pp. 331–68, and Lorrie Goldensohn, *Dismantling Glory* (New York: Columbia University Press, 2003).
8. On popular verse and its uses after 1920, see especially Mike Chasar, *Everyday Reading* (New York: Columbia University Press, 2012); see also Joan Shelley Rubin, *Songs of Ourselves: The Uses of Poetry in America* (Cambridge, Mass.: Harvard University Press, 2010). On nonelite poets and verse composition, see instead the discussion of teenaged South Boston poets in Maria Damon, *The Dark End of the Street* (Minneapolis: University of Minnesota Press, 1993).
9. Randall Jarrell, *Poetry and the Age* (1953; Gainesville: University of Florida Press, 2001), p. 317.
10. W. H. Auden, *The Dyer's Hand* (1962; New York: Vintage, 1989), p. 10.

11. For Deaf poetry and poetics in English and English translation, see Davidson, "Disability Poetics," and also John Lee Clark (ed.), *Deaf American Poetry* (Washington, D.C.: Gallaudet University Press, 2009). Two seminal works on digital, electronic, and Internet-based poetries are Loss Pequeño Glazier, *Digital Poetics* (Tuscaloosa: University of Alabama Press, 2001) and Bryan Kim Stefans, *Fashionable Noise* (Berkeley: Atelos, 2003); at the time of writing, many other resources on digital poetics appear on Web sites such as http://www.writing.upenn.edu/bernstein/syllabi/readings/digital-poetics.html (compiled by Charles Bernstein) and http://www.netpoetic.com/2009/08/some-links-to-stuff/ (compiled by Stefans).

PART I

⋆

BEGINNINGS: POETRY BEFORE 1800

Chapter 1

Remembering Muskrat: Native Poetics and the American Indian Oral Tradition

BETTY BOOTH DONOHUE

MUSKRATS DANCING
In the hole they hide
little grey souls
this is the song
they are singing in Ojibwe ...
Our cousins' bones
with the roots are roasting
while we drink swamp water
the syrup you have all forgotten.
Minobagidinigeyaang / we are good and free
ji-niimiiwaad wazhashkwedong
and dancing in the mushrooms.[1]

In the beginning, the American Indian oral tradition actuated and broke away from time. It called the world into existence and then disappeared into it. It remains there now, emanating creative power just as it did at first light. Constantly exercising its ancient ability to penetrate time and inspire human literary creations, the power of the oral tradition extends the length of the continent and guides the minds of all poets attuned to it. The Native oral tradition is an animate, creative spirit that touches all who listen. In the words of the Kiowa poet N. Scott Momaday, it is "pervasive."[2]

The earth's narrative motions began at Creation which, for Native people, is a critical reference point in time. Long ago, it is said that it was Muskrat who swam through murky floods to bring up earth in order to form a space on Turtle's back for Sky Woman and her sons. Or perhaps it was for Nanaboozhoo and his friends. For whom he did it does not matter. What does matter is that Muskrat responded to an oral imperative. He dived deep into water and carried up earth, the residing place first of narrative, and then of holy people and animal-like beings, and finally of humans. He brought them together in this visible sphere and caused them to interact. The oral tradition's various tribal creation accounts invariably link the generative word, the resulting narrative, earth, animals, and people into one great chain of Native being.

Among most traditionalists, remembering the act of creation is essential to any serious life event or narrative performance. Creation accounts are so important that some Nations, like the Osages, cause "a man who had talked with the gods" to attend a woman who had just given birth and recite a creation account to the newborn before it is allowed to nurse. The same medicine person recites the account again before the infant can have water. He is called one more time before the infant is given solid food. These recitations give the child his tribal story and the associative traditions he will be expected to uphold. The creation account sets the child on his tribal path.[3]

As part of a Native literary composition or ritual, the creation account determines a work's thematic trajectory and prepares the listeners' minds for comprehension. The ancient Sky Woman creation narrative, passages of which are common to many Iroquois and Algonquian people, is alluded to in this chapter's epigraph, written by the Ojibwe poet Margaret Noori, and it is repeated in greater detail by another Ojibwe poet, Linda LeGarde-Grover. Both poets tell of Muskrat, who in long-ago time fashioned earth. Since no ritual can begin without retelling an appropriate creation account, their versions open this one. Noori fixes our thematic course by recalling the "swamp water ... [we] have all forgotten," while LeGarde-Grover *re minds* us of the "infinite grace of this merciful earth" upon which all life depends, the life that the oral tradition called into being and sustains.

REDEMPTION

After the Great Flood, Nanaboozhoo and four animals floated on a raft looking for the Earth, and a surface on which they could live and walk. Amik (Beaver), Ojig (Fisher), and Nigiig (Otter) each exhausted their strengths diving to find where the ground originated, but they were unable to stay underwater long enough to find the bottom. As they despaired, the last and smallest animal, Wazhashk (Muskrat), asked to take a turn. Nanaboozhoo and the other animals told him that it was hopeless and urged him not to try, but the muskrat insisted on doing what he could. Because of Wazhashk's courage and sacrifice the earth was renewed.

Wazhashk, the sky watched this.
Mewinzhaa, long before the memory of mortals,
Wazhashk, the sky watched your timid, gallant warrior body
deliberate, then plunge
with odd grace and dreadful fragility

into translucent black water, [and] . . .
break the surface
>into concentric expanding disappearing rings as
>water circled your departure,
>for a moment transparently covering small soles,
>tiny seed pearl toes
>above that determined small warrior body
>that hurtled from sight then
>in an instant was pulled into cold dark depths,
>seeking the finite in the veins of a waterlocked earth.

Wazhashk, the water covering the earth watched this.
Mewinzhaa, long before the memory of mortals,
Wazhashk, when you were obscured from the sky the water watched you
(lost from the sight of the praying four
>alone on a small raft afloat on vast water)
nearly faint under crushing cold
>alone then below the waterline
>seeking the finite in the veins of a cumbrous earth
>as waterfingers intruded and invaded
>all unguarded aspects of your small warrior body
>now stiff and graceless
>pulled by will into icy dark depths.

Wazhashk, in that dark mystery
unknown and vast as the night sky
you continued your solitary plunge
>(lost from the sight of all who lived abovewater,
>who considered your size and your courage)
until in cold and exhaustion your silent voice whispered

>ninzegizi nigiikaj
>nindayekoz niwiinibaa

>I am frightened I am cold
>I am tired I must sleep

and was heard by the Great Spirit.

Wazhashk, you were heard and were answered

gawiin ni wi maajaa sin
gaawin gi ga nogan i sinoon

>have courage, have courage in the darkness
>you are not alone, I am always with you
>have courage, have courage in the darkness

til your spirit roused and spoke

I hear, I am here, I will try
　　through my despair I will

And the Great Spirit watched this and guided you.
Mewinzhaa, long before the memory of mortals,
Wazhashk, the Great Spirit guided you, and watched
　　your small curled brown fingers
　　stretch curving black claws
　　　　to grasp the muddy, rocky breast
　　　　of a waiting Mother Earth.

And today, Wazhashk, hear us breathe,
our inhalations and exhalations a continuing song
of courage sacrifice grace redemption a continuing song
since long before the memory of mortals.
With each telling of the story with each singing of the song
　　we once again rise to break the surface and seek
　　the finite beyond the grace of this merciful Earth,
　　the finite beyond the mercy of this graceful Earth.[4]

Because Muskrat has had such a long existence, it is fitting that he be regarded as emblematic of the American Indian oral tradition for purposes of this essay. He understands that summarizing the voluminous amount of information regarding Native orature carries risks. The extensiveness of the subject and the tribal markers that distinguish one Native group from another complicate the genre, but for an article of this nature, he agrees that brevity must trump both in-depth analysis and tribal specificity if a readable overview is to be presented. An old risk taker himself, Muskrat thinks the time has come to proceed, and he gives his blessing to the venture. Because the Native oral tradition operates outside time as well as in it, it resists historiography. The poetics of the oral tradition, which governs Native orality, also informs modern Native writings to the extent that there is no clear demarcation between old and new, oral and written. Because of this linkage, the oral tradition cannot be separated from the larger issue of American Indian literature; the two are inextricably tied. What a modern literary history can offer is a review of the genre along with a notation of the European American literary response to it. Present-day literary histories must also begin to acknowledge the oral tradition's effect upon European American letters. Like the wind, the tradition is invisible, but it leaves indelible marks.

At the time of Contact, literature in the Western Hemisphere was alive, copious, and dynamic. It was "practiced" by ordinary people as well as by literary specialists, who were referred to as "persons-who-know-things," or medicine people. Literature was an action that had medical, religious, social, aesthetic, intellectual, and didactic properties. It was an all-encompassing part of life. Logocentric in the extreme, American Indian literature served to instruct, to delight, and to bring forth. Generative rather than mimetic, it was, and is, vital and puissant. Simply put, American Indian literature is creative power controlled and propelled by a specialized vocabulary.[5]

Pre-Columbian Native people produced histories, orations, fables, elegies, love songs, and epics. In addition to these familiar literary modes, America's First People also composed songs or poems designed to effect protection from hurtful entities or to ensure success for particular undertakings. They created traveling songs, welcoming songs, lullabies, war chants, and battle narratives. Naming songs introduced infants to the Creator; vision recitations revealed a person's life plan or tribal obligations; coming-of-age ceremonies readied a young person for adulthood; and corn-grinding songs removed spiritual impurities from food. Rhymes, or perhaps rhythms, were composed by children at play, just as jump rope verses are created today. Death songs left something of the singer for his friends to remember. In the old world of the oral tradition, American Indian life began, was lived, and ended with poetry.

The most important of all tribal compositions were the oral formulae designed to effect change or bring about healing. I call these narratives medicine texts for the reason that they contain the poetics necessary to generate change. Navajo chants like *Ghostway or Enemyway*, the *Elohi* fragment of the Cherokees, and the *Iroquois Rite of Condolence* provide examples of such narrative configurations. Medicine, a pan-tribal concept, is many things. It is sometimes a healing potion; psychologically it can be a curative for any human problem that is out of balance with the universe. Medicine is metaphysical power that can alter reality, and it is the theme of all healing chants. Medicine, with all its simultaneous connotations, generates both the oral tradition and modern American Indian letters. Basically, medicine is literary power.

American Indian medicine texts incorporate prose accounts, songs, poetry, dance, and sacred objects in ritual form. A chant is composed of many interwoven narrative strands, and each strand is a complete story in itself. More important, each constituent narrative is essential to the entire ritual protocol. The strands that eventually become most critical to American literature are the narratives featuring ancient tribal gods, hero warriors, plants, animals, tricksters, and the earth. Embedded within the ancient texts are special songs or combinations of powerful words that enable the chant to restore balance and effect change. Humans, if they appear at all, are minor players. The colors, numbers, symbols, and occasional references to wampum or cacao used to enrich these works are usually tribally specific, while the narratives of land forms, gods, animals, tricksters, heroes, and plants, especially corn and tobacco, are common to most. Corn and tobacco are American Indian sacramentals that are essential elements of nearly all rituals and the texts that accompany them.

Drawing conclusions from works in the oral tradition presents hermeneutical obstacles. The impulse of Native literature is to create or make happen, not to represent or self-express. The ancient orality is verbal power that must be protected or kept secret in order to be effective, and it must be propelled by sound that determines meaning. Once the original language that carries the meaning is taken away, only a verbal casing remains, and it is safe to say that much, but certainly not all, of the work collected by ethnologists consists largely of fragments of long narrative cycles. These poems, often designated "songs," are something like the empty shells a locust leaves behind. They are fairly accurate replications but are devoid of animation. Not only do we now have random passages with which to deal, but these truncated sections are further obscured by the codified words, encrypted expressions, and metaphorical ciphers contained within them. A particular song's lyrics may also be broken up with vocables or modified in ways that make them unrecognizable to the uninitiated. Just as many of the verbal patterns have been "adjusted" or left incomplete by informants, they are also devoid of the ritual acts and paraphernalia that accompany them. Finally, a significant number of the cultures that surrounded the singers are either gone or transformed, so that at best we can say we have impressions of how Native poetic expressions may have been rendered. The selections we are privileged to examine, however, are beautiful and worthy of poetic attention.

The origins of some of the medicine texts, such as the Navajo chants, are uncertain, while others are said to be given to dreamers by spirits, psychic revelations, or even certain bird feathers. At one time, the Papagos, or Tohono O'odhams, believed that several illnesses, particularly those diseases that present symptoms of nervousness, were caused by the spirits of the dead. Warriors were especially susceptible to such illnesses, and so were their unborn children. The following passages are two medicine songs employed to heal warriors who had killed Apaches and had not handled their scalps as Tohono O'odham culture required. These songs are part of a series of pieces used to effect a cure for such offenses. Because the songs are removed from their original context and separated from their ritual protocols and music, it may be difficult to understand how they function as a curative purportedly provided by birds, but it is possible to appreciate their poetic grace and understand that the songs' power and meaning lie partly in their arrangements of ciphers and sounds.

THE SUNRISE
The sun is rising,
At either side a bow is lying,
Beside the bows are lion-babies,
The sky is pink,
    That is all.

The moon is setting,
At either side are bamboos for arrow-making,
Beside the bamboos are wild-cat babies,
They walk uncertainly,
    That is all.[6]

EVENING SONG
The sun is slowly departing,
It is slower in its setting;
Black bats will be swooping when the sun is gone,
    That is all.

The spirit children are beneath,
They are moving back and forth;
They roll in play among tufts of white eagle down,
    That is all.[7]

Portions of the very complicated trickster tales, the passages dealing with the con artist aspect of Trickster, are perhaps the most familiar of all the oral tradition's genres. Trickster tales usually feature Coyote, Raven, Spider, or Rabbit, depending on the Nation, and they are stories told to children for the purpose of moral instruction.[8] Originally trickster tales may have been prose interpolations found in the very lengthy healing chants. Because they are purposely designed to arouse laughter and provoke thought, they provide an engaging diversion. Because medicine chants are balanced in terms of feminine and masculine properties, they include portions that engage youths as well as adults. Trickster tales centering on a scoundrel or deceiver survive because they lack the ceremonial formalities, exalted language, and parataxis of the longer works. They are short insertions that are humorous, easily remembered, and thematically consistent. The twentieth-century Coyote, who eschews discretion, is little changed from his older, braggart brother, who once stole fire.

SONG OF COYOTE WHO STOLE THE FIRE
I am frivolous Coyote; I wander around.
        I have been the Black God's fire; I wander around.
I stole his fire from him; I wander around.
                 I have it! I have it![9]   (Navajo)

Those familiar with Coyote instinctively know that although he has the fire now, he will not hold on to it unless he keeps very quiet. And, of course, he will not. He cannot. Prudence is not in his nature.

All the significant action of a medicine text takes place at highly specific geographical sites that the hearer must remember and venerate. These locations constitute the text's land narrative, and of all the narrative strands, the land narrative carries the most interpretative weight.[10] In 1621, William Bradford, writing from Plymouth Colony, records an encounter with the oral tradition that emphasizes the genre's impulses. He relates that before the Indians came to the English to make friends, "they gott all the *Powachs* of ye cuntrie, for 3. days togeather, in a horid and divellish maner to curse & execrate them with their cunjurations, which asembly & service they held in a darke & dismale swampe."[11] Bradford's remarks indicate that the shamans were using power formulae to effect change and restore Native balance, and they were performing this ceremony in a ritually appropriate site.

Underlying the content of medicine texts are basic assumptions subscribed to by most traditional Native people. Native ethoi do not correspond to Western European literary conceptualizations. Instead they are discrete, distinctive assumptions about how the universe works through Logos and are as basic to Native texts as, for example, belief in cause and effect is to Western narrative. Three of the most important concepts are delineated here.

The first principle is that narrative, or the spoken word, created the earth and remains in it. Ancient gods presided at Creation and then went away. Nonetheless, they left their essences in the earth, in stone formations, and in bodies of water. These essences, or inner forms, are the keepers of the first creation account, or first narrative, and they retain the animating spirits of the primal forces orchestrating Creation. It follows that generative narrative force resides in the earth and maintains its primal energy. Voicing this concept is an untitled ancient Náhuatl hymn that proclaims that "the Old God / distended in the navel of the earth / dwells in waters ... [and] in the clouds."[12] The American continents are covered with geographical land forms where this energy can be approached. Lake Guatavita (Muisca), Bear Butte (Cheyenne), Nanih Waiya (Choctaw), and the Sweet Grass Hills (Blackfeet) are examples.

The earth's creative energy is in constant, transforming motion. It is not confined to sacred spots but is in heavy concentration at them.

The second principle maintains that people and the earth are the same thing. They are so closely connected that there is no difference between them. The Navajo sacred chant *Blessingway* articulates this precept: "It is the very inner form of Earth that ... remains stationary with me."[13]

The third principle holds that Native words have creative energy, perhaps something like the dark energy of quantum physics. The old gods used ritual words to bring the cosmos into being, and they have given highly specific and sacred verbal formulae to people for the purpose of maintaining it. When the balance, or beauty, is disturbed, it can be restored when the ancient words, in their proper syntactical order, are spoken. Particularly potent are proper nouns or the names of dynamic individuals or sacred sites that, when uttered, can call up the power associated with the entity dwelling there. Certain American Indian names, spoken today, still generate this primal energy. *Atakullakulla*. *Tecumseh*. Once translated into Carpenter and Panther, the words are powerless. Spoken in Cherokee or Shawnee, they invigorate. The Native convention is that the power is not in the meaning; it is in the sound. Centuries ago, an Eskimo poet articulated this verbal energy when he sang, "In the very earliest time, / ... words were like magic. / The human mind had mysterious powers. / A word spoken by chance / might have strange consequences."[14]

In many American Indian belief systems, everything that exists, both animate and inanimate, is closely related to something else, and all things are essential to the proper functioning of the universe, society, and individuals. Because only people are inclined to disrupt the system, it follows, then, that humans must work to maintain the primordial balance. Hence every aspect of Native life is surrounded with ritual. Newborn children are seen as integral components of the universe, and they must understand it and conform to it. Because the opposite is also true, each entity must recognize the other and be cognizant of the other's expectations. This recognition process begins at birth and is part of most tribal ceremonial protocols. These observances vary from Nation to Nation and range from the very simple to the complex.

THE CHILD IS INTRODUCED TO THE COSMOS AT BIRTH
Ho! Ye Sun, Moon, Stars, all ye that move in the heavens,
I bid you hear me!
Into your midst has come a new life.
Consent ye, I implore!
Make its path smooth, that it may reach the brow of the first hill! ...

Ho! Ye Winds, Clouds, Rain, Mist, all ye that move in the air,
I bid you hear me!
Into your midst has come a new life.
Consent ye, I implore!
Make its path smooth, that it may reach the brow of the second hill!

Ho! Ye Hills, Valleys, Rivers, Lakes, Trees, Grasses, all ye of the earth,
I bid you hear me!
Into your midst has come a new life.
Consent ye, I implore!
Make its path smooth that it may reach the third hill!

Ho! Ye Birds, great and small, that fly in the air,
Ho! Ye Animals, great and small, that dwell in the forest,
Ho! Ye Insects that creep among the grasses and burrow in the ground –
I bid you hear me!
Into your midst has come a new life.
Consent ye, I implore!
Make its path smooth, that it may reach the brow of the fourth hill!

Ho! All ye of the heavens, all ye of the air, all ye of the earth:
I bid you all to hear me!
Into your midst has come a new life.
Consent ye, consent ye all, I implore!
Make its path smooth – then shall it travel beyond the four hills![15]

(Omaha)

This song, performed for a child when he is eight days old, was recorded by Alice Fletcher and Francis LaFlesche (Omaha). It demonstrates the concept of interdependence noted previously. The song is "a supplication to the powers of the heavens, the air, and the earth for the safety of the child from birth to old age" and perhaps beyond.[16] The four hills suggest the four stages of life: infancy, youth, adulthood, and old age. From the portion given to Fletcher and LaFlesche, we see the repetition of four stanzas consisting of five lines interrupted by one stanza of seven lines. The numbers here are important since four is the Native "perfect" number referring to the four directions, the four seasons, the four stages of life, and the four elements: earth, wind, fire, and water. Seven is a number with "medicine" connotations varying from Nation to Nation. This narrative rite is one of many that punctuate a child's life. Among Omahas it precedes his introduction to the tribe, a ritual that is followed by yet another ceremony that takes place once the child can walk unaided and is "sent into the midst of the winds."[17] Poetic ceremonials help the child mark every event in his life, from birth to death. Such events can be daily occurrences like greeting the sun, rearing children, or performing life-sustaining tasks. Dawn is ritually greeted because it is a reenactment of Creation, itself an ongoing process. The following text is a morning prayer, given at daybreak, and it is followed by two lullabies.

PRAYER AT SUNRISE
Now this day,
My sun father,
Now that you have come out standing to your sacred place,
That from which we draw the water of life,
Prayer meal,
Here I give to you.
Your long life,
Your old age,
Your waters,
Your seeds,
Your riches,
Your power,
Your strong spirit,
All these to me may you grant.[18]   (Zuni)

PUWUCH TAWI
Puva, puva, puva
In the trail of the beetles
On each other's backs are sleeping
So on mine, my baby, thou.
Puva, puva, puva.[19]   (Hopi)

WHY DID YOU CRY?
Why did you cry; why did you cry?
Have you stepped on a thorn; have you stepped on a thorn?[20]
                                                      (Yuma)

   Just as infants were treasured, other forms of life were also crucial to human survival. Like children put to sleep by song, seeds were also placed into the ground with music. Crop cultivation was usually done by women and was attended by lengthy rituals. Some songs, like this example, were handed down through the generations, while others were composed for the moment.

CORN PLANTING SONG
I have made a footprint, a sacred one.
I have made a footprint, through it the blades push upward.
     I have made a footprint, through it the blades radiate
     I have made a footprint, over it the blades float in the wind....[21]
                                                      (Osage)

Other undertakings necessary to sustain life were likewise accompanied by songs designed to focus energy on the task at hand. Hunting songs – such as the Menominee sample noted here – were composed to attract game: "When I begin this I offer my song, so I may succeed in getting game."[22] Other hunt songs celebrate a kill or relate the details of the trip after the hunter has returned home. Some of these selections express the sadness of watching an animal expire. Because American Indians tended to believe that a kill was possible only because an animal decided to sacrifice itself for human sustenance, most hunting songs center on the animal itself, not the hunter's theoretical skill. When an animal was killed, ritual protocols were carried out to thank the animal and ensure other successful hunts.

> WALRUS HUNTING
> The walrus, I harpoon it,
> Stroking its cheek.
> You have become quiet and meek.
> The walrus I harpoon it,
> Patting its tusks.
> You have become quiet and meek.[23]　　　　　　　(Eskimo)

Courtship, marriage, and divorce rituals had their poetic expressions as well. Existing fragments of American Indian love songs continue to charm and to reveal the ancient singers' emotional states and personalities.

> WHEN I THINK OF HIM
> Although he said it
> Still
> I am filled with longing
> When I think of him.[24]　　　　　　　(Ojibwe)

> LOVE SONG
> Look oft up the river, look oft and oft.
> In spring at the breaking of the ice,
> 　　　Look oft;
> You may see me coming down in my canoe.
> Look oft up the river, look anew, anew.[25]　　　(Maliseet)

> WE MADE FIRE
> Comrade,
> 　　In the daytime when we made fire
> 　　it was pleasant.
> I understand women.[26]　　　　　　　(Mandan / Hidatsa)

Native love poems do not always articulate idyllic relationships. The following Ojibwe songs illustrate both unhappy and childishly spiteful romantic connections:

> HE IS GONE
> I might grieve,
> I am sad
> that he is gone
> my lover.[27]

> YOU DESIRE VAINLY
> You desire vainly
> that I seek you.
> The reason is
> I come
> to see your younger sister.[28]

According to the tenets of the oral tradition, it is thought that some songs were gifts given to particular individuals by birds, animals, rocks, trees, and the like. In the scheme of creation, birds and animals preceded people on the earth and often acted as their guardians. Sitting Bull, the Lakota medicine man and poet, speaks of receiving songs from birds, an eagle, and a wolf. Their advice was crucial to him at various times in his life. On one occasion the medicine man composed a song to thank yellowhammers (likely northern flickers), who in a dream warned him of a grizzly attack that subsequently took place. He avoided death by pretending to be dead and later thanked the birds:

> Pretty bird, you saw me and took pity on me;
> You wished me to survive among the people.
> O Bird People, from this day always you will be my relatives![29]

Among Native people, even today, there is an understanding that one's own songs are personal property. As such, songs can be gifts either given or received. When a song is received, it is expected that the recipient will reciprocate or "pay" for it, meaning that he will give back some token to express appreciation. The following song was supplied for this chapter by Larry Daylight (Loyal Shawnee), former art professor at Bacone College, the country's first American Indian institution of higher learning. This composition was given to Daylight by Johnny Whiteshirt (Cheyenne / Arapaho) in memory of a little girl, a student at Bacone at the turn of the century, a time when Bacone also educated elementary schoolchildren. Whiteshirt relates that when the girl's family left her at the school, she was very lonely. As she stood on the veranda of a dormitory and watched her family depart in a horse-drawn wagon, she knew that if she cried, she would anger the matron. As Whiteshirt watched the girl, he could imagine her pain, and he composed this song. Years later, he entrusted the song to Daylight in memory of the college's Cheyenne/ Arapaho alumni.

ARAPAHO VERSE
On Nay Da Zey. Hon Nay Hon Na Nawy Naw Noo. Hay Yah-Hay Yah-Hay
    Yah-Hay Aye
Yah-Hay Yah-Hay Yah-Hay Yoo.
Ewe Ne Ha Maw Bee Naw, Hay Gin Naw Taye, Yah-Aye Yah Hay Ya Yoem.

    English Free Translation
They brought her here, and now I see her standing.
Lonely and frightened, she wonders if they will ever come back for her.
    Chorus
HAY Yah-hay Ya-hay Ya-hay Yoo, Hay Yah-hay Ya-hay-Yoo.
YAH-Hay, Yah-Hay, Ya-Hay, Yah-Hay-Yah.
Yah-Hay, Yah-Hay, Yah-Hay-Yah.
Yah-Hay, Yah-Hay, Yah-Hay-Yoo.
YAH-Hay, Yah-Hay, Ya-Hay, Yah-Hay-Yah.
Yah-Hay, Yoo-Aye, Ya-Hay, Aye-Yah, Yah-Hay-Yoem.[30]

Just as the beginning of life was marked by music, so was the end, and death songs are still as poignant today as those written long ago. The following two Ojibwe songs offer examples of the genre. Ga'witayac was killed in a battle with some Lakotas. The bear had been his Manitou, or spirit guide. His friends stood by him as he sang his death song, which expresses his feeling of betrayal: "Large bear / Deceives me."[31] Namebines also was killed by Lakotas. Having been shot in the abdomen, he was too badly wounded to move. As he was dying he sang his death song and asked his colleagues to tell the women at home how he died. He further requested the men to sing his death song when they returned so that the women could dance to it as they commemorated his life: "The odor of death / I discern the odor of death / in front of my body."[32]

A feature of much American Indian poetry is its brevity, but when a song's short sentiments are expanded by repetition and vocables, the oral performance is actually much longer than it may appear when frozen in print. Expanding upon this verbal compression, in *Songs of the Teton Sioux*, Harry Paige points out that Native songs are "mere outlines of artistic expressions.... They are the stones dropped in the quiet pool which cause the ripples to spread";

moreover, these expressions are primarily intimations of feelings to which the hearer adds his own meaning.[33] In this respect, the songs conform to Native rules of narrative theory. A good story does not tell all of a story but allows the listener to create his own interpretation, given his intellectual development at the moment.[34] American Indian narrative is always a reciprocal process that involves the listener mentally adding what the singer has omitted.

Of the many works contained in the oral tradition, attraction formulae, or love charms, inevitably elicit interest. Ojibwes are especially noted for their love medicine, and Cherokees, too, have enthusiasts who admire their incantations. Jack Frederick Kilpatrick and Anna Gritts Kilpatrick (Cherokees) interpret charm poetics. They posit that Cherokee attraction chants begin with ritual power words followed by a declaration of the names of both the charmer and the person to be enchanted, as well as the clan to which each belongs, because these incantations are directed to a specific person for a particular reason. Love charms also invoke a spirit totem favored by the singer. They follow a structure based on powerful numbers, either four or seven, and they work symbolic colors into the verbal arrangement. Typically love charms are recited at dawn on seven successive mornings at a creek or river. Traditionally, Cherokees tend to enact important ritual performances near water, which, like ceremonial fire, carries power to a target. They further accompany the words with tobacco offerings. This process is called "going to water." It should be pointed out that the charms work only if they are recited in the carrier language.[35]

CHEROKEE CHARM
Listen! I am to make my appearance!
Crow, I speak well!

Now under the Morning Red, now under the treetops I
just submerged myself.
I, _____, have just laid down the Pathway.
My Red Attire, desired by Red Eyes, I have just come to spread out.

Now I have plucked them out.
They will be in my body!

You will be unable to glance away.
Your thought is not to wander.

At my back upon the Eternal White Road will be the sound
    of your footsteps.
I have come to draw away your soul!

Listen! Now You Little White Dog!

He has come to fondle your soul.
In what you have to do, you are not to desist!

This is my name, _____; these are my people, _____.[36]
(Cherokee; Adair County, Oklahoma 1882)

The Kilpatricks explain that here Crow is the spirit helper applied to. The use of the word "red" indicates the color east and victory; "white" indicates south and happiness. Within the body of the charm, code phrases referring to medicine are embedded. Actual names and clans are designated in order for the medicine to have specific application. There are seven ritual stanzas. The Kilpatricks point out that the poem can be paraphrased to mean something like the following:

Under the red sunrise, with the help of Crow, I concentrate on victory. My physical eyes I transform into mental eyes focused on winning you. I am certain that we will have a long happy life together. I will cause a small feeling of joy, like a little white dog, to come into your soul and warm your heart when you think of me.[37]

Obviously, English cannot do justice to this poem, but it is one example of power-word arrangement. Belief in word power was expressed by early Native writers, and that the notion is still accepted as a fact of Native life today is corroborated by the words of a Cherokee poet, Gladys Cardiff, who alludes to it in the following lines. Notice that she fuses her words with ceremonial fire, a constant in American Indian sacred observances.

IT HAS SOMETHING TO DO WITH FINAL WORDS
... There are words so old
they must be honored when you come
to them, and only after
can they do their work.
Fire, circled, is like that.[38]

Like Cardiff, other modern Native poets draw from the compositional impulses of the oral tradition. For example, a little Tule / Yaqui lyric collected in the nineteenth century does not differ substantially from a twentieth-century Yakama selection.

TULE LOVE SONG
Many pretty flowers, red, blue, and yellow.
We say to the girls, "Let us go and walk among the flowers."
The wind comes and sways the flowers,
The girls are like that when they dance....[39]   (Yaqui)

LOVE SONG
She is a reed swaying in blue;
Chokecherries are the color of her
skin and her feet moisten the earth....[40]

(Earle Thompson, Yakama)

Among modern Native poets, lyrical romantic expression, as in the preceding poem, is rare. Noticeably absent too are nature allusions and whimsical metaphors, like the oft-quoted Ojibwe lines, "A loon I thought it was, /
But it was my love's splashing oar."[41] In their place are old terrors and new
ambivalences. Although modern Native versifiers often seem cynical when
writing about male-female pairings, they are, nevertheless, consonant with
many twenty-first-century European American offerings. The Cree poet Beth
Cuthand is typical of today's Native poets in regard to dubious attractions.
She reconfigures romantic longings with trickster allusions for modern Native
sensibilities when she voices her interlude with a stranger. In keeping with the
old tradition, she makes good the Pima observation that "Coyote commences
singing [and] / The young woman hurries forth / To hear the Coyote songs."[42]
Of course, Coyote, who is preternaturally sexually ambitious and completely
untrustworthy, must be approached warily. In "Dancing with Rex," Cuthand
understands that while "Me and Rex are brushing the dust / off our boots. His
canine teeth / glint in the light of lightning / and his heart beats audibly in
time to the drums."[43]

Like many other ceremonial protocols, the ritual procedures surrounding
hunting continue to be performed today, as evidenced by the Mvskogee poet
Louis Oliver, Little Coon.

EMPTY KETTLE
I do not waste what is wild
I only take what my cup
        can hold.
When the black kettle gapes
        empty
and children eat roasted acorns
        only....[44]

Modern death songs – like those articulated centuries ago – even now express
the inevitable in terms of acceptance and courage. The Suquamish poet Agnes
Pratt in "Summer '76" anticipates that she will "[walk] toward death / singing
all the time."[45]

For the first several centuries of this country's existence, the oral tradition
chose to remain in relative obscurity. Preferring the company of Native people

and a select number of non-Native poets and writers, it eschewed the academy, journals, and publishing houses. Things, however, eventually changed. By the middle of the nineteenth century, it was obvious to any informed observer that American Native people were in distress. Most of the Eastern Nations had either gone into hiding or had been destroyed by the onslaught of civilization. Others had been forcibly moved West. Immediately following the Civil War, the United States government began systematically "subduing" the "hostile tribes" residing beyond the Mississippi, and in this case, "subduing" can be read as "annihilating." The oral tradition had to act; therefore, it did not object when, five years after Appomattox, a dedicated group of anthropologists, ethnologists, linguists, and ethnomusicologists, likely fearing the imminent loss of Native culture, and perhaps inspired by the previous work of Henry Schoolcraft, began fieldwork among American Indians for the purpose of collecting their songs and recording their customs. Their efforts produced literally hundreds of bulletins and brought the oral tradition to the public's attention. In 1879, Congress established the Bureau of American Ethnography, an office that became a clearinghouse for publications about American Indian culture. Researchers like Franz Boas, Daniel Brinton, Natalie Curtis, Frank Hamilton Cushing, Frances Densmore, Francis LaFlesche, Alice Fletcher, Berard Haile, Washington Matthews, James Mooney, and Elsie Parsons collected materials taken from Native sources. They, and others like them, mined their respective fields for a period extending from approximately 1870 to 1930, and it was these fieldworkers who, perhaps officially, realized the significance of their finds in terms of literary excellence. Washington Matthews and Father Berard concentrated on archiving Navajo chants, while James Mooney compiled Cherokee sacred formulae. These Native works are difficult to date but are very old. On the other hand, many of the works that ethnologists like Frances Densmore and Natalie Curtis assembled are more recent. Some of their selections are possibly contemporaneous with the various informants, while others are reported to be much older. Thus the volumes amassed by the first wave of researchers include materials ranging from ancient times to the nineteenth and early twentieth centuries.

This ethnographic research eventually led to the creation of collections of Native works. Perhaps the most well known of the first run of Native anthologies are George W. Cronyn's *American Indian Poetry* (1918), Margot Astrov's *Winged Serpent* (1946), and A. Grove Day's *The Sky Clears* (1951). These three titles are standards in the field, and they provide accessible Native poetic works adequate for pleasure reading or, with minor qualification, for introductory courses to American Indian literature.

Succeeding anthologies of works from the oral tradition like William Brandon's *The Magic World* (1971), James Houston's *Songs of the Dream People* (1972), Jerome Rothenberg's *Shaking the Pumpkin* (1972), and Brian Swann's *Coming to Light* (1994) follow the earlier models and are pan-tribal. Other poetry collections such as Ruth Underhill's *Rainhouse and Ocean* (1979), Donald Bahr's *Ants and Orioles* (1997), Nora Dauenhauer's series entitled *Classics of Tlingit Oral Literature* (1987–1994), and Miguel León-Portilla's *Fifteen Poets of the Aztec World* (1992) are tribally specific and highly detailed.

Works in the oral tradition fall roughly into four major categories: the ancient tradition that existed before Contact; the nineteenth- and twentieth-century works collected by ethnologists; the modern oral tradition, which is intentionally nonliterate; and current written works, which are closely informed by the oral tradition. Representative of the ancient works are the previously mentioned Navajo chants, the *Elohi* fragment, and the *Rite of Condolence*. The nineteenth- and early twentieth-century collections can be found in bulletins issued by the Bureau of American Ethnology with titles like *The Acoma Indians* or *Ethnology of the Kwakiutl Indians*. These volumes contain old works mixed with contemporary selections. Current powwow music, personal lyrical sentiments, and contemporary secret ceremonials, such as those performed by Southwestern Pueblos, are examples of the intentional nonliterate orature. This work presently exists, and some of it, like the powwow music, circulates. Much of it is considered private, if not secret, and it is inappropriate to access it. Certain modern Native writings, such as the two Ojibwe pieces opening this chapter, are manifestations of the oral tradition's continuing presence among us.

The first non-Native people actually to confront the oral tradition were various explorers, missionaries, and colonists. Spaniards exploring the American Southwest and Europeans traveling along the Atlantic coast and eastern waterways all reacted to Native song, and some of them recorded their impressions. For example, in January 1612, one Father Biard, a Jesuit priest working near what is now northern New York or Maine, wrote to his Provincial about an encounter he and his group had experienced with a band of Armouchiquois and the oral tradition:

> All night there was continual haranguing, singing, dancing, for such is the kind of life all these people lead when they are together. Now as we supposed that probably their songs and dances were invocations to the devil, to oppose the power of this cursed tyrant I had our people sing some sacred hymns, as the "Salve," the "Ave Maris Stella," and others. But when they once got into the way of singing, the spiritual songs being exhausted, they took up others

with which they were familiar. When they came to the end of these, as the French are natural mimics, they began to mimic the singing and dancing of the Armouchiquois who were on the bank, succeeding in it so well that the Armouchiquois stopped to listen to them; and then our people stopped and the others immediately began again. It was really very comical, for you would have said that they were two choirs which had a thorough understanding with each other, and scarcely could you distinguish the real Armouchiquois from the imitators.[46]

These observations, like the Bradford passage cited earlier, verify early cultural exchanges and reveal important attributes of the oral tradition. Both note the connection between Native poetics and the earth, the first principle of Native rhetorical theory, and they attest to its verbal power, or medicine. In these examples, the Armouchiquois are singing in a forest on the bank of a river while Bradford's *powachs* are in a carefully chosen swamp. Forests, rivers, and swamps are sources of narrative and verbal power, and verbal power is medicine. We know without doubt that the *powachs* had been conjuring with formulaic codes, but we do not know with any certainty what the Armouchiquois had been singing. Since they were men on a camping trip away from home and amusing themselves before bedtime, we can only speculate. It is not much of an imaginative stretch to see how some Frenchmen, also away from home and alone in the forest at bedtime, caught on.

Bradford's remarks, like Father Biard's, also provide accurate data about the ancient singers. The *powachs* in question were led by the famous Passaconaway, who was reportedly the most powerful of the Northeastern Algonquian medicine men. According to William Wood, a visitor to New England writing in 1634, Passaconaway could "make the water burn, the rocks move, the trees dance, [and] metamorphise himself into a flaming man."[47] Wood's report attests to the strength of Native codes. Scholars are not sure who the Armouchiquois were, but they believe that they were a very small band of Northeastern Algonquians who could have been distantly connected to the Penobscots, the Abenakis, and the Passamaquoddies.

Since Contact, Americans of one stripe or another have experienced the oral tradition in some form. Reactions to it have varied from fear to humorous tolerance and from mimicry to sincere appreciation. It is important to point out, however, that parodic or not, fearful or not, and esteemed or not, poetic conversations between Europeans and American Indians have been taking place for at least four hundred years, and these dialogues have resulted in Native modifications to the evolving American literature. Even though Passaconaway's ceremony did not bring about its desired end, it did effect changes in colonial life, thought, and discursive practices. Reactions to American Indians and the oral tradition were entered into the developing American literature and modified it. The span is short from the Ojibwe's "As my eyes / search / the prairie / I feel the summer in the spring" to Wallace Stevens's "The river is moving. The blackbird must be flying."[48]

In the period between the eighteenth and mid-nineteenth centuries, American Indians were not part of America's visible literary scene to any significant degree, even though a few Native people, like Samson Occom (Mohegan), William Apess (Pequot), Jane Schoolcraft (Ojibwe), George Copway (Ojibwe), and John Rollin Ridge (Cherokee), published. American Indians were, however, very much a part of America's invisible literary landscape. American Indian ceremonial life had not stopped in the "civilized" East or the yet-unconquered West. American poets responded, perhaps unconsciously, to the tradition's inherent power to influence. Although a clearly marked interstice that allowed Native poetics and European American discourse to meld remains elusive, it is clear that exchanges took place, and several American literary critics have noted the comingling.

In the twentieth century, at least seven literary critics, perhaps taking their cues from the late nineteenth-century anthropologists, begin to appreciate the beauty of the oral tradition and note its influence on American poetry. Scholars like Mary Austin, publishing in 1923, and Constance Rourke, in 1942, argue that American literature has Native features. Michael Castro, writing in 1983; James Nolan in 1994; and Kenneth Lincoln in 2000 have kept up the flow of critical works enlarging this position. Austin believes that Native people absorbed from the topography of America certain rhythms consonant with human experience, and these rhythms are expressed in their oral compositions. European American poets would later access these same land-generated rhythms and thus forge "relationships ... between aboriginal and later American forms."[49] Rourke posits that American Indian treaty-signing ceremonials were the first American dramas. She compares the signings to chronicle plays, complete with dramatis personae, speeches, songs, and "precise notations ... [of] ceremonial action."[50] Castro explains that the Native influence in American poetry surfaces when non-Indian poets respond to their perceptions of American Indian culture and either egregiously appropriate it or sympathetically attempt to emulate it. As they either correctly or incorrectly "interpret" their sense of Indianness, they bring the Native into their works.[51] Nolan believes that what has come to be known as "nativist" or "Americanist" poetics, such as the "cadences of Walt Whitman, Vachel Lindsay, or Gary Snyder," is largely American Indian poetics, while Lincoln maintains that styles imported from Europe have "fused" with American Indian styles and created a "hybrid literature."[52]

Amplifying these European American positions, Native poets and critics have vocalized concurrence. The Mohawk poet Maurice Kenny states that "Native American chanters and writers who support and enrich [American literature] ... are ... a strong post or two of its very foundation."[53] In his assessment of the American literary canon, the Mvskogee critic Craig Womack unequivocally states that "tribal literatures are not some branch waiting to be grafted onto the main trunk, [but they] ... are the *tree*."[54]

From American poetry's beginning, Native markers – such as American Indian characters and themes, ceremonial rhetorical protocols, Native words, and herbaceous ornamentation consisting primarily of corn, squash, and tobacco – are profuse and unmistakable in colonial poetry. Despite the heavy shadows cast by Puritan jeremiads and pious reflections, Native poetics in seventeenth-century American poetry became firmly established. Although it is true that not all European American poets absorbed and transmitted Native rhetorical formularies, those who did sufficiently discharged their errands into the wilderness. One of our earliest works, William Wood's *New Englands Prospect* (1634), provides an example of the imprint of Native poetics on American letters. *Prospect*, written by an English visitor to America, is a travelogue describing early New England. It is composed largely in prose but includes verse interpolations or short poems. These verses are framed by complex land narratives, complete with creation accounts and references to directions, seasons, bodies of water, vegetation, animals, colors, and Native people. *Prospect* incorporates lists of Native words as well as the direct discourse of Native people, many of whom were sachems. In early Native societies, the headmen or sachems interacting with colonists were first of all medicine people. Sachems were the caretakers of their tribal stories. Having internalized the Native Logos, they could summon its power. The wisdom derived from sacred tribal narratives enhanced their lives and inspired others to follow them. The headmen confronting Europeans were literary critics and wordsmiths. Their words, and their names, had enduring strength.

Wood opens *Prospect* with an acknowledgment to Native literary power when he reports on Passaconaway's previously cited verbal abilities. His decision to include the passage in his relation gives us a measure of the oral tradition's formidable strength and its allure for colonial writers. *Prospect's* verse interpolations, which are something like the holy songs in medicine texts, praise trees, animals, birds, and fish and thus encompass entities of earth, umbrage, air, and water in a ceremonial manner. In conformity with his English background, Wood's animal song begins in a slightly Anglicized fashion – "The kingly lion and the strong-armed bear, / The large-limbed mooses, with the tripping deer" – but it quickly transforms into a more Native or American rendering: "Black, glistering otters and rich-coated beaver, / The civet-scented musquash smelling ever."[55] Once Musquash, or Muskrat, is invoked by the power of the Algonquian word, *Prospect* becomes an example of American Indian poetics at work. The power word, Musquash, unlike "kingly lion," puts in place a Native presence that is not contained by European nature metaphors and conceits of royalty. It is unlikely that Wood was aware of the literary significance of his discursive strategies, but Muskrat was. *And that has made all the difference.*

American poets since Wood have continued to incorporate American Indian poetics into their works. By the beginning of the eighteenth century, European immigration to America increased, and as it did, American Indians either assimilated into what had been their old communities and moved to the cultural margins or they trekked West. They did not vanish, and neither did their literary formulae. The forces governing Native poetics seemed increasingly determined to adapt to a mode that would allow them to survive. Perhaps for that reason, Native stylistics in eighteenth-century European American poetry increase. Surfacing above the wave of the neoclassicism flooding the American literary scene are several significant works incorporating Native modes. Among them is Roger Wolcott's *Brief Account of the AGENCY of the Honourable John Winthrop, Esq; in the Court of King Charles the Second, Anno Dom. 1662* (1725). *Brief Account* is a testament to Pequot invincibility. In addition to the poem's visible Native markers and characters, American Indian poetics also regulates its structure and theme. This epyllion ostensibly celebrates the granting of a charter for Connecticut from Charles II to John Winthrop, but it is more a commemoration of the Pequot war and a celebration of the Native warriors engaged in it. In this work, the titular hero, John Winthrop, serves as narrator, detailing carefully modified particulars of the massacre at Mystic. He is, however, not the epic hero; Sassacus is: "Great was his Glory, greater still his Pride, / Much by himself and others Magnify'd."[56] The Native people are counterbalanced by the English forces led by John Mason, but Sassacus dominates the narrative, and his speeches frame the work.

By the nineteenth century, European American poets are beginning to read the land for themselves and acknowledge Native inspiration. Philip Freneau's "timorous fancy [can] see / The painted chief," while Walt Whitman can "hear America singing."[57] In these instances, the key words are "see" and "hear," and they should be taken literally as well as metaphorically. Many of the mainstream works written in this epoch show an intense preoccupation with nature, or, in Native terms, American Indians and the earth. It is as if the land narratives central to American Indian medicine texts have overwhelmed European American sensibilities and found new outlets for expression. In addition to the Native themes and stylistic devices emerging from the developing literature, various philosophical movements, such as Ralph Waldo Emerson's and Henry David Thoreau's Transcendentalism, can be seen as deriving as much from American Indian ontology and epistemology as from Kantian thought. Even though the roots of American nature poetry have long been traced to European Romanticism and prior preoccupations with Edenic metaphors, we must consider the fact that American poetry was written by persons who, perhaps subconsciously, drew their inspiration from Native geographical narrative sources and from the Native people with whom they associated.

In the nineteenth century, when the Western Nations were being militarily subdued and sensationalized by newspaper headlines, the Eastern Nations were living quietly beside their non-Indian neighbors, and the two groups associated with one another. Equally important, traditional Native people all over the United States continued to practice ancient rites, and the power those oral texts exuded filled the air. To exclude these factors from theoretical deliberations concerning the origins of American letters is to limit the scope of American literature's own creation account. As one might expect, Henry Wadsworth Longfellow, well known for his interest in Native subjects, produced Indianized texts. The most obvious is *Hiawatha* (1855), but *Evangeline* (1847) is also an example of how Native discursive strategies have embedded themselves in canonical literature. The poem's "forest primeval," prominent in Longfellow's complex and sustained land narrative, frames and controls this epic-metered dirge sung by "murmuring pines and ... hemlocks."[58] Like medicine texts, the poem orients itself directionally and stays on course for the length of the poem. Beginning and ending in the East, *Evangeline* takes a clockwise course, as action moves from Acadia to Louisiana, to the West, to Michigan, and then to Pennsylvania. The entire work is punctuated by Native interpolations, allusions, and sacramentals, particularly corn and tobacco.

The twentieth century witnessed an explosion of Native writers who draw from the oral tradition. Among them are Paula Gunn Allen (Laguna), Robert Conley (Cherokee), Louise Erdrich (Ojibwe), Joy Harjo (Mvskogee), Carter Revard (Osage), Leslie Marmon Silko (Laguna), James Welch (Blackfeet/Gros Ventre), and many others far too numerous to mention here. Despite the fact that American Indian writers are now prolific and are published globally, Native poetic devices remain a constant in twentieth-century European American poetry, and a significant amount of this verse displays the American Indian markers and discursive strategies begun in the seventeenth century. Native essences are observable in works ranging from William Carlos Williams's *Paterson* (1946–1961) to Lucille Clifton's "the message of crazy horse" (1987). In recent memory, Mary Oliver writes of "muskrats swimming / among the pads"; Carl Sandburg once saw "three muskrats swim west on the Desplaines River"; and James Wright "paused among the dark cattails and prayed / for the muskrats."[59] As we move into the early twenty-first century, we find poets like Jan Chronister, Jerah Chadwick, and Cecilia Lieder successfully combining Native poetics with European American renderings, as other non-Native poets have previously done. There is little to suggest that these compositional impulses will stop.

Whether or not it is widely acknowledged, the oral tradition persists. Native people still greet the dawn with poetry. Creation accounts are told. Lore is kept; fires tended; spirits fed; migrations recounted. Out of the darkness, the headmen give the call. The response sounds. And the circle forms. The sacred formulae move into action. Modern American Indian writers replicate the ancient oral poetics while European American writers subconsciously absorb and reshape its governing ordinances. Just as the Mesquakie poet Ray Young Bear retains the vision of "the small muskrat's clasped hands," Carl Sandburg is absolutely confident that once he "lean[ed] on an ash and watch[ed] the lights fall, the red ember glow, and three / muskrats swim west in a fan of ripples on a sheet of river gold."[60]

Notes

1. Margaret Noori, "Wazhashk Wazhashkwedong," unpublished poem, August 24, 2008. Used by permission of the author.
2. N. Scott Momaday, "The Native Voice," in Emory Elliott (ed.), *The Columbia Literary History of the United States* (New York: Columbia University Press, 1998), p. 14.
3. Alice C. Fletcher and Francis LaFlesche, note found in "The Omaha Tribe," *Twenty-Seventh Annual Report of the Bureau of American Ethnology, 1905–1906* (Washington, D.C.: Government Printing Office, 1911), p. 116.
4. Linda LeGarde-Grover, "Redemption," in *Trail Guide to the Northern Experience in Prints and Poetry* (Duluth, Minn.: Calyx Press, 2008), pp. 32–33.
5. Betty Booth Donohue, *Bradford's Indian Book: Being the True Roote & Rise of American Letters as Revealed by the Native Text Embedded in* Of Plimoth Plantation (Gainesville: University Press of Florida, 2011), pp. xiii, 5. Reprinted with permission of the University Press of Florida. An in-depth discussion of

the creative and healing power of Native poetics can be found in the preface and first chapter of this volume.

6. Frances Densmore, *Papago Music* (Washington, D.C.: Government Printing Office, 1929), p. 113.

7. Densmore, *Papago Music*, p. 114.

8. Vernida Casuse (Navajo), personal interview with the author, October 16, 2007.

9. Hasteen Klah, *Navajo Creation Myth: The Story of Emergence*, recorded by Mary C. Wheelwright (Santa Fe, N.M.: Museum of Navajo Ceremonial Art, 1942), p. 136.

10. Donohue, *Bradford's Indian Book*, p. 5.

11. William Bradford, *Of Plimoth Plantation* (Boston: Little, Brown, 1856), p. 98.

12. Miguel León-Portilla, *Pre-Columbian Literatures of Mexico*, trans. Grace Lobanov and Miguel León-Portilla (Norman: University of Oklahoma Press, 1969), p. 63.

13. Leland C. Wyman, *Blessingway: With Three Versions of the Myth Recorded and Translated from the Navajo by Father Berard Haile, O.F.M.* (Tucson: University of Arizona Press, 1970), p. 136.

14. Jerome Rothenberg (ed.), *Shaking the Pumpkin: Traditional Poetry of the Indian North Americas* (New York: Doubleday, 1972), p. 45.

15. Alice C. Fletcher and Francis LaFlesche, "The Omaha Tribe," in *Twenty-Seventh Annual Report of the Bureau of American Ethnology, 1905–1906* (Washington, D.C.: Government Printing Office, 1911), pp. 115–16.

16. Fletcher and LaFlesche, "The Omaha Tribe," p. 116.

17. Fletcher and LaFlesche, "The Omaha Tribe," p. 117.

18. Ruth L. Bunzel, "Introduction to Zuni Ceremonialism," in *47th Annual Report, Washington Bureau of American Ethnology* (Washington, D.C.: Government Printing Office, 1932), p. 635.

19. Natalie Curtis, *The Indians' Book: An Offering by the American Indians of Indian Lore, Musical and Narrative, to Form a Record of the Songs and Legends of Their Race* (New York: Dover, 1907), p. 480.

20. Frances Densmore, *Yuman and Yaqui Music* (Washington, D.C.: Government Printing Office, 1932), p. 198.

21. Francis LaFlesche, *The Osage Tribe: Rite of the Chiefs; Sayings of the Ancient Men* (Washington, D.C.: Bureau of American Ethnology, 1921), p. 296.

22. Frances Densmore, *Memominee Music* (Washington, D.C.: Government Printing Office, 1932), p. 63.

23. Originally collected by William Thalbitzer for *The Ammassalik Eskimo*. Part 2, No. 3, *Language and Folklore*, 2 vols. (Copenhagen: Reitzel, 1923). The version cited here comes from A. Grove Day (ed.), *The Sky Clears: Poetry of American Indians* (New York: Macmillan, 1951), p. 40.

24. Frances Densmore, *Chippewa Music* (Washington, D.C.: Government Printing Office, 1910), p. 154.

25. Curtis, *The Indians' Book*, p. 13.
26. Frances Densmore, *Mandan and Hidatsa Music* (Washington, D.C.: Government Printing Office, 1923), p. 174.
27. Frances Densmore, *Chippewa Music – II* (Washington, D.C.: Government Printing Office, 1913), p. 219.
28. Densmore, *Chippewa Music*, p. 218.
29. Stanley Vestal, *Sitting Bull: Champion of the Sioux* (Norman: University of Oklahoma Press, 1957), p. 21.
30. Larry Daylight, personal interview with the author, November 18, 2010.
31. Densmore, *Chippewa Music*, p. 80.
32. Densmore, *Chippewa Music*, p. 114.
33. Harry Paige, *Songs of the Teton Sioux* (Los Angeles: Westernlore Press, 1970), p. 68.
34. Randolph Jacob, personal interview with the author, October 12, 1997.
35. Jack Frederick Kilpatrick and Anna Gritts Kilpatrick, *Walk in Your Soul: Love Incantations of the Oklahoma Cherokees* (Dallas: Southern Methodist University Press, 1965; repr. 1982), pp. 3–27.
36. Kilpatrick and Kilpatrick, *Walk in Your Soul*, pp. 25–26.
37. Kilpatrick and Kilpatrick, *Walk in Your Soul*, pp. 26–27.
38. Gladys Cardiff, "It has something to do with final words," in Joy Harjo and Gloria Bird (eds.), *Reinventing the Enemy's Language: Contemporary Native Women's Writings of North America* (New York: W. W. Norton, 1997), pp. 259–61.
39. Densmore, *Yuman and Yaqui Music*, p. 199.
40. Earle Thompson, "Love Song," in Duane Niatum (ed.), *Harper's Anthology of 20th Century Native American Poetry* (San Francisco: HarperSanFrancisco, 1988), p. 254.
41. Densmore, *Chippewa Music*, p. 150.
42. George Cronyn (ed.), *American Indian Poetry: An Anthology of Songs and Chants* (New York: Ballantine), p. 125.
43. Beth Cuthand, "Dancing with Rex," in *Reinventing the Enemy's Language: Contemporary Native Women's Writings of North America* (New York: W. W. Norton, 1997), pp. 393–94.
44. Louis Oliver (Little Coon), "Empty Kettle," in Niatum (ed.), *Harper's Anthology*, p. 5.
45. Agnes Pratt, "Summer '76," in Andrea Lerner (ed.), *Dancing on the Rim of the World: An Anthology of Contemporary Northwest Native American Writing* (Tucson, Ariz.: Sun Tracks, 1990), p. 166.
46. Reuben Gold Thwaites (ed.), *The Jesuit Relations and Allied Documents: Travels and Explorations of the Jesuit Missionaries in New France 1610–1791* (New York: Pageant, 1959), vol. 2, p. 37.
47. William Wood, *New England's Prospect*, ed. Alden T. Vaughan (Amherst: University of Massachusetts Press, 1977), pp. 100–01.

48. Frances Densmore, *The American Indians and Their Music* (New York: The Womans Press, 1926), p. 71; Wallace Stevens, *Collected Poetry and Prose*, ed. Frank Kermode and Joan Richardson (New York: Library of America, 1997), p. 76.

49. Mary Austin, *The American Rhythm: Studies and Reëxpressions of Amerindian Songs* (1923; New York: Cooper Square, 1970), p. 19.

50. Constance Rourke, *The Roots of American Culture and Other Essays*, ed. Van Wyck Brooks (1942; Westport, Conn.: Greenwood Press, 1980), pp. 61–62.

51. Maurice Kenny, "Foreword," in Michael Castro, *Interpreting the Indian: Twentieth-Century Poets and the Native American* (Norman: University of Oklahoma Press, 1991), pp. xvii–xxv.

52. James Nolan, *Poet-Chief: The Native American Poetics of Walt Whitman and Pablo Neruda* (Albuquerque: University of New Mexico Press, 1994), pp. 3–4; Kenneth Lincoln, *Sing with the Heart of a Bear: Fusions of Native and American Poetry, 1890–1999* (Berkeley: University of California Press, 2000), p. xii.

53. Kenny, "Foreword," p. xiii.

54. Craig Womack, *Red on Red: Native American Literary Separatism* (Minneapolis: University of Minnesota Press, 1999), pp. 6–7.

55. William Wood, *New England's Prospect*, ed. Alden T. Vaughan (Amherst: University of Massachusetts Press, 1977), pp. 41–42.

56. Roger Wolcott, *The Poems of Roger Wolcott, Esq: 1725* (Baltimore, Md.: Public Domain Books Reprints Service, 2008), p. 37.

57. Philip Freneau, "Lines Occasioned by a Visit to an Old Indian Burying Ground," in David S. Shields (ed.), *American Poetry: The Seventeenth and Eighteenth Centuries* (New York: Library of America, 2007), p. 746; Walt Whitman, *Poetry and Prose*, ed. Justin Kaplan (New York: Library of America, 1996), p. 176.

58. Henry Wadsworth Longfellow, *Poems and Other Writings* (New York: Penguin, 2000), p. 57.

59. Mary Oliver, "The Ponds," in *House of Light* (Boston: Beacon, 1990), p. 58; Carl Sandburg, "Three Pieces on the Smoke of Autumn," in *Cornhuskers* (New York: Henry Holt, 1918), p. 25; James Wright, "Northern Pike," in *Above the River: The Complete Poems* (New York: Farrar, Straus and Giroux, 1992), p. 217.

60. Ray Young Bear, "For the Rain in March: The Blackened Hearts of Herons," in Geary Hobson (ed.), *The Remembered Earth* (Albuquerque: University of New Mexico Press, 1979), pp. 343–51; Sandburg, "Three Pieces on the Smoke of Autumn," in *Complete Poems* (New York: Harcourt Brace Jovanovich, 1969), pp. 91–92.

Chapter 2

Rhyming Empires: Early American Poetry in Languages Other Than English

SUSAN CASTILLO STREET

When European explorers and settlers began to flood into what is now known as North and South America, they were confronted not only with a bewildering variety of new experiences but also with a plethora of sensory impressions of the peoples and landscapes they encountered. Poetry in the early Americas by explorers and settlers of European origin or descent emerged at a time when sweeping changes were transforming almost every area of life in early modern Europe, with the rise of nation-states, the shift of power from monarchies underpinned by notions of divine right to powerful mercantile elites, and the economic and cultural transformations arising from expansion into the New World. By imposing poetic form on what seemed at first to them an inchoate and baffling reality, containing and giving shape to the dazzling range of images and sensations they encountered in the Americas, Europeans were able to give meaning and structure to European imperial endeavors. This chapter examines poetry written in Spanish, French, German, and Dutch in the early Americas, emphasizing the diverse ways in which the epic and lyric modes produced aesthetic meaning out of new and complex experiences.

Epic Poetry: Making Sense of Empire

In the initial phase of the colonization and settlement of the Americas, a central question for Europeans was whether or not the indigenous populations were in fact human and worthy of conversion to Christianity. In responding to these debates over the humanity of the Indians in early modern Spain, the genres of epic and mock-epic poetry enabled Europeans to articulate the ideological basis for expansion while at the same time confronting some of the troubling ethical issues raised by the stunning levels of violence against indigenous people.

David Quint has argued convincingly that the Virgilian epic, with its links to the history of a specific nation, to the notion of world domination, and to a monarchical system and in some instances a particular dynasty, was singularly well suited to simultaneously aestheticize and politicize European expansion. For Quint, however, the Virgilian epic of the victors, with its linear, end-directed teleology, also evokes a counternarrative of the vanquished in the form of romance, arising from the epic tradition of Lucan. Quint emphasizes Lucanian epic's depiction of class conflict, with a warrior aristocracy struggling against a dominant monarchy bent on limiting its power. The appeal of these literary modes for writers in the early Americas is evident: at the same time that the dominant Virgilian strand celebrates in triumphalist form a heroic narrative of imperial expansion, the Lucanian counternarrative ultimately characterizes indigenous adversaries as animals or lacking full humanity, thus legitimizing European victories.[1] Moreover, the strands of Lucanian counternarrative describing the vanquished as noble savages who, despite their courage and dignity, are nonetheless condemned to defeat allowed European writers to address, at least notionally, some of the troubling ethical issues arising from the brutality and violence of the Conquest, although ultimately reaffirming European "rights" to territorial and ideological expansion.

For Spain, the natural riches of the Americas opened up the prospect of unimaginable material wealth, but the colossal human cost of imperial expansion raised troubling ethical issues and inspired intense ideological debate in sixteenth-century Spain. One eloquent advocate of indigenous rights was the remarkable Dominican priest Bartolomé de Las Casas, who has been both exalted as a voice of conscience and denounced as a traitor to his country – as he is thought to be the principal creator of the "Black Legend" of Spanish cruelty in the colonization of the New World. He was an eyewitness to many of the key events in the conquest of New Spain, starting with the first voyage of Christopher Columbus. Additionally, he participated in the conquest of Cuba, receiving land as a reward. In 1514, however, he experienced a change of heart and came to feel that the Native peoples of America had been unjustly treated. Las Casas soon became known as the champion of Native rights, successively as a reformer at the court in Spain, an unsuccessful colonizer in Venezuela, a friar in Hispaniola, the defender of Indians in debates among ecclesiastics in Mexico, a promoter of the plan to Christianize the Indians of Chiapas by peaceful means, an advocate before the court of the Emperor Charles V in favor of legislation favorable to Indians, and the bishop of Chiapas. After returning to Spain in 1547, at the age of sixty-three, he served as attorney-at-large for the Indians during the last twenty years of his life.

Las Casas's *Historia de las Indias* offers us a remarkable view of the extraordinarily convoluted development of a Spanish discourse on the Native peoples of the New World. Las Casas was one of the first Europeans to comprehend the implications of the discovery of the Americas. After the initial sense of wonder and delight felt by Spaniards and Indians at first contact began to subside, Las Casas soon realized that the European refusal to acknowledge the humanity of the Native peoples of America would lead to the worst sort of oppression and direct violence on the part of the colonizers against the indigenous populations of America. The polemic about the humanity of the indigenous people of the Americas came to a head when Emperor Charles V ordered that a debate on this issue should take place in 1550 and 1551 between Las Casas and the eminent theologian Ginés de Sepúlveda. Concretely, two matters were to be addressed. First, was it legitimate to make war against the Native people in order to attract them to Christianity? Second, were the indigenous peoples of the New World in such a deplorable state of barbarism and inferiority in relation to other allegedly civilized nations that natural law could be invoked as a rationale for obliging them to emerge from such a state, by violence if necessary?

In his treatise *Democrates II* and in his *Apologia*, Sepúlveda's first argument (based on Aristotelian philosophy and the concept of just wars) declared that the Native people of the New World were in such a state of barbarism that it was imperative to dominate them by force in order to liberate them from this state and introduce them to Christianity. Sepúlveda's arguments were heavily based on the central premises of Aristotelian thought, and he alleged that Aristotle does not distinguish between different types of barbarism. Las Casas responded to this by citing Aristotle chapter and verse in order to invoke the different sorts of barbarism described in the philosopher's writings. The first category of barbarism was the type of action committed by cruel and inhuman men, a group into which, according to Las Casas, all too many of the Spanish conquistadores would fit very well indeed. The second category of barbarism in the Aristotelian sense comprised those who spoke a different language, while the third category was that of human beings who are not only inferior by their very nature but also incapable of self-government and righteous living. This category was prominent in Sepúlveda's arguments, but Las Casas refuted his allegations by pointing out that Aristotle himself believed that barbarians of this type are few in number, as nature always tends toward perfection. But then the doughty priest nailed his colors to the mast in no uncertain terms, stating: "Such barbarians should be attracted gently, in accordance with the doctrine of Christ. With this, let us turn our backs on

Aristotle, for we have on our side Christ's own mandate: *love thy neighbour as thyself*."[2] He then accused Sepúlveda of manipulating Aristotelian concepts for his own ends and added that the only category of barbarism (if any) that might be appropriately applied to the Native people of the New World would be the second kind. Moreover, Las Casas alleged that Sepúlveda had based his opinions on one single text, that of the historian Fernández de Oviedo, who owned Indian slaves and obviously had no interest in characterizing the Native people as possessing the right to difference and autonomy.

Sepúlveda's second argument justified war against the Indians as a punishment of their crimes against natural law, particularly idolatry and the practice of human sacrifice. In his response, Las Casas stated that Christian princes had no jurisdiction over these questions, adding that Jews and Muslims in Spain were subject to temporal laws, but not to the laws of the Church. He added that if infidels were to be punished, the disbelief of the Jews and Muslims would be far more worthy of condemnation, because they had heard the word of Christ, but the Catholic Church in Spain did not punish them. Logically, if these "infidels" living in Christian territory were not punished, it would not make sense to condemn Native people who had never been exposed to Christian doctrine.

The third argument of Sepúlveda emphasized that the Native people of the New World oppressed innocent people in order to sacrifice them to their idols or to eat their flesh. He felt consequently that armed intervention was justified in order to prevent an act contrary to natural law. Las Casas responded to this with a lengthy examination of the legitimate jurisdiction of Christian princes over conquered infidels. In support of his argument, he differentiated between the Indians and the Turks, declaring that the latter had occupied kingdoms that they had wrested from Christian princes and that the Indians (unlike the Turks) had never knowingly blasphemed against Christ or maliciously attempted to impede the preaching of the Gospel. He added: "In no way is it convenient that those who go to preach the Gospel are accompanied by armed force, and if they are, for this very reason the words of these same preachers are not worthy of belief. What has the Gospel to do with ordnance, and what have preachers of the Gospel to do with armed legions?"[3] As to the contention that Christian armies could save those who were doomed to be sacrificed and/or eaten by the Native people, Las Casas objected to sacrificing entire populations in order to free a few innocent people.

Sepúlveda's final argument justified war against infidels to prepare the way for the propagation of the Christian religion. He cited the parable of the wedding guests, who were compelled to come to the ceremony by force if necessary. Las Casas counterattacked by citing St. Augustine's exegesis of this parable in order to (once again) differentiate between heretics (those who have heard and rejected Christianity) and pagans (those who have never been exposed to the Christian faith).

These debates on the ethics of the Conquest resonated strongly with many of its protagonists. One such was Alonso de Ercilla y Zúñiga, whose epic poem *La Araucana* vividly articulates the dilemmas and contradictions of the ideology underpinning the Spanish conquest of Chile. In 1535, Diego de Almagro had led the first group of Spaniards along with their Indian allies into the lands south of Peru in search of glory and gold. They encountered fierce resistance from indigenous groups, including the Araucanians or Mapuches. Later, Pedro de Valdivia entered what is now Chile in 1541, founding the city of Santiago, but strong Araucanian resistance continued.

Alonso de Ercilla first learned of the Araucanian uprising in England, where he was part of the entourage that accompanied Philip II to negotiate marriage with Mary Tudor. The tales of Spanish heroism, adventure, and derring-do clearly appealed to the young courtier, who subsequently enlisted in Alderete's 1557 expedition, sent to reinforce his beleaguered compatriots. Ercilla was in many ways the prototypical Renaissance courtier/soldier, and he wrote his epic at a time of great creative ferment in Spanish literature. Frank Dawson comments: "Spain possessed a romantic, medieval adventurousness in her national psychology which found in the New World a marvelous outlet." He adds, "The New World with its immense riches and unusual physical phenomena was a dream become reality; as if the weird lands and animals portrayed in the popular romances of chivalry had come to life in the experiences of the *conquistadores*."[4] Ercilla would have been familiar with the *libros de caballería* in vogue at the time, and he was educated in the Italian humanist tradition, with its emphasis on classical authors; it is said that he was familiar with the works of humanists Tasso and Ariosto, and particularly with classics such as Virgil's *Aeneid*.[5] His Araucanian epic is thus a heady mixture of chivalric romance and battlefield epic, a contrast between his vision of the might and glory of Spanish arms and the courage and dignity – and indeed humanity – of their Araucanian opponents.

La Araucana is characterized by freshness and immediacy. Ercilla states that he recorded his impressions directly on the battlefield during intervals in the fighting, "often on leather due to lack of paper, and on scraps of letters, some so small that they could hold only six verses,"[6] giving his account eyewitness authority, the credibility of "I was there and saw this with my own eyes." Later, Ercilla transformed these notes into cantos made up of *octavas reales*, an Italianate verse form consisting of eight eleven-syllable lines (*endecasílabos*) with an *abababcc* rhyme scheme. The first fifteen cantos were published around 1569, followed by fourteen more in 1578, and the final section of the poem, consisting of eight cantos, in 1589.

The poem reveals a curiously divided epic sensibility, proclaiming Ercilla's dual loyalty to the ideology of the Spanish crown on the one hand and to notions of fairness and humanity on the other. One passage relates how Pedro de Valdivia, the conqueror of Chile, is captured and assassinated by his indigenous adversaries. Valdivia is brought before the assembled Araucanians:

> Caupolicán, rejoicing to see him alive,
> present in state and in person,
> with the voice of a conqueror and haughty gesture
> threatens him and questions him at close quarters.
> Valdivia, a miserable captive
> responds and begs humbly, obedient,
> that he not be killed, and promises him
> to leave the land free, in lasting peace.　　　(*LA*, pp. 20–21)

But this avails him nothing. In a temporary reversal of the conquistador–conquered binary, the indigenous leader Caupolicán "with the voice of a conqueror" condemns Valdivia to death. The Spanish leader is described as "a miserable captive" who "begs humbly" for his life. But the fortunes of the Spanish troops improve with the arrival of reinforcements, and in yet another reversal of fortune, Caupolicán, the noble Araucanian leader, is condemned to death by the invaders. He faces his executioners with remarkable courage and composure:

> Standing up above, turning his serene visage
> From one side to the other, he remained there
> Watching the great crowd of people thronging below,
> Who gazed in astonishment at this incredible event.
> They stared amazed, in fright and wonder
> That Fortune could have brought this to pass.
> He reached the pole where the atrocious sentence
> Was to be carried out, with such a countenance
> That he seemed to dismiss that terrible moment
> As though it were nothing, saying:
> Since Fate and my destiny
> Have brought me to this death,
> Let it come, it is I who want it, I who invite it.　　　(*LA*, p. 197)

Here in the midst of defeat, Caupolicán reclaims his agency as a speaking subject and asserts an unconquerable dignity. Unlike Valdivia, who had pleaded for clemency, Caupolicán repudiates victimhood and faces death with courage, insisting that it is by his own will that he chooses to accept Fate and to die.

The poem is full of memorable events and characters: fierce battles, the death of the indigenous leader Lautaro, the presence of a shaman who carries the narrator far above the earth to witness events happening elsewhere in the world, and the poignant portrayal of Glauca, an Araucanian woman searching for her husband among the dead. Ercilla was clearly aware that his description of the indigenous leaders of Chile could be considered polemical, because it engages the issues of the 1551 Valladolid debate on the humanity of the Indians and thus the morality of the Conquest. In *La Araucana*, the Aristotelian category of barbarism as the type of action committed by cruel and inhuman men seems far more applicable to the Spanish invaders than to their indigenous adversaries. What is particularly powerful, however, is Ercilla's depiction of the dignity and valor of the Araucanian leaders, which directly refutes the idea that barbarians are not only inferior by their very nature but also incapable of self-government and righteous living. Ercilla's loyalty to the Spanish crown did not prevent him from acknowledging the heroic stature of his indigenous adversaries. In the prologue to the first part of *La Araucana*, he states in no uncertain terms:

> If some feel that I am inclined to be on the side of the Araucanians, dealing with their customs and bravery in more detail than barbarians might deserve: if we look at their upbringing, customs, ways of warfare and of waging war, we shall see that few have the advantage over them, and few are those who have defended their land with such constancy and firmness against enemies as formidable as the Spanish. (*LA*, p. 1)

La Araucana was widely read, and its influence on subsequent writers was vast. In Miguel de Cervantes's *Don Quixote*, *La Araucana* is one of only three books spared from the frenzy of book burning. The epic poems of later writers imitated the neo-Virgilian model. One such was Gaspar Pérez de Villagrá's *Historia de la Nueva México* (*History of New Mexico*), published two decades later. Pérez de Villagrá had served as captain and legal officer on the 1598 expeditionary force of Juan de Oñate to New Mexico; Oñate's party consisted of both adventurers seeking precious minerals and settlers who wished to establish farms and cattle ranches. Initially, the Native Americans of Ácoma Pueblo had received the Oñate expedition well, but violence flared up when thirteen Spanish soldiers who had allegedly caused problems were killed. A punitive attack under the leadership of Vicente de Saldívar was thus mounted and sent against the Ácoma, and after a prolonged artillery attack against the city, situated strategically atop a mesa overlooking the surrounding fields, hundreds of Ácoma were killed and the survivors horribly punished: the Spanish victors amputated the right foot of every man over the age of twenty-five.

The opening lines of Pérez de Villagrá's poem draw directly on Virgil's *Aeneid*:

> I sing of arms and the heroic man,
> The being, courage, care, and high emprise
> Of him whose unconquered patience,
> Though cast upon a sea of cares
> In spite of envy slanderous,
> In raising to new heights the feats,
> The deeds, of those brave Spaniards who,
> In the far India of the West
> Discovering in the world that was hid
> "Plus ultra" go bravely saying
> by force of war and strong arms.[7]

In Pérez de Villagrá's work, the elements of Virgilian epic, with its emphasis on the imperial valor of the victors, far outweigh any Lucanian counternarrative characterizing the Indians as courageous adversaries. The Ácomas are presented as violent, barbaric, and riven by infighting. The poet denounces the intransigence of Zutacapán, one of the indigenous leaders, and describes the bloodshed in a grisly wealth of detail:

> It regrets not, that brute, the ambition
> Of that insane and lost barbarian,
> The pitiable loss and misfortune
> Which, caused by it alone, has come
> Upon the unhappy, ill-fated town
> Whose public squares and lofty walls we see
> All overflowing with fresh human blood,
> And a great store of the bodies of the dead,
> From whose deep, terror striking wounds,
> Terrible clots of blood emerged,
> Congealed and liquid blood unheard of, too,
> And bits of undigested food, as well,
> From whence also had way been made
> Through which their poor souls had escaped.

(*HNM*, pp. 136–37)

Pérez de Villagrá's poem consists of thirty-four cantos written in blank verse, with a rhyming couplet at the end of each canto. Although the poet knew Ercilla's *La Araucana*, his posture toward the indigenous people of Ácoma is very different from that of Ercilla toward the Araucanians. The only courage Pérez de Villagrá recognizes in his indigenous adversaries is in their willingness to commit mass suicide. In the following lines, there is a disturbing slippage into tropes of animality as Pérez de Villagrá describes the way in which the mother and sisters of Zutancalpo, another Ácoma leader, immolate themselves:

> So, desperate and utterly heedless,
> She cast herself backward into the flames,
> And after her the four grieving sisters
> Did also choose to be consumed there.
> Together with their dead, beloved brother.
> Thus they, with him, did hurl themselves
> In, next their mother, who burned there.　　　(*HNM*, p. 137)

The burning bodies of the women, twisting in the flames, are compared to those of poisonous snakes, writhing sinuously in a desperate attempt to escape:

> And like to the most monstrous snakes
> Or poisonous, deadly vipers,
> Who with each other intertwine
> In clinging knots and twist about,
> So these poor wretches were entwined
> Among those ashes and embers
> Which, crumbling and soft, seething
> Fiercely, did burst out in a thousand spots,
> And they, struggling up on the glowing coals
> With shoulders, hands and feet, jointly
> Attempted to get out. But all in vain …　　　(*HNM*, p. 138)

Pérez de Villagrá's grim, relentlessly teleological vision denies the humanity of the indigenous groups who dared to oppose the imperial power of the soldiers of Philip II of Spain. Although many of the Ácomas chose suicide over surrender, this is not presented as a heroic act of will as in Ercilla's *Araucana*, but rather as the desperate last act of a people doomed to be subjugated.

The Francophone Epic

The epic form took on slightly different contours in the writings of the Francophone poets of the early Americas, who also employed the power of poetry to articulate and aestheticize imperial ideologies. France had begun to consolidate its position in the Americas in the seventeenth century, after Henry IV's Edict of Nantes granted freedom of conscience to the Huguenots. In order to enhance the financial reserves of the monarchy, the king granted in 1602 a charter awarding a monopoly to a group of Rouen investors in order to build up the fur trade in what is now Canada. One supporter of these ventures, Jean de Beincourt de Poutrincourt, a noble from Picardy, sailed for Port Royal in 1604. In his expedition was Marc Lescarbot, a young lawyer and writer who was well versed in the classics and would become one of the earliest Francophone poets in the Americas. After they arrived in Canada, Poutrincourt took part in an expedition along with Samuel de Champlain and two Native leaders. On his return, Lescarbot had arranged an extraordinary spectacle to welcome him.

In the sixteenth and seventeenth centuries, the royal entry was a pageant in verse designed to mark the arrival of representatives of the European monarchies to colonized territories. Lescarbot's royal entry, titled *Theatre of Neptune*, was performed on November 14, 1606. Its protagonist, Neptune, god of the seas, was an appropriate choice to embody the might of France's maritime transatlantic empire. In the first scene, Neptune, costumed in blue and bearing his trident, was towed out to sea by a float of six Tritons to greet the returning Poutrincourt. Neptune declared:

> Pause, Sagamos, pause here before me
> And listen to a god who watches over you.
> If you do not know me, Saturn was my father,
> Jupiter and Pluto were my brothers …
> Neptune is my name, and among the gods,
> Neptune is one of those who wields
> Greatest power under the vault of heaven.[8]

Later, Neptune set out French imperial hierarchies with stunning clarity:

> Proceed joyously, and follow your path
> Wherever Fate leads you, for I see Destiny
> Preparing for France a flourishing Empire,
> And this new world, which will proclaim far and wide
> The immortal renown of de Monts and your own,
> Under the mighty reign of Henry your King.

(*TN*, p. 5)

Even Neptune, the most powerful of the gods, is subordinate to the might of the French monarch, as are de Monts and Poutrincourt, his representatives in New France.

After Neptune's greeting to Poutrincourt, the Tritons saluted him. This was followed by the offering of gifts by four "savages." The first saluted the French king and his representatives:

> ... in your hands, you who represent the Majesty
> of your Prince, may this province flourish in piety,
> in civil manners, and all else that serves to establish
> what is beautiful. (*TN*, p. 7)

A second "savage" offered a gift of beaver skins:

> Here is my hand, my bow, my arrow
> Which have made a mortal breach
> In the animal whose skin may serve
> Great Sagamos, your majesty. (*TN*, p. 9)

The third "savage" offered Poutrincourt scarves and bracelets made by his mistress, while the fourth offered to fish with his harpoon to supply the French with food. After this, cannons were fired, and Poutrincourt and his troops were welcomed to a banquet in Port Royal, with the gate to the fort decorated to resemble a royal arch. The genre of the royal entry thus enabled Lescarbot to harness the visual splendor of pageantry and performance along with the epic power of the poetic word in the service of empire.

Although the indigenous people in Lescarbot's epic drama are unequivocally seen in terms of their value to the French crown, the poet was also capable of admiring their courage. One of his poems, "To Die for the French," describes a man who died in order to help the French:

> Where would we find a courage
> Like that of the Savage
> Who to give his friends succour
> his own life did offer,
> which he felt he should expend
> to our cause defend?[9]

What is clear, however, is that Lescarbot's admiration for the subject of his poem is radically different from that of Ercilla. The valor of the "savages" is only praiseworthy when they give their lives for the French, not when they rise up in resistance.

The Mock-Epic: Dumont de Montigny

With the advent of Enlightenment rationalism, however, a different strain began to enter European poetry describing imperial endeavors. The mock-epic, with its sardonic, mocking undertones, highlights human frailties and scoffs at the foolishness of dreams of imperial grandeur. Jean-François Dumont de Montigny went as a soldier to Quebec in 1715 and not long thereafter received a commission as a sublieutenant and engineer in Louisiana. It was a turbulent time in the colony's history, in the wake of the Mississippi Bubble and the collapse of the Banque Générale Privée founded by John Law. Law had bought the Mississippi Company in 1717, which was directly linked to French colonization in Louisiana. On its collapse, many investors and colonists were left stranded in a landscape of swamps and bayous, where many died of yellow fever and malaria. Dumont continued to live in the colony, however, until 1737, moving between New Orleans, Pascagoula, Natchez, and the Yazoo River area, and frequently falling into conflict with both Bienville, the governor of Louisiana, and Chépart, the commandant of the fort at Natchez.[10]

Gordon Sayre has observed that Dumont's two-volume history of the colony, *Mémoires Historiques sur la Louisiane* (1753), was clumsily edited by a hack writer and is only loosely based on Dumont's surviving manuscripts. These contain a 4,692-line poem in four cantos that Sayre classifies as a mock-epic. The first canto tells the story of the revolt of the Natchez Indians, resulting in the death of more than 250 French. Dumont attributes much of the responsibility to Chépart, the commander of the fort:

> And through steady labors, that fertile country
> Grew many crops, and seemed to please everybody.
> But by great misfortune, this land so charming,
> Was ruled by Chépart, who thought himself a king.
> When we say as a king, we mean he was a tyrant.
> Remote from New Orleans, a hundred leagues distant,
> From court of justice and the head commandant,
> He became, in two words, tyrannic and arrogant,
> Ill treating the bourgeois and even the savages,
> Ordering the latter to vacate their villages. (DM)

In mincing couplets, Chépart is presented as both despotic and indolent, reluctant to expend the effort required to clear the land, despite the ready availability of slave labor:

> Lands of fine quality, pleasing to his sight.
> He vowed to seize them, though he lacked the right.
> He did not wish to have to clear new land,
> As others had done, when they arrived on the strand.
> Blacks he had in plenty, and had he succeeded
> He would have, at one stroke, made himself settled,

His cabins built, his storehouse erected,
His lands all plowed and cultivated.
It was a worthy plan for a wealthy French man
But his power had made him too proud and too vain.
And sadly, dear reader, it was to prove fatal,
Not only for himself but also for us all.   (DM)

When a cargo of French wine and foodstuffs arrived in Natchez in November 1729, Chépart and two other men went to visit the Sun (or principal chief) of the Natchez bearing wine and brandy, demanding after dinner that the chief give them women for the evening. Returning the morning after to the fort, Chépart and his allies were warned that the planters, officers, and interpreters of Natchez had learned from their contacts among the Indians that trouble was brewing. According to Dumont, Chépart reacted with bluster, throwing the men in jail. On November 29, a delegation of Natchez chiefs arrived bearing gifts and reiterating their good will. Chépart, in order to prove his point, ordered the jailed officials to be released, so that they could see for themselves the folly of their warnings. But shortly thereafter, a general uprising occurred. Chépart's reaction to the attack, and his subsequent demise, is presented as anything but heroic:

Chépart heard this noise, and jumped up, alert,
He shot out of his house, in just his nightshirt,
Ran into his garden, begging loudly for help.
It was too late, of course, for the Natchez now enveloped
Him, engaged in disputes over who would strike his deathblow
None wanted the honor, for no courage did it show,
To kill the man of whom they all said "He's a dog!
Unworthy to be stricken with a warrior's tomahawk."
Nonetheless, he was, for the lowest of the Natchez,
A stinkard among them, got this dubious privilege.   (DM)

The disgraced commandant met death clad in his nightshirt, begging for help, and was ultimately dispatched by a stinkard, a member of the very lowest caste among the Natchez. According to Dumont's description, Chépart was viewed with the utmost scorn by his indigenous adversaries, and only a man from the lowest social stratum would deign to kill him. Once again, the power dynamic is reversed, with the concomitant slippage into tropes of animality: Chépart's very humanity is denied by his Natchez foes, who describe him as a dog. It should also be said, however, that Dumont de Montigny does not praise the Natchez, who are depicted as duplicitous and violent, gleefully torturing their French captives. In Dumont's mock-epic, there is no glory for victors or vanquished.

As the poem draws to its conclusion, Dumont describes an episode that, although probably apocryphal, illustrates vividly the poet's capacity for corrosive satire:

> One morning, at dawn, a sergeant, quite facile
> In the ruses of war, whose name was Brinville
> Was chosen for the job of aiming the cannon
> And met with great misfortune on that one occasion.
> He wanted the enemy to be mocked and harassed
> So he lowered his britches and showed them his ass.
> But in answer, the Natchez, they shot back a ball
> Which lodged between his buttocks, a wound that was fatal.
>
> (DM)

Dumont concludes:

> For bravado, in short, he suffered mortally,
> Which should warn us how deadly are the wages of folly,
> And that the safest course on all such occasions,
> Is to have a strong heart without losing one's reason.   (DM)

And indeed that is the point of the poem. Although one senses that Dumont, despite his sardonic tone, is loyal to his country, imperial expansion becomes not so much a heroic crusade as an enterprise riven with human vanity and absurdity.

The Lyric

Unlike the epic, lyric poetry, with its emphasis on the emotions and feelings of the individual, allows us a glimpse at the daily lived experience of diverse human beings in the early Americas. Sor Juana Inés de la Cruz (1648–1695), justly considered the greatest lyrical poet of colonial Mexico, was known to her contemporaries as the Tenth Muse and the Phoenix of Mexico. She was born out of wedlock to a Basque landowner, Juan de Asbaje, and a Creole mother, Isabel Ramírez. Her father was for the most part absent from the household, and most sources indicate that she was far closer to her mother, a strong and intelligent woman who ran the family properties with great success. As a child, the young Juana Inés was passionate about education, but in Mexico at the time intellectual options for women were circumscribed; indeed, most opted for a life of marriage and childbearing. In an autobiographical memoir, she relates how, at the age of only three, she followed her elder sister to a school where girls were taught to read and managed to persuade the teacher to teach her to read as well. Sor Juana Inés states:

Being six or seven, and having learned how to read and write, along with all other skills of needlework and household arts that girls learn, it came to my attention that in Mexico City there were schools, and a University, in which one studied the sciences. The moment I heard this, I began to plague my mother with insistent and importunate pleas: she should dress me in a boy's clothing and send me to Mexico City to live with relatives, to study and be tutored at the University.[11]

Study at university level, however, was not an option for women at the time. Juana Inés thus continued her studies privately, teaching herself Latin and reading widely on subjects ranging from astronomy to rhetoric and to theology. Later, she became a lady-in-waiting at the viceregal court and quickly became a favorite due to her beauty, charm, and literary talent. At the age of twenty-one, however, she entered a convent and dedicated herself to a life of study and literary endeavor. The convent was one of the few spaces where a woman could pursue intellectual interests relatively unhindered, and in the Convent of Santa Paula, where she was to remain until her death, Sor Juana Inés assembled a considerable library. As Electa Arenal and Amanda Powell have demonstrated, life in the convent was far from austere, and Sor Juana's rooms were "more salon than cell"; there she received theologians, aristocrats, and others to discuss intellectual topics and was attended by servants and a mixed-race slave.[12] In 1690 she challenged some of the opinions contained in a sermon by the well-known Portuguese Jesuit Father Antonio Vieira. According to Sor Juana, the biblical episode in which Christ washes the feet of his disciples was proof of his love for humanity, not just an abstract affirmation of love for its own sake. Her dissent was viewed by her ecclesiastical superiors as temerity, and the bishop of Puebla, using the female pseudonym of Sor Filotea, wrote a letter demanding that she dedicate herself to her duties as a nun and give up her intellectual concerns. Clearly, the young nun felt the pressure, particularly since the Inquisition or Holy Office was still active in stamping out heresy in New Spain. She remarked ruefully,

> Women feel that men surpass them, and that I seem to place myself on a level with men; some wish that I did not know so much; others say that I ought to know more to merit such applause; elderly women do not wish that other women know more than they; young women, that others present a good appearance; and one and all wish me to conform to the rules of their judgment; so that from all sides comes such a singular martyrdom as I deem none other has ever experienced. (*SJI*, p. xvii)

Sor Juana Inés came of age as a poet at a time when Spanish baroque poetry was dominated by two literary giants, Luis de Góngora and Francisco de

Quevedo. Her own poetry shows the influence of both Góngora's *culteranista* style, which was characterized by ornate syntax and dazzling wordplay, and Quevedo's mordant *conceptista* wit and intricate conceits. Indeed, the ornate baroque aesthetic was singularly appropriate for an environment characterized on the one hand by rigid delimitations of race, caste, and gender and on the other by the conflict and eventual hybridity of different ethnicities, religions, and cultures.

One verse form that Sor Juana Inés used to great effect was the *romance*, characterized by eight-syllable lines (*octosílabas*) with the second and fourth lines in assonant rhyme. This is the poetic form that she used when a man from Peru sent her some clay vessels and suggested that she should "become a man." In her mordantly ironic response, Sor Juana comments that the Muses themselves are struck dumb on hearing this gentleman's verse, and that even the god Apollo listens rapt. She adds,

> To hear your lines, fleet Pegasus
> his lusty breathing will retain
> that no one fear his thunderous neigh
> as your verses are declaimed. (*SJI*, p. 137)

Later, she asks him to be her Apollo and her inspiration. Aware, perhaps, that her savage wit might have repercussions, she states demurely:

> You will think that I make mock;
> No, nothing further from the truth,
> To prophesy, my guiding spirit
> Is lacking but a fine hair's breadth. (*SJI*, p. 139)

She then goes on to reject any attempt to categorize or dismiss her according to gender or marital status:

> I know, too, that they were wont
> To call wife, or woman, in the Latin
> *Uxor*, only those who wed,
> Though wife or woman might be virgin.
> So in my case, it is not seemly
> that I be viewed as feminine
> as I will never be a woman
> who may as woman serve a man. (*SJI*, p. 143)

Later, she adds,

> To the degree that one is chosen
> As the target for acclaim

> To that same measure, envy trails
> In close pursuit, with perfect aim. (*SJI*, p. 143)

Although these words are ostensibly directed toward her fatuous Peruvian interlocutor, Sor Juana Inés knew all too well that her brilliance, her literary success, and her intellectual fearlessness had made her the target of backbiting and envy. In a sonnet, she describes this phenomenon:

> In my pursuit, World, why such diligence?
> What my offense, when I am thus inclined
> Insuring elegance affect my mind,
> Not that my mind affect an elegance? (*SJI*, p. 144)

For Sor Juana, wealth is not an end in itself but rather a means to cultivate her mind:

> I have no love of riches or finance,
> And thus do I most happily, I find,
> Expend finances to enrich my mind
> And not mind expend upon finance. (*SJI*, p. 144)

Another verse form used by Sor Juana Inés was the *villancico*, a Spanish lyric meant to be sung and danced, often as part of a religious drama performed within a church. Natalie Underberg has suggested that these vernacular compositions continued to retain within their form a "space" for subversive elements and thus were singularly appropriate as a vehicle for what she calls Sor Juana's "pro-woman" opinions. She adds that this is so partly because the genre was itself seen as a minor one, and partly because the fact that the *villancico* was accompanied by music and sung might distract audiences from the import of the words it contained. The most relevant element of the *villancico* genre, however, for Sor Juana's purposes, was its use of carnivalesque elements and of hagiography as "covers" for her feminist views.[13] This is particularly apparent in what is probably her most powerful *villancico*, written to St. Catherine of Alexandria, with whom she clearly identified strongly. According to popular tradition, Catherine of Alexandria was a young woman of noble birth. At the age of eighteen, she is said to have upbraided Emperor Maximinus for his persecution of Christians and attempted to convince him that it was wrong to worship false gods. The emperor detained her in his palace and summoned numerous scholars to persuade her of the flaws in her reasoning. Catherine of Alexandria, however, emerged victorious and convinced many of her learned adversaries to convert to Christianity. She was condemned to die on the wheel, but when she touched it, this instrument of torture is said to have crumbled.

She was then beheaded on the orders of the emperor. The parallels to Sor Juana Inés's situation in 1691, just after her response to Sor Filotea, are clear: as a woman under very considerable pressure from the ecclesiastical authorities to abandon her writing and her studies, the theme of the martyrdom of St. Catherine enabled her to affirm the intellectual equality of men and women, and to state that femininity and religious devotion are compatible with the life of the intellect.[14]

The *villancico* to St. Catherine was first performed in Oaxaca in 1691. The refrain is both powerful and moving:

> Victor! Victor! Catherine,
> Who with enlightenment divine
> Persuaded all the learned men,
> She who with triumph overcame
> – with knowledge truly sovereign –
> the pride and arrogance profane
> of those who challenged her, in vain,
> *Victor! Victor! Victor!* (*SJI*, p. 189)

She makes a ringing case for intellectual freedom:

> Illumination shed by truth
> Will never by mere shouts be drowned
> Persistently, its echo rings
> Above all obstacles resounds.
> *Victor! Victor!* (*SJI*, p. 189)

Sadly, however, Sor Juana Inés was forced to sell her library and was obliged to devote the rest of her life to spiritual concerns. She died after nursing her fellow nuns during an epidemic in Mexico City in 1695.

German-Language Lyric Poetry

When Germans began to settle in large numbers in North America in the seventeenth century, they brought with them a rich tradition of poetry written in High German, often on mystical or pietist themes. Probably the best known of these poets is Francis Daniel Pastorius (1651–1720?), a polymath with diverse intellectual interests. When Frankfurt became a center of the Pietist movement, which advocated the reform of Lutheranism, Pastorius was drawn into their circle; and when William Penn invited Mennonites and Pietists to emigrate to America to take part in what he called his "holy experiment," Pastorius set sail for America, where he founded Germantown. He was a remarkably prolific poet, writing poetry in Latin, Greek, French, German, and English. As a pacifist, he deplored factional strife:

> Those who with pen or sword
> Would prove their Master's word
> Durst not upon me call
> For aught save deeds of peace –
> For this I strive, nor cease
> Whatever may befall.
> Both friend and foe alike
> I wish to serve aright,
> And to turn harm from all.[15]

Life in early America, however, was far from easy. One melancholy poem dedicated to his former teacher, Tobias Schumbergius, bemoans the passing of earthly glory:

> … Hear, ye mortals, the conclusion I have drawn
> They that now are throned in power, they shall also pass away
> As there passes from our glasses imaged form or figure gay.
> Where Death's grievous hand shall leave us all beneath the churchyard stone
> Pains infernal, life eternal, we shall reap as we have sown.[16]

Lyric Poetry in New Netherland

The Dutch territories in early America were also fertile ground for lyric poetry. One early poet, Jacob Steendam (1636–1701), had published a collection of poems in Holland titled *Der Distelvink* (*The Thistle-Finch* or *The Goldfinch*); it consisted of love songs, emblems, spiritual songs, and nuptial odes. Shortly thereafter he sailed for New Amsterdam, where he established himself as a merchant, later petitioning the authorities to be allowed to import slaves from West Africa. "The Complaint of New Amsterdam," published in 1659, presents an eroticized vision of the colony as a young woman, daughter of Amsterdam, born in wartime but neglected by her sponsors, the East India Company:

> True, both simple 'twas and scant
> What I had to feed my want.
> Oft 'twas nought except Supawn[17]
> And the flesh of buck or fawn.
> When I thus began to grow
> No more care did they bestow
> Yet my breasts are full and neat,
> And my hips are firmly set.[18]

The virginal New Amsterdam appeals to her neglectful mother for protection from the encroaching English settlers, described unflatteringly as "the swine":

> But for me, – yet immature,
>   Fraught with danger; for the Swine
> Trample down these crops of mine,
> Up-root, too, my choicest land;
> Still and dumb, the while, I stand
>   In the hope, my mother's arm
> Will protect me from the harm.   (*LCA*, p. 340)

The marauding English were not the only danger the Dutch faced. Another Dutch-language poet, Henricus Selyns, in his poem "Bridal Torch" conjoins the narrative of a 1663 Indian massacre that took place at Esopus, later called Wiltswyck, with an epithalamion or poem celebrating the marriage of the rector of the local Latin school, Aegidius Luyck, to Judith Van Isendoorn. The poem begins with the line, "How soon the flame of war the flame of love destroys," setting up the central conceit of the poem. As it begins, Cupid is startled by Mars, the god of war, who is depicted as allied to Indian treachery:

> Nor does it Cupid please, who peace and love enjoys,
> And starts, at sight of arms, to hide himself from danger.
> He sees the treachery, unlooked for, but designed,
> … His words are yet still warm, and does he not behold,
> Alas! House after house, with Indian monsters posted?
> Child upon child burnt up? And pregnant women roasted?
>   (*LCA*, p. 341)

But Cupid rallies. In a curiously specular image that is (perhaps unintentionally) comic, he too fires arrows, not of war but of love, at the bridal couple, Luyck and Judith:

> Seeking to hush his wrath by thus his arms restoring
> He quickly seizes them, and draws his bow on high,
> As if he wishes to pierce some special mark above him.
> The fort, New Amsterdam, is now by all possessed;
> While Judith stands beneath, Luyck looks from the embrasure,
> And ere they see or think, he shoots Luyck in the breast.
>   (*LCA*, p. 341)

The smitten young man is rendered mute:

> Luyck speaks not, for he feels something his heart is boring.
> As all look up at Luyck, so Judith upward looks.

He shoots a second time and pierces Isendooren.
This great commotion makes, and causes, far and wide
Re-echoings of joy. While he speaks not, the cry
Resounds throughout the land: "Joy to the groom and bride,
Joy to the married pair, and joy eternally."   (*LCA*, p. 341)

In an eerie mirroring of the images of the Indian massacre of the settlers, the young Dutch couple are struck with the arrows not of war but of love. European colonization and penetration of the continent are presented as an enterprise of erotic power, institutionally legitimized.

As we have seen, explorers and settlers in the early Americas from the time of first contact gave shape and form to their experience through poetry. The epic mode, as embodied in the work of Alonso de Ercilla y Zúñiga, Gaspar Pérez de Villagrá, and Marc Lescarbot, allowed these poets to both articulate the ideological basis for European expansion and at the same time attempt to address some of the moral issues arising from the violence underpinning European expansion in the New World. The mock-epic verse of Dumont de Montigny, on the other hand, exposes the vanity and absurdity of European efforts. The lyric mode in European languages other than English gives us a glimpse of the difficulties the authors of such poems faced: for Sor Juana Inés de la Cruz, her struggle to affirm herself as an intellectual and poet despite the restrictions placed on her because of her gender; for Francis Daniel Pastorius, his awareness of the precarious character of earthly fame; and for Dutch poets like Jacob Steendam and Henricus Selyns, the vulnerability of settlers who not only were surrounded by hostile indigenous cultures but were facing factional strife in their own communities. Although all these poets were dealing with different realities, and although their aesthetic and political perspectives are often dissimilar, the thread that runs through all their verse is an awareness of the capacity of poetry to aestheticize and render intelligible the vibrant diversity of the circumstances in which they found themselves.

Notes

1.   David Quint, *Epic and Empire: Politics and Generic Form from Virgil to Milton* (Princeton, N.J.: Princeton University Press, 1993), pp. 8–13.
2.   Angel Losada (trans.), *Apología de Juan Ginés de Sepúlveda contra Fray Bartolomé de las Casas y de Fray Bartolomé de las Casas contra Juan Ginés de Sepúlveda contra Juan Ginés de Sepúlveda* (Madrid: Editorial Nacional, 1975), p. 17.
3.   Losada (trans.), *Apología de Juan Ginés de Sepúlveda*, p. 25.
4.   Frank Dawson, "Ercilla and La Araucana: Spain and the New World," *Journal of Inter-American Studies* 4:4 (October 1962), pp. 564–65.

5. Dawson, "Ercilla and La Araucana," p. 566.

6. Alonso de Ercilla y Zúñiga, *La Araucana* (Charleston, S.C.: Bibliobazar, 2009), p. 1 (hereafter cited in the text as *LA*). My translation.

7. Gaspár Pérez de Villagrá, excerpt from *History of New Mexico*, in Susan Castillo and Ivy Schweitzer (eds.), *The Literatures of Colonial America: An* Anthology (Oxford: Blackwell, 2001), pp. 132–33 (hereafter cited in the text as *HNM*).

8. Marc Lescarbot, *The Theatre of Neptune in New France* (Cambridge, Mass.: Houghton Mifflin, 1927), p. 3 (hereafter cited in the text as *TN*). Although there is an English translation in this bilingual volume, I have opted to provide my own translations of this text.

9. Marc Lescarbot, "Mourir pour les François," http://www.gutenberg.org/files/21257/21257-h21257-h.htm. My translation.

10. Gordon Sayre, "Dumont de Montigny," www.uoregon.edu/~gsayre/DM.html (hereafter cited in the text as *DM*). Gordon Sayre's translation.

11. Sor Juana Inés de la Cruz, *Poems, Protest and a Dream*, ed. and trans. Dorothy Sayers Peden (New York: Penguin, 1997), p. xxii (hereafter cited in the text as *SJI*).

12. See Electa Arenal and Amanda Powell (trans.), *Sor Juana Inés de la Cruz: Respuesta and Selection of Poems* (New York: Feminist Press at the City University of New York, 1994).

13. Natalie Underberg, "Sor Juana's Villancicos: Context, Gender, and Genre," *Western Folklore* 60:4 (Autumn 2001), pp. 297–316.

14. See Octavio Paz, *Sor Juana Inés de la Cruz, o las Trampas de la Fe* (Barcelona: Seix Barral).

15. Francis Daniel Pastorius, *Circumstantial Geographical Description of Pennsylvania by Francis Daniel Pastorius,* in Albert Cook Meyers (ed.) and Gertrude Kimball (trans.), *Narratives of Early Pennsylvania, West New Jersey and Delaware, 1650–1707* (New York: Barnes & Noble, 1912), p. 418.

16. Pastorius, *Circumstantial Geographical Description*, p. 424.

17. "*Supawn*" is boiled cornmeal.

18. Jacob Steendam, "The Complaint of New Amsterdam," in Susan Castillo and Ivy Schweitzer (eds.), *The Literatures of Colonial America: An Anthology* (Oxford: Blackwell, 2001), p. 339 (hereafter cited in the text as *LCA*).

Chapter 3

The World, the Flesh, and God in Puritan Poetry

ROBERT DALY

More than two hundred American Puritans wrote poetry that is still extant. In their worldview, the physical world was itself a book written by God to connect this world with the next, to link the lowly creatures with their creator, because "that, which may be known of God, is manifest in them" (Romans 1:20). Earthly things had divine significance. As the American Puritan Samuel Willard put it, "The things that are made lead us by the hand to him that made them."[1] In the poetics based on that worldview, metaphor was intrinsic in the world. The poet's wit and ability participated in a natural process that led to the supernatural. The lowly vehicle of each creature led to a divine tenor, and part of one's religious duty was to read that significance and contemplate that journey.

The English Puritan minister Alexander Richardson was quite clear about this duty: "And this teacheth man thus much, that he is to seek out, and find this wisdom of God in the world, and not to be idle; for the world and the creatures therein are like a book wherein God's wisdom is written, and there must we seek it out."[2] An important part of their religious life was to meditate on both scripture and the world in words. As Edward Taylor reflected in his *Preparatory Meditations*, both the created world and the Lord's Supper offered a link between nature and grace. "Dainties most rich, all spiced o're with Grace"[3] would appeal to our sensuous faculties to lead us beyond them: "And this rich banquet makes me thus a Poet" (2.110, 283). No wonder so many wrote poetry, some still worth reading. William Wood's rhyming catalogue of the wondrous creatures of New England; Edward Johnson's historic and Homeric epic, *Good News from New England*; and from many hands verse meditations, acrostics, almanac verses, anagrams, invocations of the muse, songs for the seasons filled with classical deities no longer worshipped but still invoked, and songs to celebrate and commemorate births, storms, and miraculous deliverances from dangers real and imagined – all testify to the omnipresence of Puritan poetics and poetry, the need to translate into enduring form on paper the permanent significance of transient lives. For Puritan poets form served function, and the primary function was to explore, understand, and preserve meaning. Of all this wealth of poetry, we can certainly still read Anne Bradstreet, Roger Williams, Edward Taylor, and Jane Colman Turell for pleasure and profit, and perhaps also a fifth writer, Michael Wigglesworth, whose power and long popularity merit exploration.

Yet even while Puritans wrote poetry, read it, and memorized it, they acknowledged its limitations and dangers so articulately that Puritanism and poetry may seem at first antithetical. *The Whole Booke of Psalmes Faithfully Translated into English Metre*, published in 1640 and popularly known as the *Bay Psalm Book*, was a book of religious poetry, yet John Cotton wrote a careful preface to justify the poetry primarily for the sake of religion.

Standardized prayer was criticized as a papist and Anglican ritual, because any good minister could and should "pray in the spirit," that is, think and speak in his own words. Yet "every good minister hath not a gift … to compose extemporary psalms as he hath of prayer," so the good minister was permitted to depend on others to provide standardized psalms that he could read and repeat. Yet Cotton made clear that the poetic and aesthetic were there only to serve religion: "Neither let any think, that for the meter's sake we have taken liberty or poetical license to depart from the true and proper sense of David's words in the Hebrew verses, no." Cotton assured readers that the translators had kept "close to the original text" and "attended Conscience rather than Elegance, fidelity rather than poetry." As the parallelism and balance suggest, Cotton's argument is itself well written, yet there is no irony in his precise insistence on the primacy of the religious work to be done by the book: "If therefore the verses are not always so smooth and elegant as some may desire or expect; let them consider that God's Altar needs not our polishings: Ex 20."[4]

In the Geneva Bible, the twentieth chapter of Exodus delineates what use the Israelites may and may not make of the things of this world. Verses 4 and 5 make exactly the distinction the Puritans made: "Thou shalt make thee no graven image" (Exodus 20:4) is followed by, "Thou shalt not bow down to them, neither serve them" (Exodus 20:5). This distinction is crucial. Not all images are forbidden. One must avoid images used in worship, images one must bow down to and serve, images of God. The Puritans did not, however, avoid all images. Puritan tombstones display not only engraved poetry but also a plethora of graven images: winged death's heads, skeletons, picks, shovels, scythes, coffins, death's arrow, and snuffed candles sit beside the Tree of Life, the Crown of Victory, the Palm of Righteousness, flowers, souls carried to heaven in the bellies of birds, souls figured as doves, and skulls and cinerary urns with living roots and flowers growing from them. As this abundance of religious art suggests, Puritans did not merely spurn the world and images drawn from it.

Like Augustine, they considered the creatures of the sensible world less a delusion or distraction than a gift from God. For that reason they were not ascetics, Gnostics, or Manicheans, at war with the world. Indeed, only ten years after Cotton's careful preface, other Puritan ministers revised the *Bay Psalm Book*. President Dunster of Harvard and Richard Lyon revised psalms and added their translations of other biblical verses, mostly from the intensely imagistic and beautiful Song of Solomon, "having a special eye," as they explained in their preface, "both to the gravity of the phrase" and the "sweetness of the verse."[5] Cotton Mather noted their aesthetic intentions: "It was thought that a little more of Art was to be employed upon the verses."[6] Puritans' relations to the world were complex, paradoxical, and balanced, as the prose and poetry of Anne Bradstreet (c. 1612–1672) show.

Anne Bradstreet's early poetry was taken to London by her brother-in-law, John Woodbridge, apparently without her permission and, as she wrote later, without a chance for revision. It was published there in 1650 as *The Tenth Muse Lately Sprung up in America ... by a Gentlewoman in Those Parts*. Bradstreet was, as this subtitle made clear, a "gentlewoman," the daughter of one governor of the Massachusetts Bay colony and the wife of another. Her father, Thomas Dudley, had been, in England, steward to the Earl of Lincoln, and as a child, she had access to Sempringham Castle and the earl's vast library, as well as several tutors. She drew on a great range of sources, sacred and secular, for the forms and materials from which she fashioned her own distinctive voice. Her poetry shows her reading of Guillaume Du Bartas, a French poet now obscure but then also admired by Milton and Dryden, along with Spenser, Sidney, Donne, Herbert, Raleigh, and others. A second collection published in 1678 and a third in 1758 demonstrate that her poems continued to find an audience.

Her life had hardship and loss, yet she celebrated the beauty of the world as an a fortiori argument for the generosity of a provident God, found in its nature and history warrant for both her own religion and a permanently valuable feminism, and read it through the rational sacramentalism of Calvin. But she strove to "wean" her affections from a love that terminated in the love of creatures, rather than moving from them to a love of their maker. For her, pantheism and animism were understandable and not evil, but they were merely the childish early stages of a process that continued throughout life, a process she likened, in her "Meditations Divine and Moral," to weaning. "Some children are hardly weaned" and do not wish to leave the breast for "more substantial food," so "God is forced to ... lay affliction" on them so that they may recognize the need to move on, to read the combination of beauty and affliction as a propaedeutic to adult wisdom and learn to "shake hands with the world, before it bid them farewell."[7] Even so common and earthly a thing as weaning could lead to religious enlightenment if one meditated on it.

Like other Puritans, Bradstreet meditated not only on the Bible but also on the world. The practice of meditation, of making abstract doctrine real and true to human experience through an intense focus, was itself a poetics, a way of channeling thought and feeling in language. In his *Meditations from the Creatures*, "as it was preached in Aldermanbury," the English Puritan minister Thomas Taylor collected in 1628 several sermons on this subject. He argued that there "are two great works," left for us to read, "one written in the volume of the Creatures, the other in the volume of the Scriptures." The relation between the earthly and the divine was not mutually exclusive or even dualistic: it was hierarchical. So David contemplates "the heavens and stars" because "he is led to God by them." The world is there to be read, because the "world is his book," in which there is "no letter without a part of God's wisdom in it." For that reason, "the voice of the Creatures is not to be banished out of the church." Nature is a second scripture on which to meditate: "If all Scriptures be profitable to teach and improve, then those that teach divine things from natural."[8] To be sure, Thomas Taylor was aware that he had to make an argument, that most meditation focused on the Bible, but he offered in Puritan terms an argument developed earlier, in the Middle Ages, by writers like Alain de Lille, Richard of St. Victor, John Scotus, Bernard of Clairvaux, and others: the world was, like the Bible, God's book, a fit subject for religious contemplation, and many Puritans read it as such.

As its title makes clear, Bradstreet's "Contemplations" enacts a meditative journey from the creatures to their creator, less by way of renunciation and abandonment than by way of homology. The poem begins with a speaker's looking at an autumn evening. The evening is liminal and transient, but the speaker is absorbed in its beauty: "Rapt were my senses at this delectable view" (204). Still, this speaker is not Keats, Walt Whitman, or H.D.: the image is necessary but not sufficient. She immediately thinks of its spiritual interpretation, its *glossa*, and reads the image to go beyond the image: if this earthly "excellence abide below, / How excellent is he that dwells on high, / Whose power and beauty by his works we know?" (205). The speaker phrases this linking as a question. To be sure that one has found and understood a sacramental link between the visible and the invisible worlds would be an act of presumption.

Calvin's rational sacramentalism does not claim that we can know for certain that the links we see are real, only that our minds tend to make these links, not that we do or can thereby know the mind of God. With that caveat in mind, however, we can and should read the world. What is implicit in the "Contemplations" Bradstreet makes explicit in her "Meditations Divine and Moral": "There is no object that we see, no action that we do … but we may make some spiritual advantage of all" (272).

So autumn suggests a divine beauty and excellence; the "stately oak" (205) will outlast the speaker, but even its many years "eternity doth scorn" (205). When the speaker considers the sun, the temptation to romantic pantheism grows stronger: "Soul of this world, this universe's eye, / No wonder some made thee a deity" (205). The sun, addressed in the intimate personal pronoun "thee," suggests soul and vision. Those who worshipped it are understood, and only prior knowledge keeps the speaker from joining them: "Had I not better known, alas, the same had I" (205).

Instead she joins David, the psalmist, in contemplating the creatures in order to be, in Thomas Taylor's words, "led to God by them." The sun "as a bridegroom from thy chamber rushes" (205) to court the earth and "in the womb of fruitful nature dive," bringing forth a plethora of earthly creatures whose very existence is a hymn to God. Yet when the speaker attempts to join this chorus, to "sing some song, my mazed Muse thought meet" in order that "My great Creator I would magnify," she finds that, unlike them, she cannot sing: "But Ah, and Ah, again, my imbecility!" (206). The triple medial caesura and halting alexandrine evince a difficulty not faced by "the merry grasshopper" and "black-clad cricket." These sing smoothly in flowing lines and lead the speaker to question how they can sing while "I, as mute, can warble forth no higher lays?" (207).

Her answer is the fall of Adam and Eve. Human beings fell below other creatures in the natural order of things, are weaker and more transient than they: "When I behold the heavens as in their prime, / And then the earth (though old) still clad in green," they seem "insensible of time" with neither "age nor wrinkle" on them. When they fade in winter, "A spring returns, and they more youthful made." Not so we. With two pauses, the alexandrine closes the stanza: "But man grows old, lies down, remains where once he's laid" (209). What, then, is one to do? Wordsworth, Coleridge, and other Romantics would later argue that one should affirm one's place in the order of nature, that this affirmation would bring forth the new heavens and the new earth promised in Revelation. This speaker seems to pursue the romantic argument: "Shall I then praise the heavens, the trees, the earth, / Because their beauty and their strength last longer?" They have natural advantages. "Shall I wish there, or never to had birth, / Because they're bigger, and their bodies stronger?" This speaker concludes that the wiser response to our inferiority in the order of nature is to place our hopes not in nature but in the supernatural aspect of our being. And now the halting caesuras come in the descriptions of nature: "Nay, they shall darken, perish, fade and die, / And when unmade so ever shall they lie." Their apparent death in winter is metaphoric; their return to life in spring is transient; and their final death is permanent. Now the closing line runs smoothly: "But man was made for endless immortality" (210). Where fallen human beings are below other creatures in the order of nature, redeemed ones are above them in eternity.

For that reason, when the romantic argument returns, it is phrased in the subjunctive mood as a conditional contingent on a supposition contrary to fact. The temptation to embrace nature and only nature is still there. Yet now the speaker sees the wider context. The woods and river are beautiful, "And if the sun would ever shine, there would I dwell" (210). But of course the sun will not shine forever. Nor can nature know the thoughts it occasions in us, although it can be an "emblem true of what I count the best." The fish are "nature taught, and yet you know not why, / You wat'ry folk that know not your felicity." The fish may inspire contemplation but cannot attain it themselves, cannot know the happiness and freedom of which they are unconscious metaphors. Only the speaker, "musing thus with contemplations fed, / And thousand fancies buzzing in my brain," can remember nightingales heard back in England and anticipate Keats's desire to mount the wings of poesy, to fly with them. But where he wished to fly with them forever, this speaker "wished me wings with her a while to take my flight" (211–12). Even the desire to escape time is itself temporal.

The human being is a "sinful creature, frail and vain," who "takes this earth ev'n for heav'n's bower" (213). Yet earth fades, where heaven endures. Earth's great failing is not that it is not real but that it does not last. As Bradstreet explained in "Meditations Divine and Moral," "All the comforts of this life may be compared to the gourd of Jonah" (288), a real and beautiful gift of a loving God but not to be confused with its creator. Its very transience and decay work to lead Jonah and the writer to the next step in the prose meditation, "for were earthly comforts permanent, who would look for heavenly?" (289). The contemplative speaker concludes that "Time the fatal wrack of mortal things" shows that even good things – fame, wit, and gold – will not "scape time's rust," that only "he whose name is graved in the white stone / Shall last and shine when all of these are gone" (213–14).

"Contemplations" is, then, a single poem, in thirty-three seven-line stanzas that combine and modify Spenserian stanza and rhyme royal. The Spenserian elements link her work not only to Spenser but also to the English Spenserians who tried to keep alive Elizabethan values in Stuart times. Rhyme royal links Bradstreet to English writers back to Chaucer, who used it in *Troilus and Criseyde*. It calls back fond memories of England, like the "Philomel," or nightingale, found in England but not in America.

In stanzas 1 through 6, the speaker celebrates the beauty of the physical world and the religious use of metaphors drawn from it. In stanzas 8 and 9 she considers why she cannot unselfconsciously praise God as other creatures appear to. In stanzas 10 through 17, she suggests that the fall of Adam and Eve separated human beings from the rest of nature, forcing us to dwell in consciousness and history, apart from the prelapsarian bliss of Eden. And in stanzas 18 through 33, she works out a temporal resolution and a modus vivendi. To affirm one's place in the order of nature would be to affirm one's own comparative weakness and death. Instead, one must look to the supernatural order for one's real home and end, not with nature but with Revelation. Contemplations, meditations, are parts of one's religious duty, in which nature is to be neither scorned nor worshipped, but read. Such reading will link the two books, nature and the Bible; it will lead from the world of nature to redemption and the white stone promised to "him that overcometh" in Revelation 2:17: "a white stone, and in the stone a new name written, which no man knoweth saving he that receiveth it." Like the Bible, nature contained secrets not obvious to everyone but worth careful contemplation.

So did history and science. The majority of Bradstreet's poems are not the personal reflections now frequently anthologized. Like the quaternions on the four elements, the four humors, the four ages, the four seasons, and the four monarchies, they focus on the outside world. What she wrote of her letter "To My Dear Children" applies to her poetry as well: "I have not studied in this you read to show my skill, but to declare the truth, not to set forth myself, but the glory of God" (240). Bradstreet writes public poetry that includes but goes well beyond the personal. She imaginatively reoccupies many periods in history. Doing so enables her to distinguish aspects of universal human nature from the local and transient beliefs of a particular time and place. So her famous humility about herself and her ability and willingness to look outward are not personal or poetic failings but complex philosophical and literary strategies.

In "The Prologue," for example, she begins with the conventional disclaimer about her inability to do justice to her high theme: "To sing of wars, of captains, and of kings, / Of cities founded, commonwealths begun, / For my mean pen are too superior things" (15). When the prologue is followed by poems that do exactly these things, we are tempted to conclude that the humility is merely conventional, perhaps even ironic. Yet the specific evidence suggests that she means it. Indeed the poem's treatment of those who would claim worthiness is satirical, suggesting that possessors of self-inflicted self-esteem may be, like those who cling uncritically to the things of this world, merely childish.

When she proleptically rehearses sexist arguments against her poems, she writes, "I am obnoxious to each carping tongue / Who says my hand a needle better fits." As later lines make clear, this reductive synecdoche to "carping tongue" is hardly an expression of fear and deference. The "despite they cast on female wits" is such that, "If what I do prove well, it won't advance, / They'll say it's stol'n, or else it was by chance" (16). Interestingly, these negative arguments were not made at the time. John Rogers and Nathaniel Ward praised her poetry. Her first book, *The Tenth Muse*, was a best seller in London, and even Cotton Mather, who had his doubts about both women and poetry, wrote in 1702 that "her poems … have afforded … a monument for her memory beyond the stateliest marbles."[9] Only later critics, in the nineteenth and early twentieth centuries, began to make the arguments and dismissals she answers here.

She begins by alluding to the "antique Greeks" whose muses were women: "Else of our sex why feigned they those nine / And poesy made Calliope's own child." She writes that her detractors will say, "The Greeks did nought, but play the fools and lie." It's a nice strategy. To dismiss poetry by women, one has to dismiss the Greeks, one of the great fonts of Western culture. There is no point in fighting an open battle that will end in defeat: "It is but vain unjustly to wage war." So she goes on to grant men "Preeminence in all and each" but immediately adds, "Yet grant some small acknowledgment of ours" and addresses them: "oh ye high flown quills that soar the skies, / And ever with your prey still catch your praise" (16). Now her critics, formerly "each carping tongue," are again reduced to synecdoche. Writing quills were made from the wing and tail feathers of geese and turkeys, in the Renaissance hierarchy of animals not noble parts of not noble birds, and her critics catch only their own praise. She ends with a humble request, that for her poetry "I ask no bays," the leaves used in the wreaths given to the winners in the Greek poetic competitions, as well as for cooking, but only "thyme or parsley wreath," used more for cooking than for victor's crowns (17). It may be anachronistic to call Bradstreet a feminist, yet much of her poetry can now be profitably read through this lens.

In her poem "In Honour of That High and Mighty Princess Queen Elizabeth of Happy Memory," she can be much more explicit about Elizabeth than she usually is about herself. Here the humble disclaimer includes all other writers as well as herself: "No Phoenix pen, nor Spenser's poetry, / No Speed's nor Camden's learned history, / Eliza's works, wars, praise, can e'er compact" (195). Her inability to do justice to her high theme is shared with all other writers, including those whom she admires. Her scorn for those who would attribute this inability to sex or gender is self-controlled and complete: "Now say, have women worth? or have they none? / Or had they some, but with our Queen is't gone?" (197–98). Here her learning in logic and history is brought to bear. Bradstreet lives and writes with England and America controlled by the masculine and none-too-bright House of Stuart. But it was not always so. This political situation and the habits of mind that go with it are temporal and contingent. Where her use of Spenserian and rhyme royal verse form in the "Contemplations" quietly allied her with the English Spenserians who had sung the praises of Elizabeth, where that choice of verse form was a subtle political act, here she can be more direct.

If masculine supremacy were a fact of nature, then there should be no exceptions, and this time should be like all other times. But that is not the case: "Nay masculines, you have taxed us long, / But she, though dead, will vindicate our wrong." The poem can look back on a better time and use it to alert and educate her current readers: "Let such as say our sex is void of reason, / Know 'tis a slander now but once was treason" (198). Times change, and may yet change again. By occupying various times, the poem can read what we now call sexism as local and temporary. It can look back on a time when it would have been less comfortable and forward to a time when it may disappear, a time of "the heaven's great revolution; / If then new things their old forms shall retain, / Eliza shall rule Albion once again" (198). In our own terms, neither sexism nor feminism is settled and fixed just yet. Both are contested, and Bradstreet's poetry enacts those contests.

Her prose writings, even to her children, show continual struggles and choices: "I have often been perplexed that I have not found that constant joy in my pilgrimage and refreshing which I supposed most servants of God have" (243). She expected a time of assurance and calm and sometimes achieved it, but only for a time, and her doubts are quite familiar to contemporary readers: "Many times hath Satan troubled me concerning the verity of the Scriptures, many times by atheism how could I know whether there was a God; I never saw any miracles to confirm me, and those which I read of, how did I know but they were feigned?" (243). In times of trial, then, she had no store of readymade comfort from a settled confidence in her religion. For her, Puritanism was a religion *agonistes*, a religion of struggle.

Even her coming to America, which we Americans tend to celebrate because it led to us, is phrased as change and challenge: "After a short time I changed my condition and was married, and came into this country, where I found a new world and new manners, at which my heart rose" (241). Something about the New World made her angry. Because it occurs in the same sentence with her marriage, it is tempting to think it may have been masculine supremacy, but that was hardly new or limited to America. One possibility is that it was the requirement that members of American Puritan churches had to deliver publicly, to ministers and elders, a conversion narrative and have its authenticity judged by them. This requirement was indeed new and may well have been offensive. Some evidence for this conjecture is given in the next sentence, in which whatever angered her is connected to joining the church: "But after I was convinced it was the way of God, I submitted to it and joined the church at Boston" (241). Although the cause remains debatable, the effect is revealing. She did not submit immediately, automatically, or under duress. It was only when she became convinced that it was the way of God that she chose to submit and join. She worked her way to that decision, and her submission was delayed, considered, and chosen.

One can see a similar process in her poems on her family, in her elegies, and in her last poems, in which hopes for heaven are linked to life in this world. "Before the Birth of One of Her Children" begins and ends with harsh realities. The Puritans believed that marriage ended with death. The speaker writes "farewell lines" to her husband, so that "when that knot's untied that made us one, / I may seem thine, who in effect am none." She admits that death ends the marriage and asks that her faults will be "interred in my oblivious grave," that "when thou feel'st no grief, as I no harms / Yet love thy dead who long lay in thine arms." The poem puts transient experience into a more durable form. It will outlast its writer and have a performative effect to "protect" their children "from step-dame's injury" and to preserve her memory and her request: "With some sad sighs honour my absent hearse; / And kiss this paper for thy love's dear sake, / Who with salt tears this last farewell did take" (224). The request is all the more moving for its restraint. It asks only for "some sad sighs" and a kiss. Bradstreet's poetry translates world into word in the hope of having that word affect the world.

Although Puritans did not consider marriage a sacrament, they did consider married love a religious duty and source of happiness. Puritan poetry, unlike poetry in the tradition of courtly love, is frequently addressed to spouses. In

"To My Dear and Loving Husband" the love of wife and husband is both a metaphor for God's love in heaven and a way to it: "Then while we live, in love let's so persevere / That when we live no more, we may live ever" (225). This world is linked to the next, and earthly love for husband and wife is commanded as a living metaphor for the love of God.

Misfortune, particularly the deaths of those we love, is doubly hard, because the speaker wonders how such grief can coexist with the love of a provident God. In her elegy for her grandchild Elizabeth, Bradstreet begins by bidding farewell but cannot end there. She asks, "why should I once bewail thy fate," because the child is now in heaven, but cannot end there either. She notes that, in the order of nature, "trees do rot when they are grown," and "plums and apples" fall only after they are "thoroughly ripe" (235). Puritans believed not only in the general providence of God, but also in special providences, sudden interventions in the natural order of things whose very improbability indicated their divine origin. So "plants new set to be eradicate, / And buds new blown to have so short a date" had to be "by His hand alone that guides nature and fate" (235). This acceptance depends on humility about the intentions of God but offers a third way between comforting presumption and equally blind defiance, as in her elegy on her grandson Simon Bradstreet. Simon is "Cropt by th' Almighty's hand; yet is He good" (237). There is no way to resolve this contradiction, to demand some explanation from God, or to exact vengeance for this affront, as Melville's Ahab tried to do, without much success. There is willed acceptance in the absence of understanding: "With dreadful awe before Him let's be mute, / Such was His will, but why, let's not dispute" (237). It is a choice.

A similar contingency informs Bradstreet's "Verses upon the Burning of Our House." The poem begins in terror and loss, with the hope that no one else will have to endure such fire: "That fearful sound of 'Fire!' and 'Fire!' / Let no man know is my desire" (292). The usual consolations, that the house belonged to God and that he might have taken more, are true enough, but the speaker cannot rest with either them or the harsh Manichean advice to "Raise up thy thoughts above the sky / That dunghill mists away may fly." Only when heaven itself is figured as another, better house, "With glory richly furnished, / Stands permanent though this be fled," can the speaker end, and then only with a request: "The world no longer let me love, / My hope and treasure lies above" (293). She can pray that she will eventually stop loving the world, but she has not achieved this goal yet.

In contemplating her own death in "As Weary Pilgrim," dated August 31, 1669, Bradstreet reflects that death will end "losses" and "sorrows" and that the grave that will "consume" her flesh is "the bed Christ did perfume" and the entry into marriage with him. Yet these consolations do not end the poem. It ends with a prayer and a proposal: "Lord make me ready for that day, / Then come, dear Bridegroom, come away" (294–95). Even now, she is not yet ready. Her poetry is about life on earth and the struggle to find meaning in it. The poems link biography, history, politics, and religion, the natural and supernatural orders. In them the political is the personal. Although of its time and place, her poetry still speaks to all who engage in that struggle and who look back, as she did, on a past that will help them make some sense of present and future.

Unlike Bradstreet, Roger Williams (c. 1603–1683) stayed with the ballad, a popular form intended to reach a large audience. In his *Key into the Language of America* (1643), he included thirty-two poems. These offered a complex challenge to the usual dismissals of Native Americans. For Williams they were simply other human beings with considerable natural virtues. He noted ironically that they kept many of God's commandments without knowing them, while his fellow Puritans broke these same commandments while claiming to be God's chosen people: "If Natures Sons both wild and tame, / Humane and Courteous be: / How ill becomes it Sonnes of God / To want Humanity."[10] He noted that American Indians were frequently more generous, honest, brave, altruistic, chaste, and careful of others than American Puritans, that they were born white and had become dark only through long exposure to the sun and their habit of anointing themselves with oil, and that the English had no right to their lands.

He did so, moreover, in the metaphoric, biblical language that his fellow Puritans could not help but understand, forging a linguistic community that included both groups. When he wrote that "In wildernesse, in great distresse, / These Ravens have fed me" (46), he made clear that God's providence transcended Puritan categories. When the Puritans called American Indians "ravens," they alluded to the Hebrew belief that ravens are unclean. So Williams alludes to the biblical passage in which ravens feed Elijah (I Kings 17:6) to show that God's providence includes them all.

Where most Puritans believed that typology, the belief that certain things in the Hebrew testament forecast certain things in the life of Christ, applied also to secular history and could link Israel with Massachusetts Bay and Moses with John Winthrop, Williams followed Augustine in restricting it to the Bible, so that no earthly group could claim to be the city of God or the new Israelites. In his poems he gave American Indians the language with which to charge Puritans with their pretension and hypocrisy: "We weare no Cloaths, have many Gods, / And yet our sinnes are lesse: / You are Barbarians, Pagans wild, / Your Land's the Wildernesse" (167). In these poems the Puritan logic of exclusion is turned back on them by the people they have excluded. A rich oral culture is given a voice in print. And the Puritans are charged with having brought a biblical wilderness, a moral wasteland, to a wilderness that had been merely natural.

Even now those who seek group superiority and historical exceptionalism can benefit from reading, "Boast not proud English, of thy birth and blood, / Thy brother Indian is by Birth as Good," and those who too confidently speak for God and eternity can benefit from reading, "Make sure thy second birth, else thou shalt see, / Heaven ope to Indians wild, but shut to thee" (81). Williams wrote to expand the hermeneutic networks of his time and remains pertinent in ours.

The extent to which the same may be said of Michael Wigglesworth (1631–1705) is still debated. *The Day of Doom: A Poetical Description of the Great and Last Judgment* (1662) sold out the eighteen hundred copies of its first edition within one year and remained popular in America and England for a century. *Meat out of the Eater* (1670), a long poem on the uses and meaning of affliction and solace for suffering, went through four editions in its first ten years. At that time Puritans were worried over a "declension" into confusion and secularism. In 1662, when the Halfway Covenant widened church membership and New England promptly went into a serious drought, the Puritan worldview seemed threatened by a loss of meaning and a spiritual torpor. Wigglesworth, a medical and a spiritual physician, sought to cure his flock. First in his class at Harvard, where his college oration was entitled "The Praise of Eloquence," he had turned down the presidency of Harvard because of ill health, but he was not too ill to write, and he wrote a poem to wake up his fellow Puritans, to turn familiar doctrine into intense experience. In 224 thundering stanzas of fourteener ballad in the common meter, a verse form they knew from their hymns, *The Day of Doom* summoned his considerable rhetorical and poetic skill. He used regular meter, full end rhyme, and internal leonine rhymes to hold the poem and the apparent chaos of the world together, to sing of a clearly organized supernatural order that would rule and end the confusions of the human world. "Calm was the season, and carnal reason thought so would last for ay."[11] But carnal reason would be no match for divine power. Suffering would have meaning and would end, at least for God's elect. The Puritan order would rule, if not in the individual mind, then in the final and apocalyptic analysis. This blend of poetry and rhetoric clearly persuaded its contemporary audience and was fit comfort for hard lives.

The riddles and paradoxes of *Meat out of the Eater* have more appeal to us, because "Each Paradox, is like a Box, / That Cordials rare incloseth" (143). The tone here is far more open and comforting, "That whoso will may take his fill, / And gain where no man loseth" (143). These poems pray not for better luck but for greater strength. They offer a "Light in Darkness" that "holds forth comfort from the Text, / To such as are in mind perplext" (145) and articulate clarity, comfort, and finally a sturdy resolve: "Be cheerful Suffering Saint, / Let nothing cast thee down" (275), because for the saint pain is real but temporary, while God's love is eternal. In *God's Controversy with New England*, a long poem written in 1662 but not published until late in the nineteenth century, Wigglesworth wrote a valediction in his own voice, also filled with love: "Cheer on, sweet souls, my heart is with you all, / And shall be with you, maugre Sathan's might: / And whereso'ere this body be a Thrall, / Still in New-England shall be my delight" (102). So it would remain. Generations of Puritans sought and found comfort in his poetry, particularly *The Day of Doom*. When Edward Taylor's wife, Elizabeth, was dying, the verses on her lips were not her husband's but Michael Wigglesworth's.

Despite conjectures, there is no compelling evidence that Edward Taylor (c. 1642–1729) either pursued or forbade the publication of his poetry. He did, however, preserve the poems in a large, leather-bound manuscript volume, passed down to Ezra Stiles, Taylor's grandson and president of Yale, and on to the Yale library, where Thomas Johnson found it in 1937. He published his collection in 1939. Thomas Davis and Virginia Davis collected more poetry and published it in 1981. The poems reveal yet another orthodox Puritan, but they also reveal how broad and various a category that is. Where Anne Bradstreet and Roger Williams read God's world as intrinsically metaphorical, and Michael Wigglesworth avoided metaphors not sanctioned by biblical precedent, Taylor used metaphors for their epistemological and devotional value but also explored their limits.

Like the English metaphysical poets, he went well beyond a simple description of the natural world to a wit and humor intended to surprise, to link the world to its deeper meanings, and to awaken the attention and affections of both himself and his readers. He aimed for a *discordia concors*, a discord that would lead to a deeper harmony, within both the poet and the world. Later, John Dryden and Samuel Johnson would attack this literary correlative to a worldview they did not share, yet such figures occur in both the Geneva and the King James Bible, and the notion that God had written both the scriptures and the creatures makes God look rather like a metaphysical poet, shocking us out of our inattention so that we may find the deeper harmonies within an apparently disordered world.

One reason for Taylor to follow these examples is evident in "The Ebb and Flow." A Puritan saint was expected both to have a profoundly transformative conversion experience, homologous to Saul's sudden transformation into Paul on the road to Damascus, and then to maintain that high level of commitment, clarity, and fervor throughout life. So Taylor worried about declension not only in his colony and congregation but also in himself. In that first experience of grace, "My heart was made thy tinder box" and easily flamed up at "holy Sparks of Heavenly Fire."[12] Yet now Taylor has become a minister, a role he figures through a surprising image suggestive of Catholic and Anglican priests: "But now my Heart is made thy Censar trim, / Full of thy golden Altars fire, / To offer up Sweet Incense in / Unto thyselfe intire" (470). A censer must hold fire over time and is, as every celebrant knows, always in danger of going out. Now that the original experience of affective intensity has been confirmed by a lifelong vocation with attendant duties, "If find my tinder scarce thy sparks can feel" (470).

Although every preacher, teacher, and writer has had this experience – the realization that inspiration follows its own schedule – in Puritanism this descent into the ordinary had grave portents. Perhaps the poet was deceiving himself all along: "Hence doubts out bud for feare thy fire in mee / 'S a mocking Ignis Fatuus" or merely the remains of a fire now "hid in ashes" (470). The hard realization is that, like the tides, the fire comes from, belongs to, and is controlled by God: "Yet when the bellows of thy Spirit blow / Away mine ashes, then thy fire doth glow" (470). Although the poet could not retain the fire, he could use poetry to translate it into a more enduring form that would enable him to recall that first experience of God's grace and to prepare for the next.

In *God's Determinations Touching His Elect*, finished around 1682, Taylor wrote a theologically conservative but metaphorically inventive and even comic poem, to mock pride and despair and to encourage poor, doubting Christians. From 1682 to 1725 he wrote the *Preparatory Meditations*, two series of poems to prepare himself for the Lord's Supper, given every six weeks at his church in Westfield, Massachusetts. These poems were based on the biblical passages on which he preached the sermons in church. For Taylor the Lord's Supper was Christ's metaphor for his metaphorical self and was not to be taken lightly. When he felt his own flock insufficiently prepared for communion, Taylor withheld it from them. The stakes were high, but God had offered assistance in a Bible and a world intrinsically metaphorical.

In his *Treatise Concerning the Lord's Supper*, Taylor is quite explicit about both the justification and the need for image and metaphor: "Natural things are not unsuitable to illustrate supernaturals by. For Christ in his parables doth illustrate supernatural things by natural, and if it were not thus, we could arrive at no knowledge of supernatural things, for we are not able to see above naturals."[13] Where Augustine had limited typology to the Bible itself, Taylor extended typological reading to all creation. The natural world was rich with supernatural meaning placed there by God and awaiting our attention. In the first poem of his second series of *Preparatory Meditations*, Taylor read the "glory of the world slickt up in types / In all choise things chosen to typify" (2.1, 83). Things meant, were chosen to mean, and were to be read for their supernatural meaning.

Indeed, in "The Preface," in *God's Determinations*, we see God creating a world of similes and metaphors: "Who Lac'd and Fillitted the earth so fine, / With Rivers like greem Ribbons Smaragdine? / Who made the Sea's its Selvedge, and it locks / Like a Quilt Ball within a Silver Box?" The flood of metaphors goes far beyond those used in the Bible: "Who in this Bowling Alley bowld the Sun?" (387). Even bowling has divine significance. The comic joy is necessary, because "Man at muze, and in a maze doth stand," while "still his heart for fear doth pant within" (389). But the "Almighty this foreseeing" sends aid, "makes to shine / Transplendent Glory in his Grace Divine" (399). Taylor is a skilled disputant: Christ and Satan are given good arguments and good poetry in the contest for human souls. Christ reassures in lilting rhymes worthy of Noel Coward: "Oh Cheer, Cheer up, come see. / Is anything too deare, my Dove, / Is anything too good, my Love / To get or give for thee?" (414). But Satan is a canny psychologist and knows that depravity and doubt dwell not just in theological argument but also in the human heart: "This Language of thy heart doth this impart / I am a Saint, if thou no Sinner art" (425). In other dialogues, Saint answers Soul's own doubts and those from "Satans Temptations" (441), but Satan is far from silenced. He is a wily sophist with evidence from the "Uncharitable Cariages [*sic*] of Christians" (447). Indeed, in this world, no one can finally win the argument. The conversion experience cannot be willed, only awaited and recognized.

Once it has been, the poem can end in joy. It has been a comedy all along, in both the medieval and the Renaissance senses. Like medieval comedy, it moves to a happy ending. Like Renaissance comedy, it links high and low in community. Where Herbert's notion of salvation in *The Temple* had been individual, with Christ inviting a single soul to dine, Taylor's description is communal, with a congregation of saints riding a stagecoach to heaven and singing together all the way. These are "the Saints who were / Encoacht for Heaven that sang for Joy" (458), accompanied by stringed instruments, which they help each other keep in tune: "And if a string do slip," they "set it in a more melodious Tune / And a Diviner Harmony" (459). Taylor did not restrict salvation to his own time and place: "Some few not in; and some whose Time, and Place / Block up this Coaches way do goe / As Travellers afoot, and so do trace / The Road that gives them right thereto / While in this Coach these sweetly sing / As they to Glory ride therein" (459). As the easy rhymes and smooth enjambments suggest, those finally going to heaven can "sweetly sing," but for those on earth, the singing is far more difficult.

It would seem that Taylor had everything he needed: God "Plac'd man his Pupill here, and ev'ry thing / With loads of Learning, came to tutor him" (2.41, 156). The metaphorical world could figure forth the communicable glories of God: "Thou'rt that Sun, that shines out Saving Grace" (2.68, 203). It could inspire sacred poetry: "Then Glory as a Metaphor, Il 'tende," and "my Quill shall greet / Thyselfe with Zions Song in musick Sweet" (2.100, 262–63). Salvation could be figured as saints "Padling in their Canooes apace with joyes / Along this blood red Sea" (2.78, 225) of Christ's spilling blood, an extraordinary figure that combines the Red Sea traversed by the Israelites, the crucifixion of Christ, and the canoes of Native Americans. Where Bradstreet had been inspired by "earthly comforts" that failed only because they were not "permanent," Taylor was inspired by natural beauty to think on the greater beauty of Christ. Had Christ not been more beautiful than the creatures, "true Wisdoms voice would bee, / That greater Love belong'd to these than thee" (2.120, 301).

Christ had left behind a metaphor for his metaphoric self, the Lord's Supper. "To entertain thy Guests, thou callst, and place / Allowst, with welcome, (And this is no Fable) / And with these Guests I am invited to't" (2.110, 283). This invitation led to Taylor's poetry: "And this rich banquet makes me thus a Poet" (2.110, 283). Taylor was aware that metaphor was not to be taken literally: "What feed on Humane Flesh and Blood? Strange mess! / Nature exclaims. What barbarousness is here?" (2.81, 231). To a literalist, the Lord's Supper, the notion that human beings should eat Christ's flesh and drink his blood, is cannibalistic nonsense: "This sense of this blesst Phrase is nonsense thus. / Some other Sense makes this a metaphor" (2.81, 231). Taylor was no biblical fundamentalist, and for him the words of scripture, like the sensible world, had their primary reality as metaphor.

So Taylor had no doubts that metaphor was necessary. In his *Christographia* sermons, he argues for the necessity of metaphor and links it to Christ's mediation. It is entirely appropriate that "Christ Should abound in this Sort of Speech ... and this Sort of Speech never was expected to be literally true, nor Charged to be a lying form of Speech, but a neat Rhetorical, and Wise manner of Speaking."[14] Christ was the perfect metaphor, who spoke in metaphors, and who offered us the best copy to follow in our own writing: "This is the best Example that can be: it is a Copy written by the pen of perfect Manhood, in the Unerring hand of Godhead, in Christ and wilt thou not endeavour to Write by this Copy?" (34). The answer is, of course, yes, because "these Metaphors we spiritualized / Speak out ... spirituall Beauty cleare" (2.151, 356).

Yet that endeavor turns out to be far more difficult than such justifications might lead us to believe. Having set out to imitate Christ by using metaphors, Taylor quickly discovers that they are, although necessary, hardly sufficient, even for the purposes of devotion: "My Metaphors are but dull Tacklings tag'd / With ragged Non-Sense. Can such draw to thee / My stund affections all with Cinders clag'd?" (2.36, 149). As in "The Ebb and Flow," only Christ can blow away the ashes and make the fire burn again. It is one thing to say that the natural and secular vehicle cannot be worthy of its divine tenor, but many Christians, Jesuit and Puritan, have argued that metaphors can figure the communicable glories of God. Not so Taylor.

Although metaphor works for the secular poetry of earth, "might yet serve / To hum a little touching terrene Shines" (2.82, 233), it cannot figure forth the glories of Christ, as Taylor makes clear in the *Christographia*: "All our pencils in all their drafts attain not to anything of the Excellencies of Christ's operations" (468). Verbal metaphors remain inadequate. So do natural metaphors created by God: "The Suns bright Glory's but a smoky thing" to figure forth any divine tenor, and "All other glories, that from Creatures spring / Are less than that: but both are sorry Swashes" (2.100, 262). So "the Worlds Estate's not able" (1.9, 19) to provide satisfactory metaphors. Neither is the Bible. Taylor writes of the metaphors in Canticles, or the Song of Solomon, "But yet methinks the glory of thy hands / ... / Metaphorized here too faintly stands" (2.122, 305). Taylor makes this position clear in his *Christographia*: "There are Some things whose Excellency is flourished over with metaphors. We borrow the Excellency of other things to varnish over their Excellency withall. But Grace excels all Metaphors. The varnish laid upon it doth but darken, and not decorate it: its own Colours are too glorious to be made more glorious, by any Colour of Secular glory" (253). Any and all metaphors of Taylor, nature, or the Bible were bound to be insufficient. This fact might seem a death knell for poetry, but for Taylor it became a poetics.

He had been commanded to sing and told in advance that, this side of heaven, no one song would ever be sufficient. So he kept on singing with metaphors that he knew were inadequate and therefore free. God bowls the sun; souls paddle their canoes on a Red Sea of Christ's blood. In "Upon Wedlock and the Death of Children," Taylor begins with the common figure, found also in Bradstreet, of children as flowers, beautiful but short lived and gathered to God. Yet the metaphor will not hold: "But oh! the tortures, Vomit, screechings, groans, / And six weeks Fever would pierce hearts like stones" (469). The agony of dying children is nothing like the quiet beauty of flowers. Metaphors come from nature, "and nature fault would finde / Were not thy Will, my Spell Charm, Joy, and Gem" (469). The only resolution is in the will of God, and that will is a matter of speculative realism rather than comprehensible fact. That will was figured forth in nature, history, and scripture. Taylor had, like many others, been commanded to use these in his songs.

One way to understand his sense of the limits of metaphor is to reflect that Taylor's theology was unusually Christocentric. As he explained in the *Christographia*, he believed that Christ, not the Father, had created the world: "The Father himself executes nothing: but hath committed all the executing of his Decrees unto the Son, and this wisdom executing of the Decrees appears in 1. The Works of Creation" (114). This is not heresy. Paul makes a similar suggestion in Colossians 1:16. But it is unusual, and it links all metaphor to Christ's mediation, to the struggles of this world to apprehend the next.

But "Earth is not heaven: Faith not Vision. No" (2.96, 255). Taylor "fain would something say: / Lest Silence should indict me" (1.21, 35), but even at his most enthusiastic, he can be no more sure of his song than of his election. He must make his poetry, then, on the paradox of a language he knows to be necessary but inadequate, commanded but untrustworthy. The passion is in the paradox, and at times he sounds like Samuel Beckett: "To see thy Kingly Glory in to throng. / I can, yet cannot tell this Glory just, / In Silence bury't, must not, yet I must" (1.17, 30). Not to sing at all would have been disobedience and despair. To imagine one's song satisfactory would have been presumption and pride. Thus Taylor, in many poems, yearned for death so that at last he would finally be able to sing aright the songs he had tried to sing in life.

That ambition and struggle continued in Jane Colman Turell (1708–1735), the daughter of Jane Clark and Benjamin Colman, minister of Brattle Street Church and president of Harvard College. Like Bradstreet, Turell had access to a great library and put it to good use. At age seventeen she paraphrased Psalm 137 to lament "Our lyres by us forsaken and unstrung,"[15] and in another poem,

"To My Muse, December 29, 1725," she invoked her muse to fill her mind and poetry "With rich ideas, great and unconfin'd. / Instruct me in those secret arts that lie / Unseen to all but to a poet's eye" (791). With a nice sense of wit and balance she asked, "O let me burn with Sappho's noble fire, / But not like her for faithless man expire" (791). She hoped to "be worthy of poet's name" (792) and clearly was, but when she died at twenty-seven, her husband printed only a little of her poetry, explaining, "I might add to these some pieces of wit and humor, which if published would give a brighter idea of her to some sort of readers; but as her heart was set on graver and better subjects, and her pen much oftener employed about them, so I choose to omit them, though innocent enough" (788). Her father added that "she was sometimes fired with a laudable ambition of raising the honor of her sex" (788), but the details and the poems are missing. We can only mourn what we have lost, not because of a lack of fire and ability on the part of the poet, but because of casual censorship by those who thought they knew better about what to value, even as some later readers thought they knew better about Puritan poetry.

Bradstreet, Williams, Wigglesworth, Taylor, Turell, and more than two hundred other Puritans wrote poetry, neither as a forbidden act of heretical defiance nor as a song of self-assurance, but as a part of their religion, an unending struggle to connect transient life and lasting truth, to work out the meanings of life, to connect the natural and supernatural orders. All varied. None were typical. Yet these five are linked to the hundreds of others who wrote poetry both individually distinctive and collectively recognizable as that of American Puritans. Although its forms and materials came from many places, the poetry was, from the start, American. Although its quality varied, it was, from the start, poetry, and much of it is still worth reading now.

Notes

1. Samuel Willard, *A Compleat Body of Divinity in Two Hundred and Fifty Expository Lectures on the Assembly's Shorter Catechism* (Boston: B. Green and S. Kneeland, 1726), p. 37.
2. Alexander Richardson, *The Logicians Schoolmaster* (London, 1657), quoted in Perry Miller, *The New England Mind: The Seventeenth Century* (Boston: Beacon, 1961), p. 162.
3. Edward Taylor, *The Poems of Edward Taylor*, ed. Donald E. Stanford (New Haven, Conn.: Yale University Press, 1960), p. 283. Subsequent quotations are from this edition and are documented parenthetically. Quotations from the first and second series of *Preparatory Meditations* are cited with the series number and poem number in addition to the page number.

4. John Cotton, preface to *The Whole Booke of Psalms Faithfully Translated into English Metre* (Cambridge, Mass.: Stephen Daye, 1640), quoted in Perry Miller and Thomas H. Johnson (eds.), *The Puritans* (New York: Harper, 1963), vol. 2, pp. 670–72.

5. Quoted in Miller and Johnson, *The Puritans*, vol. 2, p. 556.

6. Cotton Mather, *Magnalia Christi Americana, or The Ecclesiastical History of New England, In Seven Books* (1702), ed. Thomas Robbins (Hartford, Conn.: Silas Andrus, 1855), vol. 2, p. 406.

7. Anne Bradstreet, *The Works of Anne Bradstreet*, ed. Jeannine Hensley (Cambridge, Mass.: Harvard University Press, 1967), p. 279. Subsequent quotations are from this edition and are documented parenthetically.

8. Thomas Taylor, *A Man in Christ, or: A New CREATURE. To Which Is Added a Treatise, Containing Meditations from the CREATURES* (London: Printed for I. Bartlet at the gilt Cup in Cheapside, 1628), pp. 2–3.

9. Mather, *Magnalia*, vol. 2, p. 135.

10. Roger Williams, *The Complete Writings of Roger Williams, I – A Key into the Language of America*, ed. James H. Trumbull (New York: Russell and Russell, 1963), p. 39. Subsequent quotations are from this edition and are documented parenthetically.

11. Michael Wigglesworth, *The Poems of Michael Wigglesworth*, ed. Ronald A. Bosco (New York: University Press of America, 1989), p. 11. Subsequent quotations are from this edition and are documented parenthetically.

12. Taylor, *The Poems of Edward Taylor*, p. 470. Subsequent quotations are from this edition and are documented parenthetically.

13. Edward Taylor, *Edward Taylor's Treatise Concerning the Lord's Supper*, ed. Norman S. Grabo (East Lansing: Michigan State University Press, 1966), p. 43.

14. Edward Taylor, *Edward Taylor's Christographia*, ed. Norman S. Grabo (New Haven, Conn.: Yale University Press, 1962), p. 273. Subsequent quotations are from this edition and are documented parenthetically.

15. Jane Colman Turell, *Memoirs of the Life and Death of the Pious and Ingenious Mrs. Jane Turell … Chiefly Collected from Her Own Manuscripts (Boston, 1735, Quoted in The Heath Anthology of American Literature)*, ed. Paul Lauter, 6th ed. (Boston: Houghton Mifflin Harcourt, 2009), vol. A, p. 788. Subsequent quotations are from this edition and are documented parenthetically.

Chapter 4

Confronting Death: The New England Puritan Elegy

JEFFREY A. HAMMOND

Difficult Commemorations

As hundreds of extant specimens reveal, the funeral elegy was the quintessential poem of early New England; the passing of a pious soul virtually mandated a verse commemoration. These poems were largely ignored, however, in the revaluation of American Puritan verse prompted by the rediscovery of Edward Taylor's poetry. It is not difficult to understand why; with its sing-song prosody, formulaic images, and predictable rhetoric, the Puritan elegy has always been difficult to appreciate either aesthetically or psychologically. Given the vibrant intersection of art and mourning for which the poetry of loss is traditionally valued, we might well ask: Where is the poetry and where is the sense of loss?

Such questions were being raised while these poems were still being written. The young Benjamin Franklin, posing as the satirical Silence Dogood in his brother's *New-England Courant,* underscored the longstanding popularity of such elegies by sarcastically praising a typical example as a "new species of Poetry." Franklin comments that this lament for "a Wife, a Daughter, and a Sister," creates "a Sort of an Idea of the Death of *Three Persons,*" which "consequently must raise *Three Times* as much Grief and Compassion in the Reader."[1] Then comes Franklin's famous elegiac recipe: "Having chose the Person, take all his Virtues, Excellencies, &c. and if he have not enough, you may borrow some to make up a sufficient Quantity: To these add his last Words" and "a Handful or two of Melancholly Expressions," and pour the mix into "the empty Scull of some *young Harvard.*" After a liberal sprinkling of "double Rhimes," the recipe concludes, "you must spread all upon Paper, and if you can procure a Scrap of Latin to put at the End, it will garnish it mightily; then having affixed your Name at the Bottom, with a *Maestus Composuit,* you will have an Excellent Elegy."[2]

Parts of this chapter draw on my book *The American Puritan Elegy: A Literary and Cultural Study* (Cambridge: Cambridge University Press, 2000).

Franklin's parodic "ingredients" accurately summarize the artistic failings of the Puritan elegy as post-Enlightenment critics have defined them. Instead of the distinctive voice of an individual poet, a generic speaker recites a chant-like recitation of loss; instead of a concrete portrait of the deceased, virtues are seemingly "borrowed" to depict someone too good to be real; and instead of fresh language, standard "Melancholly Expressions" abound. William Empson once remarked that the occasion of death has always been "the trigger of the literary man's biggest gun";[3] given the performative demands of elegy, why did early New Englanders commemorate their dead in so formulaic a manner? Their choice seems especially odd given the central role of texts within Puritan culture; a seeming indifference to artistic form in elegy does not square well with the Bible-stimulated attention to language apparent in other Puritan writings, especially sermons. Moreover, educated New Englanders were acquainted with literary precedents that might have countered their rigidity in elegy. Taylor owned copies of the *Iliad*, Theocritus, and Horace and was familiar with the English metaphysicals; Anne Bradstreet read Sidney and the French Calvinist poet Guillaume Du Bartas; and many Puritans, including Cotton Mather, held Milton's poetry in high regard. When early New Englanders turned to elegy, however, they shunned Milton's example in "Lycidas" by adhering to the very conventions that gave Franklin such an easy target.

We cannot blame a lack of poetic talent – at least, not entirely. Although Edward Taylor's poetic gifts are abundantly clear from his meditative verse, there is little to distinguish his elegies from the productions of hundreds of lesser poets. Taylor's elegy for David Dewey, for example, anticipates Silence Dogood's recipe with alarming precision. Dewey is portrayed in precisely the "Three-Persons" manner that Franklin lampoons: as a father bringing his children "up to Christ," a husband whose grace "drencht" his "Consort's heart," and a citizen whose "Grace did make thy Township Neighbourhood / Among us, very pleasant, usefull, good." Franklin's critique is also borne out in a highly generalized depiction of the deceased: Dewey's "Conversation," which "gave a Shine / Of Prudence, Peace, and Piety Divine," answers the recipe's call for a recitation of abstract "Virtues" and "Excellencies." Taylor might even be accused of "borrowing" some of these virtues by reaching into an unseen realm to describe Dewey's persistence as a saint who "Cudgeld" his body of sin, never slacking the "raine" that he kept on a carnal element portrayed in equally paradigmatic terms. Smaller touches also confirm Taylor's commitment to the elegiac formula. Although he keeps "Melancholly Expressions" to a minimum, he proclaims that Dewey's survivors must borrow his "Coffin's Cambarick" to "wipe off of our Eyes the Tears of Sorrow." Taylor even manages to "procure a Scrap of Latin," as the recipe advises, to "garnish" the poem: his *"Sic flevit mastus amicus, E. T."* is an anticipatory echo of Franklin's *"Maestus Composuit."*[4]

We would expect a poet as talented as Taylor to have revealed more about Dewey the individual and less about Dewey the generic saint, whose carnal element would be raised "at the Resurrection of the Just" to rejoin the soul to sing "with Saints and Angels" in the celestial choir. Such a poem might have contained less dogma and more reflection on the cycles of nature, the power of love or memory to conquer time, or the permanence that art conveys to the deceased, whose immortality is assured by a verbal monument more lasting than bronze. Although these options were available to a poet whose Harvard schooling acquainted him with their classical precedents, Taylor made other choices. He did not see the result as an artistic failure, either; published with Dewey's writings in a commemorative pamphlet, this was the only complete Taylor poem to see print during the poet's lifetime.

Issues of Assessment

The central challenge of elegy, broadly considered, lies in negotiating the competing demands of immanence and transcendence. The paradox of observing a death in time by invoking the supposed timelessness of art helps explain why, as O. B. Hardison observed long ago, critics have never known quite what to do with occasional poems like elegies.[5] Indeed, the historical conditions of elegy work against the traditional assumption that great art somehow transcends historical conditions. The canonical elegy, from "Lycidas" on down, produces just such transcendence – or, more accurately, its illusion – by turning the occasion of death into an opportunity for seemingly timeless reflections that deflect attention from the occasion itself.

To approach the Puritan elegy on its own terms requires us to suspend formal and thematic expectations shaped by such classic poems of loss as Shelley's "Adonais," Tennyson's *In Memoriam*, and Whitman's "Lilacs" – all of which participate, more or less, in the pastoral tradition embodied in "Lycidas." As Hyatt Waggoner noted in the late 1960s, "To remember that while Puritan Milton was writing 'Lycidas,' his American coreligionists were composing acrostic elegies is to recall how provincial American Puritanism quickly became."[6] Ruth Wallerstein exposed a basic critical assumption underlying such assessments by claiming that Milton "universalizes" his grief by putting it "not in a religious form but in an artistic form."[7] Although Wallerstein's distinction between the "artistic" and the "religious" might seem valid from a New Critical perspective, early New Englanders would not have accepted or perhaps even recognized it. The intermingling of these impulses within Puritan discourse was too pervasive to permit so clean a separation.

Modern readers might find it odd that although David Dewey died at what we would consider a "young" thirty-six, Taylor does not bother to mention what killed him. The omission was typical – and reflective of a certain pragmatism surrounding the writing of elegies in early New England. The visibility of death and dying within its close-knit communities invested elegy with even higher stakes than Empson imagined; these stakes, however, had less to do with the production of art than with the reassertion of social and ideological continuities. Although the rate of infant mortality was probably lower in New England than in Old England, it has been estimated that in seventeenth-century Ipswich and Andover, one in ten children died at birth or shortly thereafter; in more densely populated areas like Boston, the rate may have been one in three.[8] As late at 1734, Franklin brooded over a contemporary calculation that "one half of Mankind" did not live to the age of sixteen, while another quarter died before reaching thirty.[9] Given these conditions, it might seem less strange that Puritans saw death not as an aberration but as a confirmation – albeit an especially poignant one – of the normal scheme of things. In their view, to "explain" death in physical terms was to offer no explanation at all; for that, one needed to turn to theology.

Puritans thus approached elegy as a situational reaffirmation of an entire belief system. On the individual level, to die was to face life's decisive question: Am I saved? On the communal level, a believer's death offered an occasion for celebrating society's chief purpose: to nurture saved souls. Theology and mission combined to make formal and thematic originality in elegy beside the point; death's disruption was to be countered with an insistent reassertion of expected patterns of doctrine and experience. Because the religio-aesthetic import of death was thought to be timeless and universal, Puritans conventionalized their elegies to the point of essential sameness, subordinating the traditional qualities of good poetry – originality in thought and expression – to the goal of demonstrating and encouraging a godly response to loss. Because this goal applied to everyone, the elegy shared a notion of audience with the plain-style sermon, especially the funeral sermon; the prosody, imagery, and themes of these poems bear out the Puritan view of elegy as an insistently democratic genre. Although poems for teachers and clergy might contain learned allusions appropriate to the deceased's occupation, elegists generally aimed to write as clearly and directly as possible for the widest conceivable audience, including those who would experience the poem through oral recitation. By one estimate, only about half of adult males in seventeenth-century New England were literate;[10] although more recent studies have suggested that this figure is too low,[11] the "double Rhimes" that Franklin mocked become more defensible in light of the oral dimension of literary experience in Puritan culture.[12]

An elegiac stress on didacticism and accessibility did not hold up well under subsequent artistic standards that privileged the formal beauty of texts at the expense of their immediate cultural function. These standards remain powerful: it is only fairly recently that critics have been able to approach elegy in light of the cultural work that it performs – as a facilitator of actual grieving within a particular historical moment. A functional approach to elegy thereby replaces the ahistorical "reader" with the historically positioned "mourner"; Peter Sacks, for example, has observed that because elegiac conventions reveal "the actual project of mourning" in an anthropological and psychological sense, elegies require attention "not so much to the figures of language as to the workings of the mind that uses them."[13] G. W. Pigman takes a similar approach to the Renaissance elegy "as part of the process of mourning rather than the poetry of praise."[14] In his study of modern elegy, Jahan Ramazani observes that "insofar as the elegy is a mimesis of mourning, psychoanalysis offers a more useful framework" than genre theory.[15] And most recently, Max Cavitch has underscored the cultural function of elegies by exploring their role in shaping social identities and categories in eighteenth- and early nineteenth-century America.

Given the predictability of its forms and the conditions of its making, the Puritan elegy is best approached neither as a universally applicable expression of loss nor as an aesthetic document aspiring to transcend time, but as a ritual script designed to orchestrate a particular process of mourning within a specific culture. Such an approach acknowledges the livelier experiential dimension of Puritanism that has emerged over the last few decades.[16] As David D. Hall has observed, "Hostile to the magic of the Catholic system, these people reinstated ritual practice at the heart of their religion."[17] Such reassertion of ritual was especially evident in funerary rites; for all their debates surrounding church polity, biblical interpretation, and the Sacraments, early New Englanders were of a mind regarding the uses and practice of elegy. For them, the value of elegiac poetry lay not in its formal beauty but in its capacity to convey religious truth. This is, of course, to state the point in modern terms. For the Puritan elegist, divine truth *was* artistic beauty; the spiritual message of elegy was both stimulus and product of its aesthetic satisfactions.

The Elegy in Early Modern England

It is in light of the ritual dimension of elegy – the notion that it can, in David Shaw's words, "comprise a kind of liturgy, releasing emotion even while controlling it"[18] – that the Puritan variant reveals its underlying nature and purposes. At root, the ritual embedded in these poems reflects the Puritan attribution of timelessness not to art but to dogma; no elegy could be a genuine *monumentum aere perennius* unless it reiterated divine truth. This view grew out of debates in Reformed England over the role that artifice and ceremony should play in commemorating the dead. Among the more radical dissenters, elaborate funerary customs were distractions from the godly duty to mourn properly. Objections among such dissenters to "Romish" funerals prompted the Westminster Convention in 1645 to endorse what had become increasingly popular practice: "Let the dead body, upon the day of Buriall, be decently attended from the house to the place appointed for publique Buriall, and there immediately interred, without any Ceremony." The opposing view is summarized in John Weever's 1631 complaint that "wee, in these days, doe not weepe and mourne at the departure of the dead, so much, nor so long, as in Christian dutie we ought."[19] This debate intensified with a rapid growth in the popularity of elegies prompted by the rise of printing and literacy, humanistic individualism, and a national pride that encouraged poets to imitate the ancients by commemorating Albion's worthies. Laments for Sidney in 1586 and for Prince Henry, son of James I, in 1612 solidified the elegy as the most common type of public verse in early modern England. A relaxation of traditional strictures on grief and its expression during the later sixteenth century contributed to this popularity,[20] as did the role played by elaborate funerary rites in shoring up the waning power of the aristocracy.[21]

Most elegists during this period took an approach to verbal mourning that drew on Elizabethan patriotism and patronage and, later, Jacobean melancholy and popular devotional traditions. This type of poem, usually called the "funeral" elegy to distinguish it from its pastoral cousin, was often incorporated into funerary rites, with the poem recited at the service and pinned to the coffin during the procession. Many Tudor and Elizabethan funeral elegies, such as the popular poems of Thomas Churchyard and George Whetstone, consisted of commemorations for nobility penned for general distribution.[22] These poems ranged from what John Draper called "Cavalier panegyric" to the more theologically oriented "Puritan lament," the latter shaped by a turn to piety and introspection influenced by Donne's 1612 "Anniversaries" for Elizabeth Drury and by the outpouring of poems at the 1646 death of the Protestant champion, the Earl of Essex. With the rise to wealth and patronage of a largely Puritan merchant class, Puritans took over the more explicitly religious elegy, stylizing its forms, intensifying its millennial fervor during the English Civil War, and using it as a vehicle for legitimizing Cromwell's rule. By midcentury, the funeral elegy was so closely associated with Puritans that an anonymous writer equated "common formall Elegies" with the "Geneva Jig."[23]

The funeral elegy posed a sharp contrast to the classically based pastoral, in which frank artifice enacted a retreat from the specific occasion of death and the mutability that it signaled into the ostensibly deathless sanctuary of art. The highly artificial and elaborate pastoral, decisively shaped by Spenser's lament for "Dido" in the "November" eclogue from *The Shepheardes Calendar* (1579) and by his poem for Sidney, or "Astrophel" (1595), was relatively rare in the nearly sixty years between the "November" eclogue and the climax of the form in "Lycidas." The subsequent canonical status of the pastoral was due, in part, to its concern with poetic vocation, a theme that culminates in "Lycidas": Milton's momentary questioning, in light of Edward King's untimely death, of his own dedication to the "thankless muse" leads to a recommitment embodied in the poem itself – a recommitment always seen, of course, in light of the subsequent achievement of *Paradise Lost*. "Lycidas" enacts an elaborately staged threat to – and recovery of – the speaker's poetic vocation, worked out through the key elements of the pastoral: an idealized landscape, nostalgia for better times, an attempt to draw on the consoling power of nature, a commingling of mourning with topical commentary, and a reassertion of continuity and purpose in response to rupture and anxiety. The emotional distancing effected by these conventions not only emulated classical restraint but enabled a shift from mourning to other tasks that could be performed *through* mourning.

English Puritans who did not share Milton's regard for the ancients or his relatively more optimistic view of human nature adhered to the more direct and "functional" sort of elegy. These poets either rejected the pastoral surface altogether or bent it back to what they saw as its religious core, as Milton himself briefly did in St. Peter's diatribe against the "Blind mouths" of corrupt clergy. Consistent with corresponding trends in preaching, liturgy, and church polity, this more severe elegiac model grounded itself more explicitly in the immediate occasion; in contrast to commemorations for "Asphodel" or "Lycidas," funeral elegies gave the real names of the deceased and focused squarely on the theological significance of the loss. Taking to heart Phoebus's lesson in "Lycidas" to shift elegiac "fame" from the realm of poetry to the realm of piety, funeral elegists rejected classical models in favor of the Bible, homiletic traditions, and the popular iconology of death embodied in funerary art, broadsides, and emblem books. Although a number of stock images – weeping willows, ministerial shepherds, and churchgoing flocks – afforded brief glimpses of a quasi-pastoral landscape, these poems took their ultimate precedent from the great biblical expressions of loss, especially David's lament for Saul and Jonathan (2 Samuel 1:19–27). Funeral elegists also saw themselves as heeding St. Paul's admonition to "rejoice with them that do rejoice, and weep with them that weep," taking care to "mind not high things" and to "be not wise in your own conceits" (Romans 12:15–16). Unlike the pastoral elegist, who was typically a university-trained man of letters speaking as a professional "poet," the funeral elegist emulated Pauline humility by presenting the poem as a frankly amateur performance that repudiated the vocational concerns of the pastoral. Although Ben Jonson, that most insistently "classical" of English poets, provided a striking example of elegiac aestheticizing by calling his son his "best piece of *poetrie*,"[24] most Puritans would have seen Jonson's trope as a tragically wrongheaded response to an occasion so momentous as death.

The Elegy in Puritan New England

At first, the more religiously explicit elegy assumed virtually identical form in both Englands. Most of the signature traits of the New England elegy appear, for example, in a poem written in 1636 by "I. L." for Reverend John Rogers of Dedham, Essex, whose grandson would become president of Harvard. Celebrating the "happy change and blessed gain" of a generalized believer, the poem ends with a call for survivors to repent in the face of a loss that signals divine disfavor with "Our sleepy formall carelessnesse, / in hearing of God's word."[25] As the Rogers family illustrates, the English audience for such poems coincided with dissenting emigrants to the New World; as a result, the plainer style of elegy proliferated there, becoming increasingly codified once the Restoration forced a sharpening of New England's cultural distinctiveness. At the same time, funerary customs grew more elaborate as a means of reinforcing a community with weakening ties to England.[26] The New England elegy also began to separate from its English counterparts by laying greater stress on the commemoration of what William Scheick has called a "collective self" that enabled survivors to absorb the deceased's piety.[27] Once it achieved definitive form, the funeral elegy enjoyed remarkable stability in New England, resisting the shift toward neoclassicism and sentimentality that marked English elegies soon after the Restoration until well into the eighteenth century.

Such conservatism reflected the social realities of New England's small communities; Boston's population at the turn of the eighteenth century was only around 7,000.[28] Puritan elegies were written for more intimate circles of readers than those addressed by the more self-consciously "literary" poems published in London and the university towns. As I have suggested, they were also written for different kinds of readers. Unlike Milton, whose poem appeared in a commemorative volume produced by and for Christian humanists intimately acquainted with classical discourse, New England's elegists eschewed literary conventions that might prove distracting to the uninitiated. Their poems were not written to be "appreciated" as art in anything like a modern sense, or even in the sense that Milton's Cambridge readers would have appreciated "Lycidas." Rather, they were written to facilitate a process of grieving that was thought to be as valid for the illiterate farmer as for the university-trained minister.

In the Puritan view, conveying the religious significance of loss did not require a poet's skill so much as a prophet's vision; indeed, the pious dead presumably offered more inspiration than even the most eloquent poet could handle. As Urian Oakes declared in his famous elegy for Thomas Shepard, Jr.,

> Poetick Raptures are of no esteem,
> Daring *Hyperboles* have here no place,
> Luxuriant wits on such a copious Theme,
> Would shame themselves, and blush to shew their face.
>   Here's worth enough to overmatch the skill
>   Of the most stately Poet *Laureat's Quill*.[29]

So hyperbolic a rejection of hyperbole reflected a determination to address loss in the real world of small towns and congregations. While the imaginary countryside of the pastoral elegy was antithetical to the actual social spaces – the court, the city, the university – where it was most popular, the Puritan elegy resisted any such deflection from the local. This social grounding is reflected in how elegies were used; poems were recited within grieving families and communities, meditated on in acts of private devotion, copied into diaries and commonplace books, exchanged by ministers, and often published as broadsides. Even unpublished elegies circulated in manuscript far beyond the time and place of their writing, thereby achieving a measure of permanence within the collective memory. Taylor, for example, sent a poem on the deaths of his two infant daughters to former college roommate Samuel Sewall, who gave a copy to Cotton Mather, who in turn reprinted two of its stanzas at the end of a sermon on the proper handling of grief. And in an elegy for Urian Oakes, Mather was able to cite seven elegists in a chain of serial commemoration that reached back more than thirty years.[30]

As Mather's commemorative chain suggests, elegists did not assert their individual roles as poets so much as they inhabited the broader paradigm of one pious soul commemorating another. The poem itself underwent a similar deflating of its status as a unique artifact by entering a larger body of oral and written texts that remained in constant circulation. This nexus of mutually reinforcing texts – other elegies, other kinds of didactic and devotional poetry, sermons, journals, prose meditations, and such popular manuals as Edward Pearse's *The Great Concern, or, A Serious Warning to a Timely and Thorough Preparation for Death* (Boston, 1705) and Cotton Mather's *Awakening Thoughts on the Sleep of Death* (Boston, 1712) – made a virtual industry of encouraging an ongoing preparation for death. The essence of the Puritan *ars moriendi* lay in Pearse's claim that *"The meditation of Death … greatly promotes our spiritual Life; therefore walk much among the Tombs, and converse much and frequently with the Thoughts of a dying hour."*[31]

The Sin of Grief and the Exemplary Deceased

For all its self-proclaimed plainness, the Puritan elegy scripted an experientially elaborate process of mourning that worked to absorb the death at hand – indeed, death's very existence – into an underlying meditative dynamic based on the conviction that although death reflected the ongoing legacy of the Fall, it also offered a portal to eternal bliss. Because the death to be truly feared was not the end of earthly life but eternal damnation, Puritans reframed the great question of elegy – Why must we die? – in terms set forth in Ezekiel: "Why *will* ye die?" (33:11). To this, Thomas Shepard, Sr., gave the standard answer: "The great cause why so many people die, and perish everlastingly, is because they will; every man that perisheth is his own butcherer or murderer."[32] The wages of sin encompassed not just death but ordinary human responses to it. Because excessive grief signaled an overattachment to the fallen world and opposition to the divine will in taking the deceased, Puritan elegies often convey ambivalence toward their reason for having been written. Although it was perfectly natural to mourn a loss, the problem lay in the fact that it *was* natural; everyone did it, whether saved or damned, but only the true believer was capable of moving from natural grief to renewed faith.

The first step in this process was to consider what, exactly, one was grieving for. Samuel Willard of Boston's Old South Church proclaimed that when saints die, "there is no greater Argument to be found that we should excite our selves to mourn by, then the remembrance that they were *Saints*."[33] The proper object of commemoration was not the individual deceased so much as the sanctity that he or she presumably possessed – the trait that made the poem worth writing to begin with. As English dissenter William Ames insisted, "inasmuch as faith is in each believer individually it is in the form of those that are called."[34] The dead appear so much alike in Puritan elegies because the goal was to make this "form" of faith as legible as possible. The resulting emphasis was not on the particularity of the deceased but on the glorified identity that all saints were destined to attain. We see this emphasis in Taylor's commemoration of Dewey as a "noble Soul refin'd, all bright."[35] At "the Resurrection of the Just," Dewey's purified body would rise

> out of the Dust,
> Transcending brightest Gold, and shining Sun
> In Glory clear; to which thy Soul shall run
> And reunite, and perfectly repair
> Thy Person spoild while 'ts parts asunder are.

By portraying the dead as distillations of piety, elegists pushed their readers toward what English Puritan Richard Sibbes called "spiritual mourning": sorrow for one's own sins. As Sibbes insisted, this was the only grief that did any good: "Every mourner and weeper is not therein blessed, except his outward losses, and crosses, and occasions, be an occasion through God's blessing and a means to bring him to spiritual sorrow and mourning."[36] Unlike natural mourning, spiritual mourning was considered a "happy estate and condition" because it increased the survivor's likelihood for salvation. Puritans thus practiced with a vengeance the truism that funerary rites are not for the dead but for the living. The belief in purgatory had been swept away by the earliest Reformers, along with the attendant practice of praying for the dead, especially those who seemed saved.[37] Why pray for someone who was now seated in eternal bliss? As Willard proclaimed, when death, "which is in it self an evil thing," comes to "a Child of God," faith transforms it into "a thing of very great worth."[38] To mourn for those who have received their reward, Willard insisted, is merely "superfluous."[39]

If mourning the dead was superfluous, heeding their spiritual example was not. "We should be so affected with the death of such," Nathanael Appleton urged, "*as to be more careful than ever, to imitate all that we saw great & excellent in them."*[40] Although the Puritan elegy might seem to have idealized the dead beyond any hope of imitation, the task of assimilating them to the broad patterns of sanctity resulted in abstract diction that made them seem more imitable. Who would not wish to become a soul who was, as Oakes portrayed Thomas Shepard, Jr., "Lovely, Worthy, Peerless," "Precious, Pleasant," "Learned, Prudent, Pious, Grave, and True," and "a Faithful Friend?" (*APS*, p. 213). So preserved, the pious dead were written into permanence as ongoing spurs to the survivors' spiritual health. Samuel Danforth II thus hoped that Thomas Leonard's "Posterity / May imitate his Virtues, and may say / His GOD shall be our GOD" (*APS*, p. 490). To that end, it was

> ... proper that to mind we call
> The Greatness of our Loss; the qualities
> And Usefulness of our deceased Friend,
> Whose Pilgrimage on Earth is at an end.
> (*APS*, p. 488)

This search for "qualities" and "Usefulness" prompted elegists to assimilate the dead to the "Pattern and Patron of Virtue" that John Norton found in Anne Bradstreet (*APS*, p. 460). Mather similarly encouraged Oakes's proper *"Use"* by his survivors (*CM*, p. 53). And in a poem for President Charles Chauncy of Harvard, Taylor extolled the deceased's ongoing value as a paradigm of holiness, "Diffusing all by Pattern, Preaching clear Rich Pray'res, & such like thro' his Practice heer."[41]

Elegists undertaking to "diffuse" this pious "Pattern" sought to provide clear evidence that the dead, as Willard put it, had "lived and died Saints": "this onely will endure and be fresh and Flourishing, when Marble it self shall be turned into common dust."[42] Perhaps surprisingly, the stress on lessons to be derived from the saintly dead applied even to deeply personal losses. How, Taylor asks in a poem for his first wife, Elizabeth Fitch, will their children and grandchildren know her "Vertuous shine" "unless I them define?" (*TMP*, p. 111). Benjamin Tompson similarly declares that he has written his elegy on his sister-in-law Mary "for the imitation of the living."[43] Generalized depictions of the dead were also common in English funeral elegies[44] and in funeral sermons on both sides of the Atlantic;[45] such portraiture had affinities with the Renaissance genre of the "character,"[46] which exerted a major influence on Puritan biography generally.[47] New England's elegists often went further, however, by depicting the dead as no longer merely human – the precise result, Puritans believed, of a saint's glorification. Mather proclaimed that even an appropriation of the biblical *ecce homo* was insufficient to describe what Urian

Oakes had become by dying: "see the *Man* / (Almost too *small* a word)!" (*CM*, p. 59). While the primary model for saintly panegyric was David's lament for Saul and Jonathan, the desired outcome came from the resurrective tropes of the New Testament, especially Jesus's words on hearing of the death of Lazarus: "This sickness is not unto death, but for the glory of God, that the Son of God might be glorified thereby" (John 11:4). By depicting the death of a saint as Christ saw Lazarus's death, New England's elegists tried to move their readers from mourning a loss to anticipating a resurrection.

Reading the Dead as Ritual Repentance

The saintly paradigm was especially evidenced by a "good death," also a standard feature in English funeral elegies.[48] The function of what Franklin's recipe listed as the deceased's "last Words" was to confirm the dying saint's eager embrace of a self whose carnal element was already "dead." Deathbed speech was invested with quasi-prophetic status, as when Taylor recorded Dewey's dying response to the weather: *"The Wind is high*, quoth hee, / *But by to Morrow I'st above it be!"*[49] Taylor provided similar witness to the "holy Counsill" and "Death Bed Charges" that emerged during Samuel Hooker's final hours: Hooker, observing his numb hands and arms, proclaims that "They are Dead, you see, and I / Have done with them" (*TMP*, p. 119). Such testimonies of deathbed stoicism brought particular consolation in poems of personal loss. Cotton Mather took immense comfort from his wife Abigail's final utterance: "I faint, till thy last words to mind I call; / Rich Words! Heav'n, Heav'n will make amends for all" (*CM*, p. 44). John Cotton attributed a similarly pious leave-taking to his daughter Sara: "Pray, my Dear Father, Let me now go Home!" (*APS*, p. 382). In their recapitulation of St. Paul's assertion that "I have finished my course, I have kept the faith" (2 Timothy 4:7), these deathbed utterances repeatedly conflated the personal with the biblical. An anonymous poet confirmed the Pauline stance in the venerable John Alden of Plymouth and Duxbury, who "with St. *Paul*, his *course* now *finished*, / Unclothed, is quietly put to bed": "His Family and Christian friends he blest / Before he did betake himself to rest."[50] An especially striking example of the neobiblical death appears in Taylor's elegy for Zecharia Symmes, an "aged Nazarite" who utters the deathbed cry, "my Head! me head!" (*TMP*, p. 22). Although Symmes's words hardly constitute a peaceful end, Taylor could not have missed their echo of the words spoken by the Shunammite's son, stricken in the fields and destined to be raised by Elisha (2 Kings 4:19).

Such blurring of current and biblical realities points to the ambiguous relation between the "real" and the "fictive" in these poems, especially those that attribute celestial speech to the deceased. John Wilson, for example, has William Tompson announce a saint's steadfastness from beyond the grave. "Do not acount me lost," the deceased proclaims: "in his righteousness i stood / Before my father just" (HP, pp. 15, 17). Benjamin Tompson has Edmund Davie assert the saint's reward with typical directness: "I'm now arriv'd the soul desired Port," Davie claims: "I've hitt the very Place I wisht at heart, / I'm fixt for ever: Never thence to part" (APS, p. 223). And Taylor's Samuel Hooker uses the joys of heaven as a goad for survivors to persevere: "In Faith, Obedience, Patience, walk a while / And thou shalt soon leape o're the parting Stile, / And come to God, Christ, Angells, Saints, & Mee" (TMP, p. 122). Puritan readers did not, of course, take such postmortem speeches as literal transcriptions – but they would not have regarded them as mere "fictions," either. As Astrid Schmitt-von Mühlenfels has noted, words from the dead had supreme biblical warrant;[51] by offering a more acceptable sacrifice than Cain, Abel "obtained witness that he was righteous, God testifying of his gifts: and by it he, being dead, yet speaketh" (Hebrews 11:4). These speeches also reinforced a sense of community that encompassed all saved souls, whether living or dead. Survivors were made to feel that they were being coaxed to glory by an ever-increasing company of saints with whom they once shared life's trials.

Ultimately, the pious dead offered more than advice from beyond the grave – they offered *selves* from beyond the grave, perfected versions of the redeemed identity for which survivors also yearned. This identity embodied what Ames called the "double form" of the true believer: "that of sin, and that of grace, for perfect sanctification is not found in this life."[52] By underscoring death's separation of the deceased's spiritual and carnal elements, elegists encouraged mourners to seek the saintly duality within themselves. Taylor thus proclaims that Dewey, "dichotomiz'd / By death's sharp Sword," is "both parted, and departed"; his soul and body now "standeth part from part" like "the *Zenith* from the *Nadir*."[53] By attesting that Dewey's natural self had been "rebellion's Kennel, Disobediences Chest," Taylor directed the survivor's grief toward an anticipation of the larger healing of a self that had also been "spoild" and rent "asunder" by sin. Although saving faith could not be mimicked, the desire to attain it could thereby be encouraged through a kind of reverse mimicry, in which the deceased's spiritual battles were shown to have been similar to the reader's. Elegists frequently attested that despite the celestial glory of the dead, the deceased had struggled, too; indeed, their struggle was inseparable from their glory. By equating the survivor's anxious present, however tentatively, with the deceased's earthly past, the Puritan elegy presented the deceased's celestial present as a hopeful harbinger of the survivor's future. Taylor thus assured readers that Samuel Hooker, for all his glory, had been beset by spiritual turmoil as difficult as theirs. The earthly Hooker's inner life had been "A Stage of War, Whereon the Spirits Sword / Hewd down the Hellish foes that did disturb" (*TMP*, p. 117). Like the pastoral "Saint" who counsels "Soul" in Taylor's *Gods Determinations*, the deceased offered supremely comforting testimony; for all the doubts that plagued survivors, he or she was made to say, "'Twas so with me."[54]

By commemorating the dead as perfected versions of the saintly paradigm, elegists exploited the widespread Puritan trope of the soul as a "text" to be studied for signs of grace. The explicated dead served as guides for survivors to read their own inner texts and gauge the degree to which they also manifested the "character" of the saved soul.[55] Because all such inner texts were to be read against the Bible as the ultimate source and arbiter of gracious experience, elegies routinely grounded the dead firmly within the pages of scripture. A frequent starting point for decoding neobiblical piety was the deceased's name, which was often rearranged into an anagram that revealed his or her redemptive essence. The anagram functioned within the elegy much as a biblical text served as the stimulus for a sermon.[56] Puritans saw the ability to decipher such messages as a gift, like wit and eloquence generally, and exercised the facility in many situations, not all of them serious.[57] When applied to elegy, however, such devices as anagrams, puns, acrostics, and biblical parallels were more than merely ornamental; they helped clarify the deceased's salvific message. In addition to proclaiming Dewey "David by Name, David by Nature," Taylor thus cites the deceased's "Dewy Tears" of repentance on a particular fast day, the "Dewy Rhymes" with which he had instructed his children, and the "Grace's Dew" that had "drenched" the hearts of the deceased and his wife.[58]

The decoded name was only a starting point for assimilating the deceased to the all-encompassing text of scripture. Occupational references frequently evoked biblical types, with the political leader lamented as a latter-day Moses or Joshua; the housewife as a Tabitha or Dorcas, whom Peter raised from the dead; and the minister as a prophet or an apostle, usually Elijah or Paul. The framing of the deceased as a neobiblical text is often quite explicit; when Benjamin Tompson commemorated his father as a thundering "Textman,"[59] he spoke to the deceased's essence not simply as an advocate for the Bible but as its anthropomorphized embodiment. Francis Drake similarly proclaimed that Jonathan Mitchell's heart contained "The *Scripture* with a *Commentary* bound" (*APS*, p. 459). And in an unusually elaborate example of deceased-as-text, Benjamin Woodbridge anatomized John Cotton as "A living breathing Bible: Tables where / Both Covenants at large engraven were" (*APS*, p. 410). Like scripture itself, the dead were to be explicated so that their redemptive message could be opened and disseminated. As Benjamin Tompson wrote of his sister-in-law Mary, "Let her example as a Coppy stand / To Childrens Children upon every hand" (*HP*, p. 5). Elegies gave literal form to the status of the dead as gracious "copies" to be circulated for the ongoing spiritual benefit of the living.

The lessons of the textualized dead, like those of scripture, were not merely private. The public dimension of the Puritan elegy emerges most clearly in the repeated assertion that God was removing pious souls from the world as punishment for the collective sins of survivors. Oakes proclaimed that "Our sins have slain our *Shepard*! we have bought, / And dearly paid for, our Enormities!" (*APS*, p. 219). At John Norton's passing, John Wilson went so far as to urge his readers to imitate the disciples' response to Christ's prediction of betrayal at the Last Supper: to search "our wayes and spirits" and "say as the Disciples did, / Lord, is it I? Is't I?" (*HP*, p. 90). With the widely perceived declension of the Puritan mission in the later seventeenth century, elegists increasingly adopted a jeremiad tone as they lamented the rapidly dwindling ranks of the godly. In a poem for John Allen, Taylor complained that the great "Spirituall Gamesters" were slipping away in alarming numbers; after delivering a roll call of fallen worthies, Taylor asked, "Shall none / Be left behinde to tell's the Quondam Glory / Of this Plantation?" (*TMP*, p. 31). As with private sin, however, elegy both lamented the crisis and performed the remedy; Taylor's ostensible pessimism was countered by the poem's very existence. Who is left to tell us New England's "Quondam Glory"? The answer was implicit in every Puritan elegy: "We" are – and we are telling that glory even as we write and read. By diminishing the distance between private grief and public reformation, elegies absorbed individual mourners into a godly community capable not only of producing souls worthy of heaven but of properly marking their translation there.[60] Marking such translations boded well for survivors who hoped someday to undergo the same change. In keeping with St. Paul's statement that "with the mouth confession is made unto salvation" (Romans 10:10), the Puritan elegiac ritual led readers through a verbal performance of mourning that opposed death's sting with renewed hopes of eternal bliss.

The Legacy of the Puritan Funeral Elegy

Like all rituals, the process of mourning scripted by the Puritan elegy had meaning only within a specific cultural and historical context. It could not survive the social, literary, and religious influences that began to filter in from post-Restoration England; by the turn of the eighteenth century, the rigid directives of elegy were loosening in accordance with ideological shifts reflective of an increasingly diverse society with multiple and often competing concerns.[61] One such shift was the growing prevalence of neoclassical aesthetic standards that broadened the goals of elegy from purely homiletic aims to a variety of concerns that echoed the wide-ranging reflections in "Lycidas." Another shift was the rise of natural religion and, with it, a sharp decline in biblical authority; nature, not scripture, was increasingly providing the chief inspiration for poetry, including elegy – and it was no longer a nature construed as fallen. With the rehabilitation of the natural realm as a source of elegiac consolation came a moral rehabilitation of the reader; Deism and Romanticism both worked, although in different ways, to render obsolete the Puritan insistence on repentance as the only appropriate response to the occasion of death. Elegy, at least in its "literary" variety, no longer worked to reaffirm dogma but instead sought to absorb loss into universal cycles that consoled without resorting to explicitly Christian beliefs and discourse. The elegiac consolations of nature came with a twist. What had served for Milton chiefly as a source of tropes was embraced, by the early nineteenth century, as quasi-scientific reality; with the full flowering of the Romantic absorption of the dead into Wordsworth's "diurnal course" came a more literal construal of death as a reintegration into natural cycles. The imagined landscape of the pastoral was thus generally eschewed for a natural landscape that was conceived – and depicted – as "real."

A clear legacy of the Puritan elegy can be seen in the fact that the social landscape of elegy remained real as well. Mourning continued to provide a prime opportunity for addressing societal concerns, although the range of these concerns broadened far beyond spiritual reformation. The social and political relevance of elegies was due, in part, to their regular appearance in the burgeoning colonial press. At the beginning of the eighteenth century, there was only one newspaper in the colonies; at the time of the Revolution, there were around forty. That popular elegies became a staple of these publications helped elegy remain the primary species of occasional verse in America well into the nineteenth century. In *Huckleberry Finn*, Twain mocked the more lugubrious of these poems through the mechanical "tributes" of Emmeline

Grangerford, who produced them obsessively until she finally succumbed to an inability to rhyme the name Whistler. Like Franklin before him, however, Twain overlooked the cultural work that popular elegies continued to perform. Despite their prosodic stiffness and verbal conventionality, the thousands of elegies written and read in post-Puritan America by all classes, including the marginalized, offered a forum for critiquing and reasserting political and social categories. The result was a collective conversation in which recurring occasions of loss generated ongoing reconstructions of American futurity. As Max Cavitch has shown, the many laments for George Washington as a "national father" exemplified an elegiac mode in which "communal expression" was "itself a kind of civic action" (*AE*, pp. 87, 92). Elegies and elegiac reflections that lamented the passing of a pristine American landscape, such as Bryant's "Thanatopsis," also played a role in assimilating the displacement of the Indians to "nature's plan" by articulating what Cavitch calls "imperialist nostalgia"; as Cavitch points out, African American elegies did important cultural work as well, lamenting an absence of lineage and thereby performing "threatened continuity as a form of identity" (*AE*, pp. 131–32, 185).

With social and political themes pervading the full range of elegiac verse, the chief distinction in American elegy became – and largely remains – between poems designed for popular audiences and those written for a more traditionally "literary" readership. Whitman's twin laments for Lincoln exemplify this distinction. "When Lilacs Last in the Dooryard Bloom'd" gives full voice to a pastoral tradition filtered through Romantic sensibilities. By attesting to "Lilac and bird and star twined with the chant of my soul," Whitman absorbs Lincoln's death into a natural cycle that does not offer immediate consolation so much as it creates a chastened sense of community with all living – and thus dying – things: "I mourn'd, and yet shall mourn with ever-returning spring." "Lilacs" employs the open prosody characteristic of most of the poems in *Leaves of Grass*; its unrhymed lines, defined by breath length, approximate the cadences of natural, though elevated, speech. When Whitman addressed the same topic for a popular audience, however, he followed the Puritan model by turning to ballad meter and a regular rhyme scheme. Published in the New York *Saturday Press* seven months after the assassination, "O Captain! My Captain!" features the accessible allegory of a ship of state and the heavy irony of a captain "Fallen cold and dead," even though "the prize we sought is won" and the "voyage [is] closed and done." "Lilacs" is clearly one of the great poems in English, but to assert, by contrast, that "O Captain!" is a bad poem is to overlook the fact that the latter is a very different kind of elegy, written for different aims and readers. I have been suggesting that a similar recognition of cultural function and rhetorical purpose applies to the Puritan elegy. Whitman's artistic choices in "O Captain!" recall Taylor's in his elegy for David Dewey; in each instance, a gifted poet writes in a conventional manner for nonelite readers. What's more, both poets succeeded in the attempt; while the Dewey elegy was Taylor's only published poem, "O Captain!" was repeatedly anthologized during the poet's lifetime.

The prosody of "O Captain!," an acoustic echo of the Puritan elegy, survives in the stock commemorative verses – usually couplets or quatrains – that still appear among the death notices in today's newspapers; many of these verses also follow the Puritan lead by asserting the traditional consolations of religion. A far more significant survival, however, lies in the continuing elegiac impulse toward communal self-examination and commentary. In the popular realm, this impulse has generally been transferred from elegiac poetry to obituary prose, in which the death of a famous person still prompts a dual recognition of rupture and continuity. When obituaries proclaim that a prominent death reflects the "end of an era," as they often do, the implication is that a new era has begun. As we have seen, the motif of succession suggested by such assertions of continuity was exploited by pastoral and Puritan elegist alike; while Milton voiced his determination to rededicate himself to the muse and carry on for the fallen Lycidas, his New England contemporaries voiced a belief that whoever commemorated the pious dead properly was likely to inherit their piety. Of course, these early modern elegists were hardly alone in their concern with lineage and inheritance; this has been – and will probably remain – a universal trait of elegy. After all, the oldest elegy that we have, David's lament for the "mighty" Saul, was sung by Saul's successor as king of Israel.

Notes

1. Benjamin Franklin, *Writings*, ed. J. A. Leo Lemay (New York: Library of America, 1987), pp. 19, 21.
2. Franklin, *Writings*, pp. 21–22.
3. William Empson, *Collected Poems* (New York: Harcourt Brace Jovanovich, 1949), pp. 58–59.
4. Edward Taylor, "Edward Taylor's Elegy on Deacon David Dewey," *Proceedings of the American Antiquarian Society* 96:1 (1986), pp. 82–83.
5. O. B. Hardison, *The Enduring Monument: A Study of the Idea of Praise in Renaissance Literary Theory* (Chapel Hill: University of North Carolina Press, 1962), pp. 107–08.
6. Hyatt Waggoner, *American Poets from the Puritans to the Present* (Boston: Houghton Mifflin, 1968), p. 13.

7. Ruth Wallerstein, *Studies in Seventeenth-Century Poetic* (Madison: University of Wisconsin Press, 1950), p. 113.

8. Peter Gregg Slater, *Children in the New England Mind: In Death and in Life* (Hamden, Conn.: Archon, 1977), p. 16.

9. Franklin, *Writings*, p. 228.

10. Kenneth Lockridge, *Literacy in Colonial New England: An Enquiry into the Social Context of Literacy in the Early Modern West* (New York: W. W. Norton, 1974), p. 13.

11. David Cressy, "Literacy in Seventeenth-Century New England: More Evidence," *Journal of Interdisciplinary History* 8 (1977), pp. 141–50; David D. Hall, "The Uses of Literacy in New England, 1600–1850," in William L. Joyce et al. (eds.), *Printing and Society in Early America* (Worcester, Mass.: American Antiquarian Society, 1983).

12. Lawrence Cremin, *American Education: The Colonial Experience, 1606–1783* (New York: Harper and Row, 1970), p. 131; David D. Hall, "Readers and Reading in America: Historical and Critical Perspectives," *Proceedings of the American Antiquarian Society* 103:2 (1994), p. 348; Charles E. Hambrick-Stowe, *The Practice of Piety: Puritan Devotional Disciplines in Seventeenth-Century New England* (Chapel Hill: University of North Carolina Press, 1982), pp. 157–61.

13. Peter M. Sacks, *The English Elegy: Studies in the Genre from Spenser to Yeats* (Baltimore, Md.: Johns Hopkins University Press, 1985), p. 22.

14. G. W. Pigman III, *Grief and English Renaissance Elegy* (Cambridge: Cambridge University Press, 1985), p. 46.

15. Jahan Ramazani, *Poetry of Mourning: The Modern Elegy from Hardy to Heaney* (Chicago: University of Chicago Press, 1994), p. 28.

16. Norman Pettit, *The Heart Prepared: Grace and Conversion in Puritan Spiritual Life* (New Haven, Conn.: Yale University Press, 1966); David Leverenz, *The Language of Puritan Feeling: An Exploration in Literature, Psychology, and Social History* (New Brunswick, N.J.: Rutgers University Press, 1980); Hambrick-Stowe, *Practice of Piety*; Patricia Caldwell, *The Puritan Conversion Narrative: The Beginnings of American Expression* (Cambridge: Cambridge University Press, 1983); Charles Lloyd Cohen, *God's Caress: The Psychology of Puritan Religious Experience* (New York: Oxford University Press, 1986); John Gatta, *Gracious Laughter: The Meditative Wit of Edward Taylor* (Columbia: University of Missouri Press, 1989); Jeffrey A. Hammond, *Sinful Self, Saintly Self: The Puritan Experience of Poetry* (Athens: University of Georgia Press, 1993).

17. David D. Hall, *Worlds of Wonder, Days of Judgment: Popular Religious Belief in Early New England* (New York: Knopf, 1989), p. 167.

18. David W. Shaw, *Elegy and Paradox: Testing the Conventions* (Baltimore, Md.: Johns Hopkins University Press, 1994), p. 229.

19. David E. Stannard, *The Puritan Way of Death: A Study in Religion, Culture, and Social Change* (New York: Oxford University Press, 1977), pp. 101, 105.

20. Pigman, *Grief*, pp. 3, 126.

21. Lawrence Stone, *The Crisis of Aristocracy, 1558–1641* (Oxford: Clarendon, 1965), pp. 572–81.

22. Dennis Kay, *Melodious Tears: The English Funeral Elegy from Spenser to Milton* (Oxford: Clarendon, 1990), pp. 17–26.

23. John W. Draper, *The Funeral Elegy and the Rise of English Romanticism* (New York: New York University Press, 1929), p. 57, ix.

24. Ben Jonson, *The Complete Poetry of Ben Jonson*, ed. William B. Hunter, Jr. (New York: W. W. Norton, 1968), p. 20.

25. John W. Draper (ed.), *A Century of Broadside Elegies* (London: Ingpen and Grant, 1928), p. 21.

26. Stannard, *Puritan Way*, 122–26; Ronald A. Bosco, "Introduction," in Ronald A. Bosco (ed.), *New England Funeral Sermons* (Delmar, N.Y.: Scholars' Facsimiles and Reprints, 1978), pp. xii–xiii.

27. William J. Scheick, "Tombless Virtue and Hidden Text: New England Funeral Elegies," in Peter White (ed.), *Puritan Poets and Poetics: Seventeenth-Century American Poetry in Theory and Practice* (University Park: Pennsylvania State University Press, 1985), pp. 290–96.

28. Carl Bridenbaugh, *Cities in the Wilderness: The First Century of Urban Life in America, 1625–1742* (New York: Oxford University Press, 1971), p. 143.

29. Harrison T. Meserole (ed.), *American Poetry of the Seventeenth Century* (1968; University Park: Pennsylvania State University Press, 1985), p. 210 (hereafter cited in notes and in text as *APS*).

30. Cotton Mather, *Cotton Mather's Verse in English*, ed. Denise D. Knight (Newark: University of Delaware Press, 1989), p. 51 (hereafter cited in notes and text as *CM*).

31. Edward Pearse, *The Great Concern, or, A Serious Warning to a Timely and Thorough Preparation for Death* (Boston: 1705), p. 65.

32. Thomas Shepard, *The Sincere Convert*, in John A. Albro (ed.), *The Works of Thomas Shepard*, 3 vols. (Boston: Doctrinal Tract and Book Society, 1853), p. 68.

33. Samuel Willard, *The High Esteem Which God Hath for the Death of His Saints* (Boston: 1683), in Bosco (ed.), *New England Funeral Sermons*, p. 16.

34. William Ames, *The Marrow of Theology*, trans. John D. Eusden (Boston: Pilgrim Press, 1968), p. 176.

35. Taylor, "Edward Taylor's Elegy," p. 83.

36. Richard Sibbes, *Spiritual Mourning*, in Alexander B. Grosart (ed.), *Works of Richard Sibbes*, 7 vols. (1862; Edinburgh: The Banner of Truth Trust, 1983), p. 268.

37. Stannard, *Puritan Way*, p. 99.

38. Willard, *High Esteem*, p. 5.

39. Willard, *High Esteem*, p. 17.

40. Nathanael Appleton, *A Great Man Fallen in Israel*, in Bosco (ed.), *New England Funeral Sermons*, p. 202.

41. Edward Taylor, *Edward Taylor's Minor Poetry*, ed. Thomas M. Davis and Virginia L. Davis (Boston: Twayne, 1981), p. 33 (hereafter cited in notes and text as *TMP*).

42. Willard, *High Esteem*, p. 18.

43. Kenneth B. Murdock (ed.), *Handkerchiefs from Paul* (Cambridge, Mass.: Harvard University Press, 1927), p. 3 (hereafter cited in notes and text as *HP*).

44. A. L. Bennett, "The Principal Rhetorical Conventions in the Renaissance Personal Elegy," *Studies in Philology* 51 (1954), pp. 110–14.

45. Barbara Kiefer Lewalski, *Protestant Poetics and the Seventeenth-Century Religious Lyric* (Princeton, N.J.: Princeton University Press, 1979), pp. 174–215, xxvi–xxviii.

46. Robert Henson, "Form and Content of the Puritan Funeral Elegy," *American Literature* 32 (1960), p. 15.

47. Josephine K. Piercy, *Studies in Literary Types in Seventeenth Century America (1607–1710)* (1939; Hamden, Conn.: Archon, 1969), pp. 68–75.

48. Bennett, "Principal Rhetorical Conventions," p. 117.

49. Taylor, "Edward Taylor's Elegy," p. 83.

50. Ola E. Winslow (ed.), *American Broadside Verse* (1930; New York: AMS Press, 1974), p. 13.

51. Astrid Schmitt-von Mühlenfels, *Die "Funeral Elegy" Neuenglands: Ein gattungsgeschichtliche Studie* (Heidelberg: Carl Winter, Universitätsverlag, 1973), p. 98.

52. Ames, *Marrow of Theology*, p. 170.

53. Taylor, "Edward Taylor's Elegy," p. 83.

54. Edward Taylor, *The Poems of Edward Taylor*, ed. Donald E. Stanford (New Haven, Conn.: Yale University Press, 1960), p. 436.

55. Hambrick-Stowe, *Practice of Piety*, pp. 157–61; John Owen King III, *The Iron of Melancholy: Structures of Spiritual Conversion from the Puritan Conscience to Victorian Neurosis* (Middletown, Conn.: Wesleyan University Press, 1983), pp. 13–82; Caldwell, *Puritan Conversion Narrative*; Scheick, "Tombless Virtue"; Hall, *Worlds of Wonder*, pp. 21–70; Hammond, *Sinful Self*, pp. 3–36; Jeffrey A. Hammond, *The American Puritan Elegy: A Literary and Cultural Study* (Cambridge: Cambridge University Press, 2000), pp. 42–68.

56. Schmitt-von Mühlenfels, *Die "Funeral Elegy,"* p. 54.

57. Jeffrey Walker, "Anagrams and Acrostics: Puritan Poetic Wit," in White (ed.), *Puritan Poets and Poetics*.

58. Taylor, "Edward Taylor's Elegy," p. 82.

59. Kenneth Silverman (ed.), *Colonial American Poetry* (New York: Hafner, 1968), p. 145.

60. Henson, "Form and Content"; Schmitt-von Mühlenfels, *Die "Funeral Elegy,"* pp. 24–31; Silverman, *Colonial American Poetry*, pp. 121–32; Hammond, *American*

Puritan Elegy, pp. 156–59, 187–89; Emory Elliot, "The Development of the Puritan Funeral Sermon and Elegy: 1660–1750," *Early American Literature* 15 (1980), pp. 151–64.

61. For later developments in American elegy, see Silverman, *Colonial American Poetry*, pp. 202–29; Schmitt-von Mühlenfels, *Die "Funeral Elegy,"* pp. 125–38; Stannard, *Puritan Way*, pp. 147–63; Elliot, "Development of the Puritan Funeral Sermon and Elegy"; Hammond, *American Puritan Elegy*, pp. 205–10; Max Cavitch, *American Elegy: The Poetry of Mourning from the Puritans to Whitman* (Minneapolis: University of Minnesota Press, 2007) (hereafter cited in text as *AE*).

Chapter 5

The Emergence of a Southern Tradition

JIM EGAN

People from a range of social positions wrote poetry in colonial Georgia, Maryland, Virginia, and the Carolinas. Indentured servants, college presidents, lawyers, tobacco merchants, schoolmasters, actors, doctors, and clergymen all tried their hand at verse. Poems appeared in a variety of different formats, including newspapers and books, but were also scribbled in diaries and letters and tacked up on fences. They were circulated to friends and, less often, enemies. Poems were incorporated into works of prose, prefaced plays, and were used to promote colonization and influence political decisions. Although the variety of writers is remarkable, so, too, are the absences. Due to powerful social forces that limited their educational opportunities and frowned on women establishing public personas, few women from these colonies published their poems during this period. Even fewer people of African descent appeared in print, although people with such lineage certainly expressed themselves in various poetic forms. Few Native Americans, either, published poetry from this region in this period, even though poetry was a rich part of many of their oral traditions. All those who did leave a legacy of poetry for us to read share a common bond. They were not southerners.

Because the South did not exist before the American Revolution, no British colonist in the Carolinas, Virginia, Maryland, or Georgia wrote southern poetry. The inhabitants of the colonies that would later make up the American South did not even consider themselves Americans until only a few years before the Revolution. They were just as British as anyone who lived in England, and they explicitly and passionately rejected being labeled as "Americans" whenever Londoners so much as hinted at it. The inhabitants of Britain's staples colonies did not feel they had given up their claim to their British identities. Instead, they cast themselves as simultaneously British and not entirely like people who lived in Britain. Living in the colonies gave the colonists, they insisted, a perspective on the world that people in Britain lacked, but residing in the wilds of America in no way compromised their status as members of what they saw as a worldwide community of British people. Before a distinctive brand of poetry from the American South could emerge, then, the South itself had to be born, and its writers had to adopt new ways of imaging their own identities so that they would embrace their status as poets writing for a national tradition that had to be built from the ground up.

Britain's colonies south of the Mason-Dixon line did share a common identity as staples colonies, as colonies, in other words, that produced valuable raw goods to be shipped back to England to be transformed into commodities that then could be sold at home and, under the right economic circumstances, around the world. The colonists' focus on commerce haunted them throughout the period, for the arbiters of taste in England wondered how poetry of distinction and refinement could emerge from a place so devoted to making money and a people who left, or whose ancestors left, the civilized confines of England to live in the savage climes next to or even amid so-called savage peoples. Great poetry, at least according to some, did not grow in a culture whose soil was fertilized by commercial activities.

Colonial poets from below the Mason-Dixon line offered no apologies for the commercial nature of their communities. They never wavered in their belief that, as Charles Hansford puts it in "My Country's Worth," "the greatest kindness to a country paid / Is to endeavor to increase its trade."[1] Instead, they challenged the theories of identity formation, of how individuals and communities develop their distinctive characteristics and abilities, used by English arbiters of taste to deny even the possibility that colonists in British America could produce poetry worth reading. In poem after poem, their verse put America's vast commercial potential on display, comparing it time and again with the most desired of goods from the most desired of regions, the East, to elevate America by connecting it with both great wealth and ancient civilizations with distinguished traditions of cultural production. When Richard Lewis compares the goods extracted from America by British labor to "India curtains" (*APSE*, p. 382), when James Kirkpatrick calls Georgia "India,"[2] or when James Sterling speaks of the virtues of "joining the Atlantic and Tartarian Wave" (*APSE*, p. 405), they are all trying to elevate American commerce and the culture that supports it by references to the place Europeans were looking for when they stumbled across America instead.

Given the inevitably social nature of commerce, the fixation on sociality we find in poetry in the staples colonies should hardly be surprising. Poets wrote about social relations between the sexes, but they also wrote about the trials and tribulations of forming social bonds between men and the manners appropriate to forming productive social bonds within a community. With some notable exceptions, only rarely does one find poetry from the staples colonies plumbing the depths of the psyche or trying to ascertain the speaker's ultimate fate in the afterlife. Poets in the staples colonies preferred to use poetry to understand interactions between people rather than to show them in solitary revelry. As such, their form of choice is social satire, a form that dominates the poems of the period. Hudibrastic poetry was extremely popular, but the colonists' desire to engage with poetic models popular among British poets of the period led them to adapt neoclassical satiric models to the colonial environment. Horace was often imitated or paraphrased (sometimes both in the same poem), georgics and Virgilian eclogues found much favor, and some meditative poems were published as well. The poets from the staples colonies wrote far fewer poems on religious topics than did their fellow poets in New England, and they relied even more heavily on Alexander Pope as a model for poetic form and subject.

From the very earliest years of colonization, promotional material routinely pitched colonization through poetry. The authors of prose tracts encouraging people in England to support efforts to plant English communities on American soil often burst into verse. As a result, poetry was inextricably linked with colonization and was a crucial ingredient in helping readers and promoters alike imagine a world in which all the activities associated with colonization – including, but not limited to, sending people across an ocean, spending huge sums of money on supplies and materials, and displacing entire communities by any means necessary – not only made sense but also, and perhaps more importantly, seemed necessary for the health of any important nation. Poetry having little explicitly to do with colonization emerged in these promotional tracts as well, and one need look no further than the most prolific promoter of English colonization of America, John Smith. Smith's most famous poem, "The Sea Marke," touches on a subject rarely covered in seventeenth-century southern verse: the spiritual life of the individual (*APSE*, p. 7). The poem appears in Smith's *Advertisements for the Experienced Planters of New-England*, a prose work devoted exclusively to Smith's views of English colonization up and down America's North Atlantic coast. In the poem, the warnings offered by a dead sailor's wrecked ship about the dangers of a particular area serve as a metaphor for the deadly fate awaiting all of us.

Ballads, one of the most popular poetic forms in early seventeenth-century England, served the purposes of colonial propagandists particularly well. Little is known of Richard Rich, the man listed as the author of one of the earliest ballads to promote Virginia, "Newes from Virginia" (1610). Rich turns tragedy into opportunity when he tells the story of a voyage of colonial reinforcements on their way to Virginia who were shipwrecked on Bermuda. Not only did the potential colonists survive their ordeal, but, in fact, they managed to reproduce on the island (he tells us that two children were born while they repaired their vessel), so when they do, eventually, make it to Virginia, they help bring new life to the inhabitants. Life in Virginia is depicted as one of abundance and possibility, where workers and food are plentiful, and where even members of the nobility have settled. In fact, the colony looks, in social structure and otherwise, like a kind of mini-England. The poem further shows that the colonial venture mixes the goal of expanding England's reach with that of glorifying God by following the claim that "Wee hope to plant a nation where none before hath stood" with the line, "To glorifie the lord tis done, and to no other end."[3]

The first wave of colonists produced little poetry, especially in comparison with the British colonists to the north. Poetry began on a high note in the staples colonies, though. The first major poetic production in the region, George Sandys's translation of Ovid's *Metamorphoses*, achieved greater stature within English poetic circles than any other work of poetry produced in the British-American colonies, even if its American origins were seldom mentioned. Born into an aristocratic family in England, Sandys came to Virginia in 1621 after his niece's husband was appointed Virginia's governor. His work as the Virginia Company's treasurer left him enough time to continue his translation of Ovid, begun while still in England and first published in London in 1626. Sandys makes the connection between his translation and his life in America in a dedicatory letter to King Charles, in which he says that although the translation "Sprung from the Stocke of the ancient Romanes," it was nonetheless "bred in the New-World, partaking of the rudenesse whereof it cannot but participate; especially having Warres and Tumults to bring it to light in stead of the Muses."[4] Indeed, the "Warres and Tumults" mentioned seem to have had a profound influence on the decisions he made as translator, shaping his portrait of the people represented in Ovid's work in such a way that he compares Native Americans to Romans (*OM*, p. 3).

Whether or not they were translating Latin poetry, few nobles of Sandys's stature chose to leave their lives in England behind to set out on the tough life to be found for English people in America. Far more common were those less fortunate, as James Revel's poem on the life of an indentured servant, "The Poor Unhappy Transported Felon's Sorrowful Account of His Fourteen Years Transportation, at Virginia, in America," illustrates (*APSE*, pp. 156–63). We know nothing of the author except what he tells us in his verse, and we are not even sure whether the author and his narrator are fictional creations of some unknown writer or composites of life in the colonies for indentured servants. The poem's story is sufficiently generic that only minor changes are necessary in an 1823 version, "The Life of James Revel," which transports the narrator to Botany Bay. The Virginia version of the ballad tells the story of a young man with loving parents and a good upbringing who falls victim to the lures of a life of crime, a mistake that leads to his arrest and transportation to the colonies, a popular punishment in seventeenth- and eighteenth-century England. Life as a laborer in the colonies helps Revel see the error of his ways, and when he is reunited with his parents in the ballad's final lines, we see that labor by wayward English subjects in America rejuvenates English families while simultaneously teaching proper work habits to those at the bottom of the social ladder. The poem provides a clear if highly compressed picture of indentured servants, who made up a significant portion of the population of the staples colonies, and it offers intriguing scenes of those servants working the fields alongside slaves brought from Africa.

The poems in George Alsop's *A Character of the Province of Mary-land* are also written from the perspective of an indentured servant, but Alsop displays a wit, poetic skill, and depth of emotion one finds in no other seventeenth-century verse from England's staples colonies. We have only a few tantalizing details about his life. Birth records suggest a London arrival in 1636, but nothing has been found to tell us when he died. The evidence indicates he was an indentured servant in Maryland for four years, beginning in 1658, and that he lived in the colony for two more years. Sometime after his return to England he became an Anglican minister, but the trail goes cold at that point. The only verse of his we have is from *A Character*, but this poetry is so distinctive that it has remained alive. For the most part, the poems are extensions of the work's efforts at promoting colonial Maryland. They appear as part of the volume's introductory materials, at the ends of chapters, and in the book's appendix, a collection of letters Alsop sent home.

Alsop's best-known poem remains "Traffique is Earth's great Atlas" (*APSE*, p. 146). The ten lines of rhymed couplets extol the value of commerce for the health of both the nation and its individual members in clear, evocative language while it advocates for a change in England's mercantilist economic policy to permit Maryland to exchange goods directly with merchants in nations other than England. "Heaven's bright Lamp, shine forth some of thy Light," included in one of Alsop's letters, expresses its support for monarchical rule by ridiculing the victors in the English Civil War (*APSE*, pp. 146–47). Alsop's disdain for his country's new Puritan leadership runs so deep that he casts England as a modern-day Sodom, where commoners have replaced true nobility in places of distinction. From the speaker's position in the New World, England, rather than America, looks like a savage and uncivilized world. In the process, Alsop provides a rare glimpse into the flip side of what would later be called the American dream when he writes, "Persons of Honour, which did before inherit / Their glorious Titles from deserved merit." Alsop makes similar use of the New World in the volume's most challenging and interesting poem, "The Author to His Book" (*APSE*, pp. 144–45). In witty and sometimes bawdy language, the speaker twists some standard figures of speech, such as the figure of the poem as the author's child, to criticize the idea that life in America literally transforms English people's bodies and minds so fundamentally that they can no longer claim to be English. In the process, the poem suggests a more flexible model of English identity.

The same concern for commerce displayed in Alsop finds poetic expression in *The Sot-Weed Factor* (London, 1708), by Ebenezer Cooke (sometimes Cook), one of the most powerful verse satires in American writing before 1820 (*APSE*, pp. 239–58). Although more is known of his life than of Alsop's, Cooke remains something of a mystery nonetheless. Probably born in England in around 1667, he moved back and forth between the New World and the Old World before settling permanently in Maryland sometime in the 1710s; there he lived until his death, sometime after 1732. *The Sot-Weed Factor* achieves its effects by playfully and bitingly employing some rather well-known satiric conventions to new ends. The poem follows the merchant on his trip through the rough-and-tumble world of colonial Maryland, where the colonists have adapted so well to the local environment that, to the narrator at least, they seem more Indian than English. The judges are illiterate, the colonists drink more often than work, and their food is inedible by those with refined tastes. While the colonists are mocked for being not English enough, the narrator is lampooned for being too English, in that he demonstrates a palate so delicate that a drink of local water renders him immobile for six months. In the end, the poem imagines English identity in terms of exchange and transformation rather than in terms of an unchanging purity of bloodlines.

Cooke went on to publish a number of other poems, although none are as good as his first, and all his subsequent publications were in Maryland. In addition to several occasional poems, Cooke published two more long poems, *The Sot-Weed Redivivus* in 1730 and *The History of Colonel Nathaniel Bacon's Rebellion* in 1731.[5] A so-called third edition of the original *The Sot-Weed Factor* appeared in 1731 as well, with only minor changes. *Redivivus* is a 540-line poem divided into three cantos, all in the Hudibrastic style. While the first *The Sot-Weed Factor* moves the reader along with one preposterous twist after another in an already ridiculous plot, *Redivivus* uses a contemporaneous controversy – the debate over the use of tobacco as a form of paper money – to hook its audience. As such, the poem is difficult for modern readers, but those able to make it through see that Cooke investigates the nature of language and collective identity in ways that extend and complicate the issues that the poet took up in *The Sot-Weed Factor* of 1708. *The History of Colonel Nathaniel Bacon's Rebellion* is also difficult because of its reliance on local details unknown to later readers, but it, too, rewards careful readers by using those details to ponder the more philosophical questions regarding leadership that grew out of this specifically colonial uprising.

Bacon's Rebellion inspired two other poems of note from the period. John Cotton of Queen's Creek has been identified by Jay B. Hubbell as the author of both of these works – found among a collection of manuscripts discovered in the nineteenth century – which present Bacon and the rebellion from diametrically opposed positions. "Bacon's Epitaph" casts Bacon as a modern Alexander by describing him as having "Marrs and Minerva both in him," a standard trope for the Greek hero, who fights for the liberty of the people.[6] In sharp contrast, "Upon the Death of G.B." charges Bacon with the misuse of his silver tongue to lead people to their deaths in the service of treason against their true protector, the king of England. Scholars have advanced various theories to explain why Cotton would lionize in one poem the same figure he lambasts in another. Some analysts contend that Cotton's two poems illustrate that he sought to rise above the fray, others argue that the poems might have been used to make the poet appealing to both sides, while still others see the poems as rhetorical exercises of the kind that were quite common in the period. Given the relative lack of information about Cotton and the context in which the poems were produced, we may never have a satisfactory answer.

If the staples colonies produced relatively little poetry in the seventeenth century, the eighteenth century witnessed a comparative explosion. Poetry was everywhere, issuing from the presses that sprang up across the region in the early eighteenth century, circulating in manuscript among members of the social clubs that came alive in the period, and appearing on the front pages of newspapers alongside foreign news and advertisements for runaway slaves. Any person in the staples colonies at this time who sought to better him- or herself simply could not avoid poetry, for the taste and refinement necessary to write and appreciate fine poetry became a sign of one's status as a civilized person. And the production of poetry by the inhabitants of the colonies showed the world, and themselves, that the colonists were as civilized as those in England who made them the butt of their jokes. Writers in the staples colonies were especially consumed with belles lettres, with the use of writing to promote sociability and conversation and pleasure, and, even more so, they were quite keen on demonstrating their regard for the very qualities belles lettres promoted. In this sense, much of the poetry in the staples colonies represents a kind of performance on paper, a performance in which the writer shows him- or herself, and the society of which he or she is a part, to be worthy of inclusion in the civilized societies of Europe, the very societies, of course, that gave value to belles lettres in the first place.

The arrival of printing presses with the financial backing to withstand the inevitable if unpredictable lean times that periodically beset the colonies helped accelerate the production of poetry. Maryland saw its first stable press in 1726 (the colony had an earlier press in the seventeenth century, one that featured a woman at the helm and is certainly worthy of further study, but it didn't last and issued nothing of relevance to the history of poetry in the region), followed by one in Virginia in 1730 and South Carolina in 1731. One man, William Parks, deserves credit for establishing the first presses in both Maryland and Virginia, and for overseeing the publication of a vast body of poetry in both these colonies. His importance to the history of poetic production in the staples colonies cannot be overestimated. Richard Lewis's 1728 poem *The Mouse Trap* earns the distinction of being, in the words of J. A. Leo Lemay, "the first belletristic book published in the South," while William Dawson's *Poems on Several Occasions by a Gentleman of Virginia* in 1736 was the first volume of poetry published in Virginia.[7] Poets even wrote poems extolling the virtues of the press for the cultural advancement of the colonies. John Markland's "Typographia: An Ode, on Printing" (Williamsburg, 1730), for instance, sees the press as a way of allowing the colonists to "pursue" the same "Vertues" as their "Fathers" when it helps them "detect" and "correct" their "Errors" as well as better "discern" "Truths" from "Falshood[s]."[8] James Sterling singles out for praise the moral good print does in his revision of a poem he had published in Britain, "On the Invention of Letters" (*American Magazine*, March 1758), a history in verse, accompanied by copious notes, of print from ancient to modern times. The poem is especially noteworthy for its self-conscious American perspective on these matters, announced in the opening lines when Sterling notes that he writes from "regions distant from maternal climes," thereby insisting that geographic space distinguishes his work from other poems on the subject.[9] Joseph Dumbleton calls "The Printer ... the Poet's Friend" in "The Paper Mill" (1744), a poem on a new paper mill established by Parks to supply his press.[10]

The books of poetry issued from these presses may have been loss leaders in comparison to the other, more profitable, materials coming off the press, but they signaled the colonists' sophistication and refinement even if they failed to recoup as much of their investment as did other works. The real poetic bonanza is to be found in the newspapers that emerged from these presses, beginning with Parks's *Maryland Gazette* in 1727. Begun in 1732, the *South Carolina Gazette* published perhaps the most poetry, and perhaps the most distinguished and accomplished poetry, of any of the periodicals issued in the staples colonies, including works by Richard Lewis, James Kirkpatrick, and James Sterling. Local periodicals were not simply outlets for regional poets. Far from it. They published writers from the other colonies as well as works of local color, and they frequently included works by British authors. Much publication was anonymous, thus complicating our ability to identify poems of American origins. The periodicals' inclusion of poetry by colonial authors marks the beginning of a poetic tradition in which the colonists themselves composed at least part, if not always all, of the imagined audience. Authors in the staples colonies were beginning to think of themselves as simultaneously British and not entirely British, simply by virtue of where they lived.

Much of the poetry published in the major periodicals of the region deals with the relations between the sexes: many poems concern courtship or take up the problems faced by lovers, spurned and otherwise. In many of these poems, women take the brunt of the criticism, although sometimes, it would seem, female authors are able to explore the foibles of men as well. An early instance of women participating in public discourse about relations between the sexes appears in issues from the *South Carolina Gazette* of 1732, in which a dialogue in verse erupts between several male and female poets. "Secretus" offers his praise for an "American pastoral nymph," which prompts "Belinda" to reply, which, in turn, produces a poem from "Dorinda."[11] Poetry on courtship allowed women a small window of opportunity, at least on occasion, to publicize their views on what constituted value in male partners, as happened, for instance, in the poetry columns of Purdie and Dixon, published in the *Virginia Gazette* of 1768–1769. Of the poetry published that appears to have been written by women, one in particular stands out: "Carolina, a Young Lady," published in the August 3, 1747, *South Carolina Gazette* by a still unidentified, although probably female, author. With considerable wit, the speaker exposes the absurdity of her father's rules – once such rules are thoughtfully examined – regarding male visitors, and, in the process, makes a case for greater autonomy for women while subtly casting such autonomy as a political issue whose implications extend beyond mere household, domestic relations.

Religious poetry appeared in the periodicals, too, as well as in books of poems, although far less often than in New England. Samuel Davies's *Miscellaneous Poems, Chiefly on Divine Subjects*, for instance, came off the Virginia press in 1752, and some of Dawson's poetry could be considered religious.[12] Thomas Cradock, a rector and schoolteacher in Maryland, wrote poetry that conformed to standards of taste and refinement derived from England. He produced devotional poetry and a number of elegies, published a new translation of the Psalms, and circulated in manuscript a pastoral poem satirizing, among other things, the unsavory behavior of some pastors as well as many aspects of social mores and structures in midcentury Maryland society. His "To Thyrsis" (published in the *American Magazine or Monthly Chronicle* in 1757), although not religious in the traditional sense of the word, has drawn some praise.[13] The almost-one-hundred-line-long poem imitates Horace's second epode and offers advice on how to live a proper life amid the trials presented in one's daily life. His most ambitious work was never published but was circulated widely in manuscript. The ten poems that comprise "The Maryland Eclogues" render life in the colonies through classical structures.[14] We witness scenes of clergymen abusing the trust of their congregants, convicts urging one another to sing of their transgressions, drunk planters reminiscing about a recently deceased planter, and Native Americans bemoaning the loss of their lands to the English. Eclogue 4 tells the tale of a male slave hoping to seduce a female slave, only to be rebuffed because she is engaging in sexual relations with her master. We should avoid labeling such couplings between people of African and European descent as miscegenation, though, for, as we will see subsequently, the modern notion of race was emergent but hardly dominant. It had different meanings and associations and operated on different principles. In the case of Cradock's master and slave, their sexual relations seem to represent merely poor management, rather than posing a threat to an as-yet-unimagined biological difference between races.

A few years after Parks left Annapolis to open a print shop in Virginia, Jonas Green established a new press in Maryland. Given his more precarious financial situation and the often dismal profits one saw from books of poetry, Green took longer to publish books of poetry in Maryland than had Parks. Nevertheless, Green's influence on poetic production in colonial Maryland was significant. The reborn *Maryland Gazette* began publishing poetry of quality in its first few issues, and it continued to publish distinguished poetry throughout Green's life.

Green was also a poet himself, but a consideration of his poetry leads us away from the world of print to club culture. While his work as a printer shows the importance of printed poems in this period, his work as a poet reveals the crucial role manuscript circulation played in the staples colonies. Green was the poet laureate for the Tuesday Club in Annapolis, a gathering of men that formed in 1746. Similar clubs formed in various colonial cities during the period and had a large influence on cultural life in the staples colonies. And wherever there were clubs, there was also much poetry. The writing of poetry required particular forms of knowledge, a well-read background, and wit, which showed – and helped produce – one's taste and refinement. Poetry promoted and produced aesthetic pleasures that were, in addition to whatever civilizing, political, and/or economic functions those pleasures produced and/or disguised, valuable to the club's members simply for the fact that they were pleasurable. Clubs, clearly, were fun for their white, male memberships, and they thrived, before the Revolutionary era helped spell their doom by casting them as necessarily tied to the very political systems the new nation sought to cast aside. Although many clubs came to life in this period, none produced works of such literary quality as the Tuesday Club. As laureate of the club, Green was, not surprisingly, responsible for its most entertaining verse. Green wrote acrostic poems and epigrams, congratulatory poems that mocked the person being congratulated and anniversary odes that lampooned the source of celebration, and mock-epics in which the heroes were always shown to be something considerably less than heroic. He did all this with great wit and poetic skill.

One particularly interesting example of manuscript poetry to emerge out of club culture can be found in writings from the 1750s of the "Dinwiddianae" group. The writers in this group, who were probably members of the Hickory Hill Club but whose most prolific contributor was almost certainly the attorney John Mercer, used satiric prose and verse to attack the policies of Governor Robert Dinwiddie and his political associates for taxes that were deemed too high and military defenses that were seen as too lax.[15] The poems included in the collection include Hudibrastic satire, mock-epics, and ballads sung to the popular "Chevy Chase," and the authors offer what by this time seems a requirement for poets in the staples colonies, namely, a direct homage to Alexander Pope amid an adaptation of Pope's formal qualities and thematic interests. The poems in the collection break the mold of midcentury staples colony poetry by rejecting the formal diction of much of the neoclassical poetry of the period. Instead, these poems favor rough rhymes and meter as well as ethnic dialects, including rather pedestrian Scottish dialect for the character meant to lampoon Governor Dinwiddie, a dialect that provides a pointed contrast to the Irish dialect used by those the poem held in higher esteem. These rhetorical choices are authorized by the many sly and not-so-sly allusions to the ancients designed to indicate with a wink and a nudge that the author might not be from quite as low a position as the poems indicate. Whatever the social position the authors of the poetry might have occupied, the poems, especially when read in relation to the collection in general, position themselves as speaking from outside the centers of power against autocratic and inattentive leaders, including those in Great Britain.

Richard Lewis not only wrote the best British-American neoclassical poem, "A Journey from Patapasco to Annapolis," but also produced the staples colonies' best body of poetic work. Few facts have emerged about the life of the region's impressive poet. The most extensive research on Lewis's life was done by J. A. Leo Lemay, who found that Lewis was probably born in Wales and most likely emigrated to Maryland in 1718 after briefly attending Balliol College, Oxford. However, no definitive record of Lewis in the colonies can be found before 1725, when he wrote a letter to the Royal Society of London about an explosion. Lewis first became visible in print with the 1728 Annapolis publication of *The Mouse Trap, or the Battle of the Cambrians and Mice*. After a preface to Benedict Leonard Calvert, the governor of Maryland, with some figures of speech worth much further study, *The Mouse Trap* offers a translation of Edward Holdsworth's Latin poem, *Musicpula*, that, like its original, presents a satiric but affectionate look at life in ancient Wales. Parks's Annapolis press issued two other works from Lewis in 1732: "Carmen Seculare," a roughly three-hundred-line celebration of the hundred-year anniversary of the colony of Maryland that ranges over the colony's history, present situation, and no doubt glorious future; "The Rhapsody," a meditative pastoral poem of approximately 125 lines that focuses the reader's attention on the natural world as an allegory of philosophical questions regarding the individual's place in the cosmos.[16]

The best of Lewis's work appears in the poems published exclusively in periodicals on both sides of the Atlantic. "Food for Criticks" not only describes the distinctive qualities of the American environment in detail but also asks the reader to value these qualities mostly for the aesthetic pleasure simply experiencing them can provide instead of for their commercial potential (*APSE*, pp. 396–400). The qualities of American nature, according to the poem, provide a peculiarly good source for poetic inspiration, a source that the poem suggests holds the potential for poetry that will surpass that produced by classical authors. This idea eventually brought Lewis some notoriety. First published in the *Maryland Gazette* in 1729, "To Mr. Samuel Hastings (Ship-Wright of Philadelphia)," an occasional poem of almost 130 lines, uses its praise of shipbuilding to challenge the common conception of the colonists as provincial ignoramuses lacking in culture. The poem's incorporation of mythological and religious figures into a carefully organized verse shows Lewis's neoclassical influences, but what is striking about the poem is the way Lewis uses the staples drawn from American nature – in this case, trees – to grant British communities in America a cosmopolitan sophistication. The traffic in goods goes more than one way, however; thus the trees shipped out of America are magically transformed into other items so that "Indian curtains screen" the colonists when they sleep (*APSE*, p. 382). Given that such screens were, in eighteenth-century England, understood as signs of cultural sophistication, this image in particular reminds his readers on both sides of the Atlantic that the colonists themselves are no less civilized than their so-called betters in England. The poem also goes on to suggest that commerce has the power to further English empire by literally transforming the "climes" where such commerce eventually ends up into English territories. Trade with other peoples shows them the virtues of English ways and so converts them into Englishmen, and all this comes about only through the transformation of the natural products found only in America.

"A Journey from Patapasco to Annapolis" bests all of Lewis's other poetic efforts (*APSE*, pp. 386–95). Although earlier printings might now be lost, the poem probably appeared first in the May 21st edition of the *Pennsylvania Gazette*, after which a number of other colonial newspapers reprinted it. Nearly four hundred lines long, the poem follows its speaker on the trip mentioned in the poem's title, taking him through a thunderstorm and past farms, all the while affording him the opportunity to convey, in vivid and moving couplets, the splendor of the natural world of America. The speaker's journey serves as a figure for the various stages of life itself and for the philosophical voyage that the narrator experiences as he travels through geographic space, using the things he sees to stimulate his meditation on the place of humans in the cosmic order. In the end, the doubts these scenes raise about man's ultimate insignificance in relation to the grandeur of the natural world, and, indeed, even about the existence of a God at all, are resolved through the speaker's carefully articulated and reasoned use of his senses to demonstrate the existence of a creator and an afterlife for the worthy.

The speaker's remarks on the hummingbird – a creature distinct to the New World, and one that had fascinated European travelers – drew, and continue to draw, the most attention. The bird's "ever-flutt'ring Wings" that "fling" what the speaker describes as "Ten thousand Colours" outward "mock the Poet's and the Painter's Skill" when its "ever-varying Dies" produce "A living

Rainbow" (*APSE*, pp. 388–89). Had Lewis stopped here, he might have been known for a fine description of a compelling creature, but he has the audacity to have the speaker postulate that, had certain classical authors witnessed the hummingbird's "wonders," it would have been the hummingbird rather than the "Phoenix" that would have been "immortalized" in verse. By then proceeding to claim that the hummingbird was "Above all other Birds – their beauteous King," Lewis has laid down the gauntlet for British neoclassical poets to defend their choice of aviary figures of poetic inspiration (*APSE*, p. 389). Alexander Pope would do so in Book IV of *The Dunciad*, in which he would make oblique reference to Lewis's image by saying that "The dull may waken to a Humming-bird."[17] Lewis had clearly struck a nerve by representing American things not simply as comparable to those from the Old World but as superior to them, and, as such, here, and in his other nature poetry, he opened up new formal and conceptual possibilities.

One of Lewis's chief rivals as most accomplished poet of the staples colonies is James Kirkpatrick, who was born in Ireland with the surname "Killpatrick" and emigrated to South Carolina in 1717 after having studied at the University of Edinburgh without earning a degree. Kirkpatrick practiced medicine in America, and he returned to London in 1742 after having caught the attention of British officials by successfully administering inoculations during a smallpox outbreak. His *Analysis of Innoculation,* published in London in 1754, earned him great renown throughout medical communities across Europe. He remained in England until his death in 1770, and his work on inoculation has kept his name alive in medical circles. Although he produced only a few poems, they are accomplished enough to merit our attention.

Kirkpatrick's "An Address to James Oglethorpe," first published in the February 3, 1733, issue of the *South Carolina Gazette*, lauds the future colony's potential to produce luxury items that might be used by English people and sold by English merchants throughout Europe. The poem's focus on, among other items, silk and perfume, which were considered valuable in part because they were exotic goods from Asia that showed the tasteful nature of those who possessed them, was rather standard poetic fare by the time "An Address" appeared in print. Kirkpatrick twists what had become a clichéd set of images into a new vision when he, through his deft and creative use of metonymy, erases the geographic distinction between America and Asia. This rhetorical sleight of hand elevates America's value in relation to Europe, which, in the end, suggests that English communities in America deserve to be ranked among the civilized communities in the world. In 1737, Kirkpatrick published *An Epistle to Alexander Pope, Esq. from South Carolina* in London; this work is surely one of the – if not *the* – best tributes to Pope in the eighteenth century.

The Sea-Piece, Kirkpatrick's most important poem, was published in London in 1750 but was written at least partly in the colonies.[18] The poem tells the story of the speaker's journey across the Atlantic from England to Carolina. The narrative, though, is really only a ruse for exploring weighty philosophical questions while also describing life at sea and the life of the sea. We are treated to lengthy digressions from the poem's putative plot to learn of the many nightmares the speaker has while onboard, nightmares prompted by the speaker's fears of what life will be like in the supposedly savage land of America. The speaker ultimately is calmed by a dream in which his father waits on the docks in America to welcome him to his new home away from home. We hear of the pirates that captured him on a previous attempt to emigrate to America, pirates who ultimately left him onshore in the town of his birth. The poem also offers detailed descriptions of nautical terms and of the different kinds of storms one encounters at sea as well as speculations on zoology and other emerging subfields of the nascent scientific movements.

In seeking to make British trade fit for eighteenth-century neoclassical forms and styles, Kirkpatrick was forging relatively new ground for British poetry. *The Sea-Piece* distinguishes itself from other "empire of the sea" poems in offering a new way of imagining British identity in a world in which every place on earth and – at least potentially – every person on earth can be made to be British. Poets writing from outside Great Britain thus offered ways of retaining one's British identity while living in a distinctly un-British environment, eating food one cannot find in Europe, and engaging in cultural practices and traditions found nowhere in the British Isles. Kirkpatrick proposes an unusual alternative model for identity in the face of British expansion across the globe. He casts Britishness itself as a mystified other at the heart of communal identity, a mystified identity used to define Britishness through its many and inevitable distortions around the world. In this way, *The Sea-Piece* makes transformation rather than conformity the criteria for inclusion in the British community. The distorted images of home found in the colonies, *The Sea-Piece* suggests, are no less a part of the definition of true Britishness for their being grotesque versions of England. Indeed, he contends, the imagined community composed of British subjects scattered across the globe living on non-British soil represents the very ideal of Britishness itself rather than an aberration.

Among those British-American poets of the staples colonies who wrote poems about the expansion of the empire, none were more prolific than James

Sterling, who was also one of the very few who immigrated to the colonies with a reputation as a poet already established. Before he came to America, indeed, by the time he was twenty years old, Sterling was a rising literary star in his native Ireland. His poetic output only increased once he arrived in the colonies, and the quality of his verse, scholars agree, also improved in the New World. Born in Ireland in 1701 and graduated from Trinity College in 1720, Sterling made his way to America in 1736, and he was ultimately assigned to a congregation in Maryland. Much of his published verse appeared anonymously and was not identified by scholars until the twentieth century, so we may yet discover that Sterling was even more prolific than we already know him to be. He published occasional poems celebrating a variety of events, and scholars now generally praise his experimentation with various rhymes and/or meters in his poetry, while finding the ideas and issues he raises in his poems more conventional and less striking. Sterling does distinguish himself in one way, at least. Few poets, if any, devoted as much verse to championing the cause of America's future glory, known as *translatio studii*, the movement of civilization from east to west. Sterling's "Occasioned by His Majesty's Most Gracious Benevolence to His British Colonies in America, Lately Invaded by the French," which appeared in the *Maryland Gazette* of December 1754, and "The Patriot," first printed in the April 1758 issue of the *American Magazine*, represent two instances in which Sterling employs this trope. Sterling tried his hand at one of the most popular forms of American neoclassical verse with "The Pastoral," a poem that adapts standard neoclassical forms to forward the cause of letters in the colonies generally.

Sterling's most noteworthy attempt to champion American things saw print in 1752. *An Epistle to the Hon. Arthur Dobbs, Esq.: In Europe from a Clergyman in America* announces on its title page the perspective it takes on British expansion. The narrator refers to himself in the body of the work as a "tuneful Savage" who writes from the "uncultured Paradise" of the New World (*APSE*, p. 405). Of course, the poem itself is designed to render these definitions ironic by showing the poet to be tuneful indeed and America to have sufficient culture to produce a great poem in the first place. Using a formalized language that sometimes seems to take itself a little too seriously, the poem, in 1,600 lines of heroic couplets divided into three sections, celebrates Dobbs's search for the Northwest Passage to emphasize the as-yet-untapped potential of America. None of Sterling's images present the natural world, or any of the subjects he takes up, in striking or surprising ways; as poetry, in other words, Sterling's poems are not especially successful. Nonetheless, they offer wonderful illustrations of the way eighteenth-century poets in the staples colonies use the people and places of the East, in particular, China, India, and Arabia, as crucial points of comparison. The poem thus illustrates one of the ways Americans in this period co-opted the figure of the East to demonstrate America's value in the face of European efforts to bypass the continent entirely so that they could reach the more lucrative markets found in Asia as quickly as possible. In the process, *An Epistle* also draws on the cultural cachet attached to the East by Europeans during this period to suggest America's own cultural sophistication.

England's Caribbean colonies would have been included in the category of the staples colonies for English readers and writers on both sides of the Atlantic, and it is in a work from these islands that one finds the most extensive engagement with slavery in poetry of the period. James Grainger's *The Sugar-Cane*, an approximately six-hundred-line, four-book georgic, offers itself simply as an instruction manual on the proper methods of planting, cultivating, and raising the sugar cane (*APSE*, pp. 492–515). It is, in fact, a meditation on the cultural benefits of the transformation of natural products into commodities. His readers would have been well aware that the colonial sugar cane that brought its owners extraordinary riches was actually cultivated by slaves, so Grainger was obliged to defend the practice and offer images of life on a colonial plantation that would show the necessity of such seemingly unsavory practices as slavery in an empire that touted its own love of liberty. Grainger's encyclopedic representation of sugar cane production lead him to devote the whole of Book IV to a detailed discussion of slaves. After lamenting the necessity of slave labor, Grainger proceeds to explain which Africans make the most productive slaves and how to manage one's slaves on the massive sugar plantations that had sprung up throughout the Caribbean. Grainger's language concerning race shows how we have to be very careful when interpreting eighteenth-century works dealing with seemingly familiar categories of collective identity. For Grainger's discussion of which Africans make the best slaves reveals the permeable, rather than fixed, nature of racial identities in this period. At the close of the poem, in fact, one of the benefits that the commercialization of natural objects found in England's overseas empires will bring England is, he says, the production of new, specifically British "races." Grainger even asserts that the appearance of these new "races" of people borne out of Britain's overseas expansion will signal the triumph of Britain throughout the globe.

The radically different notion of race, as well as other forms of collective identity, we find in poems like Grainger's reminds us of the particular care we need to take when poets in Britain's staples colonies engage racial matters. An exchange of poems in two March issues of the *South Carolina Gazette* in 1732, its first year of publication, makes this plain as well. The eight lines of "The Cameleon Lover" tells the tale of a white man's sexual relations with a woman of African descent, while "The Cameleon's Defence" one week later adopts the voice of the male lover in casting the power of love to overcome all social, rather than biological, restrictions. By suggesting that the complexion of the presumably British-American male lover literally changes after sexual relations with a woman described as possessing "the *dark* Beauties of the *Sable* Race," the first poem is especially interesting for the way it skillfully engages, perhaps even asks its readers to interrogate, the commonplace early eighteenth-century view of the malleability of a person's complexion.[19] For the dominant view of complexion at the time held that changes in a person's skin might be produced through external stimuli like the environment or sexual relations, a view in stark contrast to more modern views of the fixity of racial categories.

In the years leading up to the American Revolution, not only was Robert Bolling probably the most prolific poet from Virginia to publish, but he also has the distinction of writing one of the most humorous satires in verse of the period. He did all this in addition to producing a number of other short works that evidence his considerable poetic skill. Bolling was born into a prominent Virginian family, and, like many male children from such families at the time, he was educated in London. His experience in London, where most of his London associates were dismissive of Americans and America, can be seen in his poetry, in which he occasionally contrasts life in America with life in London to highlight the positive features of America and its social world that receive little credit in England. Bolling published his poetry in American and British periodicals, including the *Virginia Gazette* and the *London Magazine*. His considerable skills at classical languages and his wide reading of material from not just England but all over Europe gave a depth of reference to his work that one rarely finds in poetry from the staples colonies in the middle of the eighteenth century. He published translations and imitations of classical works and genres as well as many occasional poems. Indeed, one reason Bolling's writings have not become better known among scholars is because a knowledge of the intimate details of specific historical situations, events, and persons is necessary to understand them. Many of them, in other words, are so tied to the occasions of their production that they have become difficult to comprehend as the years have passed and the occasions that prompted them have faded into obscurity. Even Bolling's best poem, the mock-epic "Neanthe" in Hudibrastic verse, written probably in the early 1760s and circulated in manuscript but never published during his lifetime, suffers from the fact that the reader must know too many of the people featured in the poem for its humor to be as effective as it once was (*APSE*, p. 625). Its tale of the battle for the hand, so to speak, of a woman, Neanthe, who is the opposite of chaste and is anything but physically beautiful, retains much of its bite in part because of the absurdity of its portrait of the title character but also because of the implicit satire on courtship rituals and the idealization of feminine virtue.

Richard Beale Davis thinned the ranks of anonymous verse in the *Virginia Gazette* by one poet when, in 1971, he identified James Reid as the author of a number of poems from that periodical. Although comparatively little is known of Reid's life, we do know that he was born in Scotland and attended school there. In the colonies, Reid worked as a tutor in the late 1760s, and his writings show that he was clearly enamored of the literary life. Indeed, Reid's first identified poem, from the *Gazette* of September 1768, is labeled "To My Pen" and identifies the poet's "chiefest joy" to be "center'd in" that object.[20] Reid published a number of other short poems, writing on death and courtship, among other standard topics, but his most poignant poem seems autobiographical. In "To Ignorance," Reid speaks in the voice of a character mocked for his subpar abilities as a dancer as well as his drab clothing; he paints a compelling picture of an outsider who is made the object of ridicule by mainstream society for matters that those with the proper perspective know to be trivialities while his critics overlook qualities of far more gravity. The character of the outsider offering an unflattering portrait of American society as focused on superficialities while ignoring more weighty aspects that all humans endure as they struggle through life would have a long life in American literature. Much of the nation's most powerful literature utilizes this very structure. But as we have seen in the preceding pages, well before Reid, well before the Revolution, and well before the South emerged as a distinct community with its own ways of organizing the world, writers in this region challenged the criteria used to determine social hierarchies by presenting themselves as outsiders. Their very exclusion from the most desirable social and/or geographic spaces allowed them to see, they claimed, the world anew. It was, in part, from their position of exclusion that their poems helped give rise not only to the emergence of a southern tradition in American poetry but also to the distinctly modern ways of understanding race, commerce, and the good life with which the South became associated.

Notes

1. David S. Shields (ed.), *American Poetry of the Seventeenth and Eighteenth Centuries* (New York: Library of America, 2007), p. 131 (cited hereafter in text as *APSE*).

2. James Kirkpatrick, "An Address to James Oglethorpe," in "Two Colonial Poems on the Settling of Georgia," *Georgia Historical Quarterly* 37 (1953), p. 131.

3. Burton Egbert Stevenson, *Poems of American History* (Boston: Houghton Mifflin, 1922), p. 41.

4. Karl K. Hulley and Stanley T. Vandersall (eds.), *Ovid's Metamorphosis Englished, Mythologized, and Represented in Figures*, trans. George Sandys (Lincoln: University of Nebraska Press, 1970), p. 3 (hereafter cited in the text as *OM*).

5. Ebenezer Cooke, *Sotweed Redivivus; Or the Planters Looking-Glass* (Annapolis, Md., 1730); Ebenezer Cooke, "The History of Colonel Nathaniel Bacon's Rebellion in Virginia," in *The Maryland Muse* (Annapolis, Md., 1731).

6. John Cotton, "Bacon's Epitaph" and "Upon the Death of G.B.," in Jay B. Hubbell, "John Cotton and Ann Cotton, of Queen's Creek," *American Literature* 10 (1938), pp. 187–89.

7. J. A. Leo Lemay, *Men of Letters in Colonial Maryland* (Knoxville: University of Tennessee Press, 1972), p. 111.

8. Richard Beale Davis, C. Hugh Holman, and Louis D. Rubin (eds.), *Southern Writing, 1585–1920* (New York: Odyssey Press, 1970), pp. 242–47; Richard Beale Davis (ed.), *The Colonial Virginia Satirist* (Philadelphia: APS, 1967), p. 246.

9. James Sterling, "A Poem: On the Inventions of Letters and the Art of Printing . . . ," *American Magazine or Monthly Chronicle*, March, 1, 1758, p. 281.

10. Davis et al. (eds.), *Southern Writing*, p. 192.

11. "Belinda," "To Secretus," *South Carolina Gazette*, February 19, 1732; "Dorinda," "To Belinda," *South Carolina Gazette*, March 25, 1732.

12. Samuel Davies, *Miscellaneous Poems, Chiefly on Divine Subjects* (Williamsburg, Va., 1752).

13. Thomas Cradock, *The Poetic Writings of Thomas Cradock, 1718–1770* (Newark: University of Delaware Press, 1983), pp. 115–17.

14. Cradock, *Poetic Writings*, pp. 139–201.

15. John Mercer, "O Dinwiddianae or Select Poems Pro Patria," in Davis (ed.), *The Colonial Virginia Satirist*, pp. 15–16.

16. Richard Lewis, *The Rhapsody* (Annapolis, Md., 1732); Richard Lewis, *Carmen Seculare* (Annapolis, Md., 1732).

17. Alexander Pope, "The Dunciad, in Four Books," in Aubrey Williams (ed.), *Poetry and Prose of Alexander Pope* (Boston: Houghton Mifflin, 1969), p. 371.

18. James Kirkpatrick, *The Sea-Piece: A Narrative, Philosophical and Descriptive Poem* (London, 1750).

19. "The Cameleon Lover" and "Sable," "The Cameleon's Defence," in Kenneth Silverman (ed.), *Colonial American Poetry* (New York: Hafner, 1968), pp. 322, 323.

20. Richard Beale Davis, "James Reid, Colonial Virginia Poet and Moral and Essayist," *Virginia Magazine of History and Biography* 79 (1971), p. 11.

Chapter 6

Poetry in the Time of Revolution

KEVIN J. HAYES

As Parliament and the Lords of Trade made more demands and placed more restrictions on the American colonies in the run-up to the Revolution, the colonists lashed back in anger. The Americans ultimately expressed themselves with violence, but they also expressed themselves through verse. Poetry became an outlet for their indignation. Some poems from the Revolutionary War circulated in manuscript among like-minded readers. Others appeared in newspapers, broadsides, and pamphlets as a way of disseminating ideas and sentiments to a wider audience. The oral culture provided another method of dissemination, as many Revolutionary songs were sung in public. Oftentimes these different means of expression overlapped. A song sung in the streets would be printed in a local newspaper, reprinted in distant papers, and then sung in the streets of those distant cities. The story of poetry in the time of the American Revolution is a story of the interaction between manuscript, print, and oral culture. From the Stamp Act crisis through the Revolutionary War, colonists used poetry to vent their anger, express their political beliefs, and articulate the principles that defined the new nation.

The Stamp Act Crisis

When the news that Parliament had passed the Stamp Act reached America in May 1765, the colonists were outraged. Once the act went into effect that November, they would have to pay taxes on all kinds of printed material: almanacs, bills, legal documents, newspapers, and even playing cards. The tax itself was not the fundamental problem. What annoyed the colonists was that it was being imposed by Parliament, where they had no formal representation. Responding to their complaints, Thomas Whately, who had framed the Stamp Act, said the American colonists, like all British subjects, were "virtually represented in Parliament; for every member of Parliament sits in the House, not as Representatives of his own constituency, but as one of the August Assembly by which all the Commons of Great Britain are represented."[1]

The colonists found Whately's concept of virtual representation both absurd and callous, as "An Essay on the Virtues of the Word Virtue or Virtual" argues. An anonymous work, "Essay on the Virtues" is the earliest known poem published against the Stamp Act. It first appeared in the *New York Gazette*, July 4, 1765, and the *Boston Post Boy* reprinted it on July 15, 1765.[2] Like much American verse from the Revolutionary era, it follows the conventions of Augustan poetry established by John Dryden and Alexander Pope. Like Pope's "Essay on Man," "Essay on the Virtues" is written in heroic couplets clustered together in verse paragraphs. Paradoxically, even as the American colonists revolted against oppressive British legislation, they strictly followed the standard rules of contemporary British verse.

"Essay on the Virtues" broadens the political controversy into a semantic one. As the British stretched the meaning of the word "virtual," the poet argues, they tortured the English language, ultimately rendering words meaningless:

> Since Terms are confounded, and Words on the Rack,
> And White is oft taken for Blue or for Black,
> Since Nonsense now passes for sound Sense and Reason,
> And Words are let loose to fix what Sense you please on;
> "Tis virtual!" the same to stay here or go there,
> To breathe a free British or some other Air;
> A Freeman in London, or Vassal at Bender
> In Effect are the same – the Masculine Gender:
> Thus good Things and bad Things, and great Things and small Things,
> Are here reconciled – and virtually all Things.

During the mid-1760s, British linguists and lexicographers were seeking to fix the English language by establishing standards for the language in terms of definition, spelling, and pronunciation.[3] According to this poem, however, colonial policy made the meaning of words more vague in order to apply them to whatever arbitrary and capricious policies they wished to impose on their colonial subjects. Not only did Parliament pass arbitrary laws that restricted American political freedom, but the British also imposed arbitrary rules of language that effectively restricted freedom of speech, even freedom of thought, among their distant subjects.

In Newport, Rhode Island, the war of words over the Stamp Act that had been carried on in the local press escalated to violence when a mob hanged in effigy two men who had spoken in favor of the Stamp Act. Onto the gallows the mob posted "A New Song." The first stanza begins: "He who for a Post or Base sordid Pelf / His Country Betrays, Makes a Rope for himself." Subsequent stanzas encouraged colonists to stand their ground in defense of liberty, to maintain their rights, and to spurn all unjust taxes, concluding, "These Effigy's First, the Next the Stamp Papers Burn."[4] The effigies hung most of the day, but in the late afternoon the mob set fire to the gallows. The posted poem burned with the rest, but its physical destruction scarcely mattered. The locals had either made their own manuscript copies or committed the song to memory by singing it repeatedly.[5]

"A New Song" quickly spread outward. One Newport resident, for example, sent a manuscript copy to a Boston friend, and Bostonians soon started singing it. "A New Song" was printed on September 6, 1765, in the *Connecticut Gazette* and the *New Hampshire Gazette* and three days later in the *New York Mercury*.[6] Numerous other anti–Stamp Act poems appeared in the colonial press in the coming weeks, the most substantial being Benjamin Church's "A Dream on the Stamp Act," which appeared in the *Boston Evening Post*, October 14, 1765.

Born in Newport, Benjamin Church (1734–1778) moved to Boston in his boyhood. In 1750, he entered Harvard College, where he made his reputation writing satires on his classmates and professors. After graduation, he studied medicine locally and in London. Before 1759, he established a medical practice in Boston. For the egotistical Church, writing satirical poetry and dispensing medical advice were of a piece: both provided ways for him to build a contemporary reputation. *The Choice* (1757), which represents his finest poetic accomplishment, echoes a similarly titled poem by British poet John Pomfret celebrating the gentlemanly life. Although *The Choice* focuses largely on an affirmation of moral choices, it marks a substantial break with the Puritan verse of the past and puts New England poetry smack in the middle of the Augustan age. Church wrote little more until the Stamp Act controversy gave him an opportunity to apply his satirical powers. *The Times* (1765), published as a sixteen-page pamphlet, critiques British colonial policy in heroic couplets. The patriotic speaker of *The Times* identifies with the American land. "Wild as the soil," he is "a wild exotic neighbour to the bear." Nature is his "parent, mistress, muse and guide."[7] Church had an ear for popular rhetoric. Much of the best colonial American literature reinforced the colonists' links with the land. His sincerity remains unclear. Some see him as an American patriot, while others find him a talented opportunist who understood how to capture the attention of patriotic readers.

Church structured "A Dream on the Stamp Act" as a dream vision, a common literary device among early American authors.[8] Once the speaker of the poem falls asleep, different paper documents come alive to plead their cases – bonds, court papers, probate papers, diplomas, license papers, and newspapers. Church's use of personification is charming and effective. Responsible for granting liquor licenses, License Paper states:

> For Ages past, I've fill'd the gen'rous Bowl.
> And pour'd seraphick Pleasures on the Soul
> Of old and young, the Statesman and the Priest,
> And lull'd their troubled Mind to quiet Rest.[9]

Although the primary speaker of "A Dream on the Stamp Act" is an American patriot, Church hesitated to commit himself to the Revolution. After hostilities began, American authorities caught him corresponding with British officers. Church was taken prisoner, tried, convicted, and ordered transported to Martinique. He sailed in 1778 but perished at sea.

The Stamp Act went into effect November 1, 1765, almost bringing commercial and legal business to a standstill, as colonists refused to use the stamps. The British had greatly underestimated American resistance to the act, which Parliament repealed in March 1766, partly due to the efforts of Benjamin Franklin, who testified before Parliament against the act. Directly after the repeal Parliament passed the Declaratory Act, which gave it the right to bind the American colonies to whatever new laws it felt necessary: a legislative sword of Damocles. Colonists temporarily ignored the implications of the Declaratory Act to celebrate their victory: the repeal of the Stamp Act. They celebrated in many ways; poetry provided one medium of expression.

"The Repeal," a ninety-five-line occasional poem written in heroic couplets (but containing one odd short line toward the end for emphasis), may be the finest poem written to celebrate the Stamp Act's repeal. Although "The Repeal" appeared anonymously, Thomas Burke (1747–1783) is now recognized as its author.[10] Born in County Galway, Ireland, Burke came to America in his teens. He first settled in Virginia, contributing many poems to the *Virginia Gazette*. His most enduring poem, "The Repeal" begins by depicting ancient Greece and Rome as exemplars of freedom. With liberty secured, citizens of antiquity "Greatly unbending o'er the social bowl, / Indulged the transports of a genial soul."[11] Burke's diction recalls Church's in "A Dream on the Stamp Act." He conjures up an idealistic image of ancient culture to establish a point of comparison for colonial America, a modern society whose behavior is similarly guided by its love of freedom. The repeal of the Stamp Act gives Americans new hope. No more, Burke asserts, will the British "threat America's free sons with chains, / While the least spark of ancient fire remains."[12] The second half of Burke's poem pays homage to British politicians instrumental in the act's repeal. It ends with an image of fertility. Speaking for American men in general, the poet apologizes to their wives for ignoring them in this time of political strife: "Too long indignant tumults and alarms / Have made us heedless of your lovely charms."[13] American men and women can now come together and bring forth children into a world of freedom and liberty. Needless to say, Burke spoke too soon.

In 1772 Burke left Virginia for central North Carolina, where he became active in politics. He served as delegate to the Continental Congress from 1777 to 1781, when he was elected to a one-year term as governor of North Carolina. Despite his political ambitions, Burke continued to write poetry, leaving a volume of his verse in manuscript at the time of his death, which has since been published as *The Poems of Governor Thomas Burke of North Carolina*. This edition demonstrates Burke's fondness for love poems, pastoral verse, satirical verse, poetical dialogues, and heroic hymns to nature in the manner of James Thomson, whose writings inspired many early American poets.

Alexander Martin (1740–1807), who succeeded Burke as governor of North Carolina, was also a fair poet. *America* (1769), Martin's patriotic paean to liberty, presents a dialogue between the poet and the "Genius of America." Martin reprised the allegorical character in *A New Scene Interesting to the Citizens of the United States of America, Additional to the Historical Play of Columbus* (1798), a twelve-page verse dialogue between Christopher Columbus and the "Genius of America."[14] Martin's other writings include "A Description of Charles Town in 1769," a short satirical poem told from an outsider's point of view that critiques the natural and social world of Charleston, South Carolina.[15] "Genius of Freedom! Whither Art Thou Fled?" is Martin's poignant elegy to General Francis Nash, who died in combat during the Revolutionary War. The poem exemplifies numerous elegiac poems to emerge from the war, during which many American soldiers gave their lives.[16] That two successive governors of North Carolina would distinguish themselves as poets indicates the close ties between leadership and creative expression that existed in early America. Great leaders and great poets share some important traits: the power to think quickly, to improvise, and to imagine creative solutions under pressure.

The Poetic Circle in Revolutionary America

Not all poetry written during the Revolutionary era was politically motivated. Many people were writing more personal manuscript verse and sharing their handwritten compositions with close friends, who were busy writing verse themselves. In Pennsylvania, Massachusetts, Connecticut, and elsewhere poetic circles formed as like-minded writers came together to appreciate and critique and to encourage and promote the poetry of other members of their groups.

In the 1760s, a lively poetic culture associated with the Academy of Philadelphia emerged. The Reverend William Smith (1727–1803), the poetry-writing provost of the academy, inspired many students to start writing verse, including Nathaniel Evans (1742–1767). While at the academy, Evans formed friendships with several local poets, including Jacob Duché (1738–1798), Thomas Godfrey, Jr. (1736–1763), and Francis Hopkinson (1737–1791). Because of their passion for pastoral verse, these four became known as the Swains of the Schuylkill. Hopkinson, the wittiest poet of their circle and a distinguished musical composer, would go on to write some of the most popular ballads of the Revolutionary War, including "The Battle of the Kegs" (1778), which tells a fanciful tale of some kegs of gunpowder floating down the Delaware River that frighten British soldiers into shooting at anything and everything that floats.[17]

Many women began writing poetry during the Revolutionary era. Boston historian and playwright Mercy Otis Warren (1728–1814) is one of the best-known female poets of the time. Although she published a collection of her verse in 1790 as *Poems, Dramatic and Miscellaneous*, her Revolutionary political dramas – *The Adulateur* (1773) and *The Group* (1775) – may contain more genuine poetry than her lyric verse. In terms of literary significance, Warren's poetry and drama is overshadowed by her most substantial work, *History of the Rise, Progress, and Termination of the American Revolution* (1805). Ann Eliza Bleecker's "Written in the Retreat from Burgoyne" is a moving account of her despair at the death of her daughter when she and her family fled the British advance. She also wrote some effective lyrics, but her poems were not collected until 1793 in *The Posthumous Works of Ann Eliza Bleecker*. In Philadelphia, several Revolutionary female poets came together to share their writings. At her home, Elizabeth Graeme (1737–1801) presided over a salon that attracted many local poets, including Susanna Wright (1697–1785), Hannah Griffitts (1727–1817), and Annis Boudinot Stockton (1736–1801). The manuscript poems of these four women possess a playfulness absent from Warren's published verse. For the most part, these women circulated their poetry among themselves and a handful of other readers. Stockton created a manuscript collection of her verse, which she titled *Only for the Eye of a Friend*. Many poems from other members of their circle survive solely because Griffitts's cousin Milcah Martha Moore transcribed them in her commonplace book. The modern edition of this notebook vividly re-creates the literary world of Revolutionary America. Its contents demonstrate that the female poets of colonial Philadelphia wrote in many different verse genres: acrostics, biblical paraphrases, dream visions, elegies, meditations, occasional poems, and verse epistles.

These two poetic circles overlapped as the Swains of the Schuylkill found themselves frequently attending Graeme's salon. In addition to writing poetry of his own, Nathaniel Evans undertook the task of editing Thomas Godfrey's poetry for publication after his untimely demise. In 1765, Evans published Godfrey's posthumous works as *Juvenile Poems on Various Subjects, with the Prince of Parthia, a Tragedy*. Godfrey's lyric poetry is unremarkable, but *The Prince of Parthia* remains a landmark in American literary history. When this verse tragedy was performed in 1767, it became the first American tragedy performed on the stage.[18] Evans, in turn, died young, and Elizabeth Graeme and William Smith assumed the responsibility of editing a posthumous collection of his works, *Poems on Several Occasions, with Some Other Compositions* (1772). "To Benjamin Franklin, Esq; L.L.D.: Occasioned by Hearing Him Play on the Harmonica," for example, demonstrates Evans's technical skill as a poet. Already Franklin had established a reputation for business acumen, scientific genius, and political savvy; now he demonstrated his musical genius. Having invented and constructed from glass an instrument he called an armonica, Franklin enjoyed giving performances. Besides paying tribute to Franklin's genius, Evans indicates the power of music – and, by implication, poetry – to move the soul. Music lets man transcend the earthly, elevating himself to a higher spiritual plane. A thirty-line poem written in heroic couplets, "To Benjamin Franklin" ends with the following exclamation: "'Tis this enchanting instrument of thine, / Which speaks in accents more than half divine!"[19]

Also included in the Evans collection are verses he and Elizabeth Graeme exchanged. The playful, flirtatious manuscript poems were not originally meant for publication. Graeme kept most of her poems in manuscript, never intending them for a readership beyond her own intimate circle. Other members of her circle behaved similarly. Poetry for Graeme was a social activity; it let her ingratiate herself to other poets, gathering around her a group of like-minded souls. Yet Graeme also had personal reasons underlying what she wrote. For her, writing poetry was a kind of therapy. Her considerable output includes a metrical paraphrase, "The Psalms of David." Psalms had long been a text Graeme used for meditation as part of her closet devotions.[20] Forced to cope with the deaths of her mother and sister in 1766, Graeme returned to the psalms. The practice of versifying the psalms was not unusual. Three years earlier Francis Hopkinson had gathered numerous versified psalms for

A Collection of Psalm Tunes, with a Few Anthems and Hymns (1763). By putting psalms into verse, Graeme both diverted and comforted herself, activities that helped her to come to terms with her grief.[21]

As she and William Smith prepared Evans's collected poems for publication, Graeme realized she could not effectively publish his poems to her without publishing hers to him. Instead of signing her own name, she used her pseudonym: Laura. Evans had sent her some lines copied from Alexander Pope's "Eloise to Abelard"; she responded with "A Parody on the Foregoing Lines," which depicts the life of a country parson and implicitly critiques Evans's ministerial life. Graeme noted his studious habits – "In Greek and Latin, pious books he keeps; / And, while his Clerk sings psalms, he – soundly sleeps."[22] This poem prompted a verse response on Evans's part, "An Epistle to Laura, on Her Parody." The flirtatiousness of "An Epistle" made Graeme uneasy, as she explained in "Laura's Answer":

> Haste not to bend at Hymen's shrine;
> Let friendship, gen'rous friendship, be
> The bond to fetter you and me,
> *Vestal, Platonic* – what you will,
> So virtue reigns with freedom still.[23]

Graeme would wed Hugh Fergusson, whose loyalty to the British crown prompted others to question his wife's dedication to the American cause. They need not have. Elizabeth Graeme Fergusson remained a staunch American patriot.

While Elizabeth Graeme and other members of her poetic circle in Philadelphia shared their poems in manuscript, Phillis Wheatley (c. 1753–1784) eagerly sought to publish her verse. Wheatley's desire for publication partly stems from her lack of a close-knit circle of friends and fellow poets with whom she could share her writings. Her status as a slave, needless to say, rendered pleasant evenings reading poetry an impossibility. Yet Wheatley also sought to publish her works as a way of asserting herself, a way to efface any intellectual barriers separating her from others, and a way to insist on her humanity and her individuality in the midst of a cruel and unjust system that effaced black people's humanity and individuality.

On her arrival in a slave ship, John and Susannah Wheatley purchased Phillis as a domestic servant. They taught her to read English, mainly to acquaint her with the holy scriptures. A natural-born learner and a voracious reader, she used the Augustan poems she read as models for her early verse, which she began writing in her teens. A funeral elegy, "On the Death of the Rev.

Mr. George Whitefield," which she addressed to Whitefield's English patron, Selina Hastings, Countess of Huntingdon, gained Wheatley international renown and secured the countess's patronage. Visiting London with her master's son in 1773, Phillis Wheatley arranged publication of *Poems on Various Subjects, Religious and Moral* (1773).

In "On Being Brought from Africa to America," an eight-line poem in heroic couplets, Wheatley ponders her fate:

> 'Twas mercy brought me from my *Pagan* land,
> Taught my benighted soul to understand
> That there's a God, that there's a *Saviour* too:
> Once I redemption neither sought nor knew.
> Some view our sable race with scornful eye,
> "Their colour is a diabolic die."
> Remember, *Christians, Negros,* black as *Cain,*
> May be refin'd, and join th' angelic train.[24]

This work, though brief, demonstrates Wheatley's skill as a poet. The phrase "benighted soul" is a cliché that frequently occurs in eighteenth-century devotional literature, mainly in autobiographical narratives in which their authors explain how they received the light of Christianity. In the hands of this poet from Africa, the phrase takes on added complexity, becoming a double entendre and forming the first of four images of blackness in the poem: "sable race," "diabolic die," and "black as Cain."

John Gay coined the phrase "sable race" for *Trivia: or, The Art of Walking the Streets of London* (1716). In a blatantly racist episode, Gay uses the phrase to describe a black boy who shines shoes. The editor of a popular verse-writing handbook, *The Art of Poetry* (1762), which Wheatley may have known, gave Gay's episode greater currency by using it as an example to illustrate how to include a narrative episode within a longer poem.[25] Wheatley herself coined the alliterative phrase "diabolic die" to express the scorn some people felt toward African people. Making this phrase part of a quoted sentence, Wheatley uses direct discourse to introduce another voice to her poem – that of her oppressors – and to create a sense of drama. When the poet returns in her own voice after this quoted sentence, she appears chastened. Her use of the proverbial comparison – "black as Cain" – almost seems to accept the perspective of her oppressors. James Kilgore has compared "On Being Brought from Africa" to Paul Laurence Dunbar's "We Wear the Mask." Like the speaker of Dunbar's poem, Wheatley also wears the "mask that grins and lies."[26]

Wheatley continued writing verse through the Revolutionary era. "To His Excellency George Washington" (1776) constitutes one of the best contemporary tributes to Washington. This poem demonstrates her expertise at turning heroic couplets and brings to bear many different poetic devices – apostrophe, classical allusion, epic simile, personification – to form a moving tribute to Washington in his role as commander in chief of the Continental Army. Many other examples could be selected to illustrate Wheatley's skill as a poet, but her individual works may be less significant than her overall accomplishment. Allan Morrison finds in Phillis Wheatley the same passion and love of words as in Gwendolyn Brooks. Biographer Vincent Carretta calls Wheatley a "genius in bondage." Perhaps the most commonly used epithet is still the best: Phillis Wheatley is the mother of African American literature.

As a result of her growing renown, Wheatley formed the center of a de facto poetic circle, as other marginalized poets communicated with her either in verse or by letter. Jupiter Hammon (1711–c. 1806), the first published African American poet, made Wheatley the subject of one poem. Together Hammon and Wheatley mark a rising level of group consciousness among black people in eighteenth-century America.[27] Born into slavery on Long Island, Hammon published his first poem, "An Evening Thought: Salvation by Christ, with Penitential Cries," in 1760. His religious devotion shows in nearly all his work, including the poem to Wheatley, "An Address to Miss Phillis Wheatley, Ethiopian Poetess, Who Came from Africa at Eight Years of Age, and Soon Became Acquainted with the Gospel of Jesus Christ" (1778).

For "An Address," Hammon eschewed heroic couplets – still the predominant form of poetry in American literature – and wrote in ballad stanzas. "An Address" consists of twenty-one four-line stanzas. Hammon's diction is biblical, and he goes so far as to key his biblical allusions to specific passages of scripture. Hammon's piety is sincere, but it can be cloying. "An Address" lacks the complex ambiguity of Wheatley's "On Being Brought from Africa to America." Although she was snatched from her homeland, brought to America, and sold into slavery, Hammon sees Wheatley's odyssey as a positive one because it brought her from paganism to Christianity. The poem begins:

> O Come you pious youth! adore
> The wisdom of thy God,
> In bringing thee from distant shore,
> To learn his holy word.[28]

This seems like strange talk from one slave to another. Hammon's poem suggests that God sanctioned Wheatley's capture and enslavement. Regardless, it indicates the rhetorical power of Christianity among African American slaves. Although most were powerless to escape their condition, Christianity provided a metaphorical escape, a way they could empower themselves by working toward their eternal salvation. By accepting Christianity, slaves could find something positive in their enslaved condition.

In terms of his contribution to the history of American literature, Samson Occom (1723–1792) is best known for his sermons, but he was a fair poet as well. It was not his poetry but his bold stance against slavery that brought him into Phillis Wheatley's orbit. After reading his tirade against slavery, she initiated a correspondence with Occom, writing him a heartfelt letter to praise his outspoken views.[29] Both Mohegan Indian and Presbyterian clergyman, Occom became a missionary and brought Christianity to numerous other Native Americans. A fund-raising trip to England put him in contact with George Whitefield and the Countess of Huntingdon, who befriended him and became his patron as well.

Although a Latin elegy honoring the Reverend Thomas Thatcher by a Native American Harvard student named Eleazar, which Cotton Mather included in *Magnalia Christi Americana* (1702), deserves recognition as the first published poem by a Native American, Samson Occom was the first Native American to publish poetry in English.[30] He also edited *Choice Collection of Hymns and Spiritual Songs* (1774), an anthology of devotional poems that included several of his own composition. The imagery of "The Slow Traveller," a brief poem containing six ballad stanzas, anticipates Edgar Allan Poe's "Ulalume." Both Occom's poem and Poe's disembody the soul and then personify it, depicting the soul as an ambulatory companion to the self. The title character is the speaker of Occom's poem; his soul rushes ahead. The slower traveler urges the soul to continue forward, assuring him that he will keep him in sight as they progress toward heaven. The traveler encourages his soul to look out for him once he reaches heaven, where the two will be reunited. Like nearly all of Occom's verse, "The Slow Traveller" reflects the author's heartfelt devotion to Christian belief.[31]

While the importance of Wheatley, Hammon, and Occom has been recognized only recently, another group of poets – the Connecticut Wits – constituted the foremost poetic circle in Revolutionary America. When Elihu Hubbard Smith (1771–1798) compiled *American Poems* (1793), the very first anthology of American verse, its contents were largely devoted to the work of the Connecticut Wits. (In neglecting southern writers, Hubbard established a tradition among anthologists of American literature that continues to the present.) The Connecticut Wits came together during the early 1770s at Yale College, where John Trumbull (1750–1831), Timothy Dwight (1752–1817), David Humphreys (1752–1818), and Joel Barlow (1754–1812) all became friends.

Despite their differences in age, they came to know one another because talented students often stayed at Yale to earn their master's degrees and also to tutor undergraduate students. These four would remain active poets through the Revolutionary period. Because many published their best verse during the 1780s, their work makes a fitting conclusion to the story of poetry during the time of revolution. Trumbull, on the other hand, wrote his most renowned works in the 1770s.

Trumbull was admitted to Yale when he was seven years old, but he did not matriculate until he turned thirteen. He graduated in 1767 and took his M.A. in 1770. He remained at Yale as a tutor until 1773, when he went to Boston to read law with John Adams. As a tutor, Trumbull was inspired to compose *The Progress of Dulness* (1772–1773), a satirical poem written in Hudibrastics, that humorous form of iambic tetrameter couplets that Ebenezer Cook (sometimes spelled Cooke) and Robert Bolling had used so effectively earlier in the century. "On the Adventures of Tom Brainless," the first part of *The Progress of Dulness*, satirizes the New England college student, portraying Tom Brainless as a dunce and a dullard and attacking Yale's stagnant curriculum and stale pedagogy. The next two parts characterize a fop named Dick Hairbrain and Harriet Simper, a flighty young woman whose beautiful clothing masks her moral and mental vacuity. The first part is the strongest. While Dick and Harriet are character types derived from eighteenth-century English satire, the character of Tom Brainless is original. He is the type of insensitive and unthinking student that had been part of the American scene at least since Benjamin Franklin lampooned Harvard students in his Silence Dogood essays a half century earlier.

In August 1774, Trumbull published *An Elegy on the Times*, which chronicles the plight of Boston in the face of the Port Bill, the punitive legislation enacted in the aftermath of the Boston Tea Party. Abandoning hope of remedying injustice through official recourse, the colonists now had to rely on their own strength and perseverance. Trumbull explains:

> Ours be the manly firmness of the sage,
> From shameless foes ungrateful wrongs to bear;
> Alike removed from baseness and from rage,
> The flames of faction and the chills of fear.[32]

Trumbull's diction echoes Thomson's tragedy *Tancred and Sigismunda* (1745). Applying Thomson's language to describe the behavior and attitude of the American colonists in the face of the king's injustice, Trumbull enlarges on the positive qualities of Thomson's masculine ideal: prudence, good judgment, a belief in the importance of liberty, resistance to war unless absolutely necessary, an appreciation of the value of controlling the passions and maintaining reason, and an understanding of the importance of upholding what is right.

Trumbull soon began writing versifications, a type of political parody that involved transposing a serious work of prose into satirical poetry. The colonial tradition of travestying political speeches in verse extends back at least as far as the 1730s, when the Boston poet Joseph Green (1706–1780) versified the speeches of Governor Jonathan Belcher. Green's verse parodies circulated widely in manuscript and may have influenced Benjamin Franklin (1706–1790), whose poem "The Speech Versyfied" travesties an address by Virginia governor William Gooch in 1747.[33] On the eve of the Revolutionary War, the bombastic proclamations issued by General Thomas Gage, the royal governor of Massachusetts, provided a new impetus for verse parody. Gage's swaggering assertion of his royal authority and the heavy-handed tone of his public statements inspired Trumbull and other American satirists to undermine his authority by transforming his proclamations into satirical verse.[34] The American patriots were not the only ones to use versification to parody serious political documents. In the coming years, Loyalist poets would parody documents issued by the Continental Congress. Political pundits nowadays sometimes worry about the American public receiving its news through parody news broadcasts. Americans have been getting news through parody since the nation began.

In *A New Proclamation!*, published first in the *Connecticut Courant*, August 7–14, 1775, and subsequently as an eight-page pamphlet, Trumbull speaks in Gage's voice to demonstrate the governor's insensitivity to the plight of the American colonists. Speaking of the Battle of Lexington and Concord in this poem, Gage absolves the British regulars from culpability. They "little mischief then had done, / But kill'd eight men at Lexington." Trumbull also has Gage make fun of how the Americans reacted to the British troops: "And bragging high, as though you beat us, / No more mind Reg'lars than musquitoes."[35] Portraying American braggadocio, Trumbull good-naturedly captures an aspect that would become a defining trait of the national character and manifest itself in such characteristic American types like the backwoods braggart known as a "ring-tailed roarer."[36]

Trumbull's mosquitoes in *A New Proclamation!* constitute an important use of indigenous imagery. Throughout the history of early American literature, the mosquito had helped define whether someone had the right stuff to be a colonist. Responding to those who complained about mosquitoes in *Of Plymouth Plantation, 1620–1647*, William Bradford wrote: "They are too delicate and unfit to begin new plantations and colonies, that cannot endure the biting of a mosquito. We would wish such to keep at home till at least they be mosquito-proof."[37] The tenderfoot speaker of Ebenezer Cook's *The Sot-Weed Factor* has so little experience in the woods that he mistakes a mosquito's buzz for the sound of a rattlesnake. Complaining that "Musquitos on the Skin make blotches," the speaker of Alexander Martin's "Description of Charles Town" identifies himself as an outsider.[38] The Americans who resist the British forces at Lexington and Concord have withstood mosquitoes, and they can now withstand British regulars. Trumbull reused the motif in *M'Fingal* (1775), depicting the British regulars in much the same manner as Cook depicts his sot-weed factor. Inexperienced, they hear the sound of mosquitoes and other insects and assume they are bullets: "No more each Reg'lar Col'nel runs / From whizzing beetles, as air-guns, / Thinks hornbugs bullets, or thro' fears / Muskitoes takes for musketeers."[39]

A New Proclamation! gave Trumbull a good starting point for *M'Fingal*. He borrowed fifty or so lines from this versification, taking words he had attributed to Gage and putting them in the mouth of his eponymous hero, a supercilious and self-centered Tory. Trumbull essentially took his earlier work and used it to broaden the scope of revolutionary satire, creating a memorable character who could represent the faults of all Loyalists (*RV*, p. 510). The 1775 version of *M'Fingal* takes place at a New England town meeting. Squire M'Fingal attends to debate the legitimacy of the American rebellion. Honorius, an American patriot, defends the rebellion in the face of long-standing British oppression. Instead of denying the British treachery, Squire M'Fingal attempts to justify British behavior on the basis of self-interest (*RV*, p. 511).

Trumbull first published *M'Fingal* as a single canto, but he revised and expanded it considerably toward the end of the Revolutionary War. He split the one-canto version into two, adding a number of lines to the end of the first canto and the beginning of the second to make a smooth transition between them. He then added two more cantos, publishing the four-canto version of *M'Fingal* in 1782. The poem changed considerably because the political situation had changed considerably. With the Revolutionary War nearing its end, Trumbull recognized new satiric targets. Once Squire M'Fingal is tarred and feathered by a group of rebels, Trumbull shifts his satire to attack the issue of mob violence. Yet Trumbull's tone also changed. While the one-canto *M'Fingal* used the low burlesque conventions associated with Hudibrastic verse, the four-canto version is more elevated in tone, and it incorporates numerous allusions to the works of Homer, Virgil, and Milton (*RV*, p. 512). Trumbull's mock-epic anticipates the serious national epics that fellow members of his poetic circle would publish after the Revolutionary War.

Philip Freneau: The Poet of the Revolution

Like John Trumbull, Philip Freneau (1752–1832) travestied General Gage's proclamations by turning them into sharp-witted satiric verse. Freneau's Gage travesties include *General Gage's Soliloquy* (1775) and *General Gage's Confession* (1775). These political parodies were not his first forays into poetry, however. Freneau experimented with verse while a student at the College of New Jersey (later, Princeton). Collaborating with his classmate Hugh Henry Brackenridge (1748–1816), Freneau produced his first significant work, *A Poem, on the Rising Glory of America*, which Brackenridge read at their commencement in 1771 and which they published the following year. The poem paid homage to the spirit of Great Britain and anticipated the day when the British spirit would shine throughout America – already a commonplace theme in American literature. A few years later Freneau changed both his attitude and the poem drastically. For later editions of *Rising Glory*, Freneau revised or expurgated lines praising Great Britain. Throughout the Revolutionary period, no other poet more staunchly defended the cause of American independence.

A Voyage to Boston (1775) may be the finest of Freneau's parodies of General Gage. Echoing Alexander Martin's *America*, Freneau introduces the speaker of the poem to the "Genius of America," who provides him with a magic vest that makes him invisible and assigns him the task of using the vest to enter the "dome of state / Where Gage resides our Western potentate."[40] The poet's portrayal of Gage and his minions resembles the famous scene from *Paradise Lost* as Satan gathers the other fallen angels around him. Gage, "chief of all the Pandemonian crew," asks the others to explain the British humiliation at Lexington and Concord (*VB*, p. 10). They offer a few fatuous excuses but cannot explain how the Americans fought so well: "They fought like those who press for death's embrace / And laugh the grizly monarch in the face" (*VB*, p. 11). Gage ultimately concludes that they should attack an enemy more suited to their abilities, so they resolve to steal a sheep. As Gage and his "blackguard crew" fall asleep, the poet leaves the statehouse, returning his magic vest to the Genius of America and proceeding to celebrate the bravery of the American troops and their dedication to liberty (*VB*, p. 14).

Employment as private secretary to a prominent planter took Freneau to St. Croix in the Danish West Indies, but after he returned home, he enlisted as a private in the New Jersey militia in 1778. By no means did his military duties hinder his writing. That year he produced a strongly anti-British study, *American Independence*. Before the year's end he began serving on a coastal privateer and, while ferrying tobacco to St. Eustacia in May 1780, was captured by a British man-of-war and held for six weeks aboard the *Scorpion*, a prison ship anchored in the Hudson River. The experience inspired *The British Prison-Ship* (1781), an angry poem filled with invective that catalogues the horrors of life aboard. Although *The British Prison-Ship* has a kind of raw power, the numerous poems Freneau wrote satirizing British generals and celebrating the American patriots are much more effective both as poetry and as propaganda.

Freneau's elegy, "To the Memory of the Brave Americans under General Greene, in South Carolina, Who Fell in the Action of September 8, 1781," is one of the strongest from the Revolutionary period. Sir Walter Scott, who borrowed a line from it for *Marmion*, called it "as fine a thing as there is of the kind in the language."[41] Consisting of eight four-line stanzas, Freneau's poem exhibits great verbal economy, something that cannot be said for much of his earlier heroic verse. As Scott's attraction to the poem suggests, it possesses a Romantic quality. Overall, Freneau's poetic career spans the Augustan and Romantic eras. Although many other American poets continued using heroic couplets into the early nineteenth century, Freneau embraced the forms and sensibility of the emerging Romantic era.

After the conclusion of hostilities he wrote his best-remembered non-political poem, "The Wild Honey Suckle" (1786), which may be his crowning achievement as a poet. Consisting of four six-line stanzas that rhyme *ababcc* and taking for its subject a Carolina wildflower, the poem breaks with Augustan verse in both form and subject. The speaker initially attributes to the wildflower a beauty no man can see. Freneau thus introduces an irony: if no man can see the flower, how is the poet able to describe its beauty? The poet's presence essentially destroys what he describes. He is the snake in the garden, the one whose presence ruins Eden. As the poem continues, however, the flower becomes a symbol for man. The poet laments that this beautiful flower will wither away with the arrival of autumn: "Unpitying frosts, and Autumn's power / Shall leave no vestige of this flower." In the final stanza, the pace of the poem slackens as the poet seeks some kind of philosophical reconciliation, deciding that the flower will end where it began: "If nothing once, you nothing lose, / For when you die you are the same." After these lines, the poet closes on a melancholy note that anticipates the poetry of Robert Frost: "The space between, is but an hour, / The frail duration of a flower."[42] The wildflower functions as counterpoint to the poem itself. The flower, like man, is destined to die, but the poem endures. Through the act of writing, the poet creates something beautiful that transcends the ephemeral beauty of the wildflower.

The Quest for Epic

Throughout the eighteenth century, many readers considered Milton's biblical epic *Paradise Lost* the single greatest poem in the English language. Many British poets since Milton had sought to write epic poems themselves, with uneven results. Because nation-building had formed a prominent subject of traditional epics going back to Homer's *Odyssey*, with the success of the Revolution, many American poets turned their attention to the epic. The new nation deserved an epic poem to commemorate its founding. From Nathaniel Tucker in the South to the Connecticut Wits in New England, many poets of the Revolutionary era tried their hands at epic verse to celebrate the founding of the first modern democracy.

Coming to America from their family home in Bermuda, Nathaniel Tucker (1750–1807) and St. George Tucker (1752–1827) both looked forward to professional careers, but the two enjoyed poetry as well. Nathaniel came to Charleston, South Carolina, where he could study medicine with his older brother Thomas Tucker.[43] St. George went to Williamsburg to attend the College of William and Mary. While living in Charleston, Nathaniel wrote *The Bermudian* (1774), a topographical poem modeled on Oliver Goldsmith's "The Deserted Village" (1770). Goldsmith's poem influenced much American poetry during the final third of the eighteenth century. Before publishing *The Bermudian*, Nathaniel sent a manuscript copy to St. George, who shared it with his Williamsburg friends, a circle that included Samuel Henley (1740–1815), Thomas Jefferson (1743–1826), and James McClurg (1747–1823). These men came together as members of Virginia's first scientific organization, the Philosophical Society for the Advancement of Useful Knowledge, but all cherished poetry. Henley was a professor at the College of William and Mary who also gave public lectures about how to write poetry.[44] Henley published poetry in the *Virginia Gazette* and collected several of his poems in an appendix to his oriental tale, *The Story of Al Raoui* (1799). Dr. James McClurg dabbled in poetry. Although not known as a poet, Jefferson admitted writing some verse in his youth. The only instance of Jefferson's poetry that survives, however, is a playful verse apology written from Dolly's Chop House in London in 1786: "One Among Our Many Follies."[45]

St. George Tucker arranged for the publication of *The Bermudian* in Williamsburg, and Henley wrote an introductory poem, "To the Author: A Sonnet."[46] The form Henley chose is unusual and indicates his wide-ranging literary interests: sonnets were generally out of favor during the Augustan age.

A polymath and a student of world literature, Henley had a sixteenth-century edition of Petrarch in his Williamsburg library.[47] This sonnet also indicates Henley's knowledge of seventeenth-century English verse, as it compares *The Bermudian* to Edmund Waller's "The Battle of the Summer-Islands" (1645). The example of *The Bermudian* reveals the lively poetic culture in Williamsburg and in the South more generally. That the South produced few well-known poems during the late eighteenth century does not mean that southerners were not actively writing and sharing and enjoying one another's poetry.

The encouragement of St. George Tucker and his Williamsburg friends, followed by a London reprint of *The Bermudian* and favorable reviews in the major British periodicals, prompted Nathaniel Tucker to pursue poetry further. He settled in England to practice medicine but maintained close ties with America. At the end of the Revolutionary War, he began writing *America Delivered*, an allegorical epic patterned on *Paradise Lost*. He abandoned the work but used material from it for a masque celebrating the greatness of America that he called *Columbinus*, which he never published.

St. George Tucker was a good poet himself. He wrote such patriotic verse as *Liberty, A Poem on the Independence of America* (1788) and political satire, most notably, *The Probationary Odes of Jonathan Pindar* (1796), a pseudonymous work contemporary readers found so good that they thought Freneau had written it. But St. George Tucker really excelled when it came to writing *vers de société*, that is, poems that capture the strengths and weaknesses of people during their social interactions. For example, "The Belles of Williamsburg" (1777), which he co-wrote with James McClurg, circulated in numerous manuscript copies throughout Virginia, as its readers tried to guess which women it represented. Even after St. George Tucker turned judge, he continued to write poetry. His finest poem, "Resignation" (1807), is spoken by an old man, who regrets the loss of youth and all the wonders it represents as he faces the deterioration that comes with age. But the speaker of the poem ultimately accepts his age, realizing his pain will not last much longer and taking delight in the wisdom of a lifetime. John Adams, for one, adored this poem. He commented: "I know not which to admire most, its simplicity, its beauty, its pathos, its philosophy, its morality, its religion, or its sublimity."[48] Although Nathaniel and St. George Tucker shared a love of poetry, they approached it in very different ways. St. George enjoyed poems of the moment, those that captured special occasions, satirized political events, or described people he knew. Nathaniel chose more ambitious subjects, although his ambition outstripped his ability, as his unfinished epic *America Delivered* indicates.

Timothy Dwight chose the epic form for *The Conquest of Canaan* (1785), an eleven-book poem written in heroic couplets. Dwight saw himself as an American Milton but stopped short of Milton's use of blank verse. The heroic verse of Pope's *Iliad* and *Odyssey* Dwight found more appropriate. While Nathaniel Tucker chose a nationalistic theme for *America Delivered*, Dwight selected a biblical theme for *The Conquest of Canaan,* which retells the story of Joshua, a powerful military hero who leads the chosen people to victory. Dwight's biblical epic has numerous ties to American history. The portrayal of New England as the "new Canaan" had been an important part of Puritan literature since the early seventeenth century. Furthermore, Joshua seems remarkably similar to George Washington in both his leadership and his military expertise. Throughout *The Conquest of Canaan,* Dwight makes the analogy between the biblical story and American history explicit with reference to many heroes of the Revolutionary War.

Other members of the Connecticut Wits took inspiration from the epic. Apparently David Humphreys conceived "The Anarchiad," which he and other members of his circle wrote together. It appeared serially in the *New-Haven Gazette and Connecticut Magazine* (October 26, 1781–September 13, 1787). Inspired by mob uprisings and other threats to the fragile new democracy, "The Anarchiad" presents a series of fragments supposedly from an ancient epic about a war waged by "Anarch" to restore "Chaos and substantial night" to his nation. The phrase echoes the concluding lines from *The Dunciad* (1728–1743), Pope's scathing attack on eighteenth-century literary culture, and thus shows how deeply Pope continued to influence early American verse in terms of both metrical form and satiric tone (*RV*, p. 515).

Joel Barlow, another member of the Connecticut Wits, wrote the most renowned epic to emerge from the postwar years. *The Vision of Columbus* (1787) or *The Columbiad* (1807), as Barlow titled his revised and expanded version of the work, depicts Christopher Columbus as a sad old man dying in prison. Suddenly, an angelic figure appears – yet another version of the "Genius of America" – to demonstrate to Columbus what his great discovery had wrought, to show him the future glories of America. As Nathaniel Tucker had done in *Columbinus,* Barlow creates a gallery of allegorical characters, many derived from indigenous American mythology.[49] Like *The Conquest of Canaan* and "The Anarchiad," *The Vision of Columbus* expresses important ideas circulating in the intellectual and political worlds of post-Revolutionary America. All of these early American epics, ambitious though they may be, are more important as cultural artifacts than as literary art.

Barlow was much better when he turned from epic to mock-epic. "The Hasty-Pudding," which he wrote in France in 1793 and first published in *New York Magazine* in 1796, is his finest poem. Written in heroic couplets, "The Hasty-Pudding" reinforces the debt Revolutionary poetry owes to Alexander Pope.[50] Although its form aligns "The Hasty-Pudding" with the Augustan age, its content, especially its celebration of the folk customs and foodways of rural America, shares much with the nascent Romantic era. The speaker of the poem is an American in Paris. Homesick, he longs for some hasty pudding, the kind of cornmeal porridge he grew up eating in America. In the first of three cantos, the poet traces the history of hasty pudding, going back to pre-Columbian times. This history constitutes a characteristic device of much long Augustan verse: the progress piece. The link to pre-Columbian times lets Barlow imbue the poem with original American mythology.

In its second canto, the poem shifts from the scene of consumption to the scene of production as it describes the rituals of planting, cultivating, and harvesting corn. Throughout this canto, the poet stresses the value of hard work, which comes to fruition during harvest time. The third canto paints a picture of rural harmony, ranging from the joys of youth, to the courtship games that bring young men and women together, and to the happiness and productivity of a husband and wife working together. It ends with a close-up of a bowl filled with hasty pudding. Emphasizing how milk can enhance the taste of hasty pudding, the poet even offers a paean to the cow. He demonstrates the contentment that comes with recapturing the simple pleasures of youth.

Conclusion

Reviewing a critical study of Revolutionary verse for *Poetry* in 1916, Harriet Monroe said of the era, "It was a period which produced full-grown patriots, but its poets were extremely sophomoric."[51] Given the radical new approaches she was promoting in *Poetry*, her disdain for early American verse is understandable, but she was by no means the first to criticize early American patriotic verse. Continuing his appreciation of St. George Tucker's "Resignation," John Adams remarked, "I had rather be the author of it than of Joel Barlow's *Columbiad*."[52] Adams's remark is essentially a call to reprioritize early American verse. Those weighty national epics may be attempts at great poetry, but they are not as successful as some of the poignant lyric poems the Revolutionary poets produced, many of which started as modest poems circulating in manuscript. Although those epics are seldom read now, the impulse they reflect has continued. The long poem has become one of the defining features of

American poetry, as Walt Whitman's "Song of Myself" and Herman Melville's *Clarel* testify. Even the poets Monroe championed in *Poetry* turned to long poems to prove their poetic mettle. T. S. Eliot's *The Waste Land*, Ezra Pound's *Cantos*, and William Carlos Williams's *Paterson* – all can trace their roots to Joel Barlow's *The Vision of Columbus*. The impulse to define the meaning of the United States within an epic poem is as old as the United States itself.

Notes

1. Thomas Whatley, *The Regulations Lately Made Concerning the Colonies, and the Taxes Imposed upon Them, Considered* (London: for J. Wilkie, 1765), p. 109.
2. J. A. Leo Lemay, *A Calendar of American Poetry in the Colonial Newspapers and Magazines and in the Major English Magazines through 1765* (Worcester, Mass.: American Antiquarian Society, 1970), nos. 2042 and 2044.
3. Kevin J. Hayes, *The Mind of a Patriot: Patrick Henry and the World of Ideas* (Charlottesville: University of Virginia Press, 2008), p. 56.
4. Edward Gray, "William Almy to Elisha Story," *Proceedings of the Massachusetts Historical Society* 55 (1921–1922), p. 237.
5. Lemay, *Calendar*, no. 257.
6. Lemay, *Calendar*, nos. 2055–57.
7. Benjamin Church, *The Devil Undone: The Life and Poetry of Benjamin Church, 1734–1778*, ed. Jeffrey B. Walker (New York: Arno Press, 1982), pp. 157–58.
8. Kevin J. Hayes, *The Road to Monticello: The Life and Mind of Thomas Jefferson* (New York: Oxford University Press, 2008), p. 532.
9. Church, *Devil Undone*, p. 177.
10. J. A. Leo Lemay, "Sixty-Eight Additional Writers of the Colonial South," in Louis D. Rubin, Jr. (ed.), *A Bibliographical Guide to the Study of Southern Literature* (Baton Rouge: Louisiana State University Press, 1969), p. 339.
11. [Thomas Burke], "The Repeal," in Frank Moore (ed.), *Songs and Ballads of the American Revolution* (New York: Hurst, 1855), p. 28.
12. Burke, "The Repeal," p. 29.
13. Burke, "The Repeal," p. 31.
14. Richard Walser, "Alexander Martin, Poet," *Early American Literature* 6 (1971), pp. 55–58.
15. Kenneth Silverman, "Two Unpublished Colonial Verses," *Bulletin of the New York Public Library* 71 (1967), pp. 62–63.
16. Mary Bayard Clarke (ed.), *Wood-Notes; or, Carolina Carols: A Collection of North Carolina Poetry*, 2 vols. (Raleigh: W. L. Pomeroy, 1854), vol. 2, pp. 235–37.
17. Francis Hopkinson, *A Collection of Psalm Tunes, with a Few Anthems and Hymns Some of Them Entirely New, for the Use of the United Churches of Christ Church and St. Peter's Church in Philadelphia* ([Philadelphia: Printed by William Dunlap], 1763), pp. 169–73.

18. Jason Shaffer, "Early American Drama," in Kevin J. Hayes (ed.), *The Oxford Handbook of Early American Literature* (New York: Oxford University Press, 2008), pp. 463–64.
19. Nathaniel Evans, *George Washington's Copy of Poems on Several Occasions*, ed. Andrew Breen Myers (New York: Fordham University Press, 1976), p. 109.
20. Kevin J. Hayes, *A Colonial Woman's Bookshelf* (Knoxville: University of Tennessee Press, 1996), pp. 36–37.
21. Anne M. Ousterhout, *The Most Learned Woman in America: A Life of Elizabeth Graeme Fergusson* (University Park: Pennsylvania State University Press, 2004), pp. 111–12.
22. Evans, *George Washington's Copy*, p. 149.
23. Evans, *George Washington's Copy*, p. 154.
24. Phillis Wheatley, *The Poems of Phillis Wheatley*, ed. Julian D. Mason (Chapel Hill: University of North Carolina Press, 1989), p. 53.
25. *The Art of Poetry on a New Plan: Illustrated with a Great Variety of Examples from the Best English Poets*, 2 vols. (London: for J. Newbery, 1762), vol. 1, p. 192.
26. James C. Kilgore, "The Case for Black Literature," *Negro Digest*, July 1969, p. 66.
27. Lerone Bennett, Jr., "The Black Pioneer Period," *Ebony*, October 1970, p. 50.
28. David S. Shields (ed.), *American Poetry: The Seventeenth and Eighteenth Centuries* (New York: Library of America, 2007), p. 477.
29. Phillis Wheatley, *Complete Writings*, ed. Vincent Carretta (New York: Penguin, 2001), pp. 152–53.
30. Robert Dale Parker, *Changing Is Not Vanishing: A Collection of Early American Indian Poetry to 1930* (Philadelphia: University of Pennsylvania Press, 2011), p. 48; Joanna Brooks, *American Lazarus: Religion and the Rise of African-American and Native American Literatures* (New York: Oxford University Press, 2003), p. 78.
31. Samson Occom, *The Collected Writings of Samson Occom, Mohegan: Leadership and Literature in Eighteenth-Century Native America*, ed. Joanna Brooks (New York: Oxford University Press, 2006), p. 235.
32. John Trumbull, *The Poetical Works of John Trumbull*, 2 vols. (Hartford, Conn.: Samuel G. Goodrich, 1820), vol. 1, p. 209.
33. J. A. Leo Lemay, *The Life of Benjamin Franklin*, 3 vols. (Philadelphia: University of Pennsylvania Press, 2006–2009), vol. 2, pp. 550–53.
34. Colin Wells, "Revolutionary Verse," in Hayes (ed.), *The Oxford Handbook of Early American Literature*, pp. 508–9. This essay will be cited subsequently in the text as *RV*.
35. [John Trumbull], *A New Proclamation!* (Hartford, Conn.: Ebenezer Watson, 1775), pp. 5–6.
36. Constance Rourke, *American Humor: A Study of the National Character* (1931; New York: New York Review Books, 2004), pp. 37–69.

37. William Bradford, *Of Plymouth Plantation, 1620–1647* (New York: Modern Library, 1981), p. 159.

38. Silverman, "Two Unpublished," p. 62.

39. John Trumbull, *The Satiric Poems of John Trumbull: The Progress of Dulness and M'Fingal*, ed. Edwin T. Bowden (Austin: University of Texas Press, 1962), p. 141.

40. Philip Freneau, *A Voyage to Boston* (New York: John Anderson, 1775), p. 8. This collection will be cited subsequently in the text as *VB*.

41. Quoted in Kevin J. Hayes, "Freneau, Philip Morin (1752–1832)," in H. C. G. Matthew and Brian Harrison (eds.), *The Oxford Dictionary of National Biography*, 60 vols. (New York: Oxford University Press, 2004), vol. 20, pp. 976–77.

42. Philip Freneau, *The Poems of Philip Freneau, Poet of the American Revolution*, ed. Fred Lewis Pattee, 3 vols. (Princeton, N.J.: University Library, 1902–1907), vol. 3, pp. 306–07.

43. Lewis Leary, *The Literary Career of Nathaniel Tucker, 1750–1807* (Durham, N.C.: Duke University Press, 1951), pp. 10–13.

44. "A Course of Lectures," *Virginia Gazette*, January 2, 1772, p. 3.

45. Hayes, *Road to Monticello*, p. 314.

46. Nathaniel Tucker, *The Complete Published Poems of Nathaniel Tucker Together with Columbinus: A Mask*, ed. Lewis Leary (Delmar, N.Y.: Scholars' Facsimiles and Reprints, 1973), p. 33.

47. Hayes, *Road to Monticello*, p. 353.

48. Quoted in Charles W. Coleman, Jr., "St. Memin Portraits: St. George Tucker, Judge of the U.S. District Court for Virginia," *Magazine of American History* 7 (1881), p. 218.

49. J. A. Leo Lemay, "The Contexts and Themes of 'The Hasty-Pudding,'" *Early American Literature* 17 (1982), p. 9.

50. Lemay, "Contexts," p. 8.

51. [Harriet Monroe], "The Spirit of '76 in Poetry," review of *The Spirit of the American Revolution, as Revealed in the Poetry of the Period*, by Samuel White Patterson, *Poetry* 8 (1916), p. 267.

52. Quoted in Coleman, "St. Memin Portraits," p. 218.

★

PART II

A NEW NATION: POETRY
FROM 1800 TO 1900

Chapter 7

Asserting a National Voice

FRANK GADO

With the Revolution, our literature acquired a dramatically new role and purpose: having invented a nation, we were now to invent the terms of its distinctive expression. The noblest literary pedigree rested in poetry, and the eighteenth century, true to its penchant for taxonomic hierarchies, exalted the epic as its highest form. To be sure, Americans had written commendable lyrical poems, but these were deemed modest accomplishments. Even after a century of independence, the eminent critic E. C. Stedman would lament that the country's best poets excelled in the lyric, a genre he said suited limited ambitions. True grandeur, he asserted, would arrive "when poets of the upper cast desire to forego their studies and brief lyrical flights ... to produce the composite and heroic works that rank as masterpieces."[1] Only the emergence of an American epic would certify our credibility as a literary power and, more important, fortify our sense of nationhood.

This compulsion both inspired and crippled. As Philip Freneau mocked at the outset, "Bards of huge fame in every hamlet rise, / Each (in idea) of Virgilian size: / Even beardless lads a rhyming knack display – / Iliads begun, and finished in a day!"[2] The *Aeneid* had the major influence, principally because it pointed toward the creation of the Roman republic – the very model for the American political experiment – and in Columbus these bards perceived an analog to Aeneas as the conveyer of a declining civilization to a new land. Curiously, prior to independence Columbus had been far to the back of the public mind. He was a Catholic, after all, who had sailed for the politically repressive Spanish monarchy – the counterpart to the "tyrannical" England that the American colonists had insisted should treat them as equal subjects, entitled to parliamentary representation. Rather inconveniently, too, he had failed to recognize that this "new world" he discovered was not merely a new side to the old world of the Orient, and he never set foot on the continental mainland or on soil that would become the United States. Nevertheless, the new nation needed a mythology of its founding that rose above a dispute over taxes, shipping rights, and the participation of a minority in determining legislation, and so, regardless of the incongruence with historical fact, the Genoese navigator was pressed into service as avatar of a new age, as agent for a divinely ordered destiny. "Columbian" suddenly became a synonym for "American," and his name bespeckled the map. That he would also assume the role of epic hero was almost ineluctable.

Besides many shorter poems invoking Columbus, at least three epics bore the title *The Columbiad*, and several others were planned but aborted. Overshadowing all the rest, however, was Joel Barlow's. The young man had already resolved to vie for immortality by writing a major poem when he went off to the newly established Dartmouth College. Soon transferring to Yale, he drew close to Timothy Dwight, then a tutor who had completed (but not yet published) his epic, *The Conquest of Canaan*. By 1779, while teaching at Dwight's school in Northampton, Massachusetts, Barlow had decided on Columbus as his subject but felt unprepared to engage the full scope of an epic. Instead, he chose the scheme of a prophetic vision, a fairly common genre of that period. Eight years later, he had composed the nine books of *The Vision of Columbus*, describing the broken Great Discoverer, imprisoned by the Spanish crown, being raised from his cell by an angel to witness the wondrous future born of his four voyages. The poem seemed to augur a brilliant career. In its first five years, five editions were printed, including one in England.

Over the next two decades, Barlow continued to write poetry – including arguably his best work, "The Hasty-Pudding" and "Advice to a Raven in Russia" – but his focus fixed on foreign turmoil. His political treatises led to his being named a citizen of France after its revolution, and as American consul in Algiers from 1795 to 1797, he negotiated an important treaty with Tripoli. Even so, the intention to elevate *The Vision* into a true epic persisted – in the preface to *The Columbiad* (1807), he refers to the earlier poem as a "sketch" for the grander design. The extent of the changes was notable. A long prose "dissertation" in the earlier version recounting Peruvian history and lauding the Incan leader Manco Copac was condensed and rendered in couplets, thereby more closely stitching the story of another continent to the epic tapestry but at the cost of thematic incoherence. Similarly, previously abbreviated accounts of English settlement, French Canada, and the military history of the Revolutionary War become a progression of dioramas lacking connection to Columbus as the martyr to a vision of future greatness.

Ironically, Barlow's ambition undercut his talent, for once he departs from the tedium of long patches of merely descriptive couplets and of labored valor in the commemorative battle scenes – elements he apparently thought epic form required – his passion for human liberty excites the poem to a higher level of visionary fervor than in its 1787 precursor. The angel of *The Vision* was little more than a tour guide; reconceived here as Hesper, the genius of the Americas charged to defend the New World's claims to glory, he is a dramatic presence. When Atlas, the genius of Africa (named for the Atlas Mountains), hurls Hesper's idealism back into his teeth, angrily reminding him of the horrors accompanying the enlightenment extolled by civilization, Hesper is stripped of his pretensions. The African sharpens his attack: "Enslave my tribes!" when nature has "cast all men equal"? Human equality commands common justice: "Their fibres, feelings, reasoning powers the same, / Like wants await them, like desires inflame."[3]

This stern castigation of Hesper's blithe defense of liberty is, of course, a challenge to the reader as well. If America is to fulfill its prophecy to lead the world toward a millennial ideal, it must resolve to "purge all privations from [its] liberal code," primarily by abolishing slavery. Barlow's poem elaborates the same argument advanced in his earlier essay, "Advice to the Privileged Orders of Europe." No American writer of the federal period preaches our national exceptionalism with greater conviction, or, contrary to Washington's counsel in his Farewell Address, exhorts the new nation more ardently to meet our internationalist obligations. Our principles of equality, free elections, and federalism – a "holy Triad" – will prove a beacon for mankind that "should forever shine." The power of "Almighty Freedom," he concludes, will not only transform humanity's political institutions, sow prosperity, and foster pan-national citizenship but also release the imagination.[4] Technology will master the Mississippi's floods, create canals to permit ships to cut between continents, and invent machines for submarine and aerial travel. And the people of "Columbia" will take their destined precedence in arts and literature.

Matching the optimism for his nation, Barlow invested in a lavish printing of *The Columbiad*, confident it would assure his fortune and everlasting fame. He grossly miscalculated. Sales of the deluxe edition fell far short of expectations, and although other editions, including printings in France and Britain, fared somewhat better, critics everywhere disparaged it; it was said that few who bought the book turned many of its pages. Columbianism as the central motif for treating America's dramatic entry into history had already crested.

Virginian Daniel Bryan was no less visionary than Barlow in his opposition to slavery and his almost mystical devotion to the union. He, too, clung to neoclassical conventions in poetry. And Columbianism echoes in his constant reference to the United States as Columbia. *The Adventures of Daniel Boone* (1813), however, signaled a new direction – literally – for the epic impulse, looking west instead of east for his American apotheosis. In 1784, John Filson's popular account of Daniel Boone had presented a living symbol of the irrepressible spread of settlers through the mountain barrier, but it took three decades for our literature to seize firmly on the frontiersman as *the* national hero. That is Bryan's singular distinction. His epic unspools from the moment in Creation between Order's emergence from Chaos and the appearance of light, but its plot proceeds from Firmamental Hall on the summit of Allegany, where the angels who tend to terrestrial matters are meeting. Enterprise rises and nominates "The Hero," Boone, to explore and settle Kentucky. His candidate, the angel says, is so tender "his soul revolts / From needless cruelty, to meanest life. / He would not crush with wanton tred a fly, / Nor e'en with useless agonies of pain / Torment the poisonous snake."[5] Yet his slaying of panthers and bears in his mission to render Kentucky safe for civilized folk shows he is no St. Francis, and his rescue of a kidnapped maid he then delivers to her fiancé proves his virtue. The rough outline of the frontier adventure that James Fenimore Cooper would exploit is clearly in place here, not only in the rescue of an imperiled damsel by a natural man but also in the more important tragic theme of the hero who, in blazing the way for civilization, destroys the very Edenic wilderness he loves.

Unlike Cooper, however, Bryan skirts the compelling irony in this essential contradiction. His Boone consists entirely of deeds: no consciousness develops as a stage for dramatic resolution of meaning. More damaging, Boone's role as the roughhewn new democratic force does not conjoin with the author's involvement of angels and divine cosmological purpose cast in orotund declamations. At times, *The Adventures of Daniel Boone* veers close to spoofing the epic it purports to be. Bryan would have somewhat more success in the next decade with "The Lay of Gratitude" (1826), written to honor Lafayette during his visit to America, and "The Appeal for Suffering Genius" (1826), a plea to afford artists the means to survive, but the fruit of his aspirations never rose above tumid oration.

James Kirke Paulding, a much superior writer, also saw the West as the key to what set the United States apart, and for the better part of a decade his reputation ranked among the highest of his generation. No one defended our literary nationalism against British scorn more pugnaciously or was more steadfast in scolding British haughtiness. And no American before him had proved competent in as many genres. He advanced the art of the short story, won praise as a satirist, wrote four novels and an epistolary fiction about life in the South, and crafted a lampoon of Davy Crockett for the stage that, in two different versions, enjoyed huge success in America and England. Almost perversely, however, it is the rare literary historian who would grant credit to his poems, despite his having thought himself primarily a poet. And indeed, it was his mockery of Walter Scott's *The Lay of the Last Minstrel* in his audacious *The Lay of the Scottish Fiddle* (1813) that established his reputation.

The Backwoodsman (1818) employs none of the comic touches displayed in his other verse and some of his fiction. His venture into epic called for utmost seriousness. Although consideration of Paulding has generally restricted him to the Knickerbocker confines of New York City, his ambitions were national in scope. A fervent supporter of Andrew Jackson and a close friend of his neighbor Martin Van Buren, he offered his epic as a model for drawing the westering frontier into our literary consciousness. The epic opening lines aim directly at lofty European conventions: his tale, he announces, will be "simple" and obedient to a "humbler" muse, a manifestation of democratic pride. The "glorious feats" of "steel-clad knights, renowned in other days," he snickers, would today be crimes leading to the gallows, and he disdains "the stately dames of royal birth, / That scorn'd communion with dull things of earth." Similarly, he rejects fairies and preternatural fright figures.[6] Instead, his epic will exalt an ordinary man, Basil, driven by poverty from his New York farm to the fertile Western soil that will sustain his family in dignity.

Scenic description and a protagonist meant to be an exemplar of ordinariness, however, are unpromising basic elements in a genre virtually defined by the extraordinary, and emphasis on Basil's valor through mere multiplication of perils survived soon proves wearying. Inevitably, despite the prefatory advertisement that this would be a democratic epic celebrating the common man, Paulding bowed to the necessity of an antagonist to Basil's mission.

The reader enters Paulding's narrative squarely on the side of the white settlers, propelled by fate "To push the red-man from his solitude, / And plant refinement in the forest rude" (*TB*, p. 62). The bloody process of western expansion presumes that the establishment of civilization, serenity, and order requires the vanquishment of the savage. Midway through the poem, however, this perspective inverts: although the Indians previously characterized as "wily" and "murderous" lose none of their ferocity, they are now cast as victims rebelling against their fate. Launched as a tribute, the epic at this point becomes a tragedy. Drawing from the recent history of the Indian Wars, Paulding introduces Tenskwatawa, a sachem better known among whites as the Prophet, who totally rejects any reconciliation with the United States. In a three-day alcohol-induced trance, the Great Spirit communicates with him through a vision in which the tribes' lost hegemony is restored. This vision inflames pan-tribal war against white settlements and federal troops that intensifies until subdued by the government's superior power at Tippecanoe. Paulding, however, elaborates his version of Tenskwatawa beyond what history records. For all his preaching vengeance against the whites and the hypocrisy of their God, his more profound quarrel, ultimately, is with the injustice of the Great Spirit, who has abandoned his people and been indifferent to the destruction of their culture.

The Prophet's complexity and messianic zeal elevate *The Backwoodsman* above all other epics of this period, but his presence also creates a problem for the author. That the whites are guilty of every wrong the Prophet lists is beyond dispute, yet history prevents justice from prevailing. Not only must the Indians lose, but those who evict them from their ancestral territory must emerge as heroes if the poet is to remain true to his declared purpose. To square this circle, Paulding employs a climactic encounter between the Prophet and an old boatman preaching the Gospel who declares he has come "to lead thee to bright paths of peace and joy" through the transforming benefits of civilization. The Prophet sneers at such effeminacy. To be "the product of your Christian love," he says, would be "of every attribute of manhood shorn"; echoing the code of the Old Testament retribution, he demands nothing less than murderous repayment of the white man's evil (*TB*, p. 125). Nevertheless, the missionary's teaching of love has struck a chord of common humanity: in an ironic reversal, the Prophet spares his enemy, boasting of greater "Christian" virtue than the Christians who have slaughtered his people.

Paulding thus has it both ways: the whites, despite their treachery, are evangels of redemption and progress; the Indians, despite their cruelty, are inherently good people provoked by evil. As the war moves further west, Paulding laments the senseless carnage while stressing the valor on both sides: among the dead and dying, a German mercenary and an Irish immigrant who fought for a share of paradise in the New World embrace their equally brave fallen Indian adversaries in knightly brotherhood. The finale takes this heroic equilibrium a step further with the introduction of a scapegoat: a Briton (imported from history) who, after having fought honorably for his country, betrays his race. As the Prophet concedes the defeat of his cause, he turns on the Briton, accusing him of having taught the tribes to scalp their enemies, to dishonor their word, and to practice deceit; then, with the last of his strength, he plunges his knife into the Briton's chest. Symbolically, this act of retribution clears the way for eventual reconciliation with the good settlers. In a coda, Basil suddenly reappears, and we are informed of his rise to "judge, general, congressman, and half a score of goodly offices," while his progeny prosper in an era of peace (*TB*, pp. 173–76). With the extirpation of the serpent, the promise of Eden has been restored.

Despite its poetic deficiencies (not the least of which is its language), *The Backwoodsman* extracts a major story from events now generally ignored and invests it with mythic power. Paulding saw in the Prophet an indomitable will, a "No in thunder" that bears the potential for tragedy in the development of American literature – and indeed, much of him will be reborn in Melville's Ahab. An isolato, the Prophet "forsakes the love of woman, glory, or of gain.... All were condemned in one intense desire, / That scorched his brain and heart with quenchless fire" (*TB*, p. 91). In pursuit of human dignity, he ironically disavows community and all tempering mercies. "Sever'd from all his copper-colour'd race," he is a creature of darkness, reborn from "a dismal glen whose deep recess, / The Sun's life-giving ray never did bless" (*TB*, p. 88). The similarity is at times uncanny. He, too, is a "blasted tree" that draws down the scarring lightning from heaven to ignite defiance. And in embracing the destruction of those he champions as preferable to humiliating acquiescence, he exhibits the Promethean pride that will doom the *Pequod*: "Great Spirit! ev'n in this my dying hour, / I do defy thee, fearless of thy power. / Be it thy want of might, or lack of will, / Or one or both, I do defy thee still" (*TB*, p. 168). Poor Basil's Rotarian envoy seems pitiably sallow by comparison.

Given Paulding's close ties to the Democratic Party of Andrew Jackson, who, two decades later, would force the Cherokee onto the Trail of Tears, it is not reasonable to read this epic as providing an absolution for the sins of western expansion. Instead, the Prophet's final words warn of the nightmare being brooded by injustice:

> Hear my last adjuration – Spirit, hear!
> Let slip a race of powerful demons forth
> From the deep bosom of the blasted earth,
> To wage eternal vengeance in our name,
> To wrap the world, in one wide wasting flame,
> Sweep from their lands usurp'd the white man's fame,
> And plant still bloodier monsters in their place.

Concluding with "one last dying curse," he calls on the Spirit to "Bring thou one half of that detested race / Against the other, marshall'd face to face" until they have murdered each other – a prophecy of the Civil War forty-three years before shots would be fired at Fort Sumter (*TB*, pp. 169–70).

While Paulding was writing *The Backwoodsman*, another Knickerbocker, Robert Sands, was collaborating on an epic about an Indian subject with his college friend, James Wallis Eastburn. After Eastburn's early death left Sands to complete the task, the copyright for *Yamoyden* was issued to the deceased minister and his unidentified "friend." The long narrative poem unexpectedly proved both popular and, in its subject matter, influential. The historical content concerns Metacom, the "King Philip" who, in 1675, rallied New England's tribes to wage a bloody war against the colonists, believing that they had murdered his brother, but its story is essentially a romance about the interracial pairing of the young chief Yamoyden and Nora Fitzgerald, the Christian daughter of an irascible Puritan who had denounced their union. Because Yamoyden opposes violence, Metacom arranges to kidnap the couple's baby daughter. This sends Nora in search of her child while fighting off visions of the grisly horrors the girl may be suffering; at the same time, Fitzgerald leads a white rescue party for Nora, who is herself being pursued by the Mohegan assassin recruited by Metacom. But once the Mohegan finds Nora, her beauty converts him from his purpose, and they paddle frantically to Yamoyden. As they proceed from their canoe, the counselor of peace is ironically caught in the middle of hand-to-hand combat between an Indian band and the whites directed by Fitzgerald. A tomahawk crashes toward Fitzgerald's head, but his son-in-law deflects it into his own chest. As Yamoyden lies dying, Fitzgerald anoints him with holy chrism, and Nora clasps her husband's hand. Yet another death extinguishes the lights: "The father gazed in anguish wild, / He prest the bosom of his child, / There beat no pulse of life."[7]

The lovers' story obviously condemns bigotry, yet Yamoyden's Christian self-sacrifice also implies vindication of the whites' religious values – a question not raised by the course of preceding events. Moreover, there is no epic dimension to the mixed marriage or the threat to the family's lives. And the authors were apparently alert to the deficiency. Contradicting their portrayal of Metacom as a personification of evil, a coda presents him as a tragic king, more worthy of a crown than "the breed of palaces." Instead of advocating assimilation or brotherhood, the poem ends by restating the wrongs done to the Native peoples and, by implication, suggests that the literary exaltation of the defeated race will become the duty of our national writers. Metacom's "champion," Sands predicts, will be acclaimed "a sacred bard" everywhere that "Albion's tongue is heard, or Albion's songs resound."[8]

Despite the brief term of its success, *Yamoyden* marks a shift to the nation's westward destiny as a defining subject of our national literature. America still may have wanted to see itself as reviving classical principles – in 1824, arguing for cultural nationalism in the *North American Review*, the renowned Harvard classicist Edward Everett urged our poets to focus on "comparison of the heroic fathers of Greece with the natives of our woods" – but the international tide of Romanticism was washing over the merlons of a classically educated elite.[9] *Yamoyden*, even more than *The Backwoodsman*, is essentially a verse romance, and the ambivalence at its core about westward expansion was soon to migrate to the novel. For the immediate future, it would unfold in Cooper's Leatherstocking cycle, not in verse.

★

For Washington Allston and Richard Henry Dana, as for some others in the camp striving for literary nationalism, epic glory was a false goal. Both were intent on an aesthetic reorientation, not regression, and circumstances exposed them to the same forces of change. Allston, although South Carolina born, spent his childhood and early youth in Newport, Rhode Island, virtually in the same household as the Channing and Dana children, then in the care of their grandfather, William Ellery. Allston's close ties with Edmund Dana (Richard Henry Dana's brother) continued at Harvard, where, as admirers of Robert Southey and Ann Radcliffe, they rebelled against the dominance of neoclassicism in the school's intellectual life. After graduation, Allston left behind the provincialism of his native country, first to study painting under Benjamin West at London's Royal Academy and then to immerse himself in European art on a two-year tour, focusing on Paris and Rome. In 1809, now married to Anne Channing, he returned to England and, for the better part of the next decade, enjoyed the companionship of the Romantic poets. After his wife died, however, he yearned for her family and Massachusetts. A dozen years after his return, he married Martha Dana, another of William Ellery's grandchildren and the sister of the Dana brothers. Although chiefly recognized as a painter in the United States, "the American Titian," as he was called, was also an accomplished poet, far surpassing what his contemporary countrymen's sparse attention would indicate. The leading British poets were more generous, recognizing him as a true genius.

As cerebral in his poetry as in his art, Allston explored the nature of aesthetic effects, in course coining the term "objective correlative" (to be made famous a century later by his fellow Harvard alumnus and expatriate T. S. Eliot.) In his own writing, his espousal of the Romantics inclined him toward the sonnet, and he surpassed all previous American poets in the form. Among the nineteen he finished, those responding to particular paintings stand out. "On a Falling Group in the Last Judgment of Michael Angelo" summons "the thought of space interminable"; Raphael's *Three Angels before the Tent of Abraham* evokes the idea "of Motion ceaseless, Unity complete"; Tibaldi's *On Seeing the Picture of Æolus* stirs him to feel "Like one who, reading magic words, receives / The gift of intercourse with worlds unknown."[10] His sonnets illustrate the contesting appeals of reason and emotion, and he especially favors images of motion and imbalance, because they sharpen awareness of the shimmering boundary between earth and transcendence. "On Rembrandt; Occasioned by His Picture of Jacob's Dream" fastens on very realistic "visionary scenes" that "Yet in their random shadowings give birth / To thoughts and things of worlds to come / And fill the soul, and strike the reason dumb" (*WA*, p. 152). Perhaps his most provocative critique occurs in "On the Luxembourg Gallery," a meditation on Rubens, whom he once lauded as a liar he would rather emulate "than tell the truth in the poor, tame manner in which some painters do."

> O Rubens, thy mysterious art,
> The charm that vexes, yet enslaves the heart!
> Thy lawless style, from timid systems free,
> Impetuous rolling like a troubled sea,
> High o'er the rocks of reason's lofty verge
> Impending hangs; yet, ere the foaming surge
> Breaks o'er the bound, the refluent ebb of taste
> Back from the shore impels the watery waste.

(*WA*, p. 153)

Like this exemplar of the baroque, Allston reflects a training in classical restraint on the cusp of yielding to the dynamism of emotion. The sonnet explicates a painting that he experiences as a dramatic clash of opposing ideas and instincts. Perhaps no single poem so tersely captures the impending transformation in aesthetic concepts.

When Allston met Coleridge in Rome, the relatively unsophisticated young American found a mentor. Earlier, his enthusiasm for Romantic ideas notwithstanding, he had looked broadly to the past for formal models. "The Sylphs of the Seasons," which lent its title to his first collection (1813), employs the Scottish stanza, invented at the turn of the sixteenth century and in common use since the beginning of the eighteenth. His couplets, as in "Two Painters" and "The Paint-Kings," ring of the age of Pope in their wit, and seventeenthcentury strains emerge in such playful poems as "Thought," "A Smile," "Art," and "The Mad Lover at the Grave of His Mistress." At times, he indulges in doggerel, sharply scolding bad taste: in "Eccentricity," for example, he makes sport of several recent fads (including the raging popularity of *Childe Harold* and of the Graveyard Poets). After Rome, however, a Romantic aesthetic reigns: sentiment combines with fancy. "The Angel and the Nightingale," perhaps his best poem, presents a personal review of his artistic life, from the Wordsworthian opening lines of part II – "In childhood's dawn what bliss it is to live, / To breathe, to move, and to the senses give / Their first fresh travel o'er this glorious Earth!" – to the achievement of success and fame, and to the poisonous jealousy that then leaves him isolated, yet still pure, innocent, and fulfilled in his vocation.[11]

Richard Henry Dana, Sr., now remembered mostly as the father of the author of *Two Years before the Mast*, deserves far greater recognition as a meticulous editor and a pivotal figure in the history of American poetry. Dana spent his adolescence warmed by the foment of the Monthly Anthology Club, a group of young Federalists in the Boston area eager to promote a nationalist literature within the bounds of taste and tradition as a bulwark against abuses by a democratic culture. Like his brother Edmund and Washington Allston, members of the club's inner circle, Richard protested against slavish adherence to classical and neoclassical texts, which were to be learned by rote. A recalcitrant student, he was expelled from Harvard. But his literary passions persisted, and after a short turn at the law, he joined in founding the *North American Review*, a reincarnation of the Anthology Club publication devoted to fostering an American literature. Editorial duty honed his critical views. His review of Hazlitt's *Lectures on the English Poets* created an immediate stir by arguing for Shakespeare's superiority over Pope; soon he had established himself as the foremost advocate of Wordsworth and Romanticism in America. But Dana's zeal caused a rift among the *Review*'s editors, and although he remained in Boston, in 1821 he launched another periodical, *The Idle Man*, published out of New York.

Dana hoped New York's larger population and more receptive citizens would enable the periodical to succeed sufficiently to sustain him in a literary career. Sadly, neither contributions by Allston and William Cullen Bryant nor Dana's own well-executed essays and novellas generated enough interest to warrant its survival. But then, at the age of thirty-eight, Dana began writing poetry, and suddenly the literary career that had eluded him flourished briefly, but around 1833 his creative production faltered. Perhaps he could not meet the high standards he had set for himself: James Russell Lowell, commenting not altogether in good humor on Dana's inflexible convictions, rhymed that his fellow Bostonian was "so well aware of how things should be done / That his own works displease him before they're begun."[12] Other factors may have interfered as well. Although he attributed an almost miraculous recovery from years of fragile health to his having taken up writing poetry (and he would continue hale and fit until his death at ninety-two), his mental state over the years declined into an increasingly bitter pessimism. A religious conservative, he took issue with the Transcendentalists, even though his emphasis on spirit had much in common with their views. The nation's preoccupation with building wealth fed his despair. And the popularity of such poets as Charles Sprague, whose facile commissioned products earned many times more than Dana's carefully wrought verse, especially stoked his resentment. Yet despite his alienation, he was a significant force in the evolution of American poetry. Rufus Griswold dedicated his landmark anthology, *The Poets and Poetry of America* (1842), to Allston, but he chose Dana as one of the five great poets (along with Halleck, Bryant, Longfellow, and – particularly galling to Dana – Sprague). To be sure, Griswold's authority would diminish, yet he was not alone in awarding Dana a high place.

Most commentary on Dana's poetry agrees that "The Dying Raven" tops the rest. Its simple language subtly transforms the dying black bird who has survived the bleak winter into a metaphor for faith through suffering as necessary to life's eventual renewal. Dana would never surpass it in rich, exact description, and in the cadence of its phrasing, which anticipates his fellow New Englander, Robert Frost. His most popular work, however, displays a quite different appeal. A verse narrative, "The Buccaneer" tells a shocking story: Matthew Lee, believing himself above conscience, commits murder, but the magnificent horse Lee steals from his victim later carries the killer to his death in the sea where his master had perished. Clearly a Gothic extension from Dana's psychological fiction in *The Idle Man*, this fanciful confection of retributive justice probably fed Poe the idea for his first tale, "Metzengerstein." That said, however, there is nothing in Dana's rendering to show verse's advantage over prose. Dana's own favorite was "The Changes of Home," which is similar in theme but not in message to Wordsworth's "Michael." Returning to his origins, where he finds only unhappy outcomes, the poet rejects "the old, familiar things" for "the wide and foreign lands ... that suit the lonely soul" and sets off "for the dashing sea, the broad, full sail / And fare thee well, my own, green, quiet Vale."[13] This simple concluding choice hardly justifies the lengthy detail of the visits that precede it, however, and one must wonder whether there is a cost in cutting ties to his past. Occasionally, Dana's gloom lifts, delightfully, as in "First Love" and at the start of "Factitious Life" (in which he complains that, instead of inclining their ears to words of love, maids now prefer the talk of materialistic philosophers), but he seems unable to long resist excursions into gaumy Swedenborgianism.

★

While Boston, via a small intellectual band clustered at the *North American Review* and Harvard, was driving the debate over a national expression in literature, New York City consolidated its position as the cultural capital. The fact that Connecticut native Elihu Smith, who assembled the first anthology of American poetry (1793), established himself in New York, not Boston, indicates the way the cultural lines of force would develop. By the turn of the century, New York City had the largest population, the most wealth, the greatest sophistication, and the most dynamic mix of people. Some of its writers were natives – or nearly so; others were naturally drawn from the small towns of neighboring states to wage their careers. Unlike other cities, New York offered a vibrant array of literary and social clubs in which creative artists mingled and tested their concepts. From Italian opera to the Hudson River School in art and from novels to new periodicals, what emanated from New York caught attention in the other major cities; the flow of influence in the other direction was minimal.

No more interesting example of New York's profligate talent begs for notice than John Howard Payne, now remembered (if at all) as the author of "Home, Sweet Home." Although born in 1791 in lower Manhattan, he grew up in Boston. At fourteen he returned to New York to work as a bookkeeper, but within three months he launched his own newspaper reporting on the local stage, and in February, six weeks later, his comedy, *Julia*, opened with a notable cast at the city's principal theater. The quality of the adolescent's mind so impressed William Coleman, the owner-editor of the *New-York Evening Post*, that he secured a sponsor for Payne's college education and what Coleman was sure would be great public service in the republic. Payne had little patience for academic studies, however: after two years at Union College, he left for New York to begin an astonishingly successful acting career, and then for London and Paris, where he added translation and playwriting to his pursuits. His biographer credits him with being only a "minor poet," and both literary histories and anthologies ignore this aspect of his work, yet no American of his generation showed greater potential. Surveying "the annals of letters," Coleman judged him uniquely gifted: "Boys have sometimes appeared who wrote pretty, nay good, verses at an early age; but nothing can be found in the youthful efforts of Cowley, Pope, Milton and Chatterton evincing a [superior] strength of mind."[14]

Most of Payne's unpublished writings from his late teens and the heady years of his early stage success have presumably been lost, but what has survived is truly remarkable. An untitled poem, apparently written on his river trip north to college (although published in 1813), would suggest indebtedness to Poe's favorite devices – except that Poe was not yet born. "On the deck of the slow-moving vessel, alone," the poet watches the moon's "soft smile" light "the quivering wave." Although the ray is compared to "Christianity's gleam," the imagery implies something quite different. The "tenderness" of the "gentle," "pure" beam of light as it seems dreamily to contemplate "nature's repose" suggests a chaste lover restraining sexual desires excited by the quivering below him. The closing quatrain then reprises this repressed tumult:

> And I felt such an exquisite wildness of sorrow
> While entranced by the tremulous glow of the deep,
> That I longed to prevent the intrusion of morrow,
> And stay there forever, to wonder and weep.
>
> (*AFH*, pp. 416–17)

The title of a poem fragment apparently written at about the same age signals an intent to link the Cohoes Falls at Troy, New York, to the mythological Troy's Mount Ida, the Mountain of the Goddess – perhaps by tying suicide (or suicidal thoughts) to a frustrated suit for the favor of a local "goddess." As only a dozen lines and bits of three others remain, one can do no more than guess what the complete design might have been. Even so, the poem is worth notice. In mood and minute, sustained attention to natural movement, it evinces awareness of the Romantic redefinition of poetry at a time when *Lyrical Ballads* was barely known in the United States – and that very limited consideration mostly expressed disapproval. Payne's fragment attests either an astonishingly quick absorption of the new poetry's lessons or a precocious leap beyond his countrymen. Here Payne's protagonist, "shunning the noisy haunts of men," vividly "joy'd to mark" the Hudson's "distant waters, torn up by the crags, / Rippling and sparkling as they sprang in air"; then, after a line in which Payne seems artfully to confuse the human subject and natural object, the fragment ends with a conjunction of whelming sound and transcendent silence, of terror and reverence:

> The stream, impetuous, plunges the abyss;
> Then flows along, exulting to be free,
> With roar at which earth trembles. Here he paus'd:
> For inspiration liv'd in every wave,
> And the aw'd soul was mute. (*AFH*, p. 417)

Excepting only Bryant, Dana is often cited as America's best portrayer of nature in verse during the nineteenth century's early decades, yet nothing in Dana outshines the probative drafts of this sixteen-year-old.

Unprovidentially, Payne set too little store by his gift for poetry. Already in childhood, he strove for fame and direct, personal acclaim. Poetry could not give him that audience – or the money it brought; the stage could. By fourteen, he clearly understood the choice he faced. As he put it in the epilogue to

Julia: "If the cash be rare – / What, genius, is thy boasted lot? – despair!" Why, then, produce "a ton of verses! / If wits will write, why, let them write, and starve: / For me, thank Heav'n! I have my goose to carve."[15] To his misfortune, despite his copious production, the duplicitous practices of the theaters and his own ineptitude in business matters ensured that few geese made their way to his table. Possibly the most compact brief attesting young Payne's poetic flair lies in the conceits of this example:

> THE DEAF SEEING DANCING
>   The unexcited looker-on of love
> Is like the deaf seeing dancing. – Withheld
> The inspiration that appears to make
> The floor the light toe touches, spring to meet
> Its kiss, the wild bound looks like madness. – So
> The heart's dance seems, of the heart's music robb'd,
> A reel of bacchanals.   (*AFH*, p. 421)

Poetry's appeal to Payne did not diminish as he aged. "Silently," written when he was forty-one, deftly and delicately solicits a woman's discretion in love ("Favors, to be kind, must be / Ever granted silently.") "Star Gazing," probably from his later years, seems quite modern in its conversational speech rhythm. "Like thee, I love the stars," three of its five stanzas begin, moving the poem from aesthetic appreciation to an understanding, through the stars' distance, of "those triumphs of the little / Which makes the spirit wither up in scorn." The fifth stanza concludes with the poet, having accepted the fate the stars decreed, free again "to love the stars" purely for their beauty (*AFH*, p. 419–20). Among the unpublished poems rescued after his death in 1851, "Face to Face with Death" invites us to look on his spirit, "just ready for its flight," as it "confesses"

> Its less than nothingness; and sees with wonder
> Its once poor pathway strew'd with broken hopes
> And mad ambition's ruins: – while the forms
> Of slighted friends, hours murder'd, and the voice
> Of warning, spurn'd, and long forgotten guilt
> Call from their graves.   (*AFH*, p. 421)

Payne's judgment on himself was harsh if not altogether inaccurate. Even so, his unrecognized talents as an exceptional poet merit serious reconsideration. The pity is that so little remains for the reassessment.

William Coleman had an even greater effect on the literary fortunes of Fitz-Greene Halleck and Joseph Rodman Drake. Fortuity brought the two poets together at a dull reception where, to amuse himself, Drake wrote a few stanzas about boredom, and Halleck added lines of his own. Having enjoyed the sport, they produced several more in the same vein and submitted them to the *Evening Post*. The next day, Coleman lauded the poems in his paper and requested a visit. On arriving at the Coleman home, Drake introduced himself as "Croaker" (a name taken from a character in a Goldsmith comedy); Halleck, following his lead, extended his hand, saying, "Croaker, Jr." With that, the series acquired the tag "Croakers": the first, "To Ennui," appeared on March 13, 1819, and the rest followed at fairly regular intervals. Coleman printed the poems with great fanfare, and New York, its curiosity piqued by their anonymous authorship, delighted in these jousts against its elite.

Before year's end, Halleck, his identity still thinly veiled, published "Fanny," a long stretch of Byronic froth washing over his townsmen's foibles and follies. Among those he "sings," for example, is "a poor devil," of whom "It was not known that he had ever said / Any thing worth repeating," yet who "excelled them all / In that most noble of the sciences, / The art of making money"; consequently, his "brilliant traits of mind, and genius" shone "like the midnight lightning."[16] No poem had ever equaled it in winning an American city's favor. Copies were so coveted, they were sold and resold at up to twenty times the original price, and two years later he published a much-expanded edition.

Halleck's cleverness attracted admirers, and the city's literary arbiters boasted of him as the nation's first master satirist, but, perhaps heeding his friend (and probable lover) Drake, he expanded his poetic repertoire. His hagiolatrous tribute, "Robert Burns," mirrored America's affection for the Scottish poet. "Alnwick Castle" contrasts the valorous past with the crass present, thereafter a prominent theme. His most celebrated poem, "Marco Bozzaris," eulogized the hero of Greek independence killed in July 1823. Halleck's previously noted similarity to the Byron of *Beppo* and *Don Juan* now extended to the Byron who enlisted in the Greek cause.

The marriage of "beautiful Joe" Drake devastated Halleck, and although he tried to rationalize it as "a sacrifice at the shrine of Hymen to shun the 'pains and penalties' of poverty," he never recovered. After Drake succumbed to consumption in 1820, Halleck's bitterness continued to feed on itself until his death in 1867. (His will provided that Drake's body, along with the bodies of his family, be exhumed and buried with his.) Halleck's patently homosexual "Young America" scorned marriage while extolling what is clearly pederastic love. It was among the last poems of his ever-dwindling output.

Drake's major work, *The Culprit Fay*, preceded his collaboration in the Croakers: it was written the summer of 1819 on a dare to prove that American locales could accommodate a sustained invention about fairies as well as any in Europe. Supposedly finished in three days, it mines the same vein as Friedrich de la Motte Fouqué's *Undine*, published eight years previously, although Drake probably never read the German tale. The premise appears early, in the fifth stanza, in which the fairies hie to "the elfin court" to hear a judgment passed:

> A scene of sorrow waits them now,
> For an Ouphe has broken his vestal vow;
> He has loved an earthly maid,
> And left for her his woodland shade;
> He has lain upon her lip of dew,
> And sunned him in her eye of blue,
> Fann'd her cheek with his wing of air,
> Played in the ringlets of her hair,
> And, nestling on her snowy breast,
> Forgot the lily-king's behest.[17]

Luckily for him, she is sexually "unstained," but acquittal on the more serious charge of disobedience still requires him to perform a series of redemptive quests around the country. This device enables Drake to cram in lots of scenery, starting with the environs of West Point, where he wrote the poem. Like more insistent literary nationalists, Drake here incorporated American flora and fauna and native settings, but these attentions to calamus, sturgeon, and katydids hinder development of anything more than a superficial scheme dressed in the manner of essentially European fantasy. Ironically, this infelicitous yoking probably boosted its astonishing initial success with readers schooled to believe that European conventions were the mark of superiority. Such familiar elements from an American pen signaled that our poetry had come of age, and the poem received extravagant praise – until Edgar Allan Poe did both Drake and Halleck irreversible damage in an 1836 review. Poe mocked Drake's notion that a one-inch elf could be suspected of carnal relations with a human measuring "six feet in her stockings"; then, taking aim at Drake's putatively inventive imagery, he reduced it to a parlor game anyone could shine at.[18] The ridicule made it difficult to take Drake quite so seriously again. Poe then detailed the faults and unpoetical qualities of both Drake and Halleck. Poe did acknowledge Drake as the better poet of the two, but he also recognized that neither rose much above the level of facile wit.

The outstanding poetic talent of the period was William Cullen Bryant. A native of Cummington, Massachusetts, he won the esteem of the young literary establishment in his state, but his rise to national attention dates from his closing his law practice in the Berkshires to accept co-editorship of the newly launched *New-York Review* in 1825. The decision made him a New Yorker. Soon after that magazine and its extension as the product of a merger collapsed, William Coleman hired him as an assistant at the *New-York Evening Post*. A once passionate Federalist, Coleman probably remembered the young man as the author, at thirteen, of *The Embargo*, a best-selling anti-Jeffersonian verse diatribe, but Coleman's paper also promoted the city's culture, and Bryant's credentials, as not only a poet but also an intimate of artists, were outstanding. Whether this new career in journalism would prove felicitous, however, was uncertain – his friend Dana opposed the move. Bryant would continue to write poetry all his life, but building the *Post* and exercising political sway cut into time he might otherwise have devoted to poetry. On the other hand, working at the *Post* was "better than poetry and starvation."[19] In a short time, close association with its writers gave him a literary influence far beyond what he could have had in any other city.

Raised under the strict regimen of his maternal grandfather, a Calvinist deacon, Bryant was a sickly child who feared death's imminence and infernal punishment. But once his physician father, a pioneer homeopath, returned from his stint as a ship's doctor, he provided an anodyne to the grandfather's brimstone by teaching Cullen to love and respect nature as a source of healing for both body and soul. Later, while serving in the state legislature in Boston, Peter Bryant encountered ideas that would be refined as Transcendentalism, and he conveyed them to Cullen. Perhaps most important, as a poet manqué who had assembled one of the best verse collections in the state, Dr. Bryant also trained the boy to value poetry – especially, as did almost everyone with educated tastes, the works of Alexander Pope.

When Bryant's father submitted his son's poems to his friend Willard Phillips at the *North American Review*, his fellow editor Dana famously exclaimed, "Ah, Phillips, you have been imposed upon; no one on this side of the Atlantic is capable of writing such verses."[20] From then on, Dana became Bryant's friend, most trusted adviser in matters of poetry, and staunchest advocate. The *North American* proceeded to print some of Bryant's best early poems, as well as an essay on English metrics that surpassed any previous American scholarship on the subject, but he was still a relatively unknown outsider in the hinterlands when, in the spring of 1821, his boosters at the magazine persuaded Harvard's Phi Beta Kappa Society to invite him to speak at the college's August commencement.

Seizing the chance, Bryant, who had once planned to write an epic featuring Columbus, spent the summer composing *The Ages*, a sequence of tableaux illustrating his vision of American history. Belief in the epic as the necessary

American poem, although enfeebled, was not yet dead. *Poems*, the slim volume published on the heels of his Harvard appearance, leads with this same nationalistic hymn – as would all his subsequent collections. Even though Bryant later acknowledged that *The Ages* was inferior poetry, it advertised his aspiration to be America's bard.

"Thanatopsis," which immediately stirred the most comment, closed the volume (except for *The Ages*, the dates of composition determined the poems' order). The portion of the poem previously published in the *North American Review* had been only a fragment, beginning, "Yet a few days, and thee / The all-beholding sun shall see no more / In all his course." The next fifty-six lines of highly enjambed blank verse offered no rejoinder to its bleakness. For the *Poems* version four years later, Bryant wrote a new opening and close. Now nature, not the poet, reveals the barren fate of all that is mortal but concludes that this same death is merely obliteration of consciousness, and no more to be feared than sleep. In its denial of a hereafter, the poem becomes an affirmation of life, an exhortation to glory in existence.[21]

In denying a hereafter and a divinity beyond material nature, "Thanatopsis" should have startled the faithful, yet it set off no alarms. Perhaps "To a Waterfowl," written in 1818 while the poet questioned his choice of law as a career, served as a shield. Believers embraced that poem as affirming God's providence: the bird making its "solitary way" across the sky is in the "care" of a "Power" who will guide his creature "from zone to zone"; hence the lonely wanderer who is observing the waterfowl need have no fear about his own course in life. But the popular perception and Bryant's intention were almost certainly far apart. Bryant's Power is nature itself: if the waterfowl manifests what is inherent in its being, the observer can learn the lesson and live according to his instincts. "To a Waterfowl" and "Thanatopsis" preach the same sermon. Although later in life Bryant would accept baptism as a Unitarian and refer to a more conventional view of God in his poems, he never abandoned his trust in nature as life's absolute guide and teacher.

Recognition as his country's preeminent poet did not come until the 1832 *Poems*, published in New York and, through the intercession of his friend Washington Irving, in London. But even though the earlier collection, which had only modest success in the Boston area and sold few copies beyond it, failed to excite reviewers, it was a signal of reorientation in our national verse. Although Bryant was certainly not the first American poet to write about nature, such poems as "Inscription for the Entrance to a Wood" and "A Winter Piece" describe his scenes in the manner of a painter, defining and filling his frame; his close association with artists, particularly of the Hudson River

School, speaks to a fundamental affinity. Bryant approaches nature as a philosophical poet; a Transcendentalist well before Transcendentalism's tenets were codified, he celebrates "the eternal flow of things" through constant mutation.[22]

Equally important on another front was the sophistication he brought to the craft of poetry: not only a student of traditional English forms, he surveyed verse conventions in the several other languages he mastered and from which he translated. His early poems offer a sampler of meters and rhyme schemes, from the quatrains of "The Yellow Violet," in trimeter, and of "To a Waterfowl," in which the first and fourth trimeter lines of the quatrains enclose pentameter pairs; to the anapestic tetrameter quatrains of the remarkable "I Cannot Forget with What Fervid Devotion"; and to the inventive blank verse of "Inscription for the Entrance to a Wood." In the rhymed poems, with rare exceptions, the rhymes occur in the natural course of statement, not for the sake of the scheme, and whether rhymed or unrhymed, the verse often weaves alliteration and assonance to achieve melodic values. Again and again, he insisted that the natural rhythms and tone of speech lay at the foundation of poetry, not the confinements of metrical uniformity. Nothing Bryant wrote during these years, however, better illustrates his testing of possibilities than the opening added to "Thanatopsis" in 1821. The argument for trisyllabic feet in iambic pentameter that he had begun to advance in an 1811 essay here flowers into a strategic irregularity quite similar to what Gerard Manley Hopkins would later mean by his term "sprung rhythm." And with impressive control, he pushes meter beyond a system of stresses to attempt to orchestrate length and pitch in the sounds of his words. "Thanatopsis" is not Bryant's best poem, but it best illustrates his ingenuity in expanding the ways of poetic expression.

Bryant's influence on Robert Frost is obvious. Clearly, Isabelle Frost's requirement that her son recite "To a Waterfowl" from memory, along with other works by her favorite poet, left a lasting imprint. The two poets share a strong commitment to spoken language and to Frost's famous dictum that poetry "begins in delight and ends in wisdom."[23] Less obvious – or so one can infer from its having gone unnoticed – is Walt Whitman's deep debt to Bryant. They met as journalists in the early 1840s, and common interests brought them together for long walks. Bryant was being urged to write a long poem, in sections, about America, and perhaps with that in mind, he revived a technique he had used two decades earlier in making a poem the detailed image of the sight seen. Later, he expanded the concept to rely on lists of visual encounters. Whitman first becomes Whitman during this decade, and the similarity of the opening of "New Year's Day, 1848" to that of such a poem as Bryant's "Summer Wind" is inescapable. As Whitman draws closer to *Leaves of Grass*, the power of Bryant's example increases: "Noon," "An Evening Revery," and "Hymn of the Sea," when read aloud, show Whitman's indebtedness. That remarkable correspondence would extend to his mentor's "The Night Journey of a River." The most dramatic foreshadowing of *Leaves of Grass*, however, is in "The Prairies," which Bryant wrote on returning from a visit to his brothers in Illinois. One of his best and most exuberant uses of blank verse, this panegyric to the cycle of peoples sustained by the fecundity and beauty of the amplitude of American land expresses the epic instinct that had motivated *The Ages* and sparked the new nation's confidence in its destiny as it displaced the old Indian order.

Like many other poets, Bryant lapsed into more conventional verse as he grew older. His obligations as owner-editor of the *Evening Post* absorbed his energy, and he himself conceded that the quality of his poetry was in decline. Toward the end of his life, aware that the baton had passed to new generations of American poets, he produced graceful versions of *The Iliad* and *The Odyssey*, declaring that translation was the proper work for old poets. Even so, over the almost two decades when he was at his best, Bryant was as original and consequential a poet as his country has produced.

Notes

1. Edmund Clarence Stedman, *Poets of America* (Boston and New York: Houghton, Mifflin, 1885), p. 19.
2. Philip Freneau, *The Poems of Philip Freneau* (Princeton, N.J.: The Princeton University Library, 1907), vol. III, p. 9.
3. Joel Barlow, *The Columbiad* (London, 1809), p. 298.
4. Barlow, *The Columbiad*, pp. 301–14.
5. Daniel Bryan, *The Mountain Muse: Comprising the Adventures of Daniel Boone; and The Power of Virtuous and Refined Beauty* (Harrisonburg, Va.: printed by Davidson and Bourne, 1813), p. 45.
6. James Kirke Paulding, *The Backwoodsman* (Philadelphia: M. Thomas, 1818), pp. 7–8. Further quotations are hereafter cited parenthetically as *TB*.
7. James Wallis Eastburn and Robert Charles Sands, *Yamoyden, a Tale of the Wars of King Philip* (New York: printed by Clayton and Kingsland, 1820), p. 252.
8. Eastburn and Sands, *Yamoyden*, p. 255.
9. Edward Everett, "Politics of Ancient Greece," *North American Review* 18 (1824), p. 398.
10. Washington Allston, *The Sylphs of the Season, with Other Poems* (Boston: Cummings and Metcalf, 1813), pp. 149–51. Further quotations from this edition

are hereafter cited parenthetically as *WA*. Allston was not the only significant American artist of the period to turn to poetry: the painter Thomas Cole (1801–1848) also produced some verses of note.

11. Washington Allston, *Lectures on Art and Poems*, ed. Richard Henry Dana, Jr. (New York: Baker and Scribner, 1850), pp. 301–06.

12. James Russell Lowell, *A Fable for Critics* (Boston: Houghton, Mifflin, 1891), p. 61.

13. Richard Henry Dana, *Poems and Prose Writings* (New York: Baker and Scribner, 1850), p. 58.

14. Quoted in Grace Overmyer, *America's First Hamlet* (New York: New York University Press, 1957), p. 52; this volume will be cited subsequently in the text as *AFH*. All poems by John Howard Payne subsequently quoted here are in a brief appendix to this book, pp. 415–21.

15. John Howard Payne, *Julia, or, the Wanderer* (New York: David Longworth, 1806), p. 87.

16. James Grant Wilson (ed.), *The Poetical Writings of Fitz-Greene Halleck* (New York: D. Appleton, 1860), pp. 103–04.

17. Joseph Rodman Drake, *The Culprit Fay; and Other Poems* (New York: George Dearborn, 1836), p. 12.

18. Edgar Allan Poe, "Joseph Rodman Drake – Fitz-Greene Halleck," in G. R. Thompson (ed.), *Essays and Reviews* (New York: Library of America, 1984), p. 521.

19. Letter to Richard Henry Dana, quoted in Parke Godwin, *A Biography of William Cullen Bryant, with Extracts from His Private Correspondence* (New York: Russell and Russell, 1883), vol. 1, p. 235.

20. Frank Gado, *William Cullen Bryant: An American Voice* (Hartford, Vt.: Antoca Press, 2006), p. 11. A slightly different version of Dana's interrupted response is reported in Charles H. Brown, *William Cullen Bryant* (New York: Charles Scribner's Sons, 1971), p. 79.

21. William Cullen Bryant, *Poetical Works of William Cullen Bryant* (New York and London: D. Appleton, 1907), p. 21. A brief account of the composition of "Thanatopsis" can be found in Gado, *William Cullen Bryant*, pp. 160–61.

22. The phrase occurs in "An Evening Revery," in Bryant, *Poetical Works*, pp. 194–95. For a discussion of this key notion throughout Bryant's poetry, see Gado, *William Cullen Bryant*, pp. 179–82.

23. Robert Frost, "The Figure a Poem Makes," in *Collected Poems of Robert Frost* (New York: Henry Holt, 1939), p. 110.

Chapter 8

The Emergence of Romantic Traditions

ALFRED BENDIXEN

Calls for the creation of a national literature rang throughout the first half of the nineteenth century, but poets struggled to find verse forms capable of capturing the distinctive nature of the American landscape and American cultural life. An early fascination with the epic soon gave way to other forms, particularly those focused on detailing the specific qualities of native scenery. Narrative poetry also attracted attention but failed to produce anything coming close to the later achievements of Longfellow in this mode. The earlier examples are interesting mainly because of their treatment of frontier adventure and occasional flashes of passion. For instance, in its finest moments, John Neal's "Battle of Niagara" (1818) unites vivid description and narrative vitality into a powerful reading experience; it is certainly the most significant American literary work to emerge from the War of 1812. Neal abandoned poetry for fiction and never quite fulfilled the promise he showed in either genre, although he did play an important role in encouraging other writers. One problem facing aspiring poets was that the literary models most available to them were British works that clearly reflected the values of an aristocratic society in which order and stability were more important than fluidity and change. Thus, the many American admirers of Alexander Pope found themselves attempting to master the heroic couplet, a form whose persistent commitment to rhyme and meter seems more suited to defenses of reason and order in Augustan England than the exploration of republican values in the post-Revolutionary United States. The advent of Romanticism seemed to promise larger possibilities, with its openness to a wide range of poetic forms, its exaltation of the artist as hero, its commitment to finding meaning in nature, its emphasis on revealing the significance of the ordinary and commonplace, and its affirmation of new and bolder ways of perceiving reality.

It took a surprisingly long time for American poets to embrace the possibilities that Romantic modes offered. Emerson certainly deserves the most credit for liberating American poetry and inspiring a remarkably wide range of poets, but the emergence of a powerful Romantic tradition in the United States had a long foreground. Attention to American Romantic poetry has focused almost entirely on the Transcendentalists, but that reduces a rich field of poetic experimentation and achievement to a small part of New England culture. A number of poets practiced varieties of Romanticism that are quite different from the Transcendentalist tradition, especially in their treatment of nature, sensuality, and myth. Although many of the works discussed in this chapter are not part of the current canon of American writing, they deserve a clear place in our literary history. These authors not only attracted significant critical attention and popular acclaim but also established larger possibilities for American verse.

American Romanticism has its real beginnings in New York, not New England. The most important early examples were the work of two painters for whom poetry was a crucial means of defining and affirming aesthetic values. Washington Allston's impressive sonnets on art, most of which focus on works by Europeans, won acclaim from the British Romantics and deserve attention from any scholar interested in ekphrastic modes.[1] Allston represents the beginning of an American tradition in which the sonnet became a self-reflective form often devoted to affirming the power of artistic expression, either as a general fact or as a tribute to a specific genius. Another important artist, Thomas Cole, also produced skilled verse in a variety of forms, including some poems designed to accompany the ambitious paintings that represent the greatest achievements of the Hudson River School. Although he never quite matches Allston's mastery of phrase, Cole is unequalled in his emphasis on the power and limitations of the artistic imagination in its complex relationship to nature. In "A Painter," Cole's affirmation of nature's beauty includes an expression of regret at his own inability to match the "wild, and wondrous hues" of the mountains and woods he paints.[2] His fullest affirmation of the power of art is in "Lines Suggested by Hearing Music on the Boston Common at Night," which details the emotional impact of musical form on a sensitive listener immersed in the "Ocean of sound sublime!!" (*LOA*, p. 230). His most important poem, however, is "The Lament of the Forest," in which "the voice of the great Forest" deplores the desolation awaiting the American landscape at the hand of an emerging industrialism: "Our doom is near: behold from east to west / The skies are darkened by ascending smoke; / Each hill and every valley is become / An Altar unto Mammon, and the gods / Of man's idolatry" (*LOA*, pp. 231, 235). Cole's poem is thus part of an emerging ecological tradition in American literature that found its initial expression in popular poetry.

The American relationship to the natural world embodied a crucial conflict between reverence for the glories of a bountiful nature and the desire to convert that bounty into cash and productive industry. In this regard, George Pope Morris's "The Oak" merits special attention as one of the earliest environmental poems in our literary history to achieve immense popularity. The poem's defense of the natural world against crude materialism rests on a nostalgic affirmation of childhood memories and human connections, which were also threatened by the emergence of a commercial mentality: "Woodman, spare that tree! / Touch not a single bough! / In youth it sheltered me, / And I'll protect it now" (*LOA*, p. 251). This is not the abstract fusion of self with nature embodied in the Emersonian oversoul, but a more personal relationship to nature based both on the emotional resonance of childhood experience and on a clear insistence that a healthy relationship to the natural world entails mutual protection. The tree shelters the child, who grows into a man with the moral understanding that nature merits defending against those solely interested in monetary gain. Thus, sentiment and nostalgia join together to rebuke the worst forms of what will ultimately become industrialized capitalism. A similar vein of nostalgia runs through Samuel Woodworth's "The Bucket," which also evokes idyllic memories of a childhood immersed in the simple pleasures of nature as it transforms an ordinary object – an "old oaken bucket" – into the repository of pastoral values (*LOA*, p. 70). Both of these poems were soon turned into immensely popular songs and along with John Howard Payne's "Home, Sweet Home!" constitute a reminder that popular verse and song frequently converted the Romantic appreciation of a simple life in nature into nostalgia and sentiment, which reveal an underlying discomfort with the rise of an increasingly commercial and materialistic culture.

Not all American poets indulged in nostalgic sentiment. Of those who attracted significant attention both at home and in England, none was more daring or more original than Maria Gowen Brooks, whose lush and passionate verse earned her praise and the title "Maria Del Occidente" (Maria of the West) from the British poet laureate Robert Southey. Brooks's first book, *Judith, Esther, and Other Poems* (1820), contains a number of emotionally expressive lyrics but is especially notable for the powerful and sensuous dramatization of the Old Testament heroines in the title poems. In these works, especially "Judith," Brooks transforms the biblical framework into a vehicle for the forceful expression of female power in which heroism becomes a female virtue. Her sensuous language and fascination with erotic experience distinguish her verse, which can also be densely allusive. For example, "Written after Passing an Evening with E.W.R. A******, Esq. Who Has the Finest Person I

Ever Saw" bases its erotic longing on allusions to Sappho: "thus from the bath young Phaon came, / With that divine infusion / All glowing to the Lesbian dame, / Like a bright dream's illusion."[3]

Brooks devoted much of her Romantic fervor to the creation of a long poem, *Zóphiël: Or the Bride of Seven*, the first canto of which appeared in 1825 and then was expanded to six cantos with copious footnotes in the English edition of 1833. This remarkably ambitious work attracted significant notice and some admiration, for both its passionate verse and the blending of eroticism, unrequited love, and death at the basis of its extraordinary plot, which was drawn from the Book of Tobit in the Apocrypha. A fallen angel, Zóphiël, responds to the torments of his unrequited love for the mortal and virtuous Hebrew maiden Egla by ensuring the deaths of her first six husbands before the marriages can be consummated. The heroine finally escapes the angel and marries her destined mate, the seventh husband. The psychologically rich portrayal of Zóphiël as both angel and demon, victim and villain, adds new dimensions to the emerging tradition of the Byronic antihero. Although the book sold poorly, Brooks attracted critical acclaim; a new edition was brought out in 1879, edited by the poet Zadel Barnes Gustafson (the grandmother of Djuna Barnes).

The current critical assessment sees Brooks largely as an aberration, a solitary and undisciplined genius, a powerful voice that had no influence and left little trace. That view, however, rests on the dismissal of a number of other women poets who also dealt with passionate subjects in unladylike ways. A more generous assessment might see Brooks as the beginning of a tradition of erotic poetry by American women, a tradition that includes Mary E. Hewitt's three Sappho poems (1850), Harriet Prescott Spofford's "Pomegranate-Flowers" (1861), Adah Isaacs Menken's *Infelicia* (1868), and Ella Wheeler Wilcox's *Poems of Passion* (1883). Reading these works together suggests that Romanticism fostered a vibrant although largely neglected tradition of passionate poetry by American women that at various times has earned either considerable critical praise or a large popular audience. The most significant fact of this tradition is its insistence on recognizing the reality of sexuality, especially female sexuality, and on exalting in the fact that women can experience what Emily Dickinson calls "Wild Nights" in the poem of hers that fits most clearly in this tradition.[4] Sometimes women poets use the language of flowers and nature to explore the female body, as in Spofford's "Pomegranate-Flowers" or Lucy Larcom's "Flowers of the Fallow," thus providing an intriguing counterpart to the Calamus poems of Walt Whitman. As Emily Stipes Watts and others have noted, allusions to the classical figure of Sappho rendered sexuality into a topic fit for poetic expression, and women writers actively sought sources in mythology, as well as classical and biblical literature, that challenge the restraints of a patriarchal culture.

Recent scholarship is giving increased attention to the poets mentioned in the previous paragraph, who were either sadly missing or unfairly maligned in older literary histories. The work of recovering neglected women poets has now been going strong for several decades, resulting in impressive studies and anthologies of nineteenth-century women poets by Paula Bernat Bennett, Eliza Richards, Elizabeth Renker, Cheryl Walker, Emily Stipes Watts, Shira Wolosky, and others. Of course, nineteenth-century editors did not completely ignore women poets. In the preface to his 1849 collection, *The Female Poets of America*, Rufus Griswold singled out Maria Gowen Brooks, Elizabeth Oakes Smith, Frances Osgood, and Sarah Helen Whitman for special praise.

Elizabeth Oakes Smith became a significant feminist voice who worked in multiple genres during a long, multifaceted career, but she first gained attention with "The Sinless Child," a long poem that appeared in the *Southern Literary Messenger* in 1842. One of the defining works of the sentimental tradition in the United States, "The Sinless Child" idealizes the life and death of the virtuous child, Eva, whose incredible beauty and spiritual demeanor have the power to transform, convert, and save those who fall within her influence: "Her cheek was pale with lofty thought, / And calm her maiden air; / And all who heard her birdlike voice, / Felt harmony was there."[5] In prose headnotes introducing each of the seven parts, Oakes Smith explains her didactic purpose with excessive clarity. Thus the note for the final section explains her virtuous heroine's inevitable death: "The true woman, with woman's love and gentleness, and trust and childlike simplicity, yet with all her noble aspirations and spiritual discernments, she hath known them all without sin, and sorrow may not visit such. She ceased to be present – she passed away like the petal that hath dropped from the rose – like the last sweet note of the singing-bird, or the dying close of the wind harp."[6] Although this immensely popular work may seem quaint to twenty-first-century readers, it shaped the development of sentimental writing in its time and even inspired the depiction of little Eva in Stowe's *Uncle Tom's Cabin*. Few poems have been so influential. Oakes Smith wrote other poems that may speak more meaningfully to our time, including the remarkable "Ode to Sappho"; "The Drowned Mariner," a vivid narrative that earned a place in the "extracts" at the start of Melville's *Moby-Dick*; and a number of impressive sonnets, some of which, like "An Incident" and "The Bard," offer intriguing insights into her view of the female artist.[7]

Of the poets Griswold cites, Frances Osgood stands out as the most original and versatile, uniting in her best poems a technical mastery of rhyme and meter with an imaginative playfulness and sharp wit. Osgood's aesthetic values find fullest expression in the clever and energetic piece "A Flight of Fancy," in which the female Fancy plays havoc with the male figures of Conscience and Reason, who temporarily capture her but ultimately fail to imprison her. The poem provides a vivid defense of a female imagination with a vitality that both disturbs and defies restrictive male values. Some of her poems appear more conventional, such as those about her daughter, "Ellen Learning to Walk" and "Her Child Playing with a Watch," but even these evince an energy rarely found in poems about domestic life as well as a keen awareness of gender dynamics. Her most interesting and most original poems, however, often deal with love relationships between men and women, revealing a sharp wit and command of irony that prefigure Edna St. Vincent Millay. For instance, in "He Bade Me Be Happy," she punctures the presumption of a man who keeps returning to a woman with whom he has broken up: "He bade me 'Be happy,' he whisper'd 'Forget me,' / He vow'd my affection was cherish'd in vain. / 'Be happy!' 'Forget me!' I would, if he'd let me – / Why will he keep coming to say so again?" (*W*, p. 113). Her ironic comedy both deflates masculine conceit and questions feminine judgment in "The Lily's Delusion": a flower on a lake is beguiled by the smile of a star, unaware that "the star but smiled / To see himself reflected there" (*B*, p. 65). Osgood's remarkably fresh and sometimes daring treatment of the relationships between men and women in poetry actually led her into a public flirtation with Poe in 1845 that involved the exchange of poems published in the *Broadway Journal*. Although one rumor actually claims Poe was the real father of Osgood's third child, many scholars believe the relationship was platonic. Osgood's "The Hand That Swept the Sounding Lyre" is a noteworthy elegy to Poe, published not long before her own death from tuberculosis in 1850 (*W*, p. 131).[8]

Osgood was not the only woman whose involvement with Poe has stirred speculation. Of his flirtations with female poets, that with Sarah Helen Whitman, who claimed the title of "Poe's Helen," deserves mention. Whitman began as a follower of Transcendentalism but became the most ardent of Poe's admirers, producing a number of poems praising him, most notably "To – –," and "'The Raven.'" Her most interesting work may be the 1877 poem "Science," an attack on evolution that plays off of Poe's "Sonnet – To Science." Regarded in her own time as "the epitome of the 'poetess'" and praised for her work's "purity, its feeling for nature, and its fervent idealism" (*W*, p. 54), Whitman is a talented lyricist, but her poetry's primary value seems to be in reflecting a female counterpart to Poe's special variety of Romanticism.

Although Poe had such a distinctive metrical voice that his best works were imitated and parodied by both men and women, the responses by female poets often add intriguing insights into gender roles. Women poets seem more likely to engage Poe in verse conversation, sometimes in praise but sometimes undermining the foundations of his peculiar Romantic obsessions. Thus Phoebe Cary's comic transformation of "Annabel Lee" to "Samuel Brown" relies on switching the gender roles of the two main characters in its depiction of lost love and moving from the seaside to a town:

> The ladies not half so happy up there,
>   Went envying me and Brown;
> Yes! that was the reason, (as all men know,
>   In this dwelling down in town,)
> That the girl came out of the carriage by night,
>   Coquetting and getting my Samuel Brown.   (B, p. 98)

The parody dismisses Poe's exaltation of the death of beautiful women as the subject of great poetry and substitutes an emphasis on social realities.

In recent years, increasing attention has been paid to a number of female poets who were once popular, including Alice and Phoebe Cary, Lucretia Davidson, Emma Embury, Lucy Larcom, and Lydia Sigourney. It is no longer possible to dismiss these writers as mere sentimentalists churning out endless elegies for dead children and pretty domestic poems about home and garden. We have a larger understanding of their engagement with political and social realities and of their difficult place within a complex cultural milieu. Nevertheless, much of their verse seems graceful rather than powerful. Too often, moral reflection leads to didactic pronouncement instead of some kind of transformative vision.[9] It should, of course, be noted that a similar judgment can be made against numerous male poets who also once commanded popular audiences but are now largely forgotten, such as Charles Fenno Hoffman, Cornelius Mathews, Fitz-James O'Brien, Epes Sargent, Nathaniel Parker Willis, and William Winter. Hoffman, in fact, received twice as much space as any other poet in Griswold's groundbreaking 1842 anthology, *Poets and Poetry of America*, but has been almost completely ignored since then.

Literary historians now must confront the basic but complex issue of whether a work seems to have some enduring quality, some capacity to speak to multiple generations, or is best regarded as an artifact that reveals the interests and limitations of a specific time.[10] For instance, although there were a fairly large number of Transcendentalist poets, current literary attention has focused almost entirely on Emerson, Thoreau, Jones Very, and Christopher Pearse Cranch. Recently, scholars of Margaret Fuller, most notably Jeffrey Steele, have been attempting to establish a place for her poetry within the canon. Much less attention, however, is going to the verse of William Ellery Channing or the late sonnets of Bronson Alcott, while the poetry of William H. Furness, Charles T. Brooks, Samuel Johnson, Samuel Longfellow, Theodore Parker, and Caroline Sturgis Tappan remains largely ignored. Lawrence Buell, whose knowledge of the Transcendentalists is unrivaled, has emphasized the high quality of Ellen Hooper's poetry, which, somewhat surprisingly, is not included in the major anthologies of poetry by American women. Her artistry is demonstrated in an untitled sonnet which begins:

> Better a sin which purposed wrong to none
> Than this still wintry coldness at the heart,
> A penance might be borne for evil done
> And tears of grief and love might ease the smart.
> But this self-satisfied and cold respect
> To virtue which must be its own regard,
> Heaven keep us through this danger still alive,
> Lead us not into greatness, heart-abhorred –

Buell calls this poem "one of the neglected gems of Transcendentalist poetics: moving eloquently and surefootedly from the opening declaration to the remarkable affirmation of willingness, in effect, to be damned in order to escape from the Sahara of smugness. It is such a poem as Hester Prynne might have written."[11]

There may be reasons for Hooper's neglect, including the lack of a good critical edition of her poetry, but if Buell is right in his high assessment of her work, as I think he is, then this is clear evidence that the work of recovering the poetry of American women is still in its early stages. As efforts to explore a growing canon continue, it is almost certain that other unjustly neglected poets will be discovered. A recent edition of the unpublished writings of Jane Johnston Schoolcraft, who produced poems in formal rhymed English as well as in her native Ojibwa, certainly enlarges our appreciation of the possibilities for poetry in the early nineteenth century.[12] Schoolcraft is most interesting when she translates native oral lore into effective English, but her poems convey her personal experience with power and grace.

For a long time, it was customary to think of most of the women poets of the early and mid-nineteenth century as sentimentalists, scribbling poems about gardens and children and pretty days and producing the endless elegies that led to Mark Twain's famous satire of Emmeline Grangerford's verse in *Adventures of Huckleberry Finn*. Feminist scholars have taught us to respect the emotional power of a reader's response both to personal tragedy, such as the death of a child, and to social and political evils, particularly slavery. It is certainly true that a good bit of women's poetry does focus on the death of children, which was a more common experience in the nineteenth century than now, and that devaluing this kind of poetry seems to at least implicitly devalue the pain and suffering that was part of the lives of many American women. Nevertheless, many of the most powerful poems by women seem inspired by a different kind of Romantic impulse, one that leads these writers into more original, more engaging, and sometimes more daring confrontations with the world. Romanticism emphasizes a greater awareness of the richness of ordinary life, often exalting acts of perception that uncover the true meaning of the mundane details of human experience. In this respect, it is not surprising that some of the strongest poetry by American women focuses on a fuller apprehension of the specific kinds of work that women do. Thus, Alice Cary's "The Washerwoman" is a tribute to the working poor, and an implicit statement that a truly democratic literature must recognize the labor as well as the suffering of women. In her finest poem, "To a Shred of Linen," Lydia Sigourney offers a meditation on female creativity that moves meticulously from a contemplation of housekeeping to the issues of female authorship. Lucy Larcom's "Weaving" brilliantly uses this central metaphor to move from a single woman at the loom to the "world of women" as they engage the realities of home and nation during the Civil War (*W*, p. 229). It is not surprising that treatments of women's work often embody the act of writing poetry in clearly gendered forms of labor.

It is also tempting to point to the vast number of poems by women about the act of writing poetry in a society hostile to art, but this is a theme just as easily found in poetry by American men. It is important to stress the diversity of women's poetry in this period, which ranges from the broad comedy of Phoebe Cary's poem on women's suffrage, "Was He Henpecked?" to the abolitionist lyrics of Sarah Louisa Forten, and to the dark Romanticism of Alice Cary's tale of murder, "The Sea-Side Cave." Indeed, Romanticism's fascination with adventure and myth and the world of the fairy tale leads to a number of vigorous poems by women, including Rose Terry Cooke's powerful "Bluebeard's Closet" and the feminist rewriting of Mother Goose rhymes provided by A. D. T. Whitney. First published in 1860 and enlarged and revised in 1870 and 1882, *Mother Goose for Grown Folks* cites and responds to the traditional verse of nursery rhymes in ways that might be comic or fierce. In

"Victuals and Drink," for instance, Whitney begins: "And were you so foolish / As really to think / That all she could want / Was her victuals and drink?"[13] She ultimately compels us to recognize a process of spiritual starvation that afflicts "the famishing heart, / And the feverish brain" of women whose emotional and imaginative needs remain unmet.[14] The best of Whitney's Mother Goose poems challenge conventional assumption by establishing a fascinating dialogue with both the original nursery rhymes and the larger culture.

Romanticism's fascination with myth and adventure is, of course, not limited to female poets. William Wetmore Story's dramatic monologue, "Cleopatra," is astonishing in its delineation of the speaker's movement into "the jungle of memory" (*LOA*, p. 679), a dream world in which she can fulfill her passionate desire to become a wild animal, culminating in her calling to Anthony: "Come, as you came in the desert, / Ere we were women and men, / When the tiger passions were in us, / And love as you loved me then!" (*LOA*, p. 681). The poem combines raw sexuality and voluptuous description with a remarkable psychological portrayal of the tragic queen. Much of nineteenth-century American poetry was devoted to dramatizing the passions and intrigues of the classical past, particularly in the form of verse drama, which constitutes one of the most underexamined genres in our literary history. The range of plays in blank verse includes the first professionally produced play by an American author, Thomas Godfrey's *The Prince of Parthia* (1767); William Dunlap's historical drama, *André* (1798); James Nelson Barker's treatment of Puritan history, *Superstition* (1824); Robert Montgomery Bird's tragedy, *The Broker of Bogota* (1834); Nathaniel Parker Willis's Romantic comedy, *Tortesa the Usurer* (1839); George Henry Boker's Romantic tragedy, *Francesca Da Rimini* (1855); and Julia Ward Howe's *Leonora* (1857), which is set in early eighteenth-century Italy. In short, poetry played an instrumental role in the development of American drama, attracting both a popular audience and the talents of some highly capable poets.

A fuller literary history also requires recognizing the specific ways in which Romantic modes developed and flourished in the southern states. In general, southern writers tended to place more emphasis on polished, graceful form, on the musicality of the verse, and less on abstracting some grand philosophical truth from nature. The strongest poetic influence for most poets is Byron, and the great theme is death and loss. In fundamental ways, the poetry is less theological, less intellectual, and less political than that produced in New England. The expression of emotion is the main focus of this poetry, which is often free of the didacticism that marks much nineteenth-century American verse. The typical poet is not a professional author struggling to get by with editorial work of various kinds, but a gentleman whose income comes from the practice of law and perhaps the ownership of a plantation. Authors are much more likely to produce nature poems or fashion Romantic ballads about other times and other lands than to deal with slavery or the unpleasant reality of racism. With some notable exceptions, southern verse tends to be both more graceful and more superficial than its northern counterparts.

In addition to Poe, the principal antebellum southern figures are Edward Coote Pinkney, Richard Henry Wilde, Philip Pendleton Cooke, Thomas Holley Chivers, and William Gilmore Simms. During his short life, Pinkney produced some of the most graceful love poems of his time, particularly in "Serenade" and "A Health," both of which are devoted to praising beautiful women: "Look out upon the stars, my love / And shame them with thine eyes"; "I fill this cup to one made up of loveliness alone, / A woman, of her gentle sex, the seeming paragon" (*LOA*, p. 248). His "Italy" offers unqualified praise of that country, while "The Voyager's Song" relishes the quest for the fountain of youth without any deeper consideration of the implications of the desire to avoid aging and time. Richard Henry Wilde's most famous poem, "Lament of the Captive," is best known for its opening lines: "My life is like a summer rose" (*LOA*, p. 84); his finest work is his sonnet "To the Mocking-Bird," which is among the best of the numerous poems Americans have written about this bird.

American poets, particularly southerners, often turned to the mockingbird because their own native land lacked the bird dearest to the English poetic imagination, the nightingale. In addition to the qualities that it shares with most birds – the capacity to fly and sing – the nightingale is one of the few birds that sings boldly during the night. Furthermore, it evokes the myth of Philomela, who is transformed into a nightingale after being viciously raped by a man who cuts out her tongue.[15] Thus, both ornithological fact and mythological reference evoke the transformative power of poetry, its ability to confront the darkness of human experience and give voice to those who have been cruelly silenced. But the American landscape lacked nightingales. The principal poetic bird of our literary tradition has been the mockingbird, which possesses a vast capacity for mimicry and can be quite assertive but is not inherently tied to deeper mythological meaning. In paying tribute to the "Winged Mimic of the woods" (*LOA*, p. 85), Wilde distinguishes between the "Wit, sophist, songster, Yorick" of the day who is "Archer mocker, and mad abbot of misrule!" and the "soft, sweet, solemn, pensive strain" of the bird at night: "As if thou didst, in this thy moonlight song, / Like to the melancholy

Jaques complain, / Musing on falsehood, violence, and wrong, / And sighing for thy motley coat again!" (*LOA*, p. 86). In his blending of literary allusions (Yorick versus Jaques) and the contrasting moods of daytime mockery and nighttime complaint, the poet skillfully finds dramatic significance and philosophical depth in a bird native to the United States. Wilde's most ambitious work was the long poem *Hesperia*, which was not published until 1867, twenty years after his death, in an edition prepared by his son. In four cantos in ottava rima, the poet ranges over almost the entire American landscape, producing a peculiar and complex blend of topological epic, personal autobiography, and Byronic reflection.

During his relatively short life, Philip Pendleton Cooke earned a measure of fame with the ballad "Florence Vane," perhaps the most hardheaded of the numerous poems southerners enjoyed writing about the deaths of beautiful women, a theme that is also the basis of Cooke's "Young Rosalie Lee" (one of the inspirations for Poe's "Annabel Lee"). These were collected in his only book, the misleadingly titled *Froissart's Ballads and Other Poems* (1847), along with some mediocre nature poems and a number of narrative poems, mostly in ballad format, that convey a sense of medieval adventure (three of which are drawn from Froissart).

Among the voices who inspired Poe and shared his love for musicality and his fascination with death, none are closer in spirit or tone than Thomas Holley Chivers, who often vigorously defended Poe but accused him of plagiarizing his "To Allegra Florence in Heaven" in "The Raven." Chivers's characteristic poem mourns the death of a loved one, finds solace in the thought of a heavenly afterlife, and seeks angelic presences in this world. It is distinguished by a strong sense of rhyme and metrical form, and an emphasis on musical rhythm that sometimes values sound over meaning.

Other than Poe, William Gilmore Simms is the most important literary figure the South produced before the Civil War, but his distinction rests primarily on his fiction, particularly his historical novels. He was, however, a prolific poet who sometimes went beyond the simple nature poetry that dominated his region to produce work reflecting a significantly more complex search for meaning within a natural world that remains largely inscrutable, particularly in "The Lost Pleiad" and "The New Moon." Both of these poems take the measure of the observer's attempt to understand the heavens, of the attempt of a finite mind to comprehend an infinite universe, without indulging in the sense of loss and mourning that marks much verse. There is no grimmer, bleaker, more Gothic landscape in all of American poetry than that pictured in Simms's "The Edge of the Swamp," an unrelenting portrait of danger and despair. The complexity of nature also appears in the skillful way in which the flow of the river in his sonnet "By the Swanannoa" conveys the voice of nature in the flux of time. With the exception of Frost's "Birches," Simms's "The Grape Vine Swing" may be the most complex of the American poems in which the speaker looks back on a natural scene of his childhood. In the first stanza, the grape vine is addressed as a predator, explicitly compared to both a springing cougar and a strangling serpent, but by the second stanza, the relationship to nature becomes complex and sexual:

> Yet no foe that we fear to seek,
> The boy leaps wild to thy rude embrace;
>   Thy bulging arms bear as soft a cheek
> As ever on lover's breast found place:
>   On thy waving train is a playful hold
> Thou shalt never to lighter grasp persuade;
>   While a maiden sits in thy drooping fold,
> And swings and sings in the noonday shade![16]

It is in the poems looking back to boyhood that Simms becomes most original, especially in "Boy Lost in the Woods," a tale of "erring childhood," in which a boy's flight from home and family into the woods does not lead to the conventional moral: "It made me what I am – though it may bring me / To block or halter yet – a fearless patriot, / Ready to stand by any hapless urchin, / Doom'ed to three aunts and thirty ugly cousins."[17]

The richness of Simms's imagination also appears in some longer poems, including *Atalantis: A Tale of the Sea* (1832) and "The City of the Silent," which was composed for the dedication of a Charleston cemetery in 1850 and converts the fascination with death as poetic subject into a fully engaged and intellectually charged exploration of burial customs before moving to its affirmation of Christian immortality in its final couplet: "Show that faith still sought an upward goal, / And challenged wings for the immortal soul!" (*LOA*, p. 368). His poetry also includes a number of historical ballads and narratives, the most enduring of which has been "The Swamp Fox." His Civil War poetry reflects Confederate zeal and then despair but is not particularly distinguished. Nevertheless, Simms's best poetry reveals a mind not content with the easy glorification of natural beauty, a mind determined to seek for deeper meanings in a difficult world. He is clearly among the poets of the nineteenth century who deserve more sustained attention and who demonstrate the multifaceted nature of American poetic expression.

Notes

1. For a useful introduction to the ekphrastic, see John Hollander, *The Gazer's Spirit: Poems Speaking to Silent Works of Art* (Chicago: University of Chicago Press, 1995).

2. John Hollander (ed.), *American Poetry: The Nineteenth Century*, 2 vols. (New York: Library of America, 1994), vol. 1, p. 228. All further citations from this volume are identified in the text with *LOA* and the page number.

3. Maria Gowen Brooks, *Judith, Esther, and Other Poems* (Boston: Cummings and Hilliard, 1820), p. 43. For a perceptive account of Brooks as a transnational figure, see Kirsten Silva Gruesz, "Maria Gowen Brooks, In and Out of the Poe Circle," *ESQ: A Journal of the American Renaissance* 54 (Fall 2008), pp. 75–109. For the importance of Sappho to American women poets, see Emily Stipes Watt, *The Poetry of American Women from 1632 to 1945* (Austin: University of Texas Press, 1977), pp. 75–81.

4. For a valuable overview of this tradition, see Karen L. Kilcup, "'Wild Nights'? Approaches to Teaching Nineteenth-Century Erotic Poetry," in Paula Bernat Bennett, Karen L. Kilcup, and Philipp Schweighauser (eds.), *Teaching Nineteenth-Century American Poetry* (New York: Modern Language Association, 2007) and Paula Bernat Bennett, "Sex, Sexualities, and Female Erotic Discourse," in *Poets in the Public Sphere: The Emancipatory Project of American Women's Poetry, 1800–1900* (Princeton, N.J.: Princeton University Press, 2003), pp. 159–80. Although it does not focus on poetry, also useful is Dorri Beam, *Style, Gender, and Fantasy in Nineteenth-Century American Women's Writing* (Cambridge: Cambridge University Press, 2010).

5. Elizabeth Oakes Smith, "The Sinless Child," in *The Poetical Writings of Elizabeth Oakes Smith*, 2nd ed. (New York: J. S. Redfield, 1846), p. 35. The author's name is sometimes hyphenated: Elizabeth Oakes-Smith.

6. Oakes Smith, "The Sinless Child," pp. 85–86.

7. The most valuable representations of Oakes Smith's poetry can be found in the anthology Cheryl Walker (ed.), *American Women Poets of the Nineteenth Century* (New Brunswick, N.J.: Rutgers University Press, 1992), pp. 66–77. Poems cited from this edition hereafter will be identified with *W* and the page number. "The Drowned Mariner" may be found in the anthology Paula Bernat Bennett (ed.), *Nineteenth-Century American Women Poets* (Oxford: Blackwell, 1998), pp. 45–46. Poems cited from this edition hereafter will be identified with *B* and the page number.

8. For a fuller exploration of Poe's relationship to American women poets, see Eliza Richards, *Gender and the Poetics of Reception in Poe's Circle* (Cambridge: Cambridge University Press, 2011).

9. The most cogent attack on sentimentalism in American literature is Ann Douglas's *The Feminization of American Culture* (New York: Knopf, 1977);

perhaps the most important and influential defense of the qualities often condemned as sentimental appears in Jane Tompkins's *Sensational Designs: The Cultural Work of American Fiction, 1790–1860* (New York: Oxford University Press, 1985). For an excellent example of the revisionist scholarship that is revealing the complexity of poets once dismissed as sentimentalists, see Nina Baym, "Reinventing Lydia Sigourney," in *Feminism and American Literary History* (New Brunswick, N.J.: Rutgers University Press, 1992), pp. 151–66.

10. Thoughtful explorations of the role of values and the canon may be found in Barbara Herrnstein Smith, *Contingencies of Value* (Cambridge, Mass.: Harvard University Press, 1991) and John Guillory, *Cultural Capital: The Problem of Literary Canon Formation* (Chicago and London: University of Chicago Press, 1993).

11. Lawrence Buell, "The Transcendentalist Poets," in Jay Parini (ed.), *The Columbia History of American Poetry* (New York: Columbia University Press, 1993), pp. 113–14.

12. Jane Johnston Schoolcraft, *The Sound the Stars Make Rushing Through the Sky: The Writings of Jane Johnston Schoolcraft*, ed. Robert Dale Parker (Philadelphia: University of Pennsylvania Press, 2007).

13. A. D. T. Whitney, *Mother Goose for Grown Folks* (New York: Rudd & Carleton, 1860), p. 70.

14. Whitney, *Mother Goose for Grown Folks*, p. 73.

15. Cheryl Walker emphasizes the importance of the myth for women writers throughout *The Nightingale's Burden: Women Poets and American Culture before 1900* (Bloomington: Indiana University Press, 1982), but she relies on a different and more complex version of the myth, in which Philomela becomes a silent swallow, her sister Procne becomes a nightingale, and the rapist Tereus becomes a bird of prey; see pp. 21–22. The most common version in the English tradition has Philomela becoming a nightingale.

16. William Gilmore Simms, "The Grape Vine Swing," in James Everett Kibler, Jr. (ed.), *Selected Poems of William Gilmore Simms* (Athens: University of Georgia Press, 1990), p. 152.

17. William Gilmore Simms, "Boy Lost in the Woods," in Kibler (ed.), *Selected Poems of William Gilmore Simms*, pp. 84, 93.

Chapter 9

Linen Shreds and Melons in a Field: Emerson and His Contemporaries

CHRISTOPH IRMSCHER

On May 20, 1837, the *Albany Evening Journal* printed a poem titled "To a Shred of Linen" by Lydia Sigourney (1791–1865), now somewhat condescendingly remembered, if at all, as "the Sweet Singer of Hartford." Mrs. Sigourney, talking to a rag? Not to worry, the editor assured his readers, this poem was funny. In fact, if all literary ladies stuck to their shreds of linen, he quipped, and if they did so as beautifully as Mrs. Sigourney, then there would be fewer complaints about them.[1] Often misunderstood as an excessively sentimental and possibly not very smart poet and a writer of ponderous advice handbooks for mothers and daughters, Sigourney in this poem displayed an unexpectedly witty, even iconoclastic, streak. Not one to waste her readers' time, Sigourney, after giving us her title, proceeds to shred, literally, her very first line in two:

> Would they swept cleaner! –
>   Here's a littering shred
> Of linen left behind – a vile reproach
> To all good housewifery. Right glad am I,
> That no neat lady, train'd in ancient times
> Of pudding-making, and of sampler-work,
> And speckless sanctity of household care,
> Hath happened here, to spy thee. She, no doubt,
> Keen looking through her spectacles, would say,
> *"This comes of reading books:"* – or some spruce beau,
> Essenc'd and lily-handed, had he chanc'd
> To scan thy slight superfices, 'twould be
> *"This comes of writing poetry."* – Well – well. . . .

Establishing herself as someone who is *not* neat – who is, if truth be told, different from her pudding-producing, sampler-stitching female contemporaries, as well as from the carefully decked-out, dressed-up male ones – the speaker declares her interest in the piece of discarded cloth she has seen. Then, as if to distract the reader from too much attention to herself, the speaker demands that the piece of cloth explain itself. Which, of course, it cannot. Instead Sigourney, in metrically rocky lines that add to the conversational tone of the whole exercise, herself supplies the linen's history, beginning with the stalk of flax harvested and flailed by the New England farmer and moving on to the farmer's wife getting the bundles of fibers ready for spinning. And spun they are, by a singing maiden at her wheel, her "rustic lover" relaxing by her side. Note that while women work in Sigourney's poem, the men do nothing, or close to nothing: calculating "the mass of skeins" produced by his bride, the rustic lothario, in his excited imagination, transforms them into shelves groaning under the weight of cheese and butter (all hand-churned by his damsel), the profits from which might perchance get him a new coat someday.

Woven into a pillowcase, the newly produced linen for many years proved serviceable to different classes of people: the young, the innocent, the sick, and the sleepless, all of them at one point or another rested their weary heads on it. Think of the tears that were shed into it; think of the secrets it heard. Now all that's left is a shred, but nevertheless, the linen won't talk. Thus, in mock disgust, the speaker sends it on for recycling:

> Wilt tell no secrets, ha? – Well then, go down,
> With all thy churl-kept hoard of curious lore,
> In majesty and mystery, go down
> Into the paper-mill, and from its jaws,
> Stainless and smooth, emerge. – Happy shall be
> The renovation, if on thy fair page
> Wisdom and truth, their hallow'd lineaments
> Trace for posterity. . . .

This turn of events has important consequences. It brings the shred's life story to a conclusion. And it clears the stage for the real poetry to begin. After the tattered linen is magically and mysteriously transformed into pristine paper, it eagerly awaits the lines to be written by "wisdom and truth." Confronted with these "hallow'd lineaments" (the poetry on the page), the complaints of "the spruce beau" mentioned at the beginning of the poem are forever silenced:

> So shall thine end
> Be better than thy birth, and worthier bard
> Thine apotheosis immortalize.

But how can we forget what we just learned? How can we, faced with the near tautology in the final line ("apotheosis immortalize"), not remember that this white sheet of paper before us, about to be dignified by bardic utterance, was once a stalk of flax in a field? The real apotheosis, we can't help but feel, is not what is to come once the real poets have taken hold of the new sheet of paper. Rather, it is the one the poem has already described – the one that turns a plant into cloth and cloth into paper.

*

Ralph Waldo Emerson, too, found himself hankering after such "worthier bards." In fact, the Sweet Singer of Hartford and the Sage of Concord had more in common than standard accounts of literary history let us believe. But Emerson (1803–1882) had more in mind than just "lineaments" of truth and wisdom. In 1842, just one year after the publication of Sigourney's *Select Poems*, Emerson was working on his essay "The Poet," in which he announced, among other things, that America was still looking for her Dante, a poet liberating enough to survey, "with a tyrannous eye," the current state of the nation and celebrate it. "Our logrolling, our stumps and their politics, our fisheries, our Negroes, and Indians, our boasts, and our repudiations, the wrath of rogues, and the pusillanimity of honest men, the northern trade, the southern planting, the western clearing, Oregon, and Texas," all these were yet unsung: "I look in vain for the poet whom I describe." His lament seems even more poignant when we consider that Emerson, too, had been writing poetry, for decades.[2]

When Whitman burst on the American scene in 1855 with the first edition of *Leaves of Grass*, he looked very much like the bard whose coming Emerson had predicted. But in 1842, as Emerson found himself wishing for an American bard, Walter Whitman was still scrambling to make ends meet in New York, building houses and working for a variety of newspapers. And while Whitman was hunkering down in New York, next to his cases of type, his fingers stained with ink and his muscles taut from hard work, an "advancing multitude" of settlers (conjured up at the end of William Cullen Bryant's 1836 poem "The Prairies")[3] was continuing to push west. This was a time for loud voices, loud men, for brawn more than brain. Emerson took things into his own hands: "Merlin I" was his attempt to join the fray, his plea for a poetry written with hammer and mace, America's destiny made manifest.[4] Merlin is a composite figure, a muscular wizard-poet cobbled together from what he had read about the legendary sixteenth-century Welsh Myrrdhin and from fragments of the Arthurian romances:

> Thy trivial harp will never please
> Or fill my craving ear;
> Its chords should ring as blows the breeze,
> Free, peremptory, clear.
> No jingling serenader's art,

> Nor tinkle of piano strings,
> Can make the wild blood start
> In its mystic springs.
> The kingly bard
> Must smite the chords rudely and hard,
> As with hammer or with mace;
> That they may render back
> Artful thunder, which conveys
> Secrets of the solar track,
> Sparks of the supersolar blaze....
>
> Great is the art,
> Great be the manners, of the bard. (*CPE*, p. 92)

This is poetry that wants to say "yes, in thunder." Of course, Emerson is after flashes of insight – into the secrets of the universe, no less! – not after noise for noise's sake.[5] At the same time, it is hard to ignore the noise his own poetry makes. Lurking in the back of Emerson's mind was the Aeolian harp, favored instrument of the Romantic poets. But Emerson's harp, unlike Coleridge's, needs human players: it is not responding to the wind's gentle caresses, producing "soft-floating witchery."[6] This is magic of the rough kind: rudely plucked by the "kingly bard," the wizard harp moans, gasps, and screams. Emerson gives us not poetry slowly trembling into sound, but poetry belting out its need to be taken seriously. As Emerson's poem goes on, it becomes more and more evident that Emerson himself cannot fully play the role that he has assigned for himself. Lines *about* bad verse – about the kind of poetry a poet should never write – turn themselves into bad or at least awkward verse:

> He shall not seek to weave,
> In weak, unhappy times,
> Efficacious rhymes;
> Wait his returning strength.
> Bird, that from the nadir's floor
> To the zenith's top can soar,
> The soaring orbit of the muse exceeds that journey's length.
> Nor profane affect to hit
> Or compass that, by meddling wit,
> Which only the propitious mind
> Publishes when 'tis inclined.   (*CPE*, p. 93)

Emerson disliked poetry in which the meter influenced what the poet wants to say.[7] But in "Merlin I," as his meter adjusts and readjusts to the argument he wishes to make and as his lines alternate between three, four, and even seven beats, Emerson begins to lose focus, too. Instead of soaring to the skies,

Emerson's poetry falters, getting entangled in lines that are less than perfect. Rather than fulfilling its poetic vision, "Merlin I" talks about what the poet should *not* do, and Emerson finds himself gesturing toward a better poetry that is still to come, much as Sigourney's "To a Shred of Linen" did – poetry, in other words, that Emerson appears to admit he cannot write.

"To a Shred of Linen" was published at the beginning of the Great Panic of 1837. After British banks had raised interest rates, American banks had to scale back their loans. Businesses and farmers throughout the nation suffered grievous losses, and the price of cotton plummeted by 25 percent. These were hard times, and it's no wonder that traces of the political situation enter the poem, too – note the speaker's relief that no one sees her admiring her rag. This was not a good time to be wasting one's talents on literature. Emerson's "Merlin I" was also written at an unpropitious time, the year that the United States entered into its "shabby and to us disgraceful War" (in the words of Henry Wadsworth Longfellow)[8] with neighboring Mexico, a war that cost, some think, 15,000 American and 25,000 Mexican lives. As much as Emerson might have wanted "Merlin I" to be representative of the times, of falling trees, political stumps, and booming cannons, it wasn't even representative of the best of his own poetry. The conversational, self-mocking tone of Sigourney's "To a Shred of Linen" is more in line with the Emerson who is suspicious of what "the priest's cant / Or statesman's rant" might do to his "honied thought" ("Ode Inscribed to W. H. Channing" [1846]; *CPE*, pp. 61–62). "Merlin I" tells us little about the Emerson who is skeptical of his own orthodoxies – the same Emerson who, in *Nature*, had written that it was really hard to be a Transcendentalist when there was someone digging in a field nearby.[9]

As early as 1833, Emerson's closest ally, Margaret Fuller (1810–1850), who was then only twenty-three, had written an unrhymed poetic sketch titled "Meditations," in which the speaker faults herself for looking at nature as nothing more than a canvas on which to project her ideas of human greatness:

> In former times
> I loved to see the lightnings flash athwart
> The stooping heavens; I loved to hear the thunder
> Call to the seas and mountains; for I thought
> 'Tis thus man's flashing fancy doth enkindle
> The firmament of mind; 'tis such his eloquence
> Calls unto the soul's depths and heights; and still
> I deified the creature, nor remembered
> The Creator in his works.

Fuller offers a trenchant critique of what would become one of the corner-stones of Transcendentalist thought – the insistence on the primacy of the solitary human individual. Writing from the perspective of a disenchanted worshipper at the altar of the self ("The proud delight of that keen sympathy / Is gone"), Fuller touchingly offers a prayer in which she hopes that, given a future that now seems more uncertain, love might serve to guide her:

> But O, might I but see a little onward!
> Father, I cannot be a spirit of power;
> May I be active as a spirit of love,
> Since thou hast ta'en me from that path which Nature
> Seemed to appoint, O, deign to ope another,
> Where I may walk with thought and hope assured....[10]

Fuller's "spirit of love" quietly rebels against one of the most iconic images of Transcendentalism before Emerson had even had time to formulate it: the image of the solitary eyeball melting into the horizon, in a process of complete transformation and self-expansion that renders all human company irrelevant. Her plea that she be allowed to see just "a little onward" flies in the face of the Transcendentalist confidence in the future.

And Fuller was not alone in her doubts about the power of "man's flashing fancy." The most perfect expression of that power was Emerson's transparent eyeball fantasy – the notion (first expressed in *Nature*) that if we abandon ourselves fully to our acts of looking, we become as big as the world around us. We see fully, and we are being seen, too. It was precisely this grandiose image of the poet as larger-than-life Transcendentalist that a contemporary of Emerson's – the very funny Christopher Pearse Cranch (1813–1892), a poet, painter, and musician, and one of the most original talents of the era – wanted to undermine. Cranch was a full-fledged Emerson disciple, celebrating "the language celestial / Written all over the earth, written all over the sky" ("Correspondences" [1844]).[11] But his humor prevented him from accepting anything lofty at face value (he had, he said later, always felt that Emerson's poetry lacked "elbow room").[12] Witness his caricatures, the most famous of which glosses Emerson's transparent eyeball metaphor from *Nature* by depicting a horrifyingly engorged eyeball on spindly legs, wearing a top hat and tails and standing somewhat forlornly in a landscape, complete with mountains and clouds, that apparently refuses to melt before his gaze.[13] A lesser-known cartoon spoofs Emerson's Merlinesque supposition that greatness is a function of inner confidence: "A great man angles with himself; he needs no other bait."[14] But watch the rather scraggly-looking fish in the water that, piranha-like, snap at the great man's feet, ready to make a meal of him. The great man looks as if he is having second thoughts.

*

Such second thoughts came naturally to Emerson the poet. Although he had been writing poetry since he was able to hold a pen,[15] Emerson sometimes felt he was a mere versifier: "I am a bard least of bards. I cannot, like them, make lofty arguments in stately, continuous verse, constraining the rocks, trees, animals, & the periodic stars to say my thoughts, – for that is the gift of great poets." Orpheus he was not; if he was a poet, he was so by virtue of his proximity to the other, truly great ones.[16] Critics have tended to agree: "Poet he would have liked to be, scholar he never doubted he was," writes Lawrence Buell, in the best recent discussion of Emerson's work as a whole.[17] Yet the poems collected in the 1846 edition of his *Poems* show that the Emerson who manages to avoid lofty thoughts, who feels no desire to set the world around him into song, often achieves a surprising intimacy. This intimacy emerges more clearly when we look at his work not (as is mostly done) in terms of Emerson's own writerly ambitions but against the foil of the poems produced by his less self-consciously "bardic" contemporaries.

Take, for example, a poem by one of the most popular poets of the era, Frances S. Osgood (1811–1850), "Ellen Learning to Walk." Osgood's poem was included in *A Wreath of Wildflowers of New England*, published in 1838, when the poet and her portrait-painter husband were living in London. The Boston-born Osgood, although a fixture in New York literary salons, always considered herself a New England poet at heart: "New England's Mountain-Child," she called herself in her poetry, although she admitted that she also wanted to be seen as a "rich Magnolia" among the "woodland-gloom."[18] Emerson would have rejected any attempt to associate him with Osgood, whom he held personally responsible for keeping the bookstores stocked with her poetic "'Wreaths' and 'Flora's chaplets.'"[19] But Osgood was a shrewd and supremely self-aware poet. "Ellen Learning to Walk" unfolds a domestic drama that quickly rises beyond its apparent theme, a child's first steps, and turns into an allegory about gender. As the poet-speaker identifies with her daughter's faltering efforts, the child's father is made to seem uncooperative (although we may assume he has been told not to help) and even a bit hostile:

> My beautiful trembler! how wildly she shrinks!
> And how wistful she looks while she lingers!

> Papa is extremely uncivil, she thinks, –
> > She but pleaded for one of his fingers!
>
> What eloquent pleading! the hand reaching out,
> > As if doubting so strange a refusal;
> While her blue eyes say plainly, "What is he about
> > That he does not assist me as usual?"
>
> Come on, my pet Ellen! we won't let you slip, –
> > Unclasp those soft arms from his knee, love;
> I see a faint smile round that exquisite lip,
> > A smile half reproach and half glee, love.[20]

Metrically, this is an extremely skillful poem. Osgood alternates four-beat mostly anapestic verse in lines 1 and 3 of each stanza (sometimes propelled by an iambic substitution, as in the poem's opening line) with the extrametrical anapestic trimeter of lines 2 and 4 (again, with the odd iambic initial pushing off). Osgood's flexible handling of the four-line stanza, which evokes the 4-3-4-3 iambic beat structure of the ballad stanza, is an effective way for capturing the animated scene the poet describes for us. The substitution of a masculine ending ("love") for the feminine ending, along with the obvious fact that this is an identical rhyme ("love" / "love"), marks the mother's heightened participation in the drama as the "uncivil" father fades into the background. The poet's "I" emerges from the parental "we." Osgood's poem begins to stutter and sputter, as the stresses appear to wander too ("bráve báby"; "a bít! – trý it"). The alliteration ("foot falters forward") reveals the energy behind the daughter's attempts not to lose her balance while the mother continues to coach her:

> So! that's my brave baby! one foot falters forward,
> > Half doubtful the other steals by it!
> *What, shrinking again! why, you shy little coward!*
> > 'Twon't kill you to walk a bit! – try it!
>
> There! steady, my darling! huzza! I have caught her!
> > I clasp her, caress'd and caressing!
> And she hides her bright face, as if what we had taught her
> > Were something to blush for – the blessing!
>
> Now back again! Bravo! that shout of delight,
> > How it thrills to the hearts that adore her!
> Joy, joy for her mother! and blest be the night
> > When her little light feet first upbore her!

It becomes obvious, despite the poet's attempt to mask her involvement by referring to herself in the third person, that this is really the mother's story the poem tells ("Joy, joy for her mother!"). In the subtly gendered drama of Ellen's struggle to stand on her own feet is reflected the poet's quest for joyful independence.

Emerson, too, invoked the intuitive independence of children as a model for adult behavior, although it seems that he gravitated to the "nonchalance of boys" rather than to the fussiness of little girls: "A boy is in the parlour what the pit is in the playhouse; independent, irresponsible, looking out from his corner on such people and facts as pass by. . . . He cumbers himself never about consequences, about interests; he gives an independent, genuine verdict."[21] And in his early lecture, "Domestic Life," he imagined the change that takes place when the "little talker" becomes a little walker: "He walks daily among wonders: fire, light, darkness, the moon, the stars, the furniture of the house, the red tin horse, the domestics, who like rude foster-mothers befriend and feed him, the faces that claim his kisses, are all in turn absorbing; yet warm, cheerful and with good appetite the little sovereign subdues them without knowing it; the new knowledge is taken up into the life of to-day and becomes the means of more." These lines reflect Emerson's experiences with his own son Waldo, creative, tempestuous, funny, who had convinced him that "the household is the home of the *man*, as well as of the child."[22]

It was a disaster of mythic proportions, therefore, that befell Emerson in January 1842, when Waldo contracted and quickly died from scarlet fever. Emerson's stunned response to that death – comparable in intensity to Charles Darwin's equally traumatic loss of his daughter Annie in 1851 – has elicited much commentary, as has the movement from despair to philosophical abstraction in Emerson's memorial poem for Waldo, "Threnody" (1846; *CPE*, pp. 117–24). The knowledge, offered at the end of the poem, that heaven is not made of adamant and gold but is, instead, "a nest of bending reeds, / Flowering grass, and scented weeds," that the world is a "ruined system" watered with the tears of the bereaved, could not have consoled the poet who simply missed his "wondrous child, / Whose silver warble wild / Outvalued every pulsing sound / Within the air's cerulean round" (*CPE*, pp. 124, 117).

Missing Waldo, in "Threnody," is a matter of no longer seeing him walk. If Osgood wrote about a child's first steps, Emerson remembers his last:

> And wither now, my truant wise and sweet,
> O, whither tend thy feet?
> I had the right, few days ago,
> Thy steps to watch, thy place to know;
> How have I forfeited the right?
> Hast thou forgot me in a new delight?   (*CPE*, pp. 117–18)

Among Emerson's achingly clear memories of Waldo is his walk to the village school in the mornings, a regular parade that made a "festival" of each and every day: "When every morn my bosom glowed / To watch the convoy on the road." Waldo was the captain of that parade, and in the speaker's memory it suddenly seems as if Waldo were strutting past his window again, "Stately marching in cap and coat / To some tune by fairies played; / A music heard by thee alone / To works as noble led thee on." In the poem's next section, however, reality has set in again, and Emerson is reduced to imagining Waldo, the "deep-eyed boy," only through the places where *once* he went:

> The painted sled stands where it stood;
> The kennel by the corded wood;
> The gathered sticks to stanch the wall
> Of the snow-tower, when snow should fall;
> The ominous hole he dug in the sand,
> And childhood's castles built or planned;
> His daily haunts I well discern, –
> The poultry-yard, the shed, the barn, –
> And every inch of garden ground
> Paced by the blessed feet around,
> From the roadside to the brook
> Whereinto he loved to look.   (*CPE*, p. 119)

Emerson's painful feeling of being forever separated from Waldo is mirrored in the syntax of the passage: a heap of nouns ("sled," "kennel," "sticks," "snow-tower," "hole") combined with verbs or verb forms that do not indicate but rather obscure agency ("to staunch," "built or planned," "gathered sticks," "paced"). Waldo the maker, builder, planner, gatherer, and pacer is gone. The speaker's assertion of control is belied by the one imperfect rhyme in the passage ("well discern" / "barn"). For Emerson, Waldo's death was a "wandering away," measured by the steps that fade into the tunnel of the past, leaving the father with one thought only: "I am too much bereft" (*CPE*, p. 121).

★

Against such bereavement, against any attempt to attribute meaning to human suffering, Emerson wrote his great tribute to the medieval Persian poet Saadi Shirazi. A celebration of Saadi's sensualism and shaped by Emerson's eclectic reading of Persian poetry, "Saadi" argues precisely against a view of the world that sees darkness where there is only sunlight:

> Sad-eyed Fakirs swiftly say
> Endless dirges to decay,

Never in the blaze of light
Lose the shudder of midnight;
Pale at overflowing noon
Hear wolves barking at the moon;
In the bower of dalliance sweet
Hear the far Avenger's feet.... (*CPE*, p. 100)

The shuddering fakirs allow Emerson to give free rein to his frustration with "the wintry coldness at the heart" that some of his friends, too, associated with New England (the last line comes from a poem by Ellen Sturgis Hooper).[23] Emerson's rushed catalectic trochees, along with the aggressive fricatives and strained plosives that dominate these lines, mimic the pent-up tension that grips these Eastern Puritans. Their bodies taut with suppressed desire, Emerson's fakirs (and it's possible that Emerson wanted us to think of them as "fakers" too[24]) cannot find release except in the pain they inflict on themselves and others. "Drink not the Malaga of praise," they preach,

But do the deed thy fellows hate,
And compromise thy peaceful state;
Smite the white breasts which thee fed;
Stuff sharp thorns beneath the head
Of them thou shouldst have comforted;
For out of woe and out of crime
Draws the heart a lore sublime. (*CPE*, p.100)

Here Saadi's (and Emerson's) theology kicks in. Rejecting the implements of self-torture, he opts for sunlight, laughter, and delight in life:

And yet it seemeth not to me
That the high gods love tragedy;
For Saadi sat in the sun,
And thanks was his contrition;
For haircloth and for bloody whips
Had active hands and smiling lips.... (*CPE*, p. 100)

Thus equipped, Saadi will be a teacher to his people, a poet-healer, as Emerson suggests, in anticipation of the role that Walt Whitman would carve out for himself. Even when he writes about the night, the light of his poetry shines brighter even than the sunshine celebrated in the tributes to the day written by the later Sufi poet Jami:

Sunshine in his heart transferred
Lighted each transparent word,
And well could honoring Persia learn

> What Saadi wished to say;
> For Saadi's nightly stars did burn
> Brighter than Dschami's day.   (*CPE*, p. 101)

The poem ends with the Muse speaking to Saadi, asking him to not seek any-thing that lies beyond the walls of his own cottage. Instead, she encourages him to trust in the transformative power of his imagination, which will turn even his household servants into "blessed gods." At the same time, though, the pleasure Saadi takes in his vocation is no mere escapism; it comes with the demand that he take his immediate environment seriously. That this injunc-tion is presented to the American reader in the form of a poem honoring an old Persian poet is an irony that Emerson had fully intended. His version of localism was not meant to be a parochial one.

But this is precisely where Emerson's later poem "Hamatreya" (written in 1845 or 1846) picks up. The title reminds us again of Emerson's debt to Asian religion and literature, although the word itself cannot be found, as one of Emerson's earliest critics pointed out, with some exasperation, in any "English or foreign dictionary that the largest libraries can afford."[25] Most crit-ics acknowledge that Emerson was alluding to a sacred Hindu text, the *Vishnu Parana*, in which "Maitreya" is a disciple of Parana, who relates to his student the wisdom the earth has imparted to him.[26] Whatever the source, Emerson must have enjoyed the jarring effect that came from the contrast between the exotic word in the title and the list of names, Concord farmers all, that make up the entire first line of the poem, a self-conscious refusal to deliver poetry of the usual kind:

> Minott, Lee, Willard, Hosmer, Meriam, Flint
> Possessed the land which rendered to their toil
> Hay, corn, roots, hemp, flax, apples, wool, and wood.
> Each of these landlords walked amidst his farm,
> Saying, "'Tis mine, my children's, and my name's:
> How sweet the west wind sounds in my own trees!
> How graceful climb those shadows on my hill!
> I fancy these pure waters and the flags
> Know me, as does my dog: we sympathize;
> And, I affirm, my actions smack of the soil."   (*CPE*, p. 28)

Notice the emphasis on ownership ("'Tis mine," "my own trees," "my hill") – not an innocent topic at a time when many Americans still thought they had the right to own human beings. If Emerson has his farmers suggest that the relationship between land and landowner resembles that between a dog and his master, the irony is palpable. The next few lines spell it out: confronted with such human hubris, the earth laughs, and her amusement expresses itself in flowers (and not in the products of human agricultural labor mentioned earlier: corn, flax, wool, etc.). "Proud of the earth which is not theirs," all these farmers end up as earth themselves. Where are these men, asks the poet, and he supplies the answer, as pithy as it is chilling: "Asleep beneath their grounds" (*CPE*, p. 28). Emerson then gives his farmers another opportunity to embarrass themselves, this time as landscape architects:

> "This suits me for a pasture; that's my park;
> We must have clay, lime, gravel, granite-ledge,
> And misty lowland, where to go for peat...."
>
> (*CPE*, p. 28)

Offering his own conclusion ("Ah! The hot owner sees not Death, who adds / Him to his land"), the poet then allows the earth to strike back, in a section that is visually and metrically set apart from the rest of the poem, as blank verse yields to clipped lines that refuse to adhere to a normative beat pattern. This is no longer Saadi's Muse or the Great Heart of "Threnody," but a more commanding voice: "Mine and yours, / Mine and not yours," the earth responds, making fun especially of lawyers who draw up deeds and wills and think that one can inherit a piece of land. Says the earth:

> "They called me theirs,
> Who so controlled me;
> Yet every one
> Wished to stay, and is gone.
> How am I theirs,
> If they cannot hold me,
> But I hold them?"
>
> (*CPE*, p. 29)

By virtue of their very economy, these lines, coming after the dull, repetitive list making of the farmers, carry the weight of persuasion. But the reader is in for a surprise when, in the final section of the poem, the speaker reveals who is the one that is most affected by the earth's intervention: it is the poet himself!

> When I heard the Earth-song,
> I was no longer brave,
> My avarice cooled
> Like lust in the chill of the grave.
>
> (*CPE*, p. 29)

The poet here is no Saadi but another Concord landowner, different from his neighbors only in that he is given the benefit of insight before it is too late, at least in theory. Emerson reserves the strongest opprobrium for himself, comparing his need for ownership, his "avarice," to sexual desire. If the poet seems to have escaped death, the final image of the poem makes us doubt that he has been much luckier than his dead, boastful neighbors. If "Saadi" was about the poet able to transcend day and night, time and place, "Hamatreya" shows the poet stuck in Concord. Emerson ends the poem not cheered by the earth's laughter but chastened by rattling bones, feeling the shudder of death in the here and now. And anybody who would like to dismiss it as a persona poem would only need to remember that Emerson wrote "Hamatreya" between finalizing real estate deals in Concord.[27]

"Saadi" and "Hamatreya" remind us once again that Emerson's poetry is better than its reputation, and better than his own opinion of it. As in his essays, Emerson presents meaning as process, but without the finality of prophetic insight attached to any of its lines. His poetry remains unpredictable: sounding like doggerel in one moment, it veers into high-flying metaphors the next. It won't do to attribute such flexibility to a lack of poetical talent. Rather than celebrating the Bard, his poetry features a more low-key character: one who, like Saadi, is open to different viewpoints and who is flawed himself, like the speaker of "Hamatreya." Above all, Emerson's poetry is conversational: not only in the form of the dialogues that, often literally, inhabit his poems, but, more important, in the exchanges that his poems – such as "Saadi" and "Hamatreya" – have with one another.[28]

In his best poems, Emerson does not wish to build monuments to rival those of princes. He set the tone for this reduced vision of poetry's power early, in one of his most carefully made poems, "The Snow Storm" (lines from which John Greenleaf Whittier later used as the epigraph to *Snow-Bound* [1866]). The poem, written in 1835, details the arrival of a nonhuman force that "hides," "veils," and obscures, sending humans indoors. The first stanza imitates the kinetic, disruptive energy of the storm through the line breaks that separate subject from verb ("air / hides"; "feet / delayed") or verb from preposition ("sit / around"; "enclosed / in"). The poet invites the reader to inspect the storm's transformative energy, emphasizing how "fierce," "wild," and "savage" it is. The storm is an architect without any sense of proportion, defying the notion of "Balance-loving Nature" that Emerson invokes in "Merlin II" (*CPE*, p. 93). But more than anything the snowstorm is an ironist, mocking the human desire for decoration: hanging marble wreaths from dog kennels, shaping bushes into swans, and adding a "tapering turret" to the farmer's gate. The poem ends with breathless run-on lines describing the departure of the snowstorm and the amazement of the poet at the quick work the mad wind has done – work that takes an artist "an age" to imitate in his or her medium:

> And when his hours are numbered, and the world
> Is all his own, retiring, as he were not,
> Leaves, when the sun appears, astonished Art
> To mimic in slow structures, stone by stone,
> Built in an age, the mad wind's night-work,
> The frolic architecture of the snow. (*CPE*, p. 34)

In a sense, though, the mad snowstorm also offers an analogy for Emerson's poetry, which often seems written rapidly, infused with the knowledge of its own provisional nature, and aware of the fact that, whatever the poets might do, life elsewhere slowly goes on.

*

Given the conversational nature of his best poems, it seems odd that Emerson accepted as his disciple someone whose main effect on others seems to have been to silence them. When Jones Very is "in the room with other persons," Emerson wrote in his journal, "speech stops as if there were a corpse in the apartment."[29] Jones Very's best-known poems were written – or they happened to him, as he would have wanted his readers to think – in 1838 and 1839, when he was in a state of permanent ecstasy, teetering on the brink of insanity. When Emerson first met him, Very (1813–1880), the son of a Salem sea captain, was a student at the Harvard Divinity School and a Greek tutor to Harvard freshmen and already had a well-deserved reputation for being "cracked." He didn't help matters when he informed Elizabeth Peabody that he *was* the Second Coming and told his startled students that they should "flee to the mountains," because "the end of all things" was "at hand."[30] His eccentricities earned Very a dismissal from his Harvard teaching job and a few weeks at the McLean Asylum for the Insane.

None of which slowed him down: he continued to badger Emerson for his alleged lack of "obedience" to God, without, however, wanting to give up on his services as an editor (for the volume of Very's poems he generously published in 1839, Emerson whittled the two hundred poems Very had provided to a more manageable sixty-five).[31] Despite his irrepressible preference for formal poetry (notably the Shakespearian sonnet), Very is still considered the most "rough hewn" of the Transcendentalists.[32] However, the stereotypical image of Very as a mildly annoying – though gifted – kook, a kind of Christopher Smart redivivus, is only partially correct. He *did* feel vastly superior to his contemporaries, including Emerson, and regarded them as spiritually bereft. In "The Dead," he compared them to leafless trees, stripped not by autumn but by the distance they have created between themselves and God. They were the ones who have died, said Very, not those lying in the cemeteries: "And in their show of life more dead they live / Than those that to the earth with many tears they give" (*JV*, p. 77).

Very firmly believed that the living God was with or even within him. In "The Presence," written in his "severely monastic room in Salem," Very exclaims: "I sit within my room and joy to find / That Thou who always loves art with me here, / That I am never left by Thee behind" (*JV*, p. 78).[33] Note the odd use of "joy" as a verb, which, to be sure, has a biblical ring (as in Habakkuk 3:18 or 2 Corinthians 7:13) but also turns the experience described from an abstraction into a concrete act. However, as Very clarifies elsewhere, it is ultimately up to God to lead us to where we need to be, to guide us to the "place just right," as the Shakers would have called it:

> The hand and foot that stir not, they shall find
> Sooner than all the rightful place to go;
> Now in their motion free as roving wind,
> Though first no snail so limited and slow;
> I mark them full of labor all the day,
> Each active motion made in perfect rest ...   (*JV*, p. 193)

While our feet carry us where we must go, our eyes are free to roam. Very's poetry is rich with visual impressions. According to Very, we haven't even begun to look. "Find thee eyes and look thee there," he shouts impatiently in "Autumn Leaves," berating the reader for stepping heedlessly over the leaves on the ground, not recognizing their beauty (*JV*, p. 188). But in Very's poetry, the human eye does not, Emerson-style, expand to godlike proportions to encompass the horizon. Instead, it contracts to the level of the smallest objects: everything is worth a look. In the "The American Scholar," Emerson had suggested that our bodies, even our feet, were lined with eyes, a rather negative, Hamlet-like experience: beset with multiple insights, our minds are never at rest but keep swirling, "embarrassed with second thoughts."[34]

Where Emerson wanted to look up, Very looked down. He liked the eyes on his feet. A perfect example of that downward look is "The Columbine," a poem addressed to a small, hardy plant found in woodlands and meadows and known for the distinctive shape of its petals. As if the columbine were his friend, Very addresses her directly; if it weren't for the title, the first two lines could have been addressed to a lover. It is only in line 3 that the speaker's desire to "forget" his humanity is unveiled as a wish to become part of the world of plants. And so he does, at least for most of the poem:

> Still, still my eye will gaze long-fixed on thee,
> Till I forget that I am called a man,
> And at thy side fast-rooted seem to be,
> And the breeze comes my cheek with thine to fan;
> Upon this craggy hill our life shall pass,
> A life of summer days and summer joys,
> Nodding our honey bells mid pliant grass
> In which the bee half hid his time employs;
> And here we'll drink with thirsty pores the rain,
> And turn dew-sprinkled to the rising sun,
> And look when in the flaming west again
> His orb across the heaven its path has run;
> Here, left in darkness on the rocky steep,
> My weary eyes shall close like folding flowers in sleep.
>
> (JV, pp. 61–62)

The alliteration and internal rhyme at the beginning of the first line ("*Still, still* my eye *will*") enact the moment of deep, self-absorbed looking that triggers the quasi transformation. Gazing at the flower, the speaker *becomes* a flower (although not *the* flower). The speaker roots himself into the ground, next to the columbine, fanned by the same breeze on the hill that also touches the plant, resting "my cheek with thine." The creative blurring of human and plant worlds persists throughout the poem. However, the speaker does not substitute himself for the columbine's consciousness. In an act of respect that we would now call ecological, he joins it in a life that the next few lines render physically palpable: nodding his blossoms, heavy with pollen, thirstily drinking in the rain, waking up in the morning, "dew-sprinkled," excited to greet the sun. The transformation is not a complete one, nor was it intended to be such: the water-absorbing "pores" of the plant serve as a reminder of the speaker's former humanity, as does, in the final line, the reference to the "eyes" that close, eyes that are "like," although not the same as, the petals of the columbine folding back at night.

Similar to these acts of abandonment to the natural world are moments in Very's poetry in which the speaker finds himself longing for a kind of permanent childhood. In "The Song," for example, confronted with a landscape too wide and rivers extending too far, the speaker feels the power of poetry slipping from his grasp. He lets the tide carry him back to his childhood haunts:

When I would sing of crooked streams and fields,
On, on from me they stretch too far and wide,
And at their look my song all powerless yields,
And down the river bears me with its tide;
Amid the fields I am a child again,
The spots that then I loved I love the more,
My fingers drop the strangely-scrawling pen,
And I remember nought but nature's lore;
I plunge me in the river's cooling wave,
Or on the embroidered bank admiring lean,
Now some endangered insect life to save,
Now watch the pictured flowers and grasses green;
Forever playing where a boy I played,
By hill and grove, by field and stream delayed.   (JV, p. 70)

Readily abandoning his "strangely-scrawling pen," the speaker swims in the water, sits on the river's bank, and holds communion with the insects and flowers. If this were all, "The Song" would not be a very interesting poem: a garden-variety regressive dream, even if cast into the form of a Shakespearian sonnet. But look at his handling of syntax in the poem's final lines: the two actions described by finite verbs ("plunge" and "lean") frame a number of other activities ("insect life to save"; "watch the pictured flowers"; "forever playing"; "by field and stream delayed") that seem strangely subjectless, a perfect illustration of the kind of permanent present, the state and place of arrested development, into which the speaker projects himself, an infinitely prolonged state of happiness, stripped of the demands of adult life. Note, too, how the poem ends on the verb "delayed," a witty admission on the poet's part that, yes, he knows what he is doing: proof, of course, that the poet-speaker has never really let go of his pen. It would not be an exaggeration to say that in Very's "The Song" we see a fantasy in play that would come to dominate a much later poem, *Leaves of Grass*, composed by that leaning, loafing, lounging New York poet Walt Whitman.[35]

*

When Henry David Thoreau (1817–1862), Emerson's other great literary disciple, sought the affections of the young Ellen Sewall from Scituate, he gave her a copy of Very's poems. This was not the reason the courtship failed. In fact, Ellen said she rather liked them. In her journal, however, Ms. Sewall confessed that what had really touched her was *Thoreau's* poetry. Critics have not shared this feeling. Thoreau wrote "few, if any, great poems," declared his biographer Walter Harding.[36] And yet, readers willing to give Thoreau the poet a chance will find his verse leavened with a sense of dark humor that was unavailable to Emerson or Very. Consider this verse fragment from his journal, composed when Thoreau was holed up in Concord in the spring of 1841, frantically trying to read or write as loud sounds coming from the kitchen below kept interrupting him. Thoreau was sufficiently disturbed to speculate on the implements the people below were using. Was it tongs? Or perhaps a *shovel*? Clearly, Thoreau was no Saadi at that point, capable of transforming the "foolish gossips" down below into "blessed gods." But his reading in Eastern mysticism still came to the rescue: mentally transforming the sound of tongs-on-tea-kettle into a gong, he was able to turn his house (a "hovel"), irritating kitchen sounds and all, into an exotic place of worship:

> They who prepare my evening meal below
> Carelessly hit the kettle as they go
> With tongs or shovel,
> And ringing round and round,
> Out of this hovel
> It makes an eastern temple by the sound.

This was not the first association the poet had. Earlier, the clanging pots had reminded him of how cow bells

> Mid birches sounded o'er the open land,
> Where I plucked flowers
> Many years ago,
> Spending midsummer hours
> With such secure delight they hardly seemed to flow.[37]

In just a few lines, and with a considerable dash of wit, Thoreau's poetic sketch soars over the pots and pans in the kitchen and travels across the physical and mental landscapes that mattered to him, all anchored in a sound that could not be more trivial. Thanks to the mind's capacity to remember or to transform, a poem that starts in anger is allowed to end on a note of "secure delight."

But that delight is a past experience, a memory, not a reality, a theme Thoreau explores in another poem ("Sic Vita" [July 1841]) that revolves around a single conceit: the speaker comparing himself not to a hardy columbine but to a bunch of uprooted violets, with some sorrel and weeds mixed in, a rather unsightly "nosegay," carelessly plucked for no evident reason. He is a "parcel of vain strivings," sighs the poet, loosely tied together by a wisp of straw, subject to chance and circumstance, "Dangling this way and that." The central stanza of the poem summarizes the dilemma, ending rather drably in *ae* and *a* sounds, with the assonance of "But" and "cup" clinching the speaker's unspoken complaint.

> And here I bloom for a short hour unseen,
> Drinking my juices up.
> Which have no root in the land
> To keep my branches green,
> But stand
> In a bare cup.[38]

While some buds have been left on the severed violets, "in mimicry of life," the poet fears he will soon be known only in his withered state, and then not at all. The much-needed turn in the poem comes rather abruptly, namely as an attempt to find some ecological sense behind his uprooting and to look at it as an act of planned husbandry rather than careless displacement.

> But now I see I was not plucked for nought,
> And after in life's vase
> Of glass set while I might survive,
> But by a kind hand brought
> Alive
> To a strange place.

> That stock thus thinned will soon redeem its hours,
> And by another year,
> Such as God knows, with freer air,
> More fruits and fairer flowers
> Will bear,
> While I droop here.

From this new perspective, the humble cup turns into an ornamental vase. Or does it? Some elements in those final stanzas do seem to work against an entirely positive or, yes, "kind" reading of this final moment: not only the "strange" place where the poet (as a decaying bunch of violets) finds himself but the very language of agricultural management, which sounds almost proto-eugenic ("the stock thus thinned"). Note the lingering uncertainty ("Such as God knows") and the disconcerting final image we are left with: the drooping poet, left to die, as nature – perhaps, perhaps *not* – renews itself. Whatever alliances with nature that the Transcendentalists might have thought they had formed, they were temporary ones, reminders that while nature lives on, in "fruits and fairer flowers," humanity inevitably limps behind.

*

In one of his cartoon parodies of Transcendentalist philosophy, Christopher Pearse Cranch takes his cue from Emerson's professed wish to "expand and live in the warm day like corn and melons" and reminds us of the ridiculousness of that metaphor, which was never intended to be anything more than an image.[39] He depicts a human as a fat melon sitting on the ground, wearing a half-embarrassed smile and adorned with some impressive leaves sprouting out of his head. Cranch's half-serious poem "Bird Language" responds even more directly to Emerson's conviction that all natural facts were spiritual facts. Overhearing a conversation taking place between five bobolinks, "laughing together / Over some ornithological joke," the poet wonders what all the fuss is about. He discusses possible explanations for the birds' unrestrained laughter – a "querulous catbird," the "cawing of crows high over the trees," "some chipmunk's chatter," or perhaps a weasel, "stealthy and sly," hidden away under a stone wall – only to recognize that he just doesn't know. The next step in the poem will make sense to anyone who has ever been in a social setting surrounded by people laughing uproariously for no immediately evident reason: the poet suspects that the birds are laughing about *him*. "Or was the joke about me at my easel, / Trying to catch the tints of the sky"? Cranch's irony is quite complex: as if it were not enough that the bobolinks could be making fun of him as a poet, he now fears that they might be ridiculing his abilities as a painter, too. He rescues himself from despair by deciding that if he can't understand what the language of the birds means, he can at least appreciate the music they make. Cranch was an accomplished flutist, who once entertained the folks at Brooke Farm with his playing, and he knows how to make his poem sing the way the bobolinks do:

> Still they flew tipsily, shaking all over,
>> Bubbling with jollity, brimful of glee,
> While I sat listening deep in the clover,
>> Wondering what their jargon could be.
>
> 'T was but the voice of a morning the brightest
>> That ever dawned over yon shadowy hills;
> 'T was but the song of all joy that is lightest, –
>> Sunshine breaking in laughter and trills.
>
> Vain to conjecture the words they are singing;
>> Only by tones can we follow the tune
> In the full heart of summer fields ringing,
>> Ringing the rhythmical gladness of June![40]

Cranch's simple quatrains begin to levitate, thanks to the alliterating plosives (*b*, *t*, and *k* sounds) he employs, which suggest not only the birds' bursting into song but the poet's own participation in the music. As the poem, too, indulges in tones rather than words, Cranch builds toward the conclusion, in which poet and birds both enter into the "full heart of summer." The climactic nature of the moment is underlined by the wonderful device of repeating the present participle "ringing" while also separating it by a line break. In the final line, the *r* alliteration and *g* and *l* consonance mark the moment of final release. Interestingly, the poet still hasn't understood what the ornithological joke was that had gotten the bobolinks all a-titter. To return to Sigourney's self-deprecating "To a Shred of Linen," what we see in "Bird Language" are not the "hallow'd lineaments" of Wisdom and Truth but a tune whistled on a warm summer night, with the speaker sitting in a field "deep in the clover." And that, after all, is a place that Emerson would have enjoyed too. In his journal, Emerson described how gardening helped him forget the desire to "bite his enemies": smoothing the ground, he'd smooth his temper; pulling out the grass he didn't want, he'd pull out the splinters in his soul; and, finally, something wonderful would happen: "I can hear the Bobalink's song & see the blessed deluge of light & colour that rolls around me."[41]

Notes

1. *Albany Evening Journal* 8.2219, May 20, 1837, p. 2. The poem also appears in Sigourney's *Select Poems* of 1841.
2. Ralph Waldo Emerson, "The Poet" (published in *Essays: Second Series*, 1844), in Ralph Waldo Emerson, *Essays and Lectures*, ed. Joel Porte (New York: Library of America, 1983), p. 465.
3. William Cullen Bryant, "The Prairies" (1832), in John Hollander (ed.), *American Poetry: The Nineteenth Century*, 2 vols. (New York: Library of America, 1994), vol. 1, p. 164.
4. "Merlin I" was included in Emerson's first collection, *Poems* (1846). See Ralph Waldo Emerson, *Collected Poems and Translations*, ed. Harold Bloom and Paul Kane (New York: Library of America, 1994), pp. 91–93. Further references to this edition appear in the text, preceded by *CPE*.
5. See Paul Kane, "Ralph Waldo Emerson," in Eric L. Haralson (ed.), *Encyclopedia of American Poetry: The Nineteenth Century* (Chicago: Fitzroy Dearborn, 1998), pp. 145–50, 145.
6. Samuel Taylor Coleridge, "The Eolian Harp" (1795/1796), in E. H. Coleridge (ed.), *The Poems of Samuel Taylor Coleridge* (London: Milford, 1935), pp. 100–02.
7. See "The Poet"; Emerson, *Essays*, p. 450.
8. Henry Wadsworth Longfellow, May 27, 1846, Journal, October 1, 1845–28 February 1847, Longfellow Papers, Houghton Library, Harvard University, MS Am 1340 (200).

9. Emerson, *Nature*, chapter VII: "You cannot freely admire a noble landscape, if laborers are digging in the field hard by" (*Essays*, p. 42).

10. Margaret Fuller, "Meditations. Sunday, May 12, 1832," in Arthur B. Fuller (ed.), *Life Without and Life Within: Reviews, Narratives, Essays, and Poems* (Boston: Taggard & Chase, 1860), pp. 881–83.

11. Hollander (ed.), *American Poetry*, vol. 1, pp. 590–91. On Cranch and Emerson, see the essays by Nancy Stula ("Transcendentalism: The Path from Preaching to Painting") and David M. Robinson ("Christopher Pearse Cranch and the New England Transcendentalists") in Nancy Stula, Barbara Novak, and David M. Robinson, *At Home and Abroad: The Transcendental Landscapes of Christopher Pearse Cranch* (New London, Conn.: Lyman Allyn Art Museum, 2007).

12. See his later essay, Christopher Pearse Cranch, "Emerson's Limitations as a Poet," *The Critic* 17 (February 27, 1892), p. 129.

13. Christopher Pearse Cranch, "Standing on the bare ground . . . ," in Christopher Pearse Cranch, "Illustrations of the New Philosophy: Drawings, 1837–1839," Houghton Library, Harvard University, MS Am 1506 (4).

14. Cranch somewhat unfairly truncates a sentence from Emerson's early lecture "Domestic Life," in which Emerson argues against men pursuing wealth for its own sake: "The wise man angles with himself only, and with no meaner bait" (the lecture was published in 1870, as chapter V of *Society and Solitude*; for this quotation, see Ralph Waldo Emerson, *Society and Solitude: Twelve Chapters* [Boston: Fields, Osgood, 1870], p. 103); Christopher Pearse Cranch, "A great man angles with himself," in Cranch, "Illustrations of the New Philosophy," Houghton Library, Harvard University, MS Am 1506 (5).

15. Stephen E. Whicher (ed.), *Selections from Ralph Waldo Emerson: An Organic Anthology* (Boston: Houghton Mifflin, 1950), p. 407.

16. Emerson, *Journal VA* [February–March 1863], in Ralph Waldo Emerson, *Journals and Miscellaneous Notebooks*, ed. William H. Gilman et al., 16 vols. (Cambridge, Mass.: Harvard University Press, 1960–1982), vol. 15, p. 308.

17. Lawrence Buell, *Emerson* (Cambridge, Mass.: Harvard University Press, 2005), p. 40.

18. Frances S. Osgood, "New England's Mountain-Child," in Frances S. Osgood, *Poems* (New York: Clark & Austin, 1846), p. 190.

19. Emerson, *Nature* (1844), in Emerson, *Essays*, p. 545.

20. Osgood, *Poems*, pp. 199–200.

21. Emerson, "Self-Reliance" (1842), in Emerson, *Essays*, p. 261.

22. Emerson, "Domestic Life," in Emerson, *Society and Solitude*, pp. 88–89, 90.

23. Ellen Sturgis Hooper, "Better a Sin Which Purposed Wrong to None" (first published privately around 1872), in Lawrence Buell (ed.), *The American Transcendentalists: Essential Writings* (New York: Modern Library, 2006), pp. 478–79. Hooper (1812–1848), who was a participant in Margaret Fuller's

"conversations," left a small body of verse whose "compresse intensity" her editor Buell compares to Emily Dickinson (p. 477).

24. The earliest instance of the word "faker" as a noun cited in the *Oxford English Dictionary* dates from 1846.

25. William Sloane Kennedy, *Clews to Emerson's Mystic Verse* (New York: The American Author, 1903), p. 221.

26. See Robert Richardson, *Emerson: The Mind on Fire* (Berkeley: University of California Press, 1995), pp. 407–08.

27. In 1844 Emerson bought fourteen acres of land near Walden Pond, and in January 1847 he purchased three acres of land adjoining his Concord property; see Richard R. O'Keefe, *Mythic Archetypes in Ralph Waldo Emerson: A Blakean Reading* (Kent, Ohio: Kent State University Press, 1995), p. 20.

28. See Saundra Morris, "'Metre-Making' Arguments: Emerson's Poems," in Joel Porte and Saundra Morris (eds.), *The Cambridge Companion to Ralph Waldo Emerson* (Cambridge: Cambridge University Press, 1999), pp. 218–42, 224.

29. Emerson, Journal D, June 16, 1839, in Emerson, *Journals and Miscellaneous Notebooks*, vol. 7, p. 213.

30. Helen R. Deese, "Introduction," in Jones Very, *The Complete Poems* (Athens: University of Georgia Press, 1993), pp. xi–lviii, xvi. Further references to this edition appear in the text, preceded by *JV*.

31. Jones Very to Emerson, November 30, 1838, in Carlos Baker, *Emerson Among the Eccentrics* (1996; New York: Penguin, 1997), p. 140.

32. Paul Kane, in Kane (ed.), *Poetry of the American Renaissance: A Diverse Anthology from the Romantic Period* (New York: Braziller, 1995), p. 174.

33. Baker, *Emerson Among the Eccentrics*, p. 148.

34. Emerson, *Essays*, p. 68.

35. Note the beginning of Whitman's "Song of Myself" (1855), lines 4–5: "I loafe and invite my soul, / I lean and loafe at my ease.... Observing a spear of summer grass"; Walt Whitman, *Leaves of Grass and Other Writings*, ed. Michael Moon (New York: Norton, 2002), p. 662.

36. Walter Harding, *The Days of Henry Thoreau: A Biography*, new ed. (1970; Princeton, N.J.: Princeton University Press, 1992), p. 95. The Ellen Sewall story is recorded on pp. 98–99. See also Elizabeth Witherell, "Thoreau as Poet," in Joel Myerson (ed.), *The Cambridge Companion to Henry David Thoreau* (Cambridge: Cambridge University Press, 1995), pp. 57–70.

37. Henry David Thoreau, *Walden, The Maine Woods, and Collected Essays and Poems*, ed. Robert Sayre and Elizabeth Witherell (New York: Library of America, 2007), p. 1070. The date of the journal entry is April 4, 1841.

38. Thoreau, *Walden*, pp. 1068–69. The poem also appears, without a title, in Thoreau's *A Week on the Concord and Merrimack Rivers* (1849).

39. Emerson, *Nature*, in Emerson, *Essays*, p. 38; Cranch, "I expand and live in the warm day, like corn & melons," in Cranch, "Illustrations of the New Philosophy," Houghton Library, Harvard University, MS Am 1506 (3).

40. Christopher Pearse Cranch, "Bird Language," in Hollander (ed.), *American Poetry*, vol. 1, pp. 623–24.

41. Emerson, Journal D, June 12, 1839, in Emerson, *Journals and Miscellaneous Notebooks*, vol. 7, p. 211.

Chapter 10

Edgar Allan Poe's Lost Worlds

ELIZA RICHARDS

It has proven irresistible to identify Edgar Allan Poe the person – abandoned by his actor father, orphaned by his actress mother, disowned by his wealthy southern foster father, widowed early by his tubercular cousin and child-bride Virginia, financially defeated by his own self-destructive tendencies as well as a badly paying literary marketplace, and dead before he was forty – with his distinctly alienated and melancholy poetic personae. The incurable sorrow of the male speaker who mourns his lost Lenore, or Ulalume, or Annabel Lee, as well as the persistent, solitary questing of one who "wander[s] home but newly / From that ultimate dim Thule," and who numbly describes the apocalyptic dreamscapes of "Dream-Land," or "The City in the Sea," or "The Valley of Nis," accrue to Poe the person.[1] Starting with Marie Bonaparte, a psychoanalyst closely affiliated with Sigmund Freud, Poe has been diagnosed by dozens of critics as both a hopeless melancholic and a great poet, whose psychic pain is the source of his artistic brilliance. Poe, readers imagine, lived "out of Space – out of Time"; he inhabited the forbidding, depopulated mental geographies that he depicted in his poetry and wholly rejected the political, social, and cultural geographies that surrounded him (P, p. 344). Charles Baudelaire is just one of many readers who have concluded that the antebellum literary marketplace threatened to destroy Poe's soul: "From the midst of a greedy world, hungry for material things, Poe took flight in dreams."[2] For these readers, Poe retreated into the world inside his head, where he enacted a total rejection of the world he lived in, unrelieved by the hope of a better world to come.

Although this identification of poetic persona with poet is certainly compelling, and although it might also be justifiable, it nevertheless short-circuits the exploration and analysis of an equally compelling and less familiar aspect of Poe's work. For however maladjusted or melancholic Poe may have been, he was highly attuned to and engaged with the poetry of his predecessors and his contemporaries, European and American. He conspicuously displayed his understanding, appropriation, recombination, synthesis, and deployment of the poetic conventions, inventions, and inheritances of his day. His knowledge of the literary field was extensive; he internalized it fully, advertised it heavily, and disseminated it widely. The saturation of his verse with allusions to poetry familiar and unfamiliar, remembered and forgotten, and elite and popular is remarkable and has not yet received sufficient scholarly attention. Renowned writers of the British tradition like Shakespeare, Milton, Pope, Wordsworth, Coleridge, Byron, Shelley, Keats, and Tennyson; less familiar but popular and influential British writers such as William Cowper, Edward Young, Thomas Hood, and Thomas Moore; distinguished New England writers such as William Cullen Bryant, John Neal, Ralph Waldo Emerson, James Russell Lowell, and Henry Wadsworth Longfellow; women writers on both sides of the Atlantic such as Felicia Hemans, "L.E.L." (Letitia Elizabeth Landon), Elizabeth Barrett Browning, Lydia Sigourney, Amelia Welby, Frances Sargent Osgood, Sarah Helen Whitman, and Elizabeth Oakes Smith; and southern poets such as Thomas Holly Chivers, William Gilmore Simms, and Philip Pendleton Cooke – all these writers and many others left an impression on Poe's work. Of those living in his time, many corresponded with Poe; some were active collaborators, some were competitors, some were professional acquaintances, and some were enemies, friends, or romantic interests. Poe not only read but also wrote about the work of his contemporaries, and many of them read and wrote about his work. Poe's book reviews, his "Marginalia" and "Literati of New York" series, and his essays on poetics testify to a vibrant critical and aesthetic engagement with a vast poetic field largely unfamiliar to most readers of today, for whom poetry is usually a less central form of cultural communication than it was in the mid-nineteenth century.

Poetic literacy was at a peak in this period, and Poe was fully immersed in the social networks that produced and disseminated poetry to a wide readership. As editor of three leading literary magazines spanning the East Coast – the *Southern Literary Messenger* in Richmond, *Graham's Magazine* in Philadelphia, and the *Broadway Journal* in New York – he was fully embedded within the literary culture of his day. To suggest or assume that he simply rejected this richly varied cultural and aesthetic terrain diminishes his accomplishments. Exploring his work within the literary network of which he was a part can tell us a great deal about poetry as a form of cultural currency in the early nineteenth century. Pursuing this approach diminishes some aspects of his poetry's strangeness, idiosyncrasy, and originality, for in fact many poets of the time wrote like Poe; he is simply the one who holds the most prominent place in U.S. literary history. But by situating Poe within a broader poetic field, readers can also gain an appreciation of the complexity and sophistication of his contributions to the literary culture of his time. We can understand the place that poetic conventions of despair, dreaminess, alienation, and dislocation hold in antebellum literary culture, and then we can begin to distinguish what is truly different about Poe. For to locate Poe within the context of nineteenth-century poetic culture is not to say that he is not exceptional; closer comparisons with the work of his contemporaries help us to arrive at a more nuanced sense of what is really distinctive about his modes of poetic communication. An insistence on Poe's utter originality, in other words, can shut down avenues for understanding and interpreting his significant contributions to literary history.

For, paradoxically, it is not his consummate performance of difference that differentiates him. The isolated, tortured genius, unappreciated by his culture and thrown back on his own inner resources, was a well-known, highly recognizable figure by the time Poe assumed the persona. Byron – who, like Poe, was prone to personal scandal, wrote mellifluous poems about exotic places, and condemned social hypocrisy in satirical verse – is perhaps the closest prototype for Poe's poetic performance, although Shelley, Coleridge, Keats, Felicia Hemans, and the Graveyard Poets all leave a perceptible impression. Poe was not alone, moreover, and he was certainly not the first in the American context to adopt the type of poetic identity that made Byron a celebrity. John Neal, who early on recognized Poe as a kindred spirit, and Fitz-Greene Halleck, whom Poe reviewed rather caustically, both assumed Byronic stances before Poe.

In 1844, at the peak of his career, just before he created a sensation with the publication of "The Raven," Poe located himself within this tradition. Distinguished critic and poet James Russell Lowell had been charged with writing a biography of Poe for *Graham's Magazine* and asked Poe to write up a "sort of spiritual biography" that he could draw from. On July 2, 1844, Poe responded:

> There are epochs when any kind of mental exercise is torture, and when nothing yields me pleasure but solitary communion with the "mountains and the woods," – the "altars" of Byron. I have thus rambled and dreamed away whole months, and awake, at last, to a sort of mania for composition. Then I scribble all day, and read all night, so long as the disease endures. This is also the temperament of P. P. Cooke, of Virginia, the author of "Florence Vane," "Young Rosalie Lee," and some other sweet poems – and I should not be surprised if it were your own. Cooke writes and thinks as you – and I have been told that you resemble him personally.[3]

Here Poe not only associates himself with Byron, who craves solitary "communion" with nature and is prone to frenzied – even "diseased" – creative trances; he also attributes this same temperament as a compliment to other poets he admires – fellow southerner P. P. Cooke, whose poetry bears a striking resemblance to Poe's own, and Lowell himself. Poe implies that all true poets possess this temperament and share a common vision and practice. It may seem strange as far as other professions and pursuits go, but this behavior actually defines the practice of the true poet: it is a culturally recognizable norm for the poet to be socially aberrant.

Raymond Williams and others have noted that the figure of the "romantic artist" emerged as a feature of the "period in which the market and the idea of specialist production received increasing emphasis."[4] As Williams says,

> it is tempting to see these theories as a direct response to the actual change in relations between artist and society. Certainly, in the documents, there are some obvious elements of compensation: at a time when the artist is being described as just one more producer of a commodity for the market, he is describing himself as a specially endowed person, the guiding light of the common life.

Writers wishing to reinforce a sense of protected individuality defined themselves antagonistically in relation to their readers; this stance enabled them to publicize their work while insisting that they were not doing anything of the sort. This is not so much a kind of duplicity or hypocrisy as a way of adapting earlier modes of authorship to new economic and social conditions. But, as Williams also says, "the response is not merely a professional one. It is also ... an emphasis on the embodiment in art of certain human values, capacities, energies, which in the development of society towards an industrial civilization were felt to be threatened or even destroyed."[5]

Poe recognizes that the figure of the romantic artist negotiates complex interactions between poets, their poetic personae, and the marketplace; as a third- or even fourth-generation Romantic, living in a country that actively defined itself in terms of democratic industrial capitalism, he brings the figure to a newly compressed, intensified, and even exaggerated point that tends to expose its own contradictions. Poe's poetry repeatedly dramatizes the ways that "certain human values, capacities, [and] energies" are not only threatened but actually extinguished. The only possible human response is to look for them elsewhere, in vain. Such dramatization of impossibility paradoxically keeps these intangible qualities alive via the sense of nostalgia evoked in their negation. This is the important social and cultural work of Poe's poetry, work that he shares with his Romantic predecessors and contemporaries.

"Israfel," which Poe published repeatedly (with some revision) in magazines and books from 1831 to 1845, portrays the plight of a poet who labors to apprehend celestial beauty in a worldly environment. The earthly speaker compares himself unfavorably with the angel Israfel, "whose heart-strings are a lute, and who has the sweetest voice of all God's creatures," as Poe's epigraph from the Koran tells us (P, p. 175). According to T. O. Mabbott, Poe derived this gloss not directly from the Koran but from his primary model for the poem, *Lalla Rookh* (1817), an oriental romance by Thomas Moore (P, p. 172). While in Moore's comparison the earthly singer approaches the angel's perfection, in Poe's version the human artist falls hopelessly short. Fully aware of his inferiority, the speaker devotes the first six stanzas to unstinting praise of the heavenly angel's poetic perfection. In the two concluding stanzas, he delineates the restrictions, a result of the fact of being human, that doom his own attempts at apprehending supernal beauty. Because the poet does not find "merely – flowers" sufficient, quotidian existence drops out of view as he focuses on an impossible but laudable goal: singing like an angel (P, p. 176). His failure is ensured from the outset by his inferior resources; he must simulate celestial music by putting words on a page, whose fallen materiality cannot capture the music of the spheres. Israfel, whose heart is a stringed instrument, and whose voice is perfectly adapted to accompaniment, has an insurmountable advantage. In other words, Israfel is the ideal Romantic poet, one who can literally "sing from the heart" – the cliché underpins the poem. The impossibility of achieving that ideal leads the earthly poet to a melancholic sense of despair.

Although the poem certainly encourages readers to associate the failed earthly poet with Poe, it also conveys the irony that Poe is simultaneously trafficking in and critiquing literary conventions of tortured poetic genius. Israfel, for example, is not as angelic as he first appears, and heaven is not as starkly opposed to earth as the speaker suggests. Israfel's celestial audience behaves very much like an earthly celebrity's fan club. The stars are "giddy," and the moon is so "enamored" of Israfel that she is "tottering": they all but ask for Israfel's autograph. Israfel, moreover, seems to have a competitive streak not suited to an angel. The speaker stresses not only how well Israfel sings but also how no one can sing better; Israfel silences his competition, rendering all other heavenly inhabitants "mute." The celestial dwellers, in short, display distinctly human traits of competition, ambition, passion, and envy. These are indications that either heaven is not much different from earth, or Israfel is a projection of the poem's human speaker, designed to torture him by confronting him with his own sense of inadequacy and artistic failure. (In "The Philosophy of Composition," Poe attributes the scholar's interrogation of the raven, which he knows will always result in the response "nevermore," to "the human thirst for self-torture."[6])

Signs that the latter is the case emerge not only from his human description of the celestial spheres but also from the halting syntax, uneven rhythm, and erratic rhyming patterns that both summon a more melodic supernal realm and foreground the impossibility of representing it. The fourth stanza, for example, consists of a sentence fragment:

> But the skies that angel trod,
> Where deep thoughts are a duty –
> Where Love's a grown up God –
> Where the Houri glances are
> Imbued with all the beauty
> Which we worship in a star. (P, p. 176)

The speaker begins to tell us something about "the skies," where thoughts, love, and glances are different from ours, but then the verb is missing. Poe used off-rhymes occasionally and pointedly, for to him perfect rhymes summoned a more perfect language. The sequence of perfect rhymes in the first stanza – dwell, well, Israfel, tell, spell – degenerates by the second, as if the speaker couldn't keep it up; he starts by rhyming "love" and "above" and then adds a syllable and shifts the vowel, as if he had run out of words and had to change the rhyme. Even then, they are off: he rhymes "even" with "seven," underscoring the human poet's unheavenly propensity for linguistic dissonance. Although the lines are loosely iambic, the line lengths vary greatly, and Poe inserts a number of words that throw a wrench in the rhythmic works: "tottering" is a good example. An accomplished versifier highly sensitive to the musical qualities of language, Poe here uses his skills to fashion a certain poetic clunkiness, offering a joke for those readers for whom scansion is a pleasurable, integral part of reading poetry.

Poe thus slyly suggests that his very depictions of otherworldliness are intended to stir worldly desires; more particularly, his poem invites readers to take pity on the unnamed poet and assuage his sense of insecurity by admiring his work. If this was Poe's goal, he was successful. Seeking to comfort the speaker, readers have repeatedly responded by ousting Israfel and putting Poe in his place; in doing so, they not only erase the difference between the mirror images of earthly and angelic poets but also identify Poe with his speaker, which the poem encourages them to do. Perhaps the first to perform this alchemy was Frances Sargent Osgood in "Echo-Song," published in the *Broadway Journal* of September 7, 1845: Poe was the editor at the time and therefore responsible for Osgood's publication. In this poem Osgood, who carried on a public and eventually scandalous flirtation in an exchange of poems with Poe in the *Journal*, brings Poe's speaker's desires down to earth:

> I know a noble heart that beats
> For one it loves how "wildly well!"
> I only know for whom it beats
> But I must never tell!   (qtd. in *P*, p. 234)

Quoting Poe's description of Israfel, first Osgood recognizes the angel as an idealized projection of the earthly poet; second, she unmasks Poe's speaker as identical with himself; third, she redirects Israfel's heavenly, impersonal passion toward a particular, human, female lover. Such a response indicates the complex, nuanced engagements of readers of his time, who register Poe's own play with poetic convention and respond in kind. More earnestly, Hervey Allen entitled his biography of Poe *Israfel*, hoping to install the poet in the eternal halls of poetic fame that Israfel occupies within Poe's poem.[7]

The evocation of other worlds where flowers are not "merely – flowers" characterizes much of Poe's major work. Several of his poems – "The Valley of Unrest," "The City in the Sea," "Dream-Land," and "El Dorado," for example – describe fantastical landscapes that "resemble nothing that is ours" (*P*, p. 201). Poe's surreal landscapes mark their place in the eighteenth- and nineteenth-century revival of medieval romance that gives Romanticism its name. According to Harold Bloom, Blake, Wordsworth, Shelley, Byron, and others internalized the romantic quest narrative "in the name of a humanizing hope that approaches apocalyptic intensity. The poet takes the patterns of quest-romance and transposes them into his own imaginative life, so that the entire rhythm of the quest is heard again in the movement of the poet himself from poem to poem."[8] In his vastly popular *Childe Harold's Pilgrimage* (1812–1818), for example, Byron charts his responses to the exotic places he travels through – Portugal, the Mediterranean, and the Aegean Sea – on his self-exile from England. "Childe" is a title for a young man who is a candidate for knighthood, ironically applied in Byron's poem to a wealthy, restless young man seeking the meaning of life through aimless traveling:

> Apart he stalked in joyless reverie,
> And from his native land resolv'd to go,
> And visit scorching climes beyond the sea;

> With pleasure drugged, he almost long'd for woe,
> And e'en for change of scene would seek the shades below.[9]

Dissatisfied with all he knows, Childe Harold looks for something that will make him feel alive without knowing what it is.

Crossing the boundaries of the real in a similar quest, Poe's speakers actually do "seek the shades below" and sometimes find them. Like many of his landscape poems, "Dream-Land" invites readers to experience vicariously the speaker's trip to a place that inverts the laws of nature. As in Byron's *Childe Harold*, or Shelley's *Prometheus Unbound* – whose "Echo" choruses are one of the rhythmic, imagistic, and linguistic prototypes for "Dream-Land" – the speaker travels to an exotic land; but unlike these other poems, nothing happens once he gets there. Reporting on his travels to a place beyond the farthest point on the known horizon, the speaker cultivates an otherworldly atmosphere not only with his imagistic description but also with intensive, intricate sonic patterns:

> By a route obscure and lonely,
> Haunted by ill angels only,
> Where an Eidolon, named Night,
> On a black throne reigns upright,
> I have reached these lands but newly
> From an ultimate dim Thule –
> From a wild weird clime that lieth, sublime,
> Out of Space – out of Time.
>
> Bottomless vales and boundless floods,
> And chasms, and caves, and Titan woods,
> With forms that no man can discover
> For the dews that drip all over;
> Mountains toppling evermore
> Into seas without a shore;
> Seas that restlessly aspire,
> Surging, unto skies of fire;
> Lakes that endlessly outspread
> Their lone waters – lone and dead, –
> Their still waters – still and chilly
> With the snows of the lolling lily. (*P*, pp. 343–44)

The sonic properties substantially contribute to the poem's otherworldly impression. The repetition of vowels, consonants, morphemes, words, and whole phrases, sometimes with slight variation, encourages the reader to enter an alternative zone that defies the normal, daily, pragmatic functions of language. The adjective "lolling" seems to precede "lily," for example, first because it mirrors and doubles the *l* and *i* sounds in "lily," although the image of dying lilies is consistent with the static, "dismal," "unholy" landscape, because the lily is a conventional symbol for Christ. The dominant meter, trochaic tetrameter, is often used for chants, incantations, and the speech of supernatural beings because it inverts the normative representation of spoken English in iambic pentameter: Shakespeare's Ariel in *The Tempest* and the witches in *Macbeth* speak in trochees, for example, as do Shelley's Echoes in *Prometheus Unbound*; Poe's poem echoes these Echoes:

> By the woodland noontide dew,
> By the forests, lakes and fountains,
> Through the many-folded mountains,
> To the rents and gulphs and chasms
> Where the Earth reposed from spasms . . .[10]

The poems share anaphoric phrasing ("By the . . . By the") and disyllabic feminine end rhymes ("chasms" and "spasms" in Shelley, for example, "chilly" and "lily" in Poe). They also share the words "dew," "lakes," "mountains," and "chasms." Poe exaggerates and sustains the trance-inducing qualities of Shelley's language. His trochaic rhyming couplets, recursiveness, and repetition all encourage the reader to attend to the rhythm at the expense of the meaning of the words. These echoes of the Echoes code Poe's landscape as an extension and revision of Shelley's. It is more surreal, more remote, more forlorn, and more "melancholy."

Using spatial and temporal terminology to describe a place "out of Space – out of Time," the speaker forces language to evoke something that is beyond its ability to signify. The speaker's description is therefore a translation or approximation that dramatizes its limitations. Apocalyptic events, which usually signify the end of everything, are the ongoing norm in this strange, timeless land. The speaker observes a landscape that is, impossibly, frozen in continuous collapse: floods pour outwards, mountains fall, seas ascend to the fiery skies. Spatial terms are simultaneously asserted and negated: lakes, defined by their boundaries – they are larger than ponds, smaller than seas – "endlessly outspread," and "forms" can be discerned but not discovered, a distinction seemingly without a difference but apparently significant in a way we cannot apprehend.

The poem both evokes a world beyond the dimensional categories of human perception and seeks to convey the sense of disorientation that experiencing such a world would generate in a human visitor through an elaborate deployment of suspension and repetition. Narrative, a key mode for describing change over time, be it a physical adventure, a spiritual trans-formation, or a psychological insight, stagnates here. The speaker's modi-fying phrases describe his location but hold action at bay. The first stanza's suspension is resolved by the termination of an action: "I have reached this land." The third stanza retraces the first two, repeating phrases, syntactic structures, and descriptions: most extremely, the last four lines of the second stanza are repeated almost verbatim in the third stanza. In the first three stan-zas, in other words, Poe generates the antipode of the Romantic quest nar-rative by working within its terms. Rather than moving forward, the speaker loops back to describe what he has already described; the recursiveness disori-ents the reader in the way it stimulates a sense of déjà-vu; we wonder if we have already read what we are reading and return to reread the earlier lines, only to find that we have indeed read the same lines and are now rereading them once again.

In the second half of "Dream-Land" we finally learn that the speaker's wan-dering is motivated, consciously or unconsciously, by a preoccupation with the dead. The weird landscape serves as the stage for the traveler's encounter with ghosts of former intimates, "sheeted memories of the Past / – Shrouded forms that start and sigh / As they pass the wanderer by" (P, p. 344). He sug-gests that his "woes" are so unimaginably profound that he finds solace in this place that would leave most people "aghast." Although he finds some measure of peace, however, he cannot find resolution, for the "weak human eye" can-not bear to look directly at what the traveler wants to see: the specter of his lost loved one. The poem ends almost exactly as it began, reinforcing the hope-lessness and continued misery of the speaker, who "wandered home" just as he wandered to "this ultimate dim Thule." The almost exact repetition of the first stanza at the poem's conclusion inscribes the speaker within a doomed circle of loss; he is right back where he started from.

How does Poe's particular, rather perverse engagement with the inter-nal quest romance make sense within this tradition? What does it say not about the possibility of Poe's psychic disturbances but about what he is trying to communicate to his readers? For he published "Dream-Land" and other poems with similar themes not just once but repeatedly, in magazines as well as books, and clearly wished to reach a broad readership. In the same letter to Lowell quoted previously, Poe offers an explanation for his poetic preoc-cupation with death. It is a curiously external, even scientific explanation of a shared, religious experience that complicates Bloom's firmly individual, inte-riorized, psychological understanding of Romantic questing:

The unparticled matter, permeating and impelling all things, is God. Its activity is the thought of God – which creates. Man, and other thinking beings, are individualizations of the unparticled matter.... What we call "death" is the painful metamorphosis. The stars are the habitations of rudimental beings.... At death, the worm is the butterfly – still material, but of a matter unrecognized by our organs – recognized occasionally, perhaps, by the sleepwalker directly – without organs – through the mesmeric medium. Thus a sleepwalker may see ghosts. Divested of the rudimental covering, the being inhabits space, – what we suppose to be the immaterial universe.[11]

Poe explains that death is a transformation from "particled" to "unparticled" matter. What we understand to be spirits or ghosts is "space," and, conversely, what we understand to be space is ghosts: the two are synonymous. Mediums properly attuned – and Poe was writing at the very brink of the moment when American Spiritualists would claim to have initiated communications with other worlds – could convey to the sleepwalker's inner eye – not his physical "organ" – the animate qualities of what most people on a daily basis see as empty space.

Readers of Poe's final cosmological "prose poem," *Eureka*, will perceive the germ of that longer treatise in this passage, which throws into question the persistent tendency to think of Poe's poems as expressions of an isolated genius enclosed within his own tortured mind. Here, he portrays death and the afterlife as shared experiences: "the painful metamorphosis" is undergone by all. It is "unparticled matter," or "God – which creates," within individual persons, perhaps, but impersonally. In this understanding, the poet is a vehicle for common, shared expression. The poet's success is defined by how closely he approaches the expression of impersonal beauty; this approach offers a foretaste of the final unity of unparticled matter that we will all join after death. Poe advances his theory of poetry's role in mediating approaches to immortality in "The Poetic Principle." Poetry whets rather than appeases "a thirst unquenchable" that "belongs to the immortality of Man": "It is no mere appreciation of the Beauty before us – but a wild effort to reach the Beauty above" (*ER*, p. 77). The unavoidable drive to seek a supernal beauty known to be unattainable for the living person means, for Poe, that melancholia, a "certain, petulant, impatient sorrow," is the appropriate sentiment for poetic expression. It is not just a personal but a collective feeling, expressed by and mediated through poetry; the poet mourns his inadequacy even as he conveys "brief and indeterminate glimpses" of "divine and rapturous joys" through his poems; his readers "weep" with him, for he transports them to the edge of an experience they want but cannot have. In this respect, Poe's theory of art and individuality has something in common with Emerson's, as expressed in "The Poet," "Self-Reliance," and "The Over-Soul," regardless of how intensively they both disavowed the resemblance, and how different their means of defining transcendence. The primary difference is that Emerson (at least in those works) believes one can accomplish in human form what Poe believes is impossible: for Emerson, "poets are ... liberating gods"; for Poe, they wish they could be, but can't, so they mark the distance between the human and the divine.[12]

For Poe, the properties of poetry that stir desires for impossible beauty are the elements of language that are irrelevant, or at least secondary, to its signifying capabilities. Poetry is *"the Rhythmical Creation of Beauty.* Its sole arbiter is Taste. With the Intellect or with the Conscience, it has only collateral relations. Unless incidentally, it has no concern whatever either with Duty or with Truth" (*ER*, p. 78). In his hierarchy of the arts, music is above poetry because of its superior ability to transport the listener to the sphere of immortality; poetry holds these capabilities only insofar as it can function as music: "We are often made to feel, with a shivering delight, that from an earthly harp are stricken notes which *cannot* have been unfamiliar to the angels. And thus there can be little doubt that in the union of Poetry with Music in its popular sense, we shall find the widest field for the Poetic development" (*ER*, p. 78). This belief that music holds divine powers – a truism in the nineteenth century that Poe took very seriously – helps account for Poe's signature enhancement of the sonic properties of language to the point that it may even become difficult to focus on the meaning of the words. Words are too much of the earth; they are designed for human communication about earthly matters. Poe seeks to force words to communicate unearthly intimations, and he simultaneously dramatizes the impossibility of that task in his poetry.

Poe's theory of death and the afterlife might seem somewhat idiosyncratic, particularly his understanding of an immaterial material – "unparticled matter" – as God, creativity, action, and spirit. But Victorians were fascinated with identifying the precise boundaries between life, death, and the afterlife, and Poe's formulations resonate with many contemporary related ideas – about metempsychosis and mesmerism, for example, both of which interested him, as we can see from such short stories as "Facts in the Case of M. Valdemar," "Mesmeric Revelation," and "Ligeia." This culture-wide interest in posthumous states of consciousness suggests that Poe's poems are not simply expressions of a dark and peculiar mind that registered only emptiness, dissatisfaction, negation, and despair; rather, they are attempts at generating spiritual "effects" in his readers that offer an intimation of the collective experience of divine beauty that death will bring.

For Poe, poetic composition is motivated not by an urgent need to express one's self – he dismisses the "fine frenzy" and "ecstatic intuition" of other poets (surely Emerson is implicated in this criticism) as an emotional hoax (*ER*, p. 14) – but by a desire to generate emotional effects in readers. His consummate expression of this goal can be found in "The Philosophy of Composition," in which he tells the story of how he wrote "The Raven," his most famous poem about seeking knowledge of the dead:

> I prefer commencing with the consideration of an *effect*. Keeping originality *always* in view – for he is false to himself who ventures to dispense with so obvious and so easily attainable a source of interest – I say to myself, in the first place, "Of the innumerable effects, or impressions, of which the heart, the intellect, or (more generally) the soul is susceptible, what one shall I, on the present occasion, select?" (*ER*, p. 11)

Poe aims not only to generate an effect in a reader but to generate the same effect in all readers: "My next thought concerned the choice of an impression, or effect, to be conveyed: and here I may as well observe that, throughout the construction, I kept steadily in view the design of rendering the work *universally* appreciable" (*ER*, p. 16). Because "the province of the poem" is beauty, which only can be experienced in its absence or imperfect evocation, "melancholy is ... the most legitimate of all the poetical tones" (*ER*, p. 17). "The death ... of a beautiful woman is, unquestionably, the most poetical topic in the world," especially on the lips of "a bereaved lover," because the scenario instantiates a universal, futile desire to reach and hold beauty that lies beyond the grave (*ER*, p. 19).

It is no coincidence that Poe performed his poetic experiments in generating common feelings in periodicals during an age in which the whole trend of publication was "Magazine-ward," in his coinage (*ER*, p. 1414). Fewer people could afford books, which took longer to publish and did not promote the same sense of a collective reading experience as newspapers and magazines. Imagining thousands of people reading the same poem at the same time and receiving the same impression can itself be understood as a spiritual experience, one that bridges the gap between individual and mass, creating the impression of a group consciousness that mimics or foreshadows the transition from particled to unparticled matter, Poe's vision of divine union after death. "The Raven" was particularly suited to circulating through mass communication networks, and Poe insisted in a letter to a friend a few months after its initial publication that he devised it with that intent: "'The Raven' has had a great 'run.'... I wrote it for the express purpose of running – just as I did the "Gold-Bug," you know. The bird beat the bug, though, all hollow."[13] "The Raven" simply could not have created a public sensation if it had been first published in book form. A cultural phenomenon almost from the day of its first publication in February 1845, the poem was quickly and widely reprinted, reviewed, and imitated. According to Walter Benjamin, the purpose of "art in the age of its technological reproducibility" is "to train human beings in the apperceptions and vast apparatus whose role in their lives is expanding almost daily." For this reason, "to an ever-increasing degree, the work reproduced becomes the reproduction of a work designed for reproducibility."[14] This tautological formulation suggests that the survival and dissemination of the literary object is its primary instructive function, and indeed, Poe's most famous poem was broadly reprinted and imitated, in part because it was designed for reproducibility; these reproductive labors arguably instruct readers (some of whom become writers in turn) in ways of engaging and harnessing the expressive powers of mass print culture's "vast apparatus."

That design is first of all evident in the ways that the poem foregrounds its own acts of mimicry. More explicitly, perhaps, than other poems, "The Raven" recombines highly recognizable elements of existing poetic culture, generating an uncanny effect of recognition in readers who encounter the poem for the first time. The words "no more," "nevermore" and "evermore" are ubiquitous in the poetry of the early nineteenth century, and "The Raven" summons the echoic force of those poems in the insistent repetition of its refrain. Many of Poe's contemporaries noted the poem's uncanny similarity to a myriad of precursor poems; some went so far as to claim that Poe stole the poem, in whole or in parts, from them, or that they helped him write it.[15] Critics have identified sources for the rhythm, the story line, the refrain, the word "nevermore," and the raven (P, pp. 353–59).[16] Earlier poems that bear distinct resemblances include Thomas Holley Chivers's "To Allegra Florence in Heaven" (which shares with "The Raven" trochaic disyllabic *ing* end rhymes: "Holy angels now are bending / To receive thy soul ascending"), Albert Pike's "Isadore" (in which a bereaved lover tells about the death of a beautiful woman whose name rhymes with Lenore's), and Elizabeth Barrett Browning's "Lady Geraldine's Courtship" (which features trochaic octameter lines and definite verbal and imagistic echoes: the poems share a stirring "purple curtain," for example). Poe advertised the poem's derivative qualities rather than repudiating them. Weeks before he published "The Raven," he reviewed Elizabeth Browning's poems, drawing special attention to "Lady Geraldine's Courtship." In "The Philosophy of Composition" he refers to "an examination I once made of the mechanism of 'Barnaby Rudge,'" encouraging readers to discover an earlier version of Poe's black bird (*ER*, p. 13). While he demotes originality to the uninspired and technical exercise of recombination, he celebrates what is most tried as most true. He explains, for example, his choice of a ready-made refrain as the "pivot upon which the whole structure might turn" in terms of its efficiency and functionality, both proven by long-standing use: "The universality of its employment sufficed to assure me of its intrinsic value" (*ER*, p. 17).

Internally as well, "The Raven" foregrounds its reproductive logics. The poem opens with the speaker reading "many a quaint and curious volume of forgotten lore"; steeped in twice-told tales, he assumes their antiquated diction to describe his encounter with the raven. The bird himself seems to have stepped out of such lore and planted himself within the poem, a familiar figure from a collective repertoire of inherited myths and stories: "In there stepped a stately Raven of the saintly days of yore." Barbara Johnson has said that "it would be hard to find a poem ... which is packed with more clichés than 'The Raven': ember, remember, December, midnight, darkness, marble busts – all the bric-a-brac of poetic language is set out in jangling, alliterative trochees to hammer out a kind of ur-background of the gothic encounter." The figure par excellence of this bric-a-brac, for Johnson, is "the word 'nevermore,'" which "stands in Poe as a figure for poetic language as such."[17] Because birds, especially in the Romantic period, inevitably serve as the poet's surrogate, by selecting a highly limited mimic as his double, Poe suggests (not without humor) that writing poetry may be as simple as repeating what one hears most frequently. Duplicates proliferate, as if every aspect of the poem were prone to reproduction: "each separate dying ember wrought its ghost upon the floor," the speaker's call in the dark for Lenore summons an echo, and the raven casts his shadow over the speaker, imprisoning him eternally within the contours of a copy. The poem is saturated with sonic repetition, from its perfect trochaic octameter lines to its assonance, consonance, regular rhythms, and insistent rhymes. Each line contains a perfect, often identical, internal rhyme, and most of the lines also have end rhymes. The speaker is prone to repeating the same word multiple times. Sonic repetition serves as a mnemonic device, making the poem easily, and even inadvertently, memorizable. Editor N. P. Willis recognized this quality; he prefaced the first publication of the poem with the comment: "It will stick in the memory of everybody who reads it" (*PL*, p. 496). Indeed, the poem not only stuck in everybody's memories but also stimulated many people to write their own versions. Myriads of variations on "The Raven" were published in the weeks, months, and years following its appearance, from tributes to Poe, to advertising jingles, to political commentaries, and to Christian allegories. As editor of the *Broadway Journal*,

Poe himself published and commented approvingly on more than one rewriting of "The Raven." Made to be remade, the poem trains readers in mass media functions and encourages them to put their knowledge to use.

Poe's contemporaries celebrated the collective feeling of creepiness evoked by the poem. Elizabeth Barrett Browning told Poe that it had "produced a fit horror" throughout England (*PL*, p. 631). Another reviewer noted the appropriateness of the tone of "settled despair" as a means of ministering to "the sense of the beautiful" (*P*, p. 363). Reviewing *The Raven and Other Poems*, George P. Morris said that "tall shadows and a sighing silence seem to close around us as we read. We feel dream land to be more real and more touching than the actual life we have left" (*PL*, p. 592). Although Morris found the experience fascinating and welcome in a world of "merely – flowers," that did not prevent him from recognizing that Poe's writing was part of a Romantic tradition. For those who have difficulties appreciating Poe's work, "we recommend to him a year's regimen of monkish legends, and chronicles with which Warton and Scott fed the poetic fire" (*PL*, p. 592). Marked as a vehicle for the transmission and circulation of common feelings, "The Raven" exposes the complex relation between figures of suffering interiority and their reception. Readers may experience vicariously the claustrophobic mental state of the mournful lover, but they also take pleasure in the poem as a novel experiment in thought and feeling in which they may share. "The Raven" offers a commoditized image of private melancholy that readers can hold in common as a universally legible sign of supernal beauty. While the poem may be training its readers in the operations of print culture by reproducing reproducibility, it does so to infuse that apparatus with human impressions of the supernatural, to populate the machinery with ghosts of beauty and despair, of *"Mournful and Never-ending Remembrance"* that might otherwise be lost, buried in an unread book (*ER*, p. 25). The poem's unnerving propensity to reproduction allows it to serve as a vehicle for a range of common feelings to the present day – think of the 1990 rendition of "The Raven" in *The Simpsons* episode "The Treehouse of Horror," Lou Reed's 2003 album *The Raven*, or the 2012 film entitled *The Raven*, starring John Cusack, Alice Eve, and Luke Evans, for example.

Many of Poe's poems fall into two categories: there are the apocalyptic landscapes, like "Dream-Land," "The Valley of Unrest," and "The City in the Sea," and, perhaps more familiarly, there are the meditations on lost love, like "The Raven," "Annabel Lee," and "Ulalume." Both are characterized by Poe's particular brand of late Romantic questing, which many readers of the time recognized as a way of preserving a shared reservoir of feelings – particularly spiritual and mystical feelings – infringed on by the rise of science and industrial capitalism. The apparently distinct difference between apocalyptic scenes that suggest the destruction of mankind and personal scenes that suggest the destruction of an individual man blurs if we understand that Poe believed in a communal experience of what might be called the beauty of despair. His poetic evocations of this beauty preserve feelings and values potentially lost – the fallibility of human beings, the irrational love for another person, the dream of a fulfilling spiritual experience, the dissolution of the boundaries of the isolated self, and union with a higher consciousness – all the impractical emotions and desires that make us human.

One of the most astute contemporary critics of Poe, who was largely responsible for defending and promoting his reputation after his death and for securing his place in literary history (she was also, briefly, Poe's fiancée), Sarah Helen Whitman, offers a detailed analysis of Poe's place in a tradition of Romantic questing. In one of the earliest and most effective defenses of Poe, she arrives at a conclusion that Raymond Williams might have endorsed:

> Goethe had made his great dramatic poem an expression of the soul's craving for a knowledge of spiritual existence.... Wordsworth, in his finest imaginative poem, "Laodamia," represents and half reproves this longing. Byron iterates it with a proud and passionate vehemence in "Manfred." Shelley's sad heart of unbelief, finding refuge in a despair too deep for aspiration, stands apart ... while Keats lies sleeping, like his own Endymion, lost in dreams of the "dead Past." Then, sadder, and lonelier, and more unbelieving than any of these, Edgar Poe came to sound the very abyss. The unrest and faithlessness of the age culminated in him. Nothing so solitary, nothing so hopeless, nothing so desolate as his spirit in its darker moods has been instanced in the literary history of the nineteenth century.[18]

Williams attributes the rise of the romantic artist to an attempt to shore up aspects of the human experience threatened by the rise of industrial capitalism; in this passage Whitman charts the trajectory of such attempts. She attributes the despair in Poe's poems not, or not only, to an individual experience of personal loss but to a spiritual crisis of his age. That very hopelessness, however, contains a promise for Whitman, one that might not be immediately obvious for current readers of Poe, but that many of his contemporaries recognized, and that resonates with Poe's own theory of the afterlife, delineated in his letter to Lowell and in *Eureka*, as well as in his poems:

> Is there no evidence of a wise purpose, an epochal fitness, in the appearance, at this precise era, of a mind so rarely gifted, and accessible from peculiarities of psychal and physical organization to the subtle vibrations of an ethereal medium conveying but feeble impressions to the senses of ordinary persons;

a mind which, "following darkness like a dream," wandered forever with insatiate curiosity on the confines of that " – wild weird clime, that lieth sublime / Out of Space, out of Time! ..." seeking to solve the problem of that phantasmal Shadow-Land, which, through a class of phenomena unprecedented in the world's history, was about to attest itself as an actual plane of conscious and progressive life, the mode and measure of whose relations with our own are already recognized as legitimate objects of scientific research by the most candid and competent thinkers of our time?[19]

Whitman lived longer than Poe, long enough to witness the advent of the Spiritualist Movement, to which she alludes here, and in which she took part. She, along with other mediums, claimed to receive poetic messages from Poe's spirit, usually in the highly recognizable, otherworldly meters of "The Raven," or "Ulalume," or "The Bells." Most prominently, mediums Thomas Lake Harris and Lizzie Doten channeled Poe's communications, confirming not only that he was "seeking to solve the problem of the phantasmal Shadow-Land," as he had done in his poetry while living, but also that he was still seeking to communicate his discoveries to those left behind. Although Whitman's theory might seem like a fringe response to Poe's work, Spiritualism was a mainstream religious movement in the mid-nineteenth century with profound cultural influence. Spiritualists recognized both the communicative structure of Poe's work and a hopefulness that paradoxically emerges from his insistence on despair: after the death worm comes the butterfly, in Poe's formulation. Dying is only the farthest point in human consciousness, the verge that we can travel to before receiving knowledge of the other side. The solipsistic, melancholy despair generated by this tendency to "follow darkness" intimates by contrast the "actual plane of consciousness" that lies on the other side of death. Emily Dickinson, among other nineteenth-century poets, shares this fascination, and her own experiments with dramatizing approaches to that brink may well be influenced by Poe's earlier work.

Although "The Raven" is unsurpassed in its ability to forge relations between individual interiority and mass consumption, many of his poems share this aim, and readers recognized the strange balancing act that permitted the circulation and internalization of poetic feeling and that allowed it to become an experience held in common. "Ulalume," written after "The Raven" and often identified as one of Poe's best poems, also tells the story of the eruption of repressed mourning over a lost, loved woman, a private experience that Poe makes into a public, shared icon of the poetic ideal: a bereaved lover's tale of the death of a beautiful woman. This compressed paradox, of publicized privacy, or private publicity, is contained within the full title of the poem: "Ulalume: A Ballad." Tagging a poem as a ballad insists on its status as common property by invoking an anonymous broadside tradition. ("Annabel Lee" also advertises its status as a ballad through its close adherence to ballad meter and refrain.) In "Ulalume," the speaker walks through a weird landscape on a "sere" October evening with Psyche, his soul. He is unaware that he is propelled unconsciously to the destination of his lover's grave, on the anniversary of the day he buried her there, until they arrive on the spot:

> And I said – "What is written, sweet sister,
> On the door of this legended tomb?"
> She replied – "Ulalume – Ulalume! –
> 'T is the vault of thy lost Ulalume!"
>
> Then my heart it grew ashen and sober
> As the leaves that were crispéd and sere –
> As the leaves that were withering and sere –
> And I cried – "It was surely October,
> On *this* very night of last year,
> That I journeyed – I journeyed down here! –
> That I brought a dread burden down here –
> On this night, of all nights in the year,
> Ah, what demon has tempted me here?
> Well I know, now, this dim lake of Auber –
> This misty mid region of Weir: –
> Well I know, now, this dank tarn of Auber –
> This ghoul-haunted woodland of Weir."   (P, p. 418)

Prefiguring Freud's theory of melancholia, Poe presents us with a speaker who has repressed his loss so profoundly that it utterly controls his actions. Trying to wander freely, imagining that he is carefree, he is brought face-to-face with the evidence of the sorrow he is trying to escape. The poem is remarkable for the way it emblematizes personal feeling: the speaker's journey is recognizable as an icon of a particular state of mind. It thus depersonalizes or detaches the feelings from individual experience and renders them circulatable and shareable.

It is this quality Sarah Helen Whitman recognizes when she characterizes "Ulalume" as both an abstract depiction of an amorphous world and a highly personal "strange threnody" for Poe's wife, who had died a few months before he wrote the poem: "This poem, perhaps the most original and weirdly suggestive of all his poems, resembles at first sight some of Turner's landscapes, being apparently 'without form and void, and having darkness on the face of it.' It is, nevertheless, in its basis, although not in the precise correspondence of time, simply historical." Comparing the poem to a painting by Turner, which she understands as a representation of undifferentiated matter before creation – she cites Genesis to describe the effect of Turner's painting – Whitman recognizes the poem as a cultural artifact in an aesthetic tradition. Simultaneously and without a sense of contradiction, she identifies an autobiographical component. Revelations of self and of universal effects are not understood as conflicting or even separate. This is even clearer in the comments of a writer in the *London Critic*, who says of "Ulalume":

> What wondrous words! What a spell they wield! What a withering unity there is in them! The instant they are uttered a misty picture with a tarn, dark as a murderer's eye, below, and the thin yellow leaves of October fluttering above – exponents of a misery which scorns the name of sorrow – is hung up in the chambers of your soul forever.[20]

The critic celebrates the dismal, despairing aspects of the poem in a tone that borders on glee, and he does not understand this tone as inappropriate. The poem at once offers a portrait of "a misery which scorns the name of sorrow" and does so in a highly pleasurable, entertaining way. "Ulalume" offers readers a circulatable and transportable emblem of misery that may be "hung up in the chambers of your soul forever." Many of Poe's poems allow readers to compose the author's suffering in a way that makes it available for their own emotional purposes; it is a structure that persists, enabling Poe's poems to continue circulating and captivating readers everywhere.

Notes

1. Edgar Allan Poe, *Collected Works of Edgar Allan Poe*. Vol. 1, *Poetry*, ed. Thomas Ollive Mabbott (Cambridge, Mass.: Belknap Press of Harvard University Press, 1969), p. 344. Hereafter cited parenthetically within the text as *P*.
2. Eric W. Carlson, *The Recognition of Edgar Allan Poe: Selected Criticism since 1829* (Ann Arbor: University of Michigan Press, 1966), p. 45.
3. Quoted in Arthur Hobson Quinn, *Edgar Allan Poe: A Critical Biography* (1941; Baltimore: Johns Hopkins University Press, 1998), p. 428.
4. Raymond Williams, *Culture and Society, 1780–1950* (New York: Columbia University Press, 1983), p. 36.
5. Williams, *Culture and Society*, p. 36.
6. Edgar Allan Poe, *Essays and Reviews*, ed. Gary Richard Thompson (New York: Library of America, 1984), p. 24. Hereafter cited within the text as *ER*.
7. Hervey Allen, *Israfel: The Life and Times of Edgar Allan Poe* (New York: Rinehart, 1934).

8. Harold Bloom, "Internalization of Quest-Romance," in Harold Bloom (ed.), *Romanticism and Consciousness: Essays in Criticism* (New York: Norton, 1970), p. 5.

9. George Gordon, Lord Byron, *Childe Harold's Pilgrimage*, in Jerome J. McGann (ed.), *The Major Works* (New York: Oxford University Press, 2008), p. 24.

10. Percy Bysshe Shelley, *Prometheus Unbound*, in Sharon B. Powers and Donald H. Reiman (eds.), *Shelley's Poetry and Prose: Authoritative Texts, Criticism* (New York: Norton, 1977), p. 166.

11. Quoted in Quinn, *Edgar Allan Poe*, pp. 428–29.

12. Ralph Waldo Emerson, *Essays & Lectures*, ed. Joel Porte (New York: Library of America, 1983), p. 462.

13. Dwight Thomas, *The Poe Log: A Documentary Life of Edgar Allan Poe, 1809–1849*, ed. David Kelly Jackson (Boston: G. K. Hall, 1987), pp. 530–31. Hereafter cited within the text as *PL*.

14. Walter Benjamin, "The Work of Art in the Age of Its Technological Reproducibility: Second Version," in Michael W. Jennings, Brigid Doherty, and Thomas Y. Levin (eds.), *The Work of Art in the Age of Its Technological Reproducibility and Other Writings* (Cambridge, Mass.: Belknap Press of Harvard University Press, 2008), pp. 19–74, 26.

15. For examples and a discussion of these "thefts," see Eliza Richards, "Outsourcing 'The Raven': Retroactive Origins," *Victorian Poetry* 43:2 (2005), pp. 205–21.

16. John Ingram (ed.), *The Raven, by Edgar Allan Poe; with Literary and Historical Commentary* (London: George Redway, 1885), pp. 1–16.

17. Barbara Johnson, "Strange Fits: Poe and Wordsworth on the Nature of Poetic Language," in *A World of Difference* (Baltimore, Md.: Johns Hopkins University Press, 1987), pp. 89–99, 98.

18. Sarah Helen Whitman, *Edgar Poe and His Critics*, ed. Oral Sumner Coad (1860; New Brunswick, N.J.: Rutgers University Press, 1949), p. 75.

19. Whitman, *Edgar Poe and His Critics*, p. 81.

20. Quoted in Whitman, *Edgar Poe and His Critics*, p. 45.

Chapter 11
Longfellow in His Time

VIRGINIA JACKSON

When in 1882 Walt Whitman learned of the death of fellow poet Henry Wadsworth Longfellow, he took the occasion "for want of anything better," to "twine a sprig of sweet ground-ivy trailing so plentifully through the dead leaves" and metaphorically "lay it as [his] contribution on the dead bard's grave." That late prose ivy "sprig" was a far cry from the stunningly beautiful lilac verse "sprig" Whitman had laid at Lincoln's grave seventeen years (and a lifetime) earlier. If Lincoln became for Whitman the exemplary instance of earlier nineteenth-century American poetic ideals imagined and lost, Longfellow became the exemplary instance of bygone nineteenth-century American poetic ideals that refused to go away:

> Longfellow seems to me not only to be eminent in the style and forms of poetical expression that mark the present age (an idiosyncrasy, almost a sickness, of verbal melody), but to bring what is always dearest as poetry to the general human heart and taste, and probably must be so in the nature of things. He is certainly the kind of bard and counteractant most needed for our materialistic, self-assertive, money-worshipping, Anglo-Saxon races, and especially for the present age in America – an age tyrannically regulated with reference to the manufacturer, the merchant, the financier, the politician and the day workman – for whom and among whom he comes as the poet of melody, courtesy, deference – poet of the mellow twilight of the past in Italy, Germany, Spain, and in Northern Europe – poet of all sympathetic gentleness – and universal poet of women and young people. I should have to think long if I were ask'd to name the man who has done more, in more valuable directions, for America.[1]

We should have to think long if we were asked to name a more damning instance of faint praise than "universal poet of women and young people," unless it is "poet of the mellow twilight of the past" or poet adept at what amounts to "an idiosyncrasy, almost a sickness of verbal melody." Those compliments certainly diminish his contemporary, whose 1855 *The Song of Hiawatha* outsold Whitman's 1855 *Leaves of Grass* by far, but Whitman's Longfellow sprig is not all diminution: "What is always dearest as poetry to the general human heart and taste, and probably must be so in the nature of things" may be something for the elder Whitman to regret, but he also has to admit that such feminized, infantilized, outdated, and sugar-coated poetry was better than what the "present age in America" would imagine on its own. Perhaps a "poet of melody, courtesy, deference" was just the thing to counteract the emerging American century, to resist the "Anglo-Saxon" version of New World ambition that had begun to make of antebellum modernity something even more frightening. By not having been Whitman, in other words – or, in the younger Whitman's words, not having been the poet able to "flood himself with the immediate age as with vast oceanic tides" – Longfellow may not have realized Whitman's dream of making a better world through (of all things) poetry, but he did leave behind an Old World charm as a token of the nineteenth century's vanishing "sympathetic gentleness." It is not surprising that the Good Gray Poet offered such a condescending portrait of the most influential American poet of the nineteenth century, but it *is* somewhat surprising that Whitman's characterization of Longfellow's place in literary and cultural history seems to be the one that has stuck.

Say the words "Henry Wadsworth Longfellow was the most influential American poet of the nineteenth century" today and you are likely to hear distant if twisted echoes of Whitman's gentle elegiac acknowledgment and condescension. More than a century after Longfellow's death and Whitman's idiosyncratic evaluation, Angus Fletcher compared the two and lamented that "as a poet, competing for attention in our modern age of anxiety and irony, Longfellow has fallen from his great height."[2] Dana Gioia (later chair of the National Endowment of the Arts) went further, complaining that "when a literary culture loses its ability to recognize and appreciate genuine poems like 'My Lost Youth' because they are too simple, it has surely traded too much of its innocence and openness for a shallow sophistication."[3] In the last decades of the nineteenth century, Whitman invoked Longfellow as an antidote to a "materialistic, self-assertive, money-worshipping" American culture; in the last decade of the twentieth century, literary critics began to invoke Longfellow as an antidote to an American literary culture that no longer takes poetry to heart, in which poetry has ceased, in Gioia's words, to exercise "a broad cultural influence that today seems more typical of movies or popular music than anything we might imagine possible for poetry."[4] In the first decade of the twenty-first century, Christoph Irmscher argued that we would all "benefit ... from including Longfellow in the perennial debate about the death (or the survival) of poetry. His example will not only help us clarify what is really at stake ... it will also give us a better understanding of the hierarchies that still affect us and our thinking about literature and the arts today."⁵ But as Whitman saw clearly, Longfellow was already central to such debates in the nineteenth century; furthermore, as Whitman may not yet have seen, it was Longfellow who forged the modern literary critical version of such debates, who made the disappearance of poetry the subject of his poems, and who gave professional readers the power to bring poetry back from the brink of extinction. Whitman's somewhat grudging nostalgia for Old World innocence was Longfellow's constant theme. If for contemporary literary critics the most popular American poet in history seems to have come to represent nothing less than the disappearance of poetry, or the vanishing of a popular poetry that all Americans could understand and read without "anxiety and irony," free of the "shallow sophistication" that has come to characterize "the hierarchies" of reading that separate scholars and general readers, the poet and his public, that may be because Longfellow so effectively created so many versions of just such scenes of vanishing and recovery. For late twentieth- and early twenty-first-century professional readers, Longfellow has come to stand for a poetry that was not the property of professional readers but instead belonged to everyone, to the nation, to the world. The bygone ideal that Whitman attached to "the universal poet of women and young people" has become the bygone ideal that literary critics now attach to Longfellow. What Longfellow now represents for literary criticism is a vision of American poetry before poetry was ruined by literary criticism. Yet as it happens, Longfellow was himself the literary figure who helped to define American poetry as a common language always already lost to the very American readers who loved him most, a common language it took a professional scholar to restore.

What Whitman's version of Longfellow's comparative historical innocence and recent versions of Longfellow's "innocence and openness" share is the view that American readers cannot properly appreciate American poetry. For Whitman, that failing was evident in readers' universal embrace of Longfellow; for recent literary critics, that failing is evident in Longfellow's (and poetry's) universal disappearance. These laments are really two sides of the same coin, and both sides have Longfellow's picture on them. The truth is that Longfellow – Smith Professor of Modern Languages and Belles Lettres at Harvard, inventor of the American version of comparative literature, and best-selling American poet of the nineteenth and early twentieth centuries – was instrumental in the construction of the very hierarchies of reading later critics mistakenly believe have eclipsed him. So much of what Longfellow wrote thematized both the disappearance of cultures and the importance of turning the traces of those vanished cultures into modern poetry. It was in all ways a winning formula: in his Harvard pedagogy, the notion of the *Weltliteratur*, or concert of world literatures – a term that Longfellow borrowed from Goethe – encouraged the study of a wide variety of cultures with a view toward their progress in forming the synthetic world literature of modern America. In his popular verse, the nostalgic evocation of vanished poetries – Acadian, Ojibwe, local, rural, infantile, ancient, Semitic, colonial, Revolutionary, classical Greek, medieval, German, Norse, Spanish, Moorish, Italian, Celtic, Gaelic, French – made the poet into an expressive antiquarian, a collector of ancient lore given back to the people, whose own poetry (in the form of the poems Longfellow wrote) was in danger of becoming part of a later Americanizing and modernizing collection (as indeed it has). As my partial and haphazard list indicates, Longfellow's adoption of the umbrella trope of the *Weltliteratur* served to turn modern European nations and ancient (even mythical) cultures into a blurred verse genre in which geography and history could be confused with each other, in which the Old World was capacious indeed. That broad, multiethnic, multinational, multicultural tributary fed a much more ambitious project than either Whitman or Longfellow's recent critical champions recognized. Longfellow plundered world literary history for the materials for his immensely popular poems in order to make old literatures into modern literary currency. As the echoes between Whitman and recent defenders of Longfellow attest, it is Longfellow's currency we still exchange when we write about American poetry today.

This is to say that although Longfellow has come to represent a time gone by in which Americans loved poetry, his popularity and influence may actually be effects of the ways in which his enormous body of work lamented the passing of old worlds, old cultures, and old poetries people could love. While we tend to follow Whitman in thinking of Longfellow as representative of a more innocent poetic age, Longfellow thought of himself as a modern poet, and what marked his modernity was his distance from the distant poetic lands and ages that were his subjects. His first books emerged from the European tours on which Bowdoin and then Harvard sent the young professor in order to educate him in a new curriculum of modern languages. *Outre-Mer: A Pilgrimage Beyond the Sea* (1835) begins by invoking "the wild and romantic tales of regions so far off as to be regarded as almost a fairy land." Those tales, Longfellow tells us, "were well suited to the childish credulity of an age in which what is now called the Old World was in its childhood. Those times have passed away. The world has grown wiser and less credulous. . . . But man has not changed his nature."[6] That humanist appeal informed Longfellow's version of comparative literature at Harvard, in which literary works of various traditions could carry the freight of human progress, and it also informed all of his many publications, which increasingly took the form of single books of poetry that could make money for the first author to own his own electroplates.[7] By 1854, even before *The Song of Hiawatha* was published, Longfellow was earning enough to retire from his job at Harvard. Although everything about Longfellow's career had an enormous influence on the ways in which poetry was read and written in the United States ever after Longfellow, it is almost impossible for us to imagine that career today. His more than thirty books, ranging from early translations to the great translation of Dante's *Commedia* (1871), from the mildly abolitionist *Poems of Slavery* (1842) to ambitious anthologies like *The Poets and Poetry of Europe* (1845), and from his hugely popular *The Golden Legend* (1851) to the Native exoticism of *Evangeline* (1847) and *The Song of Hiawatha* (1855), as well as the apparently homespun New England narrative poems "Paul Revere's Ride" (1859) and *The Courtship of Miles Standish* (1858), represent such a capacious range of subjects and styles that it is difficult to believe that they were all written by the same person. It is even more difficult to believe that that person was not only America's best-selling poet but also the poet Queen Victoria once observed was admired by her palace servants. Longfellow remains one of the very few American poets to be commemorated in Westminster Abbey. Perhaps it is not so surprising, then, that his contemporaries in the nineteenth century *did* wonder whether all of the work printed as authored by Henry Wadsworth Longfellow (often in gold on the spine of fancy editions and in thousands of less fancy reprints) could actually have been written by one person; they noticed that there was something disturbing about the range of Longfellow's sources and perhaps something suspicious about the work's popular humanist assurance.

Consider Margaret Fuller's famously cutting remarks in the *New-York Daily Tribune* in 1845:

> We must confess to a coolness toward Mr. Longfellow, in consequence of the exaggerated praises that have been bestowed upon him. When we see a person of moderate powers receive honors which should be reserved for the highest, we feel somewhat like assailing him and taking from him the crown which should be reserved for grander brows.... Mr. Longfellow has been accused of plagiarism. We have been surprised that any one should have been anxious to fasten special charges of this kind upon him, when we supposed it so obvious that the greater part of his mental stores were derived from the work of others. He has no style of his own growing out of his own experience

and observation of nature. Nature with him, whether human or external, is always seen through the windows of literature.[8]

Fuller's condescension not only preceded Whitman's by almost forty years but also tells us something more about nineteenth-century perceptions of Longfellow: by 1845 (before the wild success of either *Evangeline* in 1847 or the even wilder success of *The Song of Hiawatha* in 1855), Longfellow was regarded as a crown prince of American poetry. That eminence accounts for some of his contemporaries' competitive rhetoric, but what is remarkable is how early that rhetoric escalated beyond the value attached to Mr. Longfellow to become the value attached to poetry. For Fuller, Longfellow's dependence on the history of world literature meant that he didn't write "out of his own experience," and although of course Fuller herself always saw "through the windows of literature," there could be no more damning charge. But as Fuller indicates, the more damning charges had already been filed in print before Fuller alluded to them as "special charges." Beginning in 1839 and continuing through most of 1845, Edgar Allan Poe staged a heated defense against the influx of Longfellow's scholarly poetic currency, as he saw early and often that Longfellow's *Weltliteratur* project was not just "in the modes of what is called the old school," as Whitman put it, or an attempt to see "through the windows of literature," as Fuller put it, but was instead aimed at building a new school with a new set of windows offering a different view altogether.

If for us Poe's somewhat hysterical protests (which Poe himself dubbed "the Little Longfellow War") have a certain authority granted by Poe's unlikely survival in the canon (just as Whitman's judgment on Longfellow lingers in Whitman's unlikely elevation in the canon, and Fuller's dismissal carries the Transcendentalist seal of approval), readers of Poe's 1839 review of Longfellow's *Hyperion: A Romance* (another of the books to emerge from Longfellow's early European tours) probably wondered why the stakes of Poe's disagreement climbed so high – and certainly wondered why such a minor literary figure as Poe would shake his tiny fist at the great Henry Wadsworth Longfellow over the course of a dozen increasingly manic reviews throughout six years. In the *Hyperion* review, Poe's main objection was that Longfellow included so many translations and so much material from the history of European (and especially German) poetry. When Poe reviewed the first book that was not entirely a work of translation that Longfellow had published since taking up his post at Harvard four years earlier, he began with a bang: "Works like this of Professor Longfellow, are the triumphs of Tom O'Bedlam, and the grief of all true criticism."[9] That may seem condemnation enough, but it was only the beginning. It is worth considering the remainder of that first, relatively tame review in order to appreciate how much (as Poe immediately apprehended) rode on Poe's attempt to stop Longfellow (almost a decade *before* he became the best-selling poet in American history) in his well-heeled tracks. In what would prove to be a self-defeating effort, Poe warned of "works like this of Professor Longfellow" (and Poe almost always used the academic honorific, often capitalizing it), saying that

> they are potent in unsettling the popular faith in Art – a faith which, at no day more than the present, needed the support of men of letters. That such things succeed at all, is attributable to the sad fact that there exist men of genius who, now and then, unmindful of duty, indite them – that men of genius *ever* indite them is attributable to the fact that these are often the most indolent of human beings. A man of true talent who would demur at the great labor requisite for the stern demands of high art – at the unremitting toil and patient elaboration which, when soul-guided, result in the beauty of Unity, Totality, and Truth – men, we say, who would demur at such labor, make no secret of scattering at random a profusion of rich thought in the pages of such farragos as "Hyperion." Here, indeed, there is little trouble – but even that little it unprofitably lost. To the writers of these things we say – all Ethics lie, and all History lies, or the world shall forget ye and your *works*. We have no design of commenting, at any length, upon what Professor Longfellow has written. We are indignant that he too has been recreant to the good cause. We, therefore, dismiss his "Hyperion" in brief. We grant him high qualities, but deny him *the Future*.[10]

From our contemporary perspective on Longfellow, it is hard to imagine what Poe had in mind when he accused the American people's poet of "unsettling the popular faith in Art." What the accusation turns out to mean is that Longfellow did not undertake "the stern demands of high art" and thus did not produce poetry. It was a rather brilliant performative statement on Poe's part: Longfellow has not produced what everyone acknowledges as poetry, and therefore everyone will forget that he ever pretended to write poetry. What was at stake for Poe – like Fuller and Whitman after him – was nothing less than the definition of poetry; he denied Longfellow *"the Future"* on the basis that "Ethics" and "History" would prove his claim that whatever it was that Longfellow was so successful at writing, poetry wasn't the name for it. By the end of the Little Longfellow War, Poe would bring Longfellow up on the "special charges" of plagiarism, even plagiarism of Poe himself. According to those charges, Longfellow did not write poetry, because he stole everyone else's poetry. While Poe's accusations seemed to his contemporaries increasingly crazy, we may be tempted to think that history has indeed proven

Poe right: almost two centuries later, it is Poe's (and Fuller's and Whitman's) definition of poetry as "the beauty of Unity, Totality, and Truth" that most readers wish they could embrace. If we cannot do so, it is because we have lost the Romantic ideals of the nineteenth century – or because Poe and the Transcendentalists and Whitman transformed nineteenth-century American Romantic poetics into modern American poetics. Or so the story goes. But what definition of poetry did Longfellow represent? Did the most popular and (if his somewhat resentful contemporaries are to be believed) eminent poet of the nineteenth century not believe in the Romantic ideal and not lead the way into modernism? Most readers and critics today would agree that Longfellow was indeed left behind on both fronts, but as Poe presciently apprehended, the question of Longfellow's definition of poetry was not so easily settled as we have come to believe.

Perhaps Poe was right about Longfellow, not because Longfellow wrote inferior poetry (or because he stole everyone else's work, although he certainly borrowed liberally) but because Poe apprehended something crucial about Longfellow's literary success. Poe understood not only that Longfellow was a threat to other, less successful writers (like Poe) but that the popularity of Longfellow's work threatened to introduce a new poetic economy, a system of exchange in which what counted as poetry would be changed forever. Poe was right that Longfellow's work *did* help to usher in a new way of reading poetry, although the reasons for that newness were perhaps more tangible than Poe supposed. With the benefit of hindsight, we can see what Poe could not: what the tremendous transatlantic success of Longfellow's work signaled was not (as Whitman suggested) that nineteenth-century readers were overly fond of "verbal melody," or (as Fuller suggested) that nineteenth-century readers did not appreciate originality, or (as Poe suggested) that nineteenth-century readers mistook poems for poetry, imitations for the real thing, but that nineteenth-century readers were becoming more interested in the ways to read poems than they were in the poems themselves. As Leah Price has argued, in the nineteenth century, "how one reads became more important than what," as "the conservative hierarchy of genres gave way to a reactionary hierarchy of readers."[11] What Poe was right about was that Longfellow was abstracting or blurring verse genres in ways that made it difficult for readers to tell what kind of poems they were reading. Why would readers *like* not knowing whether the poem they were reading was an ode or an elegy or a hymn or an epic or an epistle – or even if it was made up of other poets' poems? Poe, at least, was afraid that readers' embrace of Longfellow meant that people wanted to read poetry without worrying what that poetry was made of. What

Poe was identifying in Longfellow's work (without knowing it) was a symptom of the lyricization of poetry in the nineteenth century (to which Poe's own poetics also contributed).

Lyricization was basically a process that began in the late eighteenth century as the conservative hierarchy of verse genres began to dissolve and those genres began to blend into one another (think *Lyrical Ballads*); just as Bakhtin attributed the rise of the novel in this period to what he called "the novelization of genre," we might think of the rise of modern poetics as the effect of the lyricization of genre. As I have argued elsewhere, the notion that poetry is or ever was one genre is the primary symptom of that lyricization: the songs, riddles, epigrams, sonnets, epitaphs, *blasons*, lieder, elegies, marches, dialogues, conceits, ballads, epistles, hymns, odes, eclogues, and monodramas considered lyric in the Western tradition before the early nineteenth century were not lyric in the same sense as the poetry we now think of as lyric. The fact that after the nineteenth century we came to think of almost all poetry as lyric is the secondary symptom of lyricization. As we have progressively idealized poetry-as-lyric and lyric-as-poetry (an idealization that especially characterizes avant-garde poetry communities that define themselves as post- or antilyrical), the fewer actual verse genres have addressed readers in specific ways. The nineteenth century was the period in which the shift from many verse cultures articulated through various social relations gave way to an idea of poetry devoted to the transcendence of those relations. For Poe, that transcendence took the form of "the beauty of Unity, Totality, and Truth" that he claimed Longfellow's verse lacked; for Longfellow, that transcendence took another form that Poe was right to perceive but that neither he nor later critics have found a way to describe. Although most of the poetry that Longfellow wrote was in genres we would not today call "lyric," his blurring of Old World cultures and verse genres into modern American forms resulted in a generic poetry that was the effect of the historical process of lyricization. The stipulative function of the hymn or the elegy or the ode or the epistle or even the satire tends to dissolve when we think of all of these genres as "poetry," which by definition cannot have a pragmatic cultural function but must represent the receding horizon of an ideal. In all of Longfellow's work, that ideal was bound to a progressive humanism. Readers came to enjoy the pursuit of that ideal, which allowed them to feel liberated from the conservative hierarchy of genres (and, not incidentally, from hierarchies of social relations) at the same time that it did not commit them to any particular way of reading (or any particular social relations). The brilliant and tremendously influential turn in Longfellow's work was to make such an ideal the theme of his poems at the same time that he made the genres of those poems the abstract remains of the cultures that made the verse genres his modern poems blurred possible in the first place. Virtually all of Longfellow's poems – and especially the poems that made his reputation as "the first of America's poets" – abstract a traditional verse genre or lament the vanishing of a traditional culture. His most popular long poems – especially *Evangeline* (1847) and *Hiawatha* (1855) – do both at once.

In 1840 (or about the time that Poe was becoming increasingly disturbed by Longfellow's publications), Longfellow finished "The Wreck of the Hesperus" and wrote to a friend in Rome that "the *National Ballad* is a virgin soil here in New England; and there are good materials. Beside[s] I have a great notion of working on *people's feelings*. I am going to have it printed on a sheet, and sold like *Varses*, with a coarse picture on it."[12] Although published in fancy magazines and a fancy edition of *Ballads and Other Poems* and never on a cheap broadside, the poem did indeed work on people's feelings, not only as an immediate popular favorite but as a standard text for memorization and required inclusion in anthologies of American poetry well into the twentieth century. As an editor at Harper and Brothers wrote during the compilation of *The Home Book of Verse* in 1959, a "few poems like The Wreck of the Hesperus ... familiar to librarians, teachers and parents from their own childhoods – seem to us really essential: as sugar to catch flies."[13] The poem that Longfellow joked might be marketed as a broadside ballad *did* come to be marketed more than a century later as a national ballad, as a poem all Americans had in common by the middle of the twentieth century. The irony of this history is that the ballad was not "virgin soil" in New England in 1840. Whittier had been printing literary versions of ballads for more than a decade in New England newspapers by the time Longfellow wrote his poem, and of course, broadside ballads had circulated widely in early America since the late seventeenth century, becoming the most popular print genre in the Republic of Letters by the late eighteenth century. Longfellow was not, then, just expressing his "gusto at the prospect of sending his poetry further down the social ladder," as one of his twentieth-century editors has commented but was expressing his desire to have his poem received as if it were one of the people's *"Varses"* rather than as a poem by Harvard's Professor Longfellow.[14] Longfellow's strategy was to make that *as if* make all the difference, because everyone knew it *was* a poem by Professor Longfellow that looked like a broadside ballad. Longfellow's readers knew how to read ballads but also felt as if they had special skills in recognizing that "The Wreck of the Hesperus" was not just any broadside ballad. As

Poe foresaw, Longfellow's strategy worked. His faux broadside ballad came to be treated as a popular ballad by popular demand, and his imitation of a genre that had long done many kinds of work across many early American verse cultures came to replace the genre it imitated in exactly the way that Poe feared it would.

If Longfellow's lyricization of the broadside ballad in "The Wreck of the Hesperus" was exemplary of his ability to adapt a traditional verse genre for his own purposes, it was just a detail in the much larger picture of Longfellow's *Weltliteratur* and lyricization projects. "A Psalm of Life," the poem Longfellow first published in 1838 that became what one scholar calls "the most popular poem ever written in English," bore the subtitle "What the Heart of the Young Man Said to the Psalmist."[15] If twentieth- and twenty-first-century American readers have tended to forget that broadside ballads were the common national American reading matter of the eighteenth and early nineteenth centuries, they have also forgotten that psalm translation, imitation, adaptation, and recitation was a national pastime during most of the seventeenth, eighteenth, and early nineteenth centuries. Longfellow's "young man" begins the now-famous lines (currently reprinted on boxes of Celestial Seasonings herbal tea),

> Tell me not, in mournful numbers,
> Life is just an empty dream!
> For the soul is dead that slumbers,
> And things are not what they seem.
>
> (*WL*, vol. I, p. 20)

What his heart is responding to is what everyone in the nineteenth century would have recognized as not just theological *doxa* but generic verse *doxa*: rather than, as in "The Wreck of the Hesperus," imitating a popular verse genre, in "A Psalm of Life" Longfellow framed a generic alternative to a popular verse genre. The "mournful numbers" of the 1640 Bay Psalm Book, for example, were strictly 8-6 quatrains; Longfellow's numbers are the only slightly different 8-7 quatrains, extending the hymnal pattern by just one beat in the alternating trimeter lines. The effect of that single beat is to modernize traditional American psalm meter, thus literalizing in the structure of the poem the injunction of the sixth and seventh stanzas:

> Trust no Future, howe'er pleasant!
> Let the dead Past bury its dead!
> Act, – act in the living Present!
> Heart within, and God o'erhead!

> Lives of great men all remind us
>> We can make our lives sublime,
> And, departing, leave behind us
>> Footprints on the sands of time.
>>>> (*WL*, vol. I, p. 21)

The call to secular action fictively addressed to "the Psalmist" was directly addressed to readers who had learned to read and write by imitating and translating psalms. "The Wreck of the Hesperus" imitated and ultimately took the place of the broadside ballad in popular American reading culture, but "A Psalm of Life" explicitly posed as the alternative that culture should pursue. By reading the modern verse genre of "A Psalm of Life" rather than reading the common verse genres of popular psalms, Longfellow's American public was invited to imagine itself on the brink of a new and giddy literary practice that would transform everyday life – or would make everyday life make history. At the same time, the modern literary genre of Longfellow's "Psalm" reassured its public that it would do what psalms do, providing advice for living that could be taken away from its context and made portable and adaptable. In fact, Longfellow's "Psalm" takes the portability of its content as its subject, encouraging its readers to "be up and doing / With a heart for any fate" – quite literally any fate, because *what* readers are encouraged to do is left open, a blank order the reader is invited to fill (*WL*, vol. I, p. 22). If psalms were used for many different purposes in early America, Longfellow's "Psalm" was made for all possible purposes, because it could be adapted to "any fate" at will. Longfellow's first hit single not only was framed as a secular alternative to devotional reading but was itself the best possible example of such reading, because the reader could choose what sort of devotion to pursue. No wonder it is the most popular poem not translated from the Bible ever circulated in English.

"A Psalm of Life" was included in Longfellow's first book of poetry in 1839, and its generic success perhaps accounts for the generic title of his second book of poetry in 1841, *Ballads and Other Poems*. That second volume took its title from "The Wreck of the Hesperus" and from the first poem in the collection, "The Skeleton in Armor," which Longfellow's readers would have recognized as a ballad that differed from the "coarse" broadside genre of "The Wreck of the Hesperus." In his diary for January 13, 1840, Longfellow wrote that "Prescott seems to doubt whether I can imitate the Old English ballad"; for the original publication of the poem in the *Knickerbocker* in January 1841, the text was accompanied by copious marginal notes testifying to its authenticity, although as Longfellow wrote to his father, "of course I make the tradition myself" (*WL*, vol. 12, pp. 356, 379). In addition to the faux broadside ballad and faux psalm, then, Longfellow also tried his hand in this period at the faux "Old English ballad," a genre that has not translated quite so well (in spite of its debts to Coleridge's "The Ancient Mariner") across the centuries (although it would be the template for Longfellow's successor at Harvard, Francis Child, when he collected the volume *English and Scottish Popular Ballads* and founded the first Department of English in the United States later in the nineteenth century).

But two poems in *Ballads and Other Poems* have indeed become modern generic examples of Longfellow's persistence in popular American culture: "The Village Blacksmith" and "Excelsior." In fact, I was walking down a street in downtown Manhattan recently and mentioned "The Village Blacksmith" to a friend and then a moment later heard a man pipe up behind me, "Under a spreading chestnut-tree / The village smithy stands." There is a plaque (now next door to an expensive chocolate shop, on the street where Longfellow's grand house still stands in Cambridge) commemorating the tree, which was cut down in 1876; the "children of Cambridge" gave Longfellow a chair made out of wood from the tree in 1879. "The Village Blacksmith" was literally taken from Longfellow's cultural landscape and remains part of our cultural landscape, but what accounts for its staying power is not its realism but its generic inclusiveness. In his diary for October 5, 1839, Longfellow noted, "Wrote another Psalm of Life. It is *The Village Blacksmith*" (*WL*, vol. 12, p. 345). Does the note mean that Longfellow was thinking of "The Village Blacksmith" as another meta-psalm, or that he was hoping that it would equal "A Psalm of Life" as a popular success? A year later, he described the poem as "a kind of ballad on a Blacksmith" (*WL*, vol. 12, p. 374). Samuel Longfellow, the poet's younger brother and editor (and not incidentally, a writer and collector of hymns), thought that the difference between these two generic descriptions meant that "the form of the poem had been changed during the year," but it seems more likely that in "The Village Blacksmith" Longfellow took what he learned in constructing his faux psalm and faux ballads and used that technique to make a lyricized hybrid of the two (*WL*, vol. 12, p. 345).

"The Village Blacksmith" is the story of a representative individual who has taken the advice of "A Psalm of Life" to "be up and doing," has learned "to labor and to wait," and thus whose life can be cast as a national ballad and also as devotional example – that is, as a ballad and a psalm at once. In "The Village Blacksmith," the alternating tetrameter/trimeter sestets mime ballad meter as well as the hymnal meter of popular psalms, and the discourse of the first lines is explicitly the discourse of the ballad, situating the tale the following lines will tell. But the focus of the poem on this particular smithy's life story, on his role as mother and father to his children after his wife's death, shades into the discourse of the nineteenth-century sentimental novel ("And with his hard, rough hand he wipes / A tear out of his eyes") and then at the end of the poem shades unmistakably into the discourse of the secular psalm, the genre that Longfellow had just coined, as the poem turns to directly address its own subject:

> Toiling, – rejoicing, – sorrowing,
> Onward through life he goes;
> Each morning sees some task begin,
> Each evening sees it close;
> Something attempted, something done,
> Has earned a night's repose.
>
> Thanks, thanks to thee, my worthy friend,
> For the lesson thou hast taught!
> Thus at the flaming forge of life
> Our fortunes must be wrought;
> Thus on its sounding anvil shaped
> Each burning deed and thought.   (WL, vol. I, p. 66)

"The Village Blacksmith" is indeed "a new Psalm of Life," because it takes the generic frame of the (only slightly) earlier poem and fills it with the portrait of an individual. The smith is the ideal reader of Longfellow's "Psalm": he takes its advice and lives his life accordingly, thus himself becoming the object of a poem's direct address. We in turn become the objects of *this* poem's direct address, learning to read the smith as he has learned to read the "Psalm," imitating his labor so that his forge becomes a metaphor for "each burning deed and thought" of each reader's own. In "The Village Blacksmith," Longfellow not only modernized popular verse genres but also began to forge (so to speak) his own blurred genres on the basis of the verse he had taught the public to read.

Because poems were the common reading matter of the nineteenth century (and because illiteracy was also common), the early poems depended on reading practices Longfellow did not need to teach (psalm and ballad reading, in particular) in order to make his readers feel that they could read many "traditions" at once – not as if they didn't need to study with the Smith Professor of Modern Languages and Belles Lettres at Harvard in order to read poetry but as if by reading Longfellow's poetry they already *had* attended Harvard. The short poems in Longfellow's first popular volumes were accessible to all because his readers already knew how to memorize the genres already incorporated into their daily lives, but they also knew that Longfellow had abstracted those genres into something with greater cultural capital attached to it. For the most part, Longfellow's first four books of poetry used the strategy of attaching surplus value to common literary property with great success, even when, in *Poems on Slavery* (1842), Longfellow wrote about a political issue he refused to speak about publicly. Of the eight poems in the slim volume, four are faux ballads, two are faux psalms, and one is a faux hymn (the other poem, to William Ellery Channing, is a poem of dedication that invokes scriptural authority to record "This dread Apocalypse!"). As he had used common genres to make his own success, Longfellow lyricized common genres to make (as he later wrote) "the low murmur of slaves, like the chorus in a Greek tragedy," audible and legible to people (*WL*, vol. I, p. 87). These people could feel as if slavery had become a literary issue they finally knew how to read – as if sympathizing with suffering slaves gave readers access to classical literacy, a perverse version of vernacular Greek.

But Longfellow did not become the most popular American poet in history by politicizing his audience. It was not the political aim of *Poems of Slavery* that persisted in Longfellow's success but its adaptation of popular models to classical themes that persisted in the later work. The classical literacy that Longfellow's poetry made available at a discount became the subject of his two best-selling narrative poems, *Evangeline* (1847) and *The Song of Hiawatha* (1855). In 1845, Longfellow had edited an enormous collection entitled *The Poets and Poetry of Europe*, made of English versions of poems from ten languages. In 1847, Longfellow effectively combined the lyricization of traditional verse genres that had worked so well in his early poems with the *Weltliteratur* project that eventuated in *The Poets and Poetry of Europe* and that guided his creation of the first curriculum in comparative literature in the United States, held at Harvard during the 1840s. At Harvard, Longfellow often found himself in conflict with his colleagues in the Classics Department, who did not see why modern languages should be taught at the university level (could young men not simply travel in Europe to acquire French and Italian, as Longfellow himself had done?). When Nathaniel Hawthorne's friend Horace Conolly came to Longfellow with the tale of a young woman caught in the French Canadian diaspora, Longfellow (with Hawthorne's permission) took the idea and ran with it, creating *Evangeline: A Tale of Acadie*, the first of his long, narrative, book-length poems.[16] Narrative verse histories were also very familiar genres to American readers (they were especially popular in the late eighteenth century), but again Longfellow blurred the familiar genre of epic verse narrative, quite literally novelizing it, or making it very like the emerging nineteenth-century sentimental women's novels that his friend Hawthorne complained were flooding the market because of "that damned mob of scribbling women." But Longfellow also lyricized the novel: *Evangeline* borrowed the name of the heroine of Elizabeth Oakes Smith's 1842 long verse narrative, *The Sinless Child*, a name readers had already learned to associate with the feminized sympathetic identification typical of Poetess verse (an association that would be further exploited by another scribbling woman, Harriet Beecher Stowe, just a few years later, when Little Eva made her way into the genre of the novel itself). The success of *Evangeline: A Tale of Acadie* drew on the already-established value of Longfellow's popular generic sources, and especially on the popular figure of the Poetess and the popularizing position of the lady novelist, but it also derived from a much less obviously popular and apparently unlikely source: its thousands of lines were all composed in dactylic hexameter, the meter of classical epic. In *Evangeline*, Longfellow did more than give his readers more sophisticated versions of verse genres they already knew how to read, giving them instead a new kind of poetry they came to value even more: a literally novelized verse genre that offered classical literacy at a discount and that told the story of an innocent and virtuous young woman violently expelled from an Old World whose traditions survived only in the poem those readers received from Longfellow.

Part of the success of the new verse genre of *Evangeline* surely derived from the poem's insistence that it was not a poem written by Longfellow at all and that the story it told in the thousands (and thousands) of copies sold could not be found in any book:

This is the forest primeval. The murmuring pines and the hemlocks,
Bearded with moss, and in garments green, indistinct in the twilight,
Stand like Druids of eld, with voices sad and prophetic,
Stand like harpers hoar, with beards that rest on their bosoms.
Loud from its rocky caverns, the deep-voiced neighboring ocean
Speaks, and in accents disconsolate answers the wail of the forest.

This is the forest primeval; but where are the hearts that beneath it
Leaped like the roe, when he hears in the woodland the voice of the huntsman?
Where is the thatch-roofed village, the home of Acadian farmers –
Men whose lives glided on like rivers that water the woodlands,
Darkened by shadows of earth, but reflecting an image of heaven?
Waste are those pleasant farms, and the farmers forever departed!
Scattered like dust and leaves, when the mighty blasts of October
Seize them, and whirl them aloft, and sprinkle them far o'er the ocean.
Naught but tradition remains of the beautiful village of Grand-Pré.

Ye who believe in affection that hopes, and endures, and is patient,
Ye who believe in the beauty and strength of woman's devotion,
List to the mournful tradition, still sung by the pines of the forest;
List to a Tale of Love in Acadie, home of the happy.

(WL, vol. 2, p. 20)

Readers did respond in unprecedented numbers to the poem directly addressed as a fiction not of reading but of hearing a "mournful tradition" sung by the trees in six perfect three-beat feet per line. By 1847, Longfellow had already convinced his readers that they could read modern poetry using old models; in *Evangeline*, Professor Longfellow began to teach readers that they no longer needed the old models in order to read the remains only available in the modern version. Reading Greek meter without learning to read Greek, Longfellow's expanding public also read that the violence of modern warfare and genocide could be understood as natural occurrences, that a community could be "scattered like dust and leaves" and survive only in the poem – and in the readers – that kept the tradition alive. As Evangeline journeyed from Acadia down the Mississippi to Louisiana and then to Philadelphia, she traced a path from Old World social hierarchies to New World brotherly love, and although her story is tragic, its retelling (and rereading) made it the stuff of a new way of understanding American poetry.

The idea that an American poet in the middle of the nineteenth century changed the way in which we would understand poetry ever after is, of course, an idea usually attributed to Whitman rather than to Longfellow. But in 1855, the same year in which Whitman published the first edition of *Leaves of Grass*, Longfellow published another novelized verse narrative, and this one would be more influential than either *Evangeline* or any edition of Whitman's *Leaves* by a long shot. *The Song of Hiawatha* took the reading practices built into *Evangeline* and expanded them. Rather than drawing on the topos of the sentimental novel, writing large a heroine associated with the figure of the Poetess, and then combining both in the history of a displaced, vanquished population told in the meter of classical epic, Longfellow took again (as in *Poems of Slavery*) what could have been a contemporary political theme, the story of a genocide closer to home than the Acadian deportation of the mid-eighteenth century. But if the historical materials of *Hiawatha* may seem more pressing to mid-nineteenth-century Americans than those of *Evangeline* (despite the mid-century European violent revolutions to which *Evangeline* is also a response), the generic sources for *Hiawatha* were hardly popular. When Longfellow read Henry Rowe Schoolcraft's *Historical and Statistical Information Concerning the History, Condition, and Prospects of the Indian Tribes of the United States* in 1854, he was reading not popular fiction or Poetess verse but thousands of pages of state-sponsored early ethnography, partially composed to justify the Indian removal policies of the previous decades and partially part of a federal effort to passively preserve the traces of the cultures the federal government was actively destroying. Longfellow took Schoolcraft's material and adapted it to the frame of the Finnish *Kalevala*, a cycle in trochaic tetrameter that met the chronicle by the Indian agent and self-styled ethnographer where *The Poets and Poetry of Europe* had ended: the borrowed meter allowed Longfellow to render his translation of European folk song into the figures of an American translation of a foreign language already present on native soil. What proved immensely popular about *Hiawatha*, then, was not its reliance on already popular reading practices but its self-presentation as an ancient American reading practice that could claim the authority of a classical Western philological lineage and still roll off the tongue.

Like *Evangeline*'s dactylic hexameters, the trochaic tetrameters of *Hiawatha* immediately attracted an enormous critical response and generated a long line of (often brilliant) parodies (of which Lewis Carroll's "Hiawatha's Photographing" may be the most famous, but by no means the most hilarious). But whereas the controversy over the meter of *Evangeline* took up an already-established debate over the very possibility of an English hexameter (a debate that emerged from the conflict over classical quantitative and British accentual meters earlier in the nineteenth century), the furor over the meter of *Hiawatha* returned to Poe's "special charges" of plagiarism against Longfellow, because this time Longfellow's meter *was* directly lifted from a particular (rather than generic) source (specifically, from Elias Lönnrot's collection of the songs of unlettered peasants in northern Finland). By 1923, even the parodies of *Hiawatha* had become immediately recognizable objects of parody, so much so that lines like the following could be directly addressed:

> Have you ever noticed verses
> Written in unrhymed trochaics
> Without thinking as you read them,
> This was swiped from "Hiawatha"?[17]

Yet as fascinating as the branching histories of parody, plagiarism, and metrical debate that took place over the body of Longfellow's most successful book are, it is important to notice that what made such immediate parody and readerly intimacy possible was the way in which the text of *Hiawatha* returns to the instructions for reading that Longfellow's international reading public had learned to follow, precisely because so many people had been reading so much Longfellow:

Ye who love a nation's legends,
Love the ballads of a people,
That like voices from afar off
Call to us to pause and listen,
Speak in tones so plain and childlike,
Scarcely can the ear distinguish
Whether they are sung or spoken;
Listen to this Indian Legend!
To this Song of Hiawatha! (WL, vol. 2, p. 115)

Everyone *did* "listen" to "this Song of Hiawatha" in the nineteenth and well into the twentieth centuries, but not because the most popular poem in American literary history was really "so plain and childlike" as it pretended to be or as innocent as later readers have continued to believe it was, and not because everyone knew how to read Schoolcraft or the *Kalevala*, but because by 1855 everyone knew how to read Longfellow. What Longfellow's poetry made possible was a shift in modern verse-reading practices that these lines disguise as media shift: his most successful poems "call us to pause and listen" to a complex literacy, to versions of the history of Western culture made into poems that anyone can understand.

This is to say that the portrait of the popular "poet of all sympathetic gentleness" that has overshadowed Longfellow's reputation from the laments of Poe and Fuller and Whitman to the condescending nostalgia of the new century has always been a disguise. It is a pretense Longfellow himself fashioned piece by piece, and it has worked so well that we have yet to look beyond the total effect. That is a shame, not only because the illusion by which we have been distracted has made it impossible for us to recognize Longfellow's real and enduring importance to literary history, but also because so much of Longfellow's career exceeded that caricature. "Paul Revere's Ride," originally published in *The Boston Evening Transcript* in 1860, became such a standard for memorization in the American school curriculum that most readers (or reciters) give little thought to the fact that the poem's Revolutionary War details are fictionalized in order to make Revere the hero a New England on the brink of civil war needed to imagine. *Tales of a Wayside Inn* (1863) responded to the national fracturing of the war by weaving stories from different classes and regions into an imaginary union. But the great project that Longfellow undertook in the war's aftermath falls so far outside the popular myth that it has been almost forgotten. Longfellow's translation of Dante's *Divine Comedy* (1867) was in part the product of his collaboration with other members of the famous Dante Club, which began in 1865 and lasted for several years. The intellectual project of this group (which included Charles Eliot Norton, James Russell Lowell, William Dean Howells, and from time to time Oliver Wendell Holmes, among occasional others) was a far cry from the "plain and childlike" verses that made Longfellow famous. The difficulty of aligning the Longfellow that has come down to us with the Longfellow who devoted his last years to the best translation of Dante into English anyone had yet produced should give us pause whenever we are tempted to think of Longfellow as the poet for earlier readers who lacked our educated literary critical perspective. If we no longer read Longfellow, it is not because we are more modern and sophisticated than were Longfellow's contemporaries, but because Longfellow's definition of poetry as the vehicle of old cultural models that make new worlds possible is still very much our own. It is a testament to Longfellow's genius that this is true and that we still do not seem to know it.

Notes

1. Walt Whitman, "Death of Longfellow," in Justin Kaplan (ed.), *Specimen Days. Walt Whitman: Poetry and Prose* (New York: Library of America, 1996), pp. 941–42.
2. Angus Fletcher, "Whitman and Longfellow: Two Types of the American Poet," *Raritan* 10:4 (1991), p. 139.
3. Dana Gioia, "Longfellow and the Aftermath of Modernism," in Jay Parini (ed.), *The Columbia History of American Poetry* (New York: Columbia University Press, 1993), p. 85.
4. Gioia, "Longfellow and the Aftermath of Modernism," p. 65.
5. Christoph Irmscher, *Longfellow Redux* (Urbana: University of Illinois Press, 2006), pp. 5–6.
6. Henry Wadsworth Longfellow, *The Works of Henry Wadsworth Longfellow*, 14 vols. (Boston and New York: Houghton, Mifflin, 1886), pp. 19–20. This volume will be cited subsequently in the text as *WL*.
7. William Charvat, *The Profession of Authorship in America, 1800–1870: The Papers of William Charvat*, ed. Matthew J. Bruccoli (Columbus: Ohio State University Press, 1968), p. 159.
8. Reprinted in Judith Mattson and Joel Myersin (eds.), *Margaret Fuller, Critic: Writings from the New York Tribune* (New York: Columbia University Press, 2000), p. 287.
9. Edgar Allan Poe, *Essays and Reviews*, ed. G. R. Thompson (New York: Library of America, 1984), p. 670.
10. Poe, *Essays and Reviews*, p. 670.
11. Leah Price, *The Anthology and the Rise of the Novel: From Richardson to George Eliot* (Cambridge: Cambridge University Press, 2000), p. 156.

12. Henry Wadsworth Longfellow, *The Letters of Henry Wadsworth Longfellow*, ed. Andrew Hilen, 6 vols. (Cambridge, Mass.: Belknap Press of Harvard University Press, 1966–1982), vol. 2, p. 203.

13. Joan Shelley Rubin, *Songs of Ourselves: The Uses of Poetry in America* (Cambridge, Mass.: Harvard University Press, 2007), p. 248.

14. Lawrence Buell, "Introduction," in *Henry Wadsworth Longfellow: Selected Poems* (New York: Penguin, 1988), p. xviii.

15. Robert A. Gale, *A Henry Wadsworth Longfellow Companion* (Westport, Conn.: Greenwood Press, 2003), p. 202.

16. Charles C. Calhoun, *Longfellow: A Rediscovered Life* (Boston: Beacon Press, 2004), p. 180.

17. "Longfellow Unsymbolized," *Literary Digest* 77 (May 12, 1923), p. 29.

Chapter 12

Whittier, Holmes, Lowell, and the New England Tradition

MICHAEL C. COHEN

On December 17, 1877, the Boston publisher H. O. Houghton hosted a dinner honoring the seventieth birthday of John Greenleaf Whittier and the twentieth anniversary of the *Atlantic Monthly*. With Whittier, Emerson, Longfellow, and Oliver Wendell Holmes, Sr., headlining, and more than sixty of the *Atlantic's* authors attending (although none of its female contributors were invited), "certainly there has been nothing like this dinner ... for [manifesting] the swiftly growing power of the literary body in America," as the *New York Evening Post* wrote the next day.[1] As toast followed toast that long night, however, this literary body's power was challenged unexpectedly when Mark Twain tweaked Emerson, Longfellow, and Holmes in a story about three hoboes who use the poets' names to besiege a hapless California miner.[2] Although the burlesque did not seem to offend anyone at the dinner, newspapers quickly criticized it as "flat, silly, coarse, rough, and unpardonable," for Clemens, as William Dean Howells later put it, had badly underestimated "the species of religious veneration in which these men were held by those nearest them."[3]

Twain's joke refracted the veneration of the Fireside Poets by toying with the publicness of their literary personas. Standing that evening "on the shore of the Atlantic and contemplating certain of its biggest literary billows," Twain thinks back to his first attempt to "try the virtue of my *nom de plume*" during "an inspection tramp through the southern mines of California."[4] The pseudonym gains Clemens entry into "a miner's lonely log cabin in the foothills of the Sierras," but the miner complains that Twain is "the fourth littery man that's been here in twenty-four hours – I'm a-going to move" (*CT*, p. 695). The miner then explains how "Mr. Emerson," "a seedy little bit of a chap, red-headed"; "Mr. Holmes," "as fat as a balloon" with "double chins all the way down to his stomach"; and "Mr. Longfellow," "built like a prizefighter," had invaded his home, eaten his food, gambled, fought, stolen his boots, and demanded he "sing 'When Johnny Comes Marching Home' till I dropped – at thirteen minutes past four this morning" (*CT*, pp. 695–96, 698). Throughout the story, the hoboes quote poems by Emerson, Longfellow, and Holmes – "queer talk," according to the miner – usually to insult him or impose further:

Mr. Emerson came and looked on a while, and then *he* takes me aside by the buttonhole and says:

> Give me agates for my meat;
> Give me cantharides to eat;
> From air and ocean bring me foods,
> From all zones and latitudes.

Says I, "Mr. Emerson, if you'll excuse me, this ain't no hotel." You see it sort of riled me – I warn't used to the ways of littery swells. (*CT*, p. 696)

The joke ends when Twain informs his host "*these* were not the gracious singers to whom we and the world pay loving reverence and homage; these were imposters," to which the miner responds, "Ah – imposters, were they? – are *you*?" (*CT*, p. 699). Although Twain directed the punch line against himself, the humor of the speech (and the source of its offense) came from the way it split well-known poems from the genial glow of their authors: "Fancy making Mr. Emerson, even in travesty, stand for such a vulgar little scamp, and Holmes and Longfellow in such a guise," one editorialist huffed.[5] However dignified Longfellow, Emerson, and Holmes might be, even their best-loved poems could become "queer talk" in the right (or wrong) circumstances. Twain's speech therefore makes visible a conflict between the social lives of poems and the construction of a literary hierarchy in the late nineteenth century. Creating a literary elite depended on circulating certain authors and texts through sanctioned institutions and media (like the *Atlantic*, for instance), but this same circulation could destabilize the very sense of authorial presence on which canonicity depended, making every nom de plume a potential "impostor."

Twain's speech was particularly inappropriate (or appropriately wicked) for the anniversary dinner, which was meant to showcase the cultural splendor of American poetry as embodied in the Fireside Poets, a group of authors that included the guests of honor, Whittier, Holmes, Longfellow, and Emerson, along with James Russell Lowell, who was serving as ambassador to Spain, and William Cullen Bryant, who did not attend. In 1877 these poets had a popular readership, a cultural power, and a presence in public life that later poets (or contemporaries like Walt Whitman) could only dream of. As a "Western" writer struggling for legitimacy "on the shores of the Atlantic," Twain may have wanted to poke fun at the hegemony of the "Atlantic" writers, for the Fireside Poets represented both the cultural authority of "poetry" in general and a specific authority grounded in the legacy of New England. In the 1870s a new industry of American literary history books granted an exceptional place for New England's writers in the development of American literature, and the Fireside Poets frequently were identified as the best representatives of both New England and American writing.[6] By 1877 the Fireside Poets were presented as morally serious, domestic, and patriotic, and portraits of them looked down serenely from the walls of many middle-class parlors as the entire family read from any number of "Collected," "Complete," or "Household" editions of their works.

But to see the Fireside Poets simply as a dull relic of the Genteel era belies the complexity and diversity of these authors' careers, which encompass the full spectrum of nineteenth-century culture. Readers only gradually appreciated these poets as a literary legacy, for they were often controversial figures, writing pointedly on difficult, timely topics. The New England tradition was contested throughout the United States, its meanings were never monolithic, and authors like Whittier, Holmes, and Lowell are far more interesting than literary history has remembered them to be. If Twain's joke expresses a submerged hostility toward the New England tradition felt by some writers then, it also speaks to the nineteenth century's uncanny familiarity with poetry, the weird intimacy between these authors and their readers, which over time has become hard to read in its full density and strangeness.

John Greenleaf Whittier came from the most humble circumstances of any of the Fireside Poets: he was born on a farm near Haverhill, Massachusetts, in 1807, to a Quaker family that had lived in the area since the seventeenth century. His career follows a complex trajectory: in the 1830s he gained notice as a reform writer and abolitionist, associated first with Garrison and later with political antislavery. Some of Whittier's best-known antislavery poems include "The Slave Ships," "The Branded Hand," and "The Farewell of a Virginia Slave Mother," but he wrote dozens of poems, in many genres, on all aspects of the antislavery struggle. During the Civil War he supported the Union (despite the Friends' traditional pacifism), and war poems like "Barbara Frietchie," "Song of the Negro Boatmen," and "Ein Feste Burg ist Unser Gott" became popular rally songs in the North. While Whittier continued to pursue his activism, however, he also began writing legendary songs and ballads, like "Maud Muller," "Telling the Bees," "The Bridal of Pennacook," and "Skipper Ireson's Ride," that were based on the local lore, folkways, and history of New England. After the Civil War, and especially after the 1866 publication of *Snow-Bound*, his most famous poem, this portion of his work became much more celebrated and widely read. By his death in 1892, Whittier was known as the chronicler of bygone New England life, while the antislavery poems that had once made him infamous were largely forgotten.[7]

Whittier's relation to the antislavery movement was almost entirely print mediated, and in the vexed political climate of the 1830s his publications made him notorious and at times the target of violence. Thus his poems are imbued with the idiom of the era's embattled public culture: they locate agency in the free circulation of discourse (specifically antislavery speech and writing) structured by the rapid temporality of immediate publication (and immediate emancipation), in which "freedom" comes from the ability to speak and move without restrictions. Many of Whittier's antislavery poems are concerned with the suppression of *Yankee* freedoms – freedoms of speech, association, and conscience – and the poems exhort Yankee men to assert their rights or risk becoming little better than slaves. Whittier wrote few poems from the perspective or about the experiences of black slaves themselves, although one of these, "The Farewell of a Virginia Slave Mother," was often recited on the abolitionist lecture circuit (Frederick Douglass quotes the entire song in his first narrative). Much more typical of his antislavery work is a poem like "Stanzas for the Times," in which Whittier identifies those who give up their rights with "marked and branded slaves."

> Is this the land our fathers loved,
> The freedom which they toiled to win?
> Is this the soil whereon they moved?
> Are these the graves they slumber in? ...
> And shall we crouch above these graves,
> With craven soul and fettered lip?
> Yoke in with marked and branded slaves,
> And tremble at the driver's whip?[8]

By living with "fettered lip" and trembling at "the driver's whip," the poem's addressees forfeit their Revolutionary heritage and endanger the sacred value of New England's land. The rhetorical questions destabilize the collective identity constituted by a shared relation to the symbolic landscape: if "we speak but as our masters please," then this will no longer be "the land" and "the graves" of "our fathers" (*JGW*, vol. 3, p. 35). Whittier then answers these rhetorical questions:

> No! ... guided by our country's laws,
> For truth, and right, and suffering man,
> Be ours to strive in Freedom's cause,
> As Christians may, as freemen can!

Still pouring on unwilling ears
That truth oppression only fears.

(*JGW*, vol. 3, pp. 36–37)

By speaking out, the poem's readers stand up to the threat of slavery and assert themselves as the true heirs to "the memories of our dead" (*JGW*, vol. 3, p. 36). The poem concludes by assuring the "brethren of the South" that "No seal is on the Yankee's mouth, / No fetter on the Yankee's press! / From our Green Mountains to the sea, / One voice shall thunder, We are free!" (*JGW*, vol. 3, p. 38). Only by speaking freely (saying, "We are free!") can Yankees claim their rights to New England's land and history. This poem realized its intentions – free speech and circulation – by appearing in newspapers, pamphlets, and orations across the North in 1835 (it was even reprinted in Baltimore's pro-slavery *Niles' Register*). "Stanzas for the Times" gained persuasive force from a context of newsworthiness, and because the local (primarily New England) sites of its publication aligned the poem's subject with its audience. The social power of this kind of antislavery poem indicates its wide difference from the later poems in Whittier's canon with which it would be unfavorably compared after the Civil War.

Whitman Bennett has described Whittier's antislavery newspaper poems as "a very special brand – for which poetry in the accepted sense may not be quite the just word … these versified outbursts of indignation, satire, reproach, scorn, and exhortation, all mingled with specific arguments and supplications for divine aid, reached the ears and hearts of millions … who would never have read prose pamphlets or have been influenced by them."[9] The special features of the newspaper antislavery poem elicit a type of reading unique to the newspaper context, because readers encountered the poem amid articles and advertisements pertaining to the events the poem described. For instance, *The Liberator* printed "Stanzas for the Times" next to an article by Whittier that recounted how he had been attacked by a mob in Concord, New Hampshire; its place on the news page (the front page, no less) provides the poem with extratextual evidence to support its sense of urgency. In Jacksonian culture, in which readers usually encountered poems outside of books, the political work of Whittier's antislavery poems can best be understood in relation to their mobility and the uses they made of formats like the newspaper and the broadside. After Whittier joined political abolition in the 1840s, however, he wrote fewer poems about free speech, and more poems addressed to national audiences on national issues. These poems, such as campaign songs for John Fremont, poems on the Kansas-Nebraska Border War ("The Kansas Emigrants"), and poems like "Ichabod!," written after Daniel Webster endorsed the Fugitive Slave Act, appeared mostly in magazines, annuals, and books (Whittier's first authorized poetry book appeared in 1843). These formats created new meanings for his antislavery poetry, which now spoke to a multisectional audience.

In so doing, Whittier's work took on a different kind of local coloring: although he remained intimately involved in abolition, he increasingly wrote about the legends of early New England, and this localism earned him much wider admiration than the sectional partisanship of his antislavery poetry ever could. Even while being canonized as a New England elder, Whittier became known as the Barefoot Boy (a phrase taken from one of his most popular poems), a poet of regionalist memory. These poems offer a complex mixture of sentiment, nostalgia, didacticism, humor, and realism, as in "Maud Muller" (1854), a poem about a fleeting encounter between a judge riding from town and a barefoot girl mowing in the fields. Although the poem seems set up like a fairy tale that will end in a cross-class marriage, the dreams of rustic simplicity and urbane ease that each figure evokes for the other go unrealized, as both marry unhappily within their class. The poem's wistful knowledge comes too late for either party:

> Alas for maiden, alas for Judge,
> For rich repiner and household drudge!
>
> God pity them both! and pity us all,
> Who vainly the dreams of youth recall.
>
> For of all sad words of tongue or pen,
> The saddest are these: "It might have been!"
>
> (*JGW*, vol. 1, p. 153)

"Maud Muller" goes beyond evocations of barefoot boys and girls and speaks to the poet's power to weave present and past together (its popularity seems indicated by the number of parodies it prompted). This power – more than regional nostalgia – was at the source of Whittier's appeal as a New England poet. Another example is "Mabel Martin, A Harvest Idyl" (1857): despite being published in the antislavery *National Era*, this ballad about the seventeenth-century witchcraft crisis exemplifies Whittier's facility with "simple legends told ... the beautiful and old": "I call the old time back: I bring my lay / In tender memory of the summer day / When, where our native river lapsed away / We dreamed it over" (*JGW*, vol. 1, p. 196). Like many of Whittier's regionalist poems, "Mabel Martin" explicitly evokes its power to bring back lost time and return author and reader to a richer, fuller existence. These poems emphasize their historical circulation in the oral lore of the region; Whittier often invokes the telling of the tale across generations as a way to ground a poem in the deep time of its setting. "The Swan Song of Parson Avery," a ballad about a shipwreck, ends on such a note: "And still the fishers outbound, or scudding from the squall, / With grave and reverent faces, the ancient tale recall, / When they see the white waves breaking on the Rock of Avery's Fall!" (*JGW*, vol. 1, p. 192); so does "Telling the Bees," "And the song she was singing ever since / In my ears sounds on – 'Stay at home, pretty bees, fly not hence! / Mistress Mary is dead and gone!'" (*JGW*, vol. 1, p. 188). Whittier's legendary poems range across folklore from around the world (not just New England), with a formal inventiveness and generic variation that belies their simple designation as ballads. Many of those published in the 1850s and 1860s relate instances of historical injustice, whether perpetrated against the Irish ("Kathleen"), Acadians ("Marguerite"), Native Americans ("The Truce of Piscataqua"), or Quakers ("Cassandra Southwick"), making them indirectly topical to the era.

The correlation of historical incidents with contemporary events, and the focus on legendary circulation outside of books, come together in Whittier's most famous work, *Snow-Bound, a Winter Idyl* (1866), which, more than anything else, changed his persona from a sectional partisan of antislavery to a national bard keeping alive regional traditions. Although *Snow-Bound* is obviously and avowedly autobiographical, readers so intensely naturalized the relationship between the poem and the people, lore, and histories of rural New England that they granted it unique authority as the social and cultural record of a bygone folk life.[10] Such a reading plays into the poem's instructions, which direct readers to take it as the last source for a certain kind of disappearing history. *Snow-Bound* narrates the events of a blizzard during Whittier's childhood. Shut in on their farm, his family gathers by the fire, telling stories and reading to one another while the storm rages outside. The poem is framed as a series of memories: Whittier remembering the events and people of the poem, most of whom have died; family members recalling and retelling events from their own lives and history as they sit by the fireside; and the future readers of *Snow-Bound*, who, when they read it "with me by the homestead hearth," will recall their own childhoods (*JGW*, vol. 2, p. 159).

In the "lonely farm-house" where Whittier grew up, "story-telling was a necessary resource in the long winter evenings" (*JGW*, vol. 2, p. 134). The retelling of tales, memories, songs, and lore, which the narrator calls "the common unrhymed poetry / Of simple life and country ways," makes up the vast majority of the poem (*JGW*, vol. 2, p. 144). However, the stories themselves are not retold; what gets narrated are the acts of their retelling: "Our father rode again his ride / On Memphremagog's wooded side; / Sat down again to moose and samp / In trapper's hut and Indian camp" (*JGW*, vol. 2, p. 142). The "common unrhymed poetry" includes stories of religious intolerance, Indian removals, antislavery resistance, the Revolutionary War, and ecological history, along with popular legends, local superstitions, and accounts of daily life and labor in a rural community. Thus although the particular record of "my boyhood in our lonely farm-house" is compiled from the oral lore and small library of the Whittier family, this collection details a much larger history of New England, reaching outward from the Haverhill farmhouse and backward to early colonial history. As members of the family circle are introduced, the narrator reminds his readers that these folk are now dead, so that their only access to expression can come through the narrator and his retelling of them and their stories: "Henceforward, listen as we will, / The voices of that hearth are still" (*JGW*, vol. 2, p. 141). *Snow-Bound* silences the orality of the hearth in a nostalgia that is definitively written and not heard: when "the voices of [the] hearth are still," only "their written words" remain, in the form of *Snow-Bound* itself, which concludes by invoking the "Angel of the backward look" to:

> [Clasp the] brazen covers of thy book;
> The weird palimpsest old and vast,
> Wherein thou hid'st the spectral past . . .
> Shut down and clasp the heavy lids;
> I hear again the voice that bids
> The dreamer leave his dream midway.
>
> (*JGW*, vol. 2, pp. 141, 158)

While the folkways of New England once existed in the "common unrhymed poetry" of the fireside, the "Angel of the backward look" now works through the heavy materiality of the "monographs of outlived years" read by the dreamer as he sits before the fireside of memory (*JGW*, vol. 2, p. 158). In contrast to the fleeting exchanges of "common unrhymed poetry" that once made up "simple life and country ways," *Snow-Bound* finalizes its own power to circulate popular history by closing the past in the sealed pages of a book. That book is the printed poem, and it is offered to future generations of readers, who, with *Snow-Bound* in hand, will "Sit with me by the homestead hearth, / And stretch the hands of memory forth / To warm them at the wood-fire's blaze" (*JGW*, vol. 2, p. 159). *Snow-Bound* thus creates and re-creates a material shift in the circulation of poetry, from the ephemeral exchanges of "the common unrhymed poetry / Of simple life and country ways" to the solid and perennial format of the printed book, ever available for rereading in the future. In this way *Snow-Bound* allegorizes Whittier's career: his anti-slavery poems, constituted by free circulation and temporal immediacy in a local partisan context, were replaced by poems like *Snow-Bound*, which recast him as the national arbiter of New England nostalgia.[11] Reading a poem like *Snow-Bound* therefore became a way to know the popular life of bygone, rural America. The Whittier celebrated at events like his birthday dinner in 1877 was this latter-day bard, the presiding spirit of an invented national past lovingly recalled in books read by the fire.

In contrast to Whittier's marginal origins, Oliver Wendell Holmes, Sr., was born (in 1809) to a family that had been part of New England's ruling class since the seventeenth century. Holmes struggled with this legacy (as depicted in his novel *Elsie Venner*), but he also made much of it – in fact, he coined the term "Boston Brahmin." Although he wrote many poems and belonged to several literary societies while a student at Harvard in the 1820s, Holmes trained as a doctor, a profession he pursued assiduously, garnering renown and respect for his work, and eventually becoming dean of Harvard's Medical School (he also invented the word "anesthesia"). Holmes's medical training taught him to be "exact, methodical, and rigorous," and never "to guess when I can know," qualities of precision, observation, and caution that imbue many of his poems.[12]

Holmes's literary career began in earnest in the 1850s. He wrote three novels and many essays, the most famous being the Breakfast Table series that appeared in the *Atlantic Monthly* (a magazine he christened) and was later collected in three books, beginning with *The Autocrat of the Breakfast Table* (1858). These essays are the near monologues of a Holmes-like narrator speaking to fellow members of a boardinghouse, and they employ a loosely organized, digressive structure. A theme that links them is their exploration of the virtues of conversation, and, indeed, Holmes was famous as a wit and conversationalist.[13] His poetry fits into this milieu of convivial association: his poems are playful, lighthearted, and brief, and rather than writing on imaginative themes or in response to historical events, Holmes wrote most of them on request for occasions (dinners, graduation ceremonies, annual club meetings), to be read aloud to familiar audiences. These poems were published piecemeal and were not written to be collected in books with cohesive themes. The occasional, ephemeral origins of his poetry thus make it hard to measure the impact of Holmes's work, and in many ways his poems are eccentric to the "American Renaissance" narratives of literary history that emerged in the twentieth century.[14]

One of Holmes's most famous poems was also one of his earliest: "Old Ironsides" was printed in the *Boston Daily Advertiser* in 1830, after Holmes read an article that erroneously reported the navy's plan to scrap the U.S.S. *Constitution*, the frigate famed for its service in the War of 1812. The poem slid into the intense partisanship of the Jacksonian era and was reprinted in opposition newspapers in New York, Philadelphia, and Washington, D.C., creating an outcry against the proposed dismantling of the ship, and eventually saving it (the *Constitution* has never been retired from service). Holmes described the poem as "an impromptu outburst of feeling," and it deploys a rolling ballad meter and bitingly ironic tone familiar to partisan poetry of the day: "Ay, tear her tattered ensign down!" the poem begins, in mock agreement, "The meteor of the ocean air / Shall sweep the clouds no more ... The harpies of the shore shall pluck / The eagle of the sea!"

> Oh, better that her shattered hulk
> Should sink beneath the wave;
> Her thunders shook the mighty deep,
> And there should be her grave;
> Nail to the mast her holy flag,
> Set every threadbare sail,
> And give her to the god of storms,
> The lightning and the gale![15]

Although it later became a recitation piece in schoolrooms across the country, the poem speaks, sharply, the opinion of New England. The region's economy depended heavily on global trade, and the glory of Old Ironsides had come in naval battles that protected this trade and the wealth it produced in Boston and other area ports; the decision to scrap the ship, meanwhile, came from an administration deeply unpopular there. The poem never names its object, and thus its publication context explains its meaning in ways that the form and content do not. In this way "Old Ironsides" ably represents not just Holmes's work but also most of the era's poetry, like Whittier's antislavery poems, which often were tied to current events and published in newspapers, in which the surrounding articles framed the poem in more than one sense.

However popular "Old Ironsides" may have been, it was "Poetry, a Metrical Essay," delivered as an address to Harvard's Phi Beta Kappa society in 1836, that prompted Holmes to publish his first book. "Poetry" is Holmes's longest poem and arguably his most ambitious, providing a sweeping overview of history by expressing "some aspects of the *ars poetica*" and analyzing "the constructive side of the poet's function" (*OWH*, vol. 12, p. 35). "Poetry" brings

together Holmes's various interests by laying out a theory of art that is also a
theory of intellection and a brief for careful analysis and observation.

> We, like the leaf, the summit, or the wave,
> Reflect the light our common nature gave,
> But every sunbeam, falling from her throne,
> Wears on our hearts some coloring of our own . . .
> Thus Heaven, repeating its material plan,
> Arched over all the rainbow mind of man;
> But he who, blind to universal laws,
> Sees but effects, unconscious of their cause, –
> Believes each image in itself is bright . . .
> And, lost in rapture, thinks for him alone
> Earth worked her wonders.   (*OWH*, vol. 12, p. 37)

The many who cannot distinguish effects from causes never get past surface
appearances to perceive universal laws; they are "Proud of a pebble, as the
brightest gem / Whose light might crown an emperor's diadem," and they
mistake poetry as a divine gift that "sets the laws at naught / Which chain the
pinions of our wildest thought" (*OWH*, vol. 12, pp. 38, 37). Poetry, according
to Holmes, consists of intuitional inspirations – "glorious visions," "bright
auroras," fancies, visions, and passions – but these belong to all people ("if
these on all some transient hours bestow / Of rapture tingling with its hectic
glow / Then all are poets"), while only the poet can embody these flashes of
insight in language (*OWH*, vol. 12, p. 39). But because language is an imperfect
medium, and no one can "embody in a breathing word / Tones that the spirit
trembled when it heard," those who best learn the machinery of poetry – and
Holmes was a lifelong devotee of Pope – will best express the "bright auroras
of our twilight mind" (*OWH*, vol. 12, p. 39). Poetry is thus deeply linked to the
material world in its content and its form, and Holmes presents inspiration as
a product of analysis: by grasping inherent causes and separating them from
perceptible effects, a would-be poet can give voice to more durable and universal expressions. To illustrate the relation between physical circumstance
and poetic form, the poem outlines poetry's major historical epochs and concludes by celebrating the unequalled vitality and permanence of true poetry:
"One thrill of earth dissolves a century's toil / Strewed like the leaves that
vanish in the soil / . . . But one sweet tone, scarce whispered to the air, / From
shore to shore the blasts of ages bear" (*OWH*, vol. 12, p. 59).

The world may view poetry as "a mystery and a charm," but this is a mistake; poetry endures not because it rebels against universal laws but because
it adapts so thoroughly to them, making form by learning "to measure, with

the eye of art, / The wandering fancy or the wayward heart" (*OWH*, vol. 12, pp. 37–38). Indeed, grounding the phenomena of poetics in the physical universe was a lifelong project for Holmes. In "The Physiology of Versification" (1883), he argues that "two great vital movements preeminently distinguished by their rhythmical character ... the respiration and the pulse" provide the basis for meter (*OWH*, vol. 8, p. 315). "That the form of verse is conditioned by economy of those muscular movements which insure the oxygenation of the blood is a fact which many have acted on the strength of without knowing why they did so" (*OWH*, vol. 8, p. 316). Holmes again cuts through mystifications: "The reason why eight syllable verse is so singularly easy to read aloud is that it follows more exactly than any other measure the natural rhythm of respiration," while the twelve-syllable line "is almost intolerable, from its essentially unphysiological construction" (*OWH*, vol. 8, pp. 316, 317). Because he wrote nearly all his poems for oral performance, such physical considerations became even more important to him.

This materialist approach to poetics clearly differs from better-known midcentury treatises on poetry. Holmes was in many ways a late Romantic, but he was never a Transcendentalist, and works like "Poetry" – which coincided almost exactly with *Nature*, and preceded by one year Emerson's far more famous Phi Beta Kappa address, "The American Scholar" – refute Transcendental idealism. Holmes was caustic toward anything he regarded as quackery, whether it was phrenology, homeopathy, mesmerism, the Graham diet, or the fuzzy thinking he saw in Emerson, Alcott, and Fuller. "An After-Dinner Poem," delivered at Harvard in 1843, mocks Emerson, with his "Essays so dark Champollion might despair / To guess what mummy of a thought was there," and his "'many-sided' man ... Blind as a mole and curious as a lynx, / Who rides a beetle, which he calls a 'Sphinx'" (Emerson was a soft target at Harvard; his notorious 1838 address to the Divinity School banished him from there until 1865) (*OWH*, vol. 12, pp. 136, 140). The problem was Transcendentalism's fondness for grand prognostications: "oh, what questions asked in clubfoot rhyme / Of Earth the tongueless and the deaf-mute Time!"

> Here babbling "Insight" shouts in Nature's ears
> His last conundrum on the orbs and spheres;
> There Self-inspection sucks its little thumb,
> With "Whence am I?" and "Wherefore did I come?"
> Deluded infants! will they ever know
> Some doubts must darken o'er the world below.
>
> (*OWH*, vol. 12, p. 141)

Holmes later wrote an appreciative memoir of Emerson, so this poem does not completely capture their relationship, but it does measure the gap between Holmes and the orphic style of some Transcendentalist writings. Holmes could be just as scathing about the stubborn certitude of orthodox religion, whose unrelenting commitment to its own logic he saw as equally impervious to the material limits of human knowledge and power. The "Wonderful 'One-Hoss Shay'" described in "The Deacon's Masterpiece" (1855) represents the deacon's small-minded refusal to acknowledge that every human creation must have "*somewhere* a weakest spot." Such weakness is "the reason, beyond a doubt, / That a chaise *breaks down*, but doesn't *wear out*" (*OWH*, vol. 12, p. 418). When something breaks, it can be fixed: this pragmatic approach lets people adapt things to their conditions. But a worn-out carriage, like a worn-out creed, is no longer any good for anyone. Thus when the venerable deacon determines, "in such a logical way," that he will build a carriage "that *couldn'* break daown*," he sets himself up for a comeuppance that is the logical consequence of the condition of things (*OWH*, vol. 12, pp. 417, 418). Built from "the strongest oak, / That couldn't be split nor bent nor broke," the carriage lasts a hundred years, until one Sunday, just as "the parson was working his Sunday's text," it collapses in a mound,

> As if it had been to the mill and ground!
> You see, of course, if you're not a dunce,
> How it went to pieces all at once –
> All at once, and nothing first –
> Just as bubbles do when they burst.
> End of the wonderful one-hoss shay.
> Logic is logic. That's all I say.   (*OWH*, vol. 12, p. 421)

Arrogant commitments to theories (whether grandiose or small minded) in the face of facts always earned Holmes's scorn. In a famous image from the Breakfast Table series (1858), he compares the will to a "drop of water, imprisoned in a crystal": "the fluent, self-determining power of human beings is a very strictly limited agency in the universe," delimited by "organization, education, [and] condition," among other things (*OWH*, vol. 1, pp. 86, 89). The image is one in a series of comparisons, in a paper devoted to the powers of comparison, for as the Autocrat says, "just according to the intensity and extension of our mental being we shall see the many in the one and the one in the many," but, as another simile illustrates, the human capacity for comparison will never be more than "a cupful from the infinite ocean of similitudes and analogies that rolls through the universe" (*OWH*, vol. 1, pp. 83–84). These images of restricted creative agency allow for a limited poetic power:

metaphor is born from "mental being" but also from the limits placed on that being, which, like the crystal that encloses the droplet, cannot always be seen from within. These themes reemerge in the poem that concludes this paper of the Breakfast Table, "The Chambered Nautilus." To defend his point about creative agency (and, ironically, to introduce his poem), the Autocrat demurs from quoting "Cowley, or Burns, or Wordsworth" and instead from the "infinite ocean of similitudes" he pulls out the nautilus, itself a figure for similitude, because it has "long been compared to a ship" – "Poets feign" when they call it "the ship of pearl ... [that] Sails the unshadowed main" (*OWH*, vol. 1, pp. 96–97). To demystify the metaphor, he explains how the shell of the cephalopod is a perfect spiral consisting of a "series of enlarging compartments successively dwelt in by the animal that inhabits the shell":

> Year after year beheld the silent toil
> That spread his lustrous coil;
> Still, as the spiral grew,
> He left the past year's dwelling for the new,
> Stole with soft step its shining archway through,
> Built up its idle door,
> Stretched in his last-found home, and knew the old no more.
>
> (*OWH*, vol. 1, pp. 97–98)

But the demystification leads to an even greater metaphorical elaboration, the "heavenly message" of the nautilus, which sings "through the deep caves of thought":

> Build thee more stately mansions, O my soul,
> As the swift seasons roll!
> Leave thy low-vaulted past!
> Let each new temple, nobler than the last,
> Shut thee from heaven with a dome more vast,
> Till thou at length art free,
> Leaving thine outgrown shell by life's unresting sea!
>
> (*OWH*, vol. 1, p. 98)

The Autocrat jolts his fellow boarders (and readers) by asking, to conclude the paper, "Can you find no lesson in this?" (*OWH*, vol. 1, p. 97). The lesson is appropriately subtle and complex. Despite the exclamations, the model of spiritual growth provided by the shell of the nautilus continues the ambivalent tone of the essay: "the lustrous coil" that grows each year into ever-nobler temples marks the limit of the nautilus (or the spirit), which shuts it *from* heaven, rather than opening to it. Accordingly, the human spirit may develop continuously as it leaves behind outworn beliefs, but it too will never grow out of its finite being. The shell illustrates spiritual development as a work of art and beauty, but only in death, after the animal body is gone. Thus the symbol of spiritual growth and development makes its metaphorical point when it has been left behind; we read the progress of vital force in its traces. Like all earthly forms, the chambered nautilus and "The Chambered Nautilus" create meaning through indirection and comparison. But acknowledging this limit is, for the Autocrat (and for Holmes), paradoxically liberating.

Like Holmes, James Russell Lowell was born (in 1819) to an elite family; also like Holmes, he attended Harvard and was associated with Cambridge all his life. From early in his career Lowell believed that the poet had an obligation to reform society through the moral authority of his role. He sought to realize this ideal throughout his work, which ranges from acerbic satire to commemorative verse to reflective writings on nature and art. In 1843 he and Robert Carter founded the *Pioneer*, a nationalist magazine intended to elevate American literature by publishing only "original" work (no reprints) and serious criticism (no puffery). Although it brought out now-famous tales by Poe, Hawthorne, and others, the magazine folded after three issues – like many of Lowell's ventures, literary success was not matched financially. In 1844 he married Maria White, a well-known poet and antislavery activist; she pushed him to assume a more critical stance toward current events, which culminated in *The Biglow Papers*, a stinging indictment of the Mexican-American War. This poem appeared in 1848, Lowell's annus mirabilis, when he also published *A Fable for Critics*, a comic survey of the era's literary scene, and *A Vision of Sir Launfal*, an instantly popular Arthurian poem whose most famous song, "What Is So Rare as a Day in June," remains idiomatic.

In 1855 Lowell was named the Smith Professor of Modern Languages at Harvard, a position he inherited from Longfellow and would hold for twenty years. His influence on literature and culture grew over the next decade, when he edited the *Atlantic Monthly* (1857–1860) and the *North American Review* (1864–1872). He used his positions to promote serious literature, criticism, and political discussion, and also to advocate for the Union, the platform of the Republican Party, and, after 1861, Lincoln's policies. Although generally a pacifist, Lowell supported the Civil War and wrote a second series of *The Biglow Papers* that attacked the Confederacy, copperheads, and British interference. His involvement in Republican Party politics after the war led to his appointment as ambassador to Spain (1877–1881) and Great Britain (1881–1885). Although his output tapered in the postbellum decades, Lowell continued writing satirical verse that excoriated the corruption and greed of the Gilded Age, right up until his death in 1891.[16]

Lowell announced his nuanced perspective on literature in the inaugural issue of the short-lived journal the *Pioneer*:

> We are the farthest from wishing to see what many so ardently pray for – namely, a *National* literature; for the same mighty lyre of the human heart answers the touch of the master in all ages and in every clime.... But we do long for a *natural* literature ... a manly, straightforward, *true* literature, a criticism which shall give more grace to beauty, and more depth to truth, by lovingly embracing them where they may lie hidden.[17]

The dialectical distinction between "national" and "natural" literature characterizes Lowell's stance on literary value: literature becomes "national" as it becomes "natural," by growing from a global tradition; at the same time, critics (and publishers) must lovingly embrace and support this national-natural flowering. This position on value also characterizes Lowell's literary-political affiliations: he rejected the Young America movement of the 1840s but presided over the American Copyright League's efforts to establish international copyright protections. "He loved letters for art's sake; he used letters for art's sake – but also for the sake of the country," wrote *The Century* after his death; according to Henry James, Lowell wielded the "the civic lash" more effectively than any other contemporary writer because "his satiric ardor was simply the other side of ... his patriotism."[18] "Tempora Mutandur," one of Lowell's last poems, illustrates these characterizations. "Democracy, they say, / Rounds the sharp knobs of character away":

> And there's a subtle influence that springs
> From words to modify our sense of things.
> A plain distinction grows obscure of late ...
>   ... a hundred years ago,
> If men were knaves, why, people called them so ...
> In those days for plain things plain words would serve ...
> But now that "Statesmanship" is just a way
> To dodge the primal curse and make it pay ...
> Steal but enough, the world is unsevere –
> Tweed is a statesman, Fisk a financier.[19]

Gilded Age corruption springs from the decline in civic values, which are signaled and abetted by declension in language. A hundred years ago, leaders served "public duty" virtuously, and a strict morality enforced the law, while now they serve their own "private good" and are rewarded for it; a hundred years ago "plain words" described plain things, and a knave was called a knave, while now the moral line swerves away from naming things what they are.

Because language is both cause and victim of this decline, the poem launches a linguistic attack to restore the linguistic virtue that must underlie civic virtue. Lowell's plain-spoken critique derives from his patriotism and his devotion to language: as Henry James concluded, "it is difficult to recall a writer of our day in whom the handling of words has been at once such an art and such a science."[20] Lowell sharply displayed this verbal acuity in different contexts across his career. *A Fable for Critics*, his comic cutup of American poetry, was prompted in part by his irritation at the insipid state of midcentury criticism ("There are something like ten thousand bards in the nation ... whom the Review and Magazine critics call *lofty* and *true*") (*JRL*, vol. 9, p. 6). The mock fable therefore combined lacerating portraits of contemporaries with Lowell's own flamboyantly bad rhymes:

> So whenever he wished to be quite irresistible,
> Like a man with eight trumps in his hand at a whist-table
> (I feared me at first that the rhyme was untwistable,
> Though I might have lugged in an allusion to Christabel).
>
> (*JRL*, vol. 9, p. 17)

Some of the vignettes remain well known: for instance, Poe appears "with his raven, like Barnaby Rudge, / Three fifths of him genius and two fifths sheer fudge"; of Emerson, Lowell writes, "[his] prose is grand verse, while his verse, the Lord knows, / Is some of it pr – No, 't is not even prose / ... In the worst of his poems are mines of rich matter, / But thrown in a heap with a crash and a clatter" (*JRL*, vol. 9, pp. 72, 38).

Lowell's attention to the linguistic basis of satirical critique and reform finds its most complex and wide-ranging expression in the first series of *The Biglow Papers* (1846–1848). Lowell wrote the series from his belief that "our war with Mexico ... [was] a war of false pretenses.... I hated to see a noble hope [manifest destiny] evaporated into a lying phrase to sweeten the foul breath of demagogues."[21] The poem disenchants and unmasks the doublespeak of political rhetoric through its own verbal inventiveness, primarily its use of dialect. *The Biglow Papers* pioneered the extended use of dialect writing; although the papers sometimes rely on cacography or "eye dialect" (misspellings that do not change pronunciation) to mock the imperialist pretensions of the war, Lowell also worked to capture the sounds, cadences, and distinctive perspectives of a vernacular Yankee mind-set, and the success of these poems set off an explosion of dialect humor in the 1850s. *The Biglow Papers* uses dialect to pursue several lines of attack: while cacography mocks and undermines the pretensions and stupidity of a grasping but bumbling class of underlings (represented by various apologists for the war), the "plain speech" of rural yeoman like Hosea Biglow or Birdofredum Sawin cuts through such false rhetoric and dissembling bombast. According to Homer Wilbur, the papers' putative editor, the truth-telling power of the Yankee dialect inheres in its history, for "Yankee" is simply a purer form of old English, such that "it might be questioned whether [New Englanders] could not establish a stronger title to the ownership of the English tongue than the mother-islanders themselves" (*JRL*, vol. 8, p. 37). This audacious claim on the "English tongue" expresses a commitment to a set of "Anglo-Saxon" values as the source of American greatness.[22] The war's proslavery, imperial land-grab dilutes the English sources of American civic virtue, and thus Yankee dialect seeks to invigorate this wellspring by cutting through cant to return to the testamentary origins of meaning:

> Ez fer war, I call it murder –
> There you hev it plain an' flat;
> I don't want to go no furder
> Than my Testyment fer that ...
> Ef you take a sword an' dror it,
> An' go stick a feller thru,
> Guv'ment aint to answer for it,
> God'll send the bill to you.   (*JRL*, vol. 8, p. 46)

Biglow's Yankee commitment to "plain an' flat" language is based on his commitment to "Testyment"; verbal chicanery (justifying "murder" by calling it "war") cannot ultimately disguise the wrongness of an act. But these plainspoken certainties are challenged elsewhere in the series. As Sawin graphically puts it:

> Afore I come away from hum I hed a strong persuasion
> Thet Mexicans worn't human beans – an ourang outang nation,
> A sort o' folks a chap could kill an' never dream on't arter ...
> But wen I jined I worn't so wise ez thet air queen o' Sheby,
> Fer, come to look at 'em, they aint much diff'rent from wut we be,
> An' here we air ascrougin' 'em out o' thir own dominions,
> Ashelterin' 'em, ez Caleb sez, under our eagle's pinions,
> Wich means to take a feller up jest by the slack o' 's trowsis,
> An' walk him Spanish clean right out o' all his homes an' houses;
> Wal, it doos seem a curus way, but then hooraw fer Jackson!
> It must be right, fer Caleb sez it's reg'lar Anglo-saxon.
>   (*JRL*, vol. 8, pp. 58–59)

Passages like these reveal the ideological instabilities in the iconology of mid-century nationalism: the "eagle's pinions," "hooraw fer Jackson," and "reg'lar Anglo-saxon," all rhetorical staples of manifest destiny, elide the brutality and violence of the war's prosecution, and the poems expose these lies by disenchanting the militarist rhetoric with plain speech. False speaking is rife throughout the papers: Increase D. Ophace (here cacography masks the verbal joke: a "doughface" was a Northerner with Southern sympathies), a warmongering congressman, tells his constituents that "I'm willin' a man should go tollable strong / Agin wrong in the abstract . . . / But he mus' n't be hard on partickler sins, / Coz then he'll be kickin' the people's own shins" (*JRL*, vol. 8, pp. 80–81). Elsewhere, "Cunnle" Caleb (Cushing, a Massachusetts politician and warmonger) justifies the war to Sawin by saying, "Thet our nation's bigger 'n theirn an' so its rights air bigger, / An' thet it's all to make 'em free thet we air pullin' trigger" (*JRL*, vol. 8, p. 59). Such sophistries, mouthed by military and civilian leaders, lead to Sawin's nagging doubts about the war, which presage larger-scale anxieties about the meanings of phrases like "Anglo-Saxon" or "manifest destiny." The papers' failure to resolve such anxieties produces a fractured and ambivalent sense of nationalism, which ultimately breaks out in corrupted language. As Wilbur says,

> It is an abuse of language to call a certain portion of land, much more, certain personages, elevated for the time being to high station, our country. . . . Our true country is bounded on the north and the south, on the east and the west, by Justice. . . . That is a hard choice when our earthly love of country calls upon us to tread one path and our duty points us to another. (*JRL*, vol. 8, pp. 68–69)

The misuses of "our country" are fundamentally abuses of language. Yet because the notional values that define "our country" are also embodied in language, they too are susceptible to the misappropriations of false speaking. *The Biglow Papers* seeks to correct these abuses by splitting nationalist rhetoric from military aggression, and by realigning national value with the natural values that inhere in the deep English origins of the Yankee tongue. Such efforts to reestablish national values and realign them with national language were tested even more severely by the Civil War. Three of Lowell's nephews were killed in the fighting, but nevertheless he vigorously supported the war in print and defended Lincoln's controversial prosecution of it. The inconclusive outcomes of Reconstruction, however, left Lowell so ambivalent about the war that he later equivocated even on the injustice of slavery. When he was asked to contribute a poem to a memorial celebration for Harvard's veterans and war dead, he struggled to put in words his divided attitude toward the conflict, eventually writing most of his "Commemoration Ode" (1865) in the forty-eight hours before the event. The poem fights to make poetry equal to the task of finding meaning in the war's catastrophic violence, and it begins by making war poetic, an equation that quickly leads Lowell to an expressive impasse:

> Weak-winged is song ...
> We seem to do them wrong,
> Bringing our robin's-leaf to deck their hearse
> Who in warm life-blood wrote their nobler verse,
> Our trivial song to honor those who come
> With ears attuned to strenuous trump and drum,
> And shaped in squadron-strophes their desire,
> Live battle-odes whose lines were steel and fire.
>
> (JRL, vol. 10, p. 17)

When warfare becomes "squadron-strophes" written in lines of "steel and fire" with the "life-blood" of the dead, poems will only be compensatory, "A gracious memory to buoy up and save / From Lethe's dreamless ooze, the common grave / Of the unventurous throng" who survive but who therefore, paradoxically, will be forgotten, because they leave behind no martial poetic record (JRL, vol. 10, p. 17). Lowell wonders if earth is "too poor to give us / Something to live for here that shall outlive us," and his doubts mount in the face of war's poetry:

> Some day the soft Ideal that we wooed
> Confronts us fiercely, foe-beset, pursued,
> And cries reproachful: "Was it, then, my praise,
> And not myself was loved? Prove now thy truth;
> I claim of thee the promise of thy youth;
> Give me thy life, or cower in empty phrase."
>
> (JRL, vol. 10, pp. 19, 21)

War offers the opportunity "to front a lie in arms" and thereby prove faithful to "some more inspiring goal / Outside of Self" that gives a deeper meaning to existence, but this choice is presented in absolute terms: "Give me thy life, or cower in empty phrase" (JRL, vol. 10, pp. 22, 24, 21). Because poems remain for those left behind, poetry comes dangerously close to becoming the "empty phrase," the kind of moral-linguistic vacuity that Lowell elsewhere attacks *with* his poems. Poetry breaks under the strain of events, as the war's cataclysmic violence and the magnitude of its losses exceed the poem's expressive capacity, until no amount of singing can fill either the gaps in the ranks of men gathered to commemorate the dead or the gaps that break the poem's rhyme, rhythm, and structure.

As with so much Civil War poetry, the iconography of nationalism saves this faltering song by redeeming the losses exacted in the name of the state.

This ideological sleight of hand makes the united American state the ultimate outcome and meaning of the war, as though the violent pacification of the Confederacy somehow proved the inherent unity of the land. "'T is no Man we celebrate ... But the pith and marrow of a Nation / Drawing force from all her men" (*JRL*, vol. 10, p. 29). Redemptive nationalism binds together a country made "ours once more," saving both the living and the dead by making war and poetry separately meaningful.

> What were our lives without thee?
> What all our lives to save thee?
> We reck not what we gave thee;
> We will not dare to doubt thee,
> But ask whatever else, and we will dare!
>
> (*JRL*, vol. 10, p. 31)

The "Commemoration Ode" begins by imagining war – or, rather, the sacrifice of life in war – as a kind of poetry written in "warm life-blood," against which "trivial song" can never measure up; it ends by aligning death and poetry as two sacrifices made on the altar of the nation, which alone makes the violence of war meaningful while also providing a space for the commemorative work of poetry. The diminished sense of moral power in this conclusion offers a very different understanding of poetry's social function, but it accords with Lowell's ambivalent vision of the postbellum scene: imagining "our country" as a "soft Ideal" rather than "a certain portion of land [or] certain personages, elevated for the time being to high station" corrects the demagogic "abuse of language" and elicits both the poetic sacrifice of "all our lives to save thee" and poems like the "Commemoration Ode." But no temporal government, and certainly not the Radical Republican Congresses, or the administrations of Andrew Johnson or Ulysses S. Grant, could live up to such a standard, and thus Lowell's ode also marks a certain endpoint for nineteenth-century poetry. The decline of Lowell's productivity after the Civil War has been often noted, but the "Commemoration Ode" really commemorates the passing of the kind of public verse he had championed, which once shaped the social order, but which will have a much less important place in the new, postbellum world.

Notes

1. "Whittier Dinner," *New York Evening Post*, December 18, 1877, p. 1.
2. Henry N. Smith, "That Hideous Mistake of Poor Clemens's," *Harvard Library Bulletin* 9 (1955), pp. 145–80.

3. Channing, "The Whittier Dinner," *The Independent*, December 27, 1877, p. 2; William Dean Howells, *My Mark Twain: Reminiscences and Criticisms* (New York: Harper, 1910), p. 59.

4. Mark Twain, *Collected Tales, Sketches, Speeches, & Essays, 1852–1890* (New York: Library of America, 1992), p. 695. Works in this collection will be cited as *CT*.

5. N.P., "Boston," *Chicago Tribune*, December 23, 1877, p. 16.

6. Nina Baym, "Early Histories of American Literature: A Chapter in the Institution of New England," *American Literary History* 1 (1989), pp. 459–88; Joseph A. Conforti, *Imagining New England: Explorations of Regional Identity from the Pilgrims to the Mid-Twentieth Century* (Chapel Hill: University of North Carolina Press, 2001); Claudia Stokes, *Writers in Retrospect: The Rise of American Literary History, 1875–1910* (Chapel Hill: University of North Carolina Press, 2006).

7. Samuel T. Pickard, *Life and Letters of John Greenleaf Whittier*, 2 vols. (Boston: Houghton, 1894); Albert Mordell, *Quaker Militant: John Greenleaf Whittier* (Boston: Houghton, 1933); Whitman Bennett, *Whittier: Bard of Freedom* (Chapel Hill: University of North Carolina Press, 1941); Edward Wagenknecht, *John Greenleaf Whittier: A Portrait in Paradox* (New York: Oxford University Press, 1967); Michael Cohen, "Whittier, Ballad Reading, and the Culture of Nineteenth-Century Poetry," *Arizona Quarterly* 64:3 (2008), pp. 1–29.

8. John G. Whittier, *The Works of John Greenleaf Whittier*, 7 vols. (Boston: Houghton, 1892), vol. 3, p. 35. Works in this collection will be cited as *JGW*.

9. Bennett, *Bard of Freedom*, p. 85.

10. Angela Sorby, *Schoolroom Poets: Childhood, Performance, and the Place of American Poetry, 1865–1917* (Durham: University of New Hampshire Press, 2005).

11. Cohen, "Ballad Reading."

12. Quoted in Eleanor M. Tilton, *Amiable Autocrat: A Biography of Dr. Oliver Wendell Holmes* (New York: Schuman, 1947), pp. 120, 100; William C. Dowling, *Oliver Wendell Holmes in Paris: Medicine, Theology, and the Autocrat of the Breakfast Table* (Hanover, N.H.: University Press of New England, 2006).

13. Peter Gibian, *Oliver Wendell Holmes and the Culture of Conversation* (Cambridge: Cambridge University Press, 2001).

14. John T. Morse, *Life and Letters of Oliver Wendell Holmes*, 2 vols. (Boston: Houghton, 1899); Tilton, *Amiable Autocrat*; Edwin P. Hoyt, *The Improper Bostonian: Dr. Oliver Wendell Holmes* (New York: Morrow, 1979).

15. Oliver Wendell Holmes, *The Works of Oliver Wendell Holmes*, 13 vols. (Boston: Houghton, 1892), vol. 12, p. 2. Further references to poems and essays from this collection will be cited as *OWH*.

16. Edward Everett Hale, *James Russell Lowell and His Friends* (Boston: Houghton, 1899); Horace E. Scudder, *James Russell Lowell: A Biography*, 2 vols. (Boston: Houghton, 1901).

17. Robert Carter and James R. Lowell, "Introduction," *The Pioneer*, January 1843, pp. 1–2.

18. "Topics of the Time: James Russell Lowell, Poet and Citizen," *The Century*, October 1891, p. 954; Henry James, "James Russell Lowell," *Atlantic Monthly*, January 1892, p. 42.

19. James R. Lowell, *The Writings of James Russell Lowell in Prose and Poetry*, 11 vols. (Boston: Houghton, 1896), vol. 10, pp. 239–41. Works in this collection will be cited as *JRL*.

20. James, "James Russell Lowell," p. 43.

21. James R. Lowell, *Letters of James Russell Lowell*, ed. Charles Eliot Norton, 2 vols. (London: Osgood, 1894), vol. 1, pp. 333–34.

22. J. Javier Rodríguez, "The U.S.-Mexican War in James Russell Lowell's *The Biglow Papers*," *Arizona Quarterly* 63:3 (2007), pp. 1–33.

Chapter 13

Other Voices, Other Verses: Cultures
of American Poetry at Midcentury

MARY LOEFFELHOLZ

Massachusetts in the mid-nineteenth century, like the rest of the country only more so, was lousy with poets. At the apex of respectable high cultural ambitions, the *Atlantic Monthly*, founded in 1857 under the editorship of James Russell Lowell and with the nods of Ralph Waldo Emerson, Henry Wadsworth Longfellow, and Oliver Wendell Holmes among other worthies, was publishing poetry vigorously. In the 1860s alone, Lowell's Civil War revival of his seriocomic *The Biglow Papers* series, dusted off for the purpose from its original incarnation in the Mexican-American War of 1848, appeared in the *Atlantic* from 1862 through 1866, while Longfellow and John Greenleaf Whittier were also publishing in the *Atlantic* the narrative poems that would be incorporated into Longfellow's *Tales of a Wayside Inn* (1863) and Whittier's *The Tent on the Beach* (1867), sequences in their own way also marked by wartime concerns. Julia Ward Howe's "Battle Hymn of the Republic" appeared in the *Atlantic* in February 1862 and was answered by Ralph Waldo Emerson's "Boston Hymn," marking the Emancipation Proclamation, in February 1863. Writing on subjects further aside from the great matter of the war, Harriet Prescott added to the reputation she had established as the author of daring tales with the 1861 poem "Pomegranate Flowers," a dramatic monologue in the voice of a deserted seamstress; Lucy Larcom too, assisted by Whittier, found her way into the *Atlantic* in the 1860s with poems like "Skipper Ben" and the war-themed "A Loyal Woman's 'No.'" A few notches below the *Atlantic*'s cultural apex and out in the more religiously conservative townships of central Massachusetts, Josiah Gilbert Holland paused his editorial work on the *Springfield Republican* long enough to write *Kathrina* (1868), a book-length evangelical narrative poem whose nineteenth-century sales would ultimately be second only to those of Longfellow's *Hiawatha*.

Amid this blooming, buzzing profusion of print poetry were two other poets writing in central Massachusetts in the 1860s. Unaware of each other, so far as we know, both were observant amateur naturalists by disposition and, to some degree, by formal education, although both failed to complete their college educations. Both had their reading and writing interrupted from time to time by eye trouble. Both poets tracked the characteristic flora and fauna of rural New England through the seasons and memorialized that devotion not only in their poetry but also in herbariums that now reside at Harvard University's Houghton Library. Both were also of highly self-conscious literary turns, again through formal education as well as through the social networks of their professional, prosperous families, and both followed the *Atlantic* and other organs of ambitious nineteenth-century American literary culture avidly, but from a distance. Unlike Whittier and Spofford, Larcom and Holland, both were spared by family circumstances the necessity of earning a living by their pens. By the mid-1860s, both poets had accumulated a significant body of written work without a corresponding contemporary reputation, despite efforts to bring their work to the attention of influential members of Boston's literary elite.

At some point in the 1860s, each poet separately (again, so far as we know) composed a self-consciously major poem on the summer chorus of the crickets. Both poems were treated with some degree of inscriptional ceremony by their authors, who left them behind in multiple manuscript copies recording significant revisions. Unpublished during their authors' lifetimes, both poems would become the object of contested textual reconstructions in the twentieth century. Both poems also feature conspicuously high diction and formal address, and both seem mindful of poetic antecedents – locally, in Keats's sonnet "On the Grasshopper and the Cricket," and more widely, in the tradition of the Romantic ode. As Virginia Jackson observes, "Keats was already one figure for an idealized notion of poetry by the middle of the nineteenth century, especially on the American side of the Atlantic,"[1] and both poets seem to use the figure of Keats as a medium for invoking and testing such idealizations. At stake in both poems is whether an American poem can or should be *high*; might an American poem start low, translating cricket song, and mount high, as high as Keats's nightingale?

The better-known of these two poems was written down by Emily Dickinson in six copies of which some record survives, one of them now lost.[2] The longest and apparently the earliest version, sent to her friend Gertrude Vanderbilt around 1865, started with one of Dickinson's typically deferred comparative definitions: "Further in Summer than the Birds –" and developed through seven quatrains before naming the tuneful citizen of the opening quatrain's "Minor Nation" as the cricket. Dickinson rounded off this version of the poem with the high Keatsian double affirmations of stanza six, "The Earth has many keys –" (echoing, Joanne Feit Diehl suggests, Keats's "The poetry of earth is never dead")[3] and "Beauty – is Nature's Fact" (echoing Keats's "Beauty is Truth," in the "Ode on a Grecian Urn"). Her closing stanza contracts these grander harmonies to insect song: "The Cricket is Her utmost / Of Elegy, to me";[4] unlike the poet of Keats's "Ode to a Nightingale," Dickinson returns to her local earth connected to, rather than fallen away from, the natural voice of her poem's inspiration.

In later versions of the poem (including the one sent to Thomas Wentworth Higginson in January 1866), Dickinson muffled its Keatsian echoes while still, it seems, exploring the question of how self-consciously high poetry might emerge from a "minor nation." She deleted the original sixth and seventh stanzas and revised its fifth to eliminate the grammatical figure of the poem's speaker (its references to "I" and "me"), the odic affirmation that "Beauty – is Nature's Fact," and the poem's only direct reference to the cricket. The poet's marking of her individual limits as an auditor of the crickets' song ("Nor know I when it cease –") disappears in later versions, replaced by the abstract, elevated address of ritual, while the unnamed cricket migrates from the realm of nature to the realm of the sign, where it "typif[ies]" the "Druidic – Difference" of seasonal change with its "spectral Canticle." The cricket made a surprising return, however, in the last known version of the poem, sent to Mabel Loomis Todd (her brother's mistress, and later an editor of her poems) in 1883. Dickinson this time enclosed with the poem an actual cricket, as if to restore not only the cricket dropped in her revision of the poem but all the nightingales and skylarks that ever flew away in the tradition of the Romantic ode.[5] As Virginia Jackson observes of another Dickinson poem, "for Keats's lost object she substituted a found object" – a concrete reply "too intimate for print"[6] but marvelously preserved in the Amherst College archives. "Is it dead?" we can imagine the cricket's recipient asking, whether or not she recognized Dickinson's poem as a desiccated reply to Keats's affirmation of the poetry of earth.

The lesser known of these two poems, Frederick Goddard Tuckerman's "The Cricket," survives in five undated manuscript copies. By contrast with Dickinson's "Further in Summer," Tuckerman's poem, in all its versions, vests its whole faith in the form and substance of the Romantic ode as a legitimate mode of American high poetic aspiration. Composed in five irregular stanzas reminiscent of Wordsworth's metrical variations in his "Intimations" ode, "The Cricket" follows closely the central movement of Keats's "Ode to a Nightingale" while also drawing on the setting and language of Keats's "Ode: To Autumn."[7] Setting out in a natural landscape saturated with music, the poet picks out the "bright" note of the cricket "mid the insect crowd" for what he initially envisions as a compact of mutual aid: the cricket "ere day be done" shall have "his bard" while the poet "take[s] to help me in my song / A little cooing cricket."[8] Embowered within the afternoon's "sleepy" warmth, where the "dull hop" and "poppy's dark refreshing flower" combine to "Let the dead fragrance round our temples beat / Stunning the sense to slumber," he finds the power of the cricket's song increasingly overwhelming, "louder as the day declines," louder than the birds: "At hand, around, illimitably / Rising and falling like the sea, / Acres of cricks!" (SP, p. 153). Lifted up, like Keats listening to the nightingale, to follow the singing voice into a realm of inward vision, the poet finds himself not in Keats's "embalmèd darkness" listening to "The murmurous haunt of flies on summer eves" but on a harsher American shore, where the cricket's song

> bringest to me
> Always that burthen of the unresting sea,
> The moaning cliffs, the low rocks blackly start.
> These upland inland fields no more I view
> But the long flat seaside beach, the wild seamew
> And the overturning wave!   (SP, p. 154)

This unexpected "burthen" recalls him to the same realization Keats arrived at in following the nightingale: for its individual human auditor, the cricket's poetry of earth is always also the poetry of the grave.

Where Dickinson addressed this realization by canceling the elegiac "I" and "me" from later versions of her cricket poem, Tuckerman instead closes with an extended first-person meditation on alternative poetries that might emerge in response to the cricket's song. Could he, "Like the Enchanter old / ... find thy knowledge in thy song," leaping over the human limits of knowledge marked by Dickinson in the first version of her poem, he might become the cricket's "true interpreter," able to hear "articulate voices ... / In cry of beast, or bird, or insect's hum" (SP, p. 155). To do so, he acknowledges, would be to relinquish his own "quest," giving over the poet's Shelleyan responsibilities as the world's unacknowledged legislator in order to translate the cricket as "lord and lawgiver." His gain would be a naturalized poetic voice so pervasive as to be unheard, registered as "Naught in innumerable numerousness," like "The ceaseless simmer in the summer grass / To him who toileth in the windward field." Falling short of this, his consolation will be, like Wordsworth's at the end of the "Intimations" ode, to live in a natural landscape still "dear" for its associations if not transparent to the poet, who must "ignorantly" hear its voices while bearing the human knowledge that as "the Autumn goes / The shadow grows, / The moments take hold of eternity" (SP, p. 156).

What might we learn from the remarkable consonance between Dickinson's and Tuckerman's cricket poems about the "other" voices and verses of mid-nineteenth-century American poetry? Are both of these poems "other"? Neither? "Other" to what, exactly?

In view of their posthumous publication, both of these poems may qualify as "other" to the mid-nineteenth-century public print sphere as their authors knew it, although Tuckerman had earlier made his run at publicity by printing his poems at his own expense in 1860 and reprinting this volume with the well-regarded Boston firm of Ticknor and Fields in 1864. If by "other," however, we mean not conspicuous in the critical and pedagogical canon of our own day, then Tuckerman's cricket, along with the rest of his verse, earns the soft impeachment over Dickinson's. Touted by the poet-critic Yvor Winters as "probably the greatest single American poem" of the nineteenth century on its first printing in 1950 (in an essay predicting that Whitman and Poe would "shortly disappear into the twilight of queer historical phenomena")[9] and singled out for praise by other readers on the publication of the first comprehensive edition of Tuckerman's poetry in 1965, "The Cricket" has remained on the subterranean side of the emergence that Edmund Wilson in *Patriotic Gore* (1962) hopefully but, as it turned out, inaccurately forecast for Tuckerman.[10] Dickinson's "Further in Summer," by comparison, may seem to have enjoyed a speedy if not uncomplicated ascent into canonicity. Printed with relatively few editorial alterations from one of the later manuscript versions in the first posthumous volume of Dickinson's *Poems* (1891) and reconnected with its earlier version, including the final two cricket stanzas, in printings from 1945 to 1960, "Further in Summer" has been a steady citizen of pedagogical compilations like the *Norton Anthology of American Literature* and of significant critical studies of Dickinson from the 1960s forward.

If by "other," on the other hand, we mean to designate in brief something about the author's social identity – if "other" verses are critical shorthand for those authored in the United States by women, people of color, working-class writers, and peoples new to English literacy – then Dickinson's cricket is, on the grounds of the gender of its author, "other," while Tuckerman's cricket is not apparently "other" on any such grounds. That this designation upends Dickinson's and Tuckerman's relative standing in today's pedagogical and scholarly canon, however, underscores the continuing pertinence of John Guillory's reminder that canon formation "is too complex to be reduced to determination by the single factor of the social identity of the author."[11] An awkward umbrella term for a variety of social identities, the binary category of the "other" risks minimizing how much Tuckerman and Dickinson had in common by way of social circumstances. In addition to their shared race, class, region, and ethnicity, they possessed similar kinds of cultural capital and even similar modes of access to this capital: modes mediated by formal education and robust social networks, while standing apart from a professional relationship to the marketplace of letters. These similarities undergird the difference-in-likeness of their crickets and of other aspects of their bodies of work, such as their exploration of poetic sequences (Dickinson's fascicles and Tuckerman's sonnet sequences), a form difficult to break into print with unless, like Tuckerman, a poet can bear the expense of self-publication or, like Dickinson, can wait on the judgment of posterity.

In yet another possible perspective, Tuckerman's cricket represents an "other" voice in the history of American poetry exactly because its form and diction are so close to the British tradition of the Romantic ode. As Timothy Morris explains, for the last hundred years and more the most reliable route to an author's "becoming canonical" in American poetry has run through elevating an author's formal breaks with received Anglo-European poetic traditions as evidence of his or her ambitions for an original, autochthonous American literature. Dickinson's strangeness – especially the "personal grammatical short-hand" that Yvor Winters bridled at in his otherwise laudatory reading of "Further in Summer"[12] – has been absorbed into this narrative of canonization, whose cynosure remains Walt Whitman. No one reading "The Cricket," though, is ever likely to exclaim, "Here is where *we* [Americans] finally broke from England/Europe/the dead weight of the past."[13] Really "American" poetry is by this definition other to British poetry; but are we then to say, because most of the poetry actually written and published in the nineteenth-century United States would not pass any litmus test of formal estrangement from British verse of the same period, that most American poetry is un-American?

Like the shorthand use of "other" to denote social identities, this construal of what counts as the "other" voices of American poetry may blunt our capacity to discern similarities in differences among American poets, as well as our capacity to be surprised and delighted by originality that does not conform to the Whitmanian formalist-nationalist model. As evidence, consider still a third cricket from Massachusetts literary culture of the mid-1860s, one in its own way perhaps more strange and experimental than either Dickinson's or Tuckerman's. And yet this cricket, unlike theirs, saw publication in its author's lifetime, in the lofty *Atlantic Monthly* of April 1866, under the title "Were They Crickets?" Both Dickinson and Tuckerman would likely have encountered it there, Dickinson only weeks after working through the major revisions to "Further in Summer." Its unsigned author, Thomas Hill, may have been known to Tuckerman personally: he attended Harvard's divinity school during Tuckerman's time in law school and shared Tuckerman's scientific enthusiasms as well as his poetic aspirations. (Hill had self-published a book of abolitionist poems in college, contributed fugitive verses to periodicals including the *Atlantic* in the 1850s and 1860s, and would publish a book of poems at his parishioners' urging in the 1880s.)[14] At the time of his cricket's publication, Hill was Harvard's president – an extraordinary rise for a man largely self-educated, who had apprenticed to a New Jersey newspaper and then to an apothecary before entering college. Two years later he would resign, having acquired a reputation for eccentricity to which "Were They Crickets?" doubtless made a minor contribution.

"Were They Crickets?" is a prose fantasia fashioned, weirdly enough, on the generic template of the Romantic ode. Along with Dickinson's and Tuckerman's poems, Hill's fantasia asks whether American song, starting low, can mount high on the wings of cricket song. Hill's answer is yes – very high. Raptured out of his study by the spirit of Copernicus, the narrator of "Were They Crickets?" comes to himself on a grassy hill on the planet Mars, whose inhabitants, "Rational Articulates" as he eventually settles on calling them, resemble giant black crickets and whose language is an "exquisite harmony" of "polyphonous sound," a merger of sound and signification so perfect that their poetry becomes music "in the very process of utterance."[15] The narrator translates the crickets' song first in the imperfect mode of musical notation and then by devising a set of panpipes adequate to expression as well as transcription, a rudimentary poetry in which he can make himself understood to his hosts. What finally interrupts the narrator's idealization of the poetry of Mars is Martian race relations: the purple-winged dominant crickets, he learns, tolerate a "dusky" minority among them while balking at intimate social contact. The narrator's arrival disrupts this balance, forcing the issue of the minority's civil status along with his own; rather than "be the innocent cause of a civil war," he returns to earth.

Like Dickinson's gift of a cricket to Mabel Loomis Todd, "Were They Crickets?" spectacularly literalizes the pursuit of natural song in human poetry. Like Tuckerman's cricket ode, Hill's fantasia is a work of vocational doubt and exploration. The Romantic ode's generic premise of being lofted into and partly mastering a compelling alien music, only to fall back to earth, clearly figures in another key the biographical facts of Hill's own class rise, his awkward, autodidactic relationship to polite culture (recalling that of Keats), and his eventual flight from Harvard's presidency. Read with Dickinson's and

Tuckerman's poems, Hill's fantasia amplifies the latent political resonance of Dickinson's "minor nation" of crickets and Tuckerman's cricket song of "innumerable numerousness" singing in the laborer's ear, an anonymous democracy of collective poetic voice that Tuckerman entertains but resists fully entering. "Were They Crickets?" also points explicitly to the racial limit of Civil War–era American political and cultural aspirations, which can rise to Mars, can indeed become Martial (and Hill, like Dickinson, is fully alive to his etymological puns), without rising beyond racial division, racialized labor exploitation, and miscegenation panic.

The other voices of mid-nineteenth-century American poetry could scarcely be more other than Thomas Hill's transcription of Martian verse. What's uncanny, though, about Hill's American Martial poetry is its proximity to the centers of cultural authority of its own day and to poetic voices recognized as canonical in ours. The conjuncture of Emily Dickinson's, Frederick Goddard Tuckerman's, and Thomas Hill's crickets within the literary culture of 1860s Massachusetts teaches us to read for likeness-in-difference among poets at various levels of canonicity while continuing to ask how different conditions of access to authorship enable different kinds of poets and poetries. Reading for poets' connections – for what Pierre Bourdieu would call the cultural *field* of American poetry – also identifies where connections fail, as in the distance of African American poets from the *Atlantic*'s social network. Guillory usefully warns against the strategy of teaching and interpreting lesser-known writers as if they were *"intrinsically* noncanonical, ... unassimilable to the traditional canon"; this version of honoring other voices hardens the very oppositions that efforts to open the canon originally challenged.[16] To label some verses "other" is at most a contingent, roughly practical way of indicating where one network stops and another begins, or where one syllabus stops and another begins, or at its further boundary, where the syllabus stops and the archive begins. Once reading begins, though, it's crickets all the way down.

Suppose, then, that we imagine the flourishing of nineteenth-century American poetry on the model of a naturalistically accurate Darwinian bush or tree, dead limbs and all, rather than in the familiar image of the ascent of man, culminating in a luxuriantly bearded Whitman. Suppose further that we place poets genetically within this tree, connecting and contrasting them as having experienced similar and different modes of access to authorship. Some branches of the tree will feature more famous names than others, but all at some level will connect canonical figures with less familiar authors. Some branches will be significantly more hospitable than others to writers of color, women writers, writers of limited financial resources, and writers of limited formal education. Some will be distant from other branches; others adjacent and entangled. Major divisions of such a family tree for nineteenth-century American poetry might group together poetic careers rooted in educational cultures and institutions; in the learned professions (law, medicine, divinity) adjacent to higher education; in social movements; in popular journalism; or in theater and other popular entertainments. Such a thought experiment may help us better appreciate the blooming, buzzing profusion of nineteenth-century American poetry by illuminating how different kinds of poetic accomplishment tended to be fostered by different modes of access to authorship; how authors' experience of overlap, mobility, and friction among different modes of authorship spurred innovative or ambitious poetry; and how a more autonomous, aesthetically oriented sphere of poetry arose in the United States in relation to these other possibilities for authorship.

Especially prior to the Civil War, social reform movements and education offered two broad and overlapping pathways to poetic careers. Poetry based in social movements, particularly in the cause of slavery's abolition, provided women and African Americans with some of the period's most accessible paths to authorship. Although higher education remained a remote world to most Americans, the expansion of literacy and public education at the primary level and the opening of more ambitious educational opportunities to middle- and upper-class white women generated poetic possibilities as well. The expansion of access to education was in itself a social cause and a dimension of many reform movements, one with special urgency for African Americans, women, and immigrants who yoked together "Freedom of thought, and of the pen, / Free schools, free speech, free soil, free men," as the New Hampshire–born black poet James Monroe Whitfield framed these hopes in a poem celebrating the fourth anniversary of the Emancipation Proclamation.[17] Social reform movements and education together created new publication venues, audiences, and authorial identities, as well as shared thematic urgencies, for a wide range of authors.

Education provided the medium as well as the matter for the launching of Lydia Huntley Sigourney's poetic career, at its height in the 1830s and 1840s. Her first book, *Moral Pieces, in Prose and Verse* (1815), appeared while Sigourney was running a school for genteel young women in Hartford, Connecticut, and openly reflected its pedagogical origins (in the words of the *North American Review*'s notice) "as compositions, addressed to young ladies under the writer's charge."[18] Although she left schoolteaching behind as a profession on her marriage in 1819, Sigourney's subsequent poetry and prose remained deeply rooted in antebellum American cultures of both formal schooling and informal domestic tutelage. "This whole life is but one great school," she wrote in her 1837 *The Girl's Reading-Book*,[19] and her poetry was frequently both didactic in content and a celebration of the didactic routines and social relations of schooling. Sigourney memorialized her pupils and her experience of teaching them in elegies for individual students and in strings of poems like "Scholar's Tribute to an Instructor," "Teacher's Excuse," "Exhibition of a School of Young Ladies," and "On Meeting Several Former Pupils at the Communion Table." She lauded the world-historical extension of advanced learning to women: "Establishment of a Female College in New-Grenada, South America" predicts that with education women's "fragile forms, / Now trembling in their beauty and their fear, / Shall kindle with new energies."[20] The historical bent of much of her poetry reflects her republican belief that history "imparts knowledge of human nature, and supplies lofty subjects for contemplation" and so rightfully stands at the center of education;[21] a poem like "Rival Kings of Mohegan, Contrasted with the Rival Brothers of Persia" advertises its origins as a pedagogical exercise in just this kind of moral history. Her many excursions into abolitionist poetry, such as "To the First Slave Ship," and her recognition of Native American presence and rights in poems like "Indian Names," "The Cherokee Mother," and *Traits of the Aborigines of America* (1822) were continuous with Sigourney's didactic muse.

Education remained at the center of Sigourney's project in her most aesthetically ambitious works, such as "Connecticut River." Composed in heroic couplets – modeled on the eighteenth-century Anglo-American genre of the prospect poem that surveys a landscape from a distance – and replying directly to important British models in Oliver Goldsmith's "The Deserted Village" (1770) and Thomas Gray's "Elegy Written in a Country Churchyard" (1751), "Connecticut River" aims at writing an American poetry both lofty and democratic, one that can compete with "classic song." Like Tuckerman in "The Cricket," Sigourney challenges British poetic models in making them American: starting lower, perhaps to mount higher. "Though broader streams our sister realms may boast," she concedes, the citizens of the Connecticut River valley stand as "King, priest, and prophet 'mid the homes they love" (Z, p. 13) in contrast with Goldsmith's dispossessed villagers and the social hierarchies marked by Gray's "Elegy." At the heart of the village prospect as Sigourney renders it lie the school, "where village science dwells," and the graveyard, in which the history of the village's making lies uneasily buried, the dispossessed Indian in "his forfeit land" alongside the village's "patriot sires [who] with honour rest / ... Unmarked, untrophied, 'mid the soil they saved" (Z, pp. 14, 15–16). At once honored and unwritten, the condition of these forebears implies that nation building requires a simultaneous work of remembrance and forgetfulness – a complex form of historical tutelage and one enabled by distance, whether the generic distance of the prospect poem or that of the weeping frontier mother, "cheat[ing] her rustic babes with tender tales" of her native Connecticut (Z, p. 16), who closes the poem and in so doing figures Sigourney's own poetic work as a national pedagogue.

Her energetic, lifelong labors at the conjunction of poetry with the spheres of education and social reform rewarded Lydia Sigourney with popular fame, social position, and financial security. The North Carolina slave poet George Moses Horton emerged from the same conjunction, at very nearly the same time as Sigourney – his first book, *The Hope of Liberty*, appeared in 1829 – but the story of his access to authorship is far more painful. As he recounts in the autobiography prefacing his 1845 *Poetical Works*, Horton taught himself to read; driven by "anxiety for books" while denied access to formal education, he used "dim and promiscuous" fragments of textbooks and, like Frederick Douglass, the unwitting assistance of white schoolchildren to teach himself the alphabet.[22] He battened on every scrap of poetry he could pick up and began composing verses orally, a talent that brought him to the attention of the college students at Chapel Hill, who set Horton to composing acrostic verses on the names of women they were courting. His early poems were transcribed for publication by the white novelist and poet Caroline Lee Hentz; Horton himself would not learn to write until 1832. His income from poetry written at command for students – up to three dollars a week, at the rate of fifty to seventy-five cents per poem – allowed him to buy out his time and attach himself to the Chapel Hill campus, where he maintained himself in a variety of service roles, poetry included, for students and faculty.

In contrast with Sigourney's poems to her pupils and on education more broadly, Horton's poems "On the Pleasures of College Life" and "The Graduate Leaving College" (and still more his "Billet Doux [*sic*]," addressed on behalf of one of Chapel Hill's young bloods to a woman of "vermillion cheek" and "sapphire eye" [*PW*, p. 64]) memorialize vicarious experience and intimate deprivation. For Chapel Hill's students, Horton *was* one of the entitlements of college life, while many of them too clearly deprecated their own chance, denied Horton, to sit in "the rays of erudition's sun" (*PW*, p. 76). Incompetent to their college's intellectual ambitions, these students may not have appreciated the irony of Horton's exhorting them, in high heroic couplets, to "imitate [the] style" of an ideally devout "gospel prince" of graduates (*PW*, p. 84); if they could imitate models more fluently, the students would not have had to rely on Horton for their billets-doux. To the extent that Horton's own mode of access to literacy could be read as an imitation of theirs, it is an imitation that points back to its delinquent original.

Juxtaposed with Horton's poems of "anxiety for books" are his poems of social satire and vernacular observation, like "The Creditor to His Proud Debtor," addressed to a young fop whose extravagance is underwritten by the speaker's thrift, and "The Tipler [*sic*] to His Bottle," which follows the maudlin mental weavings of a drunk exalted and then cast down by his liquor. These poems shift crisply between literary diction and colloquial registers. "The Fearful Traveller in the Haunted Castle" begins as a high-flown literary nightmare, on which Horton then lifts the domestic curtain to reveal that its ghosts were only rats and cats and "Those creatures crumbling off the cheese / Which on the table lay" (*PW*, p. 28). In "The Fate of an Innocent Dog," however, the nightmare is both real on its small scale and evocative of larger terrors. Out hunting game, Tiger the dog comes upon a fatally wounded sheep and slinks away in fear; bristling at the sheep's owner, he is taken for the culprit, while the real killers, a set of human dogs armed with "powder, fire and ball" (*PW*, p. 54), go free. Through the protective distance of its animal protagonist, the poem speaks for the North Carolina countryside of Horton's origins against the depredations of the college town's careless aristocracy, while on a national scale, the fate of Horton's innocent dog calls to mind the guilt of those human packs that Whittier's famous abolitionist poem of 1835 called "The Hunters of Men."

The freeborn African American poet Frances Ellen Watkins Harper also came to authorship at the intersection of social reform movements with education. Unlike George Moses Horton, she received a formal education, at her uncle's Academy for Negro Youth in Baltimore; and in the Northern states she could participate openly, although not without personal risk, in the abolitionist movement and in efforts to open schooling to African Americans. Prior to the Civil War, the young Frances Harper moved from one teaching position to another before establishing herself as a writer and as a professional lecturer for the Maine Anti-Slavery Society.[23] Her prewar poetry, collected in *Poems on Miscellaneous Subjects* (1854; later, expanded editions added poems through 1864), brought together the multiple causes at the heart of antebellum reform, including abolition (in poems like "Bible Defence of Slavery" and "The Fugitive's Wife") and temperance ("The Drunkard's Child"). Following the Civil War, Harper dedicated her poetry, lectures, and essays to African American education at every level, from the establishment of primary schools to nation building on the largest scale among the communities of former slaves in the South. Harper's two great poetic works of this period, the biblical epic *Moses: A Story of the Nile* (1869) and the Aunt Chloe sequence in *Sketches of Southern Life* (1872), both concern themselves with what Harper in an 1875 speech called "The Great Problem to Be Solved" – the problem of educating and empowering the emancipated "four millions." *Moses* and the Aunt Chloe poems together constitute a diptych of classical and vernacular literacies, in high blank verse and colloquial ballad stanzas respectively. Like George Moses Horton's achievement, Harper's is doubled-voiced; it both narrates and performs the access of the newly emancipated to forms of cultural and social capital hitherto denied them.

Along with Lydia Sigourney, Harper yoked her advocacy for mass democratic education to an ideal of political leadership as anonymous heroism, implying that the achievement of literacy for the many entailed the unwriting of old forms of social preeminence. Her poem "Burial of Moses" echoes Sigourney's "Connecticut River" in celebrating its nation-founding hero's unmarked, untrophied "grave without a name":

> And had he not high honour?
> The hill-side for his pall,
> To lie in state while angels wait
> With stars for tapers tall,
> And the dark rock pines like tossing plumes
> Over his bier to wave,
> And God's own hand in that lonely land
> To lay him in the grave.

Democratic nation building, in Harper's vision, requires leaders ready to break the Old World molds, "with costly marble drest," of warrior, sage, and bard (*BCD*, pp. 77–78), a theme she would echo in her Reconstruction-era "Truth," another poem about the defacement of "haughty" social idols by humble forces (*BCD*, pp. 168–69). For Harper as well as for Sigourney, the great problem to be solved by American poetry is the question of what a trustworthy *democratic elevation* could look like, in poetry as well as in political leaders. The unmarked grave of Moses is Harper's answer, as cricket song in another poetic idiom was for Tuckerman and Dickinson, to the question of whether an American poetry could start low and mount high.

As the examples of Sigourney, Horton, and Harper suggest, nineteenth-century American poets emerging from education and from social reform movements, and from their conjunction, did not generally run to conspicuous formal experimentation. Educational practices of memorization and recitation favored predictably rhymed and metered forms, and educational routines of imitation encouraged replying to existing poetic models – as Sigourney does in "Connecticut River" – in their own idiom. For social movements as well, accessibility to broad audiences was a core value that favored broadcasting social innovations in familiar formal shapes.

More distinctly literary kinds of experimentation did emerge from poets who came to reform poetry from different modes of access to authorship. In *Passion-Flowers* (1853), her first collection of poems, Julia Ward Howe introduced herself as a "child of Art,"[24] in this way and in others laying claim to poetic origins in an aesthetic world apart from the more instrumental realms of schooling and reform. Where the poetry of Sigourney and Horton is overtly rooted in "anxiety for books" and the knowledge that comes out of books, Howe in *Passion-Flowers* claims the authority of direct experience of European cultural capitals, and direct experience of artistic capital more generally. The opening lines of "Rome," the volume's longest and most ambitious poem, both establish her in this high cultural realm and assert the poem's distance from the poetry of domestic duties and moral tutelage:

> I knew a day of glad surprise in Rome,
> Free to the childish joy of wandering,
> Without a "wherefore" or "to what good end?"
> By querulous voice propounded, or a thought
> Of punctual Duty, waiting at the door
> Of home, with weapon duly poised to slay
> Delight, ere it across the threshold bound.
> I strayed, amassing wild flowers, ivy leaves,
> Relics, and crusted marbles, gathering too
> Thoughts of unending Beauty from the fields . . .   (*PF*, p. 8)

What follows this opening, as Gary Williams observes, is a poem that "connects the awakening of poetic intuition with the song of a bird and an encounter with death"[25] – which is to say, still another American poem modeled at least in part on the Romantic ode and asking how and at what risk American poetry might become "high."

Howe's daring answer, in "Rome," is to map the personal elevations of the Romantic ode onto the political genre of the progress poem (central to earlier history-minded poets like Lydia Sigourney), with its concern for the rise and fall of civilizations. Howe ventures from her home into Rome not just once but multiple times, in a dialectical process of self-revision. Her first hearing (in a lover's company) of Rome's incomparable nightingale is followed by excursions that teach her how Rome's soul "widely overflowed" its boundaries into empire, and in doing so roused "The frost-bound vastness of barbaric life" to "[Sweep] her back, through all her haughty ways / To her own gates, a piteous fugitive" (*PF*, p. 15). Understanding from her immersion in Roman history that "No good survives the fitness of its time," Howe turns against the "unending beauty" that she initially sought in Rome to address both the fallen empire and the decadent (in her American Protestant eyes) Catholic Church as forms of "vampire beauty," clinging to life beyond their naturally appointed deaths: "Yield to us," she demands of them, "The wealth thy spectral fingers cannot hold; / Bless us, and so depart" (*PF*, pp. 19–20). On a visit to the Temple of the Sybil at Tivoli outside Rome, Howe at last locates the image that brings together personal passion, poetic ambition, and her peripatetic historical insight. Juxtaposing the "silent, awful oracle" of the Sybil to the rainbow-decked "Iris of the Waterfall" that like "A daring Sappho leaps . . . from the rock," Howe declares that

> the fixed Sybil sits there and decays,
> While leaping, loving human life flows on,
> And, plunging down to Chaos, is not lost. (*PF*, p. 21)

By contrast with the impersonal, universal, and pedagogically and textually mediated authority of history in Lydia Sigourney's poetry, the authority of history in Howe's poetry emerges from an antipedagogical aesthetic of self-abandonment to experience. High American song, she proposes, will be song that plunges deep: as the future potential of the United States is measured by the depth of Rome's historical fall, American poetry's potential for elevation is measured by the depth of its fortunate fall into the life of human passion.

Even when Howe spoke directly to contemporary American politics – and there is a great deal of direct political statement in *Passion-Flowers* as well as in her later collections – her authority remained grounded in the realm of the high aesthetic and high dialectical critique (she was immensely taken with Hegel), rather than in pedagogical or sentimental culture. "A Protest from Italy," for example, views the American struggle over slavery from the aesthetic distance of Italy, "Where even curses fall in words / Whose beauty heals the wounds they make." At this remove, the speaker initially counsels North and South "to part in peace." On returning to her native "icy Northern springs," however, where "The sharp steel wind doth sunder all / My silken armor of delight," she awakens to slavery as an intolerable evil that "to the social heart hath crept," whence it must be cast out – in blood, if necessary (*PF*, pp. 40–42). "A Protest from Italy" strikes martial notes that Howe would sound again, most famously in her "Battle Hymn of the Republic." By comparison with the wartime "Battle Hymn," though, "A Protest" gives fuller voice to the claims of the art world and its sensuous peace before drawing those claims into the service of another political and historical perspective. Its image of a silken dress disintegrating in a harsh wind is evocative on several levels, merging women's dress with battle-shredded pennants and metonymically rearmoring the speaker in the steely temper of the attacking wind.

For many of Howe's contemporaries, the dialectical aesthetic perspective of "A Protest," more than the univocal militancy of "Battle Hymn of the Republic," typified her poetry as a whole. Bayard Taylor's parody of Howe in "Diversions of the Echo Club" (1872) captures the distinctive elements, held in tension, of her poetic ambitions: "I tried to part / The petals which compose / The azure flower of high aesthetic art," vaunts Howe in Taylor's parody, while "blend[ing] our moral trigonometry / With Spheroids of the mind" and stretching out a hand to the "coming race" of new women and men.[26] Dedication to world-historical progress, higher learning, and the high aesthetic: for her contemporary readers, these high ambitions, coupled with what they heard as her "audacious defiance of the wholesome precedents of composition" (in the words of a contemporary *Harper's* reviewer),[27] set Howe's work apart from the school of Sigourney.

Howe's tour of ruins and relics in "Rome" spares a sympathetic glance for "the Ghetto of the hated Jew," whose "poor synagogue's simplicity" preserves "the ancient venerable word" intact under persecution (*PF*, p. 18). "Intent on reading as his fathers read," the synagogue's rabbi is both admirable for his self-abnegating interpretive fidelity and pitiable, in Howe's eyes, for his willful isolation from history. Some two decades after Howe's emergence in the 1850s, Emma Lazarus would dedicate her poetry to restoring Howe's rabbi to a place in living history, and to translating for modernity the evolving complexity – lost in Howe's patronizing sketch – of Judaism's ethical and aesthetic traditions.

At the outset of her career, Lazarus's poetry showcased her commitment to a generalized ideal of high aesthetic, cosmopolitan Euro-American culture, signaled by her juxtaposition of epigraphs from Ralph Waldo Emerson and Longfellow-style poems of the New England seashore with translations of Goethe's *Faust*. In her early poem "In the Jewish Synagogue at Newport" (1867), Lazarus represents Judaism as a "relic of the days of old," a ruin of immense beauty and pathos but not a living cultural presence.[28] Following Longfellow's "The Jewish Cemetery at Newport," Lazarus sees Newport's Jewish community as having died to human history, its cemetery full and its synagogue empty, exposing "lone floors where reverent feet once trod." In contrast with the rabbi of Howe's "Rome," whose crabbed and literal fidelity to the Old Testament is destitute of inspirational power, Lazarus does grant the rabbi of her vanished community an inspired and primary relationship to the divine word:

> A wondrous light upon a sky-kissed mount,
>> A man who reads Jehovah's written law,
> 'Midst blinding glory and effulgence rare,
>> Unto a people prone with reverent awe.

(EL, p. 50)

But this rabbi is nowhere to be seen in Lazarus's contemporary Newport. Where Howe in "Rome" honors a continuing if limited (as she sees it) Jewish exegetical tradition, the synagogue of Lazarus's poem has lost all its living links to the divine word – "the very prayers / Inscribed around are in a language dead" (EL, p. 50).

In the 1870s and 1880s, however, world events and her own experience combined to bring Jewish history, Jewish literature, and international crises in contemporary Jewish life to the forefront of Lazarus's writing. Horrified by the Russian pogroms of 1880–1881, she personally greeted refugees arriving at Ward's Island and published essays calling on American Jews to support both the "storm-tost [*sic*] European outcasts" arriving in their midst and the effort to found a Jewish homeland in Palestine (EL, p. 262). Replying to Longfellow (and to her younger self) in an essay published after his death, she declared that the trials "which our brethren still consent to undergo in the name of Judaism ... prove them to be very warmly and thoroughly alive,"[29] members of vital present communities rather than denizens of a Romantic cemetery, and she began to study in earnest the Hebrew that she had previously declared "a language dead." Lazarus's roused sense of purpose in the 1880s energized and reoriented, without repudiating, the cosmopolitan aesthetic sampling characteristic of her earlier poetry, as the grand subject of her later writing became what she called "the double cosmopolitanism of the American and the Jew" (EL, p. 264).

Lazarus's poem "The New Year" in her 1882 Songs of a Semite – dated "Rosh-Hashanah, 5643" – begins with a resounding rejection of the Christian calendar for the Jewish sacred calendar:

> Not while the snow-shroud round dead earth is rolled,
>> And naked branches point to frozen skies. –
> When orchards burn their lamps of fiery gold,
>> The grape glows like a jewel, and the corn
> A sea of beauty and abundance lies,
>>> Then the new year is born.

(EL, p. 175)

Where the Christian new year, like January's bare branches, points toward the resurrection that will lift the "snow-shroud" from the dead, the Jewish calendar by contrast begins with fruition. Its "beauty and abundance" need no resurrection, either from the social death imagined for the Jewish community by Longfellow or that offered through Christian theology. Against the privation and wretchedness widely associated with the refugees of 1880–1881 (including the "wretched [human] refuse" pictured in "The New Colossus," Lazarus's famous sonnet on the Statue of Liberty), the poem's most fundamental assertion is that Jewish time is beautiful, that it offers a lush and fully present aesthetic – as well as political and ritual – alternative to Christian eschatology. Wresting control over time itself from Christian history, Lazarus rewrites Longfellow's (and her own) image of refugees helplessly driven over the sea as a stately (in every sense of the word) and deliberate expansion of Jewish community into the globe:

> In two divided streams the exiles part,
> One rolling homeward to its ancient source,
> One rushing sunward with fresh will, new heart.
> By each the truth is spread, the law unfurled,
> Each separate soul contains the nation's force,
> And both embrace the world.
>
> (*EL*, p. 176)

Emma Lazarus's late poems and translations repeatedly affirmed Jewish culture to be authentically created in plural languages and idioms rather than bound to a specific language or site of origin. Her cosmopolitan appreciation for both diasporic communities and the first stirrings of Jewish nationalism, and her refusal to privilege one or the other as more authentically Jewish, might well guide us in better appreciating the many streams – none more authentically American than another – of poetry in the United States.

On still another branch of the family tree of nineteenth-century American poetry, Walt Whitman shares a lineage with other poets who made their way into authorship through popular journalism. The journalistic branch of American poetry was closely related to other modes of gaining access to authorship: Whitman began his authorial career in social movement writing, with a temperance novel, and John Greenleaf Whittier moved through stints as a schoolteacher and a newspaper editor before becoming one of the major poets of nineteenth-century social movements. The relationship of journalism to poetry was much closer in the nineteenth-century United States than it would be in the twentieth; most nineteenth-century American poets chose to publish in, or had their work picked up by, newspapers and popular journals.

This group of poets, however, stands out for having appeared as regular syndicated reporters in popular venues – as distinct from only contributing occasional poetry to them – or for having apprenticed themselves to literature through active editorial, managerial, and production responsibilities in popular journalistic venues – as distinct from assuming editorial responsibilities in the more rarified venues of culture and opinion, like the *Atlantic Monthly*, as a complement to an already-established literary career. In addition to Whitman, Edgar Allan Poe, Stephen Crane, Ambrose Bierce, Joaquin Miller, Eugene Field, John James Piatt, Edmund Clarence Stedman, and Bayard Taylor were a few among many poets whose writing emerged from and retained a flavor of the journalistic milieu.

This milieu was less notable for fostering the emergence of women poets. Although poems by women writers were copiously picked up and published by newspapers and popular journals, few women poets were able to mediate their access to literary careers through these kinds of editorial, managerial, and production positions in mass journalism – unless they managed "separate sphere" publications aimed at a female audience, like Sarah Josepha Hale's *Godey's Lady's Book*. African American writers similarly found, and made, these kinds of opportunities in their own community's publications but seldom in the world of mass popular journalism. The rapidly expanding sphere of popular journalism was, however, very hospitable to the emergence of poets in the western United States, in cities and towns outside the established literary centers of the East Coast, as underlined by the midwestern orbit of Eugene Field, who worked on papers in Missouri, Kansas, and Colorado before settling in Chicago; the San Francisco–based career of Ambrose Bierce; and John James Piatt's work as an apprentice printer and, later, an editor on both the northern and southern sides of the Ohio River, in Cincinnati and Louisville, Kentucky.

Poets who emerged from the sphere of nineteenth-century American popular journalism often had a freewheeling professional aesthetic, and Whitman was neither the first nor the last of them to understand the value of cultivating a celebrity persona. Relatively distant from the academic authority of received prosodic models, the journalistic sphere could be friendly to formal experimentation, often of an autodidactic character; as Jerome McGann has argued of Stephen Crane's *Black Riders*, these poets could be acutely and inventively sensitive to the modern print medium of their work as well as to the older mnemonic technologies, of meter and rhyme, on which it traveled. The same self-consciousness of their modern mass media location often led them to produce serious poetic parody and to modulate journalist notices into serious reviewing and criticism, as suggested by the careers of Bayard Taylor and

Edmund Clarence Stedman. As ambitiously practiced in Bayard Taylor's *The Echo Club*, and in Phoebe Cary's wicked *Poems and Parodies* (1854), parody could be a way of tracing poetry's social networks in the mid-nineteenth-century United States, a mode of popular literary historiography.

Taylor's "Battle of the Bards" in *The Echo Club*, a mock newspaper account of a fictional poetry slam among Walt Whitman, Bret Harte, John Hay, and Joaquin Miller, draws all these aspects of the journalistic poetry sphere into its satire. First published in the *New York Tribune* within days of Whitman's 1871 public recitation of his lengthy "Song of the Exposition," "Battle of the Bards" exhibits each poet competing against the others, not only in the distinctive formal idiom or branding (in every sense of the word) of his poetry but in ramping up the volume of his celebrity persona. Walt Whitman, in this company the dignified father of the clan, has barely finished "Straddling the Continent, gathering into my hairy bosom the growths, whatever they were," of his "Chant Democratique" before he is challenged to a "free fight" by Bret Harte, the Westerner with "the face of Raphael and ... the boots of Cinderella" and a fistful of dialect. Harte's toast to himself as "the poet / That's flattened out all the rest" is instantly challenged by Hay's melancholy, Lincolnesque frontier mien and his claim that "the real high-pressure [poetic] style" lies in the general direction of Peoria, Illinois. Finally Whitman, Harte, and Hay alike are mown down by the arrival of Joaquin Miller, who reads "In a voice loud enough to drown the whistle of ten locomotives" some galloping Western verses "from a manuscript signed JOAQUIN, written in letters of blood on the tanned hide of a Comanche princess" – "Take them and read them and yield me the crown," he yells, "And the sound of my screaming shall never die!"[30]

Taylor's appalling parody was and remains insightful about the dynamics of the mid-nineteenth-century American poetic marketplace. As Taylor's accurate reproduction of Joaquin's demi-epic, horsy, dactylic-trochaic Westering verse suggests, Joaquin Miller himself was engaged not only in self-promotion but in a kind of serious parody, a deep aggression directed more consistently against genteel Eastern poetic models than against either fictive or historical American Indian bodies. Taylor's hot-off-the-presses parody riffed on the formula Miller had most recently exploited in his 1871 *Songs of the Sierras* and anticipated both the meter and the romance plot of Miller's sprawling frontier poem of 1875, *The Ship in the Desert*. *The Ship in the Desert*, in its turn, both recapitulated and reversed the plot and the metrical form of Longfellow's mid-century demi-epic *Evangeline*. Miller's poem, like *Evangeline*, centers on a man and a woman, sundered from each other in the shipwreck of a nation, who wander over the United States and its frontiers, linked in an apparently inexorable rhythm of pursuit and flight. But where Longfellow floats Evangeline down the Mississippi and over the American West and South only to return his heroine to a life of service and a decorous deathbed marriage in Philadelphia, Miller's poem plunges up and down the Missouri, refights the Civil War to the death beside a mysterious ghost ship marooned on the shores of Utah's Great Salt Lake, and finally settles his mixed-race heroine with her lover among the Shoshone. Smackdown! The energies loosed in these journalist parodies and counterparodies remind us that defacement is a vital part of American literary culture, including its poetic culture. Like Frances Harper's *Moses* and her shorter poem "Truth," although in a very different tonal key and to very different political ends, *The Ship in the Desert* is a minor American epic of defacement, an experiment in bringing high idols low.

Among the many other objects of Taylor's parody in *The Echo Club* was Frederick Goddard Tuckerman. But unlike Whitman and Howe, Longfellow and Miller, Tuckerman – so Taylor complains – "presents only proper smoothness" to the satirist; his "verse moves onward with a step secure, / Nor hastes with rapture, nor delays with dread." At best, the *Echo* clubmen concur, he is "a conservative element in literature," useful "to keep the wild modern schools in order."[31] If Tuckerman read this (it originally appeared in the *Atlantic Monthly* in May 1872, months before his death), he may not have been entirely displeased; years before, he had cut out a local newspaper parody of his sonnet "The Starry Flower" and pasted it into his notebook (*SP*, p. xii), as if to acknowledge that for poets there is no such thing as bad publicity. But he might also have felt that the earlier parody got it more nearly right, and Taylor, wrong. The "sonnet – After F. G. T.," published in the *Springfield Republican* (which was also Emily Dickinson's local newspaper), mocked Tuckerman's "verbal mist" and "poisonous" laurels – in other words, his aspirations to a high Romantic style; the *Echo Club* parody, by contrast, complained of his "strictly classic" placidity, reading him back into the eighteenth-century models of Pope and Gray rather than next to his own idol, Tennyson. Tuckerman himself, though, in one of his sonnets, had declared his preference for "rough" criticism – even

> surgery rough as that,
> Which, hammer and chisel in hand, at one sharp blow
> Strikes out the wild tooth from a horse's jaw! –

over "ignorant praise" and pedantic flaw picking. Like his critics, he too hoped for an American poetry that would "cast out fear" and attract readers able to "touch the quick" (*SP*, p. 102).

The dialogue between this retiring and relatively little-published poet and his parodists demonstrates the vigor and connectedness of American poetry, including its lesser-known voices, at the mid-nineteenth century. Like the "wayside apple" that "drops its surly fruit" in another Tuckerman sonnet (*SP*, p. 130), or like the "harmless cur" paying his "surly" compliments in Horton's "The Innocent Dog," the family tree of nineteenth-century American poetry confounds dichotomies of the natural versus the cultured, the imported versus the indigenous, and formal versus free – dichotomies still deep-seated in the canonical formation of American literature. The wayside apple tree is no more indigenous in Tuckerman's landscape than is the sonnet form, or Horton's balladry. Its surly resilience comes not from purely autochthonous New World origins but from the incorrigible diversity of Old World genetic information (apple trees planted from seed don't run true to their parents) that the apple expresses.

This is not to say that Tuckerman's sonnet, in itself, offers any but the most anodyne of medicines for the questions of cultural resilience and survival it poses. A present-day reader will know this when she comes to sonnet IV.IX's complacent reference to walking in the footsteps of "Sagamore George," even if she doesn't know that George's Pawtucket name was Wenepoykin; that he ruled lands from Charlestown to Salem; that he was brutally disfigured in a smallpox epidemic that killed off most of his community; and that he was captured and sold off into slavery on Barbados during King Philip's War, from which in 1684 he returned to die in Natick, Massachusetts. Horton's "Innocent Dog" is far more knowing than Tuckerman's sonnet about what happens when "surly" resilience encounters guns, germs, and steel. What I am saying, though, is that Tuckerman's and Horton's poems know more together than they do separately about what burdens Anglophone poetry bore to the Americas and how poetry circulated in the nineteenth-century United States, and that what these poems, together, know remains worth retracing today.

Notes

1. Virginia Jackson, "Thinking Dickinson Thinking Poetry," in Martha Nell Smith and Mary Loeffelholz (eds.), *A Companion to Emily Dickinson* (Malden, Mass.: Blackwell, 2008), pp. 205–21, 206–07.

2. For all six versions of "Further in Summer," see R. W. Franklin (ed.), *The Poems of Emily Dickinson: Variorium Edition*, 3 vols. (Cambridge, Mass.: The Belknap Press of Harvard University Press, 1998), vol. 2, pp. 831–36.

3. Joanne Feit Diehl, *Dickinson and the Romantic Imagination* (Princeton, N.J.: Princeton University Press, 1981), p. 97.

4. Franklin (ed.), *The Poems of Emily Dickinson*, vol. 2, p. 832.

5. See Virginia Jackson, *Dickinson's Misery: A Theory of Lyric Reading* (Princeton, N.J.: Princeton University Press, 2005), p. 91.

6. Jackson, "Thinking Dickinson Thinking Poetry," pp. 210, 218.

7. On the British Romantic influences, see Eugene England, *Beyond Romanticism: Tuckerman's Life and Poetry* (Albany: State University of New York Press, 1991), pp. 197, 204–06.

8. Ben Mazer (ed.), *Selected Poems of Frederick Goddard Tuckerman* (Cambridge, Mass.: The Belknap Press of Harvard University Press, 2010), p. 152. Poems in this collection will be cited in the text as *SP*.

9. Yvor Winters, "A Discovery," *Hudson Review* 3 (1950), pp. 453, 458.

10. Edmund Wilson, *Patriotic Gore* (1962; New York: Norton, 1994), pp. 489–90.

11. John Guillory, *Cultural Capital: The Problem of Literary Canon Formation* (Chicago: University of Chicago Press, 1993), p. 17.

12. Yvor Winters, *Maule's Curse: Seven Studies in the History of American Obscurantism* (Norfolk, Conn.: New Directions, 1938), p. 159.

13. Timothy Morris, *Becoming Canonical in American Poetry* (Urbana: University of Illinois Press, 1995), p. 19.

14. William G. Land, *Thomas Hill: Twentieth President of Harvard* (Cambridge, Mass.: Harvard University Press, 1933), pp. 231–37.

15. [Thomas Hill], "Were They Crickets?" *Atlantic Monthly*, April 1866, pp. 402, 400, 403.

16. Guillory, *Cultural Capital*, p. 9.

17. Joan R. Sherman (ed.), *African American Poetry of the Nineteenth Century: An Anthology* (Urbana: University of Illinois Press, 1992), p. 87.

18. "Miss Huntley's Poems," *North American Review* 1 (May 1815), p. 111.

19. L[ydia] H[untley] Sigourney, *The Girl's Reading-Book: In Prose and Poetry, for Schools* (1837; New York: J. Orville Taylor, 1839), p. 11.

20. L[ydia] H[untley] Sigourney, *Zinzendorff, and Other Poems* (New York: Leavitt, Lord & Co., 1835), p. 102. Poems in this collection will be cited in the text as *Z*.

21. L[ydia] H[untley] Sigourney, *Letters to Young Ladies* (New York: Harper & Brothers, 1836), p. 138.

22. George Moses Horton, *Poetical Works* (1845), http://docsouth.unc.edu/fpn /hortonpoem/hortonpoem.html, pp. iv, vi. Poems in this collection will be cited in the text as *PW*.

23. See Frances Smith Foster's introduction to *A Brighter Coming Day: A Frances Ellen Watkins Harper Reader* (New York: The Feminist Press at the City University of New York, 1990), p. 11 (hereafter cited in the text as *BCD*).

24. Julia Ward Howe, *Passion-Flowers* (Boston: Ticknor, Reed, and Fields, 1853), p. 2. Poems in this collection will be cited in the text as *PF*.

25. Gary Williams, *Hungry Heart: The Literary Emergence of Julia Ward Howe* (Amherst: University of Massachusetts Press, 1999), p. 140.

26. [Bayard Taylor], "Diversions of the Echo Club (Night the Seventh)," *Atlantic Monthly* 30 (July 1872), p. 78.

27. Quoted in Williams, *Hungry Heart*, p. 137.

28. Emma Lazarus, "In the Jewish Synagogue at Newport," in Gregory Eiselein (ed.), *Emma Lazarus: Selected Poems and Other Writings* (Peterborough, Ontario: Broadview Press, 2002), p. 50. Works in this collection will be cited in the text as *EL*.

29. Quoted in Max Cavitch, "Emma Lazarus and the Golem of Liberty," in Meredith L. McGill (ed.), *The Traffic in Poems: Nineteenth-Century Poetry and Transatlantic Exchange* (New Brunswick: Rutgers University Press, 2008), p. 107.

30. Bayard Taylor, "The Battle of the Bards," in *The Echo Club, and Other Literary Diversions* (Boston: James R. Osgood, 1876), pp. 168–74.

31. Taylor, "The Battle of the Bards," pp. 97–98.

Chapter 14

American Poetry Fights the Civil War

FAITH BARRETT

On Decoration Day in May 1869, a journalist and Union army veteran named George Bryant Woods stood before a soldiers' monument in his hometown of Barre, Massachusetts, and remembered the men he had served with in 1862, when he was just eighteen. After describing the friends he caught glimpses of during the fighting at Antietam, Woods recalled how they had once recited "The Charge of the Light Brigade" as schoolboys at the town hall, never imagining that they would face the kind of combat that Tennyson's poem describes. In remembering the bravery of a young officer who died at Antietam, Woods echoed the imagery of Tennyson's poem, underlining the powerful influence this piece had over American readers. Still more importantly, echoes of Tennyson's poem in Woods's remarks also foreground the centrality of poetry to the American Civil War. When Edmund Wilson dismissed Civil War poetry as "versified journalism," he misunderstood the crucial role that poetry played in nineteenth-century culture: in the Civil War era, Americans believed that poetry could make vital contributions to the ongoing debate about the meaning of national identity.[1] Northerners and Southerners alike believed that poetry could not only reflect but also shape events that took place on battlefields.

Woods's reference to Tennyson's poem reminds us that in mid-nineteenth-century America poetry was ubiquitous. Central to schoolroom pedagogy, poetry was also read at recruitment events, in military camps and hospitals, and at memorials for fallen soldiers. It was printed in newspapers and magazines, in which it served not only as filler but also as a powerful intervention into conversations both literary and political. Americans encountered poetry in the form of broadsides, songsters, self-published collections, paper-bound books, and hard-bound volumes. Many Americans kept albums of favorite poems, and many would also try their hand at penning a few lines of verse. During the war years, reports abound of soldiers reading or singing poetry not only in camp but also as they marched into battle; newspapers offered frequent accounts of soldiers dying with poems in their pockets. Many soldiers on both sides of the conflict wrote poetry. The Civil War witnessed an extraordinary outpouring of poetry by men and women from all walks of life. In the poetry of this era, both amateur and professional writers confronted a crisis of representation, as they sought to define the changing meanings of family, home, and nation in wartime. While canonical writers like Whitman, Dickinson, and Melville might address this crisis more explicitly, studying the full spectrum of poetry from this period makes clear that popular writers, women poets, and African Americans also grappled with important representational and aesthetic challenges in their poems. This chapter, then, considers that full spectrum, ultimately arguing that Whitman, Dickinson, and Melville all responded dialogically to the work of their poetic contemporaries. Reading across the spectrum of this work underlines as well the extraordinary richness and variety of Civil War poetry.[2]

Central to poetry's remarkably broad range in this era were developments in printing and transportation technologies: poetry could now be printed and circulated quickly and cheaply. In the Northern states, magazines that printed poetry saw explosive growth during the war years; Southern publications also saw growth in their subscriptions, although shortages of paper and printing equipment ultimately proved limiting. Historians frequently note that the Civil War was one of the first wars to be shaped by the telegraph and the railroad. Because of the speed with which it could be written, printed, and distributed, poetry was a literary genre that was uniquely poised to keep pace with events taking place on battlefields, in Richmond, and in Washington.

Moreover, in both the North and the South, the avid readership for poetry worked hand in glove with interest in popular song; the boundary between these two genres would become particularly permeable during the war. Middle-class Americans with pianos in their parlors wanted sheet music; soldiers in camp sang the latest patriotic songs. Composers thus quickly set newly written poems to music, and publishers rushed to get sheet music to musicians. Julia Ward Howe's "Battle Hymn of the Republic" is a representative instance: although the poem first appeared in the *Atlantic Monthly* in February 1862, it was also distributed as a song sheet and quickly became a favorite with Union troops. During the war years, the close relationship between poetry and song allowed poets access to new audiences; women and African American writers would be particular beneficiaries of this development.

The Civil War and the years immediately preceding it proved to be a time of extraordinary variety in the range of techniques African American poets employed in support of abolition. Born a free man in Ohio, Joshua McCarter

Simpson was initially self-educated but would go on to study for four years at Oberlin. In the song-poems that he wrote in the antebellum era, Simpson uses biting satire to deride white Americans for the contradictions inherent in their vision of the nation. Writing new lyrics for the anthem "America," Simpson angrily denounces slavery:

> My country, 'tis of thee,
> Dark land of Slavery,
>   In thee we groan.
> Long have our chains been worn –
> Long has our grief been borne –
> Our flesh has long been torn,
>   E'en from our bones.[3]

Published under the pseudonym "Ella" and often attributed to Sarah Mapps Douglass, the poem "The Mother and Her Captive Boy" offers an equally angry denunciation of slavery. Yet while Simpson relies on Americans' familiarity with the anthem "America" to emphasize the satire of his biting lyrics, Ella uses a high-literary stance to heighten the bitter tone of her poem: the poem's literary sophistication strengthens the moral authority of its speaker and demonstrates definitively that black people given the advantage of education could meet or exceed the literary achievements of their white contemporaries.

Douglass's contemporary Frances Harper used both popular and high-literary stances to argue for African American rights. Born in Maryland to free parents, Harper would become one of the most successful speakers on the abolitionist lecture circuit as well as one of the most widely published black writers of her day. In "To the Cleveland Union-Savers," written in February 1861, Harper angrily denounces the Cleveland Republicans who returned a female fugitive slave to Virginia on the eve of the war. Harper uses the word "Union" to indict the white politicians for their cowardice, insistently reiterating "Union" to heighten the poem's accusatory "you." The poem concludes:

> And your guilty, sin-cursed Union
> Shall be shaken to its base,
> Till ye learn that simple justice
> Is the right of every race.[4]

Harper would frequently perform her poems from the lecture platform, and it is easy to imagine this poem's simple but powerful meter and rhyme stirring a crowd to anger.

Even as black poets were calling for emancipation, white Southern poets were laying the foundations for the Southern homeland. In the period preceding the war, the growing tension between North and South could be measured by the swelling number of white-authored paeans to an Edenic South. Emphasizing the warmth of the climate, such paeans relied on the Romantic trope of the solitary speaker who contemplates an abundant natural world. In "I Sigh for the Land of the Cypress and the Pine," Samuel Henry Dickson rhapsodizes about his Southern homeland. The poem begins:

> I sigh for the land of the cypress and the pine,
> Where the jessamine blooms and the gay woodbine;
> Where the moss droops low from the green oak tree, –
> Oh that sun bright land is the land for me!   (WH, p. 32)

Relying on Romantic conventions to represent a harmonious natural world, Dickson erases both the violence of slavery – essential to the agricultural productivity of the South – and the rise of industrialization throughout the nation at midcentury. Southern Romanticism thus looks back with longing to a pastoral ideal that had already been lost, that had never really existed. One of the most prolific and patriotic of white Southern poets, William Gilmore Simms, added crucial layers of political argument to the trope of the Southern paradise. In "Song of the South," Simms represents the Southern natural world as a female beloved for whom the speaker is willing to fight and die:

> She feels no tremors when the Danger's nigh;
> But the fight over, and the victory won,
> How, with strange fondness, turns her loving eye,
> In tearful welcome, on each gallant son!   (WH, p. 36)

Well before the outbreak of hostilities, white Southern writers were already representing the Southern homeland as a beloved woman threatened by a hostile North; in wartime, this trope would serve as the foundation for the white Southern code of masculine heroism.

The violence of the ideological collision to come could thus be read in the distance between white paeans to the Southern homeland and the stances of African American abolitionist poetry. In the last few years before the outbreak of hostilities, white audiences in both North and South laughed uproariously at the racist humor of blackface minstrelsy, which served as a kind of release valve for the escalating tension. With its catchy tune and its mock-tragic lyrics, Dan Emmett's 1859 song "I Wish I Was in Dixie's Land" was a particular favorite with white audiences. In "Dixie," the high-literary stance of the solitary

Romantic speaker is seamlessly fused with the popular racist stances of black-face. The song gives voice to the homesickness of the black speaker, who has been exiled from his Southern home:

> I wish I was in de land ob cotton,
> Old times dar am not forgotten;
>> Look away! Look away! Look away! Dixie Land.
>>> (*WH*, p. 40)

Born in Ohio, Emmett was a white performer who made his name with Dan Bryant's Minstrels in New York. With their multilayered mix of antiblack racism and nostalgia for the lost Southern homeland, Emmett's lyrics suggest that he had his finger on the political pulse of the soon-to-be-divided nation. The song's chorus points implicitly toward the Southern regional pride that would soon be sending young white men off to enlist: "In Dixie Land, I'll took my stand, / To lib an die in Dixie" (*WH*, p. 40). Although popular with whites in both North and South on the eve of the war, "Dixie" was quickly taken up as an anthem by the newly founded Confederacy, prompting a proliferation of alternate versions. Elevating the language to standard white English, an Arkansas journalist named Albert Pike gave his version the lofty title "Southrons, Hear Your Country Call You!" He also changed the singular "I" of the chorus to the crucial collective "we" of white supporters of the Confederacy: "For Dixie's land we'll take our stand, / And live or die for Dixie!"[5]

Like Albert Pike, Julia Ward Howe sought to improve on the lyrics of a popular song when she wrote her "Battle Hymn of the Republic." In her memoirs Howe tells how, on a visit to Washington, D.C., she and some friends sang "John Brown's Body" with the soldiers who marched beside them. Urged by one of her companions to write better words for the tune, Howe wrote out her own version in the predawn hours the next morning. Although "John Brown's Body" was often understood by Northerners to be a song that celebrated the martyrdom of the radical abolitionist, music historians suggest that it was originally written as a mocking comparison of the great fame of the radical abolitionist and the relative anonymity of a Massachusetts soldier who shared the same common name, John Brown.[6] This account of the song's origins makes sense of its morbid humor: even as the song insists that the radical abolitionist has ascended to heaven ("His soul is marching on"), it also suggests that the foot soldier of the same common name who dies on the field of battle may receive no recognition ("John Brown's body lies a'mouldering in the grave").[7] In revising the lyrics, Howe removed any direct reference to the radical abolitionist or to decaying bodies; she retained, however, the crucial argument that God supports the Union. Such theological arguments would abound in both North and South throughout the war. By writing her lyrics to the tune of "John Brown's Body," Howe skillfully layers the genteel white female voice of her own authorship with the voice of abolitionists and the Union soldiers' collective voice to create a still broader collective of Union supporters. The poem comes to a dramatic climax in its fourth stanza, when this collective "we" is successfully forged: "As he died to make men holy, let us die to make men free" (*WH*, p. 75). With its central image of a vengeful God endorsing the American nation, Howe's "Battle Hymn" would continue to have enduring power into the twenty-first century.

As the example of Pike's and Howe's song-poems suggests, the early years of the war witnessed an outpouring of calls to arms from both North and South. Both Northern and Southern poets called on young men to join the armies so that the freedoms established by the American Revolution could be preserved; both sides called on mothers, wives, and sisters to sacrifice young men for the good of the nation. Relying on Romantic stances to represent the human connection to nature, poets from both North and South figured the battlefield as the site of sacrifice and regeneration. With its image of sacrificial bloodshed, Howe's "Battle Hymn" was one of the most successful Northern examples of this redemptive vision of a battlefield. In "Ethnogenesis" (1861), Henry Timrod, later called the poet laureate of the Confederacy, offers a high-literary vision of the Southern nation, founded on the richness of its agricultural heritage. "Ethnogenesis" argues that the South can rely on its benevolent climate and its abundant cotton crop – "THE SNOW OF SOUTHERN SUMMERS!" – in order to establish its supremacy (*WH*, p. 313). Moving adroitly between formal complexity and direct call to arms, the poem declares that Southern men are willing to fight for this great nation.

While Southern calls to arms frequently foregrounded the Southern homeland, Northern recruitment poems often focused on Lincoln, emphasizing his strong ties to the natural world of the West. In "Three Hundred Thousand More," James Sloan Gibbons imagines generations of young men answering Lincoln's call, in July 1862, for a new round of enlistments. Positioning Lincoln as a figure of biblical and patriarchal authority, the poem opens with the soldiers' collective cry: "We are coming, Father Abraham, three hundred thousand more" (*WH*, p. 92). In stanzas 2 and 3, newly recruited men spring up bodily from the land: "If you look all up our valleys where the growing harvests shine, / You may see our sturdy farmer boys fast forming into line" (*WH*, pp. 92–93). The redemptive work done on battlefields is likened to the redemptive work of farming; Gibbons imagines a bountiful American landscape offering up a generation of young men willing to die for the nation.

Although the call to arms became one of the dominant genres of the first years of the war, other patriotic stances also played a prominent role. Another important category was that of poems praising women's contributions. Popular in both North and South and authored by both men and women, such poems represented not only women's bravery in sending their sons and husbands off to war but also their work as nurses, seamstresses, and organizers of relief efforts. The anonymously published Union poem "Soldiers' Aid Societies" represents women as taking up the "weapons" of needle and scissors to make uniforms: the women gather "To fight for their native land, / With womanly weapons girt, / For dagger a needle, scissors for brand, / While they sing the song of the shirt" (WH, p. 67). Confederate poet Henry Timrod makes a similar argument in his 1863 poem "Two Armies," suggesting that the gentler sex "by a thousand peaceful deeds, / Supplies a struggling nation's needs" (WH, p. 324). Echoing William Gilmore Simms's antebellum "Song of the South," with its depiction of a woman who urges her beloved to defend her, Timrod suggests that white Southern women give "new courage" to Confederate soldiers (WH, p. 324).

Still another dominant category in the war's early years was that of poems in praise of the leadership of generals or presidents. Celebrated by both Southern and Northern writers for his piety and his military skill, Confederate general Stonewall Jackson was a particularly popular subject. In "Stonewall Jackson's Way," Confederate loyalist John Williamson Palmer imagines "Old Blue-Light" leading his men in prayer prior to battle. A wave of Northern-authored poems lionizing Lincoln began as early as 1862. While Gibbons's "Three Hundred Thousand More" offered a popularly inflected picture of Lincoln as the father of the nation, John James Piatt's "To Abraham Lincoln" used the long literary history of the sonnet to suggest that Lincoln's leadership during the war would earn both for him and for the nation a prominent position in world history. Still other poems memorialized specific battles. In the 1861 poem "Manassas," the Mississippi writer Catherine Warfield notes with pride the shock that Northerners felt when the first major conflict, called Manassas in the South and Bull Run in the North, resulted in an embarrassing and costly Union defeat. As Warfield's poem makes clear, both sides initially felt that the war would be quickly won; only as the war dragged on into its second and third years would the broader public begin to realize how long and costly the conflict might be.

As the war moved into its second and third years, poems mourning the deaths of soldiers became more prominent. First appearing in *Harper's Weekly* late in 1861, Ethelinda Beers's "The Picket-Guard" was one of the earliest and most successful examples of a poem about the death of an individual foot soldier. Contrasting the headlines from a newspaper – "All quiet along the Potomac" – with the story of a solitary picket who is shot as he walks his rounds, Beers's poem offers no consoling pieties about the soldier's martyrdom for the good of the nation: rather, the poem uses an understated description of his death to emphasize that although it may receive little mention in the newspaper, it will have a devastating impact on his family (*WH*, p. 65). In a similarly plainspoken fashion, Confederate officer S. A. Jonas gave voice in "Only a Soldier's Grave" to the deeply rooted fear of families in both North and South that soldiers who were buried in anonymous graves could not be properly mourned. Jonas's poem begins:

> Only a soldier's grave! Pass by,
> For soldiers, like other mortals, die.
> Parents he had – they are far away;
> No sister weeps o'er the soldier's clay;
> No brother comes, with a tearful eye:
> It's only a soldier's grave – pass by. (*WH*, p. 109)

The poem concludes with the tersely worded plea that graves must be marked so that loved ones can later find them.

While Beers and Jonas relied on spare language to acknowledge the individual soldier's death, still other writers relied on the more heightened emotions of sentimentalism, a dominant literary stance in mid-nineteenth-century America. Unsettling twenty-first-century expectations about gender roles in wartime, sentimental postures were adopted by both male and female writers: just as women wrote many strident calls to arms, so too did many male writers write poems that encouraged the tearful mourning of gentle boy-soldiers. Songs mourning the deaths of soldier-boys were frequently best sellers. Written by the Kentuckian Will Hays, "The Drummer Boy of Shiloh" was one of the most popular songs – in both North and South – of the Civil War era. As Alice Fahs argues in her study of the popular literature of the war, sentimental elegies reconfirmed the worth of the individual in the face of the vast numbers of the dead; at the same time, sentimental poems of mourning represented the fallen boy-soldier as a type of martyred innocence, often reaffirming the nationalist cause for which he died.[8] While "The Drummer Boy of Shiloh" ends by evoking the vast numbers killed in the war, the middle of the song offers mourners a redemptive vision of a young man who died because he loved his country: "'I've loved my country as my God; / To serve them both I've tried,' / He smiled, shook hands – death seized the boy / Who prayed before he died."[9]

Confederate writer Caroline Ball's "The Jacket of Gray" is another sentimental poem of mourning. The poem does not shy away from graphic depiction of death: "the life-blood ooze[s] out on the jacket of gray" (*WH*, p. 125). In its insistent repetition of the refrain "the jacket of gray," however, Ball reminds her readers of the worthy nation-building cause for which the young soldier died. The poem concludes:

> Then fold it up carefully, lay it aside,
> Tenderly touch it, look on it with pride;
> For dear it must be to our hearts evermore,
> The jacket of gray our loved soldier-boy wore.
>
> (*WH*, p. 125)

Sentimental poems like "The Drummer Boy" and "The Jacket of Gray" offered models for the expression of intense grief even as they also suggested that mourners might achieve emotional closure by remembering the nation for which their loved one died.

In his 1864 poem "In the Wilderness," Northerner George Boker responded more ambivalently to sentimental conventions. "In the Wilderness" describes a badly wounded soldier who crawls across a battlefield, gathering violets:

> So, lost in thought, scarce conscious of the deed,
>   Culling the violets, here and there he crept
> Slowly – ah! Slowly, – for his wound would bleed;
>   And the sweet flowers themselves half smiled, half wept,
>   To be thus gathered in
>   By hands so pale and thin.   (*WH*, p. 143)

Boker reminds his readers of the youthful innocence of the soldier by imagining his search for the flowers; yet the violet gathering also has a macabre undercurrent, as the flowers are described as "dripping" and weeping. Moreover, the reiterated word "violets" suggests its near homophone "violence"; the "culling" of the "violets" points toward the "culling" of men in battle. The poem ends ambiguously: the wounded boy is carried from the field, but it is not clear whether he will live or die. Boker thus draws on the conventions of sentimentality but lets the image of the bleeding soldier-boy hover without narrative or ideological resolution. This refusal to fix the meaning of the image reflects the relatively late date of the poem's composition and implicitly registers Boker's horror at the staggering loss of life in the Battle of the Wilderness, which marked the start of Grant's bloody Overland Campaign.

The middle years of the war saw an increase not only in poems mourning individual soldiers but also in poems recognizing the achievements of black soldiers in the Union army. Black men were not authorized to serve in combat positions in the Union army until January 1863; while many Northern whites were initially skeptical of Lincoln's decision to allow black men to fight, by the summer of 1863, the tide of white opinion had begun to shift, thanks to reports of the bravery of the Massachusetts Fifty-Fourth, among other examples of black courage under fire. Published in May 1863 in a pamphlet designed to encourage black men to enlist, George Boker's "The Black Regiment" argues that black men are well suited to the task of fighting for the Union because they have a vested interest in the word "freedom":

> "Freedom!" their battle-cry –
> "Freedom! or leave to die!"
> Ah! And they meant the word,
> Not as with us 'tis heard,
> Not a mere party shout   (*WH*, p. 113)

Boker uses a long, narrow column of short lines down the page, the familiar meter of Tennyson's "Charge of the Light Brigade," and an abundance of trochees to evoke the sound of drums and the maneuvering of columns of troops in combat. The poem ends with a plea to white soldiers to recognize black men as their comrades-in-arms: "Never, in field or tent, / Scorn the Black Regiment" (*WH*, p. 114).

More ambivalent in its recognition of black soldiers' achievements, Charles Graham Halpine's "Sambo's Right to Be Kilt" offers a working-class Irish speaker, Private Miles O'Reilly, who observes satirically that he would be happy to let "Sambo" be "murthered" in his stead. Writing in Irish American dialect, Halpine here represents the often virulent antiblack racism of the working-class Irish immigrants who were conscripted into the army. While Halpine's speaker perpetuates racist stereotypes, the poem also expresses a grudging admiration for the black soldiers' courage, noting that Sambo's "eye runs straight on the barrel-sights / From undher his thatch of wool" (*WH*, p. 139). Frances Harper offers an angry rebuttal to Halpine in her "Lines to Miles O'Reiley." Dropping Halpine's satirical stance and his use of dialect, Harper uses a collective "we" and standard English to emphasize the dignity and bravery of black soldiers.

Following Appomattox and Lincoln's assassination, the nationalist impulses that shaped the poetry of the North and South reached a climax of ideological intensity: in the South, that crescendo took the form of poems celebrating the Lost Cause of the Confederacy; in the North, that crescendo became an outpouring of elegies for the president. George Moses Horton was just one of many African American poets who wrote a Lincoln elegy. Many Northern writers turned to the sonnet form for this task, inscribing Lincoln's name into the long literary history of the form. William Cullen Bryant's April 1865 sonnet opens by reminding Northerners that Lincoln had advocated for reconciliation with the South:

> Oh, slow to smite and swift to spare,
> Gentle and merciful and just!
> Who, in the fear of God, didst bear
> The sword of power, a nation's trust!   (WH, p. 171)

In the sonnet "The Martyr," however, Christopher Pearse Cranch argues that the spilling of Lincoln's blood eliminates the possibility of the nation reconciling peacefully:

> Rise, then, O countrymen!
> Scatter these marsh-light hopes of union won
> Through pardoning clemency. Strike, strike again!
> Draw closer round the foe a girdling flame!
> We are stabbed whene'er we spare. Strike, in God's name!   (WH, p. 173)

Calls for vengeance from the North were met with poems praising the once and future glory of the Confederacy, although calls for the South to rise again were necessarily somewhat muted in published media. Contemplating his ruined plantation, William Gilmore Simms wrote a lament that expresses both the despair and the resolve of white Southerners in the aftermath of the war:

> Tender and True, my Dixie Land!
> Though faint and few, my Dixie Land!
> We keep the Faith our Fathers knew,
> For which they bled, in which we grew,
> And at their graves our vows renew, –
> For nought is lost of truth, where Faith keeps true,
> Oh! Dixie Land! O! Dixie Land.   (WH, p. 189)

Not surprisingly, Simms opted to publish the piece anonymously in January 1867. In the summer of 1867, a twenty-five-year-old Confederate veteran named Sidney Lanier wrote a paean to the lost Southern homeland, figuring it as a beloved maternal body: in the poem's grotesque exaggeration of high Romantic imagery, Lanier registers the shame felt by Southerners at the devastation of the South, a devastation the poem implicitly represents as a rape:

> But, Mother Earth
> Of giant birth,
> Thy mother milk comes curdled thick with woe.
> Friends, blood is in the milk whereby we grow,
> And life is heavy and death is marvelous slow.   (*WH*, p. 189)

Lanier's postwar lament would not appear in print until 1916.

If the ideology of the Lost Cause was dominant among white Southerners, it was nonetheless still possible to find dissenting Southern voices – usually either white Southerners who had earlier fled the South or formerly enslaved African Americans, many of whom would also head North at the war's end. Born into a wealthy slaveholding family in Kentucky, Sarah Piatt moved to Washington, D.C., with her husband in June 1861. A keen observer of relationships in the Victorian domestic circle, Piatt was particularly successful at placing her work with prestigious Northern presses and magazines. Moreover, as Paula Bennett notes, Piatt tended to group poems about motherhood, children, and domestic themes in her published collections, reserving her explicitly political poems for the more ephemeral media of magazines and newspapers.[10] Only when we read the full spectrum of Piatt's work does her subversive use of irony become apparent.

In "Hearing the Battle, July 21, 1861," Piatt imagines a husband and wife sitting in their garden, listening to noises from a nearby battlefield and trying to imagine "the worlds unknown" of combat (*PB*, p. 4). As the poem concludes, the woman urges her beloved to join the conflict: "I shall never know / How the hearts in the land are breaking, / My dearest, unless you go." On its surface, the poem is a fairly conventional, if somewhat detached, call to arms. On closer examination, however, the poem underlines not only the detachment of the husband and wife from the suffering soldiers but also the detachment of the wife from her husband and the detachment of the wife from the sufferings of other women. The contrast between the tranquil Victorian garden and the gory scene of the nearby battle implicates both husband and wife in the hypocrisy of their genteel disengagement – a disengagement that is in striking contrast to the "passion and moan" on the battlefield (*PB*, p. 4). In "Mock Diamonds," first published in 1872, Piatt again took aim at the gender roles of the Civil War era, this time offering a withering critique of the Southern code of masculine heroism, a code sustained through the complex rituals of romantic desire between white Southern men and women.

Like his contemporary and fellow Southerner Sarah Piatt, during the postwar era, the black poet George Moses Horton offered an incisive critique of the Confederate ideology of the lost Southern homeland. Born into slavery in North Carolina at the very end of the eighteenth century, Horton published two collections of poetry while still enslaved and a third immediately following the war's end. As a young man, Horton taught himself first to read and then to write; he also persuaded his master to let him hire his own time so that he could work as a jack-of-all-trades on the University of North Carolina campus. He was particularly successful at writing love poems made to order for young white male students.[11] When the Union army arrived in North Carolina in April 1865, Horton – by now in his late sixties – finally gained freedom. For three months he traveled with the Ninth Michigan Cavalry, once again supporting himself by writing love poems made to order, this time for young white Northern soldiers for their wives and sweethearts back home. During this time, Horton also completed a third collection of poems; some time later, he moved north to Philadelphia. In "The Southern Refugee," Horton relies on a conventional Romantic stance to express the longings of many displaced Southerners – both black and white – in the aftermath of the war. On its surface, the poem reads like a fairly conventional Romantic meditation on the speaker's imminent departure from his beloved home:

> What sudden ill the world await,
> From my dear residence I roam;
> I must deplore the bitter fate,
> To straggle from my native home. (BB, p. 124)

Just beneath that surface, however, lies Horton's subtle critique of the Confederate ideology of the Southern paradise. Noting that "Eden's garden" has been "left in gloom," Horton does not make clear whether it is the violence of slavery or the violence of war that has spoiled Eden. And while the speaker's race is never made explicit, the poem's final stanza argues unequivocally that the speaker has come to terms with the necessity of his departure from the South:

> I trust I soon shall dry the tear
> And leave forever hence to roam,
> Far from a residence so dear,
> The place of beauty – my native home. (BB, p. 124)

Horton here offers a pointed rejoinder to the nostalgia of the blackface speaker in Dan Emmett's "Dixie" and also to William Gilmore Simms's lament for a fallen "Dixie Land." For a freed slave, there can be no indulgence in a utopian nostalgia for a paradise that never was.

In tracing trends in the poetry of the Civil War era, this chapter has thus far focused on poets whose pieces were well known in their time but who have received little attention since the start of the twentieth century. There are, however, three writers whose position is firmly established in the canon of nineteenth-century American literature and who offer important interventions into Civil War poetry. Walt Whitman's contribution to Civil War literature was recognized relatively early in twentieth-century criticism; only in recent decades, however, have scholars begun to attend to the Civil War poetry of Emily Dickinson and Herman Melville. So powerful was the influence of New Criticism that Dickinson was for decades seen as a poet who had little interest in contemporary events in spite of the fact that dozens of her poems focus on military tropes. Dickinson's sex no doubt also encouraged scholars to neglect the war-related arguments in her poetry. It is otherwise difficult to imagine how her extraordinary productivity during the war years could have been overlooked: Franklin's dating of Dickinson's manuscripts suggests that she wrote more than 900 poems between 1861 and 1865.

In the case of Melville's *Battle-Pieces*, the volume's improbable mix of conventional nationalism, old-fashioned Romanticism, regular meter and rhyme, densely layered allusions, and spare imagistic compression baffled twentieth-century critics almost to the same extent that it baffled nineteenth-century reviewers. In a damning *Atlantic Monthly* review in February 1867, William Dean Howells accused Melville of emotional "remoteness," of representing only his own inner "phantasms," rather than representing the war itself.[12] For many twentieth-century critics, Melville's poetry was too "remote" from modernist sensibilities in its strong attachment not only to rhyme and meter but also to nationalist ideologies. Twentieth-century scholars who admired the radicalism and innovation of Melville's novels often found little to admire in the more conservative political and aesthetic commitments of *Battle-Pieces*.

If we reposition Whitman, Dickinson, and Melville in the context of the Civil War poetry written by their contemporaries, however, this approach illuminates the extent to which all three responded to their peers. Such a strategy underlines the extraordinary range of aesthetic and political commitments in the poetry of writers now largely forgotten; it also underlines the extent to which innovations in the work of Whitman, Dickinson, and Melville have their sources in the rich and varied field of nineteenth-century poetry.

Whitman's position as the leading poet of the Civil War is well deserved not only because of the importance of *Drum-Taps* but also because he is one of the most important theorists of Civil War writing. As he made plain in his autobiographical poem "The Wound Dresser," his extensive service as an aid in the military hospitals gave him a wealth of material to reflect on. Drawn from Whitman's notebooks, *Memoranda during the War* (1875) offers incisive commentary not only on how the war changed American society but also on how it changed American writing. "The real war," Whitman famously suggests, "will never get into books."[13] As Timothy Sweet argues, Whitman addressed explicitly the crisis of representation that the war presented to American writers, as they grappled with the challenges of responding to the war's staggering scale of suffering and death. Sweet suggests that Whitman's most perceptive discussion of that crisis took place in the prose reflections of *Memoranda*; in *Drum-Taps* and its sequel, by contrast, Whitman relied on the rhetorical power of the pastoral to redeem the war's bloodshed and to reunite the divided nation.[14] Whitman's war poetry was admired by twentieth-century critics both for its innovative free verse form and for its plainspoken language. Yet if we read Whitman in relation to the dominant categories of Civil War–era poetry, his affinities with his contemporaries come clearly into focus. Whitman responded to four dominant trends in Civil War–era poetry, including the call to arms, the focus on landscapes, the soldier elegy, and the Lincoln elegy.

In editing *Drum-Taps* and its sequel, Whitman chose to order the poems in a way that re-created the war's chronology. In "Eighteen Sixty-One" and "Beat! Beat! Drums!" he reminds readers of the momentum of the war's first year, as young men joined the Union army and whole communities were swept up in the excitement. Like James Sloan Gibbons's "Three Hundred Thousand More," Whitman's "Eighteen Sixty-One" imagines male bodies springing from a generative landscape. With its dramatic imperatives and its driving rhythm, "Beat! Beat! Drums!" moves even closer to the genre of the call to arms (*WH*, p. 232). Yet both "Eighteen Sixty-One" and "Beat! Beat! Drums!" depart from the conventional call to arms in significant ways. Tellingly, neither poem uses the collective "we" for soldiers or Union supporters. Thus, rather than forging a collective "we," both of these poems instead describe the nationalist fervor that was in the air when calls to arms abounded.

Whitman's commitment to representing the American landscape is evident in the majority of his Civil War poems. In "Bivouac on a Mountain Side," he offers a description of setting up camp for the night. The poem's language is relatively detached and spare, reflecting perhaps contemporary photographic images or journalistic descriptions of military camps. In representing the relationship between the valley, the campfires, and the stars above – "far out of reach, studded, breaking out" – the poem clearly responds to Romanticism, all the while propelling that tradition forward into a new, more ambivalent poetics (*WH*, p. 234). The speaker neither endorses nor critiques the military undertaking; nor does the poem take a stand on whether or not nature endorses the war. The poem thus leaves the reader to decide how to understand the relationship between nature and human beings. It is easy to imagine why twentieth-century scholars admired the innovation of poems like this one.

It is also easy to imagine the pleasures that nineteenth-century readers took in Whitman's poems. In "Come Up from the Fields Father," Whitman draws a contrast between the plenitude of the family farm – "all calm, all vital and beautiful" – and the emotional devastation suffered by the mother when she intuits her only son's impending death in the war (*WH*, p. 235). The words of comfort the daughter offers gently echo the language of sentimental stances: "Grieve not so, dear mother." In offering an extended representation of the family's sorrow, the poem tips slightly toward the sentimental stances of Ball's "Jacket of Gray." Yet in its acknowledgment of the mother's profound depression – "O that she might withdraw unnoticed, silent from life escape and withdraw" – and in its refusal to offer its readers any solace for the mother's suffering, the poem aligns itself far more strongly with Ethelinda Beers's "The Picket-Guard," a poem that refuses to use nationalist pieties to justify wartime deaths (*WH*, p. 235). In "Come Up from the Fields," all the prosperous abundance of "teeming and wealthy Ohio" can offer little comfort to a grieving mother. Here Whitman points toward the limits of Romanticism as a means of responding to war: the natural and human worlds are painfully out of joint.

In still other poems, however, Whitman offers a redemptive vision of the relationship between human-authored warfare and the natural world. In "Pensive on her Dead Gazing," a maternal figure enjoins the land to absorb the blood shed by soldiers that new life may spring forth: "My dead absorb or South or North – my young men's bodies absorb, and their precious precious blood" (*WH*, p. 248). In the lush imagery of the Lincoln elegies, Whitman again emphasizes the redemptive powers of nature. In "When Lilacs Last in the Dooryard Bloom'd," the bird's song of grief and the painful abundance of spring flowers become a source of comfort for the grieving speaker; a speaker who initially mourns his painful disconnection from spring's plenitude is eventually able to accept that plenitude as consolation.

Like Whitman, Dickinson made Romantic stances central to her war poetry. The two dominant trends that Dickinson responded to from the spectrum of Civil War poetry are representations of battlefield landscapes and soldier elegies. Moreover, Dickinson also offered an oblique but powerful reflection on race relations in the Union army. If the first generation of Dickinson scholars overlooked her interest in the war, a second group of scholars has tended to emphasize Dickinson's radical skepticism in relation to wartime ideologies. Yet because Dickinson chose not to publish via conventional print means, she had the freedom to take a range of contradictory stances in her poems. One of the most surprising results of resituating Dickinson's war poetry in the context of work by her contemporaries is that we can see that Dickinson sometimes endorsed conventional patriotic arguments about soldiers' deaths. Like Whitman, then, Dickinson employed both skeptical and patriotic stances.

Dickinson's battlefield landscapes are among her most remarkable war poems. On the surface, these are genteel painterly representations of New England vistas; just beneath this surface, however, the poems grapple with the challenges of representing modern warfare with the imagistic repertoire of Romanticism. In "The name – of it – is 'Autumn' –" (F, no. 465), Dickinson offers a description of an autumnal landscape, tracing the movement of scarlet leaves. Already in its second line, however, the poem takes a macabre turn: the leaves are the color of "blood," and they move in patterns that resemble "an artery" and "a vein."[15] Dickinson here echoes the imagery of Howe's "Battle Hymn of the Republic" by describing a blood-drenched field, but while the dead bodies in Howe's poem are assigned a redemptive meaning ("let us die to make men free"), no particular meaning is ascribed to the carnage in Dickinson's poem. By the second stanza, the patterns of leaves have become "globules," a metaphor that makes explicit that it is a battlefield, not an autumn field, that the poem represents; the collision of the medical with the Romantic diction signals the inadequacy of Romanticism for representing war. Like George Boker's "In the Wilderness," Dickinson's poem swerves from the picturesque into the grotesque. In "Hearing the Battle," Sarah Piatt contrasts the genteel Victorian garden with a scene of nearby carnage in order to underline ironically middle-class women's separation from the field of combat. In analogous fashion, Dickinson here uses a genteel painterly stance as a veneer of irony that only half-conceals a key argument in the poem: ultimately Dickinson's poem suggests that women writers can and should respond to war.

In another of her landscape poems, however, Dickinson seems to incline toward patriotic pieties in assigning meaning to soldiers' deaths. "They dropped like Flakes –" (F, no. 545) uses a list of picturesque nature images to describe soldiers dying:

> They dropped like Flakes –
> They dropped like Stars –
> Like Petals from a Rose –

The pairing of nature images with falling bodies is somewhat jarring, but the total effect is nonetheless one of distancing aestheticization. The second stanza takes up the question of how the vast numbers of dead soldiers will be identified. So great are the numbers of the fallen, the speaker declares, that "No eye could find the place –." The poem concludes, however, with the insistent declaration that "God can summon every face / On his Repealless – List," a claim that seems to support the widely held belief that dying in battle was a sure path toward God.

In "When I was small, a Woman died –" (F, no. 518), Dickinson meditates on the reunion in heaven of a long-deceased mother and her son, who has recently died in battle. Dickinson here strongly echoes the sentimental focus on mothers' mourning. Moreover, the poem's conclusion again argues that dying in battle is a form of Christian martyrdom. The speaker declares:

> I'm confident that Bravoes –
> Perpetual break abroad
> For Braveries, remote as this
> In yonder Maryland –

Dickinson echoes this same argument in another poem composed at about the same time (spring 1863): "It may be – a Renown to live – / I think the Men who die –, / Those unsustained – Saviors – / Present Divinity –" (F, no. 524). The number of poems in which Dickinson responds to the deaths of soldiers makes clear that she was deeply engaged in responding to the war; these poems also suggest that she sometimes turned to conventional patriotic ideologies in trying to make sense of those deaths.

In still other poems that respond to soldiers' experience, however, Dickinson takes more radical positions. For example, it is possible to read "My Life had stood – a Loaded Gun –" (F, no. 764) as a meditation on the new identity a young man gains in joining the military and the adrenaline rush of opening fire on the enemy:

> And do I smile, such cordial light
> Opon the Valley glow –
> It is as a Vesuvian face
> Had let it's pleasure through –.

Moreover, in "Color – Caste – Denomination –" (F, no. 836), Dickinson seems to offer a response to the tensions that result from racial mixing in the Union army. Probably written in early 1864 – several months after black soldiers had begun to receive positive newspaper coverage for their courage under fire – "Color – Caste – Denomination –" argues that death erases all marks of racial and class difference: "Death's diviner Classifying / Does not know they are –." When Colonel Robert Gould Shaw, the white leader of the all-black Massachusetts Fifty-Fourth regiment, was buried in a mass grave with his fallen soldiers behind enemy lines in July 1863, the Confederate army's refusal to return his body was widely reported in Northern newspapers, including the *Springfield Republican*. It is possible that the circumstances of Shaw's burial may have shaped Dickinson's arguments in "Color – Caste – Denomination –"; read in relation to newspaper accounts of the military service of African Americans and their treatment in the Union army, the poem's critique of racial and class categories underlines that Dickinson was intensively engaged in responding to wartime ideologies.

Like Dickinson, Herman Melville alternates in *Battle-Pieces* between articulating skepticism about wartime policies and turning toward the consolations that nationalist ideologies offer. Torn between his desire to critique the ideologies that fueled the war and to offer comfort to a grieving nation, Melville experiments with many different stances in *Battle-Pieces*: the diverse collection includes poems that lament the carnage of war, high-literary stances that celebrate military heroism, echoes of popular patriotic songs that both endorse and critique the war's violence, and a prose supplement that exhorts Northern readers to reconcile with the South. Organized chronologically in relation to the war's events, the collection does not begin with conventional nationalist stances and move toward more radical or skeptical ones; rather, it oscillates between these positions throughout.

In "The Portent," Melville responds to popular Civil War literature on multiple levels. Working with incantatory repetition of names, he echoes poems like Gibbons's "Three Hundred Thousand More" and Palmer's "Stonewall Jackson's Way," each of which uses a hero's name to celebrate the power of an army. But while Gibbons and Palmer repeat Lincoln's and Jackson's names to urge men to join the army and to urge those armies on to valor, Melville's repetition of John Brown's name works to foreground its divisive power. The poem begins with a description of Brown's body after his execution: *"Hanging from the beam, / Slowly swaying (such the law)."*[16] As Melville's poem makes clear, the swinging of Brown's body symbolizes the dividing of the nation: Brown's name would become a rallying cry for both armies, as Southerners rebelled against Northern interference, and as Northerners – many of whom were ambivalent about abolition – joined in the collective singing of "John Brown's Body." While the popular song insists on a narrative of Christian martyrdom for the abolitionist ("His soul is marching on"), Melville's poem refuses the consolations of that nationalist paradigm, insisting instead that Brown's ultimate fate – like the fate of the nation – cannot be known: *"Hidden in the cap / Is the anguish none can draw; / So your future veils its face, / Shenandoah!"* (BP, p. 11).

In "The Cumberland," Melville again works with incantatory repetition of names, this time repeating a frigate's name to commemorate its defeat. The poem opens with a meditation on the power of names:

> Some names there are of telling sound,
> Whose voweled syllables free
> Are pledge that they shall ever live renowned.   (BP, p. 53)

Melville here describes how an act of commemoration – the reiteration of a name – can recall the bravery of men and the glory of a sunken ship, allowing both to live on in an eternal literary present. Yet in this poem, as in most *Battle-Pieces* poems, Melville carefully sidesteps the stance of the call to arms, avoids use of the collective "we," and refuses to describe the events of the battle in the present tense. The future tense he uses here is the future of commemoration, and although the poem draws from a celebratory nationalist rhetoric, what is being commemorated is not the glory of the nation as a whole but rather the glory of the men and the ship in one specific battle.

In "Donelson," Melville examines the ways that journalism and, by implication, poetry work to fan the flames of nationalism in wartime. The frame story is set in a Northern town where telegraphed bulletins about a battle are being read aloud outside a newspaper office; the poem moves back and forth between the scene of combat being described by the journalists and the town square, where the crowd reacts to each day's developments. Following the announcement of a successful round of fighting, a subsequent bulletin revises the initial impression that the battle is nearly over, making explicit the possibility for error in delivery of the news: *"(Our own reporter a dispatch compiles, / As best he may from varied sources.)"* (BP, p. 41). The couplet suggests that journalism, like poetry, can only approximate the events of the war: it cannot hope to represent them fully or accurately. When the final announcement of victory is read, there is a collective celebratory cheer from the listeners, who are constituted in the poem as a unified bloc of Union supporters. The poem concludes, however, by describing the list of the dead posted the next day, a list that will be read silently by "wife and maid"; they will weep in response to it, enduring a private suffering that will divide them from the joyous crowd of the night before (*BP*, p. 52).

While "Donelson" responds to the medium of journalism, suggesting that it will both unite and ultimately divide Northerners, "Shiloh" responds to the genre of popular song, offering a critique of the interlinked ideologies of Christian martyrdom and nationalism. Echoing the strong cultural interest in landscape depiction, "Shiloh" opens with a panoramic view of the battlefield long after combat has ended. The poem then goes on to acknowledge the "parting groan" and "natural prayer" of the dying – echoing the words of "The Drummer Boy of Shiloh," who "prayed before he died" (*BP*, p. 62).[17] At the same time, however, Melville quietly unravels the consolations of the Drummer Boy, who declares, "I've loved my country as my God." Melville's "Shiloh" argues that "fame" and "country" become irrelevant to the dying: "(What like a bullet can undeceive!)." Appearing four times in the poem, the word "Shiloh" acoustically urges the living to hush as they contemplate battlefields where men died.

Melville makes this injunction to silence explicit in "An Uninscribed Monument on One of the Battle-Fields of the Wilderness," a poem that echoes S. A. Jonas's "Only a Soldier's Grave" in its concern with unmarked graves. While Jonas worries that unmarked graves will mean unmourned soldiers, Melville insists on an uninscribed monument for an unnamed soldier, suggesting that no inscriptions and no graveside speeches can be adequate for the task of mourning the vast numbers of dead. S. A. Jonas's poem offers three stanzas of lament for anonymous graves followed by a closing stanza that enjoins the living to mark each grave; the poem thus achieves ideological closure by calling on the living to commemorate the dead both through gravestone inscriptions and – implicitly – through poems of mourning. Melville, however, talks back to the custom of graveside speechmaking and the poetry of mourning. Ultimately "An Uninscribed Monument" suggests that no text or speech can reunite a grieving nation in the aftermath of war; indeed, the poem suggests that silent and solitary mourning is the only possible response to war. The poem's speaker declares: "Thou who beholdest, if thy thought, / Not narrowed down to personal cheer, / Take in the import of the quiet here – / The after-quiet – the calm full fraught; / Thou too wilt silent stand – / Silent as I, and lonesome as the land" (*BP*, p. 173).

Battle-Pieces reveals Melville's keen awareness of the ethical challenges that a writer faces in trying to respond to a long and costly civil war. In the wartime writings of Whitman, Dickinson, and Melville, a reader finds perhaps a more fully articulated understanding of the crisis of representation posed by the war; yet in poems by Joshua McCarter Simpson, Ethelinda Beers, George Boker, and Sidney Lanier, among many others, a reader also finds an awareness that the Civil War must necessarily change the way writers respond to war's violence and the ways that they define the nation. Sarah Piatt describes overhearing the Battle of Bull Run as overhearing "the first fierce words of war" (*PB*, p. 2). What Piatt's phrase makes clear is that these writers understood their poetry as a means of intervening in the war's events. "To fight aloud, is very brave –" (F, no. 138), Dickinson writes in 1860, offering a similar claim. As the proliferation of voices and stances in Civil War–era poetry makes plain, poetry worked both to build and to divide constituencies among different audience communities. The poetry of the American Civil War shaped the rise and fall of the Confederacy, the successful fight for abolition, and the constitution of the Union as a political and military force. In the aftermath of the war, poetry would be one of the central discursive sites for grieving the war's losses; it would also be one of the central discursive sites for theorizing the reuniting of North and South. Yet the intensity and diversity of poetic voices the war produced makes clear how very difficult that work of reunification would prove to be. In American poetry, the challenges of political reunification would be signaled in part by the postbellum turn away from nationalist paeans and formal regularity, toward realism, fragmentation, and imagistic compression – the hallmarks of a modernist poetics. While these are features we recognize as characteristic in the work of Whitman, Dickinson, and Melville, they also have their roots in the extraordinarily rich body of work produced by the broader spectrum of Civil War poets.

Notes

1. Edmund Wilson, *Patriotic Gore: Studies in the Literature of the American Civil War* (New York: Oxford University Press, 1962), p. 479.

2. For a fuller discussion of this body of work, see Faith Barrett, *To Fight Aloud Is Very Brave: American Poetry and the Civil War* (Amherst: University of Massachusetts Press, 2012).

3. Faith Barrett and Cristanne Miller (eds.), *Words for the Hour: A New Anthology of American Civil War Poetry* (Amherst: University of Massachusetts Press, 2005), p. 27. Hereafter all citations from *Words for the Hour* will be quoted in the text as *WH*.

4. Frances Ellen Watkins Harper, *A Brighter Coming Day: A Frances Ellen Watkins Harper Reader*, ed. Frances Smith Foster (New York: Feminist Press at the City University of New York, 1990), p. 94.

5. William Shepperson (ed.), *War Songs of the South* (Richmond, Va.: West and Johnston, 1862), pp. 17–19.

6. See C. A. Browne, *The Story of Our National Ballads* (New York: Thomas Y. Crowell, 1919), pp. 181–99, and also Boyd Sutler, "John Brown's Body," *Civil War History* 4 (1958), pp. 251–61.

7. "John Brown's Body" (Boston: Oliver Ditson, 1861), n.p.

8. See Alice Fahs, *The Imagined Civil War: Popular Literature of the North and South, 1861–1865* (Chapel Hill: University of North Carolina Press, 2001), esp. chapter 3, "The Sentimental Soldier."

9. Will S. Hays, "The Drummer Boy of Shiloh" (Louisville: D. P. Faulds, 1863), n.p.

10. See Paula Bennett's introduction to Sarah Morgan Bryan Piatt, *Palace-Burner: The Selected Poetry of Sarah Piatt*, ed. Paula Bernat Bennett (Carbondale: University of Illinois Press, 2001). This volume will be cited subsequently in the text as *PB*.

11. For a detailed account of Horton's life and writing career, see Joan Sherman's "Introduction," in George Moses Horton, *The Black Bard of North Carolina: George Moses Horton and His Poetry*, ed. Joan Sherman (Chapel Hill: University of North Carolina Press, 1997). References to Horton's work are cited from this edition and are hereafter cited in the text with the abbreviation *BB*.

12. William Dean Howells, *Atlantic Monthly* 29 (February 1867), p. 252.

13. Walt Whitman, *Prose Works*, ed. Floyd Stovall (New York: New York University Press, 1963), vol. 1, p. 115.

14. See Timothy Sweet's incisive analysis in *Traces of War: Poetry, Photography, and the Crisis of the Union* (Baltimore, Md.: Johns Hopkins University Press, 1990).

15. Dickinson's poems are cited from R. W. Franklin (ed.), *The Poems of Emily Dickinson* (Cambridge: Belknap Press of Harvard University Press, 1998). These are hereafter cited in the text using the initial "F" and the numbers assigned by Franklin to the poems (not page numbers).

16. Herman Melville, *Battle-Pieces and Aspects of the War* (New York: Harper, 1866), p. 11. This volume will be cited subsequently in the text as *BP*.

17. Hays, "The Drummer Boy of Shiloh," n.p.

Chapter 15

Walt Whitman's Invention of a Democratic Poetry

ED FOLSOM

The place to begin with Walt Whitman is not at the beginning, with the poet's origins and the origins of his work, but rather at the ongoing end, with the remarkable response to his poetry that started during the poet's own lifetime and has grown ever since. Whitman devoted his career to defining and enacting a new poetics that would be distinctive to the American nation and its democratic aspirations. His genius was to invent a new kind of poetic address – a conversation with his reader, whom he named "you" – and to cast that "you" into the future, years or centuries beyond the poet's death, so that his poetry seems always to be intimately yet publicly addressing us as a voice from our past, speaking from his present to his future, our present. The poetry thus enacts, in an unsettlingly self-conscious way, a conversation literally across time, in which dead poet and living reader – or living poet and unborn reader – find union in the here and now of Whitman's poem, which has a palpable existence across time, allowing for the living to communicate with the dead (or the dead with the living) through the medium of poetry.

Not only has Whitman's poetic invention worked to form a vast and loyal community of readers over the many decades since its appearance, it has generated a remarkable ongoing conversation with what he called the "poets to come":

> I am a man who, sauntering along without fully stopping, turns a casual look
> upon you and then averts his face,
> Leaving it to you to prove and define it,
> Expecting the main things from you.[1]

His impact has been such that virtually all American poets after him have in some way had to engage him – to build on his ideas of what an American poet should be, or to argue against those ideas and forge a different direction. Often their responses to him involve a direct address right back to Whitman, reversing his "I" and "you": "I make a pact with you, Walt Whitman," wrote Ezra Pound in "A Pact" (1913), noting that "It was you that broke the new wood, / Now is a time for carving."[2] Twentieth- and twenty-first-century poets have carved the wood Whitman broke into a dizzying variety of shapes, but, as Pound grudgingly admitted, it was usually Whitman's original material with which these poets to come would work. His fluid address to his reader, to the promiscuous "you" that he invented (teasing out all the implications of how the second-person pronoun in English signals at once the intimacy of a lover and the distance of a stranger, how it signals at once only you, a "simple separate person," and also you, the "en masse," the world of potentially intimate strangers who always hover around us), would entice generations of poets – from Hart Crane to Langston Hughes, from Muriel Rukeyser to Robert Creeley, from William Carlos Williams to Allen Ginsberg to June Jordan, and from Federico García Lorca to Jorge Luis Borges to Cesare Pavese to Czeslaw Milosz – to respond, to talk back to him, and his influence would extend far and wide, across race and social class and ethnicity and poetic style and nationality.[3]

Whitman's influence has extended well beyond poetry. He has been examined seriously by political scientists and cultural theorists as a philosopher of democracy,[4] and he has been a central figure in gay history and queer studies, often credited with inventing the language of homosexual love.[5] His work has been set to music more often than that of any other American poet: more than five hundred composers – from Ralph Vaughan Williams to Paul Hindemith to Ned Rorem – have composed pieces using his work.[6] He has been the subject of and inspiration for innumerable songs over the past century, by songwriters from Woody Guthrie to Tom Russell to Bibi Tanga. He has been the subject of, and inspiration for, paintings and sculptures by American artists from Thomas Eakins to Ben Shahn; he has inspired the architects Louis Sullivan and Frank Lloyd Wright, photographers like Alfred Stieglitz and Edward Weston, and filmmakers from D. W. Griffith to Jim Jarmusch.[7] More than any other American poet, his presence has continued to radiate throughout the culture, and he reemerges in advertisements (most recently a television commercial for Levi's jeans that showed images of a decayed but still resilient America as the wax-cylinder recording of Whitman reading his 1888 poem "America" served as the voice-over), in politics (from Theodore Roosevelt's equating of Whitman's urban poetics to Dante's *Inferno*, to John Kennedy's decision to have Edward G. Robinson read a section of "Thou Mother with Thy Equal Brood" as the introduction to his 1960 acceptance speech at the Democratic

National Convention, and to Bill Clinton's gift of *Leaves of Grass* to his former intern, Monica Lewinsky), and in social commentary (which tends to selectively cite Whitman in support of both progressive and conservative causes, emphasizing either his radical boundary-breaking passages or his passages celebrating America as a nation destined for greatness).[8]

Such an outpouring of response from across the literary, artistic, cultural, and even political spectrum did not happen by accident. Even though his ideas and schemes could easily have failed, Whitman nonetheless set out to construct a poetry and a poetic persona that would speak to, inspire, and teach his nation – and ultimately the world – how to think democratically, in a nondiscriminating or even indiscriminate way, and how to articulate such thought in a new form that would help define an evolving democratic poetry.

Although our literary histories have tended to categorize Whitman as a poet and to focus on his shape-shifting thirty-seven-year-long book project that he named *Leaves of Grass*, it is important at the outset to keep in mind that he wrote more prose than he did poetry, and that, while he was publishing a few remarkably conventional (in both form and sentiment) poems in the 1840s, he was at that time better known for his fiction, a series of morality tales, several of which appeared in the respected *United States Magazine and Democratic Review* and a number of which were reprinted in newspapers across the country. In 1841, he published his temperance novel, *Franklin Evans*, as a supplement in the *New World* newspaper. Long dismissed as embarrassing juvenilia, several of these fictional works have in recent decades been read by critics as offering insights into Whitman's early struggles to articulate what would become key issues in *Leaves of Grass*.[9] A number of the stories, like the novel, deal with the abuse of alcohol and focus on the barroom as a place of violation and a site for new possibilities of affection. The 1841 story "The Child and the Profligate," for example, represents a symbolic homosexual rape followed by a comforting image of a night of male-male love shared between a reformed drunkard and the boy who had alcohol forced down his throat by a one-eyed sailor.[10] *Franklin Evans* is an episodic adventure following the title character as he leaves his rural life to go to New York to be seduced by the pleasures of alcohol. In the course of his wavering resolve to reform, during which he succumbs to his "fatal pleasure"[11] again and again only to reform again and again, he finds himself on a Southern plantation, where, drunk, he marries a mixed-blood slave woman.[12] Other tales have to do with violent death. We can discern in these early tales a kind of mixed brew of ideas and incidents that, over the course of his career, Whitman would develop into *Leaves of Grass*, in which death, a commitment to an ever-renewing open road that allows for one's identity to be fluid and unburdened by the past, a bravery about violating societal conventions and taboos – sexual, racial, or social – in a desire to experience the fullness and diversity of life, and a firm belief that love itself will be redefined and broadened by the experience of living in an evolving democratic society all come together in an explosive new kind of writing, a long-lined poetry that absorbs the world detail by detail, erasing the memory of what came before so as to devote the open senses to what comes now.

While he was writing his early, mostly conventional poetry and his often unconventional fiction, Whitman was also developing a career as a journalist. At twelve, he began his career as a newspaper worker, learning typesetting as an apprentice at the *Long Island Patriot* under the tutelage of master printer William Hartshorne. Late in his life, Whitman wrote a poem called "A Font of Type," in which he imagines all the "unlauch'd voices – passionate powers, / Wrath, argument, or praise, or comic leer, or prayer devout" that lie "within the pallid slivers slumbering" in "This latent mine" of the type box (*LG*, p. 509). That poem harkens back to the poet's experiences as a boy in Hartshorne's Brooklyn printing office, where he learned "the awkward holding of the stick" and "the pleasing mystery of the different letters" in the huge type cases in front of him.[13] Whitman probably never composed a line of poetry without, in his mind's eye, putting it on a composing stick. Eventually, typesetting the words of others led him to want to see his own words in print; his first signed piece appeared in the fashionable New York *Mirror* when he was fifteen. Called "The Olden Time," Whitman's little article begins by talking about how "vastly strange" it is to be told that, as "old" and "civilized" as New York City felt in the 1830s, there were still people alive who "conversed with men who once saw the present great metropolitan city as a little *dorp* or village." Whitman goes on to tell how, in 1758, a "Negro Harry," "aged at least one hundred and twenty years," had died on Long Island. He had been a slave in the same family for a hundred years. This "old oracle" carried the history of the community in a way no one else could, and he remembered New York when "there were but three houses in it."[14] The young Whitman had talked to people who knew Negro Harry and heard his amazing tales.

Whitman always carried with him this little bit of history he had picked up in his childhood and used it again, thirty years later, at the end of the Civil War, in his poem "Ethiopia Saluting the Colors," as he imagined a Union soldier on General Sherman's march through the South confronting a newly freed hundred-plus-year-old slave woman. The bemused soldier can only wonder what she must have seen during her century's journey through America, one that began with white men enslaving her and now ends with white men freeing her: "Are the things so strange and marvelous you see or have seen?" (*LG*, p. 319). From early on, Whitman knew that the best chroniclers of America's past were often those who were themselves written out of the official histories of the nation: he built a writing career, an aesthetic, on the principle of giving voice to the individuals in the society who otherwise had no public voice – the worker, the prostitute, the slave, the venerealee. As he put it in the poem that he would eventually entitle "Song of Myself":

This is the meal equally set, this the meat for natural hunger,
It is for the wicked just the same as the righteous, I make appointments with all,
I will not have a single person slighted or left away,
The kept-woman, sponger, thief, are hereby invited,
The heavy-lipp'd slave is invited, the venerealee is invited;
There shall be no difference between them and the rest. (*LG*, p. 46)

Over the years, working for and editing nearly a dozen newspapers in and around New York, Whitman produced a massive amount of journalism, writing commentary on virtually every major social issue of his day, from the need for urban green space, to the need for clean water, to the need to care for prostitutes, to the controversy over capital punishment, to the costs of war, and to the problems that the expansion of slavery into new territories would cause for white workers moving west. He went to New Orleans to edit the *Daily Crescent* for a few months in 1848, where he experienced the South's peculiar institution firsthand and saw the slave auctions that would haunt him from then on; he would take on the persona of the auctioneer and conduct a bitterly ironic inventory and valuing of the commodified human body in "I Sing the Body Electric."

He returned to Brooklyn to start a free-soil newspaper, the *Freeman*, but then, in the early 1850s, he took a break from editing and turned to the writing of *Leaves of Grass*. He gave himself time to read, and he wrote incessantly in the small notebooks he always carried with him, allowing his roiling ideas to evolve and discover a form of expression. In a burst of creative energy, still discernible in the notebooks he left behind, he discovered his revolutionary new vehicle, a long-lined free verse organized by a vast and absorptive "I" who would speak for all of America in a brash and nondiscriminating voice.

Whitman's notebooks and surviving manuscripts reveal the intensity and fluidity of the development of his poetic style. Images, phrases, and whole lines of what would become *Leaves of Grass* can be found in his prose jottings, and only a year or two before *Leaves* appeared, Whitman was unclear what shape – even what genre – his new expression would take: in one notebook from the early 1850s, in which prose lines appear that would later take their place in the poetry of *Leaves*, Whitman writes, "Novel? Work of some sort / Play? ... Plot for a Poem or other work ... A spiritual novel?"[15] Still thinking of himself as a fiction writer, Whitman initially assumed his new work might take that form. Some of his other notes indicate he thought his ideas would best emerge as speeches, and he imagined going on the lecture circuit. Only gradually do the notebooks edge toward his discovery of his poetic line, but once that discovery comes, he moves quickly toward his finished book. What is clear is that *Leaves of Grass* emerges from his early prose and has its roots there.

Whitman's thousands of poetry manuscripts have, remarkably, never been edited and are only now appearing for the first time in the online Walt Whitman Archive. The earliest of these manuscripts reveal how Whitman scoured his prose notebooks, in which he had jotted down ideas and recorded impressions of his walks through New York and Brooklyn, and began culling those descriptions for phrases that would become the core of his poetic lines. Once he discovered his line – a portable unit of perception usually generated by a first-person speaker in the present tense, with the syntax extended by the repeated use of participles – he could quickly build poems.[16] The line remained his basic building unit. Once he had a line, he tended to keep it and then move it around, testing it in different juxtapositions with other lines. As a professional typesetter, he was used to thinking of lines of type as move-able units, and, as a poet, he tended to revise by rearranging lines. Some early manuscripts are composed of lines that would later appear in *Leaves*, but that are arranged in an entirely different order. Throughout his career, he would continue to revise by literally cutting and pasting lines in new arrangements; a number of his surviving poetry manuscripts are in fact strips of paper, each containing a line of poetry, pasted together in the order he had finally shuffled the lines into. In his idiosyncratic poetic catalogues, each line adds another moment of perception without altering or modifying the previous line, both accreting detail and shifting the reader's moment of perception so that the cumulative effect is of an ever-renewing present erasing a quickly fading past. He created a syntax of continual restarting, of not letting the past accumulate and weigh down the fresh perception that was always available in the now.[17]

In July 1855, Whitman took his still-in-flux manuscript to his friend Andrew Rome, who ran a small print shop in Brooklyn and specialized in printing legal documents. *Leaves of Grass* would be the first book Rome ever printed. Setting some of the type himself, Whitman quickly altered his original plans for the book when he realized he would have to use the large, legal-sized page that the Rome shop was set up to handle; thus the first edition of *Leaves*, with its bold typeface and rough finish, looks like what it in fact is: a declaration of literary independence, a proclamation of a new kind of literature fit for a new democracy, printed words that look like they were made to be posted.[18] Omitting his name from the title page, he intensified the sense of the book as a public document. He included as a frontispiece an engraving of himself in laborer's garb, with his hat on, fixing the reader with a challenging look. The portrait is unlike any previous frontispiece representation of an author: the full-body pose, with the torso as the center of focus, suggests that *this* poetry emerges not just from the intellect but from the experience of a body at work in the world, hat on, shirt open, ready to be inspired and ready also to perspire. Blithely confident that even death will not stop him, the brash poetic "I" of the long opening poem in the 1855 edition turns these legal-form-sized pages into a last will and testament, transferring the energy of the speaker over to the reader, who is charged with carrying on the journey that he or she has, at the poem's end, literally inherited: "I bequeath myself to the dirt to grow from the grass I love, / If you want me again look for me under your bootsoles. / ... / I stop some where waiting for you."[19]

At the last minute, Whitman added a prose preface to his book, defining the new American poet. He composed the preface by culling from his notebooks passages in which he had theorized about the nature of a new American poetry, and he connected these statements with his idiosyncratic ellipses, avoiding standard punctuation for a looser and more fluid syntax controlled by a variable number of dots, the same idiosyncratic punctuation he would use in the poetry itself. In the preface, he issued commandments for both poet and reader, building a catalogue of imperative behaviors that culminate in a physically transformed body:

> This is what you shall do: Love the earth and sun and the animals, despise riches, give alms to every one that asks, stand up for the stupid and crazy, devote your income and labor to others, hate tyrants, argue not concerning God, have patience and indulgence toward the people, take off your hat to nothing known or unknown or to any man or number of men, go freely with powerful uneducated persons and with the young and with the mothers of families, read these leaves in the open air every season of every year of your life, re-examine all you have been told at school or church or in any book, dismiss whatever insults your own soul, and your very flesh shall be a great poem and have the richest fluency not only in its words but in the silent lines of its lips and face and between the lashes of your eyes and in every motion and joint of your body. (*LG* 1855, pp. v–vi)

These biblical-sounding injunctions are energized by Whitman's democratic pride and by his insistence that we know only through the body: whatever good his poetry will do, he indicates, will be manifest by its transforming effects on the flesh itself. The lines of his poetry, when read by the reader's lips, will form the "silent lines" of those lips, and its rhythms will be evident in "every motion and joint" of the reader's body. His commandments – "what you shall do" – are always, ironically, anticommandments, instructions to undermine commandment, to "hate tyrants," to "argue not concerning God," and to show subservience to no one, including, presumably, this poet who is commanding us to "re-examine all [we] have been told," including the very instructions we are reading.

Following the preface were twelve poems, the first six all called "Leaves of Grass," the last six untitled. Because Whitman was paying for the publication, he had the typesetters squeeze the last six poems tightly onto the pages so that he would not have to pay for an extra signature. He printed 795 copies, stopping the press a couple of times to correct errors and once to change an entire line, and then he had the pages bound on three different occasions in progressively cheaper bindings. It is ironic that the 1855 *Leaves* has become the most valorized of all the editions, a kind of talisman of American literature (with recently sold copies going for as much as $200,000), because it is the edition that Whitman valued the least as a piece of bookmaking: "I can't imagine why anyone would want that book," Whitman said late in his life when told that collectors were seeking it out.[20] Even the printer of the book, Andrew Rome, in 1890 would recall "the difficulties" he encountered in printing the 1855 *Leaves*, speaking of his "old press ... and of the poor job they were able to do."[21] Everything suggests that Whitman was disappointed in how that first edition looked. And it is also ironic that it became the most valorized edition because it is the one edition for which there were no plates. Rome printed the book from set type, which slipped and moved a good deal as the book was being printed; some type even broke off or fell out, notably the final period in "Song of Myself," following the last line of the poem, "I stop somewhere waiting for you." Many critics have seen the absence of that period as a significant and radical gesture on Whitman's part, indicating that his poem does not really end when the words do but passes on to the reader, who must now carry on with the journey. Compelling as this interpretation is, the recent census of all the known copies of the 1855 edition reveals that in fact seven of the nearly two hundred extant copies *do* have that final period, and clearly it was there when Whitman proofed the first sheets off the press.[22] The period fell off early in the printing, and Whitman added the period back when the 1856 edition was published. As soon as the 1855 edition was printed, the type was distributed and immediately used again for legal forms. The makeshift volume could never be reprinted.

The 1855 edition of *Leaves*, then, demonstrates the striking combination of pragmatic thinking, supple improvisation, continual reconstructing, obsessive concern for detail, and random chance that would mark all of Whitman's poetic output. He was a speculator in houses during the years he was writing *Leaves*, and he oversaw the building of new homes into which he would move his family, only to begin the building of yet another home, which he would then move his family into when he sold the previous one.[23] The building and rebuilding, the sense of never settling in one place, the experience of transience, and the fluctuation of risk, luck, and the unpredictable market all fed into a poetry that celebrated fluidity, incessant change, and open roads, and that rejected domestic stability as a condition to be valued or sought.

Whitman's addition of the prose preface to his 1855 *Leaves* marks the beginning of his career-long fascination with mixing prose and poetry, with framing and contextualizing his poetry with prose ruminations that served variously as a gloss on the poems, a counterpoint to the poetry, and often a historical contextualization of the poems. He would append to his 1856 second edition of *Leaves*, for example, a prose section called "Leaves-Droppings," containing Ralph Waldo Emerson's brief personal letter to Whitman after reading *Leaves* (in which he greets Whitman "at the beginning of a great career"),[24] Whitman's own very public and extended letter in response to Emerson, and a selection of reviews – positive and negative – of the first edition. This prose paratext put the poetry into a social debate and framed the way readers would interpret the work. Twenty years later, in his 1876 two-volume centennial edition of his writings, he experimented in one of the volumes, called *Two Rivulets*, with two separate flows of language on the same page, one poetry and one prose, inviting the reader to experiment with how to navigate two seemingly unrelated texts, in two different genres, that shared the same page. Throughout his career, Whitman was comfortable, as a journalist and newspaper editor, with a page that contained jarring juxtapositions of material, just as a newspaper page offered the reader's eye an energetic clashing field of news stories, poems, advertisements, and special interest items, each vying for a moment of the reader's attention. Genre for Whitman was a fluid concept, and he was a pioneer in testing generic boundaries, writing a poetry that many early readers perceived to be prosaic, and creating books that mixed poetry and prose in ways that anticipate the experiments of modern poets, like William Carlos Williams in *Spring and All*.

The opening poem of the first edition took up forty-three pages, beginning with "I" ("I celebrate myself, / And what I assume you shall assume") and ending its long transference of energy to the reader with "you" ("I stop some where waiting for you"). This long poem, which Whitman would title "Poem of Walt Whitman, an American" in 1856, "Walt Whitman" in 1860, and finally "Song of Myself" in 1881, became his best-known work, an epic of American individualism, setting out to expand the boundaries of the self to include all of one's fellow Americans, then the entire world, and ultimately the cosmos. In this poem, Whitman keeps probing the question of how large the self can become before it dissipates into contradiction and fragmentation, and each time he seems to reach the limit, he dilates even more: "My ties and ballasts leave me .... I travel .... I sail .... my elbows rest in the sea-gaps, / I skirt sierras .... my palms cover continents, / I am afoot with my vision" (*LG* 1855, p. 35). Cataloguing a huge array of urban and country scenes, portraying people at work in myriad occupations, incorporating vast geographical stretches, redefining life and death as one continuous and evolving dynamic process, Whitman's "I" takes the reader on a staggering journey through religions, American history, and geological and biological evolution, absorbing everything and rejecting nothing. His plea is for his readers to learn to accept and live in plurality, difference, and contradiction, which he defines as the necessary democratic condition: "Do I contradict myself? / Very well then .... I contradict myself; / I am large .... I contain multitudes" (*LG* 1855, p. 55).

The journey in this poem is one of liberation, and Whitman's concern with slavery, the burning issue in the United States during the years he wrote the poem, is everywhere evident in this first edition, from the way the "I" identifies with a captured slave ("I am the hounded slave, I wince at the bite of the dogs" [*LG* 1855, p. 39]) to the highly charged moment in the poem he would later call "The Sleepers" when the "I" turns the narration of the poem over to an incensed slave whose wife and children have just been sold down the river ("I hate him that oppresses me, / I will either destroy him, or he shall release me / Damn him! how he does defile me" [*LG* 1855, p. 74]). The whole book plays on chattel slavery as a cultural metaphor for the various kinds of enslavement – religious, economic, moral – from which all readers must craft an escape. The slave-escape core of the poem can be traced back to Whitman's notebooks, where, in the "Talbot Wilson" notebook, we find some of Whitman's earliest proto-lines, lines that led to "Song of Myself":

> I am the poet of slaves and of the masters of slaves
> I am the poet of the body

> And I am
>
> I am the poet of the body
> And I am the poet of the soul
> I go with the slaves of the earth equally with the masters
> And I will stand between the masters and the slaves,
> Entering into both so that both shall understand me alike.
>
> I am the poet of Strength and Hope[25]

From the beginning, Whitman was busy embedding deep in his poem impossible contradictions, and he always wedded opposites with his omnipresent "and." He would not be the poet of slaves nor the poet of masters but rather only the poet of slaves *and* masters. Whatever democratic voice he invented would have to speak for both, or it was doomed to be partial and thus not representative. And to stand *between* masters and slaves, of course, was to stand in a politically and sexually charged space, historically a place of rape and torture, but a place also where mixing and hybridity began. There is no easy space to inhabit in American history, and Whitman was courageous enough to insist on speaking for the full range of American identities, from the most powerful to the powerless, and to recognize that there are no slaves without slave masters, no slave masters without slaves, and that only when every individual begins to recognize the slave *and* the slave master within himself or herself could a democratic voice begin to merge and emerge.

It was, finally, nothing less than the creation of a previously unheard democratic voice that Whitman was after; he sought in "Song of Myself" to voice an "I" that would for the first time articulate just what a nonhierarchical and nondiscriminating sensibility would sound like. He was not speaking in his poem as the Walt Whitman of the mid-1850s, a man who shared many of the biases of his time, but rather as a Whitman projected far into a more perfectly realized democratic future. He was teaching Americans how to begin to think and speak democratically, in a freer and looser idiom, in a more conversational and less formal tone, in an absorptive and indiscriminate way. He achieved an uncanny combination of oratory, journalism, and the Bible – haranguing, mundane, and prophetic – all in the service of identifying a new American democratic attitude, an accepting voice that would catalogue the diversity of the country and manage to hold it all in a vast, single, unified identity. This new voice spoke confidently of union at a time of deep division and tension in the culture, only five years short of the outbreak of the Civil War, and it spoke with the assurance of one for whom everything, no matter how degraded, could be celebrated as part of itself: "What is commonest and cheapest and nearest and easiest is Me" (*LG* 1855, p. 21). His work echoed the lingo of the

American urban working class and mixed it with the diction of the rising middle-class newspaper editor, who took pride in an American language that was forming as a tongue distinct from British English.[26]

Part of that new American speech involved a much more open acknowledgment of sexuality and the body than the culture was accustomed to. "Song of Myself" was fueled by erotic energy – "Urge and urge and urge, / Always the procreant urge of the world" (LG 1855, p. 14) – and the narrator initiates his absorptive democratic journey with a bizarre sex act:

> I mind how we lay in June, such a transparent summer morning;
> You settled your head athwart my hips and gently turned over upon me,
> And parted the shirt from my bosom-bone, and plunged your tongue to my
>   barestript heart,
> And reached till you felt my beard, and reached till you held my feet.
>
> (LG 1855, p. 15)

The physical encounter here has been variously read as a homosexual union, a heterosexual intercourse, or a kind of figurative charging up of the body by the soul. Whitman is sometimes categorized as a Transcendentalist, but his beliefs are more descendentalist, the soul entering the body to energize the senses instead of the soul transcending the physical world. For Whitman, soul without body was unthinkable, and in this generative scene, the tongue is plunged into the heart, initiating a union of physical voice with the heart – both the seat of love and emotion *and* the organ of life, pumping blood to the head and hands and genitals. In "Song of Myself," the narrator's body speaks and sees and hears and touches and tastes and smells, absorbing the world through heightened senses: "Welcome is every organ and attribute of me, ... / Not an inch nor a particle of an inch is vile" (LG 1855, p. 14). This erotic drive would urge the democratic self to cross boundaries of race and gender and class: "Who need be afraid of the merge? / Undrape .... you are not guilty to me" (LG 1855, p. 17). All humans inhabit bodies, and democracy starts, Whitman believed, with a full and open acknowledgment of the body's desires and drives: they are what unify us.

Once the first edition of *Leaves* was printed, Whitman immediately began a thirty-five-year process of rethinking and revising his book: "As long as I live the Leaves must go on," he once said (WWWC, vol. 1, p. 270). The result is a textual nightmare for anyone studying the evolution of *Leaves* from 1855 to Whitman's final deathbed edition. Whitman's *Leaves of Grass* is not a single object but a bewildering array of changing book objects with the same title, in which poems are added, deleted, shuffled, and arranged in new clusters, and in which size and binding and typeface change in significant ways, until we begin to realize that what we call *Leaves of Grass* is as much a dynamic *process* as it is a "book" or a "text." And because the process is dynamic over four decades, Whitman's *Leaves* becomes thoroughly entwined with Whitman's life in a way that no other book by any other major American author does. As Whitman said in "So Long!," the poem he placed at the end of his book from 1860 on, "Camerado, this is no book, / Who touches this touches a man."[27] His book is at once a single evolving text and a shifting set of wildly various book objects. When Whitman, late in his life, was once looking through the bewildering array of photographs of himself that had been taken from the time he was in his late twenties, he found himself confused by the series of images he saw.[28] This was a common feeling among that first generation of people who had the opportunity to examine photographic traces of themselves aging over decades. "I meet new Walt Whitmans every day," the poet told friends as he stumbled on old photographs of himself; "I don't know which Walt Whitman I am." He began to wonder whether the sequence of photos finally demonstrated that his life was "evolutional or episodical": "Taking them in their periods is there a visible bridge from one to the other or is there a break?" (*WWWC*, vol. 4, p. 425). The same question can be asked about his book: was it a series of separate books, each formed by and responsive to particular historical and biographical moments, or was it in fact one evolving book, accreting new experiences while maintaining not only the same name but the same identity?

The various editions of *Leaves of Grass* each went through multiple issues, often with different bindings, different paper size, different cover designs, different typefaces, and different configurations of contents (to this day, no one is precisely sure just how many variants there are). Whitman was always experimenting with the physical appearance of his book, and his changes reflect his evolving notions of what role his writing would play in the emerging American democracy. Major historical events like the Civil War and Reconstruction had a palpable effect on the physical makeup of his books. When he published his Civil War poems in a separate book called *Drum-Taps*, for example, he constructed that book during a time of paper shortage, and the very composition of the pages reflects his desire to use every inch of space, leading to an arrangement of poems that has often been read thematically but was in fact coerced spatially, a book of war poems rationed so as to conserve paper and space.[29] After the war, as Whitman tried to figure out how to absorb his Civil War poems into *Leaves of Grass*, he began by constructing an edition in 1867 in which he had the pages of the unbound copies of *Drum-Taps* sewn into the back of the newly printed *Leaves*, a kind of bibliographical suturing that represented a first attempt to heal the vast national wound of the war. This was the beginning of a long process of postwar reconstruction of *Leaves* that mirrors the Reconstruction of the nation that was occurring at the same time. Some of the copies of the 1867 edition contain *Drum-Taps*, while others do not; the bindings change, too, and this fluidity reflects his indecision over whether *Leaves of Grass*, which originally set out to celebrate the unity of the United States, could properly contain poems chronicling the divisive war between the states. By the 1870 edition, Whitman had begun to scatter the Civil War poems throughout *Leaves of Grass* and construct a cluster of poems called "Drum-Taps" that differed significantly from the original book of that name; this process continued in the 1881 edition, in which he added poems to the "Drum-Taps" cluster (including "Ethiopia Saluting the Colors," which became the sole acknowledgment of race and slavery as an issue in the war) and moved others to new places in *Leaves*. By the final edition, the Civil War was fully woven into the book.

This is just one example of the hundreds of changes Whitman made to his books as he designed and redesigned them, each change responding to a particular biographical and cultural moment. Three of the editions (1855, 1856, and 1860) are antebellum, and three (1867, 1871–1872, and 1881) postbellum. The three editions after the Civil War struggle with absorbing Whitman's haunted war writings while retaining the celebratory sense of the first three editions, which set out to absorb and embrace the nation's differences. This episodic evolution of one of the most important texts in American literature has never been examined in detail, and there is no time to do it here, but we can indicate a few of the episodes in the evolution of the text.

Thinking back over all his editions, Whitman said late in his life,

> What a sweat I used to be in all the time over getting my damned books published! When I look back on it I wonder I didn't somewhere or other on the road chuck the whole business into oblivion. Editions! Editions! Editions! like the last extra of a newspaper: an extra after an extra: one issue after another: fifty-five, fifty-six, sixty-one, sixty-seven — oh! edition after edition. Yes, I wonder I never did anything violent with the book, it has so victimized me!

The friend to whom Whitman said this laughed and noted "how the poor victim is still making edition after edition: now, even, in eighty-eight – thirty-three years after fifty-five." Whitman answered, "We can't help ourselves: we are in a web – we are moths in flames" (*WWWC*, vol. 3, p. 562). By this time, Whitman had begun to think of the different editions almost as individual children: "They all count," he said, "I don't know that I like one better than any other" (*WWWC*, vol. 1, p. 280).

The first edition of *Leaves* had not sold more than a handful of copies, and Whitman probably gave more copies to potential reviewers than he sold. But his largesse paid off in that the book did get reviewed. Whitman wrote three anonymous, not entirely positive, reviews of it himself, and he collected all the reviews and had many of them printed up for insertion in the final issue of the 1855 edition. Meanwhile, Emerson, to whom he had sent a copy, lent the book to many friends, and the Transcendentalist grapevine worked quickly to make *Leaves* and the mysterious poet himself the topic of a number of heated conversations among figures in the Emerson circle, including Theodore Parker, Henry David Thoreau, Ellery Channing, Charles Eliot Norton, Thomas Wentworth Higginson, and Franklin Sanborn. The census of extant copies of the 1855 *Leaves of Grass* reveals, in fact, that the identifiable original owners of the first edition can largely be traced back to Emerson and his recommendations of the book to his Transcendental literary circle. Without this group of purchasers, Whitman's claim late in his life that the first edition did not sell any copies – "None of them were sold – practically none – perhaps one or two, perhaps not even that many" (*WWWC*, vol. 2, p. 472) – might in fact have been true. So, even though the meager sales did not drive a second edition, Whitman's adept manipulation of the critical response managed to put *Leaves* at the center of a heated debate about what American poetry was becoming. Anxious to move ahead with his project while the reviews of the first edition were still appearing, he quickly prepared a second edition.

Whitman had become friendly in the 1850s with the publisher, social reformer, and phrenologist Lorenzo Fowler, who gave Whitman's skull bumps a generous reading, finding him a man of large appetites.[30] Fowler's firm, Fowler and Wells, had distributed the first edition, and in 1856 they took on the publication of Whitman's second edition, although they withheld their name from the title page. This aggressive phrenological publishing firm produced endless self-help manuals, including phrenological guides on how to manipulate your own skull to discover which qualities you needed to improve. Whitman filled *Leaves* with phrenological terms like "adhesiveness" (affection between people of the same sex) and "amativeness" (affection between people of the opposite sex), as well as offering a memorable image of a kind of continental phrenological exam, as the poet examined the geological bumps around the skull of the earth in order to read each country's character: "my palms cover continents," as he put it in "Song of Myself" (*LG*, p. 61). Fowler and Wells produced many books with frank discussions of sex, and they produced guides to republican etiquette, all things Whitman included in *Leaves* and that conceivably made his book a good fit for the publishers, although finally it was too much even for this radical house, and the firm quietly backed out of reissuing it, concerned that they already were facing enough criticism from the conservative establishment for their radical list. But Fowler and Wells owned the electroplates of the book, and that was a problem for Whitman, who canvassed friends for money to see if he could raise the $200 necessary to buy them. Had he been able to raise the funds, the history of *Leaves* would likely have been much different, because plates were the key: in the second half of the nineteenth century, stereotype and electrotype plates were the spinal, enduring identity of a book. Type was set, a mold was made of the type, molten metal was poured into the mold, and permanent metal plates then emerged, with the book type permanently there, ready for printing and reprinting. Whitman would likely have begun adding supplements to this edition if he owned the plates, and *Leaves* might well have been a more stagnant and less interesting production than it turned out to be in the following years.

For the 1856 edition, Whitman added twenty new poems to the original twelve. But as the book grew in number of poems, it shrank in page size; the paper for this edition was less than half the size of that of the first edition. The new size was actually closer to the dimensions Whitman had originally had in mind for his first edition. Although critics over the years have expressed a preference for the large, legal-sized pages of the first edition, in which Whitman's lines had room to move unbroken across the page, Whitman preferred what he thought of as a "pocket-size" volume (and he never returned to the large, legal sheets of the original *Leaves*), and so the second edition is something more akin to a devotional book than a proclamation. His dream now was to have working people carry his poetry with them to read it during breaks in their workday. About a thousand copies of this edition were printed.

It is in this edition that we most clearly see Emerson's influence on Whitman. Whitman owed a great deal to Emerson, whose essay "The Poet" seemed in many ways to prophesy the poet Whitman became (some critics have argued that Whitman simply modeled himself on Emerson's essay). Whitman reportedly said that by the mid-1850s he was "simmering, simmering, simmering; Emerson brought me to a boil,"[31] and this edition represents the most furious roiling of the waters. In addition to printing the supportive letter that Emerson had sent him after reading the 1855 *Leaves* and his own twelve-page response to Emerson (addressing him as "Master"), Whitman brazenly featured Emerson's name and endorsement – "I greet you at the beginning of a great career" – on the spine of the book. In his letter to Whitman, Emerson had praised *Leaves* for its "wit and wisdom" but neglected to refer to the work as poetry, and, as if to set the record straight, Whitman now underscored the genre that he had decided to claim for himself: he titled every one of his thirty-two pieces in the new edition "Poem" ("Poem of Women," "Sun-Down Poem," "Poem of the Road," etc.), and he began his open letter to Emerson by referring to his work as "poems" seven times in the first paragraph.[32]

Two of Whitman's greatest poems first appeared in this edition – "Poem of Wonder at the Resurrection of the Wheat" (later titled "This Compost") and "Sun-Down Poem" (later called "Crossing Brooklyn Ferry"). The first poem explores the poet's deep faith in the process of composting, the idea that all of life is a resurrection out of death, an unending cycle of things breaking down to their elements, out of which new creations are made. What was true of the earth's elements was true of language, too, and the word "compost" has the same roots as "composition": Whitman, who loved the quickly expanding dictionaries of the English language that were appearing at this time, realized that every poem was a kind of composted composition, something new made up entirely of elements that were continually recirculating through the language. A dictionary, for Whitman, was the compost heap of all past and future poems. The speaker of this poem worries about how the earth can absorb so much death and not become poisonous, but the poem comes to celebrate the "chemistry" that turns that death back into life, that "grows such sweet things out of such corruptions" (*LG* 1856, p. 205). Here is the ecological mystery that lies behind *Leaves of Grass* and explains the book's title: the leaves of grass are the first sign of new life emerging from the graves of the dead, the proof that there is no such thing as death. The process of composting, Whitman knows, is the great democratic principle: everything – from plants to people to poetry – has to be broken down into its elements for new plants or people or poems to emerge. So all the insistent "I's" of the first section of the poem give way to the "the's" and "that's" and "it's" of the second section, as the self imagines its release back into the things, the *thingness*, of the world – an ecstasy of diffusion instead of a protective recoil. The earth "grows such sweet things out of such corruptions," and it "gives us such divine materials," and it accepts our "leavings" at the last (*LG* 1856, p. 205).

Here it is: Whitman's faith – spirituality as a compost heap, the soul as endlessly recycling material. He was quickly picking up the lessons of the scientists of the time whose work was expanding the concepts of time and space and eternity. "Every atom belonging to me as good belongs to you" (*LG*, p. 28): these spinning atoms that make up each of us were here at the origin of the cosmos and will be here as long as matter exists. And from some distant

ED FOLSOM

point in the universe, a telescope powerful enough to see this dust mote we call Earth would see this world before any of us were born, our present and our past translated into their future. Whitman would often address his poems to readers who would be living decades or centuries after he was dead, and his faith was that his own *Leaves of Grass* would be, like the organic leaves, the sign of ongoing identity after his physical demise.

"Sun-Down Poem" would be his great testament to the power of his poetry to transcend time and space, to allow the poet, living in his present when the poem was written, to communicate with a reader who was not yet born when the poem was written: "We understand, then, do we not? / What I promised without mentioning it, have you not accepted? / What the study could not teach – what the preaching could not accomplish is accomplished, is it not?" (*LG* 1856, p. 219). All the preaching about the afterlife could not be as effective as this poem's actual *demonstration* of an afterlife, as the living poet talks intimately to the unborn reader, as the living reader is invited to respond to the dead poet.

In the years following the 1856 edition, Whitman continued his sporadic work with Brooklyn newspapers and began frequenting Pfaff's beer hall, a Bohemian hangout on Broadway, where he socialized with Henry Clapp, editor of the *Saturday Press*, who became a great supporter of the poet, and other radical writers and artists. Since Whitman did not control the plates of the 1856 edition, he reconceived the entire project and worked hard on revising and vastly expanding *Leaves*.[33] He wrote one particularly haunting poem, called "A Child's Reminiscence," and published it in Clapp's *Saturday Press* in 1859, where it served as a controversial preview and teaser for all the recent poems he was gathering for a new edition. Retitled "Out of the Cradle Endlessly Rocking," this poem became Whitman's *Künstlergedicht*: with echoes of Edgar Allan Poe and many other poets resonating throughout, the poem evokes a child listening to the sad song of a mockingbird who has lost his mate, but in learning to translate that wordless song (made up of bits of other birds' songs), the emerging poet now comes to understand what "The sea whisper'd me": "Death, death, death, death, death." Like Poe's hearing a dark response from a bird that visited him, Whitman knows that "Never more shall [he] escape" the "solitary singer" who has taught him how to hear that "strong and delicious word" – the very word of composting, the endless rocking of life and death – that would echo more and more for Whitman in the following few years, as he became surrounded and consumed by "the million dead"[34] and had to learn to build a future on them (*LG*, pp. 252–53).

In 1860, with the country heading inexorably toward war, Whitman's poetic fortunes took a sudden positive turn. He received a letter from the Boston publishers and militant abolitionists William Thayer and Charles Eldridge, whose aggressive new publishing house specialized in antislavery literature; they wanted to become the publishers of the new edition of *Leaves of Grass*. Whitman, feeling confirmed as an authentic poet now that he had been, for the first time, offered royalties, readily agreed, and Thayer and Eldridge invested heavily in the stereotype plates for Whitman's idiosyncratic book – more than 450 pages of varied typeface and odd decorative motifs, a visually chaotic volume all carefully tended to by Whitman, who traveled to Boston to spend his days with the typesetters and oversee the printing. Emerson came in from Concord to see Whitman and tried to talk him out of including his new "Enfans d'Adam" cluster of poems (later "Children of Adam"), which celebrated sex in remarkably direct terms ("O hymen! O hymenee! Why do you tantalize me thus?"; "It is I, you women, I make my way, / ... I pour the stuff to start sons and daughters fit for these States – I press with slow rude muscle") (*LG* 1860, pp. 313, 303). Emerson worried that the poems would sensationalize the book and blind readers to the wisdom there, but Whitman argued that sex was central to his vision and that to cut the sex out of *Leaves* would be to destroy it.

And sex was exuded everywhere in this edition of *Leaves*. While the 1855 edition had featured a cover with the title in floriated letters, with roots and leaves growing out of the type and forming a lush and fertile foliage, and with the period at the end of the title transformed into a germinating seed, his third edition clearly upped the ante. On the cover and spine, instead of floriated letters, we find letters that sport spiraling tails, as if they are wriggling and swimming and have been momentarily captured in some tentative arrangement. When we open the book to the title page, the letters now sport spermatozoa tails, and the period at the end of the title is no longer the germinating seed of the 1855 cover but rather another kind of seed: a clear representation of a sperm cell, swimming from beneath the final "S" to take its place at the conclusion of the title. With the word "GRASS," Whitman creates what we might call a spermatoid typeface; instead of the letters actually being the spiraling creatures themselves, here the sperm have swum onto the letters.[35]

This striking visual introduction to his book underscores Whitman's radical concept of democratic reading. His sexual imagery was integral to the act of reading he was proposing. He believed his *words* were the seeds for new ideas, a new nation, and a new conception of democracy, but, to have an effect, his words would need to penetrate readers and fertilize their imaginations.

Whitman worked with the typesetters to get those curling tails and tendrils to extend from the letters on his cover and title page to suggest how the words would move, attach, and cling, find nurturant ground so they could fertilize and grow into something new. Whitman imaged, then, the act of reading as a sexual act, an act of fertilizing, inseminating. The "process of reading," Whitman would write in *Democratic Vistas* (1871), is "an exercise, a gymnast's struggle," and the democratic reader "must himself or herself construct indeed the poem, argument, history, metaphysical essay – the text furnishing the hints, the clue, the start or frame-work," because what is needed for democracy to flourish is "a nation of supple and athletic minds" (*PW*, vol. 2, pp. 424–25). His words were the seeds, but the womb in which the seed would grow and form was the reader's mind, and the ovum belonged to the reader too: the poet's job was to cajole, seduce the reader until the seminal ideas could flow into a receptive mind and join with the reader to construct a future unexpected and strong, deriving its strength and character from the reader as much as from the poet. When he wrote poems evoking the sexual joining of the poet with the female reader, then, or the affectionate physical contact of the poet to the male reader, his explicit imagery was always in the service of an erotics of reading. He evoked the process in "Calamus 13,"

> Love-buds, put before you and within you, whoever you are,
> Buds to be unfolded on the old terms,
> If you bring the warmth of the sun to them, they will open, and bring form,
>   color, perfume, to you,
> If you become the aliment and the wet, they will become flowers, fruits, tall
>   branches and trees,
> . . .
> They have come slowly up out of the earth and me, and are to come slowly
>   up out of you.
>
> <div align="right">(<i>LG</i> 1860, pp. 359–60)</div>

This was part of the physicality of the book for Whitman: it had a body, a spine, a face, and folds, and it received a reader's actual physical touch, just as the reader was touched by the book (in physical and emotional ways). "O how your fingers drowse me" (*LG* 1860, p. 455): Whitman's words speak from the face of the page into the reader's face, as the reader's fingers trace the lines, caressing the face, perhaps mouthing the words. Whether he imagined the book astride the reader's hips or nestled against the reader's breast ("thrusting me beneath your clothing, / Where I may feel the throbs of your heart, or rest upon your hip" [*LG* 1860, p. 346]), Whitman wanted his reader to be aware that he (and, metonymically, his book) was intimately close to "whoever you are, holding me now in hand" (*LG* 1860, p. 344). There's an anonymous intimacy, a democratic, ever-shifting intimacy, as one reader puts the book down and another picks it up, a cruising intimacy that makes readers keenly aware that the "you" Whitman so privately addresses is at once no one but you and yet also everyone who has ever read or is now reading or will read his book. The book is inexhaustible in its potential for intimacy, and its seminal fluid is there on the title page of the 1860 edition for every reader to see as the book waits patiently yet urgently to plant its seed.

The new cluster of poems in the 1860 edition that would alter Whitman's book more than any other is one that Emerson did not comment on: "Calamus," a group of poems that explored male-male affection. Deriving from a sonnet-like sequence of poems that Whitman uncharacteristically left only in manuscript, called "Live Oak, with Moss," these poems seem to trace a love affair between the poet and a young man, identified in recent years as Fred Vaughan, a friend of Whitman's in the 1850s.[36] In order to create his "Calamus" cluster, Whitman rearranged the "Live Oak" poems and supplemented them with other new poems; the sequence caused little reaction at the time, although toward the end of Whitman's life and throughout the twentieth century these poems would come to be read as Whitman's admission of or endorsement of homosexuality; in recent decades, they have been read as a courageous early articulation of gay identity and as Whitman's brave new vision of a transformed America, in which same-sex affection would be openly expressed and publicly recognized. Whitman described these poems as his most political; in an age of advancing U.S. capitalism, he realized that something would have to offset the fierce competition that males were increasingly taught was crucial to their success. Whitman's solution was what he called "camaraderie," an intense affection between men that would temper competition and bind the nation through love. Democracy could not thrive, he believed, in a brutal competitive economic environment: men needed to learn to love one another for the republic to endure.

The 1860 *Leaves*, carrying this innovative message of men loving men, appeared in May 1860, less than a year before the outbreak of the Civil War. Whitman had put the date "1860–61" on the title page of this edition of *Leaves*, and the broken date proved prophetic, because it marked the transition between a troubled but still unified nation and a nation fractured. Suddenly, Whitman's "Calamus" poems took on a greater urgency, as American men began killing other American men: fathers killing sons; sons, fathers; brothers, brothers. And the war had another immediate impact on *Leaves*: after a promising start of sales for the 1860 edition, Thayer and Eldridge, like so many publishers after the beginning of the Civil War, went out of business by the end of the year. Once again, the all-important plates of the book slipped from Whitman's control: Thayer and Eldridge sold the electrotyped plates at auction. The publisher Richard Worthington bought the plates for the 1860 edition in 1879 (after they had passed through a number of other hands), and he began in 1880 to reissue the book, much to Whitman's dismay, because it appeared just as Whitman was preparing his final authorized edition of *Leaves* and would for many years appear on bookshelves as a cheaper competitor.

Whitman stayed in New York until the end of 1862, continuing to go to Pfaff's, but also visiting hospitals where wounded soldiers were already being brought from the battlefields. When he learned that his brother George had been wounded in the battle of Fredericksburg, he went to Virginia to check on him, and, in another characteristically impulsive move, he simply abandoned New York and settled in Washington, D.C., so that he could be at the political heart of the war. During the next two years, Whitman lived in a series of rooming houses, worked as a clerk in the army paymaster's office, served as a correspondent for New York newspapers, and almost daily visited the ubiquitous war hospitals that filled the nation's capital. He once estimated that he visited up to 100,000 wounded soldiers, for whom he would write letters, run errands, provide treats, and offer comfort.

Still keeping notebooks, he jotted down the battlefield stories the young soldiers told him. Out of those notes emerged a series of poems about the Civil War, unlike any poems he had written before – quieter, more somber, with a more subdued "I" who now witnessed and observed and nursed and listened. Often, the "I" of some of the poems shifts from his usual absorptive poetic "I" to specific personae, sometimes particular soldiers, as in "A Sight in Camp in the Daybreak Gray and Dim," which captures the thoughts of a soldier as he lifts the blankets off the faces of three dead comrades, coming finally to the last one: "I think this face is the face of the Christ himself, / Dead and divine and brother of all, and here again he lies" (*LG*, p. 307). The soldier voices a Christian realization, but the point is not that this dead soldier is unique and Christlike but rather that every one of the deaths is as significant as the Crucifixion, is in its own way the Crucifixion enacted again and thousands of times again; each dead soldier on the battlefield is a lost piece of the divine, and this young soldier's death is as equally significant as any in history.

Whitman had written some early Civil War poems when he was still in New York, but these had been boisterous recruitment poems – like "Beat! Beat! Drums!" – almost giddy in their excitement over the impending war. After he had seen the battlefield at Fredericksburg and a pile of amputated limbs outside the battlefield hospital there, his tone changed, and poems like "The Wound-Dresser" (originally called simply "The Dresser") turned the war inside out, shifting our attention from the battlefield to the hospital, from heroic deeds in battle to the horrific aftereffects of those battles: "The crush'd head I dress, (poor crazed hand tear not the bandage away,) / ... (Come sweet death! Be persuaded O beautiful death! / In mercy come quickly.)" (*LG*, p. 310). Death, cast in the earlier *Leaves* as a vital part of the composting process, churning up new life, was now putting Whitman's compost-faith to its sternest test, as hundreds of thousands of young Americans decomposed in the soil, rivers, and seas of the North and South. Out of this vast compost, Whitman realized, America would have to grow its future. As he put it in one of the longest sentences he ever wrote, a four-hundred-plus-word sentence that appears in his prose *Memoranda During the War* but that began in manuscript as a poem, the "infinite dead" of the war now left "the land entire saturated, perfumed with their impalpable ashes' exhalation in Nature's chemistry distill'd, and shall be so forever, in every future grain of wheat and ear of corn, and every flower that grows, and every breath we draw" (*PW*, vol. 1, p. 115). We can feel in such passages how Whitman created a syntax of mass death: he entitled this section of his *Memoranda* "The Million Dead, Too, Summ'd Up," using his characteristic contraction-apostrophe, which here creates a haunting ambiguity, because the sentence – with all its embedded statistics, its death data – does give us the Civil War dead *summed up*, but the contraction also invites us to fill in a few more letters, as we realize this death sentence literally *summons up* the dead, reminding us of their actual physical presence throughout the landscape, north and south, and insisting on their physical emergence in everything that grows from the soil they dissolved into. It is a vast national compost. It is the million dead summoned up. Whitman's catalogue is a summing and a summoning, and the summons is not just of the dead but also of the living, who are being summoned to witness this mass death and, grotesque as it may seem, ingest it, take communion with it, live off of it, make a future out of it.

His extraordinary hospital service took a toll on Whitman's own health. He took sick leave for the last half of 1864 and returned to his mother's house in Brooklyn, where he continued to write short war poems, some of them based on newspaper accounts of battles. He returned to Washington in early 1865, in time for Lincoln's second inauguration, and took a new job as a clerk in the Indian Bureau of the Department of the Interior. He now turned his attention to *Drum-Taps*, his book of poems about the war. This book, another self-published work, had been almost entirely set in type by the time that Lincoln was assassinated. Whitman quickly added a brief poem, "Hush'd Be the Camps

To-Day," acknowledging the assassination and had a few copies bound before deciding to put the publication on hold so that he could absorb the ending of the war and the momentous events surrounding it.

That summer he wrote two of his best-known poems, "O Captain! My Captain!" and "When Lilacs Last in the Dooryard Bloom'd," both elegies to Lincoln. The first was written in conventional meters and rhymes, perhaps capturing the voice of a sailor imagining the loss of Lincoln in terms of a ship losing its captain. The second poem is one of the greatest elegies in the language, beginning with a complex evocation of the moment the poet first heard of the assassination: Whitman was with his mother in Brooklyn and went outside to her dooryard, where the early lilacs were in bloom; inhaling deeply out of his grief, his senses registered the smell of lilacs and forever bound that aroma with Lincoln's death and the deaths of all the soldiers of the war. The poem – with its talismanic images of the drooping evening star and the hidden thrush that sings, from deep in the swamp, a death carol the poet must translate into lasting language – became Whitman's great statement of faith in the composting process. Following Lincoln's death train across the blooming spring landscape of America, the poem is finally drawn deep into the swamp, the very site of composting, and the poet finds there "retrieve-ments out of the night" (LG, p. 337), fragments on which he will build a future, based on the natural fact that the lilacs will continue to bloom in the annual cycle of renewal, carrying in their aroma the memory of death bound always to the hope of a fresh beginning. He would even go back to his 1856 compost poem, which he named "This Compost" in 1867, and poignantly add a half line to his long catalogue of nature growing out of death: "the lilacs bloom in the door-yards" (LG, p. 369).

Whitman printed a sequel to "Drum-Taps," containing these two ele-gies along with other late Civil War poems, including his powerful call for a national healing, "Reconciliation," in which he (or a soldier persona) kisses the corpse of his enemy, trusting again in the powerful process of compost: "Beautiful that war, and all its deeds of carnage, must in time be utterly lost; / That the hands of the sisters Death and Night, incessantly softly wash again, and ever again, this soil'd world" (LG, p. 321). On the title page, he dated the sequel "1865–6," marking another transitional moment in American his-tory, the break between the last year of the Civil War and the first year of reconciliation.

"Sequel to Drum-Taps" marks the end of Whitman's great poetic output. He would continue to write for the next twenty-five years, and he would produce a few memorable poems, like "Passage to India" (1871), with its increasingly global concerns, along with innovative and important prose works like *Democratic Vistas* (1871), his meditation on the failures of and hopes for American democracy, and his analysis of how democracy would have to expand from a form of government to a way of life, penetrating every aspect of Americans' behavior, habits, and ways of thinking. He also wrote *Specimen Days* (1882), his self-described "wayward, spontaneous, fragmentary book" (*PW*, vol. 1, p. 1), which contained his previously published *Memoranda During the War* (1875–1876), the prose account of his encounters with soldiers during the last years of the conflict. But his major poetry was now behind him.

In 1865, Interior Secretary James Harlan dismissed Whitman from his job, and, although Whitman was quickly hired in the attorney general's office, the firing became a national scandal thanks to Whitman's passionate friend and supporter, William Douglas O'Connor. O'Connor, a government worker and writer, was outraged at Harlan's actions and was sure Whitman was the victim of Harlan's conventional and cramped morality. Harlan had found Whitman's working copy of the 1860 *Leaves* in his desk and had been shocked at some of the language. O'Connor wrote a diatribe against Harlan and called it *The Good Gray Poet: A Vindication* (1866), portraying Whitman as a kind of saint because of his service in the Civil War hospitals and extolling the "intellectual and moral grandeur of this work."[37] Whitman soon *became* the Good Gray Poet, less and less the radical and outrageous artist and more and more the sage old prophet. His poetic diction changed from a journalistic idiom and edged toward a more Latinate and even biblical vocabulary. He devoted most of his creativity to rearranging and revising what he had already written. Where earlier he had viewed his poetic line as a moveable unit, cutting and pasting poems in different arrangements of the same lines, he now viewed individual poems themselves as portable units, and he experimented with new clusters of poems, new arrangements of previous clusters, and new juxtapositions of clusters and poems. Even as he continued to write new poems, his real imaginative energy was focused on the larger arrangements and rearrangements of *Leaves of Grass*.

He had hoped to attract a commercial publisher for his postwar arrangement of *Leaves*, but the publishing world was still shaken by the aftereffects of the war, and many publishers were put off by Whitman's raw descriptions of sexuality. One friend, trying to convince publishers to take on Whitman's book, wrote that "the chief objection raised by everyone I talked with was on account of the too seminal element everywhere jetting out from the 'Leaves.'"[38] Whitman ended up self-publishing the 1867 edition, and he had it set in the same type that *Drum-Taps* had appeared in, so that he could sew the Civil War poems into the volume as a kind of appendix. By 1870, he had hooked up with J. S. Redfield, whom Whitman had encountered back in the 1840s and 1850s, when Redfield was the well-known publisher of Edgar Allan Poe and William Gilmore Simms. Redfield, like Thayer and Eldridge, had gone out of business just before the war began in 1860, but he reentered the publishing world in the very late 1860s and agreed to publish three Whitman books in order to generate some controversy about his new publishing venture – the new edition of *Leaves* (with *Drum-Taps* now fully absorbed into the revised arrangement of poems), a new book Whitman called *Passage to India* (which he thought of as a book of the soul to balance the emphasis on the body in *Leaves*), and *Democratic Vistas*. These were published in a matching paperback edition; Redfield's arrangement with Whitman gave the author control of the plates, and so Whitman quickly combined *Leaves* with *Passage to India*, once again deciding that *Leaves* was large enough to absorb it all. But, because he finally owned the plates, he simply bound the *Passage* book in as an annex to *Leaves*. In 1876, when he issued a centennial edition of *Leaves*, he separated out *Passage* once again and bound it into a separate volume called *Two Rivulets*, which also contained *Democratic Vistas, Memoranda During the War*, and other material, new and reprinted. As long as he had usable plates of *Leaves*, his impulse was to add on, supplement, and annex material instead of resetting the type and making expensive new plates.

The year 1873 was Whitman's worst. He suffered a stroke, followed quickly by the death of his mother, and he went to Camden, New Jersey, where his brother George lived. As abruptly as he had left New York for D.C., he now left Washington behind and took up residence in Camden, first with his brother and then in a small house of his own. It was in Camden that he worked on *Specimen Days* and his 1881 edition of *Leaves*, in which he achieved the final ordering of his poems and created the version of *Leaves* that most readers after his death would come to know. After 1881 he would again add poems to *Leaves*, but, harkening back to his house-building days, only as what he called "annexes"; he would never again rearrange the poems of the main book nor have them reset in type. The 1881 edition was published in Boston by the prestigious firm of James R. Osgood, but the book was immediately attacked by moral reformers in the city and was ruled obscene and banned from the mails. Osgood tried to get Whitman to expurgate the book, and, when the poet refused, Osgood transferred the plates to Whitman, who had the book printed in Philadelphia, which became his publishing home for the rest of his life. Fueled by the banned-in-Boston scandal, sales of *Leaves* were more robust than ever before. The plates were now everything, and he used these Osgood plates to print a dizzying array of issues of *Leaves of Grass*, from a cheap paperback version to a monumental merging of his poetry and prose in a volume entitled *Complete Poems and Prose*.

Living in very modest surroundings in a dirty industrial city, visited by a growing number of admirers and disciples from the United States and abroad, and steadily declining in health, Whitman continued appending poems to *Leaves* up to his death in 1892, including some moving brief poems on his aging body. These late annex poems have generally been dismissed as the tired last vestiges of a poetic career, but in recent years they have been read as powerfully evocative articulations of old age and impending death. The poet Robert Creeley's final published essay before his own death was about Whitman's last poems: "The common sense is that Whitman's poems faded as he grew older, that their art grew more mechanical and that the poems themselves had rarely the power of his more youthful writing. The life, however, is finally the poetry, the issue and manifest of its existence – . . . literally so." These poems, Creeley argues, teach us "that age itself is a *body*, not a measure of time or record of how much one has grown."[39] In these last poems, Whitman records unflinchingly how his aged body, with its "Ungracious glooms, aches, lethargy, constipation, whimpering *ennui*, / May filter in my daily songs" (*LG*, p. 510). Facing death and dissolution in "Song of Myself" had seemed exhilarating – "I depart as air, I shake my white locks at the runaway sun, / I effuse my flesh in eddies, and drift it in lacy jags" (*LG*, p. 89) – but now, while recognizing death's inevitability, the poet wants to linger in the "twilight," the "opiate shades": "(I too will soon be gone, dispell'd,) / A haze – nirwana – rest and night – oblivion" (*LG*, p. 532)

What is most striking about these last poems is the gradual disappearance of the "I" on the page, as in the poem that concludes the first annex, "After the Supper and Talk," in which Whitman sets up what promises to be a simile: the poet's departure from his readers is "As a friend from friends his final withdrawal prolonging." The simile, however, never materializes, and the "I" we expect to enter into the poem never appears except as it is buried in the homophonic "aye": "Soon to be lost for aye in the darkness – loth, O so loth to depart! / Garrulous to the very last" (*LG*, p. 536). The "I" is already forever lost in the darkness, diffused and no longer able to materialize as it speaks its final garrulous word. To the very end, Whitman maintained his faith in composting and dissolution, although the tonality and register of his voice faltered and altered as he revised and added to *Leaves* in the months before he died. Asked how the 1892 last issue of *Leaves of Grass* would differ from the earlier ones,

Whitman, on his deathbed, answered, "Why, *in being complete* – which is difference enough" (*WWWC*, vol. 9, p. 546).

Notes

1. Walt Whitman, *Leaves of Grass: Comprehensive Reader's Edition*, ed. Harold W. Blodgett and Sculley Bradley (New York: New York University Press, 1965), p. 14. This volume will be cited subsequently in the text as *LG*.
2. For a gathering of poets talking back to Whitman, see Jim Perlman, Ed Folsom, and Dan Campion (eds.), *Walt Whitman: The Measure of His Song* (Duluth, Minn.: Holy Cow!, 1998). Pound's "The Pact" can be found on p. 111.
3. For a gathering of international writers talking back to Whitman, see Gay Wilson Allen and Ed Folsom (eds.), *Walt Whitman and the World* (Iowa City: University of Iowa Press, 1995).
4. For a recent collection of essays on Whitman by political scientists, see John E. Seery (ed.), *A Political Companion to Walt Whitman* (Lexington: University Press of Kentucky, 2011).
5. See, for example, Jonathan Ned Katz, *Love Stories: Sex between Men before Homosexuality* (Chicago: University of Chicago Press, 2001).
6. For a collection of essays on Whitman's influence on music, see Lawrence Kramer (ed.), *Walt Whitman and Modern Music* (New York: Garland, 2000).
7. The most extensive examination of Whitman's relationship to painters is Ruth L. Bohan, *Looking into Whitman: American Art, 1850–1920* (University Park: Pennsylvania State University Press, 2006); for Whitman and architects, see John F. Roche, "Democratic Space: The Ecstatic Geography of Walt Whitman and Frank Lloyd Wright," *Walt Whitman Quarterly Review* 6 (1988), pp. 16–32, and Kevin Murphy, "Walt Whitman and Louis Sullivan: The Aesthetics of Egalitarianism," *Walt Whitman Quarterly Review* 6 (1988), pp. 1–15; for Whitman and film, see Kenneth M. Price, *To Walt Whitman, America* (Chapel Hill: University of North Carolina Press, 2004), chapter 6 ("Whitman at the Movies").
8. See Ed Folsom, "'What a Filthy Presidentiad!': Clinton's Whitman, Bush's Whitman, and Whitman's America," *Virginia Quarterly Review* 81:2 (2005), pp. 96–113.
9. See, for example, Michael Moon, *Disseminating Whitman: Revision and Corporeality in Leaves of Grass* (Cambridge, Mass.: Harvard University Press, 1991), chapter 1 ("Rendering the Text and the Body Fluid: The Cases of 'The Child's Champion' and the 1855 *Leaves of Grass*").
10. Walt Whitman, *The Early Poems and Fiction*, ed. Thomas L. Brasher (New York: New York University Press, 1963), pp. 68–79.
11. Whitman, *Early Poems and Fiction*, p. 153.

12. For an exploration of the novel in relation to "fatal pleasure," see Michael Warner, "Whitman Drunk," in Betsy Erkkila and Jay Grossman (eds.), *Breaking Bounds: Whitman and American Cultural Studies* (New York: Oxford University Press, 1996), pp. 30–43; see also Martin Klammer, *Whitman, Slavery, and the Emergence of Leaves of Grass* (University Park: Pennsylvania State University Press, 1995), chapter 1 ("The Construction of a Pro-Slavery Apology").

13. Walt Whitman, "Brooklyniana," in *The Uncollected Poetry and Prose of Walt Whitman*, ed. Emory Holloway, 2 vols. (New York: Doubleday, 1921), vol. 2, p. 247.

14. Walt Whitman, *The Journalism*, ed. Herbert Bergman, Douglas A. Noverr, and Edward J. Recchia, 2 vols. (New York: Peter Lang, 1998–2003), vol. 1, p. 3.

15. Walt Whitman, *Daybooks and Notebooks*, ed. William White, 3 vols. (New York: New York University Press, 1977), vol. 3, p. 775.

16. The best examination of Whitman's discovery of his line is Matt Miller, *Collage of Myself: Walt Whitman and the Making of Leaves of Grass* (Lincoln: University of Nebraska Press, 2010).

17. See Wai Chee Dimock, "Whitman, Syntax, and Political Theory," in Erkkila and Grossman (eds.), *Breaking Bounds*, pp. 62–79, for an analysis of how Whitman's language demonstrates "the renewability of syntax but not the sedimentation of meanings" (p. 75).

18. See Ed Folsom, "What We're Still Learning about the 1855 *Leaves of Grass* 150 Years Later," in Susan Belasco, Ed Folsom, and Kenneth M. Price (eds.), *Leaves of Grass: The Sesquicentennial Essays* (Lincoln: University of Nebraska Press, 2007), pp. 1–32.

19. Walt Whitman, *Leaves of Grass* (Brooklyn, New York, 1855), pp. v–vi. Available on the Walt Whitman Archive (whitmanarchive.org). This volume will be cited subsequently in the text as *LG* 1855.

20. Horace Traubel, *With Walt Whitman in Camden*, 9 vols. (Various publishers, 1906–1996), vol. 9, p. 174. Available on the Walt Whitman Archive (whitmanarchive.org). These volumes will be cited subsequently in the text as *WWWC*.

21. J. Johnston and J. W. Wallace, *Visits to Walt Whitman in 1890–1891* (London: George Allen, 1917), p. 138.

22. See Ed Folsom, "The Census of the 1855 Leaves of Grass: A Preliminary Report," *Walt Whitman Quarterly Review* 24 (2006–2007), pp. 71–84.

23. For an investigation of how Whitman's real estate activities affected his writing, see Peter J. L. Riley, "Leaves of Grass and Real Estate," *Walt Whitman Quarterly Review* 28 (2011), pp. 163–87.

24. Walt Whitman, *Leaves of Grass* (Brooklyn, New York, 1856), p. 345. Available on the Walt Whitman Archive (whitmanarchive.org). This volume will be cited subsequently in the text as *LG* 1856.

25. Walt Whitman, *Notebooks and Unpublished Prose Manuscripts*, ed. Edward F. Grier, 6 vols. (New York: New York University Press, 1984), vol. 1, p. 67.
26. For a detailed study of Whitman's class-inflected diction, see Andrew Lawson, *Walt Whitman and the Class Struggle* (Iowa City: University of Iowa Press, 2006).
27. Walt Whitman, *Leaves of Grass* (Boston: Thayer and Eldridge, 1860), p. 455. Available on the Walt Whitman Archive (whitmanarchive.org). This volume will be cited subsequently in the text as *LG* 1860.
28. For Whitman's ideas about photography and his views about photographs of himself, see Ed Folsom, *Walt Whitman's Native Representations* (Cambridge: Cambridge University Press, 1994), chapters 4 and 5.
29. For a detailed examination of the economics of printing and arranging *Drum-Taps*, see Ted Genoways, "The Disorder of Drum-Taps," *Walt Whitman Quarterly Review* 24 (2006–2007), pp. 98–116.
30. The best discussion of Whitman's relationship to Fowler and Wells, and to phrenology in general, remains Madeleine B. Stern, *Heads and Headlines: The Phrenological Fowlers* (Norman: University of Oklahoma Press, 1971).
31. John Townsend Trowbridge, "Reminiscences of Walt Whitman," in Joel Myerson (ed.), *Whitman in His Own Time* (Iowa City: University of Iowa Press, 2000), p. 173.
32. For a provocative discussion of the tense messaging going on between Emerson and Whitman, see Jay Grossman, "Rereading Emerson / Whitman," in Steven Fink and Susan S. Williams (eds.), *Reciprocal Influences: Literary Production, Distribution, and Consumption in America* (Columbus: Ohio State University Press, 1999), pp. 75–97, and Jay Grossman, *Reconstituting the American Renaissance: Emerson, Whitman, and the Politics of Representation* (Durham, N.C.: Duke University Press, 2003).
33. For detailed work on Pfaff's beer hall, see Christine Stansell, "Whitman at Pfaff's: Commercial Culture, Literary Life and New York Bohemia at Mid-Century," *Walt Whitman Quarterly Review* 10 (1993), pp. 107–26; Mark A. Lause, *The Antebellum Crisis and America's First Bohemians* (Kent, Ohio: Kent State University Press, 2010); and Joanna Levin, *Bohemia in America, 1858–1920* (Stanford, Calif.: Stanford University Press, 2010).
34. Walt Whitman, *Prose Works 1892*, ed. Floyd Stovall, 2 vols. (New York: New York University Press, 1963–1964), vol. 1, p. 114. These volumes will be cited subsequently in the text as *PW*.
35. See Ed Folsom, "'A spirt of my own seminal wet': Spermatoid Design in Walt Whitman's 1860 *Leaves of Grass*," *Huntington Library Quarterly* 73 (2010), pp. 585–600.
36. On Whitman's relationship to Fred Vaughan, see Robert Roper, *Now the Drum of War: Walt Whitman and His Brothers in the Civil War* (New York: Walker,

2008), pp. 111–16, and Gary Schmidgall, *Walt Whitman: A Gay Life* (New York: Dutton, 1997), pp. 193–98.

37. Jerome Loving, *Walt Whitman's Champion: William Douglas O'Connor* (College Station: Texas A&M University Press, 1978), p. 172.

38. Rufus A. Coleman, "Trowbridge and O'Connor: Unpublished Correspondence, with Special Reference to Walt Whitman," *American Literature* 23 (1951), p. 326.

39. Robert Creeley, "Reflections on Whitman in Age," *Virginia Quarterly Review* 81:2 (2005), p. 262.

Chapter 16

Emily Dickinson: The Poetics and Practice of Autonomy

WENDY MARTIN

Although Emily Dickinson published only a few poems in her lifetime, she has since emerged as one of the two most important nineteenth-century American poets, along with Walt Whitman. Dickinson was a reclusive poet who has been the focus of much mythologizing over the years. In addition to being described as "a partially cracked poetess," she has been portrayed as a neurasthenic invalid; as an agoraphobic or, at best, neurotically shy; as morbidly death obsessed; and as a lovelorn spinster who dressed in white and isolated herself from the world to mourn unrequited love.[1] Since the emergence of feminist criticism in the 1970s, Dickinson's work and life have been reexamined. We now understand that Dickinson was a lively and fiercely independent woman with a loving family and a deeply loyal community of lifelong friends. We also know that she dedicated her life almost entirely to her family, friends, and poetry, which she wrote with passionate commitment. Although she has been portrayed as someone who was removed from the world, we now understand that Dickinson was immersed in the world to an unusual extent.

Emily Dickinson seems to stand alone, yet she was someone we might have known as a friend, classmate, or neighbor. She loved to cook, and her recipe for gingerbread is famous; even more, she loved to garden and was an expert horticulturalist (her much-admired herbarium, a collection of plant specimens, has been published by Harvard University Press). She was a steadfast friend, and her emotional wisdom, empathic understanding, and humorous quips were appreciated by all who knew her. Finally, she was a loyal daughter and sister and a beloved aunt to her nephews and nieces. Although she knew "the shore is safer," Dickinson loved to "buffet the sea," as she wrote to her childhood friend Abiah Root (*EDL*, p. 104). She devoted her life to the exploration of even the most intimidating aspects of the world around her, including love, religious doctrines and the existence of God, nature, the meaning of war, and perhaps most famously, death and the afterlife. Dickinson was stubborn, rebellious, and utterly committed to being a poet. As a young woman, she confided in a friend that she wanted to achieve greatness, and she did just that. She has had a profound influence on many poets who followed and on American poetry as a whole.

Born in 1830, Emily Dickinson was the second child and eldest daughter of Edward Dickinson and Emily Norcross, who were married and settled in Amherst, Massachusetts, in 1828. Dickinson's elder brother, Austin, was born in 1829, and her younger sister, Lavinia, was born in 1833. Edward Dickinson was a respected lawyer, acted as treasurer of Amherst College, served in the Massachusetts House of Representatives and the U.S. Congress, and represented Amherst in the General Court of Massachusetts. Early in the Dickinson marriage there were financial hardships, which eventually led to the sale of the family home, called the Homestead, when Emily was nine. The Dickinsons lived in a house on West Street for several years, but in 1855, when Emily was twenty-five, her father was able to buy back the Homestead property and to build the Evergreens, a house for Austin and his wife, Susan Gilbert Dickinson, on the same lot. The Homestead was a large, stately house with enough private bedrooms for all of the Dickinson children, as well as separate servants' quarters, and it represented the increasing wealth of the upper middle and professional classes in nineteenth-century New England. The Homestead's library, garden, and grounds reflected the growing leisure of the women who inhabited them and the financial success of their husbands and fathers.

In many respects, the senior Dickinsons were a conventional Victorian couple. Edward Dickinson was the strict head of his household; he issued edicts about domestic order and child-rearing practices, while his wife submitted to his authority. Indeed, Emily Norcross Dickinson languished in the confinement of her home and spent much of her adult life as an invalid, reclining on a sofa, as did many affluent Victorian women. This extreme passivity might be seen as a physical acting out of the Victorian adage to women to "suffer and be still"; this was an ironic embodiment of the invalid status of the Victorian housewife, whose life was limited to the domestic realm. It may well be that this was Emily Norcross Dickinson's way of resisting and even subverting her husband's authority, but her languor and inattention alienated her daughter, Emily, who declared that she "never had a mother" (EDL, p. 342b). When Mrs. Dickinson's health declined in the mid-1850s, Emily and Lavinia had to bear the burdens of both caring for their mother and running the household, including cooking, cleaning, managing household staff, and entertaining Edward Dickinson's frequent guests.

The concept of separate spheres for men and women was codified in Coventry Patmore's *Angel in the House* (1854), which was published in England

and widely read in the United States. In Patmore's view, the wife and mother in the Victorian household should aspire to angelic, self-sacrificing behavior. Her first priority was to nurture her husband and children and to create a home that was a haven from the cares of the world. Even though Dickinson had a copy of Patmore's book on her bookshelf, she clearly did not subscribe to his prescriptions. As Adrienne Rich observes, "Dickinson's life was organized on her own terms";[2] even in her youth, years before her famous seclusion, Dickinson demonstrated a resolve to obey the dictates of her spirit rather than Victorian society.

Perhaps nowhere was this more evident in her young life than in Dickinson's resistance to conversion and the strong Puritan religious influence in Amherst, which began in her school years. Beginning at age nine, Dickinson attended Amherst Academy, where she was an outstanding student with many friends. In that same year, a religious revival passed through Amherst; seven more would follow in the next twenty-two years, including major revivals in 1845 and 1850, when Dickinson was a teenager. Amherst caught the fervor, and numerous citizens, including Edward and Lavinia Dickinson, made public professions of faith as a sign of their being "chosen" by God – but Emily did not. In spite of intense social pressure and many letters from concerned friends and relatives with well-meaning but patronizing fear for the fate of Emily's soul, she held out. The pressure to publicly acknowledge Christian faith increased when, at sixteen, Dickinson entered Mount Holyoke Female Seminary, which emphasized religious training in its curriculum. It was a matter of deep self-examination for Dickinson, one over which she agonized – the social and familial pull of the church was so strong that she continued to attend the First Church in Amherst until her late twenties – but she ultimately came down on the side of uncertainty. "You may be surprised," she wrote to Abiah, "but I am not happy, ... that I did not give up and become a Christian. It is not now too late, so my friends tell me, so my offended conscience whispers, but it is hard for me to give up the world" (*EDL*, p. 67). For Dickinson, conversion meant relinquishing the joys of this life, which she treasured; for her classmates, teachers, and society, her refusal meant Dickinson was "one of the lost ones." But in spite of her fear of alienation from God and her peers, she could not accept the conventional notions of sin, salvation, and eternity.

Dickinson's poetry addresses the social ostracism she experienced as a religious skeptic. With the full understanding that her decision made her a kind of outcast at school and in the Amherst community, Dickinson accepted the consequences of her decision and explored them carefully in verse. "What is – 'Paradise'" asks whether she can expect social interactions in heaven to be as unkind as those in Amherst and suggests that if there is a "'a Father' – in the sky –" perhaps in heaven "Ransomed folks – won't laugh at me – / Maybe – 'Eden' a'n't so lonesome / As New England used to be!"[3] The possibility that the mere absence of mocking laughter in "Eden" will make it less "lonesome" than New England demonstrates how socially isolated Dickinson felt. In another poem, she describes the aftereffects of her decision in starker terms:

> I'm banished – now …
> How foreign can that be –
> You'll know – Sir – when the Savior's face
> Turns so – away from you –
>
> (*EDP*, p. 117, no. 256)

Dickinson feels not only exiled but abandoned, so distant from God that even "the Savior's face" has turned away. Dickinson's remarkable commitment to her own personal convictions and experience in the face of this hard treatment reveals her determination to be true to herself and her understanding of the world, no matter what the cost.

Dickinson's later poetry increasingly reflects her religious skepticism. In some poems, she uses religious and biblical language but undercuts it by using punctuation and physical format to emphasize its dubious qualities. Some boys "believe," but "Other Boys are 'lost' –" one poem remarks doubtfully (*EDP*, p. 644, no. 1545). In another poem, she says that following death

> there's Heaven –
> The *Good* Man's – "*Dividend*" –
> And *Bad* Men – "go to Jail" –
> I guess –
>
> (*EDP*, p. 107, no. 234)

Dickinson's quotation marks question the rewards and punishments associated with the Christian afterlife; she also capitalizes and italicizes "Good" and "Bad" men, as if to mock the distinction between the two. Further, she employs the language of commerce to equate going to heaven with a profitable and possibly questionable business transaction – one that could just as easily land someone in "Jail." And the final line, with its lack of conviction and abrupt ending, implies not just skepticism but flat disbelief.

The fact that Dickinson did not embrace organized religion does not mean she had no faith, only that the doctrines of the churches she had attended throughout her life did not adequately encompass her beliefs. As an adult, she essentially created her own religion, one that combined elements of her Calvinist upbringing with beliefs based on her own experience. Instead of anticipating an afterlife in heaven, Dickinson celebrated the joy of the moment, particularly as found in the company of her friends. In her letters, she often expressed this feeling using biblical imagery and language, inverted in potentially blasphemous ways. "If prayers had any answers to them, you were all here to-night, but I seek and I don't find, and knock and it is not opened," she wrote to her close friends the Hollands, playing with the language of Matthew 7:7 and suggesting that its promise of answered prayers is a false one (*EDL*, pp. 263–64). In another letter to Susan Gilbert, who would become her sister-in-law, Dickinson describes not God but "Susie" as her "sweet shelter [and] covert from the storm" (*EDL*, p. 181). And in one poem, she reproaches a friend who "forgot – and I – remembered," comparing this lapse to Christ's betrayal by Peter (*EDP*, p. 95, no. 203). As can be seen in these examples, Dickinson relied on her friends for comfort and protection, sought their presence, and loved them fervently. Her dedication to her friends represented a transfer of the idea of devotion from God to the men and women she loved, those capable of making a heaven of her earth.

Dickinson's day-to-day experiences in nature also brought this divine joy and sense of the eternal. She spent hours outside, particularly in her garden, and she meticulously recorded her experiences. In numerous letters and poems, she elevates the natural world to a religious, transcendental level. "Oh, Matchless Earth –," she wrote in one letter, "We underrate the chance to dwell in Thee" (*EDL*, p. 478). A later poem affirms that "Earth is Heaven – / Whether Heaven is Heaven or not" (*EDP*, p. 602, no. 1408). She cannot envision a heaven more glorious than the earth, which is full of "Awe" and "Rapture" (*EDP*, pp. 280–81, no. 575). In her worship of nature, Dickinson invests even tiny details with divine significance. She closes one poem by praying, "In the name of the Bee – / And of the Butterfly – / And of the Breeze – Amen!" (*EDP*, p. 14, no. 18), replacing the members of the Christian trinity. Hers is not the Romantic love of nature that seeks overwhelming grandeur but an adoration that finds beauty in its subtle processes and intricacy. To Dickinson, these minute revelatory elements are worthy of careful attention and veneration. They take the place of scripture, and they place the divine squarely on earth.

For all her appreciation, Dickinson was no naïve worshiper of nature. She saw its beauty, but she also saw its potential for cruelty, its darker rhythms. The details in which she often experienced the divine could just as easily prove grimly dangerous. One poem describes a "certain Slant of light" in the winter that "oppresses, like the Heft / Of Cathedral Tunes," causing a "Heavenly Hurt" in the observer (*EDP*, pp. 118–19, no. 258). In the language of this poem, nature brings sorrow, despair, and a heaviness comparable to the religious rituals Dickinson has sought to escape. Elsewhere, she describes how "Nature – sometimes sears a Sapling – / Sometimes – scalps a Tree," highlighting the potential for destructive power that coexists with natural beauty (*EDP*, p. 148, no. 314). Importantly, Dickinson does not shy away from depicting these aspects of nature, even though they in some ways contradict her other representations of it; she does not "repress the darker aspects of her vision in order to create the illusion of control."[4] Instead, she allows herself the freedom to see all parts of the natural world. In other poems, such as "The Sky is low – the Clouds are mean," she explores the mean, petulant side of nature, characterized by "A Narrow Wind" that "complains all Day." Like us, Dickinson tells her reader, Nature "is sometimes caught / Without her Diadem" (*EDP*, p. 488, no. 1075). Her willingness to record the unpleasant as well as the uplifting aspects of nature shows Dickinson's ability to embrace each moment for itself and to accept contradictions as an inescapable part of experience.

Dickinson has often been portrayed as a victim of Victorian social conventions, but her life, like her poetry, was a declaration of independence from the limitations of prescribed behavior. Just as her poetic style rebuffed Victorian aesthetic practices and her religious beliefs rejected Puritan theology, Dickinson's life choices represented an ironic protest against the constraints of "true womanhood" – purity, piety, and passivity. Victorian society dictated that women should be dutiful caretakers of the home, models of decorum and propriety, and above all, devoted wives and mothers. They were not expected to be creative, productive, innovative, or intellectual. Dickinson consciously adopted a subversive approach to these limitations, using the resources of her family, home, and network of friends and relatives to carve out a space of personal, spiritual, and artistic rebellion and gaining the time and the space to write.

Perhaps the most important – and most famous – element of this subversion was Dickinson's gradually increasing separation from outside society. This separation began with her deliberate choice to become "a woman in white," wearing the color exclusively from the 1860s onward. There are many possible reasons she made this choice, such as the practicality of white for laundering, its symbolic resonances suggesting mourning or virginity, and its use as a kind of uniform; in any case, it was unusual and excited a great deal of comment. Her unorthodox behavior suggests that Dickinson was not submitting to domestic confinement; instead, this choice signaled a commitment to independence with regard to both her personal relationships and her poetry. So great was this desire for independence and the chance to "make a little destiny" of her own that she could not accept the idea of marriage, even though it was the primary expectation for women of her time; she could not bear the thought of being "yielded up" to the will of another person (*EDL*, pp. 144, 210). She had suitors, and even a late romance with Judge Otis Lord, but her overwhelming desire even then was for independence and control of her selfhood.

Around 1869, when Dickinson was thirty-nine, she began to stay at home more and more, which seems to have been a conscious decision. As her seclusion became complete, she observed, "I do not go away, but the Grounds are ample – almost travel – to me" (*EDL*, p. 349). A year later, she wrote, "I cannot tell how Eternity seems. It sweeps around me like a sea while I do my work" (*EDL*, p. 86). Dickinson's isolation may have been partially motivated by a decline in health, including trouble with her eyesight and perhaps the first symptoms of Bright's disease, the kidney disorder that was the eventual cause of her death. However, it seems in large part to have been related to her quest for greater personal and artistic autonomy, perhaps a transformation of the Victorian custom of "confinement" from a patriarchal mandate that shut out pregnant women from society to an expression of individual freedom through which Dickinson could give birth to her poetry without the hindrances and distractions of social interaction. Whatever the reasoning, whether Dickinson made a virtue of a health-related necessity or willfully chose seclusion, what is clear is that she embraced her confinement and devoted herself to her poetry, thereby subverting the patriarchal order that kept women at home and away from intellectual and creative endeavors. "The Soul selects her own Society," which describes the soul as a zealous guardian, reveals Dickinson's impulses for isolation as a means of gaining control over her time:

> I've known her – from an ample nation –
> Choose one –
> Then – close the Valves of her attention –
> Like Stone –   (*EDP*, p. 143, no. 303)

In this depiction, Dickinson's self-imposed isolation can be seen as obedience to the dictates of her soul, a particular entity to which she gives complete allegiance. In this withdrawal from the world, behind "Valves" closed "Like Stone," the soul has the privacy to do what it pleases. It is invisible to society, free from its demands and dictates. The poem is an imaginative illustration of the personal liberty for which Emily Dickinson longed.

These choices would not have been possible had Dickinson not had the support of her family. Although as a teenager Emily was afraid of her domineering father, with his strict views of femininity, as she grew older they seemed to develop a more complex relationship characterized by Edward's greater understanding of his talented, unusual daughter. As an adult, Emily won some concessions from him that allowed her to devote herself to her writing, including the use of the best bedroom in the house and the ability to retreat from society as she saw necessary. Lavinia, too, lent essential support, overseeing the household staff of servants (including a cook, maid, and gardener) and running interference between Emily and various visitors. In general, the family seemed to agree that Emily was gifted and should be able to define her own schedule in the service of her work.

The clearest symbol of this tacit family agreement was Emily's bedroom, the largest and most private bedroom in the Homestead. Located in the front corner of the second floor, it was relatively protected from the sounds of household activities. Two of the three windows looked over the lawn to the south and had a view of Main Street in Amherst.[5] The other window faced west, toward the Evergreens, the home of her brother and sister-in-law. The room was Dickinson's retreat. She spent many hours there writing poetry, as well as letters to friends and relatives. On the walls she hung portraits of Thomas Carlyle, Elizabeth Barrett Browning, and George Eliot. It was her sanctuary as well as her writing studio; it allowed Dickinson to have her energy and power under her control rather than in service as a wife and mother. As she once said to her niece Martha upon entering her room, "Matty: here's freedom."[6]

Although the image of Emily Dickinson as a spinster recluse has taken more than a century to dissipate, it was always at odds with her actual life. Dickinson had warm and affectionate relationships with her family members, particularly with her sister, Lavinia; her sister-in-law, Susan; and her niece and nephews, and she was very much in touch with political and economic events. Her appetite for news was immense, even in her youth. While away at Mount Holyoke when she was sixteen, she wrote to her brother, Austin, begging for information about the presidential candidate and the Mexican-American War, humorously complaining that at school "I dont know anything more about affairs in the world, than if I was in a trance" (*EDL*, p. 49). In 1852, while her father was at a national Whig convention, Dickinson wondered, "Why cant I be a Delegate to the great Whig Convention? – dont I know all about Daniel Webster, and the Tariff, and the Law?" (*EDL*, p. 212). This ardent desire for knowledge continued throughout her adult life. Her family subscribed to many newspapers and magazines, which she read on a daily basis, and the language and tropes of contemporary political and economic culture found their way into her writing as frequently as natural and domestic images did. One poem imagines "Revolution" as a pod whose seeds are scattered by the

"Winds of Will" (*EDP*, p. 490, no. 1082); another addresses industrialization and declares a preference for "A Letter chief to me" over news of "The Stock's advance and Retrograde / And what the Markets say" (*EDP*, p. 493, no. 1089). Although Dickinson may have physically withdrawn from the social world, intellectually and creatively she remained very much engaged.

The Civil War in particular became both a focus and impetus for much of Dickinson's poetry. She followed the war battle by battle and was deeply distressed by the senseless loss of life and the widespread tragedy of war. Significantly, the years of the Civil War (1861–1865) were Dickinson's most productive years for her poetry and are often referred to as her "flood years." At her peak in 1862, when she was thirty-two, she averaged a poem a day. Many poems use explicit battle images and were written in response to specific Civil War campaigns, as Alfred Habegger, Shira Wolosky, and others have noted.[7] In one famous poem, the speaker imagines her life as a "Loaded Gun" with the potential to be a "deadly foe" having "the power to kill" enemies (*EDP*, pp. 369–70, no. 754); in another, she ponders the nature of "Victory" and observes that defeat is "populous with Bone and stain – / ... And Chips of Blank – in Boyish Eyes – / And scraps of Prayer – / And Death's surprise" (*EDP*, p. 316, no. 639). One of the most searching of Dickinson's Civil War poems was written after the 1862 death of Frazer Stearns, the son of the president of Amherst College and a good friend of Austin Dickinson. A devastated Emily wrote to her cousins that "Brave Frazer" had been "killed at Newbern. ... His big heart shot away by a 'minnie ball.' I had read of those – I didn't think that Frazer would carry one to Eden with him" (*EDL*, pp. 397–98). Dickinson's deep knowledge of world affairs, including advances in military technology, gave an excruciating edge to the details of Stearns's death and surely prompted her questioning of progress and the purpose of war in the elegy she wrote for him. In it, Dickinson despairs at the tragic loss of life and wonders whether any war is worth the cost. "It feels a shame to be Alive – / When Men so brave – are dead –" she laments, asking:

> Are we that wait – sufficient worth –
> That such Enormous Pearl
> As life – dissolved be – for Us –
> In Battle's horrid Bowl?   (*EDP*, p. 213, no. 444)

Although Dickinson doesn't diminish the valor of the dying men, she questions whether the objectives and outcomes of war are worth the sacrifice of the "Enormous Pearl" of life. Does society – those who "wait" while the war is waged – deserve its liberty at this cost? In an antebellum poem Dickinson had asserted that only the "defeated – dying –" could truly understand the meaning of victory (*EDP*, p. 35, no. 67); here, she suggests that death and defeat reveal that the value of victory is insignificant compared to its price, and she deplores the waste of life that produces such an ugly and painful knowledge. For Dickinson, then, physical isolation did not keep her from being profoundly changed by the war. As with so many of her generation, the Civil War affected her not only in deeply personal ways as she dealt with the loss of loved ones but also intellectually, imaginatively, and philosophically as she grappled with the larger issues of life, death, and liberty it raised.

Although not a political activist, Dickinson followed the women's rights movement as closely as she did the war. The Seneca Falls Convention for women's rights was held in 1848, when Dickinson was seventeen. Although it is doubtful that Dickinson would have drawn a connection between herself and the Seneca Falls women at that age, she was already forming strong views about independence and female education. As a teenager, she keenly felt the difference in her father's treatment of his son and daughters. While Edward encouraged Austin to read voraciously, he monitored Emily and Lavinia's reading material; as a result, Emily sometimes had to read in secret. "[Father] buys me many Books –" Emily wrote to a friend, "but begs me not to read them – because he fears they joggle the Mind" – likely a reference to the Victorian belief that the womb and the brain were inversely related, so that if a woman read or wrote too much, her brain would impair her fertility by consuming the vital energy necessary for the womb to bear children (*EDL*, p. 404). Given this understanding, Dickinson's father was clearly conflicted about whether his daughter should be allowed to read or write poetry with such passionate energy. And unlike her brother Austin, who was pushed to pursue a law career, Emily and her sister were allowed only one year at college, after which they were expected to take up household duties in preparation for marriage. Even Emily's year at college was marred by an illness. She was determined to hide it from her family so she could stay in school; however, on being informed of the sickness by a family friend, Edward Dickinson dispatched Austin, who "arrived in full sail, with orders from head-quarters to bring me home at all events," in spite of Emily's "desperate battle" to stay (*EDL*, p. 65). This thwarting of her desire for independence and autonomy rankled for young Emily, even as she obeyed her father's wishes. As she grew older she was frequently exposed to the views of the closely aligned abolitionist and suffragist movements through her father's political connections and the hospitality of Austin and Sue, who hosted such luminaries as Harriet Beecher Stowe and Wendell Phillips. In addition, many of the close friendships Dickinson developed later in life were with ardent advocates for increased civil rights and liberties, including Thomas Wentworth Higginson, Samuel Bowles, and Helen Hunt Jackson. Abolition and women's rights were causes to which the Dickinson family was committed, and Emily Dickinson was well aware of the issues at stake.

In addition to her engagement with local, national, and international events, Dickinson had a wide circle of beloved friends and relatives. As a young woman, Emily Dickinson was especially passionate about her relationships. She was ferociously possessive of her friendships and romantic love interests and expected similar devotion from her intimate friends. Susan Gilbert Dickinson, Emily's sister-in-law, was an extremely close friend (and, some have argued, a lover).[8] Cousins Louise and Emily Norcross, early friends like Abiah Root and Jane Humphrey, and later Mary Bowles and Elizabeth Holland were also among her dearest friends.

Dickinson corresponded regularly with this circle of friends via letter, the primary form of keeping in touch with family and friends in her lifetime. There were strict rules governing the decorum of epistolary exchanges, but rather than being discreetly polite as was the order of the day, Dickinson was frequently direct, candid, and intimate in her observations. She was in touch with her circle of friends often several times a week. There were multiple mail deliveries every day in Amherst and frequent train service from Amherst to Boston, so Dickinson could send flowers from her garden along with her letters and poems, in which she shared her deepest thoughts. Many of her letters include lines that later were incorporated into her poetry, and her lines from her poems often became part of her letters – so much so that her letters often seem like poems, and vice versa. "The Frogs sing sweet – today – They have such pretty – lazy – times –" she wrote on one occasion; in another letter, she describes her beloved natural world: "The Violets are by my side, the Robin very near, and 'Spring' – they say, Who is she – going by the door –" (*EDL*, pp. 406, 333). Eminent Dickinson scholar Thomas Johnson and others have determined that she circulated about five hundred of her poems in her letters to more than forty correspondents, and some poems were sent to more than one person at a time. With her voluminous correspondence, Dickinson created a lively personal, intellectual, and artistic community for herself that persisted long after her seclusion.

An important part of this community for Dickinson was the group of men she called her "Preceptors." From childhood on, she searched for mentors. Her first was Benjamin Franklin Newton, who was nine years older than Dickinson and studied with her father. They had long conversations about poetry, and he gave her a book of Emerson's 1847 poems. The Reverend Charles

Wadsworth was another important preceptor, with whom Dickinson carried on an extended correspondence after meeting him in Philadelphia while traveling with her father. Samuel Bowles, editor and owner of the *Springfield Republican*, was also an extremely important mentor, and they shared a long and intimate correspondence, one that was sufficiently intimate for some critics to speculate that Bowles was the recipient of Dickinson's anonymous, impassioned Master Letters. Finally, Thomas Wentworth Higginson, writer, abolitionist, and supporter of women's rights, and the editor of the *Atlantic Monthly*, became a lifelong friend and mentor as well. Dickinson first wrote to Higginson in response to his essay of advice to young writers in the April 1862 *Atlantic Monthly*. She asked him very directly, "Is my Verse Alive?" and she enclosed four poems: "Safe in their Alabaster Chambers" (*EDP*, p. 100, no. 216); "I'll tell you how the Sun rose" (*EDP*, p. 150, no. 318); "The nearest Dream recedes – unrealized" (*EDP*, pp. 150–51, no. 319); and "We play at Paste" (*EDP*, p. 151, no. 320). Dickinson goes on to explain that "The Mind is so near itself – it cannot see, distinctly – and I have None to ask –" (*EDL*, p. 403). Higginson responded ten days later, and their lifelong correspondence began.

In writing to Higginson, Dickinson was looking for guidance from a male authority regarding the value of her poetry. Unfortunately, she did not get a very encouraging response from Higginson, who advised that she "delay" publication; this must have been extremely disappointing – even devastating – to the young poet. After all, two editors had asked her for poems for publication, and writing poetry was at the core of Dickinson's being. But instead of expressing her sadness, Dickinson developed an elaborately defensive posture in an effort to save her pride, writing back to say that the idea of publication was "as foreign to my thought as Firmament to Fin." She claimed that she was not even interested in public recognition, protesting that "If Fame belonged to me / I could not escape her –" (*EDL*, p. 408). At the same time, she gently mocks Higginson's criticism that her work is unruly and rough – "wayward" – in her now-famous quip, "You think my gait spasmodic: – I am in danger – Sir –" (*EDL*, p. 409). Indeed, Dickinson was in danger – after Higginson's criticism she never attempted to publish her poems. She wrote more prolifically than ever, but she developed her own private method of preparation and compilation. As has been documented by major biographer Ralph W. Franklin and scholar Eleanor Elson Heginbotham, Dickinson carefully copied her poems in ink on folded stationery and sewed them by hand into fascicles (a small bundle of clustered pages), which she placed in a drawer in a chest in her bedroom and never circulated.[9] And yet despite Higginson's distressing criticism of her work, she continued to send him her poetry and to confide in him, and he was one of the few visitors she saw after her seclusion. The relationship was clearly a valuable and important one to Dickinson; they remained friends until she died, and he gave a eulogy at her funeral.

From the perspective of the twenty-first century, the fact that Dickinson accepted Higginson's judgment of her poems, even though other editors had praised her work, is deeply disturbing. However, it is important to understand Emily Dickinson as a Victorian woman subject to the customs and constraints of her society. At the same time, it is necessary to locate Dickinson in American literary history, in which she takes her place in a long line of intensely independent nineteenth-century American writers, including Henry David Thoreau, Ralph Waldo Emerson, Mark Twain, Herman Melville, and Walt Whitman. Like them, Dickinson was a highly original artist who departed from nineteenth-century social and artistic conventions. By taking into account this historical trajectory, it is easier to understand why Dickinson might have withdrawn from public consideration and competition: the anxiety of the necessary self-assertion in the public sphere in a time when women were expected to remain in the private sphere was too daunting for Dickinson to manage.

While it is true that many women activists and writers of her era entered the public realm in spite of intimidating public exposure and criticism, Dickinson was not among them. Even though Dickinson knew very well that women suffragists like Elizabeth Cady Stanton, Susan B. Anthony, Lucretia Mott, and many others were a vibrant part of American politics, she did not follow their lead. Similarly, there were a substantial number of American women writers, like Susanna Rowson, Judith Sargent Murray, Margaret Fuller, Louisa May Alcott, Julia Ward Howe, Lydia Sigourney, Harriet Prescott Spofford, Fanny Fern, Harriet Beecher Stowe, and Helen Hunt Jackson, who were well known or were gaining widespread recognition, demonstrating that women could achieve literary success. In fact, Helen Hunt Jackson was persistent in urging Dickinson to give her poems to publish, but Dickinson wasn't willing to put herself forward.

Given the traditional values of the Dickinson household with regard to gender roles and the immense emphasis placed on feminine gentility and decorum, Dickinson's reluctance to seek public attention and approval is understandable. It would have been acceptable if an esteemed male authority like Higginson had taken her under his wing and protected her from criticism by presenting her as his protégée. It would have been quite another matter for a woman to seek attention for herself. There was no financial necessity for Dickinson to publish, as there was for Louisa May Alcott, who desperately needed the money from her writing to buy food and clothing for her family, so it was much easier for Dickinson to demur and remain in the private sphere. Instead of publishing in local newspapers and magazines in the hope of gaining wider recognition for national publication, Dickinson sent her poems privately to her friends. In many respects, one might say this was a high price to pay for gentility, but the imperative of piety, passivity, and passionlessness as the core elements of womanhood was deeply internalized by most women in the nineteenth century.

Higginson's criticism, and Dickinson's subsequent unwillingness to publish, were influenced by another consideration too: her commitment to her artistic vision. Emily Dickinson's poetry broke the mold of nineteenth-century aesthetic conventions; instead of heavily rhymed long lines of poetry, she wrote in short, syncopated, sometimes abrupt, and often enigmatic stanzas that often omitted rhyme. Some poems were only two or three lines long. Many words within the poems were capitalized irregularly. Numerous poems ended not with periods but with dashes, or with no punctuation at all. In thus abandoning the poetic traditions of her time, Dickinson in her poetry paralleled the movement of Transcendentalists such as Emerson and Whitman away from received traditions both poetic and spiritual. Indeed, this poetic departure mirrored Dickinson's personal movement toward Transcendentalist ideals and away from received traditions, as has been observed by Karl Keller.[10] To Higginson she suggested that the received structures of poetry disguised and constricted her ideas like too-confining clothing: "While my thought is undressed – I can make the distinction," she told him, "but when I put them in the Gown" of conventional language and structure, "they look alike, and numb" (*EDL*, p. 404). Numbness was the opposite of what she believed poetry should induce in its reader. According to Higginson, Dickinson defined poetry in a vivid, visceral way: "If I read a book [and] it makes my whole body so cold no fire ever can warm me I know *that* is poetry. If I feel physically as if the top of my head were taken off, I know *that* is poetry. These are the only way I know it. Is there any other way" (*EDL*, pp. 473–74). These were the feelings Dickinson wanted to convey in her writing – an almost physical sensation, and the awakening of specific emotions tied to the moment described. Her unusual choices in syntax, structure, and punctuation were attempts to do just this.

Dickinson's poetry was powerfully original. She rebelled against the rules of Victorian poetics that required heavily rhymed and metered lines. Instead, Dickinson's poems capture a thought in motion that anticipated the stream of consciousness that would arise in the early twentieth century. Dickinson's poetry is now understood to be avant-garde; she was a modernist poet decades before modernism became a literary movement. Her signature style, full of slant rhymes, colloquial language, staccato phrasing, and what often seems like jumbled syntax punctuated by dashes, captures the multivalent vibrancy of each specific moment and defies the reductive effect of social and artistic practices that insisted on predictability and regularized order. This defiance in the service of creative freedom was extremely important to Dickinson. Higginson's criticism had been preceded by a few early, unpleasant brushes with publication, in which she saw her punctuation, capitalization, and stanza structure standardized; her slant rhymes regularized; and her meanings altered by the addition of titles and other editorial choices. Her decision to circulate her poems only privately among her friends, then, left her with the freedom to write to her own aesthetic standards. She came to view formal publication as an unacceptable moral and artistic compromise, describing it in one poem as "the Auction / of the Mind of Man" and suggesting that it might be better to endure "Poverty" rather than "reduce" the "Human Spirit / To Disgrace of Price –" (*EDP*, pp. 348–49, no. 709). Creativity and thought, Dickinson felt, were the expressions of the individual soul, and to assign a monetary value to it was to engage in an immoral trade. It should be noted that it was Dickinson's status as a secure member of the middle class that allowed her to maintain this position without compromise, unencumbered as she was by the necessity of having to support herself through her work. Nevertheless, in standing against contemporary social and artistic practices, Dickinson also saw herself as standing against the increasingly mercenary values of the world around her.

Looking back, it seems clear that Dickinson was convinced that if her poems were indeed worthy of publication, her sister, Lavinia, and her sister-in-law, Susan Gilbert Dickinson, as well as the friends with whom she shared her poems, would make certain that they were published. The fact that the poems were so carefully sewn into fascicles and stored neatly in piles in a drawer to be discovered by Lavinia after Dickinson's death was no accident. It was a great risk to take, a gamble on the willingness of her loved ones to tend to and preserve her work – and yet it speaks to her intense craving for artistic autonomy that she was willing to leave her poetic legacy to chance in this way. This commitment to autonomy both artistic and personal was not easy for Dickinson, and her poetry reveals that she had to first wage a personal civil war to resolve the conflict between the cultural edict of female submission and her desire to be an autonomous, thinking woman and poet. The famed Master Letters, and the poetry she wrote contemporaneously, offer one of the clearest demonstrations of this internal battle.

After Dickinson's death, three drafts of letters to someone identified only as "Master" were found among her correspondence. No other records of her letters to the Master survive, but the language of the three drafts suggests an ongoing relationship. The last of these drafts is dated 1861, at the beginning of Dickinson's "flood years." The letters clearly show her wrestling with a passionate but unrequited love that dominates her will, in spite of her desire to remain independent. They are a portrait of overwhelming and self-abnegating love: "I used to think that when I died – I could see you – so I died as fast as I could," she wrote in one (*EDL*, p. 374). The theme of sacrificial love is reiterated over and over to the point of obsession; it is as though in writing these letters Dickinson has to experience the eclipse of self in its most extreme form before she can find herself again. In her final Master letter, Dickinson begs for recognition again and again in the language of self-abasement. Describing a "love so big it scares her, rushing among her small heart – pushing aside the blood and leaving her faint and white in the gust's arm," she begs for some acknowledgment: "Oh, did I offend it ... who bends her smaller life to his, meeker every day – who only asks – a task – something to do for the love of it – some little way she cannot guess to make that master glad" (*EDL*, p. 391). She repeatedly declares her smallness and desire to serve and suggests that even the most meager response will satisfy "all she asks" or needs. Dickinson then begs for forgiveness for an unknown offense and asks the Master to "teach her, preceptor grace – teach her majesty" (*EDL*, p. 391). She submits herself completely to the Master's instruction and guidance, asking him to reshape her, to remake her in his image. She continues to grovel, asking that he "punish dont banish her – shut her in prison, Sir – only pledge that you will forgive sometime – before the grave" (*EDL*, p. 391). This willingness to accept so little in return for her whole self is both an act of self-humiliation and a cry for love and acceptance.

The extraordinary emotional intensity and self-abnegation of Dickinson's Master Letters has been a topic of critical debate for many decades, and there has been much speculation about the identity of the recipient of these letters. Samuel Bowles, Thomas Higginson, and Susan Gilbert Dickinson have all been suggested as the person to whom Dickinson wrote these letters. More important than the identity of the Master is the fact that Dickinson experiences such intense agony in this relationship. For example, she writes in the closing lines of one letter, "I've got a Tomahawk in my side but that don't hurt me much [If you] Her master stabs her more" (*EDL*, p. 391). It is an image of helpless vulnerability to great wounding. The Master's failure to return her love hurts her almost to the point of destruction. In the letters we see

Dickinson in the throes of despair and misery, with almost no will or strength of her own, and it is a disheartening sight.

But the Master Letters reveal much more than this. In them, Dickinson shrinks almost to invisibility, but she survives. She does not "extinguish herself" but finds within herself the strength to reclaim her will from the Master's power; the letters record the grief and rage of a painful rejection, but as can be seen in the poems written during this period, her sense of self survives.[11] There is some scholarly disagreement about the dating of some of Dickinson's poetry;[12] however, if we follow Johnson's dating, the poems that were written during this time demonstrate that Dickinson in fact emerged from the struggle a stronger, more self-possessed person. "Title divine – is mine!" she proclaims in one poem, identifying herself as the "Empress of Calvary! / Royal – all but the Crown!" Dickinson finds in herself the authority and power of royalty, even if it has come at the cost of suffering as the "Empress of Calvary." She rejoices that she is not "Born – Bridalled – Shrouded – / In a Day" as married women are (EDP, p. 487, no. 1072). "I'm ceded – I've stopped being Theirs –" is in effect her declaration of independence, in which she rejects "The name They dropped upon my face – / With water" and asserts that she has received a new baptism, "this time, consciously, of Grace – / Unto supremest name – Called to my Full" (EDP, p. 247, no. 508). And in "To be alive – is – Power," Dickinson takes control of her life and claims her ontological energy for herself, describing "Existence" as "Omnipotence – Enough" and arguing that

> To be alive – and Will!
> 'Tis able as a God –
> The Maker – of Ourselves – be what –
> Such Being Finitude!   (EDP, p. 335–36, no. 677)

In these poems, Dickinson claims complete autonomy. She casts off the constraints of patriarchy, including the names conferred on her by her father, the church, and society; rejects marriage as the only way for women to achieve a measure of power; and even arrogates to herself the divine power of self-creation. Her assertions of personal liberty and authority in these poems are a far cry from the self-abnegation of the letters; they are pervaded by a sense of triumph and freedom.

As evidenced by her experience with the Master, Dickinson was deeply committed to confronting the full range of her emotions, however frightening the experience. She devoted herself both in her personal life and in her poetry to exploring what she called "Circumference," not just the center of life but all of its edges; she wanted to experience all that she could of each moment, whether pleasurable or painful (*EDL*, p. 412; *EDP*, p. 313, no. 633). This willingness to approach life with a wide perspective allowed her to accept the inevitable coexistence of grief and joy, of despair and hope, and of the potential for danger and the possibility of great power. She described this process of abandonment to the emotion of each moment as a careful balancing act:

> I stepped from Plank to Plank
> A slow and cautious way
> The Stars about my Head I felt
> About my Feet the Sea.   (*EDP*, pp. 416–17, no. 875)

This poem evinces Dickinson's simultaneous commitment to exploration of each moment and her awareness of how this commitment imperils her and puts her at the risk of descent into chaos and destruction. While she gazes with wonder at the beauties of the night sky, she can feel the pull of the sea at her feet. And yet Dickinson remains open. She moves forward inch by inch on unknown terrain, ready to encounter both agony and ecstasy in her determination to find out the fullness of experience the world offers. Her awareness of these tensions and her willingness to risk everything in order to feel each moment gives her poems an authenticity that rings true to contemporary readers.

Emily Dickinson's poems explore a wide range of emotions ranging from fury to ecstasy; much of her poetry focuses on love, autonomy, nature, and death. To the contemporary reader, it might seem as though Emily Dickinson was death obsessed, but we have to keep in mind that the mortality rate was much higher in her lifetime than it is now. Her bedroom in the family home on West Street overlooked a church graveyard, and Dickinson had ample opportunity to observe the patterns and rituals of death. Later in her life, in 1874, when Edward Dickinson collapsed while giving a speech in Boston and died soon afterward, Emily began to confront the brevity of life in very concrete ways. In the ten years immediately following, many of her family members and closest friends died, including Samuel Bowles in 1878; Reverend Charles Wadsworth in 1879; and Dickinson's mother, Emily Norcross Dickinson, in 1882. Soon after, Judge Otis Lord, with whom Dickinson had a very intimate relationship, died, as did the poet Helen Hunt Jackson, who had remained a close friend from their school days. When her eight-year-old nephew, Gib, died of typhoid fever in October 1883, Dickinson became despondent. With so much death in her immediate circle, it is no wonder that reflections on the end of life took up a large part of her work.

As in her work on other subjects, in her poetry Dickinson subverted Victorian sentimental norms about death as a passage to the afterlife. Rather than depicting death as a gentle lover or angel escorting the faithful to heaven, as was common in Victorian poetry and fiction, Dickinson emphasizes that death is a "Riddle, at the last," making it clear that death is decidedly unromantic, and that what happens after death is inherently unknowable and mysterious (*EDP*, p. 243, no. 501). In a letter after the death of Judge Lord, she remarked that his death was "a Sleep that ended with a smile, so his Nieces tell us, he hastened away, 'seen,' we trust, 'of Angels' – 'Who knows that secret deep' – 'Alas, not I –'" (*EDL*, p. 816). And one of Dickinson's most famous poems, "I heard a Fly buzz – when I died," interrupts the "Stillness" and solemnity of the deathbed room to follow a common fly and ends not with a vision of heaven or the afterlife but with a refusal of vision altogether: "And then the Windows failed – and then / I could not see to see –" (*EDP*, pp. 223–24, no. 465). The presence of the fly undercuts any sentimentality in the moment and suggests the anticlimactic nature of death, and the abruptness of this ending underscores death's inscrutability.

Dickinson's poetry explores the experience of death not only for the dying but for those left behind to mourn the dead, and her purpose is not to sanitize or sentimentalize it but to record it. She was committed to describing the experience of mourning with all its variations, no matter how unpleasant. In one poem she describes the physical sensations of grief, including "great pain," followed by a "formal feeling" in which the "Nerves sit ceremonious" and the "stiff Heart questions" while the "Feet, mechanical, go round"; it is, for the mourner,

> ... the Hour of Lead –
> Remembered, if outlived,
> As Freezing persons, recollect the Snow –
> First – Chill – then Stupor – then the letting go –

> (*EDP*, p. 162, no. 341)

In this description, those who "outlive" their loved ones move through the world empty and numb, scarcely feeling at all after the initial pain. Grief steals over them like cold, gradually and inevitably, and the emptiness it leaves behind is a kind of death of the soul that hints at the ends that await the mourners too. But pain is not the only emotion Dickinson explores; she also examines the anger and guilt that come with death. "How dare the robins sing," she asks,

> When men and women hear
> Who since they went to their account

Have settled with the year! –
Paid all that life had earned
In one consummate bill
And now, what life or death can do
Is immaterial.   (*EDP*, p. 700, no. 1724)

That robins can continue to sing when the dead can no longer hear them is an insult to their memory, and a source of bitter guilt for their loved ones. The dead have paid the "consummate bill" for life, but it is the living who are allowed to hear and enjoy the beauty of nature. In these poems, Dickinson acknowledges the variety of emotions that accompany death for both the dying and their mourners. She does not attempt to soften death; she experiences it – both imaginatively and, as a mourner, literally – and presents it in all its complexity.

Dickinson accepted the inevitability of death, and her poems celebrate her deepest convictions that life should take on intense meaning in the context of mortality. In one such poem, she describes her first outing after a long illness and concludes,

My loss, by sickness – Was it Loss?
Or that Ethereal Gain
One earns by measuring the Grave –
Then – measuring the Sun –

(*EDP*, pp. 279–80, no. 574)

Consistent with her belief that the heaven promised in the Christian afterlife can be found in the joys of earthly life, Dickinson suggests that paradise can be hastened if one faces the possibility of death and accepts that it will come, if one "[measures] the Sun" with the perspective gained by first measuring the "Grave." In this respect, the "loss" of time spent in nature is not a loss but an "Ethereal Gain," a way of bringing heaven-on-earth closer. For Dickinson, the seeming omnipresence of death and the impossibility of knowing what followed it served to make life infinitely dear.

In the mid-1880s, when Dickinson was in her early fifties, her life was seriously circumscribed by increasingly serious health problems, including an eye condition that brought increasing light sensitivity and Bright's disease, a kidney ailment that was associated with fluid retention, incontinence, and eventual kidney failure. When she lost consciousness for the first time in August 1884, Dickinson described it as a "revenge of the nerves," a diagnosis applied to many ailments in the nineteenth century, and she was told to rest. This treatment was consistent with the commonly prescribed "Rest Cure" treatment for "nervous diseases of women" made famous by prominent neurologist S. Weir Mitchell; the cure involved seclusion and bed rest, minimal social and intellectual engagement, and a mild diet of warm milk and bread. In a letter to Helen Hunt Jackson, Dickinson recounted that she "took [her] summer in a Chair" and optimistically announced that she had since "taken [her] Nerve by the Bridle" (*EDL*, p. 937). Dickinson's recovery was short lived; a year later she was confined to her bed. In the spring of 1886, she wrote to Higginson, "I have been very ill, Dear friend, since November [1885], bereft of Book and Thought, by the Doctor's reproof, but begun to roam in my Room now" (*EDL*, p. 1042). This setback was the beginning of a serious decline in Dickinson's health that ended with her death in 1886.

Throughout her life, Dickinson rejected social convention and the comforts of religion. This commitment to self-reliance meant that she had to explore uncharted emotional terrain, which involved confronting fears of rejection on all fronts – family, friends, love interests, teachers, editors, readers, and religious and community leaders – as well as the ultimate fear of death. In undertaking this courageous journey, Dickinson left behind traditional comforts and assurances, perhaps most powerful among them the promise of salvation and eternal life, to navigate choppy existential waters alone. Relinquishing the comforting assurances provided by filial piety, traditional marriage, or faith in an afterlife, Emily Dickinson struggled with the complexities and contradictions of her emotions. Finally, she rejected all patriarchal authorities – her father, potential husbands, literary mentors, and an all-powerful God. Her poetry and letters form a chronicle of her challenging, and often dramatic, adventure.

Ultimately, Emily Dickinson spurned a cosmology defined by absolute and authoritarian certainties and instead created a personal vision in which consciousness itself was a gift, ecstasy was the joy of being alive, human love was a form of grace, nature was heaven, home was paradise, and art created eternal life. As a young girl, Emily Dickinson proclaimed that she was not afraid to pick "Satan's flowers," to explore and know the intimate nature of things others considered dangerous. Her determination to live her life in this way, without the traditional comforts of marriage and certainties of religion, gave her the understanding necessary to write powerful and timeless poetry.

Notes

1. Thomas Higginson, quoted in Emily Dickinson, *The Letters of Emily Dickinson*, ed. Thomas H. Johnson (Cambridge, Mass.: Harvard University Press, 1986),

p. 570. Letters in this collection will subsequently be cited in the text as *EDL* followed by the page number.

2. Adrienne Rich, "Vesuvius at Home: The Power of Emily Dickinson," *Parnassus: Poetry in Review* 5:1 (1976), reprinted in *Adrienne Rich, Selected Prose, 1966–1978* (New York: Norton, 1979), p. 161.

3. Emily Dickinson, *The Complete Poems of Emily Dickinson*, ed. Thomas H. Johnson (New York: Little, Brown, 1960) p. 99. Poems in this collection will subsequently be cited as *EDP* followed by the page number and poem number (e.g., *EDP*, p. 99, no. 215). Johnson and R. W. Franklin are considered the two major scholars in the editing and publication of Dickinson's poetry and letters. Johnson's three-volume edition of Dickinson's poetry (1951) was a landmark publication in that it was the first major collection of Dickinson's work that attempted to present her poems in their original formatting and style, with minimal editorial intervention in punctuation, capitalization, and ordering. He also published a variorum edition in 1955 and a single-volume reading edition in 1960. Franklin later built on Johnson's work and in various editions (beginning in 1981) has attempted to make the published texts resemble Dickinson's manuscripts as closely as possible. There is some variation in dating and order between Johnson and Franklin; Johnson's 1960 reading edition is cited here for ease of reference.

4. Wendy Martin, *An American Triptych: Anne Bradstreet, Emily Dickinson, Adrienne Rich* (Chapel Hill: University of North Carolina Press, 1984), p. 121.

5. Diana Fuss, *The Sense of an Interior: Four Writers and the Rooms That Shaped Them* (New York: Routledge, 2004), pp. 55–56.

6. Quoted in Rich, "Vesuvius at Home," p. 158.

7. See Alfred Habegger, *My Wars Are Laid Away in Books: The Life of Emily Dickinson* (New York: Modern Library, 2002) and Shira Wolosky, *Emily Dickinson: A Voice of War* (New Haven, Conn.: Yale University Press, 1984).

8. See John Cody, *After Great Pain: The Inner Life of Emily Dickinson* (New York: Belknap, 1971) and Marietta Messmer, *A Vice for Voices: Reading Emily Dickinson's Correspondence* (Amherst: University of Massachusetts Press, 2001).

9. See Ralph W. Franklin, *The Editing of Emily Dickinson: A Reconsideration* (Madison: University of Wisconsin Press, 1967) and Eleanor Elson Heginbotham, *Reading the Fascicles of Emily Dickinson: Dwelling in Possibilities* (Columbus: Ohio State University Press, 2003).

10. See Karl Keller, *The Only Kangaroo Among the Beauty: Emily Dickinson and America* (Baltimore, Md.: Johns Hopkins University Press, 1979).

11. Martin, *An American Triptych*, p. 102.

12. The poetry is difficult to date because of the nature in which it was stored, and the way the materials were handled following Dickinson's death. Some poems were bound into fascicles; many were written on a wide variety of scrap papers and materials; for many, it was difficult to tell whether the poems

were drafts or final versions; almost all were undated. Some poems could be dated based on their inclusion in letters, but for the most part they were in no discernible order. To add to the confusion, after Dickinson's death the fascicles were unbound and separated by well-meaning relatives attempting to order the poems, further obscuring any organization Dickinson might have intended.

Chapter 17

The South in Reconstruction: White and Black Voices

JOHN D. KERKERING

"Reconstruction" is the term traditionally used to designate the period and process by which the defeated Southern states were reintegrated into the United States after the U.S. Civil War. The period typically extends from the close of hostilities in April 1865 to the withdrawal of federal troops from the South in 1877. The process included two major plans for reintegration, first that of the president (Andrew Johnson) and second that of the Republican Senate, and it produced such major legislation as several civil rights acts and three amendments to the Constitution – the Thirteenth, Fourteenth, and Fifteenth Amendments.[1] The social and political turmoil of the Civil War and Reconstruction periods could not help but be evident to poets writing during this time, and their responses to this turmoil took a variety of forms, but the overall shape of this period witnesses a shift by poets away from a focus on regional affiliation to an increasingly strong confrontation with the issues of race. In other words, the conflicts between North and South come to have less centrality than those between black and white people.

The Southern poet Henry Timrod was briefly enlisted in service of the Confederacy before poor health dictated that he turn his activities in a more literary direction, which he pursued as assistant editor of the Charleston *Mercury* in 1863. During the early years of the Civil War he wrote poems like "Carolina" (now the state's official song) that championed his native state and reflected the commitment to states' rights associated with the Southern cause: "They shall not touch thy noble heart, / Carolina!"[2] As the war waged on, however, his poems referenced the conflict but tended not to champion one side over another; thus, Timrod's concern with regional divisions between North and South ultimately reflects a studious avoidance of drawing poetry into the fray.[3] For instance, in "Spring" he laments the coming of that season – normally a welcome event – because it will bring with it a resumption of military hostilities: "Yet not more surely shall the Spring awake / The voice of wood and brake / Than she shall rouse, for all her tranquil charms, / A million men to arms" (*CPT*, p. 124). In the poem "Christmas" he asks, "How shall we grace the day? / Ah! Let the thought that on this holy morn / The Prince of Peace – the Prince of Peace was born, / Employ us, while we pray!" (*CPT*, p. 117), suggesting a shared religious sentiment uniting both sides. In "The Two Armies" the conceit portrays a single army of men doing the fighting and a single army of women supporting them and waiting for the fighting to end, so he divides the opponents by sex rather than by region. Insofar as they look toward reconciliation, these sentiments anticipate the values necessary for Reconstruction to succeed.

An exception to Timrod's martial restraint is the exhilaration inspired by Confederate victories that led to the poem "Carmen Triumphale": "Our foes are fallen! Flash, ye wires!" (*CPT*, p. 128). The South would soon, however, suffer military setbacks at Vicksburg and Gettysburg, and Timrod's poems often express the mourning that goes along with such losses. This proves especially true of his poems in the early days of Reconstruction. For instance, in 1866 he wrote an occasional poem for the dedication of the Charleston cemetery for Confederate dead, a poem that takes a universalist rather than regionalist tone: "Stoop, angels, higher from the skies! / There is no holier spot of ground, / Than where defeated valor lies / By mourning beauty crowned" (*CPT*, p. 130). Here "defeated valor" is a description that could apply as well to combatants on either side of the Civil War. Timrod's view of Reconstruction is partial, because he only lived a couple of years into the process (he died in 1867), but one of his latest poems registers – albeit obliquely – a fear common among the former Confederates, a fear that the defeated South would be at the mercy of the triumphant North. Thus the poem "Storm and Calm" expresses the following concern: "Awake, thou stormy North, and blast / The subtle spells around us cast; / Beat from our limbs these flowery chains / With the sharp scourges of thy rains!" (*CPT*, p. 139). Here the "calm" South is harassed by the stormy North in an allegory in which the contrasting seasons stand in for political differences, with Northern storms threatening Southern tranquility. Timrod died too soon, however, to have the experiences of Reconstruction that would lead him to write more poems in this register of complaint. What we primarily see from Timrod, then, is a profound awareness of the losses of the war and a tendency to use poetry not as a means of fomenting the conflict but instead as a way of mourning those losses.

A desire to preserve Timrod's name and reputation motivated Paul Hamilton Hayne, himself a Southern poet, to produce an edition of Timrod's writings in 1873, with a biographical sketch that remains an important resource. Like Timrod, Hayne was also a poet of wartime, and several of his works express sentiments associated with the experiences of both victory and defeat,[4] but Hayne, in living and continuing to write until his death in 1886, had greater opportunity to write about Reconstruction.

Some of his poems complain about the way the defeated South was being treated by the victorious North. "South Carolina to the States of the North" has an opening footnote that reads: "This Poem was composed at a period when it seemed as if all the horrors of misgovernment ... would be perpetuated in South Carolina. It was a significant and terrible epoch; a time American statesmen would do well to remember occasionally as a warning against patchwork political re-constructions" (PH, p. 297n). In the poem itself Hayne mixes strategies of personalization and personification: to personalize, the speaker complains of "these hands with iron fetters banded" and "Your tyrant's sword [that] shone glittering at my throat!"; to personify, the speaker refers to the abstract concept of "Freedom" as a "sweet goddess" whose "outraged form [is] receding" (PH, pp. 297–98). To close the poem, the speaker threatens a reversal of fortunes at the time of divine judgment, when he "May mock your ruin, as ye mocked at mine!" (PH, p. 299).

If this poem envisions an ultimate and divinely sanctioned revenge, other Hayne poems took a softer tone, seeking reconciliation with the North rather than vengeance. For instance, "The Stricken South to the North" acknowledges the goodwill of particular Northern friends like Oliver Wendell Holmes (to whom the poem is dedicated) so that, even as it complains of wrongs ("Behold her now – the scourged and suffering South!"), the poem envisions "A voice of manful cheer and heavenly trust / A hand redeeming breaks the frozen starkness" (PH, p. 299). This redemption is, as in the earlier poem, associated with divine judgment – "Ah! Still beyond the tempest smiles the Christ!" (PH, p. 300) – but here the redemption is to be attained in this world rather than the world to come: "Whose voice? Whose hand? Oh, thanks, divinest Master, / Thanks for those grand emotions which impart / Grace to the North to feel the South's disaster, / The South to bow with touched and cordial heart!" (PH, p. 300). Here it is a sentimental reconciliation, or "emotions" and "feeling," based on religious humility and "love," that Hayne envisions as allowing the two sections to reunite: "Now, now at last the magic words are spoken / Which blend in one two long-divided lands!" (PH, p. 300). These "magic words," from Holmes to Hayne, are quoted from a private letter excerpted at the beginning of the poem ("We are thinking a great deal about the poor fever-stricken cities of the South, and all contributing according to our means for their relief" [PH, p. 299]). In other poems Hayne envisions reconciliation in other terms than religious feeling. For instance, "The King of the Plow" foresees a time after the war when "The war-cloud has hurled its last light-ning" and there rules, instead, the monarch of agriculture: "What monarch rules blissfully now? / Oh! Crown him with bays that are bloodless, / The king, the brave king of the plow!" (*PH*, p. 311). The geographic sections are thus unified here by their shared subservience ("All climes to his prowess must bow") to this "homely, but bountiful God" (*PH*, p. 311) of agricultural pro-duction who rules over North and South alike. In yet another poem, "On the Death of President Garfield," Hayne expresses a shared sorrow that joins both North and South as one nation: "North," "West," and "South" are "Thus by the spell of one vast grief united" (*PH*, p. 313).

Reconciliation of North and South would eventually become the explicit goal of another Southern poet, Sidney Lanier, who was chosen to partici-pate in the 1876 centennial celebration in Philadelphia by writing the lyrics to a work composed jointly by a Southerner and a Northerner: Lanier would write the words, and a Northerner, Dudley Buck of Boston, would write the music, with the conjunction of music and words in a harmonious whole rep-resenting reunion. This disposition toward reconciliation, however, did not come easily to Lanier, who took until 1876 to reach this view. Lanier, who had been a Confederate soldier, had similar views to Hayne about the abuses of the North against the South. Thus in an 1868 poem called "Laughter in the Senate" Lanier responds to the shift from a presidential to a congressional plan of reconstruction, complaining that the new plan makes light of the South's ills: "The tyrants sit in a stately hall; / They jibe at a wretched people's fall."[5] More sinister is Lanier's 1870–1871 poem "Them Ku Klux," in which a conver-sation between a Southerner and a "Yankee" leads to oblique praise of the ter-rorist conspiracy that this group perpetrated against Southern black people. In this poem, Ulysses S. Grant is imagined as the "leader" and "breeder" of the Klan insofar as he set up the postwar conditions that prompted Klan violence (*PPO*, p. 193). In the 1874 poem "Civil Rights," a dialect speaker complains of the equality envisioned for African Americans in the proposed Civil Rights Act (enacted in 1875). "Them Yanks had throwed us overboard from off the Ship of State. / Yes, throwed us both – both black and white – into the ragin' sea / With but one rotten plank to hold," and the speaker warns, "*I'll push the nigger in*" (*PPO*, pp. 41–42), making explicit reference to rising racial conflict in the postwar South. As this hostile language demonstrates, Lanier was quite will-ing to use poetry to express his pain and anger at the way the white South was being treated in Reconstruction.

But if Hayne was interested in reconciliation by the means we've seen – via Christian love, the common harvest, or shared grief – then Lanier was interested in reconciliation of the warring sections by a different means, that of racial identity. Hayne, for his part, used the word "race" to mean generation – thus he referred to someone as belonging to a "time and race gone by" ("To Alexander H. Stephens" [*PH*, p. 293]). But Lanier saw "race" as a term expressing the persistence through time of a particular people – in his case, Anglo-Saxons. Lanier thus looked further backward – to the Anglo-Saxon past – in order to look further forward – toward an ultimate resolution of sectional conflict on the grounds of racial unity. African Americans would be excluded from Lanier's vision of a reunited United States.

Lanier's views about the shared Anglo-Saxonness of the North and South are evident in his extensive prose writings about poetry. Lanier's racial logic begins by establishing that poetry is to be understood as music rather than language. In his view, music and language are two distinct phenomena, the one (language) concerning itself with conveying meanings, or the contents of individual consciousness, and the other (music) evoking emotion without communicating any conscious ideas whatsoever. Here is Lanier's emphatic declaration of the point in a fragment of writing on Wagner:

> Wagner is again wrong in his fundamental assertion that music "speaks a language intelligible by all." The truth is that *as language* (i.e. as that which conveys the contents of one consciousness into another consciousness; or that which makes *you* aware *pro tanto* of *me*) [music] is not intelligible to any save in the most limited degree. If you shall play me your improvisation, I can tell whether you mean a funeral dirge, or dance music, I can apprehend to some degree the state of your soul: but within these widely separated extremes lies a vast domain of tone which when I come within its influence does not bring me the least intelligible report of your consciousness: and you shall play to me by the hour without increasing my definite accessions of matters drawn from your consciousness however thoroughly your music may penetrate my heart.[6]

Lanier's next logical step argues that poetry is not just music but racial music. He does this by asserting that Anglo-Saxon poetry from the eighth century to the present has employed the same rhythmic basis, what Lanier calls three-rhythm. Thus, in his *The Science of English Verse* (1880), Lanier writes, "we find the English love for 3-rhythm not only unabating after more than twelve hundred years' use of it, but the most modern English verse tending into the very specific forms of 3-rhythm used by our earliest ancestral poets."[7] Lanier identifies this as "the typic rhythm of Anglo-Saxon poetry" (*SEV*, p. 120) and asserts that it "never varies from the beginning to the end of what we may call Anglo-Saxon poetry" (*SEV*, p. 120). According to Lanier, Anglo-Saxon poets have been making the same music for more than a thousand years; the fact that poets make this same rhythmic music – and not whether they follow the rules of language (which have changed over time) – is what makes them count as Anglo-Saxon. Even such radical formal experiments as those produced by Walt Whitman can, according to Lanier, be subsumed under the banner of Anglo-Saxon music.[8]

This point about U.S. racial unity achieved via poetry-as-music gives us an insight into Lanier's 1876 centennial cantata, mentioned previously. In a letter to the editors of the *New York Times* in which Lanier defends his cantata text against widespread criticism, he writes that he deliberately chose "abrupt vocables" of "short, sharp, vigorous Saxon words" for his poem's lines, thus making his poetry – that is, his music – Anglo-Saxon.[9] There is a tension between the racial music of the poem and its national text: the cantata text is entitled "The Centennial Meditation of Columbia"; thus its overt reference is 1776 and the New World goddess – Columbia – who presides over the new nation, but the form that the poem embodies – because it is not language but music – is not national but racial, and the race it embodies is the Old World race of Anglo-Saxons, the race the poem imagines as colonizing the New World at Plymouth and Jamestown. Understood in this way, the performance of this text at the 1876 centennial celebration in Philadelphia effectively endorsed Lanier's vision for Reconstruction, a solution to the sectional conflict that unified whites to the exclusion of African Americans.

This commitment to Anglo-Saxon racial identity provides the background for many other poems whose themes are not ostensibly political or racial. An example is Lanier's Christian poem "A Ballad of Trees and the Master" (1880), which uses Lanier's characteristically Anglo-Saxon three-rhythm to depict the sympathy of woodland nature as Christ spends time in the wilderness and, subsequently, is crucified on a tree: "From under the trees they drew Him last: / 'Twas on a tree they slew Him – last / When out of the woods he came" (*PPO*, p. 144). The longer poems for which Lanier is best known include "Corn" (1874), "The Symphony" (1875), and "The Marshes of Glynn" (1878). The first of these articulates a tension between cotton, which is presented as a mere commodity in the fickle marketplace, and corn, which is presented as a steadfast companion and counterpart to the poet-speaker: "Thou lustrous stalk, that ne'er mayst walk nor talk, / Still shalt thou type the poet-soul sublime" (*PPO*, p. 36), and "Fitly thou playest out thy poet's part" (*PPO*, p. 37). In this way corn, although just as much a commodity as cotton, becomes an extension of Romantic nature – an eternal resource for the foundation of human dignity. "The Symphony" further develops the critique of a commercial culture that reduces life to mere commodities: "'O Trade! O Trade! would that thou wert dead! / The Time needs heart – 'tis tired of head: / We're all for love,' the violins said" (PPO, p. 46). With a series of orchestral instruments serving as speakers, the poem makes its case for an elevation of loving heart over trading head: "'Trade! is thy heart all dead, all dead? / And hast thou nothing but a head? / I'm all for heart,' the flute-voice said" (PPO, pp. 51–52). The poem concludes that "Music is Love in search of a word" (PPO, p. 56). Lanier's emphasis on poetry as music recognizes that words are capable of serving either head or heart and insists that words must become musical in order to achieve the status of "Art" (PPO, p. 51) and overcome vile trade. This theme of commerce is also present in "The Marshes of Glynn," in which "the trowel of trade is low" (PPO, p. 119) and, by contrast, the majesty of nature is wholly present to a speaker who watches a day unfold in the marshland: "Oh, like the greatness of God is the greatness within / The range of the marshes, the liberal marshes of Glynn" (PPO, p. 121). In addition to tracing the passage of noon to night, the poem's speaker stands watch as the high tide arrives: "The tide is at his highest height: / And it is night" (PPO, p. 122). Here the land and sea unite in a full measure of divine creation. What unfolds in these lines is a drama of rapt spectatorship as the marsh is invested with all the grandeur of natural divinity: "I will fly in the greatness of God as the marsh-hen flies / In the freedom that fills all the space 'twixt the marsh and the skies" (PPO, p. 121). Throughout this poem Lanier experiments with the musicality of an anapestic line, one fully in keeping with his notion of an ancestral Anglo-Saxon three-rhythm.

In his approach to poetry – treating it as music, and treating that music as inherently racial – Lanier effectively closes out the representation of African Americans from his vision of postwar national unity. By contrast, an explicit effort to represent black people in poetry is exemplified by Walt Whitman's 1871 poem "Ethiopia Saluting the Colors," in which Whitman embeds a black speaker who suggests the relationship that "Ethiopia" – an aged "dusky" woman who stands in for all black people – bears to "the Colors," or the flag of the federal union. The poem begins,

> Who are you dusky woman, so ancient hardly human,
> With your wooly-white and turban'd head, and bare bony feet?
> Why rising by the roadside here, do you the colors greet?
>
> ('Tis while our army lines Carolina's sands and pines,
> Forth from thy hovel door thou Ethiopia com'st to me,
> As under doughty Sherman I march toward the sea.)

> Me master years a hundred since from my parents sunder'd,
> A little child, they caught me as the savage beast is caught,
> Then hither me across the sea the cruel slaver brought.[10]

Here a remnant from the other Old World – Africa – is presented as an embedded speaker in the poem, so a black voice is mediated by Whitman's white one. There is thus an effort here to envision someone speaking on behalf of black people, much as Lanier sought a voice speaking on behalf of white people (or Anglo-Saxons). This effort to articulate a racialized poetic voice for black people would be taken up more extensively by the poets Frances Ellen Watkins Harper, Paul Laurence Dunbar, and Albery Allson Whitman.

Harper's effort to speak on behalf of black people extended back before the Civil War, when she agitated in favor of freedom for African American slaves. This agitation found voice in her prose writings as well as her poetry. In the poem "To the Cleveland Union-Savers: An Appeal from One of the Fugitive's Own Race" (1861), for instance, Harper chastises those who, for the sake of saving the federal union, would call for returning Southern fugitive slaves to their masters, calling instead on these Union advocates to give freedom to black people: "And your guilty, sin-cursed Union / Shall be shaken to its base, / Till ye learn that simple justice / Is the right of every race."[11] A similar viewpoint motivates Harper's longer narrative poem *Moses: A Story of the Nile* (1869). Writing in 1859, Harper had asserted, "I like the character of Moses. He is the first disunionist we read of in the Jewish Scriptures" (*BCD*, p. 103). But in this postwar poem Harper focuses more on devotion to one's race than on the drama of freedom obtained, for the Jews can be freed only if Moses – who is of a different class than the slaves of his race – chooses to breach class distinctions and identify with the lowly slaves. Near the end of *Moses*, Harper writes, "His life had been a lengthened sacrifice, / A thing of deep devotion to his race" (*BCD*, p. 163). Harper's Reconstruction poetry often advocates the identification of upper-class black people with lower-class black people, a goal that also takes center stage in her 1892 novel *Iola Leroy*.

What we've seen, then, is that following the Civil War and the freedoms won for African Americans, Harper shifted her focus from freedom for slaves to civil rights and uplift for black citizens. During a tour of what she calls "the unreconstructed states" in July 1867 Harper writes, "so far as the colored man is concerned, I do not feel particularly uneasy about his future. With his breadth of physical organization, his fund of mental endurance, and his former discipline in the school of toil and privation, I think he will be able to force his way upward and win his recognition even in the South" (*BCD*, p. 124).

Her collection *Poems* (1871) set out to be a spur to this kind of uplift. In "Lines to Hon. Thaddeus Stevens," a prominent congressional advocate of black civil rights, she writes, "There is hope in God's great justice, / And the negro's rising brain" (*BCD*, p. 167). The threat to this hope was to be found in the ambitions of the former "traitor" to the nation, the Southern white, and the proof against this threat was to be the solidarity of the rest of the nation with black people, who, during the war, "were faithful to the end" ("An Appeal to the American People" [*BCD*, p. 167]). Harper put her hopes in those "Americans" to whom she appeals, but she also took solace from legal milestones, as indicated by her poem "Fifteenth Amendment": "With freedom's chrism upon thy head, / Her precious ensign in thy hand, / Go place thy once despised name / Amid the noblest of the land" (*BCD*, pp. 189–90).

Harper presented speakers in her 1872 collection *Sketches of Southern Life* who were both regional and racial: black Southerners. This was a pioneering foray into racial representation in poetry. Central to this collection is the energetic voice of a frame narrator, Aunt Chloe, in a series of impressive poems: "Aunt Chloe," "The Deliverance," "Aunt Chloe's Politics, "Learning to Read," "Church Building," and "The Reunion." Frances Smith Foster describes Aunt Chloe as a folk character who speaks in dialect and thus represents a contribution to the literature of local color, but it is striking how standard the English is in the Aunt Chloe poems, especially when compared to the dramatically nonstandard dialect rendered in the poetry of Paul Laurence Dunbar, which would be published three decades later (*BCD*, p. 137). An example is "The Deliverance," which depicts the divergence of views on the Civil War between the slave quarters and the master's house: "Mistus prayed up in the parlor / That the Secesh all might win; / We were praying in the cabins, / Wanting freedom to begin" (*BCD*, p. 200). The poem goes on to discuss the slave quarters' reaction to the death of Lincoln ("we had one awful sorrow") and its hopes for the new president: "I'd vote for him for breaking up / The wicked Ku-Klux Klan" (*BCD*, p. 202). The subject of voting leads Aunt Chloe to address the circumstance of some former slaves selling their votes and the negative reactions of their wives to this practice: "You'd laughed to seen Lucinda Grange / Upon her husband's track; / When he sold his vote for rations / She made him take 'em back" (*BCD*, p. 204). African Americans were widely criticized for selling their votes (which was taken as a sign that they did not appreciate their newly won liberty), and Aunt Chloe ends "The Deliverance" with reassurances that most former slaves refused to sell their votes and properly valued the right to vote; they "know their freedom cost too much / Of blood and pain and treasure, / For them to fool away their votes / For profit or for pleasure" (*BCD*, p. 204).

Other Aunt Chloe poems include "Aunt Chloe's Politics" and "Learning to Read." The former laments the "mighty ugly tricks" perpetrated by those who "talk so awful sweet," concluding level-headedly that political corruption is a "loss we all must share" (*BCD*, pp. 204–05). The latter addresses an important aspect of Reconstruction's racial uplift project, the dissemination of education to the former slave population. "Well, the Northern folks kept sending / The Yankee teachers down; / And they stood right up and helped us, / Though Rebs did sneer and frown" (*BCD*, p. 206). Despite her age ("rising sixty" [*BCD*, p. 206]), Aunt Chloe insists on learning to read her Bible, and this quest for intellectual independence is paralleled by independent living in a room of her own: "Then I got a little cabin – / A place to call my own – / And I felt as independent / As the queen upon her throne" (*BCD*, p. 206). The poem "Church Building" underscores another important aspect of Reconstruction for African Americans, the construction of independent churches as institutions of stability within the community. Aunt Chloe relates, "Uncle Jacob often told us, / Since freedom blessed our race / We ought all to come together / And build a meeting place" (*BCD*, p. 206), and Uncle Jacob goes on to "the promised land" – which, here, is not freedom (as it was often described prior to Reconstruction) but a Christian heaven. The final poem in the Aunt Chloe sequence is "The Reunion," which represents the effort to reconstitute African American families that had been torn apart by slavery – particularly, by the separation of slave mothers from their children. Thus Aunt Chloe says to her newly discovered son, whose search for her has finally succeeded, "Old Mistus got no power now / To tear us both apart" (*BCD*, p. 208). This ambition to reconstitute families during Reconstruction would be a prominent part of the plot of Harper's 1892 novel *Iola Leroy*, but the Aunt Chloe sequence is different and distinctive insofar as it gives a central role as speaker to a former slave and resident of the slave quarters.

In her speeches from this period Harper continued to underscore the notion of racial uplift, a concept that would gain its greatest notoriety through the writings of Booker T. Washington, particularly his autobiography, *Up from Slavery* (1895). Harper states in an 1866 speech that "Society cannot afford to neglect the enlightenment of any class of its members" (*BCD*, p. 217), suggesting that racial classifications should not be a basis for differential treatment of black and white people. She continues, "This grand and glorious revolution which has commenced, will fail to reach its climax of success, until throughout the length and brea[d]th of the American Republic, the nation shall be so color-blind, as to know no man by the color of his skin or the curl of his hair" (*BCD*, p. 218). This ambition for an absence of racial distinctiveness within the U.S. nation would prompt criticism from later writers who sought an autonomous racial identity, setting black people apart from white interference. Such later writers – notably, W. E. B. Du Bois – resisted the idea that the African American, or "Negro," was a "problem" to be solved. This, however, is how Harper phrases the situation in her speech "The Great Problem to be Solved":

> The great problem to be solved by the American people, if I understand it, is this – whether or not there is strength enough in democracy, virtue enough in our civilization, and power enough in our religion to have mercy and deal justly with four millions of people but lately translated from the old oligarchy of slavery to the new commonwealth of freedom: and upon the right solution of this question depends in a large measure the future strength, progress, and durability of our nation. (*BCD*, p. 219)

According to Harper, race, as an operative distinction between black and white peoples, should give way to a shared American national identity. Ironically, Harper often wrote from a racially distinct voice in order to advocate the vanishing of that racial distinctiveness. Harper envisioned racial uplift – and in particular the assistance of white toward black people – as sufficient to bring justice in this earthly world.

The earthly world coexists, for Harper, with a sacred world beyond it, and Christian themes are prominent in Harper's poetry. In "Jesus," which appeared in Harper's 1871 collection *Poems*, Harper's speaker states, "I need the grand attraction / That centres 'round the cross, / To change the gilded things of earth / To emptiness and dross" (*BCD*, p. 189). Harper was known, however, to mix her notions of divinity with this world; thus, the Civil War could be seen as divine retribution for the worldly sins of slavery, and the end of slavery could be a worldly manifestation of arriving at the promised land. We see the former notion in the poem "Retribution" (from *Poems* [1871]): "As a warning to the nations, / Bathed in blood and swathed in fire, / Lay the once oppressing nation, / Smitten by God's fearful ire" (*BCD*, p. 190). Here the aftermath of divine judgment isn't the kingdom of heaven but the worldly hell of punishment for slavery's evil ways. Another example sees the end of slavery as itself the promised land: "O ransomed race! Give God the praise, / Who led thee through a crimson sea" ("Fifteenth Amendment" [*BCD*, p. 190]). But Harper's eschatology was also geared toward setting aside the earthly world – whether it be a site of divine punishment or a site of divine reward – in favor of a distant heaven to be sought after in spite of this world's successes or failures.

Thus in the poem "Light in Darkness," the speaker states, "And we thanked the chastening angel / Who shaded our earthly light, / For the light and beautiful visions / That broke on our clearer sight" (*BCD*, p. 195). In "I Thirst," this divinity, although remote from worldly concerns, is made proximate to one's inmost heart: "Within, in thee is the living fount, / Fed from the springs above" (*BCD*, p. 209). The poem "A Dialogue" draws an "Inquirer" away from "Wealth," "Fame," and "Pleasure" and toward "Religion ... As the guide and the solace of man" (*BCD*, p. 215). And the speaker of "Saved at Last" rejoices that "Behind me were life's fetters, / Its conflict and unrest; / Before me were the pearly gates, / And mansions of the blest" (*BCD*, p. 215).

Christianity would be a far less explicit theme in the poetry of Paul Laurence Dunbar, whose collection *Complete Poems* of 1913 uses special categories to describe his poetry – thus he includes poetry "of lowly life," "of the hearthside," "humour and dialect," "of love and sorrow," and "of sunshine and shadow" – but who did not include among these a category of poetry of religion. Although Dunbar lists "humour and dialect" as the focus of a single section in *Complete Poems*, he in fact included humor and dialect poetry together in his earlier collections, which included eleven volumes between 1893 and 1905. As Martin Griffin notes, Dunbar is often remembered for his dialect poetry alone, but it should be noted that, at least in terms of gathering his poems for publication, he did not distinguish the one group from the other, the dialect from the standard.[12] As already noted, Dunbar's dialect is much more pronounced than that of Frances Harper's speaker, Aunt Chloe. Harper has Chloe use abbreviations such as "agin'" (for "against") or contractions such as "'Twould" (for "It would") (*BCD*, p. 205), but these are few and far between; Dunbar, by contrast, makes much more pervasive use of these devices in his dialect poetry. An example is a line in "Accountability" in which nearly every word is modified (and all of the lines of the poem show similar dialect alteration): "Nuthin's done er evah happens, 'dout hit's somefin' dat's intended."[13] In an early review of Dunbar's poetry, the influential novelist and literary critic William Dean Howells singled out his dialect poems for special praise, and an emphasis on this aspect of his work has continued in subsequent treatments of his poetry.[14]

Dunbar's eleven collections of poetry appeared in the period that also saw the rise of Jim Crow segregation, which became the law of the land when the *Plessey v. Ferguson* U.S. Supreme Court decision of 1896 enshrined "separate but equal" as federally sanctioned practice. Dunbar protested against the racial prejudice of his time in his magazine and newspaper writings. In an 1898 newspaper article entitled "The Race Question Discussed" (an article prompted by the Wilmington race riots of that year) Dunbar writes the following:

> Thirty years ago the American people told the Negro that he was a man with a man's full power. They deemed it that important they did what they have done few times in the history of the country – they wrote it down in their constitution. And now they come with the shot gun in the South and sophistry in the North to prove to him that it was all wrong.[15]

Dunbar would be even more caustic in his tone in an essay published on July 10, 1903, in the *New York Times*, entitled "The Fourth of July and Race Outrages." There he writes,

> The papers are full of the reports of peonage in Alabama. A new and more dastardly slavery there has arisen to replace the old. For the sake of reenslaving the Negro, the Constitution has been trampled under feet, the rights of man have been laughed out of court, and the justice of God has been made a jest and we celebrate. (*SG*, p. 293)

This phrase, "and we celebrate," becomes a refrain for this newspaper piece, which chastises all parties involved for complacency on the matter of "race outrages."

Dunbar resists this complacency not only through his journalistic essays but also through several of his "protest poems."[16] Perhaps the best known of these is the poem "We Wear the Mask," in which the speaker anticipates W. E. B. Du Bois's notion of "double consciousness," suggesting that life for the "we" of the poem – African Americans – involves a duplicitous concealment of their struggles with racial segregation. The mask is worn in the presence of whites, but its "grins and lies" conceal the human hurt that segregation brings: "We smile, but, O great Christ, our cries / To thee from tortured souls arise. . . . But let the world dream otherwise, / We wear the mask!" (*CPD*, p. 71). Another example of Dunbar's protest poetry is the poem "Ode to Ethiopia," which opens his first collection of poems (*Oak and Ivy* [1893]) but sets out a very different tone from the one we saw previously in Whitman's "Ethiopia Saluting the Colors." Although she is represented, as in Whitman's poem, as a female figure, Ethiopia, in Dunbar's poem, is not an ancient relic but a vital maternal force: "O Mother Race! To thee I bring / This pledge of faith unwavering, / This tribute to thy glory" (*CPD*, p. 15). The final stanza of the poem looks to the future less with an interest in racial uplift (which we saw in Harper, and which emphasizes moving from lowly status to that of dignity) than with an interest in racial prowess and triumph:

> Go on and up! Our souls and eyes
> Shall follow thy continuous rise;
>> Our ears shall list thy story
> From bards who from thy root shall spring,
> And proudly tune their lyres to sing
>> Of Ethiopia's glory. (*CPD*, p. 16)

The kind of triumph that Dunbar attributes to African Americans here is made concrete in his poem "The Colored Soldiers," which celebrates the role played by black soldiers in the Civil War. "So when War, in savage triumph, / Spread abroad his funeral pall – / Then you called the colored soldiers, / And they answered to your call" (*CPD*, p. 50). "And their deeds," the poem continues, "shall find a record, / In the registry of Fame; / For their blood has cleansed completely / Every blot of Slavery's shame" (*CPD*, p. 52).

But this tone of triumph is less common in Dunbar's protest poems than a tone of chastisement and reproach. The latter is evident in Dunbar's "The Haunted Oak," in which the speaker is an oak tree whose branches were used to lynch a black man accused of, but never tried for or convicted of, rape. Lynching was on the rise in the post-Reconstruction United States, particularly in the South, and Dunbar's speaker – the oak tree – becomes, in its death, a reproach to those who participated in the lynching:

> I feel the rope against my bark,
>> And the weight of him in my grain,
> I feel the throe of his final woe
>> The touch of my own last pain.
>
> And never more shall leaves come forth
>> On a bough that bears the ban;
> I am burned with dread, I am dried and dead,
>> From the curse of a guiltless man. (*CPD*, p. 220)

Dunbar brings his tone of reproach directly to bear on the South in "To the South; On Its New Slavery." Here Dunbar's target is debt peonage, a legal and economic condition that held African Americans tied to the soil as workers in a manner that resembled slavery because, as they fell further and further into debt, black farmers became chained to the land by these financial obligations – obligations typically owed to white owners of the land. Dunbar's speaker asks, "Did Sanctioned Slavery bow its conquered head / That this unsanctioned crime might rise instead?" (*CPD*, p. 218)

But part of Dunbar's technique in "To the South" seems to run counter to his protest message, for he uses the poem to praise the Southern past – the past of sanctioned slavery – by contrast to the Southern present: "Oh, Mother South, hast thou forgot thy ways, / Forgot the glory of thine ancient days, / Forgot the honor that once made thee great, / And stooped to this unhallowed estate?" (*CPD*, p. 218). This tactic of praise for a prior South involves Dunbar in a nostalgic invocation of the condition of slavery, a nostalgia he envisions even for slaves: "For him no more the cabin's quiet rest, / The homely joys that gave to labor zest; / No more for him the merry banjo's sound, / Nor trip of lightsome dances footing round" (*CPD*, p. 218). And it is this nostalgic stance toward the slave past that Dunbar is often criticized for depicting. As Joanne M. Braxton puts it, "Dunbar's work began to decline in popularity during the 1920s after New Negro critics accused him of accommodating negative stereotypes of life in order to sell his poems to white readers."[17] Dunbar's accommodationist stance is most often associated with his dialect poetry, in which the use of dialect is seen as participating in stereotypes about African Americans' uneducated speech and thus in denigrating African Americans generally.

Dunbar's dialect poetry nevertheless seeks to capture the moments of positive emotion shared among African Americans under conditions of enslavement. These moments, few and far between as they may have been, might well be considered as genre scenes, in which – as in European styles of painting – domestic life is placed on display. Dunbar's purposes in this display were varied and may include a desire to express nostalgia for the antebellum past, a wish to refute such nostalgia, or a broader attempt to affirm the beauty of black experience under slavery; see, for instance, his poems "A Banjo Song," "An Ante-bellum Sermon," "When de Co'n Pone's Hot," "A Plantation Portrait," "Noddin' by de Fire," "When Sam'l Sings," "When Malindy Sings," "Scamp," and "The Old Homestead." Dunbar writes in his journalistic prose that he is enamored of the life of the middle classes in England, and he wishes this kind of life for African Americans:

> Our peasantry, if such the laboring blacks may be called, in condition is much like that of England; but in realization and acceptance of their lot, how different. The novel message of freedom has been blown into their ears with such a ringing blast that the din has for the moment confused them. Every man reads his own destiny in the stars, and sees only greatness there. (*SG*, p. 255)

Here the personal ambitions to "greatness" of newly freed African Americans seem to be questioned in comparison to an "acceptance of their lot," a lot Dunbar nevertheless knew to be quite painful for many black Southerners (*SG*, pp. 268–70). Dunbar continues, reflecting on his own travels to England, "The beauty and perfection of a pure family life is one thing which, say what we will, the Negro needs greatly to learn. I must confess that no phase of English social observance struck me more forcibly than this" (*SG*, p. 253). It is this "pure family life" that Dunbar attributes to African Americans in his dialect poetry, in which genre scenes display less an individuality than a communal set of relations.

The notion of communal life has the effect, in Dunbar's poem "Chrismus on the Plantation," of casting black and white people as one big family, and the question the poem raises is whether the former slaves, now being paid for their labors, will stay on and work once their former master runs out of money to pay them. The dilemma is summarized in the voice of a slave named "ol' Ben":

> Look hyeah, Mastah, I's been servin' you' fu' lo! dese many yeahs,
> An' now, sence we's got freedom an' you's kind o' po', hit 'pears
> Dat you want us all to leave you 'cause you don't t'ink you can pay.
> Ef my membry has n't fooled me, seems dat whut I hyead you say.
> Er in othah wo'ds, you wants us to fu'git dat you's been kin',
> An' ez soon ez you is he'pless, we's to leave you hyeah behin'.
> Well, ef dat's de way dis freedom ac's on people, white er black,
> You kin jes' tell Mistah Lincum fu' to tek his freedom back.
>
> (*CPD*, p. 137–38)

This notion that "white" and "black" are in something other than a wage relation rehearses an idealized Southern white view of the slave past: instead of acting out of market-based self-interest, the laborers that ol' Ben envisions are motivated by loyalty prompted by demonstrations of their master's kindness. This is one example of the favoring of a set of emotional over commercial interests, which runs throughout much Southern writing in the late nineteenth century. Much of Dunbar's dialect poetry is accommodationist in this sense, reflecting a nostalgic projection of emotional reciprocity on the antebellum past of slavery. Additional examples of this dynamic include the poems "The Deserted Plantation," "The Party," "Lullaby," "Chrismus is a-Comin'," "A Cabin Tale," "To the Eastern Shore," and "The Old Cabin."

Not all of Dunbar's dialect poetry employs Southern "Negro" dialect; he experiments with other regional speech as well, as is evident in poems like "Possum Trot" and "James Whitcomb Riley." Indeed, formal experimentation is a salient feature of Dunbar's poetry, a quality that is particularly apparent in his numerous explorations of the dramatic monologue. Also a hallmark of Dunbar's verse is technical experimentation. For instance, he uses a variety of stanza forms and a variety of rhyme schemes (using rhyming couplets at times [*aabbcc*] and at times an alternation of rhyming lines [*abab*]). Dunbar's line forms are, by contrast to Harper's, quite various, including blank verse, iambic pentameter, trochaic tetrameter, and anapestic pentameter, tetrameter, and dimeter. He even experiments with quadruple meter in his lines (as in "A Back-Log Song"). For additional musical effect, he makes frequent use of a refrain (as in the line "I know why the caged bird sings" in "Sympathy") and even repeats lines (as in "A Song"). In one poem, "Whistling Sam," Dunbar embeds musical notation at intervals over the course of the poem, thus allowing the interjection of purely musical intervals in the poem's presentation. Although Dunbar did not share Lanier's strong view that poetry is itself indistinguishable from music, he felt a strong enough kinship between the two that he made frequent use of musical poetic effects.

Somewhat surprisingly, Dunbar's poems almost never invoke the musical form we now call "spirituals" – what he called "old plantation music" in his 1899 essay "Negro Music" (SG, pp. 271–73). There he writes, "The strange, fantastic melody of the old plantation music has always possessed a deep fascination for me. There is an indescribable charm in it – a certain poetic sadness that appeals strongly to the artistic in one's nature" (SG, p. 271). Although he associates this music with the "old plantation," Dunbar has a theory about its origins that traces it back even before the rise of the plantation; according to his view, this music is a remnant of the imported slaves' African past: "If my hypothesis be correct, the man who asks where the negro got all those strange tunes of his songs is answered. They have been handed down to him from the matted jungles and sunburned deserts of Africa, from the reed huts of the Nile" (SG, p. 272). This is a view shared by W. E. B. Du Bois, who popularized the notion that African American spirituals – what he called "sorrow songs" – are remnants of African cultural practice. In his 1903 collection of essays The Souls of Black Folk, Du Bois devotes the final chapter to a treatment of the sorrow songs, and he uses sorrow songs as epigraphs to each of his chapters. Du Bois's The Souls of Black Folk would become an important document for writers of the Harlem Renaissance, who increasingly looked to Africa as a repository of cultural resources for bolstering their notion of what it means to be a "New Negro." While Dunbar and Harper were commonly viewed by those of the Harlem Renaissance as examples of an "Old Negro" (Harper for her ambition of color-blind uplift and Dunbar for his use of nostalgic dialect poetry), Dunbar at least was clearly thinking about the spirituals in ways that were to become commonplace in African American thought. Dunbar writes, "Let black composers – and there are such – weave those [old plantation] melodies into their compositions" (SG, p. 272), a view set out prominently by the Harlem Renaissance writer James Weldon Johnson in his Autobiography of an

Ex-Colored Man (1912, 1927), in which composing music based on songs including "Swing Low, Sweet Chariot" (the very same spiritual invoked at the end of Dunbar's poem "When Malindy Sings") becomes the central character's main ambition as a way of contributing to the good not of his region but of his race.

Current scholarship continues to emphasize the role of race in nineteenth-century American literary culture and to seek for previously neglected voices. One of the recent rediscoveries is Albery Allson Whitman, who was born a slave in Kentucky in 1851 and who, following emancipation, received sufficient education to inspire him to pursue poetic composition. Whitman's numerous works, published between 1871 and 1901, are proving to be of interest to scholars for a variety of reasons. For instance, like Lanier and Dunbar, Whitman was – as Ivy G. Wilson has recently asserted – "consumed with the aesthetics of sound," a fact made evident through his use of a variety of line and stanza forms, often in imitation of British poetic models.[18] In addition to his musical forms, Whitman's social and historical themes have also prompted the interest of recent scholars. Whitman's long narrative poems *Not a Man, and Yet a Man* (1877) and *The Rape of Florida* (1884), for instance, portray the complex dynamics of race relations on the U.S. frontier, a topic of increasing importance to scholars studying transnational borderlands. And Whitman's final long narrative poem, *An Idyl of the South* (1901), aspires, as he asserts in the poem's preface, to shed light on "the sociological conditions suggested by the narrative," which features "the story of an Octoroon," the term used at the time for a person with one-eighth "black blood."[19] Like Whitman's exploration of geographical borderlands in his earlier works, this poem's examination of corporeal racial boundaries within hybrid persons and between interracial lovers promises to expand our growing understanding of how citizenship and personhood were configured in the late nineteenth and early twentieth centuries. Finally, scholarly attention to Whitman promises to restore to prominence the individual who was featured along with Fredrick Douglass and Paul Laurence Dunbar during the designated "Colored American Day" at the 1893 World's Columbian Exposition in Chicago.[20] There Whitman recited his poem "The Freedman's Triumphant Song," which references wartime heroism as a basis for inclusion of African Americans within a single national narrative:

> Hurrah for him! Let caste's old mouth
> Keep still about a "North and South"
> The Negro's dark intrepid brow
> Shall wear the hero's laurels now.[21]

Whitman's desire here to push beyond affiliations with the North or South exemplifies, as we have now seen, the effort of poets during and after Reconstruction to replace regional with racial solidarities, thus setting the stage for the problem of the color line that, as W. E. B. Du Bois famously asserted, would dominate the century to come.

Notes

1. See Eric Foner, *Reconstruction: America's Unfinished Revolution, 1863–1877* (New York: Harper and Row, 1988).

2. Henry Timrod, *The Collected Poems of Henry Timrod; A Variorum Edition*, ed. Edd Winfield Parks and Aileen Wells Parks (Athens: University of Georgia Press, 1965), p. 111. This collection will be cited subsequently in the text as *CPT*.

3. See Edd Winfield Parks and Aileen Wells Parks, "Introduction," in Timrod, *The Collected Poems of Henry Timrod*, p. 9.

4. See the section "Poems of the War, 1861–1865" in Hayne's 1882 collection *Poems of Paul Hamilton Hayne* (New York: AMS Press, 1970), pp. 65–86. This collection will be cited subsequently in the text as *PH*.

5. Sidney Lanier, "Laughter in the Senate," in Charles R. Anderson (ed.), *The Centennial Edition of the Works of Sidney Lanier*. Vol. 1, *Poems and Poem Outlines* (Baltimore, Md.: Johns Hopkins University Press, 1945), p. 14. This collection will be cited subsequently in the text as *PPO*.

6. Sidney Lanier, "Appendix: Wagner's Beethoven," in Paull Franklin Baum (ed.), *The Centennial Edition of the Works of Sidney Lanier*. Vol. 2, *The Science of English Verse and Essays on Music* (Baltimore, Md.: Johns Hopkins University Press, 1945), pp. 338–39.

7. Sidney Lanier, *The Science of English Verse*, in Baum (ed.), *The Centennial Edition of the Works of Sidney Lanier*, vol. 2, p. 137. This collection will be cited subsequently in the text as *SEV*.

8. See Sidney Lanier, *The English Novel*, in Clarence Gohdes and Kemp Malone (eds.), *The Centennial Edition of the Works of Sidney Lanier*. Vol. 4, *The English Novel and Essays on Literature* (Baltimore, Md.: Johns Hopkins University Press, 1945), p. 54.

9. Sidney Lanier, "The Centennial Cantata," in Baum (ed.), *The Centennial Edition of the Works of Sidney Lanier*, vol. 2, pp. 272–73.

10. Walt Whitman, "Ethiopia Saluting the Colors," in Michael Moon (ed.), *Leaves of Grass and Other Writings* (New York: Norton, 2002), pp. 267–68.

11. Frances Ellen Watkins Harper, *A Brighter Coming Day: A Frances Ellen Watkins Harper Reader*, ed. Frances Smith Foster (New York: Feminist Press, 1990), p. 94. This edition will be cited subsequently in the text as *BCD*.

12. Martin Griffin, *Ashes of the Mind: War and Memory in Northern Literature, 1865–1900* (Amherst: University of Massachusetts Press, 2009), p. 176.

13. Paul Laurence Dunbar, *The Collected Poetry of Paul Laurence Dunbar*, ed. Joanne M. Braxton (1913; Charlottesville: University Press of Virginia, 1993), p. 6. This edition will be cited subsequently in the text as *CPD*.

14. Joanne M. Braxton, "Introduction: The Poetry of Paul Laurence Dunbar," in Dunbar, *The Collected Poetry of Paul Laurence Dunbar*, pp. xvi–xvii.

15. Paul Laurence Dunbar, "The Race Question Discussed," in Shelley Fisher Fishkin and David Bradley (eds.), *The Sport of the Gods and Other Essential Writings* (New York: Modern Library, 2005), p. 263. This edition will be cited subsequently in the text as *SG*.

16. See Braxton, "Introduction," p. xviii.

17. Braxton, "Introduction," p. xxix.

18. Ivy G. Wilson, "Introduction: Reconstructing Albery Allson Whitman," in Ivy G. Wilson (ed.), *At the Dusk of Dawn: Selected Poetry and Prose of Albery Allson Whitman* (Boston: Northeastern University Press, 2009), p. 6.

19. Albery Allson Whitman, "Preface to *An Idyl of the South* (1901)," in Wilson (ed.), *At the Dusk of Dawn*, p. 309.

20. See Wilson, "Introduction," pp. 1, 13–14.

21. Albery Allson Whitman, "The Freedman's Triumphant Song," in Wilson (ed.), *At the Dusk of Dawn*, p. 295.

Chapter 18

The "Genteel Tradition" and Its Discontents

ELIZABETH RENKER

The terms "genteel," "genteel poetry," and "genteel tradition" appear frequently in American literary histories and criticism, typically as rhetorically negative terms indicating conventional forms of literature that respect, and adhere to, the cultural, social, and economic status quo. To call poetry "genteel" is to imply that it is safe, traditional art, ideologically suspect because it affirms cultural hegemony. My concern in the pages that follow is not this more generic designation of gentility but instead the historically specific place and time to which George Santayana (1863–1952) was responding when he coined the influential phrase "the genteel tradition" in 1911.[1] For him, the term described the dominant American cultural formation at the close of the nineteenth century, a vague and intellectually weak form of idealism that he scorned. Santayana's "genteel tradition" had a powerful legacy. His formulation came to stand as a negative emblem of nineteenth-century American culture's complacency and intellectual vapidity. In such accounts, modernism became the triumphant and long-awaited new movement in art that would finally kill off the genteel, renewing poetry at last from stale convention. The inverse relation between conventionality and greatness that both Santayana and then the modernists articulated (as in Ezra Pound's famous dictum "make it new") was only to grow more central in twentieth-century aesthetics, particularly with the emergence and increasing institutional power of New Criticism. The allegedly genteel poets receded farther and farther into the background of poetry studies as embarrassing grandparents. Santayana's formulation and the generalizations it fed inaccurately simplified the poetic practices of the latter half of the nineteenth century for much of the twentieth.

Although it has long been standard to portray American verse between Whitman and Dickinson and the modernists as a wasteland, the historical record presents a substantially distinct picture. Scores of poets published during this era, in a broad array of styles, genres, and venues. The poetry of the period is not uniformly "genteel" but replete with conflicting impulses about what Edmund Clarence Stedman would call (in his 1892 volume by the same title) "the nature and elements of poetry." Such impulses are legible not only from poet to poet but sometimes within the careers of individual poets or even within a single poem. In sum, rather than a monolithic era of bland gentility awaiting redemption by the modernists, "the genteel tradition" warrants redefinition as a thriving index to the changing cultural meaning of poetry actively transpiring all around it.

One particular group of poets that literary history has long identified as emblematic of the genteel tradition is the New York School. (Like the poets themselves, the term "the New York School" is now mostly archaic. The twentieth century gave the same label to a group of its own poets, including Frank O'Hara, John Ashbery, and Kenneth Koch, and the former designation mostly vanished.) Core members of the group included George H. Boker (1823–1890), Bayard Taylor (1825–1878), Richard Henry Stoddard (1825–1903), Edmund Clarence Stedman (1833–1908), and Thomas Bailey Aldrich (1836–1907). One index to their gentility is their self-conscious attachment, as possible heirs, to the cultural throne of the New England poets, including (at that time) Ralph Waldo Emerson (1803–1882) and the so-called Fireside Poets: Henry Wadsworth Longfellow (1807–1882), John Greenleaf Whittier (1807–1892), Oliver Wendell Holmes (1809–1894), and James Russell Lowell (1819–1891). Note that the oldest New York poet (Boker) was only four years younger than the youngest of the New England poets (Lowell). The New York poets talked a good bit among themselves about these national figures and about their aspirations for their own poetry in the wake of these towering, iconic forebears.[2] Although their desire for national acclaim kept them mindful of the Fireside Poets, they were aesthetically most devoted to the British Romantics and their Victorian successors. Stedman described his "lyrics and idylls" as "keyed to the note, and reminiscent of Wordsworth, Shelley, Keats, and above all, Tennyson, my master who had drawn the best from all," an apt general description of the New York School overall.[3]

Taylor, Boker, and Stoddard initially met as young men in the thrilling atmosphere of Manhattan in 1848, soon adding Aldrich and Stedman to their circle. They saw New York as the literary future, overtaking in primacy the long-standing rank of Boston as the center of American letters.[4] (Not all were to stay in New York; Aldrich, for example, left for Boston in 1865, and Boker built an estate outside Philadelphia.) All used their contacts and influence to place one another's poems and collections with publishers and magazines, wrote positive reviews of one another's work, and, in general, did one another literary favors.[5]

They wrote prodigiously in a broad array of genres, including poetry of many kinds, newspaper journalism, travel narrative, drama, prose fiction, criticism, translation, correspondence, and lectures. Taylor in particular produced what Richard Cary calls "staggering" amounts of writing, including travel books and encyclopedias, novels, poetry, poetical drama, literary histories, translations, histories, short stories, critical essays, and parodies. His early travel narratives (especially *Views A-Foot* [1846]) were widely popular. Also generically versatile, Boker gained particular distinction in Romantic blank verse tragedy, such as his *Francesca da Rimini* (1855; revived in 1885), based on the story of Paolo and Francesca. Stoddard was best known for his critical essays and his poetry, particularly his lyric poems – whose temper was indebted to Keats – in such volumes as *Songs of Summer* (1857), but his range encompassed such works as *Abraham Lincoln: An Horatian Ode* (1865) and eighteen "translations" of Chinese poems published between 1850 and 1880, including *The Book of the East* (1871). Translation was a routine and highly esteemed poetic practice during this era, construed to be a vital source for the development of poetry in the English tongue. The term was used elastically, reflecting a case-by-case mix of strict translation, work with other translations, interpretation, and origination; Stoddard, for example, did not work from any original Chinese sources.[6] His active work in this poetic genre, with its complex layers of translation and allusion to other languages and cultures, is only one of many examples of "genteel" precedent for allegedly modernist practice. Stoddard was also husband to novelist and poet Elizabeth Drew Barstow Stoddard (1823–1902), whose intense work exploring subjectivity, sensuality, gender, and domesticity included the searing and experimental realist novel *The Morgesons* (1862) as well as poems published in highly regarded periodicals (such as "Mercedes," in *The Atlantic Monthly* [1858], and "Before the Mirror," in *Harper's* [1860]) and later in book form (*Poems* [1895]). Elizabeth Stoddard's razor-sharp critique of the poetry by her husband and his friends as inadequate to their time left them all reeling and provides another solid indication that poetry of the age contained its own crosscurrents and self-critique.[7]

The New York group revered poetry as a sacred office. Still at the top of the literary hierarchy of prestige, poetry was nevertheless under increasing pressure from the novel, which (as poets were nervously aware) seemed only to accrue power in the form of mass readership. As Dino Franco Felluga has argued of nineteenth-century Britain, as the novel claimed a large popular market, and as a (threatening) lower-class readership grew, Victorian culture carved out a more restricted, elite space for a "pure" poetry predicated on its otherworldliness from the contaminations of mundane, market-driven reality.[8] By embracing a highbrow arena, poets could validate their distance from the masses as a sign of aesthetic fineness, rather than accepting it as a simple sociological loss of market share. Feelings of uncertainty run as a fine thread through the New York poets' correspondence and published writing. While emotionally attached to the most elevated poetry they could imagine, their own practical generic versatility, including popular work they devalued, is certainly part of the transatlantic history of the stratifications of genre.

Their privileged aesthetic was mostly what the era itself called "ideality" or "idealism," a conception that poetry's proper domain was the higher sphere of the soul and of transcendent beauty. As Aldrich put it in his 1907 poem "Enamored Architect of Airy Rhyme," the poet is a "worker in sublime / And heaven-sent dreams."[9] The words "romantic" and "romance," also common in literary debates of the era, designated a realm, often associated with divinity ("heaven-sent dreams"), beyond or better than the actual world of material fact. Forms of the words "ideality" and "romance" are often synonymous in discourse of the time. Literary history's current consensus declares that this commitment to Romanticism in art left them out of step with the energies of their own day. Such energies included, most pressingly, science and realism in particular, to which the New York poets reacted with distress and disgust. Stedman in particular repeatedly reflected on the scientific temper of the age as a devastating threat to poetry. Within the domain of literature, they also fought realism as a vulgar abdication of art's highest charge: to elevate the soul of mankind to its highest aspirations.[10] The conventional account of the school is that its death grip on the waning aesthetic power of Romanticism was so repressive, and so institutionally powerful in the literary magazines and publishing houses in which they were well connected, that they inadvertently gave birth to the modernist revolt.

A fuller picture of the complex currents of poetic history must address the ways in which these poets were not merely forces of stodgy conservatism. For example, they passionately advocated the value of art amid a postbellum society aggressively invested in the ideology of "practical work" or "the world's work" (two terms that circulated widely in public discourse). In addition, Stedman's influential criticism was instrumental in carving out a new poetic canon even as he remained allied with a passing aesthetic mode. His 1900 *An American Anthology 1787–1900* includes many poets of great interest to scholars today, such as Emerson, Poe, Whitman, Melville, Elizabeth Stoddard, Rose Terry Cooke, Alice and Phoebe Cary, Emily Dickinson, and Sarah Piatt. Even Harriet Monroe, whom Stedman befriended when she was a young poet, appears; in 1912, she would found the revolutionary little magazine *Poetry*, typically hailed as an origin of modernism. Stedman devotedly advocated the work of Poe and Whitman at a time when both were disreputable figures in American letters.[11] His 1885 volume *Poets of America*, for example, insisted on their importance to the development of the art of poetry, beyond the issues of personal titillation or moral outrage that both tended to attract. We might remember, with due irony, that it was Santayana who disliked Whitman, while Stedman defended him. Stedman was also foundational to recasting Emerson's reputation, moving him from his cultural association with the Fireside group into alignment with the poetic energies of Whitman instead.[12]

However distressed (Stedman) or officious (Aldrich) they were by the prospect, the New York poets saw that their own poetic mode was expiring, and they marked it.[13] Given their cultural stature, their elegiac mode was crucial to how their era thought about the status of poetry, and this elegiac mode is in fact one of their most influential legacies; it created a climate that opened doors to change. In *Victorian Poets*, Stedman wrote, "At present, skepticism, analysis, scientific conquest, realism, scornful unrest. Apollo has left the heavens." Nevertheless, he insisted that the era of "scientific iconoclasm" was simply a transitional period on the way to better things for poetry.[14] Indeed, the modernist poets who were little boys as Stedman's ideas were circulating would have been familiar both with his laments and with his call for a new poetry. As one of the most famous men of letters of the day, Stedman was in a position to make pronouncements that readers would heed. His critical works *Victorian Poets* (1875) and *Poets of America* (1885); his 1885 essay "The Twilight of the Poets" (*Century Illustrated Magazine*); his Turnbull Memorial Lectures, which inaugurated that series, at Johns Hopkins University in 1891 (collected as *The Nature and Elements of Poetry*); and his *An American Anthology* were all widely reviewed and cited as authoritative in his own time. Michael Cohen forcefully traces Stedman's influence in conceptualizing a "Victorian" period and a "transatlantic" field of poetics, new frameworks that contested the increasingly philological models for literary study defining the higher study of poetry in the new university culture.[15]

Indeed, the single concept for which Stedman remains best known is his characterization of the poetic era as an "interregnum" or "twilight." His 1885 title phrase "the twilight of the poets" became a catchphrase of the late nineteenth century. Poets and reviewers immediately picked it up, circulating it widely as an accurate description.[16] Although Stedman likely picked up the specific word "twilight" from Whitman's 1881 essay "The Poetry of the Future," it was Stedman's use of the term that caught on. Even poets like Edwin Arlington Robinson, whom literary history has loved to position in opposition to Stedman and his "genteel" ilk, used Stedman's twilight aura in his own poem, "Sonnet": "Oh for a poet – for a beacon bright / To rift this changeless glimmer of dead gray." Robinson sounds an awful lot like Stedman here, rather than like his antithesis. Stedman was not simply a figure to be surpassed by new poets. He was cultivating terms they would embrace.

A rigid concept of the genteel tradition has prevented us from seeing a more complex matrix of related poetic practices, both across the era more generally and within the careers of individual poets. For example, the poems that brought Stedman his fame were not genteel at all: they were sensational newspaper verses about current events and politics. He published "The Diamond Wedding," a 218-line verse satire, in the New York *Tribune* in 1859. In a to-the-minute social commentary about the garish, mercenary wedding of a young blond New York belle to a Cuban slave-holding "foreigner" three times her age, Stedman deflated the wedding, whose lavish expenditures the New York press had tracked with gossipy fascination. Composed, by Stedman's own description, in one night, it caused an instant sensation, leading to the threat of a libel suit. Stedman himself called the poem "a metrical screed" (*LL*, vol. 1, pp. 186, 188). A friend in Italy reported that she had shared the poem with Elizabeth Barrett Browning and Harriet Beecher Stowe, who, she reported, "have expressed the highest admiration" (*LL*, vol. 1, p. 198). The *Tribune* also published Stedman's political, eighteen-stanza narrative poem "John Brown's Invasion" (November 12, 1859; later retitled "How Old Brown Took Harper's Ferry"), hardly a poem of ideal beauty ("I tell you that the flagon, / Filled with blood of Old Brown's offspring, was first poured by Southern hands").[17]

Some of his other popular poems poked fun at idealist impulses. "Pan in Wall Street," published in the *Atlantic Monthly* (January 1867), depicts a street musician whom Stedman called "the man who plays the real Pan's pipe around the Wall Street district." (Stedman was, by profession, a broker and member of the New York Stock Exchange.) Here Stedman creates a pastoral demigod visiting the modern scene. The title points to his playful combination of romantic and realistic worlds. In this urban recasting of a conventional pastoral, modern "bulls and bears" stand mesmerized by Pan's music, until a police officer shoos him away as a "vagrant."[18] Another popular comic work, "The Ballad of Lager Bier," extols in twenty-one stanzas the fun of drinking "Glass after glass in due succession" (*PW*, p. 60). It ends with a similar ironic deflation of the romantic imagination. He and his drinking buddy soar into the empyrean realm that he spoke of elsewhere, with reverence, as poetry's domain, but his drinking ballad ironizes its own terms. Once drunk, each becomes "a priest and seer" undergoing a "misty change" in which "Things look, as in a moonlight dream" (*PW*, pp. 60–61). Finally, his inebriated buddy soars so high – "higher yet, in middle Heaven, / Your steed seems taking flight, my friend" – that he leaves the beer hall without paying, and the speaker is stuck with the bill (*PW*, p. 63).

At the age of twenty-six, Stedman was surprised and uncertain about how to handle his sudden fame. He wondered whether his "lyrics and idylls" modeled on Wordsworth, Shelley, Keats, and Tennyson, written "in the realms of high art," should "be subordinate to the mere notoriety so strikingly aroused by the production of a newspaper skit, so easy for me to write, and so utterly out of my desire?" (*LL*, vol. 1, p. 188). Stedman himself saw that the cultural life of poetry entailed various readerships, venues of publication, and social spheres of taste. As Virginia Jackson has trenchantly argued, among the powerful legacies of New Criticism, the "lyricization" of poetry – that is, reducing the genre to the lyric, itself an elastic term but often defined as a self-contained poem in which a speaker meditates on a matter of the interior life – pushes into oblivion the vast scope of poetry's actual historical forms.[19] When Stedman pitted his "lyrics and idylls" against the prospect of what he called "popular work," he called the former "high art" in contradistinction to his writing as a satirist and public sensation. Satire was, in his words, "a poetic heresy" opposed to "my graver, more aesthetic work" (*LL*, vol. 1, p. 197–98). Taylor, too, after winning an 1850 songwriting contest sponsored by P. T. Barnum, wrote to Boker that he had "defiled the temple of divine Poetry" and would never do so again (*BT*, pp. 82–85). Even Aldrich made his early career at age nineteen on a popular smash, the ballad of Baby Bell.

Preoccupied with poetry's sacred sphere and their own reputations, the New York poets only nervously comprehended that the social status of poems and poets were moving targets in this era of profound change. In 1894, reflecting at age sixty-one on the breakout sensation of his career as poet thirty-five years prior, Stedman saw the sphere of popular poetry in a more appealing light: "If I had been wise in my generation, and more a man of the world, I would have pushed my luck, as my friend Bret Harte did with his 'Chinese cheap labor' and would have accepted some of the offers for 'popular' work which 'The Diamond Wedding' brought me" (*LL*, vol. 1, p. 198). Stedman imagines his road not taken as that of Bret Harte (1836–1902), journalist, editor, and author of what was then and is now called "local color" poetry and fiction, that is, a form of realism treating specific locales, their dialects, and their ways of life. Harte was well known for his work on California and the gold mines. His most famous comic ballad, initially published as "Plain Language from Truthful James" (1870), portrays a conniving game of euchre among mutual cheats. It suited the era's attraction to (often racist) depictions of populations it construed as ethnic others, in this case, the Chinese. In the many pirated republished versions that swept American culture, it was popularly christened "The Heathen Chinee" (1870).

One of Harte's achievements was to step out of the poetic diction and idealist orientation of the New York poets, and into the world as it was changing in the tumultuous postwar decades. Norman Foerster aptly calls the idealist poetic mode of the New York poets the "poetry of beauty," a mode that contrasted starkly with the work of Harte and other dialect poets, like fellow "Westerners" James Whitcomb Riley and Joaquin Miller as well as Paul Laurence Dunbar, known for his "Negro" dialect poems. Taylor and Aldrich excoriated dialect poetry as the hated opposite of their literary ideal. Its aggressively unlovely language – and its popularity on that vernacular account – drew only their scorn.[20] Although Stedman believed that realism's greatest threat to poetry arose from prose fiction, dialect poetry posed that threat from within the genre of poetry itself. When Stedman described the twilight interval, he failed to comprehend that his own fellow poets were already leveling a foundational challenge to "the nature and elements of poetry" as he defined them. Whitman's diagnosis in 1881 was, unsurprisingly, spot on: the "fatal defect" hampering "our American singers," he said, was "the beauty disease."[21]

An array of Stedman's contemporary poets in fact wrote in, or shifted to, poetic practices that challenged the "poetry of beauty" in the decades following the Civil War, poems often aligned with the antigenteel aesthetics of realism and naturalism. One of our most profound realist poets is the Kentucky-born Sarah Piatt, born Sarah Morgan Bryan and married into the Ohio Piatt family. Her status as spouse to one of the era's genteel poets – her husband, J.J. Piatt, co-authored *Poems of Two Friends* with William Dean Howells in 1860 – had the effect until the mid-1990s of obscuring her own poetic achievement, and of lumping her into the genteel group, where she in fact belongs only as a voice of complex interlocution. Widely known in postbellum literary circles, Sarah and J.J. both actively published and appeared routinely in anthologies of the era. Both mostly vanished from twentieth-century literary history. Paula Bernat Bennett's 2001 *Palace-Burner: The Selected Poetry of Sarah Piatt* sets out to "put Piatt's reputation as a genteel poet (and nothing more) permanently to rest."[22] She argues that Piatt's vast body of poems includes very successful genteel-style lyrics (Piatt published thirty poems in the *Atlantic Monthly*, for example, which John Timberman Newcomb calls "the institutional epicenter of genteel culture")[23] as well as poems that challenge the genteel ethos. These poems plunge into what Bennett calls "the real," the "everyday dramas of family and social life and the life of the nation" (*PB*, pp. xxviii, xxxiii). Piatt wrote in and out of the genteel tradition.[24]

Inspired by the dramatic monologues of Robert Browning, Piatt pushed the form in new directions, experimenting with multiple speakers, shifts in perspective, fragmented speech, evasions and omissions, and an often bewildering array of juxtapositions, not only between two or more speaking voices but also between what one speaker says and another thinks, or what a single speaker says out loud and then thinks to herself – sometimes all in a single poem. The effects of simultaneous multiplicity and fragmentation, innovative and complex, left many readers baffled. Taylor's comical volume *The Echo Club* (1876), in which the New York poets, under fantasy names, amuse themselves by writing parodies of their contemporaries, includes a parody of "Mrs. Piatt," to whom the group jokingly (and revealingly) refers simply as "The 'Woman,'" an allusion to her 1871 volume *A Woman's Poems*.[25] Utterly missing the point, Taylor's parodist (fittingly named with the romance moniker "Galahad") describes her poems as "dreams" whose fault is that they lack "a distinct reality."[26] Given the literary climate in which Piatt worked, it makes sense that, among her complex experiments with competing perspectives, she frequently explored the gaps between idealist and realist perspectives, gaps that sometimes play themselves out in dialogues between persons who don't understand each other. The fact that she often depicted mothers and children or husbands and wives in these roles of misperception led readers to see her as a "domestic poet" or a "Woman" rather than a poet who ironizes (as Bennett has powerfully argued) her own immediate poetic culture of gentility.[27] The New-York-School Galahad, complete with his fantasy name, simply can't see the "distinct reality" she offers.

One of four poems Piatt herself chose to represent her work for an 1886 collection was "A Prettier Book," nine stanzas of iambic tetrameter in her signature form, the dramatic dialogue. In some ways, it resembles the poem for which she is currently most famous, "The Palace-Burner," in which a mother and son look at illustrations from what the poem's subtitle calls the "newspaper," including one of a Frenchwoman on her way to execution for her role in the Paris Commune in 1871. Like "The Palace-Burner," "A Prettier Book" also opens with unidentified voices:

> "He has a prettier book than this,"
> With many a sob between, he said;
> Then left untouched the night's last kiss,
> And, sweet with sorrow, went to bed.

> A prettier book his brother had? –
>> Yet wonder-pictures were in each.
> The different colors made him sad;
>> The equal value – could I teach?[28]

Piatt, in a way utterly typical of her poems, puts her reader in the uncertain position of figuring out who the unidentified speakers are. Her poems sometimes provide adequate internal evidence for doing so, and sometimes don't. Here, we can identify the speaker as the boy's mother. Before a reader might decide to dive into the poem's complex terrain, he or she could just as easily stop at the surface level, with prettiness, kisses, family relationships, and sweet sorrow, and conclude that this is a conventional domestic poem. Indeed, the poem works well as a domestic poem in which a mother struggles to teach her child how to understand his own pain in a world that, seemingly capriciously, favors some and not others.

Closer inspection yields an additional, metapoetic poem about two "books." Both books contain "wonder-pictures," but only one of them is "pretty." Here she juxtaposes their respective contents:

> A peasant, seeking bitter bread
>> From the unwilling earth to wring,
> Is in my book; the wine is red,
>> There in my brother's, for the king. (RP, p. 508)

Like "The Palace-Burner," this poem depicts an ostensibly domestic scene in which a mother and son look at printed material, among other things, together; poverty and starvation stand alongside material wealth; and a mother's initial instinct to dismiss the child's concerns fails, and she ends up confronting threatening, unwelcomed, dark knowledge.

Only two lines in this poem appear in quotation marks: the opening line, introducing the stanza that sounds conventionally domestic, and the penultimate line, "My brother has a prettier book" (RP, p. 508). While at first glance these similar lines look like a simple near repetition, in part serving to round out a formal symmetry, in fact something very important has changed. The boy's opening question has led his mother to meditate on the "value" of the respective books. Although she initially plans to teach that their value is "equal," by the last stanza, she has come over to her boy's position.

> Put out the lights. We will not look
>> At pictures any more. We weep,
> "My brother has a prettier book,"
>> And, after tears, we go to sleep. (RP, p. 508)

The quoted line is no longer her son's alone: she weeps it with him. It's initially odd that line 1, "He has a prettier book than this," is more pronominally elastic than the penultimate line. That is, while either a mother or brother could refer to another child as "he" (as in stanza 1), the penultimate line specifies the referent as "my brother," appearing to clarify the speaker as a sibling and not a parent. Yet it is at this point that, with apparent illogic, the mother and her son become a plural first person: "We will not look / At pictures any more." We must wonder who is "brother" to the mother, and here we can hear the echo of the second tale Piatt tells in this poem, about the adult speaker's relationship to her own "brother"-poets with their "prettier" books.

The intervening stanzas, which juxtapose scenes from each of the two books, in fact read as an image-by-image catalogue of Piatt's own poems alongside images from her genteel peers. For example:

> I see, through fierce and feverish tears,
>   Only a darkened hut in mine;
> Yet in my brother's book appears
>   A palace where the torches shine.   (RP, p. 508)

Piatt depicts the "darkened huts" of poverty in poems like "The House Below the Hill" (1877) and "From North and South" (1878). Indeed, in "A Prettier Book," her own poems are, polemically, not the ones the title names; they stand against poems like Stedman's 1869 "The Blameless Prince," with its palaces, consorts, and, as Stedman himself puts it in the prelude to the poem, "Old romance ... / Ancient names of King and Queen, / Knightly men and maidens fair" (PW, p. 187).

Another realist poet whose poems are mostly unknown is the dean of realism himself, William Dean Howells. Although central to literary history primarily for his realist fiction and his editorial crusade on its behalf, Howells was also an active poet, with poetic works dating back to *Poems of Two Friends* (1860). His early poems are mostly sentimental and romantic treatments of conventional subjects such as death, passion, love, and nostalgia. By the 1890s, Howells's poetry had changed substantially in attitude. He published thirty-nine poems in *Harper's Monthly* between 1889 and 1895. He then added four and published them in the dark, ironic, and despairing 1895 volume *Stops of Various Quills*.[29] Abandoning the late-romantic ethos of his early poems, Howells, as Edwin H. Cady puts it, "joined poetry now to his realistic positions." He also pushed poetic form onto a spectrum of experimentation from "lawful to outlaw."[30]

As a way into Howells's poetry of 1895, let's return to Aldrich, who published a new volume of poems the same year, titled *The Unguarded Gates*. While the title speaks to Aldrich's broader sense at this time of poetry under attack by mongrel forces, the title poem more explicitly addresses his horror over the unclean races entering the United States. Unsurprisingly, his poem is full of romantic figures of Arabs and Norsemen, standard figures in which Taylor's travel writing in particular had specialized.[31] Nevertheless, the poem pushes aside the romantic exotics abroad and turns to fear about the influx of "tiger passions" brought by "a wild motley throng" onto the terrain of the homeland. The speaker finally bursts out: "O Liberty, white Goddess! is it well / To leave the gates unguarded?"[32] Aldrich's stance of highbrow retrenchment deplores changes in American society and their relation to the genre of poetry. In this sense, the title trope of unguarded gates applies not only to immigration but also to the function of literary gatekeepers like himself. (He was the editor of the *Atlantic Monthly* from 1881 to 1890.)

The Unguarded Gates also included one of Aldrich's disgusted commentaries on the state of poetry, this one called "Pessimistic Poets":

> I little read those poets who have made
> A noble art a pessimistic trade,
> And trained their Pegasus to draw a hearse
> Through endless avenues of drooping verse.[33]

The accusations here about "pessimism" are standard in the antirealist diatribes of the era. For Aldrich, a technical perfectionist and exquisitely skilled craftsman (ironic given his jibe at poetry as "trade"), "drooping" means declining, weakening, and dispirited. It implies dejection of mood and languishing physical condition as well as limping or hampered gait, of great consequence to Aldrich in light of his pristine sense of the poetic foot. The empyrean flight of Pegasus pulled down and chained to the realities of earth is a fitting image indeed for Aldrich's rejection of new directions in poetry. Meanwhile, Whitman, Howells, Crane, Sarah Piatt, Melville, and other genteel discontents were pushing against the restricting gates (and gaits) of formal convention.

For an example of a "drooping" poem directly contemporary to "Pessimistic Poets," let's consider Howells's "The King Dines" from *Stops of Various Quills* (1895). Howells leads with a hyper-romantic image, the world of (British) royalty, which runs throughout genteel verse of the period as one of the primary fantasy locales for American anglophilia. Moving from the title to the first line, "Two people on a bench in Boston Common," we find a gap: a quick, surprising shift of locale. Although the title momentarily promises a genteel verse of lordly fantasy, in line 1 we find ourselves, instead, at home. Still – there's a moment of hope for the Aldrich set – Boston Common was a locale with cultural shine: Boston was the traditional center of effete New England culture (and home to Aldrich), and Boston Common was the site of Emerson's "transparent eyeball" vision, an idealist flight into the spiritual world. When we hit line 2, though, all hope is lost:

> An ordinary laboring man and woman,
> Seated together,
> In the November weather
> Slit with a thin, keen rain;
> The woman's mouth purple with cold and pain . . .[34]

The poem thus tactically scatters the two layers of illusion with which it deliberately led: first, the fantasy world of romantic verse as Howells's poetic contemporaries still purveyed it and, second, the fantasy world of upper-class Boston. Part of the artistic polemic of "The King Dines" inheres in its bifurcation of perspective. As in Piatt's "A Prettier Book," Howells works with a bifurcation of perspective specifically between a genteel and a realist aesthetic. (Howells knew Sarah Piatt's poems. Because she has been invisible in American literary history, her possible influence on such a towering figure has remained unexplored.) Howells flags, and rejects, the stock genteel tropes of the fantasy king.

His laboring man "gnaw[s] at a bent bone like a dog, / Following its curve hungrily with his teeth, / And his head twisted sidewise."[35] Here Aldrich's vision of the poet's lordly control of "his" Pegasus devolves into an uncertain distinction between human and animal, the human naturalistically meeting animal instincts in a way that genteel writers deplored as vulgar, atheistic scientism. Formally, we find that Howells has pushed conventional poetic forms, the sonnet in particular, into more limber gaits. A single stanza of eighteen lines, "The King Dines" is composed of six couplets followed by a sestet rhyming *abbacc*. The rhymes are sometimes perfect (rain/pain) and sometimes slant (newspaper/brought with her). The meter ranges from dimeter to pentameter, hovering in particular around iambic pentameter, to which it alludes without regularity. In Aldrich's terms, this poem would be a crippled, modern "poem of pessimism" or, as he put it in his equally disgusted poem "Realism," "To-day we breathe a commonplace, / Polemic, scientific air" (*PTB*, p. 273), vivisecting the nightingale and leaving the Muse to wander "in alien ways remote" (*PTB*, p. 274).

As in the case of Howells, the poetry of Rose Terry Cooke (1827–1892) has mostly been overshadowed by her fiction, although she, too, wrote actively in both genres. She published more than two hundred periodical poems and two volumes of poetry (1861, 1888), but her recovery after the canon wars focused on her realist, local-color tales, often about the narrow lives of New England women. Her poetry has been largely dismissed as "romantic" and conventional, an assessment fed by her use of traditional poetic forms. A handful of critics have called bracing corrective attention to her poetry's phantasmagoric, violent, gothic, and sensual currents, pointing out that its "romance" elements are profoundly tied to the actual conditions of women's lives.[36] In "Arachne," a spider who spins in her corner evokes woman the housekeeper; in "Bluebeard's Closet," the domestic realm is a "red" chamber where "Silence and horror / Brood on the walls."[37] In "Fantasia" (in her first volume, *Poems* [1861], which she published under the name Rose Terry), a superficially romantic veneer belies a scene of horror that the speaker relishes and aestheticizes (*RT*, pp. 78–79). The poem appears to be an imaginative flight in which the speaker enjoys fantasizing that she is a sea flower, in stanza 1; a sea bird, in stanza 2; and a sea wind, in stanza 3. The word "fantasia" connotes musical performance, fancy, and passion. The tone and diction create an atmosphere of freedom and loveliness, exploring wish fulfillment, cool green tides, rocking billows, merriment, and singing.

Yet, as the inhuman speaker soars in unfettered fashion from sea to sky – dreaming of freedom from human form – her subtext is an accelerating and increasingly disturbing picture of human, specifically male, trauma. The surf rushing on black rocks in stanza 1 becomes "lee-shore's thunder / Mocking the mariner's cry" (*RT*, p. 78) in stanza 2. In stanza 3, we face the crying mariners, while the speaker blows merrily through "the sails and rigging" (*RT*, pp. 78–79).

> The crew shall be like dead men
> White with horror and woe;
> Then I'll sing like a spirit,
> And let the good ship go.   (*RT*, p. 79)

Cooke stages her spree of mirth and simultaneous horror in the realm of the familiar. Fantasies are psychically particular, and this speaker tells us the precise terms of her fantasy: "When I am a sea-wind, / I'll watch for a ship I know" (*RT*, p. 78). She then delights in the horror she can create in this "known" male world. She is now inhuman and, significantly, immaterial and beyond touch. Her power to threaten and terrify is implicitly greater in fantasy than what she possesses in real life. The source of her song is a revenge delirium of escape from the domestic world on shore and from her own female body.

Cooke's deceptive aestheticization of the sea provides a bridge to a related poetic experiment of the era, Melville's deceptive aestheticization of flowers. Although Melville wrote and published novels for only a little more than a decade (1846–1857), he wrote and published poems for more than thirty years. His first volume failed to find a publisher in 1860; he then published four volumes, left one volume in manuscript, and produced a substantial body of unpublished poems that are mostly still unknown to both readers and scholars. Standard accounts of his career mistakenly construe the three decades during which he wrote poetry to be an unfortunate dark period during which he lost touch with his real talent, writing fiction.

His first published volume, *Battle-Pieces and Aspects of the War* (1866), reflected on the Civil War in seventy-two formally and conceptually complex and oblique poems. Moving from a national to a transnational sphere, *Clarel: A Poem and Pilgrimage in the Holy Land* (1876), a Victorian long narrative poem of faith and doubt, follows an American divinity student as he grapples with the crumbling legacy of Western Christianity in the aftermath of theories of evolution and the Higher Criticism. Neither book fared well in the marketplace, and Melville published his next two volumes privately, in editions of twenty-five copies: *John Marr and Other Sailors with Some Sea-Pieces* (1888) and *Timoleon, Etc.* (1891). Both continued his significant experimentation with poetic occasion, form, diction, and voice but were now circulated by him only to a hand-picked audience.

The volume of poems he left unpublished at his death, *Weeds and Wildings Chiefly: With a Rose or Two*, is Melville's response to the poetry of beauty. Its title depicts his poems as "weeds and wildings chiefly," explicitly contrasted with "a rose or two." While weeds and wildings are both uncultivated, wild plants, for both nineteenth-century gardeners and genteel poets the rose emblematized high cultivation. Cooke is a worthy compatriot on this point, specifically working from the domain of gender: she opens her poem "Truths" this way: "I wear a rose in my hair, / Because I feel like a weed; / Who knows that the rose is thorny / And makes my temples bleed?" (*RT*, p. 86). Poetic value (to return to Piatt's term in "A Prettier Book") is indeed the subject that Melville encodes in this entire volume's insistent roster of botanical poems. It is in these terms that we can understand his repeated depictions of reception scenarios, in which viewers reject or otherwise somehow fail to "see" the botanical specimens right in front of them (for example, "Field Asters," "The American Aloe on Exhibition," and "A Way-Side Weed").

Melville's formal strike against the poetry of beauty and the way it delivered meaning was to cultivate, through exacting art, something that looks like a poem of beauty, but whose alluring surface then turns out to be nearly opaque. This opacity, in turn, foregrounds the relation between viewer and page, because the former seeks recognizable meaning in the latter, but the poem counters that expectation. In Melville's metapoetics, this scenario becomes a drama of engagement in which the reader hits the wall. The poetry of beauty implodes. Only a complete recasting of one's expectations from poetry can avert that fate. His common-looking specimens, if assessed by conventional standards of poetic value, truly can't be seen at all. His field asters in the poem by that title are "Wild ones every autumn seen – / Seen of all, arresting few." The next stanza begins: "Seen indeed."[38]

Weeds and Wildings takes the idea of the rose in particular and estranges it from the poetic matrix that had cultivated it to the point of collapse. In this sense, Melville concurs with Whitman's diagnosis of "the beauty disease." Let's consider an emblematic (and, emblematically, a highly resistant and off-putting) poem, "A Ground-Vine Intercedes with the Queen of Flowers for the Merited Recognition of Clover." The title stages an aesthetic debate as an issue of botanical hierarchy. A literally lowly plant, "a ground-vine," approaches the high-born rose (the "Queen of Flowers") on behalf of a third party, Clover. The title summarizes the polemic: that Clover deserves but does not receive "recognition," certainly not from the Queen.

The poem opens with a stance of apparent obsequiousness directed at both the Queen and the poetic tradition:

> Hymned down the years from ages far,
> The theme of lover, seer, and king,
> Reign endless, Rose! for fair you are,
> Nor heaven reserves a fairer thing.　　　　(WW, p. 22)

The age-old "theme" of roses provides the occasion for the speaker's own hymn. The vine dares to speak his case before the Queen, despite his status as "a groundling" (WW, p. 22). The political edge in this self-description becomes more palpable when we note that, for Melville, the word "groundling" invokes his beloved Shakespeare. Although the opening stanza associates the Rose with "heaven" – a common genteel trope for the world of airy, idealist, romantic perfection, as in Aldrich's "heaven-sent dreams," discussed earlier – the ground-vine wants to bring her down to earth:

> O Rose, we plants are all akin.
> Our roots enlock; each strives to win

> The ampler space, the balmier air.
> But beauty, plainness, shade and sun –
> Here share-and-share-alike is none! (*WW*, p. 22)

What started out as obsequiousness in the pretty world of gardens turns into a dog-eat-dog scene of survival. Although the ground-vine leads his appeal with what sounds like an egalitarian plea based on common interests, it quickly turns into a blunt description of the battle for resources. His initial posture of petition to a botanical better thus gives way to a warning to the Queen about her tentative status. Because "plants are all akin," she had best not simply assume the necessity of her own exalted position.

The penultimate stanza evens out the terrain between Rose and Clover:

> And, ranked with grass, a flower may dwell,
> Cheerful, if never high in feather,
> With pastoral sisters thriving well
> In bloom that shares the broader weather;
> Charmful, mayhap, in simple grace,
> A lowlier Eden mantling in her face. (*WW*, p. 22)

The ambiguity of the phrase "a flower" is stark in a poem obsessed with particular, named plants and their "rank" relative to one another. The tactical ambiguity of "a flower" sustains two possible referents, part of the poem's larger challenge to categories of botanical and poetical value. The first is Clover; indeed, Clover already dwells amid the lowlier botanical ranks "with grass." But just as the previous stanza has imagined a world in which plants are "all akin," we also find implicit in this stanza a notional space in which the "Queen of Flowers" has been demoted to the status of "a flower," imaginatively transplanted over the garden wall into the broader world of plants with "enlocked" roots. Thus running through the ostensible hymn to the "endless" reign of the Queen of Flowers is a fantasy – and a threat – that she will lose her place. (Recall Cooke's fantasia of power.) The ground-vine confronts the Queen of Flowers to "recognize" that she may be brought down to his level with the other groundlings, such that she is no longer "high in feather," but just another "flower," "ranked with grass" and subject to the fight for "the ampler space, the balmier air" (*WW*, p. 22).

Just as its surface conceit challenges botanical hierarchies, the poem simultaneously troubles its own ostensible genre as a hymn or song of praise. The verbal undercutting becomes most overt in the last stanza:

> My Queen, so all along I lie,
> But creep I can, scarce win your eye.

> But, O, your garden-wall peer over,
> And, if you blush, 'twill hardly be
> At owning kin with Cousin Clover
> Who winsome makes the low degree.   (*WW*, p. 23)

The ground-vine "lies" and "creeps" along the ground, as ground-vines do; but both of these words also suggest a position of duplicity – of verbally lying "all along" as part of a stealthy attack. Lyon Evans has persuasively traced duplicity as a mode in other sections of *Weeds and Wildings*, and Vernon Shetley incisively calls Melville's ironic use of familiar nature tropes "negative pastoral."[39] We have seen that the dynamic in the title, which promised a plot in which the vine appeals to the Queen to raise Clover up in status, turned out to be a false lead. At the same time, the poem's ostensible genre, a hymn to the Rose in an "endless" tradition handed down by the ages, is a generic false lead as well. We saw in "The King Dines" that Howells created a bifurcation of perspective between the generic genteel promise of regal fantasy in his title and his polemical form and content. Melville leads as if writing a hymn to ideal beauty and then overturns, from within, the entire aesthetic of the poem.

The proper place for this poem in the standard categories of American literary history is in fact naturalism, typically defined as a second-generation, darker wave of realism focused on evolutionary struggles and biological drives, competition for resources, and an evisceration of human agency. Here we can turn to another of the era's hidden poets, someone whose career is rarely placed alongside Melville's: Theodore Dreiser, whom conventional literary history has identified almost completely with prose fiction, naturalism in particular. Dreiser, too, was an active poet, publishing many periodical poems in the 1890s up through a book of poems, *Moods: Cadenced and Declaimed*, in 1926. One of the challenges to recovering Dreiser as poet has been that he often published his periodical poems anonymously or pseudonymously.[40] Nancy Warner Barrineau points out that his pseudonyms in *Ev'ry Month*, a magazine he ran and for which he did almost all the writing, allowed him to experiment "with a series of narrative voices"; the same is certainly true of the poems he published there as well, under names such as "S. J. White," "Theodore Dreiser," and "The Poet."[41] Judgments of his late nineteenth- and early twentieth-century poems as "done in the manner of the 'genteel tradition'"[42] remain automatic and uninterrogated.

In *Ainslee's Magazine* (1899), for example, we find the twelve-line poem "Bondage," which, although written in rhymed iambic pentameter, is hardly genteel; it's a naturalist poem about enslavement to desire. It concludes: "Its slave you are. Denying is so vain. / Someone hath touched you saying: 'Feel desire.' / His will you do – you run, you run, aspire!"[43] Although the male pronoun in the final line indicates a male person, importantly a nearly anonymous "someone" who has the power to call up your biological sexual instincts regardless of your choice, your individuality, or your human connections, it also refers to "desire" itself as a more general human drive. The word "desire" in fact sets the poem in motion in the first two lines: "We only know we're caught within the stream, / And feel the ceaseless drag of all desire" (*AM*, p. 26). But "His" in the final line has a third meaning that is the most radical of all. It refers back to a completely unidentified male pronoun in line 4: "We only know of toil food [*sic*], sleep and dream, / And as we bow, so we escape His ire" (*AM*, p. 26). The capitalized "His" here connotes the Christian God, but the actual referent for this pronoun is desire itself, Dreiser's polemical replacement. Desire is true lord and master. Only by bowing to "His" dictates, by following the lead of your drives, can you escape desire's insistent wrath.

The fact that this poem appeared a year before the first edition of *Sister Carrie* (1900) only dramatizes the fact that Dreiser's naturalism was not transpiring exclusively, or even first, in the genre of prose fiction. We thus find another dramatic indication that the genteel tradition narrative is an ideology that has been mistaken for a history. The era was not a barren one, awaiting later modernist redemption. An imprecise generalization even when Santayana coined the term, its repeated invocation has served to obscure the complexity of actual poetic practices during the decades in question.

Notes

1. George Santayana, "The Genteel Tradition in American Philosophy," *University of California Chronicle* 12:4 (1911), pp. 357–80; George Santayana, *The Genteel Tradition: Nine Essays by George Santayana*, ed. Douglas L. Wilson (1915; Cambridge, Mass.: Harvard University Press, 1967), pp. 72–76.
2. John Timberman Newcomb, *Would Poetry Disappear? American Verse and the Crisis of Modernity* (Columbus: Ohio State University Press, 2004), pp. 14–15.
3. Laura Stedman and George M. Gould, *Life and Letters of Edmund Clarence Stedman*, 2 vols. (New York: Moffat, Yard, 1910), vol. 1, p. 188 (hereafter cited in the text as *LL*).
4. Albert H. Smyth, *Bayard Taylor* (Boston: Houghton Mifflin, 1896), p. 63 (hereafter cited in the text as *BT*).
5. Richmond Croom Beatty, "Bayard Taylor and George H. Boker," *American Literature* 6:3 (1934), pp. 316–27; John Tomsich, *A Genteel Endeavor: American Culture and Politics in the Gilded Age* (Stanford, Calif.: Stanford University Press, 1971), pp. 9, 120; Andrew Dubois and Frank Lentricchia, "Prologue," in

Sacvan Bercovitch (ed.), *The Cambridge History of American Literature*. Vol. 5, *Poetry and Criticism 1900–1950* (Cambridge: Cambridge University Press, 2003), pp. 11–14, 11.

6. William Purviance Fenn, "Richard Henry Stoddard's Chinese Poems," *American Literature* 11:4 (1940), pp. 417–38.

7. Beatty, "Bayard Taylor and George H. Boker," pp. 325–26.

8. Dino Franco Felluga, *The Perversity of Poetry: Romantic Ideology and the Popular Male Poet of Genius* (Albany: State University Press of New York, 2005), p. 143.

9. Thomas Bailey Aldrich, "Enamored Architect of Airy Rhyme," in *The Poems of Thomas Bailey Aldrich* (1858; Boston: Houghton, Mifflin, 1885), p. 207. Poems in this collection will be cited in the text as *PTB*.

10. Howard Mumford Jones, *The Age of Energy: Varieties of American Experience 1865–1915* (New York: Viking, 1970), p. 238.

11. G. E. DeMille, "Stedman, Arbiter of the Eighties," *PMLA* 41:3 (1926), p. 766; Willard Thorp, "Defenders of Ideality," in Robert E. Spiller et al. (eds.), *Literary History of the United States*, 3rd ed. (New York: Macmillan, 1963), p. 815; Martha Edelsberg Passe, "Criticism of Poetry in America During the Nineties" (doctoral dissertation, Ohio State University, 1957), pp. 67–80.

12. Newcomb, *Would Poetry Disappear?*, p. 112.

13. DeMille, "Stedman, Arbiter of the Eighties," p. 762.

14. Edmund Clarence Stedman, *Victorian Poets* (1875; Boston: Houghton, Mifflin, 1889), pp. 14–15.

15. Michael Cohen, "E.C. Stedman and the Invention of Victorian Poetry," *Victorian Poetry* 43:2 (2005), pp. 166, 168–69.

16. Edmund Clarence Stedman, "The Twilight of the Poets," *Century Illustrated Magazine*, September 1, 1885, American Periodicals Series Online, ProQuest; Elizabeth Renker, "The 'Twilight of the Poets' in the Era of American Realism, 1875–1900," in Kerry Larson (ed.), *The Cambridge Companion to Nineteenth-Century American Poetry* (Cambridge: Cambridge University Press, 2011), pp. 135–53.

17. Edmund Clarence Stedman, "How Old Brown Took Harper's Ferry," in Burton Egbert Stevenson (ed.), *Poems of American History* (New York: Houghton Mifflin, 1908), p. 393.

18. Edmund Clarence Stedman, "Pan in Wall Street," in *The Poetical Works of Edmund Clarence Stedman* (Boston: Houghton Mifflin, 1884), pp. 250–52. Poems in this collection will be cited in the text as *PW*.

19. Virginia Jackson, *Dickinson's Misery: A Theory of Lyric Reading* (Princeton, N.J.: Princeton University Press, 2005).

20. Richard Cary, *The Genteel Circle: Bayard Taylor and His New York Friends* (Ithaca, N.Y.: Cornell University Press, 1952), p. 27; Norman Foerster, "Later Poets," in William Peterfield Trent et al. (eds.), *The Cambridge History of American Literature*, 3 vols. (New York: Macmillan, 1946), vol. 3, pp. 37, 41, 31.

21. Walt Whitman, "The Poetry of the Future," *The North American Review*, February 1881, p. 195.

22. Sarah Morgan Bryan Piatt, *Palace-Burner: The Selected Poetry of Sarah Piatt*, ed. Paula Bernat Bennett (Urbana: University of Illinois Press, 2001), p. xxxiii (hereafter cited in the notes as *PB*).

23. Newcomb, *Would Poetry Disappear?*, p. 7.

24. My formulation that Piatt wrote "in and out of" the genteel tradition is indebted to Kirsten Silva Gruesz's important formulation about Maria Gowen Brooks, in Gruesz, "Maria Gowen Brooks, In and Out of the Poe Circle," *ESQ: A Journal of the American Renaissance* 54 (2008), pp. 75–109.

25. Bayard Taylor, *The Echo Club, and Other Literary Diversions* (Boston: James R. Osgood, 1876), p. 136.

26. Taylor, *The Echo Club*, p. 147.

27. Paula Bernat Bennett, *Poets in the Public Sphere: The Emancipatory Project of American Women's Poetry, 1800–1900* (Princeton, N.J.: Princeton University Press, 2003).

28. Sarah Piatt, "A Prettier Book," in Jeannette Leonard Gilder (ed.), *Representative Poems of Living Poets, American and English, Selected by the Poets Themselves* (New York: Cassell, 1886), pp. 507–08. This collection will be cited in the text as *RP*.

29. Julie Bates Dock, "William Dean Howells," in Eric L. Haralson (ed.), *Encyclopedia of American Poetry: The Nineteenth Century* (Chicago: Fitzroy Dearborn, 1998), pp. 226–27.

30. William Dean Howells, *Pebbles, Monochromes, and Other Modern Poems, 1891–1916*, ed. Edwin H. Cady (Athens: Ohio University Press, 2000), pp. xxvii, xxix.

31. See Bayard Taylor, "El Khalil," in *The Poetical Works of Bayard Taylor* (1854; Boston: Houghton Mifflin, 1875), pp. 61–62; Bayard Taylor, "The Norseman's Ride," in *The Poetical Works of Bayard Taylor*, p. 17; Aldrich, *The Poems of Thomas Bailey Aldrich*, pp. 17–18.

32. Thomas Bailey Aldrich, "Unguarded Gates," in *Unguarded Gates* (Boston: Houghton Mifflin, 1895), pp. 15–17.

33. Aldrich, *Unguarded Gates*, p. 119.

34. William Dean Howells, "The King Dines," in *Stops of Various Quills* (New York: Harper, 1895), n.p.

35. Howells, *Stops of Various Quills*, n.p.

36. Paula Bernat Bennett (ed.), *Nineteenth-Century American Women Poets: An Anthology* (Malden, Mass.: Blackwell, 1998); Karen Kilcup, "Rose Terry Cooke," in Haralson (ed.), *Encyclopedia of American Poetry*. Cheryl Walker (ed.), *American Women Poets of the Nineteenth Century: An Anthology* (New Brunswick, N.J.: Rutgers University Press, 1992).

37. Rose Terry Cooke, *Poems* (New York: Geo. Gottesberger Peck, 1881), pp. 101–03; Rose Terry, *Poems* (Boston: Ticknor and Fields, 1861), pp. 20–23. Poems in the 1861 collection will be cited in the text as *RT*.

38. Herman Melville, *Weeds and Wildings Chiefly: With a Rose or Two*, in Robert C. Ryan (ed.), "Weeds and Wildings Chiefly: With a Rose or Two. By Herman Melville. Reading Text and Genetic Text, Edited from the Manuscripts, with Introduction and Notes" (doctoral dissertation, Northwestern University, Evanston, 1967), p. 14. Poems in this collection will be cited in the text as *WW*.

39. Vernon Lionel Shetley, "A Private Art: Melville's Poetry of Negation" (doctoral dissertation, Columbia University, 1986), p. 150.

40. Donald Pizer, Richard W. Dowell, and Frederic E. Rusch, *Theodore Dreiser: A Primary Bibliography and Reference Guide* (Boston: G. K. Hall, 1991), p. 29.

41. Nancy Warner Barrineau (ed.), *Theodore Dreiser's Ev'ry Month* (Athens: University of Georgia Press, 1996), pp. xx, 25, 98.

42. Robert Palmer Saalbach (ed.), *Selected Poems (from Moods) by Theodore Dreiser* (New York: Exposition Press, 1969), p. 6.

43. Theodore Dreiser, "Bondage," *Ainslee's Magazine*, April 1899, p. 293 (hereafter cited in the text as *AM*).

Chapter 19

Disciplined Play: American Children's Poetry to 1920

ANGELA SORBY

"Can children's poetry matter?" When Richard Flynn posed this question in 1993, he was paraphrasing Dana Gioia's famous challenge to readers of poetry in general, but he was also upping the ante.[1] Children's poetry is often seen as a marginal subfield within the already-somewhat-marginal field of poetry. It is barely studied and barely taught, except as an instrumental teaching tool in colleges of education. And yet, ironically, nineteenth-century verses for children ("A Visit from St. Nicholas," "Mary's Lamb") are among the best-known and most culturally influential texts in American literary history. To examine the popular success of such texts, it is necessary to ask not whether children's poetry can matter but how and why it has continued to matter so much, for so long, to so many readers.

What, exactly, is children's poetry? The idea of childhood is notoriously malleable, as many historians have pointed out. In *Huck's Raft*, Steven Mintz argues that although contemporary childhood is defined by fixed stages (start school at five, drive at sixteen, etc.), pre-twentieth-century lives were "far less regularized or uniform. Unpredictability was the hallmark of growing up, even for the children of professionals and merchants."[2] Certainly in America, and especially before the Civil War, the line between childhood and adulthood was blurry and heavily dependent on class, race, religion, and personal circumstance. Very young children were offered alphabets and nursery rhymes, often drawn from the oral tradition. But just as older children shared adult responsibilities, so too did they share adult reading materials; this is evident, for instance, in the proliferating "household" editions of poets such as Lydia Sigourney and Henry Wadsworth Longfellow. The idea of household or mixed-age readership had a profound influence on pre-twentieth-century American poets, from Sigourney to Emily Dickinson to Paul Laurence Dunbar. It is necessary to understand children's literature and children's reading, not because it was a separate sphere but because it was so thoroughly integrated into the commercial and literary life of pre-twentieth-century America. In other words, it may be deceptive to say that children read adult poetry or vice versa; instead, one could argue that most pre-twentieth-century popular poetry was not age graded; it was instead intergenerational in ways that affected its composition, circulation, and horizons of interpretation.

In early Puritan communities, older children read poems written for a broad readership, such as Michael Wigglesworth's spine-tingling "Day of Doom" (1662), which much later would serve as a model for Clement Clark Moore's "A Visit from St. Nicholas" (1823). However, Puritans were also among the first to produce rhymes aimed at young children, because they believed that they must learn to read as soon as possible to gain direct access to biblical salvation. Beginning readers were given rhymed, illustrated alphabets such as those in the *New England Primer*. Indeed, the *Primer* alphabet, beginning "In Adam's fall / We sinn'd all," is probably one of the earliest English-language American poems, although its precise origins are murky. The Boston-based printer Benjamin Harris likely derived the first *New England Primer* (1686) from an ABC book, *The Protestant Tutor*, which he had published in England in 1679. Although the *Primer* was the most widely distributed American-authored book throughout the seventeenth, eighteenth, and early nineteenth centuries, few editions survive, not because they were unpopular but because they were overused; even Emily Dickinson scissored her copy to pieces when she wanted to illustrate her verses with woodcuts.

As a poem, the *Primer*'s alphabet evolved, like folk material, in response to changing cultural conditions. For instance, as Clifton Johnson notes, the rhyme for K ("King Charles the good, / No Man of blood") became, by the later eighteenth century, "Queens and Kings / Are gaudy things."[3] Patricia Crain's *The Story of A* describes how the *Primer* contributed to the "alphabetization" of America: "The verbal and visual tropes that surround the alphabet cloak the fact that the unit of textual meaning – the letter – lacks meaning itself. The alphabet represents a threat to orthodoxy, for into this space competing meanings may rush."[4] Although the image/text combination of the alphabet is theologically Calvinist, it also draws on competing discourses, from tavern signs to Renaissance emblems to nursery rhymes. Moreover, unlike the *Bay Psalm Book*, with its strict hymnal meter, the *Primer*'s prosody is ragged and changeable, without a uniform meter to make the letters cohere. Ironically, the hybrid *New England Primer* is aesthetically compelling precisely because it fails at orthodoxy; it reflects, as Crain notes, an emerging mercantile economy in which flexibility is key.

Beyond the *Primer*, few influential American children's poems appeared in the seventeenth, eighteenth, and early nineteenth centuries, although the rapidly expanding printing trade flooded the market with tiny children's chapbooks that were hawked as toys. Poems in such volumes were often nursery or street rhymes (*Tommy Thumb's Song-Book*; *Melodies of Mother Goose*), copied from John Newbery and other Britons. Such secular materials supplemented soberer works like the *Primer*, initiating tensions between oral and written texts, and between didacticism and entertainment, that would enliven children's poetry through the nineteenth century and beyond.

American children's poetry, like American literature more generally, took on distinctive characteristics after about 1820, as more work was written and published (as opposed to pirated) by Americans. The reasons for this are manifold: the demand for consumer goods rose; holiday traditions were codified; magazines and newspapers proliferated; romantic and sentimental discourses venerated childhood; middle-class mothers had the leisure to be readers and even writers of poetry; and public schools became common and eventually mandatory. Social and material conditions favored the circulation of sentimental or didactic poems that could be read aloud, memorized, and repeated by children in the company of adults.

Clement Clark Moore's "A Visit from St. Nicholas" (1823) was the earliest secular children's poem to achieve mass-cultural popularity, and it is a bit of an outlier: its author was not a professional writer, and it is neither sentimental nor didactic, although it does lend itself to oral reading. Moore, an academic specializing in Hebrew, drew on Dutch folklore (including Washington Irving's *Knickerbocker's History of New York*) to write perhaps the most famous opening couplet in American history: "'Twas the night before Christmas, when all through the house / Not a creature was stirring, not even a mouse."[5] In *The Battle for Christmas*, Stephen Nissenbaum argues that Moore's poem draws on, and contributes to, an invented tradition only tangentially related to its European sources. Nissenbaum suggests that "A Visit from St. Nicholas" adjudicates between carnivalesque working-class Christmas bacchanals and the more staid traditions of upper-class New Yorkers. St. Nicholas himself is transformed from a patrician bishop to a "pedlar / just opening his pack," but as a benevolent elf he sheds the illicit connotations of itinerancy and works to contain class tensions that elites like Moore found threatening.

Although Nissenbaum's analysis is meticulous, it is perhaps too localized to account for the poem's uncannily wide circulation. Structurally, the work parallels Wigglesworth's "Day of Doom," while offering domestic, materialistic pleasures in place of the old Puritan apocalypse. Moore's jarringly secular vision of Christmas is thus couched in a reassuringly established frame; like much successful popular culture, it makes something new feel natural. The poem was first published in the (Troy, New York) *Sentinel* in 1823 but was widely copied in other newspapers. In 1848 it made its début as a stand-alone picture book, with woodcuts by Theodore Boyd; at this point, it was explicitly identified as "a present for good little boys and girls." Indeed, gift-giving practices (rather than the containment of class tensions) seem key to this poem's popularity: it both celebrates gifts and can also serve as a gift. In the poem, as at Christmastime, gifts from an adult authority to a child stress the intergenerational bonds that poems can build, and that are central to sentimental domestic ideology. In *Revolution and the Word*, Cathy Davidson emphasizes that "every work of art operates both within a market economy and a gift economy," and even when readers buy books, they experience them, to some degree, as gifts.[6] Although Davidson is arguing for the importance of the novel, a poem like "A Visit from St. Nicholas" proves her point even more directly, because poems (like St. Nicholas in his sleigh) are remarkably mobile and were often packaged as giftbooks. And indeed, if memorized, they did not even require a print text in order to be transmitted from household to household.

The gradual shift from church-based to home-based holidays also spurred the popularity of Lydia Maria Child's "The New-England Boy's Song About Thanksgiving Day," which first appeared in Child's commercial giftbook *Flowers for Children*, in 1844:

> Over the river and through the wood
> To grandfather's house we go;
> The horse knows the way,
> To carry the sleigh
> Through the white and drifted snow.   (*OB*, p. 38)

Like "A Visit from St. Nicholas," "The New-England Boy's Song" is ultimately about consuming desires: "Hooray for the fun! / Is the pudding done? / Hooray for the pumpkin pie!" (*OB*, p. 39). In both poems, desires are framed as fulfilled in domestic space; the whole thrust of "The New-England Boy's Song" emphasizes that the sleigh should rush as quickly as possible toward the gratifications of the warm house and kitchen. As versions of Child's poem were reprinted very widely in giftbooks and school readers, stanzas and phrases appeared and disappeared, mimicking the dynamic of an oral tradition. This is one quality specific to children's poetry, seen much less often in elite "adult" poems: the verses tend not to be stable or sacralized, but rather open to playful modification as they are repeated in daily life. For example, *The*

Mary Dawson Game Book (1916) proposes a game of "Hooray for the Pumpkin Pie!" that uses Child's poem as a jumping-off point.[7] Not surprisingly, given the powerful cult of domestic motherhood, "grandfather's house" gradually became "grandmother's house," and by the mid-twentieth century this matriarchal substitution seems to have become the dominant variant.

The household unit was also celebrated in the output of the so-called sentimental women poets, whose work has been recovered in the late twentieth century by scholars including Paula Bennett, Cheryl Walker, Elizabeth Petrino, and Karen Kilcup. Because recovery work is aimed at taking women writers seriously – and because children's literature is often *not* taken seriously – the intergenerational quality of this oeuvre has generally been downplayed so that other qualities, such as subversiveness or eroticism, can be highlighted. And yet, nineteenth-century women poets, including Lydia Sigourney, Hannah Flagg Gould, Emily Dickinson, Lucy Larcom, Alice and Phoebe Cary, Sarah Piatt, and most others, published volumes that mix juvenile and adult work indiscriminately, making these categories themselves seem irrelevant or inadequate. For instance, in *Select Poems* (1841), Lydia Sigourney juxtaposes "Birthday Verses to a Little Girl" with "Farewell to the Aged," as if to stress – in typically market-savvy Sigourney style – the range of her reach. This very fluidity of voice and of audience is a productive force within the poems and within nineteenth-century poetry writ large.

Hannah Flagg Gould was probably the most prolific antebellum producer of poems aimed partly (although not exclusively) at children. One poem, "The Child's Address to the Kentucky Mummy," seems to muse on the issue of audience:

> And now, Mistress Mummy, since thus you've been found
> By the world, that has long done without you,
> In your snug little hiding-place far under ground –
> Be pleased to speak out, as we gather around,
> And let us hear something about you!

The child puzzles over the mummy and her history, finally concluding:

> Say, whose was the ear that could hear with delight
> The musical trinket found nigh you?
> And who had the eye that was pleased with the sight
> Of this form (whose queer face might be brown, red or white,)
> Tricked out in the jewels kept by you?[8]

Janet Gray's recent close reading of Gould's poem supports a thesis about veiled abolitionism, but Gray's observations can also work as a comment on the tensions within nineteenth-century children's verse:

Adopting the persona of a child boldly trying to initiate a public discussion, she looks back at an estranged version of herself – a woman buried with a musical instrument, an oral performer from an alien culture – and exposes the incoherence of her relationship with her audience.... A figure over six feet tall folded into fetal position, the mummy would have conveyed to viewers both largeness and smallness, the forms of adult and child bound together in death's imitation of birth.[9]

Just as the adult and child are bound together in "The Child's Address," so too are "the forms of adult and child bound together" in Gould's *Poems*, generating fertile instances of heteroglossia as she code-switches between younger and older voices.

The practice of addressing adults and children together in volumes of poetry spanned the whole nineteenth century, although it was slightly more common during the antebellum period. Most scholarly work on the childlike qualities of women authors stresses that, although the voice seems innocent, it is "really" an adult voice making an adult point. In her groundbreaking introduction to *The Palace-Burner*, Paula Bennett underscores the seriousness of Sarah Piatt, a mid- to late nineteenth-century writer: "Very much like Fanny Osgood and Emily Dickinson ... Piatt uses 'naïve' speakers to make 'sensitive' adult points."[10] Bennett's emphasis on Piatt's fundamental adulthood makes sense in the context of a twenty-first-century critical environment that continues to marginalize children's literature; after all, Bennett is rescuing Piatt from the margins. However, a close reading of Piatt suggests that her engagement with childhood is not a strategic mask but is in fact integral to her literary agenda and to her voice. Like many other poets of the era, if she is not merely a children's poet, she is just as assuredly not simply a poet for adults. "Trumpet-Flowers," for instance, appeared in the family paper the *Youth's Companion* in 1883:

> They light the green dusk with their fire-like glow,
> And the brown barefoot boys laugh out below.
>
> The wind wakes in the grass and climbs the tree,
> The wind – ah, what a trumpeter is he:
>
> He blows them in the leaves above my head
> So low, so long, that he might wake the dead.
>
> He blows them, till a child they cannot see
> Hears them, and plays with that brown company.   (PB, p. 111)

This poem is free of the entertainment-versus-didacticism battle that dogs some nineteenth-century children's verse, because it aspires to be neither funny nor preachy. Instead, it uses its own playfulness, and the playfulness of the "barefoot boys" (a trope that would be familiar to readers of Whittier) to meditate on the relationship between death and play: Can the dead awaken? Are children closer to the spirit world? The poem does not answer its own questions, except by imagining that a child who can be neither seen nor heard might be stirred from death by the trumpet flowers. Piatt, at her best, neither excludes children nor condescends to them, and in "Trumpet-Flowers" children are aligned with the wind that climbs a tree (like a child) and that acts as the animating agent of the poem.

Emily Dickinson's child voice has generated discussion about the extent to which she can or should be read as a children's poet – again, partly because twenty-first-century readers are used to drawing boundaries around children's literature. Elizabeth Philips, for instance, notes that "Some of the poems, about trifles and 'little things,' suggest that Dickinson, like Swift, Twain, and a number of women contemporary with her, had an interest in writing for children as well as adults."[11] Philips believes that Dickinson's juvenile verse is "not always among the best poetry she wrote," and that it only sometimes rises to the level of "superior light verse."[12] The trouble, here, is one of genre: What is an "adult" poem? Must it exclude the child's perspective? Must it eschew playfulness? Or is adulthood in poetry simply a matter of complexity? And if so, what counts as a trifle or little thing? The few poems that Dickinson published in her lifetime appeared mostly in intergenerational venues, like the Springfield *Republican*, that routinely published poems for a child/adult mixed readership. And posthumously, although some of her work appeared in the *Atlantic*, it was also deemed appropriate for the *Youth's Companion*. A case can be made that Dickinson's power derives in part from her intergenerational voice and the tensions it produces, and that this intergenerational perspective pervades many if not most of her poems. Paul Crumbley, for instance, advances a subtle analysis in *Inflections of the Pen*, arguing that "I'm Ceded – I've stopped being Theirs" "demonstrates that the child's voice must be thought of in dialogue with other voices. To hear the child is also to hear the voices that instruct, curse, comfort, and punish an innocent, unformed consciousness."[13] In other words, the discursive condition of intergenerational dialogue saturates Dickinson's poems, just as the poems themselves were "addressed" (literally, in letters) to correspondents of all ages, and just as they continue to address adults and children today – like Piatt, without condescension.

The male Fireside or Schoolroom Poets, most prominently Henry Wadsworth Longfellow and John Greenleaf Whittier, achieved iconic celebrity status in ways that would have been unthinkable for women poets. Ultimately, however, they too functioned as intergenerational poets, and much of their fame rested on their ubiquity in schoolrooms. As I argue in *Schoolroom Poets*, the growth of a public education system based on rote recitation meant that virtually all children educated in the United States learned the same popular canon of poems, including, for instance, Longfellow's "A Psalm of Life," "The Village Blacksmith," and "Paul Revere's Ride" and Whittier's "Barefoot Boy." Children learned these poems in school, and adults recalled them with nostalgia. Like popular songs, schoolroom poems became repositories of personal memories even as they also served to bind schoolchildren into imagined communities:

> Listen, my children, and you shall hear
> Of the midnight ride of Paul Revere;
> On the eighteenth of April in seventy-five,
> Hardly a man is now alive
> Who remembers that famous day and year.　　(*OB*, p. 45)

All children, in this poem, are posited as Longfellow's children, gathered close enough to hear his voice even as they are widely dispersed across the nation. Public school classrooms often displayed busts or portraits of Longfellow beside George Washington, cementing the nationalist aims of public school educators. Especially in their dotage, Longfellow and Whittier were hailed, in countless articles, as children's poets and above all as children's paternal friends. Both increasingly addressed themselves directly to this constituency, and when Whittier edited a commercial volume of *Child-Life: Poetry* (1871), Longfellow and the other Fireside Poets featured prominently.

Within an ambiguously intergenerational milieu, anthologies helpfully identify what literary qualities – including frankness, humor, and colloquial speech – were considered childlike. Ralph Waldo Emerson's "A Fable," for instance, appeared in *Child-Life* and in many other children's anthologies:

> The mountain and the squirrel
> Had a quarrel;
> And the former called the latter "Little Prig."
> Bun replied,
> "You are doubtless very big;
> But all sorts of things and weather
> Must be taken in together,
> To make up a year
> And a sphere.
> And I think it no disgrace
> To occupy my place.

If I'm not so large as you,
You are not so small as I,
And not half so spry.
I'll not deny you make
A very pretty squirrel track;
Talents differ; all is well and wisely put;
If I cannot carry forests on my back,
Neither can you crack a nut."   (*OB*, p. 39)

In his 1872 study *Americanisms*, Maximillian DeVere notes that "Bun" is New England slang for "squirrel."[14] Although Emerson pushed for American colloquialisms – stumps and boasts – in his essay "The Poet" (1840), his own verse often resorts to elite literary language. The squirrel's boasting brings "A Fable" closer to the oral tradition than most of Emerson's work, making it a popular children's recitation piece. Moreover, its humor and colloquialisms also bring it closer to Emerson's own stated literary ideals, suggesting that perhaps intergenerational audiences helped nudge American poetry away from archaism and artifice.

Child-Life was meant for household use, but the most influential disseminators of poetry – not just children's poetry but any poetry – throughout the nineteenth century were school anthologies, particularly the McGuffey's Reader series. These graded American schoolbooks, beginning with the *Primer* and ending with the *Sixth Reader*, draw as often from the annals of adult poetry as from the archive of specifically children's verse, again establishing crossover hits that were quickly naturalized as part of a popular intergenerational canon that "everyone" supposedly knew. A list of McGuffey's selections includes most of the poems now understood to be nineteenth-century children's classics, including, for example, Longfellow's "Paul Revere's Ride," Celia Thaxter's "The Sandpiper," Edgar Allan Poe's "The Raven," and Bryant's "Lines to a Waterfowl." It also includes memorable poems by less remembered authors, such as Sarah Roberts's "The Voice of the Grass," which predates Whitman's grass:

Here I come, creeping, creeping everywhere;
  By the dusty roadside,
  On the sunny hillside,
  Close by the noisy brook,
  In every shady nook,
I come creeping, creeping everywhere.[15]

As "The Voice of the Grass" (and the flocks of ravens, sandpipers, and waterfowl) suggests, McGuffey's reigning aesthetic was overwhelmingly pastoral, reflecting romantic assumptions about youth and nature that steered the course of much children's poetry throughout the nineteenth century.

If a handful of textbook poems were frequently repeated in schools and parlors, American magazines and newspapers took the opposite tack, trumpeting new poems in every issue. Antebellum American children's magazines that published poems aimed specifically at young readers included, inter alia, the *Juvenile Miscellany* (edited by Lydia Maria Child and later Sarah Josepha Hale), *Parley's Magazine* (edited by Samuel Goodrich), the *Fireside Miscellany* (edited by Hannah Flagg Gould and Darius Mead), the *Southern Rose Bud* (edited by Caroline Gilman), and many others, although adult magazines, such as *Godey's*, also published children's verses. This list of editors reads as a who's who of children's poetry – perhaps in part because the editors were compelled to fill gaps with poems they wrote themselves.

The most famous children's poem to emerge from antebellum magazine culture was Sarah Josepha Hale's "Mary's Lamb," which, with its fleece "white as snow," remains so familiar that it barely needs quoting. "Mary's Lamb" first appeared in the *Juvenile Miscellany* in 1830, when Lydia Maria Child was still the editor. It was widely reprinted in newspapers, and its fame was cemented when McGuffey's included it in the 1836 *First Reader*, ensuring that it was among the very first poems that young children memorized. Elsewhere, I have read "Mary's Lamb" as an animal rights poem, because kindness to animals was a constant refrain in children's magazines, reflecting a sentimental/political imaginary that aligned children, animals, slaves, and women. However, and perhaps even more importantly, "Mary's Lamb" registers Hale's strong commitment to female education. Mary, after all, takes her lamb to school, and although this violates pedagogical norms, it results in a useful lesson:

> "What makes the lamb love Mary so?"
>   The little children cry;
> "Oh, Mary loves the lamb you know,"
>   The teacher did reply.
> "And you each gentle animal
>   In confidence may bind,
> And make it follow at your call,
>   If you are only kind."   (*OB*, p. 19)

Without Mary's female influence, the school would be a more orderly but less gentle place. As Mary Kelly put it in her classic study of literary domesticity, many antebellum women asked that women be educated, not because they were like men but "because they set 'a purer, higher, more excellent example,' as Sarah Josepha Hale told the readers of the *American Ladies Magazine* in 1835."[16] As a girl venturing into the public sphere of the public schoolroom, Hale's Mary is precisely such an exemplar: "purer, higher, and more excellent" because of her feminine capacity for empathy. Indeed, Mary represents the ideology of many antebellum children's poems (by poets of both sexes), which were steeped in the politics and sensibilities of sentimental culture.

After the Civil War, children's poetry became relatively less concerned with useful lessons and more concerned with sales. This trend was energized by the expanding fields of age-graded commercial marketing, nature study, illustration and photography, "nonsense" literature, and folklore studies. Although intergenerational poetry was still being written, it was increasingly rivaled by poetry and giftbooks aimed at specific demographics. The circulation and influence of children's magazines, particularly *Youth's Companion* and *St. Nicholas Magazine for Boys and Girls*, grew, but so did the market for individual books, particularly at Christmastime. Poetry for children became less didactic and more ludic as play came to be seen as both a marketable commodity and a developmentally productive activity. In contrast to most antebellum texts, children's poetry of the post–Civil War era increasingly explores, and even fetishizes, the material culture(s) of childhood. Toys and dolls take center stage and literally come alive, as in "The Duel" by the hugely popular poet Eugene Field. "The Duel" begins:

> The gingham dog and the calico cat
> > Side by side on the mantle sat;
> 'Twas half-past twelve and – what do you think?
> > Nor one nor t'other had slept a wink!
> > The old Dutch clock and the Chinese plate
> > Appeared to know as sure as fate
> There was going to be a terrible spat.
> > (*I wasn't there; I simply state*
> > *What was told to me by the Chinese plate!*)   (OB, p. 161)

This uneasy scene, with its mix of imperial imports and homespun animals, plays (like many Field poems) with boundaries: between the bought and the made, between objects and people, between children and adults. There is no moral at the end of the poem; instead, the two stuffed animals simply devour each other in an entertaining example of consuming appetites run amok.

As a counterweight to Gilded Age consumerism, some educators promoted "nature study" as a way for youngsters to escape the effects of industrialization. This dovetailed with the work of women regionalist writers (Celia Thaxter, Mary E. Wilkins Freeman, Sarah Orne Jewett, and others) who – when they wrote children's poems – tended to focus on the flora and fauna of their environs. Most nature-study poetry is reverent, encouraging close observation, as in Clara Doty Bates's poem "Grass Gypsies," about spiders:

> Why, here is a camp in the wayside grass!
> Let's look at the tents before we pass.
> Beaded with dew is every one –
> Ah, 'tis only webs the spiders have spun.[17]

Discussing this poem, the *Kindergarten-Primary Magazine* suggested that it be taught as children observe real spiders through a microscope, and, more generally, nature poems were recruited to teach scientific observation skills.

Because children's poetry was so market driven, however, it is deceptive to link poets too closely with specific styles: Eugene Field wrote material culture poems, but he also wrote poems derived from folklore and anachronistic sentimental-mourning poems. Clara Doty Bates wrote nature-study poems, but she also churned out faux fairy-tale epics. And Mary E. Wilkins Freeman was neither regionalist nor scientific in her treatment of the ostrich:

> The ostrich is a silly bird,
> With scarcely any mind.
> He often runs so very fast,
> He leaves himself behind.
>
> And when he gets there, he has to stand
> And hang about all night,
> Without a blessed thing to do
> Until he comes in sight.   (*OB*, p. 173)

The vastly expanding children's marketplace of the later nineteenth century sparked a kind of stylistic anarchy: poets wrote what children would read, or what their parents would buy, rather than focusing on developing a unified voice.

The market, combined with emerging print technologies, also spurred new text/image combinations. Illustrated rhymes had been a staple in children's poetry since the woodcuts in the *New England Primer*, but after the Civil War, illustrators began to make art central to children's poetry – paving the way for twentieth-century comic strips and picture books. For instance, Peter Newell's *Topsys and Turvys* (1893) depends on pictures and rhymes that reinforce one another. Accompanied by an illustration of an African horned animal, one verse begins, "The koodoo stays alone and dreams of loved ones far away"; then line 2, printed upside down, concludes: "The Seal invites two lovely snakes to come and spend the day."[18] The koodoo's horns have turned into snakes, and his head is now a seal's. Like the duck/rabbit illusion described at length by Newell's exact contemporary, the American psychologist Joseph Jastrow (and later appropriated by Wittgenstein), Newell's verse/picture combinations play on the ways that language puts pressure on visual perception.

Newell saw his illustrations and his physical books as extensions of his verses; registering one of several patents for oddly shaped books, he wrote:

> I, Peter S. Newell of Leonia, in the State of New Jersey, have invented certain new and useful Improvements in Illustrated Books and Pamphlets. . . . As such books have been heretofore made it has been usual to form or shape them in rectangular configuration, with the result that no, or but little, variety in the form of the books could be obtained, and the constant uniformity of such books in such forms, fails to meet the desire for change and variety which is strong in many persons, especially in children and young people.[19]

The Slant Book is thus a parallelogram, down which a child's runaway go-cart can careen, accompanied by anarchic verses as the cart hits an oompah band, an egg peddler, and even a policeman: "But down the go-cart swiftly sped / And smashed that cop completely / And as he sailed o'er Bobby's head / Bob snipped a button, neatly!"[20]

The Slant Book also reflects a newly irreverent or even subversive tone in children's poetry – suddenly, after the Civil War, books and magazines were full of bad boys and even the odd bad girl. Naughtiness was a gold mine, and a number of poet/illustrators cashed in, creating serial works like Palmer Cox's Brownies and Gelett Burgess's Goops. The Goops series was a mass-cultural phenomenon that poked fun at conduct manuals. The Goops had a long run: they appeared first in Burgess's San Francisco–based magazine, the *Lark*, and then in the *Burgess Nonsense Book* (1901), in *St. Nicholas Magazine for Boys and Girls*, and as a stand-alone series of books, the latest of which was released in 1951, five decades after the original. *Goops and How to Be Them* (1900) bills itself as "A Manual for Polite Infants Inculcating many Juvenile Virtues both by Precept and Example, with 90 illustrations." The Goops are grotesquely baby-faced characters who wreak havoc in poem after poem:

> The Goops they lick their fingers,
> And the Goops, they lick their knives;
> They spill their broth on the tablecloth,
> Oh! They lead disgusting lives.[21]

The Goops' "sins" are always secular, and their punishments progressive: they are sent to bed, not to hell. Burgess's didacticism is self-reflexive: it is present, but it is also ironic.

Burgess's most viral contribution to American poetry, "The Purple Cow," appeared in the first issue of the *Lark*, in 1895: "I never saw a purple cow / I never hope to see one ..." (*OB*, p. 209). The *Lark* was the locus of a new American interest in nonsense. Other practitioners included Oliver Hereford, Carolyn Wells, and Laura Richards. Wells, in the introduction to her groundbreaking *Nonsense Anthology* (1902), attempts a taxonomy of nonsense: it is not just silly or meaningless verse but a specifically "pure" kind of absurd poetry, practiced most perfectly by Edward Lear and Lewis Carroll. To be nonsense, she argues, language must not be teleological; it must have no purpose apart from its own play. In Wells's opinion, no American rose to the standards of Lear and Carroll, although she and her contemporaries made forays into nonsense. Laura Richards, for instance, seems to both mark and parody imperial expansion in "Harriet Hutch":

> Harriet Hutch, her conduct was such,
> Her uncle remarked it would conquer the Dutch.
> She boiled her bonnet, and she breakfasted on it,
> Then she rode to the moon on her grandmother's crutch!
> (Oh, she rode to the moon, yes she rode to the moon, and she rode to the
>   moon on her grandmother's crutch.)[22]

However, "Harriet Hutch," like "The Purple Cow," is more broadly humorous than properly absurd. Both Richards and Burgess place their "nonsensical" characters in commonsense contexts, rather than in the anarchic parallel linguistic universe of, say, "Jabberwocky."

If the age of American pragmatism did not lend itself to nonsense, it did support the emerging disciplines of ethnography and folklore, and many of the most powerful nineteenth-century children's poems draw on these discourses. For instance, Olive A. Wadsworth's work is mostly mired in nineteenth-century conventions (*Heavenward Bound: Words of Help for Young Christians*), but she had one bona fide hit when she transcribed and standardized a southern Appalachian counting-out rhyme:

> Over in the meadow
> In the sand, in the sun
> Lived an old mother toadie
> And her little toadie one.
> "Wink!" said the mother,
> "I wink!" said the one,
> So they winked and they blinked
> In the sand, in the sun.

Over in the meadow
Where the stream runs blue
Lived an old mother fish
And her little fishes two.
"Swim!" said the mother,
"We swim!" said the two,
So they swam and they leapt
Where the stream runs blue.[23]

This poem is full of unadorned action, eschewing the arch romanticism of so much nineteenth-century nature writing. Number ten is a mother spider ("'Spin!' Said the mother / 'We spin!' said the ten ..."), and the rhyme implicitly encourages children to use their fingers or toes to keep track. Thus it not only mimics an oral tradition but also invites, through its infectious rhymes, readers to speak the poem aloud and to perpetuate the tradition.

The American ethnographic imagination also inspired dialect humorists, such as Will Carleton, Artemis Ward, and Whitcomb Riley, who performed their work on live tours. Riley, in particular, embraced the cult of the child while appealing to intergenerational crowds. His most famous poem, "Little Orphant Annie," recounts the arrival of a spooky native informant into a Hoosier household:

Little Orphant Annie's come to our house to stay,
An' wash the cups and saucers up, an' brush the crumbs away.
An' shoo the chickens off the porch, an' dust the hearth, an' sweep,
An' make the fire, an' bake the bread, an' earn her board-an'-keep;
An' all us other children, when the supper things is done,
We set around the kitchen fire an' has the mostest fun
A-list'nin' to the witch tales 'at Annie tells about,
An' the Gobble-uns 'at gits you
            Ef you
          Don't
        Watch
      Out![24]

Like much dialect literature, "Little Orphant Annie" marks the authenticity of the story by ventriloquizing a lower-class regional speaker. Riley articulates this reality effect more plainly in a prose defense of dialectal literature for children, which concludes, "All other real people are getting into literature: and without some real children along will they not soon be getting lonesome, too?" To "sound real," to Riley, is to speak in dialect.

Riley also understood children's speech to be its own dialect, as in "The Bear Story," which has a three-year-old speaker:

> W'y, wunst they wuz a Little Boy went out
> In the woods to shoot a Bear. So, he went out
> 'Way in the grea'-big woods – he did. – An' he
> Wuz goin' along – an' goin' along, you know,
> An' purty soon he heerd somepin' go "*Wooh!*" –
> Ist thataway – "*Woo-ooh!*" An' he wuz *skeered*,
> He wuz. An' so he runned an' clumbed a tree –
> A grea'-big tree, he did, – a sicka-*more* tree.   (*CR*, p. 179)

In some ways, "The Bear Story" tips Riley's political hand by showing the ways that children were bundled together with regional others such as African Americans, "Hoosiers," and Irish immigrants. The child is charming, but his speech also makes him an "other" whose cuteness stems partly from his cultural and linguistic incompetence. This bundling is also evident in the burgeoning toy industry, which made heavy use of ethnic types, especially Native Americans and African Americans, on the assumption that they were childlike and comical.

Riley's friend and admirer Paul Laurence Dunbar worked within and against dialectal conventions. His many poems for children (and their parents) perpetuated oral, intergenerational traditions but also raised issues of representation and "reality" that were heightened by American racial politics. As Kate Capshaw Smith has noted, Dunbar's use of dialect was criticized by some Harlem Renaissance intellectuals, but he inspired affectionate readings and performances in ordinary African American communities. Thus Arna Bontemps recalls his own childhood circa 1910:

> The name of Paul Laurence Dunbar was in every sense a household word in the black communities around Los Angeles when I was growing up there. It was not, however, a bookish word. It was a spoken word. And in those days it was associated with recitations that never failed to delight when we heard them or said them at parties or on programs for the entertainment of church-folks and their guests.[25]

Dunbar, then, did not just depict an oral tradition but to some degree melted into it. For instance, as Henry Louis Gates points out, the opening lines from "Sunday Morning" ("Lias! Lias! Bless de Lawd!") became a playful way for parents to rouse children from bed.[26]

As Dunbar and Riley were composing literary renditions of oral traditions, folklorists were documenting them directly. William Wells Newell's *Games and Songs of American Children* (1883) is a landmark volume recording what Joseph Thomas has called the "playground" tradition of American poetry: that aspect of children's verse that is embedded in their jump rope rhymes, their counting-out rituals, and even their taunts. Rhymes that early American chapbooks had simply transcribed were now "folklore" to be classified and compared to other national traditions. Newell's introduction describes both his methodology and his conviction that children's folk poetry, like other primitive arts, is disappearing: "A majority of the games of children are played with rhymed formulas, which have been handed down from generation to generation. These we have collected in part from the children themselves, in greater part from persons of mature age who remember the usages of their youth; for this collection represents an expiring custom."[27] Newell hypothesizes that the most nonsensical counting-out rhymes are the oldest, which have been "corrupted" beyond recognition from European sources:

> Onery, unery, ickery, a,
> Hallibone, crackabone, ninery-lay,
> Whisko, bango, poker my stick,
> Mejoliky one leg!   (Massachusetts; *GS*, p. 200)

Despite its antiquity, "Onery, unery" points children's poetry in a bracing new direction: away from sentimentalism and didacticism, but also away from commercialism. It implies that the best poems are not just oral but participatory and subject to spontaneous revision. Many violate spelling or grammatical rules:

> Monkey, monkey, bottle of beer,
> How many monkeys are there here?
> One, two, three,
> You be he (she)!
>   (Massachusetts to Georgia; *GS*, p. 202)

This poem takes pleasure in the internal rhyme ("You-be-he") and privileges play over sense. And despite Newell's social Darwinian pessimism, playground rhymes remained among the most adaptable forms of American poetry through the twentieth century because they were enmeshed in daily-life activities such as choosing who will be "it" in a game of tag.

In *Games and Songs*, Newell focuses heavily on rhymes that originated in England and the Continent. In 1922, the African American folklorist Thomas Talley broadened the picture with his *Negro Folk Rhymes: Wise and Otherwise*. Like Newell, Talley relied mainly on adults' recollections of their post–Civil War Southern childhoods. Along with work and dance songs, he gathered a substantial collection of children's poems, including some that he traces to African origins, such as "Tree Frogs":

> Shool! Shool! Shool!
> I rule!
> Shool! Shool! Shool!
> I rule!
> Shool! Shacker-rack.
> I shool bubba cool.
>
> Seller! Beller eel!
> Fust to tree'l!
> Just came er bubba.
> Buska! Buska-reel![28]

Talley's collection owes debts to the minstrel and plantation traditions, as well as to Africa, and was seen as problematic even in the 1920s. But through Talley and other folklorists, poets such as Langston Hughes gained access to an oral heritage that was lively, flexible, and intergenerational. Hughes himself wrote poems for children, as have many – if not most – prominent twentieth-century African American poets, from Gwendolyn Brooks to Elizabeth Alexander to Kwame Dawes. Indeed, African American poets have remained attuned to the needs of young readers and of broad community audiences even as poets in general have narrowed their focus to address adults within the academy.

Early twentieth-century modernism, as epitomized by Ezra Pound and T. S. Eliot, did not so much squelch children's poetry as banish it to a separate sphere, as evidenced by the radically different voices that Eliot uses when writing *The Waste Land* (for adults) and *Old Possum's Book of Practical Cats* (for children). It can be argued that while twentieth-century adult poetry became increasingly invisible to readers outside the academy, American children's poetry stayed visible and audible, in the classroom, on the playground, and at home. This was due partly to its embeddedness in oral and playground traditions and partly to the lively multimedia mixes of text and image that had been pioneered by poet/illustrators like Peter Newell. As the twentieth century progressed, American poetry found a secure popular niche in the children's picture book format. Poet/illustrators such as Theodore Geisel (Dr. Seuss) and Shel Silverstein extended the Newell tradition, while author/illustrator teams such as Margaret Wise Brown and Clement Hurd created memorable images: "In the great, green room, / there was a telephone, / and a red balloon ..."[29] *Goodnight Moon* is certainly a playful lyric rather than a prose narrative – and it should not be surprising that Clement Hurd also illustrated Gertrude Stein's sole children's book, *The World Is Round*. *Goodnight Moon*, like a Gertrude Stein poem, enacts repetitive linguistic rituals that readers are invited to share, both metaphorically and literally. It offers, through words and images, an accessible context for poetry – a way to make it part of daily life without diluting its play value. The best American children's poetry has always worked this way, and its survival and popularity can perhaps serve as an object lesson for "adult" poets who struggle to find readers.

Children's literature can be innovative, but it is also conservative, because adults control what is purchased – if not what is read – and are inclined to perpetuate what they themselves enjoyed as children. As new forms of poetry such as picture books emerged, old favorites like "A Visit from St. Nicholas" continued to circulate. And even today, many children know a (British Puritan) Isaac Watts prayer ("Now I lay me down to sleep ...") that was included in the *New England Primer*. Perhaps more than other subgenres, then, children's poetry must be seen not as a time line in which one movement supersedes another but rather as an expanding circle of coexisting texts that are simultaneously vital, playful, and memorable.

Notes

1. Richard Flynn, "Can Children's Poetry Matter?," *The Lion and the Unicorn: A Critical Journal of Children's Literature* 17:1 (June 1993), p. 37.
2. Stephen Mintz, *Huck's Raft: A History of American Childhood* (Cambridge, Mass.: Harvard University Press, 2006), p. 75.
3. Clifton Johnson, *Old-Time Schools and School-Books* (New York: Macmillan, 1904), p. 82.
4. Patricia Crain, *The Story of A: The Alphabetization of America from the New England Primer to the Scarlet Letter* (Stanford, Calif.: Stanford University Press, 2003), p. 18.
5. Donald Hall (ed.), *Oxford Book of Children's Verse in America* (New York: Oxford University Press, 1990), p. 15. Poems in this collection will be cited as *OB*. On the role of Christmas in poetry, see Stephen Nissenbaum, *The Battle for Christmas: A Cultural History of America's Most Cherished Holiday* (New York: Vintage, 1997).
6. Cathy Davidson, *Revolution and the Word: The Rise of the Novel in America* (New York: Oxford University Press, 1986), p. 72.
7. Mary Dawson, *The Mary Dawson Game Book* (Philadelphia: D. McKay, 1916), p. 794.
8. Hannah Flagg Gould, *Poems* (Boston: Hilliard and Gray, 1836), vol. 2, p. 172.
9. Janet Gray, *Race and Time: American Women's Poetics from Antislavery to Racial Modernity* (Iowa City: University of Iowa Press, 2004), p. 88.
10. Sarah Morgan Bryan Piatt, *Palace-Burner: The Selected Poetry of Sarah Piatt*, ed. Paula Bernat Bennett (Urbana: University of Illinois Press, 2001), p. xliv. Poems in this collection will be cited as *PB*.

11. Elizabeth Philips, *Emily Dickinson: Personae and Performance* (State College: Pennsylvania State University Press, 2004), p. 159.
12. Philips, *Emily Dickinson*, p. 159.
13. Paul Crumbley, *Inflections of the Pen: Dash and Voice in Emily Dickinson* (Lexington: University Press of Kentucky, 1996), p. 98.
14. Maximillian DeVere, *Americanisms* (New York: Scribner, 1872), p. 448.
15. William Holmes McGuffey (ed.), *McGuffey's Eclectic Reader*, 6 vols. (1879; Hoboken, N.J.: Wiley and Sons, 1997), vol. 6, p. 83.
16. Mary Kelley, *Private Woman, Public Stage: Literary Domesticity in Nineteenth-Century America* (1984; Chapel Hill: University of North Carolina Press, 2002), p. xiii.
17. Clara Doty Bates, *From Heart's Content* (Chicago: Morrill, Higgins, 1892), p. 88.
18. Peter Newell, *Topsys and Turvys* (New York: Century, 1893), n.p.
19. Peter Newell, "Illustrated Book and Pamphlet," U.S. Patent 970,943, September 20, 1910.
20. Peter Newell, *The Slant Book* (New York: Harper Brothers, 1910), n.p.
21. Gellet Burgess, *Goops and How to Be Them* (New York: Stokes, 1900), n.p.
22. Laura Richards, *In My Nursery* (New York: Little, Brown, 1892), p. 88.
23. John Greenleaf Whittier, *Child-Life: A Collection of Poems* (Boston: Houghton Mifflin, 1871), pp. 51–52.
24. James Whitcomb Riley, *Child-Rhymes* (New York: Grosset and Dunlap, 1905), p. 23. Poems in this collection will be cited as *CR*.
25. Kate Capshaw Smith, *Children's Literature of the Harlem Renaissance* (Bloomington: Indiana University Press, 2006), p. 123.
26. Mark C. Carnes (ed.), *Invisible Giants: Fifty Americans Who Shaped the Nation but Missed the History Books* (New York: Oxford University Press, 2003), p. 67.
27. William Wells Newell, *Games and Songs of American Children* (New York: Harper Brothers, 1884), p. 1. Poems in this collection will be cited as *GS*.
28. Thomas Washington Talley, *Negro Folk-Rhymes: Wise and Otherwise* (New York: Macmillan, 1922), p. 168.
29. Margaret Wise Brown, *Goodnight Moon* (New York: Harper Collins, 1947), n.p.

Chapter 20

Dialect, Doggerel, and Local Color: Comic Traditions and the Rise of Realism in Popular Poetry

DAVID E. E. SLOANE

American poetry served a host of diverse functions throughout the nineteenth century. Poetry could provide a way of coping with grief and loss and personal pain, or a means of appreciating the glories of the natural world, or a mode for political expression. For some it was a way of expressing the noblest emotions and attaining a higher truth about the transcendent place of humanity in God's universe. Often, poetry was regarded as the highest of the literary arts, a form to be composed by the educated and refined for the educated and refined. But there was also another strain of popular American poetry that performed cultural work of a very different kind. Much of the most interesting comic poetry relied on dialect and doggerel to deflate the pretensions of those who failed to value the egalitarian nature of democratic life. These poets wrote in opposition to those who thought that meaning lay in philosophical abstractions instead of the physical details of the real world. America's comic tradition in poetry was fundamentally skeptical of abstractions, suspicious of all pretense, open to linguistic experimentation, and inclined to both irreverence and nostalgia in its treatment of everyday life. The subject matter of these poems was "low," and their style frequently forced or awkward. Sentiment predominated over the sublime, but the insistence on the value of flesh-and-blood individuals and the social circumstances of the American democratic experience made the writing of comic poets popular for generations. This poetry rarely won acclaim from critics or genteel academics, but it earned a substantial place in the newspapers and popular publications of the time and did much to both express and shape the American literary imagination, particularly in its embrace of forms of realism.

American popular poetry often fuses local color with dialect and doggerel. It is marked by several distinguishing characteristics. The authors address a popular audience, focusing their work on unique characters, local scenes, specific events, and social issues, sometimes with an emphasis on social or political satire. Their poetry sought to be consciously "American" in voice, setting, and style, featuring "American" stories, often of the frontier but also from villages; or regions of the North American continent, including Canada and Alaska; or the new urban frontiers populated by immigrant speakers, slums, and the marketplace. They often see their function as partly historical: to capture and represent the egalitarian experience, whether present or past. The egalitarian mood causes them to emphasize individual actions portraying human connectedness, many times leading to openly sentimental portrayals. Alternatively, they burlesque, caricature, or humble the financially well-to-do, parvenus, politicians, and capitalists, who often appear innately opposed to common human sympathy. Finally, they write downward to the mud in the streets rather than upward to some higher transcendent reality in the clouds, and they are more likely to deal with the local poor and working classes than with some abstract symbol that unites the soul with nature. In short, popular poetry often exemplifies the qualities associated with literary realism.

The new popular tradition was born in the common regions of American life, both agrarian and urban, using language and images that were simple, earthy, local, and comic. It was democratic in nature and skeptical of formal art, manners, or beliefs. It was openly vulgar, vernacular, or plainspoken, as the subject dictated to the individual author. Its practitioners came from every corner of life, from those employed in the fields of mining, engineering, and newspaper writing to prison convicts, ploughmen, and cart drivers. An untitled eight-line doggerel verse from George Helmbold's Philadelphia *Tickler* in 1811 displays some of these characteristics:

> I am a merchant bold,
> On South Wharves is my store,
> Hard times like these for honest folks,
> None can too much deplore.
> With Tongue as smooth as oil,
> Each day untruths I tell,
> Look sharp for fools to take them in,
> Charge twice for mackerell.[1]

The merchant's gleeful avarice is happily hypocritical. The language is plain. The verse scheme is effective and appropriate in its rhyme and brevity, and the end word – a smelly "mackerell" fish – lowers and degrades the mood.

The symbolic mackerel reappears as the heroine's married name in Mrs. M. V. Victor's social caricature, "The Stilts of Gold," in the January 1867 *Beadle's Monthly*.[2] The heroine, sitting in the back of her husband's grocery, with the smell of fish and other goods, learns from her near-hysterical husband that they have become rich by inheritance: "A million pounds of solid gold / One would have thought would have crushed them dead; / But, dear, they bobbed, and courtesied, [*sic*] and rolled / Like a couple of corks to a plummet of lead. / 'Twas enough the soberest fancy to tickle / To see the two mackerels in such a pickle!" Mrs. Mackeral, like the character speaking Helmbold's doggerel, is the perfect symbol for parvenu greed and ostentation, and she soon stands higher in society by acquiring, as her most outlandish trapping of wealth, a pair of golden stilts to further elevate her social position. Throwing a grand ball for herself, Mrs. Mackeral suddenly begins pirouetting out of control as her stilts take on supernatural characteristics. Finally, as she whirls above the crowd, her stilts take on a bluish light and carry her, like a witch on a broom, out of the hall to an unknown destination. Her fellow parvenus are left to the realization that they must better use "their dollars and sense" to chasten their social pretension. Lawless in its comic action, the doggerel verse shows hostility toward those who detach themselves from the working classes. The poem revels in its subject's degradation by ostentation. The popular poets who wrote dialect, doggerel, and local color comic verse are well represented by this rejection of tawdry show.

A rich potential for comic poetry, whether doggerel, dialect, or local color, had early on been identified in new American artifacts, which readily lent themselves to genre pictures. Joel Barlow's "The Hasty-Pudding" (1793) builds on the details of cooking and eating cornmeal mush to create a comic genre painting of the most egalitarian of Yankee foods, elevated by his skilled mock-heroic rhetoric into a Yankee icon. American words are notable at crucial comic moments. American language from the new continent's word-stock included "squaw," "Indian corn," "mush," "succotash," "maize," "raccoon," and "skunk," among others. Barlow's mock-heroic comedy derives from playing Romantic terms against these more common terms of factual, local reality. Barlow rhapsodizes over an Indian maid, some "tawny Ceres," but she is also comically degraded to a "squaw" who "cracks the maize."[3] Barlow even turns the satire on himself; he is pleased when milk cools the mush, for it "saves the pains of blowing while I eat," a provocative statement for a poet. Other acclaimed American poets also participated in this movement with more serious poetry. John Greenleaf Whittier's *Snow-Bound* (1866) demonstrates how homespun elements could depict in simple language an imaginary world contained within the glow of fireside family experience. The poem enfolds both success – the bells of the oxen and plows – and failure – in the life of the maiden aunt and in Whittier's painful closing nostalgia over the loss of all of the beloved actors but the final two. Its language is plain, but a wide gap of time is evoked. Descriptions are rooted in the pictorial, as in the fireside scene, the boy's impressions as his father reads, and the snow plowing. The world is densely populated by sympathetic figures, farmers and schoolteachers from farm and village experience, not kings. The aunt and the schoolmaster are vignettes of New England figures in photographic detail, captured in retrospective objectivity. Few poems in American literature can match Whittier's simple portraiture and sense of place and pride. As a representative of American historical vision, *Snow-Bound* was taught in American school editions for a hundred years after its composition, testimony to the force of its tradition. Throughout the continental United States and Canada, a vast number of popular writers attempted to capture and interpret, as did Whittier, the precious moments of common experience, and the credos and beliefs at their foundation. Their works appeared in newspapers, periodicals, and homegrown volumes of poetry whose publication was urged by friends.

The Fireside Poets were notable for, and are now somewhat undervalued for, their ability to give poetic meaning to the apparently ordinary details of daily life by fusing wit, irony, and metrical skill with a simple everyday language that conveyed the distinctive quality of specific American scenes. In Oliver Wendell Holmes's "The Deacon's Wonderful One-Horse Shay," the sudden dissolution of a wagon provides a satirical picture of the failings of Puritan theology. The local, the intellectual, and the ironic assume new dimensions in the verses of dialect humor produced by James Russell Lowell, especially the political satire of *The Biglow Papers*. Lowell's "The Courtin'," in which "Zekel crep' up, quite unbeknown, / An' peeked in thru the winder," soon capturing the kiss that led to the marriage bans being read next Sunday, gently burlesques the social habits of subliterary Yankees in a way that was humorously sympathetic even while defining its author's patrician distance. In their experimentations with the vernacular, the comic, and the portrayal of everyday life, the Fireside Poets created a highly respectable and imitable model for American popular poetry.

The dialect, doggerel, and local verse writers sometimes openly declared that they did *not* write poetry at all. They intended a far more comprehensive cultural statement that contradicted the sublime ideals and eloquent style of the "poets" whom they felt were "above" them in terms of literary pretension. Foreword after foreword in their published volumes declare that they present these "verses" humbly with only the claim of the approbation of authorial friends or local readers. "Poetry" to them is a stilted thing of artificial language and bloodless abstractions. John Byers Wilson, in his preface to *Reminiscent Rhymes and Other Verse*, writes that his "untrained fingers" had swept the lyre to produce notes that were inspiring, no matter how "inharmonious." His poems were gathered from a life of labor, often hard and barren – not intended to conceal thought in artistic mysticism but rather to offer simplicity and true poetry from the heart of the common man, whom Byers claims, is independent and iconoclastic.[4] Ellen P. Allerton, the very popular midwestern author of *Walls of Corn and Other Poems* (1894), offers "My Ambition": "– it is not / To mount on eagle wings and soar away / ... Scorning the griefs and joys of every day; / I would be human – toiling like the rest / With tender human heartbeats in my breast."[5] She was largely successful in writing placid verses expressing the God-given beauty of the plains states, and her signature poem "Walls of Corn" concludes that industry has made the desert fertile and brought wealth to rich and poor alike through the rippling breezes brushing the "walls of corn." The tercet that concludes her twenty-two couplets notes that the wise men would have laughed in scorn at prophets who foresaw this vaguely patriotic richness in the rippling "banners" of corn.[6] Will Carleton, in the opening preface to his six-volume chronicle of American farm and urban experience stretching from 1870 to 1900, apologizes for his "crude and unfinished" poems, noting that "he has often wandered ... from the established rules of rhythm, ... but he believes The People are, after all, the true critics."[7] The people approved, and Will Carleton's rural Michigan verses became some of the most popular of the post–Civil War era. The "Peasant Bard" (Josiah D. Canning) prefaces *The Harp and Plow* with the humble statement, "Content will he be should his readers discover a vein of homely but honest COMMON SENSE." God and "PATRIOTISM" cause him to write, even though the roughness of his farm life does not admit, nor incline, him to aspire to be "the exquisite poet," or to reach for "the unintelligible profoundness of the laureate bard."[8] The literary comedian Doesticks (Mortimer Thomson), according to his verse preface, found his epic satire *Pluri-bus-tah* (1856) in a coat pocket of his "uncle," slang for a pawnbroker. Its low origin leads to even lower doggerel, satirizing a national hypocrisy driving the country toward disaster. Each of these authors knew that conventional poetry lay in the realm of the ideal, sublime, and transcendent, but the "humbler poets"[9] were democratic revolutionaries, empowered by identification with the American egalitarian vision. Walt Whitman understood his "barbaric yawp" similarly.

A drive to express America's distinctive places, people, ideals, and, most of all, achievements dominated much of this poetry. Many poems identified the importance of steam, machines, and electricity as uniquely expressive of industrial America and democratic strength. Heroic stagecoach drivers brought their wagons through Indians, robbers, and storms. Breakdowns in marital relations and family life came out in the numerous ballads and drunken first-person narratives of tramps and derelicts. Instead of subtle wit, these poems offered slapstick burlesque or depicted scenes of barroom vulgarity; for their subjects, they looked not to the lost Lenore but rather to the starving prostitute and the frontier wife. Drunks, crooked politicians, burlesque abstractions of gods and financial manipulators, inventors, technical entrepreneurs, steamboat pilots, slaves and freedmen, and wily Chinamen populated their works. Dialect was a dominant medium. Their milieu ranged from mountains and seashore to small towns and agrarian life, and even into the technical and the urban. If sentimentalism overreaches what later readers find comfortable, it was to them an acceptable mood, and perhaps even a preferred mood, for it reflected a wide social sympathy in opposition to the greedy landowners, the political manipulators, and the socially mobile, elites from which they were barred. Formal dignity represented not just pomposity but also hypocrisy, greed, insincerity, and, sometimes, outright egocentric viciousness and disregard for the common claims of humanity. The inhabitants of popular poetry did not suffer from moral pretension: Their language was coarse; their professions were dirty and low; their hands were covered with dust and sweat; and their hearts and eyes were unashamed to cry real tears of sympathy.

Their poetry, however, often made real and uncomfortable demands on middle- and upper-class readers. Not all readers welcomed the scribblers of Pike County as their moral arbiters. Many of the localist writings burlesqued social customs that were widespread, although fair game for literary comedians like William Allan Butler in "Nothing to Wear" (1857), a satire on women's frivolity over fashion. However, Butler's satire bred other satires on itself, such as one by "Doesticks" (Mortimer Thomson), "Nothing to Say," which asserted that the fashionable would find plenty to do if they nursed the suffering victims of the Yellow Fever epidemic in Charleston, South Carolina. The message was an attack on upper-crust critics who already found their educational goals devalued, or so they thought, by the irrepressible slang and bad grammar of the lower-caste personae inhabiting this poetic realm.

When the furious battle over dialect poetry broke out, it seemed to be over language and its social implications as much as about patriotism or ownership of the American ethical vision. The great argument of 1871 was a superficial controversy over the primacy of Bret Harte's "Heathen Chinee" or John Hay's "Jim Bludso of the Prairie Bell" as the "first inventions" of Pike County dialect poetry. The two authors together, in only a handful of poems, brought the American dialect poem into the center of literary life. Both Hay's and Harte's poems featured dialect speech as their mode of discourse. Both maintained a pious skepticism, but both also took their subjects on their own terms, and the Pike dialect they employed was symbolic language to assert that fact. The characters were models of a very special kind. Jim Bludso of the steamboat *Prairie Belle* "were n't no saint, – them engineers / Is all pretty much alike, – / One wife in Natchez-under-the-Hill / And another one here in Pike." The Natchez area referred to was notorious for its brothels and gambling. Jim is a "low" character; he is careless in his talk, handy in a fight, "But he never flunked, and he never lied." "And if ever the Prairie Belle took fire, – A thousand times he swore, / He'd hold her nozzle agin the bank / Till the last soul got ashore." When the ship does burst into flame, Jim Bludso turns her toward the bank and yells out through the cursing and running that he will hold her nozzle against the bank "Till the last galoot's ashore." When the smokestacks fall, after Jim, through sheer dedication to his role, has saved every passenger, his "ghost went up alone / In the smoke of the Prairie Belle":

> He warn't no saint, – but at jedgment
> I'd run my chance with Jim,
> 'Longside of some pious gentlemen
> That would n't shook hands with him.
> He seen his duty, a dead-sure thing, –
> And went for it thar and then;
> And Christ ain't a going to be too hard
> On a man that died for men.[10]

Hay is deft at foreshadowing. The word "soul" is transformed to "galoot" to involve the spiritual and the vulgar in Jim's signature phrase. The closing octet expands on the theme of the rough man with a human heart devoted to others. Hay's verse boldly affirms working men who serve as clear alternatives to the refined members of higher classes. Hay's religion is subversive to the standard culture, including the readers who represent the very group Hay is targeting. The last line of the octet – the climax of Hay's message – is the only line completely without a trace of dialect, assuring its impact.

In "Banty Tim," Sgt. Tilman Joy confronts the white bigots of Spunky Point, Illinois, who want a Black veteran known as Banty Tim run out of town. Sgt. Joy counters with historical fact, noting that Tim had rescued him from the frightful rebel crossfire at Vicksburg: "That nigger ... was crawlin' to me / through that fire-proof, gilt-edged hell." Tilman Joy tells them they may "rezoloot" all they want at their meeting, but if one of them touches the boy, "He'll wrastle his hash to-night in hell." The use of the racist language is purposeful throughout, emphasizing that behavior, not color or status, determines rights. The mob's principles, such as they are, crumble in the face of heroism, no matter how low the hero's status. Hay's poem is one of many such democratic verses in this tradition that masquerades as a merely colorful incident. Mark Twain's portrayal of Huck Finn coming to grips with Jim as a human being follows this theme to its logical conclusion.

Bret Harte's poems show local characters engaged in trivial cheating, card playing, or aping their betters. His treatment of "Truthful James" and the "Heathen Chinee" is slightly more satirical than Hay's style. The narrator, like others in the poem, is a poser, opportunist, and hypocrite, but his stories are engaging. Comic types and stereotypes abound, speaking in their Western argot, free from cultural censorship. The effect, as in Hay's verse, is realistic comedy with an outcome that rewards readers with a new idea of what "success" includes. If the Chinaman is a cheater at cards, the only way he is discovered is by the other Anglo-Saxon players holding copies of the same cards to cheat him. Racial prejudices are satirized, fitted to San Francisco rather than Pike County. Harte offered a wider range of poems than Hay in this medium, but the "In Dialect" section of his collection *Poems* in 1871 still amounted to a mere forty pages, including some tall tales, light irony, and narratives of school scenes and spelling bees. He also composed more formal verses, a few of which paint interesting portraits of the western regions and California, but "Plain Language from Truthful James" and "The Society Upon the Stanislaus," the most famous of his vernacular poems, helped revolutionize the poetry of the time. Contained in their own milieu without any outside moral context or lesson, cheaters are cheated, sharpers are comically dull, and would-be scientists are defeated by their own ignorance and small-time competitiveness. The battle between Harte's paleontologists offers a slapstick travesty of more educated brawls held at the higher levels of American social, economic, and academic life.[11]

The Harte-Hay controversy followed the actual initiation of dialect poetry by Charles G. Leland of Philadelphia with *Hans Breitmann's Ballads*. Leland published his first Hans Breitmann poem as a prose paragraph in 1857 to fill space in a journal he was editing, but more poems began appearing in verse during the Civil War, and James R. Lowell, among others, urged Leland to publish them as a book as early as 1866.[12] "Hans Breitmann's Party" displays the mix of vulgarity and sentimentalism that fixed the German immigrant personality as a comic type:

> Hans Breitmann gife a barty
> We all cot troonk ash bigs.
> I poot mine mout to a parrel of bier
> Und emptied it oop mit a schwigs.

Und denn I gissed Madilda Yane
Und she shlog me on de kop,
Und de gompany fited mit daple-lecks
Dill de coonshtable made oos shtop.

Hans Breitmann gife a barty –
Where ish dat barty now!
Where ish de lofely golden cloud
Dat float on de moundain's prow?
Where ish de himmelstrahlende Stern –
De shtar of de shpirit's light?
All goned afay mit de Lager Beer –
Afay in de ewigkeit![13]

The action is vulgar and unregulated by the standards of the Victorian American parlor. Hans's party is a drunken beer brawl with a slight suggestion of sex to top it off. The language is uneducated dialect, but the sentiments are quite educated, and the German dialect is sophisticated in the shades of meaning it supplies, including the Romantic appeal to lost times past. Leland had called for a literature to match our "steam-engine whirling realism" in a little book titled *Sunshine in Thought* in 1862;[14] Hans was his own bluff answer, hijacking the nostalgic theme of Romantic loss in favor of a descent to drunken sexual behavior. Leland was later recognized as one of the founders of modern sociology with his studies of the Romany (Gypsy) people. More serious observation lies behind these supposedly comic studies than their titles and comic illustrations suggested, further evidence of the underlying urge toward realist portraiture.

Many critical writers expressed disgust at the dialect poem almost from its "invention." "P. R. S." (Peter Remsen Strong) was one of the most detailed in raging against the genre in *"AWFUL," and Other Jingles*. Strong inadvertently provides a comprehensive definition of the genre in his diatribe against it in "A Recipe for a Poem 'in Dialect'":

I.
Take, for your hero, some thorough-bred scamp,
Miner, or pilot, or jockey, or tramp –
Gambler (of course), drunkard, bully, and cheat,
"Facile princeps" in ways of deceit;
So fond of ladies, he's given to bigamy,
(Better, perhaps, if you make it polygamy);
Pepper his talk with the raciest slang,
Culled from the haunts of his pestilent gang;
Season with blasphemy, lard him with curses,

Serve him up hot in your "dialect" verses.
Properly dished, he'll excite a sensation,
And tickle the taste of our delicate nation.
II.
Old Mother English has twaddled enough:
Give us a language that's ready and rough!
Who cares, just now, for a subject Miltonian?
Who isn't bored by a style Addisonian?
Popular heroes must wear shabby clothes!
What if their diction is cumbered with oaths?
That's but a feature of life Occidental,
Really, at heart, they are pious and gentle.
Think, for example, how solemn and rich is
The sermon we gather from dear "Little Breeches"!
Isn't it charming – that sweet baby-talk,
Of the urchin who "chawed" ere he fairly could walk?
Sure 'tis no wonder bright spirits above
Singled him out for their errand of love!
III.
I suppose I'm a "fogy" – not up to the age –
When a real inspiration (divinus afflatus)
Could be printed without any saving hiatus;
When humor was decently shrouded in rhyme,
As suited the primitive ways of the time;
And we all would have blushed, had we dreamed of the rules,
Which are taught us to-day in our "Dialect" schools.
IV.
It may be all right, though I find it all wrong,
This queer prostitution of talent in song;
Perhaps, in our market, gold sells at a loss,
And the public will pay better prices for dross –
Well! 'twere folly to row 'gainst a tide that has turned,
And the lesson that's set us has got to be learned;
But I'll make one more desperate pull to be free
Ere I swallow the brood of that "Heathen Chinee."[15]

Sam W. Smith's *Gems from the Tailings*, in "The Judge's Poetic Venture," took the same ground as Strong in *"AWFUL"* but reversed the conclusion, making a positive assertion for roughness and reality in poetry, even though he suggests that Harte had lost his touch by the mid-1870s. Smith's Judge goes to "the city" one summer to write and sell poetry but becomes "blue" when hearing a lecturer pontificate: "But a miner, could not be a poet; / Their thoughts ar' too low and grov'lling, / For truth of the point, he could show it, / In dirt they ar' always shov'lling." But the Judge chanced to meet "Mr. Hart [*sic*]" and thought he played cards (an allusion to his most widely read poem, "The Heathen Chinee"), and the Judge called him "one o' my pards." Before he gives up on poetry and the sublime to return to the mines, the Judge learns Hart's secret: "We dickered, I sold him my trash, / To most any terms would agree; / I asked him: 'Whar'd you get all that cash?' / He whispered, a 'Heathen Chinee.'"[16] Harte was the center of the storm over dialect, in which a rather simple surface argument about language and class sometimes reveals a deeper concern with character and ethical behavior. The democratic foundation underlying much popular verse is well established by the wide variety of references to the fact that the roughhouse style and characters, despite their low status, were moneymakers for the authors who employed them.

P. R. S. would have been even less pleased by stronger portraits yet to come. *Rustic Rhymes and Ballads* by Mrs. E. T. Corbett offers, among other varied topics, "The Deacon's Lament" and "The Village Sewing Society," the latter filled with venomous small-town gossip in ignorant dialect. "What Biddy Said in Police Court" appears in thick Irish brogue from Biddy's mouth. The cause: Tim came home drunk, broke up the furniture, and scared his daughters screaming into the halls, all in response to his wife asking him for the rent money. Biddy is a battered woman, and for relief from domestic violence she has had her husband arrested. An urban low-class figure, she exhibits her reality without any authorial framing:

> Yis, luk at me now, if ye can, Tim:
> Luk in me face if you dare!
> It's bruised an' it's ugly – I know it –
> But sorra a bit do ye care,
> Ye dhrunken – I'm ready, yer Honor;
> I'll show ye's the mark of Tim's fist,
> An' the black an' the blue bruise on me shoulder
> Where he pushed me agin the ould chist.

When the judge fines Tim ten dollars, battered Biddy pays his fee with her cash from "washin' an' clanin'."[17] We know her name only from Corbett's title: "What Biddy Said in the Police Court." The battered wife syndrome raises its ugly head in comic guise. This verse is close enough to prose realism to stand with it. Other poems in urban slum dialect appeared in volumes by various authors, in addition to the comic Irish dialect satirizing the reverse logic of this paradoxical social tragedy.

Corbett's "The Foreclosure of the Mortgage" lays out a widow's convincing lament in New England dialect over her hard and thankless work, her ingrate children, and her husband Caleb's death. Finally, in a reversal, Caleb's old friend, "the Deacon," appears, buying up the mortgage so that she can stay in her battered and poorly maintained farmhouse, which is better than being thrown into the street.[18] If the escape from poverty seems sentimentalized, however, the recognition and acceptance of poverty is not. The first-person conversation offers appropriate language and regional diction as it goes on to critique urban wealth and absentee capitalist ownership. Corbett's "Old Abel's Experience" narrates how Abel's tragic, pointless, and dreary life resulted from a failing marriage, bad choices, and his wife's death in childbirth.[19] The lengthy narrative lines, primarily iambic hexameter, are end-stopped, rhymed couplets. No sense of lyric joy or freedom intrudes on the matter-of-factness in Abel's delivery of his narrative to a young man who ironically is about to be wed. Corbett's world is a stark one, *despite* its comic devices and sentiment, providing a sharp contrast to what might be expected from the conventional hackneyed image of the nineteenth-century female poet.

In spite of powerful work by authors like Corbett, female poets were often burlesqued for mawkish sentiment and inept technical skills, perhaps most notably in the ghastly effusions of Emmaline Grangerford in Twain's *Adventures of Huckleberry Finn*. Marietta Holley, writing satirically as "Josiah Allen's Wife" between 1870 and 1910, made her poetaster, Betsy Bobbett, appropriately addlebrained. Although there is a clear foundation for these satiric portrayals in the work of some sentimental poets, there is an alternative tradition that relies on sharp wit and pointed satire. For example, Sarah M. B. Piatt's sardonic reinterpretations of domesticity have sharp edges. Her poetic images are twisted into the reflections of a woman's psychological pain. "That New World," the title poem of her 1877 collection, doubts the existence of any heaven and skeptically asks for a whiff of a heavenly flower or the echo of a heavenly seashore to *prove* it, blunt atheism for that period.[20] "If I Had Made the World" allows that she would make Washington, Columbus, and Shakespeare but concludes by saying she would not have made the world *at all* if she had her way.[21] It was another twenty-five years before even such a personage as Mark Twain dared put such nihilism in print. Poem after poem twists mundane, sentimental topics to reject the premises of conventional middle-class life. "The Sad Story of a Little Girl" suggests a psychological progression as arresting as Gilman's "The Yellow Wallpaper" in its treatment of a girl distancing herself from her mother and the mother's unhappiness and sense of loss.[22] "A Tragedy in Western Woods" is a Poesque poem located in frontier experience but progressing psychologically.[23] As a psychological realist, Mrs. Piatt has few, if any, equals, but others of less power could be cited.

For instance, Mrs. S. L. Oberholtzer's *Daisies of Verse* (1886) explores poverty in "The Coal-Pickers," among other poems with social content in a volume with a misleading title.[24]

First among all equals, male and female, however, is Will Carleton, now ignored but arguably the most notable American poet in the early 1870s, with the publication of "Over the Hill to the Poorhouse," which permanently embedded the title phrase in the American imagination. Carleton (1845–1912) covered the wide spectrum of American democratic aspirations and sympathies in local settings and plain colloquial speech. The preface to the sixth volume of his Farm and City series of books on agrarian and urban American life laid out his philosophy explicitly. His motive was to make people better, and he vowed to reach this end by writing in a spirit that was deep and sincere. His realist orientation appears in his commitment to speech that is plain, direct, and simple and has no more errors than uneducated people make naturally. His egalitarian stance requires characters who must be accessible to general readers.[25]

The poems that launched his national reputation are "Betsy and I Are Out" and "Over the Hill to the Poorhouse," which appeared in the popular *Harper's Magazine* in 1871 and 1872, respectively, and then in Carleton's first major volume, *Farm Ballads*.[26] In each, a folksy dialect speaker is drawn from Michigan farm or village experience. In "Betsy and I Are Out," a garrulous old farmer explains how he and his wife continuously fight over religious doctrine: "Draw up the papers, lawyer, and make 'em good and stout; / For things at home are crossways, and Betsy and I are out." His quatrains, varying iambic and anapestic feet in *aa/bb* rhymes, and his lengthy lines, allowing for a conversational narrative, develop the scenes of farm life and household quarreling as the farmer's monologue. In "How Betsy and I Made Up," the tone is sustained; the colloquial language continues. He feels "blue" going home; his "hosses" pull steadily as he reminisces over scenes of his past farm life. When Betsy realizes that the divorce agreement gives her everything, she kisses her husband for the first time in twenty years. In another poem, a widow who is sent over the hill to the poorhouse has a sharp tongue, which she vents on her snobbish son and daughter-in-law until they put her on the town. In the sequel, her scapegrace horse-thief son returns from somewhere out west to join with her happily in a little cottage of their own. Readers adored his poems. Carleton's biographer, A. Elwood Corning, reports that William Dean Howells was impressed by Carleton's "homely realism," but when he requested a poem, Howells found the work he supplied too sentimental and artificial to print.[27]

Carleton understood the changing American experience and thought early on of combining his style and characters with the images and events of cities.

In a number of poems spread over several volumes, "Farmer Stebbins" supplies country-style skepticism as he comments on the pretensions and social, economic, and practical frauds that he finds in the urban environment. "Arthur Selwyn" is his invented educated spokesman – a young poet seeking his subject matter in the urban world. By this device Carleton allows harsh subjects to be framed by the sensibility of his persona, as in the boxing poem, "The 'Slugging'-Match": "Hands gloved – to comply with the law; / Gloves hard – to comply with the crowd; / Fists savage as murder could draw; / Cheers heavy and fervent and loud." Selwyn's voice can ascend the scale of diction and historical references while maintaining his character, and so Carleton allows his pictorial impressionism to draw in Rome through a reference to the Tiber and even discovers that the "glittering spoil" was more than a teacher or preacher "could earn / In years of the hardest of toil."[28] Elsewhere in Selwyn's "Note-book" interludes, voices of the city, factories, and even walls and roads call out, "What did we cost?" The answer is toil; labor; machines run by poor, pale-faced children; and prostitution, all that labor for the sake of wages that disappear – "Where do your earnings go?" The implied answer is to capitalist exploiters representing all the forces that the local color and dialect writers frequently battle with their genre painting and sentimental conventions of human interaction.

Carleton wrote directly to plain folk, lower-class and middle-class readers, and small-town locals. *Farm Festivals* (1881), the third book in his six-volume cycle, offers titles for local experience treated as populist festivals, including the festival of melody (the singing school), the festival of industry (the county fair), the festival of injustice (the lawsuit), and the festival of dis-reason (the debate). Carleton's strength lay in his ability to start with a local premise; generalize it, as these titles suggest; and then return to local description and language to present it as a genre painting of the American spirit. "The Festival of Reminiscence; or, The Pioneer Meeting," a poem written in four segments, begins with "Song of the Axe," which claims to "strike the key-note of the national song … For I am the pioneer of pioneers." "The First Settler's Story," Carleton's own favorite, begins, "It ain't the funniest thing a man can do – / Existing in a country when it's new."[29] With an ill-considered rebuke, the pioneer husband says unkind words that lead to his innocent and grief-stricken wife's death. He becomes an isolated hermit in an unforgiving wilderness – a far cry from earlier happy endings. "The Second Settler's Story," placed in the winter of 1843, involves a sleigh ride home after dark with an attack by famished wolves. The drama of the chase and final victory by the settler is sheer action in iambic trimeter and tetrameter. The farmer kills the lead wolf with an axe and sees him devoured by his own pack, gaining the riders the few extra seconds they need to reach their cabin, where the storyteller chases the animals off with flaming brands snatched from his own hearth and clutched in his blistered hands. The story has another story wrapped inside it, as the farmer reveals that the wife he won from her favored suitor had treated him civilly but not lovingly: "A woman half-won is worse than none, / ... It's nothin' to gain her body and brain, / If she can't throw in her heart."[30] The farmer now wins her heart and provides his listeners with an interpretation in plain language of the personal involvement of local experience with history, noting that a man will "go far to plant a star" but further to hear a woman say she loves him for her own.[31] The cycle Carleton created is close to an American epic, only diminished by its lack of Whitman's bardic power and euphoric vision.

An epic impulse is at the foundation of much American writing, both serious and comic. Native Americans played an important role in the development of poems with characteristically American themes. Indian maidens at the falls, best if they were the Niagara Falls – an obvious natural symbol – and Indian tribal history in the face of change offered wide scope for romantic imagery, nostalgia, and adventure plots in extended narrative poems. Henry Wadsworth Longfellow's *Hiawatha* in 1855 was based on Henry Schoolcraft's serious research into the sociology of American Indians, and his choice of the metric scheme of the Finnish *Kalevala* provided a bardic style that gripped both American readers and American satirists. In a different vein, Pope's exclamation, "Lo, the poor Indian," from "Essay on Man," was easy fodder for the sarcastic Bohemian wits of Pfaff's Cellar in New York, who sometimes converted him into a wretched drunken victim, renamed "Lo," a degraded caricature of the noble stature of Romantic beliefs. Other authors took the opposite side and satirized his vicious treatment at the hands of greedy Christian whites who covet his land and deny him civil rights, as Peter Peppercorn (Emanuel Price) satirized the case in 1884 in "Mr. Lo!": "As Congress does not seem to know / How to dispose of Mr. Lo, / It may, if he don't choose to go – / Kill him off!"[32] As for Longfellow's serious epic, it was immediately the center of a firestorm of doggerel burlesques from all corners of the country, including political satire, social burlesque, commentaries on local events, and sheer nonsense; abroad, Charles Lutwidge Dodgson even took a crack at him. Longfellow's Indian epic also inspired one of the two greatest of the American doggerel epics, *Pluri-bus-tah* (1856), a sarcastic burlesque of American "progress" up to the events leading to the Civil War, by Mortimer Thomson, better known as Q. K. Philander Doesticks, P. B. The other significant doggerel epic, *The New Yankee Doodle* (1868), by E. Jane Gay, writing under the male pseudonym "Truman Trumbull, A. M.," describes the horrors of the Civil War.

Pluri-bus-tah is an eight-hundred-line doggerel verse narrative of the history of America from the arrival of the first Puritan settlers to the apocalyptic destruction of white America in the battle over "Cuffee," the condescending name for the character representing American slavery in Thomson's allegory. Pluri-bus-tah, the central figure, is depicted as an ugly Puritan entrepreneur, cavorting with Mistress Liberty to rape the new continent. Every aspect of the mock-heroic epic shows degradation. Doesticks even claims to have found the manuscript history in the pocket of a coat left by a starving writer in the care of his "uncle," slang for pawnbroker. The poet then invokes the cast of characters by vulgarizing juxtapositions: "Ye, who want to see policemen, / Roman heroes, modern Bloomers, / Heathen gods of every gender, / News-boys, generals, apple-peddlers, / Modern ghosts of ancient worthies, / Editors, and Congress members / With their bowie knives and horsewhips, / Saints and scoundrels, Jews and Gentiles."[33]

The story is that Jupiter, sitting on a slop-pail smoking, cross-legged, like Mrs. Bloomer at the women's rights convention, snuggles with the Yankee goddess America and sends Pluri-bus-tah to her for a mate. Pluri-bus-tah promptly ambushes the Indians, who drink his whiskey, roast his women, and kill and scalp his children, but he reshapes their land to his Yankee notions: "On the mountain streams built sawmills, / Then he dragged the lofty pine-trees, ... / Dragged them to his cruel sawmills, / Sawed their heads off, sawed their hearts out. / Sawed them into slabs and scantling, / To make wigwams for his people." After dispatching "Johnny Taurus," he admires his iron steamers, monster post roads, matchless clippers, northern cornfields, and southern rice fields.[34] His greatest love, however, is not for his free-love wife and partner Liberty but for the ALMIGHTY DOLLAR, so he combines her face with his idol:

> Potent and ALMIGHTY DOLLAR,
> Dirty, filthy, greasy DOLLAR!
> And he would have loved as truly,
> Hugged as closely, kissed as fondly,
> Had the female image on it
> Been a dog or been a jackass.[35]

His son Younga-Merrikah unfortunately decides to enslave Black "Cuffee." Why? Because "I am white and I am stronger." At this, the allegorical Miss Liberty and her sister Thrift depart in a huff. An apocalyptic war breaks out as

Liberty, swindled and betrayed by the Yengah nation, marches out for good, wringing the neck of her eagle as she goes. Younga-Merrikah is finally crushed under a gigantic replica of his father's idol, the Yankee dollar, and Cuffee lies down in the ashes and sings his death song, accompanied by the tune of "Yankee Doodle" on the banjo. Doesticks writes imagistically and in the lawless argot and Bohemian images of the New York Bowery. His irony is raucous, and his mock-heroic allegorization of events is outrageously clever. Predicting the Civil War five years before its outbreak, Doesticks identifies the causes and the outcome without seeming ponderous or bardic. As American doggerel poetry, the work is a classic that shows the characteristics of American self-critical skepticism at its best.

E. Jane Gay's *The New Yankee Doodle*[36] is a 341-page history of the American Civil War in "Yankee Doodle" verse. Gay had been a Yankee schoolmarm in the South before leaving hurriedly for Washington, D.C., in 1856. During the war she nursed the wounded and became the secretary-amanuensis for Dorothea Dix. As a governess to the children of major Washington figures, Gay held an insider's perspective on the events she laid out in fascinating detail, recounting the emotional agony of Northerners, but in reportorial language, which makes her angry irony even more compelling. Old Abe and Yankee farmers are plainspoken figures drawn in the comic mode, and the Southern politicians play their foils. Necessarily, the poem's details include battle-maimed soldiers at the most catastrophic battle scenes; the flight of slaves from the South, and Northern generals turning them back; Andersonville; political conniving by rebels and patriots alike; and the multitude of bloody battles on land and sea – all in the staccato "Yankee Doodle" verse, with its brief lines and hurried metric. Unfortunately, the texture of her poem does not lend itself to the citation of extracts, and it is difficult to capture the intense vitality, satiric energy, and appropriateness of her chosen voice for the events she records. Francis Hopkinson used the "Yankee Doodle" tune in "The Battle of the Kegs" (1778) and Ebenezer Cooke caught the sarcastic spirit in "The Sot-Weed Factor" (1708), but Gay's sustained fusion of irony, historical events, representative local and historical figures, satire, and parody is unique in our literary history. Her accomplishments as a comic poet merit more attention.

Writers of the second rank also achieved a great deal in capturing the American experience, although none rise to the level of the two epics just discussed. In "The Emigrant's Story," James T. Trowbridge provides a well-executed narrative about a farmer's survival of a natural catastrophe; the work has elements of sympathy and humor. His "The Vagabonds" is a sentimental poem about the lost love of a drunken fiddle player, mostly told in first-person voice; it was often published as a stand-alone gift volume. Trowbridge's characters use dialect cleverly, and the poem's counterpart, "Old Simon Dole," is a similarly realistic narrative of the unsatisfying marriages of a brother and a sister who like each other better than their spouses. It is worthy of Edward Arlington Robinson's Tilbury Town residents, but without their desperation. Trowbridge's burlesque of Yankee ingenuity and invention, "Darius Green and His Flying-Machine," remained a comic recitation classic for a century after its composition.

Toward the end of the nineteenth century, Sam Walter Foss, a librarian living in Somerville, Massachusetts, brought out several series of poems of village life and vernacular experience. The two poems most often cited are "The Calf Path" – a poem about following trails of thought that might have triggered Robert Frost's "The Road Not Taken" – and "The House by the Side of the Road," where the poem's speaker would be a friend to man. Neither poem is particularly representative of his creation of local characters and situations. His volumes, *Whiffs from Wild Meadows*, *Dreams in Homespun*, and *Back Country Poems*, include varied local characters and scenes, usually with a moral, as exemplified by the speaker in "Chet Golder and His Whale."[37] Chet is backed into realizing his own tall fish tale is a hoax. He sadly concludes, "This unbelivin' age, yer see, / So loves to poke an' pry, / 'Twon't let a poor ol' man like me / Believe in his own lie." The poem is comic dialect; the outcome is more world-aware realism. Foss's work as a representation of popular experience and American egalitarian ambition has been undervalued, but together with Trowbridge, he did as much to document New England experience as Carleton did for the Midwest. Sidney Lanier's economic poems, such as "Thar's More in the Man than Thar Is in the Land" and "Jones's Private Argyment," gave the southern farmer acknowledgment for practical intelligence, or its lack, but his "Farmer Jones" poems "Corn" and "The Symphony" are too few in number to depict the South as well.

African American poetry provides another pool of materials, authors, and viewpoints with a variety of critical complications. The origins of the "Minstrel Show" supposedly date from the appearance of various forms of "Etheopean" singers in the 1830s, often in "black-face," although the tradition of "blacking up" appeared on the London stage well before 1800; but the literary dialect poetry and the Minstrel Show are not identical. Slave songs and African-derived materials were noticed early, not as literature but as a more direct product of experience. Eric Lott's *Love and Theft: Blackface Minstrelsy and the American Working Class* provides authoritative coverage of the subject as a complex American social phenomenon. Some later Black dialect verse was created by white writers, who also produced dialect verse in German, Italian, Hebrew, Chinese, and any other language that was easily adapted to comic stereotyping. Post–Civil War Black verse often aimed to capture the sentimentalism of the "Lost Cause" by picturing innocent and happy slaves "befo' de Waw," or by providing condescendingly cute doggerel on "pickaninnies." Such genre portraits appear in the poems of A. C. Gordon and Thomas Nelson Page's *Befo' de War* (1888), Ruth McEnery Stuart's *Daddy Do-Funny's Wisdom Jingles* (1913), and Mary Fairbanks Childs's *De Namin' ob de Twins* (1908), and into the 1920s in Benjamin Batchelder Valentine's *Ole Marster and Other Verses* (1921) and well beyond. Unhappily, readers' predilection for the folksy racism of the Negro stereotype made it difficult for African American writers to gain serious attention for any other form of work through the 1950s.

Distinguishing artificial poetry from "real" expressions of dialectal local poetry is no simpler in African American experience than elsewhere. One certainty is that astute critics often found Black dialect song to be uniquely American. For instance, "A Talk about Popular Songs" from *Putnam's Monthly Magazine* expresses the mixed qualities of a national poetry derived from a working man's democracy: "We are a timber-tuned people. We are not given to trilling and quavering. The pioneer in the forest wont sing the song made for him by a young lady; he speculates with his axe, on the constitution for the territory and the new governor. ... It is the same all round."[38] Dismissing Whittier and the "White lyrists of the North," the Putnam critic turned to "a poetry, really indigenous, and, in a certain degree, racy of the soil," derived from the "poor serfs" of the African race. Passing the racks of printed ballads for sale weekly on Broadway by St. Paul's Churchyard, the writer took home three hundred and found "about one third of them were negro melodies, either in their lingo, or on 'darkey' subjects ... another third were in the American style," with a remainder composed of thirty British works, forty Irish works, and half a dozen works that put moral or religious themes to profane tunes.[39] The subject of African American dialect remains controversial, because it is enmeshed in all the complications of racial portrayal that mark much of American writing, but it is important to remember that some major writers, perhaps most notably Langston Hughes, used dialect with great effect in both poetry and prose as a realistic tool for projecting the experience of African American life.

The dialect poetry of Paul Laurence Dunbar, the most notable of a number of Black dialect writers in the 1870–1920 period, was once severely criticized for its apparently nostalgic portrayal of happy darkies on the plantation. Recent critics, however, have emphasized both the vitality of African

American experience that is represented in many of the plantation poems and the clear political and social messages of other powerful poems. Perhaps the most intriguing of these dialect poems is "An Ante-Bellum Sermon," in which a minister's references to the Old Testament repeatedly raise the issues of freedom and slavery. The poem ironically interprets history in terms of the egalitarian message associated with other dialect writers:

> So you see de Lawd's intention,
> Evah sence de worl' began,
> Was dat his almighty freedom
> Should belong to evah man,
> But I think it would be battah,
> Ef I'd pause agin to say,
> Dat I'm talkin' 'bout ouah freedom
> In a Bibleistic way.

The irony of the poem is posed elsewhere in plain, nondialectal verse in "We Wear the Mask," in which the emotional pain of the African American's personal invisibility is expressed in lyric form. As elsewhere in the dialect and local color tradition, Dunbar's work can serve the uses of history, social observation, nostalgia, and protest – the offices of American literary realism, generally.

The South is also represented by one of the best of the local, dialect, and genre poets, Frank L. Stanton, the Georgian author of *Songs of the Soil* (1894), whose work reflects his newspaper background. Most significant in Stanton's work is his successful solution, lying somewhere between dialect and poetic diction, of a means to elevate localist themes and enhance their seriousness. Diction and inversion that make other poets seem stilted and artificial are controlled in Stanton's relatively short lines and plain words. As with many dialect poets, his "Mighty Lak a Rose," advocating its readers to "Keep A-Goin!" despite life's thorns, was a hit when put to music. It typifies his optimism, but it is otherwise unrepresentative of his better dialect poems, which offer effective depictions of southern Black people and white farmers, even when sentimentalized. "Lynched" is a brief example of the powerful images Stanton at his best could capture:

> The tramp of horse adown a sullen glen;
> Dark forms of stern, unmerciful masked men:
> A clash of arms, a cloven prison door,
> And a man's cry for mercy! ... Then high o'er
> The barren fields, dim outlined in the storm,
> The swaying of a lifeless human form.
> And close beside, in horror and affright,
> A widowed woman wailing to the night.[40]

The power of the subject matter, the stark couplets, and the prevailing mood of color and image subsume the one or two less natural word choices that maintain the metric scheme and imagery. In other poems, Stanton combines this skill with a mastery of comic narrative, producing effective genre paintings in verse. "The Feast at Waycross" describes in dialect a successful camp meeting in a Georgia town.[41] The caricature of the inept inventor-farmer in "Jones's Cotton Planter" focuses on the mechanical components, bellows, and mechanical devices in relation to Jones's frustrated wife and starving children; the dialect enhances the scene's comic realism.[42] The portrait of the individual, both in himself and as a type, is the fusion of voice and vision that many local color writers sought as the alternative to elevated poetry. Another lynching poem, "At Devil's Lake," in *Comes One with a Song* (1899), holds a similar power; the mists at the site of the lynching are "crawling o'er the pines," loading the fog image with the sinister word.[43] A few of the poems in *Comes One with a Song* are in the voice of Negro children "before the war," but Stanton created mostly plainspoken genre scenes of personal experience, varied with nature lyrics, or poems in what was then called (without malice) "cracker" dialect.

The middle of the continent offers its own style, often from popular poets of their time who are remembered more for their children's poems or popular lyrics than their serious writing. Eugene Field, author of *Hoosier Lyrics*, is commonly cited for his children's poetry, but like other versifiers from the newspaper world, he was often devoted to political events and urban experience. His poem "Hoosier Lyrics Paraphrased" goes directly to the political: "We've come from Indiany, five hundred miles or more, / Supposin' we was goin' to get the nominashin, shore; / For Col. New assured us (in that noospaper o' his) / That we could hev the airth, if we'd only tend to biz."[44] The vulgar voice and egocentric ideology from "Indiany" show low-life gullibility not childish purity. "The Color That Suits Me Best" openly rejects "acres and acres of Art" in Italy, Germany, and France: "Marines I hate, madonnas and / Those Dutch freaks I detest! / But the peerless daubs of my native land – / They're red, and I like them best!" To cover the ground of "culture," he continues, "we can't abide / The tastes that obtain down east," either, in favor of the "critical west."[45] Field rejects formal culture, burlesques the political, and depicts a deeper layer of midwestern life than children's poems would suggest.

When Hamlin Garland interviewed Eugene Field for *McClure's Magazine* in 1893, Garland praised the "boy life" poems, which he placed in the realm of "Veritism," his own homegrown form of realism. Field evaded the label. As with other writers in this tradition, he insisted that he did not write poetry, but rather "verses," and he skirted Garland's appreciation of his reminiscences of

boy life to contend that satire was where he had done his best work, "illustrating the foolery of these society folks." Although his stories were invented, he
said flatly, "I like the probable. I like the near at hand."[46] *A Little Book of Western
Verse* included plenty of sentimental poems of home and hearth. However,
the sprinkling of Colorado dialect verse is based in the mining country of
"Red Hoss Mountain," featuring a modified cowboy Pike dialect. The values
are "Western," describing the country of "Casey's Table D'Hote" as a place
and time "When the money flowed like likker, 'nd the folks was brave 'nd
true!"[47] Another poem, "Prof. Vere De Blaw," takes up a Western event – the
coming of a "steenway gran' piannyfort" to a mining camp – that was a popular frontier theme, playing working-class people against high culture. The
coming of pianos was a major Western theme, reflecting, perhaps, the West's
yearning for cultural acceptance reinvented in local color caricature. About
the same time, William DeVere, "Tramp Poet of the West," titled his 1897
volume *Jim Marshall's New Pianner and Other Western Stories* and played up the
clash between high and low culture similarly.[48] In Field's poem, the Eastern
tenderfoot musician plays the songs of "Home, Sweet Home" to excite the
appropriate responses in the rough miners: "The homestead in the States 'nd
all its memories seemed to come / A-floatin' round about me with that magic
lunty-tum." An unknown, hollow-eyed stranger, who had not found surcease
"from sorrer in a fur, seclooded spot," waltzes up to the bar "an' demand[s]
whiskey straight"; the stranger then gets "outside" the whiskey, and the door
holding back a freezing storm, into which he disappears. What is left of him
is found a few months later, "associated with a tree, some distance from the
ground": "And Husky Sam, the coroner, that set upon him, said / That two
things wuz apparent, namely: first, deceast wuz dead; / And, second, previously had got involved beyond all hope / In a knotty complication with a yard
or two of rope!"[49] Despite ending on a laugh line, the local color dialogue
makes a realist point; the event stands on its own as unsentimentalized fact.
These poems may be about social and economic status as much as regional
culture; Sam Walter Foss offered a more sentimentalized version of the outcast musician in "The Volunteer Organist." Foss's New England derelict also
leaves the hall to freeze to death in a snowstorm after wringing the hearts of
his audience with his playing. The poems together might be taken as a reflection of local color and dialect poetry itself as an outcast form of expression.

Like Carleton, Field was also able to take up the urban scene and include
realistic artifacts within the poetic framework. Field's mock-pastoral "April"
illustrates again the ability of local color and dialect poetry to include the low
and the ugly, create a social message, and reflect a "real" environment. April

with its sweet showers rouses last summer's vigorous breath, while "The rau-cous-throated frog ayont the sty / Sends forth, as erst, his amerous vermal croak" [*sic*]; in the second quatrain, only the word "sty" drops unnoticeably out of place, along with "vermal," which the reader likely retranslates as a typographical blunder for "vernal," rather than attaching it to the cerebellar vermal region of the brain. The quatrain also lumps in "pots and pails" in place of streams and fields. The third quatrain then delivers us into the world of Goose Island, with its yowling dogs and cats, where "John Murphy's wife outpours her slop":

> With gurgling glee the gutter gushes by,
> Fraught all with filth, unknown and nameless dirt –
> A dead green goose, an o'er-ripe rat I spy;
> Head of a cat, tail of a flannel shirt.
> . . .
>
> So in Goose Island cometh April round;
> Full eagerly we watch the month's approach –
> The season of sweet sight and pleasant sound,
> The season of the bedbug and the roach.[50]

Field did not reinvent the mock-pastoral, but he captures urban argot and twists it together with pastoral language to envision a disgusting place: an artificially created industrial island in a notoriously polluted river in Chicago, occupied by tanneries, breweries, and soap factories. "Amerous," yet another word that is likely to be thoughtlessly converted (to "amorous"), signified a person who lies about another, although it also appears in the opening of the 1532 English translation from Boccacio of "Guystarde and Sygysmonde," two lovers put to death by the lady's father. From its opening until its perfect emphatic closure on the sound-word "roach" in the last, slightly halting line, the poem is dense, clever with misdirection, and unflinchingly urban, the per-fect example of realism in comic doggerel poetry.

James Whitcomb Riley remains one of the most widely remembered of the dialect and local color poets, but his poetry lacks the bite of Field's best poems. Neighborly poems and dialect sketches were his hallmark, and Hoosier Indiana his heritage, but the strand of sentimentalism in his work overpowers the folksy stories, genre painting, and local dialect of such poems as "The Old Swimmin'-Hole," "The Barefoot Boy," "Little Orphant Annie," and "When the Frost Is on the Punkin'." Although his satire of Whittier's "Maud Muller" rivals one by Bret Harte, the closing couplet is cute rather than blunt. He tried for, but missed, satiric formulation, making his works vulnerable to clever burlesques. In his time, though, as his critical biographer Elizabeth J. Van Allen notes, he was a very effective performer on the lecture circuit who also produced one of the most successful books for children, *Rhymes of Childhood* (1891).[51]

The movement of dialect, doggerel, and local color poetry stretches from at least the early 1800s, reaches its culmination in the late nineteenth century, and continues up to the present in various folk verse writers and the cowboy poetry movement.[52] New England poetry is represented by Holman F. Day, Sam Walter Foss, Joseph C. Lincoln, and others preceding Edwin Arlington Robinson. From the urban slums comes Charles Follen Adams's *Leedle Yawcub Strauss*, Henry Blake Fuller's *Lines Long and Short*, David L. Proudfit's *Love Among the Gamins, and Other Poems*, and Wallace Irwin's *Chinatown Ballads*. In the Midwest, *Ben King's Verse* was popular. Edgar Guest and James Whitcomb Riley still maintain a regional, and national, readership, but Will Carleton's more concrete and pictorial narrative poems are largely forgotten. "Black" dialect poetry is readily found in volumes such as Valentine's *Ole Marster and Other Verses* and A. C. Gordon and Thomas Nelson Page's *Befo' De War, Echoes in Negro Dialect*, and in many of the best poems of Paul Laurence Dunbar. Joaquin Miller practically invented the wild Western cowboy poet and turned his frontier persona into a traveling road show to England and the Continent, but a host of rougher versions followed him. Representing the West among cowboy poets are titles like Elva Irene McMillan's *Lyrics of the West*, James W. Foley's *Tales of the Trail*, and Sam W. Smith's *Gems from the Tailings*. Typical titles of other works from across America include John H. Flagg's *Lyrics of New England*, Charles P. Green's *Ballads of the Black Hills*, Edward McQueen Gray's *Alamo and Other Verses*, and Dr. L. C. Hiegel's *Rhymes from a Hill Billy*. Literary comedians writing in this genre range from William Allen Butler, John G. Saxe, Benjamin P. Shillaber, and Charles G. Halpine; through Charles Francis Adams, Benj. F. Taylor, and Bert Leston Taylor; and past the turn of the century, when Grantland Rice and Damon Runyon published volumes of "hooligan" dialect verse. Dorothy Parker's Algonquin cynicism provides a female counterpart.

As the Fireside Poets, one by one, disappeared from the American literary scene, the plaint was often heard that their like would never be seen again. It may be, however, that popular American and Canadian poets had already taken over many aspects of their work to express their broadly egalitarian ethic. The poets of the popular traditions produced gritty realist verse, portraits of "real life," political histories and political satire in vulgar and vernacular voices, and effective natural lyrics, as well as comic narratives with unique regional flavors, aspiring in some cases to the status of vulgar doggerel epics, both during their time and after. William Dean Howells addressed the issue of the disappearance of such poetry in a 1912 speech. Speaking of the great American poets he had known, Howells said,

> Longfellow and Bryant and Emerson and Whittier and Lowell and Holmes … belonged to an idealistic period when man dreamed of human perfectability through one mighty reform. Their dream was that if the slaves were freed there could hardly be sorrow on the earth which our good-will could not easily assuage. Now long ago the slaves were freed, but through the rift of the poets' broken dream the faces of underwaged women and overworked children stare at us.… Has the real frightened the ideal from us? Is poetry so essentially of the ideal that it must go into exile with it? … I am ready, almost ready, to say that as much good poetry is written in this time as in the time that is past; but it is not the poetry of the few, it is the poetry of the many. We no longer have supremacies, we no longer have primacies; the gods, the half-gods, the heroes are gone, I hope not to return; and it is the high average which reigns in this as in all American things. Amidst the misgivings of our excellence in poetry, we may console ourselves with the fact that the average in it is higher than ever before.[53]

Howells's observation applies to the poets under consideration here. Not all succeeded in transmuting bombast into meaningful verse. An impressive number nevertheless turned native materials into comic and serious verse that was readable and absorbing. They merged American voices, dialects, settings, and characters into a vast national kaleidoscope that included both sentiment and satire, often illuminating social issues and historical realities, and sometimes successfully bringing forward dramatic moments of realistic intensity and enriching our literary history.

Notes

1. *The (Philadelphia) Tickler*, September 4, 1811.
2. Mrs. M. V. Victor, "The Stilts of Gold," *Beadle's Monthly* III (January 1867), pp. 60–64.
3. Joel Barlow, esq., *The Hasty-Pudding, a Poem, in Three Cantos* (New Haven, Conn.: William Storer, 1838), p. 2.
4. John Byers Wilson, *Reminiscent Rhymes and Other Verse* (Cincinnati, Ohio: Press of Jennings & Graham, 1911), pp. 5–6.
5. Ellen P. Allerton, *Walls of Corn and Other Poems*, ed. and with memorial sketch by Eva Ryan (Hiawatha, Kans.: Press of the Harrington Printing Co., 1894), pp. 5–6.
6. Allerton, *Walls of Corn*, pp. 2–3.
7. Will Carleton, "Preface," in *Farm Ballads* (New York: Harper & Brothers, 1873), n.p.

8. [Josiah D. Canning], *The Harp and the Plow* (Greenfield, Mass.: M. H. Tyler, 1852), pp. iii–iv.

9. The phrase "humbler poets" was used by Slason Thompson in 1885 for his anthology *The Humbler Poets: A Collection of Newspaper and Periodical Verse*. The publisher, A. C. McClurg and Company, published at least seven editions in the first year, and many more later revised editions.

10. John Hay, "The Pike County Ballads," in *Poems by John Hay* (Boston: James R. Osgood, 1871), pp. 13–28.

11. Bret Harte, *Poems* (Boston: Fields, Osgood, 1871), pp. 47–88.

12. Elizabeth Robins Pennell, *Charles Godfrey Leland, a Biography* (Boston: Houghton Mifflin, 1906), vol. 1, pp. 285–300.

13. Charles G. Leland, *Hans Breitmann's Ballads* (Philadelphia: T. B. Peterson & Brothers, 1869), pp. 5–6.

14. Charles G. Leland, *Sunshine in Thought* (New York: Charles T. Evans, 1862), p. 4.

15. P. R. S. [Peter Remsen Strong], *"AWFUL" and Other Jingles* (New York: G. P. Putnam & Sons, 1871), pp. 14–17.

16. Sam W. Smith, *Gems from the Tailings* (San Francisco: C. W. Gordon, 1875), pp. 21–23.

17. Mrs. E. T. Corbett, *Rustic Rhymes and Ballads* (New York: Gillis Brothers, 1883), pp. 49–51.

18. Corbett, *Rustic Rhymes*, pp. 9–13.

19. Corbett, *Rustic Rhymes*, pp. 14–17.

20. Mrs. S[arah] M[organ] B[ryan] Piatt, *That New World and Other Poems* (Boston: James R. Osgood, 1877), pp. 13–15.

21. Piatt, *That New World*, pp. 111–14.

22. Piatt, *That New World*, pp. 119–21.

23. Sarah M. B. Piatt, *Palace-Burner, the Selected Poetry of Sarah Piatt*, ed. Paula Bernat Bennett (Urbana: University of Illinois Press, 2001), pp. 90–91.

24. Mrs. S. L. Oberholtzer, *Daisies of Verse* (Philadelphia: Lippincott, 1886), pp. 14–19

25. Will Carleton, "Preface," in *City Festivals* (New York: Harper & Brothers, 1892), pp. vii–viii.

26. Will Carleton, *Farm Ballads* (New York: Harper & Brothers, 1873), pp. 17–26, 51–62.

27. A. Elwood Corning, *Will Carleton, a Biographical Study* (New York: Lanmere, 1917), p. 35.

28. Will Carleton, *City Ballads* (New York: Harper & Brothers, 1885), pp. 130–31.

29. Will Carleton, *Farm Festivals* (New York: Harper & Bros., 1881), pp. 16–17.

30. Carleton, *Farm Festivals*, p. 33.

31. Carleton, *Farm Festivals*, p. 40.

32. Peter Peppercorn [Emanuel Price], "Mr. Lo!," in *The Poetical Works of Peter Peppercorn* (Philadelphia: David McKay, 1884), pp. 224–25.

33. Q. K. Philander Doesticks, P. B. [Mortimer Thomson], *Pluri-bus-tah* (New York: Rudd and Carleton, 1856), pp. xxii–xxiii.

34. [Thomson], *Pluri-bus-tah*, pp. 110–12.

35. [Thomson], *Pluri-bus-tah*, pp. 120–21.

36. Truman Trumbull, A. M. [E. Jane Gay], *The New Yankee Doodle* (New York: Wm. Oland Bourne, 1868).

37. Sam Walter Foss, *Dreams in Homespun* (Boston: Lothrup, Lee & Shephard, 1897), pp. 100–02.

38. "A Talk about Popular Songs," *Putnam's Monthly Magazine* VII:4 (April 1856), pp. 401–15, 411.

39. "A Talk About Popular Songs," p. 411.

40. Frank L. Stanton, *Songs of the Soil* (New York: D. Appleton, 1894), p. 7.

41. Stanton, *Songs of the Soil*, pp. 154–56.

42. Stanton, *Songs of the Soil*, pp. 189–91.

43. Frank L. Stanton, *Comes One with a Song* (Indianapolis, Ind.: The Bowen Merrill Co., 1899), pp. 186–87.

44. Eugene Field, *Hoosier Lyrics* (Chicago: M. A. Donohue, 1905), p. 9.

45. Field, *Hoosier Lyrics*, pp. 106–07.

46. Hamlin Garland, "Interview with Eugene Field," *McClure's Magazine* 1:3 (August 1893), pp. 195–204.

47. Eugene Field, *A Little Book of Western Verse* (New York: Charles Scribner's Sons, 1893 [1890]), pp. 1–7.

48. William DeVere, *Jim Marshall's New Pianner and Other Western Stories* (New York: M. Witmark & Sons, 1897). Also worth noting is another poem in this volume, "Jeff and Joe. A True Incident of Creede Camp, Colorado," which describes the friendship of two cowboys over thirty years. One critic, Paul Constant, has labeled this as a portrait of homosexuality, although various respondents to his assertion demur (see http://www.thestranger.com/slog /archives/2010/04/13/brokeback-mountain-the-prequel and http://soapy smith.net).

49. Field, *A Little Book of Western Verse*, pp. 161–70.

50. Field, *Hoosier Lyrics*, pp. 116–17.

51. Elizabeth J. Van Allen, *James Whitcomb Riley: A Life* (Bloomington: Indiana University Press, 1999), pp. 216, 268–69.

52. David Stanley and Elaine Thatcher (eds.), *Cowboy Poets and Cowboy Poetry* (Urbana: University of Illinois Press, 2000).

53. William Dean Howells, "Mr. Howells's Speech," in Rudolf and Clara Marburg Kirk (eds.), *Criticism and Fiction and Other Essays* (New York: New York University Press, 1959), pp. 371–72.

Chapter 21

Political Poets and Naturalism

TYLER HOFFMAN

In the last two decades of the nineteenth century, following the lead of the French novelist Émile Zola and in the face of perceived mounting social injustices in the United States, some American poets began to write according to a theory known as "naturalism," a deterministic philosophy that holds that man is subject to universal forces that are wholly indifferent to his survival. It is a bleak world that they depict, one Darwinian in nature, with the fate of man determined by social and biological factors beyond his control. As free market capitalism expanded in America in the Gilded Age, and the country experienced a growing disparity between rich and poor, many of these naturalists became politically engaged, looking to forms of socialism for relief while speaking out against the systematic degradation of fellow humans and advocating for reform.

Although a great deal of critical attention has been paid to naturalism in fiction, not as much has been paid to the movement's impact on poetry, perhaps in part because naturalist poets themselves appeared most successful in other genres, especially fiction and social science. In fact, though, a significant strand of American verse written around the turn of the twentieth century expresses the tensions or contradictions within naturalism that the critic Donald Pizer identified as occurring in fiction, namely, although the world of the naturalist is that of "the commonplace and unheroic," she nonetheless "discovers in this world those qualities of man usually associated with the heroic or adventurous, such as acts of violence and passion"; and, although the naturalist "describes his characters as though they are conditioned and controlled by environment, heredity, instinct, or chance[,] ... he also suggests a compensating humanistic value in his characters or their fates which affirms the significance of the individual and of his [or her] life."[1] In this way, life is given some meaning notwithstanding the harsh and oppressive forces that impinge on men, women, and children in an increasingly complex, dehumanizing, and strictly regulated American cultural milieu.

Several of the most important and influential American naturalist poets – Charlotte Perkins (Stetson) Gilman, Edwin Markham, and Stephen Crane – were writing for a popular press, with the line between muckraking journalism and poetry at times significantly blurred. Occasionally, their work was criticized for being unartful, for being too didactic, or too ideologically freighted. In some cases, these writers do not even refer to themselves as poets or to what they write as poetry, preferring to think of themselves as political activists first and foremost, or somehow as outliers, rather than as artists committed to a traditional ideal of Beauty. Just as they espoused political causes that were radical in their day, so too did the performance of their work strike the world as daring and subversive. Their often sharp-tongued verse protests the brutality of both the natural and the civilized worlds and our lack of control over the course of our lives in them, at least if the status quo were to prevail.

Charlotte Perkins Gilman first broke into print as an author (under her married name of Stetson) with her book of poems, *In This Our World* (published in four editions between 1893 and 1898). She published more than five hundred poems in her lifetime, some of which appeared in her self-published magazine the *Forerunner* (1909–1916), in which she also wrote columns on the pressing political issues of the day from a socialist and feminist perspective; the suffrage weekly *Woman's Journal*; and *Cosmopolitan*. Her socialism was influenced in part by Edward Bellamy's enormously popular utopian science fiction novel *Looking Backward* (1888), and her own 1915 utopian novel *Herland* (also set in America in the year 2000) is indebted to it. Gilman took a decidedly feminist perspective on science and socialism and exposed what she regarded as the economic dependence of women on men, arguing that women should support themselves economically and find worth outside of the menial, unremunerated labors of the home. Despite her sense of the debilitating effects of patriarchy, she voiced great confidence in social progress, in our collective ability to improve conditions not only for women but for others who are downtrodden and oppressed by custom and law.

The sectional organization of *In This Our World* speaks to Gilman's wide-ranging social conscience and activist agenda: "The World"; "Woman"; and "The March" (originally "Our Human Kind"). In her poems she works through a variety of fixed poetic forms and uses these traditional structures (limericks, ballads, rondeaux, heroic couplets, and blank verse, to name a few) to interrogate in very untraditional ways the paradigms of the dominant culture. Gilman was well known in her day for her lampoons in particular, with an early supporter, the realist writer William Dean Howells, hailing her for her civic satire in support of radical social reform: "You speak with a tongue like a two edged sword," he told her.[2] *In This Our World* was praised by Horace Traubel, a committed socialist and friend of Walt Whitman, who played down her art and trumped up her politics: "She is neither past nor present master of phrases and verbal dress suitings. But the effect she achieves is wonderful.... *In This Our World* touches at some point every problem of our time."[3] Gilman herself was pleased to be regarded primarily as an activist in her verse, going so far as to say of *In This Our World*, "I don't call it a book of poems. I call it a tool box. It was written to drive nails with"; as she elsewhere insisted, "I am not a poet. I'm only a preacher whether on the platform or in print."[4] Her definition of herself makes clear the public stance that she assumes as a writer, someone performing on the stage and on the page in an effort to reach audiences with her revolutionary gospel. When some try to rescue her from the charge of not being literary or artistic enough, they tend to turn to her nonpolitical lyrics – her nature and city poems – which stand squarely in the Romantic tradition. In fact, though, there is a high degree of artfulness in her most politically charged poems, and although she might distract from her own aesthetics, many of her poems turn on her careful use of forms with particular historical generic associations.

In "Homes," subtitled "A Sestina," in *In This Our World* Gilman ironically comments on both male and female entrapment: while the homes that couples work to maintain are deceptively "smiling" and "comfortable," they severely curtail personal freedom. When they ask "Are we not homes? And is not all therein?" we know what the answer is, because we have seen in the poem that men learn to worship homes instead of God and women do not in fact find there the "perfect world" that fulfills all their natural desires.[5] Gilman's decision to write in the highly prescriptive form of the sestina, and to foreground that fact, is meant to figure the condition of being tightly bound by bourgeois convention. Gilman's feminism is pronounced throughout the book, but especially so in the second section, in which she asserts the need for women to develop an independent economic identity from men, to reinvent the delimiting roles of wife, housekeeper, and mother. In "In Duty Bound" the speaker viscerally feels the trap shutting on her, with

> No chance of breaking out, except by sin;
>   Not even room to shirk –
>   Simply to live, and work.
>
> An obligation pre-imposed, unsought,
>   Yet binding with the force of natural law.
>
> (*ITOW*, pp. 33–34)

Gilman puts her finger on the "wasting power" of the imprisoned, domesticated woman and seeks to break with the patriarchal ideology that produces it (*ITOW*, p. 34). The metrical break in the poem (with iambic pentameter suddenly giving way to a trimeter couplet) symbolizes the break (or "breaking out") that she seeks; the reimposition of iambic expresses the iron "law" that is so hard to undermine or escape.

In poem after poem Gilman takes to the barricades, asserting her sense of the injustices that rule the world but also her conviction that that rule can be challenged and changed. In the tripping meters of light verse, Gilman mocks women who find comfort and security in the domestic sphere, as in "The Housewife":

> Here is the House to hold me – cradle of all the race;
> Here is my lord and my love, here are my children dear –
> Here is the House enclosing, the dear-loved dwelling place;
> Why should I ever weary for aught that I find not here?[6]

Her feminism is again in bloom in "Six Hours a Day," in which she portrays the degradation of women in the kitchen, women who must spend six hours a day cooking for their family, "Struggling with laws she does not understand / Of chemistry and physics, and the weight / Of poverty and ignorance besides." Women, she sees, are "Toiling without release, no hope ahead," and "to refuse to cook is held the same / As to refuse her wife and motherhood." Her fate is predestined, as "the slow finger of Heredity / Writes on the forehead of each living man, / Strive as he may, 'His mother was a cook!'" (*ITOW*, pp. 136–37). It is this determinism that she seeks to interrupt.

Gilman was not content to allow anyone to choose not to become involved in political protest; according to her, all people, but especially fellow women, were responsible for helping in the fight for change. In "To the Indifferent Women," another sestina whose title seeks to activate politically all mothers of the world, she states forthrightly that "The one first duty of all human life / Is to promote the progress of the world." The speaker tells her audience, who are happy in their bourgeois trappings, that they cannot rest content in their "domestic peace," that "the neglected, starved, unmothered world" needs them to add their "power of love" to man's in order "to care for all the world" (*LP*, pp. 114–15). "The Anti-Suffragists" more harshly criticizes the various types of women who are content with what they have, and who keep up an ignorance of the world, unmotivated to fight for female enfranchisement. She ends the poem by calling out these women who have turned against their sex: "who shall measure the historic shame / Of these poor traitors – traitors are they all – / To great Democracy and Womanhood!" (*ITOW*, p. 154). Gilman did not pull her punches, and sometimes, as here, she embarrasses people into doing the progressive thing. When suffrage finally is won, she pens "A Chant Royal," hailing that political triumph in a form associated with heroic subject matter since Chaucer, and in the envoi the speaker addresses her "Sisters" thus: "To make a better world and hold it so / Women are free at last in all the land" (*LP*, p. 110).

The poem that Gilman became best known for in her lifetime was the 120-line "Similar Cases," dubbed a "great campaign document" for the socialist movement of Nationalism by her uncle, the Unitarian minister Edward Everett Hale (*LP*, p. 28). The satiric verse was published in the April 1890 issue of the *Nationalist* and was reprinted in newspapers and magazines all across the country. In the poem she jabs at conservatives who believe that man's nature is fixed for all time, and she retraces the stages of evolutionary history, demonstrating that change is fully part of our nature, not inimical to it. We first meet Eohippus, who is small in size and proclaims he is going to become a great big horse; his peers laugh at him, mocking, "*Why! You'd have to change your nature!*" Next is Anthropoidal Ape, who is "Far smarter than the rest" and says he is going to be a man, for which he, too, is jeered and mocked. Finally, Neolithic Man is upbraided for his vision of modern humanity ("We shall be civilized! We are going to live in cities!"):

> Said One, "This is chimerical!
>   Utopian! Absurd!"
> Said another, "What a stupid life!
>   Too dull, upon my word!"
> Cried all, "Before such things can come,
>   You idiotic child,
> *You must alter human nature!*"
>   And they all sat back and smiled.
> Thought they, "An answer to that last
>   It will be hard to find!"
> It was a clinching argument
>   To the Neolithic Mind!   (*ITOW*, pp. 95–100)

Gilman satirizes the conception that change is unnatural, charging that we indeed are capable of progress, as proved already by the evolution of man, and her position is perfectly in line with Nationalism's sense of the need for the slow evolution of economic, social, and political reforms in the effort to effect social change.

Often in her verse Gilman wryly places the human order against the animal and thereby shows that what is deemed "natural" in patriarchy is not in fact. In "Females," for example, she states that in the animal world the male and female are equally "representative of race": one is deemed as capable as the other. The only female occupying "a parasitic place / Dependent on the male" is, Gilman argues, the human female. Imagining the retort of her critics that she simply is slandering mothers and wives, who "earn their living" in such occupation, she parries, "A Human Creature is your state, / And to be human is more great / Than even womanhood!" (*ITOW*, pp. 169–71). Gilman also invokes the animal kingdom when she trains her sights on the social ill of child labor; in a poem entitled "Child Labor [No. 2]" she makes her appeal to her audience with ironic incisiveness:

> Only the human mother,
> Degraded helpless being
> Will make her little children work
> And live on what they bring.
>
> No fledgling feeds the father-bird,
> No chicken feeds the hen,
> No kitten mouses for the cat,
> This glory is for men.

She ends the poem on an optimistic note, fully believing that it is possible for Americans to "awake, rebuild, remake, / And let our children grow" (*LP*, p. 43).

Although Gilman can be very pessimistic at times in her poems, as in "The Mother's Charge," which closes in the ironic heroic couplet "She died, as all her mothers died before. / Her daughter died in turn, and made one more," she often turns a degrading, controlling environment into a political opportunity, pointing up the ways in which some progressive action could change the world and make it less oppressive an environment for all (*ITOW*, p. 161). In "One Girl of Many," she treats the problem of the female prostitute, who is "Hungry from her birth / Half-fed. Half-clothed. / Untaught of woman's worth." Her heart feels pain "as keenly as your own," Gilman's speaker tells us; she has human worth but ignorantly chooses to sell her body because it seems to promise a better life: "She had no knowledge of our nature's laws." Her fate is to descend, in shame, to death, but her very existence is a "Social necessity": "Men cannot live / Without what these disgraceful creatures give." When at one point in the poem the speaker states, "And so she – sinned. I think we call it sin," she reveals the sanctimony that dooms the girl to a living hell, exposing the destructiveness and falsity of our moral codes (*LP*, pp. 115–16).

Gilman framed life as a Darwinian struggle, and she paints a grim picture of the efforts of the working class, regardless of gender, to endure. In "The Wolf at the Door," that title figure relentlessly threatens the hopeless inhabitants of a home with extinction unless they get out of bed, "To work! To work!" (*ITOW*, p. 177). In "The Survival of the Fittest," she represents the growing disparity between rich and poor, describing the way the polar bear adapted to survive in cold climes by growing fat and how the modern millionaire has done much the same: "Where Poverty and Hunger are, / He counts his bullion by the car. / Where thousands suffer, still he thrives, / And after death his will survives." But in the end, the speaker notes, man slays the bear for his fat and fur, and so too will the millionaire meet his demise, as the "simple common Human Race," "so wise, so strong, so many," asserts itself (*ITOW*, p. 209). Gilman is not shy about stoking class warfare, urging average citizens to seize their own rightful inheritance, and in her poem "Work and Wages" she protests in satirical tones the poor pay of the worker, whose hard labor simply allows the rich to get richer: "It does not seem exactly straight / That he who serves so well the state / Should just be kept alive"; she goes on to ask pointedly, "why should one man feed the earth, / Enriching it by all he's worth, / If Rockefeller eats it?" (*ITOW*, p. 176). Gilman raised concern about urban workers denied the right to strike and saw the American labor scene degenerating into European conditions, with increasing distance between the haves and have-nots; in her opinion, no one had the right to sit idly by: "We have no place for lookers on / When all the world's at war!" (*ITOW*, p. 184). And her call "To Labor" is clarion:

> Then rise as you never rose before!
> Nor hoped before!
> Nor dared before!
> And show as was never shown before,
> The power that lies in you!
> Stand all as one!
> See justice done!
> Believe, and Dare, and Do! (*ITOW*, p. 194)

In "A Hope," she looks forward to the creation of the fraternal state that the uprising of labor will secure: "Be of good cheer the end is near / You have not worked alone!" (*ITOW*, p. 90). It is, Gilman insists, through such solidarity that the world's woes will be remedied, if ever.

In the scope of her career, Gilman satirically addressed a range of specific social problems in her verse that stem from an industrial capitalism run amok, and she sometimes assumed in her poetry the role of consumer protector. In several poems about the meat-packing industry, she exposes its corruption and the crimes that are being committed by it against humanity, with no one ultimately held accountable. A poem that alludes to fellow muckraker Upton Sinclair, "How About the Man?," accuses:

> Somebody did it. Somebody knew –
> Somebody excellent profits drew
>> From this public poisoning plan;
> They are pushing a Bill to finish the fun, –
> But think of the mischief that has been done! –
> Is there no blame coming to any one?   (*LP*, p. 49)

In her sonnet "To the Packer" she concludes her diatribe against this type with the couplet, "His hands with gold uncounted we have filled / While he, safe, secret, subtle, killed and killed" (*LP*, p. 51). "I Would Fain Die a Dry Death," composed in anapestic lines ironically recalling the light verse tradition, complains of the American public's willingness to accept oppression and manipulation by big corporations: "We submit to be killed by our railroads, / We submit to be fooled by our press, / We can stand as much government scandal / As any folks going, I guess" (*LP*, p. 48). But the line must be drawn, she insists, at tolerating the poisoning of our food supply. As for being "fooled by our press," in her poem "Hyenas" she lambastes yellow journalism, decrying the increasing tabloidization of newspaper reportage, which, for profit, greedily digs up the bodies of dead heroes to drag them through the mud.

Gilman's politics build on a foundational naturalism: while individuals are controlled by their environment, she also believes that that environment is susceptible to change. In the first of three scenes in "Nature's Answer," a man who has built a house in an idyllic setting suddenly is beset by fever and dies:

>> "how could I know
> That death was lurking under this fair show?"
>
> And answered Nature, merciful, and stern,
> "I teach by killing; let the others learn!"

The same brutal lesson is taught to a maid in the poem's final tableau, a maid who thinks that, "in the holy name of wife," she will find "greater joy"; what she finds, though, is unremitting pain – "work as brainless slaves might do, / By day and night, long labor, never through." When she dies, Nature's refrain remains the same: "I teach by killing; let the others learn!" (*ITOW*, pp. 3–4). This hostile universe also bares its teeth in her poem "The Rock and the Sea," in which those two contending forces show no concern at all for the plight of man: "What is the folly of man to me? / I am the Sea!" (*ITOW*, p. 11). It is in this context that Gilman's socialism operates, as she searches for ways to overcome the crushing circumstances of "Nature," especially the foolish "Nature" of our own making.

Similarly progressive in spirit, Edwin Markham knew Gilman well, and he was part of her California literary salon. The poets shared a commitment to political reform and concentrated their artistic efforts on seeking remedy for the downtrodden, both of them looking to a future when social justice would be served. Also like Gilman, Markham became widely famous for a single blockbuster poem. He read it on New Year's Eve 1898 to the editor of the *San Francisco Examiner* and on January 18, 1899, "The Man with the Hoe" was published on the front page of that newspaper; it became one of the most talked-about poems of the nineteenth century and was republished in more than ten thousand newspapers and magazines and translated into more than forty languages. Inspired by Jean-François Millet's painting *Man with a Hoe*, which depicts a French peasant in a field bent over the harvest, the poem spurred a broad debate about not only agrarian reform but also labor conditions in all segments of American society.

In the poem Markham uses blank verse, a form associated with the epic by way of Milton, to petition on behalf of his title figure, one "Bowed by the weight of centuries," wearing "The emptiness of ages in his face, / And on his back the burden of the world." The farmer is "dead to rapture and despair / A thing that grieves not and that never hopes, / Stolid and stunned, a brother to the ox." The responsibility for the perversion of man is laid at the feet of the world: this "Slave of the wheel of labor" has been stripped of all dreams, hopes, and aspirations, brutalized by "masters, lords and rulers in all lands." As Markham contends, the hoe man will come back to haunt capitalists and politicians, posing a revolutionary danger to the world:

> How will it be with kingdoms and with kings –
> With those who shaped him to the thing he is –
> When this dumb terror shall rise to judge the world,
> After the silence of the centuries?[7]

Markham himself sought to explain the intended purpose and effect of his poem in later years, stating that Millet's toiler "is the type of industrial oppression in all lands and in all labors. He might be a man with a needle in a New York sweat-shop, a man with a pick in a West Virginia coal-mine.... The Hoeman is the symbol of betrayed humanity, the Toiler ground down through ages of oppression, through ages of social injustice." The figure represented "the slow, sure, awful degradation of man through endless, hopeless and joyless labor." Markham himself saw "The Man with the Hoe" as a poem of hope, a call to the conscience of the ruling class, even as it refuses to turn away from "rugged and savage reality."[8]

But if Markham's poem is without irony, its rhetorical strategy of dehumanizing the worker is not. As Cary Nelson points out, Markham takes it on himself to speak for the hoe man, thereby forgetting the history of labor protest and song in workers' own voices, and it is the "relentless *othering* of the worker" that gave his poem such "remarkable cultural warrant": the mute sufferer was acceptable to the tastes of the dominant culture.[9] William Dean Howells referred to the poem in a letter to the author as "great and noble."[10] It was a favorite poem of the labor leader Eugene V. Debs as well. Samuel Gompers of the American Federation of Labor was strongly enough impressed by the image to comment on it in a formal report, stating that he was looking forward to the day of "the intelligent worker, standing erect, looking his fellow man in the face, demanding for himself, and according to all, the full rights of disenthralled manhood."[11]

Markham's poem did not sit well, though, with the well-known satirist Ambrose Bierce. In San Francisco in 1893, Markham made his way into Bierce's circle and became his protégé. Bierce was supportive of Markham early on but turned against him when "The Man with the Hoe" appeared. In the pages of the *Examiner*, the same newspaper that first ran the poem, Bierce called it "in structure, stiff, inelastic, monotonous," comparing the execution of the blank verse unfavorably to Milton's; he especially objected to "the thought that the work carries," that is, its socialist strain:

> The thought is that of the labor union – even to the workworn threat of rising against the wicked well-to-do and taking it out of their hides.... The notion that the sorrows of the humble are due to the selfishness of the great is "natural," and can be made poetical, but it is silly. As a literary conception it has not the vitality of a sick fish.[12]

In a private letter to Markham, Bierce accused him of propounding "a doctrine of hate." Markham replied, "I believe in sympathy.... I believe also in the practice of the Golden Rule as the supreme law in all human affairs.... I wish to arouse but one hatred – the hatred of injustice." Bierce was far from satisfied and in another column in the *Examiner* charged his former friend with attacking the principles of capitalism and flatly stated that "the stuff" Markham was writing and publishing "is not poetry," but rather "demagogy."[13]

Markham was undeterred. He kept writing verse in form and theme similar to "The Man with the Hoe," appeared in public in support of labor, and began writing articles for the *Examiner* on related social issues (for instance, in August 1899 he published "The Epidemic of Strikes and the Remedy," in which he argues for government ownership and worker solidarity). His poem "The Man under the Stone" first appeared at the top of the first page of the official American Federation of Labor monthly magazine, the *American Federationist*, for July 1899. In this poem the poet's class sympathies are again front and center in his portrait of a benighted figure, stripped of his very humanity:

> When I see a workingman with mouths to feed,
> Up, day after day, in the dark before the dawn,
> And coming home, night after night, through the dusk,
>
> Swinging forward like some fierce silent animal,
> I see a man doomed to roll a huge stone up an endless steep.

The toiler in the shadow of the rock is perceived as "twisted, cramped, misshapen," physically and spiritually distorted by the work he must perform to eke out an existence.[14] The speaker of the poem does not let us know whether or not the worker will be ultimately crushed by the rock. In "A Harvest Song" Markham again paints a bleak picture of the situation of American laborers, who have filled up the granaries, but who then are deprived of the fruits of the harvest: "And now the idle reapers lounge against the bolted doors: / Without are hungry harvesters, within enchanted stores." The laborers are reduced to "strolling beggars"; out of season, they are out of work, with the harvest being but "A little while their hope on earth, then evermore their tomb" (*P*, p. 36).

In his pessimistic lyric "The Rock-Breaker," also in *The Man with the Hoe and Other Poems* (1899), Markham likens the "labor-blasted toiler" not to a crouching animal this time but to a tree, isolate and vulnerable:

> So have I seen, on Shasta's top, a pine
>   Stand silent on a cliff,
> Stript of its glory of green leaves and boughs,
>   Its great trunk split by fire,
> Its gray bark blackened by the thunder smoke,
>   Its life a sacrifice
> To some blind purpose of the Destinies.   (*P*, p. 34)

The pine tree stands (barely), a victim of fate. The lyric immediately following "The Rock-Breaker" in the book (and the last of the poems) is "These Songs Will Perish," in which Markham makes the case that art and the artist will not endure, but the broader socialist message of both will: poetry, he asserts, stands in service of "Truth," who "cried to man of old / To build the enduring, glad Fraternal State," and it is that cry that cannot be silenced (*P*, p. 164). The tenor of the poet, then, is key, and in "The Toilers," in which the laborers' "blind feet drift in the darkness, and no one is leading," Markham conjures the Romantic poet Percy Shelley's ideal of the poet-legislator from "A Defence of Poetry" as he insists on the artist's involvement in the conduct of the state, his public charge, as a way to break from the unjust feudal arrangements that somehow seem to persist in an industrialized economy: "Shelley, where are you – where are you? our hearts are a-breaking!" (*MHOP*, pp. 112–13).

In *Lincoln and Other Poems* (1901) Markham continues to dwell on these issues, exposing the corrupting force of greed in "The Wall Street Pit" and singing again the praises of "The Muse of Labor," that is, "The Muse of the Fraternal State," in bathetic lines: "the builders have no part – / No share in all the glory of their hands."[15] In his blank verse poem "Lincoln, the Man of the People," which he read at the dedication of the Lincoln Memorial in Washington, D.C., in 1922, he extols the slain president for his commitment to social justice, drawing a direct line between his farm labor and his statesmanship: "The grip that swung the ax in Illinois / Was on the pen that set a people free" (*P*, p. 82). In "The Angelus," a poem suggested by another Millet painting, Markham similarly ennobles the work of men's hands in the field – "their day-long sacrament of toil" – and in closed heroic couplets exalts their "comrade kindness" and their service to God, who "finds no labor mean": "More than white incense circling to the dome / Is a field well furrowed or a nail sent home" (*P*, p. 38).

Markham felt the plight not only of the man in the field but of female workers. In his Petrarchan sonnet "A Leaf from the Devil's Jest-Book," which also harks back to Milton and his turning of that form to political subjects, he shines a light on the seamstress "bowed" over her stitching, "chained and bent," toiling for a woman of means: "They stitch for the lady, tyrannous and proud / For her a wedding-gown, for them a shroud" (*MHOP*, p. 44). Another poem about women laborers was intended specifically to help finance a political cause: "The Friendly Door" was "Written at the request of the New York women struggling to raise $3,000,000 to erect Y. W. C. A. buildings as homes for working girls." In the poem these struggling women are said to be "on the battle-line early and late," women who "take their chance in the fight with Fate."[16] They are victims of the forces of nature and man, but the very act of writing the poem serves as an attempt to ameliorate their conditions, to provide them respite.

Throughout his life, Markham took aim at laws and codes that he believed undercut the rights and freedoms of the working class, and he actively lent his support to trade unions and other progressive causes in an effort to relieve the suffering of the common man. He published journalistic essays in such magazines as *Cosmopolitan* on the horror of child labor and co-wrote a book-length exposé of child labor in America titled *Children of Bondage* that was published in 1914. Later on, Markham wrote "The Ballad of the Gallows Bird," a long dramatic narrative poem published in 1926 that is narrated by a man who is hanged to death for his crimes. Conceptually indebted to Bierce's short story "An Occurrence at Owl Creek Bridge" (1890), it stands as an expansion of Markham's reflections on social justice, staging as it does an existentialist conflict between right and wrong in rather gruesome imagery. In the words of the poet George Sterling, who extolled Markham in an anthology of verse in tribute to him on his seventieth birthday, Markham possessed "Homer's head and Milton's art / Shelley's soul and Lincoln's heart!"[17] As with Gilman, his naturalism did not rule out but rather set the groundwork for a utopian vision.

When Stephen Crane learned of the proposed American Academy of Arts and Letters, he chose Markham as the leading candidate to become its first member, because that poet was "of that virile manhood which expresses itself by appearing in public in its shirt sleeves; a strong man, mark ye; no apish child of fashion; a veritable eagle of freedom, and, withal, kindly, tender to the little lame lamb – aye, bold, yet gentle, defiant of all convention, and yet simple in his manner even to kings."[18] Clearly, he recognized Markham's twin streaks of unconventionality and progressivism. Like Markham, Crane wrote according to a theory of naturalistic determinism, exposing the corrupted institutions and false morality of the world, but through a different rhetorical technique: whereas Markham fills his poetry with pathos, Crane bites with irony and so sounds more like Gilman or Bierce, who first praised Crane before turning against him (just as he had done with Markham). Crane's usual sidestepping of specific social issues and problems in his verse, in favor of a general condemnation of sin and hypocrisy, also sets him apart from both Gilman and Markham, whose political reference points usually are much more definite. His humorous statement of his political philosophy also is at an angle to theirs; as Crane put it, "I was a Socialist for two weeks but when a couple of Socialists assured me I had no right to think differently from any other Socialist and then quarrelled with each other about what Socialism meant, I ran away."[19] This comment highlights his aversion to institutional thought and predicts some of the strong countercurrents running through his poetic lines.

Despite this disavowal, Crane's fiction, especially *Maggie: A Girl of the Streets* (1893), represents a decidedly progressivist point of view. He worked as a journalist as well, and in his 1894 article "In the Depths of a Coal Mine" in *McClure's* he announces his sympathy for miners and the brutal conditions they face daily in a way that points to both leftist politics and naturalistic philosophy: "Man is in the implacable grasp of nature. It has only to tighten slightly, and he is crushed like a bug. His loudest shriek of agony would be as impotent as his final moan to bring help from that fair land that lies, like Heaven, over his head." It is the "sinister struggle far below" that these workers enjoin, lorded over by the coal-breaking machine, an "imperturbably cruel and insatiate, black emblem of greed, and of the gods of this labor" that constitutes, for Crane, a "grim, strange war."[20] These symbols show up again in his poetry, which created quite a stir when it was published.

Crane's first book of verse, *Black Riders and Other Lines* (1895), contains sixty-eight short poems in free verse, each set high up on its own page in capital letters and identified not by titles but only by Roman numerals. Its strange formatting drew critical complaint and certainly contributed to the riddling, or orphic, quality of the lines, which resembled on the page the script of a telegram or newspaper headline. The poet claimed to like the book better than his own novel *The Red Badge of Courage*, published earlier that year, but he often hedged away from calling its contents "poems," preferring instead "pills" or "lines," as if to suggest that they were so unconventional as to demand generic reclassification. One reviewer wondered whether the lines in *Black Riders* were in fact "poetry," and William Dean Howells pronounced that Crane had "done the most striking thing of the year" in *Black Riders*; however, he took exception to Crane's refusal of traditional poetic form, asking how his "fresh" thought "would have been any less so if it had been cast in the mould which need not have been broken to secure them [the poems] the stamp of novelty."[21] As the story, perhaps apocryphal, goes, Crane started writing his verse after Howells read some of Emily Dickinson's gnomic verse to him. Certainly, the brevity of his poems – their epigrammatic terseness – resonates with Dickinson's lyrics.[22] A review in the *Nation* similarly noted the unruliness of Crane's verse, stating that the book "is an attraction which makes young people learn it by heart, carry it into the woods with them, sleep with it under their pillows, and perhaps suggest that it should be buried with them in their early graves." It goes on to claim that in "its rhymelessness and covert rhythm" it appears as "a condensed Whitman or an amplified Emily Dickinson."[23] To invoke these two poets – and lodge Crane between them – suggests something of the perceived eccentricity of his art.

Generally, reviewers found the book to be "rebellious," "modern in the extreme," "blasphemous," or "satiric." In a letter to his editor, who wanted to cut out several poems from the book, especially those calling into question the existence or goodness of God, Crane argued that "the ethical sense" of *Black Riders*, which is grounded in its "anarchy," that is, his open defiance of cultural norms, would be spoiled.[24] In the poems of *Black Riders*, we encounter a dark world pervaded by sin and faithlessness; the landscape that man walks through proves a vacant desert. He is lost in darkness, and, when there is any flash of color, it is a Darwinian phantasmagoria, "red in tooth and claw," as Tennyson imagined it. The titular black riders come charging out of the sea in the first poem, with "clang" and "clash," armed to do battle with "sin."[25] In poem 3 of the book the monstrous aspect of nature comes into full focus: "a creature, naked, bestial" is discovered eating his own heart (*SCP*, p. 4). Crane's naturalism is on full display here, as his speaker finds himself in a world where man is beast, caught in a jungle that allows for no hope and no comfort in any guiding light.

Despite (or perhaps because of) the fact that Crane was a Methodist minister's son, he attacked religiosity with fervor, and his early Bohemianism – and the rhetoric of rebellion that is part and parcel of it – flows out of his involvement in the New York Art Students' League beginning in 1888, when he first started writing verse. In the nihilistic poem 6, "God fashioned the ship of the world carefully," God is depicted as having built that vessel only to turn away from it "at fateful time": when he does so, it "slipped slyly" away, "forever rudderless,"

> Going ridiculous voyages,
> Making quaint progress,
> Turning as with serious purpose
> Before stupid winds.
> And there were many in the sky
> Who laughed at this thing.   (*SCP*, p. 5)

As Crane's speaker perceives, God leaves man to his own devices, totally uncaring and even derisive of man's mistaken sense that he has a purpose. The speaker's animus toward God becomes more palpable in poem 12, where he spits,

> Well, then, I hate Thee, unrighteous picture;
> Wicked image, I hate thee;

> So, strike with Thy vengeance
> The heads of those little men
> Who come blindly.
> It will be a brave thing.   (*SCP*, p. 8)

Crane's blasphemy continues unabated in later poems in the sequence, in which we encounter a "Blustering god" who is a "Liar!" and "Fat with rage" (*SCP*, pp. 33, 35, 31). In poem 32, "Two or three angels," his attack is not so much on God as it is on institutionalized religion. When the angels came to earth, he writes, "They saw a fat church," and the "Little black streams of people" going in to worship perplex the angels, who cannot figure out "why the people went thus, / And why they stayed so long within" (*SCP*, p. 19).

Throughout these poems, Crane posits that we inhabit a universe that we cannot hope to control, one that is at best indifferent to our fate. In poem 22 demonic nature rears its head, and man's chances for survival are uncertain:

> Once I saw the mountains angry,
> And ranged in battle-front.
> Against them stood a little man;
> Aye, he was no bigger than my finger.
> I laughed, and spoke to one near me,
> "Will he prevail?"   (*SCP*, p. 13)

In poem 37 we find another mountain ominously bearing down on insignificant man, with "the peaks assembled" against him (*SCP*, p. 21). In poem 66 the sky is seen as "a vast blue, / Echoless, ignorant"; there is no divinity, only emptiness. The very next poem, "God lay dead in Heaven," underlines that absence: angels' wings are "drip-dripping / With blood," and the earth a "groaning thing." Monsters, "livid with desire," appear as part of this apocalyptic landscape, and man is about to go down to "the jaws of the final beast" (*SCP*, p. 41). In the poems "Should the wide world roll away" and "If I should cast off this tattered coat," God also is figured as wholly absent or indifferent. In the final poem of *Black Riders*, the speaker implores God, but to no avail, and is forced to conclude, "Ah, there is no God!" at which "A swift hand, / A sword from the sky, / Smote him, / And he was dead" (*SCP*, p. 42). The speaker's faithlessness is promptly rewarded with God's wrath.

The closest Crane comes to tackling a specific social problem is in his poem on the plague of yellow journalism, which Gilman also addresses. As he writes in poem 11,

> In a lonely place,
> I encountered a sage

Who sat, all still,
Regarding a newspaper.
He accosted me:
"Sir, what is this?"
Then I saw that I was greater,
Aye, greater than this sage.
I answered him at once,
"Old, old man, it is the wisdom of the age."
The sage looked upon me with admiration.　　(*SCP*, p. 8)

These lines resonate with a poem in his next book that begins baldly "A newspaper is a collection of half-injustices," and goes on to state with irony that "A newspaper is a court / Where everyone is kindly and unfairly tried," that

A newspaper is a symbol;
It is fetless life's chronicle,
A collection of loud tales
Concentrating eternal stupidities,
That in remote ages lived unhaltered,
Roaming through a fenceless world.　　(*SCP*, p. 52)

For Crane, the newspaper is filled with sensational stories and thus has no legitimacy. It features a lurid and irresponsible journalism that is meant to make profit but has nothing to do with fact and contributes nothing to man's wisdom of the world.

In Crane's second and final volume of verse, *War Is Kind and Other Lines* (1899), there are twenty-seven untitled poems. Here he begins to use refrain and rhyme for the first time, but the poems remain short and often cryptic. The critical appraisal of the book was mixed. One reviewer insisted, as Howells had done, on treating the pieces as prose. Willa Cather, who said she found *Black Riders* "a casket of polished masterpieces when compared with *War Is Kind*," argued against its darkly militaristic stance. At least one critic found the irony of the title all too obvious, but that irony is a primary trope in the book, weaving through many of its lyrics, is not in doubt.

The first poem features the short-lined refrain: "Do not weep. / War is kind." It rings with irony in the context of surrounding scenes of horror and despair: "Because your father tumbled in the yellow trenches, / Raged at his breast, gulped and died." Under the pageantry of the "Swift, blazing flag of the regiment, / Eagle with crest of red and gold," we hear of "the virtue of slaughter," "the excellence of killing," against a corpse-strewn battlefield (*SCP*, p. 45). We are made to experience the romantic inflation of war and its discrepancy with the reality of death through the speaker's detached point of view. In a later poem, "To the Maiden," Crane articulates the notion that an individual's feelings about the universe depend largely on his or her point of view; to the maiden, "The sea was blue meadow, / Alive with little froth-people / Singing," but

> To the sailor, wrecked,
> The sea was dead grey walls
> Superlative in vacancy
> Upon which nevertheless at fateful time,
> Was written
> The grim hatred of nature.   (*SCP*, p. 47)

Which view is accurate? Which is the Truth? Both and neither. Through the maiden's joyful eyes, the world is joyful; to the shipwrecked sailor, who is fighting for his life, the world presents as malevolent. We ultimately are captive to our own circumstance. In another poem from *War Is Kind*, Crane returns to the cynical questioning of *Black Riders*:

> What?
> You define me God with these trinkets?
> Can my misery meal on an ordered walking
> Of surpliced numbskulls?
> And a fanfare of lights?
> Or even upon the measured pulpiting
> Of the familiar false and true?
> Is this God?
> Where, then, is hell?
> Show me some bastard mushroom
> Sprung from a pollution of blood.
> It is better.
>
> Where is god?   (*SCP*, p. 47)

As John Blair argues, this is not a poem that denies God or religion; rather, it rejects the customs of worship, or the institutions of religion, that intervene in our experience of God.[26]

We find a similar indictment in Crane's poem "A man adrift on a slim spar," which was not published until after his death. The sea surrounding this shipwrecked sailor is hostile, too, with "waves rearing lashy dark points" and "growl after growl of crest." The stark, three-word refrain, "God is cold," is repeated four times (*SCP*, p. 83). In critical commentary on the poem, there is some disagreement as to whether God is culpable, refusing to intervene to help man, or merely leaving man room to exercise his free will, making him accept responsibility for his own fate. Is the poem a damning of God, then, or simply an expression of the pathos of man against an indifferent nature? From the shipwrecked sailor's perspective, God is at fault, but his vision is not necessarily reliable.[27]

In another posthumously published poem, the question of man's ability to recognize good and evil is brought into question:

> The patent of a lord
> And the bangle of a bandit
> Make argument
> Which God solves
> Only after lighting more candles.　　　(*SCP*, p. 90)

Here Crane's Christian belief would seem intact, as we sense from these lines that God will enlighten us in death, and that we must have faith in God, not question divine will. Clearly, he is no longer simply denying God, as he does in his early verse. Crane also expresses his belief in God in "When a people reach the top of a hill" (uncollected in his lifetime) and "Each small gleam was a voice" (in *War Is Kind*):

> Small glowing pebbles
> Thrown on the dark plane of evening
> Sing good ballads of God
> And eternity, with soul's rest.　　　(*SCP*, p. 60)

Even so, man is not able necessarily to count on any succor in life but instead is consigned to uncertainty and seemingly random chance. Crane's pessimistic determinism is probably best and most succinctly exemplified by a squib in *War Is Kind*:

> A man said to the universe:
> "Sir I exist!"
> "However," replied the universe,
> "The fact has not created in me
> "A sense of obligation."　　　(*SCP*, p. 57)

This terse dialogue stands as the very sign and symbol of naturalism, serving as the definitive statement of man's total insignificance and nature's utter disregard.

Together, these three naturalist poets helped set the tone for a number of American poets to come, their legacy of rebellion in politics and art making an indelible cultural impression. Edgar Lee Masters's book of epitaphic poem-portraits, *Spoon River Anthology* (1915), represents a range of men and women who in life were trapped in a narrow social environment and whose fates were determined for them. Sarah N. Cleghorn, in poems such as "The Golf Links" and "The Survival of the Fittest," along with other largely forgotten leftist poets of the early twentieth century, also follows in the wake of the probing of social injustice in Gilman, Markham, and Crane. Upton Sinclair's *The Cry for Justice: An Anthology of the Literature of Social Protest*, first published in 1915, rounds up the work of many of these poets, from Morris Rosenfeld's "A Cry from the Ghetto" ("I do not ask, or know. I only toil") to Florence Wilkinson Evans's "The Flower Factory," a poem that describes the struggle of child laborers, who "will dream of cotton petals, endless crimson, suffocating, / Never of a wild rose thicket or the singing of a cricket, / But the ambulance will bellow through the wanness of their dreams, / And their tired lids will flutter with the street's hysteric screams."[28] In addition, Carl Sandburg, in poems like "Mamie" and "Muckers" in *Chicago Poems* (1916), paints a picture of the circumscribed lives of workers, trapped in dehumanizing economic and social conditions, even as he writes verse that suggests the ability of man to retain his essential dignity in the face of brute labor (as in the case of Markham's "The Man with the Hoe"). Theodore Dreiser, best known for his stirring naturalist novels, also wrote in that vein in his poetry. "The Factory," for instance, takes a fatalistic view of inequality, with the laborers' "deepest, darkest moods repressed"; when the speaker finds "one who dreams a dream," that dream quickly dissipates ("trembling, fleeing thoughts!") at the sound of the shoe factory whistle.[29] Other of Dreiser's poems, however, seem to suggest the opportunity of man to rise above his conditions through spiritual belief. In all of these naturalist poets, we sense the tension between the affirmation and denial of the self interlacing their political and cultural critiques.

Notes

1. Donald Pizer, *Realism and Naturalism in Nineteenth-Century American Literature* (1966; Carbondale: Southern Illinois University Press, 1984), p. 11. In his two-pronged understanding of naturalism, Pizer follows Charles C. Walcutt's *American Literary Naturalism: A Divided Stream* (1956).
2. Quoted in Cynthia J. Davis, *Charlotte Perkins Gilman: A Biography* (Stanford, Calif.: Stanford University Press, 2010), p. 130.
3. Horace Traubel, review of *In This Our World*, *Conservator* 9 (September 1898), p. 109.
4. Quoted in Charlotte Perkins Stetson [Gilman], *The Later Poetry of Charlotte Perkins Gilman*, ed. Denise D. Knight (Newark: University of Delaware Press, 1996), p. 28.

5. Charlotte Perkins Stetson [Gilman], *In This Our World* (1893; New York: Arno Press, 1974), pp. 7–8. This volume will be cited subsequently in the text as *ITOW*.

6. Stetson [Gilman], *The Later Poetry of Charlotte Perkins Gilman*, p. 73 (hereafter cited parenthetically in the text as *LP*).

7. Edwin Markham, *Poems of Edwin Markham*, ed. Charles L. Wallis (New York: Harper, 1950), pp. 30–31. This volume will be cited subsequently in the text as *P*.

8. Edwin Markham, *The Man with the Hoe* (New York: Doubleday and McClure, 1900), p. 23. This book comes with an extensive note by Markham on the circumstances surrounding the writing of the poem.

9. Cary Nelson, *Revolutionary Memory: Recovering the Poetry of the American Left* (New York: Routledge, 2001), p. 17.

10. William Dean Howells, *Selected Letters*, ed. George Warren Arms (Boston: Twayne, 1979), vol. 1, p. 202.

11. Quoted in Joseph J. Kwiat and Mary C. Turpie, *Studies in American Culture: Dominant Ideas and Images* (Minneapolis: University of Minnesota Press, 1960), p. 66.

12. Ambrose Bierce, *The Collected Works of Ambrose Bierce* (New York: Neale, 1911), vol. 10, pp. 141, 142, 143.

13. Quoted in Jesse Sidney Goldstein, "Edwin Markham, Ambrose Bierce, and 'The Man with the Hoe,'" *Modern Language Notes* 58:3 (March 1943), p. 174.

14. Edwin Markham, *The Man with the Hoe and Other Poems* (New York: Doubleday and McClure, 1899), p. 119. This volume will be cited subsequently in the text as *MHOP*.

15. Edwin Markham, *Lincoln and Other Poems* (New York: McClure, Phillips, 1901), p. 60.

16. Markham, *The Shoes of Happiness and Other Poems* (New York: Doubleday, 1919), p. 164.

17. *A Wreath for Edwin Markham: Tributes from the Poets of America on His Seventieth Birthday April 23, 1922* (Chicago: Bookfellows, 1922), p. 16.

18. Stephen Crane, *The University of Virginia Edition of the Works of Stephen Crane*, ed. Fredson Bowers (Charlottesville: University of Virginia Press, 1973), vol. 8, p. 759.

19. Quoted in John Berryman, *Stephen Crane* (New York: William Sloane, 1950), p. 141.

20. Crane, *The University of Virginia Edition of the Works of Stephen Crane*, vol. 8, pp. 599, 600, 591.

21. George Monteiro (ed.), *Stephen Crane: The Contemporary Reviews* (Cambridge: Cambridge University Press, 2009), p. 18.

22. Richard M. Weatherford (ed.), *Stephen Crane: The Critical Heritage* (London: Routledge, 1973 [1997]), p. 81.

23. Monteiro (ed.), *Stephen Crane*, p. 16.

24. Quoted in Berryman, *Stephen Crane*, p. 92.

25. Stephen Crane, *The University of Virginia Edition of the Works of Stephen Crane*, ed. Fredson Bowers (Charlottesville: University of Virginia Press, 1975), vol. 10, p. 3. This volume of the edition will be cited subsequently in the text as *SCP*.

26. John Blair, "The Posture of a Bohemian in the Poetry of Stephen Crane," *American Literature* 61 (1989), pp. 215–29.

27. In his study *The Poetry of Stephen Crane* (New York: Columbia University Press, 1957), Daniel Hoffman observes that "this poem is Crane's most complete denial of God – not only of the God of vengeance, but, worse, of the God of mercy" (p. 96); this view of an uncaring deity stands against Patrick K. Dooley's sense of Crane's construction of a "finite God, a quiet, caring father" in the poem – one who "sometimes does not intervene" because he is not omnipotent (Patrick K. Dooley, *The Pluralistic Philosophy of Stephen Crane* [Urbana: University of Illinois Press, 1993], p. 127).

28. Upton Sinclair (ed.), *The Cry for Justice: An Anthology of the Literature of Social Protest* (1915; New York: Lyle Stuart, 1963), pp. 43, 419. Markham's "The Man with the Hoe" and "The Man Under the Stone," Gilman's "Child Labor," and Crane's "Have you ever made a just man?" from *War Is Kind* also make appearances in this anthology.

29. Theodore Dreiser, *Moods, Philosophic and Emotional Cadenced and Declaimed* (New York: Simon and Schuster, 1935), pp. 234, 235.

PART III

★

FORMS OF MODERNISM,
1900–1950

Chapter 22

The Twentieth Century Begins

JOHN TIMBERMAN NEWCOMB

Soon after 1890, poetry in the United States entered a period of serious crisis in which commentators routinely doubted its continued survival, presuming it destined to become a pathetic orphan in modern cultural economies dominated by mass-marketed ephemera such as popular songs and dime novels. This decline in status had been precipitous. As late as 1875, poetry was without question the central genre of American literary culture. Its foremost living practitioners, the "Fireside Poets" Longfellow, Lowell, Emerson, Bryant, Holmes, and Whittier, were lionized as the nation's greatest creative spirits. But by the time the last member of this canon died in 1894, it was evident to most that they had few if any worthy successors. Measured against these "tremendous Absences," as William Dean Howells put it in 1899, contemporary poets amounted to little more than dilettantes and feeble imitators.[1] Meanwhile, the genteel custodians of the nation's elite literary institutions, deploring the unpoetic times, clung to the formal and tonal conventions of decades or even centuries earlier, insisting on portrayals of American life couched in nostalgic pastoral imagery – as if keeping urban-industrial modernity out of poetry could nullify its destabilizing force on the world. Poetry had come to function as an anticommodity, the genre most antithetical to modernized conditions that threatened to reduce all works of art to an endless parade of ephemeral commodities. These circumstances generated fervent idealization of past genius but virtually precluded any institutional or economic support for living writers. Anything that smacked of bureaucratic organization, career planning, or worldly reward was likely to be condemned as a corruption of poetry's pure nature. Given the burgeoning support for civic artistic institutions in the United States during these same years, this refusal to support poetry was not the sign of a populace with no money or goodwill to spare for the fine arts, but a psychic and ideological imperative, an expression of resistance to the commercializing and professionalizing forces transforming American culture.

By 1900, these circumstances had thrown American poetry's discursive infrastructure into desperate disarray. In contrast to the intensive institutional organization taking place in other cultural genres and professional disciplines, no one took sustained responsibility for the publicizing and reviewing of new books of verse, the identification of emerging authors and trends, or the preservation of periodical verses past their immediate moment of publication. No serial publications were devoted to the work of living American poets. No ongoing national contests or awards remunerated them. In the twelve years following the publication of Edmund Clarence Stedman's *American Anthology* in 1900 – years in which the overall number of books published in America exploded – not a single anthology of serious literary verse by living Americans appeared.[2] Support was especially lacking for younger or lesser-known writers, who had little hope of seeing a volume of their work unless they financed it themselves. The nascent discipline of academic literary scholarship, seeking institutional legitimacy from the quasi-scientific methods of historical philology, ignored the words of living writers. Not only was the writing of poetry not taught in institutional contexts, as architecture and painting and music now were, but an entrenched account of poetic genius insisted that it could not be taught at all, that poets were not made but born.

Far from professing regret at the plight of the contemporary poet, many turn-of-the-century commentators demanded that poets embrace poverty and neglect as character-building virtues, claiming that they could not realize their full potential *without* being unhappy and ignored. Thus an 1893 piece in *Poet-Lore* described the poet's lot as to "be silent and quietly ... wait in the calm assurance that any word with truth and beauty in it will always find its audience, 'fit though few,'"[3] while another in *The Forum* hoped that "there will never be a society for the prevention of cruelty to poets," because "the spectacle of a snug, self-sufficing existence can be no inspiration to him who yearns for greatness and for glory."[4] Those who complained were met by a rhetoric of canonical plenitude that held that all the great poems had been written already, that the productions of contemporary poets were merely so much waste paper. As late as February 1911, *The Dial*, not yet the champion of modernism it would become in the 1920s but still a vocal defender of the genteel tradition, insisted that American poets were provided not too little opportunity but too much, because it seemed that every speaker at ceremonial public occasions summoned forth execrable effusions in rhyming couplets or blank verse.[5] *The Dial* concluded by ridiculing the notion that these "Misguided Poets" should be supported or even encouraged, suggesting sardonically that most should be rewarded only for promising not to write anything more.[6] If, as *The Dial* opined in a similar editorial of 1914, "the tendency after one has waxed fat is to turn unto false gods,"[7] then conditions keeping poets on the edge of starvation could be seen as enhancements to the nation's cultural life.

The Dial's position turned on a familiar modern paradox in which improving levels of education and financial security in the overall population eventually generate so much artistic aspiration that the value of all works seems diminished – at least from elite perspectives. This same irony defined the situation of poetry in the dramatic expansion of the American book publishing industry after 1902. Annual compilations by Publishers' Weekly of the number of books published in America suggest that even during the worst of poetry's crisis between 1900 and 1910, more books of verse were being issued each year. And yet this increase in the sheer number of volumes clearly did not signal a more hospitable publishing climate for poetry. Indeed, in January 1911, surveying a year in which the number of volumes Publishers' Weekly classified as "poetry and drama" leaped to the highest level yet,[8] the editors were moved to complain that "pure literature perhaps never made a poorer showing than this year, poetry of promise being especially lacking."[9] During these years even the most respected and high-toned firms routinely demanded subventions for volumes of verse, a practice that likely became a self-fulfilling circuit in which publishers, having guaranteed themselves a break-even result or small profit from the author's contribution, felt little impetus to market volumes of verse energetically, which merely reinforced their assumption that poetry had no market potential. Just two years before she issued the first number of Poetry: A Magazine of Verse, Harriet Monroe had written to Houghton Mifflin about issuing a book of her verse, which they firmly declined on "any other basis than the commission one," citing "the present state of public inattention to anything in verse form," which they stated as "a condition, not a theory."[10] The complacent certainty of these phrasings suggests that publishers had thoroughly internalized poetry's economic unviability as an iron law of the modern literary marketplace.

These converging forces created an impasse in which contemporary poems were routinely derided as stale imitations of revered figures and forms of the past, yet nearly all attempts at innovation in form or subject matter were greeted with corrosive skepticism. The young American poets writing between 1890 and 1910, doubting that their work would be appreciated or even seen, produced self-reflexive verse poignantly marked by a sense of belatedness and dispossession. And yet this phase of anxiety and apparent futility made poetry in the United States modern. After 1912 the participants in the explosion of creative and institutional activity that they called the "New

Poetry" or the "New Verse" would rediscover an ebullient conviction in the vocation of poetry. But it was their "lost" predecessors of the previous two decades who first broke modern ground, articulating a poetics of skepticism toward received ideas and conventional expressive strategies, making such "modernist" qualities as ambiguity, marginality, and irony central to their aspirations as artists. Underneath the conventional surfaces and archaic imagery of much turn-of-the-century poetry, moments of violent rebellion simmer, anticipating the ferocious iconoclasm of Ezra Pound and other avant-gardists of the post-1912 renaissance. In "Les Bourgeois" (1902), for example, George Cabot Lodge (1873–1909) portrays the American middle classes as ruled by fear, weakness, and hypocritical desire, living lives no more significant than those of "gaudy flies that play and perish" in a single day, who are, "Once vanished, like a stupid dream / That never was." Lodge ends by urging his bourgeoisie to "Be something, good or bad! Be real!,"[11] embracing the modernist ideal of authenticity at any transgressive cost.

The continuity between the young American poets of the 1890s and the most prominent figures of the 1910s comes into clearer focus when we see both as comprising a single generation born between the end of the Civil War and the mid-1880s. Richard Hovey, Francis Brooks, William Vaughn Moody, Stephen Crane, George Cabot Lodge, Paul Laurence Dunbar, Ellen Glasgow, Trumbull Stickney, and Alice Dunbar-Nelson, born between 1864 and 1875, were essentially chronological contemporaries of Edgar Lee Masters, Amy Lowell, Robert Frost, Carl Sandburg, Vachel Lindsay, and Wallace Stevens, born between 1868 and 1879. Yet with just one exception, the first group, publishing actively in the 1890s and 1900s, had either died prematurely or given up writing verse by 1910. The second group published almost nothing of note before 1910, becoming significant forces in the New Poetry only in their late thirties and forties. Edwin Arlington Robinson (1869–1935) is the only poet to overlap substantially between the two groups. The middle-aged avant-gardists of the 1910s were more oriented toward the exploration of new forms than were their turn-of-the-century predecessors, but both groups exhibit qualities that mark them as modern in outlook: sardonic, sometimes furious antagonism toward traditions and predecessors; an affinity for irony, historical reference, and self-reflexivity; a persistent interest in placing poetry into formal and thematic dialogue with other literary genres and art forms; and a growing sense of engagement with the material conditions and psychological dynamics of twentieth-century urban experience.

The exclusion and purposelessness felt by younger American poets between 1890 and 1910 became a primary subject of their work, which often poignantly reveals how they had themselves internalized the prevailing philistine stereo-type of verse writers as idlers and parasites. "A Common Plaint" by Alice Dunbar-Nelson (1875–1935), written around 1900 but ironically not published until 1988, announces in its title her generation's shared sense of dispossession and futility. Worrying that she should be attempting some saleable potboiler in prose, "A tale of thrilling things," the speaker complains with some disgust "And here, I scribble rhymes" instead.[12] Yet despite her real need ("A check looms large into my sight"), she "cannot write" because she knows "No edi-tor will heed my plight, / I've proved that scores of times" (PD, p. 76). The speaker sticks with poetry not because it alone can express her feelings but because its derided status best symbolizes her belief that she will be rejected and ignored no matter what she writes: "I'd rather dream than work; / Then what's the use, let's take to-night / For luxury of shirk. / Those editors would send it back, / I cannot write, ah, well, alack" (PD, p. 76). Another verse of 1900, "Play Up, Piper!" by Josephine Preston Peabody (1874–1922), articulates the plight of the turn-of-the-century poet by asking sardonically why anyone still bothers to write verse in the absence of any purpose or reward: "But tell us of the wage, man, / You had for this hard day; / Play up, play up, dear Piper, / And tell us why you play!"[13] The demand "tell us why you play," implying that poetry's existence must now be continually justified even or especially by those who ought to value it most fervently, became the overriding concern of American verse during these two decades.

These concerns were often articulated through self-reflexive personae that positioned the modern poet as a vagabond wandering through landscapes that have lost all comprehensible markers of coherence, tradition, or ethics. The imagery used by Lizette Woodworth Reese (1856–1935) in 1909 to charac-terize her speaker-poet – "A wayfarer blown to and fro"[14] – echoed through a vast number of turn-of-the-century poems. Perhaps the most widely popular poets of the American 1890s were the "Vagabondians"– Richard Hovey (1864–1900) and the Canadian native Bliss Carman (1861–1929) – who took this persona as their entire identity and credo. The untitled envoi on the inner cover of their volume More Songs from Vagabondia (1896) evokes such predecessor works as Longfellow's Tales of a Wayside Inn (1860–1873), but the Vagabondians insist that now everyone – and particularly the modern poet – is "an alien and a vagabond," merely "a lodger for the night / In this old wayside inn of earth." Some, including the most important African American poet before 1910, Paul Laurence Dunbar (1872–1906), sought to emphasize the more sanguine aspects of the vagabond topos. In "Morning" (1905), for example, Dunbar portrays his "wanderer" as a "careless-free" figure who "fares right jauntily, / For towns and houses are, thinks he, / For scorning, for scorning."[15] But young turn-of-the-century poets found expressing scorn for the domestic and conventional much easier than articulating viable alternatives. The often aimless character of their rebellion was expressed most directly by William Vaughn Moody (1869–1910) in "Road-Hymn for the Start" (1901), which begins with a seemingly unequivocal repudiation of American genteel poetry – "Leave the early bells at chime, / Leave the kindled hearth to blaze"[16] – but then sets its wandering personae adrift on the road with no clear object or destination: "We have heard a voice cry 'Wander!' / That was all we heard it say."[17]

The trope of modern poet as wanderer or exile reached its ironic apogee in the work and lives of a group of ill-fated young writers, including Moody, Lodge, Robinson, Trumbull Stickney (1874–1904), Francis Brooks (1867–1898), Philip Henry Savage (1868–1899), and Hugh McCulloch (1869–1902), who matriculated at Harvard University between 1889 and 1895, most of them gravitating toward a charismatic young instructor, George Santayana (1863–1952, class of 1886). Although these "Harvard poets" seemed to have sufficient talent, ambition, and pedigree to claim leading roles in the American literary world, they were hampered in varying degrees not only by the inhospitable conditions in contemporary poetry described previously, but also by their own obsessive quest for some form of "spiritual idealism" intransigently opposed to the despoiling materialism of urban-industrial modernity. The opening image of one of Santayana's 1894 sonnets evokes this urgent desire for insular self-exile: "A wall, a wall around my garden rear, / And hedge me in from the disconsolate hills."[18] Idealizing the elite college as a quasi-monastic space, this enclosure serves to protect the speaker from the contaminating force of a modern mass man.[19] Such urgent need for self-quarantine against modernity tempted the Harvard poets to wander through fetishized fantasy versions of biblical, classical, or medieval cultures, while restiveness with the stifling canonical traditions of American poetry led them to agonistic identification with monumental mythic figures who struggle nobly against an insurmountable force: Prometheus (Stickney, Moody), Heracles (Lodge, McCulloch), Cain (Lodge), and Julian the Apostate (Stickney).

The most consistently successful poets who emerged from this "exile" culture of 1890s Harvard were Brooks, Moody, and Robinson, who in their stronger moments found that dispossession might lead not only to frustration and self-pity but to the freedom to explore new forms and subject matter. Their most fully modern poems discard overheated rhetoric and bookish nostalgia, working instead toward a poetics of close observation of the phenomenal, material, or social world. Francis Brooks died before he could publish even a second volume, but in the title and themes of *Margins* (1896), he addressed the exile of the contemporary poet, revealing a capacity for striking natural imagery and phenomenological complexity that went well beyond the conventions of that moment. "Titular," the work that best embodies his distinctive poetics, begins with an elegant mosaic of visual images, spatial relationships, and emotional impressions – "Margins of the mere and moor, / Margins of the sea by shell / Convoluted, many-hued, / Mosses manifold, defined; / Margins of the furrowed fields, / Daisy-decked, and aster-starred" – that portrays the poet's marginality as a liminal state offering access to "untraveled worlds."[20]

William Vaughn Moody, unlike Brooks and Robinson, was an insider in literary Harvard, remaining a lifelong friend of the New England Brahmins George Cabot Lodge and Trumbull Stickney. Yet he had grown up an orphan in small-town Indiana and in 1895 would relocate to the new University of Chicago, joining the socially progressive upper-middle-class milieu from which came the editorial staff and many of the financial guarantors for *Poetry: A Magazine of Verse*. Although Moody would write widely, from the obligatory verse closet drama on classical themes (*The Fire Bringer* [1904]) to a prose "Western" play that enjoyed notable success on Broadway and the London stage (*The Great Divide* [1906]), he found his strongest voice as a dissident social critic in two major poems condemning the American occupation of the Philippines, "Ode in a Time of Hesitation" and "On a Soldier Fallen in the Philippines."

The ode was first published in the *Atlantic Monthly* in May 1900 after months of debate concerning the authenticity and propriety of newspaper stories publishing clandestine letters from soldiers recounting atrocities by American forces on the Filipinos. It quickly became the best-known American poem on the Spanish-American War and its aftermath, quoted widely by anti-imperialist speakers, editors, and congressmen. The poem is cast as a fall into disillusioned understanding, from naive pride at America's stated commitment to Cuban freedom in 1898 to bitter awareness that the subsequent occupation of the Philippines was nothing but imperialist oppression, "pure conquest put to hire."[21] Moody finds an inspired symbolic locus for this critique: Augustus Saint-Gaudens's bronze bas-relief on the Boston Common honoring the Massachusetts Fifty-Fourth regiment, the first African American combat troops in the American military, and their young abolitionist commander, Colonel Robert Gould Shaw, who were devastated in a near-suicidal attack on a Confederate fort in 1863. As it would for Robert Lowell sixty years later in "For the Union Dead," the statue becomes for Moody a symbol of American idealism undermined by ongoing selfishness and injustice, the African

American soldiers representing the foreign non-Caucasian peoples who had sought America's aid toward their own self-rule but were instead subjected to its imperial ambitions. Measuring himself against a dissident poetic tradition personified by Whittier and Whitman, the speaker confesses he has "striven to evade" the moral imperative to create a "swift and angry stave" indicting the nation's drift into imperialist mendacity. Although he still shrinks from the task ("Too sorely heavy is the debt they lay / On me"), the "resolute ghosts" on the statue and in the news haunt his escapist desires as they reveal the nation's shame, and finally he gathers his moral indignation into forceful lines that evoke Whittier's abolitionist jeremiads: "For save we let the island men go free, / Those baffled and dislaureled ghosts / Will curse us from the lamentable coasts / Where walk the frustrate dead."[22] Just as in 1860, America's moral crucible in 1900 concerns the bondage or self-determination of a racial other.

"On a Soldier Fallen in the Philippines," written later the same year and published in *The Atlantic* in February 1901, converts another traditional poetic form, the eulogy, into an incisive analysis of the dishonorable realities underneath the idealistic rhetoric the United States had used to justify its takeover of the islands. As its dead native son is returned, the soldier's hometown barely pauses from the endless "roar" of commerce to honor him. Yet the fiction that his sacrifice was made for a worthy cause must be maintained even in death ("never a whispered hint but the fight he fought was good"), because now the soldier, embalmed in the trappings of honor, has become part of the "grists of trade," a multilayered phrase that suggests the booming demand for military commodities enriching American industry, the imperialist goal of opening vast new markets for American goods, and the operation of the war-propaganda mills of the new century, trading in human bodies as patriotic symbols. The poem ends with bitter prophecies of "evil days" ahead, when "the nation, robed in gloom," will rue its imperial misdeeds.[23] Moody's two great anti-imperialist poems offer a model of the modern poet as a dissident patriot, expressing love of country by decrying the damage done to its ideals by the ominous convergence of expansionist capitalism and nationalist ideologies. They are among the earliest manifestations of a defining tendency of twentieth-century American poetry, away from long-standing homiletic and patriotic traditions celebrating normative social values, and toward the elaboration of oppositional subject positions.

E. A. Robinson (as he preferred to be known), the product of a desperately unhappy middle-class family of Gardiner, Maine, could muster the funds for only a two-year sojourn as a "special student" at Harvard (1891–1892) and never felt entirely comfortable in that rarefied milieu, although exposure to its literary circles afforded early publishing opportunity and helped him to imagine himself as a serious poet. Typical of his Harvard roots, Robinson was mesmerized by medievalism throughout his career, as such voluminous narrative works as *Merlin* (1917), *Lancelot* (1920), and *Tristram* (1927) attest; but his comic-melancholy self-portrait "Miniver Cheevy" (1910), about a dreamer who "eyed a khaki suit with loathing" and "missed the medieval grace / Of iron clothing,"[24] shows he also maintained some sardonic distance from these potentially disabling obsessions. His saving grace as a poet was his deeply felt, if often morose, response to a specific sociomaterial milieu, the chronically declining villages of northern New England, to which his strongest poems returned well after he had permanently departed Maine for New York City in the late 1890s. Although he published nearly thirty books of poetry, the most admired of his works are the earlier Tilbury Town verses in *The Children of the Night* (1897) and *The Town Down the River* (1910), which, although composed in graceful metrical and rhyming forms, brought into American poetry the influence of realist fiction, particularly the strain of New England regionalism exemplified by Sarah Orne Jewett and Mary Wilkins Freeman. In lyrics such as "The Clerks" and "The House on the Hill" (both published in 1897), Robinson's vivid portrayals of the village's dusty surfaces, decaying structures, and ossified social relations anticipated the close observation and precise description that would be emphasized by the Imagists, and the investment in the local espoused by such modernists as William Carlos Williams.

Robinson's Tilbury Town poems also evoke the contemporary realist novel in their emphasis on complex characterization, at times anticipating Edgar Lee Masters's *Spoon River Anthology* (1915) by extending intersecting biographies across multiple poems. Balancing narrative and meditation, such character poems as "Reuben Bright" (1897), "Flammonde" (1915), and "Mr. Flood's Party" (1921) emphasize ironic reversals, lost connections, and unfulfilled hopes within a modernizing social milieu of eroding communitarian values. Although a lifelong bachelor, Robinson was also capable of great insight into the complexity of intimate relationships; in "Eros Turannos" (1914) he sketched with economy and empathy the shifting power dynamics and the underlying desperation shaping the lives of an unnamed married couple. Many Tilbury poems are narrated by a collective persona ("We") that articulates a choral perspective of the village on the particular characters and situations being portrayed, but these references often seem calculated to emphasize a modernist distance between the community's imperfect knowledge and the cryptic or unfathomable truths known only to the individuals involved: why the outwardly fortunate subject of "Richard Cory" (1897) was miserable enough to "put a bullet through his head,"[25] or how to measure the private visions of bliss experienced by the woman of "Eros Turannos" against her apparent marital misery.

At a moment when most poets, even those who yearned to be "modern," remained ensnared by the assumption that poetry gained in power and nobility as it increased in rhetorical intensity, Robinson rediscovered the great potential of understatement. Even where he comes closest to the declamatory lyric mode predominant in American verse before 1910, Robinson maintains a delicate tonal restraint, as in "Luke Havergal" (1897), a poem that suggests the influence of Yeats's "twilight" work of the 1890s as translated into a distinctive American vernacular, understated yet emotionally intense: "Go to the western gate, Luke Havergal, / There where the vines cling crimson on the wall, / And in the twilight wait for what will come. / The leaves will whisper there of her, and some, / Like flying words, will strike you as they fall; / But go, and if you listen she will call."[26] Despite its limited range of moods, Robinson's work demonstrated how traditional forms could be reoriented away from the conventions of exalted sentiment and poetic diction, toward a poetry expressive of the voices, hopes, and disappointments of everyday life. In that sense, much as Whitman can be considered the progenitor of modern free verse, Robinson stands behind all twentieth-century American formal poets, most immediately Robert Frost, but thereafter Millay, Ransom, Bishop, Jarrell, Wilbur, and Justice, among many others.

Although the climate of crisis and anxiety in American poetry would not ease substantially until 1912, some attempt to renew interest in contemporary verse can be detected from the middle of the first decade of the century. These early initiatives sought to assuage crippling absences of access to print, to time and money, to readers and peers, or to a viable national poetic tradition. In 1905 in the Boston *Evening Transcript*, a young African American poet and journalist, William Stanley Beaumont Braithwaite (1878–1962), began publishing summaries of the thousands of verses appearing in American periodicals. He continued these annually through 1912, and then from 1913 published an expanded version in book form as the *Anthology of Magazine Verse* (yearly through 1929, with occasional volumes thereafter). Although Braithwaite's own tastes ran to elevated tonalities and fairly traditional forms, his earnest effort to read and evaluate all the nation's magazine verse reasserted the premise that contemporary poems might be worth preserving as more than ephemeral page fillers. In late 1909 a group based in New York led by Jessie B. Rittenhouse and Edward J. Wheeler sought to organize poets into an institutional entity analogous to the quasi-official bodies recently created to support and regulate nearly every intellectual and artistic discipline. The result of their efforts, the Poetry Society of America, would be dominated by a group of pedestrian East Coast versifiers who would play little role in the New Verse movement, but its model of a national network of poets, emulated over the next twenty years by affiliated societies in nearly every state, helped to establish modern poetry's place in a professionalized disciplinary culture.

In early 1912, Braithwaite and Wheeler agreed to serve as judges in another institutional innovation, a contest and anthology featuring one poem each by one hundred poets. *The Lyric Year* failed to become an annual ongoing project as originally planned, yet the single volume published in late 1912 was still something of a landmark, the first significant contest for American poetry in decades, and the first anthology of serious contemporary verse since Stedman's volume of 1900. By the standards of a few years later, its verses show little evidence of stylistic experiment, but several poems portraying the material and experiential textures of urban-industrial modernity, including the first-prize winner, "Second Avenue" by Orrick Johns, anticipated the embrace of modern subject matter that would characterize the New Verse movement. *The Lyric Year* also gave early support to several younger writers who would become important in the New Verse, such as Witter Bynner, Sara Teasdale, Arthur Davison Ficke, Vachel Lindsay, Louis Untermeyer, James Oppenheim, and the sensational twenty-year-old Edna St. Vincent Millay, whose "Renascence" narrowly missed winning a prize, creating the controversy that launched her meteoric career and earned her a private scholarship to Vassar College.

Although these early initiatives have been largely obscured by the transformative events of the following decade, they were significant challenges to the dominant view of modern poets as preposterous dilettantes, and they were arguments for imagining them instead as productive twentieth-century artists. The editor of *The Lyric Year*, Ferdinand Earle, closed his preface by noting the staggering fact that ten thousand verses by almost two thousand writers had been submitted to the contest.[27] If nothing else, this enormous response belied complacent assumptions that poetry in America was silently withering away. Harriet Monroe (1860–1936), who began issuing her magazine *Poetry: A Magazine of Verse* in October, two months before *The Lyric Year* appeared, remarked that the contest showed "how eager is the hitherto unfriended American muse to seize any helping hand."[28] She must have been greatly encouraged by this confirmation of her belief that American poetry would grow in volume and quality if poets were offered some hope of recognition and financial support. As she prepared the first issues of *Poetry* in mid-1912, neither Monroe nor anyone else could have confidently predicted the boom times just ahead for poetry in the United States. Yet barely a year later, she had firmly established something American poets and poetry lovers had long assumed to be impossible: a stable and vigorous space that publicized virtually all the significant books of American and British verse, defended experiments in both versification and subject matter, and even insisted on paying poets for their work. *Poetry*'s immediate and lasting success vindicated the motivating premise of Monroe's work – that to immerse American poetry in the discursive practices and economies of the modern metropolis would not ruin but energize it. The astonishing period of rejuvenation that began in October 1912 indicates that the conditions of crisis described previously had decisively debilitated previous norms of poetic practice – that American verse in the old nineteenth-century sense was indeed dead.

After October 1912, American poetry's reversal of fortune was remarkably swift. By Christmas, *The Lyric Year* and the first three issues of *Poetry* were being perused on the shelves of bookstores and discussed in the pages of magazines. A poem in *Poetry*'s January 1913 issue, "General William Booth Enters into Heaven" by Vachel Lindsay, created a sensation like no American poem since Edwin Markham's "The Man with the Hoe" in 1899 and was quickly reprinted in multiple venues sensitive to popular demand, including the March issues of *Current Opinion* and *The Literary Digest*, and *The Independent* for March 13. Meanwhile, scandalous verses by Ezra Pound in early issues of *Poetry* were beginning to galvanize the rebellious energies of young American poets who had long chafed against the genteel-middlebrow American readership that Pound disparaged as a "mass of dolts" in "To Whistler, American."[29] By July 1913, *The Literary Digest* had begun to speak of "a boom in poetry," singling out the reception of Lindsay's "General Booth" and citing "periodicals devoted exclusively to poetry, an increasing popular demand for volumes of verse, more and more space given up to poems in the popular magazines, and an improvement in the economic conditions of the poets themselves."[30] By year's end, Braithwaite had stepped into the void left by the disappearance of *The Lyric Year* and published his first yearly *Anthology of Magazine Verse*, while Houghton Mifflin had brought out an anthology of American poetry since 1900 edited by Rittenhouse, *The Little Book of Modern Verse*, which sold beyond anyone's expectations.

The momentum accelerated further throughout 1914. In *The Literary Digest* for April, in a piece called "Poets Again Best Sellers," the president of Macmillan, George P. Brett, remarked on a notable "change in the public's attitude toward literature" that had produced such surprises as Rabindrinath Tagore's 1913 volume of verse *The Gardener*, whose U.S. sales of more than 100,000 had not been seen "since the heyday of Tennyson."[31] These changes in the market for poetry had come, according to Brett, "with disconcerting suddenness."[32] The following month, short free verse poems by the pseudonymous "Webster Ford" about the lives and deaths of small-town Midwesterners began appearing in the St. Louis magazine *Reedy's Mirror*, to immediate national acclaim. When these verses were collected into a Macmillan volume issued in April 1915, Edgar Lee Masters's *Spoon River Anthology* became that rarest of things, a poetry best seller. A new publishing economy for modern American poetry had begun to emerge that would have seemed an impossible dream to the morose commentators of just a decade earlier. Over the next five years, many volumes, including Lindsay's *The Congo and Other Poems* (1914), Amy Lowell's *Sword Blades and Poppy Seed* (1914), Robert Frost's *North of Boston* (1915), Carl Sandburg's *Chicago Poems* (1916), and Edna St. Vincent Millay's *Renascence and Other Poems* (1917) – all issued by prominent commercial presses without subvention – would find sizable markets and help to make their authors full-scale literary celebrities.

In its heyday between 1913 and 1919, the New Verse was published and publicized and attacked, defended, and wondered at across a wide range of sites, including mass-marketed general magazines (such as *Munsey's* and *The American Magazine*), monthlies and bimonthlies oriented toward the literary culture (*The Bookman*, *The Dial*, *Reedy's Mirror*, *The Forum*, and *The Independent*), certain academic journals (*Yale Review* and *Sewanee Review*), publications of cultural reportage (*Current Opinion* and *The Literary Digest*), urban-chic magazines (*The Smart Set* and *Vanity Fair*), and even the old "quality magazines" that had borne the standard of genteel culture (particularly *The Atlantic* and *The Century*). Important volumes of poems were issued by many different publishers, both younger firms such as Mitchell Kennerley, Alfred A. Knopf, Boni & Liveright, and B. W. Huebsch and old-guard houses such as Houghton Mifflin, Macmillan, Harper's, Henry Holt, and Scribner's. But above all, the creative energies of the New Verse were catalyzed in the "little magazine," a distinctively modern publishing format made possible by the convergence of falling production costs and emerging practices of niche marketing. A little magazine required minimal capital outlay and could be advertised and distributed relatively easily, if not widely, through distinctive subcultural venues such as the "advanced" literary bookstores then found in nearly every major American city. An individual publication might be read by very few people and might last for only a few numbers, but after 1912 the little magazine remained vigorous and stable as a field of literary production.

Poetry: A Magazine of Verse, published in Chicago by Harriet Monroe and her successors since 1912, was not only the first little magazine in the United States devoted to contemporary poetry but the first successful manifestation of a modern American avant-garde. Redefining poetic "genius" from some vague mystical afflatus into an exhilarating interchange between experimenting authors and open-minded audiences, *Poetry* challenged the authority of established cultural institutions and sponsored verse in experimental styles and modern subject matter. It was quickly joined by a scrappy group of other magazines featuring contemporary verse, all of them in different ways and proportions both socially engaged and aesthetically experimental. The most important of these included *The Masses* (1911–1917), a New York–based organ of revolutionary socialism that published more than four hundred verses in an eclectic mix of styles, mingling avant-garde ironies with the most urgent political issues of the day. Although its circulation was much greater than that of a little magazine, the NAACP-sponsored periodical *The Crisis* (1910–present) published verse by contemporary African American poets and began to play a major role in the Harlem Renaissance after Jessie Fauset became its literary editor in 1919. *The Little Review* (1914–1929), begun in Chicago by Margaret Anderson, moved to New York and finally to Paris, becoming a key impresario of European experimental modernism, lionizing the work of Eliot, Pound, and Joyce, among many others. Alfred Kreymborg's *Others* (1915–1919) passionately pursued new styles of free verse expressive of the unprecedented material and social landscapes of the twentieth-century city, achieving a canonical impact drastically disproportionate to its tiny circulation. The five issues of Robert Coady's *The Soil* (1917) marshaled verse by Wallace Stevens, Mina Loy, Maxwell Bodenheim, and others into an intriguing synthesis of experimental artsiness and open-hearted enthusiasm for modern mass culture. *The Seven Arts* (1916–1917), a magazine poised between avant-garde and mainstream, began by proposing a utopian synthesis of modernist aesthetics and American progressivism but after April 1917 undertook an all-consuming and courageous opposition to the nation's war policy, demonstrating how poetry could be used as a powerful vehicle of dissent in a time of world-historical crisis.

The variety of these initiatives and the common ground among them suggests the remarkable synergy between the New Poetry and the little magazine format. Some publications, notably *Poetry* and *Others*, took verse as their primary object of attention, while others set verse alongside material from a wide range of genres. Both approaches contributed to the dramatic rejuvenation of American poetry during the 1910s. The former challenged the long-standing and damaging assumption that publications founded on contemporary

American verse were economically impossible dreams, insisting on poetry's self-sufficient identity in the modern literary scene. The latter treated poetry not as some aestheticist backwater but as an integral part of their ambitious syntheses of modern culture and politics.

The New Verse movement has often been treated as a revolution in form, but of equal importance was its radical expansion of poetic subject matter. In the early 1910s, poets writing in a wide variety of forms rejected stifling genteel prohibitions against topical entanglement and delved enthusiastically into the distinctive technologies, spaces, social dynamics, and political problems of twentieth-century life. Finding few useful poetic predecessors in this effort, they drew instead from contemporary developments in fiction, painting, photography, cinema, advertising, and other forms of material culture. By embracing the modern and urban conditions that genteel orthodoxy had condemned as incorrigibly unpoetic, these writers showed that poetry could still speak not only to rarefied emotions and private fantasies but to the public, the profane, the political – to every aspect of twentieth-century experience. Dozens if not hundreds of Americans contributed to this new poetics of modern life – many of them now quite deserving of scholarly recovery – but the most immediate to the transformative impact of the New Verse were the poets sometimes called "popular modernists," including Masters, Lindsay, Lowell, Sandburg, Frost, and Millay. Although their work varied widely in tone, form, and theme, all worked to pare away genteel poeticisms from American verse. They drew on regional and colloquial diction, conversational syntax, and realist modes of verbal representation to generate a poetry of everyday experience that was widely accessible to nonspecialists yet still complex and nuanced enough to attract the admiration of connoisseurs and professionals.

The earliest of these poets to achieve this wide impact were two who used the places and voices of their downstate Illinois upbringing to create a modern verse vernacular of the American Midwest, Edgar Lee Masters (1868–1950) and Vachel Lindsay (1879–1931). Working as a lawyer in Chicago from the 1890s, Masters had self-published verse and plays extensively before 1912, but not until he went back imaginatively to the place of his origin – northwest of Springfield near the village of Lewistown – did he find an individual poetic voice. *Spoon River Anthology*, consisting of first-person commentaries by the residents of a small-town cemetery on their lives and times, evoked the classical epitaph at the level of the individual poem, while in overall structure resembling the *Greek Anthology*. This quasi-classical structure, combined with Masters's command of laconic midwestern accents, colloquial diction, and conversational free verse rhythms, created an effect of sensational iconoclasm for readers of 1914–1915, who devoured the poems in *Reedy's Mirror*, and then in the Macmillan volume, as they would such sardonic portrayals of bourgeois American life in fiction as Sinclair Lewis's *Main Street* a few years later.

Although each Spoon River poem is designed to create its own self-contained effect, Masters cross-references the stories of more than two hundred residents, allowing readers to build from the book a comprehensive picture of the history and character of a representative American town. Employing an ironic mode more cutting and iconoclastic than Robinson's, Masters empathizes with those nonconformists destroyed by the narrow-mindedness of small-town life, such as the title character of the poem "Margaret Fuller Slack," whose novelistic ambitions were thwarted by the old untenable choice forced on women: "celibacy, matrimony, or unchastity."[33] And he celebrates those few who withstood these pressures and lived rich lives, including the subject of the poem "Lucinda Matlock" (based on his own grandmother), who raised twelve children, all the while "shouting to the wooded hills, singing to the green valleys."[34] Although he published prolifically for three decades thereafter, Masters never again approached the popular or artistic success of *Spoon River Anthology*. Some of his later work, such as *The New Spoon River* (1924), was taken as transparently imitative of the original, while his more ambitious projects such as *The Domesday Book* (1920) and *The New World* (1937) tended to drift back toward the lumbering rhetorical modes of the pre-1910 era, suggesting that in his heart Masters had never fully accepted the formal and tonal breakthroughs of 1913–1916, despite having been one of their main instigators.

Younger than Masters by a decade, Vachel Lindsay, based mostly in his hometown of Springfield, also served an extensive apprenticeship of self-publishing during the 1900s, illustrating his rhapsodic verse with mystical-primitive artwork somewhat in the manner of Blake. After 1905 he converted his visionary aspirations for realizing the social value of poetry into action, repeatedly walking hundreds of miles across the countryside – the last time from Illinois to New Mexico – as a modern vagabond-troubadour, bartering his poems for food and lodging. Despite these strenuous efforts, Lindsay was still virtually unknown until he broke through to a new vernacular energy in "General William Booth Enters into Heaven," an idiosyncratic synthesis of the vigorous vocal rhythms of the Christian camp meeting with a social-democratic gospel celebrating the outcasts who populate a raucous Salvation Army parade into paradise led by its founding "General," the crusading British clergyman who had died in 1912. The poem's form is equally idiosyncratic, so closely following the strong regular rhythms and rhymes of the marching song that Lindsay even inserts instrumental cues and sound-effect words into section headings and margins, advising readers to sing the poem to the tune of the well-known spiritual "The Blood of the Lamb." As with Masters's use of the epitaph, these formal adaptations made the poem seem boldly modern to its early readers. Lindsay's emphasis on poetry as oral declamation and singing, complete with flailing gesticulations and sound effects belted out at full volume, became central tenets of a poetics he termed the "Higher Vaudeville."

Lindsay followed his sensational début with exuberant public recitations that supported several financially successful volumes, but after touring almost continuously for nearly a decade, he collapsed from exhaustion in early 1923. Thenceforth his life was shadowed by financial anxieties, a difficult marriage to a much younger woman, psychological breakdowns, and declining literary reputation, all of which contributed to his suicide in 1931. Unquestionably, Lindsay played an important role in the revival of American poetry's energies in the mid-1910s, but his extremely mannered style of writing and performance, once established, became a straitjacket preventing him from developing as an artist. Compared to the other popular modernists, all of them in their own ways notably thoughtful, even calculating, Lindsay suffered from severe deficiencies of intellect and self-possession that were exemplified by perhaps his most popular poem and certainly his most controversial, "The Congo" (1914), which (although it was probably intended to express sympathy and support for "the Negro") employed wholesale racial stereotyping in its portrayal of black races as irredeemably other, even savage. Although much of the poem's imagery and characterization resembles that used by other white poets and even some African American writers of the period, the contemporary critical consensus is that Lindsay failed more thoroughly than most to comprehend the pitfalls and responsibilities of representing other races in poetry.

The Bostonian Amy Lowell (1874–1925), the deeply unconventional daughter of a famous American family (and cousin to a revered poet of the previous century, James Russell Lowell), was prevented by inhibiting parental circumstances and adverse cultural conditions from establishing herself as a poet until she was nearly forty. But once embarked on a literary career, she made the most of the dozen years left to her, benefited greatly by the emotional and practical support she received from the actress Ada Dwyer Russell, her lover and domestic partner from 1914. Often unfairly resented by Ezra Pound and others for her inherited wealth, forceful personality, and flair for self-promotion, Lowell exerted herself as tirelessly as anyone on behalf of the New Verse. She published her own verse prolifically, reviewed the work of others generously, sponsored and edited the annual anthology *Some Imagist Poets* (1915–1917), gave popular and controversial public lectures on the

New Verse throughout the country, and produced the first large-scale critical study of the movement, *Tendencies in Modern American Poetry* (1917), which devoted well-informed chapters to the work of Robinson, Frost, Masters, and Sandburg.

In less than fifteen years, Lowell published more than six hundred poems in an ever-changing mix of styles, many of which remain to be assimilated. But the ongoing recovery of a substantial vein of intensely erotic lesbian love poems written to and about her muse Russell – many grouped together in the section entitled "Two Speak Together" in *Pictures of the Floating World* (1919) – has begun to challenge long-standing assumptions of Lowell as a decorative miniaturist. She often explored questions of female experience and self-expression in ways that make her work valuable to feminist critical approaches. "The Sisters" (1922), for example, addresses the relation of the modern individual talent to a tradition of female poetic artistry extending back to Sappho, while "The Captured Goddess" (1914) considers the ambivalent desire to be an artist in a culture that forcibly elevates women into inert art objects.

Lowell's stature as both an experimental modernist and an insightful social poet is also growing. She first established herself through association with the *imagiste* movement of Pound, H.D., and John Gould Fletcher, becoming its driving force as Pound sulked away toward Futurism and Vorticism. By 1914, in collaboration with Fletcher, she had developed an experimental mode called "polyphonic prose," which they saw as a modern form for epic poetry that would counterpoint the smaller scale of most Imagist verse. She used polyphonic prose to explore a variety of themes, including the impressionistic textures of the modern city in "Spring Day" and "Towns in Colour," both published in 1916. And in *Can Grande's Castle* (1918), she presented four long historical narratives that prefigure or allegorize aspects of twentieth-century life, most notably the challenging "Guns as Keys: And the Great Gate Swings," which examines Western imperial ambitions in Asia by portraying the forcible "opening" of Japan by Commodore Matthew Perry in 1853–1854. Although never expressing public doubt over the Allied cause in the Great War, Lowell also produced a thoughtful body of allegorical antiwar verse, including "Flotsam" (1916) and "Orange of Midsummer" (1917), both of which portray the forces drawing America into the war as seductive but destructive objects of erotic desire. Perhaps her best-known single poem is the allegorical narrative "Patterns" (1915), which condemns the rigid conventions of class and gender that lead a passionately loving aristocratic couple to follow their tragic duty – he to fall in battle "in Flanders," and she to mourn and wander through her mazelike gardens, forever encased in whalebone corsets that constrict and

contort the natural contours of her body.[35] Lowell departs from her characteristic allegorical mode for more direct statement in the moving free verse
lyric "September 1918" (1919), which presents a perfect late summer day of
apparent serenity but then darkens as the image of boys lying prone on the
ground, gathering bright red berries into a box, becomes a visual trace of the
torn and bloody male bodies on the western front, a turn that Lowell confirms
by shattering the poem's imagistic poise with the line "Some day there will
be no war." She hopes that on that day she will remember the peace of this
afternoon, but right now, even harmless play signifies only what the war has
destroyed, such that "I have time for nothing / But the endeavour to balance
myself / Upon a broken world."[36]

Like Lowell's, the verse of Carl Sandburg (1878–1967) offers a great deal more
variety and artistry than it has been given credit for. Another early discovery
of Harriet Monroe's, Sandburg advanced a forceful working-class perspective
on twentieth-century city life in well-wrought free verse cadences that spoke
to avant-garde poets and popular audiences alike. His earliest important publication was the sensational series Chicago Poems in *Poetry* for March 1914, the
first poem of which became a self-defining editorial statement for that proudly
Chicagoan magazine and supplied the city with two memorable nicknames,
"Hog Butcher for the World" and "City of the Big Shoulders."[37] Introducing
into American poetry a new note, perhaps more aggressively modern and
urban than anything that had preceded it, "Chicago" was condemned by genteel gatekeepers who found it an "impudent affront to the poetry-loving public," in the outraged words of *The Dial*.[38]

As Robinson and Masters built a modern poetics through an intense focus on
the American small town, Sandburg built his from the industrialized metropolis. The verse collected in three vital volumes, *Chicago Poems* (1916), *Cornhuskers*
(1918), and *Smoke and Steel* (1920), chronicles Chicago as a distinctive geographical, material, and social terrain using methods akin to those of the realist
photographer. This realist methodology is elaborated in "Halsted Street Car"
(1916), an empathetic portrayal of the spatially segregated working-class experience that begins by urging artists who seek to capture the modern city to
"Hang on a strap with me here / At seven o'clock in the morning / On a
Halsted Street car" and "Find for your pencils / A way to mark your memory"
of the visages of surrounding riders, who even at "cool daybreak" are "Tired
of wishes, / Empty of dreams."[39] The "way" that Sandburg's artist-poet seeks,
the method of portrayal, comes not through adherence to any particular style
but through a willingness to inhabit the same physical spaces as those he writes
about. In poem after poem from this period, Sandburg recorded the effects of

the industrial city on its populace as honestly and intensely as any American poet ever has. In "Clean Curtains" (1920), for example, he dramatizes the stifling effects of the densely built metropolis on class aspiration, describing how the new occupants of a house at the corner of Congress and Green streets (in the working-class district southwest of the downtown Loop) place pristine curtains like "white prayers" in their windows. But in this intersection the impulses toward hygiene and genteel domesticity are ill starred, because "One way was an oyster pail factory, one way they made candy, one way paper boxes, strawboard cartons," and all types of "wheels whirled dust" constantly on the windows (*CP*, pp. 167–68). The poet's reference to "the winds that circled at midnights and noon listening to no prayers" (*CP*, p. 168) portrays industrial capitalism as so all-encompassing that it may as well constitute the very air the working class breathes, threatening to blunt its self-ameliorating efforts. The white curtains last all of "five weeks or six" (*CP*, p. 168).

However bleak such city verses may sometimes seem, in their forceful articulation of the problems of working-class metropolitan life they serve an activist purpose for Sandburg, as necessary steps toward any sort of progressive change. Much like his idol and formal model Walt Whitman, Sandburg sustained a balance between gritty, often harshly critical realism and a fundamental optimism for the possibilities of modern life throughout a long, varied, and celebrated career as poet, journalist, folksinger, biographer (of Abraham Lincoln), and populist cultural icon. The literary reputation of all the popular modernist poets, Sandburg's in particular, was eroded, especially in the academy, by the ascendancy of New Criticism and high modernism from the 1930s. Even now, after the canonical expansion in American poetry of the past two decades, these poets are in the paradoxical position of being at once overly familiar in broad outline and inadequately known in the details of their poetic output. But no one did more during the 1910s to demonstrate that contemporary poetry was no longer merely a pastime for an idle evening or a filler for a half-empty magazine page, practiced and appreciated by leisured idlers detached from the lives of ordinary people.

In *Poetry* for April 1916, looking back on just three and a half years of her magazine, Harriet Monroe described a startling change in American poetry's fortunes, "as though some magician had waved his wand – presto, the beggar is robed in scarlet."[40] The change had been so abrupt that she fretted it was merely a fad, but despite the moderating reputation of some of the decade's poetic stars and the constricted economic and political climate after America's entry into the Great War, by 1920 poetry in America had been thoroughly rejuvenated. Poets were finding publishers for their work, making money from public readings, competing for a growing number of prizes, and assuming posts at periodicals, publishing companies, and universities. A sizable core of men and women fervently committed to contemporary verse presided over a group of stable institutional sites that would provide continuity and renewal for several subsequent generations of writers and readers. In one remarkable decade, the participants in the New Verse Movement had transformed a mawkish refuge for dilettantes into a vital, expressive form of twentieth-century life.

Notes

1. William Dean Howells, "The New Poetry," *North American Review* 168 (1899), p. 591.
2. John Timberman Newcomb, *How Did Poetry Survive? The Making of Modern American Verse* (Urbana: University of Illinois Press, 2012), pp. 264–65.
3. Francis B. Hornbrooke, "What Should Be the Poet's Attitude Toward His Critics?," *Poet-Lore* 5 (1893), p. 140.
4. Charles Leonard Moore, "The Future of Poetry," *Forum* 14 (1893), p. 776.
5. "Misguided Poets," *Dial* 50 (1911), pp. 113–14.
6. "Misguided Poets," p. 114.
7. "Poetry and Prosperity," *Dial* 57 (1914), p. 329.
8. John Tebbel, *A History of Book Publishing in the United States*, 4 vols. (New York: R. R. Bowker, 1975), vol. 2, p. 721.
9. Quoted in Tebbel, *History of Book Publishing*, vol. 2, p. 700.
10. Harriet Monroe, letter of March 8, 1910, Personal Papers, Regenstein Library, University of Chicago.
11. George Cabot Lodge, *Poems and Dramas*, 2 vols. (Boston: Houghton Mifflin, 1911), vol. 1, p. 134.
12. Alice Dunbar-Nelson, *The Works of Alice Dunbar-Nelson*, ed. Gloria T. Hull (Oxford: Oxford University Press, 1988), vol. 1, p. 75. Poems in this collection will be cited as *PD*.
13. Josephine Preston Peabody, *Fortune and Men's Eyes* (1900; Boston: Houghton Mifflin, 1911), p. 98.
14. Lizette Woodworth Reese, *A Wayside Lute* (Portland, Maine: Thomas Mosher, 1909), p. 44. Italics in original.
15. Paul Laurence Dunbar, *Lyrics of Sunshine and Shadow* (New York: Dodd, Mead, 1905), p. 51.
16. William Vaughn Moody, *Poems* (Boston: Houghton Mifflin, 1901), p. 9.
17. Moody, *Poems*, p. 10.
18. George Santayana, *Sonnets and Other Verses* (New York: Duffield, 1894), p. 17.
19. Santayana, *Sonnets*, p. 17.

20. Francis Brooks, *Margins and Other Poems* (Chicago: Searle & Gorton, 1896), pp. 5–6.

21. William Vaughn Moody, "An Ode in Time of Hesitation," *Atlantic Monthly* 85 (1900), p. 598.

22. Moody, "An Ode," p. 598.

23. William Vaughn Moody, "On a Soldier Fallen in the Philippines," *Atlantic Monthly* 87 (1901), p. 288.

24. Edwin Arlington Robinson, *The Town Down the River* (New York: Scribner's, 1910), pp. 97–98.

25. Edwin Arlington Robinson, *The Children of the Night* (1897; New York: Scribner's, 1905), p. 35.

26. Robinson, *The Children of the Night*, p. 22.

27. Ferdinand Earle (ed.), *The Lyric Year* (New York: Mitchell Kennerley, 1912), p. viii.

28. Harriet Monroe, review of *The Lyric Year*, ed. Ferdinand Earle, *Poetry* 1 (1913), p. 130.

29. Ezra Pound, "To Whistler, American," *Poetry* 1 (1912), p. 7.

30. "A Boom in Poetry," *Literary Digest*, July 5, 1913, p. 19.

31. "Poets Again 'Best Sellers,'" *Literary Digest*, April 25, 1914, p. 987.

32. "Poets Again 'Best Sellers,'" p. 987.

33. Edgar Lee Masters, *Spoon River Anthology* (1915; New York: Macmillan, 1944), p. 48.

34. Masters, *Spoon River Anthology*, p. 229.

35. Amy Lowell, *Complete Poetical Works* (Boston: Houghton Mifflin, 1955), p. 75.

36. Lowell, *Complete Poetical Works*, p. 75.

37. Carl Sandburg, "Chicago Poems," *Poetry* 3 (1914), p. 191.

38. "New Lamps for Old," *Dial* 56 (1914), p. 231.

39. Carl Sandburg, *Complete Poems* (New York: Harcourt Brace, 1950), p. 6. This volume will be cited subsequently in the text as *CP*.

40. Harriet Monroe, "Down East," *Poetry* 8 (1916), p. 85.

Chapter 23

Robert Frost and Tradition

SIOBHAN PHILLIPS

Robert Frost seems like a traditional poet. Robert Frost thus seems like a literary anomaly. Born three years after Marcel Proust, one before Thomas Mann, and two before F. T. Marinetti, Frost appears to stand apart from the modernist ranks that these and other writers constitute. Ezra Pound urged poets to "make it new," but Frost distrusted an age that "ran wild in the quest of new ways to be new."[1] While William Carlos Williams broke from iambic pentameter to explore free verse, Frost composed in metered lines and found new uses for the sonnet; while Wallace Stevens wrote philosophical tercets about a "supreme fiction," Frost wrote poetic narratives about witches and hired men; while T. S. Eliot moved to London to analyze urban malaise through verse that quotes great European literature, and Langston Hughes moved to Harlem to write of African American experience in poems adapting jazz and blues, Frost settled in New England to write about rural couples in lines using their own colloquialisms. While Eliot insisted that poetry of his time "must be *difficult*," Frost wrote verse that was lucid.[2]

That verse was widely read, moreover, refuting a modernist division between high art and mass culture. Many writers of the era spurned middlebrow success for the approval of little magazines and limited editions, but Frost courted fame on the widest scale and became by some measures the most well-known English-language poet of the twentieth century. He advertised himself as common rather than avant-garde, claiming that his "inspiration" came from the "wholesome life of the ordinary man," in a tactic that divided him from literary peers and estranged him from academic critics as it endeared him to a general readership.[3] Frost's choice was deliberate. "There is a kind of success called 'of esteem,'" he wrote in a letter early in his career, "and it butters no parsnips" (*FCP*, p. 667). It was also deliberately anachronistic. Frost took much from a nineteenth-century heritage of popular, often feminine or feminized poetry, as Karen L. Kilcup has shown, and he admired Francis Palgrave's *Golden Treasury*, a best-selling anthology of the late 1800s. His first volume, *A Boy's Will*, takes its title from Longfellow, and its opening work, called "Into My Own," presents a speaker who would be "only more sure of all I thought was true" (*FCP*, p. 15). In this and other instances, Frost seems to be content with the familiar rather than ambitious for the novel.

Oppositions of tradition and modernity crumble quickly, however, when considering Frost. The categories mixed in his own time: that debut volume looking back to Longfellow was promoted by Pound himself. The categories are even more intertwined now, when modernism has become a contradictory tradition and when Frost's Fireside forebears are no longer dismissed as merely sentimental.[4] Frost's verse may be featured on samplers and quoted in self-help columns, but that does not preclude its depth or reach. His traditional themes use common settings to debate humanity's place in a world of natural alterity – an inquiry as contemporary as other poets' questions. And his traditional forms use rhyme and meter to demonstrate the power in ordinary conversation – a strategy as daring as free verse imagism or bricolage quotation. Frost tests or estranges the customary as much as he endorses it. He aims to "suggest formulae," as he wrote in one early letter, "that almost but don't quite formulate" (*FCP*, p. 692). He adds that he would "like to be so subtle at this game as to seem to the casual person altogether obvious."

That subtlety makes Frost's work both inviting and tricky. In "Mending Wall," for example, the oft-cited formula that "good fences make good neighbors" comes as the questionable opinion of the speaker's own neighbor (*FCP*, pp. 39–40). The speaker is unconvinced, concluding that

> "Before I built a wall I'd ask to know,
> What I was walling in or walling out,
> And to whom I was like to give offense.
> Something there is that doesn't love a wall,
> That wants it down." I could say "Elves" to him,
> But it's not elves exactly, and I'd rather
> He said it for himself. I see him there
> Bringing a stone grasped firmly by the top
> In each hand, like an old-stone savage armed.
> He moves in darkness as it seems to me,
> Not of the woods only and the shade of trees.
> He will not go behind his father's saying,
> And he likes having thought of it so well
> He says again, "Good fences make good neighbors."

(FCP, p. 40)

An enduring human practice of boundary building, passed from father to son, meets an even more intractable natural force that upsets stability: the opposition touches on the authority of divisions, meanings of property, and persistence of monuments or covenants. Yet the poem does not settle these questions with a simple refutation of the neighbor's maxim. "Mending Wall" manifests a practice of wisdom getting as much as the substance of wisdom gotten, and the neighbor must say "for himself" any new truth. Practice, in turn, keeps any new truth perpetually indefinite. After all, the speaker cannot "exactly" formulate "for himself" what brings down a wall, and despite his questions, he may be as much invested in fences as his neighbor (it is he who initiates repair).[5] He seems less interested in refuting his neighbor's beliefs than in engaging them.

Frost's poem aspires to similar engagement with the reader through its conversational register. This tone is vital to Frost, even in works that do not dramatize people talking to each other. He believed that good writing captures the "sentence-sounds" in ordinary speech (FCP, p. 675). One could perceive this "sound of sense," Frost explains in letters, when listening to "voices behind a door that cuts off the words," and the recognizable music, "gathered by the ear from the vernacular," can be "brought into books" by skillful writers (FCP, pp. 664, 675). The skillful poet, in particular, will set colloquial rhythms against the standard patterns of metered verse, "breaking the sounds of sense with all their irregularity of accent across the regular beat of the metre" (FCP, p. 665). The resulting "strained relation" is Frost's signature delight: "I like to drag and break the intonation across the metre as waves first comb and then break stumbling on the shingle," he writes (FCP, p. 680). One can see the result in "Mending Wall," in which phrases like "Spring is the mischief in me," or "In each hand, like an old-stone savage armed," or "He is all pine and I am apple orchard" each find a different pattern of stressed syllables and different affect of common speech within lines that are steadily, poetically iambic. Frost's versification uses consistency to reveal inconsistency – the wall, perhaps, to reveal a force that tumbles it.

This strategy is central to Frost's work in general, proving the concept of tradition to be useful to analysis of that work even after one recognizes his innovations. From "Into My Own" forward, Frost emphasizes self-definition, yet he finds that the strongest individual freedom comes through an individual's management of constriction. Frost's best critics describe versions of this animating tension, as Frank Lentricchia, Richard Poirier, Katherine Kearns, Mark Richardson, Elisa New, and others chart the varying interdependence of what Frost called "formity and conformity" (FCP, p. 735).[6] Trusting in this vital combination, Frost would neither discard nor submit to any established rule, whether that rule be natural, artistic, or cultural. Nor would he endorse the catalytic, impersonal approach of Eliot's "Tradition and the Individual Talent," although Frost's practice is closer to Eliot's than might at first appear.[7] To Frost, traditions and conventions are useful means for defining oneself as an independent voice and a viable will, allowing demonstrations of "prowess" in a world that could easily make human "achievement" seem negligible (*FCP*, p. 890). When Frost dismisses free verse as "tennis with the net down," therefore, the analogy is not flippant (*FCP*, pp. 735, 809). Only a game with rules lets players prove their skill.

The outcome is more than a tennis score, just as "Mending Wall" is more than "just another kind of outdoor game." As "Two Tramps in Mud Time" explains with unfortunate didacticism, Frost aims for a state in which "work is play for mortal stakes" (*FCP*, p. 252). These stakes acknowledge a nihilism present in Frost, as in others of his era: "The background is hugeness and confusion shading away from where we stand into black and utter chaos," he writes in his "Letter to *The Amherst Student*" (*FCP*, p. 740). Frost goes on to say, however, that humans can resist confusion through creation, because the world "admits," even "calls for," the "making of form." "When in doubt there is always form for us to go on with," he writes. Rather than Eliot's dubiously reassuring fragments, then, Frost confidently cites "any small man-made figure of order and concentration." A poem is one such figure. In "Desert Places," for example, when a snowy night threatens to subsume the "absent-spirited" speaker into a state of "nothing to express," expression of this very "nothing" resists the waste lands around him (*FCP*, p. 269). "Empty spaces" cannot overwhelm him, he concludes: "I have it in me so much nearer home, / To scare myself with my own desert places." A now-perilous game of frightening oneself effects the self-assertion manifest in the poem's formal achievement, and a final, feminine rhyme of spaces/places can claim what was, in the title phrase, an external reality – now definitively, if just as terrifyingly, "my own." Writerly craft domesticates chaos without denying its power.

This craft is detailed in Frost's great prose meditations, "Education by Poetry," "The Figure a Poem Makes," and "The Constant Symbol." Here he explains that "every poem is an epitome of the great predicament; a figure of the will braving alien entanglements," and here he describes how each poem creates a "momentary stay against confusion" (*FCP*, pp. 787, 777). The best and bravest stay, he believes, comes through the literary habit of saying one thing in terms of another, confronting material with "a gathering metaphor to throw it into shape and order" (*FCP*, p. 724). To Frost, therefore, all poetry is "simply made of metaphor" (*FCP*, p. 786). Indeed, all thinking is metaphoric, its product less units of perception than "feats of association" (*FCP*, p. 892). Cognition does not apprehend the world so much as work on and in it, Frost believes, through the effortful links by which one turns the alien and unknown into the significant and owned. This process, as Frost describes it, not only blurs the divide between poetry and other language use; it also conflates the lessons of verse with the lessons of general meaning-making.[8] "The person who gets close enough to poetry," Frost asserts, "is going to know more about the word *belief* than anybody else knows, even in religion nowadays" (*FCP*, p. 726). Frost's feats of metaphor are also acts of faith.

Frost's modernist skepticism cautions this faith when he explains that metaphors are forever "break[ing] down" (*FCP*, p. 723). Achieved meaning is a brief reprieve in an ongoing process, and "the figure a poem makes" is a moving figure: "It begins in delight and ends in wisdom," Frost describes, just like "love"; "it begins in delight, it inclines to the impulse, it assumes direction with the first line laid down, it runs a course of lucky events, and ends in a clarification of life" (*FCP*, p. 777). The contingency of the lucky clarification, however, is not entirely regrettable. It makes the achieved poem a new experience for each reader: "Read it a hundred times: it will forever keep its freshness as a metal keeps its fragrance" (*FCP*, p. 778). Moreover, contingency assigns ongoing work to each writer.[9] The activity is as important as any result, for a poet who believes that "there is nothing more composing than composition," and Frost's relish for this process nourished his sense of pleasure in his occupation (*FCP*, p. 808). It also bolstered his belief that pleasurable, composing composition could be "everybody's sanity," because "no forms are more engrossing, gratifying, comforting, staying than those lesser ones that we throw off … our individual enterprise"; these include "a basket, a letter, a garden, a room, an idea, a picture, a poem" (*FCP*, p. 740). Frost practiced poetry as one instance of a general and continual human endeavor.[10]

This conviction offers an explanation of his poems' appeal that does not rely on their simplicity. It may suggest, too, why Frost persisted in his vocation through years of little encouragement: he was a popular writer who did not publish a book until he was nearly forty. He was also a New England figure born in California, a rural sage who grew up in a city, a campus eminence who had little patience with his own schooling, and a farmer-poet who mostly failed at farming. Frost lived in San Francisco for the first eleven years of his life, during which time his father tried to work as a reporter and politician before dying of tuberculosis. Nearly penniless, Frost's mother then took him and his sister to Lawrence, Massachusetts, where Frost's grandparents lived, and where

Frost attended school regularly for the first time. By the time he graduated, he shared valedictory honors with Elinor White, to whom he would soon be engaged, but he left college after less than a term at Dartmouth, troubled over Elinor's refusal to marry immediately. Depression even drove him to a possibly suicidal sojourn in Virginia's Dismal Swamp. He returned north and worked while waiting for his bride. He also wrote poems and saw his first professional publications. After marrying, he entered Harvard, although he did not finish a degree there either, leaving after two years to take up poultry farming with his wife and two children. When the eldest died from cholera in 1900, the tragedy plunged both parents into depression, and Frost soon moved again, to a farm in Derry that his grandfather bought. It was perhaps the most stable home he would ever have, and there he wrote much of the poetry in his first two books as he also farmed desultorily and taught school. By 1912, however, discouraged at his lack of literary success, he decided to move to England and write full time while he lived on his grandfather's legacy. He settled with his family in Buckinghamshire, later in Gloucestershire, where he enjoyed the company of other "Dymock poets" and a deep friendship with Edward Thomas.

In London, Frost also met Pound, among other writers, and found a publisher. When Frost returned to America in 1915, his first two volumes had found an American publisher, too, and favorable reviews of *North of Boston* were already swelling the poet's reputation. Frost's most important book, this collection assembles the narratives of New England life that define his aesthetic and includes the masterpieces "Mending Wall," "Home Burial," "A Servant to Servants," "After Apple-Picking," and "The Wood-Pile." His next book, *Mountain Interval*, appeared in 1916, its poems more varied in type but almost as uniformly high in quality. From this point on, Frost lived on several farms in New Hampshire and Vermont while reading, teaching, and serving as poet in residence at different institutions, among them Amherst College, the University of Michigan, Dartmouth, and the Bread Loaf School of English. Collections called *New Hampshire*, *West-Running Brook*, and *A Further Range* followed in the 1920s and 1930s, during which time Frost's sales, honors, and salaries steadily increased. When he lectured at Harvard in 1936, more than a thousand attended. Yet even as Frost managed this successful career, he came to rue the effects of his public life on his family relationships, which presented a series of tragedies in later life. His daughter Marjorie died of puerperal fever in 1934, his wife from heart failure in 1938, and his son Carol by suicide in 1940. In 1947, his daughter Irma entered a mental hospital. Frost continued to write, however, and *A Witness Tree*, published in 1942, is perhaps his best collection since *Mountain Interval*. It won the last of Frost's record-setting four Pulitzer

Prizes. Frost also continued to speak and teach, maintaining his schedule and stature unremittingly until he died in 1963.

During his last decades, Frost often used that stature to press his conservative, nationalist political views: after a trip to the Soviet Union in 1962, for example, Frost invented a comment by Khrushchev that described Americans as "too liberal to fight" (*FCP*, p. 954). A similar pugilism is evident even in his famous appearance at the Kennedy inauguration. His poem for the occasion hails a "golden age of poetry and power" (*FCP*, p. 437). Prevented by the sun from reading this piece, Frost instead recited "The Gift Outright," a better, older poem that nonetheless suggests its own troubling politics; it chronicles America's manifest destiny without concern for the imperialist presuppositions of expansion – or for the effect on native peoples (*FCP*, p. 316). In the context of politics, Frost's focus on form-making prowess can overlook the self-questioning doubt and interpersonal awareness so vital to his earlier works. These are present in the two-sided fence tending in "Mending Wall," for example, or the two-sided debate in "The Death of the Hired Man," both of which Frost later describes as political (*FCP*, p. 885).[11] The strengths of these and other poems explain why Frost's work continues to sway writers and readers whose views and backgrounds differ greatly from his.

To understand those strengths further, however, and to appreciate Frost's ongoing presence in various poetic traditions, it may be helpful to look more closely at some of the traditions that influenced Frost, among them a poetic lineage of classical and romantic pastoralism and a philosophical heritage of Darwinism, Transcendentalism, and pragmatism. Frost's engagement with these strains deepens the thoughts and feelings in seemingly straightforward work.

"Mowing," an important poem from Frost's first collection, makes the question of work central when it sets the labor of farming against the dreams of literature:

> There was never a sound beside the wood but one,
> And that was my long scythe whispering to the ground.
> What was it it whispered? I knew not well myself;
> Perhaps it was something about the heat of the sun,
> Something, perhaps, about the lack of sound –
> And that was why it whispered and did not speak.
> It was no dream of the gift of idle hours,
> Or easy gold at the hand of fay or elf:
> Anything more than the truth would have seemed too weak
> To the earnest love that laid the swale in rows,

Not without feeble-pointed spikes of flowers
(Pale orchises), and scared a bright green snake.
The fact is the sweetest dream that labor knows.
My long scythe whispered and left the hay to make.

(FCP, p. 26)

Frost was deeply read in English-language poetry and knew classical literature in the original; his uniquely rhymed sonnet recalls a Virgilian georgic tradition manifest also in Marvell's and Wordsworth's verse. "Mowing" invokes this strain, it seems, to challenge a common comparison of poetic and agricultural production: the scythe's whispering is not a dreamy lyricism. The strength of actual efforts forbids the weakness of literary fancy. Yet the speaker of "Mowing" knows the value of what he excludes, which is "anything more" and not "anything less" than the truth, and he finds, perhaps, a way to include it. When the "fact" of actuality is professed to be the "sweetest dream that labor knows," the formula blends truth and untruth even as it cautions the latter. Poetry must yield to labor, but that labor might become poetry; in the very refusal of imaginative indulgence, empiricism includes the sweetness of the unreal. It also includes the sweetness of love, as mowing's connotations of mortality, emphasized by the Shakespearean "heat of the sun," accommodate hints of sexuality, emphasized by "orchises" and "snake." The creativity promised in the poem's conclusion seems literary, corporeal, and agricultural at once, its "making" manifest in careful, generative rows of verse as well as earnest, harvesting rows of the scythe. Frost emphasizes that earnestness with a final two lines, each containing one declarative sentence. Through their respect for a factual dream, these lines join the poet-farmer's labor to more natural endeavors, so that he can leave the hay, and perhaps his poem, to finish without him.

This poem could thus counter worries that a twentieth-century worker lacks the inspiration of poetic predecessors in pastoral, georgic, and Romantic traditions. At times, Frost implies that the source of verse may be as obscure as the spring on top of "The Mountain," which refigures Parnassus as a Vermont peak, or as dry as "Hyla Brook," which is "run out of song and speed" by June of each year (FCP, pp. 47–48, 115–16).[12] When Frost describes the brook's "faded paper sheet / Of dead leaves stuck together by the heat," the desiccated page of once-flowing music suggests a withered lyricism (FCP, p. 116). Frost's response holds to the truth that "Mowing" champions, using that facticity to continue nature poetry even when one is uncertain about the inherent poetry of nature.[13] The speaker of "Hyla Brook," for example, turns away from the literary dreaming of "brooks taken otherwise in song" to accept the actuality of the brook before him, and he concludes that "we love the things we love for what they are." As in "Mowing," though, regard for fact includes some admission of fancy. Loving the water in its real absence depends on maintaining the water as a mental presence: "Hyla Brook" is a "brook to none but who remember long."[14] The "song" of this poem could therefore compare to the song of "The Oven Bird," in which the titular artist-figure continues his task through a dry season (*FCP*, p. 116). "The question that he frames in all but words," Frost concludes here, "is what to make of a diminished thing." Like the scythe that knows in working not to poeticize, the oven bird "knows in singing not to sing," and his unaesthetic artistry creates something from his very doubts about creation.

What to make of diminishment is one lesson that Frostian singers learn. Another is what to make of indifference. "The Need of Being Versed in Country Things," for example, rebukes a desire for nature's empathy: it describes a burned homestead, then cites the worldly processes that continue in spite of human sorrow (*FCP*, p. 223). For the birds, Frost's speaker reminds himself, "there was really nothing sad." The poem concludes, however, with the ambiguous assertion that "One had to be versed in country things / Not to believe the phoebes wept." Although rural truths rightly refuse to anthropomorphize, and although the word "versed" locates such truths in poems like this one, Frost uses a carefully managed rhyme scheme and contradictory concluding statement to end with "the phoebes wept" – lingering, then, on the chance or hope of sympathy.[15] "The Most of It" is more severe, perhaps, toward the hopes of a protagonist who is frustrated by "mocking" natural echoes to his cries (*FCP*, p. 307). The scene recalls a famous passage from Wordsworth's *Prelude* in which a boy who mimics the calls of owls begins a happy "concourse" that ends in profound communion.[16] In Frost's poem, the speaker wants similar evidence of "counter-love, original response." But his human voice is followed by "nothing." Or rather, it is followed by something uncertain: the poem describes a potential "embodiment" in a "great buck" that emerges, swims across a lake, and crashes through brush out of sight. "And that was all," Frost ends, leaving readers to wonder what "all," or even "the most of it," was. Among other things, the ambiguity seems to rebuke the protagonist's initial wish, and Frost may have written this poem in an estranging third person to challenge that demand. Nature does not conform to human desires, even to human desires that nature be original. Nature instead schools human desires, refusing direct response to provide uncertain opportunity.

The deepest human desire, perhaps, is the yearning for meaning, and the most fervently hoped-for reply a revelation of significance. One possible obstruction of significance, in Frost's time, was Darwinian evolution. Frost's scientific knowledge surpassed that of most American writers in his era or since: during high school, he studied botany and astronomy with his friend Carl Burrell; in college, he took geology and read Darwin, Lyell, Spencer, and Huxley, among others; in a talk, he cited *Scientific American* as one of two "great magazines" in his country.[17] Frost's interest made him acutely conscious of what his post-Darwinian situation could present: a world governed by survival of the fittest, such that deathly competition directs universal action, and a world barren of benevolent purpose, such that unthinking processes drive strictly material change. The sonnet "Design" suggests the magnitude of possible horror at these conditions through its description of a miniature scene (*FCP*, p. 275). As the poem's speaker watches a spider and its prey on a "heal-all" flower, his matter-of-fact diction reports a fatal morning routine, in which the white color of the players ironically emphasizes their dark implications. The poem finishes with a traditional couplet rendered untraditional by its subversion of any summative point: "What but design of darkness to appall? – / If design govern in a thing so small." Natural malevolence appalls the viewer, perhaps turning him as pale as the play before him. But even malevolence may be evacuated from nature's blank, because the universe may admit no intentions at all.[18] Any teleology one could discover, moreover, may register on so large a scale as to be immaterial to the insects or human beings who are equally small in evolutionary terms.[19]

These conclusions make belief difficult. But Frost would not always endorse pure scientism, nor would he always employ the playfully grim tone of "Design." The speaker of "For Once, Then, Something," a quasi-sonnet of beautifully lilting hendecasyllabics, refuses to resign himself to meaninglessness (*FCP*, p. 208). Instead, he makes a habit of peering into well water, continually seeking a revelation that may never come. Although often stymied, he reports, by the obstruction of his own surface reflection, he did *"once"* catch sight of a "white" hint in the depths. This alluring glint of ambiguity revises the appalling pallor of "Design." It may be no more than a "pebble of quartz," another of those quizzical facts that frustrate quests for intelligibility. Yet it might also be "Truth," the capitalized beginning of a poetic line suggesting more than ordinary veracity. For Frost, this chance is belief enough, as he relies on the possibility of "something" not quite compassed by strictly material explanations.[20] In the underappreciated "A Star in a Stone-Boat," for example, Frost recalls the rocks in "Mending Wall" and even predicts the pebble in "For Once, Then, Something" when he imagines finding a fallen star among the boulders of a fence (*FCP*, pp. 162–64). This meteorite is the "one thing palpable besides the soul / To penetrate the air in which we roll," he writes. Frost's playfully audacious comparison of souls, stars, and stones would discern heavenly ethereality and human spirituality in the most seemingly inert of earthly substances. The "worldly nature" of facts is also otherworldly.

That combination emphasizes Frost's dualism.[21] Frost criticized those Platonists who describe anything earthly as a deficient imitation of heavenly excellence, and in his gorgeous poem "To Earthward," Frost welcomes the flaws of a mundane situation (*FCP*, pp. 209–10). But Frost's refusal of ultimate perfection is not a refusal of any purpose, and his refusal of pure idealism is not an endorsement of sheer materialism. He would perceive and maintain a dynamic balance between mind and world, idea and substance. The "height" of metaphoric formalism, to Frost, is "the attempt to say matter in terms of spirit and spirit in terms of matter" (*FCP*, pp. 723–24). His respect for both terms fed his enthusiasm for Henri Bergson, for example, whose notion of a "creative evolution" served Frost as an important counterargument to any mechanical model of Darwinian development. His respect for both terms also directed Frost's response to an American philosophical tradition. Raised by a Swedenborgian mother who told him that he had clairvoyant powers, Frost appreciated the Transcendental impulses in Thoreau's and Emerson's writings; both come to mystical convictions through material evidence.[22] The poet of "Mowing" would have agreed with Thoreau that a "true account of the actual is the rarest poetry" or with Emerson that "a fact is true poetry, and the most beautiful of fables."[23] Emerson's "Nature," however, holds that facts reveal a "real higher law," and Frost stops short of the quasi-religious monism inherent in Emerson's conviction.[24] A "melancholy dualism is the only soundness," Frost cautions (*FCP*, p. 860). Frost's work is less concerned with an Emersonian "Over-Soul," which gathers the material world into unifying spirit, than with his own singular soul, which confronts the material world with spirited individualism.

Frost's poetic thought, then, is even more indebted to the work of Emerson's great philosophical heir, William James, whose books Frost read with care and admiration. Like Frost, James would face a Darwinian universe without yielding to its potential effacements, and, like Frost, James responds to inherited dualisms by refusing to choose between the terms. With regard to the crucial dualism of free will versus intransigent reality, both would preserve mental independence through its accommodation of effective facts rather than through its transcendence of an unknowable world.[25] Frost shows his faith in that shaping particularly through his Jamesian emphasis on personal choice: in the strange, underread poem called "The Trial by Existence," for example, one's earthly life is the result of an individual decision that no human is allowed to remember, and in the lucid, overexposed poem called "The Road Not Taken," one's earthly path is the result of an individual decision that one will someday recall (*FCP*, pp. 28–30, 103).[26] If this latter poem seems to argue for nonconformity, it also troubles the ease of that moral. Frost's speaker notes that his two routes are "really about the same" and that he wants to take both. The ruling between them may be as much arbitrary or willful as valiant or principled.[27] The mere fact of choice seems to make the difference in the final lines, as the speaker foresees a retrospective significance to his progress. By claiming responsibility for what has been or what must be, humans turn universal purposelessness into unique purpose and natural inevitability into conscious freedom.

The result can be a fluency evident in "Birches," which presents a dualistic game of swinging between earth and heaven (*FCP*, pp. 117–18).[28] Frost's speaker wistfully imagines some boy practicing the skill: "So was I once myself a swinger of birches," he writes. "And so I dream of going back to be." He adds that he would

> ... like to get away from earth awhile
> And then come back to it and begin over.
> May no fate willfully misunderstand me
> And half grant what I wish and snatch me away
> Not to return. Earth's the right place for love:
> I don't know where it's likely to go better.
> I'd like to go by climbing a birch tree,
> And climb black branches up a snow-white trunk
> *Toward* heaven, till the tree could bear no more,
> But dipped its top and set me down again.
> That would be good both going and coming back.
> One could do worse than be a swinger of birches.

The boy of this poem, swinging on "his father's trees," replaces the commandments of divine paternalism with the lessons of a created world. These teach a vital balance, an escape from earthly "considerations" that never leaves those concerns altogether and an aspiration "*toward* heaven" that prompts the very force setting one down again. Such paradoxically driven alternation is both means and end; to "subdue" trees finally, or to be subdued by them, is to prevent the fun of further swinging.[29] Frost would inhabit a practice that sees good in, and performs well at, both "going and coming back." His game therefore revises the Dantean ascent to paradise that allusion to a "pathless wood" suggests. Yet in the "poise" of Frost's process is the grace of his own religious feeling, which discovers transcendence through the superfluities of immanent phenomena – through a water-glass meniscus, for example. Frost's earth may be sufficiently heavenly merely by allowing this kind of sensing.

"Birches," however, prizes earth for its allowance of "love," and this emphasis distinguishes Frost's thought from James's as it deepens the implications of Frost's many poems about couples. To Frost, eros is the most important manifestation of a spiritualized materialism. "To Earthward," for example, considers the pain of love specifically, and "Bond and Free" describes a divide between earthly "love" and ethereal "thought" before deciding that mundane affection has all the "beauty" of transcendent cognition (*FCP*, pp. 116–17). In other poems, love discovers this beauty through a creativity akin to worldly generation: as Poirier emphasizes, romantic union can set the Frost speaker in a harmonious affinity with material process.[30] The sonnet "Putting in the Seed," for example, describes a couple whose "springtime passion for the earth" makes agricultural work a fellowship with the soil as well as each other (*FCP*, p. 120). A similar accord pervades "Two Look at Two," in which paired confidence counters the solitary despair of "The Most of It": the hero of the latter poem lacks "someone else," and the "great buck" embodiment could even serve to question a masculine arrogance that keeps "the universe alone," but the couple of "Two Look at Two" come upon a doe and buck for a moment of serene, if still ambiguous, interaction (*FCP*, pp. 211–12). When they conclude that "this *must* be all," the phrase seems far from "that was all" in "The Most of It." The "Two" feel "as if the earth in one unlooked-for favor / Had made them certain earth returned their love." To be part of a pair is to be at home in a universe of pairings.

Yet Frost's homes and marriages are not always communions with natural creativity. They are often defenses against natural chaos, as "Storm Fear," among other works, demonstrates (*FCP*, p. 19). Homes and marriages, moreover, can corrode from within through that very resistance.[31] In Frost's work, domestic neurosis presents the underside of domestic generativity, hardening households into deathly stasis rather than sustaining them through vital making. In the quietly terrifying "A Servant to Servants," for example, a wife tells two visitors how desperately tired she is of "doing / Things over and over that just won't stay done," although her husband merely responds that "the best way out is always through" (*FCP*, pp. 65–69). Their grim symbiosis of determination and compliance shows human work devolved from high-stakes play into futile compulsion. The imagination denied by that automatism then sours into insanity: when the servant describes her threatening tendency to "have ... fancies," she compares herself to a mad uncle who was locked up for years in the family attic. He raved about lost love, the servant recalls, and "just when he was at the height,"

> Father and mother married, and mother came,
> A bride, to help take care of such a creature,
> And accommodate her young life to his.
> That was what marrying father meant to her.

The "meaning" underlines the impossible choices of this poem: a dangerous wildness or a drudging domesticity, the madness of thwarted emotion or the monotony of unfeeling marriage. The two terms turn into each other, and while the servant is "glad to get away" from the space of her uncle's imprisonment, the space of her own relationship seems to foster the lunacy she escaped. Home becomes asylum, and security becomes insanity, its hysteria staved off incompletely only by a routine "over and over."

Frost's dualism opposes an abstract, masculine control and a material, feminine disorder.[32] But (as Katherine Kearns has shown) Frost seems most interested in showing the difficult relation of these opposed qualities within a person or couple.[33] Relations are never more difficult than in the marriage of "Home Burial," probably Frost's greatest poem, which reports the conversation of a husband and wife whose child has recently died (*FCP*, pp. 55–58). With its reference to a humble interment, the title also comes to imply the destruction of home that results, even the destruction implicit in homemaking itself, by which a "momentary stay against confusion" could become the permanent stay of death. Creativity and mortality mingle in any earthly work. Frost suggests this as early as "Mowing," and when the husband of "Home Burial" notices that his family graveyard is "not so much larger than a bedroom," his offhand comparison presses a pervasive link of generation and destruction. To the pair of "Home Burial," however, destruction seems final and divisive, because the two differ on how to respond to loss: the wife wishes to perpetuate mourning, the husband to finish it. The difference is most stark, perhaps, when she remembers his comment just after digging his child's grave:

> "I can repeat the very words you were saying.
> 'Three foggy mornings and one rainy day
> Will rot the best birch fence a man can build.'
> Think of it, talk like that at such a time!
> What had how long it takes a birch to rot
> To do with what was in the darkened parlor.
> You *couldn't* care! ..."

She finishes with a refusal to abandon grief and go "back to life," a position that seems almost neurotically melancholic. Yet the husband, by contrast, can seem almost unfeelingly sane; he follows the above speech, for example, with "There, you have said it all and you feel better." With this, his insensitivity and her intractability not only forbid better feelings but also preclude an answer to the wife's question about the relationship of rotting wood and human death. As failed love hinders connections between humanity and nature, the collapse also seems to render futile all one's endeavors, from building a fence to conceiving a child.

"Home Burial" shows this futility through ineffectual speech: as many critics have noticed, the poem emphasizes the difficulty of the talk it records. Indeed the husband seems correct when he states that his "words are nearly always an offense." His wife tells him flatly that he doesn't "know how to speak," and the husband is even driven to propose "some arrangement / By which I'd bind myself to keep hands off / Anything special you're a-mind to name." When he adds, however, that this would make married life impossible, he diagnoses an underlying problem. His marriage may be failing less by its disagreements than by its refusals to let disagreements converse: although the wife of "Home Burial" scorns the notion that "talk is all," her poet knows talk to be quite a bit. The emphasis goes further even than Frost's affection for "sentence sounds," although "Home Burial" provides many instances of spoken and poetic rhythms in productive relation: the husband's "you must tell me, dear," in which metrical arrangement points out an awkward endearment, or the wife's "Don't, don't, don't, don't," in which a contrast of bifurcated iambic foot and single repeated imperative manifests intransigence. Frost's focus on verbal exchange also reveals his general preference for double-minded "repartee" over single-minded argument.[34] This predilection links his thought to some findings of ordinary-language philosophy, as Walter Jost and Christopher Benfey show, and especially to the work of Stanley Cavell, who uses elements of Austin's and Wittgenstein's theories to describe a salutary ordinariness that is dependent on conversation and manifest in marriage.[35] The beneficial matrimonial talk of "West-Running Brook," for example, contrasts with that of "Home Burial" when it allows a couple to "go by contraries" harmoniously (*FCP*, pp. 236–38). The pair thereby mimics the forward-and-backward progress of a stream, human relationship again securing an accord with worldly movements – and securing a resistance, as well, to deathly flux. When the wife ends "West-Running Brook" by predicting that "today will be the day of what we both said," she institutes an anniversary that may foresee renewal in saying itself.

The question of this renewal marks one final philosophical theme that pervades Frost's poetry and deepens particularly his poems of marriage. When considering time, his work often sympathizes with the "backward motion" of the west-running brook or the "standing still" of "The Master Speed," another matrimonial poem that opposes temporal advance (*FCP*, p. 273). In "Spring Pools," for example, a speaker cautions oncoming foliage not to "blot out" the reflective waters of an early season, perhaps worried that progression will erase the reflections of human consciousness as well (*FCP*, p. 224). Yet Frost also acknowledges the appeal of oncoming insentience: in "Stopping by Woods on a Snowy Evening," for example, the speaker nearly yields to the "lovely" darkness of winter (*FCP*, p. 207). "After Apple-Picking" extends Frost's ambivalence through an equally hypnotic poem of human and earthly falls; here, a speaker tired of harvesting looks ahead to a "winter sleep" that seems at once his day's rest, year's hibernation, and life's end (*FCP*, pp. 70–71). In lines and rhymes both unexpected and regular, dreams and facts mix like the metaphoricity or dualism of the poem's "two-pointed ladder," as the protagonist considers loads of apples and accumulations of experience. The working dreams of "Mowing," however, become troubled recollections of labor in "After Apple-Picking," and when the speaker holds up a "pane of glass" that he "skimmed this morning from the drinking trough / And held against the world of hoary grass," he invokes Corinthians while questioning the biblical implication of a more beneficent vision to come. Our "afters," even our "afterlife," may be human rather than heavenly in their remembrance of flawed effort, and the poem foresees their foreboding inevitability.

Yet retrospection need not always be final. As Frost himself asserts in his high school graduation speech, the "after-thought of one action is the forethought of the next" (*FCP*, p. 637). The formulation suggests new beginnings, and Bonnie Costello has shown that Frost opposes "evolutionary" advance not just with a "lyric time" of arrest or resistance but also with a "pastoral time" of cycles and continuance.[36] In "The Onset," for example, a speaker refuses the despair of a snowy landscape with his knowledge that spring will return (*FCP*, p. 209). Similar assurance imbues the matrimonial "day" concluding "West-Running Brook" and the coupled "round" of "In the Home Stretch" (*FCP*, p. 114). The ongoing life of natural-human efforts, moreover, seems especially potent in another poem uniting marriage, voice, time, and possible falls: the great sonnet "Never Again Would Birds' Song Be the Same." Here an Adam-like figure lovingly affirms his wife's "influence on birds" when he remembers how Eve's "call[s]" and laughs added an "oversound" to the songs of Eden (*FCP*, p. 308). Mixed with indigenous voicings, Eve's tones form an enduring poetry, its permanence guaranteed by an evolving artistry of voices "crossed" with each other. Such combination lets human making join a natural making that extends agency beyond temporal limits. "He would declare and could himself believe," the poem begins, and it ends by rounding on itself to declare and believe the title: "Never again would birds' song be the same. / And to do that to birds was why she came."

Not the least important function of these "woulds" is their perpetual rewriting of Eve's purpose, as she who once effected a descent into sin and death instead perpetuates an ascent into communion and creativity. Trust in ongoing time seems to forbid any definite fall. Frost scorned those writers, in fact, who saw their eras as postlapsarian: "You will often hear it said that the age of the world we live in is particularly bad," he writes in his "Letter to *The Amherst Student*," whereas he believes that "it will always be about equally hard to save your soul" (*FCP*, p. 739). It will always be equally possible, too, through the form making dramatized by his poems.

Frost's insistence on the historical uniformity of soul saving, however, tends toward an apolitical disregard for particular souls' situations, and his insistence on the individual duty of salvation supports a conservative aversion to collective remedies.[37] These leanings are evident in Frost's poetry, especially his later poetry. "Provide, Provide," for example, argues against New Deal policies that in his view vitiated free will and personal responsibility. The poem describes a typical fall from fame to obscurity and urges one's own preventive steps: "Better to go down dignified," it ends, "With boughten friendship at your side / Than none at all. Provide, provide!" (*FCP*, p. 280) The voice is triumphant in its very bitterness. Yet while its harsh individualism recommends self-help, the poem does not reject the difficult need for others' regard, even if it is "boughten." Viewed this way, "Provide, Provide" suggests a politics more general and subtle than any response to Depression-era legislation.[38] Marit J. MacArthur uncovers a related ambiguity in "The Gift Outright," citing its wary assessment of both American citizens, "such as we were," and the American land, "such as she was."[39] Written originally during the Depression, this poem may celebrate Kennedy's inauguration by suspecting its historical premises.

Ambivalence also marks Frost's most influential public role, as teacher and speaker in American universities. Frost's talks on campus were a new genre, a partly spontaneous mixture of linked thoughts and poetic recitation, and criticism has only begun to mine these productions as both a source for Frost's theories on various topics and a manifestation of his ideas on conversation and performance. Frost's teaching methods were even more unconventional, favoring education "by presence" rather than formal instruction, and criticism has only begun to describe his complicated example for the increasing number of writers on campus during the post–World War II era.[40] It is clear, however, that Frost's stints as resident poet demonstrate the inescapable tensions of institutionalizing a creativity that is valued precisely for its anti-institutional proclivities.[41] Frost's case shows that if the problem cannot be solved, it can nonetheless be productive. His distrust of academia seemed only to augment his popularity as an academic. Resistance to professional definition helped to consolidate his fame.

That fame, meanwhile, shaped the academic and critical reception of Frost's work, letting early reviewers scorn or ignore what they found to be its easy and affirmative tendencies. Malcolm Cowley, for example, wrote two 1944 essays that explain "the case against Mr. Frost" by disparaging the Frost partisans who want an "optimistic, uncritical" national literature.[42] Exceptions to this attitude, however, were notable and catalytic. In essays of 1947 and 1952, Randall Jarrell describes the "other Frost," a great modernist writer whose wisdom is misrepresented by anthology pieces and conservative bromides.[43] A later tribute by Lionel Trilling similarly dismantles the popular image with descriptions of a "terrifying poet."[44] This darker side of Frost gained detail from Lawrance Thompson's three-volume biography, published from 1966 to 1976; although Frost had appointed him, Thompson grew more and more disillusioned during research, and the resulting chronicle emphasizes Frost's personal failings. It also draws further attention to the contradictions of his poetry, and later, better biographies by William H. Pritchard and Jay Parini present a more balanced assessment without erasing the troubling and troubled elements of Frost's life and work – adding to a literary criticism that has increasingly considered Frost's depth.[45]

Twentieth-century American poetry, meanwhile, shows Frost's continuing and various importance to other writers. Poets as different as Gwendolyn Brooks, Robert Lowell, and Muriel Rukeyser wrote poems about him, and a panoply of others' work bears signs of his influence. For many of the generation born in or just before the 1920s, Frost's verse modeled forms and themes that other modernists pass by, and verse by William Meredith, Howard Nemerov, James Wright, and Richard Wilbur, among others, capitalizes on the example. Several noteworthy poets of the 1920s generation, moreover, extend Frost's poetics with work less obviously similar in style: with poems like "The Yucca Moth," A. R. Ammons reverses the terrifying implications of "Design" into a celebration of humanity's involvement in nature.[46] In poems like "Clearing the Title," James Merrill's deployment of conversation and cliché recalls Frost's "sentence sounds" while also rewriting his marriage poems in descriptions of homosexual partnership.[47] In his pivotal *Three Poems*, John Ashbery uses the paradigmatic situation of Frost's "The Road Not Taken" to question the capacity for choice in a game of postmodern uncertainty.[48] The work of younger American poets continues to recall Frost's legacy in lines that may diverge from his forms and diction. With the "opposite / directions" of "Salmon," for example, Jorie Graham turns the "contraries" of "West-Running Brook" into a meditation on human sexuality and natural process during an era of ecological endangerment.[49] With "Interpretation of a Poem by Frost," Thylias Moss revisits the familiar scene of "Stopping by Woods on a Snowy Evening" with a "young black girl" as protagonist.[50] In "Winter Fear" and other works, Kay Ryan extends Frost's themes into reticent meditations on the paradoxes of common sayings. Ryan's selected poems, *The Best of It*, even nods to Frost in its half-resigned, half-assertive title.[51]

Unexpected affiliations map Frost's presence in world literature, too, which seems increasingly important to his legacy as American literary criticism looks beyond established borders. Although Frost was a regional poet with nationalist politics, his poems have proven useful to writers far from New England settings and distanced from American values, as appreciations by Derek Walcott and Joseph Brodsky demonstrate.[52] These and other poets locate Frost's self-questioning of conservative assumptions in the conversing, contradictory voices of his verse.[53] The Irish poets Tom Paulin, Seamus Heaney, and Paul Muldoon have all taken Frost as an important forebear in their negotiations of key paradoxes – a globally relevant regionalism, a written speech, and a responsible freedom.[54] In addition, both Heaney and Muldoon use Frost's poetic "game" to mitigate the potential burden of a social role or literary heritage, as Heaney's treatment of "Directive" suggests.[55]

"Directive" also shows, once more, the possibilities in Frost's sense of tradition. Frost's last great poem, this work was written in the 1940s yet seems to refuse its moment. Its speaker leads the reader on a walk toward a deserted farm at the location of two former villages (*FCP*, p. 341). The traveler must make himself "at home" in this abandoned scene, passing the site of children's make-believe and the spot of a vanished house "in earnest," before finally coming to a "lofty and original" brook. There, one can fill a cup that has been hidden in a nearby tree. "Drink and be whole again beyond confusion," the poem concludes. "Directive" thus inscribes a characteristic temporal pattern, as the narrative charts a "backward motion" of resistance that becomes a forward quest for renewal, as well as a characteristic tonal register, as Frost's version of *The Waste Land* transforms the literary-religious allusions of its modernist predicament into familiar and factual terms.[56] Moving from the complications of a world that is "now too much for us," a plain-speaking voice provides purifying waters from a genuine stream and a holy "grail" from the objects of childhood play. Yet the ambiguities within wholeness remain: this comforting escort "only has at heart your getting lost," this consolation is under a spell "so the wrong ones can't find it," and this salvation comes from a broken cup at a no-longer-inhabited imaginary home. Attenuation emphasizes the provisionality and uncertainty of Frost's place "beyond confusion." The challenges of achieving a "momentary stay" are as perennial as the need for such assurance, and throughout, Frost's poetry is more powerful for including both.

Notes

1. Robert Frost, *Collected Poems, Prose, & Plays*, ed. Richard Poirier and Mark Richardson (New York: Library of America, 1995), p. 741. This collection will be cited subsequently in the text as *FCP*.

2. T. S. Eliot, *Selected Prose of T. S. Eliot*, ed. Frank Kermode (New York: Houghton, 1975), p. 65.

3. Edward Connery Lathem (ed.), *Interviews with Robert Frost* (New York: Holt, Rinehart, 1966), p. 47; Frank Lentricchia, *Modernist Quartet* (Cambridge: Cambridge University Press, 1994), pp. 106–07; Mark Richardson, *The Ordeal of Robert Frost: The Poet and His Poetics* (Urbana: University of Illinois Press, 1997), pp. 19–22.

4. Karen L. Kilcup, *Robert Frost and Feminine Literary Tradition* (Ann Arbor: University of Michigan Press, 1998), pp. 22, 243; John Timberman Newcomb, *How Did Poetry Survive?* (Urbana: University of Illinois Press, 2012), p. 5.

5. Frank Lentricchia, *Robert Frost: Modern Poetics and the Landscapes of Self* (Durham, N.C.: Duke University Press, 1975), pp. 105–06; Richard Poirier, *Robert Frost: The Work of Knowing* (Stanford, Calif.: Stanford University Press, 1990), pp. 104–05.

6. Lentricchia, *Robert Frost*, p. xii; Poirier, *Robert Frost*, pp. 52–53, 97, 258; Katherine Kearns, *Robert Frost and a Poetics of Appetite* (Cambridge: Cambridge University Press, 1994), pp. 1–2; Richardson, *The Ordeal of Robert Frost*, pp. 2–15, 67, 174–80, 213–22; Elisa New, *The Line's Eye: Poetic Experience, American Sight* (Cambridge, Mass.: Harvard University Press, 1998), pp. 24–25.

7. Richardson, *The Ordeal of Robert Frost*, pp. 186–87.

8. Reuben Brower, *The Poetry of Robert Frost: Constellations of Attention* (Oxford: Oxford University Press, 1963), p. 242; Lentricchia, *Robert Frost*, p. 128; Guy Rotella, *Reading and Writing Nature: The Poetry of Robert Frost, Wallace Stevens, Marianne Moore, and Elizabeth Bishop* (Boston: Northeastern University Press, 1991), p. 62.

9. Poirier, *Robert Frost*, p. 258.

10. Poirier, *Robert Frost*, p. 24.

11. Tyler Hoffman, *Robert Frost and the Politics of Poetry* (Hanover, N.H.: Middlebury College Press, 2001), p. 76.

12. Helen Bacon, "Frost and the Ancient Muses," in Robert Faggen (ed.), *The Cambridge Companion to Robert Frost* (Cambridge: Cambridge University Press, 2001), pp. 75–100, 80–81.

13. Rotella, *Reading and Writing Nature*, pp. 71–72.

14. On "Hyla Brook," see especially Brower, *Poetry of Robert Frost*, p. 83; Judith Oster, *Toward Robert Frost: The Reader and the Poet* (Athens: University of Georgia Press, 1991), p. 174; Rotella, *Reading and Writing Nature*, pp. 76–78.

15. William H. Pritchard, *Frost: A Literary Life Reconsidered* (New York: Oxford University Press, 1984), p. 168.

16. William Wordsworth, *The Prelude, 1799, 1805, 1850*, ed. Jonathan Wordsworth, M. H. Abrams, and Stephen Gill (New York: Norton, 1979), p. 172.

17. Reginald Cook, *Robert Frost: A Living Voice* (Amherst: University of Massachusetts Press, 1974), p. 69. Robert Faggen and Robert Bernard Hass have detailed the consequences of this avidity: see Robert Faggen, *Robert Frost and the Challenge of Darwin* (Ann Arbor: University of Michigan Press, 1997); Robert Bernard Hass, *Going by Contraries: Robert Frost's Conflict with Science* (Charlottesville: University Press of Virginia, 2002).

18. Brower, *Poetry of Robert Frost*, p. 107.

19. Faggen, *Robert Frost and the Challenge of Darwin*, pp. 85–88; Randall Jarrell, *Poetry and the Age* (1953; Gainesville: University Press of Florida, 2001), pp. 46–49.

20. Hass, *Going by Contraries*, p. 20.

21. On Frost's dualism, see especially Peter J. Stanlis, *Robert Frost: The Poet as Philosopher* (Wilmington, Del.: ISI Books, 2007).

22. Jay Parini, *Robert Frost: A Life* (New York: Henry Holt, 1991), p. 15.

23. Henry David Thoreau, *A Week on the Concord and Merrimack Rivers, Walden; Or, Life in the Woods, the Maine Woods, Cape Cod* (New York: Library of America, 1985), p. 266; Ralph Waldo Emerson, *Essays and Lectures* (New York: Library of America, 1983), p. 48.

24. Brower, *Poetry of Robert Frost*, p. 86.

25. Lentricchia, *Robert Frost*, p. 8.

26. Poirier, *Robert Frost*, pp. 150–52; Richardson, *The Ordeal of Robert Frost*, p. 215.

27. Pritchard, *Frost*, p. 127; Richardson, *The Ordeal of Robert Frost*, pp. 182–83.

28. New, *The Line's Eye*, pp. 24–25.

29. Lentricchia, *Robert Frost*, p. 112.

30. Poirier, *Robert Frost*, pp. 62–72, 176, 206, 222.

31. Lentricchia, *Robert Frost*, p. 60; Poirier, *Robert Frost*, p. 123; Kearns, *Robert Frost*, p. 87.

32. Kearns, *Robert Frost*, pp. 1–31, 112, 188.

33. Kearns, *Robert Frost*, p. 97.

34. Robert Frost, *The Notebooks of Robert Frost*, ed. Robert Faggen (Cambridge, Mass.: Harvard University Press, 2006), pp. 45, 48.

35. Walter Jost, *Rhetorical Investigations: Studies in Ordinary Language Criticism* (Charlottesville: University of Virginia Press, 2004); Christopher Benfey, "Dark Darker Darkest: Frost in His Notebooks," *The New Republic* 236:4 (2007), pp. 24–28, 26.

36. Bonnie Costello, *Shifting Ground: Reinventing Landscape in Modern American Poetry* (Cambridge, Mass.: Harvard University Press, 2003), pp. 38–40.

37. Poirier, *Robert Frost*, p. 233.

38. Richardson, *The Ordeal of Robert Frost*, pp. 2–15, 136–37; Mark Richardson, "Frost and the Cold War: A Look at the Later Poetry," in Earl J. Wilcox and Jonathan N. Barron (eds.), *Roads Not Taken: Rereading Robert Frost* (Columbia: University of Missouri Press, 2000), pp. 55–77, 67–72.

39. Marit J. MacArthur, *The American Landscape in the Poetry of Frost, Bishop, and Ashbery: The House Abandoned* (New York: Palgrave Macmillan, 2008), pp. 62–70.

40. Lathem, *Interviews with Robert Frost*, p. 67.

41. Richardson, *The Ordeal of Robert Frost*, pp. 90–95.

42. Malcolm Cowley, "Frost: A Dissenting Opinion," *The New Republic* 110 (September 11, 1944), pp. 312–13, 312.

43. Jarrell, *Poetry and the Age*, pp. 28–69.

44. Lionel Trilling, "A Speech on Robert Frost: A Cultural Episode," *Partisan Review* 26 (1959), pp. 445–52, 451.

45. For influential work on Frost not discussed elsewhere in this chapter, see especially Donald G. Sheehy, "(Re)Figuring Love: Robert Frost in Crisis, 1938–1942," *New England Quarterly* 63:2 (1990), pp. 179–231; James Sitar, "Selected Lectures of Robert Frost" (dissertation, Boston University, 2008).

46. A. R. Ammons, *Corsons Inlet* (Ithaca, N.Y.: Cornell University Press, 1965), p. 41.

47. James Merrill, *Collected Poems*, ed. J. D. McClatchy and Stephen Yenser (New York: Knopf, 2001), pp. 406–10.

48. John Ashbery, *Collected Poems 1956–1987* (New York: Library of America, 2008), p. 306.

49. Jorie Graham, *The Dream of the Unified Field: Selected Poems 1974–1994* (Hopewell, N.J.: Ecco, 1995), pp. 38–39.

50. Thylias Moss, *Rainbow Remnants in Rock Bottom Ghetto Sky* (New York: Persea, 1991), p. 44.

51. Kay Ryan, *The Best of It: New and Selected Poems* (New York: Grove, 2010), p. 165.

52. Joseph Brodsky, Seamus Heaney, and Derek Walcott, *Homage to Robert Frost* (New York: Farrar, Straus, and Giroux, 1996).
53. Hoffman, *Robert Frost*, pp. 204–220.
54. Rachel Buxton, *Robert Frost and Northern Irish Poetry* (Oxford: Oxford University Press, 2004).
55. Seamus Heaney, *The Redress of Poetry* (New York: Farrar, Straus and Giroux, 1995), pp. xiv–xv. Paul Muldoon's lecture on "The Mountain" also analyzes Frost's verbal legerdemain; see *The End of the Poem* (New York: Farrar, Straus and Giroux, 2006), pp. 53–81.
56. Costello, *Shifting Ground*, p. 49.

Chapter 24

T. S. Eliot

CHARLES ALTIERI

T. S. Eliot was the figure who defined modernist poetry for educated Americans. He refused pastoral settings for urban realities, replaced rhetoric and ornament by precise diction like "measured out my life with coffee spoons,"[1] transformed regular rhythms into an elaborate musicality composed by phrasal relationships, and replaced on a large scale coherent argument and narrative by the application of montage principles. Building poems by juxtaposition, he foregrounded how indefinable meanings could provide textures of echoes and implications that could only be completed by a reader's emotional commitments to the rendered situations. Then Eliot was to define modernist poetry again to a generation of post–World War II poets weary of his authority and trying to produce a postmodernism free of what, through Eliot, had become critical demands for a poetry that cultivated complex acts of mind abstracted from common life and bound to a social conservatism that ironically provided a mirror for the age that it refused to confront directly. In 1930 it seemed every ambitious poet had to either imitate Eliot or rage about his dominance (as William Carlos Williams did); in 1970 it seemed that being contemporary required rejecting everything Eliot stood for.

Eliot was born on September 26, 1888, in St. Louis to an old New England family displaced by his father's career as an industrialist. Eliot's childhood seemed a contented one but must have been difficult psychologically. He was the youngest of seven children, five of them female, and suffered from a congenital double hernia that kept him from sports and caused him to spend much of his time reading. Worse, his mother had all sorts of ambitions for him, and his father had the immense task of living up to a legendary father of his own, William Greenleaf Eliot, who combined New England exemplary righteousness with tremendous entrepreneurial inventiveness. In 1932–1933, Eliot gave the Charles Eliot Norton lectures at Harvard, named for one of his ancestors. But the young man who went to England for graduate study in philosophy in 1914 felt "immature for my age, very timid, very inexperienced."[2]

His isolated childhood had produced considerable alienation from quotidian society, making it necessary for him ultimately to find a sense of belonging only in a relation to transcendental domain.

If we rely on the evidence of the poetry Eliot wrote at Harvard – from which he graduated in 1910, after only three years (and where in his first year he was put on probation for poor grades) – his childhood taught him two things that he would put to excellent use as a writer. One was to protect his many vulnerabilities by cultivating masks through which he could protect himself from judgment while achieving a distanced critical consciousness that could roam freely within the domain of social appearances. The other was a capacity from the start to see through the limitations of those appearances to justify something like a constant stance of infinite longing. In "Opera," written in 1909,

> Life departs with a feeble smile
> Into the indifferent.
> These emotional experiences
> Do not hold good at all,
> And I feel like the ghost of youth
> At the undertaker's ball.[3]

Inspired by Arthur Symons's *The Symbolist Movement in Literature*, Eliot in 1908 had started to read modern French poetry. This poem offers explicit homage to Jules Laforgue, with its distanced perspective on the action, its shifts of levels of experience in the second stanza, and above all its critical self-consciousness, which will not allow the self-ennoblement of identifying with tragic seriousness. For Laforgue, as for Eliot in this poem, humans lead lives of quiet desperation, barely holding off "the indifferent" that establishes man's metaphysical condition. But even as a junior at Harvard, Eliot's writing showed considerable promise that he would distinguish himself. The leap from the labor of the instruments to "love torturing itself" would become characteristic of his imaginative mobility. And he was already a master of pacing, moving elegantly from the Laforguian "feeble smile" to the strong, flat statement, "These emotional experiences / do not hold good at all." The final image is even more striking: lesser poets might come up with the figure of the ghost of youth or attendance at the undertaker's ball, but both together betoken a great deal of promise, and a great deal of pain, for this twenty-year-old writer.

Despite its borrowing from Laforgue's hypersophisticated poses, Eliot's Harvard poetry lacked substance – both in philosophical heft and in the imaginative fluidity to expand and combine the states of feeling he could already name so witheringly. At least subliminally aware of what his poetry still lacked, Eliot felt he needed experience that would excite and extend his imagination, and he decided to spend a year in Paris, at a time when the American dollar could go a very long way in Europe. Paris did little for Eliot's tendencies to withdraw into isolated distances from what he felt was a tawdry, mechanical world. But he did make one very close friend, Jean Verdenal, who was to die in World War I and be memorialized in the dedication to *Prufrock and Other Observations* (1917). His year in Paris also allowed Eliot to pursue two sharply conflicting philosophical interests – in the vitalist thought of Henri Bergson, whose lectures Eliot attended, and in the reactionary writings of the Catholic monarchist Charles Maurras. One might think of Eliot's passion for Bergson as fostering his acute attention to the dynamics of sensation in his poetry, and his passion for Maurras as cultivating his critical distance from those very sensations as he interpreted what experience offered against the backdrop of a belief in the decline of Western civilization.

Bergson's vitalism stressed the flow of duration in which experiences fused together into dynamic complexes that could not be pieced out by the spatializing mind or, implicitly, grasped by the synthetic ironic attitudes that Laforgue exemplified. With this in mind, compare "Opera" to the opening of "The Love Song of J. Alfred Prufrock":

> Let us go then, you and I,
> When the evening is spread out against the sky,
> Like a patient, etherized upon a table;
> Let us go, through certain half-deserted streets,
> The muttering retreats
> Of restless nights in one-night cheap hotels
> And sawdust restaurants with oyster shells:
> Streets that follow like a tedious argument
> Of insidious intent
> To lead you to an overwhelming question . . .   (*ECP*, p. 3)

Most striking is the new fluidity of mind and of verse. The opening is dramatic, shaped more by Donne's aggressive overtures than Laforgue's laconic evasiveness. But the deliberate vagueness of this "you" puts that assertiveness within Laforgue's indefinite social space. The poem will have to define its possible audience by coming to terms with the contradictory desires its speaker cannot escape. Then there is a new concern for the texture of sensation, which gets converted into metaphorical intensity. Modern American poetry can almost be said to be born in the expansion from the bland descriptive metaphor of the evening "spread out against the sky" to the figure based on this patient "etherized upon a table." It is as if the imagination took the liberty to interpret the full range of the initial figure by hearing what "spread out" implied, in order to follow an order sponsored more by imaginative affinities than by any accuracy to the particular scene. This poem definitively makes the night far more frightening psychologically than was the custom in the pastoral poetry dominant in Eliot's literary culture. Now night is inseparable from a decaying urban environment that in its turn is inseparable from an imaginative atmosphere which acknowledges responsibility only to the intricacies of the psyche. Formally, this freedom is registered by breaking from the equal weights of the lines in "Opera" to a much more fluid sense of the line as finding its own rhythm and playing with strange rhyming possibilities (even posing the question of whether "table" rhymes with anything at all). This is free verse in the full sense, in that it claims the capacity to build on its own gathering energies rather than following a prescribed form.

Eliot's poem goes on also to adapt principles of juxtaposition and montage that were just emerging in the visual arts as overt conditions of a modernist spirit unwilling to be bound to the continuities of logical space. Juxtaposition builds a marvelous cross between physical and psychological qualities. The yellow fog that "curled once about the house, and fell asleep" (*ECP*, p. 3) mixes the alienating industrial gloom of London evenings with the figure of a cat, expressing Prufrock's fantasies that he might find some secure and loving place for rest. And the poem's structure treats time itself as the condition wherein the psyche stands exposed by having its fantasies laid bare and, worse, by having to confront its own impotence:

> Would it have been worth while, ...
> If one, settling a pillow or throwing off a shawl,
> And turning toward the window, should say:
>> "That is not it at all,
>> That is not what I meant at all."   (*ECP*, pp. 6–7)

Yet there is no moralizing. Eliot shows that poetry can simply render complex psychological states that seem beyond judgment because they capture the speaker's essential characteristics. Art claims the privileges held by moral judgment.

But, as his capacity to so fully imagine Prufrock indicates, Eliot was not one to leap into the profession of poet. He lacked self-confidence and feared that his work would not be accepted by a world for which he had little respect. How could the son of a New England industrialist take up so indulgent a profession? He returned to Harvard as a graduate student in philosophy, the one profession that might fit his interests in self-reflection and still be sufficiently respectable for his father and for what Eliot still internalized as the kind of work displaced aristocrats like the Eliots might profess. In his three years of study at Harvard he pursued two interests that would shape the course of twentieth-century American poetry. First, he let himself explore his passionate curiosity about what William James called "the varieties of religious experience." Eliot even studied Sanskrit and took a special interest in Hindu and Buddhist texts. No longer would Eliot's imagination be trapped within the alienated psychodramas of Laforguian individual self-consciousness. Instead, the alienation could turn metaphysical and become not just a mark of social failure but a means for exploring the possible religious significance of both private and public experience. Second, he chose to do a dissertation on F. H. Bradley, in part because Bradley tried to work out how the intricacy of individual self-conscious states could take on a public dimension. Bradley envisioned an absolute in which consciousness could assign a significant place for the varieties of individual experience. Eliot rejected that claim to an absolute because it seemed to rely only on an idealist faith in spirit. But he developed from Bradley a related synthetic idea of "degrees of reality," which for him provided a continuum between his fascination with solipsistic hallucination and aspects of objectivity provided by the fact that many subjectivities had to attribute significance to given objects. The garden in a dream only matters as a sign of individual obsession; the garden that people talk about takes on reality because of its place in a shared life, where it might also become an effective symbol of further possibilities for sharing ideal worlds.

The academic year 1914–1915 saw an even more propitious series of events, at least for Eliot, and for the course of modern poetry. He was awarded a traveling fellowship to study philosophy in Germany and then could not return to the United States because war had broken out. Instead he went to Oxford, where he began a close friendship with Ezra Pound that was to have enormous effects on his future. Pound worked on Eliot's self-confidence by trying to convince him that he could and should make a living as a poet. It was typical of Pound that once he was convinced of Eliot's talent, he worked tirelessly to convince others. Pound's enthusiasm eventually persuaded Harriet Monroe to publish "Prufrock" in the June 1915 issue of *Poetry*: that was also the month when Eliot married a young English woman, Vivien Haigh-Wood. The decision to marry in England enabled Eliot to stand up to his parents' requests that he return home to take up the career of philosopher. And when Eliot did decide to return, at least to defend his thesis on Bradley in 1916, the voyage had to be canceled because of fears of German submarines. Meanwhile, Eliot had taken a position as a teacher, had begun to lecture for money, and eventually settled in a position with Lloyd's Bank in London, where he stayed eight years, achieving considerable success in their international finance department.

Curiously, the years after Eliot decided to make his living as a poet were not very good years for his poetry. Instead, his most effective creative labors were in developing a distinctive style as a critic-essayist and a body of general ideas about what a modern poetry might look like. *Prufrock and Other Observations* was published in 1917, but the book's best poems had for the most part been written close to the time of "Prufrock" and share its cross of a laconic sense of reality with a disturbing lushness of sensual imaginings. The ending of "Preludes" offers one of the richest moments in Eliot's work, literally producing the "I" as a source of hopeless lyricism that will inevitably invite its dialectical other, the mind's harsh lucidity about its own imaginary investments:

> I am moved by fancies that are curled
> Around these images, and cling:
> The notion of some infinitely gentle
> Infinitely suffering thing.
>
> Wipe your hands across your mouth, and laugh;
> The worlds revolve like ancient women
> Gathering fuel in vacant lots.   (ECP, pp. 14–15)

The poems to be collected in Eliot's second volume, *Ara vos Prec* (1920), extended that lucidity but had little imaginative sympathy to mollify the satires on everything that might tempt belief. Notice the keen intellect and grasp of the expressive power of syntax in this passage from "Gerontion," which is limited only by the fact that the intricate syntax has to expel any lyrical possibilities for imaginative caring, leaving only its analytic intensity as the locus of lyric emotion:

> After such knowledge, what forgiveness? Think now
> History has many cunning passages, contrived corridors
> And issues, deceives with whispering ambitions,
> Guides us by our vanities. Think now
> She gives when our attention is distracted
> And what she gives gives with such supple confusions
> That the giving famishes the craving.   (ECP, p. 30)

One might argue that this is cultural criticism attempting to be raised to the level of poetry. And one would be right, at least to the extent that the powers Eliot gained in his early London years were primarily powers to deploy distanced critical stances with a suppleness that would make this work influential in shaping an ideology for a modernist revolution. Eliot needed the money he could make from lecture courses for working people, so he developed a style that could make complex and intense thinking available without patronizing that audience. He became an exemplar of a new sensibility, shaped by four fundamental critical ideas. If we treat these ideas as a logical thematic set, we have to begin with Eliot's claim that the mind of Europe in the mid-seventeenth century, not coincidentally the time of the flourishing of Protestantism, experienced a dissociation of sensibility in which writing could no longer feel thought as a direct experience but broke down into periods of thinking and periods of feeling, with precious little fusion of those capacities.[4] With a single stroke, Eliot seems to have clarified why eighteenth-century poetry offered masterpieces distinguished by their affinities for prose reasoning, while the nineteenth century seemed increasingly to rely on mawkish sentiment without much thinking that could hold up in a prose world now dominated by empiricist methods.

No wonder, then, that Eliot's three other basic concepts came to dominate critical accounts of modernist values, in part because Pound was developing somewhat analogous concepts in very different tonal situations. Eliot's call for the importance of tradition promised to resist the dissociation of sensibility by attacking its therapeutic core – the idea that value is primarily a construct based on individual sensibilities and interests. An ideal of tradition offers writers "a feeling that the whole of the literature of Europe from Homer and within it the whole of the literature of his own country has a simultaneous existence and composes a simultaneous order" (*SE*, p. 4). The fullest measure of the writer's significance for the present is his or her capacity to modify our sense of the past so that it now has to include this imaginative act if witnesses are to make sense of the whole history for which the text takes responsibility. For if there are degrees of reality, tradition helps make sure that the poet is engaging what has occupied many other literate minds and so is worthy of being taken seriously.

The essay "Tradition and the Individual Talent" realizes that if writers are to submit to tradition as a test of originality, there must also be a very different model of what poets try to accomplish in their texts. In its second part it proposes moving from Romantic expressivist models stressing the concerns of the poet to stressing the manifest qualities of the work considered as an impersonal composition organizing disparate energies. To exemplify this shift, Eliot makes a simple gesture with enormous consequences. He turns to science for an analogy with the life of spirit and in effect aligns art with science in terms of the pursuit of objectivity. Poetry need not offer opinions or emotional reactions to historical circumstances. Rather, poetry can actually make history by fusing emotions and feelings together under pressure so that they can take new and unpredictable forms – look again at how "Prufrock" first presents a metaphor of the evening being "spread out against the sky," then fuses that metaphor into the more radical figure of "the patient etherized upon a table," and then fuses this with the street that leads to a tedious argument. Eliot would have called this the logic of the metaphysical conceit, the last style in Europe that successfully challenged the dissociation of sensibility. Here "a degree of heterogeneity of material compelled into unity by the operation of the poet's mind is omnipresent in the poetry[:] ... idea and simile become one" (SE, p. 243):

> In Chapman especially there is a direct sensuous apprehension of thought, or a recreation of thought into feeling, which is exactly what we find in Donne.... Tennyson and Browning are poets, and they think; but they do not feel their thought immediately as the odour of a rose. A thought to Donne was an experience; it modified his sensibility. (SE, pp. 246–47)

An ideal of impersonality pervades all three arguments I have been developing, because Eliot saw that European culture was doomed to embrace therapeutic values that would substantially change its moral ideas by embracing the primacy of subjective needs over objective values. But it was only in "Hamlet and His Problems" that Eliot developed a powerful figure for his own conservative morality. That figure was the "objective correlative." In art, as in life, there can be felt an imperative to make the object of expression adequate to the feeling. That means there is no residue, no claims about a needy subject that demands sympathy for a "personality" that can claim importance for the self even though it cannot quite take the forms of responsibility that involve making that self fully articulate: "Hamlet's bafflement at the absence of an objective equivalent to his feelings is a prolongation of the bafflement of his creator in the face of his artistic problem" (SE, p. 125). The measure of Hamlet's sickness is his inability to articulate feelings for his mother that in the play she is too weak a character to compel. So we get only his subjectivity on display in a desperate search for something inexpressible that might give relief. The play fails to transcend its fascination with subjectivity. And Eliot shows by his critical sympathy that, in the words of another essay, "only those who have personality and emotions know what it means to want to escape from those things" (SE, p. 11). St. Louis continues to take its toll.

All these essays cultivate an intimate relation to art crossed with a sense of frightening distance from the society that art addresses. In this context Eliot's interest in foreign and ancient religions should not be surprising. But all Eliot could do with this concern for religious traditions was to use it as a context enabling an impersonal stance toward what he had come to see as the spiritual vacuousness of his contemporary society. He had to stop writing the satires that came so naturally to him and begin articulating in poetry a collective sense of the suffering that this world, so easy to satirize, produced. And he had to do that without turning to Hamlet's replacement of the objective world with figures of his personal pain. He had to be objective and critical, yet also sympathetic with the deepest levels of his culture's suffering.

It was those qualities, mixed with residues of Eliot's smug ironies, that Ezra Pound encountered late in 1921 when he was given some drafts of passages that would eventually take form as *The Waste Land* (1922). Pound cut most of the satiric ugliness and the adolescent attitudinizing to produce intricately woven textures combining several levels of scenic objectification, from the visionary to the domestic. There are numerous useful critical accounts that use the footnotes added to the poem for book publication to establish how the plot of this poem embodies elaborate allegorical structures. The footnotes identify allusions and indicate a level of action that echoes the structure of primitive fertility myths, especially the story of the fisher king, recently studied by the anthropologist Sir James Frazier in *The Golden Bough* (1890–1915). The poem begins with a society wounded and cut off from life-giving waters and then explores possibilities that this culture can find some equivalent of the fisher king's struggles to restore a spiritual life to this wasteland. In the poem, however, that renewal cannot occur: the patterns of allusion dramatize how far the West has strayed from the times when imagination could permeate the facts of experience. Now renewal depends on the non-Western religions that fascinated Eliot, especially in fragments from the Upanishads. Most critics agree that the desired renewal does not take place in the poem. But they also agree that the spiritual terrors rendered by this poem ultimately proved fundamental for the conversion in 1927 that led Eliot to be baptized into the Church of England.

Here I can only outline one path through the allegory while concentrating on how the poetry develops sufficient concrete power to compel our attention to the allegorical level. Notice first how the opening of the poem preserves the lush, imaginative mobility of "Prufrock" while projecting a spiritual crisis far more deep and pervasive than Prufrock's psychological problems. *The Waste Land* renders an entire culture coming to self-consciousness of the historical forces shaping its deficiencies and its painfully reduced range of available voices:

> April is the cruellest month, breeding
> Lilacs out of the dead land, mixing
> Memory and desire, stirring
> Dull roots with spring rain....
> Summer surprised us, coming over the Starnbeergersee
> With a shower of rain; we stopped in the colonnade,
> And went on in the sunlight, into the Hofgarten
> And drank coffee, and talked for an hour....
> In the mountains, there you feel free.
> I read much of the night, and go south in the winter.
>
> What are the roots that clutch, what branches grow
> Out of this stony rubbish? Son of man,
> You cannot say, or guess, for you know only
> A heap of broken images ...   (ECP, p. 53)

There is immense scope, because the season affects everyone and indicates a collective malaise. And the allusion to the hopeful opening of Chaucer's *Canterbury Tales* becomes here a profound mistrust of instinct, because the spring that should bring hope brings only awareness of a despair that cannot make human consciousness resonate with seasonal forces. There is no personality to blame or to shield by imaginary projection from these bare facts of the human condition; there is only the impersonal measure of change from conditions the culture could once celebrate. But Eliot is also careful to register particular intimate qualities of that malaise, especially in how the rain is used, in the cadence that makes us feel drums beating into our heads, and in the lovely suspended participles that produce five of the opening six line endings. These participles make syntax a vital expressive feature of the poem by suspending the mind in a present tense abstracted from the physical scene and by creating a space hovering about the scene that will soon be filled by echoes of religious values. It is as if syntax could capture a sense of physical process and transition between states that contrasts sharply with the trapped defensiveness that permeates the human interactions.

I use ellipses in citing the opening passage so that I can illustrate how the poem moves quickly from the season to how representative human agents respond to their situation. The quiet passage about summer introduces human speaking, crucially in the first-person plural, which the author's impersonality can bring into focus. Here we enter a domain of lyrical possibility within the casual world that anticipates the more elaborate memories of the hyacinth garden soon to come. There is rain, although the protagonists do not yet know how much they will need it, and there is sunlit peacefulness. But the agents see neither the intensity possible in those physical states nor the symbolic dimension making them valuable. So they consume the time (rather than redeem it) in casual talk. Then the casual talk seems largely a defensive shield, as the next passage presents particular voices pervaded by a fearfulness and evasiveness that can only understand freedom as the capacity to read much of the night and go south in the winter.

I add the opening of the second stanza of the poem's first section to indicate the shock Eliot wants to create as we move from "civilized" and repressed evasiveness to the competing voice of the prophet, demanding that the citizens take stock of the lives that work so hard to evade lucid self-consciousness. Now the world of broken images has to be seen in relation to the possibility of accounting for our lives in relation to the symbolic and transcendental orders that they represent, and that they violate. The prophet demands responses that engage all that "Son of man" has come to mean in Christianity. (The heap of broken images may be read as a mark of how far this poem is from Pound's Imagism, which was all the rage only a decade before; and so the broken images demand a very different kind of poetry.) Now we experience the need to work out how the overall plot will interpret the contrasts of the intimate versus the public, the image versus the symbol, and acts of attention versus acts of protective denial.

The Waste Land has five sections (beautifully correlated with the movements of Beethoven's quartets). Each builds on juxtapositions and allusions to reflect a different aspect of spiritual crisis. The first section maps the distance between the ordinary life of citizens and what has become symbolic detritus (like tarot packs, churches, intense personal memories, and spring itself). Here the poem creates an imperative for consciousness to be open to the symbolic realm even while it has to distrust the culture's use of those symbols. A heap of broken images cannot be fixed by building another heap: there must be a difference in reading that allows us to hear the prophet and recognize "fear in a handful of dust" (*ECP*, p. 54). In contrast to the multiple worlds of the first section, the second concentrates on developing the sterility that pervades all classes of London life, which prove utterly unalike, except in this shared sense of distance from any vital principle. Eliot is especially playful and pervasively ironic in this section because he wants his language and his allusions to mime that sterility. The more we capture the allusions, the more we feel the uselessness of this knowledge, just as the portrayal of rape on the aristocratic lady's mantle has none of the urgency or impact of what it represents.

The third section of *The Waste Land* turns from psychology to the landscape of broken images, insisting now that we find psychology echoed there as well. It is entitled "The Fire Sermon" to emphasize the dry thirst that water can bring when it cannot bring life. The central section has seven units. It begins with an empty landscape echoing biblical psalms of desperation; builds to a central unit staging a complete failure of sexual connection as the bored typist submits without receiving, or giving, anything but her consent; and reaches a climax in a conjunction of Saint Augustine with Buddha's fire sermon. At the figurative core of this wasteland is an internal hell. But this hell can be experienced in two somewhat different ways: one can simply register or defend the self from despair, and one can try to read the situation in purgatorial terms as a call for efforts at purification by coming to terms with the text's allusions and realizing what we have lost as we adapt to secularity. These options are intensified in the poem's short fourth section, which displays the sea's picking the bones of Phlebas the sailor in whispers, far from the sounds of lamentation or the traces of redeeming prayer.

The poem asks whether there is an alternative to this death by water, and so whether there is any possibility of reading water as baptismal. Because there might be that possibility, we have to go through another dimension of purgatory, presented by a visionary confrontation with the symbolic implications of the landscape in the final section, as if the fisher king had to surmount this final – here impossible – challenge before bringing the kind of water that could bring life to the wasteland.

At the dramatic center of this section there is an echo of Christ's journey to Emmaus, during which he speaks with two disciples who do not recognize him until he reveals himself:

> Who is this third who walks always beside you?
> When I count there are only you and I together
> But when I look ahead up the white road
> There is always another one walking beside you ...

> (*ECP*, p. 67)

For Eliot this is the ultimate test of faith. It offers itself not in visionary splendor but in the casual processes of living, in which spiritual truth seems just the other side of appearances. But how do we get to the other side when our relation to appearance is simultaneously so needy and so insensitive? How do we not confirm the wasteland by repeating its empiricist mantras, suspicious of all belief? The one hope seems to be to find possibilities of belief in the spiritual world by turning to specific passages in religious texts that have yet to be distorted and travestied by believers and unbelievers alike. So the poem turns to three commands from the Upanishads – "Dattta," "Dayadhvam," and "Damyata." The text, mired in modernity, still has the power in the footnotes to give these terms literal translations – "Give," "Sympathize," and "Control." But moral imperatives have to be translated into possibilities for practice. And in this respect the poem can only respond with memories. There is no way to make the imperatives present and operable:

> Dayadhvam: I have heard the key
> Turn in the door once and turn once only
> We think of the key, each in his prison
> Thinking of the key, each confirms a prison
> Only at nightfall, aethereal rumours
> Revive for a moment a broken Coriolanus   (*ECP*, p. 69)

After engaging the three imperatives, the poem shatters into fragments, concluding with the mad Hieronymo's cry in the Renaissance poet Thomas Kyd's *Spanish Tragedy*, "Why then Ile fit you" (*ECP*, p. 69). In Kyd's play, Hieronymo is pretending madness and promises to write a play accommodating the desires of those who murdered his son, a play in which he writes himself a part that allows him to take revenge. But these lines in Eliot's poem mark the maddening frustration that there is no fit for this age that does not become an aspect of its spiritual vacuity: to attempt to change the culture is to be co-opted by it on the deepest psychological levels. So Eliot's poem can end only with what most critics think is an echo of a formal ending to an Upanishad, "Shantih, Shantih, Shantih," now reduced to a ritual promise of peace that covers over but does not resolve the spiritual turmoil.

After *The Waste Land* Eliot was done with trying by secular poetry to establish a spiritual core for his culture. Indeed he was done with a distinctive modernist poetics. He devoted his secular energies to founding and editing the review *The Criterion*, which from 1922 to 1939 tried to represent the best writing in Europe about its cultural dilemmas. (For Eliot, Marxism and Christianity were the only fully serious discourses because they both took seriously the plight of European culture.) But his imaginative energies were devoted primarily to looking toward his own salvation, which included freeing himself of his wife, from whom he separated in 1932, and whom he put into a mental hospital in 1938. (The movie *Tom and Viv* gives a sensitive picture of their hopes and their conflicts.) Eliot had a distinctive view of his conversion – that it was the result not of faith but of the surrender to a humility and a sense of need that could take a path on which faith might ultimately be found. That need was for him defined against humanism, as he made clear in the powerful essay "Second Thoughts about Humanism" (1928). There he criticized humanism both because it could not produce an ethics and because it had to make ethics the ultimate value in how we judge human lives. Humanism could not produce an ethics because it was committed to honoring all imaginatively rich human products. It had an aesthetics, but it had far too much diversity to provide any strict principles or even fealties to specific cultural traditions. The lesson of humanism in this regard was that one could not idealize experience in itself or pursue universals based on abstractions from the variety of human practices. One had to determine what in experience mattered most to a given individual and to find ultimate values that one could commit to as this individual. And one had to recognize that morality could never reach much further than a highly civilized aesthetics based on distaste for evil rather than confrontation with sinfulness:

> Mr Foerster's Humanism, in fact, is too ethical to be true. Where do all those morals come from? One advantage of an orthodox religion, to my mind, is that it puts morals in their proper place. I cannot understand a system of morals which seems to be founded on nothing but itself – which exists, I suspect, only by illicit relations with either psychology or religion or both, according to the bias of the mind of the individual humanist.... Mr. Foerster is more likely to end in respectability than in perfection. (*SE*, pp. 32–33, 35)

Eliot's defining Christianity against humanism shaped his literary career after 1927. While he became a more generous literary critic, even finding ways to praise Milton, most of his criticism, like *After Strange Gods* (1934), *The Idea of a Christian Society* (1940), and *Notes Towards a Definition of Culture* (1948), was devoted to somewhat strange and chilling speculations on what it might take to revive a distinctive Christian culture. He turned to the theater as a test of whether spirituality could still play a part on the modern stage, in plays like *Murder in the Cathedral* (1935), *The Family Reunion* (1939), and *The Cocktail Party* (1949). And he continued to write noteworthy poetry. "Ash Wednesday" (1930) maps a meditative path to possible salvation. And *Four Quartets* (1935–1942) develops a marvelous rewriting of *The Waste Land*: its engagement in the culture becomes a tale of England subject to German bombing, and its allusive complexity centers on the evocation of Christian mystical writing as the tradition offering a discipline of the spirit that can show an individual the way of salvation:

> The dove descending breaks the air
> With flame of incandescent terror

Of which the tongues declare
The one discharge from sin and error.
The only hope, or else despair
Lies in the choice of pyre or pyre –
To be redeemed from fire by fire.

Who then devised the torment? Love.
Love is the unfamiliar Name
Behind the hands that wove
The intolerable shift of flame
Which human power cannot remove.
We only live, only suspire
Consumed by either fire or fire.   (*ECP*, p. 207)

Conversion is elemental and total, allowing the mind to see all four of the elements – earth, water, fire, and air – as redemptive reversals of the alienating resistance to spirit they embodied in *The Waste Land*. And, above all, *Four Quartets* transforms the tormenting gap between the present and the allusions it evokes into the capacity completely to accept the present and to speak decidedly Christian sentences that believers can offer to a secular world without either embarrassment or righteousness.

The earthly aspect of Eliot's torment ended on January 4, 1965.

Notes

1. T. S. Eliot, *Collected Poems 1909–1962* (New York: Harcourt Brace, 1970), p. 3. This collection will be cited subsequently in the text as *ECP*.
2. T. S. Eliot, *The Letters of T. S. Eliot, Vol. 1: 1898–1922*, ed. Hugh Haughton and Valerie Eliot (London: Faber and Faber, 2009), p. xvii.
3. T. S. Eliot, *Inventions of the March Hare: Poems 1909–1917*, ed. Christopher Ricks (London: Faber and Faber, 1996), p. 17.
4. T. S. Eliot, *Selected Essays* (New York: Harcourt, Brace, 1950), p. 247. This collection will be cited subsequently in the text as *SE*.

Chapter 25

William Carlos Williams: The Shock of the Familiar

BOB PERELMAN

"But that sounds just like my husband! ... You mean to stand there and tell me that *that's a poem?*" – a teacher enrolled in a poetry workshop in the 1970s has just been introduced to what many readers will recognize as the erstwhile kitchen table note William Carlos Williams scrawled to his wife, Flossie. It has become one of Williams's most familiar poems. First, the confession:

> THIS IS JUST TO SAY
> I have eaten
> the plums
> that were in
> the icebox

The second stanza displays a bit of sympathy for the wronged party, who was "probably / saving" the plums "for breakfast." The final stanza starts with a bare-bones apology – "Forgive me" – but then shifts to a recollection of the guilty pleasure: "they were delicious / so sweet / and so cold."[1]

The teacher's reaction to the poem is a small moment situated well outside the circles of critical expertise, but it makes a telling emblem of the current situation of Williams in the twenty-first century. The anecdote appears in an essay concerned with teaching poetry in schools;[2] it involves a reader who is neither poet nor critic, and her reaction is out of sync with the standard critical histories. But this is appropriate for Williams, who himself was out of sync with the reigning paradigms of his day. He remains anomalous with regard to contemporary poetic expectations of our day, although this is masked by his ubiquitous influence on poets and his presence in anthologies and on syllabi. In accounts of American poetry, Williams is a basic marker of the development of modernism, of the avant-garde, and of a democratic art of everyday speech.[3] However, although he has become important to these literary chronologies, he fits awkwardly into them all. The imagery from one of his own typically off-the-cuff critical remarks can be applied to his current reception: "Forcing twentieth-century America into a sonnet – gosh, how I hate sonnets – is like putting a crab into a square box. You've got to cut his legs off to make him fit."[4]

This is not to say that attaching any literary label to Williams's work is some kind of mutilation. He is a crucial American modernist who developed a stripped-down, flexible language that has been more influential than that of any other twentieth-century American poet; he experimented tirelessly with formal dimensions of poems – lineation, punctuation (or lack thereof), incorporation of everyday speech and visual icons, and mixing of passages of syntactic continuity with disjunctive moments; and he wrote a major modernist epic, *Paterson* (1946–1958). Given his lifelong attack on received poetic convention and his insistence on the new, it seems wrong not to associate him with the avant-garde. His prose-poetry hybrids *Spring and All* (1923) and *The Descent of Winter* (1928) as well as the unconventional prose of *Kora in Hell* (1920) and *The Great American Novel* (1923) show him as an excited experimenter; lines like the following are clearly addressed to avant-garde arenas: "where bridge stanchions / rest / certainly / piercing / left ventricles / with long / sunburnt fingers" (*WCPI*, p. 212). But, to move to the third category, much of Williams's writing is inescapably democratic in vocabulary, in subject matter, and in immediacy of address. The prose of his fifty-plus short stories, four novels, five plays, and *Autobiography* (1951) is conventional: for example, "In half an hour I was back at the house again, as agreed. There was an old black-and-white cat lying in the sunny doorway who literally had to be lifted and pushed away before I could enter" (*FD*, p. 326). However, such everyday texture is rarely placed in the service of narrative tension. Then again, passages of the most ordinary language appear throughout his most experimental work – all of which is to say that basic categorical separations have been, and continue to be, difficult to maintain when reading Williams's work. His attack on the sonnet is modernist – compare it with Ezra Pound's oft-quoted line "(to break the pentameter, that was the first heave)" – and his defense of the crab is Romantic, a version of Wordsworth's "We murder to dissect."[5] Is the poem a made thing that must reflect the latest poetic advances, or is it a natural outgrowth that must not be deformed?

The teacher in our opening anecdote is not thinking in terms of literary historical categories, but she is, in a way, reinventing them, reinscribed in a democratic (unprofessional) context: to her, the poem seems scandalously unpoetic, simply a scrap of real life masquerading as art. Such a reaction could put us in mind of earlier, more notable shocks occasioned by T. S. Eliot's *The Waste Land*

(1922) or Marcel Duchamp's *Fountain* (1917). *Time* magazine, reviewing Eliot's poem in its initial issue, quoted the last eight lines of Eliot's poem as if they were self-evident nonsense and concluded, "It is rumored that *The Waste Land* was written as a hoax."[6] If we emphasize the origin of "This Is Just to Say" as a kitchen table note, the closer parallel might be a Duchamp readymade, in which a snow shovel, bottle rack, or, most famously and provocatively in the case of *Fountain*, an upside-down urinal was exhibited as art.

A strict chronological perspective would disallow such comparisons. By 1970, the era of modernist and avant-garde shocks was long past, and the poem that shocked the teacher had become something of a literary chestnut.[7] Kenneth Koch's affectionate parody "Variations on a Theme by William Carlos Williams," published ten years before in *The New American Poetry*, assumes the Williams poem as an obvious reference; otherwise Koch's violent humor loses much of its bite: "We laughed at the hollyhocks together / and then I sprayed them with lye. / Forgive me. I simply do not know what I am doing."[8]

The minimalism and undisguised everydayness of "This Is Just to Say" might, in 1970, have surprised a neophyte like the teacher, but even at its publication in 1934 it would have looked, to a knowledgeable reader, merely "modern" (unrhymed, *vers libre*, no punctuation). The stripped-down, quasi-regular quatrains are a far cry from the daunting literary reach and cultural range of *The Waste Land*; nor are the poem's communicativeness and domesticity avant-garde in the slightest. In fact, the poem is currently being used as a writing prompt for eighth graders.[9] As with *The Rite of Spring* going from scandal at its 1913 Paris premiere to Disney soundtrack in 1940, here is an example of how quickly the shocks of artistic advance, whether large or small, are neutralized and repurposed for domestic use.

However, such knowledgeable divisions between new and belated make only partial sense of Williams. Naïve as the teacher's reaction must seem from informed perspectives, it shows us a quality of Williams's work that has affected its reception for many decades: its unstable mix of the ordinary and the new. If we attend carefully to what she says – and Williams is the poet who has been crucial in showing how everyday speech can be a primary material for poetry – we will find more than some dim echo of avant-garde or modernist impacts. In fact, what first strikes her about the poem is its utter familiarity: "But that sounds just like my husband!" For her, the shock of the new arises reflexively from what we might term the shock of the familiar.

In the pedagogical context in which the anecdote appears, the teacher is no longer a half century behind the times; rather, she becomes a figure of the expansive future of Williams's work: her reaction in the 1970 workshop remains a teachable moment on the twenty-first-century website of the Academy of American Poets. A myriad of similar events have enabled Williams to outflank the larger reputations that, during his writing life, were well ahead of him. A laggard according to the modernist calendar, Williams's staying power is better measured in terms of social breadth rather than via tropes of aesthetic advance. It participates in dissynchronous chronologies, making its relation to literary history labile.

This does not mean the work is, in any sense, timeless. Often the ever-widening gap of actual years is quite clear, as in the widely taught "The Young Housewife" (1916). The questions the poem raises about male voyeurism are vivid to twenty-first-century readers, but the following lines, which present the object of the doctor's fantasy coming into actual view, also present a puzzle to the contemporary reader: "Then again she comes to the curb / to call the ice-man, fish-man, and stands / shy, uncorseted" (*WCPI*, p. 57). What were corsets, ice-men, and fish-men at the moment the doctor-poet was driving by? Many things, clearly; but few contemporary readers will have any sense of them. Williams's success in addressing his present with appropriate poetic quickness remains apparent, but it is also clear that the poem is a century old.

The poetic horizon that Williams often evokes – a primal opposition between a young United States and an adult Europe, pitting a jejune chaos against a culture of varied sophistication – is a phenomenon from the first half of the twentieth century. Williams voices the conflict loudly:

> God I would like to see some man, some one of the singers step out in the midst of some one of Aida's songs and scream like a puma.... I am a beginner. I am an American. A United Stateser. Yes, it's ugly.... I hate you [Europe], I hate your orchestras, your libraries, your sciences, your yearly salons, your finely tuned intelligences of all sorts. (*IM*, pp. 174–76)

Williams's sense of his own cultural deficit may be a constant, but even his (rhetorical) yelling shows us that he was keeping up with the latest manifestos from Europe.

When we think of Williams staying in New Jersey, we should remember that for him the local included nearby New York City, where he assiduously kept up with poets and painters. Despite his complaints about isolation in the provinces, Williams interacted with many significant artists, writers (Pound, H.D., Mina Loy, Marianne Moore, Wallace Stevens, Robert McAlmon, Elsa von Freytag-Loringhoven, Nathaniel West, Louis Zukofsky, Robert Creeley, Denise Levertov, and Allen Ginsberg), and visual artists (Duchamp, Man Ray, Charles Sheeler, Marsden Hartley, Charles Demuth, Alfred Stieglitz). Such a list only begins to suggest the range of his contacts. His poems often show the influence of innovations from the visual arts, much as Gertrude Stein's writing reflects Picasso or the poetry of Frank O'Hara and John Ashbery reflects the New York painting scene in the 1950s. And, it should be remembered, the fact that he was a doctor with a full-time general practice gave him access to more different people, classes, and types of event than any other American poet. For example: "The girl who comes to me breathless, staggering into my office, in her underwear a still living infant, making me lock her mother out of the room." This is not meant as a dramatic climax; Williams introduces it as part of his routine (*A*, p. 361). Williams's combination of wide social experience and artistic sophistication is, in hindsight, remarkable.

But the narrative that mattered to Williams involved a frustrating pursuit of those who, he felt, were ahead of him: Pound and Eliot, primarily – although Duchamp merits mention here as well. Late in life Williams said, "Before meeting Ezra Pound is like B.C. and A. D."[10] From their meeting as teenagers, Pound, younger, confident, and knowledgeable, assumed the role of Williams's teacher, a pattern that was to continue for half a century. Williams soon saw through some of Pound's intellectual pretentions – in *Kora* Williams outs Pound, so to speak, by quoting him as saying, "It is not necessary ... to read everything in a book in order to speak intelligently of it. Don't tell everyone I said so" (*IM*, p. 10). Nevertheless Williams remained daunted. Three decades later, in *Paterson*, he quotes pedagogic letters that he was still receiving from Pound: "Read all the Gk tragedies in / Loeb. – plus Frobenius, plus Gesell" (*P*, p. 138). Throughout his life Williams made irregular progress toward emancipating himself, declaring in one of his last poems, "To My Friend Ezra Pound" (1956), "Your English / is not specific enough / As a writer of poems you show yourself to be inept not to say / usurious" (*WCPII*, p. 434) – the last word a most knowing thrust naming the cardinal sin in Pound's poetic politico-theology. But such moments of confident equality are not the rule. From our perspective it is no surprise that Williams, who associated with the likes of Duchamp and Alfred Steiglitz, would be a more sophisticated figure than Pound. But for Williams, Pound's erudition was always a problem, as we will see in the discussion of *Paterson*.

Williams was not a figure such as Eliot, Pound, or Duchamp who could declare, authoritatively, what mattered and what didn't. This authority was brought about by their creative work but just as significantly by their critical dicta: Duchamp's rejection of what he termed "retinal art"; Pound's division of poetry into *melopoeia*, *phanopoeia*, and *logopoeia*;[11] and Eliot's pronouncements that Joyce's "mythical method" was something that "others must pursue after him"[12] or that "poetry in our civilization, as it exists at present, must be *difficult*."[13] Such statements, regardless of how accurate or prophetic they turned out to be, were powerful in setting the terms for inexorably forward-moving aesthetic chronologies.

According to such reckonings, Williams was behind the times, both in his writing and in his situation as a full-time doctor in New Jersey. Often enough, Williams himself shared this perception. In *Spring* he critiques his performance in *Kora*: "Their [i.e., the Improvisations'] fault is their dislocation of sense, often complete. But it is the best I could do under the circumstances" (*WCPI*, p. 203). Decades later, at the beginning of *Paterson*, his deficits are emphasized:

> To make a start,
> out of particulars
> and make them general, rolling
> up the sum, by defective means –
> Sniffing the trees,
> just another dog
> among a lot of dogs.   (*P*, p. 3)

His despair at the publication of *The Waste Land* is well known: "It wiped out our world as if an atom bomb had been dropped upon it. . . . I felt at once that it had set me back twenty years" (*A*, p. 174). A less remarked encounter with Duchamp produces a similar result. "I finally came face to face with him as we walked about the room and I said, 'I like your picture[.]' . . . He looked at me and said, 'Do you?' That was all. He had me beat all right, if that was the objective. I could have sunk through the floor, ground my teeth, turned my back on him and spat" (*A*, p. 137). Williams did not react to these defeats in similar fashion. He paid the most serious attention to Duchamp, whose radically playful senses of art stayed with Williams throughout his career.[14] His aversion to Eliot, on the other hand, was unnuanced and unchanging.

Williams assembled the manuscript of *Spring and All* (1923) in reaction to *The Waste Land*.[15] The two works are now, of course, widely considered of the most signal importance to the history of American poetry. But at the time, in contrast to the impact of *The Waste Land*, the publication of *Spring* was a complete nonevent: most of the three hundred copies printed in Dijon were destroyed by U.S. customs.[16] The single meeting between the two poets, in 1948, furnishes a fitting conclusion to Williams's inverse trajectory vis-à-vis Eliot. By this point, Eliot ruled poetry in English, stylistically, critically, and, as senior editor at Faber and Faber, logistically; he would receive the Nobel Prize a month later; Williams's omission from Conrad Aiken's 1945 anthology of American poetry makes a suitable counter-emblem.[17] Eliot's one recorded remark was the following: "Williams, you've given us some good characters in your work, let's have more of them."[18] By pointedly praising the short stories (faintly, to be sure), Eliot was confirming Williams's status as a nonpoet.

Eliot's triumph set the terms for Williams's critical reception during his lifetime and for decades afterward. To parse the battle schematically: on the victor's side there would be the major poem (*The Waste Land*, *The Cantos*), authoritative criticism, and established protocols of knowledge requiring the services of professional academics to be circulated. Eventually, Williams could approximate these accomplishments: *Paterson* was crucial to his wider acceptance; Marjorie Perloff calls it his "major work, the poem that finally made him famous."[19] To match the critical terms of Pound and Eliot there would be Williams's variable foot.[20] But where Eliot and Pound had spawned critical industries devoted to explication, Williams's work was always open to charges of confusion if not simplemindedness. Randall Jarrell's rave review of the first book of *Paterson* had been most responsible for Williams's success; but when Williams concluded Book 2 with eight pages of a Marcia Nardi letter, Jarrell's reaction was incredulousness: "What has been done to them to make it possible for us to respond to [Nardi's letters] as art and not as raw reality? ... I can think of no answer except: *They have been copied out on the typewriter* [emphasis in original]."[21] As for the variable foot, despite some smart and generous attempts to grapple with what Williams meant,[22] the term has always been vulnerable to commonsense dismissal. If the variable foot is taken as referring to syllables heard in real time, a skeptic would ask if the following units from one of Williams's stairstep lines were really intended to be similar in duration: (1) "even" and (2) "an initiation, since the spaces it opens are new places" (*WCPII*, p. 245).[23] The editor of the current *Oxford Anthology of American Poetry* writes, affectionately but dismissively, "One of the secrets of modern American poetry is that no one knows what 'the variable foot' really is."[24]

In a letter that Williams quotes in the preface to *Kora*, Pound gives Williams the left-handed compliment of "opacity," which Pound thinks comes from Williams's mixed ancestry. It is rather close to saying that Williams is dense: "And America? What the h – l do you a blooming foreigner know about the place.... You thank your bloomin gawd you've got enough Spanish blood to muddy up your mind.... The thing that saves your work is opacity, and don't forget it" (*IM*, p. 11). Pound's perception of Williams hardly changed: in a 1930 review, he praises (again) Williams's "opacity" and the "lack of celerity of his process"; *Kora*, Pound finds, is "Rimbaud forty years late."[25] Such condescension carries through to Charles Olson, who complained to Robert Creeley that "Bill, with all due respect, don't know fr nothing abt what a city *is*."[26] In a private letter, he was harsher: "Bill's own lack of intellect is sabotaging . . . all our positions."[27]

One might ascribe such swipes to the contentiousness of poetic rivals. But senses of Williams as untutored, a bit of a bumpkin, are not hard to come by: throughout his work, one finds moments of naïveté, pugnaciousness, clowning, blunt crudity, foregrounded gaps, and mistakes – all manifestations of his aversion to authority and prestige. In *Kora* Williams quotes a letter from H.D. deploring his lack of seriousness, "the hey-ding-ding touch . . . as if you mocked at your own song" (*IM*, p. 13), and then seems to prove her right by declaring, "There is nothing sacred about literature, it is damned from one end to the other" (*IM*, p. 13). Although Book 5 of *Paterson* (1958) contains much valedictory lyrical seriousness, the lines likeliest to lodge in memory are, "Paterson, / keep your pecker up, / whatever the detail!" (*P*, p. 231).

Such moments can't be separated out from what is most serious in his work. The foregrounded silliness of the opening of *Spring* and the brokenness of the prose throughout are not a turning away from the challenge that Eliot's poetics posed: they are part of Williams's answer. However, Williams's turn away from cultured language does not always guarantee vivid liveliness. One of his most famous poems, "To Elsie,"[28] begins memorably – "The pure products of America / go crazy –" (*WCPI*, p. 217) – but is soon full of cliché: "devil-may-care-men who have taken / to railroading / out of sheer lust of adventure." This could be read as an unannounced switch into the diction of adventure magazines; such a reading would make Williams a bit of a Joycean[29] (and such a reading could be supported by many similar moments of juxtaposed diction in *Paterson*). But the lines can also be taken simply as ordinary (careless) phrasing. "The Black Winds" (poem V) in *Spring* begins with imagery that can only be called hackneyed: "Black winds from the north / enter black hearts. Barred from // seclusion in lilies they strike / to destroy –" (*WCPI*, p. 189–90). Yet the poem ends with a crisp modernist credo: "How easy to slip / into the old mode, how hard to / cling firmly to the advance –" (*WCPI*, p. 191).

Williams began by writing bad Keatsian pastiche ("For I must read a lady poesy / The while we glide by many a leafy bay" [*WCPI*, p. 21]) and in a few years had progressed into a modernist mode: free verse, no capitals at the beginnings of lines, and everyday language and images. The seventh section of "January Morning" reads in its entirety: "– and the worn / blue car rails (like the sky!) / gleaming among the cobbles!" (*WCPI*, p. 101). But Williams's advance is never chronologically pure. The expressive subject from his belated Romanticism has not disappeared into modernist objectivity: throughout his work, Williams's subjectivity is hard to miss. Often the poet's enthusiasm is betrayed by exclamation marks, which Williams consistently uses more than any other modernist. The end of "January Morning" makes the subjective dimension blatant, as Williams addresses his mother: "All this – / was for you, old woman. / I wanted to write a poem / that you would understand. / For what good is it to me / if you don't understand it? (*WCPI*, p. 103).

Another poem from this period, "Portrait of a Lady," shows Williams's advancing compositional sophistication, as he conceives of the poem as an event in its own right, free from any need for description. The opening lines mix sarcastic imagery, distanced but genuine eroticism, and an aggressive appropriation of art history: "Your thighs are appletrees / whose blossoms touch the sky. / Which sky? The sky / where Watteau hung a lady's / slipper." A few lines later Williams is playing with the conceits he has invented: "Ah, yes – below / the knees, since the tune / drops that way, it is / one of those white summer days, / the tall grass of your ankles / flickers upon the shore – / Which shore? – / the sand clings to my lips –" (*WCPI*, p. 129). Such a passage, neither description nor interior monologue, illustrates a point Williams would make later: "The poet thinks with his poem" (*A*, pp. 390–91). However, the subjectivity of the poet is hardly absent here, as the poem is also an erotic colloquy between poet and "lady."

During the 1920s Williams began publishing substantial amounts of prose, with *In the American Grain* (1925) garnering the most contemporary attention. It is a highly personal account of American history, focusing on an archipelago of representative figures: Columbus, De Soto, Cotton Mather, Daniel Boone, Washington, and Poe, among others. Making no attempt at an objective history, Williams writes from a quasi-identificatory position, continually telling a similar story: the unfinished creation of an American culture, a process involving the falling away of European norms under the shock of physical contact with the unknown New World. This was a scenario that applied closely to Williams's own attempts to fashion a modernist poetic idiom in America while resisting European sophistication. Poe was the exemplar: "It is NOT culture to oppress a novel environment with the stale, if symmetrical, castoffs of another battle.... Poe could look at France, Spain, Greece and NOT be impelled to copy."[30] One could read "Williams" for "Poe" there without much distortion of meaning.

Williams's experimental prose and prose-poetry pieces of the period, *Kora*, *Spring*, *The Great American Novel*, and *The Descent of Winter*, have, since their republication in *Imaginations* (1970), been highly esteemed by generations of innovative poets and pro-innovative critics. But their initial impact was minimal: in addition to their paltry circulation, Williams's experiments blatantly revealed the spontaneity of their composition. As its title makes clear, the pieces in *Kora* were improvised. The book was a yearlong series of daily prose pieces, scribbled at odd hours in the midst of his medical practice. For example: "Awake early to the white blare of a sun flooding in sideways. Strip and bathe in it. Ha, but an ache tearing at your throat – and a vague cinema lifting its black moon blot all out.... There's no dancing save in the head's dark" (*IM*, p. 66). About the preceding excerpt, Williams comments: "In the mind there is a continual play of obscure images which coming between the eyes and their prey seem pictures on a screen at the movies.... The wish would be to see not floating visions of unknown purport but the imaginative qualities of the actual things" (*IM*, p. 67).

It is easy to read Williams's best-known poetic slogan, "No ideas but in things," as rejecting everything save physical description. However, although Williams almost always rejected the vague interiority of "the head's dark," it was never the pure exteriority of "actual things" that his poems aimed to reveal: it was the middle term that he valued, "the imaginative qualities" of what he perceived. In the broken prose of *Spring*, a constantly occurring word is "imagination," which could provide "an escape from crude symbolism, the annihilation of ... ritualistic forms designed to separate the work from 'reality' – such as rhyme, meter.... The work will be in the realm of the imagination as plain as the sky to a fisherman – A very clouded sentence. The word must be put down for itself" (*IM*, p. 18). The prose of *Spring* is almost always "very clouded": Williams never settles on what he means by imagination, but the poems, in their variousness, give a sense of its capaciousness. There is his best-known poem, "The Red Wheelbarrow," whose minimalist focus on the physical can obscure its form (three-word / one-word stanzas) and its verbal dexterity (breaking "wheelbarrow" into its two constituent nouns and decomposing rain into process, "rain," and material, "water"). Other poems show Williams's interest in Cubism and Dada: "The sunlight in a / yellow plaque upon the / varnished floor // is full of a song / inflated to / fifty pounds pressure" (*WCPI*, p. 196). "Shoot It Jimmy!" lineates American speech: "Our orchestra / is the cat's nuts – // ... // That sheet stuff / 's a lot a cheese" (*WCPI*, p. 216). "To Elsie" is a complex poem that, despite Williams's anti-Eliot stance, now can be read as an American equivalent to *The Waste Land*. Here, Williams is as unhappy with modernity as Eliot is; Elsie, who surfaces in the middle of the poem, is as bleak a figure as Eliot's Lil or the young man carbuncular. But where Eliot uses scorn to distance himself (and his readers) from such unappealing personages, Williams allows Elsie to be emblematic of

the present, which includes poet and reader: she "express[es] with broken //
brain the truth about us." Where the end of *The Waste Land* gestures, however
ironically, toward some transcendent conclusion ("Shantih shantih shantih"),
"Elsie" leaves us in an open-ended present, in a moving car careening toward
an unknown future: "No one / to witness / and adjust, no one to drive the
car" (*WCPI*, pp. 218–19).

In the teens and 1920s it was easy for modernists as different as Pound and
Stein to imagine that innovative writing had a real social impact. In the 1930s,
the Depression and the rise of fascism made such confidence obsolete. In the
1920s one can see Williams collaging different social perspectives in poems;
in the 1930s emblematic social figures appear, for instance, in "Proletarian
Portrait," which presents a "big bareheaded woman / in an apron" – although
Williams is careful to avoid the heroism of proletarian poetry, as this woman
merely takes off her shoe and "pulls out the paper insole / to find the nail /
That has been hurting her" (*WCPI*, p. 384). She has the power to improve her
own situation in this small way; improving the world is another matter. In
"The Yachts," one of his major poems of the period, Williams maintains the
tension between the exquisite calibrations of fine art and unnuanced human
needs. At first the yachts "appear youthful, rare // as the light of a happy eye,
live with the grace / of all that in the mind is fleckless, free and / naturally to
be desired." But in the latter half of the poem the yacht race becomes a "horror," and our attention is turned away from the triumphal elegance of the
yachts toward the supporting medium, the water, which is seen as "an entanglement of watery bodies / lost to the world bearing what they cannot hold"
(*WCPI*, pp. 388–89). Incidentally, here is another example of Williams aiming
to register "imaginative qualities," rather than simply "things."

Williams's notion of a poem as a made thing rather than a personal expression finds its most memorable expression in the introduction to *The Wedge*
(1944), in which we are told that a poem is a "machine made of words" (*WCPII*,
p. 54). However, "machine" shouldn't be taken as implying standardization,
which Williams dismisses two paragraphs later: "all sonnets say the same
thing of no importance." While many of his best poems of the 1940s, such as
"Burning the Christmas Greens" (*WCPII*, pp. 62–65) and "The Clouds" (*WCPII*,
pp. 171–74), hardly seem machinelike and in fact are discursive, Williams often
makes his poems meditations on what a new poetics might require: "Let the
snake wait under / his weed / and the writing / be of words, slow and quick,
sharp / to strike, quiet to wait, / sleepless." Note that the image representing
the poem is not a machine, but a living thing:

> Compose. (No ideas
> but in things.) Invent!
> Saxifrage is my flower that splits
> the rocks. (*WCPII*, p. 55)

Some of Williams's most celebrated poems were written in the latter part of his career. "The Desert Music" (1951) is something of an *ars poetica*, containing a mix of modes typical of Williams: vulgarity – "an old whore in / a cheap Mexican joint in Juárez, her bare / can waggling crazily" (*WCPII*, p. 281) – appears side by side with eloquent gratitude for the human capacity for writing: "And I could not help thinking / of the wonders of the brain that / hears that music and of our / skill sometimes to record it" (*WCPII*, p. 284). A stern sense of poetic exactitude – "Only the counted poem, to an exact measure: / to imitate, not to copy, nature" (*WCPII*, p. 272) – is counterpointed by the following answer as to why one writes a poem: "I am that he whose brains / are scattered / aimlessly" (*WCPII*, p. 282).

"Asphodel, That Greeny Flower" (1953) is Williams's longest poem outside of *Paterson* and one of his best known, primarily due to these lines: "It is difficult / to get the news from poems / yet men die miserably every day / for lack / of what is found there" (*WCPII*, p. 318). Originally conceived as belonging to Book 5 of *Paterson*, "Asphodel" mixes direct address to Flossie with a series of meditations on the power of poetry to confront the newly unleashed atomic bomb. Williams's dealings with Flossie have received a mixed reception. Although it is touching to read what is essentially love poetry written by a frail old man to his wife of four decades, many readers have found Williams's confession of his infidelities to be maudlin and self-serving.

Williams and women is not a topic to be clarified in a few paragraphs. Williams was terrifically interested in women, and, as a son (whose mother lived in close contact with him until her death at 102), husband (for more than fifty years), serial philanderer, and obstetrician who delivered 2,000–3,000 babies, his experiences with them were intimate, multitudinous, and lifelong. Given his candor and aggressive refusal of decorum, it is not surprising that many readers have found moments, passages, and, in the case of *Paterson*, whole poems to be offensive. Moments of objectification are everywhere: in the often-commented-on line break in *Spring* – "a girl with one leg / over the rail of a balcony" (*WCPI*, p. 206) – or in the more "Cubist" (in a homegrown sense) poem that uses "the Police Sergeant wife's perfect thighs" (*WCPI*, p. 154) as a repeating compositional element. More generally, it is the undisguised presence of Williams's excitement that has seemed untoward: "– she / opened

the door! nearly / six feet tall, and I ... / wanted to found a new country –"
(*WCPI*, p. 331; ellipsis in original).

Debaters could trade passages and poems endlessly to convict or exon-
erate, but it should be noted that some of the most intense reactions to
Williams have come from women, starting in the 1920s with Else von Freytag-
Loringhoven's vituperations against Williams, in which she insisted that the
experimental *Kora* was nothing more than the hypocritical high jinks of a suburban husband, and extending to Alice Notley's *Doctor Williams' Heiresses* and
Rachel DuPlessis's "Pater-Daughter."[31] DuPlessis and Notley praise and censor
Williams intensely. For Notley, he is the most useful poet, "How could you not
use him since he was the greatest one?"; although she is also emphatic that, at
times, his "reasoning was specious and enraging."[32] DuPlessis is also emphatic
in her praise, saying that *Spring* is "an amazing new document of change, of
challenge, of difference"; but she finds its conclusion, a clichéd apostrophe to
an "Arab / Indian / dark woman" who is "rich / in savagery" (*WCPI*, p. 236),
to be dismal: "It returns us to the 'savagery' of sameness. Oldness. A conventional vocabulary of race and gender."[33] This critique of *Spring* applies on a
larger scale to *Paterson*.

Paterson resists summary, although Williams did present a number of simple
schemes for it – in this, contradicting a basic practice of his writing, which was
predicated on discovery rather than fleshing out of prior thinking. *Paterson*
was to follow the course of the Passaic: "the river above the Falls, the catastrophe of the Falls itself, the river below the Falls and the entrance at the end to
the great sea" (*P*, p. xiii). The roar of the falls seemed "a language which we
were and are seeking." Another primary theme is announced in Book 1: "A
man like a city and a woman like a flower / – who are in love. Two women.
Three women. / Innumerable women, each like a flower. // But / only one
man – like a city" (*P*, p. 7). Williams did not stick closely to such plans – for
which many readers will be grateful. Naturalized gender roles and rivers representing life cycles are turgid thematic notions, especially when compared
with the rapid multifariousness of Williams's non-epic work. It seems the lifelong traumatic challenge that Williams projected onto Pound and Eliot called
for the epic, and the epic, in turn, called for such hoary props.

Each of the five books contains three sections, some of which are focused
around specific locales or narratives. The first section of Book 2, "Sunday
in the Park," is organized around the protagonist, sometimes referred to as
"Paterson," walking amid Sunday picnickers; a large part of the second section is given over to the futile, enthusiastic harangues of a Salvation Army
preacher. The second section of Book 3 focuses on the fire that destroyed the

Paterson library; the opening section of Book 4, subtitled "An Idyl," narrates, in jumpy, intercut fashion, the relations between three figures: a New York socialite (rather mockingly called "Corydon") with lesbian longings toward her working-class masseuse ("Phyllis"), who does not reciprocate but who does appear to be having a sporadic affair with a doctor ("Paterson"). However, such capsule summaries miss the coruscating line-by-line, page-by-page texture of the poem. Any page might interweave reference to other material in the poem; the verse is constantly interrupted by chunks of miscellaneous prose: bits of nineteenth-century histories of Paterson, local weather reports, flyers, and letters from literary and nonliterary contemporaries.

At times, the prose is thematically apropos: in the midst of the "Beautiful Thing" passage in Book 3 – a fraught, lyrical meditation on an African American prostitute who has been beaten up at a party – Williams interposes a savagely unfeeling colonial account of French explorers torturing Native Americans. But often quotations will offer no symbolic recuperation, as in the letter from Alva N. Turner discussing family matters in minute detail (P, p. 26).

Paterson was to be "a reply to Greek and Latin with the bare hands" (P, p. 2), challenging Pound's and Eliot's conservative erudition. But the extensive collaged quotations in *Paterson* would have been unthinkable without Pound's example. The difference between how the two use the collaged elements is significant. In *The Cantos*, the quoted language is always integrated into Pound's compositional and rhythmic purposes. Williams's quotations, on the other hand, have struck many as problematically long. It is as if readers are put into the position of virtual doctors listening to patients.

The Nardi letters, which dominate Book 2, are an extreme example, as well as being ethically controversial. Is Williams exploiting her? Is he giving her a public platform for her eloquent and sometimes obsessive complaints about the difficulties of getting support for writing when one is a woman? The inclusion of so much of the letters also raises issues of authorship, as Book 2 becomes as much Nardi's as Williams's. Mike Weaver takes a judicious approach when he writes that Nardi and other figures "are not represented in *Paterson* because they are neurotic, but because their veracity as thwarted human beings – their unimpaired though distorted vigour"[34] is a supreme value for Williams.[35]

Throughout Book 1 the roar of the falls is apostrophized as a source of genuine language that cannot be harnessed: "... no words. / They may look at the torrent in / their minds / and it is foreign to them" (P, p. 12). Occasionally the description of the falls is physical: "And the air lying over the water / ... / parallel but never mingling, one that whirls / backward at the brink and curls invisibly / upward, fills the hollow, whirling, / an accompaniment – but apart" (*P*, pp. 24–25); more often the falls furnish a pervading metaphoric backdrop, as in the following, in which Williams applies imagery of falling water both to the hair of two young girls and to the air surrounding them. "Two – / disparate among the pouring / waters of their hair ... one – / a willow twig pulled from a low / leafless bush in full bud in her hand, ... holds it, the gathered spray, / upright in the air, the pouring air, / strokes the soft fur – / / Ain't they beautiful!" (*P*, p. 18).

The unsophisticated aesthetic enthusiasm of the girls reads as a critique of the excessive lyricism of the previous lines, although Williams constantly laments the failure of language in general terms: "the language / fails them / They do not know the words / or have not / the courage to use them" (*P*, p. 11). But when actual speech is quoted, it is unpretentious and lively, a source of poetic energy rather than a symptom of failure: "Hi, open up a dozen, make / it two dozen! Easy girl! / You wanna blow a fuse?" (*P*, p. 137). In his *Autobiography* Williams is explicit about this, boasting that he got his language "from the mouths of Polish mothers" (*A*, p. 311). The tacit polemic here is directed against the refinement of Pound's language and the traditionalism of Eliot's.

Paterson does not come to anything like a neat conclusion. In fact, near the end of Book 4, Williams disparages coherence: "Waken from a dream, this dream of / the whole poem" (*P*, p. 199). As it progresses, *Paterson* opens up more and more to its present context; the first section of Book 5 contains a letter from the young Allen Ginsberg that comments on the preceding parts of the poem, saying, among other things, that Williams doesn't know much about the actual city of Paterson in the present. The second section ends with an excerpt from an interview in which the journalist Mike Wallace grills Williams on the apparent eccentricities of modern poetry. The poem becomes something of a bulletin board for younger generations – a contemporary instantiation might be *Paterson: A Blog*.

The best readers of Williams, starting with Hart Crane and Louis Zukofsky in the 1920s, have been the subsequent generations of poets, for whom his writing remains centrally instructive. Frank O'Hara named Williams, Crane, and Whitman the only American poets who were "better than the movies"; for Robert Pinsky, Williams is the poet who best "takes up [Whitman's] vision of poetry as a central national art."[36]

Williams has been frequently invoked at the beginning of literary initiatives. Donald Allen's introduction to the pathbreaking anthology of nonacademic poetic movements, *The New American Poetry* (1960), begins its list of notable modernist ancestors with Williams – Eliot is omitted. Robert Grenier's "On Speech" (1971) is often cited as a key opening articulation of the poetics of Language writing, attacking the presumed naturalism of everyday language. There, Williams is invoked as a prior limit to be superseded, with Grenier looking for "the progression from Williams"; but Williams is also used as the model for what is to come next. *"To me, all speeches say the same thing, or: why not exaggerate, as Williams did, for our time proclaim an abhorrence of 'speech' designed as was his castigation of 'the sonnet'"*[37]

Charles Bernstein's polemic "The Academy in Peril: William Carlos Williams Meets the MLA" (1983) makes Williams's career emblematic of a century-long division between innovative and conservative writing: "Williams, more than almost any other American poet of his time, took an activist position ... – his work is an intervention ... against static forms of knowledge.... Official verse culture is no more hospitable to Williams's literary politics now [1983] than it was fifty years ago."[38]

Ten years later, Hank Lazer gave a succinct rundown of "the two Doctor Williamses," posing Bernstein's textual poet against Williams as "the poet of common objects, immediate description, and common life."[39] This is where things stand in the twenty-first century, but the larger point is that Williams doesn't fit into such a binary struggle. To give a less abstract sense of what this means, let us list some of the different historical inflections and temporal sequences that can be detected in "This Is Just to Say."

The poem's simple vocabulary, narrative economy, and realism – in the sense that Williams actually ate those plums and then scrawled those lines – make it suitable for eighth grade pedagogy. However, this referentiality was problematized by deconstructive critics in the 1970s. As Jonathan Culler put it:

A note left on a kitchen table which read "This is just to say I have eaten the plums which were in the icebox and which you were probably saving for breakfast. Forgive me, they were delicious: so sweet and so cold" would be a nice gesture; but when it is set down on the page as a poem the convention of significance comes into play.... The value affirmed by the eating of the plums ... transcends language and cannot be captured ... except negatively (as apparent insignificance), which is why the poem must be so sparse and superficially banal.[40]

Readers with more sensitivity to nuances of erotic relations have not found the poem to be (even superficially) banal. (In an interview in his old age, Williams himself called it "practically a rape of the icebox!"[41]) But first, note Culler's transcription: not his elimination of the lineation (which is his point), but his addition of normative punctuation. When Culler writes, "Forgive me, they were delicious: so sweet and so cold," the apology and the memory of the transgression are kept punctiliously separate; the colon in "delicious: so sweet and so cold" anatomizes the guilty pleasure into its subsidiary sensations. Williams's quatrain, on the other hand, achieves complexity via the absence of punctuation.

Although the scribbling of the actual note may well have taken no more than one minute, it had taken Williams more than a decade to establish a form that was clearly syntactic but did not use punctuation. It does not appear in his work until the poems of *Spring*. In "To Elsie," although there are no periods, new sentences begin with capital letters:

> while the imagination strains
> after deer
> going by fields of goldenrod in
>
> the stifling heat of September
> Somehow
> it seems to destroy us
>
> It is only in isolate flecks that
> something
> is given off
>
> No one
> to witness
> and adjust, no one to drive the car
>
> (*WCPI*, pp. 218–19)

If we read "This Is Just to Say" with this template in mind, we get the following sentence: "Forgive me they were delicious so sweet and so cold." This run-on does not distinguish between the atonement and the vivid restatement of the crime; this in turn expresses a complex of possible emotions, from narcissism to sadism to intimacy with the addressee. Readings of such a complex will vary widely: the fact that the poem is an artifact of address utterly embedded in real life adds as much to the lability of poetic sense as any of the formal devices.

One more compositional element should be mentioned: the title, which does not function as a caption but begins the syntactic statement of the poem: that is, "This is just to say I have eaten . . ."; the title is thus both part of the poem and outside it. Williams seems to have invented this specific form, although he does not use it all that often.[42] But the aesthetic implications of being able to gesture both inside and outside the frame of the poem are important throughout his work, especially in *Paterson*. In regard to "This Is Just to Say," the effect is the opposite of the run-on "Forgive me / they were delicious": it bespeaks a detachment on the part of the author.

If there are two Williamses currently being used as emblems for opposing poetries, his own work, if cited judiciously, can prove him a textualist or a realist. But, as we have seen repeatedly, Williams does not fit easily into such dichotomies. The interview with Mike Wallace in *Paterson*, Book 5, shows the two approaches superimposed. Wallace, rather like our teacher in the opening anecdote, is upset by modern poetry, which is both obscure and too close to real life. He confronts Williams with an e. e. cummings poem as an example of obscurity:

> (im)c-a-t(mo)
> b,i;l:e
>
> FallleA
> ps! . . .

The contemporary reader can strip away the typographic high jinks to produce the rather cute "I'm cat-mobile. Fall leaps!" But Williams admits to Wallace that he can make nothing of Cummings's lines. Wallace stays on the attack, quoting some of Williams's own lines – ". . . a Dungeness crab / 24 hours out / of the Pacific / and a live-frozen / trout / from Denmark . . ." – and exclaiming, "Now, that sounds just like a fashionable grocery list!" At first Williams simply yields to the accusation, "It is a fashionable grocery list," but he then continues, "Rhythmically it's organized as a sample of the American idiom. . . . [I]f you treat that rhythmically, ignoring the practical sense it forms a jagged pattern. It is, to my mind, poetry." But then, undoing the opposition he has just made between linguistic pattern and practical sense, he says that both are to be perceived: "In poetry, you're listening to two things . . . [ellipses in original] you're listening to the sense, the common sense of what it says. But it says more" (*P*, p. 222).

Williams, as the writer being interviewed, offers a synthesis of reading for sense and attending to nonlinguistic music. But the author of *Paterson*'s Book 5 is posing more complex framing. We are reading, as part of *Paterson*, a quoted interview, a conversation between a poet and a reader, and an example of a poem narrating its own reception, as Mike Wallace, reporter for the *New York Post*, expresses the public's incredulity. Williams is showing himself as much object of history as subject.

And there is one more layer: the excerpt comes from one of the most emotional poems Williams ever wrote, "Two Pendants: For the Ears," an account of Williams tending his dying mother. One of the many strands of the poem involves coaxing the dying mother to eat. She has little appetite but occasionally eats an eccentric assortment of items: oysters, a banana, ice cream. Thus when Williams lists what someone brought home from the market, "2 partridges / 2 Mallard ducks ..." it reads as a moving attempt to amuse his mother and to pique her desire in the particulars of the world she is about to quit (*WCPII*, p. 208).

When Williams first admits to Wallace that "it is a fashionable grocery list," he is admitting to the basic problem that has plagued – and piqued – his readers. What he allows into his poem is too obviously real. But patterning, framing, and reframing make it art. This is akin to the paradox in the Duchamp readymade, which is how Henry M. Sayre reads "The Red Wheelbarrow." But Sayre wants art to be uncontaminated: "It is crucial that Williams' material is banal, trivial: by placing this material in the poem, Williams underscores the distance the material has traveled, and the poem defines a radical split between the world of art and the world of barnyards."[43]

It is just such a split that Williams never accepted. For him, art could not begin without the artist's attentive imbrication with the matters of everyday life. One of his short stories, "Comedy Entombed," furnishes a final example.[44] The story involves a woman who is having a slow-moving miscarriage. The quotidian details – discussions with the husband and interactions with the children – do not betoken any narrative drama. And yet at the end, when the husband asks about the sex of the dead fetus and is told it would have been the girl he was hoping for, his sadness and his wife's odd callousness create a powerful tableau.

At one nondramatic juncture (and at 4:30 in the morning), the doctor has a revelation:

> The whole place had a curious excitement about it for me.... There was nothing properly recognizable, nothing straight.... Tables, chairs, worn-out shoes piled in one corner.... I have seldom seen such disorder and brokenness – such a mass of unrelated parts of things lying about. That's it! I concluded to myself. An unrecognizable order! Actually – the new!
>
> And so good-natured and calm. So definitely the thing! And so compact. Excellent. And with such patina of use. Everything definitely "painty." Even the table, pushed off from the center of the room. (*FD*, p. 327)

One could call this a democratic readymade, if that term be thought of as encompassing everyday use along with its commitment to perfected abstraction. Note how Williams's recognition of "the new!" doesn't end things: his aesthetic elation extends into effervescent commonalities: "So definitely the thing!" and so on. The room looks like an exciting painting due to its "patina of use" – its being lived in. It is both new and used: its use adds to its newness. Williams is no demiurge: he didn't make this new order; he merely recognized it. His stock of knowledge has not been increased, just his openness. This openness is "the new" for the doctor in the story, for Williams as he wrote the story, and for readers today.

A Note on Gertrude Stein

It is interesting – and there is just enough room – to apply the oxymoronic notion of a democratic readymade to the other major antischolarly and American-identified modernist: Gertrude Stein. This is not to say Stein wrote readymades; there are no readymades but Duchamp's, and the Duchamp readymade is the opposite of democratic.[45] Anyone can buy a snow shovel; only Duchamp could buy what became *In Advance of the Broken Arm*. But the democratic readymade, however incorrect the term, dramatizes an issue basic to Stein's work. The scandal of the readymade was to commandeer the common as a sign of the singular. Stein did something like this, deploying common words and everyday objects for highly singular ends. She repeatedly created difference out of sameness and is today widely identified with the trope of using the same word differently: "Rose is a rose is a rose is a rose";[46] "there is no there there."[47]

But her provocation went beyond making difference palpable. Turning a snow shovel into *Broken Arm* was a gesture of separation meant to shock the bourgeoisie; Stein's gestures were more pervasively unsettling: their singularity was not in the service of separation. Stein commandeered the common with the aim of becoming part of the everyday world – an important part, an eminent one, but very much of that world. She may have written and acted like a genius who was ahead of her time, but hers was an avant-garde of the ordinary: both her early notoriety and her later popularity index this.

The scale and seriousness of her writing and the persistence with which she addressed her work (and herself) to the public produced complex aesthetic and social effects. Early and late, her range was wide. Consider the stylistic distances between "Melanctha" (1909) and *Tender Buttons* (1914): the former with its tortuous, not-quite-repetitive syntax and basic but ambiguous vocabulary continually suggesting but never resolving complex emotional turmoil and the latter a playful, at times erotically charged, venture into quasi-Cubist, polysyntactic portraiture of the everyday lifeworld. Another disparate pair would be the best-selling *Autobiography of Alice B. Toklas* and the uncompromisingly abstract *Stanzas in Meditation*, both written in 1932. However, a fundamental concern threads through her various procedures: the coincidence of the ordinary and the different.

In "Composition as Explanation" (1926), Stein continually presents her own genius as almost indistinguishable from everyday modernity and yet as completely distinct. The play of sameness/difference begins with the opening clause: "There is singularly nothing that makes a difference a difference ..." A range of detractors, from reporters to competing modernists like T. S. Eliot and Wyndham Lewis, scorned such language, dismissing it as nonsense or an attempt at nursery rhyme. But Stein is juxtaposing the two differences to compactly demonstrate a word being either charged or empty: some differences don't make any difference. Then again, some do, and there is singularly nothing like them.

The materials of Stein's work are ordinary words and familiar things, but she puts them to unfamiliar use, as when, in the next paragraph of "Composition," she contrasts war with genuine creativity. War is old-fashioned, "prepared" beforehand, and thus academic; it is the same as bad writing and painting, which are produced by "those ... who don't make it as it is made." Counterpoised to these are the celebrated heroes: "the few who make it as it is made."[48] We might translate Stein's praise as promoting artistic process over product, but she uses more elementary words ("make," "made") to keep this activity both commonly available and mysterious. Bad artists fail to unite make and made; Stein activates what is almost, but is not, a tautology.

A well-known pleasantry in *The Autobiography of Alice B. Toklas* shows more of the complex imbrication of high art and the everyday. Toklas (that is, Stein writing as Toklas) tells us, "You cannot tell what a picture really is ... until you dust it every day."[49] The lightness and paradox are blatant – how quaint to put dusting above careful looking, especially when the objects being dusted are so valuable. But more is implicit here. Toklas is claiming authority: she knows what the Picassos and Cezannes *really* are. Then, too, note how the quintessentially bourgeois activity of dusting becomes the prime aesthetic act. And, furthermore, this bourgeois normativity presents, without disguise, the scandal of Stein and Toklas's unsanctioned but very proper lesbian marriage.[50]

"Scandal" will seem a dated term to many, although some have pushed for "re-scandalization," with Stein's stance toward the Vichy regime as the smoking gun. There's not much smoke there, however, beyond Stein's self-protective myopia.[51] Stein's often patrician political and historical opinions, while part of the record of her celebrity, are epiphenomenal to her self-enabling egotism. More remarkable is the writing that her behavior made possible. Her work remains an exciting exemplar for contemporary poets, with Bernadette

Mayer, Joan Retallack, Juliana Spahr, and Lee Ann Brown as notable examples. And her impact extends beyond the literary into the other arts.[52] Her work is shaping poetic and cultural history in ways that generic categories and evaluative scales have not succeeded in containing. DJ Spooky's mash-up of Stein reciting "If I Told Him: A Completed Portrait of Picasso" with DJ Wally makes one striking emblem of this incomplete, open-ended condition.

But this conjunction of Stein and recombinatory turntable music can be reconstrued to match T. S. Eliot's nearly century-old complaint, in which we are told that Stein's work was neither "improving," "amusing," or "interesting"; that it had a "kinship with the saxophone"; and that it portended a "future ... of the barbarians."[53] This is one of Eliot's least prophetic pronouncements, calling up anxious notions of Prufrock, crashing surf, and peaches. A more apt emblem of Stein's continuing pertinence could be brought forward by considering her catchphrase quoted at the beginning of this note: "there is no there there."

Consider how widely used this Steinianism is: it is a staple of political blogs, sports pages, and fashion shows – any context in which opinions contend. It is a highly portable, pragmatic rhetorical tool, using language – "there there" – to highlight the volatility of words and thus to incite linguistic vigilance against bogus claims of presence.

The original context of the phrase does more than this. Stein describes returning, in 1935, to the scene of her adolescence: "anyway what was the use of my having come from Oakland it was not natural to have come from there yes write about it if I like or anything if I like but not there, there is no there there."[54] Note the differences in these "theres": the first is fraught (a Freudian might even say "uncanny" – but not *there!*); the second is colorless, purely linguistic (the "there" of "there is"); and the last two perform the basic Steinian utopian move, in which the ordinary word becomes charismatic.

Notes

1. William Carlos Williams, *Collected Poems*, ed. A. Walton Litz and Christopher MacGowan (New York: New Directions, 1986), vol. I, p. 372. This collection will be cited subsequently in the text as *WCPI*. Other writings by Williams will be cited by abbreviations as follows: *A = Autobiography* (New York: New Directions, 1967); *WCPII = Collected Poems*, ed. Christopher MacGowan (New York: New Directions, 1988), vol. II; *FD = The Farmers' Daughters* (New York: New Directions, 1957); *IM = Imaginations*, ed. Webster Schott (New York: New Directions, 1970); *P = Paterson*, ed. Christopher MacGowan (New York: New Directions, 1992).

2. Bill Zavatsky, "Everything You Always Wanted to Know About Poetry," *The Whole Word Catalogue* 2 (1977), reprinted on the Academy of American Poets website, http://www.poets.org/viewmedia.php/prmMID/16062.

3. "Modernist," "avant-garde," and "democratic" are used here as simplified markers of differentiation: modernist indicating expertise (e.g., Joyce, Eliot); avant-garde indicating provocation (e.g., Duchamp, Tristan Tzara); and democratic indicating communicativeness (e.g., Frost).

4. Linda Wagner (ed.), *Interviews with William Carlos Williams* (New York: New Directions, 1961), p. 30.

5. Ezra Pound, *The Pisan Cantos*, ed. Richard Sieburth (New York: New Directions, 2003), p. 96; William Wordsworth, *The Oxford Authors: William Wordsworth*, ed. Stephen Gill (New York: Oxford University Press, 1984), p. 131.

6. "Books: Shantih Shantih Shantih," *Time*, March 3, 1924, http://www.time.com/time/magazine/article/0,9171,881419,00.html.

7. Although Lionel Trilling "wished to emphasize the subversive power of modern literature," he had to report the demise of such power: "When the term-essays come in, it is plain to me that almost none of the students have been taken aback by what they have read: they have wholly contained the attack." Trilling, "On the Teaching of Modern Literature," in Neil Jumonville (ed.), *The New York Intellectuals Reader* (New York: Routledge, 2007), pp. 223–41, 238.

8. Kenneth Koch, *Collected Poems* (New York: Knopf, 2007), p. 135.

9. Writing Tutor, "Writing Test Sample: Grade 8, Narrative Writing," http://written.co/2011/02/writing-test-sample-grade-8-narrative-writing.

10. William Carlos Williams, *I Wanted to Write a Poem: The Autobiography of the Works of a Poet*, ed. Edith Heal (Boston: Beacon Press, 1958), p. 5.

11. Ezra Pound, *ABC of Reading* (New York: New Directions, 1960), p. 37.

12. T. S. Eliot, *Selected Prose*, ed. Frank Kermode (New York: Harcourt, 1975), pp. 178–80.

13. Lawrence Rainey (ed.), *The Annotated Waste Land with Eliot's Contemporary Prose* (New Haven, Conn.: Yale University Press, 2005), p. 199.

14. David E. Chinitz speaks of Williams's "Thirty Years' War on Eliot." Chinitz, *T. S. Eliot and the Cultural Divide* (Chicago: University of Chicago Press, 2003), p. 144. On Williams's interest in Duchamp, see Henry M. Sayre, "Ready-Mades and Other Measures: The Poetics of Marcel Duchamp and William Carlos Williams," *Journal of Modern Literature* 8:1 (1980), pp. 3–22.

15. *Spring* contains sardonic echoes of Eliot's vocabulary in some of the poems, as well as a prose diatribe against "THE TRADITIONALISTS OF PLAGIARISM" (Williams, *Imaginations*, p. 97).

16. See Paul Mariani, *William Carlos Williams: A New World Naked* (New York: McGraw-Hill, 1981), p. 209. The radical mix of poetry and often-broken prose of *Spring* did not make a perceptible impact on American poetry until its republication in 1970.

17. William Rose Benet and Conrad Aiken (eds.), *An Anthology of Famous English and American Poetry* (New York: Modern Library, 1945).

18. This quote is taken from Williams's note. Quoted in Mariani, *William Carlos Williams*, p. 831n7.

19. Marjorie Perloff, *The Poetics of Indeterminacy: Rimbaud to Cage* (Evanston, Ill.: Northwestern University Press, 1983), p. 148.

20. Williams never defined the variable foot clearly. His letter to John C. Thirlwall is one of his most sustained discussions. He points to his own poem "The Descent" (Williams, *Collected Poems*, vol. II, p. 245), mentions Gerald Manley Hopkins and Whitman as antecedents, and speaks of Einstein's relativity – but does not offer a definition. William Carlos Williams, *Selected Letters of William Carlos Williams*, ed. John Thirlwall (New York: New Directions, 1957), pp. 334–36.

21. Charles Doyle (ed.), *William Carlos Williams: The Critical Heritage* (London: Routledge, 1980), p. 239. When the remarks are reprinted in *Poetry and the Age*, the italics are removed: see Randall Jarrell, *Poetry and the Age* (London: Faber, 1953), p. 230. For Jarrell's earlier rave, see Doyle, *William Carlos Williams*, pp. 174–79. Williams continues to be accused of fundamentally confusing life and art. In a current anthology, Lawrence Rainey complains of "Williams's truculent and dogmatic belief that poetry could offer unmediated access to the world": see Lawrence Rainey (ed.), *Modernism: An Anthology* (Oxford: Blackwell, 2005), p. 500. Williams's use of such swathes of Nardi's prose can be thought of as anticipating contemporary appropriation poetry such as Kenneth Goldsmith's.

22. See especially Mary Ellen Solt, *Toward a Theory of Concrete Poetry*, ed. Antonio Sergio Bessa (Buffalo: OEI, 2010) and also Stephen Cushman, *William Carlos Williams and the Meaning of Measure* (New Haven, Conn.: Yale University Press, 1985).

23. In the latter stages of his career, Williams often set his lines in staggered groups of three. For example:

> The descent beckons
>> as the ascent beckoned.
>>> Memory is a kind
>> of accomplishment, [Williams, *Collected Poems*, vol. II, p. 245]

This is often referred to as his stairstep line.

24. David Lehman (ed.), *The Oxford Book of American Poetry* (Oxford: Oxford University Press, 2006), p. 277.

25. Ezra Pound, "Doctor Williams' Position," in T. S. Eliot (ed.), *Literary Essays of Ezra Pound* (New York: New Directions, 1968), pp. 392–94. Williams, who was echoing a Pound letter, had already made a similar observation in *The Great American Novel* (Williams, *Imaginations*, p. 167).

26. Charles Olson, *Selected Writings*, ed. Robert Creeley (New York: New Directions, 1967), p. 84. In the Poundian shorthand Olson employs, "fr" equals "from" and "abt" equals "about."

27. George F. Butterick (ed.), *Charles Olson and Robert Creeley: The Complete Correspondence* (Los Angeles: Black Sparrow, 1987), vol. 7, p. 84.

28. Here I am referring to the titles Williams used later; in *Spring*, the poems were merely numbered.

29. "Joycean" is used here to connote the stylistic shifts of the latter half of *Ulysses*.

30. William Carlos Williams, *In the American Grain* (New York: New Directions, 1956), p. 225.

31. Else von Freytag-Loringhoven, "Thee I Call Hamlet of Wedding-Ring," *Little Review* 7:4 and 8:1 (1914), reprinted at http://www.modjourn.org/render .php?view=mjp_object&id=LittleReviewCollection; Alice Notley, *Doctor Williams' Heiresses* (Berkeley: Tuumba Press, 1980); Rachel Blau DuPlessis, *The Pink Guitar: Writing as Feminist Practice* (New York: Routledge, 1990).

32. Notley, *Doctor Williams' Heiresses*, n.p.

33. DuPlessis, *The Pink Guitar*, p. 41.

34. Mike Weaver, *William Carlos Williams: The American Background* (Cambridge: Cambridge University Press, 1977), p. 133.

35. See also Marcia Nardi, *The Last Word: Letters between Marcia Nardi and William Carlos Williams*, ed. Elizabeth Murrie O'Neil (Iowa City: University of Iowa Press, 1994).

36. Frank O'Hara, *Collected Poems*, ed. Donald M. Allen (New York: Knopf, 1971), p. 498; Robert Pinsky, *Poetry and the World* (New York: Ecco, 1988), p. 18.

37. Robert Grenier, "On Speech," *This* 1 (1971), n.p. Grenier is referring to Williams's "To me, all sonnets say the same thing of no importance."

38. Charles Bernstein, *Content's Dream* (Los Angeles: Sun & Moon, 1983), pp. 243–51, 244, 246.

39. Hank Lazer, *Opposing Poetries*. Vol. 2, *Readings* (Evanston, Ill.: Northwestern University Press, 1996), p. 21.

40. Jonathan Culler, *Structuralist Poetics* (Ithaca, N.Y.: Cornell University Press, 1975), pp. 175–76.

41. Wagner, *Interviews*, p. 17.

42. Some examples are "New England" (Williams, *Collected Poems*, vol. I, p. 249), "March Is a Light" (Williams, *Collected Poems*, vol. I, p. 266), and "The Moon –" (Williams, *Collected Poems*, vol. I, p. 326). Brian Reed, in conversation, notes that Marianne Moore's "The Fish" has precedence.

43. Sayre, "Ready-Mades and Others," p. 12.

44. This has already been quoted at the opening of this chapter, as an example of ordinary prose: the "old black-and-white cat lying in the sunny doorway."

45. For discussion of Stein and Duchamp, see Marjorie Perloff, "Of Objects and Readymades: Gertrude Stein and Marcel Duchamp," *Forum for Modern Language Studies* 32:2 (1996), pp. 137–54.

46. Gertrude Stein, "Sacred Emily," *Stein: Writings 1903–1932* (New York: Library of America, 1998), p. 395. It also appears in Gertrude Stein, *The Autobiography of Alice B. Toklas*, in *Stein: Writings 1903–1932*, with an initial article that obscures the proper name: "a rose is a rose is a rose is a rose" (p. 798).

47. Gertrude Stein, *Everybody's Autobiography* (Cambridge, Mass.: Exact Change, 1993), p. 298.

48. Stein, "Composition as Explanation," *Writings*, p. 520.

49. Stein, *Writings*, p. 776.

50. Wanda M. Corn and Tirza True Latimer, *Seeing Gertrude Stein: Five Stories* (Berkeley: University of California Press, 2011), p. 237: "Stein and Toklas put a well-mannered, mature face on lesbian sexuality.... They embodied American ideals of domesticity and family."

51. See Janet Malcolm, *Two Lives* (New Haven, Conn.: Yale University Press, 2007) and Barbara Will, *Unlikely Collaboration: Gertrude Stein, Bernard Faÿ, and the Vichy Dilemma* (New York: Columbia University Press, 2011); contra, see Charles Bernstein, "Gertrude Stein's War Years: Setting the Record Straight: A Dossier," *Jacket2*, https://jacket2.org/feature/gertrude-steins-war-years-setting-record-straight.

52. See Corn and Latimer, *Seeing Gertrude Stein*, chapter 5.

53. T. S. Eliot, "Charleston, Hey! Hey!" *Nation and Athenaeum*, January 29, 1927, p. 595.

54. Stein, *Everybody's Autobiography*, p. 298.

Chapter 26

Finding "Only Words" Mysterious: Reading
Mina Loy (and H.D.) in America

CRISTANNE MILLER

Mina Loy (1882–1966) is an anomalous addition to a history of "American" poetry – a fact perhaps most obvious in the frequent claiming and questioning of Loy as American, starting with Ezra Pound's 1918 assertion that Loy's verse has something "distinctly American in quality."[1] Born in England, Loy spent only slightly more than two years in the United States until 1936, when she was fifty-four, and only became a naturalized citizen in 1946. Most of the early poetry by which she is best known was written in Florence, Berlin, or Paris. U.S.-born expatriates like Gertrude Stein, Ezra Pound, H.D., and T. S. Eliot are invariably included in American literature anthologies, despite the fact that H.D. became a British citizen as early as 1912 and Eliot did the same in 1927. H.D. repeatedly identified herself as American and struggled to regain her citizenship – successfully in 1956. Others are understood to be American primarily because their formative years were spent in the United States. By the latter reasoning, Loy is distinctly English, and recent work on Loy considering her childhood or published in the United Kingdom suggests that her English roots may soon become a more prominent aspect of Loy criticism.[2]

At the same time, Loy regarded herself as aesthetically and ethically aligned with "America." Loy turned to her American friends and editors to publish; she was enabled by her sojourns in New York to move in new directions with her poetry and art; her primary influence has been on American poets – noted already in her warm reception by New York's most radical writers and artists in 1916; and she developed simultaneously a perception of American culture, modern aesthetics, and her own life and writing as emerging from a "melting pot" and "mongrel." Loy wrote as an Englishwoman of Jewish / Anglican heritage who had studied art in Munich from 1899 to 1901, studied and painted in Paris from 1903 until 1906, and then lived in Florence until the fall of 1916. She spoke German, French, and Italian; may have learned Spanish during her year with her second husband, Arthur Cravan (Fabian Lloyd), in Mexico City; and traveled extensively in Europe after returning there (by way of Argentina) at the end of 1918. Yet the two major changes of direction in her work occur around 1920 and then after 1936, in response to her experiences in New York.

First, Loy's ties to avant-gardism end sometime between December 1917, when she left New York City for Mexico to marry Cravan, and March 1920, when she returned to New York. During this period, Loy left satirical auto-mythologies behind and began to focus on aesthetics, eventually resulting in her articulation of an aesthetic of mongrel poetry in the epic-lyric "Anglo-Mongrels and the Rose." This poem also marks Loy's first representation of her Jewishness as significant to both her life and her poetry. Published in the same year as the final section of "Anglo-Mongrels," Loy's 1925 essay "Modern Poetry" gives expository and more explicit form to some of the ideas in her poem, while identifying the "new" verse as American in origin. Her work written up to the mid-1920s makes Loy among the most important poets of early modernism, although critics are also increasingly finding her late work and her visual art, drama, and fiction significant.

This chapter follows the trajectory of Loy's writing life from its beginnings in distinctly European avant-gardes through the influence of her early visits to the United States to a late poem titled "America * A Miracle." Primary characteristics of Loy's writing are shaped by her engagement in distinctly European avant-gardes, but after 1920, I argue, the directions of her creative energy are powerfully illuminated by being understood in an American context and through her own mapping of the "American." Loy's writing moves along a spectrum from reaction against Futurist precepts in the language and style of European artistic movements to a late articulation of similar principles, this time in a language of nationalism presenting the United States as an almost Whitmanian ideal location in which feminism, passion, and art can thrive.

Although modernism is rightly understood as international, what this meant at the beginning of the twentieth century was different from what it means to readers more than a century later. When Loy first began writing her poetry in Florence and publishing it in New York, mass media like newsreels and television had not been developed. Beginning in 1914, Loy mailed handwritten poems and her "Aphorisms on Futurism" in letters that traveled by ship from Florence to New York, asking her friends – especially Carl Van Vechten but also Mabel Dodge (Luhan) and Alfred Stieglitz – to place her work. Loy's poems were known as part of New York's early modernist scene, even though she was still in Florence.

Generally, in the early twentieth century, local communities of production had unique identifying characteristics.[3] Loy's early poems place themselves distinctly in such a local sphere, satirizing gender iniquity not universally but in response to the particular forms of misogyny and cultural restriction she experienced and witnessed in Florence. Loy herself calls attention to their local grounding through titles, epigraphs, or internal reference, in "Italian Pictures"; "Virgins Plus Curtains Minus Dots" – which begins with the epigraph "Latin Borghese" ("bourgeois" in Italian); "At the Door of the House" – with its reference to Tuscan marble and Italian names; and "The Black Virginity." These poems mark themselves as written in response to gendered patterns of life in a traditional small Italian city as witnessed by someone who is not Italian and whose experiences in London and Paris stand in strong contrast to those of the "Latin Borghese."

The specificity of the location of this critique becomes more apparent in comparison with that of the women poets who were Loy's most significant peers: Gertrude Stein (1874–1946), Marianne Moore (1887–1972), and H.D. (Hilda Doolittle, 1886–1961). Although Loy is least often compared to H.D., this comparison is in fact most striking in looking at the development of both poets' writing in relation to their lives. None of these American poets would imagine representing women in 1914 as housebound, requiring dowries, or dominated by hierarchies of the Catholic Church, although there are of course intersections among their economic, political, religious, and sexual critiques of gendered institutions and systems. H.D.'s "Sheltered Garden," for example, like Loy's "Virgins Plus Curtains" and "At the Door of the House," represents women through metaphor as protected, bound by borders. Rather than describing women as ready to "scratch" from behind a "locked" door ("Virgins Plus Curtains"), however, H.D. implicitly calls for women and men to reconceive aesthetics and the feminine: "beauty without strength, / chokes out life. / I want wind to break, / scatter these pink-stalks, / snap off their spiced heads."[4] "O to blot out this [sheltered] garden," she exclaims, and instead "find a new beauty / in some terrible / wind-tortured place."[5] While the long-honored trope of women as flowers suggests H.D.'s impatience with the "pink" loveliness of traditionally feminine women, she does not call for a literal snapping off of women's "spiced heads" but for eradicating the environment that produces such cultivated or artificial weakness as beautiful.

H.D.'s poems of the early 1910s refigure the feminine through natural landscapes that emphasize the need to alter gendered modes of perception and value, often by praising the vegetation that thrives in or on the shores of the rough, uncontrolled sea as her preferred model for beauty ("Sea Rose," "Sea Lilly," "Sea Poppies," "Sea Violet"). In an American city such as H.D.'s Philadelphia, women circulated in social, educational, and other public spheres; on public transportation; and in other ways that allowed them to be

relatively independent of male escort or permission – at least opening the possibility of experience closer to that of a primal seascape than that of a locked
house. H.D. also, however, imagines women declaring radical independence
even from within constrained circumstances. This is most strikingly exemplified in "Eurydice," in which from the world of the dead she tells Orpheus
"Against the black / I have more fervor / than you … I have more light; … I
have the flowers of myself, / and my thoughts, no god / can take that" (*HDCP*,
p. 55).

Loy's early poetry is equally marked by her location among European avant-
gardes. *Épater le bourgeois* was a rallying cry of French and English decadents
such as Baudelaire, Rimbaud, Oscar Wilde, and Aubrey Beardsley in the late
nineteenth century, and only somewhat less explicitly of the later proponents
of Futurism and Dada. Loy's early satires relish the shocking, in concert with
transnational avant-gardes. Similarly, her shifting devotion to various arts may
suggest her greater interest in avant-garde making than in the craft of any
single art. During her lifetime she was celebrated as both a visual artist and
a poet. Her work was accepted in the prestigious Paris Salon d'Automne in
1906. She also designed clothing; designed and made hats, lampshades, and
other decorative objects; and created three-dimensional art or junk sculptures;
in 1959 she won a Copley Foundation Award for Outstanding Achievement in
Art. Loy spent relatively few years writing poetry, composing almost all her
verse around 1914–1916 in Florence, between 1919 and 1925 in various places,
and in the 1940s in New York. Loy also more than once eschewed the title
"poet." She wrote Van Vechten that "to maintain my incognito, the hazard I
chose was – poet" and decades later responded to would-be "rediscoverers":
"I was never a poet" (*LoLB*, p. xii). In a late interview, Kerker Quinn reports
that "Miss Loy says she is a painter," not a poet.[6] The partial truth of these self-
representations illuminates the fragility of her earliest forays into publishing.
Although it seems probable that Loy would not have been animated to write
without her contact with Futurism, it also seems likely that she would not
have published without the encouragement and support of the Americans
she met in Florence, such as Carl Van Vechten, Mabel Dodge, and Gertrude
Stein.

In New York, modernists were less interested in outraging cultural norms
and less political in opposing specific cultural institutions than European avant-
gardists. Rather than producing manifestos, American modernists trumpeted
their inclusivity. Their little magazines, salons, and exhibitions were organized
by individuals who could find funding – from Stieglitz's 291 Gallery and *Camera*

Work; to the 1913 Armory Show; to the Arensbergs', Mabel Dodge's, and other salons; and to little magazines like *Others*, whose editor proclaimed that its contributors were not "members of a group, a school" and "collectively or separately ... eschew everything which approximates is-mism."[7] Similarly, the *Little Review* and the *Dial* avoided aligning themselves with specific movements or principles; as editor of the *Dial*, Marianne Moore remembers, "individuality was the great thing"; "we certainly didn't have a policy, except I remember hearing the word 'intensity' very often."[8] Man Ray, who famously photographed Loy and H.D., claimed "pleasure and liberty were the words I used [in New York], as my goals" – goals Rudolf E. Kuenzli describes as evidence of "fiercely individualistic Americans' resistance to yet another European label."[9] Alfred Kreymborg also stresses individuality in his previously quoted 1918 editorial, asserting that at *Others* the editors ask only to "be permitted to evolve their own individualism, if they possess any, and to allow other folk to evolve theirs."[10] New York's innovative individualism attempted to conceive aesthetic and literary community free of the boundaries of gender, class, and (to a lesser degree) race; hence it was exceptionally open to women's leadership in literature and the arts.[11] This may have been another reason for Loy's continuing ties to the United States. Although H.D.'s early writing gained attention in part through Pound, H.D. was typical of American modernists in regarding her writing as independent of all even loosely formal groups or movements, following Imagism's brief flare.

Much has been written about Loy's early association with Futurism. Her first publication was "Aphorisms on Futurism" (*Camera Work* [1914]) and several of her early poems and plays and her unpublished novel "Brontolivido" deal with Futurists, most prominently "The Effectual Marriage," "Sketch of a Man on a Platform," "Giovanni Franchi," "Human Cylinders," and her play "The Sacred Prostitute." Stylistically this early verse is equally indebted to what Loy calls the "inimitable Explosive" of Futurism and the profuse eroticism and artifice of the earlier decadent movement, which can also be seen in Loy's painting.[12] Futurism influences the exaggerated pronouncements, irregular capitalization, and visual spacing of Loy's poetry and manifestos: "THUS shall evolve the language of the Future. / THROUGH derision of Humanity as it appears – / TO arrive at respect for man as he shall be," Loy writes in "Aphorisms" (*LoLB*, p. 152). More significantly, her experimentation with the use of white space mid-line – what Suzanne Churchill calls her "signature formal device" – may develop from Futurism's visual play with the space of the page.[13] In the 1914 "Parturition," Loy writes:

```
Locate an irritation      without
It is                     within
                          Within
It is without
The sensitized area
Is identical     with the extensity
Of intension                              (LoLB, p. 4)
```

Similar spatial gaps occur in most of Loy's poems written before her first stay in New York and in "Anglo-Mongrels and the Rose." Such use of white space continues in a few poems of the 1920s, but after "Anglo-Mongrels," mid-line spacing largely disappears from her work, as does Futurist typography – with the primary exception of "Time-Bomb," which presents words widely spaced, as though an explosion has blown them apart (c. 1945). Because the manuscript copies of several poems are lost, we cannot be certain where spatial gaps have been edited out. Marissa Januzzi notes that many spaces between words are closed or reduced in typescripts for her 1958 *Lunar Baedeker and Time Tables* edition, but it is likely that *Others* and the *Dial* published her lines as she wrote them.[14]

Loy's stylistic innovation in part imitates and in part extends Futurist aesthetics, just as she is both inspired by Futurist practices of art and energized to formulate her rejection of its ideas. As she writes to Mabel Dodge in 1914, "I am in the throes of conversion to Futurism – But I shall never convince myself – there is no hope in any system that 'combats le mal avec le mal.'"[15] The same year she writes to Van Vechten, "If you like you can say that Marinetti influenced me – merely by waking me up – [but] I am in no way *considered* a Futurist by futurists" (*LoLB*, p. 188).

The Sacred Prostitute (1914) sheds some light on this initiating moment. Early in this play, a stage direction reads: "FUTURISM *arrives on the scene*" (*SEML*, p. 193). Futurism then functions as a character, spouting irrational sexist clichés to another character, "Love." Following the internationally popular sexologist Otto Weininger, Futurism proclaims, "I shall reach your soul through the medium of your body ... for women are only animals, they have no souls" (*SEML*, p. 199). The character Love (perhaps a figure for Loy) both humors Futurism and is enamored of him, desiring to be "galvanized by the force of [his] undiluted masculinity," and claiming she can remember and realize "nothing but you –" (*SEML*, pp. 212, 213). In what the Procuress (another Loy figure) calls "the play 'Man and Woman'" within Loy's play, Futurism seems to conquer Love, but he also disappears, and the play ends with the "Directors of the World Brothel," who appear to manipulate all male-female relationships in economic ratios of "supply" and "demand" (*SEML*, p. 215).

Loy was intrigued, amused, and annoyed by Futurist sexism and hypermasculinity, even while she seems to have enjoyed the sexual attention of particular Futurists. Love, as romantic thralldom, however, was as dangerous to women as any domineering man was. Women must choose "between *Parasitism, & Prostitution* – or *Negation*," she writes in her 1914 "Feminist Manifesto," representing marriage as nothing more than a legalized exchange of women's sexual freedom for economic support. "Leave off looking to men to find out what you are **not** – seek within yourselves to find out what you **are**," she more mildly recommends. Yet she also adopts a Futurist outrageousness in recommending "the *unconditional* surgical *destruction of virginity* through-out the female population at puberty" as a "protection against the man made bogey of virtue" and further demands that women "must destroy in themselves, the desire to be loved" (*LoLB*, pp. 154, 155).

Loy's attraction to stylistic features of decadence may represent her desire to construct a femininity that has the aggressive presence ascribed to masculinity without sacrificing an aesthetics of plenitude and fanciful flair. Futurism rejects all things feminine or foppish more than it rejects women per se, although these categories are entangled in complex ways in all sexological tracts of the period. The widespread influence of Weininger's *Sex and Character*, for example, reveals itself in proclamations like Filippo Tommaso Marinetti's "scorn for women" in his 1909 manifesto but also in Dora Marsden's controversial promotion of some of Weininger's ideas in *The Freewoman* in 1912 – a periodical Loy could have seen during her fall 1912 visit to London.[16] In 1916–1917, H.D. became literary editor of this periodical, renamed *The Egoist*. In contrast to Futurism's aggressive masculinity, in decadent art like that of Aubrey Beardsley, Loy would have found an artificiality so ostentatiously contrived that it blurs natural categories of gender and sexuality while celebrating the erotic in a way inclusive of what sexologists dismissed as "feminine" materiality. Similarly, Loy's language use is above all artificial. Often described as abstract, it combines various registers, favors obscure or highly specialized vocabularies – often contrasted with slang or other colloquial usage – borrows from Loy's multilingualism, and manipulates alliteration and other forms of language play at times with such exaggeration as to all but cancel its lyrical effects.[17] One hears such exaggeration in Loy's depiction of a literally decadent scene in "Café du Néant," in which candles on its coffin tables "[lean] to the breath of baited bodies" and one woman "Prophetically blossoms in perfect putrefaction" (*LoLB*, pp. 16, 17). Similarly, in "Lunar Baedeker," "Delirious Avenues ... lead / to mercurial doomsdays / Odious oasis / in furrowed phosphorous – – – / / the eye-white sky-light / white-light district / of lunar lusts"

(*LoLB*, p. 81). Although aspects of this style continue throughout her verse, it is most pronounced in her poems of the 1910s and 1920s; the poems of the 1940s typically have a less abstract, less recondite, less alliterative compression of thought and syntax.

This extravagantly mannered style, rich with archaic and erudite vocabulary, stands in distinct contrast to the various kinds of language play and innovative aesthetics being developed simultaneously by H.D., Stein, and Moore. Albeit in wholly distinctive ways, each of these poets developed aspects of her style under the influence of American pragmatism and popular literary traditions that eschewed both avant-gardism and mannerism for the more direct intensity of what Moore, only in part satirically, called "plain American which cats and dogs can read!"[18] Again, a comparison with H.D. is most telling – although even Stein, whose *Tender Buttons* involves multilingual punning and a contrived grammar, similarly unpunctuated, maintains an edge of plainness in her vocabulary and choice of subjects (food, objects, rooms). In 1915, Loy infamously and alliteratively presents the "Spawn of Fantasies / silting the appraisable / Pig Cupid his rosy snout / Rooting erotic garbage" (*LoLB*, p. 53). In contrast, between 1912 and 1914, H.D. uses a condensed directness of repetition, syncopated rhyme, and a contrasting fullness of sound to produce an intense lucidity of presence that is strikingly different from Loy's profusion of images and associations. "If I could break you [O rose] / I could break a tree. // If I could stir / I could break a tree – / I could break you," she writes in "Garden" (*HDCP*, pp. 24–25). H.D. soon abandoned Imagism, but she maintained the intensely compressed syntax and repetition of her early poems just as Loy maintained most aspects of her more stylized and erudite manner.

Given that H.D. was a devoted reader of Algernon Charles Swinburne, one might think that her language would have taken on more of the lushness of the decadents rather than echoing the plain style patterns of her Moravian childhood. As Cassandra Laity points out, however, what Swinburne modeled for H.D. was not the richly verbalized eroticism attractive to Loy but the exploration of "alternate forms of desire" in a "psychic landscape" and a "rejection of external constraints in his passionate mythology of the elements," especially the sea.[19] From the start, H.D.'s style has a stoic simplicity, already clear in her 1912 "Hermes of the Ways," in which "The hard sand breaks, / and the grains of it / are clear as wine" (*HDCP*, p. 37). In "The Wind Sleepers," she writes, "Tear – / tear us an altar. . . . When the roar of a dropped wave / breaks into it, / pour meted words / of sea-hawks and gulls / and sea-birds that cry / discords" (*HDCP*, p. 15). The frequently reprinted "Sea Rose" begins with a light slant rhyme occurring at inconsistent intervals to represent the stark beauty of its unloveliness:

> Rose, harsh rose,
> marred and with stint of petals,
> meager flower, thin,
> sparse of leaf   (*HDCP*, p. 5)

Like Loy, H.D. is committed to a poetics of female desire and to the negation of structures envisioning or encouraging women's romantic thralldom to phallic and patriarchal (and for H.D. heterosexist) norms.[20] Especially in her poems about nature, she uses the language of violence to represent the force with which old forms must be broken (breaking, cutting, marring, rending). Her poems construct alternative visions or mythologies through the portrayal of nature, through dramatized lyrics of soliloquy or address, and through impassioned meditation, not through Loy's style of satire, witness, or automythologies.[21]

There are many similarities between Loy's and H.D.'s lives and creative concerns – including that both were expatriates, unconventional mothers, creative in several fields in addition to poetry, and feminists. Like Mina Lowy / Loy, Hilda Doolittle / H.D. published under a name independent of the patronymics of her father and husbands. Both greatly admired Freud – although H.D. underwent extensive analysis, and we know only that Loy sketched him in Vienna and later described him as a "Saviour": "When the Gentile world required a Saviour they nailed up the Christ. When it required a second Saviour to counteract the effects of the first, Freud was at its service."[22] Both engaged in religious or spiritual quests and articulated religious, sexual, and philosophical concerns in part through the language of electromagnetism.[23] Both also wrote significant long poems and influenced the early directions of modernism, in particular influencing Pound's and Williams's experimentation with highly compressed language and the line.[24] Pound gave high praise to both Loy's and H.D.'s early poetry: he included H.D. in his 1914 *Des Imagistes* anthology and in 1918 wrote about Loy (and Moore) as having developed a "dance of the intelligence among words and ideas," or *prosopoeia*, which became the model for his own later writing. H.D. influenced the development of Pound's early writing through her condensed presentational style, and Loy influenced him through her satires, enabling his "Hugh Selwyn Mauberley."[25] Still, these two poets could hardly be more different in the modes and styles of their own early verse, and both reflect their upbringing in developing that style. How then does Loy's aesthetic develop such that it may be understood as "American"?

Initially, Loy appeared foreign to American readers. Alfred Kreymborg recalls that a "curious woman, beautiful and exotic, came to New York from foreign shores: the English Jewess, Mina Loy [whose] clinical frankness and sardonic conclusions, wedded to a madly elliptical style scornful of the regulation grammar, syntax, and punctuation, horrified our gentry and drove our critics into furious despair."[26] During her first year in the city, Loy's primary affiliation remained a transnational avant-garde, particularly the Dada artists/performers Marcel Duchamp, Francis Picabia, and Arthur Cravan. Loy collaborated in editing and writing articles for the Dada publications *The Blind Man* and *Rongwrong* and participated in Dada events, but she wrote no new poems during this period, and after 1918 she had no involvement with the avant-garde apart from loose ties to surrealists in Paris, who heroized Cravan after his death. Yet in the February 1917 *Evening Sun* interview of this "English Poetess," Loy is described as being "particularly proud" of having been "discovered by America"; according to the reporter, her "last word" was, "No one who has not lived in New York has lived in the Modern world."[27]

In 1919, after returning to Europe, Loy again began writing poetry.[28] In these years she turned from writing automythological narratives or gender satire to portraits of artists she admired and of anonymous performers. Cumulatively, Loy's poems written during the 1920s reveal her attempt to articulate an aesthetic independent of any movement, perhaps in response to her strong association with *Others* and the *Dial* or generally with New York modernism. A polemic she wrote in 1918 in Buenos Aires reveals a midpoint in this turn, in which she both outlines the "purpose" of the "International Psycho-Democratic Party" and declares that, in contrast to "most movements," "we move away from all fixed concepts in order to advance" (*LaLB*, pp. 276, 278). "*Psycho democracy is* / Democracy of The Spirit, government by creative imagination, participation in essential wisdom – Fraternity of Intuition, the Intellect and Mother Wit," she writes, in Futurist capitals reminiscent of her earlier manifestos, subtitling her essay "Mina Loy's Tenets" to underline that it expressed her own and not a group's convictions (*LaLB*, p. 277). Loy's poems of the 1920s do not mention this "Party" but in effect define the "Fraternity" she imagined.

When writing of the "meteoric" Joyce ("James Joyce's Ulysses"), of Stein's irradiate purifying of consciousness in language ("Gertrude Stein"), of the folk arts of the circus ("Crab-Angel") and street performers ("Der Blinde Junge"), and of the pathetic social performance of an "abbess-prostitute" ("Lady Laura in Bohemia"), Loy does not distinguish art from artists. Art, she thereby suggests, blooms or radiates from the individual's uninhibited rejection of standardizing, constricting, or prudish norms; the artist lives in a "lunar" rather than daylight landscape and "crushe[s] / the tonnage / of consciousness / ... to extract / a radium of the word" (*LoLB*, p. 94). Although Loy may have seen herself, like Lady Laura, as "Trained in a circus of swans" (*LoLB*, p. 98), she rejects this bourgeois upbringing, in which a woman "learned," as she puts it in a draft, "Queen's walk and courtesies" by turning to an art and to artists of what she calls "absolute act[s]" (Ms6, box 7, folder 188; *LoLB*, p. 79). Such acts are simultaneously outrageous and spiritual, or "immaculate," because their "Spirit" reveals itself in "Flesh" and a vitality of form ("Perlun," "James Joyce's Ulysses," *LoLB*, pp. 75, 88).

"Apology of Genius" describes this company of artists by mapping that which distinguishes "we" artists from "you" – the rest of the world and specifically the lawmakers, the censors, and those who see art as suspicious: "magically diseased ... sacerdotal clowns," "we forge the dusk of Chaos / to that imperious jewellery of the Universe / – the Beautiful." Although "you" may be our spouses or parents, "we" are "beyond your laws," the "chances of your flesh," and your perception of our art as ready for the "censor's scythe" (*LoLB*, pp. 77–78). This poem's first line – "Ostracized as we are with God" – sounds a recurring note of the divinity of the artist – secular, sexualized, or debased as that divinity may be. Constantin Brancusi's "Golden Bird" is "As if" formed by "some patient peasant God" and an "immaculate conception"; "James Joyce's Ulysses" presents either the author or his creation as the "voice and offal / of the image of God," "The word made flesh / and feeding upon itself / with erudite fangs" (*LoLB*, pp. 79, 80, 88, 89); and Wyndham Lewis's "The Starry Sky" blows out "celestial conservatories" and makes "The nerves of Heaven / [flinch]" in the "austere theatre of the Infinite" (*LoLB*, p. 91). Even the blind victim of war, "Void and extinct," plays his harmonica in a "planet of the soul" that "strains ... in static flight upslanting" (*LoLB*, p. 83). "The Spirit / is impaled upon the phallus," she writes of *Ulysses* (*LoLB*, p. 88). The body as phallic or female, sexual, and desiring, but also as decomposing, diseased, and in pain, constitutes Loy's route to "the Beautiful." Like the "Eros" of bourgeois love, "obsolete" because it is conventional, for Loy beauty is without interest unless it is "Pocked with personification," formed in "the raw caverns of the Increate" (*LoLB*, pp. 82, 78). While these poems include Loy's most intensified alliterations and juxtaposition of the erudite with slang or punning registers, they reflect the aesthetic programs of Futurism and Dada only in their continued condemnation of middle-class normality.

Loy articulates a fully original aesthetic first in "Anglo-Mongrels and the Rose," a poem influenced in two ways by her brief years in the United States.

First, it was not until her second trip to New York in 1920 that Loy had any experience of significant interaction with a large Jewish population. In England, Loy was raised in the Anglican church and encouraged to condemn her father's Jewishness. In Florence, according to Carolyn Burke, Jewishness was typically unacknowledged or approached with ambivalence within the Anglo-American expatriate community.[29] In New York City, however, during her second stay, Loy lived in Greenwich Village, which abutted the Lower East Side, with its dominant population of Yiddish-speaking immigrants. With her knowledge of German, Loy would have had some understanding of spoken Yiddish, but, more to the point, she would have rubbed elbows with Jewish artists, writers, and playwrights. After leaving New York in the summer of 1921, Loy traveled in the spring of 1922 to Vienna and then to Berlin, the European metropolis whose Jewish population was most thoroughly integrated with its artistic and cultural community. Second, Loy came to an understanding of her aesthetic as "mongrel" through her time in New York, although she had long written in a multilingual or hybrid style. As early as 1914, in "To You," Loy addressed a semi-autobiographical protagonist in New York who becomes hybrid by writing: "Plopping finger / In Stephen's ink / Made you hybrid-negro" (LaLB, p. 89). The essay "Modern Poetry" implies both these influences in its attention to the multiple ethnicities and languages of New York's Lower East Side. It was in Berlin and in the context of her recent life on the Lower East Side that she composed the first parts of "Anglo-Mongrels and the Rose."[30]

Before turning to the poem itself, it is useful to consider how Loy theorized her changed ideas about hybridity in "Modern Poetry." In 1927, Loy wrote to Julian Levy that she "was trying to make a foreign language because English had already been used."[31] In "Modern Poetry" she characterizes American English in particular as a "composite language," and therefore "a very living language, it grows as you speak" (LoLB, p. 159); this, in other words, is not a language "already used" but one constantly in the process of remaking itself – as her own had been since 1914. In the United States, "a thousand languages have been born," constituting an "English enriched and variegated with the grammatical structure and voice-inflection of many races"; "the true American appears to be ashamed to say anything in the way it has been said before," instead at "every moment" "coin[ing] new words for old ideas." This "unclassifiable speech," Loy asserts, arises from an American "melting-pot" that loosens the "tongue" of "modern literature" (LoLB, pp. 158, 159). By the terms of this description of American modernism, there is indeed no more "true American" than Mina Loy. While Pound described Loy and Moore as "producing something distinctly American in quality," poetry with "the arid clarity, not without its own beauty, of le temperament de l'Americaine,"[32] Loy identifies all of the "new poetry of the English language" as having "proceeded out of America" because of the kind of language she heard there on the street (*LoLB*, p. 157).

For Loy, "the structure of all poetry is the movement that an active individuality makes in expressing itself"; in it, one hears "the evocation of speech" (*LoLB*, p. 157). The particular speech that initiates modern verse, in her view, comes from what she calls the "baser avenues" of New York – as Rachel Blau DuPlessis points out, clearly the Lower East Side, with its large immigrant populations.[33] This linguistic fluidity comes from the "triple rhythm" of an individual's race, citizenship, and personality, she asserts. Both "the high browest modern poets and an adolescent Slav" have had to adapt "to a country where the mind has to put on its verbal clothes at terrific speed if it would speak in time . . . the ear that has listened to the greatest number of sounds will have the most to choose from when it comes to self expression, each has been liberally educated in the flexibility of phrases" (*LoLB*, p. 159).

Such "flexibility" and adaptation through familiarity with "the greatest number of sounds" was a hallmark of Loy's verse from the start. Although she uses few outright coinages and there is sparse evidence of the many languages she knew besides English in her earliest poems, she even so gives birth (to use her metaphor) to a "composite" language, containing such a high ratio of abstract, Latinate, and rarely used words that it sounds foreign. The 1914 "Italian Pictures" provides an early example of what would be Loy's increasing play with mixed registers. Here she combines Latinate derivatives with the Anglo-Saxon roots of Middle English in "Fluidic blots of sky" and "SPLOSH / Pours something / Viscuous / Malefic / Unfamiliar" (*LoLB*, pp. 11, 12–13). By 1915, Loy's language is looser in its play with forms and sounds. In "The Effectual Marriage, or The Insipid Narrative of Gina and Miovanni," Gina is "more than" a "female"; she is "an incipience a correlative / an instigation of the reaction of man / From the palpable to the transcendent / Mollescent irritant of his fantasy," lending monogamy a "changeant consistency" – although we later discover that this woman "with no axis to revolve on" other than her husband is also "mad" (*LoLB*, pp. 36, 38, 39). In her New York experience of living among immigrants of several countries and languages, Loy finds a theoretical formulation for her own triple rhythm as born of a melting pot experience that is symbolically, albeit in her case not literally, American, or, as she comes to call it, "mongrel."

In "Anglo-Mongrels and the Rose," Loy traces this "flexibility of phrases" or "changeant consistency" as it leads the toddler Ova (another Loy figure) from an initial understanding of sounds to a transcendent experience of language, and through the witness and critique of various models for art. In particular, the child Ova finds "only words / mysterious" and "nothing objective new" (*LaLB*, p. 139). While Ova is not yet under the pressure of needing to "put on [her] verbal clothes at terrific speed," she is learning that language marks identity and that words are both given and plastic:

> Sometimes a new word comes to her
> she looks before her
> and watches
> for its materialization
>
> ...
>
> A
> lucent
> iris
> shifts
> its
> irradiate
> interstice
>
> glooms and relumes
> on an orb of verdigris
> An unreal
> globe terrestial
> of olive-jewel
> dilates
>
> evaporates
> into the Increate   (*LaLB*, pp. 139, 141–42)

Just as "we" artists in "Apology of Genius" forge chaos into "imperious jewelry" in "the raw caverns of the Increate" (*LoLB*, p. 78), Ova witnesses a "globe ... of olive-jewel" disappear into that "Increate" cavern of energy from which poetry will eventually be born. That the word she hears in relation to this creative intensity is "diarrhea" signals both the comic misunderstandings of childhood and Loy's conviction that spirit is always embodied.

Ova experiences the mysteriousness of language, experiments with ways to bridge the distance between chaotic embodiment and feeling on the one hand and articulate meaning on the other, and identifies her allies according to their relationships with language and the "Increate," or that source from which individuals can give birth to their own creativity. This "mongrel-girl / of Noman's land," like the "arrested artists / of the masses ... made moon-flowers out of muck / and things desired / out of their tenuous soul-stuff"

(*LaLB*, pp. 143, 142). In contrast, Esau – a character representing Loy's first husband – "absorbs the erudite idea" that beauty exists only "posthumously to itself / in the antique" (*LaLB*, p. 143). For him there is nothing "mysterious" in language's "materialization."

Bearing no stylistic relation to Loy's satirical narrative of familial relations and development, and focused on spiritual and psychic being rather than language, H.D.'s *Trilogy* nonetheless takes on similar questions about the gestation of art from experiences of chaos and embodiment. This three-part poem was written and published in individual sections: "The Walls Do Not Fall" (1944), "Tribute to the Angels" (1945), and "The Flowering of the Rod" (1946). Susan Stanford Friedman refers to it as H.D.'s "war and peace," a "cosmic mythmaking" expression of her spiritual hunger to keep a dream of peace alive in a world of chaos and violence, acknowledging that "we are voyagers" without a map but holding out the hope that "possibly we will reach haven, / heaven" (*HDCP*, p. 543).[34] In "The Walls Do Not Fall," that which initially has only a "small, static, limited // orbit" makes itself "indigestible" to "the shark-jaws / of outer circumstance ... so that, living within, / you beget, self-out-of-self, // selfless, / that pearl-of-great-price" (*HDCP*, p. 514). In the bombed-out streets of London, H.D. finds a kind of "Increate" (to use Loy's word) or "spell" (to use her own) that both promises and grows from "Dream, / Vision"; through such vision, poets may also become prophets moving the world toward spiritual rebirth (*HDCP*, p. 519). In words that echo Loy's phrases from several of her poems in the 1920s, H.D. also finds "companions / of the flame," or a community of artists wrapped in the same "mystery" or "Presence ... rare as radium" as she is, "aloof" from conventional "good and evil" (*HDCP*, pp. 521, 520). In a sequence of parables of origin and creative regeneration and reflections on World War II, H.D. gives psychic and symbolic form to her hope that art will endure and creative forces outlive destructive ones. In her earlier narrative of individual mythologizing, Loy expresses less hopefulness. Even as a child, Ova receives "Illumination," an experience of spiritual transcendence in which she is "conscious / not through her body but through space," yet it results in an "indissoluble bliss / to be carried like a forgetfulness / into the long nightmare" of the rest of her upbringing, or perhaps human history (*LaLB*, p. 164).

Neither H.D. nor Loy writes a poetic of documentary or makes explicit reference to the social and political events of the twentieth century. Their deep concern with the "long nightmare" of life or history, however, becomes clear during World War II. This war brings to a climax the conjunction of H.D.'s antimilitaristic ethos and religious convictions. Witnessing the war's terrors and devastation sharpens her intuitions about the integrity of spiritual survival and the principles and strength required to enable a humane psyche to survive. The war also brings H.D. to extraordinary productivity, which is primarily manifest in *Trilogy*, one of the great modernist long poems, but also in her verse epic *Helen in Egypt*, written in the early 1950s. In *Helen*, H.D. goes even further in constructing a cosmic mythology that enacts the conflicts of attempting to live embodying the forces of creative (not romantic) love and fulfillment in a world that glorifies masculine prowess and war. H.D. also turns in her late poetry to an affirmation of the duplicity or multiplicity of language and its fluidities, moving closer to Loy's embrace of language that reveals itself as permeable to multiple influences and therefore in "movement," "living" (*LoLB*, pp. 157, 159).[35]

Loy, in contrast, reaches the peak of her vision for human creativity in the 1920s in "Anglo-Mongrels." In her late feminism, she turns to portraits of street people, finding in them manifestations of both beauty and divinity.[36] Consequently, it is unclear whether it is the war that inspires her last burst of writing and art making or whether it is the more general conditions of aging, dependence (on her daughters), and poverty. In this period Loy does, however, reiterate a similarly antimilitaristic ethos and celebrate what both she and H.D. identify in various forms as the power of love.

Nearly a quarter century after writing "Anglo-Mongrels," Loy writes a poem of nationalist celebration that returns full circle to her early protests against (Futurist) masculinism, but this time she identifies a feminized "America, Heroica" rather than the overthrow of patriarchal institutions or a language of quick fluidity as the focus of what she there called her "magnetic horizon of liberty" (*LaLB*, p. 170). Sentimental and patriotic rather than satirical and polyglot, "America ☆ A Miracle" both addresses and describes this idealized new power. "America" is "a flash of lightening, / a stroke of genius" because of its "willpower," engineering know-how, inventions of "electric conjury," and "bountifulness" to the world's sufferers (*LaLB*, pp. 227, 229). Presenting Abraham Lincoln's "urgent promise" as epitomizing the country's past, Loy asserts that "the power of the man-of-prey, / the living robot" that "roars abroad / *wavers*" in the face of the American "people" (*LaLB*, pp. 229, 231, my emphasis). Americans are a "people resolute," who "in a resurgence of ardour / oppose the mechanized monster" of combative military aggression or any kind of power without spirit. With this act, "Supremacy is at last ... an outcome of vision"; "the mightiest" are made so, presumably, by their "ardour," through "keeping a pact with Deity / made in Lincolnian love of this nation."

This idealizing affirmation echoes the optimism of Allied victory – making it likely that this poem (first published posthumously) was written around the end of the war.

"America * A Miracle" has none of the poetic force of "Songs to Joannes" or "Anglo-Mongrels and the Rose," and none of the brilliant satire of jingoistic empire building of the latter, but in it Loy gives materialized form to her earlier critique of both patriarchal authority and the stale purity of language she associated with university professors. By resisting fascism, America "might," in Loy's eyes, resist historical privilege, military power, secrecy, and silence: "the echoes of your voice / are Earth's antipodes whispering together" (*LaLB*, p. 229). In 1918, Loy described *"Power"* as "a secret society of the minority," or the singular "Dominator" (*LaLB*, p. 280). While in art or aesthetics Loy always favored a minority that stood above a bourgeois or common populace incapable of understanding its "imperious jewellery of the Universe," in politics she was democratic. "International Psycho-Democracy" calls for an "evolution" of habits, ideas, and psychology that will overturn "the *belligerent masculine* social ideal" (*LaLB*, p. 281). In "America * A Miracle," Loy identifies this evolutionary ideal with the United States: America's "whispering" and echoing voices seem to come from the "antipodes" or farthest reaches of the earth in their multiplicity and inclusiveness.

During the 1940s, Loy wrote primarily about poverty in the Bowery, that region "Beyond a hell-vermilion / curtain of neon" where she lived among "the vanquished," "faces of Inferno," "prophet[s] of Babble-on" (*LoLB*, pp. 133–35). As Linda Kinnahan argues, her whole corpus of poetry can be read as an extended critique of gender systems in relation to economics, religion, sex, and domestic relations, a critique made explicit in her Bowery poems.[37] She knew the problems of American society, including its class and racial prejudices and economic injustice. Nonetheless, Loy apparently felt more affirmed as an immigrant artist and poet in a land where she could hear at least "echoes" of "Earth's antipodes" or an "English enriched and variegated with the grammatical structure and voice-inflection of many races" than in the other lands of her expatriate domicile or her London home. From her earliest years of writing, Loy objected to institutions of privilege, especially as they affected women, and she cultivated a style of flamboyant inclusiveness, eventually articulating this fluidity of language play in relation to peoples and ethnicities rather than exclusively in relation to gender and languages. Her articulation of this aesthetic, developed among international avant-gardes in England, Germany, France, and Italy, depended on her experience of the United States.

Notes

1. For general discussion of Loy as American, see Lara Vetter, "Theories of Spiritual Evolution, Christian Science, and the 'Cosmopolitan Jew': Mina Loy and American Identity," *Journal of Modern Literature* 31:1 (2007), pp. 47–63, and Matthew Hart, *Nations of Nothing but Poetry: Modernism, Transnationalism and Synthetic Vernacular Writing* (New York: Oxford University Press, 2010), passim. For Pound's comment, see Ezra Pound, "Others," *Little Review* 4:11 (1918), p. 57.

2. Alex Goody, *Modernist Articulations: A Cultural Study of Djuna Barnes, Mina Loy, and Gertrude Stein* (Hampshire: Palgrave Macmillan, 2007); Rachel Potter and Suzanne Hobson (eds.), *The Salt Companion to Mina Loy* (Cambridge: Salt, 2010); Mina Loy, *Stories and Essays of Mina Loy*, ed. Sara Crangle (Champaign, Ill.: Dalkey Archive Press, 2011), cited subsequently in the text as *SEML*.

3. Cristanne Miller, *Cultures of Modernism: Marianne Moore, Mina Loy, Else Lasker-Schüler: Gender and Literary Community in New York and Berlin* (Ann Arbor: University of Michigan Press, 2005).

4. Mina Loy, *The Lost Lunar Baedeker*, ed. Roger L. Conover (New York: Farrar, Straus and Giroux, 1996), pp. xii, 23; Mina Loy, *The Last Lunar Baedeker*, ed. Roger L. Conover (Highlands, N.C.: Jargon Society, 1982), p. xv. *The Lost Lunar Baedeker* (1996) will be cited subsequently in the text as *LoLB*. *The Last Lunar Baedeker* (1982) will be cited as *LaLB*. Loy's unpublished manuscripts and letters are quoted with the permission of Roger Conover, Mina Loy's editor, who also serves as literary executor of Loy's estate. Unpublished material is cited from the Mina Loy Papers, Yale Collection of American Literature, Beinecke Rare Book and Manuscript Library, Yale University.

5. Hilda Doolittle [H.D.], *Collected Poems 1912–1944*, ed. Louis L. Martz (New York: New Directions, 1983), pp. 20, 21. This collection will be cited subsequently in the text as *HDCP*.

6. Colby Emmerson Reid, "Mina Loy's Design Flaws," *FACS* 10 (2007–2008), pp. 109–49, 112.

7. Alfred Kreymborg, [Untitled editorial], *Others* 5:1 (December 1918), p. 1.

8. Marianne Moore, *The Marianne Moore Reader* (New York: Viking, 1961), p. 266.

9. Rudolf E. Kuenzli (ed.), *New York Dada* (New York: Willis Locker & Owens, 1986), p. 5.

10. Suzanne Churchill, *The Little Magazine* Others *and the Renovation of American Poetry* (London: Ashgate, 2006).

11. Miller, *Cultures of Modernism*.

12. Rowan Harris, "Futurism, Fashion, and the Feminine: Forms of Repudiation and Affiliation in the Early Writing of Mina Loy," in Potter and Hobson (eds.), *The Salt Companion to Mina Loy*, pp. 17–46, 27.

13. Churchill, *The Little Magazine* Others *and the Renovation of American Poetry*, p. 188.
14. Marisa Januzzi, "'Reconstru[ing] Scars': Mina Loy and the Matter of Modernist Poetics" (doctoral dissertation, Columbia University, 1997), p. 199.
15. Carolyn Burke, *Becoming Modern: The Life of Mina Loy* (New York: Farrar, Straus and Giroux, 1996), p. 157.
16. Harris, "Futurism, Fashion, and the Feminine," p. 21.
17. Marjorie Perloff, "English as a 'Second' Language," in Maeera Shreiber and Keith Tuma (eds.), *Mina Loy: Woman and Poet* (Orono, Maine: National Poetry Foundation, 1998), pp. 131–48; Reid, "Mina Loy's Design Flaws."
18. Marianne Moore, *Complete Poems* (New York: Viking, 1981), p. 46.
19. Cassandra Laity, "H.D.'s Romantic Landscapes: The Sexual Politics of the Garden," in Susan Stanford Friedman and Rachel Blau DuPlessis (eds.), *Signets: Reading H.D.* (Madison: University of Wisconsin Press, 1990), pp. 110–28, 114, 115.
20. H.D.'s stories and novels developed a more excessive and in part more experimental style than her poetry and were more explicit in their feminist critique. Diana Collecott, *H.D. and Sapphic Modernism* (Cambridge: Cambridge University Press, 1999).
21. Susan Stanford Friedman, *Penelope's Web: Gender, Modernity, H.D.'s Fiction* (Cambridge: Cambridge University Press, 1990).
22. Burke, *Becoming Modern*, p. 313.
23. Vetter, "Theories of Spiritual Evolution."
24. Linda Kinnahan, *Poetics of the Feminine: Authority and Literary Tradition in William Carlos Williams, Mina Loy, Denise Levertov, and Kathleen Fraser* (Cambridge: Cambridge University Press, 1994).
25. Peter Nicholls, "'Arid clarity': Ezra Pound, Mina Loy, and Jules Laforgue," in Potter and Hobson (eds.), *The Salt Companion to Mina Loy*, pp. 129–45.
26. Alfred Kreymborg, *Our Singing Strength* (New York: Coward-McCann, 1929), pp. 488–89.
27. "Mina Loy, Painter, Poet and Playwright, Doesn't Try to Express Her Personality by Wearing Odd Looking Draperies – Her Clothes Suggest the Smartest Shops but Her Poems Would Have Puzzled Granma," *Evening Sun*, February 17, 1917, n.p.
28. This observation is determined by publication dates and reference in letters; several of Loy's poems do not exist in manuscript and those that do are not dated.
29. Burke, *Becoming Modern*, pp. 112, 131.
30. Cristanne Miller, "Feminist Location and Mina Loy's 'Anglo-Mongrels and the Rose,'" *Paideuma* 32:1–3 (2003), pp. 75–94; Cristanne Miller, "Tongues 'Loosened in the Melting Pot': The Poets of *Others* and the Lower East Side," *Modernism/Modernity* 14:3 (2007), pp. 455–76.

31. Burke, *Becoming Modern*, p. 361.
32. Pound, "Others," pp. 56–58.
33. Rachel Blau DuPlessis, *Genders, Races, and Religious Cultures in Modern American Poetry, 1908–1934* (Cambridge: Cambridge University Press, 2001), p. 165.
34. Susan Stanford Friedman, "Teaching *Trilogy*: H.D.'s War and Peace," in Annette Debo and Lara Vetter (eds.), *Approaches to Teaching H.D.'s Poetry and Prose* (New York: Modern Language Association, 2011), pp. 135–41, 133.
35. Helen V. Emmitt, "Forgotten Memories and Unheard Rhythms: H.D.'s Poetics as a Response to Male Modernism," *Paideuma* 33:2–3 (2004), pp. 131–54.
36. Maeera Shreiber, "Divine Women, Fallen Angels: The Late Devotional Poetry of Mina Loy," in Shreiber and Tuma (eds.), *Mina Loy: Woman and Poet*, pp. 463–82.
37. Linda Kinnahan, "Economics and Gender in Mina Loy, Lola Ridge, and Marianne Moore," in Cary Nelson (ed.), *The Oxford Handbook of Modern and Contemporary American Poetry* (New York: Oxford University Press, 2012), pp. 143–72.

Chapter 27

Marianne Moore and the Printed Page

ROBIN G. SCHULZE

In many ways, the world of print that Marianne Moore and her modernist peers entered offered an embarrassment of riches when it came to publishing. Moore started her writing life at the same time that a host of new American publishing venues sprang up in the years before the First World War. Throughout her career, Moore's powers as a poet developed as she struggled to meet the physical and commercial demands of the venues that published, and refused to publish, her work. Her experience proves a vital window into the ways in which modernist poets negotiated the changing demands of early twentieth-century print culture.

Between 1890 and 1916, American print culture underwent an unprecedented expansion, due in part to an immigrant-fueled increase in the nation's population, in part to urbanization and a consequent rise in literacy rates, and in part to technological advancements in printing that lowered the prices of and improved access to print materials. Indeed, Frank Luther Mott estimates that between 1890 and 1916, no fewer than 7,500 new magazines entered the American market.[1] American print culture of the early twentieth century, then, seemed expansive and varied enough to accommodate any emerging author.

Changes were afoot, however, that had dramatic consequences for those seeking to get on what Robert Darnton has dubbed a "communications circuit" of print culture that runs "from the author to the publisher (if the bookseller does not assume that role), the printer, the shipper, the bookseller, and the reader."[2] As James L. W. West notes, in the years before the turn of the twentieth century, American book publishing was a "clubby," politically conservative, Ivy League affair of family-owned houses that took pride in their mission of cultural uplift.[3] Although long-standing houses such as Harper, Appleton, Scribner, Putnam, and Holt were certainly in the business of making money, they were run on what Michael Winship terms an "ad hoc" basis that did not employ modern business models of internal organization.[4] The established publishers knew their authors personally and aimed their products at the well heeled and the well educated. The book market in turn drove the periodical market. Houses such as Harper and Scribner created expensive, high-toned magazines that served primarily as teasers for their books and more generally as the public faces of the houses that issued them. Subsidized "book magazines" routinely ran in the red.

By the turn of the twentieth century, though, this old world was swept aside by a new business model in publishing. Demographic shifts inspired entrepreneurial publishers to conceive of periodicals as vehicles for advertisements aimed at a growing middle-class audience.[5] At the end of the nineteenth century, the American middle class remained a reading market lost between the relatively expensive and high-toned book magazines aimed at America's educated elite and the lowbrow penny "story papers" pitched at the working classes. All this changed in the face of a series of industry-shifting price wars based on the premise that a magazine's price could be subsidized by the sale of advertising. Publishers could sell magazines for far less than it cost to produce them, increasing circulation, which would in turn attract more advertisers. General magazines such as *Munsey's*, *McClure's*, and *Ladies' Home Journal* became mass-market periodicals, selling not 10,000 or 20,000 but 500,000 copies. Circulation of monthly magazines rose from 18 million in 1890 to 64 million in 1905.

By the time modernist poets such as Marianne Moore, Hilda Doolittle, Ezra Pound, T. S. Eliot, and William Carlos Williams were undergraduates, then, American print culture, formerly focused on the book, was driven by the periodical. The increasing status of art as commodity and publishing as big business meant that both American artists and the venues that printed them needed to think harder than ever before about the audiences they wished to attract. Publishers needed to focus less on what they wanted to print and more on what readers in particular market segments wanted to read.

The proliferation of periodical literature and the parsing of readers into market segments had profound effects both on the content of American books, newspapers, and magazines and on their material features – what Jerome McGann terms their "bibliographic codes." In McGann's view, all texts are made up of two sets of codes: linguistic codes, the syntactic array of words on a page, and bibliographic codes, the book cover, dust jacket, trim size, typography, font, illustrations, paper, and ink that constitute a text's material presentation. Products of the socializing processes of printing that make texts palatable and saleable, bibliographic codes are just as important as linguistic codes in determining the meaning of a given text.[6] Bibliographic codes send social signals about the genre, audience, and subject of printed matter that direct the processes of decoding words on a page before such processes even begin at the level of syntax. With so many periodicals, newspapers, and books on the market vying for consumer attention, the act of signaling what a reader would encounter in any particular book or periodical took on a new urgency. The drive to attract and engage an audience before a single word of linguistic content was consumed led to a brave new world of material codes, such as colorful book dust jackets, screaming banner newspaper headlines, and full-page halftone photographs.

Critics of the new ad-driven system pictured American culture as a subject of tyrannical consumer preference. American art, they complained, was doomed to be determined by the mediocre democratic mass. One common reading of "modernist" literature situates such grumblings in the emergence of the difficult, genre-bending, experimental work that critics have retrospectively granted the "modernist" label. Andreas Huyssen famously argued that literary modernists worked hard to produce art that could avoid the "contamination" of mass culture, which was gendered female. Modernists consciously produced works hard to read and impossible to sell in an elitist bid to rise above the consumer culture they despised as intolerably cheap and degraded. They also established an alternative print culture – "little magazines," bookshops, small presses – to share work while keeping art out of the hands of those who would sully it. With its "paranoid view of mass culture," modernism, Huyssen contends, "begins to look more and more like a reaction formation."[7]

Scholars of modernist print culture, such as Mark Morrisson and Sean Latham, have spent the last decade or so revising Huyssen's perhaps misleading vision by demonstrating how literary modernists participated, willingly and hopefully, in the literary marketplace. As Morrisson puts it so well, "the institutional adaptation of promotional culture by young modernists suggests an early optimism about the power of mass market technologies and institutions to transform and rejuvenate contemporary culture."[8] Indeed, Marianne Moore's experience, reading practices, and poetry suggest that not all the modernists who participated in the alternative print world of the modernist little magazine were averse to reading and publishing in mass-market periodicals. Moore's archive reveals her love of periodicals of all kinds, including those of the mass market. In one of her early reading diaries, she records snippets of text from such mass-market publications as *Literary Digest*, *Littell's Living Age*, *Life*, *Munsey's*, *Good Housekeeping*, and *Ladies' Home Journal*. The same diary, however, contains references to numerous "book periodicals," including *Harper's*, *Atlantic Monthly*, and *Century*, as well as manifesto-driven modernist little magazines, including Ezra Pound and Wyndham Lewis's *Blast* and Margaret Anderson and Jane Heap's *Little Review*. Moore was equally catholic when it came to the ways in which she made use of what she read. She employed periodicals to direct her reading, relying on reviews to point her to books of interest. As a hopeful reviewer herself, she also used magazines and newspapers to model her critical prose. Most importantly, mass-market and book periodicals frequently provided not only the inspiration for but also the *substance* of her poems. While Pound and Eliot were apt to make poetic allusions to works of high Western culture, Moore was more likely to reference a picture she cut out of the *National Geographic* or a story she read in the *New York Times*. She grabbed direct quotes from her periodicals, employing bits of language in quotation marks that captured common habits of thought that she wished to examine or expose.

Perhaps even more surprising, however, was Moore's desire, at the start of her career, to participate as both an editor and content provider in the ad-driven communications circuit of mass-market print that Ezra Pound claimed he had fled to London to escape. Moore was, in the eyes of her modernist peers, a "poet's poet." From her earliest days, her work was difficult – unique in ways that drove many readers to distraction. Eschewing traditional verse forms, Moore constructed her poems in syllabic stanzas, choosing to hold them together with intricate patterns of full, light, and off rhyme. Eschewing traditional poetic subjects and symbols, she wrote poems about curious plants, animals, and objects that often seemed wholly descriptive. Eschewing emotional rhetoric and the lyric "I," her poems seemed treatises rather than testimonies of feeling – as Ezra Pound wrote, "a mind cry rather than a heart cry." How Moore imagined such work would play well in Peoria in the early twentieth century is something of a mystery. And yet, at the beginning of her national career, she did.

As her archive attests, at the start of her career Moore privileged popular venues over modernist little magazines when it came to the submission of her poems. At the same time that she was reading modernist little magazines such as the *Egoist* and *Blast*, she was submitting her work to high-circulation magazines such as *McClure's*, the infamous purveyor of "muckraking" journalism, with a circulation of 400,000 in 1906, and *Everybody's Magazine*, a digest of literary gossip, features, short stories, and poetry with a circulation of more than 750,000 in 1908. Her poem "A Fool, a Foul Thing, a Distressful Lunatic," which takes a loon, a vulture, and a goose as its subjects, went out first to the *Youth's Companion*, a weekly magazine aimed at adolescent boys and girls with a circulation of more than 300,000 before World War I. Moore reported to her brother in July 1915 that she was "trying to sell" her "gander" to the *Youth's Companion*, but, if the magazine did not take the poem, she would forward it to Alfred Kreymborg, editor of the modernist little magazine *Others*, who could not afford to pay.[9]

Indeed, the ultimate publication of Moore's "A Fool, a Foul Thing, a Distressful Lunatic," first printed under the title "Masks," demonstrates just how far she was willing to go to join the world of mass-market print. At the beginning of her career, Moore's goal was to be not just a poet but a "man of letters." She needed to work to support her family (Moore lived with her mother her entire life, in part because her father left the family before she was born), and she wanted to do so by writing essays, comments, and reviews that would contribute broadly to the public life of the arts. She also, unlike some of her wealthier peers, needed to sell her work to venues that would pay for it.

In the ten years following her graduation from Bryn Mawr College in 1909, Moore tried hard to put together a life as a paid writer. At the same time that she was publishing her poems in modernist little magazines, she was making serious attempts to "get on" as a critic at the *Boston Evening Transcript* and the *Philadelphia Public Ledger*, two of the largest newspapers in the East. She wrote to her brother:

> I feel sure I can get a job with the *Ledger*, not by pulling Mr. [Samuel Duff] McCoy's leg (he is on the *Ledger* and revised some of my poems for *Contemporary Verse*) but by my concentrated exertions in the past. I am just as sure of getting it as I am of eating, if I could only see them.[10]

Moore was not above thinking about connections that might advance her career, particularly when it came to the *Philadelphia Public Ledger*. In 1916, Samuel Duff McCoy, a Princeton graduate who was working as both a poet and a journalist on the *Public Ledger*, founded *Contemporary Verse*. McCoy liked didactic and often frankly sentimental verse with strict form and full rhyme. Moore sent *Contemporary Verse* "A Fool, a Foul Thing, a Distressful Lunatic," which McCoy, as Moore states, "revised." By way of comparison, here is the poem as Moore produced it in a pre-1916 typescript.

> With webs of cool
>   Chain mail and his stout heart, is not the gander
>   Mocked and ignorantly designated yet,
> To play the fool?
>   "Egyptian vultures, clean as cherubim,
>   All ivory and jet," are they most foul?
> And nature's child,

ROBIN G. SCHULZE

> That most precocious water bird, the loon – why
> Is he foremost in the madman's alphabet;
> Why is he styled
> In folly's catalogue, distressful lunatic?[11]

Moore's typescript version of the poem bears many hallmarks of her early verse. Her poem constitutes a challenge to those who allow conventional thinking to dictate their approach to experience, particularly of the natural world. Waging an assault on dead metaphors that keep humans from marking the true value of the organic world around them, Moore's speaker calls on her audience to rethink a "silly goose" as a composed battle-ready knight, a "dirty vulture" as an angel, and a "crazy loon" as a creature of rare ability. Stylistically, the poem also resembles Moore's other work of the early 1910s in its carefully wrought collections of syllabic lines, many of which flirt with metrical regularity but ultimately reject it in favor of complex, conversational rhythms. The line breaks of "A Fool, a Foul Thing, a Distressful Lunatic" work to emphasize the play of rhyme – full, light, and slant – that holds the poem together: "cool," "fool," and "foul"; "child," "why," and "styled"; and "yet" and "alphabet." Also characteristic are Moore's insistent questions, which she often employed to interrogate misguided interlocutors or, in a more rhetorical vein, the flaws of her culture.

The poem that appeared in *Contemporary Verse* in 1916 under the title "Masks" is a very different piece. It begins:

> "Loon" .... "goose" .... and "vulture" ....
> Thus, from the kings of water and of air,
> Men pluck three catchwords for their empty lips.
> Mock them, in turn, wise dumb triumvirate!
> You, gander, with stout heart tooled like your wings of steel,
> What coward knows your soul?[12]

Under McCoy's hand, Moore's poem became not an address to those determined to use a "madman's alphabet" at the expense of their relationship with other living things but an address to the birds themselves. The poem urges the loon, goose, and vulture to "mock" the men who label them. The two questions that remain in the poem are posed not to the offending parties who need to be corrected, Moore's usual practice in her early poems, but to the injured parties. The birds, too, acquire characteristics that do not specifically argue against the terms used to demean them. The loon appears as a "precocious" child in Moore's typescript, a word that emphasizes its unusual maturity and positions the bird as the antithesis of a mad, foolish "lunatic." In McCoy's version, the loon becomes instead a symbol of triumphant and scornful individuality – a "water bird, / That shouts exultantly among lone lakes" and "laugh[s]" at its oppressors. McCoy disrupts the rhyme so ubiquitous in Moore's early verses, as well as the play of enjambment that makes the sonic relations between Moore's words so prominent.

My point here is not to scold McCoy but to suggest what Moore was willing to do to make her way into the paying literary world she wanted so badly to inhabit. She accepted McCoy's revisions to her "gander" poem, as her letter to Warner suggests, for the sake of her chances at the *Public Ledger*. Her note to Warner reveals that she did not, as of 1916, see an unbridgeable gap between her literary life in modernist little magazines and her potential literary life as a critic and poet in popular venues. For Moore, the ad-driven world of periodical print culture was a continuum rather than a realm divided into "modernist" and "other." When considering her potential reading public, Moore did not begin by considering her work as particularly subversive or experimental. Only as the rejection slips from mass-market venues mounted did she start to think of her poems as somehow unsuited for a mass market.

By the end of 1919, Moore had reached a crossroads. At the age of thirty-two, she had made a name for herself as a poet and made many literary friends and acquaintances, but she still had not managed to translate her talents into regular paying work. Both of her most supportive periodicals, the *Egoist* and *Others*, ceased publication in 1919, leaving Moore without a regular venue. In the summer of 1919, she tried one last time to find employment at the *New York Times Book Review*. Her brother Warner secured an interview for Moore that resulted in an invitation to pen some sample reviews of recent books. But when she did not hear back from the *Times*, she wrote to Warner:

> As for the *Times*, ... I hope you will not do anything about it further. And don't have it in mind to get a hearing for me anywhere else – I think I could do such work and am sure of it in fact but I don't believe I fit in with the program of the average daily and will have to get at the matter some other way.

She added reflectively:

> The more I think of it, the more I think it is a matter of temperament, that editors for large crowds of people don't want fine distinctions and meditative comment they want something practical and colorless that would not draw attention to itself or seem contentious. And the more play I had in what I wrote the more offensive uncompromising I would be, so I will have to let things go as they are for a while.[13]

Unable to secure a position as a man of letters, Moore took a part-time job at the Hudson Park branch of the New York Public Library. Moore did not turn her back on mass publishing until it seemed that mass publishing had turned its back on her, a narrative that poses a distinct challenge to readings of modernist production as either a heroic stick in the eye of a more conservative bourgeois culture or a frightened and elitist rejection of a feminized mass culture. Moore wanted "in" to the paying world of the average dailies. She only began to think of her work as in any way "contentious," difficult, and temperamentally unsuited to large crowds when constant rejections made any other view untenable. At the beginning of her career, Moore became an aesthetic "radical," to use Harriet Monroe's derogatory term for her work, because only the most experimental journals would publish her work.[14] It was her experience in negotiating the communications circuit that constructed her literary identity.

Enter the *Dial*

Ultimately, it was Scofield Thayer and J. Sibley Watson who both saved and made Moore's career. Thayer and Watson purchased the *Dial* magazine in 1919 and set to work turning it into a premier journal of modern art and culture. Thayer and Watson were willing to spend big money to buy the art they deemed representative of "advanced cultural life," regardless of whether or not it sold the magazine. As Lawrence Rainey points out, however, Thayer and Watson were not simply altruistic supporters of the arts. They were canny investors. In identifying the works they printed as valuable examples of "advanced cultural life," they set out to create a consumer demand for the cultural capital that they were themselves purchasing.[15] Thayer, in particular, was an avid collector who well understood the investment potential of art. All he needed to do, he surmised, was to make other people value the works he loved, and their commercial value would increase. As editor of the *Dial*, he had a plan for how to accomplish his mission. Thayer wrote in his "Statement of Purpose" for the *Dial* that the goal of the magazine was to place "radical creations" by younger artists in conversation with more "traditional" works by older and established artists so that "the enlightened public" might see the continuity between the two. Of course, the scheme was contingent on having the money to purchase works by "accepted artists," works that had a much higher commodity value than those by unknown youngsters.[16] The expense was worth it, however, from the standpoint of raising the stock of those more experimental artists who were in the habit of giving their work away.

As Rainey makes clear, patron-investors like Thayer and Watson rescued literary modernism from a consumer-driven model of publishing, even while they strove to invest literary modernism with a new form of commodity value. This new model, however tenuous, solved several problems for Moore. First, Thayer and Watson paid well for her work out of their own pockets. Second, the *Dial* published prose as well as verse, and Thayer and Watson let Moore explore the sorts of "meditative" criticism that she could not sell to the average dailies. Third, the *Dial*, although not aimed at a mass audience, had a much larger circulation than either the *Egoist* or *Others*. By 1922, the *Dial* had 6,374 subscribers and a monthly circulation of 9,200 copies.[17] Finding herself published alongside Yeats and Conrad, Moore gained a cultural imprimatur that proved vital to her career. The *Dial*, with its glossy photographs of "modern" art, long pieces by "serious" and "established" authors from around the globe, and high price tag, coded her work as a lasting contribution to what Thayer and Watson termed the "advanced cultural life." Ultimately, eleven of the fourteen new poems Moore published between January 1920 and December 1924 appeared in the *Dial*. Just as important, the *Dial* printed the bulk of Moore's critical prose from 1921 to 1924.

The *Dial* not only granted Moore a new artistic peer group but also changed both the style and substance of her art. The *Dial* granted Moore a larger trim size that gave her room to experiment with ever-longer lines. Starting in 1921, she abandoned her syllabic stanzas; her tight, ubiquitous rhymes; and her complex indents in favor of long, free verse lines anchored against the left margins. She also began to experiment with what were, for her, very long poems, which the *Dial*, unconcerned about expense, would print. Her verses also began to ruminate on an important subject that the *Dial* made evident. Featured alongside a range of established modernist writers and artists from England, France, and Germany, Moore fashioned a number of poems that considered the differences between the aesthetic approaches of various nations. In "New York," Moore compared her city's roughness, the "savage's romance," to the overcivilized urbanities of Europe as a means to explore America's potential as a breeding ground for art. In "People's Surroundings," she compared the living spaces that people of different regions and cultures create in order to reflect on what aesthetic models might be best to follow and why. In "Novices" she measured the work of brash young American artists whose false sophistication and egotism appalled her against the lively and honest verses of the ancient Hebrews. The *Dial* inspired her to consider whether or not aesthetic cosmopolitanism was a good idea.

Moore by the Volume

By 1919, Moore's colleagues sensed that she was doing something unique. They also felt, however, that they needed to see her work en masse in order to make sense of it. Her growing circle of literary friends began to urge her to publish a book. Moore certainly had options. Book historians frequently refer to the period from 1915–1940 in the United States as the golden age of publishing: readership soared, and brash, talented new publishers entered the market. B. W. Huebsch, Alfred Knopf, Horace Liveright, and Alfred Harcourt, for example, all started publishing firms in the early twentieth century. As George Bornstein has pointed out, many of these men were Jews who found it hard to advance in the frankly WASPy world of the traditional American East Coast publishing houses.[18] Out on their own, they were in stiff competition for good things to print and were often willing to take chances on modernist texts that proved risky for the bigger houses.[19] In addition, several of the patron-investors behind the little magazines also opened "little presses," inverting the book-magazine model of pre-twentieth-century publishing firms (books first, then magazines to support them). In 1923, Scofield Thayer and Sibley Watson started the Dial Press to support the *Dial* magazine. In keeping with the art-as-investment model that drove the patron-investors, the stock in trade of the little presses was the luxury limited edition – the book designed for wealthy collectors that would sell out quickly, thus enhancing its future potential as a bankable commodity. Also, older, more traditional firms in both America and Britain, such as Henry Holt, Macmillan, and Houghton Mifflin, sometimes took chances on experimental poetry.

The choice of book publisher, however, had just as many consequences for a poet's career as the choice of periodical venues when it came to coding a poet's work for consumption. While the small commercial firms had chutzpah, they did not necessarily promise the stability, or the respectability, that many artists craved. The larger, more established firms flirted with experimental poets, but only to a point. The patron-investor presses generally produced beautiful limited editions, but, as Rainey has demonstrated, by their very nature they did not provide access to a wide readership.[20]

Moore had tough decisions to make when it came to her first book prospects, but she ultimately did not get the chance to decide for herself. H.D., Bryher, and Harriet Shaw Weaver took the matter of Moore's book publication into their own hands. After Moore had politely declined their offer to make up a volume of her verse, the three went ahead and published a small book entitled *Poems* from the Egoist Press without Moore's consent. The book arrived in Moore's mailbox on July 7, 1921, a beautiful limited edition with thick papers and an ornate cover. Moore knew the gift was a labor of love, but she was upset about having the decision of where, when, and how to publish a book made for her. As she wrote to Bryher: "I had considered the matter from every point and was sure of my decision – that to publish anything now would not be to my literary advantage; I wouldn't have the poems appear now if I could help it and would not have some of them ever appear and would make certain changes."[21]

A product of the segmented world of early twentieth-century print culture, Moore sensed that her "literary advantage" was inevitably tied up with the social signals that both the material and institutional codes of a particular publication would send. Moore had managed to find a well-paying outlet in the *Dial* that placed her work in the company of those who published books regularly with established commercial houses. As a regular *Dial* author, Moore had reason to hope for better than the Egoist Press. As she revealed to Bryher in the context of turning down her services as a publisher, she also still had the desire to open her verses out to more readers. "If the poems were to be published," she stated, "I think there ought to be more of them and I think that there ought to be among them some that are easy to understand and that are beyond doubt, alluring."[22]

Unfortunately for Moore, *Poems* coded her as a poet suited for only the smallest of educated coterie audiences. Richly produced with a brightly colored, patterned cover that invoked a Byzantine mosaic, Bryher and H.D.'s volume positioned Moore's poems as the gorgeous products of an archeological dig. Inside the cover, the book employed a font full of ligatures that consciously referenced an earlier age of print. By titling the book simply *Poems*, Bryher and H.D. encouraged readers to anticipate that they would find texts between the covers that would be recognizable to most readers as traditional verse – a problematic strategy considering the experimental, genre-bending contents.

Moore's publishers, however, were perhaps less concerned about the contradictions inherent in the volume's bibliographic coding because they were not producing the book to sell. Bryher printed *Poems* as an expensive calling card for Moore, something to give away. Bryher's strategy as Moore's patron was one that many of Moore's modernist peers adopted on their own behalf: Ezra Pound, Vachel Lindsay, and Edwin Arlington Robinson all published a volume at their own expense in order to shop their work to potential reviewers and future publishers. The strategy backfired in Moore's case, however, precisely because Bryher was not focused on the issue of Moore's marketability.

Harold Child of the *London Times Literary Supplement* savaged the volume, laying emphasis on the sheer obscurity of the poems. "She writes ... a clumsy prose," wrote Child, "and tries to give an adventitious effect to it by tricks of printing which only obscure her meaning."[23] Writing for the *Nation*, Mark Van Doren declared that Moore's "manners" were "those of the absurder coteries."[24] Bad notices were not an entrée to the sort of publishing house with whom Moore wished to work. When Bryher, who remained Moore's good friend, asked for help in publishing her novel *Adventure*, Moore made the following list of suggested presses: "Macmillan, Doran, Knopf, Huebsch."[25] Her first choice was not a press that would produce a luxury edition, or one of the upstart firms, but the staid and long-established Macmillan.

Upset with the response to her *Poems*, Moore retreated from book publication. Once again, Thayer and Watson rescued Moore's career. In mid-1924, Thayer urged the editor of the fledgling Dial Press, Lincoln MacVeagh, to approach Moore about putting together an American volume. Thayer assured Moore that the Dial Press was "a business house" that would undertake the publication of her book "with hope of financial gain." "Although," he added, "I trust you will believe me, not only with that purpose."[26] Secure in the notion that Thayer believed her book was potentially marketable, Moore set to work putting together the manuscript of *Observations*. Thayer's interest in Moore's book marked one of his most savvy ploys as a patron-investor. Archival evidence reveals that, before ever approaching Moore about a book, Thayer and Watson had already decided to award the annual Dial Prize for 1924, a magnificent sum of $2,000, to Moore. The awarding of the prize would sell the book, Thayer surmised, enriching the Dial Press. The sale of the book would, in turn, sell Moore and the *Dial* magazine.[27]

Thayer's patron-investor strategy, partly conceived to promote Moore's poems, partly conceived to promote the *Dial*, left Moore $2,136.25 richer in prize money and royalties. The sales of *Observations* were good enough to prompt a second edition. The Dial Press was not a commercial press by the standards of the day, but it allowed Moore to imagine that her work, while still subsidized by Thayer and Watson, had a viable paying audience. Thayer also coded Moore's book for a readership beyond a coterie. Unlike the ornate *Poems*, Thayer's book was typographically simple. The cover he selected was a plain black cloth with a small black-and-white label. He also employed a limited-run dust jacket of gold foil that positioned Moore not as an excavation of lost artistry but as a *winner*. The cover was a product not of a vision of the book as art but of a marketing strategy based on the Dial Prize. Moore chose the title *Observations* for her volume, and Thayer included a full set of notes to her poems as well as an index to the subject matter in her verses. Together, the title and the apparatus suggested that Moore's poems were as much information as they were art.

Unlike *Poems*, *Observations* received wide reviews that were at least mixed, including a full-page spread by Herbert Gorman, with Moore's picture, in the *New York Times Book Review*. Gorman noted that both Moore's Dial Prize and her Dial book "gave inordinate pleasure to an audience of readers which had long since overgrown the limitations of a coterie." He was happy to see that Moore at last had a book "issued in a trade way and between cloth covers" and hoped that the award and the book would "quite definitely aid her in widening her audience."[28] Gorman admitted to reading Moore's Egoist Press *Poems*, but he did not review Moore until the prize and the book "issued in a trade way" made her a worthy subject for the *New York Times*.

The *Dial* not only gave Moore credentials as a trade author but also made Moore, at last, a man of letters. In 1925, she took over as acting editor from Alyse Gregory and later became editor in chief alongside Sibley Watson when Thayer, plagued by mental illness, could no longer manage the job. Between 1925 and 1929, she directed the content of the magazine and wrote constantly for its pages, producing a vast corpus of reviews, essays, and comments. As the editor of the *Dial*, Moore became a figure to be consulted and contacted. She drew a regular salary from the *Dial* and, for the first time, felt financially secure in her chosen profession.

The *Dial* also gave Moore her first true taste of editorial control. Throughout her early career, Moore decided very little when it came to the material presentations of her poems. As the editor of the *Dial*, however, she had serious input into the content and presentation of a major publication. She had a taste of the power to manage the material codes that defined her literary identity – a power that many of her modernist peers were willing to do just about anything to get. Pound was constantly searching for a wealthy backer who would allow him to create a magazine in which the linguistic and bibliographic content of every page would express his aesthetic program. Writing beyond the pale of recognizable literary genres, modernists such as Pound, Moore, Williams, and Eliot – all of whom served as editors – had a larger stake than more traditional artists in creating material codes that could carry the burden of signaling how their work should be read. For many modernist poets, editing a successful magazine was a holy grail because, in the absence of recognizable generic markers (no rhyme, no regular meter, and no traditional poetic form), material codes (the ordering of poems, the placement of lines, the illustrations, and the typographic cues, such as dashes, ellipses, bold type, and expressive fonts) proved vital to the intelligibility of their work.

In 1929, however, the *Dial* closed its doors: Thayer's mother no longer wished to pay for the magazine that her son was too sick to edit. From Moore's literary perspective, the collapse of the *Dial* was both good and bad. Editing a major periodical left Moore little time to devote to her own verse. Between 1925 and 1931, she published no poems. Once the *Dial* had shut down, she returned to her own poetry, and many critics now see her expansive, complex verse of the 1930s as the capstone of her career. But Moore again faced the uncomfortable task of making a living, made all the more urgent by the global economy's collapse.

The 1930s, the "Real" Presses, and One Last Bit of Luxury

Moore's editorship of the *Dial* had put her at the center of the modernist cultural production of the late 1920s. The economic chaos of the early 1930s, however, made it very difficult for Moore to capitalize on the literary reputation that she had built throughout the end of the decade. In the wake of the financial collapse, many modernist little magazines established in the 1910s and 1920s failed. As the Depression deepened, a new set of agenda-driven political magazines replaced them. Little magazines like the *New Masses*, the *Anvil*, *Dynamo*, the *Partisan Review*, the *Modern Quarterly*, and *transition* considered the verse they printed as part of their political programs. Although Moore had certainly written a fair amount of political poetry throughout her life – her many poems decrying the carnage of the First World War and her poems that make reference to the Irish Troubles, for example – she despised the fleering, propagandistic tone of many of these new publications. "Judged by our experimental writing," Moore complained in a review of three anthologies of new poetry in the 1930s, "we are suffering today from unchastity, sadism, blasphemy, and rainsoaked foppishness."[29]

The politicizing of the 1930s little magazine scene meant that, once again, Moore found herself in a tenuous position when it came to outlets for her work, although there were still a few paying little magazines in America and England, such as Lincoln Kirstein's *Hound and Horn* and T. S. Eliot's *Criterion*, that considered Moore's *Dial* editorship to be bankable cultural capital. The most important of such outlets for Moore in the 1930s was Harriet Monroe's *Poetry*, which published eight of Moore's nineteen new poems between 1932 and 1936. Moore's experience with Monroe at the start of her career had not been happy. Monroe published a handful of Moore's poems in 1915 but disliked her style and told her so. Monroe's 1922 review of *Poems* stated frankly that Moore's poetry was not poetry at all. A decade later, however, Monroe and Moore found themselves on the same side in the battle against leftist backlash. Chided throughout the early 1930s for being ignorantly detached and apolitical, Monroe defended her editorial policy of "aesthetic value" at *Poetry*. "We cannot believe," she wrote in her reply to Stanley Burnshaw, "that it is our duty to accept and spread before our readers such half-baked efforts at class-consciousness poetry as the *New Masses*, the *Anvil*, *Partisan Review*, *Dynamo*, . . . and other enthusiastic organs of the Left groups . . . may perhaps legitimately use."[30] Like Monroe, Moore hated the idea of baldly polemical thinking where art was concerned.

Again, Moore's poems evolved in response to the venue that published them. Monroe was very conscious of the ordering of poems in her magazine and asked her authors to think about the arrangement of their verses. She also asked them to provide overarching titles for the groups of poems she printed. Monroe's practice of thinking of poems as sets prompted Moore to do the same. The poems that Moore sent to *Poetry* in 1932 constituted her first major poetic sequence, "Part of a Novel, Part of a Poem, Part of a Play." Composed of three poems, "The Steeple-Jack," "The Student," and "The Hero," Moore's extended meditation on American character and the role of art and learning in American culture was the first of several carefully composed sequences.

Perhaps most important, Moore's appearances in *Poetry* positioned Moore's work as belonging to what critics of the time saw as Monroe's apolitical aesthetic program. In 1922, Monroe claimed that Moore's art was a misguided "rallying point for radicals."[31] As true political radicals began to take to the artistic field in the early 1930s, however, the aesthetic radicalism of the 1920s began to look tame by comparison. Moore's poems of the 1930s were among her most stylistically challenging work. They were just as geometric and cryptic, just as lacking in conventional emotional climax, as her earlier poems. They were also, in their own way, political. Yet, because they were poems that took pelicans, pangolins, and peaches as their subjects, they appeared more engaged with aesthetic matters than with the "real" political and economic crises that dominated the headlines. At the height of her career as a technically advanced "difficult" poet, Moore became aesthetically palatable to Harriet Monroe and the centrist little magazine that had rejected her verse ten years earlier.

The repositioning of Moore's poems as something other than radical had one very important result: once Moore was regularly represented in the pages of *Poetry*, a breeding ground for Macmillan authors, Harold Latham, the lead acquisitions editor for the New York office of Macmillan, sought her out in early 1933.[32] Moore responded that she lacked sufficient material for a new book but promised to send her next volume his way. Only a few months later, T. S. Eliot, then an editor at Faber and Faber, contacted Moore about the possibility of giving a volume of verse to his press. Having depended on presses that were not business houses to produce her volume work of the 1920s, she now had two business houses vying for her services. Moore ranked Macmillan first among her own choice of publishers and did not want to break her promise to Latham. She also, however, did not want to turn down Eliot and forgo the obvious advantage of having him, a valued colleague with growing literary celebrity, involved in the project. She was also comforted by the fact that a book for Faber would be not a favor but a commercial product. "The commercial superstition is such that one does need a certain financial recognition," she wrote to Eliot, "and I should be entirely pleased with the royalty you mention."[33]

Eager to sign Moore, T. S. Eliot sent fellow Faber and Faber director, Frank Morley, to call on her. Moore was thrilled. "*There* is 'a man,'" she wrote to her brother admiringly: "He and T. S. Eliot, and Mr. Latham are, so far, my first experience of real publishers. Ask me about this, and you shall hear; and of Paul Revere at Macmillan's also."[34] Morley impressed Moore as an industry insider who, along with Latham, Moore could not help but picture as a rescuer. Moore must have explained the situation with Macmillan to Morley, who took the logical step of contacting Latham directly. Ultimately, T. S. Eliot agreed to both select and supply an introduction to a book of Moore's poems that would include both new work and previously published poems. Macmillan in turn agreed to publish an American edition, leaving the English edition to Faber. When all was said and done, Moore's *Selected Poems*, with an introduction by T. S. Eliot, appeared first in the United States from Macmillan and then a few months later from Faber and Faber in England.

Selected Poems secured the career that the *Dial* had launched, not by making Moore easier to read but by making her harder. Eliot let Moore select her verses, but he ordered them. He chose to put Moore's most challenging new poems at the start of the volume, a group of poems on animal subjects that Moore dubbed her "animiles" when she saw them together. His decision, as he wrote to Moore, was specifically designed to separate the wheat from the chaff when it came to her readers:

> I want to start with the new poems hitherto uncollected, and shove some of the slighter pieces toward the end. At your simplest, you baffle those who love "simple poetry," and so one might as well put on difficult stuff at once, and only bid for the readers who are willing and accustomed to take a little time over poetry.[35]

Eliot's introduction echoed his strategy to market Moore through her difference and difficulty.

Moore's entrée into the house of Macmillan again changed her mode of literary production. In December 1934, after Moore was already working with Latham and Eliot, H.D. contacted Moore about making up a small book for Bryher's Brendin Publishing Company. Funded by Bryher, the Brendin Press was the antithesis of a commercial venture. Like the Egoist Press, also supported by Bryher's wealth, the Brendin Press specialized in small-run luxury editions, roughly eight times the price of high-end trade books of the period. Given Moore's drive to work with "real" presses, it seems odd that she should turn to Bryher and the Brendin Press on the brink of the appearance of *Selected Poems*. She had a standing contract with Macmillan, and Latham had an option on anything she wished to print next. Latham's promise, however, was just the security Moore needed in order to experiment with a luxury book. Latham assured her that publishing with Brendin would be no obstacle and that he would gladly print the poems she gave to Bryher again in a longer volume whenever Moore wished. Such assurances gave Moore the freedom to do what she had longed to do her entire career – exert real control over the bibliographic codes of a volume of verse. One enticement that Bryher used to lure Moore to the Brendin Press was the promise that George Plank, a highly successful graphic artist, would illustrate her book. The luxury edition also allowed Moore to explore her new preoccupation with poetic sequences born of her 1930s relationship with Monroe's *Poetry*. At the time of H.D.'s query about a book for Brendin, Moore had four new poems – "Pigeons," "Bird-Witted," "Half-Deity," and "The Pangolin" – that remained uncollected. As Heather White tells the story, Moore sent the poems to Eliot, asking him, once again, to help her with the arrangement.[36] But by the time Eliot responded to her initial plea for help, Moore had already reorganized her poems, along with the new "Virginia Britannia" (originally entitled "Jamestown"), into a sequence entitled "The Old Dominion":

I
Jamestown

II
Bird-Witted

III
Half-Deity
Pigeons
The Pangolin[37]

She ultimately removed "Pigeons" and inserted "Smooth Gnarled Crape Myrtle." She also removed "The Pangolin" from the "Old Dominion" sequence and left it to stand alone at the end of the volume. The final table of contents for *The Pangolin and Other Verse* read:

The Old Dominion
    Virginia Britannia
    Bird-Witted
    Half-Deity
    Smooth Gnarled Crape Myrtle

The Pangolin[38]

George Bornstein argues that both the ordering of the poems and the George Plank illustrations in *The Pangolin and Other Verse* bring the commentary on colonial race relations in "Virginia Britannia" front and center.[39] As Bornstein notes, the volume begins with a Plank illustration that pictures outstretched hands, one black, one white, attempting to meet in a handshake. Between them, Plank interposes the early American Gasden flag, which pictures a coiled rattlesnake over the legend "Don't tread on me." The flag tropes on Benjamin Franklin's cartoon depicting the American colonies as a snake cut into segments. Together, the cartoon argues, the colonies will be deadly to tyranny; un-united, they will die. In her poem "Virginia Britannia," Moore invokes the flag as evidence of her country's strange progression from colony to colonizer. In Virginia, the home of Jamestown, the first permanent colony in the New World, the English settlers encountered the tidewater natives of the Pamunkey nation, including the princess Pocahontas. The meeting resulted in a strange new amalgamation from which, Moore contends, America – neither English nor native – was born. The "feminine / odd Indian young lady," Pocahontas, is no odder, Moore suggests, than the "Odd / thin / gauze-and-taffeta- / dressed English " mistress who sets up house in the New World.

Terrapin
meat and crested spoon

feed the mistress of French
plum-and-turquoise-piped chaise-longue;
of brass-knobbed slat front-door and
everywhere open
         shaded house on Indian-
         named Virginian
streams, in counties named for English lords. The
    rattlesnake soon

said from our once dashingly
undiffident first flag, "don't tread on
        me," tactless symbol of a new republic.[40]

The meeting of "Pamunkey princess" and English mistress results in a new breed. The English woman's "odd," too-dainty ways transform by necessity: the silver spoon with the family crest now holds not consommé but turtle meat. From such an audacious mixture, the idea of America arises – a separate country that is at once spunky and sadly lacking in humility. Under the rattle-snake flag and the motto "don't tread on me," the "new republic" of America forgets all too quickly what it feels like to be placed beneath another's boot soles.

         the dwarf
      fancying Egyptian, the American,
  the Dutch, the noble
         Roman, in taking what they
         pleased – colonizing as we say –
  were not all intel-
    lect and delicacy.[41]

Moore lumps the new Americans together with the ancient imperial Romans and Egyptians. The colonized have become, she laments, the imperial colo-nizers, purchasing their power at the expense of the "savages" – black people and Native Americans (those subject to Powhattan's "deer-fur Crown") – that they consider expendable animals. In the last stanza of the poem, however, Moore concludes that there is still hope for her nation. Against the setting sun, the various trees outside her Virginia window, both native species and those imported by settlers, "lose identity / and are one tree." Ultimately, "Virginia Britannia," while holding out hope for a future marked by amity, endorses a vision of American history that does not erase the violence bound up in the nation's founding.

    Moore's sequence title in *The Pangolin and Other Verse*, "The Old Dominion," suggests that not only "Virginia Britannia" but all four of the poems under heading question America's relationship to various forms of tyranny. Do ⌐rms of "old dominion" still hold sway? Has America fulfilled its potential or its promises of freedom? With such questions in mind, the other poems in Moore's set become considerations of how Virginia's chosen symbols and mottoes might be productively recontextualized and reread. On the heels of the "Old Dominion" sequence, "The Pangolin," Moore's "armored animal," with "sting-proof scales," made "graceful by adversities, con- // versities," becomes a symbol of eternal vigilance, a reminder that tyranny is an ever-present threat and that the beauty that emerges through struggle is the only viable form of self-protection.[42]

Bibliographic control, the freedom Bryher granted Moore to order her poems and collaborate with her illustrator, gave Moore the means to consider how she might forge a more direct political identity as a poet. The experiment, however, was one that few would ever see. Bryher priced the book, in a print run of only 120 copies, at fifteen dollars, a price that Moore deemed appalling. The lesson of how to produce an effectively ordered small volume of verse, however, was one she took with her into the 1940s. In 1941, Moore published her next volume, *What Are Years*, with Macmillan. As she had promised Latham, she took all the poems from *The Pangolin and Other Verse* into her new book, most of them heavily revised. She also included ten uncollected poems published between 1936 and 1941. The new book looked nothing like the Brendin Press collection, particularly where the "Old Dominion" sequence was concerned. Moore still grouped the four "Old Dominion" poems together, but she moved "Virginia Britannia" to the end of the group. She then placed the four poems in the middle of the volume and removed the identifying sequence header, effectively obscuring the relations between the poems that she had worked so hard to build in *The Pangolin and Other Verse*.

White reads Moore's new arrangement for *What Are Years* as a move to a more personal poetic that reflects her family struggles of the 1940s, especially the declining health of her beloved mother.[43] *What Are Years* ends not with "The Pangolin" but with "The Paper Nautilus," Moore's ode to the power of motherly love. In his analysis of Moore's 1941 volume, Bornstein argues that "the stripping of the *Pangolin* volume's bibliographic codes for the plainer production of commercial publication significantly reduced the political bite of ['Virginia Britannia.']"[44] But there is a wider point to be made. Moore's reordering of her poems for her trade press does not so much personalize or depoliticize her poems as repoliticize them in the context of another eloquent arrangement. In the wake of the eruption of global war, the second in Moore's lifetime, the tyranny that Moore deemed a threat in *The Pangolin and Other Verse* became an all-too-present fact. *What Are Years* is a volume that takes the question of survival in a brutal world as its central subject. Drawing on her earlier experience of sequencing her poems, Moore began *What Are Years* with four newer poems that unflinchingly face the fact of mortality, and possible extinction.

In the lead poem, "What Are Years?," Moore begins with a pointed question, "What is our innocence, / what is our guilt?" Moore surprisingly answers that, from the standpoint of the current conflict, the question of guilt or innocence is immaterial – all creatures "are / naked, none is safe."[45] The poem and the three that follow are a call to action, a plea for American intervention in the war. In "Rigorists," Moore appreciates the survival skills of the reindeer, "adapted / / to scant reino," whose transportation to Alaska by the intercessory Sheldon Jackson prevented "the extinction / of the Esquimo."[46] In "Light Is Speech," Moore laments the tragic fall of France to Nazi forces in 1940. As Cristanne Miller argues, the poem doubles as an attempt to "stimulate the French and non-French into action."[47] In "He 'Digesteth Harde Yron,'" Moore considers the ostrich, the world's largest bird, who, although flightless and mercilessly hunted throughout history, has managed to avoid extinction. "Heroism is exhausting," she states of the bird's gallant actions in defending its young, "yet / it contradicts a greed that / did not wisely spare / the harmless solitaire / / or great auk in its grandeur."[48] Extinction awaits all those unprepared to be heroes.

Selected Poems, its order determined by Eliot, had presented Moore as a frankly "difficult" poet; *What Are Years*, the first trade volume whose order Moore determined herself, recoded Moore in wartime as a *relevant* poet. The recoding had measurable results. In his review of the 1943 anthology *New Poems*, which included Moore's verse, Kimon Friar wrote that, in contrast to most of the poets represented in the volume, Moore "faces the hatred and carnage of our times with searing directness and with greatest personal distress. . . . In her masterful poem 'What Are Years,' Miss Moore departs from her usual exact description of external objects by which the theme is suggested, to write . . . [a poem] in which the theme is explicitly and even emotionally stated, a change courageous and welcome."[49] Friar was not alone in his assessment. After the appearance of *What Are Years*, Moore found herself with access to the two most important weekly journals of anti-isolationist liberal opinion in America, the *Nation* and the *New Republic*.

Moore's rehabilitation from cruelly difficult modernist to liberal moralist, one engineered in part by Moore's ordering of her 1941 volume, again had repercussions. In Moore's next small volume, *Nevertheless* (1944), Macmillan drastically changed the bibliographic codes they had put into play in the mid-1930s to market her work. The dust jacket cover Macmillan had chosen for *What Are Years* mimicked the cover of the American edition of her 1935 *Selected Poems*. The title of the book and Moore's name appeared in large, white block capitals with minimal serifs on a black field, a restatement of the cover of *Selected Poems* that testified to Moore's difficulty and seriousness. The bibliographic codes of Moore's 1944 volume, however, were much softer. The trim size for the book was a scant five and one half by seven and one half inches, a bow to wartime scarcity and to the slimness of Moore's output of only six new poems. For the jacket, Macmillan chose an elegant, slanted white italic font that left ample open space on a navy blue field. The initial "N" of the title *Nevertheless* was beautifully curved, with a vine detail crossing the letter. The codes of the volume positioned Moore not as a difficult writer but as a calm, uncomplicated center of a global storm. Macmillan ultimately printed four thousand copies of *Nevertheless*, the largest print run that Moore had garnered to date.[50]

Sadly, just as Moore had truly achieved the broad public appeal that she had always hoped for her poems, her mother died, and Moore entered a period of depression that left her with little energy to write. Moore's last act as a Macmillan author was the preparation and publication of her 1951 *Collected Poems*, which won the Pulitzer Prize, the National Book Award, and the Bollingen Prize and catapulted Moore into a whole new level of literary fame.

Moore's career is a testament to the ways in which access to the various institutions that constituted the circuit of modernist publishing shaped the writing lives of those who entered it.

Throughout her career, Marianne Moore inhabited a number of different subject positions as an author, positions determined in large part by the venues that published her work. Her poems were, by turns, collectible and companionable, cruelly difficult and calmly reassuring, cutting edge and conservative, and unsellable and widely marketable. The venues that published Moore's work made it legible through the bibliographic codes they employed and the institutional definitions of the genre of poetry they enacted, codes and definitions that Moore could never wholly control.

Notes

1. F. L. Mott, *A History of American Magazines 1885–1905* (Cambridge, Mass.: Belknap Press, 1957), p. 11.
2. Robert Darnton, "What Is the History of Books," in D. Finkelstein and A. McCleery (eds.), *The Book History Reader* (New York: Routledge, 2006), p. 11.

3. J. L. W. West III, "The Expansion of the National Book Trade System," in C. Kaestle and J. Radway (eds.), *A History of the Book in America*. Vol. 4, *Print in Motion: The Expansion of Publishing and Reading in the United States, 1880–1940* (Chapel Hill: University of North Carolina Press, 2009), p. 79.

4. M. Winship, "The Rise of a National Book Trade System in the United States," in Kaestle and Radway (eds.), *A History of the Book in America*, vol. 4, p. 57.

5. Richard Ohmann, *Selling Culture: Magazines, Markets, and Class at the Turn of the Century* (London: Verso, 1996), pp. 25–30.

6. Jerome McGann, *The Textual Condition* (Princeton, N.J.: Princeton University Press, 1991), pp. 48–68.

7. Andreas Huyssen, *After the Great Divide: Modernism, Mass Culture, and Postmodernism* (Bloomington: University of Indiana Press, 1986), p. 53.

8. Mark Morrisson, *The Public Face of Modernism: Little Magazines, Audiences, and Reception, 1905–1920* (Madison: University of Wisconsin Press, 2001), p. 6.

9. Marianne Moore to J. W. Moore, July 20, 1915, Marianne Moore Collection, Rosenbach Museum and Library, Philadelphia (hereafter cited as Rosenbach).

10. M. Moore to J. W. Moore, December 16, 1915, Rosenbach.

11. M. Moore, typescript of "A Fool, a Foul Thing, a Distressful Lunatic," folder 1: 02: 06, Rosenbach.

12. Marianne Moore, "Masks," in Marianne Moore, *Becoming Marianne Moore: Early Poems 1907–1924*, ed. Robin Schulze (Berkeley: University of California Press, 2002), p. 186.

13. M. Moore to J. W. Moore, October 5, 1919, Rosenbach.

14. Harriet Monroe, "A Symposium on Marianne Moore," *Poetry* 19 (January 1922), p. 208.

15. Lawrence Rainey, *Institutions of Modernism: Literary Elites and Public Culture* (New Haven, Conn.: Yale University Press, 1998), p. 87. See Lawrence Rainey's account of the general role of patron-investors in modernist production, pp. 1–9, and his detailed account of Thayer's and Watson's patron-investor strategies at the *Dial*, pp. 77–106.

16. Scofield Thayer, "*The Dial*: Statement of Purpose," Dial/Scofield Thayer Papers, YCAL MSS 34, series II, box 9, folder 309, Beinecke.

17. Lawrence Rainey, "The Cultural Economy of Modernism," in M. Levenson (ed.), *The Cambridge Companion to Modernism* (Cambridge: Cambridge University Press, 1999), p. 48.

18. George Bornstein, "Textual Scholarship and Diversity: Which Needs Affirmative Action More," *Textual Cultures: Texts, Contexts, Interpretation* 3:1 (2008), p. 72.

19. See Catherine Turner's account of the problems faced by the upstart presses in their search for publishable materials in *Marketing Modernism Between the Two World Wars* (Amherst: University of Massachusetts Press, 2003).

20. See Rainey's account of the effect of coterie luxury edition publishing on H.D.'s career in *Institutions of Modernism*, pp. 146–68.

21. M. Moore to Bryher, July 7, 1921, in B. Costello, C. Goodridge, and C. Miller (eds.), *Selected Letters of Marianne Moore* (New York: Knopf, 1997), p. 164.

22. M. Moore to Bryher, October 15, 1920, in Costello et al. (eds.), *Selected Letters of Marianne Moore*, p. 133.

23. H. Child, "Poems by Marianne Moore," *Times Literary Supplement* (London), July 21, 1921, p. 471.

24. Mark Van Doren, "Women of Wit," *The Nation* 113:2938 (October 26, 1921), in E. Gregory (ed.), *The Critical Response to Marianne Moore* (Westport, Conn.: Praeger, 2003), pp. 33–34.

25. M. Moore to Bryher, August 31, 1921, in Costello et al. (eds.), *Selected Letters of Marianne Moore*, p. 178.

26. S. Thayer to M. Moore, August 18, 1924, Dial/Scofield Thayer Papers, YCAL MSS 34, series IV, box 35, folder 974, Beinecke.

27. See my account of this arrangement in Moore, *Becoming Marianne Moore*, pp. 29–38.

28. H. S. Gorman, "Moore's Art Is Not a Democratic One," *New York Times*, February 1, 1925, p. BR5.

29. M. Moore, "Courage, Right, and Wrong," *The Nation* 143 (December 5, 1936), in P. Willis (ed.), *The Complete Prose of Marianne Moore* (New York: Penguin, 1987), p. 341.

30. H. Monroe, "Comment: Art and Propaganda," *Poetry, A Magazine of Verse* 44:2 (July 1934), p. 212.

31. Monroe, "A Symposium on Marianne Moore," p. 208.

32. Sheila Kineke, "T. S. Eliot, Marianne Moore, and the Gendered Operations of Literary Sponsorship," *Journal of Modern Literature* 21:1 (1997), p. 131.

33. Costello et al. (eds.), *Selected Letters of Marianne Moore*, p. 317.

34. M. Moore to J. W. Moore, March 1, 1934, in Costello et al. (eds.), *Selected Letters of Marianne Moore*, p. 319.

35. T. S. Eliot to M. Moore, July 20, 1934, Rosenbach.

36. See Heather Cass White's account of Moore's production of *The Pangolin and Other Verse* in her introduction to the facsimile edition of the book Heather Cass White (ed.), *A Quiver with Significance: Marianne Moore, 1932–1936* (Victoria, B.C.: ELS Editions, 2008), pp. 15–30.

37. White (ed.), *A Quiver with Significance*, pp. xviii–xix.

38. White (ed.), *A Quiver with Significance*, p. 11.

39. George Bornstein, *Material Modernism: The Politics of the Page* (Cambridge: Cambridge University Press, 2001), pp. 112–17.

40. M. Moore, "Virginia Britannia," in White (ed.), *A Quiver with Significance*, p. 17.

41. M. Moore, "Virginia Britannia," in White (ed.), *A Quiver with Significance*, p. 18.

42. M. Moore, "The Pangolin," in White (ed.), *A Quiver with Significance*, pp. 27–29.

43. White (ed.), *A Quiver with Significance*, pp. xxi–xxii.

44. Bornstein, *Material Modernism*, p. 115.

45. Marianne Moore, *What Are Years* (New York: Macmillan, 1941), p. 1.

46. Moore, *What Are Years*, pp. 2–3.

47. Cristanne Miller, *Marianne Moore: Questions of Authority* (Cambridge, Mass.: Harvard University Press, 1995), p. 161.

48. Moore, *What Are Years*, p. 8.

49. Kimon Friar, "The Action of Incorrigible Tragedy," *Poetry* 64:2 (November 1944), pp. 89–90.

50. Craig Abbott, *Marianne Moore: A Descriptive Bibliography* (Pittsburgh, Pa.: University of Pittsburgh Press, 1977), p. 27.

Chapter 28

The Formalist Modernism of Edna St. Vincent Millay, Helene Johnson, and Louise Bogan

LESLEY WHEELER

Modernism claims the new for itself. Because a fractured, spare, allusive free verse is modernist poetry's signature style, formal verse has often been regarded by poets and critics as modernism's antithesis. Received forms, according to this logic, are feminine, retrograde, and populist, while the disjunctive modernist aesthetic occupies a violently masculine world, manifests innovative genius, and subverts the cheap sentimentality of mass culture. For example, expatriates H.D. and Ezra Pound cast themselves as rebels against the stifling values of the American bourgeoisie. From New Jersey and Harlem, William Carlos Williams and Langston Hughes posed challenges to their audiences that entwined aesthetic and cultural critique. The early work, at least, of Marianne Moore and T. S. Eliot is satirically resistant to the social and poetic status quo.

This is the dominant narrative of the twentieth-century critical response to modern poetry, even though the most prestigious U.S. poets of this era admired W. B. Yeats's formal genius enormously, wrote verse haunted by metrical patterns, and were, as Louise Bogan put it, "engaged in a task of restoration as well as of originality."[1] Modernism's "story of experimentalist triumph" has been successfully critiqued by Cary Nelson, Suzanne Clark, Joseph Harrington, and others, and the "new modernist studies" is temporally and spatially expanding the period's scope.[2] The political and aesthetic meanings of rhythm and rhyme during modernism nevertheless deserve further analysis. *Vers libre*, although enormously important and influential, was only one of the revolutions affecting poetry's sound and shape, its production and reception, during the first half of the century.

A great deal of formal verse was in circulation during the same decades – in newspapers and periodicals, on the radio, in live recitation, and elsewhere, doing "vital cultural work."[3] Much of it was meant to uplift, comfort, and reaffirm traditional order in a time of race riots, war, and rapid technological and cultural change. In other cases, however, technical mastery could in itself be a controversial testament to the full humanity of the writer, proof that a member of an excluded group deserved respect as an artist. Received forms empowered poets, delivered them to new audiences, and in themselves constituted a radical message. Sometimes, too, meter was the object of innovation, as poets tested contemporary language and attitudes against inherited verse structures. Could less common verse forms be put to modern use, as Pound and Edna St. Vincent Millay did with Anglo-Saxon measures? Could English prosody accommodate a casual voice, as in W. H. Auden's poems? Could American music be mined for new poetic structures, as Langston Hughes did in his blues poetry? Could a sonnet be a call to arms, as in Claude McKay's work, or a closet, as for Countee Cullen? Could a woman put on sonnet conventions as if donning a man's armor, as in Elinor Wylie's verse, or a male soldier's uniform, as in one sequence by Gwendolyn Brooks?

Several modernist-era poets who worked largely in meter and rhyme were innovators: their use of received forms was an integral part of their response to modernity. Sound-driven lyricism retains a connection to oral cultures that were receding during the advent of mass media – especially the displacement of local entertainments, including music and recitation. Invocations of a listening audience by Millay and others anticipate later eruptions of oral structures and a performance orientation into U.S. verse during the Beat, Black Arts, antiwar, feminist, ethnopoetics, and spoken word movements, and in the poetic practice of indigenous Americans in the late twentieth and early twenty-first centuries.

Modernity is characterized by alienation: as communication and travel technologies developed rapidly, new modes of connection seemed to obviate immediacy and proximity. Radio broadcast began in the United States in 1920, for example, and announcers' voices began to displace reading aloud by the hearth. Accordingly, the period generated many poetic explorations of the dialectic between presence and absence, an issue that is as old as the printed lyric but that gained new urgency in the twentieth century. Not only did print, a distancing technology in itself, enable poets to reach audiences over temporal and geographical gaps, but in the 1920s and 1930s, poets began to negotiate other media, including radio and recording. Even as Eliot sketched out his poetics of impersonality, U.S. audiences were responding eagerly to the relatively new phenomenon of well-known print poets delivering programs of their own verses in public spaces – a spectacle dependent less on the skill of the performer, as in nineteenth- and early twentieth-century displays of elocution, than on the identity of the performer.[4] The most innovative and successful poet-performers were as likely to be practitioners of free verse (Amy

Lowell, Carl Sandburg, Hughes) as of meter and rhyme (Robert Frost, Millay, Vachel Lindsay). This very fact suggests an alternate way of organizing canons and perceiving resemblances among writers. Instead of grouping poets chiefly by their relation to traditional English prosody, one might ask: Who recorded work at the Harvard Vocarium, and how did they approach the task? Who toured the literary societies or experimented with radio broadcast, and who maintained chaste, silent seclusion? The answers to these questions, too, indicate communities of experiment and resistance.

Themes of presence and absence recur in the verse of this period, whether or not the poet was a platform entertainer or an aficionado of rhyme and meter. However, sound-driven poetry is particularly insistent in its appeal to the physical body. This physicality, further, implies a larger role for race, gender, and sexuality in verse. Print disembodies the poet entirely, although readers reconstruct a sense of textual voice and therefore, to some degree, of the presence of the poet through rhythm, other acoustic effects, diction, syntax, punctuation, and typographical elements. A live reading, conversely, manifests gendered and racial bodies strongly, in both a visual and auditory way. Recording and broadcast separate physical voice from real-world presence but can still convey gender and race, although less reliably. It is no wonder, then, that women were among the most successful users of poetry's new platforms and that the same women became marginal to the modernist canon. A poetics of presence responds to the same crisis as does a poetics of impersonality – both are undergirded by a critique of the estrangements of modern life.

Andreas Huyssen argues that "mass culture has always been the hidden subtext of the modernist project" and that "mass culture is somehow associated with woman while real, authentic culture remains the prerogative of men."[5] According to Clark, modernist discourse banishes domestic culture by designating women's writing as "sentimental."[6] Sandra Gilbert and Susan Gubar likewise find that modernist innovations not only contrast but are motivated by the popular and critical successes of female writers.[7] Certainly, many women lyricists of the era – Sara Teasdale, Elinor Wylie, Georgia Douglas Johnson – wrote work that, for all its beauty and value, was fundamentally opposed to the project of poetic modernism. However, in other cases, this binary fails. Formal verse can be modernist, addressing in its concerns and in its very style what it meant to live and work in the United States early in the twentieth century.

This chapter concentrates on formal verse by women that explicitly engages the modern world, in large part by exploring sound, presence, and physicality amid technological alienations, revolutionized gender roles, and racial oppression. "Form" and "formalism" are contested terms, but in this context they indicate adherence to sound patterns borrowed from a preexisting prosodic tradition rather than invention of new aural structures. These established forms can include syllabic and accentual verse as well as accentual-syllabic meter, used strictly or loosely; however, most of the poems discussed here deploy meters and stanza shapes that have been common in English-language poetry since the Renaissance.

The lyric poetry of Millay, Helene Johnson, and Bogan is in conversation with modernist experiments, although each of these poets emphasized different aspects of twentieth-century politics and culture and, at least to some extent, aspired to reach different audiences. Millay had wide popular appeal during her career and is still read beyond the academy; Johnson has always been obscure beyond her literary circle; and Bogan was better known as a critic than a poet and is now read chiefly by other writers. Much of their work is also marked, like the free verse of H.D. and Mina Loy, by candid portrayals of female sexual desire. Millay cultivated and capitalized on an intensely feminine public persona, but her poems highlight self-construction rather than self-expression and depict her struggle to restore physical presence to the printed lyric. Johnson uses rhyme and meter to intensify her invocation of beautiful African American bodies and to convey erotic drive. Most of Bogan's work stresses the deadly silence of the printed poem, the stoppage of communication, and the occultation of identity and feeling; however, her later work features uncanny incursions of sound and presence. All these poets find in received forms ways to embody convention, disjunction, and conflict, particularly the physical experience of modernity. Meter is not the only way to emphasize sound in poetry, and emphasizing sound is not the only way to conjure presence and embodiment. However, to argue that modernism precludes formalism is to sideline some of the most powerful, interesting, and radical poetry of this era.

Edna St. Vincent Millay (1892–1950) was considered by many contemporaries to be a premier American poet – one of "the two and only two great things in the United States," according to Thomas Hardy, along with the skyscraper.[8] Then and since, she has also been received as a lyric poet in a Romantic vein with particular achievements in the sonnet form, as a promiscuously rhyming bohemian, as a gifted entertainer with a highly theatrical and elocution-influenced performance style, as a "female female impersonator" who parodies gender roles in order to critique "a tradition predicated upon her silence," and as a hysterical propagandist.[9] Millay's poetry also constitutes a direct response to a range of international crises and to the conditions of modern American life, especially to urbanization, the rise of mass culture, and women's increasing sexual and political freedom.

Like Frost, she built a popular audience by delivering poetry's familiar pleasures through a familiar persona but also charged those forms and stereotypes with colloquial energy and uncomfortably dark perceptions of human relationships and the natural world. Her performance of the femme fatale occurred both on the page and on the stage; she was immensely popular as a reader, her long gowns and dainty frame described rapturously in countless news reports. Also like Frost, Millay published her most difficult and interesting poems amid much more conventional lyrics. Both poets have a complex relation to modernism, standing outside it in their strong commitments to aural order, but, with the so-called high modernists, perceiving and sometimes mourning the erosion of other organizing paradigms, such as religion and community. Unlike Frost, however, Millay has not been fully restored to literary history as a creator of complex, beautiful, disturbing poems that have had a substantial impact on writers and readers.

Although Millay made her name with the extended lyric "Renascence" in 1912, and although a high proportion of her work is pastoral in setting and elegiac in tone, she is better known now for the urban seductress poses she strikes in verses such as "First Fig" and "Only until this cigarette has ended." She married in 1923 but was notorious for her sexual affairs with men and women; some of her love poetry uses second-person address to obscure the gender of the beloved. Her work ranges in length from memorable epigrams and brief lyrics, through mid-length narrative poems such as the "Ballad of the Harp Weaver," to sonnet sequences – one of them, *Fatal Interview*, is book length. As her poetic success developed, Millay maintained serious interests in other media: she was an accomplished pianist, worked for a stint with the Provincetown Players, had verse dramas and radio plays produced, and published short fiction. The character and range of her work was conditioned not only by ambition, predilection, and talent, but by her economic situation. Millay was raised in poverty in Maine by a divorced single mother; her Vassar education was paid for by a wealthy woman impressed by Millay's talent; and although, in 1923, she was only the second woman to earn the Pulitzer Prize in Poetry, she struggled to attain financial security. Millay lacked the family funds that underwrote young H.D. and Eliot. Rather than pursuing a bourgeois profession as Wallace Stevens or Williams did, Millay made the same choice as Frost and Hughes: she sought to earn a living as a writer.

Millay's poetic oeuvre is remarkable for the variety of received, modified, and invented forms she employs, but she is most admired for her dexterity with the sonnet. She used both the English and Italian varieties throughout her career, most often on the failure of romantic love; her books regularly end with a set of poems in this form. "Bluebeard" and a few other sonnets create distinct personae, but in most, the speaker resembles some version of Millay herself. Sometimes the diction is elevated and the rhymes predictable. However, Millay also produced many striking examples of sonnets in fluently natural voices, full of references to subways and advertisements, using the form's architecture brilliantly. "If I should learn, in some quite casual way," for example, suspends a single sentence over three quatrains and a couplet.[10] The speaker imagines reading of a lover's death in a newspaper, suppressing her grief, and deflecting her attention to journalistic advice on "where to store furs and how to treat the hair." The tension between sentence and form suggests one painfully prolonged moment; the crowded urban setting pressures her to maintain the neutral face of a busy consumer; and the syntax, knitted together by dashes, dramatizes both this "formal" behavior and the strain it causes. Millay highlights how one constructs a public self and the disjunctions inherent in this activity – the absence in her presence.

Millay dramatizes such paradoxes at the level of diction and meter, too. "Oh, think not I am faithful to a vow!" in *A Few Figs from Thistles* (1920) ends with the couplet: "So wanton, light and false, my love, are you, / I am most faithless when I most am true" (*EMCP*, p. 570). Every line in the poem presents some variation to the iambic pentameter pulse; only the penultimate line is perfectly, satisfyingly regular. As Millay reflects that it would be illogical to remain faithful to this errant lover, or to received gender norms more generally, she enacts this noncompliance on an acoustic level. Obedience to social or poetic rules constitutes treason to feeling, an inherently unruly condition. The next poem in the book ends, likewise, with cynicism: "Whether or not we find what we are seeking / Is idle, biologically speaking" (*EMCP*, p. 571). The shift from conventionally poetic to scientific diction deflates the poem's emotional intensity. Because the sonnet is strongly associated with male pursuit of a female beloved, Millay presses at its boundaries in the very act of performing female sexual desire. She characterizes this yearning as a physical instinct that may exist quite apart from love. Both this scientific-mindedness and her address to an ungendered "you" unsettle the heterosexual order. Millay's sonnets often invoke heterosexual romance only to subvert it or make space for same-sex love, thus participating in a countertradition of queering the form.[11]

Other forays into sonneteering bend the poem's technical parameters. "Sonnets from an Ungrafted Tree," a seventeen-poem sequence often cited as among her best work, tells of a young woman nursing her dying husband in rural isolation. Millay highlights her critique of marriage as an institution by closing each sonnet with a heptameter line that variously reaches into an imagined future ("Who planted seeds, musing ahead to their far blossoming"), laments the monotony of the woman's condition ("That here was spring, and the whole year to be lived through once more"), and presents the complexity and mysteriousness of each partner's interior life ("But the oak tree's shadow was deep and black and secret as a well") (*EMCP*, pp. 606, 616, 615). The latter sequence is a particularly powerful achievement, but Millay never stopped experimenting with the sonnet's rules. Later in her career, Millay published "Three Sonnets in Tetrameter," using an abbreviated line to depict the violent foreshortening produced by war (*EMCP*, p. 694).

Perhaps her most radical takes on the form occur in the 1939 volume *Huntsman, What Quarry?* The fourteen lines of "Rendezvous" and "The Fitting" are so elongated and rhythmically irregular that the rhyme pattern is almost undetectable (*EMCP*, pp. 340–43). "Rendezvous" cites Milton, rhymes "Greek" wittily with "chic," and remarks caustically on visual appearances: overly decorated rooms, overly scrubbed skin. The tryst it presents is strained by the speaker's sense that authentic connection – that moment when "you are you" – is difficult to achieve. The excess, talky length of many lines could be read as overdecoration that compensates for a lack of intimacy, but this poem also anticipates a shift in what authenticity sounds like: not harmonious verses but loose vernacular. The long lines of "The Fitting" give the latter poem a similar complexity, especially because, paradoxically, it concerns diminishment. "The Fitting" depicts French seamstresses fussing over the speaker's thin figure, altering her dresses to fit her shrinking frame. This encounter between women's bodies is both intimate and alienating, as the clash of languages within the poem emphasizes. Elision of emotional detail, the unpretty frankness of sensory imagery ("smelling of sweat," "her knuckles gouged my breast"), and casual language all show Millay finding common ground between modernist aesthetics and the sonnet form. The subject matter also manifests her concern with presence, the way the body withdraws from the language as the poem's aural order dissolves.

Although most of Millay's poetry is iambic, she organized her lines in a wide range of ways throughout her career. Each book moves a little further away from the strict formalism of her early publications; her last books mix received forms, free verse, and heterometric iambic poems (the uneven lines of these pieces look random, but meter is often present). However, Millay employed free verse occasionally, even early on. For example, the lead poem in *Second April* (1921), "Spring," uses ragged, angry rhythms to depict what Eliot would soon call "the cruellest month." In fact, the crux of Millay's complaint is the same as Eliot's – the rebirth of beauty in the spring tortures the half-dead, disillusioned speaker – although, unlike the expatriate poet, she personifies April as an Ophelia figure, "babbling and strewing flowers" (*EMCP*, p. 53). Elsewhere Millay deploys less common meters or establishes an accentual-syllabic pattern. For example, the falling rhythms of trochees evoke the elusive nymph in "Daphne" and the decline of summer in "Autumn Chant" (*EMCP*, pp. 141, 152). Deviant long lines in "Visiting the Asylum" suggest the uncanniness of the "queer folk" who reside there, and in "The Plum Gatherer," they dramatize the asymmetry of the past and present (*EMCP*, pp. 166, 248).

Finally, Millay was well read in the English tradition and resourceful in her use of nonmetrical sound patterning. One example in her lyric poetry is the hypnotic "Recuerdo," in *A Few Figs from Thistles* (*EMCP*, p. 128). This three-stanza poem, whose title could mean "I remember," "memory," or "memento," depicts a late-night adventure in her friendship with Nicaraguan poet Salomón de la Selva. "Recuerdo" is full of returns and exchanges: between the two poets who go "back and forth all night on the ferry" between Manhattan and Staten Island; between the revelers and street vendors of fruit and morning papers; and between the poor bohemians (who are nevertheless "very merry") and a more profoundly poor woman to whom they give their apples, pears, and "all our money but our subway fares." Its lines are accentual – six beats with a medial caesura and occasional alliteration – rather than accentual-syllabic, as is meter in English verse. Accentual measure is characteristic of oral poetry in English, from nursery rhymes to spoken word. Not surprisingly, Millay also employed it in her opera libretto, *The King's Henchman*, based on a tale of love and treachery from the *Anglo-Saxon Chronicle*. The libretto closely adheres to her Anglo-Saxon sources, employing heavy allusion and two- and four-beat lines. She even sent a telegraph to the composer, Deems Taylor, to insist that the title not be changed because she was carefully designing the libretto's diction: "KINGS MESSENGER ABSOLUTELY IMPOSSIBLE FOR THIS REASON THE WORD MESSENGER WAS BROUGHT INTO ENGLISH BY THE NORMANS AND I AM WRITING MY ENTIRE LIBRETTO IN ANGLOSAXON THAT IS TO SAY THERE IS NOT A WORD IN THE LIBRETTO WHICH WAS NOT KNOWN IN ONE FORM OR ANOTHER IN ENGLISH A THOUSAND YEARS AGO."[12] Her awareness of the history and context of language and verse was high.

Millay's poetry both employs received forms and deforms them, just as she both defies feminine stereotypes and deploys them strategically. Her best poetry is starker than that of the nineteenth-century "songbirds" she might be compared to, but it doesn't represent a clean break from that tradition: as a prosodist, she renews rather than reinvents. She is most modern stylistically in her attitudes toward poetry's media. Her experiments in performance and broadcast were forward-looking and nostalgic simultaneously. In reading her poems for a national radio series in 1933, she approached a technology that listeners found both exciting and threatening and discovered in it a new way of delivering the seductive illusion of presence to audiences.[13] Millay conceived of print as only one of poetry's media, and not the primary one. She transformed the oral tradition she had received – poems memorized and recited at home and at school for the betterment of the soul and the citizenry – for the new conditions of mass culture, the incursions of radio broadcasters into domesticity, and the increasingly intense phenomenon of national celebrity.

Form remained political for Millay, a way to counter alienation and enact progressive views. While there was always a latent critique of poverty and injustice in her work, by the late twenties she used lyric to address political crises directly, dismaying some readers. "Justice Denied in Massachusetts," for example, appeared in the New York *World* on the afternoon before Sacco and Vanzetti's executions, and later poems forthrightly address World War II. She is both too politically progressive and too formally conservative to fit some definitions of modernism, and yet she could hardly have been more engaged with the cultural crises of her time.

Most women poets associated with the Harlem Renaissance period wrote frequently, although not exclusively, in rhyme and meter. Alice Dunbar-Nelson (1875–1935), Georgia Douglas Johnson (1880–1966), Jessie Redmon Fauset (1882–1961), Anne Spencer (1882–1975), Effie Lee Newsome (1885–1979), Gwendolyn Bennett (1902–1979), Gladys May Casely Hayford (1904–1950), and others practiced formalism with an edge of racial protest. At the time, Georgia Douglas Johnson was compared to Millay and Teasdale, but now the work of Harlem Renaissance women is too rarely considered alongside the formalisms of white women poets.[14] Helene Johnson (1906–1995) was one of the youngest among these African American women, and her work contrasts with the regular iambs and familiar sentiments of her elders: although her career fizzled early, she wrote free verse of especial boldness and energy. Meter and rhyme, however, are far more pervasive in Helene Johnson's work than is generally acknowledged. For Johnson, aural patterns provided an important background for rebellion as well as a way to re-create sound and presence. There is no evidence that these two New York City poets met or read each other's work, but Millay and Johnson both bring defiant sexuality, deep commitment to sound, and an experimental edge to formal poetry.

Helene Johnson was a promising early light in the Harlem Renaissance: in 1925, at nineteen, she won an honorable mention for "Trees at Night" in *Opportunity*'s annual contest; she earned three more in the 1926 competition, judged by Robert Frost. She had received a top-notch education in Brookline, Massachusetts, where she was unconventionally raised by her mother and a cadre of aunts, most of whom worked "in service," as maids. Johnson eventually moved to New York with her cousin, author Dorothy West, where James Weldon Johnson and Zora Neale Hurston encouraged her writing. In 1933 Johnson married, in 1935 she published her last poem, and she ceased writing for many years as she worked as a correspondent for Consumer's Union to support her child. Her verse was not collected in book form until Verner Mitchell edited *This Waiting for Love*, a volume of poems and selected letters published in 2000.[15] Many women writers of that era vanished after early success, but Johnson's disappearance was compounded by her fiercely private temperament. For example, she dwelled in New York City for nearly all of her adult life but operated well under the radar of scholars and poets researching the Harlem Renaissance. When asked to give a public reading in 1987, she sent in a tape recording instead.

The forty-seven poems in *This Waiting for Love* are both sound driven and lyric. Although Mitchell writes that Johnson's "preferred form was the free verse of Whitman or Hughes," twenty-six of these poems use meter or rhyme in a prominent way (*TWL*, p. 12). Several of those are sonnets; quatrains are also common, although many regular ballad stanzas are broken visually into more than four lines. Like Millay, Johnson tropes constantly on song, drawing attention to aural structures even as she disguises them, and writes often about sexual desire and transgression. Although some of these erotically charged pieces conjure black bodies vividly, others tease out an almost-presence.

Johnson's free verse is shot through with irregular rhyme; conversely, the music of her formal poetry is highly varied. "The Road," for instance, compares a dusty highway first to a thrush's "single singing line of dusky song" and then to the "trodden pride" of her race (*TWL*, p. 25). The tone is rapturous as she exhorts the road, in the poem's final line, to "Rise to one brimming, golden, spilling cry!" Although this poem is imagistic and its diction recalls Romantic poetry, especially Keats and Whitman, it is also distinctly political. "The Road" celebrates racial beauty, decries oppression, and, in that last line, urges uprising, at least through artistic expression.

Johnson magnifies the poem's latent tension by establishing iambic pentameter and then disturbing that pattern. It begins with a fully rhymed couplet, but while the end rhyme creates harmonies, the word "song" lacks a partner, and

the poem ends on an assonantal slant rhyme ("pride" / "cry"). The line length
fluctuates, too. The fourth and fifth are three and seven feet long, respectively.
Together they add up to two pentameter lines, but the variation accents a contrast between song and silence: the short line ends in a "drowsy hush," and the
longer culminates in that extended description of "dusky song." Another formal variation is more subtle. Of the eighteen polysyllabic words in the poem,
all but one are trochees. Johnson creates a falling rhythm within and against
the rising iambs. While poets commonly use trochaic words in iambic poems,
the strategy is strikingly predominant here. The conflicting rhythms perhaps
imitate the undulation of the road, its "leaping clay hill," but they also build a
sound of loss or ambivalence into a forward-looking poem, a memory of pain
within its optimism.

In "The Road," Johnson uses the color brown to link dust and clay with
"my race." In fact, she often rhymes the natural landscape, particularly earth
itself, with human flesh or depicts a person in erotic contact with the soil to
convey the fertility and beauty of both. In the quatrains of "Fulfillment," for
example, the speaker desires to "dig my hands deep into the pregnant earth,"
and to "melt the still snow / with my seething body / And kiss the warm earth
tremulous underneath" (*TWL*, p. 28). In other pieces, even less conventionally beautiful aspects of the cityscape incite arousal. In "A Missionary Brings
a Young Native to America," a woman's body is invaded by the sound of
stampeding pedestrians, the "city grit upon her tongue," and a "steel-spiked
wave of brick and light" (*TWL*, p. 43). Although she is initially fearful, by the
end of the Petrarchan sonnet's overflowing octave (nine lines balance against
five here, rather than eight against six), songs "surge" within her, and she
must recite prayers and litanies to contain her "young abandon" and defuse
her "Unholy dreams." The swallowed urban dust becomes, by nightfall, an
aphrodisiac.

One of Johnson's boldest embodiments occurs in "Sonnet to a Negro in
Harlem," another apostrophic poem, this time addressed to a "disdainful and
magnificent" man. The power of his character is so great that Harlem melts
away around him in favor of "palm trees and mangoes" – the poet's eye and
ear focus only on him. Johnson frankly admires the man's "perfect body" and
angry posture. Paradoxically, however, this sonnet suggests the pointlessness
of writing sonnets. Johnson accuses this Negro in Harlem of being "incompetent / To imitate those whom you so despise": she insists on his difference
without specifying the possible grounds for imitation, but other moments in
the poem hint that African American use of European forms is on her mind.
Metrical puns come to the fore when Johnson lingers on attributes of his "gait."

Because "Scorn will efface" any mark he tries to make, she says, he refuses to "urge ahead [his] supercilious feet" (*TWL*, p. 40). Although Johnson reverses the sonnet's usual gendered dynamic and produces a poem that praises much more intensely than it mocks, she raises questions here about what it means to be a desiring woman and how received forms modulate the expression of that desire.

"Sonnet to a Negro in Harlem" is one of several poems by Johnson that invoke the power or beauty of black male bodies, especially those of dancers. They contest a white vision of African American identity – the vision of a jazz club tourist in Harlem – by re-deploying primitivist tropes. "Poem," featuring a "little brown boy" whose song suggests African tom-toms, is one such piece, its free verse structured by anaphora and the repeated apostrophe, "Gee, boy" (*TWL*, pp. 38–39). The swelling free verse lines of "Bottled," too, invoke Africa as they depict a man who, as Rachel Blau DuPlessis puts it, is a "tricked-out figure being tricked yet being trickster ... a black person doing blackface minstrelsy" (*TWL*, pp. 85–86). Johnson demonstrates a persistent interest in such blurred identities, performances layered over performances, even as she insists on physicality: her poems "both assert and refute the idea of authenticity."[16] The presence Johnson seeks to materialize through her poems is always black and always explicitly gendered, but it is not typically the speaker's or the author's.

As one might expect given Johnson's ambivalence about publicity, the women in her poems are sometimes half-hidden, as in the couplets of "Night" (*TWL*, p. 26), or conceal erotic secrets, as in the slant rhymes of "The Little Love" (*TWL*, p. 30). Elsewhere she expresses a preference for night's mysteriousness over daylight's revelations (*TWL*, p. 42). Night can be a racial signifier in African American poetry, a way "to assert the primacy of blackness," although it suggests concealment as well.[17] Other poems, however, exhibit an open, exuberant physicality. The "Widow with a Moral Obligation," for instance, begs to repeat a failed seduction attempt, promising to overcome her feeling of being haunted by her dead husband. In the process of repudiating shyness, she twice promises to "have my hair unbound, / My gown undone" (*TWL*, p. 59). The fully rhymed quatrains, in short lines of two or three beats, convey a playful lightness as the sexually alive speaker materializes to displace the dead man's jealous specter. Johnson can't deliver full presence even through this vivid, sound-saturated writing, but many of her poems aspire toward that consummation. Contemporary urban settings, celebrations of female desire, and explorations of racial tension mark Johnson's engagement with modernity, but so does her work within and against rhyme and meter.

In a well-known essay, Louise Bogan (1897–1970), a formalist in her own poetry, praises how

> the cluster of lyric poets that appeared on the American scene just before and after 1918 restored a genuine and frank feeling to a literary situation which had become genteel, artificial, and dry. Sara Teasdale's later verse; the best of Edna Millay's early rebellious songs and meditations; Elinor Wylie's ability to fuse thought and passion into the most admirable and complex forms; the sensitive, intellectual poetry of Leonie Adams – all these poetic productions helped to resolve hampering attitudes of the period.[18]

Bogan believed that "the large and true poetic talents, in Europe, England, and America, since before 1914, have either worked in form or toward the discovery of form."[19] Her many reviews convey particular esteem for the technical achievements of Yeats and Auden. However, at other times Bogan expresses skepticism about twentieth-century formalism as an enterprise. She suggests that adherence to received forms deadens contemporary writing, cautioning May Sarton away from sonnet cycles in a 1961 letter. Bogan warns that "I do not think that such sequences can be written, nowadays, with any hope of effectiveness," citing sequences by Millay and Wylie as exemplary failures.[20] Familiar measures can "force poets into stock attitudes, usually of pomposity or gloom." Addressing poetry by women, she suggests that "there is no basic reason for women to excel in the art of poetry by producing the same sort of poetic structures as men" and cites the bold experiments of Gertrude Stein, H.D., and Moore as examples of aesthetic revolution. Change is paramount: "The whole encumbered ground must be cleared." This is true even of successful metrical verse – it must represent a real break from the work preceding it. For example, she finds Auden's poetry so forceful because he can be "casual in tone" even as he employs regular couplets or a "disused Byronic stanza form": this change is not a superficial one, she judges, but the result of a profound reexamination of modern poetry's "intellectual pretension, and spiritual gloom."[21] Bogan is more often claimed as a modernist than other women writers who work primarily in meter, in part because of her commitment to "reducing the lyric to its essentials," but her critique of formalism is another important credential.[22]

While Johnson is a more formal poet than readers have recognized, Bogan may be less so. Most of Bogan's poems employ rhyme, and many are metrical; however, Bogan produced free verse as well, and even poems arranged into rhymed verses can be rhythmically irregular enough that one can barely discern an underlying meter. Nor does Bogan link formalism with sexual liberation and empowered female desire, as Millay and Johnson do. Bogan certainly resisted the strictures of her Catholic upbringing and describes her teenaged self as a "radical and a Fabian." However, although she wrote in one unsent author questionnaire, "I also like love-making, when it is really well-informed," another statement from the same piece is more representative: "I prefer to draw the veil over my experiences, sexual and otherwise from the age of nineteen, when I married for the first time, to the present."[23] Her poetry, too, even when it clearly springs from personal suffering, is more deflective than revelatory. Her verses are typically economical, engaged in what Gloria Bowles describes as an "aesthetic of limitation."[24] Bogan does share common ground with the other poets treated in this chapter, nevertheless. Like Millay and Johnson, she investigates the connections between gender and form, and in particular the ability of the lyric to convey authorial presence. For the most part, the self performed in them is insubstantial, half-hidden, inaccessible. Bogan's later poetry, however, emphasizes the authentic gestures and residues that give a poem life.

Bogan was born to working-class parents in Maine in 1897, suffered an unhappy childhood, and discovered writing when a benefactor subsidized her education at a girls' Latin school. She spent a year at Boston University and, after much struggle, was able to earn her living as a writer of poetry, fiction, and nonfiction prose. Her three slim poetry volumes were published between 1923 and 1937, their selections overlapping in part; most, but not all, of these verses are collected in *The Blue Estuaries: Poems 1923–1968*, which remains in print. Her verse was well received in her lifetime, but she was at least as highly lauded for her thirty-eight-year stint as poetry reviewer for the *New Yorker*.

Bogan has a reputation for misogyny. She often resisted reviewing other women poets. Although she argued that "to separate the work of women writers from the work of men, is, naturally, a highly unfeminist action," she regarded women's poetry as essentially different from men's, as discussed subsequently.[25] Her early poem "Women" identifies the whole sex with stifling containment. Women do everything wrongly, feel too much, and think too little. They are "Content in the tight hot cell of their hearts / To eat dusty bread," but even when they step out of those cells, Bogan alleges in the last stanza, they do so at the wrong moment, when they should be accepting their exclusion from "life."[26] The steady pattern of full rhymes in the quatrains – most of the rhyme words are single syllable – reinforces this predictability. With this poem, Bogan sets herself apart from her sex. She speaks as if from beyond gender, seeing and hearing what real women fail to perceive, measuring all their shortcomings. This outsider stance is typical of her work, marked by dissociation and solitude.

While "Women have no wilderness in them," however, these stanzas do. The apparently locked-up quatrains are less regular than they appear in a visual assessment. Lines fluctuate unpredictably, with the weightier first and third lines of the ballad stanzas ranging in length between four and five feet, the second and fourth between two and three. Although the poem is rhymed and iambic, the lineation is unruly. The sound of "Women," in other words, runs contrary to meter's reason. Is this a mark of unreasonable femininity? In any case, the little cells or rooms of this poem are deformed, as if by women's frustration, or Bogan's own.

Bogan is generally less likely to criticize women in her poems than she is to mock those who seek to confine them. Her first volume, *The Body of This Death* (1923), is full of characters who look at women, trying and failing to control them with a steady gaze: "The Frightened Man," "Portrait," "The Romantic," and "Statue and Birds." The female presence in each piece escapes domination, or at least seeks escape. Bogan's best-known and most discussed meditation on vision and power is "The Medusa," a piece formally similar to "Women" and from the same book – arranged in rhymed quatrains, it contains both anapestic lines and roughly iambic ones, and the line lengths vary to an unusual degree. The speaker of this piece, whose gender is not identified, has glimpsed Medusa and is now trapped in a "dead scene" of permanent stasis (*BE*, p. 4). "What is glimpsed by the poem's speaker," according to Clark, "is a shadow of herself, a feminine subjectivity that is unspeakable and uncanny."[27] Medusa's apparition occurs in the single five-line stanza, again as if the power of the goddess deforms the poem's scheme.

The Body of This Death contains many references to time's breakdown, but in "Medusa" and other poems the stoppage is not paradisiacal but deadly. It is also profoundly silent: bells can never toll, the "rusted mouth" cannot speak, wind is "arrested" (*BE*, pp. 3, 17). When the air does vibrate, the sound is hypothetical and faint, as in the evocative closure of "Men Loved Wholly Beyond Wisdom," when the speaker imagines "Listening to the prisoned cricket / Shake its terrible, dissembling / Music in the granite hill" (*BE*, p. 16). Bogan draws a contrast between vision and sound that resonates with Millay's sense of the lyric. Printed, a poem is a lasting monument, but it is deathly quiet. It encodes longing for physical voice.

Bogan was no populist performer but an intensely reserved person who suffered from depression and alcoholism and was "temperamentally and aesthetically hostile to display."[28] Her poems betray horror at the persistence of the body – mixed with some wry humor. "The Alchemist," for example, seeks to burn away matter in favor of "passion wholly of the mind," but what the fire leaves behind is in fact not some pure spiritual essence but "unmysterious flesh" (*BE*, p. 15). The poem's initially steady rhythm starts to disintegrate as the speaker recognizes the staying power of physical emotions. In "The Crows," an "old" woman continues to experience love and desire, but a sense of age and mortality inflects those feelings; the final line of each quatrain is foreshortened to suggest the diminished time remaining. What should be "heart's laughter" turns into the raucous crying of those unbeautiful birds, as if sexuality in a mature woman is repulsive, unseemly (*BE*, p. 17).

When Bogan's poetry depicts the wild strength of the body and its drives, physical presence is sometimes half-hidden. *Dark Summer* (1929), her second collection, uses images of secrecy and latency that resemble the concealments in Johnson's verses. *Dark Summer* also depicts separations between writer and reader as if poetry has no communicative function. The emblem it offers for the lyric poem is a mirror in an "abandoned chamber," in which natural beauty changes and dies with no one to observe it (*BE*, p. 34). A still later poem, "Man Alone," addresses a man who seeks his own face in books and mirrors and finds only strangers there. "The printed page gives back / Words by another hand," Bogan writes, insisting on literature as a construction made of words rather than a space of recognition or relationship (*BE*, p. 75). Metrical disruptions mimic the cognitive ones, and sight rhyme in the last stanza creates additional dissonance: the look of the words is betrayed by their sound.

Bogan suggests, nonetheless, in the 1933 essay "Managing the Unconscious," that writing can involve some uncanny manifestations. Her advice seems both a way to conquer writer's block and a mechanism for channeling "richness" into poetry: get up early and write while one is still half-dreaming, she instructs; write anything, without consideration of audience; "forget that you have any critical faculty."[29] This process may or may not have generated "Medusa" and other surreal poems in Bogan's canon, but Bogan certainly, in a subset of her verses, imagines the lyric as haunted by mysterious power and impossible presence.

"Homunculus," for example, offers a very different metaphor for poetic production than the unwatched mirror in "The Cupola." The speaker describes the little man of the title, with some delight, as "A delicate precious ruse / By which death is betrayed," a perfect bit of trickery, "fine," "strong," "wise," and "young" (*BE*, p. 65). However, like a golem or Dr. Frankenstein's monster, the homunculus requires animation: "It lacks but life: some scent, / Some kernel of hot endeavor." The homunculus is the poem – in this case, one possessing a regular iambic heartbeat, ligaments of alliteration, and symmetry in its stanza pattern. The end rhymes suggest that its creator devised it as a cunning bid at immortality: "made" / "betrayed," "ruse" / "use," "endeavor" / "forever." Although the process of animation occurs in the present tense and is not completed, this poem does, in fact, possess weird force, uncanny liveliness.

In other poems, "life" in art comes explicitly from personal sources. In "The Dream," four quatrains of anapestic tetrameter, the speaker is about to be trampled by a terrible horse and cowers in terror. A braver woman leaps in: "Give him, she said, something of yours as a charm" (BE, p. 103). Although the speaker despairs of salvation, she obeys, pulling the glove from her right hand and flinging it at him; the horse submits and assumes a posture of devotion. Bogan invites psychoanalytic reading by plainly labeling the poem as a dream. The reticent woman has another, bolder self who can help the speaker strip away her prim covering, give of herself, and thereby conquer fear and receive love. Her fierce muse in "The Daemon" also demands self-exposure: the speaker must "show outright / The bruise in the side" (BE, p. 114). The syntax and structure are simple, involving quatrains of alternating full rhymes and pared-down dimeter lines. For Bogan, however, self-expression is not a straightforward project. The poem mingles personal and religious revelation, alluding to Jesus's side pierced by soldiers after the crucifixion (John 19:33–37). How can one express a self that is so layered, so ruptured?

Inner division, paradoxically, enables the poet to "speak" and "tell" (BE, p. 114), to move the metaphorical "rusted tongue" on the very first page of her first collection. In "The Sleeping Fury," for instance, vision displaces sound. The speaker watches "my scourge, my sister" slumbering, analyzing from a calm distance the Fury's beauty and destructive power (BE, p. 78). This poem, along with much of Bogan's other work, suggests a woman's struggle against her own unmanageable will, her disappointment in the world, and painfully acquired knowledge assessed from an isolated vantage. The "clamor" of repressed force is both present and absent. In a later poem, "Little Lobelia's Song," Bogan reverses this situation. An embodied dream, given a diminutive name, is estranged and seeks a way back to the mind that generated it; the poem consists entirely of her voice, although she "can barely speak," and the poem's brief verses depend on repetition and tightly limited diction: "Else I weep, weep, / Else I cry, cry" (BE, p. 133). Poetry erupts from all this fierce grieving and partakes of its eerie, half-formed presence.

The psychological thrust of Bogan's later work suggests the midcentury poetics of Lowell, Sylvia Plath, or Anne Sexton more than it resembles modernism, formalist or otherwise. The hide-and-seek of the self in her poems, though – ambivalence about the divide between author and audience and a persistent drive to restore at least the illusion of co-presence – marks Bogan's work as modern. The point of this chapter, and of many recent retellings of literary history, is that the poetic production of this period is too robust and heterogeneous to be captured in any one narrative. The quest to manifest impossible presence nevertheless suggests a through-line with as much explanatory power as what Nelson calls the "story of experimentalist triumph" and makes room for a wider range of practice.

An important context for these three writers and all modern poetry is the more traditional rhymed and metered verse produced by Georgia Douglas Johnson, Sara Teasdale (1884–1933), Elinor Wylie (1885–1928), Léonie Adams (1899–1988), and others. Georgia Douglas Johnson was the most anthologized woman poet of the Harlem Renaissance – she was part of the old guard against whom Helene Johnson, Langston Hughes, and others rebelled but was still critical of the constrictions women faced in their professional and affective lives.[30] Teasdale and Wylie were literary celebrities, and Wylie was an object of social scandal. The latter deserve discussion here for their achievements and their influence, although they might reasonably be labeled antimodernist. Proximity to modernism, after all, is not the only measure by which poetry of this era succeeds or fails.

Teasdale's formalism is marked by nostalgia for chivalry and the classical world, and her most common subject is romantic love, often failed, faded, or thwarted by circumstance. Like Georgia Douglas Johnson, she is faithful to the traditional territory of women's verse, both in form and theme. Her poetry started appearing in print in 1907, earlier than the works of other writers discussed here, and she was certainly one of the popular writers against whom the modernists took their highbrow stand. Yet Teasdale's language itself is straightforward and modern. She wrote about the contemporary urban world as well as nature and romantic historical scenes; a poem about the New York City subway, for example, appears in her 1915 collection.[31]

Teasdale's poetry is predicated on lack or absence, a trope that is common in Bogan's work and, to a lesser extent, in Millay's. However, Teasdale does not counter it with attempts to manifest physical presence. In "Vox Corporis," the mind holds the body (or "beast") firmly back (*STCP*, p. 38). In fact, physical intimacy turns out to be a disappointing experience. In "The Kiss," Teasdale observes the disjunction between idealized romance and the reality of heterosexual coupling: "His kiss was not so wonderful / As all the dreams I had" (*STCP*, p. 28). Elsewhere she gives her lover the "gift" of her absence (*STCP*, p. 5) and predicts, in "Land's End," that "none will care" about the disappearance of her footprints from the sand. In "The Tree," she wishes to be transformed, through a series of displacements, into words on a page. She begins, "Oh to be free of myself," imagining her heart "as bare / As a tree in December," fearless and unburdened. Her plaint ends with the desire to be "heedless / If anyone pass and see / On the white page of the sky / Its thin black tracery" (*STCP*, p. 156). In other words, she would disappear into her poems with complete indifference to the work's audience. The impulse behind this poem could not be further from Millay's urgent renewal of connection between author and audience through the figure of voice.

Teasdale redirects sensual passion toward language itself. "Indian Summer," a poem in four Sapphic stanzas from *Rivers to the Sea* (1915), suggests the kind of music that resonates in Teasdale's work. "Indian Summer" apostrophizes "lyric night," a twilight scene during the last moments of summer heat. Sound triumphs over vision: the fields are "shadowy," but the night is full of song. "Never a bird" calls, she observes, rejecting that common figure for the lyric poet in favor of the "passionless chant of insects," "The grasshopper's horn," and "the wheel of a locust leisurely grinding the silence" (*STCP*, p. 61). These voices are not expressing feeling but producing a disembodied sound in increasingly mechanical metaphors. When Teasdale shifts gears to apostrophize the "little insects" fighting the "heartless" winter and compares this listening to gazing into the eyes of a departing loved one, the poem loses some energy and vividness. The stock first-person mourning woman is less compelling than the link Teasdale had earlier forged between her own falling rhythms and the weird persistence of inhuman sound.

Elinor Wylie, like Teasdale, uses an impressive range of metrical and stanzaic patterns and received forms with exceptional fluency and was widely read during this period. Wylie's contemporaries admired both her technical skill and the intelligence at work in her verses. Her tonal range is similar to Millay's in that it includes lyric ecstasy, philosophical meditation, and sharp satire – the satirical poems, often in couplets, are thick with witty, incongruous polysyllabic rhymes such as "alarums" / "bar-rooms."[32] While some of her poems convey frustration at traditional feminine roles, though, most are otherworldly, chivalric, classical, or otherwise removed from modernity. There is no reference more current than trolley cars or the American Civil War in her entire *Collected Poems*, no phrase that could not have been uttered in the nineteenth century.

Cheryl Walker identifies Wylie as a "woman warrior" and "the angriest woman in the nightingale tradition" and hears echoes of her outrage in Anne Sexton and Sylvia Plath.[33] Wylie's strategy for coping with hostile conditions was to ride out in masks and armor. She constructed a masculine, knightly persona while nevertheless adhering to the nineteenth-century notion of separate spheres. Wylie, raised an Anglophilic American aristocrat, preferred a pose of modest reticence even in her public art. The motif governing *Black Armour*, for instance – a collection divided into sections called "Breastplate," "Gauntlet," "Helmet," and so on – both draws attention to the body and conceals it. Again and again, she describes herself as "a spiritual savage caged" by lowly flesh, emphasizing the purity of word and spirit in contrast to the "carnal mesh."[34] Occasionally her imagery has a racial cast as she imagines a fleeting absent whiteness in contrast to dark embodiment. In "August," she unfavorably compares a Negro pushing a cart of bright "smouldering daisies" to the hypothetical creamy coolness of white lilies "Plucked from some hemlock-darkened northern stream / By fair-haired swimmers." More subtly, in "Self-Portrait," the mind is a "lens of crystal" and "the little rest / A hollow scooped to blackness in the breast."[35] Here the true speaker, an intellectual essence, is not so much concealed as transparent or insubstantial, and the residue is a hollowed-out black body. The effect, despite resurgent anger, is resistance to the noisy, urban, racially mixed world she dwelled in, and to the sexual adventure celebrated by Millay and Johnson. Wylie declares her physical removal from her own elegant lyrics.

Surveying the history of verse by U.S. women in her 1947 essay "The Heart and the Lyre," Bogan offers sweeping generalizations about the gifts and handicaps of women poets: "They are not good at abstractions and their sense of structure is not large"; forced to become adults early, "they are practical, intense ... and they are natural singers." "In women, more than men," she writes, "the intensity of their emotions is the key to the treasures of their spirit." She finishes by lamenting current trends toward a distant, logical style in the poems of younger women poets, although she cites only Elizabeth Bishop by name, and urging these women to keep "the emotional channels" of literature open.[36]

Formalist modernists do create an effect of expressiveness, of authorial presence that defies modern alienation. They also subvert, interrogate, and unsettle this illusion in part by manipulating traditional English prosody, using form as a resource in social critique and to remediate modern ills. Millay, Johnson, and Bogan tackle the same material canonical modernists engage: shifting gender codes; isolation amid urban crowds; racial pride and conflict; estrangement from religion, except through numinous nature; consciousness riven by buried drives; the debasement of language and the failure of human connection; and science, politics, and the terrible costs of twentieth-century warfare. In their shared insistence on aural patterns and the power of sound, they also sustain a connection to the past *and* anticipate the rebellions of U.S. poetry at midcentury and beyond.

Notes

1. Louise Bogan, *A Poet's Alphabet: Reflections on the Literary Art and Vocation*, ed. Robert Phelps and Rith Limmer (New York: McGraw-Hill, 1970), p. 12.
2. Cary Nelson, "The Fate of Gender in Modern American Poetry," in Kevin J. H. Dettmar and Stephen Watt (eds.), *Marketing Modernisms: Self-Promotion, Canonization, Rereading* (Ann Arbor: University of Michigan Press, 1996), pp. 321–60, 323; Douglas Mao and Rebecca L. Walkowitz, "The New Modernist Studies," *PMLA* 123:3 (2008), pp. 737–48, 737–38.
3. Cary Nelson, *Repression and Recovery: Modern American Poetry and the Politics of Cultural Memory, 1910–1945* (Madison: University of Wisconsin Press, 1989), p. 23; see also Joseph Harrington, *Poetry and the Public: The Social Form of Modern U.S. Poetics* (Middletown, Conn.: Wesleyan University Press, 2002).
4. Lesley Wheeler, *Voicing American Poetry: Sound and Performance from the 1920s to the Present* (Ithaca, N.Y.: Cornell University Press, 2008), pp. 3–13.
5. Andreas Huyssen, *After the Great Divide: Modernism, Mass Culture, Postmodernism* (Bloomington: Indiana University Press, 1986), p. 47.
6. Suzanne Clark, *Sentimental Modernism: Women Writers and the Revolution of the Word* (Bloomington, Ind.: Indiana University Press, 1991), pp. 1–2.
7. Sandra M. Gilbert and Susan Gubar, *No Man's Land: The Place of the Woman Writer in the Twentieth Century*, 3 vols. (New Haven, Conn.: Yale University Press, 1988, 1989, 1994), vol. 1, p. 131.
8. Elinor Wylie, "A Nightingale at the Court of King Eadgar," *New York Herald Tribune*, February 20, 1927, pp. 1–6, 1.
9. Sandra M. Gilbert, "'Directions for Using the Empress': Millay's Supreme Fictions," in Diane P. Freedman (ed.), *Millay at 100: A Critical Reappraisal* (Carbondale: Southern Illinois University Press, 1995), pp. 163–81, 170; Stacy Carson Hubbard, "Love's Little Day: Time and the Sexual Body in Millay's Sonnets," in Freedman (ed.), *Millay at 100*, pp. 100–16, 102; Susan Schweik, *A Gulf So Deeply Cut: American Women Poets and the Second World War* (Madison: University of Wisconsin Press, 1991), pp. 59–69.
10. Edna St. Vincent Millay, *Collected Poems*, ed. Norma Millay (New York: HarperCollins, 1956), p. 565. This collection will be cited in the text as *EMCP*.
11. David Caplan, *Questions of Possibility: Contemporary Poetry and Poetic Form* (New York: Oxford University Press, 2005), pp. 61–85.
12. Nancy Milford, *Savage Beauty: The Life of Edna St. Vincent Millay* (New York: Random House, 2001), p. 282.
13. Wheeler, *Voicing American Poetry*, pp. 46–58.

14. Gloria T. Hull, *Color, Sex, and Poetry: Three Women Writers of the Harlem Renaissance* (Bloomington: Indiana University Press, 1987), p. 179.

15. Helene Johnson, *This Waiting for Love: Helene Johnson, Poet of the Harlem Renaissance*, ed. Verner D. Mitchell (Amherst: University of Massachusetts Press, 2000), pp. 125–27. This collection will be cited in the text as *TWL*.

16. Katherine R. Lynes, "'A Real Honest-to-Cripe Jungle': Contested Authenticities in Helene Johnson's 'Bottled,'" *Modernism/Modernity* 14:3 (2007), pp. 517–26, 523.

17. Maureen Honey (ed.), *Shadowed Dreams: Women's Poetry of the Harlem Renaissance*, 2nd ed. rev. (New Brunswick, N.J.: Rutgers University Press, 2006), p. xlv.

18. Louise Bogan, *A Poet's Prose: Selected Writings of Louise Bogan*, ed. Mary Kinzie (Athens: Ohio University Press, 2005), p. 319.

19. Bogan, *A Poet's Alphabet*, p. 12.

20. Bogan, *A Poet's Prose*, p. 184.

21. Bogan, *A Poet's Prose*, pp. 223–27.

22. Elizabeth Frank, "A Doll's Heart: The Girl in the Poetry of Edna St. Vincent Millay and Louise Bogan," in Martha Collins (ed.), *Critical Essays on Louise Bogan* (Boston: G. K. Hall, 1984), pp. 128–49, 128.

23. Bogan, *A Poet's Prose*, pp. 63–65.

24. Gloria Bowles, *Louise Bogan's Aesthetic of Limitation* (Bloomington: Indiana University Press, 1987).

25. Bogan, *A Poet's Alphabet*, pp. 431–32.

26. Louise Bogan, *The Blue Estuaries: Poems 1923–1968* (New York: Farrar, Straus & Giroux, 1968), p. 16. This collection will be cited in the text as *BE*.

27. Clark, *Sentimental Modernism*, p. 117.

28. Frank, "A Doll's Heart," p. 137.

29. Bogan, *A Poet's Prose*, p. 85.

30. See Georgia Douglas Johnson, *Selected Works*, ed. Henry Louis Gates, Jr. (New York: G. K. Hall, 1997), and especially Claudia Tate's introduction.

31. Sara Teasdale, *Collected Poems* (New York: Macmillan, 1937), p. 58. This collection will be cited in the text as *STCP*.

32. Elinor Wylie, *Collected Poems* (New York: Alfred A. Knopf, 1932), p. 59.

33. Cheryl Walker, *Masks Outrageous and Austere: Culture, Psyche, and Persona in Modern Women Poets* (Bloomington: Indiana University Press, 1991), pp. 67–69.

34. Wylie, *Collected Poems*, p. 47.

35. Wylie, *Collected Poems*, pp. 8, 69.

36. Bogan, *A Poet's Prose*, pp. 318–19.

Chapter 29

The Romantic and Anti-Romantic in the Poetry of Wallace Stevens

GEORGE S. LENSING

No other poet of modernism makes a claim such as this from Wallace Stevens: "It was in the earth only / That he was at the bottom of things / And of himself. There he could say / Of this I am."[1] Many poets of the Romantic tradition have imputed a salvific and restorative efficacy to the natural powers of the earth, yet we are struck at once by the injection of the adverb "only": *only* in the earth – nowhere and with no one else – does the speaker find "the bottom of things / And . . . himself." The mysterious "he" of the poem may include a potential everyone, including the reader, but it is a typical disguise whereby Stevens slightly camouflages himself.

In these opening lines of the poem "Yellow Afternoon," a poem written mid-career, in 1940, one's inclination is to identify the setting of the poem with earth's bounty in spring and summer – like a Virgilian georgic or Wordsworthian "pastoral farms, / Green to the very door" – an earth of fruition and renewal.[2] But, Stevens hastily adds, "This reposes alike in springtime / And, arbored and bronzed, in autumn," as if the possession of the earth in *all* its climates and seasons, all its blooms and decays, is equally requiting.

Stevens's poem, however, makes an even greater claim: the earth is held as the object of his perfect and compulsory "love." Stevens's "he" must love the earth because it demands no less, and it remains his "only" love. Even for the poet, the wordsmith, "The odor / Of the earth penetrates more deeply than any word." The poem's conclusion pushes his claims even further, as if Stevens must now check himself by duly noting that similar compensations have come in the past from "men" and "in a woman," although they, in the end, are lesser things, perhaps more inconstant than the gifts of the earth:

> The thought that he had found all this
> Among men, in a woman – she caught his breath –
> But he came back as one comes back from the sun
> To lie on one's bed in the dark, close to a face
> Without eyes or mouth, that looks at one and speaks.

The haunting, even shocking, conclusion leaves the speaker and his "he" on the lover's bed beside a spectral presence obviously not the woman who caught his breath: "close to a face / Without eyes or mouth, that looks at one and speaks." The eyeless and mouthless figure on the bed, skeletal and cold, momentarily disrupts the poem's confident affirmations. The poem ends with these words, but the ghostly lover on the bed, the earth's very personification, has already become his eager substitute. If it is the earth "only" that returns his love, what can it speak? Nothing. The earth has already been defined in the poem as "mute" and "Around which silence lies on silence." The mouthless lover speaks the silence of the faithful earth. The "he" has found "unity" not in the woman but in the earth – "as one loves that / Of which one is a part as in a unity." What has brought about these circumstances? Have men and women somehow failed the speaker? And, if so, how can the recompenses of the earth placate those failures?

The life of Stevens (1879–1955) has its center in three different places: Reading, Pennsylvania, where he was born and spent his first eighteen years; New York, where he lived after three years as a student at Harvard and where he eventually studied law, began to practice it, and lived with his wife, Elsie Kachel; and Hartford, Connecticut, where he lived for almost forty years as an attorney for the Hartford Accident and Indemnity Company and eventually a vice president in charge of surety claims. In each of these three settings, Stevens sought and found his pastoral retreats, a part of the earth where "he was at the bottom of things / And of himself." They, more than home or office, became the central loci of his life.

At the time of his engagement to Elsie, while she was back in Reading and he was in New York, he gave her a glimpse into that home country – Mount Penn, Mount Neversink, the fields of Oley, and the Schuylkill, Perkiomen, and Tulpehocken Rivers – as a personal arcadia: "I always walked a great deal, mostly alone, and mostly on the hill, rambling along the side of the mountain."[3] When he was nineteen, doing farm work at home in Pennsylvania after his second year at Harvard, he recorded in his journal: "One finds immense satisfaction in studying the lyrics of song-sparrows, catbirds, wrens and the like. A valley choked with corn assumes a newer and more potent interest when one comes to notice the blade-like wind among the leaves."[4]

Stevens's journals during his New York years are all but devoid of reference to his study and practice of law or to the city itself, except to record concerts, museums, and plays he attended or to lament the coldly impersonal life of the urban mass that surrounded him. He seized every opportunity, especially on weekends and vacations, to return to Reading or to get out of the city and hike along the nearby Hudson River paths and the surrounding New Jersey countryside. Most of his hikes were solitary and sometimes of twenty or thirty miles or more. Collecting twenty of his own short and undistinguished poems for his fiancée's birthday, he included these words from "Song": "A month – a year – of idle work, / And then, one song. / Oh! all that I am and all that I was / Is to that feeble music strung, / And more." The poem ends as another voice from forest and capes "calls me to it without choice, / Alone" (*SCP*, pp. 503–04), just as the earth of "Yellow Afternoon" mandated that "it must be loved." At the age of twenty-two, Stevens acknowledged that his love of nature was assuming a religious significance and upending the Presbyterianism of his youth: "Last night I spent an hour in the dark transept of St. Patrick's Cathedral," he noted in his journal, "where I go now and then in my more lonely moods. An old argument with me is that the true religious force in the world is not the church but the world itself: the mysterious callings of Nature and our responses."[5] It was not long after this that Stevens abandoned his Christian faith, although never his love of churches and religious rituals.

In 1916 Stevens and his wife left New York and moved to Hartford, the city where he would spend the second half of his life, eventually to become "the dean of surety-claims men in the whole country" and a vice president of the company.[6] Seven years later, Stevens and his wife became the parents of their only child, Holly. After purchasing what would become his permanent home on Westerly Terrace, he made it his daily practice to walk the two miles that separated him from the office and then again to return home on foot at the end of the day. That journey skirted Elizabeth Park, a large public park that enclosed a wooded area, large pond, rock gardens, greenhouses, and winding paths. It became Stevens's favorite part of the city, and he often paused there. A neighbor would later recall: "As he walked I could almost see him composing in his mind. He had a very interesting walk. It was slow and rather symmetrical. He almost walked in cadences. Every Sunday he used to walk over to the park. Rain, or sometimes it'd be sleeting, he'd walk over. He'd spend an hour; all kinds of weather."[7]

I cite these examples of Stevens's pastoral predilections to illustrate what the "earth" of "Yellow Afternoon" meant to the poet himself. It is not just that Stevens, like other Romantics, found solace and strength in the natural world, but that he loved it with a passion as if it were a lover and that, in truth, it became a kind of eyeless and mouthless lover. Helen Vendler was among the first to call attention to Stevens's "inner world" and "human loneliness."[8] Shortly before his marriage to Elsie, in 1909, he wrote: "The truth is, it gets to be a terror here. Failure means such horror – and so many fail. If only they knew of the orchards and arbors and abounding fields, and the ease, and the comfort, and the quiet. –One might preach the country as a kind of Earthly Paradise."[9] Writing in his journals when he was in his mid-twenties and living in New York, Stevens described his own state of mind, including "loathing" and "disillusionment," but he also laid out a course of consolations for his personal future as well as that of his poetry. I reproduce the entry in its entirety:

> I am in an odd state of mind today. It is Sunday. I feel a loathing (large & vague!), for things as they are; and this is the result of a pretty thorough disillusionment. Yet this is an ordinary mood with me in town in the Spring time. I say to myself that there is nothing good in the world except physical well-being. All the rest is philosophical compromise. Last Sunday, at home, I took communion. It was from the worn, the sentimental, the diseased, the priggish and the ignorant that "Gloria in excelsis!" came. Love is consolation, Nature is consolation, Friendship, Work, Phantasy are all consolation.[10]

His loathing of "things as they are" points to the future modernist's need to transform them through the projection of his imagination. In his future work, the phrase itself becomes a kind of catchword for a manifestation of reality that is sometimes found wanting: "'Things as they are / Are changed upon the blue guitar'" (*SCP*, p. 135). Indeed, "Phantasy," with its interior power to change things as they are, is already identified as one of his "consolations" just as "Nature" is his exterior consolation. If there is "nothing good in the world except physical well-being," one might suspect that such robust and blood-coursing physicality exists to allow him to bring himself into greater company with the earth itself.

Notably missing from his list of consolations is religion itself, although he was still taking communion. Ten years after this Sunday entry laying out his consolations, Stevens would publish one of his best-known poems, "Sunday Morning," in which he proclaims that for his post-Christian woman, lounging among her physical luxuries on a more secular Sunday morning, "Divinity must live within herself." Although in "contentment" she still feels "The need of some imperishable bliss," she nonetheless surrenders the fixed and static imperishable of "paradise" for the dynamically perishable "earth ... remembering / The bough of summer and the winter branch." All physical things take on an urgent and heightened beauty in the cycle of life and death: "Death is the mother of beauty," and "from her, / Alone, shall come fulfillment to our dreams." In place of God, "Sunday Morning" concludes, there remains the earth, where "the quail / Whistle about us their spontaneous cries" and "Sweet berries ripen in the wilderness" (*SCP*, pp. 53–56).

Stevens's estrangement from religious faith set him at odds with the evolving orthodox traditionalism of a poet like Eliot: "After all, Eliot and I are dead opposites and I have been doing about everything that he would not be likely to do," Stevens wrote in 1950.[11] Feeling sharply the absence of God, Stevens attempted to construct a kind of substitute for him and thus to clear his own modernist path. As he said in one letter, "It is not possible merely to disbelieve [in God]; it becomes necessary to believe in something else.... It is easier to believe in a thing created by the imagination" (*LWS*, p. 370).

One such fictional object of belief is Stevens's concept of the hero. In a letter to his friend Henry Church in 1943, Stevens hinted at his growing dissatisfaction with humanism: "The chief defect of humanism is that it concerns human beings. Between humanism and something else, it might be possible to create an acceptable fiction" (*LWS*, p. 449). The hero as final man, final poet, and final substitute for God could only be imagined as a projection of the future, an eschatological figure both human and more than human, substantial and insubstantial, real and fictional: "Unless we believe in the hero," he asks in "Examination of the Hero in a Time of War," "what is there / To believe" (*SCP*, p. 246)? The hero is the counterpart of Stevens's conception of a "supreme fiction," to which he can write only "notes." Like the supreme fiction, the hero remains an "impossible possible"; he is

> The man who has had the time to think enough,
> The central man, the human globe, responsive
> As a mirror with a voice, the man of glass,
> Who in a million diamonds sums us up.   (*SCP*, p. 227)

In the early journal entry already cited, Stevens defined his five consolations: love, nature, friendship, work, phantasy. Each was posited on the foundation of "physical well-being," there being "nothing good in the world" except it.[12] By the time he wrote "Yellow Afternoon," Stevens seemed to possess the consolations only of nature and phantasy. What of love and what of work and what of friendship? "Yellow Afternoon" suggests that he had found, at least for a while ("Among men, in a woman – she caught his breath") just such consolations in friendship and love, and yet the "he" of the poem returns to the spectral presence of an eyeless and mouthless lover, the earth itself.

Personal friendships did not come easily for Stevens. In the interviews conducted by Peter Brazeau and collected under the title *Wallace Stevens Remembered: An Oral Biography*, Stevens's business associates invariably found him distant and sometimes rude. One of them remembered: "Most executives, whenever they are free to do so, love to sit around and chat, relax, unwind, lollygag. Stevens was not that kind of person. He was not receptive." And another colleague commented, "He had difficulty relating to people; he was not oriented toward being able to see their problems."[13] (Some of the younger associates whom he guided and promoted at the Hartford company remembered him more warmly.) There were other kinds of acquaintances, such as those from his literary world, but they were largely epistolary in nature. Stevens collected such friends from all parts of the world, and he relished the kinds of artifacts, foods, and even postcards they sent him, but he saw them in person hardly at all, if ever. Having never left North America in his lifetime, this most cosmopolitan of poets brought the world to him through his correspondence: "I survive on postcards from Europe" (*LWS*, p. 797). As for the work itself, Stevens brought to it intelligent competence, hard work, and persistence. One cannot escape the impression, however, that he derived little real pleasure in it, just as, during the New York years, he did "not exist from nine to six, when I am at the office" (*LWS*, p. 121).

From his parents and four siblings in Reading he became all but completely estranged, especially after his marriage to Elsie Kachel. The wedding in Reading was attended by none of the Stevens family, after an altercation between Stevens and his father, and the estrangement continued until his father's death and almost his mother's. Elsie herself, almost eight years his junior and a dropout from high school after attending only her first year, was a gifted pianist but seemed to have little sympathy for his mature poetry and dissociated herself from his business world. The two came to live separately in the house on Westerly Terrace. Poems like "Red Loves Kit," "Arrival at the Waldorf," "World without Peculiarity," and "Good Man, Bad Woman" hint at these strains.

In editing her father's journals, Holly Stevens remarked on the isolation of the family: "We held off from each other – one might say that my father lived alone."[14] He increasingly withdrew into the sanctum of his own room on Westerly Terrace, his books, his music, his letters, and his visits to the park. The consolations of work, friendship, and love wore thin and sparse. Three years before his death, he wrote a favorite correspondent: "The truth is that one gets out of contact with people during the summer and feels the immense need (of which one is not conscious in other seasons) of people for other people, a thing that has been in my thoughts for a long time, in one form or another" (*LWS*, p. 759). Left in large part with the consolations of nature and the powers of the interior phantasy, Stevens in many ways lived out his most intense and personal life through his poems. Again and again, he would hint at his personal recourse to art as "our salvation," "my piety," "life's redemption," and "the better part of life" – and, finally, he wrote, "I have no life except in poetry. No doubt that would be true if my whole life was free for poetry" (*SCP*, p. 652; *LWS*, p. 473; *SCP*, pp. 901, 913).

Beginning with the poems of his first volume, *Harmonium* (1923), and continuing through his *Collected Poems* (1954) and other poems written before his death the following year, his poems play an orchestral point and counterpoint, deriving from that interior world of thought and will and sensory abstraction, but drawing toward and seeking harmony with the outer world of the earth itself. Invariably, the words "imagination" and "reality," words of Stevens's own choosing, have become for his readers the great polarities of what he once called his "grand poem." Even so, the words themselves are sometimes confusing, because, for one thing, the imagination possesses its own reality and, for another, reality itself can never be known except by abstracting it into consciousness and thus making it an irreality: "According to the traditional views of sensory perception, we do not see the world immediately but only as the result of a process of seeing and after the completion of that process, that is to say, we never see the world except the moment after" (*SCP*, p. 857). I prefer the definition he laid out in brief remarks on one of his poems, called "Les Plus Belles Pages," in which the terms are applied more expansively, in contrast to the sometimes mechanical application of them by his readers:

> Les plus belles pages are those in which things do not stand alone but are operative as the result of interaction, interrelation. This is an idea of some consequence, not a casual improvisation. The interrelation between reality and the *imagination* is the basis of the character of literature. The interrelation between reality and the *emotions* is the basis of the vitality of literature, between reality and *thought* the basis of its power. (*SCP*, p. 867; emphasis added)

When using the term "imagination," Stevens sometimes seems to mean consciousness itself, all the agencies of perception: the senses, the will, and the complete synthesizing powers of perception. One might equate it with the composite subject. Its counterpart consists of all that is the object of perception, reality as the thing itself, all that is outside consciousness. At times the abyss that separates the two forces dissolves, and they meet naturally and spontaneously in harmony: "In the presence of extraordinary actuality, consciousness takes the place of imagination" (*SCP*, p. 905).

More typically, Stevens refers to imagination and reality in more restricted ways. Although reality, for example, may afford us the moments of "visible and responsive peace," as "Yellow Afternoon" would have it, at other times reality does not present itself so invitingly (*SCP*, p. 216). Reality is the "malady of the quotidian," in "The Man Whose Pharynx Was Bad"; or the disorder of "meaningless plungings of water and the wind," in "The Idea of Order at Key West"; or even social cataclysm: a "body in rags" and "streets ... full of cries," in "Mozart, 1935" (*SCP*, pp. 81, 105, 107–08). In the face of these confusions, Stevens boldly enlists the imagination to combat ennui, disorder, ugliness, and social eruptions, to become "a violence from within that protects us from a violence without" (*SCP*, p. 665).

At the foundation of Stevens's oeuvre is the supposition that by remaking his pastoral world into the words of his poems, he could share with others the very power of the earth that had sustained him. I emphasize here the social dimension of Stevens's project, because he never intended it as a sealed-off, private world.

> The deepening need for words to express our thoughts and feelings which, we are sure, are all the truth that we shall ever experience, having no illusions, makes us listen to words when we hear them, loving them and feeling them, makes us search the sound of them, for a finality, a perfection, an unalterable vibration which it is only within the power of the acutest poet to give them. (*SCP*, pp. 662–63)

He then adds that the ability of the imagination's power to combat the less desirable aspects of reality and its pressures "seems, in the last analysis, to have something to do with our self-preservation; and that, no doubt, is why the expression of it, the sound of its words, helps us to live our lives" (*SCP*, p. 665).

Stevens was conscious that the exercise of the imagination placed him within the tradition of English and American Romanticism. At the same time, he knew that his place within it had to be modern. "Sailing after Lunch" suggests the paradox of the necessity of the Romantic versus the need to deny it:

> Mon Dieu, hear the poet's prayer.
> The romantic should be here.
> The romantic should be there.
> It ought to be everywhere.
> But the romantic must never remain,
>
> Mon Dieu, and must never again return.   (*SCP*, p. 99)

In one of his essays on the poetry of Marianne Moore, he recognizes that the term itself ("Romantic") "in the pejorative sense merely connotes obsolescence" (*SCP*, p. 777). There remained, however, another sense: "It is absurd to wince at being called a romantic poet. Unless one is that, one is not a poet at all.... It means, now-a-days, an uncommon intelligence. It means in a time like our own of violent feelings, equally violent feelings and the most skil-ful expression of the genuine" (*SCP*, p. 778). In a sense, modern Romantic verse had to reclaim the genuine with violent feelings and an uncommon intelligence; it must dissociate itself from what had come to be regarded as the excesses of Romanticism – dissociation from what T. S. Eliot abhorred in Swinburne as "an hallucination of meaning" or from the mannerisms of Tennyson that Ezra Pound loved to parody.[15]

I have been implying that Stevens's self-defined mode of survival depended on his consolation of phantasy, all the powers of the imagination acting on his consolation of nature, the earth itself. But one cannot discuss for long the poetry of Stevens without taking into account the varieties and complexities of both consolations. The assembly of his collected poems discloses a vast conge-ries of associations of self with world, modulations and nuances of inner and outer connections. The poet's shifting responses are deeply rooted in his own fascination with epistemology itself: the world outside seems rooted in philo-sophical realism, but the processes of perception reshape our knowledge of it into a Kantian idealism. At times, the frangibility of the world and its unknow-able essences push him toward a kind of solipsism: "There never was a world for her / Except the one she sang and, singing, made" (*SCP*, p. 106). Other philosophers, known by Stevens from his Harvard years (1897–1900), pointed him in another direction. In the year before Stevens's arrival at Cambridge, William James published his essay "The Will to Believe," which Stevens knew and absorbed into his own will to know the "volatile world": "There was a will to change, a necessitous / And present way, a presentation, a kind / Of volatile world, too constant to be denied" (*LWS*, p. 443; *SCP*, p. 344). George Santayana, whom Stevens knew well during his Cambridge years – the two even exchanged rival sonnets – was an even greater influence. His *Scepticism and Animal Faith* (1923) invokes the same Stevensian skepticism that rises from the Cartesian chasm between knower and known. At the same time, "animal faith," like the will to believe, is the means whereby one affirms the "exis-tence" of a world that conceals its "essence." Such a world may be "false," but we nonetheless accede to a faith that "there is a future, that things sought can be found, and things seen can be eaten – [even though] no guarantee [of their verity] can possibly be offered." For Santayana, such a faith in life's empiri-cisms "launches the adventure of knowledge."[16]

The elusiveness and shifting allegiances of Stevens point to another way in which he redefined Romanticism. When he talks about believing for a while in the imagination but then turning to believe in reality, he hints at two powerful strains, each running counter to the other in his poetry. The former is closer to Stevens's joyous self-enfolding on the world that he so proudly loved, as he describes it in "Yellow Afternoon." But the latter – the desire to possess the pure and unmediated, or nearly unmediated, real – requires a rigorous self-abnegation, a less Romantic and more classical subjugation of the self, with all its qualities of phantasy and fiction making. Remaking the world into words makes it a tentative and copied thing; this is especially dangerous for the poet, for whom words are his only resource: "It is a world of words to the end of it" (*SCP*, p. 301).

Stevens's tentative verbal gestures toward the world prompt Angela Leighton to conclude: "[Stevens's] delight in words which move and express movement for its own sake, rather than for description's sake, is the key to his work."[17] That part of Stevens that distrusted the movement of language for its own sake has had a strong appeal to poststructuralists under the influence of Derrida at the end of the twentieth century. If the ground of reality is unattainable and unknowable, only the poet's schema remains to cover over the widening abyss. Writing on Stevens, J. Hillis Miller puts it this way: "Without the production of some schema, some 'icon,' there can be no glimpse of the abyss, no vertigo of the underlying nothingness. Any such scheme, however, both opens the chasm, creates it or reveals it, and at the same time fills it up, covers it over by naming it, gives the groundless a ground."[18] Stevens's pursuit of the real at "the exactest point at which it is itself" releases his more classical side (*SCP*, p. 402). Aware that his poetics pushed toward a purely verbal world, he was no less hasty to retreat to the very descriptiveness of the sensual world that Leighton finds wanting: "We keep coming back and coming back / To the real: to the hotel instead of the hymns / That fall upon it out of the wind. We seek // The poem of pure reality" (*SCP*, p. 402).

Balancing back and forth between the claims of the real and the imagined, Stevens never allows himself to rest for long with either. Just as the imagination, for example, modifies reality, so by the same measure it distorts it, ultimately to its own disadvantage. The aggregation of Stevens's poems eventually makes up a kind of journey of revisitations – often keyed to the four seasons of the year. Fearful of those very exaggerations of the imagination, the poems of autumn give vent to the poet's disavowal of the imagination's previous fiction making, a de-creation that is coterminous with the stripping of the leaves themselves. Here Stevens as anti-Romantic comes into play. The mind reorients itself in the direction of the real. "The imagination loses vitality as it ceases to adhere to what is real," he says in one place, and in another, "The real is only the base. But it is the base" (*SCP*, pp. 645, 917). In the poems of winter, he seeks to draw as near to the pure and unmediated reality as his abstracting and transforming perception will permit, nature itself as cold, white, and denuded. It is in their pursuit of "the thing itself" that the modernist poetics of Stevens and William Carlos Williams converge and mark both poets as heirs of Imagism. Quoting the whole of Williams's short, four-line poem "El Hombre," Stevens's poem "Nuances on a Theme by Williams" upholds Williams's "ancient star," stripped of anything that a distorting "you" could lend it. Addressing the same star, Stevens then rewrites Williams: "Lend no part to any humanity that suffuses / you in its own light. / Be not chimera of morning, / Half man, half star" (*SCP*, p. 15).

Stevens's longing for the real, however, could never be as complaisant for him as it came to be for Williams. The poems of spring release the imagination to the beginnings of its newly awakened life, while those of summer transport him into a brief but idealized unity and harmony with a now-mediated world – the harmony that "Yellow Afternoon" defines. Having rediscovered "reality" in the poems of autumn and winter, the poet then makes it "the footing from which we leap after what we do not have and on which everything depends" (*LWS*, p. 600). Yet, one quickly notes, the imagination's evolving distortions can make illusions into delusions, and the cycle must be relaunched by returning to autumnal suppressions of the imagination's impositions. The poems of winter and summer become his polarities; those of autumn and spring, his transitions.

In "Autumn Refrain," Stevens moves from high melody to something approaching desolate stillness, from the "measureless measures" of the nightingale – although, for him personally, such measures are "evasions," ones "I have never – shall never hear." The American grackle and its harsher "skreak and skritter" are also dismissed. What remains is the grackles' "residuum" of minimal sound, the something that remains when evasions are nullified: "The stillness is all in the key of that desolate sound" (*SCP*, p. 129).

The poems of the season that coalesce around "Autumn Refrain" share the quality of impoverishment, a self reduced to a lesser thing, a radical, sometimes painful disengagement of the mind from its actions on a diminished world. We are left with an empty house and cast-off dress in "The Beginning," a "barbarous green" of the last plant of "The Green Plant," or "the evening's one star" in "One of the Inhabitants of the West" (*SCP*, pp. 431, 428). The "finally human" of "Lebensweisheitspielerei" is reduced to "indigence" and "poverty":

> Little by little, the poverty
> Of autumnal space becomes
> A look, a few words spoken.
>
> Each person completely touches us
> With what he is and as he is,
> In the stale grandeur of annihilation.
>
> (*SCP*, pp. 429–30)

"Montrachet-le-Jardin" arrives at "the naked man in a state of fact," while in the often-anthologized "The Plain Sense of Things," "The great structure has become a minor house. / No turban walks across the lessened floors," leaving only the "inevitable knowledge" of the shrunken imagination to behold the rat, muddy pond, and silence (*SCP*, pp. 237, 428). "The Auroras of Autumn," a longer meditation and the title of Stevens's 1950 volume, places a viewer gazing at the aurora borealis as it "leaps through us, through all our heavens leaps, / Extinguishing our planets, one by one" and leaving, as in "Autumn Refrain," a "shivering residue" (*SCP*, pp. 355–63). The various cantos of the poem introduce other tropes of collapse: a deserted cabin, the dissolved mother, "a time of innocence / As pure principle":

> So, then, these lights are not a spell of light,
> A saying out of a cloud, but innocence.
> An innocence of the earth and no false sign
>
> Or symbol of malice. That we partake thereof,
> Lie down like children in this holiness
> As if, awake, we lay in the quiet of sleep.   (*SCP*, p. 360)

In "Metamorphosis," the poem itself seems to disintegrate as it moves from "Sep-tem-ber" to "Oto-otu-bre" to "Fro-Niz-nil-imbo." Deep into autumn, November is a cryptogram of diminution: frozen, in limbo, and the nil of nothing (*SCP*, pp. 238–39).

If the poems of autumn leave the poet in a state of limbo, those of winter seek the "nothingness" that can only be imagined, a "pure principle" of reality shorn of all human intrusions. The nothingness of winter is the pure something, even though it remains nothing to the absented human beholder. Such a beholder could only be the snowman, or (phonetically) "this no man," who, as the poem of that title demands, is "nothing himself." Enigmatic and riddling, "The Snow Man" continues to fascinate us (*SCP*, p. 8). How, we ask, can the bareness of winter convey such searing beauty ("junipers shagged with ice," "spruces rough in the distant glitter") and, at the same time, harshly dissolve the human "One" (the first word of the poem) into a dehumanized snowman possessing "nothing" and "nothing himself"? It seems to be a poem violently beautiful and cruelly purifying, costing, as Eliot would say, "not less than everything."[19] Indeed, if it necessitates the very forfeiting of one's humanity, it truly costs no less than everything. Still, "the nothing that is" is the poem's final and exigent prize, an immaculate and pristine thing in its intrinsic and unmarred essence. If in "Yellow Afternoon" Stevens affirms that "Everything comes to him / From the middle of his field," and if it is "this that I could love," one should note that it is not only the effulgence of summer but, equally, the nothingness of winter that engages his passion for the earth (*SCP*, p. 216).

But we are not snowmen; we have not forfeited our humanity, even though Stevens once wrote, "I want, as poet, to be that in nature, which constitutes nature's very self" (*LWS*, p. 790). Other poems of winter draw as near "nature's very self" as a chastened perception will allow. A lonely "syllable" remains, and it "Intones its single emptiness" in "No Possum, No Sop, No Taters" (*SCP*, pp. 261–62). The "One," otherwise violently dismembered in the first stanzas, enters the scene as a minimal self, joining the malicious crow at the end of that poem, "But at a distance, in another tree." A state of "complete simplicity" is attained in "The Poems of Our Climate," in opposition to the "evilly compounded, vital I." But now, "At the end of winter," the beholder is allowed a tincture of color, a cold, porcelain bowl of "Pink and white carnations." The "never-resting mind," awakening to its own new life, desires more than the faint colors of the carnations, "More than a world of white and snowy scents," where "scents" is also "sense" (*SCP*, pp. 178–79).

Spring is an awakening from sleep, as well as a sexual awakening to the promiscuous earth, itself budding with new life. It is a journey commenced, open to the earth's redolent pleasures. But the long-suppressed mind is tentative, experimental, and childlike, settling for the minimum, but also eager, anticipatory, and resolute. The previous program of harshly stern self-denials has come to an end. Having earned its proximity to an undistorted real, "The imagination wishes to be indulged" (*SCP*, p. 901). Penelope, yearning for the return of Ulysses in "The World as Meditation," enters the poem at daybreak and at a time when "winter is washed away." While it is his "arms" that "would be her necklace / And her belt," such a consummation must now be deferred. Instead, the rising sun itself becomes for the lonely and beleaguered Penelope a "Someone," a "form of fire," and a "savage presence [that] awakens the world in which she dwells." So powerful is the "barbarous strength within her" that Penelope "meditates" her husband's presence and mediates it through the sun: "It was Ulysses and it was not. Yet they had met." At the end of the poem, Penelope is "repeating his name with its patient syllables," much as the poem's first line overtly repeats his name in rhythm and sound: "Is it Ulysses ... approaches ... east" (*SCP*, pp. 441–42). Penelope's combing and repeating at the end becomes an enactment of the decelerated and floating meditation that constitutes the style of the whole poem: caesuras in seventeen of the poem's twenty-four lines; ostensible repetitions in lines 2 and 10, 9 and 20, and 1, 16, and 19; an anaphora in lines 14 and 15; and chiasmus in lines 7 and 8. Everything in the poem works toward the fluidity of thought in motion.

An awakening similar to Penelope's occurs in "Not Ideas about the Thing but the Thing Itself." The cry of leaves "that do not transcend themselves" from "The Course of a Particular" now becomes the "scrawny cry" of a bird at dawn (*SCP*, p. 460). Like Penelope, the "he" of the poem awakens to the sun at daybreak. The cry is "not from the vast ventriloquism / Of sleep's faded papier-mâché." Both bird and sun are "outside," but, heard and seen, they are also inside. The poem's title – and the qualifying "like" of "It was like / A new knowledge of reality" – notwithstanding, the poem's "he" has internalized both the sound of the bird and the rings of the sun: "He knew that he heard it" (*SCP*, pp. 451–52). His ideas about the thing, his "new knowledge," now cancel the "inert savoir" of "The Plain Sense of Things" (*SCP*, p. 428).

When Ulysses symbolically returns, when the scrawny cry is full throated, other tropes define the mind in perfect appeasement with the earth, and these poems often occur in the season of high summer. As even its title suggests, "Credences of Summer" is a set of propositions calling for something like religious faith in the season's accord for those who seek it (*SCP*, pp. 322–26). As Stevens wrote in one essay, "While it can lie in the temperament of very few of us to write poetry in order to find God, it is probably the purpose of each of us to write poetry to find the good which, in the Platonic sense, is synonymous with God" (*SCP*, p. 786). In this poem he finds that "good" in an intense momentary cessation of time and space: "Things stop in that direction and since they stop / The direction stops and we accept what is / As good" (*SCP*, p. 323). Throughout the poem's ten cantos, the speaker commemorates the time when "the mind lays by its trouble" and indulges the effulgent world, "this and the imagination's life" (canto I). Even the "consolations" that had eluded Stevens in his own private life are now reinstated: "these fathers standing round, / These mothers touching, speaking, being near, / These lovers waiting in the soft dry grass" (*SCP*, p. 323). The poet's entanglements with the world always suggest change. If in "Credences of Summer" it is "the last day of a certain year" (canto I), the succeeding days will inevitably dislodge him from that station and push him toward a different one. Indeed, the poem's final cantos are already pointing to some kind of rupture of the ideal moment: "A complex of emotions falls apart, / In an abandoned spot," as "last year's garden grows salacious weeds" (*SCP*, p. 326). The cycle of the seasons is about to be replayed again.

Stevens's pastoralism inevitably invites comparisons with Robert Frost. Stevens, who knew Frost from his business trips to Key West, Florida, once accused him of writing a poetry of "things," to which Frost retorted that Stevens wrote poems of "bric-a-brac."[20] There is more of the decorative in Frost and more thingness in Stevens than either poet seems to have allowed. But both created a poetry of the seasons, an engagement of the mind reaching out to a world in flux and fluidity – often inviting, sometimes forbidding. But unlike Frost, Stevens is more dedicated to ferreting out the world, possessing it joyfully and relinquishing it ruefully; he is less interested in deducing the "truths" of nature than in attaining nature.

Having noted Stevens's seasonal transitions, the reader quickly becomes aware that the poems themselves resist easy and mechanical applications of such a formula. Stevens's poems, like those of no other modernist, often tend toward the machinations of thought itself in all its spontaneity and discursiveness. As a result, such poems take on a quality of tentative and speculative drift, as these titles suggest: "*Notes* toward a Supreme Fiction," "Like *Decorations* in a Nigger Cemetery," "*Prologues* to What Is Possible," "*Variations* on a Summer Day," "*Repetitions* of a Young Captain," "*Extracts* from Addresses to the Academy of Fine Ideas," and so on (emphases added).

In generalizing, we have come to associate the poetry of Stevens with a certain kind of formal stateliness, a diction of luxuriant elegance, and a syntax of parataxis and apposition like the movements of thought itself. His cadences favor something like blank verse but not so rigorously as Milton or Wordsworth: "My line is a pentameter line, but it runs over and under now and then" (*LWS*, p. 407). I want to argue, however, that Stevens's voice has a quality of the unpredictable about it. If, in its composition, a poem's "true subject" and "poetry of the subject" are brought into tension, as he suggests, we expect in Stevens's poetry a quality of caprice, playfulness, dislocation, and surprise (*SCP*, p. 785). For all his formality, Stevens can sometimes adopt the spontaneity of a wide-eyed child: "People ought to like poetry the way a child likes snow & they would if poets wrote it," he once insisted (*LWS*, p. 349). Especially in his poems from his first volume, *Harmonium*, come interjections like "Chieftain Iffucan of Azcan in caftan / Of tan with henna hackles, halt!" (*SCP*, p. 60). The comparison of cock versus dove plays to the advantage of the latter in "Depression before Spring": "But ki-ki-ri-ki / Brings no rou-cou, / No rou-cou-cou" (*SCP*, p. 50). As early as 1926, with *Harmonium* her only specimen, Marianne Moore thought that "Wallace Stevens' sensory and technical virtuosity was perhaps the 'new' poetry's greatest ornament."[21]

There is one line in "Yellow Afternoon" that I have not yet cited; it occurs in the poem as part of his claim to be "a part [with the desirable earth] as in a unity." For the lover of earth, his life consists of "all the lives that comprise it," as if the speaker brings all aspects of his life and personality to bear on his loving "unity" with the earth. The poem then adds an illustration of such diversity and multiplicity of lives: "So that one lives all the lives that comprise it / As the life of the fatal unity of war" (*SCP*, p. 216). The poem poses the possibility here that such a "fatal unity" may be different from "A unity that is the life one loves." How, in fact, can one love the earth when it is co-opted by a devastation like war? That question remains unanswered in "Yellow Afternoon," even as it is laid before us.

Stevens's personal political loyalties are difficult to categorize. In the middle of the Great Depression, he had found himself "headed left, but there are lefts and lefts, and certainly I am not headed for the ghastly left of [NEW] MASSES" (*LWS*, p. 286). Later, writing after the upset victory of Truman (a Democrat) over Dewey (a Republican), he confessed:

> As to Truman: I am of two minds about the result of the election. So far as I am personally concerned his election is probably a misfortune because he is one of those politicians who keep themselves in office by taxing a small class for the benefit of a large class.... On the other hand, I recognize that the vast altruism of the Truman party is probably the greatest single force for good in the world today. (*LWS*, p. 623)

In the presidential election four years later, he declared that "Stevenson [a Democrat] was not my man." He favored Eisenhower (a Republican): "We ought to have a little prose in the White House after all the poor poetry" (*LWS*, p. 765).

Stevens's poetry, spanning the first half of the twentieth century, included the time of the Great Depression, two world wars, the Spanish Civil War, the Korean conflict, and some of the most menacing years of the Cold War, as weapons of mass destruction were added to national arsenals. Stevens wrote poems that addressed each of these menaces. How, in the face of such catastrophes and threatened catastrophes, could poetry even justify itself without appearing irrelevant? At the same time that he wrote "Yellow Afternoon," Stevens wrote another poem called "Of Modern Poetry," the poem that begins, "The poem of the mind in the act of finding / What will suffice." Such a poem, by its very modernity, becomes indentured to historical circumstance, war itself:

> It has to think about war
> And it has to find what will suffice. It has
> To construct a new stage. It has to be on that stage
> And, like an insatiable actor, slowly and
> With meditation, speak words that in the ear,
> In the delicatest ear of the mind, repeat,
> Exactly, that which it wants to hear.   (*SCP*, pp. 218–19)

How could such poetry avoid "affectation" even as it contained the mind in a state of war (*SCP*, p. 654)? (At this time, America's direct entry into World War II was still more than a year away.) In each decade of his writing, Stevens asked similar questions about the other national and international events that created massive human suffering. The question is part of the larger one that seems to recur in every generation about how poetry, and art in general, can engage with historical threats and calamities as they are "occupying our thoughts and feelings to the exclusion of anything except the actual and the necessary" (*LWS*, p. 365). Can and should poetry be an arm of political ideology? Even as he viewed the "misery of Europe" after the end of World War II, Stevens noted that a proposed new literary magazine was likely to appear "academic and unreal" and even acknowledged that at such times, "one is inclined, therefore, to sympathize with one's more unsympathetic critics" (*LWS*, p. 525).

Stevens's position in the face of these questions and issues was remarkably consistent throughout his life. While a student at Harvard, Stevens dismissed "art all alone, detached, sensuous for the sake of sensuousness" as "inexcusable rubbish." He then added, "Art must fit with other things; it must be part of the system of the world. And if it finds a place in that system it will likewise find a ministry and relation that are its proper adjuncts."[22] The position outlined here would be substantially unchanged for the rest of his life. His political poetry would walk a fine line – avoiding the sensuous self-indulgence of an art of social disengagement, at one extreme, while abjuring any particle of propagandistic or nationally ideological side taking, on the other. For both disavowals, he would suffer criticism.

Even in his own lifetime, charges of insufficient sensitivity to contemporary social and political disruptions occasionally stirred him to poetic response. When Stanley Burnshaw condemned the poems of *Harmonium* in 1935 as "the kind of verse that people concerned with the murderous world collapse can hardly swallow today except in tiny doses," Stevens responded with his poem "Mr. Burnshaw and the Statue," originally the second part of the longer poem "Owl's Clover" in its first publication. Later, the accusation that he was a poet of merely "charming distemper" by an anonymous soldier at the front in World War II discomfited Stevens enough to lead to his composition of "Esthétique du Mal."[23]

The "sudden rightnesses" that Stevens called on the poet to deliver in "Of Modern Poetry" can perhaps best be demonstrated by examples from the poems themselves (*SCP*, p. 218). I want to mention only two, "Mozart, 1935" and "Contrary Theses (I)," one of which is from the time of the Great Depression and the other from World War II. "Mozart, 1935" lays out a time of social disorientation and violence, leaving only the date in the title to suggest the historical circumstance. Unidentified people "throw stones upon the roof"; they "carry down the stairs / A body in rags" and "the streets are full of cries." It is a time of "angry fear" and "besieging pain." Far from addressing a political panacea to such times of desperation, he addresses a "poet," commanding that person to be "seated at the piano." What poetry-music could he possibly play? The answer is Mozart, but not a Mozart of evasion or distraction. "Strike the piercing chord. // ... Be thou, be thou / The voice of angry fear, / The voice of this besieging pain." The poet-musician must absorb the "wintry sound" itself. Only then can he create a momentary surcease "By which sorrow is released, / Dismissed, absolved / In a starry placating" (*SCP*, pp. 107–08). The poet-musician does not influence the immediate circumstances of the Great Depression; his contribution is more to those individuals who are victimized by social circumstances, the victims and perpetrators of anger and pain. He offers them an almost religious ("Be thou, be thou") alternative, a momentary calming against the forces of enveloping distress.

A few months after Pearl Harbor and America's entry into World War II, Stevens wrote "Contrary Theses (I)." The immediate circumstances seemed to call for a poetry of defiant outrage and patriotic fervor. Stevens, however, wrote a different kind of poem. An anonymous soldier, of any era or nationality, "walks before my door" and then "stalks before my door" (*SCP*, p. 239). The stalking soldier tramps over all attempts to push him aside in favor of autumnal ripeness or even "seraphs" and "saints." Five times in the poem's twelve lines the soldier's arrival at the door is announced – as disruptive to the poem as it is to the speaker. As a contrary thesis, the soldier cannot be dismissed or forgotten. The figure only presages the violence he represents: "Blood smears the oaks." It could be any war in any century; the soldier could be a German soldier at the door of an American home or an American soldier at the door of a German home. Even the poem's rhythm enacts the soldier's footsteps: "Befóre, befóre, befóre my dóor." Domestic peace is disrupted by the contrary thesis of war; to expose that menace seems to be the poet's dramatic purpose.

Only the order imposed by the poem on the scene and the circumscribed form of the six couplets counter the disorder and fear that it evokes. Both "Mozart, 1935" and "Contrary Theses (I)" offer a "violence from within" to act against the "violence without" (*SCP*, p. 665).

In the larger context of Stevens's poetry of reality and the imagination, the consolations of nature and phantasy are Stevens's only consolations. In the end, he asks, "What is there here but weather, what spirit / Have I except it comes from the sun?" (*SCP*, p. 104). His "sense" of the world and his "sense" of the poem are one: "Weather is a sense of nature. Poetry is a sense" (*SCP*, p. 902). And in a letter he states: "We are physical beings in a physical world. . . . The state of the weather soon becomes a state of mind" (*LWS*, p. 349). For a poet whose life was made up of so many personal abstentions and withdrawals – from faith in God, from parental ties, from a distant wife, and from friends and associates (although each of these absences requires a degree of qualification) – Stevens could not escape the larger social and political cataclysms that intruded on him. What remained was the earth in all its weathers, in all its seasons – and words. "In poetry, you must love the words, the ideas and images and rhythms with all your capacity to love anything at all" (*SCP*, p. 902). For this poet, who, according to his daughter, "lived alone," one feels compelled to ask if words, in the end, were enough. Was the earth enough? Was the eyeless and mouthless lover enough? Even Stevens had his moments of doubt, as he questions himself in "World without Peculiarity": "What good is it that the earth is justified, / That it is complete, that it is an end, / That in itself it is enough?" Then, in the following line, he offers his only response to that question, "It is the earth itself that is humanity" (*SCP*, p. 388). Was it enough? For this loneliest of poets, one can only ask the question. What remains is Stevens's renewed Romanticism – always followed by its accompanying disavowals and reconstitutions – evolving into his own amassing "grand poem" and marking his unique testimony to modernism in the last century.

Notes

1. Wallace Stevens, *Collected Poetry and Prose*, ed. Frank Kermode and Joan Richardson (New York: Library of America, 1997), p. 216. This collection will be cited in the text as *SCP*.
2. William Wordsworth, *Poems*, ed. John O. Hayden (New Haven, Conn.: Yale University Press, 1977), p. 358.
3. Wallace Stevens, *The Contemplated Spouse: The Letters of Wallace Stevens to Elsie*, ed. J. Donald Blount (Columbia: University of South Carolina Press, 2006), p. 134.

4. Wallace Stevens, *Souvenirs and Prophecies: The Young Wallace Stevens*, ed. Holly Stevens (New York: Knopf, 1977), p. 48.

5. Stevens, *Souvenirs*, p. 104.

6. Peter Brazeau, *Parts of a World: Wallace Stevens Remembered* (New York: Random House, 1977), p. 67.

7. Brazeau, *Parts of a World*, p. 239.

8. Helen Vendler, *Wallace Stevens: Words Chosen out of Desire* (Knoxville: University of Tennessee Press, 1984), pp. 5, 7.

9. Stevens, *The Contemplated Spouse*, pp. 199–200.

10. Stevens, *Souvenirs*, p. 146.

11. Wallace Stevens, *Letters of Wallace Stevens*, ed. Holly Stevens (New York: Knopf, 1966), p. 677. This collection will be cited in the text as *LWS*.

12. Stevens, *Souvenirs*, p. 146.

13. Brazeau, *Parts of a World*, pp. 22, 27.

14. Stevens, *Souvenirs*, p. 4.

15. T. S. Eliot, *Selected Essays* (London: Faber and Faber, 1951), p. 327.

16. George Santayana, *Scepticism and Animal Faith* (New York: Dover, 1955), pp. 180–81.

17. Angela Leighton, *On Form: Poetry, Aestheticism, and the Legacy of a Word* (Oxford: Oxford University Press, 2007), p. 187.

18. J. Hillis Miller, *The Linguistic Moment: From Wordsworth to Stevens* (Princeton, N.J.: Princeton University Press, 1985), pp. 399–400.

19. T. S. Eliot, *The Complete Poems and Plays, 1909–1950* (New York: Harcourt, Brace, 1958), p. 145.

20. Lawrence Thompson, *Robert Frost: The Years of Triumph, 1915–1936* (New York: Holt, Rinehart & Winston, 1970), p. 666.

21. Marianne Moore, "'New' Poetry since 1912," in Stanley Braithwaite (ed.), *Anthology of Magazine Verse for 1926* (Boston: B. J. Brimmer, 1926), pp. 172–79, 175.

22. Stevens, *Souvenirs*, p. 38.

23. Stanley Burnshaw, "Turmoil in the Middle Ground," *New Masses* XVII (October 1, 1935), p. 42; quoted in John Crowe Ransom, "Artists, Soldiers, Positivists," *Kenyon Review* 6 (1944), p. 276.

Chapter 30

Ezra Pound, William Carlos Williams, and the East Coast Projectivists

MATTHEW HOFER

As radical innovators throughout their careers and also the main sponsors of the major American avant-garde movements launched in 1931 (the Objectivist generation) and in 1950 (the projectivist generation), Ezra Pound and William Carlos Williams have often been figured as the authors of a counterculture in American poetry. Once expedient, perhaps even sensible, that persistent account of an outsider twentieth-century literary history is no longer viable in the twenty-first century. It is surely no longer necessary. Critics as well as poets increasingly agree that the contributions of these modernist inventors fall much nearer the center of the art than its margins. Among projectivist writers the influence of Pound and Williams is openly acknowledged. These East Coast poets affiliated with Black Mountain College – including Charles Olson, Robert Creeley, Denise Levertov, and Larry Eigner – have owned this debt and occasionally struggled with it, particularly when confronted with Pound's erratic and offensive political pronouncements. However, Pound's and Williams's poetic techniques resonate demonstrably in the finest work of subsequent generations.

Friends and rivals from their days at the University of Pennsylvania (1902) through old age, Pound and Williams constantly praised, critiqued, promoted, and contested each other. They shared more than a few ideas and goals, but not a poetics. Neither was prone to compromise, and their various engagements, although often productive, were rarely genteel. The prologue to *Kora in Hell* (1917) recounts what was for Williams an exemplary dispute between hungry young poets, in which "I contended for bread, he for caviar. I became hot. He, with fine discretion, exclaimed: 'Let us drop it. We will never agree, or come to an agreement.' He spoke then like a Frenchman, which is one who discerns."[1] Williams's equivocation is not trivial. In fact, his adept assessment of their relative temperaments is no less sensitive than the subtle linguistic play that informs his anecdote: its jibe turns on a historical conflation of the Old French terms *discern*, "to separate or distinguish," and *decern*, "to decide or decree." By Pound's cool acquiescence Williams depicts the future expatriate as both mediator and polemicist, a traditional critic with an avant-garde bent, and anything but American.

Of course, Pound's attraction to Continental culture was by no means restricted to Gallic discernment, and his decision to expatriate figures centrally in his extended debate with Williams about the appropriate course for modern (American) poetry. In a reply to Williams's early complaint to his "old friend" about "hurt feelings," Pound exhorts, "I demand of you more robustezza. Bigod sir, you show more robustezza, or I will come over to Rutherford and have at you, *coram*, in person."[2] Even in praise of an early masterpiece like *Kora* – "the best you have done" – Pound urged above all a fierce independence: "ANYHOW blaze away, and more power to yr. elbow. Dont listen to any one else, and above all dont listen to me." However, with reference to Williams's express goal of establishing a "representative American" writing, Pound did share the reasonable insight that it "will be that which can be translated in foreign languages without appearing ridiculous to us after it has been 'accepted'" and, moreover, that it "will appear new" to those outside the United States.[3]

Neither disagreement nor hurt feelings precluded solidarity. When Pound called from London "to break the pentameter" and formulated the three tenets of Imagism, he solicited Williams's poem "Postlude" for inclusion in his revolutionary anthology, *Des Imagistes* (1914). This memorable love lyric begins with a proposition as unsentimental as it is precise, invoking cyclical nature and sequential history in order to explain transitory human relations in terms appropriate to architectural monuments:

> Now that I have cooled to you
> Let there be gold of tarnished masonry,
> Temples soothed by the sun to ruin
> That sleep utterly.[4]

Appropriately for a postlude, this poem begins right "now"; it begins, that is, in the present tense, and the speaker's emotions, although they endure, are past perfect. Following the comparatively muted and reflective negotiation of the first strophe (in which "masonry" insistently evokes "memory"), the second rises to meet the first tenet of Imagism – the "direct presentation of the 'thing' whether subjective or objective" – head on in terms that render the modern affair commensurable to a little-known yet much-conquered ancient city: "Your hair is my Carthage / And my arms the bow," "our words arrows / To shoot the stars" (*WCPI*, p. 3). While successfully avoiding strict rhythm, tight rhyme, and elevated diction, the chiming of end words such as "bow" and "arrows" intensifies the presentational metaphor, which provides a homophonic undertone of eros as well as an attendant cupidinous image. This underscores the Imagist rebuke to "use absolutely no word that does not contribute to the presentation" (tenet 2) as well as the insistence "to compose in the sequence of the musical phrase, not in sequence of a metronome" (tenet 3).[5]

A mediated contact with Imagism did much to modernize Williams, and "Postlude" showcases several qualities he retained from this style, although its classical references and foreign flourishes – typical of H.D., Richard Aldington, and Pound – are of course remote from the American idiom the obstetrician-poet would later famously claim to have gotten "from the mouths of Polish mothers." Pound, a key figure among the original Imagists, quickly broke with the movement after Amy Lowell commandeered it (rendering it "Amygism"), because, as Hugh Kenner notes, any coterie "in part defines one's company, and Imagism ... soon entailed negotiating with dim and petulant people."[6] Williams, however, whose company and identity never risked being determined by his loose association with the Imagist, Objectivist, or projectivist writers, maintained his persistent adherence to the principles of Imagist writing, selectively at least, throughout his career. He even proposed, in a 1953 letter to Creeley, that his dedication to the poetic image was what precluded him from fully appreciating Olson's comparatively imageless poems.[7] Yet an appreciation of a style was for Williams no more constrained by systems or institutions than was the use of it; his sense of affiliation, almost always cast as a commitment to the local, particular, and "new," was more fluid than that.

Pound's and Williams's essays on each other's work are remarkably perceptive, and although their criticism can be severe, their praise, however sardonic, is also genuine. For example, in "Dr. Williams' Position," Pound extols the accurate observation and pragmatic expertise of Williams's art. However, in his estimation, those qualities stemmed from the biological, cultural, and linguistic hybridity that simultaneously "provided the infant William with material sustenance" and relegated him to the position of "the observant foreigner" (*LE*, p. 391). "In his verse," Pound cautions readers, "Williams' integrity passes for simplicity."[8] While his work is by no means simple, Williams was prepared to run the risk of allowing it to appear so; simple was, for him, a less compromising quality than conventional. Thus Williams could mordantly profess to "praise those who have the wit and courage, and the conventionality, to go direct toward their vision of perfection in an objective world where the signposts are clearly marked, *viz.*, to London" and yet earnestly wish to "confine them to hell for their paretic assumption that there is no alternative but their own groove" (*IM*, p. 27). In response to Pound's seeming compliance with this general paresis – and despite publishing his own first commercial volume of poems, *The Tempers* (1913), with Pound's London publisher Elkin Mathews – the nativist modernist proclaimed the preeminent expatriate to be "the best enemy United States verse has" (*IM*, p. 26). The promise of an identifiably American modernism was for Williams always worth the effort.

Just as Williams's abiding interest in concrete imagery did not make him a holdover from the original Imagist movement, so Pound's Vorticism is not merely Imagism by another name. The success of an Imagist poem is gauged by its capacity to present "an intellectual and emotional complex in an instant of time," which "instantaneously ... gives that sense of freedom from time limits and space limits; that sense of sudden growth, which we experience in the presence of the greatest works of art" (*LE*, p. 4). Pound's celebrated Imagist poem "The Garden" achieves this effect by a series of deft and swift comparisons that characterize "the *end* of breeding" – that is, its purpose and its limit. In it, a pair of perfectly calibrated sibilant adjectives, "excessive and exquisite," particularize the redundant yet highly refined boredom of an aristocratic woman, repeating the syllable "ex-" not only for the dense sound structure it generates but also to recall its typical etymological function as a prefix that emphasizes a degree of dignity, an inviolate singularity, and an inevitable obsolescence. The logic of the Imagist poem – "This thing, that hath a code and not a core" – allows for a series of static associations that maintain their distinctiveness even in the moment of most insistent association.[9] A toney woman walking in the public-private space of Kensington Gardens is like (but is not) a "skein of loose silk blown against a wall." Her perceptible if incremental death from "a sort of emotional anaemia" stands in sharp contrast to the encroaching (but still separate) crowd of "filthy, sturdy, unkillable infants of the very poor." Finally, her altogether visible boredom is figured as a desire to be addressed that nearly justifies (but fails to entice) an incursion by the modern artist: "She would like some one to speak to her, / And is almost afraid that I / will commit that indiscretion" (*PT*, pp. 264–65). These tropes are far from ornamental; they present the woman's movement, situation, and status precisely. Imagism remains distinct from symbolism because "the symbolist's *symbols* have a fixed value, like numbers in arithmetic," but the "imagiste's images have a variable significance, like the signs a, b, and x in algebra."[10] Such variables give rise to a sensation of freedom or sudden growth when their meaning suddenly becomes apparent in relation to one another. But nothing, in the poem, actually happens.

Against the backdrop of the coming world war, the specific advance that Vorticism made on Imagist practice entails a renewed commitment to representational energy, figured materially as a dynamic spiral "from which, and through which, and into which, ideas are constantly rushing" (*GB*, p. 92). Whether swelling to the national level ("The Great English Vortex") or focusing down to the individual practitioner ("Vortex: Pound"), Vorticism extends to painting, sculpture, and music; its figure of spiral-patterned energy with an unmoving center amplifies the preceding literary movement. Unlike Imagism, the Vortex asserts the energy of the diagonal as opposed to the stasis of gridded binaries, and, unlike Italian Futurism, it posits no divorce from history. Pound, building on the analogy that had distinguished symbolism from Imagism, frames a distinction between Imagism and Vorticism in terms of that between algebra (which exceeds the "arithmetic" power of symbolism) and analytical geometry (which equally exceeds the "algebraic" power of Imagism). Applied to Vorticism, the theory of analytical geometry provides a universal idiom, complex and elegant, that points to a "new way of dealing with form" (*GB*, p. 91).

From a literary perspective, the Vorticist "one-image poem" concentrates the intensity of the poetic event in an effort "to record the precise instant when a thing outward and objective transforms itself, or darts into a thing inward and subjective" (*GB*, p. 89). This is how the signature transformation of faces into petals occurs in Pound's poem "In a Station of the Metro":

> The apparition   of these faces   in the crowd   :
> Petals   on a wet, black   bough   .[11]

While the title serves as a necessary first line – providing orientation via its prepositional phrases as well as a sense of a modern, urban, and technologically advanced setting – the disarticulated colon (later rendered as a semicolon) that separates and links these disparate images visibly marks the moment of radical transformation that Pound's prose articulates. Conspicuous blank spaces, closed up in later presentations, help to structure the first version of this poem – which was published in *Poetry* (1913) – governing the rhythm of the change. The spaces usefully highlight what a successful Vorticist poem invariably does: it channels the syntactic movement from one image to the next, compartmentalizes attention, focuses power, and defers completion. That is to say, although something is manifestly happening here, nothing is being consumed in the process. Rather, the "precise instant" of transformation from the objective to the subjective thing is made literal, material, and powerfully present. This is how art handles life in the Vortex.

The nascent Vortex benefited from Pound's receipt in 1913 of Ernest Fenollosa's papers, which simultaneously confirmed the evolution of his post-Imagist poetics and expanded his cultural scope, finally giving rise to the ideogrammic method of the cantos (arranging what Pound previously called the "luminous details" of short lyrics into larger structural units, and so making the long poem possible). Scholars rightly, if pedantically, argue that Fenollosa's study of Chinese writing lacks linguistic accuracy with regard to the ideogram, yet the poetic theory adapted from it reveals a great deal about English, which is, like Chinese, uninflected. Edited by Pound as *The Chinese Written Character as a Medium for Poetry*, the essay relates the transference of force in writing, and the "flash of lightning" stands in as the prime sentence that can "redistribute force" within "a regular and flexible sequence, as plastic as thought itself."[12] From this perspective, Fenollosa posits that the conventional sentence form is impoverished, distracting, and unnatural, given that nature cannot support the concept of an abstraction, a negation, a truly *completed* action, or an action (verb) that is separate from an actor (noun). These insights effectively authorized the modernist revolution in poetic syntax as parataxis.

For Pound's poetics – as for the projectivists' sense of the open field that extends (or supplants) free verse – the freshly liberating observation is that nature has "no grammar." Cleaving to the processes of nature rather than being constrained by artificial forms for making meaning allows poets to rediscover forgotten yet vital mental processes in which relations become "more real and important than the things which they relate." Moreover, as a "time art," poetry promises simultaneous access to "the vividness of painting" and "the mobility of sounds," although "it is, in some sense, more objective than either, more dramatic."[13] The drama that Fenollosa identifies here corresponds to a version of the energy that defines the Vortex. However, even a cursory look at the short-lived Vorticist journal *BLAST* (1914, 1915) also suggests how the correlation of illumination to an energizing, renewing, or sanitizing violence was informed by a practical naïveté about the horrors of total war. When these horrors became evident and unavoidable, the radical drive of modernism could neither reconcile its logic nor survive its losses. The resultant Thermidor did much to suppress poetic experimentation prior to the 1950 salvo of Olson's "Projective Verse" manifesto, the critical demonstration piece that theorized the practice of open field composition and inaugurated the New American poetics.

The concept of ideogrammic juxtaposition was integral to the development of an open field method of projectivist composition. For Creeley, the "*ordering of expression*" that the formal innovation made available to poetry "duplicates

the differentiation of force in actuality *as* consequence leading to *new consequence.*" The *Chinese Written Character* essay also led Olson to posit that while
the use of adjectives can produce a "logic of time, as event," this logic is "viti-
ating because it is inherently descriptive"; however, he contends that a metamorphosis in time and space is possible by way of the pressure adverbs place
on verbs "to change them, to move them," and, he later adds, "*thus* ourselves –
changed."[14] This understanding of ideogrammic theory, predicated on illumination and a sense of the spatial as well as the temporal elements of a poem,
helps to confirm the terms of Pound's distinction of Vorticism from Imagism.
However, to the extent that Creeley and Olson are concerned with the articulation of language as spoken, it also anticipates a corrective Olson thought
to provide in open field poetics "on this biz of, expression versus illumination.
All the way thru I find em (including Ez's absolute ARS POETICA) half right.
(They leave out one side of the thoroughfare, much-travelled side.)" (*CC1*,
pp. 137–38). The much-travelled side involves the resources of rhetoric, which
are oral, prosaic, and pedagogical. Olson's drive to explain and systematize
required that he prioritize the communication of content (expression) in a discursive poetics that is often more tightly controlled than his expository prose.
In this and in his masculinist attitudes toward art, Olson resembles Pound –
the predecessor whom he sedulously rejects in "GrandPa, Goodbye" – more
closely than he could, or in any case ever did, acknowledge.

*

An urgent desire to make writing new motivated both Pound and Williams,
each after his own fashion. Kenner's early sense of the high modern poet-critics balances Pound's passion for activity against Williams's underrated "tena-
ciousness," dismissing, with a sidelong swipe, T. S. Eliot's supposed careerist
drive: "Where Mr. Pound reads his contemporaries to find out if they are still
alive, and Mr. Eliot to see if they merit introductions, Dr. Williams reads and
rereads them to find out what they mean."[15] Reading and rereading Pound's
work, Williams recognized achievements that he sought to adapt for his own
writing. As early as 1913 he (like most open form poets) denied writing "free
verse" and claimed not to "believe in vers libre," since in any poem "the motion
continues or it does not continue, either there is rhythm or no rhythm."[16] He
considered "formal invention" crucial because he held that only in "intimate
form" do "works of art achieve their exact meaning ... to give language its
highest dignity, the illumination in the environment to which it is native."[17]
For Williams, who disdained the "beautiful illusion" and all things mimetic,
"poetry has to do with the crystallization of the imagination – the perfection

of new forms as additions to nature" (*IM*, p. 140). Materiality, while not necessarily inimical to clarity or precision or euphony, came to mean more to Williams than those qualities. Although Williams was capable of remarkable precision, he was often opaque, as Pound observed ("The thing that saves your work is opacity, and don't forget it") (*IM*, p. 10). To him, traditional features, sustained by linear continuity, plot, and connectives, were the elements of the bound thinking that he sought, in his writing, to unbind. This, too, is evident as early as the genre-defying experiment *Kora in Hell*, in which the artist's process is described in terms of a struggle to represent reality as a conscious product of the active imagination: "The stream of things having composed itself into wiry strands that move in one direction, the poet in desperation turns at right angles and cuts across currents" (*IM*, p. 17).

The contour of these early insights helps explain the shape of the successive experiments of *Spring and All*, *The Descent of Winter*, and the triadic structure of late poems composed with the variable foot. The technologies of Cubist composition intensified Williams's prioritization of perception over meaning and flatness over depth. This is explicit in the metonymic experimentation of *Spring and All*, in which Williams asserts, "the word must be put down for itself, not as a symbol of nature," and insists that "words freed by the imagination affirm reality by their flight" (*IM*, pp. 102, 150). The early texts push toward, even if they do not fully achieve, the openness of a process poem; they gesture powerfully toward key features of what will become the projectivist practice of privileging energy, body, and sound. Some of Creeley's most memorable compositions, including the open field seriality of *Pieces*, pursue and develop Williams's insights.

Pound imagined poetic vocabulary differently, prizing *cheng ming*, the principle of the rectification of names, which points to the revelatory clarity of words that are, so to speak, unwobbling pivots. This faith in words as solid referents is a key distinction between Pound's and Williams's approaches to modernism. For Pound, and for Olson too, the deep history of linguistic evolution was as true a history as culture workers could ever approach: Pound went back to the Greek and Chinese classics, and Olson's ambition drove him deeper still to the ancient "E on the stone," the "navel stone" at Delphi, which is given as the oldest glyph extant – predating Greek civilization – in "The Kingfishers."[18] Olson elaborates on his intellectual suspicion of punning and linguistic play in a letter to Eigner about Robert Duncan's "arbitrary etymologies" as irresponsible fabrication. In it he stipulates that "what's most needed right now is an *Indo-European* Dictionary – roots, so one can feel that far back along the line of the word to its first users – what they meant, in *inventing* it" (*COSA*, p. 78). Here "inventing" means to come upon, find out, discover – never to make up.

Pound's association of vital language with historical thought aims to discover "the gristly roots of ideas that are in actions" (*Paideuma*).[19] It also informs the two liberative themes of *The Cantos* that were singled out by Williams: "a closed mind which clings to its power – about which the intelligence beats seeking entrance" and the idea that "all men are contemporaries, in whatever time they live or have lived, whose minds (including the body and its acts) have lifted them above the sordidness of a grabbing world" (*SE*, pp. 106, 167). This gets close to what Pound demanded in his credo "make it new": a regenerated, intensified, and so relevant sense of tradition as the "tale of the tribe" (*Sagetrieb*).[20] Making it new, Pound and Olson agree, is not making it up.

A less sympathetic, perhaps more anxious reader of *The Cantos*, Olson began from insights similar to Williams's but reached rather different conclusions. Williams understood the transformation effected by the poem as a move "away from the word as a symbol toward the word as reality," by which he meant that Pound was effectively employing each word as "an objective unit in the design – but alive" (*SE*, p. 107). This is an act of will exercised at the level of the word. However, in the course of their instructive conversation in letters about projective verse, Olson advises Creeley that "to undo free verse" will require poets to "hammer each line out as purely as each SYLLABLE, or we're dead ducks, like / / the Amygists, / or even EZ, when, as so often, in the Cantos, he / goes by his will, thinks / that it will carry him, he's / so strong. It don't, & / IT WON'T" (*CC1*, p. 126). In his Mayan Letters, written to Creeley, Olson elaborates on this critique, concluding that *The Cantos* originates in a flawed method that results in a largely failed project:

> Ez's epic solves problem by his ego: his single emotion breaks all down to his equals or inferiors.... Which assumption, that there are intelligent men whom he can outtalk, is beautiful because it destroys historical time and thus creates the methodology of the Cantos, viz, a space-field where, by inversion, though the material is all time material, he has driven through it so sharply by the beak of his ego, that, he has turned time into what we must now have, space & its live air. (*CC5*, p. 49)

What remains available for poets of the 1950s to use – historical time transformed into a space-field – appears, on this account, to be incidental, even accidental. This liberation from time, as Robert von Hallberg explains, permits Olson to compose didactic poems that can "shift idioms abruptly, without warning, without explanation," and to do so without committing, as Pound did, to the "nonrational psychology and rhetorical strategy" of the ideogrammic method (*COSA*, pp. 19, 3). The theory of projective verse is finally irreconcilable to an ideogrammic model that harmonizes disparate images, voices, and ideas within a horizontal chord (found also in Arabian music and Provençal metrics), which gives rise to a meaning-making order elaborated in a claim from *Antheil and the Treatise on Harmony*, in which Pound posits that "any chord can follow any other."[21]

During the 1930s, as Pound's economic, political, and racial statements grew increasingly strident, Williams strove to keep their exchanges as literary as possible. With the depression raging and the prospect of a second world war in Europe looming, he had only partial success, at best. As he attempted to explain, "When you go off the handle about the economic situation, though I acknowledge you may be in the right, you are all wet to me. But when you write as you have written in the preface to the *Active Anthology* you are superb. You do hold the lamp and it is lit."[22] Pound's *Active Anthology* (1933) – which included fifteen poems by Williams – was meant in part to direct and in part to counter Objectivist writing as represented by Louis Zukofsky's special issue of *Poetry* magazine (February 1931) and his *"Objectivists" Anthology* of 1932. Pound was then losing faith in the aesthetic of objectification, characterized by "sincerity" and the "totality" of "perfect rest," because it seemed to him increasingly remote from the orientation it had initially taken from Imagism and Vorticism.[23] A late limerick published in the *European* recalls his concern about abstraction succinctly:

> This is the grave of old Zuk
> who wasn't really a crook
> but who died of persistence
> in that non-existence
>   which consists in refusing to LOOK.
>
>   (*PT*, p. 1200)

The grave, like the theft, is metaphorical only: Zukofsky lived and wrote well, albeit in relative obscurity, until 1978. But some of Pound's 1930s cantos do begin to display a tendency to revisit or even revise history that does not always go in fear of abstraction. This is less a refusal to look than an increasingly biased tendency to seek out and accumulate evidence that betrays traces of conspiratorial thinking. The poems are made vulnerable to that tendency by the easy connection of unlike events, people, and concepts facilitated by a less than ideally careful application of the ideogrammic method.

Pound's best cantos of the 1930s remain thematically focused, concrete, and also continue to display his signal use of end-stopped lines and rhythmic regularity to bring the lines to a felt conclusion, after which the beginning of the next line will "catch the rise of the rhythm wave" (*LE*, p. 6). Consider, for example, the fully achieved canto 45, which stages its lyrical condemnation of usury in what Peter Makin has termed "the grand prophetic style: terse, emphatic, and denunciatory."[24] If few poems are so well suited to Pound's contemporaneous advice for learning about the art while avoiding the boredom of "professorial documentation" – "LISTEN to the sound that it makes" – few, too, have been as compellingly analyzed by critics.[25] This terrestrial inferno documents "sin against nature" and also against art – which is neither "made to endure nor to live with / but it is made to sell and sell quickly" – and so, Pound indicates, the extent of economic corruption can be gauged from the quality of art produced during a given era: "with usura the line grows thick / with usura is no clear demarcation" (*C*, p. 229). This is followed in canto 49 by a rare ideogrammic "glimpse of paradiso" that makes use of many of the same formal resources. Known as "The Seven Lakes Canto," this free translation creatively adapts material from a series of eight Chinese poems and paintings from a Japanese manuscript volume that came to the poet through his parents in 1928.[26] The sonorous and image-rich approach to a capacious *personal* history inspired by the heirloom extends a familiar sense of thematic anonymity, beginning in canto 1 with an Odyssean descent into hell, which nonetheless retains individuality in the expression of a style. Canto 1 demands that there be no interruption, no distortion of that style as a result of translation (in this case of Homer's Greek into Latin), in the lines "Lie quiet Divus. I mean, that is Andreas Divus, / In officina Wecheli, 1538, out of Homer" (*C*, p. 5). The opening line of canto 49, "For the Seven Lakes, and by no man these verses," is, besides the closing distich, one of four interpolated Poundian lines.[27] The balance is carried over from the composite source.

"Translation," broadly construed, is an integral term of an authorial process responsive to a demand to "make it new," one that seeks out and adapts source material that represents origins or perfections wherever those may be. Such capaciousness, which exceeds individuality, sometimes appears contrarian. For example, Pound's early interest in what resources a poem like "The Seafarer" might offer to modern English from the Anglo-Saxon tradition came about while he was building a reputation as an expert in Romance languages and literature. A similar interest is recapitulated in the inspired and obscure carrying-over of canto 36, which reprises Italian poet Guido Cavalcanti's canzone "Donna mi pregha" in its fine realization of the Provençal troubadour tradition. In "The Seven Lakes Canto" this interest produces a glimpse of paradise in parallax that proceeds from a depiction of dignified and harmonious but altogether ordinary events and routines: wholly apart from – yet not exclusive of – our three dimensions, Pound finds "The fourth; the dimension of stillness. / And the power over wild beasts," a divine (Dionysian) power that is granted only on rare occasions to special humans (C, p. 245).

The stylistic distinction between Pound and Williams as incipient open form poets relevant to projectivist writers is a matter of individualized structures and distinctive rhythms. The modern impulse to establish new forms in addition to breaking conventional ones – canto 81 recalls, "To break the pentameter, that was the first heave" – finds support in Pound's observation that the regular use of symmetrical stanzas "naturally HAPPENED when a man was singing a long poem to a short melody which he had to use over and over."[28] Both Pound and Williams avoided the constraints of external symmetries and meters, but where Pound often finds ways to bring his lines to a kind of resolution, Williams depends on radical enjambment and intensifications of syntax to construct rhythms that either describe the action of his poems or serve to make their meaning apparent. Williams exhibits textual strategies for the representation of energy and motion in the formally distinguished "Poem" ("As the cat / climbed over / the top of // the jamcloset"), which demonstrates a style largely compatible with the projectivist emphasis on kinetics, in which content dictates form (WCPI, p. 352). Not unlike his ideal verbal cat, the four tercets that compose Williams's unpunctuated one-sentence poem embody precarious balance as well as purposeful motion. Remarkably modest at the level of the word, "Poem" begins in the middle of an act less tentative than intense, which makes the past tense of the action feel present and the language seem solid. The consequence of the act it describes – climbing over leads to stepping down – is all but inevitable. There is nothing extraneous here to distract from the progression, yet each line is unpredictable based on the ones that precede it. "Poem" resists easy paraphrase because its form commands all the significance of its content. Although the poem provides orientation via prepositions, precision via verbs and adverbs, and weight via nouns, these words in this order generate a formal sense of movement capable of producing surprise.

Williams's emphasis on movement and form clarifies his definition of the art of poetry, because "to write or to comprehend poetry the words must be recognized to be moving in a direction separate from the jostling or lack of it which occurs in the piece" (IM, p. 146). This insistence on kinetics – which enjoins readerly participation – pertains to the development of open or organic verse to the extent that the projectivists defined composition by field by expressly rejecting "the inherited line, stanza, over-all-form, what is the 'old' base of the non-projective."[29] In taking modernist experimentation to its logical limit, Olson and Creeley declare that the open poem operates on a *"principle"* that "FORM IS NEVER MORE THAN AN EXTENSION OF CONTENT" and by a *"process"* that shapes the energies of the one "right form" into a "high-energy construct, and, at all points, an energy discharge," stipulating that "one perception must must must MOVE, INSTANTER, ON ANOTHER" (*COPr*, p. 240).

For "projective or OPEN verse" poets, form requires movement, and the manifesto opens with the constellation of terms "projectile," "percussive," and "prospective," all in opposition to the verse that "print bred," which continues to dominate both American and English poetry "despite the work of Pound & Williams" (*COPr*, p. 239). In a projective poem, form is determined by content but is also unique to its author, given that it is shaped by "the HEAD, by way of the EAR, to the SYLLABLE" as well as by "the HEART, by way of the BREATH, to the LINE" (*COPr*, p. 242). "That's the whole biz," as Creeley wrote Olson, "I mean / is precise, exact: what all Ez's negatives were trying to push to / in the Imagist biz. Look & see" (*CC2*, pp. 60–61). The varied appearance of open form poems on the page – that is, Creeley's poems look nothing like Olson's – is attributable to the physical makeup of each writer. That is, the voice comes from the body, "speech is the 'solid' of verse, the secret of a poem's energy," and particular speech reifies the poem so that "everything in it can now be treated as solids, objects, things" (*COPr*, p. 244). A poet, declares Olson, who is inclined to "sprawl" will "find little to sing but himself," yet one who "stays inside himself" is "able to listen, and his hearing through himself will give him secrets objects share. And by an inverse law his shapes will make their own way. It is in this way that the projective act ... leads to dimensions larger than the man" (*COPr*, p. 247). The significance of such a claim is not only stylistic but also mystical, bridging a gap between the physical and metaphysical, accessing "that place where breath comes from, where breath has its beginnings, where drama has to come from, where, the coincidence is, all act springs" (*COPr*, p. 249). Williams, in *Spring and All*, praises Marianne Moore on similar terms: her poems also reject the "shapes" and "meter" of verse, and some may be "diagrammatically informative," yet they come "invariably from the source from which poetry starts" (*IM*, p. 145). And then, of course, they *move*.

Williams's poems of the 1930s continued to experiment with kinetics and form, in terms of the motion of feet and movement across lines, anticipating his 1940s move toward what he called a "variable foot" in a triadic stanza. This gives rise to a model of the poem as a dance – a model that Olson, whose "Tyrian Businesses" raises the question of "how to dance / sitting down," shares.[30] For both poets, a tendency to employ radical enjambment, syntax-driven rhythms, and a rich, trim, local, and particularized language renders such a model not only viable in theory but sometimes remarkably successful in practice. In his introduction to Williams's *Selected Poems*, the poet Charles Tomlinson – professing a desire to be "the second Englishman to read [Williams] aright" (the first was D. H. Lawrence) – further relates Williams's practice to projectivist composition. He contends that the best of these poems makes manifest "a vivid sense of what Olson calls 'the elements and minims of language,' down to the syllabic components or 'the dipthong / ae.'"[31] Although Tomlinson's aptly chosen example is from poem VI in *Spring and All*, the process is also on display in "The Dance," a masterful ekphrastic poem that reproduces in a single sentence the movement of a painting via the music of lyrical language. As the sounds – consonants and vowels – accrue and advance with an almost ritualistic sureness, the poem captures in just twelve lines of tripping, falling rhythm (made primarily of wraparound dactyls) the manner in which sixteenth-century village "dancers go round, they go round and / around, the squeal and the blare and the / tweedle of bagpipes, a bugle and fiddles" (*WCPII*, p. 58). Ultimately, when the first line, "In Breughel's great picture, The Kermess," repeats as the last, to halt the movement and signal its completion, Williams's motivated, stylized, purposeful repetition is anything but redundant. It is efficient.

Repetition is not only present in but integral to Williams's body of work: ideas, phrases, and sometimes whole poems are recapitulated in new contexts. As Williams happily acknowledges, his own position is diametrically opposed to that of "the extractors of genius" like Eliot, because in his work he is "making a modern bolus" destined to be "the mass in which some other later Eliot will dig" (*SE*, p. 285). His principle of accretion depends on a method that is articulated in the preface to *Paterson*, Book 1 (1946):

> To make a start,
> out of particulars
> and make them general, rolling
> up the sum....[32]

Consider, for example, the well-known phrase "no ideas but in things," which makes its way into *Paterson*, Book 1, part 1, by way of the first lyric of *The Wedge* (1944), "A Sort of Song" (*WCPII*, p. 55). The earlier presentation of "No ideas / but in things" in *The Wedge* responds to the overwhelming fact of America's then-current war against fascism, dismissing any relevance of metaphysics, and expressing its key aesthetic concepts as "two bald statements: There's nothing sentimental about a machine, and: A poem is a small (or large) machine made of words." The poet's focus on particulars demands special attention to the relations between parts, and this process requires Williams to seek materials that are close at hand and to arrange them precisely "into an intense expression of his perceptions and ardors that they may constitute a revelation in the speech that he uses" (*WCPII*, pp. 53–54). However, after the war, the opening book of *Paterson* sought to isolate and then "unravel" a "common language" that is composed of these very words, and in the process to recover the "miraculous" prospect of thoughts that are – and must be – "divorced from [our] minds" (*P*, p. 12).

The accomplishment of Williams's variable foot, which is perhaps his most important contribution to the open field poetics of the projectivists, may be approached by way of another repetition. Poems that attempt to marshal a variable foot too often fail to epitomize the form in the (rather vague) critical terms Williams used to describe it, but "The Descent," first printed in *Paterson*, Book 2, part 3 (1948), and reprinted as the opening to *The Desert Music* (1951), embodies its possibilities nicely. The poem, which begins as a kind of ersatz poetics statement, warrants attention and analysis, although its formal intricacies – as with "Poem" or "The Dance" – intend to frustrate selective quotation. It ends:

> No defeat is made up entirely of defeat – since
> the world it opens is always a place
>   formerly
>   unsuspected. A
> world lost,
>   a world unsuspected
>   beckons to new places
> and no whiteness (lost) is so white as the memory
> of whiteness   .   (*WCPII*, p. 245)

In depicting the gain that follows from loss, like a victory taken from defeat, Williams's lines stand witness to global as well as personal history. They attest that, in postwar America, poetry retains relevance as a tool of discovery, a strategy for preserving memory, and even a species of action. Measure may be the only reality modern humans can know, but poetic measure in particular can open up new places, concepts, perceptions, and even places "formerly // unsuspected."

Williams's art (like Creeley's) is principally an art of linguistic making, whereas Pound's art (like Olson's) typically prioritizes teaching or explaining. But those two goals are by no means mutually exclusive. Williams expounded on his newest poetic ideas and their general relevance just two years prior to Olson's publication of "Projective Verse," calling for "a revolution in the concept of the poetic foot" that would result in "sweeping changes from top to bottom of the poetic structure" (*SE*, p. 281). In his unstinting focus on the syllable as "the minimum and source of speech" in an effort to undo "the smothering of the power of the line by too set a concept of foot," Olson was the one to make the attack – and Williams subsequently reprinted Olson's "Projective Verse" in his *Autobiography*, appreciably increasing its audience (*COPr*, p. 241). In a late interview, Williams agreed that Olson's theorization of the syllable and line followed in the same Whitmanian tradition as his variable foot with regard to "the spacing of the verses," but admitted that he had "been trying to approach a shorter [measured] line which I haven't quite been able to nail."[33] These statements relate to the claim that field poetics ultimately generates active force via form: the two halves are the language of illumination ("the HEAD, by way of the EAR, to the SYLLABLE") and the kinetics of the poet's body ("the HEART, by way of the BREATH, to the LINE") (*COPr*, p. 240).

The variable foot was a significant if not uniformly successful quantitative experiment in flexible cadence that, despite an ongoing critical expression of not unreasonable skepticism, poets – certainly projectivist ones – found useful. The standard critical responses to the variable foot pithily dismiss it as a "rubber inch" (after Kenner) or elaborately attempt a degree of technical precision that risks generalizing it into meaninglessness as "one heavily accented syllable, an unlimited number of unaccented syllables, and an unlimited number of syllables of secondary accent" (after Yvor Winters).[34] Marjorie Perloff offers a fresh perspective by proposing that it was scored to the eye rather than the ear (*NSE*, p. 25). Among the poets, Levertov vindicates it explicitly, insisting that it is "temporal and auditory," that each segment has the same duration in time, and that the "variations in *speed*" as well as the pauses in each foot (or segment) "have expressive functions to fulfill – waiting, pondering, or hesitating" (*NSE*, pp. 24, 25). Williams also commends Levertov's comprehension of the "unity" of his own "metrical arrangement of lines," crediting her with being "very much more alert to my feeling about words."[35] This alertness, however, also extends beyond her sense of the rhythmic possibilities of the variable foot; as von Hallberg recounts, "Levertov is one of the few people to observe that much of what 'Williams said about the American idiom is not really borne out in his poetry because much of it rises way above the American idiom as it is commonly used. It's a kind of high language'" (*COSA*, p. 74).

The claim for the memory of whiteness in "The Descent," which seems carefully calibrated to the capacity assigned to whiteness in Pound's *Pisan*

Cantos to preserve and synthesize, suggests a relevant thematic connection between Williams's and Pound's postwar work. Written from a cage in the U.S. Army's detention training center near Pisa, with no access to research materials, these may of necessity be the most American as well as the most personal of Pound's cantos. The questions they pose are at once formal, historical, public, and private. The lines to which Williams responds are found near the beginning of canto 74:

> What you depart from is not the way
> and olive tree blown white in the wind
> washed in the Kiang and Han
> what whiteness will you add to this whiteness,
> > > what candor?
> "the great periplum brings in the stars to our shore."

> > > > > (*C*, p. 445)

"Candor" is a powerful term that speaks to the prospects for art and memory after defeat, denoting not only a brilliant illumination (or literal whiteness) but also integrity, sincerity, and freedom from bias. Whether these nostalgic, troubled cantos constitute an attempt to atone for Pound's wartime activities (adherents to this position promote as evidence the lines near the end of canto 81 that repeat the insistent refrain "Pull down thy vanity") or to explain and vindicate them ("But to have done instead of not doing / this is not vanity") has been contested. If there is a degree of contrition, it is certainly intermittent. However, a clear measure of fellow feeling and mutual appreciation persists in the tense times after World War II. Williams – who had expressed annoyance to Zukofsky at being absent from Pound's epic when so many others were present – finally makes his début at the end of canto 78, during a scenic description that ultimately recalls the dictum "no ideas but in things" and pays tribute to the achievement of "The Red Wheelbarrow":

> and as for the solidity of the white oxen in all this
> perhaps only Dr Williams (Bill Carlos)
> ~~will understand its importance,~~
> its benediction. He wd/ have put in the cart. (*C*, p. 503)

Although Pound and Williams never again collaborated as closely as they did in the years prior to World War I, and although in 1939 Williams publicly accused Pound of anti-Semitism in his review of *Guide to Kulchur*, their persistent regard for each other's literary work helped sustain a friendship. They shared not only an editor – James Laughlin of New York's New Directions – but also mutual interests in representations of American history in literature, theories of social credit, and the development of emerging American poets such as Olson and Creeley. Postwar publications brought new celebrity and acclaim to both poets, particularly through Pound's celebrated and contested *Pisan Cantos* and the earliest installments of Williams's five-part long poem, *Paterson*. In the wake of World War II, during the twelve-year period when Pound was incarcerated at St. Elizabeths in Washington, D.C., Williams remained skeptical about the plea of mental incompetence that had excused Pound from standing trial on charges of treason. But he nevertheless visited Pound in the asylum and provided what support he could, until his flagging health prevented him from doing more.

Olson, who had recently resigned from a promising political career in the Roosevelt administration to begin his career as a poet, still lived in Washington, D.C., after the war and visited Pound at St. Elizabeths. "The K," the early poem in which he publicly tenders his resignation from politics ("Take, then, my answer . . ."), not only declares the continuity of his public commitments ("The affairs of men remain a chief concern") but also posits the importance of place as well as the cyclical nature of change ("There! is a tide in the affairs of men to discern").[36] In light of his focus on the role of political art, Pound's ideas and conversation proved unsurprisingly inimical to Olson's liberalism, and he told Creeley bluntly in the summer of 1950 that his "big struggle, after the decision to leave politics (THE K), was to leave Ez" (*CC1*, p. 136). The praise Olson offers in "GrandPa, Goodbye," the essay that officially records his decision to "leave Ez," is qualified, ambivalent: while Olson finds *The Cantos* overly personal and even nostalgic, he also asserts that Pound himself was "an extraordinary ear of an era, and did the listening for a whole time, the sharpest sort of listening, from Dante down. (I think of Bill Williams' remark: 'It's the best damned ear ever born to listen to this language!')" (*COPr*, p. 146). Creeley, too, established a correspondence with Pound at St. Elizabeths, first ostensibly through Dorothy Pound and then directly with the incarcerated poet (who, for a time, was signing his letters "Anon E. Mouse"). Creeley did not elect to "leave Ez" after Olson's strident fashion, although his real ambivalence is evident in a letter to Cid Corman that embraces the "man who pushed prosody in specific uses" and "who demanded Joyce, Williams, Eliot, etc. should be READ" but cautions against the "man who delights in conspiracy / & the resulting superiorities," whom "one sd damn well stay clear of," concluding that he is describing "A tightrope granted / but one you have to walk."[37] In Creeley's "have to" the senses of both need and inevitability are deeply felt.

Olson's commitment to renewal, to change as evolution or revolution, is a focal issue even in his earliest open verse experimentation. "The Kingfishers," written in 1949, is a both sustained and overt meditation on this relation, beginning with the universal and ahistorical proposition paraphrased from Heraclitus, "What does not change / is the will to change." In Olson's usage a slash becomes a symbol that marks not a line break but "a pause so light it hardly separates the words" (*COPr*, p. 245). To develop a means of punctuation that separates sounds without either affecting the semantic meaning of the line or slowing its progress is crucial, because, in a projective poem, "one perception must must must MOVE, INSTANTER, ON ANOTHER!" (*COPr*, p. 240). Precise and regulated typewriter composition – which requires monospaced type with an augmented range of punctuation marks – affords the poet for the first time "the stave and bar that a musician has had," and the projective writer is therefore able to "indicate exactly the breath, the pauses, the suspensions even of syllables, the juxtapositions even of parts of phrases" (*COPr*, p. 245). Musicality here is more than a convenient analogy; the achieved ability to record the music of speech without recourse to the devices of rhyme and meter is central to Olson's theory of projective verse. While the poems may be pedagogical or didactic, the knowledge that Olson seeks to transmit is absolutely not available in facts alone and is antithetical to ornamentation and fancy. It depends on a repeatable performance that is derived from the acts of the body rigorously listening to its voice and transcribing the syllables and lines meticulously on the page. As Olson himself emphasizes, the "personal and instantaneous" recording of "the meaning and the breathing" is what enables "the already projective nature of verse as the sons of Pound and Williams are practicing it" (*COPr*, p. 246).

Olson's long and insistently active poem *Maximus* is an epic of the local, "Root person in root place," and it is concerned with an isolated conjunction of perceptions, concepts, and events that can be brought together only by the imagination of the poet (*MP*, p. 16). This conjunction animates the projective poem. Its operation is powerfully revealed in "Letter 3," a poem that elucidates the particular sense of locality that drives the epic. The root here is literal, that of the tansy plant, which is given at the outset as "Tansy buttons, tansy / for my city / Tansy for their noses" (*MP*, p. 13). However, the concept of the local in *Maximus*'s Gloucester is a condition of the possibility presented by the harbor and the sea and, as such, does not preclude an idea of mobility. Tansy is, in fact, a figure for both rootedness and mobility, because it simultaneously characterizes Gloucester as a particular place from which to sing yet also as one to which the singer (and the herb) are not native. As Olson recalls, tansy was brought to the area in an accident of commerce on the bottom of sacks, and its disappearance from the place was "due to more efficient mowers, and the desire (like blacktop) to have anything smooth and of one sort or character," which prompts the poet to "celebrate TANSY MORE THAN BEFORE."[38] Formerly common in Gloucester and rare elsewhere, tansy is reminiscent of the more familiar goldenrod; it has extremely limited commercial use and is in no conventional sense important, which is exactly what renders it an ideal repository of cultural value for Olson. The pungent herb becomes indistinguishable from the smell of freedom, "of all owners," "of all of us," which is expressly opposed to slavery and the commercialism of "mu-sick": the object assumes value because its referent is known and mutually prized, unlike "those who use words cheap, who use us cheap." Even when the young Olsonian speaker – here distinguished from Olson's "Tyrian" (one source for this compound hero is the second century A.D. philosopher Maximus of Tyre) – as a boy, newly arrived in Gloucester, rolled in tansy from Cressy's Beach on Freshwater Cove "and didn't know it was tansy," he did appreciate "how rare it was" (compared to Worcester, where he was born) (MP, pp. 13, 14). Knowledge of a locale, like definition, is communal; inclusion in community is synonymous with an ability to recognize it as your own.

Olson's *Maximus*, which essentially agrees with Pound's ideas about vocabulary and pedagogy but with Williams's ideas of syntax and structure, is an American depiction of the Greek polis (city-state), a local setting that is defined by the quality of relations among citizens rather than the fact of a group dwelling in a particular place. This differs clearly from the standard definition of the nation, and Olson's estimation of the difference is clear in *Maximus*'s appeal to the heterogeneous city: "o tansy city, root city / let them not make you / as the nation is." The goal of the poem is to achieve and maintain the unity of polis, a totality mirrored by that of the citizens who compose it, in the coherence that can be revealed by a rare scent, by "a few" who remain sensitive to "a word":

and that word meant to mean not a single thing the least more than
what it does mean (not at all to sell any one anything, to keep them anywhere,
not even
in this rare place.   (*MP*, p. 15)

Although Williams's *Paterson* does not share this emphasis on civic relations, the concept of a long poem dedicated to a single city ("the LOCAL") was as important to Olson as what he derived from Pound's methodology ("the RAG-BAG"), and he clarifies this debt to Corman in 1953:

> Or put it that pat: EP the verb, BILL the NOUN problem. To do. And who, to do. Neither of them: WHAT. That is, EP sounds like what, but what his is is only more methodology, in fact, simply, be political. Politics – not economics – is him. And validly. For (1) politics is a context wide as nature, and not only what we call "politics"; and (2) its essence is will. Which latter – will – is what EP cares abt.[39]

For Creeley the concern about methodology was inextricable from a concern about structure, as he came to recognize following an abortive attempt to read the philosophy of Alfred North Whitehead that had moved Olson so profoundly. As he explains to Pound, his effort to comprehend Whitehead was codified by *The Chinese Written Character* essay: "I'd been reading Whitehead, and came out, finally, with not much more than this sentence, 'The only endurances are structures of activity ...' And I felt it, then, a warping of his own emphases to so isolate it. But here, in the Fenollosa, it is altogether clear and unequivocal (page 60 – 'a true noun, etc.'); it falls precisely to hand."[40]

Forms – or "structures of activity" – are integral to projectivist practice, and particularly so to Creeley's remarkable diverse compositions and collaborations, from early to late. When Creeley, whom Olson ordained as "the figure of Outward" in the dedication of *Maximus*, left Harvard to drive an ambulance for the American Field Service in Burma, he took with him copies of *The Wedge* and *The Cantos*. These were happy choices. Yet achival research led George Butterick to realize that "much of Creeley's earliest verse is poetry aching toward definition," because the poet disarticulated the lines of the verse he wrote in the late 1940s that was composed in regular stanzas – for example, "Still Life or" and "Sanine to Leda" – revising that work "for *Le Fou*, his first collection, in accordance with his understanding of poetics as they had begun to emerge from the discussion with Olson underway."[41] The words remain virtually unchanged, as these 1940s poems were recast from conventionally closed forms to open ones, and Creeley's projective practice continued to develop through the 1950s into the 1960s. The poet Robert Grenier puts a point on this observation when he declares – in a piece called "I HATE SPEECH," published in the first issue of *This* – that "'PROJECTIVE VERSE' IS **PIECES** ON," suggesting that the projective element of Creeley's writing dominates in the 1968 volume *Pieces* and everything after.[42] Creeley neatly sums up the force of this development as personal revelation: "Sometime in the mid-sixties I grew inexorably bored with the tidy containment of clusters of words on single pieces of paper called 'poems' – 'this will really get them, wrap it up. . . . ' I could see nothing in my life nor those of others adjacent that supported this single hits theory."[43] Of the fresh seriality of *Pieces*, Creeley recalls how a shift from composing on the typewriter to *"scribbling"* in notebooks of various sizes opened up "many senses of possibility" because "such notebooks accumulated the writing and they made no decisions about it – it was all there, in whatever state it occurred, everything from addresses to moralistic self-advising, to such notes as I now find in the smallest and first of them":

> This size page forces the
> damn speciously gnomic
> sans need for same
>   – it
>   it –[44]

The point, for Creeley, is that this provides access to "the truth, however unreal," a more accurate and meaningful representation of experience that is not only personal but also public and communal. This transformation of writing is one also of thinking about when the process "began to lose its specific edges, its singleness of occurrence, and I worked to be open to the casual, the commonplace, that which collected itself. The world transformed to bits of paper, torn words, 'it/it.' Its continuity became again physical" (*RCE*, p. 575). The lines that open *Pieces* describe the structure as well as the purpose of the new process poem:

> As real as thinking
> wonders created
> by the possibility –
>
> forms. A period
> at the end of a sentence
> which
>
> began *it was*
> into a present,
> a presence
>
> saying
> something
> as it goes.   (*RCP1*, p. 379)

This combination of qualities – definite and indefinite, present and absent, intimate and impersonal, developing and completed – is captured by a pronoun that is variously anticipatory, deictic, and exclamatory. "It" stands in as an abstract concrete, an unrestrained order. That is what Creeley strives to present, beginning with a proposition in the past tense, *"it was,"* and then defining, modifying, and reifying it as "it goes" into the present.

Creeley attests that the very "intent of the poem" is "a process of definition" and explicitly attributes his sense of the revelatory nature of the art to Williams's comment in the *Autobiography* that "the poet thinks with his poem, in that lies his thought, and that in itself is the profundity."[45] A poet insistently of the local – rather than the "small" or "modest" – he is compelled by ideas of range and perception and thinks about the open field in terms of its boundaries. This becomes the source of measure as well as the value of chance in any complex locality: the "unequivocal order" to which poetry obtains, and by which activity the poet can "as Charles Olson says, come into the world" (*RCE*, pp. 486, 488). One limit case for such a world is available in the "so sparely present" high desert of New Mexico, a place that, as Creeley approvingly quotes, "is less 'nature' than a concept, a place that swallows up boundaries" (*RCE*, p. 441). The spare, tight, irregular couplets of "For John Duff" assess and critique the place the poet professes to wish to leave: "not a tourist's paradise," "not the solar / energy capital // of the world, not," in the harsh light of day, "your place in the sun" (*RCP2*, p. 169). The night, however, offers other possibilities, recalling conversation with a sculptor (Duff) about the shapes, forms, colors, and company that define a place. A place, and its history, is of the mind; the closest rhyme offered by any couplet in the poem – "a *menhir* – / remember" – makes this point insistently. The *menhir*, here a boundary stone near an arroyo, marks the inexplicable prehistory of culture or making that persists without clear purpose beyond its existence, which is given and is sufficient. For Creeley in the New Mexican desert, this rhyme raises a question about the relation of local culture to myth, history, and, a favorite term, *company*:

> a *menhir* –
> remember
>
> that oar
> you could screw into
>
> ground, say,
> here I'll build a city?
>
> No way.   (*RCP2*, p. 170)

The vision of "a quiet // grey column" elicits a reference to the well-made oar that Tiresias had prophesied that Odysseus (restored as the king of Ithaca) must carry inland until its function was no longer discernible by the locals, at which time he would plant it and there establish new residence. In rejecting this prophecy, the poem flatly rejects the literal and concomitantly literary referent as well. A combination of the concrete and the abstract, the spatial and the temporal, and a continuous present and an inevitable (but not yet) past instead provokes a discovery that is central to the "it" of Creeley's projectivist poetics:

> And this *it*
> you gave us:
>
> *here*
> *is all the wonder,*
>
> *there*
> *is all there is.*   (*RCP2*, p. 172)

★

To the extent that they are defined stylistically, the key writers of the projectivist and Objectivist generations have long been associated with Pound and Williams but not with one another. The generations are as uneasily close to the modernist masters as they are uneasily removed from one another. Explicitly unconcerned with issues of originality and influence, Creeley was proud of the company he kept and had reason to claim that Objectivism – especially the work of his friend Zukofsky – forged a continuity between Pound and Williams and the East Coast projectivist poets.[46] Yet Zukofsky conceived of the connection quite differently, complaining in a letter to Edward Dahlberg, Olson's predecessor at Black Mountain College, that "Projective Verse," which he derides as Olson's "Projectile," derived directly (if imperfectly) from his own poetic theories in the February 1931 Objectivist issue of *Poetry* magazine.[47] "If anything," he alleges, Olson's manifesto was "a steal," and it was "bungled up" in the process. Olson gives surprisingly little serious thought to the Objectivists in "Projective Verse" or more generally. He acknowledges almost incidentally that "it is no accident that Pound and Williams both were involved variously in a movement which got called 'objectivism,'" attempts to shelve it as a (formerly) "necessary quarrel … with 'subjectivism,'" and then proposes "objectism" as "a more valid formulation for present use" (*COPr*, p. 247). Although it is uncertain whether Zukofsky's charge of plagiarism is warranted, he was surely justified in challenging this blunt misunderstanding and curt dismissal of Objectivism.

The development and practice of open form poetics does give rise to questions of influence and originality. On these grounds, Perloff has criticized Olson more comprehensively than any other major critic, in an article that takes its title from Olson's repudiation of Pound and Williams as "inferior

predecessors." Here she persuasively demonstrates that "Projective Verse,"
the central demonstration piece, mainly paraphrases theories established by
Pound and concludes that it "is thus not as revolutionary as Olson's admirers
have professed it to be."[48] Ralph Maud works to ameliorate the appearance of
Olson being "arrogant and ungrateful" by recuperating the context in which
the attribution "inferior" was used in a literal sense of what is "below or underneath … as a scaffold," suggesting that any meaningful predecessors (including precedent versions of the self) may be understood as a means of giving
"backing from the past, which can be considered a layer under the present."[49]
In any case, few now would disagree that the practitioners of projective verse
are rightly known for amplifying and extending – or, more dismissively, for
imitating – the innovations that distinguished Pound's and Williams's modernism. Such derivations, in *Maximus*, are frequent, important, and wholly
unembarrassed: borrowings and allusions from Williams's and Pound's work
are abundant.

Given Olson's and Creeley's propensity to affirm – if also to qualify –
literary allegiances, the question of influence may be intriguing, but it is
not as damning as it might otherwise seem. When Gerard Malanga asked
Olson shortly before his death whether he could have written *Maximus* without having known Williams's and Pound's work, the poet replied, "That's
like asking me how I could have written without having read."[50] This is, of
course, neither a statement of value (relative or absolute) nor an admission that his work has nothing new to offer; to the contrary, Olson intimates that *Maximus* "was created to put me out of business, as well as my
friend, the lovely Dr. Williams, as well as Mr. Pound."[51] The evidence of
an Objectivist struggle to be recognized as the generation that followed
Pound and Williams, entirely left out of Olson's account, became apparent
when the projectivist generation of 1950 was gaining notoriety. In "Third
Wave Objectivism," Ron Silliman argues that the return of the Objectivists
to active publication was in part inspired by the very public successes of
the projectivist writers and a desire not to be eclipsed by those successes.[52]
Rachel Blau DuPlessis explains this historical argument with reference to
Silliman's claims, positing that a second phase of Objectivist writing after
1929–1935 is defined by the very absence of Objectivist poets, "which created
an extremism in the New American Poets of the 1950s as they tried to formulate an 'open-form, speech-based' poetics that would connect them to
Williams and Pound."[53]

Objectivist writing is conventionally understood to be about writing itself,
and projectivist writing is about the act of performance, which emphasizes

speech, or breath and body "telling a brain," as Olson puts it (*COPr*, p. 243). This appears to present a relatively clear choice to subsequent writers, whose preference shapes the contours of literary history – but the choice is not so simple. In 1929 Zukofsky tried to express to Williams the risks of collaboration both within and across generations: "What bothers you I suppose is that [Pound is] always wanting to button your overcoat – as you say – but after all he has a beard, and that's his privilege. Somehow my allegiance – if I have any – is all your old friend's after all."[54] By 1950 Williams had a beard too, and Olson, whose professed allegiance ran the other way, then proposed to him that the projectivists must "love, not imitate, you and ez."[55] When influence is at stake, such choices are fluid, complex, often misleading, and just as often misunderstood.

The difficulty even to identify the key members of the East Coast projectivist generation beyond the Olson-Creeley core exacerbates this misunderstanding. Spending time at Black Mountain College is not a useful criterion for inclusion, because some of those who were there fit the model less easily than, say, Levertov or Eigner, who never so much as visited the place. Style is more telling. In "Maximus, to Himself" the "wind / and water man" sits at the harbor and speaks of the as-yet "undone business" of apprehending "the known," which cannot be discovered but must be given, as "a life, love, and from one man / the world" (*MP*, pp. 57, 56). (This one man is Creeley, who expressed the sense of the "world" as, etymologically, the span of a life [*RCE*, p. 66].) He entertains questions about his superiority, his process, and his contribution, but not about his presence, "with the sea / stretching out / from my feet," or "the stem of me," which circumscribes place and polis (*MP*, p. 57). This relation of presence to projection allows for an expression of cultural power as a measurement of the song and the singing self, as Maximus relates in "Letter 9":

> I measure my song,
> measure the sources of my song,
> measure me, measure
> my forces.   (*MP*, p. 48)

Olson's image of projection is usefully complicated by the actual demands of the breath and body when the facility of those qualities can no longer be taken for granted. If stylistic consonance rather than proximity defines the group, Eigner can help. His best poems press projectivist principles about form and content – about the syllable and the line, the ear and the breath – to their logical limits. This is because, although Eigner was palsied from hard birth, his

poems are not merely a vocal prosthesis, an expression of his physical limitations. Eigner's emphasis on slowness, parataxis, and the motion of individual
phonemes resembles the movement of the triadic line for Williams and the
physical dimensions of the page for Pound's *Cantos*.

Eigner's work clarifies the relation of song, sources, and forces as well as
the measurement that corroborates them. In his poems, Eigner consciously
aims to produce "a piece of language in verse, measured, deliberated," that is
really "a stretch, process of thinking, one thought really attained, in a second
or longer time, leading to another, a math of everyday life, penetrating or
anyway evaluative."[56] Privileging intensity rather than alacrity, Eigner uses the
"immediacy and force" of poetic composition to achieve projective thought
in which, as Olson specifies, "our management of daily reality as of the daily
work" gets on.[57] Consider, in this regard, what may be his most famous poem,
"Again dawn," from *another time in fragments*. It ends:

<pre>
                    nowhere

          empty the blue

                stars

      our summer
                    on the ground
          like last night another
                        time

            in fragments[58]
</pre>

Here the "invisible whiteness" of the sky (invoked earlier in the same poem)
occludes the blue of the stars, simultaneously presented as center of the text
yet absented from it, to fragment time and displace memory. This is not, however, any conventional act of preservation; Eigner's fragments are not being
shored against the ruin of anyone or anything. These fragments, which for
Duncan encompass "melodies of perception" that "raise the very body of a
world whose reality we sought in poetry," cannot stand in to protect or salvage
an integral experience, precisely because they are the experience.[59] For Charles
Bernstein, this "other" time "extends and deepens the always present present,
created by the algebra of constellated (or multiplied) moments of perception,"
resulting in "a kind of hyperperceptual poetry."[60] These stars stand as the only
experience available to us, the one witnessed at the center of the poem, the
dropping, passing out, and emptying that, together, "we saw." Thus a season,
like a night, is memorable only for its evanescence and its repeatability, and
the space-field (here "nowhere") of the modern gives way once again to what

Olson called "space & its live air" ("Again dawn") (*CC5*, p. 49). In 1993 this poem was carved into the façade of the Berkeley University Art Museum.

Together Pound and Williams offered future generations of American poets access to a spirit of radical innovation as well as a precedent for effecting change, but they also provided distinctive theories about how vocabulary, syntax, lineation, rhythm, and even history and thought operate in a (late) modern poem. What Pound and Williams made possible for these writers and those who followed – Language writers of the late twentieth century and conceptual writers of the early twenty-first – is a particular way of understanding poetic language, not as a mode of communication but as a material practice pitched between speech and music. This, as Kenneth Goldsmith intriguingly argues, is finally the end of modernism and the beginning of something else, something conceptual and apparently postmodern: "Real speech, when paid close attention to, forces us to realize how little one needs to do in order to write. Just paying attention to what is right under our noses – framing, transcription, and preservation – is enough." Goldsmith insistently iterates the mantra "I LOVE SPEECH" throughout an essay dedicated to "methods of disorientation" that require us to "reimagine our normative relationship to language," marking a new return to speech, as opposed to writing or composition, even.[61] This radical shift positions experimental predecessors such as Pound, Williams, and the projectivists nearer the main line of American writing, and it makes their experiments appear to be conventionally "literary" in the process. It also demands that we ask whether that is, in the final analysis, a more interesting place to be.

Notes

1. William Carlos Williams, *Imaginations* (New York: New Directions, 1970), p. 26. This collection will be cited in the text as *IM*.
2. Ezra Pound and William Carlos Williams, *Pound/Williams: Selected Letters of Ezra Pound and William Carlos Williams*, ed. Hugh Witemeyer (New York: New Directions, 1996), p. 31.
3. Pound and Williams, *Pound/Williams*, pp. 42, 44.
4. William Carlos Williams, *Collected Poems: Volume I, 1909–1939*, ed. A. Walton Litz and Christopher MacGowan (New York: New Directions, 1986), p. 3. This collection will be cited in the text as *WCPI*.
5. Ezra Pound, *Literary Essays of Ezra Pound*, ed. T. S. Eliot (New York: New Directions, 1968), p. 3. This collection will be cited in the text as *LE*.
6. Hugh Kenner, *The Pound Era* (Berkeley: University of California Press, 1971), p. 191.

7. Robert von Hallberg, *Charles Olson: The Scholar's Art* (Cambridge, Mass.: Harvard University Press, 1978), p. 208. This volume will be cited in the text as *COSA*.

8. Ezra Pound, "Praefatio aut Tumulus Cimicium," in Ezra Pound (ed.), *Active Anthology* (London: Faber and Faber, 1933), p. 400.

9. Ezra Pound, "An Object," in Richard Sieburth (ed.), *Poems and Translations* (New York: Library of America, 2003), p. 236. This collection will be cited in the text as *PT*.

10. Ezra Pound, *Gaudier-Brzeska: A Memoir* (New York: New Directions, 1970), p. 84. This volume will be cited in the text as *GB*.

11. Ezra Pound, *Personae: The Shorter Poems*, ed. Lea Baechler and A. Walton Litz (New York: New Directions, 1990), p. 251.

12. Ernest Fenollosa, *The Chinese Written Character as a Medium for Poetry*, ed. Ezra Pound (San Francisco: City Lights, 1936), pp. 12, 7.

13. Fenollosa, *Chinese Written Character*, pp. 16–17, 22, 9.

14. Charles Olson and Robert Creeley, *The Complete Correspondence*, 10 vols., ed. George F. Butterick (vols. 1–8) and Richard Blevins (vols. 9–10) (Santa Barbara, Calif.: Black Sparrow Press, 1980–1994), vol. 9, pp. 229–30. This collection will be cited in the text as *CC1–CC10*.

15. Hugh Kenner, *Gnomon: Essays on Contemporary Literature* (New York: Obolensky, 1958), pp. 58–59.

16. Barry Magid and Hugh Witemeyer (eds.), *William Carlos Williams and Charles Tomlinson: A Transatlantic Connection* (New York: Peter Lang, 1999), p. 95.

17. William Carlos Williams, *Collected Poems*. Vol. II, *1939–1962*, ed. Christopher MacGowan (New York: New Directions, 1988), p. 55. This collection will be cited in the text as *WCPII*.

18. Guy Davenport, "Scholia and Conjectures for Charles Olson's 'The Kingfishers,'" *Boundary 2* 2 (1973–1975), pp. 252–53.

19. William Carlos Williams, *Selected Essays* (New York: New Directions, 1954), p. 109. This collection will be cited in the text as *SE*.

20. Ezra Pound, *The Cantos of Ezra Pound* (New York: New Directions, 1995), pp. 53, 264. This volume will be cited in the text as *C*.

21. Ezra Pound, *Antheil and the Treatise on Harmony* (1924; New York: Da Capo, 1968), p. 20.

22. Pound and Williams, *Pound/Williams*, p. 139.

23. Louis Zukofsky, "An Objective," in Mark Scroggins (ed.), *Prepositions+: The Collected Critical Essays*, rev. and expanded ed. (Middletown, Conn.: Wesleyan University Press, 2000), pp. 12–13.

24. Peter Makin, *Pound's Cantos* (London: Allen and Unwin, 1985), p. 205.

25. Ezra Pound, *ABC of Reading* (1933; New York: New Directions, 1960), p. 201.

26. Carroll F. Terrell, *A Companion to The Cantos of Ezra Pound* (Berkeley: University of California Press, 1993), p. 190.

27. Hugh Kenner, "More on the Seven Lakes Canto," *Paideuma* 2 (1973), p. 46.

28. Pound, *ABC of Reading*, pp. 199–200.

29. Charles Olson, *Collected Prose*, ed. Donald Allen and Benjamin Friedlander (Berkeley: University of California Press, 1997), p. 239. This collection will be cited in the text as *COPr*.

30. Charles Olson, *The Maximus Poems*, ed. George F. Butterick (Berkeley: University of California Press, 1983), p. 39. This volume will be cited in the text as *MP*.

31. Magid and Witemeyer (eds.), *William Carlos Williams and Charles Tomlinson*, p. 95.

32. William Carlos Williams, *Paterson*, ed. Christopher MacGowan (New York: New Directions, 1992), p. 3. This volume will be cited in the text as *P*.

33. Walter Sutton, "A Visit with William Carlos Williams," *Minnesota Review* 1 (1961), pp. 309–24, 310.

34. Denise Levertov, *New and Selected Essays* (New York: New Directions, 1992), pp. 25, 23. This collection will be cited in the text as *NSE*.

35. Sutton, "A Visit with William Carlos Williams," p. 311.

36. Charles Olson, *The Collected Poems of Charles Olson*, ed. George F. Butterick (Berkeley: University of California Press, 1997), p. 14.

37. Robert Creeley to Cid Corman, July 17, 1950, Robert Creeley correspondence, The Lilly Library, Indiana University, Bloomington, Ind. Reproduced courtesy of the Lilly Library, and by permission of the Robert Creeley Estate.

38. George F. Butterick, *A Guide to The Maximus Poems of Charles Olson* (Berkeley: University of California Press, 1980), pp. 22–23.

39. Charles Olson, *Letters for Origin: 1950–1956*, ed. Albert Glover (New York: Cape Goliard Press, 1970), p. 129.

40. Robert Creeley to Ezra Pound, September 28, 1951, Robert Creeley Papers, Stanford University, Department of Special Collections and University Archives – Manuscript Division, Stanford, Calif. Reproduced courtesy of Stanford University Libraries, and by permission of the Robert Creeley Estate.

41. George F. Butterick, "Robert Creeley and the Tradition," in Carroll F. Terrell (ed.), *Robert Creeley: The Poet's Workshop* (Orono, Maine: National Poetry Foundation, 1984), pp. 120–21.

42. Robert Grenier, "I HATE SPEECH," *This* 1 (1971), n.p.

43. Robert Creeley, *Collected Essays* (Berkeley: University of California Press, 1989), p. 574. This collection will be cited in the text as *RCE*.

44. Creeley, *Collected Essays*, pp. 535, 536; Robert Creeley, *Collected Poems*, 2 vols. (Berkeley: University of California Press, 1982, 2006), vol. 1, p. 391. Volumes 1 and 2 of *Collected Poems* will be cited in the text as *RCP1* and *RCP2*, respectively.

45. Creeley, *Collected Essays*, p. 473; William Carlos Williams, *The Autobiography of William Carlos Williams* (1951; New York: New Directions, 1967), pp. 390–91.

46. Robert Creeley, *Contexts of Poetry: Interviews 1961–1971*, ed. Donald Allen (Bolinas, Calif.: Four Seasons, 1973), p. 14.

47. Sandra Kumamoto Stanley, *Louis Zukofsky and the Transformation of a Modern American Poetics* (Berkeley: University of California Press, 1994), p. 147.

48. Marjorie Perloff, "Charles Olson and the 'Inferior Predecessors': 'Projective Verse' Revisited," *ELH* 40 (1973), pp. 285–306, 288.

49. Ralph Maud, *Charles Olson at the Harbor: A Biography* (Vancouver, B.C.: Talon, 2008), p. 169.

50. Gerard Malanga and Charles Olson, "The Art of Poetry XII," *Paris Review* 49 (1970), pp. 176–205, 198.

51. Malanga and Olson, "The Art of Poetry XII," p. 197.

52. Ron Silliman, "Third Phase Objectivism," *Paideuma* 10 (1981), pp. 85–89.

53. George Oppen, *Selected Letters*, ed. Rachel Blau DuPlessis (Durham, N.C.: Duke University Press, 1990), p. 364.

54. William Carlos Williams and Louis Zukofsky, *The Correspondence of William Carlos Williams and Louis Zukofsky*, ed. Barry Ahern (Middletown, Conn.: Wesleyan University Press, 2003), p. 39.

55. Charles Olson to William Carlos Williams, April 21, 1950; quoted in James E. B. Breslin, "Introduction: The Presence of Williams in Contemporary Poetry," in William Carlos Williams, *Something to Say: William Carlos Williams on Younger Poets*, ed. James E. B. Breslin (New York: New Directions, 1985), p. 28.

56. Larry Eigner, *Areas Lights Heights: Writings 1954–1989*, ed. Benjamin Friedlander (New York: Roof Books, 1989), p. 25.

57. Eigner, *Areas Lights Heights*, p. 135; Olson, *Collected Prose*, p. 240.

58. Larry Eigner, *another time in fragments* (London: Fulcrum Press, 1967), p. 2.

59. Robert Duncan, jacket note for Eigner, *another time in fragments*, n.p.

60. Charles Bernstein, "How Empty Is My Bread Pudding," in Louis Armand (ed.), *Contemporary Poetics* (Evanston, Ill.: Northwestern University Press, 2007), p. 9.

61. Kenneth Goldsmith, "Postlude: I Love Speech," in Marjorie Perloff and Craig Dworkin (eds.), *The Sound of Poetry/The Poetry of Sound* (Chicago: University of Chicago Press, 2009), pp. 285–90, 286.

Chapter 31

Langston Hughes and His World

DAVID CHIONI MOORE

African American poetry flourished in the early twentieth century – key figures included James Weldon Johnson, Claude McKay, Jean Toomer, and Countee Cullen – giving African American poets a more established but still marked presence, seen not as American poets (who were Negro) but as Negro poets. Much the same obtained in African American poetry's next major florescence, in Black Arts–era writers like Amiri Baraka, Nikki Giovanni, and the elder Gwendolyn Brooks. Their markedness, or status as an inevitably raced collective, can be seen in a 1993 precursor to the present volume, Jay Parini's *Columbia History of American Poetry*. Parini's *History* offers single-author chapters for Longfellow, Dickinson, Whitman, Poe, Frost, Pound, Eliot, Stevens, Williams, Crane, and Auden – all there individually as poets, but not as whites. In contrast, the volume assigns the seven African American poets named previously, plus Langston Hughes, to three chapters set aside for black poets: "Early African American Poetry," "The Poetry of the Harlem Renaissance," and "The Black Arts Poets."[1] "Official" recognition that African American poets could stand unclustered and be seen as integral rather than supplementary to "general" or white American traditions arrived a decade later in Sacvan Bercovitch's eight-volume *Cambridge History of American Literature*, whose chapter "Langston Hughes: The Color of Modernism" argued for the individual importance of at least one raced poet, and for his position in a seemingly unraced literary movement.[2]

Thus the present chapter, part of a next-stage consideration of African American poetry, is titled "Langston Hughes and His World." This title suggests many things. "World," for one, is a capacious term, far larger than (for example) "circle," and it includes but exceeds the United States. "World" is also not "era" or "age" and so argues that Hughes's long career is framed as well by space as it is by time. "World," too, is in the singular, reflecting Hughes's conviction, and the evidence of his work, that Harlem piano players, Georgia mothers, conscript Moors, Spanish Negroes in the cane fields, and even Chinese workers in the foundries can all find voice in one poetic oeuvre. The title's "his" suggests not that Hughes owned the world, but that he considered it his artistic home. In that broad light, this chapter surveys and assesses the poet Langston Hughes in the context of his many worldly links. More specifically, it proposes four frameworks through which Hughes and his many diverse works, especially his poems, can productively be viewed: the bardic-demotic, left-internationalist / Afro-planetary, professional, and sublimated-closeted frameworks.

The great African American poet and man of letters James Langston Hughes was born February 1, 1902, in Joplin, Missouri, into an uncertain future.[3] Although descended on his mother's side from distinguished African American activists and leaders, Hughes was abandoned early by his father, who hated U.S. racism and became a prosperous if cold-hearted businessman and landowner in Mexico. Hughes was likewise not well cared for by his mother. His childhood was spent living with different relatives (and sometimes his mother) in Missouri, Kansas, and finally Ohio, where he attended Cleveland's burgeoning multicultural Central High School, graduating in 1920 as the class poet. Sent by his father to study engineering at Columbia University in New York – an unusual distinction for an African American of that era – Hughes dropped out after one year and took up work as a messboy on an ill-maintained freight ship that plied the coast of Africa. In his first published autobiography, Hughes said he tossed all his books overboard as the ship left New York, but he confessed in a draft that he had kept one volume: Whitman's *Leaves of Grass*. After a brief return to the United States, Hughes shipped out again for Europe, where he spent several vagabond months before repairing again to New York. Throughout the 1920s, Hughes divided his time among Europe, Harlem (the great center of Negro cultural life in New York), Washington, D.C., and the small but distinguished historically black Lincoln University in Pennsylvania, where he received his B.A. in 1929. (In deference to Hughes's lifelong usage and self-identification, this chapter will often use the respectful term "Negro," preferred in American speech through at least Martin Luther King, Jr.)

Hughes saw himself as a poet from a young age. Although he claimed an accidental origin for this vocation (he was the only Negro in his grade school class, and because Negroes were supposed to have rhythm, he was elected class poet), he self-identified primarily as a poet (or a "social poet") from his late teens until his death. He published his first and eternally most famous poem, "The Negro Speaks of Rivers," in the W. E. B. Du Bois–edited official magazine of the NAACP, the *Crisis*, in June 1921, when he was just nineteen. During the

1920s, Hughes rapidly became a major figure in the Harlem Renaissance, publishing a growing body of verse in prominent black and white periodicals, and enjoying emerging connections with noted black and white figures such as the philosopher Alain Locke and the litterateur Carl Van Vechten. All this led to the publication of Hughes's first volume, *The Weary Blues*, in 1926, and his second, *Fine Clothes to the Jew*, in 1927, by the young yet elite firm of Alfred A. Knopf.[4]

As a rough characterization, African American poetry in the few decades prior to Hughes came in two main styles: a genteel tradition, composed largely in the staid, formulaic rhyme schemes found in mainstream white poetry of that time, and a "dialect" tradition, rendered in a caricatured version of African American peasant speech, which, often double voiced, wryly explored the race relations of the day. Many poets wrote both; some were dismayed that the latter sold better, as when Paul Dunbar complained that the world preferred "a jingle in a broken tongue."[5] Themes and subjects ranged across slavery, freedom, dignity, resistance, uplift, song, race, the South, and Christian figures and motifs, including suffering, redemption, deliverance, the cross, Daniel, Judas, Cain, and Christ.

Important poets of this era, such as James Weldon Johnson, Claude McKay, and, intensely but briefly, the modernist Jean Toomer, began to surpass predecessor traditions. Johnson (1871–1938) was by turns a teacher, lawyer, song lyricist, U.S. diplomat in Venezuela and Nicaragua, novelist, and scholar. His poems richly invoked African American folk and spiritual musical traditions, as in "O Black and Unknown Bards":

> O black and unknown bards of long ago,
> How came your lips to touch the sacred fire?
> How, in your darkness, did you come to know
> The power and beauty of the minstrel's lyre?
>
> . . .
>
> Who heard great "Jordan roll"? Whose starward eye
> Saw chariot "swing low"? And who was he
> That breathed that comforting, melodic sigh,
> "Nobody knows de trouble I see"?[6]

His 1900 poem "Lift Every Voice and Sing," later set to music by his brother, the composer John Rosamond Johnson, is known to this day as the Negro (or black or African American) national anthem. No reader of American poetry could then have anticipated the recitation of its last stanza, 109 years later, at the start of the Reverend Joseph Lowery's benediction for Barack Obama's presidential inauguration. Claude McKay (1889–1948), a novelist and activist as well as poet, was Jamaica born but a U.S. resident and international traveler from his early twenties to his death. After two 1912 books of poems in Jamaican English, McKay moved to the United States and began to combine conventional verse forms in standard English with a franker, more militant voice and new urban settings. His critique of prostitution in "Harlem Shadows" speaks bitterly of "dusky, half-clad girls of tired feet" who trudge, "thinly shod, from street to street," to "bend and barter at desire's call." His bold 1919 sonnet "If We Must Die," first published in the radical magazine *Liberator*, galvanized a generation of African American readers. It began by asserting that "If we must die, let it not be like hogs / Hunted and penned in an inglorious spot" and ended thus: "Like men we'll face the murderous, cowardly pack, / Pressed to the wall, dying, but fighting back!"[7]

Langston Hughes arrived on this scene in 1921 at age nineteen, his best poems suffused with unusually mature insight and historical and geographic scope. We must reproduce his first-published and most enduring poem, "The Negro Speaks of Rivers," in full:

> I've known rivers:
> I've known rivers ancient as the world and older than the
>   flow of human blood in human veins.
>
> My soul has grown deep like the rivers.
>
> I bathed in the Euphrates when dawns were young.
> I built my hut near the Congo and it lulled me to sleep.
> I looked upon the Nile and raised the pyramids above it.
> I heard the singing of the Mississippi when Abe Lincoln
>   went down to New Orleans, and I've seen its muddy
>   bosom turn all golden in the sunset.
>
> I've known rivers:
> Ancient, dusky rivers.
>
> My soul has grown deep like the rivers.[8]

Other early Hughes poems offered a keen sense of voice beyond his own, in both age and gender, such as the celebrated "Mother to Son" from 1922:

> So boy, don't you turn back.
> Don't you set down on the steps
> 'Cause you finds it's kinder hard.
> Don't you fall now –
> For I'se still goin', honey,
> I'se still climbin',
> And life for me ain't been no crystal stair.[9]

As a formal matter, Hughes's earliest published verse owed much to his acknowledged models Sandburg and Whitman. Thus, although acutely attuned to meter, form, and sound, Hughes shunned the high-culture English verse conventions still favored by others such as Countee Cullen and McKay. As the twenties wore on, his work steered to the adaptation of African American song forms, especially the blues – as here in "Bound No'th Blues" from 1926:

> Goin' down de road, Lawd,
> Goin' down de road.
> Down de road, Lawd,
> Way, way down de road.
> Got to find somebody
> To help me carry dis load.[10]

Thematically, Hughes's first decade of published work ranged widely. Dreams loomed large and would remain for his entire career, from his 1923 injunction to "hold fast to dreams"[11] to his 1950s meditations, later invoked by figures from Martin Luther King, Jr., to Barack Obama, on "a dream deferred." Hughes's frank celebration of blackness and Africa ("I am a Negro: / Black as the night is black, / Black like the depths of my Africa"[12]) had few precedents, even if Hughes's positive African image first tended to stereotyped tom-toms and jungle moons. Hughes also added to African American poetry's long-standing confrontation with the rural South by unflinchingly addressing the formerly taboo topic of race mixing, as in this wrenching triply voiced excerpt from his 1927 "Mulatto":

> The scent of pine wood stings the soft night air.
>   *What's the body of your mother?*
> Silver moonlight everywhere.
>   *What's the body of your mother?*
> Sharp pine scent in the evening air.
>   A nigger night,
>   A nigger joy,
>   A little yellow
>   Bastard boy.[13]

Despite all of these varied subjects, Hughes is best remembered for his engagement with the urban Negro North, especially Harlem. His poems robustly portray the dancers, piano players, hustlers, prostitutes, and other "low-down folk" who constituted a new center of gravity in African American life. The title poem of his first volume, *The Weary Blues*, sets its raceless speaker as both auditor and omniscient observer of an iconic Harlem scene:

Thump, thump, thump, went his foot on the floor.
He played a few chords then he sang some more –
   "I got the Weary Blues
   And I can't be satisfied.
   Got the Weary Blues
   And can't be satisfied –
   I ain't happy no mo'
   And I wish that I had died."
And far into the night he crooned that tune.
The stars went out and so did the moon.
The singer stopped playing and went to bed
While the Weary Blues echoed through his head.
He slept like a rock or a man that's dead.[14]

In this and many other poems, Hughes's 1920s were indissolubly linked to the cultural flourishing of the Harlem Renaissance, for which competing terms then included the "New Negro Movement," "New Negro Renaissance," and "Negro Literary Renaissance." Encompassing music, theater, writing, and the visual arts, the Harlem Renaissance captured national attention, including that of white elites. In his memoir *The Big Sea*, Hughes durably termed the era "when the Negro was in vogue."[15] Beyond new voices like Cullen and Hughes, somewhat older poets like Johnson and McKay were key: Johnson was admired for his landmark 1922 anthology *The Book of American Negro Poetry* and his own 1927 collection *God's Trombones*, which did for the Negro sermon what Hughes had done for blues; and McKay, for his 1922 collection *Harlem Shadows* and his 1928 novel *Home to Harlem*.[16] Another new voice, Jean Toomer, was celebrated for his 1923 composite *Cane*, which blended poems, stories, and vignettes and is seen today as a modernist success.[17] Nearly everyone discussed previously, plus others such as W. E. B. Du Bois, Walter White, Anna Julia Cooper, Eric Walrond, Zora Neale Hurston, and Nella Larsen, as well as the electrifyingly controversial pan-Africanist Marcus Garvey, were either born or spent significant time outside the United States.[18]

Against this backdrop, and to invoke the four-part framework outlined early in this chapter – of bardic-demotic, left-internationalist, professional, and closeted-elusive viewpoints – Hughes's 1920s were spent largely in the bardic-demotic mode, in which he spoke primarily of, as, and for the ordinary Negro. Adapting but never mocking common Negro speech, and mobilizing the most vernacular of Negro song forms, Hughes voiced the travails and achievements of his people. Despite his own early Atlantic travels and those of Harlem Renaissance figures around him, the impact of internationalism on

Hughes's poems was still modest: Paris served as something of an imagined refuge, the Afro-diasporic Caribbean remained marginal, and Africa itself, despite Hughes's coastal encounters, was still largely an idea. As for the professional, Hughes was still in his twenties and glad for monetary prizes, white patrons, college scholarships, and a semivagabondish style. In the 1920s, writing was Hughes's life, but not yet his profession.

If Hughes had a poetic rival in the 1920s, it was the NYU- and Harvard-educated Countee Cullen (1903–1946), with his sustained command of historically lauded forms. In "Heritage" he asked, "What is Africa to me: / Copper sun or scarlet sea, / Jungle star or jungle track, / Strong bronzed men, or regal black / ... / Spicy grove, cinnamon tree, / What is Africa to me?"[19] In the protest-focused "From the Dark Tower," Cullen asserted that "We shall not always plant while others reap / The golden increment of bursting fruit, / Not always countenance, abject and mute / That lesser men should hold their brothers cheap."[20] But Cullen's most creative phase lasted less than a decade; his political and social vision was less compelling than that of, for example, McKay; and his brilliance in traditional European forms captured neither the variety of African American speech nor the embrace of its newest literary generation.

A far more demotic (but not bardic) poet, Sterling Brown (1901–1989), is often associated with the Harlem Renaissance, but as a lifelong non–New Yorker and Renaissance skeptic, he embodied an alternative tradition. Although educated at the elite Dunbar High School in Washington, D.C., Williams College, and Harvard, Brown spent most of the rest of his life in or near the American South, studying black folk traditions as a professor at Howard University. Brown's work thus resonates with that of folk-inflected figures ranging from Robert Burns, Carl Sandburg, Zora Neale Hurston, and Alan Lomax to the white poets of the Popular Front. The title poem for Brown's vernacular- and blues-based 1932 volume *Southern Road*, a convict blues, included this:

> Doubleshackled – hunh –
> Guard behin';
> Doubleshackled – hunh –
> Guard behin';
> Ball an' chain, bebby,
> On my min'.
>
> White man tells me – hunh –
> Damn yo' soul;
> White man tells me – hunh –
> Damn yo' soul;

Got no need, bebby,
To be tole.[21]

Brown's alternative tradition, however, sparked little interest among contemporary readers and appeared in book form only after his era's 1920s peak. He thus devoted himself to teaching, scholarship, and commentary but enjoyed a late-life revival, warmly embraced (and freshly published) by poets of the 1970s.

Although Langston Hughes was not a "theoretical" poet, his 1926 essay "The Negro Artist and the Racial Mountain," published in the influential white leftist magazine the *Nation*, became the literary manifesto of the Harlem Renaissance. In it, Hughes criticized the white-aspiring preferences of the Negro middle and upper classes, defended his portraits of "the low-down folks," rejected sterile respectability, and concluded by asserting the right of his generation to "express our dark-skinned selves without fear or shame.... If white people are pleased we are glad. If they are not, it doesn't matter.... If colored people are pleased we are glad. If they are not, their displeasure doesn't matter either. We build our temples for tomorrow, strong as we know how, and we stand on top of the mountain, free within ourselves."[22]

For all the majesty of this declaration – one of Hughes's rare published statements on his writerly profession – Hughes *did* care deeply what his colored readers thought. To be sure, he had a taste, especially in his twenties and thirties, for upsetting pieties, but as an emerging professional, he worked tirelessly to reach ever-wider audiences. Some of this is seen in his substantial work as an anthologizer, discussed subsequently, and in his lifelong commitment to national poetry-reading tours, which emphasized Negro venues. His publisher correspondence contains frequent requests for inexpensive editions he could sell while on the road, and hundreds of his personal letters mention an enclosed gift volume of his verse. Here we see the fusion of the demotic and professional Langston Hughes. In sharp contrast to near-contemporary white modernists like Eliot, Cummings, Stevens, and Pound; the noted black modernist Melvin B. Tolson; or the later African American poet Robert Hayden, almost all of Hughes's nearly 900 published poems could be readily understood by a reader (or listener) of limited formal education. Indeed, one of the best-known moments in Hughesian reception history came in Jonathan Kozol's 1967 critique of American schools, *Death at an Early Age*, which recounted Kozol's firing from a public elementary school in Roxbury, Massachusetts, for assigning his black fourth graders poetry by Hughes.[23] To return to Hughes's "Racial Mountain," Hughes would not have cared if white principals (or Negro parents) *disliked* his poems, but he cared immensely if anyone, especially ordinary readers, were *barred* from coming to his work.

Langston Hughes's 1930s differed sharply from his 1920s and can be characterized as the radical-global phase of both his writing and his life. He gained his first extended exposure to the Francophone and Hispanophone Caribbean with visits to Cuba in 1930 and Haiti in 1931 – spaces he considered brethren within the African diaspora. There he met the Cuban *négrismo* poet Nicolás Guillén and the Haitian indigenist poet, novelist, and ethnologist Jacques Roumain. Hughes translated both into English, and they returned the favor in French and Spanish. Thus by January 1932, at age twenty-nine, Hughes had already traveled to four continents – unprecedented for an African American writer of his era – and, with the 1929 German volume *Afrika Singt*, had appeared in at least four languages.[24] The more he learned about the United States and the black Atlantic, the more he adopted a radical leftist account of the whole world's injustice. In a U.S.-focused mode, his critique of the abuse of religion by the powerful was never stronger than in the riveting poem "Christ in Alabama" (from *Contempo* in 1931), which begins:

> Christ is a Nigger,
> Beaten and black –
> *O, bare your back.*
>
> Mary is His Mother –
> *Mammy of the South,*
> *Silence your mouth.*[25]

Such U.S.-focused poems aside, the 1930s most profoundly marked the emergence of Hughes's third major mode, beyond the already described bardic-demotic and professional: the left-internationalist. For example, his protest poem "Scottsboro," also published in December 1931, began "8 black boys in a Southern jail. / World, turn pale!" but then moved rapidly to invoke not just standard Euramerican martyr figures like Christ, John Brown, and Jeanne d'Arc but also the Haitian revolutionary Dessalines, the black insurrectionist Nat Turner, the controversial young Gandhi, the anti-U.S. Nicaraguan revolutionary Sandino, and "Lenin with the flag blood red."[26] "Left-internationalist," however, is too vague a word for what Hughes became. He is best termed a *rooted Afro-planetarist*, meaning that, whether reporting on a Moscow visit, analyzing changes in the Uzbek poetic tradition, or reflecting on Japan's role in World War II, Hughes and his poems saw the world through what he termed "Negro eyes."[27]

In this connection, in March 1932, while in California on the final leg of a cross-country poetry-reading tour, Hughes got an invitation from the New York–based African American activist and editor Louise Thompson to join a Negro artists and musicians group traveling to the Soviet Union to serve as screenwriter for a Soviet motion picture, *Black and White*, about the oppression of African Americans in the U.S. South. Soviet Moscow was a relatively race-free revelation, but the film project soon fell apart. Hughes, however, remained and received permission to travel to largely forbidden Soviet Central Asia, which he saw as the USSR's own colored, dusty, cotton-growing South. There he wrote poems, met literary and cultural elites, and toured (often with Arthur Koestler) factories and collective farms.[28]

In this phase of his career, Hughes was at his worst a bad propagandist. There is little to cherish, politically or poetically, in poems that begin like this: "Put one more S in the U.S.A. / To make it Soviet. / One more S in the U.S.A. / Oh, we'll live to see it yet."[29] One of his most strident 1930s poems, "Goodbye Christ," later caused him massive troubles when repeatedly reprinted by his detractors in the 1940s and 1950s.[30] Indeed it is unclear whether one should classify some of Hughes's 1930s compositions, such as the "mass chants" he wrote for rallies, as poetry. But the thirties also saw Hughes write initially little-noted poems that would be interpreted decades later as important modernist interventions, such as the 1934 "Cubes." Its first stanza begins, "In the days of the broken cubes of Picasso," and ends, unexpectedly, "I met on the boulevards of Paris / An African from Senegal." The poem links France's long historical entanglements with "the cubes of black and white, / black and white, / black and white" to a long roster of colonial and economic sorrows.[31] Even a poem with a title as wince-worthy as "Ballads of Lenin" was, on closer inspection, a moving and heterodox claim to include the worldwide colored poor in a white-dominated leftist pantheon.[32] Hughes's internationalist commitments were furthered by his 1937 work as an Associated Negro Press journalist reporting from the Spanish Civil War. During this era, Hughes poems such as "Letter from Spain" – which began "We captured a wounded Moor today. / He was just as dark as me. / I said, Boy, what you been doin' here / Fightin' against the free?" – illustrate the widely divergent estimations of his work.[33] For some critics, "Letter from Spain" embodies both vernacular eloquence and a far-seeing awareness that prefigures later global political configurations like the Non-Aligned Movement. Such critics hold that Hughes's Afro-planetarism supplies substantive depth, while his mild vernacular bespeaks demotic strength.[34] For others, such as Hughes's unsurpassed biographer and most influential critic Arnold Rampersad, "Letter from Spain" is a "maudlin dialect poem" characteristic of the "proletarian doggerel" Hughes would go on publishing "for years to come."[35]

In the broadest sense, Hughes's 1930s poetry is indissoluble from his linkages to the American and international left. Figures with whom Hughes interacted included white poets such as Muriel Rukeyser, the black poet Frank Marshall Davis, and Mike Gold, who, as editor of *New Masses*, regularly solicited and published poetry by Hughes. But for all his internationalism, Hughes – unlike figures such as James Baldwin, Richard Wright, and at times Paul Robeson and W. E. B. Du Bois – never simply abandoned the United States. Indeed Hughes's engagement with America's unmet promise was never deeper than in his long 1936 poem "Let America Be America Again," which conversed with classic American voices like Whitman and Woody Guthrie and diverse patriotic anthems to rhapsodize that "I'm the one who left dark Ireland's shore, / And Poland's plain, and England's grassy lea, / And torn from Black Africa's strand I came / To build a 'homeland of the free.'" Then the poem's subsequent two-word stanza starkly asks, "The free?"[36]

It is appropriate here, at the midpoint of this essay and of Hughes's life, to speak to Hughes's vast literary career beyond his poems, not least to underscore his professional dimensions. After his groundbreaking 1926 and 1927 poetry collections, Hughes next published a gentle midwestern coming-of-age novel, *Not Without Laughter*. A penetrating, stylistically diverse, and accurately titled short story collection, *The Ways of White Folks*, was written just after his return from the Soviet Union and appeared in 1934. Indeed, some of its draft pages have its U.S.-set short stories on one side and draft magazine essays on Soviet Central Asia on the other. Hughes also wrote extensively for the theater; he completed some sixty-three pieces, including radio plays, operas, gospel musicals, and dramas for venues from major Broadway houses to regional Negro theaters.[37] One of these, the musical *Street Scene*, was co-written with Kurt Weill, while another, *Mule Bone*, was co-written with Zora Neale Hurston but not produced until 1991 due to a bitter authorship dispute. Although Hughes had been asked to write a memoir as early as 1926, his first, *The Big Sea*, would not appear until 1940; its last section remains the most valuable firsthand portrait of the Harlem Renaissance that we have. A second autobiography, *I Wonder as I Wander*, a retrospectively mild recounting of Hughes's radical 1930s, followed in 1956.[38]

Through his weekly column in the nationally circulated Negro paper the *Chicago Defender*, Hughes reached an enormous audience (and received a steady paycheck) from 1942 to 1962, commenting on political, social, literary, and artistic topics in the United States and abroad. About one-fourth of those columns launched Hughes's career as a humorist. In these columns, a usually unnamed but bland, formal, educated narrator chats at a local bar with his loquacious, grammar-bungling folk genius friend, Jesse B. Semple, known as Simple. Hughes gathered his Simple stories into five books from 1950 to 1965. Also worth naming, for their both professional and demotic dimensions, are Hughes's books for children: a 1932 story, *Popo and Fifina*, co-written with Arna Bontemps; a 1932 collection of verse for younger readers, *The Dream Keeper*; and five didactic "first books" on Africa, the West Indies, rhythms, jazz, and Negroes.[39] Hughes also had a serious career as an anthologist, with *The Book of Negro Folklore*, *The Book of Negro Humor*, *Famous American Negroes*, and two groundbreaking photo histories with the visual archivist Milton Meltzer.

Returning to poetry proper, Hughes's sense of himself in the history of African American verse was consolidated by his 429-page anthology, co-edited with Arna Bontemps, *The Poetry of the Negro, 1746–1949*, which innovatively contained a rich selection of "tributary poems by non-Negroes" including Whitman ("The Runaway Slave" and the Civil War–themed "Ethiopia Saluting the Colors"), Blake, Browning, Wordsworth ("To Toussaint L'Ouverture"), Longfellow, James Russell Lowell, Melville, Vachel Lindsay, Hart Crane, Sandburg ("Jazz Fantasia"), and Elizabeth Bishop ("Songs for a Colored Singer").[40] Among the first books to recognize the complex poetic linkages between African America and the West Indies, the anthology also offered a long selection of Caribbean poets, including translations from Roumain, Nicolás Guillén, and the *négritude* co-founders Aimé Césaire and Léon Damas. Interestingly, Hughes and Bontemps placed Claude McKay in their Caribbean section, although McKay lived most of his adult life in the United States. *The Poetry of the Negro* included just one poet from anywhere in Africa, Aquah Laluah, the pen name for the prominent Anglo–Sierra Leonean Gladys May Casely Hayford; we will return to Hughes and Africa subsequently.

Hughes translated (in part with Ben Carruthers Guillén and Roumain), notably recasting (with co-translator Mercer Cook) Roumain's peasant novel *Masters of the Dew* into U.S. southern rural speech.[41] He translated Federico García Lorca at least twice: the *Gypsy Ballads* in 1951 and, in a manuscript unpublished until 1994, the landmark play *Blood Wedding*.[42] Hughes was also the first substantial translator of the Chilean Nobel laureate poet Gabriela Mistral.[43] Further afield, Hughes translated Louis Aragon's Soviet-themed poetry from the French and, with assistance, Vladimir Mayakovsky's Cuba-set poems from the Russian and some Central Asian folk poetry from the Uzbek.[44]

Hughes did not achieve financial stability until relatively late in life, and he frequently referred to himself, in letters to Arna Bontemps, as "a literary sharecropper."[45] Yet Hughes was the first African or African-descent writer in English to make his living exclusively from his published words. But Hughes's wide-ranging prolificness was motivated by much more than money. Theatrical writing, for one, is a notoriously unreliable way to wealth; it functioned for Hughes instead as a way to reach more people. Translation proved so nonmunificent for Hughes that his exasperated agent Maxim Lieber once ordered him to stop. A similar analysis can be applied to Hughes's tireless 1950s promotion of African writing. The fastest, richest writing job he ever had – as Hollywood co-screenwriter, along with Clarence Muse, for the forgettable 1939 RKO musical *Way Down South* – was so artistically and politically unsatisfying that he never sought such work again.[46] Instead, anthologizing, children's writing, translation, drama, and the promotion of African writing gave Hughes ways to present ever-fuller U.S. and global materials to an ever-wider range of readers, to further enhance his cultural depth and literary craft, and often to speak through other authors' pens or names: the bardic-demotic, internationalist, professional, and sublimated all at once.

With this, we move to the 1940s, during which period Hughes began a steady withdrawal from the overt Left and carefully balanced support for American involvement (including heroic African American involvement) in the antifascist fight with critique of the irony that an internally race-oppressing nation battled racism overseas. His 1942 *Shakespeare in Harlem*, much like his 1927 *Fine Clothes to the Jew*, offered a wide portrait of African American life in the idiom of blues, but shorn of his 1930s political commitments. A poem that began obscurely as an aria in his late-1930s libretto for a Haiti-themed opera co-written with the composer William Grant Still became, with multiple later printings, one of his most enduring statements:

> A world I dream where black or white,
> Whatever race you be,
> Will share the bounties of the earth
> And every man is free,
> Where wretchedness will hang its head
> And joy, like a pearl,
> Attends the needs of all mankind –
> Of such I dream, my world![47]

More darkly, his 1942 "The Bitter River" recast prior positive imagery of dreams and rivers to protest a Mississippi lynching. The poem's sustained anger is only partly captured by the first of its many stanzas:

> There is a bitter river
> Flowing through the South.
> Too long has the taste of its water
> Been in my mouth.
> There is a bitter river
> Dark with filth and mud.
> Too long has its evil poison
> Poisoned my blood.[48]

Toward the end of the decade, Hughes's 1947 "Trumpet Player: 52nd Street" deepened his long history of poetry on jazz. It begins with this:

> The Negro
> With the trumpet at his lips
> Has dark moons of weariness
> Beneath his eyes
> Where the smoldering memory
> Of slave ships
> Blazed to the crack of whips
> About his thighs.

Then shifts to unusually (for Hughes) sexual imagery:

> The music
> From the trumpet at his lips
> Is honey
> Mixed with liquid fire.
> The rhythm
> From the trumpet at his lips
> Is ecstasy
> Distilled from old desire –

Several stanzas later it closes by blending images of heroin, style, and release: "The Negro / With the trumpet at his lips ... Does not know / Upon what riff the music slips // Its hypodermic needle / To his soul."[49]

Hughes's next strong poetic achievement came in 1951, with *Montage of a Dream Deferred*, whose eighty-six separate elements form a coherent whole. Marking a fresh musical influence, Hughes's preface stated that "this poem on contemporary Harlem, like be-bop, is marked by conflicting changes, sudden nuances, sharp and impudent interjections, [and] broken rhythms ... of the music of a community in transition."[50] Its opening section, "Dream Boogie," accordingly plays with reader expectations, in both emotional and metrical uncertainty:

Good morning, daddy!
Ain't you heard
The boogie-woogie rumble
Of a dream deferred?

Listen closely:
You'll hear their feet
Beating out and beating out a –

> *You think*
> *It's a happy beat?*

Listen to it closely:
Ain't you heard
something underneath
like a –

> *What did I say?*

Sure,
I'm happy!
Take it away!

> *Hey, pop!*
> *Re-bop!*
> *Mop!*

> *Y-e-a-h!*   (*MDD*, p. 3)

In subsequent pages, *Montage's* segments, ranging from eight short words to several dozen lines, voice the earnest student, sassy neighbor, dramatic preacher, and simple Harlem witness. Its "Theme for English B," of interest to any teacher-reader of this volume, may be the most perceptive short text ever written on the relationship between black students and white professors. A poignant short poem, "Casualty," speaks of shell-shocked veterans of any era, including ours: "He was a soldier in the army, / But he doesn't walk like one. / He walks like his soldiering / Days are done. // Son! ... Son!" (*MDD*, p. 59). Another brief entry, "Dime," puts Hughes's cherished and affirming 1922 "Mother to Son" in a much more bitter light:

Chile, these steps is hard to climb.

> *Grandma, lend me a dime.*

Montage of a dream deferred:

> *Grandma acts like*
> *She ain't heard.*

Chile, Granny ain't got no dime.

> *I might've knowed*
> *It all the time.*   (MDD, p. 62)

Montage's most widely reproduced poem, "Harlem," begins by repeating the volume's standard question, "What happens to a dream deferred?" and then, uncertain in reply, asks yet further questions that would supply, eight years later, the title of Lorraine Hansberry's celebrated play: "Does it dry up / like a raisin in the sun? . . . Maybe it just sags / like a heavy load. / *Or does it explode?*" (*MDD*, p. 71). Hughes's *Montage* had a mixed reception in its day, especially among elites. Arthur P. Davis noted coolly in the *Journal of Negro History* that it had "recaptured some of the magic" of *The Weary Blues*, while Babette Deutsch of the *New York Times* disparaged its "facile sentimentality" and "contrived naïveté."[51] If Hughes had once been glad to upset reviewers with his fidelity to Negro life, he was far from glad to hear reviewers say his art had been surpassed. For in ways it had been surpassed, in both quality and elite acclaim, most significantly by Gwendolyn Brooks, fifteen years his junior and the beneficiary of Hughes's generous support when she was young. Brooks's formal versatility ranged from urban vernacular to modernist free verse to the sonnet, as in "The Children of the Poor," from her 1949 Pulitzer Prize–winning *Annie Allen*:

> What shall I give my children? who are poor,
> Who are adjudged the leastwise of the land,
> Who are my sweetest lepers, who demand
> No velvet and no velvety velour;
> But who have begged me for a brisk contour,
> Crying that they are quasi, contraband
> Because unfinished, graven by a hand
> Less than angelic, admirable or sure.[52]

Another segment from *Montage*, although little noted at the time, offered Hughes's first express poetic reflection, thirty years into his career, on homosexuality:

> *Café: 3 A.M.*
>
> Detectives from the vice squad
> with weary sadistic eyes
> spotting fairies.
>
> > *Degenerates,*
> > some folks say.
>
> > But God, Nature,
> > or somebody

made them that way.

Police lady or Lesbian
over there?

Where?   (*MDD*, p. 32)

This poem offers a good starting point for consideration of Hughes's sexuality, and with it, the closeted-sublimated dimension of Hughes's work noted at the outset. Hughes has, especially in the past two decades, frequently been referenced as a gay or queer or homosexual poet – three overlapping but not identical designations. Hughes's unsurpassed biographer, Arnold Rampersad, has noted that, even in his exhaustive reading of the vast Hughes archive and lengthy interviews with dozens who knew Hughes, he found no serious evidence of any sustained sexual or affective relationship between Hughes and anyone, female or male, in his entire life. Rampersad concludes that Hughes was largely "asexual," or that his sexual desire had been "not so much sublimated as vaporized."[53] Aware that Hughes's sexuality was long subject to question – after all, Hughes was a bachelor, poet, and former bohemian and sailor – Rampersad finds no "concrete evidence" of Hughes's sexual disposition, beyond perhaps a lack thereof, and asserts instead what Hughes's close friends felt was its "maddening elusiveness."[54]

Critics and scholars reading Hughes as gay have responded that the overwhelming power of the closet in the United States from the 1920s to the 1960s, especially among African Americans, would have deterred Hughes from leaving any clear trace of his orientation. Noting Hughes's long-standing friendships with numerous less-closeted gay men, including Carl Van Vechten, and the degree to which Hughes's commitment to effectiveness in (and income from) the public sphere would have precluded his endangering that effectiveness, such scholars instead focus on reading Hughes's poems for their gay or queer inflections. Exploring the "homoeroticism and other gay markings" in these poems,[55] these Hughes scholars detail "Hughes's lyric archive of queer sociality"[56] both directly, in poems such as "Café: 3 A.M.," "Curious," and "Desire," and obliquely, in Hughes's many tales of racial (rather than sexual) passing.

The charge of affectional sublimation resonates with many other Hughesian self-suppressions. Politics is Hughes's other great axis of suppression, only with undeniable evidence of his 1930s leftism, despite his later attempts to recast and suppress it. But of course the literary question is not "was Hughes a self-suppressor," "was he in the closet," or "was he gay," but rather "can his works productively be read as queer or gay," and "how and to what effect do his writings re-channel what he could or would not say?" The answers to these questions vary.

Remarkably, Hughes seems never to have attempted a full-fledged love poem in a half-century literary career.[57] Yet elsewhere Hughes's personal re-channeling produced some of his most vivid creations, from his fearless alter ego Simple to the sassy, uncompromising "Madam" Alberta K. Johnson. At some level, however, reading the sublimated Hughes often requires pursuit of the not-said, never more explicitly than in the 1933 poem "Personal," which begins, "In an envelope marked: / *Personal* / God addressed me a letter," and then describes, or does not describe, Hughes's "answer," also "In an envelope marked: / *Personal*."[58]

At this juncture, a discussion of the place of Hughes's primary biographer and major critic, Arnold Rampersad, is required. After publishing a superb literary biography of W. E. B. Du Bois, Rampersad arranged with George Houston Bass, Hughes's last private secretary and co-executor of his literary estate, to write Hughes's biography, based in good measure on access to the trove of papers held at Yale's Beinecke Library and only later opened to all scholars. The resulting two-volume *Life of Langston Hughes* (1986 and 1988) set a nearly unsurpassed standard for American literary biography. No scholar, past or present, commands as full an understanding of Langston Hughes as Arnold Rampersad. What is more, as co-executor, Rampersad has been involved in the continued publication of Hughes's extant and archival works, often penning introductions to fresh Hughes volumes edited by others.

In consequence, current readers and scholars of Langston Hughes, the author of the present chapter included, engage not simply Hughes's literary history but the literary history of Rampersad's Langston Hughes. Thus (to choose one example), proponents of gay or queer interpretations of Hughes's verse also contend with Rampersad's view of Hughes. Likewise, admirers of Hughes's radical-internationalist poems make claims not just on Hughes but also against Rampersad's negative framing of Hughes's radical-internationalist incarnation. I do not mean to suggest a negative relationship or effect – indeed, to the contrary. But never has the literary afterlife of a major American poet been so thoroughly inflected by his leading biographer, scholar, successor co-executor, and critic.

The standard Hughes volume today is the 1994 *Collected Poems of Langston Hughes*, co-edited by Rampersad and David Roessel. Rampersad and Roessel follow standard practice by printing the last published version of each poem authorized by the poet in his life. But Hughes was far from the same poet in 1959 or 1967 that he had been in 1926 or 1931. Early in this chapter, for example, one finds a portion of Hughes's "Bound No'th Blues" as originally printed in the National Urban League's magazine *Opportunity* and Hughes's *The Weary Blues* in 1926. But the *Collected Poems* version comes from his 1959 *Selected Poems*, which "whitened" the voice by shifting "de" and "dis" to "the" and "this." Although many of Hughes's changes are described in the *Collected Poems*'s notes, others are not. A good example is Hughes's "Christ in Alabama," discussed previously. The poem first appeared in the leftist Chapel Hill magazine *Contempo* in December 1931, and then in Hughes's now-rare 1932 *Scottsboro Limited: Four Poems and a Play in Verse*. But today's readers typically know "Christ in Alabama" only in its milder 1967 version. This more recent version differs, among other things, in capitalization, italicized voice, an "us" changed to "Him," and the closing line breaks: the first six lines of the later version, for example, replace dashes with colons, remove all italics, and add an exclamation point in line 3.[59]

Hughes's 1930s past would haunt him. Called to testify before Senator Joseph McCarthy's subcommittee in 1953, Hughes endured a withering assault on his prior radical verse, especially "Goodbye Christ," and nearly saw his writing life destroyed. Although his brief public testimony suggests a mild, even "supine" posture before the committee,[60] the recently released transcript of his long private interrogation reveals that Hughes mobilized a vast range of rhetorical strategies and tactics, decidedly not including defiance or anger, to defuse the committee's ire.[61] And he named no names. He emerged with his reputation diminished on the left but in general intact. Still, he engaged in even greater self- and retrospective suppression for the remainder of the decade. The balance of Hughes's 1950s was not devoted to new poems; he focused instead on his second memoir (1956), the *Langston Hughes Reader* (1958), *Selected Poems* (1959), and many more workmanlike or semicommercial publications. His creative reputation was far below its peak; the most damaging evidence of this was James Baldwin's brutal *New York Times Book Review* account of Hughes's *Selected Poems*, which began with this: "Every time I read Langston Hughes I am amazed all over again by his genuine gifts – and depressed that he has done so little with them."[62]

On a far more affirming note, the 1950s also saw Hughes's deep internationalism reignite, now in direct exchange with Africa. In 1923, Hughes had visited many African ports as a menial sailor. He thematized the continent in often stereotyped ways in the three decades to follow, penned a scathing poem on the Johannesburg mines in 1925, and kept vaguely aware of the continent's anticolonial struggles. But that was about the extent of his involvement. Although he was revered by the Francophone *négritude* movement and by many Anglophone African poets from the early 1930s on, Hughes himself was barely aware of their existence.[63] Hughes's African consciousness reawakened in 1953 when he received, out of the blue, an invitation to judge an Africa-wide short story contest for the widely distributed, black-oriented South African magazine *Drum*. Impressed by the entries, Hughes determined to assemble an African anthology for the U.S. and British markets at a time when African writing of any kind had a microscopic presence in both nations. It took nearly a decade, endless correspondence, and heavy triangulation between emerging African writers and American and U.K. publishers before Hughes came out with the multigenre *African Treasury* in 1960 and *Poems from Black Africa* in 1963.[64] Nearly every notable Francophone and Anglophone African poet and writer of the 1950s and early 1960s corresponded warmly with Hughes, the most widely known black writer in the world, before his death in 1967.

Hughes traveled to the continent five times during this period, at times as a U.S. State Department cultural ambassador. In November 1960, with Hughes in the audience, his short, uplifting 1924 poem "Youth" ("We have tomorrow / Bright before us / Like a flame") was recited by his old Lincoln University schoolmate Nnamdi Azikiwe at the close of Azikiwe's inauguration as the first governor-general of independent Nigeria.[65] Hughes's post-1953 re-cognition of himself as a pan-African or Afro-planetary internationalist fueled his last major poetry achievement, the luxuriously produced 1961 *Ask Your Mama: 12 Moods for Jazz*. Conceived as a single poem, *Ask Your Mama* takes its impetus from the comic/bitter African American insult ritual called "the dozens," as here:

> IN THE QUARTER OF THE NEGROES
> WHERE SIT-INS ARE CONDUCTED
> BY THOSE YET UNINDUCTED
> AND BALLOTS DROP IN BOXES
> WHERE BULLETS ARE THE TELLERS
>
> THEY ASKED ME AT THANKSGIVING
> DID I VOTE FOR NIXON?
> I SAID, VOTED FOR YOUR MAMA.[66]

Despite its origin in the dozens, *Ask Your Mama* goes far beyond its insult-driven seed. It was conceived, like Hughes's 1951 *Montage*, as a multifocal portrait of a Negro world, although 1961's portrait was much more densely allusive, violent, and global than any before. Accompanied by narrative musical cues in its right-hand column, *Ask Your Mama* begins:

IN THE
IN THE QUARTER
IN THE QUARTER OF THE NEGROES
WHERE THE DOORS ARE DOORS OF PAPER
DUST OF DINGY ATOMS
BLOWS A SCRATCHY SOUND.
AMORPHOUS JACK-O'-LANTERNS CAPER
AND THE WIND WON'T WAIT FOR MIDNIGHT
FOR FUN TO BLOW DOORS DOWN.[67]

A few score additional lines in the same voice then invoke, among other great African American figures, "Leontyne Sammy Harry Poitier / Lovely Lena Marian Louis Pearlie Mae," and then George S. Schuyler, "Jimmy Baldwin," "Arna Bontemps chief consultant," and "Lieder, lovely lieder / And a leaf of collard green." But then *Ask Your Mama* veers to a global, anticolonial mode:

IN THE SHADOW OF THE NEGROES
   NKRUMAH
IN THE SHADOW OF THE NEGROES
   NASSER NASSER
IN THE SHADOW OF THE NEGROES
   ZIK AZIKIWE
CUBA CASTRO GUINEA TOURÉ
FOR NEED OR PROPAGANDA
   KENYATTA
AND THE TOM DOGS OF THE CABIN
THE COCOA AND THE CANE BRAKE
THE CHAIN GANG AND THE SLAVE BLOCK
TARRED AND FEATHERED NATIONS
SEAGRAM'S AND FOUR ROSES
$5.00 BAGS A DECK OR DAGGA.

. . .

AND THEY ASKED ME RIGHT AT CHRISTMAS
IF MY BLACKNESS, WOULD IT RUB OFF?
I SAID, ASK YOUR MAMA.[68]

Needless to say, this differs sharply from any prior poetry by Hughes, not only in its sustained intensity but also in its reliance on specific knowledge. For understanding *Ask Your Mama* requires a vast grasp not only of African American references but also of mid-twentieth-century African, Afro-diasporic, and global Third World events and persons. Although massively internationalist and Afro-planetary, it is one of the few *nondemotic* poems Hughes ever wrote. To choose but one of the preceding uncommon terms, "dagga" is the

Afrikaans- and Kohekohe-derived South African English term for marijuana –
something few American readers knew in 1961. Unsurprisingly, contemporary
reviews of *Ask Your Mama* ranged from laudatory to derisive to confused.
The keenest came from the pioneering Africana studies scholar John Henrik
Clarke in the black progressive journal *Freedomways*. Stating correctly that
the poem represented Hughes's estimable outreach to "a second generation,"
Clarke concluded by noting that if this second generation wished to know
what the first Negro generation thought of Hughes, the task was simple: "Ask
Your Mama."[69]

Hughes wrote little notable poetry in the remaining six years of his life.
To be sure, his poems responded to the tumult of the 1960s: they marked
the emergence of independent African nation-states, sang a "backlash blues"
about white opposition to what he still termed "Negro advancement,"
engaged the heightened strife in northern cities, and revisited long-standing
themes. But Hughes broke no new formal or stylistic ground. Whatever thunder he still held could not compete with the profane intensity of the Black Arts
Movement poets, especially Amiri Baraka, who until the last year of Hughes's
life still went by LeRoi Jones. The two writers had a mutually respectful if
increasingly distant relationship across their generational divide; their distance flowed from Jones's sense of Hughes's political and stylistic datedness,
and Hughes's reactions to poems such as Jones's 1966 "Black Art."

Apart from a highly successful late career as the originator of yet another
genre, the gospel musical or gospel play – key achievements being *Black
Nativity* and *Jerico Jim Crow* – Hughes's 1960s had a senior-statesman flavor,
replete with the NAACP's Spingarn Medal, induction into the National
Institute of Arts and Letters (preceded among African Americans only by Du
Bois), European leisure travel, and an invitation to a White House luncheon
hosted by President Kennedy to honor visiting Senegalese president Léopold
Senghor. Langston Hughes died in New York on May 22, 1967, at sixty-five,
of complications following prostate surgery. His jazz-infused Harlem funeral
was heavily attended.

Hughes's poetic afterlife has taken on many guises. Among ordinary
American readers (especially but not only African Americans), his presence
has been unbroken. For the white public in particular, this has flowed from his
continual assignment in American schools. The widespread popular embrace
of Hughes's poems, as well as his memoirs, short stories, and other writings, contrasts with an older, eroding, but still extant academic notion, based
perhaps on insufficiently examined standards, that Hughes was less literar-
ily important than the midcentury African American prose writers James

Baldwin, Ralph Ellison, and Richard Wright and midcentury white poets like Wallace Stevens, T. S. Eliot, or Ezra Pound. In this light, it is worth suggesting that Hughes's tremendously wide and profuse professional literary output may have masked his depth. One wonders what critical reputation Hughes would have today if he had had, like his near contemporary Elizabeth Bishop, the monetary resources and personal inclination to concentrate on poems only, or if today we read, as we do with Bishop, only the best 105 of the nearly 900 poems Hughes put in print.

Also important here is history's fluctuating view of mandarin versus bardic-demotic verse – with Hughes's poems decisively in the latter camp – and of social-political versus personal or abstracted poetry, with Hughes's Afro-planetary commitments again putting him on the wrong side of most elite and academic taste. As for the fourth assessment framework offered in this chapter, the closeted-elusive, the literary question is again not "was Langston gay but in the closet" but rather "how productively did Hughes re-channel what he would or could not say?" And the answer is, again, quite mixed. In all of these domains, historical shifts in reader interests, canons of taste, and scholarly understanding of movements such as modernism have continually refreshed our view of Hughes. Throughout it all lies a core view of Langston Hughes – a professional, bardic-demotic, and Afro-planetarist writer who might have had a lot to hide and a descendent of Whitman, Sandburg, and a complex Negro tradition – as the most committed, innovative, sympathetic, and deeply rooted poetic exponent of African American life, and the most globally engaged major American poet of any kind. In Hughes's words, and in Hughes's world, it's not so far from here to yonder.

Notes

1. Jay Parini and Brett C. Millier (eds.), *The Columbia History of American Poetry* (New York: Columbia University Press, 1993).
2. Irene Ramalho Santos, "Langston Hughes: The Color of Modernism," *The Cambridge History of American Literature*. Vol. 5, *Poetry and Criticism 1900–1950*, ed. Sacvan Bercovitch (Cambridge: Cambridge University Press, 2003).
3. Much of Hughes's biography is multiply attested, well known, and naturally relies on Hughes's two memoirs: *The Big Sea* (1940) and *I Wonder as I Wander* (1956). Still, the authoritative source for Hughes's life, on which this chapter substantially relies, is Arnold Rampersad, *The Life of Langston Hughes*. Vol. I, *1902–1941: I, Too, Sing America* (New York: Oxford University Press, 1986), and Rampersad, *The Life of Langston Hughes*. Vol. II, *1941–1967: I Dream a World* (New York: Oxford University Press, 1988).

4. Langston Hughes, *The Weary Blues* (New York: Alfred A. Knopf, 1926), and *Fine Clothes to the Jew* (New York: Alfred A. Knopf, 1927).

5. Paul Laurence Dunbar, "The Poet" (1903), in Herbert Woodward Martin (ed.), *Selected Poems* (New York: Penguin, 2004), p. 152.

6. James Weldon Johnson, *Writings*, ed. William L. Andrews (New York: Library of America, 2004), pp. 817–18.

7. Claude McKay, *Harlem Shadows* (New York: Harcourt, Brace, 1922), pp. 22, 53.

8. Langston Hughes, "The Negro Speaks of Rivers," *The Crisis* (June 1921), p. 71.

9. Langston Hughes, "Mother to Son," *The Crisis* (December 1922), p. 87.

10. Langston Hughes, "Bound No'th Blues," *Opportunity* (October 1926), p. 315.

11. "Dreams," first published in 1923, here from Langston Hughes, *The Dream Keeper and Other Poems* (New York: Alfred A. Knopf, 1932), p. 4.

12. Langston Hughes, "The Negro," *The Crisis* (January 1922), p. 113, and later published as "Proem" in Hughes, *The Weary Blues*, p. 19.

13. Langston Hughes, "Mulatto," *Saturday Review of Literature* (January 29, 1927), p. 547.

14. Hughes, *The Weary Blues*, pp. 23–24.

15. Langston Hughes, *The Big Sea* (New York: Alfred A. Knopf, 1940), p. 223.

16. James Weldon Johnson, *God's Trombones: Seven Negro Sermons in Verse* (New York: Viking, 1927); James Weldon Johnson (ed.), *The Book of American Negro Poetry* (New York: Harcourt, Brace, 1922); Claude McKay, *Harlem Shadows* (New York: Harcourt, Brace, 1922), and *Home to Harlem* (New York: Harper & Brothers, 1928).

17. Jean Toomer, *Cane* (New York: Boni and Liveright, 1923).

18. Brent Hayes Edwards, *The Practice of Diaspora: Literature, Translation, and the Rise of Black Internationalism* (Cambridge, Mass.: Harvard University Press, 2003), p. 4.

19. Countee Cullen, "Heritage," in *Color* (New York: Harper & Brothers, 1925), p. 36.

20. Countee Cullen, "From the Dark Tower," in *Copper Sun* (New York: Harper & Brothers, 1927), p. 3.

21. Sterling A. Brown, "Southern Road," in *Southern Road* (New York: Harcourt, Brace, 1932), p. 47.

22. Langston Hughes, "The Negro Artist and the Racial Mountain," *The Nation* (June 23, 1926), pp. 692–94.

23. Jonathan Kozol, *Death at an Early Age* (Boston: Houghton Mifflin, 1967), chapters 17–20.

24. Anna Nussbaum (ed.), *Afrika Singt: Eine Auslese neuer afro-amerikanischer Lyrik*, trans. Hermann Kesser, Josef Luitpold, Anna Siemsen, and Anna Nussbaum (Vienna: Speidel, 1929).

25. Langston Hughes, "Christ in Alabama," *Contempo* (December 1931), p. 1.

26. Langston Hughes, "Scottsboro," *Opportunity* (December 1931), p. 379.

27. Langston Hughes, *I Wonder as I Wander: An Autobiographical Journey* (New York: Rinehart, 1956), p. 116.

28. Hughes, *I Wonder as I Wander*, pp. 101–90, although Hughes's autobiographical account of this period plays down his most radical dimensions.

29. Langston Hughes, "One More 'S' in the U.S.A.," *Daily Worker* (April 2, 1934), p. 7.

30. First published without Hughes's permission in *The Negro Worker* (November–December 1932), p. 32.

31. Langston Hughes, "Cubes," *New Masses* (March 13, 1934), p. 22.

32. Langston Hughes, "Ballads of Lenin" (initially published as "Ballad of Lenin"), *Anvil* (May 1933), p. 17.

33. Langston Hughes, "Letter from Spain," *Volunteer for Liberty* (November 15, 1937), p. 3.

34. See, for example, Cary Nelson, *Revolutionary Memory: Recovering the Poetry of the American Left* (New York: Routledge, 2003), pp. 186–207.

35. Rampersad, *Life of Langston Hughes*, vol. 1, p. 351.

36. Langston Hughes, "Let America Be America Again," *Esquire* (July 1936), p. 92, and in different form in Langston Hughes, *A New Song* (New York: International Workers Order, 1938).

37. Susan Duffy, *The Political Plays of Langston Hughes* (Carbondale: Southern Illinois University Press, 2000), pp. 2, 201.

38. J. Saunders Redding, "Travels of Langston Hughes: Events as Seen in Passing," *New York Herald Tribune* (December 23, 1956), p. 7.

39. In chronological order, the titles of these books are as follows: *The First Book of Negroes* (1952), *The First Book of Rhythms* (1954), *The First Book of Jazz* (1955), *The First Book of the West Indies* (1956), and *The First Book of Africa* (1960; rev. ed. 1964).

40. Langston Hughes and Arna Bontemps (eds.), *The Poetry of the Negro, 1746–1949* (New York: Doubleday, 1949).

41. Nicolás Guillén, *Cuba Libre*, trans. Langston Hughes and Ben Frederic Carruthers (Los Angeles: Anderson & Ritchie, 1948). Jacques Roumain, *Masters of the Dew*, trans. Langston Hughes and Mercer Cook (New York: Reynal & Hitchcock, 1947).

42. Federico García Lorca, *Gypsy Ballads*, trans. Langston Hughes, *Beloit Poetry Journal*, chapbook no. 1 (1951). Federico García Lorca, *Blood Wedding*, trans. Langston Hughes (New York: Theatre Communications Group, 1994).

43. Gabriela Mistral, *Selected Poems of Gabriela Mistral*, trans. Langston Hughes (Bloomington: Indiana University Press, 1957).

44. Louis Aragon, "Magnitogorsk," trans. Langston Hughes, *International Literature* 4 (1933–1934), pp. 82–83. The typescripts of Hughes's and Lydia Filatova's joint translations of Vladimir Mayakovsky's "Syphilis" and "Black and White" are held in the New York Public Library's Schomburg Research

Center, Sc. 891.7-M. Ghafur Ghulom, "On the Turksib Roads," translated from the Uzbek by Langston Hughes with the assistance of the author and Nina Zorokovina, *International Literature* 5 (March 1933), pp. 67–69.

45. See, for example, Charles H. Nichols (ed.), *Arna Bontemps-Langston Hughes Letters, 1925–1967* (New York: Dodd, Mead, 1980), pp. 277, 282, 283, 292, 408.

46. Langston Hughes, "Statement in Round Numbers Concerning the Relative Merits of 'Way Down South' and 'Don't You Want to Be Free' as Compiled by the Author Mr. Langston Hughes." Typescript "sent to Louise, Loren, Arna," November 6, 1939. Langston Hughes Papers, Beinecke Rare Book and Manuscript Library, JWJ Mss 26 367.5927.

47. Langston Hughes, "I Dream a World," in Langston Hughes, *Collected Poems*, ed. Arnold Rampersad and David Roessel (New York: Alfred A. Knopf, 1994), p. 311.

48. Hughes, *Collected Poems*, pp. 242–44.

49. Langston Hughes, *Fields of Wonder* (New York: Alfred A. Knopf, 1947), pp. 91–93.

50. Langston Hughes, *Montage of a Dream Deferred* (New York: Henry Holt, 1951), p. 1. This text will subsequently be cited parenthetically as *MDD*.

51. Arthur P. Davis, "Review of *Montage of a Dream Deferred*, by Langston Hughes," *Journal of Negro History* 36:2 (April 1951), pp. 224–26. Babette Deutsch, "Waste Land of Harlem: Review of *Montage of a Dream Deferred*, by Langston Hughes," *New York Times Book Review*, May 6, 1951, p. 12.

52. Gwendolyn Brooks, *The Essential Gwendolyn Brooks*, ed. Elizabeth Alexander (New York: Library of America, 2005), p. 49.

53. Rampersad, *Life of Langston Hughes*, vol. 1, p. 69.

54. Rampersad, *Life of Langston Hughes*, vol. 2, p. 336.

55. Karl L. Stenger, "Langston Hughes (1902–1967)," in Emmanuel Nelson (ed.), *African American Dramatists* (New York: Greenwood, 2004), pp. 226–46, 228.

56. Shane Vogel, "Closing Time: Langston Hughes and the Queer Poetics of Harlem Nightlife," *Criticism* 48:3 (2006), pp. 397–425, 400. See also Anne Borden, "Heroic 'Hussies' and 'Brilliant Queers': Genderracial Resistance in the Works of Langston Hughes," *African American Review* 28:3 (1994), pp. 333–45; and also Juda Bennett, "Multiple Passings and the Double Death of Langston Hughes," *Biography* 23:4 (2000), pp. 670–93.

57. Tellingly, the closest he came seems to have been a handwritten poem given to the beautiful Afro-Chinese Trinidadian Soviet dancer Si-Lan (Sylvia) Chen, to whom Hughes could not commit: "I am so sad / Over half a kiss / That with half a pencil / I write this." See Rampersad, *Life of Langston Hughes*, vol. 1, p. 265.

58. Langston Hughes, "Personal," *The Crisis* (October 1933), p. 238.

59. The versions quoted here are from *Contempo* (December 1931), p. 1, and Hughes, *Collected Poems* (1994), p. 142.

60. This is the interpretation of Rampersad, *Life of Langston Hughes*, vol. 2, p. 219.

61. "Testimony of Langston Hughes (Accompanied by His Counsel, Frank D. Reeves)," *Executive Sessions of the Senate Permanent Subcommittee on Investigations of the Committee on Government Operations*, vol. 2, Eighty-Third Congress, First Session, 1953, made public January 2003 (Washington, D.C.: Government Printing Office, 2003), pp. 972–98.

62. James Baldwin, "Sermons and Blues," review of *Selected Poems of Langston Hughes. New York Times Book Review*, March 29, 1959, p. 6.

63. For example, late in the editing of his 1949 anthology *The Poetry of the Negro*, a letter came to Hughes from the Howard University French professor Mercer Cook advocating inclusion of the Senegalese poet and politician Léopold Senghor. But Hughes had never heard the name and couldn't insert Senghor in time. Correspondence between Langston Hughes and Mercer Cook, August 9, 10, and 11, 1948. Langston Hughes Papers, Beinecke Rare Book and Manuscript Library, box 47, folder 867.

64. Langston Hughes (ed.), *An African Treasury* (New York: Crown, 1960), and Langston Hughes (ed.), *Poems from Black Africa* (Bloomington: Indiana University Press, 1963).

65. Langston Hughes, "Youth," *The Crisis* (August 1924), p. 163. See Rampersad, *Life of Langston Hughes*, vol. 2, p. 325.

66. Langston Hughes, *Ask Your Mama: 12 Moods for Jazz* (New York: Alfred A. Knopf, 1961), p. 70.

67. Hughes, *Ask Your Mama*, p. 3.

68. Hughes, *Ask Your Mama*, pp. 5–8.

69. John Henrik Clarke, "Book Reviews," review of Langston Hughes, *Ask Your Mama, Freedomways* 2 (January 1962), pp. 102–03.

Chapter 32

The Objectivists and the Left

MARK SCROGGINS

Over the course of the depression that followed the stock market crash of October 1929, American poets on the left wrote an enormous amount of often passionate poetry addressing their social contexts. Such writing initially addressed the economic, racial, and gender inequalities these poets perceived in American capitalism and called for radical reforms, even revolution on the model of the Soviet experiment in Russia. In the latter part of the decade, many leftist poets turned their attention to the Spanish Civil War, where the conflict between left-leaning democracy and fascism presented itself in bold relief. In the pages of *New Masses* and other Communist-linked periodicals, readers might be hailed by voices drawing their attention to bread lines and foreclosures, unfair labor practices, and harsh economic inequities, and calling them to revolution. If they moved in the circles of the East Coast avant-garde, readers could trace the doctrines of Marx in complex, fugal juxtaposition with contemporary events, or they could read sharply elliptical, personalized portraits of the intransigent conflicts of capital in crisis. Or if a reader were lucky enough to know Lorine Niedecker, living quietly in rural Wisconsin, she or he might be able to read utopian aspirations cast in the gentle, questioning tones of Mother Goose:

> Scuttle up the workshop,
> settle down the dew,
> I'll tell you what my name is
> when we've made the world new.[1]

The reigning ideologues of the Communist Party–connected literary Left, under the influence of the cultural offices of the Soviet Comintern, tended to promote an aesthetic of socialist realism in both poetry and prose, which led in practice to a poetry of easily apprehensible political content and overt persuasive or hortatory intent. Such writing was diametrically opposed to the various innovative forms and rhetorics American modernist poets had pioneered in the first decades of the century. But although it might be convenient to divide American poetry of the 1930s between a straightforward, rhetorically transparent leftist poetry and a politically quiescent (or even reactionary) modernism, in reality the forms and modes of American leftist poetries were as varied as those of less politically engaged writing. The boundary between aesthetic experimentation and social commitment (always, one suspects, an artificial distinction) was never less than porous, and in many cases poets would assert a direct connection between their formal innovations and their revolutionary fervor.

*

Perhaps the most familiar model of the politically engaged poem is epitomized in the refrain of Shelley's "The Mask of Anarchy" – the hortatory poem, that which calls on the oppressed to rise up and seize what is rightfully theirs: "Rise like Lions after slumber / In unvanquishable number ... Ye are many – they are few."[2] There were many poems in this vein published during the 1930s, like Edwin Rolfe's "These Men Are Revolution" ("Come brother, come millhand, come miner, come friend – / we're off! and we'll see the thing through to the end"), Richard Wright's "I Have Seen Black Hands" ("I am black and I have seen black hands / Raised in fists of revolt, side by side with the white fists of white workers"), or H. H. Lewis's "The Sweeter Our Fruits ..." ("Before 1918 we were 'visionaries,' / Socialism 'against human nature,' / But now / We point / To Red Russia").[3] Mike Gold, among the most prominent of left-wing literary figures and an editor for New Masses (a self-appointed successor to the 1911–1917 leftist journal the Masses, edited by Max Eastman), argued for muscularity and clarity in writing: the poet should avoid "verbal acrobatics," which are "only another form for bourgeois idleness. The worker lives too close to reality to care about these literary show-offs, these verbalist heroes" (NM, p. 208). The "verbalist heroes" Gold derides, presumably, are such modernist figures as T. S. Eliot, Ezra Pound, and Wallace Stevens. But revolutionary American poetry of the 1930s was inevitably written in the atmosphere of the modernist formal revolution. Poems like those of Rolfe, Wright, and Lewis cited previously, straightforward exercises in preaching to the choir or raising the consciousness of the downtrodden, were by no means the inevitable staple of 1930s leftist poetry (as the literary scholar Cary Nelson has shown in his expansive surveys of the field); nor, some would argue, were they the majority of radical poetry.[4]

For poets on the left, the rapidly forming modernist canon sometimes offered itself as an object of scorn and ridicule. The symbolically dense and formally heterodox works of the "high" modernists, although they might be revolutionary in a strictly *literary* sphere, in reality expressed the decadence of a dead-end bourgeois culture. Eliot in particular, whose *Waste Land* (1922) had so rocked the poetic landscape, had in 1928 declared himself "classicist in literature, royalist in politics, and anglo-catholic in religion."[5] Stanley Burnshaw attacked him in his 1934 "Mr. Tubbe's Morning Service":

> The priceless Mr. Waldo Tubbe
> And all his little Tubbes now dare
> Approach the world they long to snub,
> Well insulated with despair.   (*NM*, p. 64)

And Sol Funaroff refunctioned *The Waste Land* itself into a revolutionary screed, "What the Thunder Said: A Fire Sermon," in which the thunder of part V of Eliot's poem becomes the harbinger of an explosive eruption of new social forms, "the synthesis of new worlds ... worker palaces of art and culture ... higher bonds of social union."[6] These poets derided the cultural despair they read in Eliot's work, and they regarded the overtly reactionary politics of Pound's poetry as positively repugnant, but many of them had nonetheless learned from and been influenced by the *poetics* of the modernists. If one leaves aside the hard-nosed socialist realism of *New Masses* and similar outlets, one finds that ideological debates over leftist poetry, such as that between Burnshaw and Wallace Stevens in 1935, sometimes centered less around accusations of obscurantism and decadence than around the precise degree to which a poetic work could be read as properly "committed."[7] But the forms that commitment took over the 1930s were varied indeed, and many of them partook of the innovations of the first generation of modernists or responded to modernity by forging new, hybridized poetic forms.

Kenneth Fearing (1902–1961) grew up in the Midwest but after college moved to New York City, where he published pseudonymous pulp fiction and wrote poetry that was deeply imbricated in the urban culture of the Roaring Twenties and the Great Depression. Even *New Masses* liked his work, which combines acute social observation, often gleeful satire, and hard-boiled realism in an electric, fast-moving style. In 1921 Eliot had observed how Stravinsky's *Rite of Spring* had transmuted "the scream of the motor horn, the rattle of machinery, the grind of wheels, the beating of iron and steel, the roar of the underground railway, and the other barbaric cries of modern life" into music.[8] One might argue that Fearing's verse, at its most energetic, packs a similar panoply of contemporary life – with the addition of newspaper headlines, radio news, and film newsreel text – into verse. In "1933," for instance, an unnamed "you" has beheld

the faith, the union of rags, blackened hands, stacked carrion, breached
   barricades in flame,
no default, credit restored, Union Carbide 94 3/8, call money 10%, disarm,
   steel five points up, rails rise, Dupont up, disarm, disarm, and heard again,
ghost out of ghost out of ghost out of ghost....[9]

In passages like this, Fearing presents modernity as a barrage of information, a sift of unsorted indices to the enormities being perpetrated on the
working classes – whom he presents, inevitably, in the person of an ordinary
man or woman. Fearing plays out the class struggle in the same deadpan,
affectless register as the hard-boiled detective novels he would write from the
late 1940s. There is always a touch of the surreal in such poems, however, as
when the poet addresses the businessman in "Portrait of a Cog": "When they
dig you up, in a thousand years, they will find you in just this pose, / One hand
upon the buzzer, the other reaching for the phone, eyes fixed upon the calendar, feet firmly on the office rug."[10] It is easy to see how Fearing's poems, with
their terrifying vision of the boredom of modern life, their electric sequences
of connection, and their moments of revolutionary uplift, would appeal to a
leftist readership seeking an emphatically *contemporary* idiom. But Fearing's
epic catalogues, as exhilarating as they may be in moderate doses, often spend
themselves out in trivialities, and his Whitmanian rhetoric (sometimes satirically deflated, but just as often painfully earnest) wears rapidly threadbare.

A more compellingly modern voice from the Left, perhaps, is that of Muriel
Rukeyser (1913–1980). A native New Yorker, Rukeyser was only twenty-two
when her *Theory of Flight* won the Yale Younger Poets Prize; that book already
evinced her leftist leanings, nurtured by her education at the Ethical Culture
Fieldston School and Vassar College. Rukeyser's most startling achievement
(her career included volumes of criticism, history, and biography, as well as
poetry) is the 1938 poem *The Book of the Dead*. The poem drew on Rukeyser's
investigations into the town of Gauley Bridge, West Virginia, the site of the
Hawk's Nest Tunnel Disaster. The company responsible for this hydroelectric
project, Union Carbide, drilled through the tunnel's seam of silica "dry" in
order to save time. It did not use water, which was customarily used to prevent
the spread of dangerous silicate dust, and neglected to provide its workers
with proper protective gear; hundreds of miners contracted debilitating or
fatal silicosis.

Rukeyser's poem – really a sequence of twenty shorter poems – takes its title
from the ancient Egyptian *Book of the Dead*, or *The Book of Coming Forth by Day*,
a series of spells to assist one's entry into the afterlife. Rukeyser alludes to that
text on a number of occasions, but her own *Book of the Dead* is more broadly

a memorial to the men who died (or who were dying) from the effects of the silica dust, and a scathing exposure of the corporate interests that caused their demise. What sets the poem apart from other poems on industrial disasters – there were no doubt any number of poems written about the Triangle Shirtwaist Factory fire of 1911, for instance – is its daring, genre-crossing structure. From section to section, Rukeyser shifts from pastoral travelogue, to interviews with tunnel workers (or their widows), to court testimony, and to the intimate, lyrically rendered voices of Gauley Bridge inhabitants. The poem in effect marries a sort of late-born symbolism to the gritty documentary style emerging in such works as James Agee and Walker Evans's *Let Us Now Praise Famous Men* (then in progress), and in the oral history and ethnography being produced under the auspices of the Federal Writers' Project.

Rukeyser does not burst forth in invective against Union Carbide; she lets the company's representatives be indicted in their own words, and in the transcribed (but edited and lineated) words of the congressional committee investigating the disaster. The poem's overall shape is that of a descent into, and then reascent from, the Inferno. It begins with an address of invitation to an unnamed American "you" – "These roads will take you back into your own country. / Select the mountains, follow rivers back, / travel the passes. Touch West Virginia" – an invitation that leads, down highways and through history, to Gauley Bridge and Hawk's Nest Tunnel.[11] It ends, after hundreds of lines of personal tragedy and industrial betrayal, on a note of solidarity and optimism:

> fanatic cruel legend at our back and
> speeding ahead the red and open west,
>   and this our region,
>
> desire, field, beginning. Name and road,
> communication to these many men,
> as epilogue, seeds of unending love.[12]

The abstraction of such an ending might not have pleased Rukeyser's associates in the Communist Party; her focus is on the minute human details of the mine disaster, rather than the capitalist system that made it occur. But the power of the crosscut lyricism and documentary realism of *The Book of the Dead* is undeniable, and the work Rukeyser produced over her long career would make her an important elder figure for both leftist and feminist poetic traditions. In particular, her poems exploring feminine subjectivity in by turns mythopoeic and quotidian terms have been deeply influential on such contemporaries as Adrienne Rich.

*

The Romantics clearly associated their formal poetic innovations and their republican political sympathies – Wordsworth would call *Lyrical Ballads* an experiment, written "with a view to ascertain how far the language of conversation in the middle and lower classes of society is adapted to the purposes of poetic pleasure."[13] But the Objectivists, by far the most interesting group of American poets to emerge in the 1930s, wrote in the shadow of and built on the achievements of a generation of modernist poets, Pound and Eliot most notably, whose formal innovations were often in the service of quite conservative, even reactionary political agendas. Far from being a rebel, Eliot seemed to aim at being absorbed into and playing a leading role in English conservative culture; and since 1924 Pound had been living in Italy, where he had become a fervent admirer of Mussolini's fascist regime, continuing regularly to issue cantos whose reactionary political implications were far from subtle.

The Objectivists themselves – Louis Zukofsky, George Oppen, Carl Rakosi, Charles Reznikoff, and Lorine Niedecker – were nothing if not second-generation modernists, writing in the immediate tradition of *The Waste Land, The Cantos*, and the innovations of William Carlos Williams, James Joyce, and (to a certain extent) Gertrude Stein. Pound and Eliot, however, for all the formal modernism of their verse, can be classified ideologically as "restitutionist Romantics," as Michael Löwy and Robert Sayre define the term: they partake in the general Romantic revulsion at the social changes brought about by maturing capitalism and, like Thomas Carlyle and John Ruskin, look back with longing on an imagined precapitalist, medieval past.[14]

The Objectivists, in contrast, are thorough-going modernists, looking forward in both aesthetic and political terms. The work of these five poets is widely divergent, but it is safe to describe it, as Rachel Blau DuPlessis and Peter Quartermain do, as "a non-symbolist, post-imagist poetics, characterized by a historical, realist, antimythological worldview."[15] Michael Heller sums up these poets' commonalities rather nicely when he calls the Objectivists "a flying poetic truth squad."[16] "*No myths*," writes Hugh Kenner, "might be the Objectivist motto."[17]

It is misleading to speak of the Objectivists as a "group" or "movement" in any formal sense, on the model of the Pound-led Imagists or of André Breton's tightly policed Surrealists. DuPlessis and Quartermain aptly describe them as a "nexus," a group of writers "conjoined through a variety of personal, ideological, and literary-historical links."[18] The term "Objectivists" first appeared in the February 1931 issue of *Poetry: A Magazine of Verse*. Ezra Pound had persuaded *Poetry*'s editor, Harriet Monroe, to allow his young New York correspondent Louis Zukofsky to edit a "special number" of the magazine; she agreed but insisted that Zukofsky present his selection of poets under the banner of a new "movement." Zukofsky was somewhat nonplussed – he was unaware of participating in any such movement – but he complied, retooling an essay he had earlier written on the work of his friend Charles Reznikoff, "Sincerity and Objectification," into a theoretical statement that could describe what he found most vital in the rather disparate work of the twenty-odd poets published as "'Objectivists' 1931."

Zukofsky's Objectivist "manifesto" – which he had drafted before he knew it would serve as such, and which was written without consulting any of the other poets who would come to be known as Objectivists – is in large part a restatement of the principles Pound had presented in support of the Imagists back in 1913; where "Sincerity and Objectification" differs from and goes beyond Pound is in its emphasis on the poem's overall *form*. "Sincerity" is a kind of poetic *askesis*, a writing that hews closely both to the poet's experience and to the quality of his words; it is writing "which is the detail, not mirage, of seeing, of thinking with the things as they exist, and of directing them along a line of melody." "Objectification" is a formal principle, "the resolving of words and their ideation into structure," a tangibility in which the readerly mind can attain "rested totality."[19]

Movement manifestos, of course, rarely capture the range of practices within a group. "Sincerity and Objectification" describes Zukofsky's conception of his own writing, and of what he deems worthwhile in any poetry, more than it does the work he collected in the February 1931 *Poetry* issue, or in An *"Objectivists" Anthology*, which he edited in 1932.[20] Indeed, Zukofsky was at pains to dissociate the term "Objectivist" from any organized "movement": "The interest of the [*Poetry*] issue was in the very few recent lines of poetry which could be found, and in the craft of poetry," he wrote in the preface to the *Anthology*, "NOT in a movement. The contributors did not get up one morning all over the land and say 'objectivists' between tooth-brushes."[21]

There were some two dozen poets in the "'Objectivists' 1931" issue of *Poetry*, and fifteen in the *Anthology*. The five who would come to be identified as the core "Objectivists were associated through a tenuous web of personal ties. Four of them were Jews, to some degree outsiders in an overwhelmingly Anglo-Saxon American literary culture. Zukofsky and Reznikoff (a decade older than the others) had been friends for some time; Oppen had discovered Zukofsky's work while flipping through a magazine in a bookstore and then met Zukofsky himself shortly afterward in New York; Rakosi's relationship was with Zukofsky and was primarily epistolary, as Zukofsky had discovered his poetry in the little magazines and had written him (he was then living in Houston) for work to include in the *Poetry* issue. Niedecker was the latecomer: she was so taken with the writing in *Poetry* that she contacted Zukofsky from her remote Wisconsin home, visited him in Manhattan, and established a close, lifelong friendship.

These poets' work, however, was various indeed. Charles Reznikoff (1894–1976) was born in Brooklyn to immigrant parents and pursued his poetry in relative solitude. In the face of almost entire public indifference – a number of his early books were typeset and printed by the poet himself – Reznikoff honed a minutely detailed poetics of observation, drawing on the sonorities of the King James Bible, the lyrics and epigrams of the *Greek Anthology*, and the formal precisions of the Imagists and William Carlos Williams. Reznikoff was an inveterate, even obsessive, walker, and his poems vividly depict the sounds, sights, and smells of New York in the first part of the century. With a remarkably keen eye for detail, he is able to fashion endlessly resonant images out of the welter of everyday perceptions: "Among the heaps of brick and plaster lies / a girder, still itself among the rubbish."[22]

Other Reznikoff poems explore the gritty, everyday reality of urban life – the struggles of minor artisans, office workers, and small businessmen – and dwell in a melancholy key on his own sense of isolation within the polis, both as a Jew within a culture that defined itself overwhelmingly as classical and Christian and as a Jew who found himself estranged from his own tradition. "How difficult for me is Hebrew," Reznikoff writes, "even the Hebrew for *mother*, for *bread*, for *sun* / is foreign. How far have I been exiled, Zion."[23] In "Hellenist," the poet laments the slowness of his own access to the richness of Gentile culture: "As I, barbarian, at last, although slowly, could read Greek, / at 'blue-eyed Athena' / I greeted her picture." The awkward, stumbling phrases of the first line mime the poet's stumbling encounter with *glaukopis Athene*, while the last clause – "the beautiful lips slightly scornful" – captures his timidity in an image of cold classicism.[24]

When he was not writing short lyrics, Reznikoff was much engaged in recasting biblical stories, or retelling Jewish tales from the intertestamental period. Many of his poems also present narratives of contemporary life; they are practically short stories in verse, often haunting in their obliquity. Reznikoff had been trained as a lawyer and had a keen eye for the human drama concealed beneath legal evidence. His work as a researcher on the *Corpus Juris* legal encyclopedia would contribute immensely to his long poem *Testimony: The United States (1885–1915), Recitative*. This sprawling work presents edited and versified excerpts from thirty years of courtroom testimony across the nation and lays out a sometimes dreary panorama of injustice, inequality, and violence. Reznikoff understood "Objectivist" as referring to the necessary objectivity of the judge or the courtroom reporter: his "testimony" stands unalloyed and uncommented on and is all the more scarifying in its nakedness as objective social commentary.

Carl Rakosi (1903–2004) was born in Berlin, his parents immigrated to the Midwest when he was seven, and he grew up in Chicago and Indiana; he knew Kenneth Fearing when he attended the University of Wisconsin. In sharp contrast to Reznikoff, Rakosi rarely essays narrative verse, or poems longer than a page or two. His verse is distinguished in turn by a plainspoken formal care, an almost finical attention to enjambment and stanza break reminiscent of the Williams of *Spring and All*, and alternately by a florid, ornate diction strongly redolent of Wallace Stevens, as in "Salons," with its "lines of peridot," "cairn-gorm pomp," and "refinements of the clavichord."[25] Rakosi is an unabashedly *lyrical* poet, but with a propensity toward satire that often aims at (but rarely skewers) social targets. When he openly expresses his political sentiments, as in "To the Non-Political Citizen," the result is no more subtle than *New Masses*'s common fare: "When will you become indignant / and declare yourself / against the wrongs of the people?"[26] More than anything else, Rakosi's poems seek to *see* the world in its fresh and colorful detail; the social structures of that world rarely engage his attention for long.

Louis Zukofsky (1904–1978) was a poet of large if often frustrated ambition. He was the first American-born child of immigrant Lithuanian Jews; his father worked as a pants presser in the Manhattan garment district, a life of back-breaking drudgery that Zukofsky was determined to escape. And escape it he did, graduating from Columbia University with a master's degree at twenty-two, and striving throughout his life to make the Western cultural inheritance his own. Zukofsky's first major work, "Poem beginning 'The,'" is a 330-line parody of *The Waste Land* that draws on contemporary American Yiddish verse, and that asserts, in the face of the anti-Semitism of Eliot's shorter verse, Zukofsky's stubborn pride in his own Jewishness. "Poem beginning 'The'" ends with a moment of most un-Eliotic optimism, hope in the Russian Bolshevik experiment. Zukofsky's early short poetry veers between moments of chiseled, almost finically crafted free verse observation and political statements distinguished largely by their obliquity; this was verse that, whatever its merits in formal precision and intellectual density, could be of little *use* to the Left.

From early on Zukofsky intended to write a long poem, and he began his twenty-four-section *"A"* in 1928, expecting it to occupy no more than a few years. In the event, he would labor at the poem for almost five decades.

"A" begins much in the mode of Pound's *Cantos*: each movement of verse concatenates materials from the present, the historical past, and the general cultural record, aiming to elicit a larger movement or meaning from the juxtaposition of the discrete elements. (Zukofsky himself liked to describe the formal structure of the early movements of "A" as in some sense "fugal.") But where *The Cantos* tend to contrast historical shifts and events with timeless, mythological moments, "A" is concerned with tracing the dialectics of history, the inconsistent relationship between a capitalist system in crisis and artists' repeated reaching for timeless beauty, a utopian moment continually undermined by economic inequity. Marx is a major presence in the early movements of "A"; the first half of "A"-9 (1938–1940) is an adaptation of the Renaissance Italian poet Guido Cavalcanti's canzone "Donna mi priegha" (a poem Pound had translated repeatedly), adopting the original's complex meter and rhyme scheme to present a restatement of the passage from *Capital* in which Marx defines value in the voice of the commodity itself.

If "A" had begun as something of a Marxist *Cantos*, as the poem progressed into its middle sections, it became increasingly a showcase for Zukofsky's formal experiments, his attempt to fashion the materials of his historical moment, his wide reading, and his personal life into a bewilderingly various larger whole – what he called "a poem of a life."[27] Zukofsky's work would come to be a set of modernist limit texts, the pushing to extremes of radical condensation and the ruthless excision of bridge passages, connectives, and all materials of less than "first intensity";[28] translation as an instrument for the poet's taking on unfamiliar voices, and as the discovery of new formal "templates" for verse (most notably in Zukofsky's translation – with his wife Celia – of Catullus); and quotation, the creation of the poem out of widely disparate but cunningly joined fragments of others' writing.

Like Rakosi, Lorine Niedecker (1903–1970) hailed from the Midwest, but her own upbringing was a rural one, and apart from her visit to New York City she would spend most of her life in the marshy, lake-spotted Wisconsin area where she was born. During the first years of her association with Zukofsky, she was deeply interested in Surrealism, in exploring the various levels of individual consciousness through techniques of semi-"automatic" writing and dream exploration. In a pair of sets of poems published in 1935, for instance, she sought to tease out successive "planes of consciousness": in the "Beyond what" set, those of the "subconscious," "toward monologue," and the "social-banal" (*LNC*, p. 370). This is in some sense Freud, of course (id, ego, and super-ego), but it is edging toward political commentary, especially in its final lines:

"the stars and stripes forever / over the factories and hills of our country / for the soldier dead" (*LNC*, p. 34).

Over the course of the second half of the 1930s, Niedecker's verse became sparer and sparer. Turning from the expansive innerscapes of her Surrealist work, she pursued the potentials of a stripped-down language of startling clarity, and the formal possibilities of traditional vernacular verse forms – folk songs and nursery rhymes. This direction in her work culminated in the formidable achievement of the *New Goose* collection (published in 1946, but including work dating back to the mid-1930s). *New Goose* includes poems of personal experience, deep meditations on the privations and riches of Niedecker's rural existence: "Remember my little granite pail? / The handle of it was blue" (*LNC*, p. 96). In a poem about her mother – one of many – Niedecker writes, "I've wasted my whole life in water. / My man's got nothing but leaky boats. / My daughter, writer, sits and floats" (*LNC*, p. 107). Other pieces touch on historical characters – John James Audubon ("Tried selling my pictures. In jail twice for debt. My companion a sharp, frosty gale"), Vincent van Gogh ("At times I sit in the dunes, / faint, not enough to eat"), and the fur trader John Baptiste DuBay (*LNC*, pp. 107, 108).

As her citations from Audubon and van Gogh indicate, Niedecker took note of the economic hardship all too often suffered by the artist, and that hardship, other poems of the collection imply, is part and parcel of a system of private property and capitalist competition. As the Sauk chief Black Hawk holds,

> In reason
> land cannot be sold,
> only things to be carried away,
> and I am old.

But the Sauks are dispossessed by the expanding United States, "and to this day, Black Hawk, / reason has small room" (*LNC*, p. 99). Niedecker's political commitments are quite evidently leftist and are as evidently on display throughout *New Goose*; but she rarely strays into sloganeering. Instead, her social and political commentary is embedded in wry, Mother Goose–like quatrains, its impact all the sharper for its playful tone. The "folk" idiom of *New Goose* is a continuingly impressive achievement: Niedecker's vernacular vocabulary and sharp eye for the patterns of ordinary rural conversation (often quoted seemingly verbatim) speak to a wide range of readers, while her minutely calibrated line breaks and deliberate syntactic obliquities reward the closest repeated attention.

In one poem, the nineteenth-century naturalist Asa Gray writes to his colleague Increase Lapham, "pay particular attention / to my pets, the grasses" (*LNC*, p. 105). Such language would seem to forecast the future of Niedecker's own interests. Both Gray and Lapham were celebrated nineteenth-century naturalists; Lapham is known as the first great cataloguer of Wisconsin's flora and geography, and Gray's injunction to him – to pay special attention to the natural phenomena around him, the "grasses" under his feet – is one that Niedecker would take to heart.

George Oppen (1908–1984) grew up in a more than well-to-do family in downstate New York and San Francisco, but by 1928, when he met Louis Zukofsky and Charles Reznikoff in New York City, he had turned his back on that milieu, hitchhiking across the country with his wife, Mary, and working odd jobs. Oppen's only book of the 1930s, *Discrete Series* (1934), is perhaps the most obdurate, unaccommodating work of the first wave of Objectivist poetry. "I see the difference between the writing of Mr. Oppen and Dr. Williams," Pound writes in his preface to the volume; "I do not expect any great horde of readers to notice it."[29] The angular, eloquent line breaks of Williams's free verse, as well as the spare observations of the Imagists, are perhaps the most evident influences on Oppen's poetics. But the poems of *Discrete Series* aim to go beyond the Imagists' presentational aesthetics: as Oppen's editor Michael Davidson puts it, to link "the phenomenal object with an experiencing, language-using subject" (*GONC*, p. xxx).

In practice, this means that there are no poems of pure observation in *Discrete Series*; every phenomenon the poet observes is mediated through a keen awareness of its position within a social order. Driving "our car … on a higher road," the poet notes that

> Nothing can equal in polish and obscured
> origin that dark instrument
> A car
> (Which.
> Ease; the hand on the sword-hilt   (*GONC*, p. 8)

The car, then as now the quintessential emblem of American freedom and masculinity, attracts by its "polish," its easy instrumentality, but those very aspects make it near kin to the premodern emblem of manhood, the sword. Just as the "Frigidaire" hides its inner workings behind a polished enamel surface, or the soda jerk making an egg cream cracks eggs out of sight of the customer – "the prudery / Of Frigidaire, of / Soda-jerking" – "big-Business" occludes itself "Above the / / Plane of lunch, of wives" (*GONC*, p. 7), removes itself from quotidian consciousness, even as it continues to manipulate the social order that allows one a lunch hour during which one might step out for an egg cream.

This is perhaps as close as *Discrete Series* comes to outright social commentary, save for another brief poem that freezes a Depression snapshot: amid automobile traffic, "By the elevated posts / And the movie sign," "A man sells postcards"(*GONC*, p. 30). Oppen's verse is simultaneously a sensory and an intensely cerebral poetry: his poems seem to stammer their way through the shifting experience of "the world, weather-swept, with which / one shares the century" (*GONC*, p. 5). They dramatize a search for certainties in a society that seems in terminal crisis, and while they register the rumbling movement of larger social forces, they refuse to settle for easy answers. Poetry, Oppen found, was – like philosophy – the process of discovering the words to ask the big questions; and as Marx had charged in his "Theses on Feuerbach," the time had perhaps come for the philosophers to set aside "explaining" the world in order to *change* it.

*

In the wake of the February 1931 "Objectivists" issue of *Poetry* magazine, Zukofsky, Oppen, and Reznikoff sought to prolong the public attention focused on their "movement" with a pair of publishing ventures: To Publishers, bankrolled by Oppen and edited by Zukofsky, which issued *An "Objectivists" Anthology* and volumes of prose by Pound and Williams, and the Objectivist Press, a collective venture that published Williams's *Collected Poems 1921–1931*, Oppen's *Discrete Series*, and four volumes by Reznikoff. (Williams's presence in both of these lists as a fully participant Objectivist both demonstrates the ductility of the Objectivist moniker and underlines the movement's continuity with an older generation of modernism.) Neither of these presses was very successful, and as the Depression deepened, more and more of the little magazines that had printed these poets were forced to close. *New Masses* continued publication, and for a while Zukofsky made some editorial contributions to it and even placed a couple of poems there; but he ultimately found that he could not convince Mike Gold and the other editors of the value of his own intransigent modernism, however authentically Marxist his ideological stance might be. As the 1930s wore on, Zukofsky and Niedecker found themselves almost entirely without publishing outlets.

Rakosi similarly found that, although he was a committed leftist, the left-wing magazines had no use for his lyrics, and after he married in 1939 he stopped writing, mostly out of sheer lack of time. Oppen made an even cleaner break. Unable to reconcile his commitments to poetry and social activism, after the

publication of *Discrete Series* he joined the Communist Party, on whose behalf
he worked as an election campaign manager and strike organizer. He entirely
gave up poetry, unwilling to write the sort of poems the party demanded. He
fought as an infantryman on the western front in the Second World War, but
in 1950 moved with his wife Mary to Mexico to avoid harassment by the FBI on
account of his earlier political activities.

As a "movement," and as individual poets, the Objectivists had been largely
forgotten by the end of the 1930s. Oppen and Rakosi had ceased writing,
and Reznikoff had to some extent forgone poetry for prose writing. While
Zukofsky and Niedecker continued writing poems, they had extraordinary
difficulty getting their work published. Their first book collections were issued
during the 1940s and were received with resounding silence. By the postwar
years, it was as though these poets had never existed.

*

But the poets of the Objectivist nexus experienced a remarkable public resurgence over the 1960s. In 1958 Oppen, after a quarter century away from poetry
and eight years in self-imposed exile in Mexico, began writing again and moved
back to the United States. Rakosi returned to writing in the 1960s after a similar
hiatus, and Reznikoff turned his attentions back to poetry. These three poets
found a wider audience than heretofore, as they were now published by New
Directions, Pound's and Williams's publisher. Even Zukofsky, who had issued
a series of small press (and self-published) books over the 1940s and 1950s,
by the late 1960s found his poetry being published by the trade firm W. W.
Norton. A new generation of American avant-garde poets, inspired largely by
Charles Olson's "Projective Verse" manifesto – among them Robert Duncan,
Robert Creeley, Cid Corman, and Denise Levertov – began rediscovering the
Objectivists. At first these younger poets looked to Zukofsky and Oppen as
still-living relics of an earlier generation of experimental writing, a surviving
direct link to the heroic first generation of high modernism. But soon enough,
it became clear that these poets were by no means museum exhibits but were
writing some of the most vital poetry of the postwar decades.

Of course, if the Objectivists had ever really been a group back in the 1930s,
by the 1960s they were a heterogeneous set of poets who shared little besides
memories and past associations. Rakosi's own return to writing had been
spurred by the English poet Andrew Crozier's contacting him in 1965, but he
had been out of touch with the others for years. Zukofsky and Oppen had
tried to reestablish their once intimate friendship when Oppen moved to New
York in 1958, but the two men found themselves radically incompatible on

both aesthetic and personal bases. By the mid-1960s they were no longer on speaking terms. Niedecker and Zukofsky alone, carrying on their epistolary relationship over the decades, sharing personal news and poems, constituted a "movement" of two. Niedecker in the 1950s and early 1960s was more isolated than ever, her primary contacts with the literary world her correspondence with Zukofsky and, later, with the poet and editor Cid Corman.

Although James Laughlin of New Directions had used the Objectivist connection to promote the books he published by Oppen, Rakosi, and Reznikoff, the notion of the Objectivists as a group of four – those poets and Zukofsky – was crystallized by their appearance together in a 1969 feature in *Contemporary Literature*, "The Objectivist Poet: Four Interviews." The texts of those interviews, indeed, demonstrate rather decisively how loose any conceptual commonalities of the original "movement" had been: the very term "Objectivist" becomes a kind of Rorschach blot, eliciting four different definitions from the four poets. The young poets of 1931 were now poets in their late middle age. More crucially, the subject matter, forms, and techniques of their work had blossomed in new, provocative directions that were to prove an instigation to younger poets through the rest of the century.

One index of the shift in Zukofsky's concerns is the second half of "A"-9 (1948–1950), written a decade after the first. The poem is still an adaptation of Cavalcanti, his internal and end rhymes and meter intact. But where the first half uses the words of *Das Kapital* to define *labor*, the second half uses the words of Spinoza's *Ethics* to define *love*. Between 1938 and 1948 Zukofsky had become a husband and a father, and to a large degree the focus of his work shifted from political engagement to the more immediate sphere of his family life. That he rewrote "A"-9's first half, however, preserving its original rhyme words, indicates the degree to which Zukofsky had become obsessed with formal experimentation. Indeed, the later movements of "A" can be read as a series of increasingly strange and recondite formal challenges issued by the poet to himself: to excavate a poem out of *Paradise Lost*, preserving Milton's words in their original order, but distributed in two-word lines ("A"-14); to open a poem on the death of John F. Kennedy with a passage from the book of Job, its Hebrew homophonically translated into barely grammatical – but *very* strange-sounding – English ("A"-15); to write an elegy for his friend William Carlos Williams, using only the words he had previously written about or to Williams ("A"-17); to translate Plautus's *Rudens* (*The Rope*) into a slangy vernacular, keeping to one five-word line for each line of Latin hexameter, and preserving as much of the sound of the original as possible; and to plot a pair of geological, linguistic, and cultural histories of the world on the structure of one thousand five-word lines ("A"-22 and -23). These last movements are indeed, as some of their final lines put it, a "never- / Unfinished hairlike water of notes / vital free as Itself – impossible's / sort-of think-cramp work x."[30]

Zukofsky's late work presses the very limit of the intelligible. His final collection, *80 Flowers*, published shortly after his death in 1978, is a series of strictly formal short poems – eight five-word lines – each one addressing a given plant or flower, each one a collage of quoted, translated, or transliterated words. The opening lines of "Bearded Iris," for instance – "Gay ore geek con candlelows / driveway west fanswordleaves equitant stride" – condense passages from Virgil's *Georgics* (whose Greek title, *Georgikon*, is transliterated in the first words) and from *Gray's Manual of Botany*, crosscutting them with direct description ("fanswordleaves," "driveway west") and allusions to one of Zukofsky's recurrent images, that of the poet as laboring "horse" ("equitant stride").[31] Zukofsky could not have expected his readers to be able to unwind these condensed miniature labyrinths of reference: these are not the late *Cantos*, in which a single talismanic word alerts us to a reference to Justinian or Confucius. Rather, these forty-word lyrics function as nodes of alluring indeterminacy, challenging the reader to test their alternatives of syntax and meaning, and to wonder at their ghosty, half-perceived depths of resonance.

Already by the 1960s there were a number of poets whose voices were deeply influenced by Zukofsky's angular lyricism, Robert Creeley, Robert Kelly, John Taggart, and Ronald Johnson among them. His fantastically impacted, obdurate late writing would have a deep impact on an even younger generation – the poets of the Language Movement, among them Lyn Hejinian, Ron Silliman, Charles Bernstein, and Barrett Watten, who looked to Zukofsky's early writing as one model of a politically engaged modernism, and to his late work for models of nonlinear and semantically indeterminate lyricism.

The poems George Oppen made when he returned to writing in the late 1950s are quite unlike his early Objectivist work in both texture, intensity, and scope. His keen eye for detail is the same, as is his halting, almost stammering lyricism, but there is a philosophical depth only hinted at in *Discrete Series*. His first posthiatus collection, *The Materials*, opens with an epigraph from Jacques Maritain – "We awake in the same moment to ourselves and things" (*GONC*, p. 38) – and this preoccupation with the very state of *being* in the world, which Oppen also found brooded on by Heidegger, is at the center of Oppen's mature work. "I am no longer sure of the words," he writes in "Leviathan" (whose title evokes Thomas Hobbes's political meditation), "The clockwork of the world. What is inexplicable / / Is the 'preponderance of objects.' . . . We must talk now. Fear / Is fear. But we abandon one another" (*GONC*, p. 89). The poems of Oppen's later collections from *The Materials* (1962) to 1978's *Primitive* are a series of approaches to very basic questions: What does it mean that we, as language-using creatures, are living in a world of objects and animals? In what ways do those seemingly dumb phenomena among which we live speak to us? And how can we manage to live with one another, given our propensity for violence and self-destruction?

Oppen's late work is an inescapably political poetry, but it is political in a deep sense that transcends divisions of party: what does it mean that the human being is (in Aristotle's phrase) a *zoon politikon*, a "political animal," one who by rights lives in a polis, a community? The issue is explored most extensively in the long title poem of *Of Being Numerous* (1968), which moves and circles back in numbered sections from a meditation on the objects among which we live, to memories of Oppen's military service in the Second World War, and to the present state of the American republic, at once engaged in a war of imperialist aggression in Vietnam and lacerated by civil dissent at home. The fundamental American paradox, to form a single polis out of inviolable individualities ("*e pluribus unum*"), is at stake here, the significance of "being numerous":

> Obsessed, bewildered
>
> By the shipwreck
> Of the singular
>
> We have chosen the meaning
> Of being numerous.   (*GONC*, p. 166)

In order to confront the horrors and paradoxes of his time, the poet must somehow, through his word skill, through his passion of his thought, rise above the common level; at the same time, he must retain his vital connections to others, must avoid "the bright light of shipwreck" (*GONC*, p. 173), the solipsism of those who have detached themselves from their fellows and direct the helicopters against the rice paddies.

The poet's primary responsibility, in Oppen's eyes, is to confront the world as openly and keenly as possible, and then to speak what he sees with the utmost clarity possible:

> Clarity
>
> In the sense of *transparence*,
> I don't mean that much can be explained.
>
> Clarity in the sense of silence.   (*GONC*, p. 175)

The problems the poet confronts may be at the very limits of our understanding, ultimately intractable, but the poet's duty is to speak them as plainly as possible. What this ethos gives rise to in Oppen's later work is a poetry in which questions of staggering philosophical weight are revolved and pondered in fragments of sometimes inarticulate questioning and flashes of great lyric beauty. It is something like Heidegger in verse, but without Heidegger's serene confidence in the surety of his own intuitions.

Oppen's emphasis on clarity no doubt contributed to his break with Zukofsky; he saw the increasing hermeticism and formal complexity of Zukofsky's later work as no better than a series of formal flourishes, evidence of Zukofsky's having turned his back on the readers with whom Oppen so desperately wished to communicate. Oppen's own poetry found many readers indeed over the 1960s; they were attracted in part by the poems' willingness to confront the pressing political issues of the day. (*Of Being Numerous* was awarded the Pulitzer Prize in 1969, much to Oppen's discomfiture.) But Oppen has become a central influence on succeeding generations of writers, moved by his work's craggy lyricism, its utter sincerity, and its intransigent thoughtfulness. His writing has spoken not merely to adherents of various avant-gardes, such as the Language poets, but to such "mainstream" poets as Sharon Olds.

Niedecker's early poetry had explored her own experience as one exemplar of class relations and struggle. Over the course of the postwar decades, her work came to dwell more insistently on her own relationship to her midwestern setting, and to explore the natural, even geological histories of her surroundings. And although she continued to compose in the tight, compact forms she had evolved over the 1930s, she gradually abandoned the evocations of traditional folk forms, developing a wonderfully spare and evocative vernacular, free verse idiom. Her 1968 collection *North Central* contains several striking longer poems or sequences, in which she works to build larger wholes out of her mostly self-sufficient shorter units.

"Lake Superior," for instance, a poem based on a car trip she took around that lake in 1966, is at once travelogue, geological exploration, and history lesson. As Niedecker rounds the lake, she evokes the French explorers who first opened up the region to European settlement and the Indians who lived there before them, and she meditates on the importance of iron deposits and iron shipping routes, on the various rock formations she encounters, and on the succession of names given to points on the lake's environs: the lake itself becomes a palimpsest of history, reaching back beyond its human inhabitants. "Wintergreen Ridge" is another tour de force of naturalistic description, moving from geological observation to a minute tracking of flora, all interspersed with personal reflection and cultural allusion. In the midst of meditation on time and falling leaves, Niedecker notes that

Nobody, nothing
   ever gave me
     greater thing

than time
  unless light
    and silence

which if intense
   makes sound   (*LNC*, p. 253)

These lines would seem beautifully to sum up Niedecker's quiet, penetrating aesthetic.

Zukofsky was given to comparing Niedecker to Emily Dickinson (while at times he compared himself to Walt Whitman). The grounds of the analogy are clear, if unfortunately sexist: the isolated female poet, cut off from the world of literary commerce, piecing out her "letter to the world" in mostly unread lyrics. Perhaps that stereotype has been reinforced by the critical attention paid to "Paean to Place," a late, longish (for Niedecker) poem that dwells much on the poet's forebears and her Wisconsin environment, and that displays little of the range of cultural references that so inflects most of Niedecker's poetry. But "Paean to Place" is indeed a masterpiece of self-reflection and natural observation. Midway through, Niedecker describes her own lyrical gift:

I was the solitary plover
a pencil
   for a wing-bone
From the secret notes
I must tilt

upon the pressure
execute and adjust
   In us sea-air rhythm
 "We live by the urgent wave
of the verse"   (*LNC*, p. 265)

Niedecker is neither an autodidactic hermit nor a self-obsessed spinster but an immensely subtle and sophisticated poet who brings a formidable mastery of sound, lineation, and diction and a deep knowledge of poetic tradition to bear on a sometimes deliberately limited set of subject matter. Of all of the original Objectivists, her work is perhaps most widely known and valued by a broad readership, forty years after her death.

★

Leftist poetry in 1930s America flourished in response to a particular historical moment, just as many thousands of antiwar poems were written during the Vietnam War. What is most fascinating about the politically engaged poetry of the 1930s, however, and what sets it apart from similarly engaged work written during, say, the American Revolution or the English Commonwealth, is that it was written in the wake of a large-scale formal revolution in English-language writing. Leftist poets of the 1930s wrote in relation both to the possibility of political revolution and to modernism, a "revolution of the word" that had radically redefined the terms of poetry itself. Some committed poets essentially ignored modernism or dismissed it as bourgeois decadence; others, like the Objectivists, sought to make their politico-rhetorical interventions in the forms and modes pioneered by the modernists, and to extend those modernist modes.

In fact, it might be argued that the Objectivists advance what amounts to a fundamentally *materialist* poetics, in which their relentless foregrounding of the materiality of the poem – the graphic shapes of the words and lines out of which it is made and the aural sounds of its words – becomes a sustained analog for the representation of conditions of objects and persons in the world. The political charge of Objectivist poetry lies less in the specifically political stances taken up within the poems – although much of the Objectivists' work, especially their early work, is very committed indeed – than in the forms and idioms of that work, which ceaselessly question the accepted order of things and which might even be read as restlessly hunting for the utopian in the nooks and crannies of a capitalist world order.

It is possible to speak of a "second generation" of Objectivist poets, those who knew and have been directly influenced by the original Objectivists, and whose works are both grounded in the Objectivists' projects and extend those projects in new directions: Michael Heller, Rachel Blau DuPlessis, Norman Finkelstein, and Hugh Seidman would be among such poets. But the Objectivists' influence has become far more widely diffused than their relatively modest success during their lifetimes would indicate. However belatedly – certainly the Objectivists' impact has paradoxically lagged behind that of Charles Olson and the poets associated with his "Projective Verse" (Robert Creeley, Robert Duncan, and Denise Levertov) – literary history has begun to recognize the Objectivist nexus as one of the central instigations of twentieth-century American poetry.

Notes

1. Lorine Niedecker, *Collected Works*, ed. Jenny Penberthy (Berkeley: University of California Press, 2002), p. 87. This collection will be cited in the text as *LNC*.

2. Percy Bysshe Shelley, *Shelley's Poetry and Prose*, ed. Donald H. Reiman and Sharon B. Powers (New York: W. W. Norton, 1977), p. 305.

3. Joseph North (ed.), *New Masses: An Anthology of the Rebel Thirties* (New York: International Publishers, 1969), pp. 56, 58, 66. This collection will be cited in the text as *NM*.

4. Cary Nelson, *Repression and Recovery: Modern American Poetry and the Politics of Cultural Memory, 1910–1945* (Madison: University of Wisconsin Press, 1989); Cary Nelson, *Revolutionary Memory: Recovering the Poetry of the American Left* (New York: Routledge, 2001).

5. T. S. Eliot, *For Lancelot Andrewes: Essays on Style and Order* (London: Faber and Gwyer, 1928), p. vii.

6. Nelson, *Repression and Recovery*, p. 215.

7. James Longenbach, *Wallace Stevens: The Plain Sense of Things* (New York: Oxford University Press, 1991), pp. 135–47; Harvey Teres, *Renewing the Left: Politics, Imagination, and the New York Intellectuals* (New York: Oxford University Press, 1996), pp. 116–33; and, more generally, Alan Filreis, *Modernism from Right to Left: Wallace Stevens, the Thirties, and Literary Radicalism* (Cambridge: Cambridge University Press, 1994).

8. T. S. Eliot, *The Annotated Waste Land with Eliot's Contemporary Prose*, ed. Lawrence Rainey (New Haven, Conn.: Yale University Press, 2005), p. 189.

9. Kenneth Fearing, *Selected Poems*, ed. Robert Polito (New York: Library of America, 2004), p. 43.

10. Fearing, *Selected Poems*, p. 101.

11. Muriel Rukeyser, *Out of Silence: Selected Poems*, ed. Kate Daniels (Evanston, Ill.: Triquarterly Books, 1992), p. 10.

12. Rukeyser, *Out of Silence*, p. 40.

13. William Wordsworth, *William Wordsworth: The Oxford Authors*, ed. Stephen Gill (Oxford: Oxford University Press, 1984), p. 591.

14. Michael Löwy and Robert Sayre, *Romanticism Against the Tide of Modernity*, trans. Catherine Porter (Durham, N.C.: Duke University Press, 2001).

15. Rachel Blau DuPlessis and Peter Quartermain (eds.), *The Objectivist Nexus: Essays in Cultural Poetics* (Tuscaloosa: University of Alabama Press, 1999), p. 3.

16. Michael Heller, *Conviction's Net of Branches: Essays on the Objectivist Poets and Poetry* (Carbondale: Southern Illinois University Press, 1985), p. 7.

17. Hugh Kenner, *A Homemade World: The American Modernist Writers* (New York: Knopf, 1975), p. 187.

18. DuPlessis and Quartermain, *The Objectivist Nexus*, p. 2.

19. Louis Zukofsky, *Prepositions+: The Collected Critical Essays*, rev. and expanded ed. (Middletown, Conn.: Wesleyan University Press, 2000), p. 194.

20. Louis Zukofsky (ed.), "Objectivists," special issue, *Poetry* 37:5 (1931), http://www.poetryfoundation.org/poetrymagazine/toc/221; Louis Zukofsky (ed.), *An "Objectivists" Anthology* (Le Beausset, Var, France: To Publishers, 1932).

21. Zukofsky, *Prepositions+*, p. 214.
22. Charles Reznikoff, *Poems 1918–1936: Volume I of the Complete Poems*, ed. Seamus Cooney (Santa Barbara, Calif.: Black Sparrow, 1976), p. 121.
23. Reznikoff, *Poems 1918–1936*, p. 72.
24. Reznikoff, *Poems 1918–1936*, p. 107.
25. Carl Rakosi, *Poems 1923–1941*, ed. Andrew Crozier (Los Angeles: Sun & Moon, 1995), p. 87.
26. Rakosi, *Poems 1923–1941*, p. 140.
27. Zukofsky, *Prepositions+*, p. 228.
28. Ezra Pound, "Vorticism," in *Early Writings: Poetry and Prose*, ed. Ira B. Nadel (New York: Penguin, 2005), p. 281.
29. George Oppen, *New Collected Poems*, ed. Michael Davidson (New York: New Directions, 2002), p. 4. This collection will be cited in the text as *GONC*.
30. Louis Zukofsky, *"A"* (1978; New York: New Directions, 2011), p. 563.
31. Louis Zukofsky, *ANEW: Complete Shorter Poetry* (New York: New Directions, 2011), p. 345.

Chapter 33

"All the Blessings of This Consuming Chance": Robert Lowell, John Berryman, Theodore Roethke, and the Middle-Generation Poets

DAVID WOJAHN

At the time of his death in 1977, Robert Lowell was the most esteemed American poet of his era, enjoying a reputation comparable to that of his great modernist predecessors T. S. Eliot and William Butler Yeats. Like them, he had come to be seen as not only a strikingly original and influential poet but also a public figure whose import far surpassed that of other poets of his generation. As early as 1965, critic Irvin Ehrenpreis could declare "the Age of Lowell."[1] This adulation began very early in Lowell's career. He was not yet thirty when he received the Pulitzer Prize for his second collection, *Lord Weary's Castle* and was barely in his forties when his greatest and most influential collection, *Life Studies*, appeared.

During the years since his death, Lowell's reputation has waned, although he remains a writer of considerable interest among readers and scholars; he has been the subject of two biographies. Lowell is now seen less as the dominant poet of his time than as a leading member of the so-called middle generation of American poets born between roughly 1905 and 1920, whose ranks include such formidable names as John Berryman, Theodore Roethke, Randall Jarrell, George Oppen, Muriel Rukeyser, Robert Hayden, Lorine Niedecker, Delmore Schwartz, Stanley Kunitz, Weldon Kees, and above all Elizabeth Bishop – Lowell's closest literary associate, whose reputation has now eclipsed that of her generational peers. The middle-generation poets represent various aesthetics and schools, but all of the names on this list share a particular unease toward what they came to regard as the excessively programmatic high modernism of Eliot, Pound, Moore, and Stevens. Yet the middle-generation poets emphatically regarded themselves as the successors of the modernists, seeking less to depart from their example as to vary, refine, and individualize a manner that came to be seen by them as rarefied and aesthetically restrictive. Lowell may not today be regarded as the greatest poet of his era, nor even the most significant talent among the middle generation, but he is arguably the poet most representative of the middle generation's particular aesthetic and personal anxieties. And, if the desire for stylistic change can be regarded as a primary hallmark of ambition, then he is perhaps the most ambitious American poet of his time, his work falling into at least four distinct periods; few other poets have so successfully made such radical changes.

Furthermore, Lowell's influence on later generations continues to be felt, and of the middle-generation poets he is second only to Bishop in this regard. Perhaps the most enduring legacy of Lowell's work is that his seminal collection, *Life Studies*, gave several generations of American poets permission to write an overtly autobiographical poetry that appeared to derive directly from experience, often the experience of emotional extremity. These topics included accounts of mental breakdowns, marital strife, dysfunctional family histories, and drug and alcohol abuse, subjects considered indelicate at best, even taboo. The critic M. L. Rosenthal dubbed such writing "confessional poetry," a label that displeased Lowell, and one that came to have a slightly pejorative import.[2] By the end of the 1980s, the style began to fall into disfavor. Still, without Lowell's example, the careers of as diverse a group of American poets as Sylvia Plath, Anne Sexton, Adrienne Rich, Frank Bidart, C. K. Williams, Robert Pinsky, Robert Hass, Frederick Seidel, Louise Glück, Mark Doty, Jorie Graham, Sharon Olds, and Yusef Komunyakaa would be hard to imagine. Lowell's influence on Anglophone poetry in the British Isles and elsewhere is similarly considerable. Figures such as Seamus Heaney, Derek Walcott, Tony Harrison, Paul Muldoon, and Geoffrey Hill all owe, in differing ways, a considerable debt to Lowell.

Yet Lowell is a more complex and challenging figure than any of the poets on this list, not merely because he allowed autobiographical testimony to return to poetry after its diminishment in the era of the modernists, but also because he drew little distinction between his desire for scrupulous self-examination and his ambition to speak as a public figure of authority, addressing – in a tone sometimes merely stentorian but at best authentically prophetic – the complacency and conformity of the Eisenhower era, the Cold War and its threat of nuclear annihilation, and the hubris that lead to the U.S. involvement in the Vietnam War. Although Lowell felt decidedly ambivalent about his New England predecessors, the Transcendentalists, Lowell epitomizes the sort of American poet whom Emerson envisioned when he called for a "genius ... with tyrannous eye, which knew the value of our incomparable materials" and could above all confront the "barbarism and materialism of the times."[3]

Lowell was drawn to address the turmoil of his era in no small measure because his own life was itself manifestly turbulent. Not long after the publication of *Lord Weary's Castle* in 1946, he was diagnosed with severe bipolar disorder, a disease that at the time was little understood and difficult to treat with the psychotropic drugs then available. During Lowell's manic attacks, which occurred on an almost annual basis from the 1950s until the time of his death, his behavior could be highly delusional and sometimes violent, and his stays in mental hospitals – which he wrote about with disarming frankness in *Life Studies* and in his final collection, *Day by Day* – became so frequent as to amount to ritual. He was married three times, first to the novelist Jean Stafford, then to the novelist and essayist Elizabeth Hardwick, and finally, after his move to Great Britain in the 1970s, to the fiction writer Lady Caroline Blackwood. Each of these relationships was strife ridden, and Lowell's insistence on writing about them in sometimes lurid detail resulted in perhaps the greatest controversies of his career. Bidart, Lowell's amanuensis and editor of his posthumous *Collected Poems*, has labeled Lowell a "transgressive" writer, a canny label that suggests both Lowell's bravery – which was considerable – and his indiscretion, which some would regard as equally considerable.[4]

To fully appreciate Bidart's characterization of Lowell as an artist of transgression, one must also take into account other aspects of his writing. The first two arise from his biography. Few American poets have been as concerned with how family history intersects with personal history, and this concern is partly explained by Lowell's unusual background, at once quintessentially American and democratic and on the other hand deeply elitist. Lowell's mother's family, the Winslows, could trace their ancestry back to the Mayflower pilgrims. His father's ancestors included such luminaries as the poets James Russell and Amy Lowell, and the astronomer Percival Lowell. The poet was keenly aware both of the burdens of his ancestry – in the *Life Studies* poem "Waking in the Blue," he characterizes himself as a "Mayflower screwball" – and of his ability to exploit it.[5] In his poems he often regards himself as the heir of a fraught New England legacy composed of repressive Calvinism, Romantic and Transcendentalist naïveté, and a pronounced sense of moneyed privilege. This position permitted Lowell to speak with authority in political-historical poems such as "For the Union Dead" and "Near the Ocean." But it also allowed Lowell to exploit a more self-satisfied element of his character. The blank verse sonnets of the collection he entitled *Notebook*, which were later published in a revised form and many yet again in *History*, at times grow benumbing as Lowell name-checks his acquaintances with the likes of Robert Kennedy, Norman Mailer, and Jacqueline Kennedy Onassis.

Yet Lowell's snobbery was tempered by poems and letters that show an abiding devotion toward his many literary friends and mentors. Indeed, his published correspondence, especially the letters exchanged with Bishop, are one of the most bracing elements of his legacy.

Coming as he did from a New England saturated with the Calvinism of the Bay Colony, on the one hand, and the Romantic subjectivism of Emersonian thought, on the other, it is no wonder that theology was also one of Lowell's abiding concerns, informing some of his best but also some of his most gothic and inflated writing. The arc of Lowell's spiritual questioning also invites the adjectives "tumultuous" and "transgressive." In his twenties, Lowell became an ardent convert to Catholicism, although it might be said that Lowell's conversion was to a kind of *literary* Catholicism in the manner of his mentor, the poet and critic Allen Tate, or of Flannery O'Connor. Still, the religious feeling that dominates Lowell's first three books, particularly *Lord Weary's Castle*, gives them a tone of stern apocalyptic dread that is an uncompromising and strangely appropriate response to the carnage of the Second World War and the tension of the Cold War that succeeded it. The world is bent out of shape, and Lowell seems willing to take it on himself not so much to right it as to warn us of even greater tribulation to come. Still, the sincerity of Lowell's Catholic phase should not be too strongly questioned: in 1943, distressed by the Allies' bombing of civilian targets in Europe, Lowell refused induction into the army and spent several months in jail as a conscientious objector. (Characteristically, this decision was announced via a haughty personal letter to President Franklin Roosevelt.) Lowell's Catholic phase was fairly short-lived, and by the early 1950s he had written a farewell to the Catholic Church in "Beyond the Alps," the fiercely ironic poem that opens *Life Studies*. "Much against my will," he laments in the poem, "I left the City of God where it belongs" (*RLCP*, p. 113). From this point on, the poet was a nonbeliever, ascribing to a position very much akin to the stoically self-reliant stance of existentialism in vogue within the literary circles of Lowell's day. Yet this position is haunted by a poignant nostalgia for the stability of Christian belief, one that informs some of his best work, most notably the poems "Skunk Hour," "For the Union Dead," and "Near the Ocean." The latter poem offers a couplet that tidily encapsulates Lowell's later stance toward belief and spiritual reckoning: "O that the spirit could remain / tinged but untarnished by its strain" (*RLCP*, p. 384).

It is in Lowell's approach toward composition and his evolution as a stylist that his identity as a transgressive artist is most pronounced. Lowell had a remarkable capacity to repeatedly remake himself as a poet. Beginning as a formalist whose work could display his ability to offer a prosodic tour de force while at the same time retaining a roughhewn insistence, Lowell then remade himself as a highly idiosyncratic free verse poet in much of *Life Studies* and in *For the Union Dead*. Yet in 1967's *Near the Ocean*, he returned to traditional form, employing an almost preposterously restrictive tetrameter couplet he had modeled after Andrew Marvell. *Near the Ocean* also reflects Lowell's abiding interest in classical literature and includes a set of deeply ironic adaptations of Juvenal and Horace – poems offered in part to emphasize the parallels between the arrogance of imperial Rome and the messianic recklessness of American Cold War policy. Then, in the late 1960s and early 1970s, he began to compose the hundreds of unrhymed sonnets that make up *Notebook* and the trilogy of books that grew out of it. But in his final collection, *Day by Day*, Lowell returned once again to free verse, this time employing a loose and fluent line much different from the free verse of his earlier books. These prosodic changes do not arise from a mere desire for expressive variety; they are adapted to reflect the searching and restless changes in Lowell's stance toward politics, religion, history, and above all self-revelation. Lowell's newfound interest in vernacular speech seems essential to capture the immediacy of the autobiographical disclosure that characterizes *Life Studies*, just as his return to rhyming couplets in *Near the Ocean* helps Lowell to frame the rhetoric of the odd jeremiads that blend the personal with a searing condemnation of American imperialism during the height of the Vietnam War. Lowell was able to enact these stylistic transformations partly because of a dizzyingly vast knowledge of the literary tradition, and partly because, as so many of his fellow poets who read his work in manuscript have attested, he was a dogged reviser of his poems. Prolific though he may have been, he was reluctant to let go of his work. Although Lowell had a careerist streak, he had an uncalculating and helpless ambition to be a great poet; the sheer urgency of this ambition is perhaps the most instructive legacy Lowell left to the generations of poets that followed him. Lowell felt deeply competitive with many of his peers, particularly Berryman and Roethke, and, in a more complicated way, Bishop. But his overriding desire was to compete with his pantheon of great English-language poets, with Milton, Wordsworth, Browning, Hopkins, and Pope, to name just a small group of the figures who influenced and provoked him. The fact that Lowell's mental illness and his tumultuous public and private life may well have prevented him from achieving his ambitions haunts all of Lowell's poems and increases their level of pathos, if not their ultimate value. The concept of greatness is of course highly suspect today, but Lowell steadfastly – and some would say tragically – believed in its existence and sought it for himself.

Perhaps the best way to offer evidence of Lowell's enduring importance is to chart his development, which falls into four periods: the early work, up to *Life Studies*; the controversial, celebrated books from *Life Studies* to *Near the Ocean*; the books of sonnets (1968–1973); and the final volume, *Day by Day*.

Like that of many of his fellow middle-generation poets, Lowell's early work was written at a time when modernism had retreated from the prosodic and thematic experimentation that characterized its "heroic" era of the 1920s. The lengthy, fragmented, collage-like, and often densely allusive work of Eliot in *The Waste Land*, Pound in his early cantos, and – in a different way – Williams in works such as *Kora in Hell* and *Spring and All* had been replaced by a more domesticated brand of modernist writing, one best exemplified by W. H. Auden, the most influential poet of the 1930s. Furthermore, the 1930s saw the rise of the poet-critic, first in the form of Eliot's highly influential and often very prescriptive essays, and later in the work of figures such as Lowell's mentors John Crowe Ransom and Allen Tate. New Critical approaches to reading poems lent themselves especially well to analysis of the dense intricacies of the metaphysical poets, particularly John Donne, and later figures such as Gerard Manley Hopkins, whose work had only recently become available. At this particular moment, Lowell was able to offer precisely what this literary establishment wanted – work compacted, formal, brimming with biblical and literary allusion, and exemplifying a kind of stern orderliness whose import was as much ideological as aesthetic, reflecting modernism's growing political and prosodic conservatism. The closing words of Allen Tate's introduction to Lowell's first volume, *Land of Unlikeness*, state the cause alarmingly well: "In a young man like Lowell, whether we like his Catholicism or not, there is at least the memory of the spiritual dignity of man, now sacrificed to mere secularization and a craving for mechanical order" (*RLCP*, p. 860).

Published in a fine press edition in 1944, when Lowell was only twenty-six, *Land of Unlikeness* is a work of rhetorical brio that does not coalesce into a coherent artistic statement. Steven Gould Axelrod rightly notes that the book is concerned with "three related themes ... history, current events, and God. In one form or another, these subjects continued to haunt and nourish [Lowell] throughout his career, but in *Land of Unlikeness* they are handled ineffectively."[6] "On the Eve of the Feast of the Immaculate Conception" illustrates Axelrod's point all too convincingly, mixing topical reflections on the Second World War with a portrayal of the Virgin Mary as a kind of comic book superheroine:

> Freedom and Eisenhower have won
> Significant laurels where the Hun
>   And Roman kneel
> To lick the dust from Mars' bootheel
> Like foppish bloodhounds; yet you sleep
> Out our distemper's evil day
>   And hear no sheep
>   Or hangdog bay!   (*RLCP*, p. 866)

But one cannot completely dismiss *Land of Unlikeness* as the work of a tyro. It earned respectful reviews from the likes of the then-esteemed poet Conrad Aiken, and a prediction by Randall Jarrell, the finest poet-critic of the middle generation, that Lowell would write "some of the best poems of the next years."[7] More importantly, several of the most successful poems of the collection were later reprinted – and sometimes substantially revised – in 1947's *Lord Weary's Castle*.

The themes of *Lord Weary's Castle* do not differ from those of *Land of Unlikeness*. But the writer who pursues them is a far more able technician. Witness these lines from "The Holy Innocents":

> King Herod shrieking vengeance at the curled
> Up knees of Jesus choking in the air,
>
> A king of speechless clods and infants. Still
> The world out-Herods Herod; and the year,
> The nineteen-hundred forty-fifth of grace
> Lumbers with losses up the clinkered hill
> Of our purgation ...   (*RLCP*, p. 10)

Several of the hallmarks of Lowell's mature style are in evidence here. The poet's willingness to counterpoint metrical regularity with dissonance is especially impressive. "A king of speechless clods and infants. Still" is a strict pentameter, but it is complicated by the caesura after "infants" and the strategic enjambment of "Still." "Lumbers with losses up the clinkered hill," with its trochaic substitutions and the oddball adjective choice of "clinkered" displays a typically Lowellian metrical variation and approach to syntax.

Long and rangy sequences in the high modernist mode were a sort of rite of passage in the early work of the middle-generation poets – we see evidence of this in Roethke with his "The Lost Son," Berryman with *Homage to Mistress Bradstreet*, and Schwartz with *Shenandoah*. These poems are in certain respects the middle generation's attempt to beat the modernists at their own game, and in "The Quaker Graveyard in Nantucket" Lowell joins them. Yet the 147-

line poem incorporates other influences as well, most notably Melville's *Moby Dick*, Milton's *Lycidas*, and even borrowings from Thoreau.[8] Like Milton's poem, "The Quaker Graveyard" is an elegy, mourning the death at sea of the poet's cousin Arthur Winslow. By giving the poem a specific occasion, one that is at least nominally personal, Lowell is able to rein in the brooding theological rhetoric of his other early poems. I suspect, however, that what impresses most readers about "The Quaker Graveyard" is its formal gravity and enthralling music. Most of the sections are written in heavily enjambed couplets that move the poem along at a rather dizzying speed. Most kinetic of all is the opening section, which describes Winslow's burial at sea. Written in irregular rhyme and meter, with a distant source in Thoreau, the movement is propulsive, even while Lowell embellishes the section with some of his most intricate metaphors:

> A brackish reach of shoal off Madaket, –
> The sea was still breaking violently and night
> Had steamed into our North Atlantic Fleet,
> When the drowned sailor clutched the drag-net. Light
> Flashed from his matted head and marble feet,
> He grappled at the net
> With the coiled, hurtling muscles of his thighs:
> The corpse was bloodless, a botch of reds and whites,
> Its open, staring eyes
> Were lustreless dead-lights
> Or cabin windows on a stranded hulk
> Heavy with sand. (RLCP, p. 14)

Lord Weary's Castle made Lowell something of a celebrity. The book garnered the Pulitzer Prize, and Lowell was appointed to the prestigious post of poetry consultant to the Library of Congress. He was even the subject of a photo spread in *Life* magazine. But the next few years were also troubling ones for Lowell, seeing the end of his marriage to Jean Stafford and his new marriage to Elizabeth Hardwick, the death of his mother while she was visiting Italy, and the onset of his mental illness. *The Mills of the Kavanaughs* (1951), the book of Browningesque monologues and gothic character studies that emerges during these years of triumph and turmoil, is Lowell's least successful collection. The book's best efforts, "Mother Marie Therese" and "Falling Asleep over the Aeneid," are artfully rendered but today seem affected and quaint. Lowell had worked the intricacies of his early style to exhaustion.

Eight years separate *The Mills of the Kavanaughs* and Lowell's next collection, 1959's *Life Studies*. Lowell undertook a long and painstaking struggle to revamp his style and adopt new subject matter. Although many of the *Life Studies* poems hew to traditional form – "Inauguration Day: January 1953," one of Lowell's most scathing political poems, is a tautly rendered sonnet, as is a biting monologue spoken in the voice of Hart Crane – the book replaces the mandarin utterances of Lowell's earlier work with a vernacular mode that Lowell claimed was borrowed in no small measure from William Carlos Williams, with whom he had long maintained a friendship. Yet *Life Studies* represents a loosening of Lowell's previous style, not a complete abandonment of it. Although Lowell was aware of the Beat poets, he was interested in the *appearance* of immediacy, not in actual improvisation. Indeed, Lowell said in 1961 that his wryly ironic elegy for his father, "Commander Lowell," was originally composed "in perfectly strict four-foot couplet[s]" but altered to a looser form because its "regularity just seemed to ruin the honesty" (*RLCPr*, p. 243). The poems seem less conversational than diary-like, and this mode seems the only one that will do justice to the concerns of *Life Studies*, which include (among others) family history, the workings of memory, the loss of religious faith, and mental and marital instability. The predominant tone is elegiac, not in the formal sense of the word as it pertains to a poem such as "The Quaker Graveyard in Nantucket," but as it applies to a particular American male of the 1950s as he enters middle age. Of course, Robert Lowell is by no means a typical American male of his time; he feels the burdens of his peculiar aristocratic family history and especially his personal failings. Lowell further cements the book's autobiographical intentions by including a prose memoir, "91 Revere Street," modeled on Elizabeth Bishop's bittersweet prose recollection of her own childhood, "In the Village." Indeed, it is possible to view *Life Studies* as a lengthy prose autobiography subjected to erasure, the events of the poet's life offered as fragments and distillations selected for their dramatic intensity and psychological penetration. Behind the poems we sense the ruin of a larger work – an effect that may well have been intentional, a manifestation of what Richard Tillinghast has called the "damaged grandeur" that is to him the central element of Lowell's writing.[9]

On the level of the book's individual poems, this flawed grandeur emerges through ruthless self-appraisal, through vividly rendered images that possess nothing of the Byzantine quality of Lowell's earlier figurative language, and thanks to a large measure of self-deprecating humor. The book's most famous poems begin in duress: "Memories of West Street and Lepke" recalls the jail where Lowell was incarcerated as a conscientious objector; "Skunk Hour" charts the speaker's dark night of the soul in a Maine resort town; "Sailing Home from Rapallo" records Lowell's journey to Italy to bring his mother's body back to New England; and "Waking in the Blue" is set in a ward at Mclean's, an upscale Boston mental hospital. Yet the most memorable and haunting elements of the poems are often their mordant wit. "Czar Lepke," the Mafioso in "Memories . . ." is a far cry from the stereotypical crime boss: "Flabby, bald, lobotomized / he drifted in a sheepish calm, / where no agonizing reappraisal / jarred his concentration on the electric chair" (*RLCP*, p. 188). "What use is my sense of humor?" Lowell asks in the opening stanzas of "Waking in the Blue" (*RLCP*, p. 183). One is tempted to answer his question by saying that the humor creates a tonal edginess and unpredictability. Self-mockery gives way to pathos; irony gives way to dread. As "Waking in the Blue" progresses, we are offered portraits of fellow inmates. The descriptions are brisk and absurdist: "Bobbie," "a replica of Louis XVI / without the wig – / redolent and roly-poly as a sperm whale" (*RLCP*, p. 183). Yet in the closing stanza of the poem, the speaker can no longer maintain his distance from his fellow "Mayflower / screwballs" (*RLCP*, p. 184). As in so many of Lowell's poems, its closing suggests an imminent apocalypse, but in this case it is acutely and tragically personal: Lowell can

> see the shaky future grow familiar
> in the pinched, indigenous faces
> of these thoroughbred mental cases,
> twice my age and half my weight.
> We are all old-timers,
> each of us holds a locked razor.   (*RLCP*, p. 184)

Bishop and Tate had seen the book in manuscript, and while Bishop immediately understood the book's importance, Tate brutally dismissed the poems as having "no public or literary interest."[10] Reviews tended toward extremes: the British poet Thom Gunn complained of "trivial autobiographical details, rambling and without unity," but John Thompson, in perhaps the most perceptive appraisal of Lowell's work to that time, recognized an artistic triumph, "a major expansion of the territory of poetry."[11]

In 1961, Lowell published a small anthology of translations – many of them very freely adapted – entitled *Imitations*. Lowell's selections ranged from Homer and Sappho to twentieth-century European poets, most notably Eugenio Montale, Boris Pasternak, and Rainer Maria Rilke. The volume's supporters regarded the collection as a form of self-portraiture, reflecting, in Ben Belitt's words, Lowell's "irascible and inquiring genius."[12] But more than one critic found Lowell's deliberate lack of what they saw as even minimal fidelity to the originals to be troubling.[13] Fifty years on, now that attempts at equivalent and freely rendered rather than literal translations of European verse into English have become something of the norm, the charges leveled against Lowell's approach in *Imitations* seem rather beside the point. The book also helped to form tastes, offering the first widely circulated English translations of such seminal figures as Montale and Giuseppe Ungaretti.

If *Life Studies* is Lowell's best individual collection, then the title piece of his next volume, 1964's *For the Union Dead* may be seen as Lowell's greatest individual poem. (The poem was in fact added as the closing effort of a 1960 paperback edition of *Life Studies*.) "For the Union Dead" is the poet's most sustained attempt at synthesizing personal and public history. Like so much of Lowell's work, the poem's overriding concerns are eschatological, epitomizing the unique sort of dread that haunted American culture at the dawn of the 1960s, with the escalation of the nuclear arms race and the placid conformity of the Eisenhower years about to be challenged, most notably by the civil rights movement. As the poem unfolds, Lowell insinuates that the carnage of that earlier conflict is but a foretaste of a greater carnage to come. Lowell answers the reactionary solemnities of Tate's "Ode to the Confederate Dead" – a poem much admired in its time – with a series of implicit but urgent questions, ones that depart radically from traditional approaches to the formal ode. Can we survive what we now are facing? What can we take from the past that will sustain us? The poem investigates these questions in a mode of imagistic juxtaposition, offering a fugue-like repetition of its central motifs, and through a kind of apotheosis of its central character, Colonel Robert Gould Shaw, who died leading one of the first black regiments of the Union army and is memorialized with them in a famous monumental sculpture by Augustus Saint-Gaudens, which sits near the State House on Boston Common.

As Mark Rudman notes, Lowell turns the Common into "the symbolic center of America."[14] It is here that Lowell recalls the Boston Aquarium that so mesmerized him in his childhood, now dismantled and replaced by an underground parking garage. It is a landscape of the most abject desolation, given dignity only by Shaw and his troops. Yet theirs is a vexed nobility. Their monument "sticks like a fishbone / in the city's throat," more an object lesson than a representation of valor. And Shaw, the prototype of the solitary existential hero, suggests to us that it may no longer be possible for bravery to be a collective endeavor: Shaw "rejoices in man's lovely / peculiar power to choose life and die" (*RLCP*, p. 377). The catalogue of images that complete the poem offers little by way of solace, but it is a breathtakingly ironic tour de force. A "commercial photograph" shows "Hiroshima boiling // over a Mosler safe," television shows "the drained faces of Negro school-children" facing violent resistance to integration, and "Everywhere / giant finned cars nose forward like fish; / a savage servility / slides by on grease" (*RLCP*, pp. 377–78).

Written largely in a rhyming free verse, the individual lyrics of *For the Union Dead* continue the loosening of style and approach that began in *Life Studies*. As with *For the Union Dead*'s title poem, their method tends to be associative and image driven. The orderly retrospective intentions of the earlier book are replaced by a desire to chart the shifts and vagaries of consciousness as it moves from sensation to sensation, from self-recrimination to rueful self-acceptance, and from nostalgia to more troubled reckonings with the past. "Eye and Tooth" begins with a painstakingly rendered description of the speaker's scratched cornea but concludes with Lowell bemoaning a larger failure of vision, one characterological and psychological. "I am tired," he writes in the poem's final line, "everyone is tired of my turmoil" (*RLCP*, p. 335). The volume's poems achieve their success because we sense how mightily the speaker is struggling against the forces that bedevil him. Lowell, in an interview with Stanley Kunitz, suggested that "some readers have turned to my poems because of the very things that are wrong with me. I mean the difficulty I have with ordinary living, the impracticality, the myopia. Seeing less than others can be a great strain."[15]

Near the Ocean (1967) completes a kind of trilogy that began with *Life Studies*. The book's genesis can be traced to an event that represents a typically Lowellian mixture of the public and the personal. In the summer of 1965, as a gesture of protest against the war in Vietnam, Lowell declined to attend a White House event in celebration of the arts. Lowell composed a letter to President Lyndon Johnson that warned that the United States was "in danger of imperceptibly becoming an explosive and suddenly chauvinistic nation, and may even be drifting on our way to the last nuclear ruin" (*RLCPr*, p. 371). Lowell released it to the *New York Times*, and twenty leading figures in the arts, unbeknownst to Lowell, signed a statement endorsing his position. The *Times* ran a front-page story on the controversy. The event is further evidence of how slyly Lowell was able to manipulate his public image. Yet what Lowell termed his "dismay and distrust" at the nation's misadventure in Vietnam was deeply felt, manifesting itself in his later support for antiwar Democratic presidential candidates Eugene McCarthy and Robert Kennedy, and in his avid participation in antiwar protests.

"Near the Ocean" is a flawed sequence, veering from urban melodrama ("Central Park") to a chatty verse epistle to Lowell's cousin Harriet Winslow ("Fourth of July in Maine") and ending with its title piece, an unsettlingly ambivalent love poem to Hardwick. Yet the sequence's opening section, "Waking Early Sunday Morning," closely rivals "For the Union Dead" in its ability to incorporate both the domestic and the political and to investigate the question of faith in a world where religious belief is deemed impossible. Although the section's tetrameter couplets are sometimes less then dexterous, the abruptness of their enjambments befits the poem's immense shifts in scale, evoking a world gone wrong on microcosmic and macrocosmic levels. After some Swiftian description of Johnson and his cabinet, "Waking Early Sunday Morning" moves to a heartfelt passage in which Lowell's familiar themes of gloom and doom are not so much replaced as freighted with a weary abjection. In the penultimate stanza, rhetoric gives way to a purer form of lamentation:

> Wars
> flicker, earth licks its open sores,
> fresh breakage, fresh promotions, chance
> assassinations, no advance.
> Only man thinning out his kind
> sounds through the Sabbath noon, the blind
> swipe of the pruner with his knife
> busy about the tree of life . . .   (*RLCP*, p. 386)

Like most of Lowell's best poems, "Waking Early Sunday Morning" concludes with a gesture of fraught prophecy: the "pruner with his knife" is not the bucolic reaper familiar to us from the pastoral tradition but the Grim Reaper; and in the poem's final stanza, the legacy bestowed by imperialist America on future generations is seen as a terrifying one: "until the end of time / to police the earth, a ghost / orbiting forever lost / in our monotonous sublime."

Beginning in 1967, Lowell wrote the hundreds of largely blank verse sonnets that were eventually gathered in his 1973 trilogy of collections: *History*, *For Lizzie and Harriet*, and *The Dolphin*. On the one hand, the sonnet trilogy is the culmination of Lowell's decades-long struggle to admit immediacy, improvisation, and serendipity into his method – because he is the most willful of writers, this goal is by no means easy to attain. On the other hand, Lowell, like many of his fellow middle-generation poets, was always a writer in search of a masterwork, a grand poetic statement that could compete with the long poems of the modernists. In a eulogy for John Berryman, whose *Dream Songs* surely influenced the sonnet trilogy, Lowell wonders if the middle generation were merely the "uncomfortable epigoni of Frost, Pound, Eliot, Marianne Moore, etc." (*RLCPr*, p. 115). Indeed, one might argue that the most notable thing about the sonnets is how acutely they attest to this discomfort: the result is an almost helpless drive to alchemize small gestures into ostentatious ones, and to manipulate desultory reportage into rigorously plotted drama. This desire is evidenced even in the books' bewildering publishing history. The trilogy derives from three published editions of a work that Lowell originally entitled *Notebook*, which appeared in a U.S. edition in May 1969, then in a revised British edition in July of that year, and in yet another, much revised and expanded, edition in 1970. *Notebook* was originally intended to be a kind of poetic journal, in which, in Lowell's own words, "accident threw up subjects and the plot swallowed them."[16] Some of the poems are highly immediate responses to events of the turbulent late 1960s, particularly the continued escalation of the Vietnam War and the protest movement against it. We are offered poems on the killings of Martin Luther King, Jr., Robert Kennedy, and Che Guevara, and poems occasioned by the 1968 Democratic Convention in Chicago, alongside historical vignettes and portraits of figures ranging from Lincoln to King David to Attila the Hun. Lowell also adds poems about Hardwick and their daughter Harriet, elegies for fellow writers such as Randall Jarrell and I. A. Richards, and poems of memory and retrospection in the mode of *Life Studies*. "At the Dentist" is a loopy monologue spoken in the voice of the poet's dentist; "Words for Muffin, a Guinea Pig" is related by Lowell's daughter Harriet's pet. At their best, the *Notebook* poems abundantly display Lowell's seemingly boundless capacity to concoct startling metaphors and striking adjective-noun combinations; and they hinge on searching and jittery statements that seem to arise from the intricacies of consciousness rather than from rhetoric. "To Allen Tate 3. Michael Tate: August 1967–July 1968," an elegy for Allen Tate's infant son, showcases all of these qualities:

> his small gravestone,
> his *one-year* common as grass in auld lang syne
> is beyond our scale of faith ... and Michael Tate
> gagging on your plastic telephone,
> while the new sitter drew water for your bath,
> unable to hear you gasp. They think: if there'd been
> a week or two's illness, we might have been prepared.
>
> (*RLCP*, p. 518)

This is the 1973 version of the poem, published in *History*, and it differs in several small but significant ways from the version published in the third revision of *Notebook*.[17] And "Michael Tate" is but one example among many of Lowell's obsessive tinkerings as *Notebook* grew larger and was then recycled and expanded once again. *History* became the repository for the historical and topical poems of *Notebook*; *For Lizzie and Harriet* bracketed the *Notebook* poems that Lowell had composed for Hardwick and the couple's daughter.

The Dolphin was an entirely new sequence, devoted to the breakup of Lowell's marriage to Hardwick and his subsequent marriage to Caroline Blackwood.

During the trilogy's composition, Lowell's personal life was once again in upheaval. Although Lowell had involved himself in a number of extramarital affairs during his years with Hardwick, these attachments were usually linked to the onset of Lowell's bipolar episodes, and Hardwick came to be wearily tolerant of them as yet another manifestation of Lowell's mental disorder. But Lowell's involvement with Lady Caroline Blackwood – which began in 1970 while Lowell was in Britain at the University of Essex – was different. Soon Lowell and Blackwood were living together, and in 1971 Blackwood gave birth to the couple's son, Robert Sheridan Lowell. The collapse of Lowell's marriage to Hardwick and his new involvement with Blackwood is narrated, sometimes obliquely, sometimes with a frankness disarming even for Lowell, in the poems that make up *The Dolphin*. Lowell's wholesale quotation from the letters Hardwick wrote him during their breakup is dubious on ethical terms, surely, but also on aesthetic ones, for the quoted passages seem merely to give authenticity, veering from prosy incidentals ("I'm off / to Dalton to pick up Harriet's grade and record") to hurt sentimentality (*RLCP*, pp. 661, 663). The book does not so much unfold a plot as continually complicate the speaker's crisis; his self-recriminations about leaving Hardwick and their daughter Harriet are too manifold, and his uncertainties about his future with Blackwood are too grave. *The Dolphin*'s final sonnet is tinged with the same sort of regret that characterizes the closing of *For the Union Dead*'s "Eye and Tooth." Yet where that earlier poem evokes its speaker's remorse with a pained directness that gives it considerable rhetorical power, the concluding lines of the newer poem seem oddly self-aggrandizing, however exquisite their syntax and parallelism:

> I have sat and listened to too many
> words of the collaborating muse,
> and plotted perhaps too freely with my life,
> not avoiding injury to others,
> not avoiding injury to myself –
> to ask compassion ... this book, half-fiction
> an eelnet made by man for the eel fighting –
>
> my eyes have seen what my hand did. (*RLCP*, p. 708)

Adrienne Rich made this passage the fulcrum of her excoriating review of *The Dolphin*. "I have to say," Rich writes, "that I think this is bullshit eloquence, a poor excuse for a cruel and shallow book, that it is presumptuous to balance injury done to others with injury done to myself."[18] Vicious as this critique may be, it is not entirely unfair – Lowell's stance in the book is indeed presumptuous, yet in the nearly forty years that have elapsed since the book's publication, its characterological shortcomings seem somewhat less scandalous. Richard Tillinghast's 1995 appraisal of *The Dolphin* is perhaps the most measured and accurate assessment and might be extended to the trilogy: "As flawed and problematic as it is, it still has a measure of greatness."[19] Lowell never again wrote sonnets.

Lowell published his final collection, *Day by Day*, in September 1977, just weeks before his death from a heart attack. The poet had determined to end his marriage to Blackwood, and return to Hardwick. On his way from Kennedy Airport to Hardwick's Manhattan apartment, Lowell died in a taxicab; beside him on the seat was a small portrait of Blackwood rendered by her first husband, the renowned British painter Lucian Freud.

During his years in England, the poet's bipolar episodes continued to result in hospitalizations, and in January 1977, he was hospitalized after a heart attack and diagnosed with congestive heart failure. It is impossible to read the weary and mortality-obsessed poems of *Day by Day* without seeing them as premonitions of Lowell's death. The ironically entitled mental hospital poem "Home" is a kind of prolix rewrite of "Waking in the Blue." The wit and sprightliness of the earlier poem is replaced by a tone of exhaustion and fear:

> The immovable chairs have swallowed up the patients
> and speak with the eloquence of emptiness.
> By each the same morning paper lies unread....
>
> Less than ever I expect to be alive
> six months from now –
> 1976,
> a date I dare not affix to my grave ...   (*RLCP*, p. 825)

In its form, "Home" is typical of *Day by Day*. Written in a leisurely free verse that eschews the enjambments and linguistic pyrotechnics of his earlier work, the poems at times seem flaccid, but the best of the book's writing possesses a sober and unhurried gravity. The poems tend to revisit subjects treated earlier. Lowell's hectoring mother makes yet another appearance, as does Lowell's first wife, Jean Stafford, and the collection contains a somber elegy for John Berryman, who committed suicide in 1972. Perhaps the most striking element of the book is that certain of the poems seem finally to achieve the lyric immediacy that Lowell had so long sought. Yet this immediacy is bittersweet, because it is found mainly in poems such as "Last Walk?" and "Runaway," which foretell the end of Lowell's marriage to Blackwood. In *Day by Day*, a poet whose signature mode is of grand designs and even megalomania is forced to reinvent himself as a writer of diminishment, of discontinuity, one who struggles for insight but who ultimately meets largely with "lost connections." Still, as Helen Vendler insists, Lowell's "unfailing gift for images" let him "invent a style incorporating inertia and death," in part through mere "glimpses" in place of developed narrative, and in part through conspicuous "subtraction," lines and sentences with something clearly left out.[20]

"Notice" is a good example of the method that Vendler describes. The poem begins with the promise of drama, the memory of a mental ward psychiatrist who confesses that his treatments will be of little help (*RLCP*, p. 828). Yet by the second stanza of the poem, Lowell leaves the hospital dialogue behind:

> The doctor's name is forgotten now
> like a friend's wife's maiden name.
> I am free
> to ride elbow to elbow on the rush hour train....
>
> Then home – I can walk it blindfold.
> But we must notice –
> we are designed for the moment.   (*RLCP*, p. 828)

Although the poems of *Day by Day* often begin in recollection, in what Lowell calls a "downlook," they soon, as Vendler notes, become a subspecies of the carpe diem poem.[21] To embrace the moment must serve as change enough, and in order to achieve this, Lowell must also look back on his life and work with an acceptance that is considerably more restrained than the often self-lacerating gestures that had previously characterized his work. Like *The Dolphin*, *Day by Day* closes with an *ars poetica*, but the bombast of the earlier book is replaced in "Epilogue" with a stance that is querulous and chastened. Lowell yearns to make "something imagined, not recalled," but he fears that the "threadbare art" of his autobiographical vision has made his legacy one of mere snapshots, pictures that are "lurid, rapid, garish, grouped / heightened from life but paralyzed by fact. / All's misalliance" (*RLCP*, p. 838). The lines are archetypal Lowell: even in one of his most abashed self-assessments, he cannot resist a pyrotechnical catalogue of adjectives or a grandiloquent statement. As the poem moves to its closure, the poet's self-doubts are eased, although by no means erased:

> We are poor passing facts,
> warned by that to give
> each figure in the photograph
> his living name.   (*RLCP*, p. 838)

A few months prior to his death, the journal *Salmagundi* published a fest-schrift to honor Lowell's sixtieth birthday; in it the poet offers a short and self-deprecating essay about the development of his work that is remarkably similar to the "Epilogue" of *Day by Day*. The concluding paragraph of the piece sometimes even employs some identical word choices and syntax, and the key phrases of both works are tellingly liturgical: "I pray that my progress has been more than recoiling with satiation and disgust from one style to another, a series of rebuffs. I hope there has been an increase in beauty, wisdom, tragedy, and all the blessings of this consuming chance" (*RLCP*, p. 991).

It is unlikely that Robert Lowell will ever regain the position of preeminence that he enjoyed during the middle years of the last century. Yet any serious reader of Lowell (and he will always find such readers) is likely to conclude – even when confronted with Lowell's overreaching, infelicities, grandiosity, and occasional exhibitionism – that Lowell's final prayers were answered. No other American poet has examined the workings of his inner life with such ruthless penetration. Yet at the same time no other American poet has engaged historical force with a greater degree of urgency; and of America's great political poets, Lowell is the one whose vision, from *Life Studies* onward, is least burdened and muddled by ideology. Furthermore, Lowell was a consummate technician; no other figure among the middle-generation writers save for Bishop can be regarded as his equal in this respect. And finally, in a manner that is at once paradoxical and characteristically American, Lowell ranks among our greatest poets in part because of his very willingness to fail – to fail in a way that is at once grand and humbling.[22]

The careers of John Berryman and Theodore Roethke parallel that of Lowell in several crucial ways. Although both were slightly older than Lowell – Roethke was born in 1908, and Berryman in 1914 – they rose to their greatest prominence, as Lowell did, in the 1950s and 1960s. They shared with Lowell many of the major prizes and awards: Roethke received a Pulitzer Prize in 1954 for his fourth collection, *The Waking*, and Berryman too was given the Pulitzer, for the first installment of his major work, *The Dream Songs*, in 1965. Also like Lowell, their literary reputations were far more substantial during their lifetimes than they have been since. Roethke and Berryman possessed Lowell's driving ambition – as well as his careerism. Although Lowell did not share with Berryman or Roethke the abiding literary friendship he possessed with Elizabeth Bishop, he held both writers in high regard. Most importantly, the three poets shared a desire to construct personal mythologies; all three made from the autobiographical impulse poems of great individuality and formal ingeniousness. Sadly, in the case of Berryman and Roethke just as much as in that of Lowell, self-interrogation and formal innovation derived in no small measure from trauma and psychological suffering. Like Lowell, Roethke was afflicted with an acute bipolar disorder during an era when the condition was little understood. He endured numerous stays in mental hospitals and was subjected at least once to electroshock therapy. Berryman too lived a disordered and troubled existence. Married three times, his domestic life was turbulent, not least because of his lifelong struggle with alcoholism. Hospitalized on several occasions, Berryman's inability to overcome his condition was a deciding factor in his suicide in 1972, at the age of fifty-seven. Although Berryman and Roethke are less read today than they deserve to be, they are – despite the marked eccentricities of their mature styles – among the best and most characteristic voices of the middle generation.

The future John Berryman was born in Oklahoma in 1914. John Allyn Smith, his father, was a banker. But a move to Florida in 1925 for that state's real estate boom proved disastrous for Berryman's father, who suffered a series of business failures. In 1926, John Allyn Smith was found shot dead outside the family home. Although the death was ruled a suicide, the poet harbored a lifelong suspicion that his father was in fact murdered by his mother and her lover, John McAlpin Berryman. The pair were married only a few weeks after his father's demise; the young poet was given his stepfather's last name and was packed off to boarding school. Berryman remained rather uncomfortably close to his mother throughout his life, and the death of his father became one of the overarching concerns of *The Dream Songs*.

At Columbia University, the poet Mark Van Doren encouraged both Berryman's poetry and his interest in Shakespeare. In 1937 he was awarded a scholarship to Clare College, Cambridge, and he began the kind of literary career that typified his generational peers. He held academic appointments at Princeton, the University of Cincinnati, the University of Iowa, and eventually the University of Minnesota, where he taught from 1955 until his death. He authored a biography of Stephen Crane and worked for many years on a book (published posthumously) about Shakespeare. Very derivative of Yeats and to a lesser extent of Auden, *The Dispossessed* (1948) is best read as a skillful representation of its period's style. More daring is the sequence of 120 sonnets that he wrote in 1947, during the throes of an illicit love affair with the wife of a Princeton colleague. These poems, finally published twenty years afterward, are affected and uneven and often seem less to do with erotic fervor than with the desire for subject matter to exploit. Yet the sonnets' stylistic and syntactical eccentricities – revealing a considerable debt to Hopkins – would later be refined in *The Dream Songs*.

Berryman's first major work is his long poem, *Homage to Mistress Bradstreet*, published in book form in 1956. It is Berryman's entry into the modernist long poem sweepstakes, indebted to Eliot's *The Waste Land* and to Crane's *The Bridge*. It is nominally a character study of the seventeenth-century American poet Anne Bradstreet, alternating between the voice of Bradstreet and that of the poem's narrator. However, as with the later *Dream Songs*, the poem is characterized by abrupt and often unattributed shifts in speaker and person, and the willful archaism of the poem's style and syntax help to make it a cramped but impressive tour de force. The poem's most famous passage, narrated by Bradstreet as she gives birth to a daughter, is a good representation of the poem's tonal complexity and devotional ardor:

> No. No. Yes! everything down
> hardens I press with horrible joy down
> my back cracks like a wrist
> shame I am voiding oh behind it is too late
>
> hide me forever I work thrust I must free
> now I all muscles & bones concentrate
> what is living from dying?
> Simon I must leave you so untidy
> Monster you are killing me Be sure
> I'll have you later Women do endure
> I can *can* no longer
> and it passes the wretched trap whelming and I am me
>
> drencht & powerful, I did it with my body!
> One proud tug greens Heaven. Marvelous,
> unforbidding Majesty.
> Swell, imperious bells. I fly....[23]

Homage was a critical success. For his next work, Berryman projected a long poem of several hundred sections, each comprised of three rhyming stanzas of six lines each. The poem would build on the structural and narrative methods of his earlier sonnet sequence, but its scope would be much larger. One of Berryman's biographers, Paul Mariani, draws on Berryman's unpublished notes:

> He wanted the poem to deal with the human condition, but channeled through the life of one man. Each poem would have at least "one stroke of some damned serious humor." He wanted a "gravity of matter," but he wanted it wedded to a "gaiety of manner."... He also meant to get all the sexual longing and lust into his poems he could.... He would use the old iambic norm, but jazz it up and make it freer, mixing it with "rocking meter,

anapests, spondees, iambs, trochees, dactyls" until he drove the prosodists "right out of their heads."[24]

This project, which eventually became *The Dream Songs*, does not fulfill the poet's epic intentions, but Berryman's intended mixture of thinly veiled auto-biography, gallows humor, prosodic variety, and "sexual longing" is every-where. The poet's alter ego, "Henry Pussycat," sometimes speaks in the first person, is sometimes discussed in the third, and frequently engages in dialogue with an unnamed companion who speaks in blackface dialect drawn from the minstrelsy tradition, addressing Henry as "Sir Bones" or "Mr. Bones." The diction of the poem wavers violently between a kind of mock-Elizabethan mode and contemporary slang, and as with *Mistress Bradstreet*, the poem is filled with syntactical inversions, archaic spellings, and neologisms concocted to fulfill the rhyme scheme.

Few significant American poets have adopted a style as mannered or as extreme. Berryman can sustain this argot for hundreds of pages, making the style supple enough to incorporate not only Henry's skewed self-portraiture but also elegies for his contemporaries (especially Randall Jarrell and Delmore Schwartz) and topical poems, as well as tender poems in praise of Berryman's / Henry's children. Also, despite *The Dream Songs*'s many contrivances, the effect of the individual sections can be quite immediate and visceral – and as often as not discomforting. Berryman's emotional intentions seem to shift not just from section to section and stanza to stanza but often from line to line. The mannerisms and buffoonery so often present in the poem's sections almost invariably give way to an abjection that, within the framework of Berryman's verbal pyrotechnics, can seem little short of shocking. *Dream Song* 29, one of the book's many anguished attempts to reckon with the suicide of Berryman's father, shows us the poet at his very best: it begins,

> There sat down, once, a thing on Henry's heart
> só heavy, if he had a hundred years
> & more, & weeping, sleepless, in all them time
> Henry could not make good.
> Starts again always in Henry's ears
> the little cough somewhere, an odour, a chime.[25]

Berryman's finest writing can be found in *77 Dream Songs* (1963); the much longer concluding volume, 1968's *His Toy, His Dream, His Rest*, shows a marked falling off. During the last years of his life, Berryman published two additional volumes, *Love and Fame*, a series of autobiographical poems in free verse that suffer in comparison to *The Dream Songs*, and the uneven *Delusions Etc.*, which was in press at the time of the poet's death. In a review of *77 Dream Songs*, Robert Lowell paid eloquent homage: "All is risk and variety here. This great Pierrot's universe is more tearful and funny than we can easily bear" (*RLCPr*, p. 111).

Theodore Roethke was born in Michigan in 1908; his father was the owner of a prosperous greenhouse establishment. The elder Roethke, a stern but loving parent of German extraction, died of cancer when the poet was fifteen; as with Berryman, Roethke came to regard the loss of his father as a crucial event in his life, and he returns to the subject repeatedly in his poetry. Roethke's greenhouse-keeping father becomes in his poetry inextricably identified with the forces and cycles of nature. Indeed, Roethke is often called a nature poet, but his treatment bears little resemblance to the pantheism of Wordsworth. Roethke at his best is a poet of spiritual yearning in the tradition of figures such as the metaphysical poets George Herbert and Henry Vaughan and later poets such as Hopkins, Christopher Smart, and especially Yeats, all of whom Roethke read with special seriousness. Like Yeats, he seems to have been motivated to create a theology through his poetry. But the mandarin occultism of Yeats's philosophy bears little resemblance to the worldview that Roethke formulated, which was roughhewn and might best be described as animistic – nature for Roethke is a realm of highly charged and undisciplined spiritual forces, nominally controlled by a father figure whose powers are sometimes dynamic, sometimes insignificant. This symbolic vocabulary draws significantly from Freud and especially Jung, despite the poet's disclaimers.[26]

When Roethke's do-it-yourself cosmology is matched with the animated and urgent pacing of his best writing, he shows himself to be a poet of great originality and invention. But Roethke, like Berryman, was a decidedly uneven writer, prone to self-imitation and excessively dutiful imitations of the poets who inspired him, particularly Yeats. A large, gregarious man of great appetite and considerable charisma, Roethke was also a gifted teacher, and his students at the University of Washington – where he taught for the last fifteen years of his life – included James Wright, David Wagoner, Richard Hugo, Tess Gallagher, and Carolyn Kizer, all of whom went on to notable careers as poets.

The poems collected in Roethke's first volume, 1940's *Open House*, are skillful but very formally constrained lyrics in the manner of Stanley Kunitz, who formed a long friendship with the poet, and Louise Bogan, with whom he had had a short but intense love affair. Roethke's second volume, *The Lost Son*, develops his characteristic style. Written in both fixed forms and a supple free verse, the poems of *The Lost Son* are a carefully plotted cycle, a spiritual autobiography charting birth, death, and the poet's tentative rebirth. Beginning with poems that energetically describe the greenhouse flora of his childhood, and culminating with the book's title poem, with its mixture of childhood memories, recollections of the poet's father, and renderings of spiritual yearning and regression, the collection is notable for both its lyric particularity and its haunting replication of a child's sensibility. Within a few lines, the style of the poems can veer from Whitmanian catalogues to the cadences and vocabulary of nursery rhymes. As with Berryman's *Dream Songs*, the poems are characterized by radical shifts in tone. In the title poem, the poet recalls a childhood night spent alone in his father's greenhouse:

> There was always a single light
> Swinging by the fire-pit,
> Where the fireman pulled out roses.
> The big roses, the big bloody clinkers . . .
>
> Scurry of warm over small plants.
> Ordnung! Odnung!
> Papa is coming!
>
> A fine haze moved off the leaves;
> The rose, the chrysanthemum turned toward the light.
> Even the hushed forms, the bent yellowy weeds
> Moved in a slow upsway . . .[27]

"Ordnung" is German for "order," and the father's emergence at the end of the section, giving purpose once again to the unruly world of the greenhouse, is a gesture often repeated in Roethke's poetry. A later poem, "Otto," employs these motifs even more explicitly. Here is the poem's closing section:

> In my mind's eye I see those fields of glass,
> As I looked out at them from the high house,
> Riding beneath the moon, hid from the moon.
> Then slowly breaking whiter in the dawn;
> When George the watchman's lantern dropped from sight
> The long pipes knocked: it was the end of night.
> I'd stand upon my bed, a sleepless child
> Watching the waking of my father's world –
> O world so far away! O my lost world![28]

Roethke issued four collections in the 1950s, and some of his strongest work can be found in 1964's posthumously published *The Far Field*. Yet Roethke, like Berryman in *The Dream Songs*, found it difficult to overcome the expressive constraints and peculiarities of the style he had forged. As Adam Kirsch observes, "*The Lost Son* is the peak of Roethke's inventiveness as a poet, but his attempt to extend its discoveries into a series of poems exposed the limitations of his style: without the momentum of narrative, it quickly grows static."[29] Still, Roethke's literary influence was considerable. The Deep Image poets who emerged in the 1960s, particularly James Wright and Robert Bly, are especially indebted to Roethke in their insistence on the primacy of metaphor in their poetry. Roethke's influence was felt in England as well: the violence and mystical atavism of the natural world in Ted Hughes's poetry owes much to Roethke's example. Just weeks prior to Roethke's death, Robert Lowell sent his fellow poet a letter whose troubled and valedictory tone seems prophetic: not simply of Roethke's own death but of the way that Lowell and all of his middle-generation peers would be viewed in the future:

> We couldn't be more different, yet how weirdly our lives have gone the same way. Let's say we are brothers, have gone the same journey and know far more about each other than we have ever said or will say. It's a strange fact about the poets of roughly our age, and one that doesn't exactly seem to have always been true. It's this, that to write we seem to have to go at it with such single-minded intensity that we are always on the point of drowning.... There must be some kind of glory to it that people coming later will wonder at. I can see us all being written up in some huge book on the age.[30]

Notes

1. Irvin Ehrenpreis, "The Age of Lowell," in Michael London and Robert Boyers (eds.), *Robert Lowell: A Portrait of the Artist in His Time* (New York: David Lewis, 1970), p. 155.
2. Robert Lowell, *Collected Prose*, ed. Robert Giroux (New York: Farrar, Straus and Giroux, 1987), pp. 286–87. This collection will be cited in the text as *RLCPr.*
3. Ralph Waldo Emerson, *Essays: Second Series* (Boston and New York: Houghton Mifflin, 1876), p. 37.
4. Frank Bidart, "Foreword," in *Robert Lowell: Selected Poems* (New York: Farrar, Straus and Giroux, 2006), p. xiii.
5. Robert Lowell, *Collected Poems*, ed. Frank Bidart and David Gewanter (New York: Farrar, Straus and Giroux, 2003), p. 184. This collection will be cited in the text as *RLCP.*
6. Steven Gould Axelrod, *Robert Lowell: Life and Art* (Princeton, N.J.: Princeton University Press, 1978), p. 44.
7. Axelrod, *Robert Lowell*, p. 49.
8. On "The Quaker Graveyard" and its sources, see especially Vereen Bell, *Robert Lowell: Nihilist as Hero* (Cambridge, Mass.: Harvard University Press, 1983), pp. 10–32.

9. Richard Tillinghast, *Robert Lowell's Life and Work: Damaged Grandeur* (Ann Arbor: University of Michigan Press, 1995), p. 43.

10. Ian Hamilton, *Robert Lowell: A Biography* (New York: Random House, 1982), p. 238.

11. Hamilton, *Robert Lowell*, pp. 272, 271.

12. Ben Belitt, *"Imitations:* Translation as Personal Mode," in London and Boyers (eds.), *Robert Lowell: A Portrait of the Artist in His Time*, p. 114.

13. See especially John Simon, "Abuse of Privilege: Robert Lowell as Translator," in London and Boyers (eds.), *Robert Lowell: A Portrait of the Artist in His Time*, pp. 143, 141.

14. Mark Rudman, *Robert Lowell: An Introduction to the Poetry* (New York: Columbia University Press, 1983), p. 137.

15. Hamilton, *Robert Lowell*, p. 309.

16. Robert Lowell, *Notebook*, 3rd rev. ed. (New York: Farrar, Straus and Giroux, 1970), p. 262.

17. Compare this passage with Lowell, *Notebook*, p. 251.

18. Paul Mariani, *Lost Puritan: A Biography of Robert Lowell* (New York: W. W. Norton, 1994), p. 422–23.

19. Tillinghast, *Robert Lowell's Life and Work*, p. 105.

20. Helen Vendler, *Last Books, Last Looks: Stevens, Plath, Lowell, Bishop, Merrill* (Princeton, N.J.: Princeton University Press, 2010), pp. 71–72.

21. Vendler, *Last Books, Last Looks*, p. 71.

22. Hayden Carruth, *Selected Essays and Reviews* (Port Townsend, Wash.: Copper Canyon Press, 1996), p. 88.

23. John Berryman, *Selected Poems*, ed. Kevin Young (New York: Library of America, 2004), p. 36.

24. Paul Mariani, *Dream Song: The Life of John Berryman* (New York: William Morrow, 1990), p. 301.

25. Berryman, *Selected Poems*, p. 107.

26. Theodore Roethke, *Selected Letters*, ed. Ralph J. Mills (Seattle: University of Washington Press, 1968), p. 360.

27. Theodore Roethke, *Selected Poems*, ed. Edward Hirsch (New York: Library of America, 2005), p. 28.

28. Roethke, *Selected Poems*, p. 109.

29. Adam Kirsch, *The Modern Element: Essays on Contemporary Poetry* (New York: W. W. Norton, 2008), p. 176.

30. Robert Lowell, *The Letters of Robert Lowell*, ed. Saskia Hamilton (New York: Farrar, Straus, and Giroux, 2005), pp. 427–28.

Chapter 34

Elizabeth Bishop, Randall Jarrell, and the Lost World of Real Feeling

RICHARD FLYNN

On October 29, 1964, at a reading at the Guggenheim Museum celebrating Elizabeth Bishop's $5,000 fellowship from the Academy of American Poets, Randall Jarrell read Elizabeth Bishop's poems and his own because Bishop was unable to leave Brazil to receive the award. Robert Lowell, a longtime friend of both poets, introduced the reading, and his introduction reflected his estimation of each poet's reputation, an estimation that would remain the conventional wisdom for years to come. Speaking first of his good friend Bishop, he noted that her poetry differed both from the "standardized somewhat machine-made Academic poem," and from poetry that "comes through with a sort of shocking vulgarity and coarseness of mind." Echoing Jarrell's review of *North & South* (1946) as well as his own, Lowell praised Bishop's "eye" and her "tolerance and humor" and noted the "beautiful formal completeness" of her poetry. He also repeated the unfortunate sexism of his own review, noting that Bishop was "one of the two or three best women poets in the language." Introducing his friend Jarrell, Lowell described him primarily as a brilliant critic who had once written some of the finest poems about World War II and as the "last of the great critics."[1] Although he praised Jarrell's recent poetry for its "Chekhovian directness and subtlety," one senses that Lowell (and indeed Bishop) would not have disagreed with Helen Vendler's judgment that Jarrell put his "genius into his criticism and his talent into his poetry."[2]

Although both Jarrell and Bishop were well respected, their work was somewhat overshadowed by flashier postmodernist innovators, not just by the New York School, Beat, projectivist, or other New American poets but by the linguistic pyrotechnics of John Berryman, the personal revelations of confessional poets like W. D. Snodgrass and Anne Sexton, and, perhaps, more than anyone else, by Lowell himself. Bishop had a coterie following as what John Ashbery would later call a "writer's writer's writer" and Jarrell was considered a strong critic whose most recent poems bordered on the sentimental.[3] Both poets resist the orthodoxies of their time. Accounts of the affinity between

775

Jarrell and Bishop, at least since the 1990s, have served as correctives to what James Longenbach and others have criticized as "the breakthrough narrative," in which Lowell's *Life Studies* represents a turning point when a caricature of modernist "impersonality" is replaced by "free verse and free thinking"; as Longenbach notes, this story is "often cast in terms of masculine fortitude," which cannot account for writers like Bishop nor for writers like Jarrell concerned with traditionally feminized or childlike points of view.[4] Langdon Hammer has argued convincingly that "the world of [Jarrell's] poems is unreal, eccentric, or 'lost' (the title of Jarrell's final book of poems is *The Lost World*) because he self-consciously created it in opposition to the world in which he lived and worked, the 'real' world where literature and power were very intimately linked."[5] Hammer argues that the "manifest excesses" of Jarrell's poetry are deliberate, "evidence of his dissatisfaction with the boundaries ... defined by New Criticism's canons of taste."[6] Despite concerted advocacy, Jarrell's conversational style and unfashionable late subject matter (fairy tales, children, and housewives) have often been attacked as sentimental, "soppy or sloppy if you skim it instead of reading it," as Stephen Burt puts it.[7] Critical of "academic, tea-party, creative-writing-class poets" whose poems Jarrell described as "at bottom, social behavior calculated to satisfy a small social group of academic readers, editors and foundation executives," Jarrell insisted that one ought to write poems that come "out of life," acknowledging that this aesthetic seemed to violate "the rules or standards implicit in ... 'the best modern practice.'"[8]

Bishop, as Lowell's commentary at the 1964 reading notes, was also a poet who refused to write the "standard" academic poem fashionable at midcentury, nor did she write the kind of "confessional" poem that was quickly supplanting it. Despite her admiration for Lowell's *Life Studies* (1959) and Sylvia Plath's *Ariel,* which she read in the 1965 British edition, she resisted the notion of confessional poetry, even as her poetry was becoming more personal. In the 1967 *Time* cover story on Lowell, she made her now-famous dismissal of Lowell's "confessional imitators": "The tendency is to overdo the morbidity. You just wish they'd keep some of these things to themselves."[9] Bishop herself, who once jokingly described herself as "a minor female Wordsworth," was also troubled about her slow production of poems, and in her late years, according to Frank Bidart, was increasingly "diffident about her work and reputation":

> She felt that because she had been out of the country so long she was unfashionable, half-forgotten. (Years later, visiting my apartment, she plucked *The*

Modern Poet, a volume of essays edited by Ian Hamilton, off my shelves. There were essays on Lowell, Plath, Berryman, Jarrell – nothing on her. She scanned the table of contents, then putting the book back said, with woe in her voice: "It's like being buried alive.")[10]

Far from being unfashionable or half-forgotten, Bishop's work has steadily risen in the regard of readers and critics of poetry since her death in October 1979. She is now widely considered a canonical poet – the major poet of her circle – and one of the most important figures of the mid-twentieth century. Jarrell, whose poetry was truly unfashionable during his lifetime, continues to be undervalued precisely because his poems frequently violate normative expectations of both gender and genre. As Alan Williamson has argued so cogently, Jarrell's intense exploration in his poetry of "the earliest, most forgotten experiences of life and with the senses of identity, relationship, and gender that begin to form there" is what makes his work unique. It is also, Williamson argues, the reason that "at its most incandescent moments, it completely transcends the accusation" of sentimentality.[11]

Jarrell himself was the first to recognize his affinity with Bishop, noting an uncanny, "queer feeling" that they were "very different but *did* come from the same planet."[12] Jarrell expressed "awed wonder" at seeing in Bishop's poems such as "Manners" (1955) and "Sestina" (1956) "some phrases feeling to me a little like my own phrases, in your poems," noting that they shared the ability to "really remember childhood"; he wrote Bishop that he was "particularly interested in the 'more subjective, personal interior life-kind'" of poems that became more prominent in Bishop's later career.[13] The personal dimension had attracted him to Bishop's work all along, and it was this same dimension that, when displayed in his own work, provoked critical controversy. Since the 1990s, critics have demonstrated the affinity between the two poets, in terms of both style and subject matter.[14] But to most readers in the 1940s, 1950s, and 1960s, their poetry seemed very different on the surface. Bishop's star rose (albeit slowly) during this period because her poetry resisted received notions of feminine poetry by virtue of its objective, impersonal eye, whereas Jarrell's reputation declined as he increasingly rejected conventionally masculine authority in favor of a personal and conversational style that he himself attributed, in a 1939 letter to Allen Tate, to his "poetic and semifeminine mind."[15]

Both poets experienced childhood dislocations that influenced their work. Jarrell, who was born in Nashville, Tennessee, on May 6, 1914, spent much of his childhood in Los Angeles and Long Beach, California. When his parents separated in 1924, he moved with his mother to Nashville but later spent a year between 1926 and 1927 in the "blue wonderland" of Hollywood with his paternal grandparents and great-grandmother before returning to Nashville, a period commemorated in his poem "The Lost World" (1963). Jarrell frequently expressed a feeling of estrangement from his mother's side of the family and also felt a sense of betrayal when his grandparents made him return. At Vanderbilt University he studied with Robert Penn Warren, Allen Tate, and John Crowe Ransom. Moving to Kenyon College in 1937 to follow Ransom, Jarrell worked as an instructor and roomed in Ransom's attic with Robert Lowell. After completing his M.A., he taught at the University of Texas, where he met and married fellow instructor Mackie Langham in 1940. By the time Jarrell enlisted in the U.S. Army Air Forces in 1942, he had become well established as a critic and had published *Blood for a Stranger* (1942) and *Little Friend, Little Friend* (1945).

Bishop's early dislocations were more profound. Born in 1911 in Worcester, Massachusetts, Bishop lost her father when she was eight months old. Moving to Great Village, Nova Scotia, in 1915, Bishop lived with her maternal grandparents; when she was five years old, her mother was committed to a public mental hospital in Nova Scotia. Bishop never saw her again. Brought back to Worcester "unconsulted and against my wishes," she lived first with her paternal grandparents and then her aunt Maud Shepherdson and suffered from eczema and asthma.[16] At Vassar College, she met lifelong friends who helped her cultivate her writing. Marianne Moore became an early mentor, choosing some of Bishop's poems, including "The Map," for the anthology *Trial Balances*. Bishop traveled widely and wrote slowly until her first manuscript of poems received the Houghton Mifflin Literary Fellowship in 1945.

The two poets first met shortly before Jarrell reviewed that first book, *North & South* (1946), when Jarrell, just discharged from the army, was replacing Margaret Marshall for a year as literary editor of the *Nation*. In January 1947, he introduced Bishop to Robert Lowell, who became her most important literary friend. In the fall of that year, Jarrell accepted a faculty position at the Woman's College in Greensboro (now the University of North Carolina at Greensboro). Throughout the forties his reputation as a critic was legendary, while his reputation as a poet was still insecure. Shortly after his third book, *Losses*, was published, the September 1948 issue of *Poetry* magazine led off with a selection of seven Jarrell poems followed by both a negative and a positive review of the volume, under the title "Jarrell's 'Losses': A Controversy." The negative reviewer, W. S. Graham, faulted Jarrell's poems for wishing to connect "poetic experience" with its "verifiability in the 'real' world," describing as faults what most sympathetic readers of Jarrell today see as defining characteristics of his style:

> As an addition to his intended verisimilitude Mr. Jarrell sprinkles his poems full of little conversational phrases trailing off to dots, which, as a device, have a loosening effect upon a poetic line which is, in the first place, conceived at too low a tension. He also employs dashes liberally, although not consistently, sometimes to do the work of commas, other times of periods. The whole would seem to represent a revolt against the "poetic," and urge to deal with an honest thorny reality.[7]

Graham, no doubt, would have been unsympathetic to Jarrell's later aesthetic credo: "Art matters not merely because it is the most magnificent ornament and the most nearly unfailing occupation of our lives, but because it is life itself."[18] In keeping with this belief, Jarrell would later criticize (somewhat unfairly) the ending of Richard Wilbur's "The Death of a Toad": "You think with a surge of irritation and dismay, 'so it was all only an excuse for some Poetry'" (*PA*, p. 251). Interestingly, Bishop thought this review more than fair, remarking to Lowell that Jarrell's "reviews infuriate me and yet that activity and that last minute *devotion* to criticism is really wonderful. I think he admires Richard Wilbur too much, though."[19] Clearly, however, Bishop shared Jarrell's ideal aesthetic, his belief that a moral commitment to accurate observation and an allegiance to "life" were more important than the mere technical facility of "Poetry." This aesthetic is exemplified in his praise for the lines from the middle of section 33 of Whitman's "Song of Myself," beginning with "I understand the large heart of heroes" and concluding, "All this I swallow, it tastes good, I like it well, it becomes mine, / I am the man, I suffered, I was there." "These lines are so good," writes Jarrell, "that even admiration seems like insolence, and one is ashamed of anything that one might find to say about them. How anyone can dismiss or accept patronizingly the man who wrote them, I do not understand" (*PA*, p. 127).

Jarrell's praise for William Carlos Williams's *Paterson*, Book 1, and for the poems of Bishop's *North & South* is predicated on a similar aesthetic. "The subject of *Paterson*," Jarrell writes in his 1946 omnibus review that included both poets, "is: How can you tell the truth about things? – that is, how can you find a language so close to the world that the world can be represented and understood in it?" (*PA*, p. 228). His famous and still influential assessment of Bishop's first book works in a similar vein:

> Instead of crying, with justice, "This is a world in which no one can get along,"
> Miss Bishop's poems show that it is barely, but perfectly possible – has been,

that is, for her. Her work is unusually personal and honest in its wit, perception, and sensitivity – and in its restrictions too; all her poems have written underneath, *I have seen it*. She is so morally attractive in poems like "The Fish" or "Roosters," because she understands so well that the wickedness and confusion of the age can explain and extenuate other people's wickedness and confusion, but not, for you, your own; that morality, for the individual, is usually a small, personal, statistical, but heartbreaking or heartwarming affair of omissions and commissions the greatest of which will seem infinitesimal, ludicrously beneath notice, to those who govern, rationalize or deplore. (*PA*, p. 235)

As James Longenbach has argued, Jarrell here "seems to be describing the ideals of his own poems."[20] The critical ambivalence about *Losses* surfaced in part because Jarrell's postwar subject matter was emerging in that volume, in poems such as "Moving" (1948). Like Jarrell's late poem "The Lost World" (1963), "Moving" also frames the perceptions of the child (in this case a little girl) against the more jaded reflections of the adult. In many ways the innocent reflections of the child in "Moving" resemble those of Bishop's later children, such as the child in "Sestina" (1956), who perceives the kitchen animistically and "draws another inscrutable house," or the child in "First Death in Nova Scotia" (1962).

For Bishop, the period between 1948 and 1951, when she left for Brazil, was extremely difficult, marked by an almost unwelcome visibility as poetry consultant at the Library of Congress (1949–1950) as well as a number of personal upheavals. Her decision to stay in Brazil and the stability of her relationship with her partner, Lota de Macedo Soares, allowed her to begin developing her later style and subject matter, in which exploring questions of childhood, "questions of travel," and the "art of losing" became more urgent (*BPL*, pp. 74, 166). Although she continued to think of Jarrell as a good friend, their correspondence became sporadic during the 1950s, and they saw each other only during Bishop's infrequent visits to the United States. Paradoxically, it is during this period that the two poets' work shares similar concerns and strategies. Writing to Bishop after a long silence, in 1957, Jarrell told Bishop that he saw Jarrell-like phrases in Bishop's poem "Sestina" (1956). Mary Kinzie, in a convincing comparison of Jarrell's and Bishop's styles, notes that both poets "address an earlier state of being with a later mind and resources"; Kinzie points to "the astonishing resemblances in their nearly simultaneous discovery of the child among its objects."[21] For both poets, "adult ease only intensifies the illusion of young wonder and unmediated freshness, which, in turn, rescues the commonplaces, makes authentic (hence poetic) the self-evidential, approximate, halting, interrupted, and fussily circular utterances that pepper the style of both."[22]

Temperamentally, the poets were indeed very different: Jarrell loved teaching, was reputedly quite a performer in the classroom, and relished his role as a public intellectual as poetry consultant at the Library of Congress. More than any poet in his circle, he experienced suburban culture from within, both in Greensboro and in northwest Washington, D.C. After his second marriage, to Mary Von Schrader in 1952, his life – at least outwardly – was typical of the new Cold War ideal of the heterosexual nuclear family: he had both a devoted wife and stepdaughters. While he wrote scathing indictments of consumer culture, he also seemed to celebrate and enjoy the professional life of what Karl Shapiro would soon call (in capital letters) "the Bourgeois Poet."[23] In contrast, Bishop was terrified of teaching and even of reading her poems in public, and her year as poetry consultant was perhaps the most miserable year of her life. Living on a modest trust fund and fellowships until the late 1960s, she was, for much of her career, an American living outside of American culture. As Camille Roman has shown, Bishop's long-distance relationship with the United States compounded the profound sense of alienation that she felt so acutely in the late 1940s.[24] While Jarrell was frequently critical of American culture, he criticized it from within.

Bishop admired Jarrell's poetry, calling him "a fine poet ... and the best and most generous critic of poetry I have known," but she had reservations (*BPL*, p. 717). In particular, she was troubled by what she was to describe years after his death as "his understanding & sort-of-over-sympathizing with the lot of women" (*WA*, pp. 741–42). Bishop's discomfort with Jarrell's cross-gendered performances may have stemmed from her objection to the outright sexism in poems like "Woman," which Bishop hated both in its early version in *Botteghe Oscure* (1953) and in its 1964 version, included in *The Lost World*. While she rightly criticizes the poem for perpetuating "all those clichés about women," her discomfort also seems somewhat bound up with her vigilance about sentimentality, which oddly takes the form of her insistence on preserving rather than disrupting conventional notions of gender. Even as early as 1948, she had not known how to respond to one of Jarrell's most successful cross-gendered poems, "The Night before the Night before Christmas," which she characterized as *"limp and more suited for a short story"* (*WA*, p. 73). In 1960 in a letter to Lowell, Bishop expressed her disdain for what she characterized in Anne Sexton as "the 'our beautiful old silver' school of female writing" and, later, for its male equivalent in the work of W. D. Snodgrass (*WA*, pp. 333, 359). She then reassured Lowell that his own work in *Life Studies* was "really 'masculine' writing – courageous and honest" (*WA*, p. 360). Bishop seemed to understand that Jarrell was deliberately pushing the boundaries of sentimentality. Writing to Anne Stevenson in 1964, she commented, "Randall, I think – well, I think that sentimentality is deliberate, you know – he is trying to restore *feeling* perhaps – but I just don't think we can believe in it these days."[25] In addition, Jarrell's obsession with aging undoubtedly contributed to her uneasiness. Writing to Lowell in 1975, she implores him, "Please, *please* don't talk about old age so much, my dear old friend! You are giving me the creeps" and goes on to say that what "Lota admired so much about us North Americans was our determined youthfulness and energy" (*WA*, p. 778). Often tying self-pity about aging in her friends like Lowell and Jarrell to her general disdain for what she perceived to be the sentimental excesses in "lesser" poets like Sexton and Snodgrass, she nevertheless defined the drawbacks of midcentury verse in terms of an absence of "real feeling." Writing to Lowell in 1960, Bishop complains about merely "adequate" poetry:

> I get so depressed with every number of POETRY, *The New Yorker*, etc.... so much adequate poetry all sounding just alike and *so* boring – or am I growing frizzled small and stale or however you put it? There seems to be too much of everything – too much painting, too much poetry, too many novels – and too much money, I suppose. (Although I certainly welcomed mine.) And no one really feeling anything much. (*WA*, p. 344)

For Bishop, who was a severe censor of her own work, Jarrell's poems may have had *too much* feeling – may have been too distinctive sounding and more disturbing than boring. They were also, Bishop insisted, "truly American":

> You are truly "American," too – if again one can leave out all the unfortunate possible meanings of that word – You make me feel almost homesick and disloyal. – I should go back and live it all over again – except that I always was an expatriate of sorts, from the beginning, and I suppose that's why your poems amaze me so with their realer USA than any I ever knew – (*BPL*, p. 868)

Bishop, living in Brazil, often characterized herself as "3/4ths Canadian" (*BPL*, p. 852) and wrote to Lowell that Jarrell "does write about a class of American life that is strange to me – perhaps it is the 'west.' He makes me feel scarcely American at all, and yet I am, through and through" (*WA*, p. 573). Responding to "The Lost World," she writes Jarrell, "I'm naturally fascinated by the autobiographical ones – I really have to read them more as poems, though – right now I am so amazed at how very different our lives were that that's what strikes me most of all" (*BPL*, p. 868).

Lowell wrote to Bishop that he admired Jarrell's now widely anthologized poem "Next Day" (1963). The poem, spoken by a middle-aged suburban house-wife in the supermarket, stood in a long line of monologues spoken by aging women through whom Jarrell expressed his own loss of vitality. The woman's predicament hearkens back to Jarrell's polemical essays criticizing American consumer culture, as she wanders the aisles of the supermarket among the detergents "Cheer," "Joy," and "All," vainly seeking their emotional equiva-lents. Bishop did not share Lowell's enthusiasm for "Next Day," but she had little firsthand experience of the consumer culture that gave rise to the speak-er's – and Jarrell's – sad heart at the supermarket. Neither did she, like Jarrell, have extensive experience as an educator of young women, many of whom, like the speaker of "Next Day," might well have ended up in supermarkets, quoting William James to themselves, because they had few opportunities to make use of their college educations in their conventional marriages. Bishop was to maintain an idyllic – some would say naïve – view of Brazil itself as a lost paradise, recommending it to Jarrell as an antidote. Brazil, Bishop wrote Jarrell, is "a country where one feels closer to real old-fashioned life":

> With all its awfulness and stupidities – some of the Lost World hasn't quite been lost here yet, I feel, on the days I still like living in this backward place. – This is true particularly when one gets away from Rio, or the coast. – The peo-ple in the small poor places are so absolutely natural and elegantly polite. – I'm not really off the subject of your poems – it is that I think the things you feel a sense of loss for aren't entirely lost to the world, yet. I gather up every bit of evidence with joy, and wish I could put it into my poems, too – (*BPL*, pp. 870–71)

Much of what Bishop learned of the United States between 1951 and her first extended return visit in 1957 she learned from the popular magazines, such as *Time* and the *Saturday Evening Post*, representatives of the "instant culture" that Jarrell had begun railing against.

Although she shared Jarrell's criticism of the direction of postwar America, Bishop, for the most part, had viewed it from afar. During Bishop and Soares's only extended visit to the United States (March 31–October 15, 1957), although Jarrell was getting a lot of attention as a public intellectual, he was also in the depths of what he described as depression, unable "to write on poems, criticism, or anything."[26] Bishop, seeing the proliferation of "superhighways" and "automobiles" since 1952, asked whether "it's just some lack of vitality in myself that makes me feel so hopeless about my own country.... I really can't *bear* much of American life these days – surely no country has been so filthy rich and so hideously uncomfortable at the same time" (WA, pp. 228–29). But it is clear that Jarrell felt his own dismay far more keenly. Writing not as an expatriate but from within Eisenhower's America, he lamented the fundamental difference between the American postwar present and the American past:

> The climate of our culture is changing. Under these new rains, new suns, small things grow great and what was great grows small; whole species disappear and are replaced. The American present is very different from the American past: so different that our awareness of the extent of the changes has been repressed, and we regard as ordinary what is extraordinary – ominous perhaps – both for us and for the rest of the world.[27]

Jarrell's cultural pessimism was compounded by a feeling that his poetry was not being read or appreciated. Despite winning the National Book Award for Poetry for *The Woman at the Washington Zoo* (1960), he had also suffered a poetry writing block for a number of years; the award-winning volume contained a large number of translations and few genuinely new poems. So he must have been dismayed when, in a 1962 article titled "Poetry in English: 1945–62," the anonymous author(s) of *Time* declared Lowell and Bishop (along with Theodore Roethke) the most important poets of their generation. To be sure, the article described their work in stereotypical terms; Lowell's career was described in terms of the emerging breakthrough narrative as that of someone who had changed from a poet with "a driving religious concern and a nervously aggressive masculine line" to a poet who, in *Life Studies*, "limbered his forms and strengthened a strong and even peculiar personal tone that sounds a little like cubistic Browning." Bishop was described as "limited and proficient": "The cool, eely slickness of her poems is sometimes repellent. They have little human warmth, no specific temperature. She seldom writes about people or their feelings." But Jarrell received only a passing mention as one of four poets who were "moved to describe their military experiences in rough-edged verse that some did not like but all could understand."[28]

Later that year, insult was added to injury when *Time* introduced excerpts from Jarrell's lecture "Fifty Years of American Poetry" in a way that surely must have stung: "Poets' opinions of other poets are often unintelligible to anybody except a poet. But Minor Poet Randall Jarrell is also a witty critic who can sometimes be more eloquent in prose than he is in verse."[29] During the last year or so of his life, Jarrell suffered from severe mania and depression brought on by the careless prescription of the newly marketed antidepressant Elavil, but his condition was also aggravated by a vicious attack in the *New York Times Book Review* charging his last book of poems, *The Lost World* (1965), with "an indulgent and sentimental Mama-ism."[30] When Jarrell was struck by a car in October 1965, the mystery surrounding his death unfortunately deflected attention away from his work. But despite some of her reservations, Bishop, in a letter Jarrell may not have received, recognized the unique value of his last poetry: "You're both very sorrowful, and yet not the anguish-school that Cal seems innocently to have inspired – the self-pitiers who sometimes write quite good imitations of Cal! It is more human, less specialized, and yet deep" (*BPL*, p. 867).

By the time Bishop returned to live permanently in the United States – on Christmas Eve, 1967, after Soares's suicide – she had been living abroad so long that she experienced culture shock, living in San Francisco with a much younger partner. Brett Millier notes that Bishop "was not quite prepared for San Francisco the winter following the Summer of Love."[31] Bishop wrote to Louise Crane expressing a bewilderment worthy of the speaker of Jarrell's "Next Day," albeit with a much better sense of humor:

> Now I have a little flat, little car, somebody else's little boy, and have joined the great lower-middle-class American public in spending a lot of time looking for a place to park. It is a strange sensation. I had never been in a laundromat before. I'm getting used to it now, but at first when I went to the Supermarket I spent hours because I wanted to read what it said on all the packages.[32]

She wrote to May Swenson in November 1968 that the United States was "all pretty new to me, after 17 years away. I really was awfully out of touch I find."[33] Despite her sojourn in what was not quite Randall Jarrell's "west," her feelings of displacement from American culture seem to have made her "Questions of Travel" ever more urgent.

As Bishop worked on her late poetry, particularly that in *Geography III*, she worked hard to negotiate the line between sentimental excess and "real feeling" in her own work. The drift in Bishop studies toward an insistence on the poet as more personal than the reticent, modest poet for whom "restraint, calm and proportion" (*PA*, pp. 234–35) are paramount has given the general reader access to letters, drafts, and ephemera previously available only to scholars willing to travel to various archives. But the publication of this material has been somewhat controversial. Alice Quinn's edition, *Edgar Allan Poe and the Juke-Box: Uncollected Poems, Drafts, and Fragments*, outraged Vendler, who castigated the publication of "these maimed and stunted siblings" of Bishop's published poetry.[34] One need not share Vendler's outrage to concur with her judgment that the draft pages from Bishop's aborted "Elegy," written for Lota de Macedo Soares, pale in comparison to the masterpiece "Crusoe in England." And with a handful of exceptions, one sees in the fragments and drafts that producing a poem of "real feeling" was for Bishop an act of intense craftsmanship – the relatively banal and prosaic first draft of "One Art" is a case in point. Like her Crusoe, Bishop understood the temptation to "[give] way to self-pity," but by the time that impulse made its way into a finished poem, the poet distanced herself from raw emotion in such a way that real feeling could emerge:

> What's wrong about self-pity, anyway?
> With my legs dangling down familiarly
> Over a crater's edge, I told myself
> "Pity should begin at home." So the more
> Pity I felt, the more I felt at home. (*BPL*, p. 153)

Crusoe's monologue is leavened with this sort of wry humor throughout; as in much of Bishop's best work, her poetic voice captures the characteristic combination of "awful but cheerful" that she first invoked in "The Bight" (1949). Bonnie Costello has offered a provocative reading of Crusoe in which she criticizes what she sees as biographical reductiveness in the burgeoning Bishop industry, but I'd like to point to a draft Bishop abandoned in order to illuminate what Jarrell saw as the point of connection between himself and Bishop: the great poems and stories about childhood that Bishop wrote in the 1950s and early 1960s.[35] Certainly, Bishop abandoned the draft "Where are the dolls who loved me so" (from the early 1950s) because she detected that it gives way to self-pity in the way that finished poems like "Sestina" (1956) or "First Death in Nova Scotia" (1962) do not. The dolls, with their "blank crotches, / and / play / wrist-watches, / whose hand moved only when they wanted –" possess a

> stoicism I never mastered
> their smiling phrase for every occasion –
> ~~They went their rigid little ways~~
>
> To meditate in trunks or closets
> To let [life and] unforeseen emotions
> ~~Glance off their glazed complexions.~~ (*BPL*, p. 235)

The elements of early childhood animism that are the key to the finished poems remain unprocessed here. Indeed, the fragment seems almost to be a preliminary note for the 1953 autobiographical story "Gwendolyn," and little more. This story and the much more accomplished "In the Village" (1953) lay the groundwork not only for the poems about childhood in the "Elsewhere" section of *Questions of Travel* but for poems such as "In the Waiting Room" and

"The Moose" in *Geography III*. That the doll fragment was abandoned shows Bishop's good judgment about her own writing. But it also shows a fear of allowing herself too much emotional excess in her writing, censoring herself just when the messy feelings in the draft threatened to spin out of control.

Bishop was always protesting that she was not a critic, but she appears to be an astute (and specific) critic to Lowell and others in her letters. Given her ambivalence about Jarrell's work, she was often more dismissive than astute in her judgments of his poetry, and she often withheld those judgments from Jarrell. However, despite her frequent complaints about Jarrell's aging women, one poem of his she praises is "The Player Piano" (1964). Her praise is not without qualification, but it is clear that she admires the poem more than other cross-gendered performances by Jarrell. Nevertheless, her praise continued to emphasize her difference from Jarrell:

> Right now I am so amazed at how very different our lives were that that's what strikes me most of all. It is too bad, perhaps, that "The Player Piano" didn't get in this book, too. The ending of that is marvelous – Heavens – I remember the false armistice – but, for some reason, not the real one. However, I don't seem to mind growing old at all, or rarely. – I just get bored because any stories need longer explanations than they used to, because so many people are now younger – I suppose that means one should stop telling them. But not your kind – these are invaluable, and the *only* poems I know that do tell any of these things. (*BPL*, p. 868)

A monologue spoken by yet another of Jarrell's aging women, the poem engages the lost Southern California landscape of Jarrell's childhood. Although it is doubtful that he himself would have remembered the false armistice, which took place when he was four years old (Bishop was seven), the poem certainly contains autobiographical elements, like "The Night before the Night before Christmas" (1948), "The Face" (1950), "The Woman at the Washington Zoo" (1960, but first sent to Bishop in 1957), and monologues such as "Next Day" (1963) and "The Lost Children" (1965). "The Player Piano" is, as Stephen Burt has demonstrated, "one of Jarrell's last and best poems about the life course,"[36] so its excellence may have overcome Bishop's general aversion to Jarrell's women. Here is the ending of the poem Bishop praised:

> Here are Mother and Father in a photograph,
> Father's holding me.... They both look so *young*.
> I'm so much older than they are. Look at them,
> Two babies with their baby. I don't blame you,
> You weren't old enough to know any better;

If I could go back, sit down by you both,
And sign our true armistice: you weren't to blame.
I shut my eyes and there's our living room.
The piano's playing something by Chopin,
And Mother and Father and their little girl

Listen. Look, the keys go down by themselves!
I go over, hold my hands out, play I play –
If only, somehow, I had learned to live!
The three of us sit watching, as my waltz
Plays itself out a half-inch from my fingers.[37]

"The last two stanzas," Bishop wrote in a postscript to Jarrell,

> remind me just a little bit of one I think is still just about Roethke's best – "My Papa's Waltz" – but more, they suddenly brought back to me one of my very favorites of Hardy's – "The Self-Unseeing" – one of his most beautiful little poems, I think. (I've even been trying to write a poem *about* it.) But yours has a stranger and more contemporary – although still past – mystery to it – those *keys*.... And the word "keys" itself seems to be so full of ambiguity. (*BPL*, p. 869)

Bishop's connection of Jarrell's poem with Hardy's small masterpiece is indeed more apt than any superficial resemblances the poem might have to "My Papa's Waltz." The mystery of Jarrell's poem might seem more "contemporary," but what Burt identifies as Jarrell's sophisticated management of repetition and time scales is indeed reminiscent of the Hardy poem, with its "ancient floor, / Footworn and hollowed and thin," and its "former door / Where the dead feet walked in":

> Childlike, I danced in a dream;
> Blessings emblazoned that day;
> Everything glowed with a gleam;
> Yet we were looking away![38]

David Bromwich connects Hardy's poem (the third stanza in particular) with Bishop's concept of "a self-forgetful, perfectly useless concentration" necessary for both experiencing and creating a work of art, from the famous "Darwin Letter" to Anne Stevenson (*BPL*, p. 861).[39] The correspondence with Stevenson is now available in its entirety in *Prose*, and the Darwin Letter was begun on January 8, 1964, and finished on January 20, a little more than a month before Bishop's letter to Jarrell about "The Player Piano" (*BPL*, pp. 855–65). So it would appear that what resonated for Bishop in the Jarrell poem touched the heart of her own fundamental creative principles – one might even say, paraphrasing "Poem" from *Geography III*, that their "looks" coincided here.

One might also say that, alone among the handful of Jarrell's posthumously published poems, "The Player Piano" might have pointed to Jarrell's poetic future. Certainly, the aesthetic that Bishop touches on in the Darwin Letter reflects her understanding that the recently completed *Questions of Travel* represented a shift in the direction of her work. Given Bishop's working habits, it was a shift that began in 1952 with her move to Brazil and discovery of a "de luxe Nova Scotia" (*WA*, p. 676) in writing both poems and stories about early childhood and poems about Brazil. Jarrell had undergone a significant shift in both subject matter and style in the late forties and early fifties and then again from 1962 until his death. Bishop learned from Jarrell that she could let her guard down a little. She would confront her childhood (and adult) losses more directly and more discursively. And although she was still suspicious of Jarrell's apparent sentimentality, she learned that adopting Jarrellian personae (Crusoe, for instance) allowed her to express emotion more directly as well. Jarrell learned from Bishop to pay closer attention to concrete particulars in his poems and to manage their music more skillfully: although he had learned much of this already from Robert Frost, Bishop's example also helped him discover the unobtrusive yet masterful music of the terza rima of "The Lost World" and of the children's poems from *The Bat-Poet*, as well as that of "The Player Piano." Writing about *The Lost World* and *The Bat-Poet*, Bishop says, "you are the real one and only successor to Frost. Not the bad side of Frost, or the silly side – the wisdom of the ages side, etc. – but all the good. The beautiful writing, the sympathy, the touching and real detail" (*BPL*, p. 867).

Both poets strove to pay attention to facts while remaining open to the possibility of "sinking or sliding giddily off into the unknown" (*BPL*, p. 861). For Bishop, this involves bridging the apparent split between conscious and unconscious states: "There is no 'split.' Dreams, works of art (some), glimpses of the always-more-successful surrealism of everyday life, unexpected moments of empathy (is it?), catch a peripheral vision of whatever it is one can never really see full-face but that seems enormously important" (*BPL*, p. 861). If Darwin was Bishop's hero, Freud was Jarrell's. And while it seems that he placed more stock in works of art as wish fulfillments, the trajectory of his work points to the importance of empathy and intersubjectivity; in similar ways, the trajectory of Bishop's work points to what Victoria Harrison terms "relational subjectivity," especially as Bishop turns to childhood as a subject, beginning in 1952.[40] Perhaps one difference between the two poets in terms of their interest in psychoanalysis is that Bishop found the object-relations theory of Melanie Klein more significant than Freudian theory.

The epigraph to Bishop's last book of poems, *Geography III* (1976), was drawn from a book John Ashbery had given her, *First Lessons in Geography* (1884), and ends with a dizzying series of questions. Reading the epigraph on Susan Howe's Pacifica Radio show, Bishop says, "Then the book gets rather hysterical":[41] "*In what direction is the Volcano? The Cape? The Bay? The Lake? The Strait? The Mountains? The Isthmus? What is in the East? In the West? In the South? In the North? In the Northwest? In the Southeast? In the Northeast? In the Southwest?*" (*BPL*, p. 148). In her early work, such as "The Map" (1935), "topography displays no favorites": "More delicate than the historian's are the map-maker's colors"; in her late work, the poet finds herself answering the dislocation suggested by the epigraph by returning to what Jarrell called "The Elementary Scene."[42] The epigraph's first lessons have no conclusive answer except for the "un-rediscovered, un-renameable" lost world of "In the Waiting Room" (1971) and "Crusoe in England" (1971) (*BPL*, p. 151). "Was there / a moment when I actually chose this?" asks Crusoe – and Bishop. Perhaps I chose it that moment in the waiting room on "the fifth / of February, 1918" when nearly seven-year-old "*Elizabeth*" discovers she is an "*I*" and therefore "one of *them*" (*BPL*, p. 150).

Reviewing Walter de la Mare's anthology *Come Hither* in *Poetry* magazine in 1958, Bishop connects de la Mare's selection of verse for "the young of all ages" with Jarrell and Crusoe: "[De la Mare] loves 'little articles,' home-made objects whose value increases with age, Robinson Crusoe's lists of his belongings, homely employments, charms and herbs. As a result he naturally chose for his book many of what Randall Jarrell once called 'thing-y' poems, and never the pompous, abstract, or formal" (*BPL*, p. 700). There are a number of poems and passages in Jarrell's work – for example, his own 1949 Crusoe poem "The Island" and the passage in "The Lost World" on Barrie's play *The Admirable Crichton* – that appear to have influenced "Crusoe in England," which Bishop began writing in 1964.[43] As with Jarrell's beloved objects – the children's arms in "The Lost World" that "arm, for a child's wars, the child" but are ineffective "in the sands / Of age in which nothing grows, where all our friends are old" – "the living soul has dribbled away" from Crusoe's "home-made" objects, which are now mere museum pieces: "How can anyone want such things?" he asks (*BPL*, p. 156). If talk about old age gave Bishop "the creeps," perhaps it is because her understanding of old age and of loss is far bleaker than Jarrell's. For Jarrell, there is a tentative rapprochement between child and adult – as in "Thinking of the Lost World," in which adult emptiness is traded for the emptiness of the child, an emptiness that seems to be marked by a potential for wonder, imagination, and creativity. There is a transaction, however evanescent, between the lost world and the world of the poem's present.

But unlike the ending of "Thinking of the Lost World," the ending of "The Player Piano" resembles the conclusion of "Crusoe" in its bleakness. "If only somehow I had learned to live," laments Jarrell's speaker; "How can anyone want such things?" cries Bishop's Crusoe. Lowell pointed out to Bishop the presence of Jarrell's late style in the poem:

> Jean Valentine sent me (what I'm really writing about) your long "Crusoe in England" – maybe your best poem, an analogue to your life, your "Ode to Dejection." Nothing you've written has such a mix of humor and desperation; I find bits of the late Randall, his sour witty downgrading of his own jokes, somehow this echo, if it is, makes the poem still more original and sealed with your voice. (WA, p. 755)

The ambiguity of those "keys" Bishop noticed, as the speaker's waltz plays itself out, emphasizes that those treasured objects that once "reeked of meaning" are no longer alive (BPL, p. 156). A piano roll playing Chopin, snatches of the 1918 popular song "Till We Meet Again," a memory of Fatty Arbuckle before the scandal, and the false armistice: while they appear to be shared, "live," and "touching in detail / – the little that we get for free, / the little of our earthly trust" – these objects are ultimately "Not Much" (BPL, p. 166).

One particular passage from Jarrell's last book of poems that Bishop admired were the lines from "The One Who Was Different": "I feel like the first men who read Wordsworth. / It's so simple I can't understand it" (BPL, p. 870). The twenty-first century understands that Bishop's great poems that articulated the art of losing resonated within and beyond the noisier, messier 1960s and 1970s. Jarrell's early death has obscured for too long our understanding of his idiosyncratic and original poetic style – tentative, conversational, qualified, irrational, tender, and aggrieved. Bishop wrote in her memorial tribute that she and Jarrell, despite the occasional quarrel, "really were in agreement about everything that matters" (BPL, p. 717). In the same "Inadequate Tribute" she describes her friend as "difficult, touchy, and oversensitive to criticism" as well as "constantly tuned up to concert pitch that most people, including poets, can only maintain for short and fortunate stretches" (BPL, pp. 717–18). Although we were deprived of the poems Jarrell might have written in the 1960s and 1970s, he was, like Bishop, an inveterate explorer of the lost world of real feeling in poems that our century could benefit from reading as attentively as we have learned to read hers.

Notes

1. "Randall Jarrell Reading the Poems of Elizabeth Bishop and His Own Poems." Academy of American Poets Reading. Solomon R. Guggenheim Museum, New York, October 29, 1964. 2 CDRs.

2. "Randall Jarrell Reading the Poems of Elizabeth Bishop and His Own Poems"; Helen Vendler, "Randall Jarrell, Child and Mother, Frightened and Consoling," *New York Times Book Review*, February 29, 1969, pp. 5, 42, reprinted in Suzanne Ferguson (ed.), *Critical Essays on Randall Jarrell* (Boston: G. K. Hall, 1983), pp. 37–41.

3. John Ashbery, "Second Presentation of Elizabeth Bishop," *World Literature Today* 51:1 (1977), pp. 8–11, 8.

4. James Longenbach, *Modern Poetry After Modernism* (New York: Oxford University Press, 1997), p. 8.

5. Langdon Hammer, "Who Was Randall Jarrell?" *Yale Review* 79:2 (1990), pp. 389–405, 392.

6. Hammer, "Who Was Randall Jarrell?," p. 403.

7. Stephen Burt, "A Pure Reader," *Yale Review* 88:3 (2000), pp. 148–58, 154.

8. *National Poetry Festival: Held in the Library of Congress. October 22–24, 1962, Proceedings.* (Washington, D.C.: Library of Congress, 1964), p. 135.

9. "Poets: The Second Chance," *Time*, June 2, 1967, http://www.time.com /time/subscriber/article/0,33009,902090,00.html.

10. Frank Bidart, "Elizabeth Bishop," *Threepenny Review* 58 (1994), pp. 6–7, 7.

11. Alan Williamson, *Almost a Girl: Male Writers and Female Identification* (Charlottesville: University Press of Virginia, 2001), p. 11.

12. Randall Jarrell, *Randall Jarrell's Letters*, ed. Mary Jarrell, rev. ed. (Charlottesville: University of Virginia Press, 2002), p. 420.

13. Jarrell, *Randall Jarrell's Letters*, pp. 420, 422.

14. Mary Kinzie, *The Cure of Poetry in an Age of Prose: Moral Essays on the Poet's Calling* (Chicago: University of Chicago Press, 1993); Longenbach, *Modern Poetry After Modernism*; Thomas Travisano, *Midcentury Quartet* (Charlottesville: University of Virginia Press, 1999); Jeredith Merrin, "Randall Jarrell and Elizabeth Bishop: 'The Same Planet,'" in Suzanne Ferguson (ed.), *Jarrell, Bishop, Lowell, and Co.* (Knoxville: University of Tennessee Press, 2003), pp. 41–57.

15. Jarrell, *Randall Jarrell's Letters*, p. 19.

16. Elizabeth Bishop, *Poems, Prose, and Letters*, ed. Robert Giroux and Lloyd Schwartz (New York: Library of America, 2008), pp. 402–09, 413. This collection will be cited in the text as *BPL*.

17. W. S. Graham, "It All Comes Back to Me Now," *Poetry* 72:6 (1948), pp. 302–07, 303.

18. Randall Jarrell, *Poetry and the Age* (1953; Gainesville: University Press of Florida, 2001), p. 22. This collection will be cited in the text as *PA*.

19. Elizabeth Bishop and Robert Lowell, *Words in Air: The Complete Correspondence Between Elizabeth Bishop and Robert Lowell*, ed. Thomas Travisano with Saskia Hamilton (New York: Farrar, Straus and Giroux, 2008), p. 130. This collection will be cited in the text as *WA*.

20. Longenbach, *Modern Poetry After Modernism*, p. 58.

21. Kinzie, *The Cure of Poetry*, pp. 93, 66.

22. Kinzie, *The Cure of Poetry*, p. 93.

23. Karl Shapiro, *The Bourgeois Poet* (New York: Random House, 1964).

24. Camille Roman, *Elizabeth Bishop's World War II-Cold War View* (New York: Palgrave Macmillan, 2001).

25. Elizabeth Bishop, *Prose*, ed. Lloyd Schwartz (New York: Farrar, Straus and Giroux, 2011), p. 421.

26. Richard Flynn, "Jarrell's Wicked Fairy: Cultural Criticism, Childhood, and the 1950s," in Ferguson (ed.), *Jarrell, Bishop, Lowell, and Co.*, pp. 93–112, 95.

27. Randall Jarrell, *A Sad Heart at the Supermarket* (New York: Athenaeum, 1962), p. 86.

28. "Poetry in English: 1945–62," *Time*, March 9, 1962, pp. 92–95, http://www.time.com/time/magazine/article/0,9171,939990,00.html.

29. "View from Parnassus," *Time*, November 9, 1962, http://www.time.com/time/magazine/article/0,9171,829367,00.html.

30. Joseph Bennett, "Utterances, Entertainments and Symbols," *New York Times*, April 18, 1965, BR 24.

31. Brett C. Millier, *Elizabeth Bishop: Life and the Memory of It* (Berkeley: University of California Press, 1993), p. 399.

32. Elizabeth Bishop, *One Art: Letters*, ed. Robert Giroux (New York: Farrar, Straus and Giroux, 1994), p. 394.

33. Bishop, *One Art*, p. 500.

34. Elizabeth Bishop, *Edgar Allan Poe and the Juke-Box: Uncollected Poems, Drafts, and Fragments*, ed. Alice Quinn (New York: Farrar, Straus and Giroux, 2006); Helen Vendler, "The Art of Losing," *The New Republic*, April 3, 2006, pp. 33–37, 37.

35. Bonnie Costello, "Elizabeth Bishop's Impersonal Personal," *American Literary History* 15:2 (2003), pp. 334–66.

36. Stephen Burt, *Randall Jarrell and His Age* (New York: Columbia University Press, 2002), p. 259.

37. Randall Jarrell, *The Complete Poems* (New York: Farrar, Straus and Giroux, 1969), pp. 354–55.

38. Thomas Hardy, *Poems of the Past and Present* (London: Macmillan, 1903), pp. 211–12.

39. David Bromwich, "Poetic Invention and the Self-Unseeing," *Grand Street* 7:1 (1987), pp. 115–29.

40. Victoria Harrison, *Elizabeth Bishop's Poetics of Intimacy* (Cambridge: Cambridge University Press, 1993), p. 17.

41. Susan Howe and Charles Ruas, "Elizabeth Bishop: Reading and Interview on WBAI (NY) Pacifica Radio," PennSound (April 19, 1977 [misdated 1979]), http://www.writing.upenn.edu/pennsound/x/Howe-Pacifica.php.

42. Jarrell, *The Complete Poems*, p. 231.

43. Burt, *Randall Jarrell and His Age*, p. 259.

Chapter 35

Writing the South

ERNEST SUAREZ

John Crowe Ransom, Allen Tate, and Robert Penn Warren laid the foundations for twentieth-century southern poetry at Vanderbilt University in the twenties. Their writings resulted in two verse traditions that responded to broader American trends and developed within universities. One tradition is tied to Ransom's turn away from politics and return to aesthetics after *I'll Take My Stand: The South and the Agrarian Tradition* (1930) drew allegations of fascist tendencies from reviewers. Ransom's emphasis on form and local settings influenced a line of lyric poets, including Donald Justice and Charles Wright, whose verse largely remained outside the sociopolitical arena. Another tradition grew out of Tate's and Warren's embrace of modernism, but this tradition transformed in the forties, when modernism's influence diminished, and World War II served as a catalyst for Warren's and Randall Jarrell's turn toward more accessible, psychologically oriented narrative verse, a tendency that continued with James Dickey. During the second half of the century, southern poets absorbed and modified techniques associated with confessional and other midcentury movements but did not participate in them. Instead, a long succession of relationships within the academy led Wright, Dave Smith, and a new generation of southerners to extend and alter their predecessors' creative practices.

Before discussing these developments, it's important to consider how a lack of academic opportunities helped determine southern poetry's history. Without exception, the South's most accomplished poets met at universities, where they studied, earned a living, influenced one another, and formed alliances. When Ransom entered Vanderbilt in 1903, the South was the poorest and most backward region in the United States. For much of the century, its legacy of poverty made obtaining an education that might result in literary accomplishment difficult for anyone except the well-to-do; its history of discrimination made such an education almost impossible for people of color. Ransom and Warren came from relatively humble backgrounds, and

Tate's parents went bankrupt when he was a teenager; but all three men were academic overachievers who found the means to cultivate their talents. However, African Americans and women faced much more daunting barriers and were largely denied faculty positions, which made practicing the poorly compensated craft of poetry even more difficult (James Weldon Johnson of Jacksonville, Florida, and Sterling Brown of Washington, D.C., are exceptions treated in other chapters). While a number of women flourished as prose writers, except for Margaret Walker's *For My People* (1942), no significant collection of verse by a woman appeared until Eleanor Ross Taylor's *A Wilderness of Ladies* (1960). This situation didn't change until the final decades of the twentieth century, when faculty trained after the gains of the civil rights and women's movements reached maturity, and African American and female poets achieved greater access to the academy.

*

John Crowe Ransom's (1888–1974) emphasis on traditional forms and local settings had its most substantial influence on southern poetry after World War II, but his greatest period of poetic creativity was from 1916 to 1927, after which he published a small handful of original poems, revised previous work, and primarily dedicated himself to writing criticism and editing *The Kenyon Review*. The son of a Methodist minister from Pulaski, Tennessee, he entered Vanderbilt University at age fifteen. His studies in philosophy and classical literature at that university, and as a Rhodes scholar at Oxford University, led him to believe that people had become marred by a disassociation between rationality and sensibility; cultural rituals, including art, could serve as restoratives. Those convictions informed his writing for the rest of his life. Ransom believed form and subject were ontologically bound, inseparable components of a textured, nuanced rite.

Chills and Fever (1924) and *Two Gentlemen in Bonds* (1927) featured carefully modulated and intricately crafted poems that reflected Ransom's disdain of abstraction, his love of the concrete, and his commitment to traditional forms. Two widely celebrated poems, "Bells for John Whiteside's Daughter" (1924) and "Janet Waking" (1927), suggest how Ransom controls irony to balance tone in relation to subject. The former poem concerns a traumatic event, the death and funeral of an energetic young girl, and consists of five quatrains that develop according to the three-stage progression of the elegy, moving from lament to praise to consolation. The first stanza opens with the observation, "There was such speed in her little body," and proceeds to shift between images of motion and stillness, presenting the girl in her coffin and the narrator's reaction: "It is no wonder her brown study / Astonishes us all."[1] The use of "wonder" and "astonishes" is characteristic. In most contexts these words would not be associated with understatement, but here they invoke surprise and only imply pain and grief. The three middle stanzas shun the melodramatic, providing a tongue-in-cheek description of the rambunctious girl's pursuit of geese. The final stanza returns to images of motion and stillness, but the surprise expressed in the first stanza is replaced with an acceptance of reality.

> But now go the bells, and we are ready,
> In one house we are sternly stopped
> To say we are vexed at her brown study,
> Lying so primly propped.

The mourners are set in motion by the bells and are now "ready." However, that declaration is quickly modified when they are "sternly stopped" by the somber image of the dead girl. As Robert Penn Warren observed, the word "vexed" summarizes the mourners' reactions: astonishment, anger, grief, and consternation, all underscored by the wrenchingly ironic image of the once-active girl now "Lying so primly propped."[2]

Similarly, "Janet Waking" concerns the shock of death, but the poem's tone is altered to fit a far less tragic situation, a young girl's response to her pet hen's death. Instead of understatement, Ransom heightens emotion to portray the child's reaction and create humorous affect. After a night of restful sleep in her secure, happy home, she goes "Running across the world upon the grass," a phrase that suggests her innocence and inexperience.[3] Janet discovers her pet has been killed by a "transmogrifying bee." Janet, "weeping fast as she had breath," implores her parents to wake the bird. She is unready to "be instructed in how deep / Was the forgetful kingdom of death."[4]

Whether addressing tensions between body and spirit, reason and imagination, or past and present, Ransom consistently privileges aesthetic experience. At times, particularly when science is his nemesis, his poems can be overly schematic. Ransom's more successful poems that address the need for a rich imaginative life rely on subtle, contradictory pressures. "Morning" involves a relatively common decision, whether to spend the day having fun or attending to mundane responsibilities. Cast in three seven-line stanzas with near-identical metrical patterns and rhyme schemes, the poem opens with Jane waking Ralph "so gently" that he remains in bed.[5] Jane's tenderness and the alluring scenery entice him to consider spending the day with her, "walking / Through the green waves," "singing not talking." But in the last stanza the "dutiful mills of" his "brain" begin to "whir with their smooth-grinding wheels," and "man-liness" returns "entire to Ralph," phrases that suggest the stern demands of adult responsibilities. The poem ends as Ralph rises from bed and grudgingly but stoically accepts that it is "Simply another morning."

Ransom's student John Orley Allen Tate (1899–1979) of Winchester, Kentucky, shared his teacher's skepticism of a materially oriented culture and also portrayed science as the imagination's bête noire. Where Ransom relied on traditional forms, realistic settings, and irony, Tate wrote allusive verse heavy with pro-vocative, sometimes idiosyncratic, metaphors. He believed that modern poets' tendency to experiment could be likened to modern painters' rejecting the "tyr-anny of representation" in order to remake the "constituted material world" in a subjective manner that expressed the artist's interior reality.[6] In "Morning" and other poems, Ransom's characters entertain imaginative possibilities, but their experiences aren't fantastic or surreal. In "Last Days of Alice" (1932), Tate draws on Lewis Carroll's *Alice in Wonderland* and *Through the Looking Glass* to cast mod-ern humans as "Alice grown lazy, mammoth," a ghoulish projection of people who passively accept science's power to turn the physical world into abstract theorems, "all infinite, function, depth and mass / Without figure, a mathemat-ical shroud / Hurled at the air – blessèd without sin!"[7]

As an undergraduate, Tate's enthusiasm for modernism led him to reject Ransom's literary practices. Their acrimonious rift over T. S. Eliot's *The Waste Land* helps clarify their differences and points to similarities Tate shared with Eliot. When Ransom's scathing review of *The Waste Land* appeared in the *Literary Review* of the *New York Evening Post* on July 14, 1923, Tate reacted angrily. Ransom asserted that art's vitality depended on critics' ability to expose aes-thetic defects. He went on to disparage Eliot's capacity to reconcile the poem's disparate themes, allusions, and techniques. The twenty-three-year-old Tate fired off a letter to the *Literary Review*, accusing his former teacher of violating the "principle of free critical inquiry" by using an important poem to advance his own critical agenda. Tate declared that Ransom wasn't really an individual; he "is a *genre*."[8] Their acerbic exchange resulted in several years of personal tension, during which they slowly reconciled, but as Ransom wrote to Donald Davidson in 1926, Tate's enthusiasm for modernism served to "destroy any illusion that we are a 'school of poets' with unity."[9]

Tate and Ransom's disagreements were formal, not ideological. Like Eliot and many modern writers, they both believed that the dissolution of traditional religion and culture had fractured humans' relationship to the past, nature, and the metaphysical, resulting in alienation and a loss of a coherent sense of self. Tate's disdain for cultural relativism led him, like Eliot and Ransom, to embrace classicism, particularly in the form of Greco-Roman culture, a characteristic evident in "Aeneas at Washington," "The Mediterranean," "To the Lacedemonians," and other poems. His best-known poem, "Ode to the Confederate Dead" (1927), is cast in the irregular rhymes of Milton's "Lycidas" and employs Eliot-like imagistic stanzas that disrupt the narrative. In the poem, a modern man enters a graveyard and compares his existential uncertainty to Confederate soldiers' resolve. Four of the five imagistic stanzas contain slightly varied images of "leaves," that "flying, plunge, expire," an allusion to Glaucus's words to Diomedes in *The Iliad*, part VI: "Just as the generation of leaves, so is that also of men. The wind scatters the leaves upon the earth, but the forest as it flourishes, puts forth others when spring comes."[10] But in Tate's poem there's no hope of regeneration; only the "ravenous grave" awaits – a sentiment that recalls *The Waste Land*. In his essay on the poem, "Narcissus as Narcissus" (1938), Tate invokes the Greek myth of a handsome young man who peers into a pool of water and perishes because he falls in love with his own image. In "Ode to the Confederate Dead" Tate uses the myth to point out that modern humans are their own worst enemies; their loss of faith and inability to connect with the past or with nature, including their own nature, has resulted in a devastating form of self-consciousness and has reduced life to a series of trivial routines – "And in between the ends of distraction / Waits mute speculation, the patient curse / That stones the eyes."

Robert Penn Warren's ability to change and challenge his own artistic and political beliefs over a long and prolific career led him to become the South's most influential poet and one of the United States' most celebrated literary figures. Born in Guthrie, Kentucky, Warren (1905–1989) shared Ransom's and Tate's suspicion of romantic idealism, but his interest in naturalism modified his nostalgia for antiquity and was in stark contrast to their emphasis on traditional, ritualistic religion. The son of a bank clerk and a schoolteacher, he entered Vanderbilt in the fall of 1921 after an eye injury prevented him from accepting admission to the U.S. Naval Academy. Ransom was his freshman English teacher, and as Warren later recalled, he became "like a father to me."[11] Warren read Ransom's *Poems About God* (1919), which is set in middle Tennessee, and felt the "world that I knew around me to be the stuff of poetry."[12] But Tate introduced him to Eliot's work in the summer of 1922. When *The Waste Land* appeared in *Dial* that November, Warren was "completely overwhelmed" and memorized the entire poem.[13] The 1923 August–September issue of the *Fugitive* – a literary magazine named after a group of Vanderbilt faculty, students, and others who gathered to discuss philosophy and poetry – featured Warren's "After the Teacups," an allusion to "The Love Song of J. Alfred

Prufrock." On one afternoon of that same year, Tate returned to Wesley Hall and was thrilled to discover that Warren had painted four murals from *The Waste Land* on their dormitory walls.

Eliot's and Ransom's influences on Warren would be enduring. For the next quarter century, his diction and imagery often echoed Eliot's, and his poems reflected the metrical regularity Ransom advocated, a combination that sometimes resulted in mannered and derivative verse. An overly prophetic tone and persistent world-weariness plague *Thirty-Six Poems* (1935). Naturalism, via Thomas Hardy and Theodore Dreiser, inflects the more successful poems, including the "Kentucky Mountain Farm" sequence and "The Return: An Elegy." But Eliot's influence is pervasive, as in these lines from "The Return": "rain creeps down the loam again / Where the blind and nameless bones recline. / they are conceded to the earth's absolute chemistry."[14]

Despite their disagreement over verse techniques, Ransom and Tate united in the South's defense as the region came under greater national scrutiny, particularly in regard to *The State of Tennessee v. Scopes* (1925), a trial in which Clarence Darrow defended a high school teacher's right to teach the theory of evolution. Ransom, Tate, and Donald Davidson began planning the essay collection *I'll Take My Stand: The South and the Agrarian Tradition* (1930), which endorsed the virtues of a less materialistic, pastoral way of life in opposition to the threats they believed communism and corporate capitalism posed. Most of the essays support family ownership of small sectors of land and local businesses and are informed by the assumption that industrialization and centralized power undermine a sense of community. Richard Gray points out that "even while clinging" to "Southern mythologies," the Agrarians "had to reinvent them, reinterpret them according to their needs."[15] In their essays Ransom and Tate draw close parallels between preindustrial Europe and the South, characterizing their home region as the last bastion of a traditional culture unified by religion and a personal relationship to the land. Warren, still in his early twenties, wrote an essay that would later trouble him. "The Briar Patch," which Tate and Davidson thought too liberal, was an evasive defense of racial segregation. Warren invokes Booker T. Washington's "emphasis on vocational education" and considers how an agrarian society offers a rich life for black and white people alike. He acknowledges the shortcomings of a separate-but-equal ideology yet asserts that the "negro" should "sit beneath his own vine and fig tree."[16]

Robert Brinkmeyer has shown that many reviewers associated the Agrarians' agenda with feudalism and fascism, charges that led to the group's disintegration, and dramatically changed southern poetry's direction.[17] After publishing another controversial collection of essays, *Who Owns America? A New Declaration of Independence* (1936), Ransom withdrew from political commentary and devoted himself to literary criticism that examined what he called the "ontological" relationship between form and content in poetry. In his essay "Art and the Human Economy" (1945) he declared that Agrarianism had been a mistake, and the few poems he wrote later in his career used politically neutral contexts and echoed themes he'd emphasized in the twenties. "Painted Head" (1945) describes the portrait of a relatively young man and stresses the split between mind and body, and between the material and the aesthetic. In contrast, Tate continued to use modernist verse techniques and to engage social matters. His best-known poem of the period, "Seasons of the Soul" (1944), invokes World War II and employs literary and religious allusions to link humans' penchant for violence to what Eliot called a "dissociation of sensibility," the rupture between mind and spirit.

Ransom's return to aesthetics proved influential, particularly as university creative writing programs became widespread, and Tate's reputation waned as a younger generation shunned modernist techniques. However, Warren changed in a radical manner. Unlike Ransom and Tate, whose poetics and themes remained consistent from the twenties to the end of their careers, Warren became dissatisfied with his previous creative practices and questioned his political convictions. Late in the summer of 1939, Warren and his wife departed for Italy, despite warnings of impending war. During his stay abroad he worked on a verse play – *Proud Flesh* – that became the basis for *All the King's Men* (1946), a novel set in the American South that examines the dynamics of demagoguery. "Terror," the final poem of *Eleven Poems on the Same Theme* (1942), moves from iambic pentameter to free verse and employs irregular rhymes, techniques designed to reflect humans' unpredictability. The poem's distraught narrator listens "by radio" to how the "brute crowd roars or the blunt bootheels resound / In the Piazza or Wilhelmplatz" (*CPRPW*, pp. 77–78).

Selected Poems, 1923–1943 (1944) contained new works – "The Ballad of Billie Potts" and the sequence "Mexico Is a Foreign Country: Five Studies in Naturalism" – that continue to experiment with verse forms. "The Ballad of Billie Potts," which Warren called an attempt to "make a tie between modernism and balladry and make them both stack up to a kind of view of American history *and* a kind of interplay of styles," used looser, more conversational verse laced with looping rhyme schemes, dialogue, and a strong narrative.[18] The poem's narrative sections contain playful, singsong rhythms – "Little Billie heard hoofs on the soft grass, / But he squatted and let the rider pass" – that differ from the prophetic tone he'd adopted from Eliot, but the parenthetical philosophic passages are laden with Eliot-like diction: "And the waitress says, 'Will that be all, sir, will that be all?' / And will not stop. / And the valet says, 'will that be all, sir, will that be all?'" (*CPRPW*, pp. 81–92). Warren remained prolific – publishing novels, criticism, and the verse play *Brother to Dragons* (1953) – but "The Ballad of Billie Potts" was the last new poem he would finish for more than a decade. In a 1957 interview with Ralph Ellison, Warren expressed the frustration he'd felt in the forties and early fifties, observing that he "quit writing poems for several years; that is, I'd start them, get a lot down, then feel that I wasn't connecting somehow ... they felt false."[19]

Warren's use of the word "false" reflected his belief that both modernist and formalist literary practices had come to seem contrived, and like many American poets at midcentury, he sought a fresh style. During his hiatus from poetry, he watched his friend and former student Randall Jarrell (1914–1965) become the first southern poet – and one of the first American poets – to make the transition toward conversational, neo-Romantic verse that explored the nature of identity. Jarrell's verse would have a wide influence on southern poets, and the development of his career suggests changes that took place in southern poetry during the middle of the twentieth century. Jarrell, Warren, and a new generation of southern poets participated in American poetry's shift toward more personal, conversational verse, but they did not take part in the major contemporary movements – Beat, confessional, Black Mountain, Deep Image, and New York School – that arose after World War II. Instead, southern poetry divided along two lines: one associated with Ransom's emphasis on aesthetics, and another that examined the self within competing social and philosophical contexts.

Jarrell influenced the latter trend, largely due to his differences from his mentors. Jarrell studied with Warren, Ransom, and Davidson at Vanderbilt in the thirties and was particularly close to Tate, who paved the way for the publication of his first book, *Blood for a Stranger* (1942); but Jarrell, who was born in his parents' native Tennessee and spent his youth moving back and forth between Nashville and California, did not see himself as a southern poet, and his Marxist political sympathies were in sharp contrast to the Agrarians' conservatism. In the early forties, Jarrell pulled away from Tate, and in his essay "The End of the Line" (1942), he declared that the modernism of Eliot, Tate, and others was "dead."[20]

Jarrell's military experiences during World War II contributed to changes in his verse. Stephen Burt asserts that "Jarrell derived his concerns about postwar conformity from his experiences of the Second World War," prompting him to explore themes of loneliness and loss by creating highly individualized characters.[21] In *Little Friend, Little Friend* (1945) and *Losses* (1948), Jarrell, who served as an aerial navigation instructor in Arizona, often focused on Air Force personnel. In *The Seven-League Crutches* (1951) Jarrell widened his explorations of characters' psychology, an approach that would impact southern poets – including James Dickey and Eleanor Ross Taylor – for decades to come.

In the fifties Warren followed Jarrell's example and turned toward stylistically looser poetry that examines the nature of the self. Warren, who had published more than twenty of Jarrell's poems in the *Southern Review*, later recalled that Jarrell would visit him and "brutally criticize my poems. I would listen carefully. He was so often right."[22] After reading Warren's *Selected Poems* of 1944, Jarrell made an astute observation that indicates his dissatisfaction with Warren's verse. In a letter to a friend he contended that Warren's poetry tended to be too abstract, "the world and everything in it ... is so purely Original Sin, Horror, loathing, morbidness, final evil ... whereas the practice he lives by says the exact opposite."[23]

Changes in Warren's personal life, particularly his divorce from Cinina Brescia in 1951 and marriage to author Eleanor Clark in 1952, would lead him to the more concrete, personal qualities Jarrell felt his verse lacked. In 1954 Warren resumed publishing lyric poetry, resulting in *Promises* (1957), a book that reflects his later verse's tendency to address the personal within larger cultural or philosophical contexts. Some poems are composed in irregular meters, and others are experiments with irregular rhyming free verse, with diction that is variously idiomatic and formal. The book displays Warren's practice of organizing many of his later collections as carefully plotted, interrelated series of poems. *Promises* opens with "To a Little Girl, One Year Old, in a Ruined Fortress." The five-poem sequence is dedicated to Warren and Clark's daughter Rosanna and is set at La Rocca, a decaying fortress the Warrens frequented on an Italian peninsula. Warren largely abandons modernist distance, but a naturalistic outlook still permeates the verse. For instance, part III concludes with a reference to Rosanna – "I think of your goldness, of joy" – but the mood is tempered by a deterministic perspective: "how empires grind, stars are hurled. / I smile stiff, saying *ciao*, saying *ciao*, and think: this is the world" (*CPRPW*, p. 104).

In the mid-1960s Warren's interest in American pragmatism, particularly the thought of William James and Sidney Hook, led him away from a relatively strict naturalistic perspective, and a vigorous dialectic between determinism and idealism began to drive his verse. Change and transformation – characteristics that marked his career – became important themes in his poetry and were informed by pragmatism's emphasis on ideas' practical consequences.

Where the naturalistic perspective that shaped his early verse often resulted in expressions of Weltschmerz, in his later poetry Warren became a self-described "yearner" who seeks insight into existential dilemmas, rejecting any single answer as insufficient. The result was an outburst of poetic creativity. Harold Bloom has claimed that, from 1966 to 1986, "between ages sixty-one and eighty-one," Warren enjoyed a "poetic renaissance fully comparable to the great final phases of Thomas Hardy, William Butler Yeats, and Wallace Stevens" (*CPRPW*, p. xxiii).

The new poems in *Selected Poems: New and Old, 1923–1966* display an increasingly accessible style, and the collection contains several sequences central to Warren's canon. "Homage to Emerson, on Night Flight to New York" is a guarded tribute that suggests how Warren distinguished between the dangers of idealism as a guiding philosophical concept and its value as a way of confronting the mysteries of existence. John Burt points out that Warren had disparaged Emerson's thought since the 1920s, viewing it as an American style of Romanticism that unwittingly led to destructive national impulses, including the concept of manifest destiny.[24] In "Homage to Emerson" the narrator is in an airplane, and "Emerson – / The essays, on my lap, lie." The metaphorical use of "lie" alludes to Emerson's confidence in human perfectibility. The narrator asserts that at "38,000 feet Emerson / Is dead right" – a phrase that acknowledges Romantic idealism's danger and appeal – and warns that "at 38,000 feet you had better remember something specific, if / You yourself want to be something specific." Emerson is pictured as someone who had naïvely "forgiven God everything," but memories of a wart on the narrator's finger and of a drunk, disabled man serve as reminders that life isn't an idealistic "allegory." However, the poem ends by contemplating humans' responses to natural beauty and people's feelings for one another. The narrator declares "there must be / A way by which the process of living can become Truth" (*CPRPW*, pp. 194–97).

The relationship between determinism, idealism, and pragmatism also informs Warren's concept of individual autonomy, an issue he regarded as central to American democracy. *Audubon: A Vision* (1969) is widely considered his most important poem and ranks with *All the King's Men* as his greatest literary achievement. The poem explores the conflict between an individual's quest for self-fulfillment and deterministic circumstances. Composed in diction that wends between the philosophical and the vernacular, the poem mixes narrative and lyric modes over some 440 lines, arranged in 27 sections.

Audubon begins by examining a specific character's identity but moves toward greater amplification. The poem opens by announcing that, contrary to rumor, Audubon was not the "lost dauphin," the offspring of Louis XVI and Marie Antoinette; instead he was "only / Himself, Jean Jacques, and his passion." Vivid descriptions of the natural world establish how nature serves as a major source of Audubon's identity. In the second stanza, Audubon watches a heron glide over the horizon at dawn, "long neck outthrust, wings crooked to scull air, moved / In a slow calligraphy, crank, flat and black against / The color of God's blood spilt." Warren's use of spondees to create resistance and to compel the reader to absorb the imagery suggests how he alters his rhythms to pace the narrative. In a typical turn, Warren ends the first section with a line that extends the poem's meaning. The question "and what is your passion?" enlarges the context to include the reader (*CPRPW*, pp. 253–67).

In contrast to the two lyrics that set up the poem's major themes, part II, "The Dream He Never Knew the End Of," presents a dramatic, suspenseful narrative. Audubon finds himself in a shoddy cabin, the domain of an ugly, witchlike woman and her two sons. The woman takes Audubon's gold watch, hangs it around her neck, and fondles it, making Audubon's "gut" twist "cold. He cannot bear what he sees. / Her body sways like a willow in spring wind. Like a girl." The ensuing sections make it clear that Audubon's reaction does not result from the woman's unattractive physical appearance. That night, pretending to sleep, Audubon listens to the woman and her sons whisper to one another as they drink and ominously sharpen a knife. Audubon – "gun by his side, primed and cocked" – thinks "Now," knowing "What he must do, do soon," but he is overcome by "lassitude," leading him to wonder "what guilt unmans him," a scene that underscores how Audubon's desire to act and define himself butts up against something within his nature. At that moment, three men break into the cabin and administer frontier justice, hanging the woman and her sons the next day. Unlike the sons, who pray and "blubber," the woman remains true to her identity "And is what she is." In contrast to the scene in which Audubon is repulsed by the woman playing with his watch, her actions during the hanging attract him to her. Unlike Audubon, who can't act because of a gap between his desires and his nature, resulting in an amorphous sense of self, the woman's identity achieves a kind of permanence. Audubon "suddenly sees," she is "beautiful as stone, and / So becomes aware that he is in the manly state" (*CPRPW*, pp. 253–67).

Warren's declaration in the poem's final section that the "name of the story will be Time / But you must not pronounce its name" reflects his long-held belief that "Time" provides the fundamental framework for comprehending the human condition, and that narrative supplies the scaffolding for exploring an individual's plight within that context. Warren regarded poetry and other literary forms as a "laboratory for living." In his essays "Literature as Symptom" (1936), "Pure and Impure Poetry" (1943), "Democracy and Poetry" (1975), and other works, he advocated art that dramatized the concrete and the paradoxical as a means of emphasizing individual autonomy and resisting ideology. Time and circumstance – "this century, and moment, of mania" – help determine one's story and help shape the tensions between Audubon's desires, nature, and actions, resulting in a mixture of free will, fortune, and destiny.

Warren's next book of verse, *Or Else: Poem/Poems 1968–1974* (1974), is a meticulously crafted long poem composed of individual poems interrupted by a series of interjections. The book contains some of Warren's strongest verse, including "The Nature of a Mirror," the surrealistic "I Am Dreaming of a White Christmas: The Natural History of a Vision," and "Homage to Theodore Dreiser." "Rattlesnake Country," one of Warren's most compelling examinations of the dynamic between Romantic and naturalistic impulses, ends with a meditation on time, memory, and the self, the "compulsion to try to convert what now is *was* / Back into what was *is*" (*CPRPW*, pp. 294–97).

In the 1960s and 1970s the issue of race continued to tug at Warren and other southern poets, particularly Tate, who was embarrassed by the publication of a letter he wrote to editor Lincoln Kirstein in 1933. In *The Hound and the Horn: The History of a Literary Quarterly* (1966), Leonard Greenbaum quoted Tate's claim that the "negro race is an inferior race.... A white woman pregnant with a negro child becomes a counter symbol, one of evil and pollution."[25] Tate, who had converted to Roman Catholicism in the 1950s and had gradually begun to reverse his attitudes on race (his correspondence reveals a mixture of guilt and defensiveness), had surprised the literary community by writing an introduction to Melvin Tolson's *Libretto for the Republic of Liberia* (1953) and by giving a speech announcing his support for Martin Luther King, Jr., in 1959. One of his finest late poems, "The Swimmers" (1960), was inspired by a childhood memory of seeing the corpse of a lynched black man. The poem describes his reaction at encountering evil for the first time and concludes by declaring the community's complicity: "This private thing was owned by all the town, / Though never claimed by us within my hearing."[26] Tate casts the poem in Dante's terza rima, and shuns his often idiosyncratic use of myth and metaphor in favor of a straightforward, quickly paced narrative. But his racist past hovered over him, further eroding his already diminished reputation.

Warren drew criticism in 1972 when Sterling Brown, a distinguished African American poet and critic, chastised him in print for his naturalistic depiction of a black character in "Pondy Woods," a poem published in the 1920s. Warren was also willing to chastise himself. Nearly two decades after *Promises*, Warren addressed the changes he underwent during that period in one of his most important works, "Old Nigger on One-Mule Car Encountered Late at Night When Driving Home from Party in the Back Country." The poem was first published in the *New Yorker* and later collected in *Selected Poems: 1923–1976* (1977) in a section titled "Can I See Arcturus from Where I Stand? Poems 1975." The section's title comes from the poem's last line. At the end of the poem, the narrator wonders if he can see Arcturus, the brightest star in the constellation Bootes. The question comes from the point of view of a person confronting the extent to which the panorama of time has resulted in self-knowledge, and it links the changes in Warren's poetry to changes in his racial assumptions.

One of Warren's most celebrated later books, *Now and Then: Poems 1976–1978* (1978), is divided into two sections, "Nostalgic" and "Speculative," and most of the poems explore relationships between past and present. The verse is conversational and rhymed and unrhymed, without metrical regularity. "American Portrait: Old Style" describes an encounter with Warren's childhood friend Kent Greenfield, a crack rifleman and Major League pitcher. Like much of Warren's later poetry, the collection shows a keen awareness – as he states in "Identity and Argument for Prayer" – "that old *I* is not I anymore," a dynamic that led to a career of perpetual change, growth, and accomplishment (*CPRPW*, pp. 372–73).

James Dickey's and Donald Justice's careers demonstrate how southern poetry divided along two distinct lines for much of the later twentieth century. Previous southern poets influenced both writers, but in starkly different ways. Dickey (1923–1997) was born into a well-to-do Atlanta family and served in the U.S. Air Corps during World War II, an event that profoundly shaped his outlook. After the war he enrolled at Vanderbilt. Davidson was the only remaining faculty member who had been associated with the *Fugitive*, but Dickey soon realized that Jarrell, a fellow veteran, was the southern poet who "appealed to me most," and he turned away from "language" that was "too busy" and filled with "rhetorical effects" and concentrated on creating accessible narratives.[27]

Dickey continued Warren's and Jarrell's tendency to probe the paradoxical nature of identity. His poems present disparate points of view – including those of soldiers, women, suburbanites, laborers, criminals, children, religious fanatics, and animals – to investigate how attempts to relate the self to elemental situations can serve as a vital, but potentially destructive, catalyst for endowing life with meaning. His first three books, *Into the Stone* (1960), *Drowning with Others* (1962), and *Helmets* (1964), feature heavily cadenced poems that use dactyls, anapests, and trochees to propel the action. "The Performance" and

"Between Two Prisoners" are based on the executions of Dickey's fellow soldiers Donald Armstrong and Jim Lalley, who were captured by the Japanese. As in most of Dickey's verse, the focus is on individual revelation. The common bonds of war and death unite the characters, a situation the narrator of "Between Two Prisoners" asserts is not desirable – "I would not wish to sit / In my shape bound together with wire" – but that results in knowledge otherwise unattainable.[28] Similarly, "The Heaven of Animals," a near-perfect lyric, presents an idealized cycle of predators and prey fulfilling their destinies. "Cherrylog Road" describes two young lovers in a junkyard, where their lovemaking energizes them and restores life to the symbolic wasteland.

In *Buckdancer's Choice* (1965) Dickey uses longer lines and experiments with "split lines" of sonic and imagistic clusters, for example, in "The Firebombing," "The Shark's Parlor," "The Fiend," and "Slave Quarters." In these poems Dickey creates a poetic stream of consciousness to regain ground he felt poetry had ceded to prose. His masterful and controversial "The Firebombing" presents a former American pilot confronting his "guilt at the inability to feel guilt" at having bombed Japanese civilians during World War II. In order to induce the guilt he believes he should feel, the narrator recalls participating in an "anti-morale" mission but can only remember being "Deep in aesthetic contemplation, / Seeing the ponds catch fire / And cast it through ring after ring of land," a sensation he identifies as "this detachment / The honored aesthetic evil, / The greatest sense of power in one's life" (*WM*, pp. 193–200). He can only confront the destruction he committed by imagining his American suburb firebombed: he can't conceive of anything that isn't as "American as I am, and proud of it," a conclusion that points to the paradox of committing officially sanctioned atrocities in a war worth fighting. *Buckdancer's Choice* won the National Book Award, but trouble arose when Dickey's old friend and editor, Robert Bly, denounced Dickey's alleged support of the Vietnam War. In "The Collapse of James Dickey," Bly used "The Firebombing" as evidence and interpreted the poem as if it concerned Vietnam instead of World War II. Dickey was widely identified as a prowar poet, despite his support for and friendship with Eugene McCarthy, an antiwar presidential candidate. Dickey made matters worse by striking macho poses, sometimes playing the southern redneck, and inventing tall tales, including an oft-repeated story in which he parachuted from a plane and was rescued by a submarine.

Dickey's *Poems 1957–1967* included "May Day Sermon to the Women of Gilmer County, Georgia, by a Woman Preacher Leaving the Baptist Church" and "The Sheep Child," forays into what he called "country surrealism." "Falling," perhaps his best-known poem, is based on a *New York Times* account describing the death of a twenty-nine-year-old stewardess who plunged to her death when an airplane's emergency door opened mid-flight. Dickey, who was much influenced by French existentialism, used the circumstance as an analogy for an individual's descent through life, in which every moment brings one closer to death. During her fall the stewardess engages in what Dickey called "creative lying," assuming various roles, and clinging to the possibility of survival. Her final words, "AH, GOD," are deliberately ambiguous, suggesting a plea for immortality and the uncertainty of life after death.

The 1980s and 1990s were decades of literary experimentation for Dickey, but unlike Justice, whose formal gymnastics and apolitical themes met critics' expectations of him, Dickey provoked controversy. *Puella* (1982), a series of sonically complex verses written from the perspective of a young girl coming into womanhood, confused critics who had known him as a singularly masculine writer. In the early 1990s he experienced a creative resurgence, publishing a fine book of verse, *The Eagle's Mile* (1990), and *The Whole Motion: Poems 1945–1992* (1992). "Daughter," one of his best later poems, celebrates the birth of a child from his second marriage and presents his conception of the "real God." The narrator holds his newborn and tells her "you are part / Of the flowing stone: understand: you are part of the wave, / Of the glacier's irrevocable / Millennial inch" (*WM*, pp. 446–48). Similarly, "The Eagle's Mile" envisions Supreme Court justice and outdoorsman William O. Douglas soaring like a bird over Appalachia, his "death drawing life / From growth / from flow, as in the gill-cleansing turn / Of the creek," a fantasy that reflects Dickey's stress on the essential union between fundamental natural forces and the imagination (*WM*, pp. 444–46).

Justice's sense of lyric restraint and tendency to foreground technique – qualities he inherited from Ransom – were in sharp contrast to Dickey's dramatic narratives and willingness to engage controversial topics. Justice, whose parents were raised on small Alabama farms, was born in Miami, Florida, and never ventured outside the South until age eighteen. As an undergraduate at the University of Miami, he studied with composer Carl Ruggles, whose love of music influenced Justice's verse, and befriended poet George Marion O'Donnell, who introduced him to Ransom's poetry. In 1947 he took an M.A. at the University of North Carolina with a thesis titled "The Fugitive-Agrarian 'Myth'" and then briefly enrolled at Stanford University, where he audited Yvor Winters's class and "learned a good deal about the meters."[29] At age twenty-six he entered the University of Iowa and honed his formal practice under the direction of Robert Lowell, who had been mentored by Ransom, Tate, and Warren, and John Berryman, who had studied with Tate.

Justice's manipulations of the sestina in his first book, *The Summer Anniversaries* (1960), suggest how his verse's self-conscious, meditative qualities invite the reader to linger over his poems' designs. In "The Metamorphosis" the repetends consist of half rhymes rather than repeated words; in "Here in Katmandu" shortened lines of varying length replace iambic pentameter; and "Sestina on Six Words from Weldon Kees" is based on the end words "others / voyage / silence / away / burden / harm."[30] Justice's second book, *Night Light* (1967), contains prose poems and experiments with free verse, but whereas Dickey used split lines to dramatize his themes, Justice remained focused on technique. In "Early Poems" he announces his dissatisfaction with his previous work, declaring "How fashionably sad those early poems are! / ... The rhymes, the meters, how they paralyze!" (*DJC*, p. 87). "Memos from the Desk of X" and "For a Freshman Reader" address stylistics from a professional writer's perspective. In "The Grandfathers" and "Elsewheres," Justice depicts the South in terms of relatives and domestic scenes – a vivid contrast to Dickey's "Slave Quarters," which presents a contemporary white southerner's vision of a man lusting after his female slave and confronting a son he doesn't acknowledge but owns. Justice's *ars poetica*, "The Thin Man," is a subtly sculpted lyric that consists of two three-line stanzas with five syllables per line. In the first stanza Justice observes, "I indulge myself / In rich refusals. / Nothing suffices" (*DJC*, p. 88). The word "indulge" indicates his poetry's playful characteristics, and the phrase "rich refusals" suggests his preference for spare, evocative verse that spurs the imagination through understatement. Similarly, the final stanza – "I hone myself to / This edge. Asleep, I / Am a horizon" – reflects his desire to imply more by saying less. Two of Justice's finest poems are cautious meditations on bourgeois conformity. "Men at Forty" likens the onset of middle age to the unsteady sensation of standing on a ship's deck. "Bus Stop" consists of six stanzas of syllabic verse that move between haunting, Edward Hopper–like imagery – "Lights are burning / In quiet rooms" – and suggestive interpretation of the images – "Where lives go on / Resembling ours" (*DJC*, p. 100).

The title of *Departures* (1973) indicates its differences from Justice's previous poetry, as well as his tendency to use others' work as inspiration. "ABC," a poem about poetry – "A syllable with skin, / Tough and saurian, / Alive in the sewer's mouth" – recalls Baudelaire (*DJC*, p. 123). Three poems – "On the Night of Departure by Bus," "White Notes," and "Cool Dark Ode" – are loosely modeled on poems by Rafael Alberti. "Variations on a Text by Vallejo" plays off the line "me moriré en París con aguacero" and presents a whimsical reverie cast in anapests of the day "I will die in Miami in the sun" (*DJC*, p. 158).

A night of poker with the composer and writer John Cage led Justice to experiment with "chance" poems, in which he "made up three large decks of 'vocabulary' cards – one deck each for nouns, verbs, and adjectives – and a smaller fourth deck of 'syntax' cards" and shuffled the cards to create poems.[31]

Selected Poems (1979) won the Pulitzer Prize, helping bring Justice the acclaim that largely had been reserved for his teaching and his students' success. New offerings included "Memories of the Depression," a suite of lyrics concerning places his family lived. His most highly regarded book, *The Sunset Maker* (1987), consists of interrelated poems, stories, and memoirs, including the sonnet sequence "My South." But despite his use of personal materials, Justice never embraced the confessional mode. His poems refrain from including intimate details and, like Ransom's, maintain a well-mannered distance. A series of largely tongue-in-cheek poems is presented under the heading "Tremayne," a character who is often viewed as a surrogate for Justice. In contrast to the rough-and-tumble image Dickey projected, Justice describes his alter ego as a quiet, slightly obtuse poet who "as usual, misquotes, / Recalling adolescence and old trees / In whose shade once more he memorized that verse / And something about 'late flowers for the bees'" (*DJC*, pp. 224–26).

The new poems in *New and Selected Poems* (1995) and *Collected Poems* (2004) continued to involve music, painting, and the South of his youth, and to highlight formal dexterity. "The Miami of Other Days" describes a time when the "city was not yet itself" but still a relatively small town where people danced on the beach to the "new white jazz / of a Victrola on its towel in the sand" and "crackers down from Georgia (my own people) / Foregathered on the old post office steps" (*DJC*, pp. 247–48). *Collected Poems*, published two weeks before Justice passed away, closes with "There is a gold light in certain old paintings." The poem invokes Orpheus, a figure Justice sometimes used to address the poet's craft. Justice's fondness for nostalgic reminiscence is suggested as Orpheus hesitates "beside the black river / With so much to look forward to he looked back . . . / At least he had seen once more the beloved back" (*DJC*, p. 278). As a poet and teacher, Justice bequeathed to southern poetry – and American letters – an acute awareness of stylistics and of spare, chiseled verse's resonance. His student Ellen Bryant Voigt remarks, "Any time I put an adjective in a poem . . . I hear Don Justice asking why it's there."[32]

The last three decades of the century produced what Charles Wright called a "flowering" of southern poetry. In 1998 Wright, a lyric poet and student of Justice's, asserted that from "Dickey / Warren to Smith / Bottoms . . . Almost everyone who's thought of as a southern poet is a narrative poet" (*SI*, p. 49). Narrative's predominance can largely be attributed to the power of Warren's and Dickey's verse, which inspired a new generation, including Dave Smith, David Bottoms, Fred Chappell, Andrew Hudgins, Betty Adcock, T. R. Hummer, Rodney Jones, and Kate Daniels. Like Warren's and Dickey's poetry, Smith's verse examines the self's relationship to a range of social circumstances. Smith (b. 1942) sees himself as a "regionalist" in "my deepest sense of self" and asserts that he "learned to write a drama" from Dickey, adding, "Dickey's use of folk narratives to ennoble and elevate lower-class, blue collar disempowered people was particularly important to me" (*SI*, pp. 28, 34). Many of the poems in Smith's early books, collected in *Floating on Solitude: Three Volumes of Poetry* (1996), are set in his native coastal Virginia and are plotted in the style of Dickey's longer poems. He uses a technique he calls "orchestration" (the "exfoliation of imagistic constructs which reinforce each other in such a way that the reader is led to perception by repeating signals") to create complex narratives with multiple, often contradictory, layers of meaning (*SI*, p. 23). Helen Vendler has claimed that "Smith's narrative poems ... require quotation in full to display their (often stunning) cumulative effect."[33] "Night Fishing for Blues" concerns racial tensions. In the poem, a contemporary white southerner fishing near a family of black southerners at Fortress Monroe, a Civil War battle site, is forced to confront paradoxical feelings associated with his southern heritage. As in many of his poems, Smith's muscular, polyphonic Anglo-Saxon rhythms – "the big-jawed Blue-fish, ravenous, sleek muscle slamming / at rock, at pier legs, drives into Chesapeake shallows" – create resistance, forcing the reader to slow down and ponder obstinate emotional quandaries.[34] Another significant early poem, "Cumberland Station," describes a man's return to an economically depressed town for his grandfather's funeral. The narrator's conflicted sense of guilt leads him to confront painful memories without resolution.

In the 1980s, Smith claims, he "switched allegiances" from Dickey to Warren, moving away from an emphasis on action and toward reflective narratives (*SI*, p. 33). *The Round House Voices* (1985) spans seven previous collections and includes twenty-two new poems. In the title poem an adult narrator addresses his dead uncle and remembers how as a boy he'd sneak into a railroad yard and play baseball with him. Various voices – of the narrator at different stages of life, the uncle, and a guard – inhabit the poem and mix to form an intricate mediation on death, social class, and the artist's urge to combat loss. "The Tire Hangs in the Yard," a poem dedicated to Warren, involves an adult narrator's visiting a place that represents the "end / of the childhood road."[35] The poem divides into a series of five interrelated memories concerning time and identity. *The Wick of Memory: New and Selected Poems* (2000) gathers work from seventeen previous collections, including a series of haunting thirteen-line near sonnets from *Fate's Kite* (1996).

Ransom's and Justice's influence can be seen in Wright, Miller Williams, and Voigt's lyric practices. Wright (b. 1935), of Pickwick Dam, Tennessee, studied under Justice at the University of Iowa and was influenced by his emphasis on spare, imagistic language. But Wright takes his teacher's – and Ransom's – tendency to foreground the aesthetic over the social in another direction. While they worked with a variety of forms, Wright composes in unaccentual syllabics and favors odd-numbered syllable counts in order to avoid traditional meters. Thematically, he fashions an aesthetic of perception reminiscent of Wallace Stevens. An awareness of the subject/object split consistently informs his verse and creates a fluid dynamic between his narrator's observations and the world outside the self. In poem after poem, Wright explores his totem subject, the relationship between "landscape, language and the idea of God."[36] Relatively early in his career Wright realized the interconnectedness of his poems and began to assemble what critics often call a "trilogy of trilogies."

Italy and the poetry of Dino Campana and Eugenio Montale, whose works Wright translated, were important influences on Wright. His first trilogy, *Country Music* (1982), was conceived as a "small time *inferno, purgatorio,* and *paradiso*" (*SI*, p. 56). But unlike the *Divine Comedy*, *Country Music* doesn't contain a readily identifiable narrative. Instead, Wright drew on Gerard Manley Hopkins's concept of "inscape" and developed a technique he calls the "under-narrative ... the story line that's underneath the imagistic line on the top. ... The story line is what the poem is about, the journey you are reminded of each time you come back out to the landscape" (*SI*, p. 49). "Clear Night" begins with the narrator observing the "thumb-top of a moon" against "a back-lit sky" and moves from description to prayerlike yearning: "I want to be bruised by God. / I want to be strung up in a strong light and singled out."[37] "Snow" reflects Wright's desire to meld "an exterior world and an interior world" in order to create "an *It* which is a combination of the two": "If we, as we are, are dust, and dust, as it will, rises, / Then we will rise and recongregate / In the wind, in the cloud, and be their issue."[38]

In his next trilogy, *The World of the Ten Thousand Things* (1990), Wright lengthens his lines and uses the "dropped line" as means of keeping the verse "line from breaking under its own weight" while maintaining the "integrity of the single line musically."[39] Wright's interest in art and oriental thought are more pronounced than in his first trilogy, and his explorations of the relationship between perception, landscape, and language extend as the book progresses. The collection's penultimate section, *Zone Journals*, is a freewheeling long poem filled with metaphysical speculations that are constantly asserted, undercut, and modified. His spiritual quest often settles into a quasi-Buddhist position, the "Immeasurable emptiness of all things."[40]

Wright's move to the University of Virginia in 1983 had a substantial effect on his verse. His return to the South led him to conceive of his final trilogy, *Negative Blue* (2000), as an "Appalachian Book of the Dead" that explores the possibility of "trying to bring what's not there into terms of what is visible in the visible world" (*SI*, p. 57). The book begins with a typical situation. The narrator sits in his backyard and attempts "To answer the simple arithmetic of my life" by contemplating his surroundings.[41] He observes that "This object and that object / Never contained the landscape / Nor all of its implications." In the collection's final poem, "Sky Diving," Wright notes,

> I've talked about one thing for thirty years,
> > And said it time and again,
> Wind like big sticks in the trees –
> I mean the still, small point at the point where all things meet;
> I mean the form that moves the sun and the other stars.[42]

Characteristically, Wright presents an image – "Wind like big sticks in the trees" – that melds into a search for the interrelatedness of all things. But instead of discovering an answer, he ends the trilogy by inviting the reader to let the starlit sky "swallow us," and to join him and "open our mouths" to the heavens, a summons that suggests the symbiotic nature of the relationship between the perceived and the perceiver, the world and the imagination. The final line – "I mean the form that moves the sun and the other stars" – echoes the last line of the *Divine Comedy* – "l'amor che move il sole e le altre stele" – and reaffirms the link between Wright's trilogy and Dante's. Wright's description of his subsequent books as a "long goodbye" to his trilogy of trilogies indicates his subject matter's consistency.[43] In a poem from *Scar Tissue* (2006), "The Minor Art of Self Defense," he asserts, "Landscape was never a subject matter, it was a technique / ... Language was always the subject matter, the idea of God / The ghost that over my little world / Hovered."[44]

The late twentieth and early twenty-first century signaled a shift in southern poetry, largely due to increased opportunities within the academy for women and people of color. Female and African American poets were influenced by previous southern poets but brought different perspectives to their materials. The achievement of southern women – including Voigt, Adcock, Daniels, Sonia Sanchez, C. D. Wright, Brenda Marie Osbey, Claudia Emerson, and Natasha Trethewey – in the late twentieth and early twenty-first centuries helped reawaken interest in Eleanor Ross Taylor (1920–2011). Taylor, born in rural North Carolina, studied at the University of North Carolina–Greensboro with Tate and his first wife, novelist Caroline Gordon, who helped her get a scholarship to Vanderbilt, where she took courses from Davidson. Jarrell helped edit and secure a publisher for her first book, *A Wilderness of Ladies* (1960), but Taylor's poetry attracted little attention until the century drew to a close and other southern women poets affirmed her importance. Betty Adcock calls Taylor the mother of subsequent southern female poets, and Ellen Bryant Voigt claims that it's "no surprise to find so many pioneers" in her verse "since she herself is one."[45]

Like Jarrell, Taylor often writes monologues and uses female personae. But unlike Jarrell, who rarely wrote about the South, or other previous southern poets, Taylor emphasizes rural, southern white women. She describes her materials as "back-woods Southern characters, the poverty of the rural South during the Depression years, handed down family stories, and the echoes of hymns and Scripture from Southern country churches."[46] Taylor was also influenced by Emily Dickinson's elliptical lyrics and Edna St. Vincent Millay's emphasis on "current, everyday life."[47] In *A Wilderness of Ladies*, "Sister" starts in medias res and uses colloquialisms – "And we two alone here in this peace pan / Are ever strolling uphill to the old-house-place" – to express a country woman's regret at the life she feels she missed.[48] "Woman as Artist" employs taut, Dickinson-like lines – "I'm mother. / I hunt alone." – and compares the giving and caring of life to the creative process.[49]

Taylor's next book, the Vietnam-era collection *Welcome Eumenides* (1972), displays her preference for allusive, modernist techniques. The book's title comes from an entry in Florence Nightingale's diary, and several poems stress the ravages of war. The ambitious title poem draws from Nightingale's biography and vividly dramatizes her war-torn consciousness in imagistic language akin to Hilda Doolittle's. "After Twenty Years" presents the thoughts of a woman whose son was killed during World War II and whose husband subsequently committed suicide. Taylor notes that "A Few Days in the South in February (A Hospitality for S. K. Wightman, 1865)" is modeled on Wightman's "account of his pilgrimage to North Carolina reprinted from family papers in *American Heritage* February 1963," which details a perilous journey he undertook to retrieve his dead son's body. Richard Howard has called it the "best poem since Whitman about the war between the states."[50] Taylor's later poetry, collected in *Days Going/Days Coming Back* (1991) and *Captive Voices: New and Selected Poems, 1960–2008* (2009), addresses her upbringing on a farm that lacked plumbing or electricity but was filled with religion and an emphasis on education.

Yusef Komunyakaa (b. 1947) provides another example of how southern poets rearranged their relationships to literary and social trends. Komunyakaa studied at the University of California–Riverside with Wright and was "drawn to" his "patterns of images" (*SI*, p. 141). Warren and Dickey also impacted his verse. *Promises* furnished "a sense of place" that seemed "somewhat more inclusive than John Crowe Ransom and much of Allen Tate" (*SI*, p. 136). Komunyakaa studied Dickey's "attention to detail ... the precise naming of things. I knew those names, the nuances of language" (*SI*, p. 138). But he notes that as an African American he had a different relationship to the South than those poets. Komunyakaa, born James William Brown, Jr. (he later took his great-grandparents' surname), was born and raised in Bogalusa, Louisiana, a city once infested by the Ku Klux Klan. In "Chair Gallows," from *Dedications and Other Darkhorses* (1977), the narrator reads of a lynching and declares, "I know war criminals / live longer than men lost between railroad tracks / & crossroad blues, with twelve strings / two days out of hock."[51] "How I See Things," from *I Apologize for the Eyes in My Head* (1979), involves violence perpetrated on black people during the civil rights era. A contemporary narrator recalls "Men run twelve miles into wet cypress / swinging bellropes" and asks "Have we earned the right / to forget, forgive / ropes for holding / to moonstruck branches?" (*NV*, p. 89). *Magic City* (1992), perhaps his strongest book, recounts his youth in racially charged Louisiana and continues to explore slavery's devastating legacy.

Komunyakaa's use of blues and jazz rhythms was influenced by Langston Hughes and Sterling Brown, poets associated with the Harlem Renaissance but with ties to the South, and by Bob Kaufman of New Orleans, associated with the Beats and the San Francisco Renaissance. In contrast to Warren and Dickey's emphasis on broad philosophical contexts and narrative dramatics, Komunyakaa writes "tonal narratives" in which a series of compressed images unfold into a "sped-up meditation." He draws on musical patterns to inject multiple perspectives into his verse and create visceral relationships between images. He shuns the didactic and strives for poems that "one person may see ... as blasphemous, and another ... as sacred or a song of praise" (*SI*, p. 133). His tonal narratives often generate complexity by presenting a central story with other stories within it. "Blues Chant Voodoo Revival," collected in *Neon Vernacular: New and Selected Poems* (1993), reflects blues songs' tendency to "talk around a subject or situation" involving emotional pain (*SI*, p. 133). The poem's terse lines "chant ... my story," "your story," "this story," and "our story" through images of items – "feathers from a crow," "honey locust leaves," "the speaking skull," "the seventh son's mojo hand" – used in vodun rituals (*NV*, pp. 81–83). "Change; or, Reveries at a Window Overlooking a Country Road, with Two Women Talking Blues in the Kitchen" consists of two parallel columns of verse. The first column draws on gospel and blues music's call-and-response format to present a conversation between two women. The second column mimics improvisational jazz through irregular punctuation and free association: "Rhythms / like cells multiplying … language & / notes made flesh. Accents & stresses, / almost sexual. Pleasure's knot" (*NV*, pp. 8–10). In "Song for My Father" fourteen quatorzains play off of one another to portray a son's conflicted relationship with his parent. Komunyakaa's celebrated Vietnam War poems tend to shun overt political commentary and present individuals' struggles with the psychological and emotional consequences of war. "You and I Are Disappearing" juxtaposes a series of imagistic similes – "She burns like a cattail torch / dipped in gasoline. / She glows like the fat tip / of a banker's cigar" – to convey the narrator's memories of a woman being incinerated (*NV*, p. 142). In *Taboo: The Wishbone Trilogy, Part One* (2004) Komunyakaa writes in tercets and explores black people's relationship to Western culture, particularly through instances of miscegenation. Thomas Jefferson sits "at his neo-classical desk / musing, but we know his mind / is brushing aside abstractions / so his hands can touch flesh."[52]

Southern poets' absence from histories of contemporary American poetry suggests what makes their poetry distinctive and is linked to the Agrarians' political demise. In the years before World War II, critics and reviewers' association of the Agrarians' agenda with fascism and racism motivated Ransom's move away from politics and back toward poetics, leading to a line of lyric poets who emphasized the aesthetic over the social. Critics' charges and events involving World War II led Warren to question his political assumptions and helped spark changes in his verse. Warren's and Jarrell's shift to more personal verse that explored issues of identity within various social contexts helped generate a branch of narrative poets who distrusted ideology and stressed the paradoxical.

Contemporary southern poets have enjoyed a good deal of individual recognition, but Warren and Dickey's emphasis on competing philosophical contexts and Justice and Wright's on aesthetics differ from the values and poetics often associated with Beat, confessional, Deep Image, Black Mountain, and New York School poetry. The South's history of racism and poverty, and the Agrarians' legacy and missteps, helped create a poetry dominated by white men who were wary of certainties, a situation that changed in the late twentieth century as a more diverse group of southern poets gained increased access to the academy and negotiated their relationships to their predecessors, southern history, and an evolving cultural landscape.

Notes

1. John Crowe Ransom, *Selected Poems* (New York: Alfred A. Knopf, 1964), p. 11.
2. Cleanth Brooks, R. W. B. Lewis, and Robert Penn Warren, *American Literature: The Makers and the Making* (New York: St. Martin's Press, 1973), vol. II, p. 2654.
3. Ransom, *Selected Poems*, pp. 58–59.
4. Ransom, *Selected Poems*, pp. 58–59.
5. Ransom, *Selected Poems*, p. 65.
6. Allen Tate, "Whose Ox?" *The Fugitive* I (December 1922), pp. 99–100.
7. Allen Tate, *Collected Poems: 1919–1976* (New York: Farrar, Straus and Giroux, 1977), pp. 38–39.
8. See John Crowe Ransom, "Waste Lands," *Literary Review, New York Evening Post* 3, July 14, 1923, pp. 825–26, and Allen Tate, "Waste Lands," *Literary Review, New York Evening Post* 3, August 4, 1923, p. 886.
9. Thomas Daniel Young, *Gentleman in a Dustcoat: A Biography of John Crowe Ransom* (Baton Rouge: Louisiana State University Press, 1976), p. 176.
10. Tate, *Collected Poems*, pp. 20–23.
11. Floyd C. Watkins and John T. Hiers (eds.), *Robert Penn Warren Talking: Interviews, 1950–1978* (New York: Random House, 1980), p. 287.
12. Joseph Blotner, *Robert Penn Warren: A Biography* (New York: Random House, 1997), p. 33.
13. Watkins and Hiers, *Robert Penn Warren Talking*, p. 180.
14. Robert Penn Warren, *The Collected Poems of Robert Penn Warren*, ed. John Burt (Baton Rouge: Louisiana State University Press, 1998), pp. 33–35. This volume will subsequently be cited in the text as *CPRPW*.
15. Richard Gray, *Writing the South: Ideas of an American Region* (Cambridge: Cambridge University Press, 1986), p. 125.
16. Robert Penn Warren, "The Briar Patch," in *I'll Take My Stand: The South and the Agrarian Tradition* (1930; Baton Rouge: Louisiana State University Press, 1977), p. 264.
17. Robert H. Brinkmeyer, Jr., *The Fourth Ghost: White Southern Writers and European Fascism, 1930–1950* (Baton Rouge: Louisiana State University Press, 2009).
18. Interview with Warren, conducted by David Farrell on May 9, 1978. *Robert Penn Warren Oral History Project*, Department of Special Collections and Archives, University of Kentucky.
19. Robert Penn Warren, "The Art of Fiction No 18," interview conducted with Ralph Ellison and Eugene Walter, *Paris Review* 16 (Spring/Summer 1957),

collected in Floyd C. Watkins, John T. Hiers, and Mary Louise Weaks, *Talking with Robert Penn Warren* (Athens: University of Georgia Press, 1990), p. 34.

20. Randall Jarrell, "The End of the Line," *The Nation*, February 21, 1942, p. 226.

21. Stephen Burt, *Randall Jarrell and His Age* (New York: Columbia University Press, 2002), p. 55.

22. Robert Penn Warren, "A Reminiscence," in John Edgerton (ed.), *Nashville: The Face of Two Centuries* (Nashville, Tenn.: Media Plus, 1979), p. 218.

23. William H. Pritchard, *Randall Jarrell: A Literary Life* (New York: Farrar, Straus and Giroux, 1990), p. 149.

24. John Burt, *Robert Penn Warren and American Idealism* (New Haven, Conn.: Yale University Press, 1989).

25. Leonard Greenbaum, *The Hound and the Horn: The History of a Literary Quarterly* (The Hague: Mouton, 1966), pp. 145–48.

26. Tate, *Collected Poems*, pp. 132–35.

27. James Dickey, *Self-Interviews* (New York: Doubleday, 1970), pp. 34, 85.

28. James Dickey, *The Whole Motion: Collected Poems, 1945–1992* (Middletown, Conn.: Wesleyan University Press, 1992), pp. 94–95. This volume will subsequently be cited in the text as *WM*.

29. Dana Gioia and William Logan (eds.), *Certain Solitudes: On the Poetry of Donald Justice* (Fayetteville: University of Arkansas Press, 1997), p. 178.

30. Donald Justice, *Collected Poems* (New York: Alfred A. Knopf, 2004), pp. 16–17. This volume will subsequently be cited in the text as *DJC*.

31. Gioia and Logan (eds.), *Certain Solitudes*, p. 178.

32. Ellen Bryant Voigt, in Ernest Suarez, *Southbound: Interviews with Southern Poets* (Columbia: University of Missouri Press, 1999), p. 66. This volume will subsequently be cited in the text as *SI*.

33. Helen Vendler, "Catching a Pig on the Farm," review of *The Wick of Memory: New and Selected Poems 1970–2000* by Dave Smith, *New York Times Review of Books* 48:4, March 8, 2001, p. 45.

34. Dave Smith, *Floating on Solitude* (Urbana: University of Illinois Press, 1996), pp. 112–16.

35. Smith, *Floating on Solitude*, pp. 260–63.

36. Charles Wright, *Quarter Notes: Improvisations and Interviews* (Ann Arbor: University of Michigan Press, 1988), p. 123.

37. Charles Wright, *Country Music: Selected Early Poems*, 2nd ed. (Middletown, Conn.: Wesleyan University Press, 1991), p. 152.

38. Wright, *Country Music*, p. 112; Suarez, *Southbound*, p. 40.

39. Wright, *Quarter Notes*, pp. 79–80.

40. Charles Wright, "Virginia Reel," in *The World of the Ten Thousand Things: Poems 1980–1990* (New York: Farrar, Straus and Giroux, 1990), p. 17.

41. Charles Wright, *Negative Blue: Selected Later Poems* (New York: Farrar, Straus and Giroux, 2000), p. 3.

42. Wright, *Negative Blue*, p. 201.

43. Joe Moffett, *Understanding Charles Wright* (Columbia: University of South Carolina Press, 2008), p. 105.

44. Charles Wright, *Scar Tissue* (New York: Farrar, Straus and Giroux, 2006), pp. 33–39.

45. Betty Adcock, unpublished audiotaped panel discussion with Ernest Suarez, Millennial Gathering of Southern Writers, Vanderbilt University, April 7, 1999; Ellen Bryant Voigt, "Foreword," in Eleanor Ross Taylor, *Captive Voices: New and Selected Poems, 1960–2008* (Baton Rouge: Louisiana State University Press, 2008), p. xiii.

46. Eleanor Ross Taylor, "Eleanor Ross Taylor Transcends Place," *The Women's Review of Books* 16:10/11 (July 1999), p. 19.

47. Susan Settlemyre Williams, "An Interview with Eleanor Ross Taylor," *Blackbird: An Online Journal of Literature and the Arts* 1:1 (2002), http://www.blackbird.vcu.edu/v8n2/nonfiction/williams_s/taylor_page.shtml.

48. Taylor, *Captive Voices*, pp. 8–9.

49. Taylor, *Captive Voices*, pp. 14–15.

50. Richard Howard, "Eat Some, Drink Some, Bury Some," *The Kenyon Review* 14:4 (1994), p. 186.

51. Yusef Komunyakaa, *Neon Vernacular: New and Selected Poems* (Hanover, N.H.: Wesleyan University Press, 1993), p. 38. This volume will subsequently be cited in the text as *NV*.

52. Yusef Komunyakaa, "Monticello," in *Taboo: The Wishbone Trilogy, Part One* (New York: Farrar, Straus and Giroux, 2004), pp. 27–28.

PART IV

★

BEYOND MODERNISM:
AMERICAN POETRY, 1950–2000

Chapter 36

San Francisco and the Beats

STEPHEN FREDMAN

In the 1950s San Francisco acquired a reputation, which it has since maintained, as a mecca for poetry. In the popular imagination, San Francisco poetry is synonymous with the Beat Movement, which first rose to prominence there. Ironically, the writers most responsible for launching the Beat Movement as a social phenomenon, Allen Ginsberg and Jack Kerouac, came from the East Coast and left California after only a few years, but the effect of those years, especially on Ginsberg, was decisive. Prior to the arrival of Ginsberg and Kerouac, an experimental poetry scene, anchored by Kenneth Rexroth, Robert Duncan, and Jack Spicer, had been afloat in the Bay Area for a decade. It was this scene into which the new poets entered and found a place. After the Beat phenomenon took off, readers lost sight of the extent to which the San Francisco scene was a single milieu in which all of these poets participated. This chapter presents the salient features of that milieu and then discusses what have been seen as the two strains within it: the spontaneous and the hermetic. From the spontaneous wing, Ginsberg and Bob Kaufman are discussed in detail; from the hermetic wing, the chapter addresses Spicer and, to a lesser extent, Duncan. Finally, a consideration of Gary Snyder, who partakes of both tendencies, argues again for the unity of the San Francisco scene.

San Francisco in the mid-twentieth century promised fertile ground for the flowering of a poetry renaissance. A city of striking natural and architectural beauty, isolated from the Eastern cultural establishment, San Francisco had a history of permissive social mores and radical politics, which encouraged sexual, political, and mystical shoots of varieties rare in postwar America. The arts in particular flourished: the Fillmore District was home to a vibrant jazz scene; the screenings of the Art in Cinema Society helped make the Bay Area a breeding ground for independent film; the California School of Fine Arts (later the San Francisco Art Institute) fostered new departures in painting and sculpture; Anna Halprin's epoch-making Dancer's Workshop took off in the late 1950s; and budding poetry circles, including the Berkeley Renaissance of the late 1940s (headed by Duncan, Spicer, and Robin Blaser) and Rexroth's highly influential "at-homes," devoted to poetry and anarchism, had begun to blossom. Out of this cross-fertilization of geographic, political, social, and artistic strains arose the San Francisco Renaissance in poetry, composed of poets who became associated with the Beat Movement, such as Ginsberg, Kerouac, Kaufman, Snyder, Lawrence Ferlinghetti, Philip Whalen, Lew Welch, and Diane di Prima; those who congregated around Spicer and Duncan, including Blaser, William Everson, Joanne Kyger, and Helen Adam; and those who traveled easily between these two groups, such as Rexroth, John Wieners, Philip Lamantia, David Meltzer, and Michael McClure. Although di Prima, Kyger, Adam, and other women were active in San Francisco poetry, the milieu had the hallmarks of a boys' club. It took forty years to acknowledge women writers' substantial contribution, most notably through the publication of two anthologies, *Women of the Beat Generation* (1996) and *A Different Beat* (1997).[1]

A glance at the landmark 1960 poetry anthology, Donald Allen's *The New American Poetry*, shows the poets mentioned previously located in four of the five groupings around which Allen organized his volume – the Black Mountain School, the San Francisco Renaissance, the Beat Generation, the New York School, and a group of unaffiliated younger poets – of these groups, only the poets of the New York School were not represented in San Francisco. Although Allen's designations have proven durable for half a century, he admits in his preface that the groupings are more arbitrary than they seem and that their main function is to create "some sense of milieu" and thus prevent relegating the then-unheralded poets to an undifferentiated miscellany. These heuristic labels have reified over time, and readers have lost sight of the extent to which the poets in Allen's anthology share an aesthetics he characterizes as third-generation modernism, following, as did the Objectivists of the second generation, "the practices and precepts of Ezra Pound and William Carlos Williams" (to which list of decisive precursors one would wish to add Hart Crane, D. H. Lawrence, and Surrealism).[2] Allen's labels also obscure the extensive degree to which poets falling under different headings met and conversed with, corresponded with, gave readings with, published with, learned from, disagreed with, and defended one another. In the 1950s, the two major geographical lodestones for the New American poets were San Francisco and New York City – along with the outlier of Black Mountain College, situated in North Carolina but occupying a predominantly literary space through *Black Mountain Review*.

From a sociological perspective, though – a perspective prompted by attention to the intricate interaction of poets in San Francisco – it would be possible to apply a single capacious label to all of the poets in the Allen anthology: Beat. The origins of the term are controversial, but it emerges from the hipster culture inspired by jazz, in the physical gesture of snapping one's fingers to keep a beat. The Beat Movement also took on two opposing metaphorical extensions of the word "beat": "beaten," as in downtrodden, and "beatific." As participants in the aesthetic reaction to the social and political conformity mandated by a fearful American society during the Cold War, these poets explored, in styles ranging from the most cosmopolitan to the most vernacular, the dark underside to America's rise to economic and political domination, and they joined in currents of personal, sexual, religious, and political liberation that inspired the larger social movements of the 1960s. Writing in a 1956 letter that accompanies an early version of "Howl," Ginsberg informs his former mentor, Columbia University professor Lionel Trilling, about an historic shift in literary taste:

> I think what is coming is a romantic period (strangely tho everybody thinks by being hard-up and classical they are going to make it like Eliot which is silly). Eliot & Pound are like Dryden and Pope. What gives now is much more personal – how could there be now anything but reassertion of naked personal subjective truth – eternally real? Perhaps Whitman will be seen to have set the example and been bypassed for half a century.[3]

Ginsberg puts his finger on the newly emerging dividing line in the American cultural imaginary between the Beat and the square, the hipster and the social conformist; he sees the Beat ethos as a return to the prophetic stance of Romanticism and to Whitmanian democratic comradeship after the political and aesthetic conservatism of the previous twenty years. If we look at the Beat Movement as an antiestablishment culture in the late 1950s and early 1960s, in which writers joined with jazz musicians, action painters, existentialist philosophers, and Buddhist seekers, then all of the New American poets (regardless of the very real differences among them) would have been regarded by American society at the time as Beats, as seemingly incomprehensible outsiders.

Although the writers who have been seen as the vocal leaders of the Beat Generation – Jack Kerouac, Allen Ginsberg, and William Burroughs – met in New York in the mid-1940s, the inaugural public manifestation of Beat aesthetics was a poetry reading that took place in San Francisco at the Six Gallery on October 7, 1955. The Six Gallery was launched in September 1954 on Fillmore Street by Spicer and five of his students from the California School of Fine Arts. In addition to showing the most avant-garde San Francisco art, the gallery hosted poetry readings and staged a notorious production in January 1955 of Duncan's play *Faust Foutu* (*Faust Fucked*).[4] Duncan, Spicer, McClure, and Adam all read parts in this contemporary setting of the Faust legend, at the climax of which Duncan disrobed in order to display the power and vulnerability of the poet. Duncan's gesture had a decisive impact on one member of the audience, Ginsberg, who learned the rhetorical value of nakedness as a form of truth telling – which he then espoused not only while stripping at his own poetry readings but by championing emotional nakedness as a fundamental virtue in writing. An earlier venue, the King Ubu Gallery, had opened at the end of 1952 in the same cavernous auto repair garage that would house the Six Gallery. Named for the eponymous hero of a play by Alfred Jarry, the King Ubu Gallery was founded by Duncan and two artists (including his life partner, Jess); it produced exhibits by local painters and sculptors and poetry readings by Duncan, Spicer, and Blaser, as well as the first public screening of films by Stan Brakhage. In this grimy garage on Fillmore Street, the poets and artists created a locus for artistic happenings, poetry readings, jazz, film screenings, and theater.

One of the artists who ran the Six Gallery, Wally Hedrick, met McClure on the street and suggested he organize a poetry reading as a follow-up to *Faust Foutu*. McClure agreed but turned over duties to a recent acquaintance, Ginsberg, who was eager to take on the task. Ginsberg had arrived in San Francisco a year earlier with a letter of introduction to local poets from William Carlos Williams. Learning that Duncan and Jess had decamped for Europe and that Spicer had gone to New York and Boston (he participated in the reading via a letter urging someone in the audience to find him a job so he could return from exile), Ginsberg arranged for Rexroth to act as master of ceremonies and for a group of largely unpublished poets – McClure, Lamantia, Whalen, Snyder, and himself – to read.[5] Lamantia, who already had a reputation as an American Surrealist, was the only poet who had published a book, and he chose to read work by a friend who had recently died in Mexico. The Six Gallery reading has acquired the status of legend, recounted countless times in memoirs by participants and fictionalized in Kerouac's novel *The Dharma Bums*.[6] For most of the poets, this was their first public reading; the audience, which included Kerouac, Ferlinghetti, and Neal Cassady (hero of Kerouac's as-yet-unpublished *On the Road*), had no idea what to expect. Ginsberg, the penultimate reader, got off to a slow start, nervous about whether he could propel the prophetic tenor of his poem and worried that its humor would undercut its serious intent. He began in a Whitmanian vein, projecting a self capable of communing with the souls of his fellow Americans

and ascertaining their deepest conflicts: "I saw the best minds of my generation destroyed by madness, starving hysterical naked, / dragging themselves
through the negro streets at dawn looking for an angry fix, / angelheaded
hipsters burning for the ancient heavenly connection to the starry dynamo in
the machinery of night."[7]

The opening lines of "Howl" have achieved emblematic status as the abject
testimony of self-exiled outsiders who sought a shamanic vision into the
recesses of the American spirit (often through the agency of drugs), but when
Ginsberg first uttered these lines to an audience, they fell a bit flat. It wasn't
until he picked up the beat from the anaphoric "who," which leads off nearly
all of the succeeding "strophes" (as Ginsberg called his verse paragraphs), that
he began to read the long lines as if he were taking a full-breathed, ecstatic,
and unpredictable saxophone solo in the mode of the iconic bebopper Charlie
Parker. Kerouac immediately understood and began shouting "Go! Go!" –
urging Ginsberg on as he would an artfully improvising instrumentalist. As
the reading gathered intensity, the audience joined with Kerouac in voicing
encouragement and approval. The effect was transporting, as if both poet and
listeners were witnessing the discovery of a new form of rhythmic truth telling. When Ginsberg finished with an invocation of a self "speechless and intelligent and shaking with shame, . . . the madman bum and angel beat in Time,"
who "rose reincarnate in the ghostly clothes of jazz in the goldhorn shadow of
the band and blew the suffering of America's naked mind for love," he broke
down in tears, having reduced the collective body to stunned silence.[8]

"Howl" was a breakthrough poem in many ways. For Ginsberg, it was a stylistic and confessional revolution. He reports writing the first section in a furnished room at 1010 Montgomery Street, only a few blocks from Ferlinghetti's
City Lights Bookstore. Using "a secondhand typewriter, some cheap scratch
paper," he typed

> not with the idea of writing a formal poem, but stating my imaginative sym-
> pathies, whatever they were worth. As my loves were impractical and my
> thoughts relatively unworldly, I had nothing to gain, only the pleasure of
> enjoying on paper those sympathies most intimate to myself and most awk-
> ward in the great world of family, formal education, business and current
> literature.[9]

The style that crystalized from this relaxed exercise, combining collage,
Surrealism, anecdotes, and prophecy, was unprecedented in midcentury
American poetry; its most direct affiliations reach back through Crane to
Whitman. In personal terms, the poem constituted Ginsberg's coming out

as a homosexual and his avowal of empathetic connection to various forms of madness, drug addiction, high jinks, and economic destitution. In San Francisco, he had had the rare good fortune to meet with a young psychiatrist, Dr. Philip Hicks, who, during a year of therapy "to overcome a block in his writing," was able to convince the poet that he was not mentally ill, that it was fine to explore his homosexuality, and that writing itself could be therapeutic.[10]

More than a half century after its composition, the poem continues to pack a wallop to first-time readers. Ginsberg's incantatory exposé of his own fears, transgressions, and erotic desires and those of his friends, coupled with his denunciation of a rapacious capitalist culture in the form of the devouring god Moloch, has made "Howl" an epoch-defining poem. Delivered exactly a hundred years after Whitman's ecstatic assessment of American promise in the first edition of *Leaves of Grass* (1855), "Howl" endeavors to take the spiritual pulse of the nation after the lapse of a century. Employing the prophetic cadences, exuberant declarations, and omniscient catalogues of Whitman, "Howl" maintains a darker tone that pits individual anarchic actions and perceptions against an overweening social conformism painted as far more restrictive in the contemporary United States. At the same time, the poem harks back to T. S. Eliot's *The Waste Land* (1922), building on it as a model for the postwar reassessment of a wounded culture. Ginsberg was so insistent on analogies between his poem and Eliot's, which was the most prestigious modern American poem during Ginsberg's lifetime, that he compiled a text to demonstrate the similar stature of the two poems. Just as Valerie Eliot caused a scholarly sensation in 1971 by printing a facsimile edition of the manuscripts of *The Waste Land* (showing Ezra Pound's heavy editing), Ginsberg hoped to prompt a reassessment of "Howl" by assembling, thirty years after its first edition, *Howl: Original Draft Facsimile, Transcript & Variant Versions, Fully Annotated by Author, with Contemporaneous Correspondence, Account of First Public Reading, Legal Skirmishes, Precursor Texts & Bibliography* (1986).[11] Another measure of the poem's impact can be found in the obscenity trial that greeted the initial release of *Howl and Other Poems* in the City Lights Pocket Poets series. The trial catapulted the book's sales far beyond what the publisher, Ferlinghetti, could have dreamed (it remains the press's best-selling title), and the verdict finding against obscenity in *The People of California v. Lawrence Ferlinghetti* became a landmark in civil liberties law and helped open wide the door to freedom of expression, especially with respect to sexual frankness.

★

The publication of *Howl and Other Poems* in 1956 drew nationwide attention to the San Francisco poetry scene. *Evergreen Review*, edited by Barney Rosset (publisher of Grove Press) and Donald Allen, provides a timely snapshot of the "San Francisco Scene" a year later, just prior to the publication of Kerouac's *On the Road* (1957). The second number of the magazine contains writing by everyone who had read at the Six Gallery except for Lamantia (who temporarily abjured publishing); by poets who attended the reading – Rexroth, Ferlinghetti, and Kerouac; by other acknowledged eminences of the Bay Area – Duncan, Spicer, Brother Antoninus (William Everson), James Broughton, and Josephine Miles; by a transplanted student from Black Mountain College – Michael Rumaker; and by a tutelary spirit living in Big Sur – Henry Miller. The editors round out the picture of San Francisco as a cultural capital with the "San Francisco Letter" by Rexroth, a tour of "the San Francisco Jazz Scene" by local jazz critic Ralph J. Gleason, an evaluation of "the San Francisco School" in visual art by *New York Times* critic Dore Ashton, and a gallery of portraits of eight poets by photographer Harry Redl.[12] Rexroth's "Letter" is particularly fascinating because it discusses the "San Francisco Renaissance and the New Generation of Revolt"[13] – which will soon be called the "Beat Generation" – as a single phenomenon.

Rexroth begins by complaining that there has been "so much publicity recently about ... Our Underground Literature and Cultural Disaffiliation that I for one am getting a little sick writing about it, and the writers who are the objects of all of the uproar run the serious danger of falling over, 'dizzy with success.'" He explains that for "ten years after the Second War there was a convergence of interest – the Business Community, military imperialism, political reaction, the hysterical, tear and mud drenched guilt of the ex-Stalinist, ex-Trotskyite American intellectuals," and the ascendancy of the southern poets and critics associated with the New Criticism; this "ministry of all the talents formed a dense crust of custom over American cultural life – more of an ice pack. Ultimately the living water underneath got so damn hot the ice pack has begun to melt, rot, break up and drift away into Arctic oblivion." San Francisco he characterizes as the only "Mediterranean" city in North America, where the warm spirit of *"laissez faire* and *dolce far niente"* makes a cultural revolt conceivable. Then, employing a hipster rhetoric that imagines a strict demarcation between the cognoscenti and the legions of benighted conformists, he chastises anyone who doesn't understand that San Francisco is the *only* city where the ice pack of custom could be breached: "But – like all squares if you don't know already you won't know anymore than you did before." Discussing countercultural currents such as mysticism and Surrealism among "disaffiliated" writers in San Francisco, he gives the most extensive treatment to "Howl," which the issue reprints. He claims that *"Howl is much more than the most sensational book of poetry of 1957"* and foresees that it epitomizes the generational revolt that will continue to gather momentum during the next decade: "Listen you – do you *really* think your kids act like the bobby sox-ers in those wholesome Coca-Cola ads? Don't you know that across the table from you at dinner sits somebody who looks on you as an enemy who is plan-ning to kill him in the immediate future in an extremely disagreeable way?" Arguing against the critics and commentators who denounced the poem as merely an angry screed filled with nihilism, Rexroth insists, *"Howl is the con-fession of faith of the generation that is going to be running the world in 1965 and 1975 – if it's still there to run."*[14]

The "San Francisco Letter" marks the last moment in which Rexroth had the unquestioned authority to speak as an elder and mentor for the San Francisco poetry scene. "Noretorp-Noretsyh," his poem that accompanies the letter, contrasts "the brilliant Pacific sky," "the cry of the peacocks" in Golden Gate Park, and his lover's "incomparable thighs" with the grim polit-ical reality of the 1956 Hungarian Revolution; harking back to earlier revolu-tionary moments, Rexroth imagines brigades of anarchists and poets arriving in Budapest to defeat the Soviets.[15] With the publication of *On the Road* and the emergence of the Beat Generation as a full-fledged cultural phenome-non, Ginsberg and Kerouac soon greatly overshadowed Rexroth, and his historic commitment to political anarchism looked instantly old fashioned. Duncan and Spicer, too, grew envious and resentful of the sudden renown of the Beats, finding their own acknowledged prominence questioned and the San Francisco Renaissance hijacked by the recent arrivals from New York. In Kerouac's hurriedly written follow-up novel, *The Dharma Bums* (1958), he enshrines the Six Gallery reading as the defining moment in San Francisco poetry and focuses on Snyder, Ginsberg, and himself as the major figures, with Whalen and Rexroth as minor adjuncts. From this moment forward, the rupture within the San Francisco scene caused by the rapidly spreading fame of the Beat Generation split the poets into two camps – which, although they share many qualities in common, can be labeled the "spontaneous" and the "hermetic." Employing what Kerouac called "spontaneous bop prosody" (as outlined in his "Essentials of Spontaneous Prose"), the spontaneous wing wrote a vernacular poetry inspired by jazz; in addition to an improvisational writing style, many of these poets developed a jazz-inflected performance style.[16] Making a virtue of eschewing fame, the hermetic wing turned inward, viewing the scene of writing as akin to magic or séance – in which spirits might direct the making of poetry – and addressing the poem principally to a group of like-minded initiates.

The vogue for poetry readings as verbal performances spread rapidly outward from San Francisco. After the Six Gallery reading and other celebrated renditions of "Howl" around the Bay Area, Ginsberg gained confidence in his performing abilities. Over the course of his career he honed a bardic style of declamation and cultivated the related modes of chant and song. Bob Dylan, an assiduous student of Ginsberg and Kerouac, taught Ginsberg to accompany himself on the harmonium and brought the poet with him on several musical tours. For a time during the 1960s and 1970s, Ginsberg himself was able to fill auditoriums and stadiums around the world with avid listeners. In San Francisco, Kerouac and Ferlinghetti, whose million-selling *A Coney Island of the Mind* (1958) embodies a commedia dell'arte style of physical humor and satire, read poetry to jazz accompaniment, and Meltzer and his wife, Tina, formed an early rock band.[17] McClure created a "beast language" for his *Ghost Tantras* (1967), roaring into the face of lions at the San Francisco zoo; he also collaborated with Jim Morrison and the Doors and continues to perform with one of the members of the Doors, Ray Manzarek.[18] He has made a major contribution to American theater as one of the first playwrights to bring over the entire European tradition of Dada, Surrealist, and absurdist drama that begins with Alfred Jarry's *King Ubu*. McClure's play *The Beard* (1965), which stages an extended tête-à-tête in eternity between Jean Harlow and Billy the Kid that ends in a simulated sex act, was prosecuted unsuccessfully for obscenity and helped break open American theater in the same way that "Howl" had shattered the sexual taboos in American poetry. From the East Coast, ex-convict Gregory Corso made his way to San Francisco and wrote "Ode to Coit Tower," using elements of jazz and Surrealism to pair the phallic monument near North Beach with the fortress prison of Alcatraz in San Francisco Bay: "Ah tower from thy berryless head I'd a vision in common with myself the proximity of Alcatraz and not the hip volley of white jazz & verse or verse & jazz embraced but a real heart-rending constant vision of Alcatraz marshaled before my eyes."[19] The performative style that grew out of the readings and plays at the King Ubu and Six Galleries was also embraced by street poets in the Bay Area, who could be found declaiming spontaneous verse in coffee houses, in bars, and on street corners. Over time, this style contributed to the national rise in the 1980s of poetry slams and freestyle rap.

The best-known poet in San Francisco to embrace the spontaneous style wholeheartedly was Bob Kaufman, an African American improvisational performer who became in many ways the epitome of a Beat poet. Born in New

Orleans with a mixed African American heritage that included a Jewish ancestor, Kaufman joined the Merchant Marine while still a teenager and became a radical labor organizer in New York City. He moved to San Francisco in the 1950s and spent most of the rest of his life there, often holding court in the early days at the Coffee Gallery and the Coexistence Bagel Shop. Like his mentor Langston Hughes, Kaufman was steeped in jazz and drew poetic inspiration from Whitman and Federico García Lorca; like many of the Beats, his other major poetic precursor was Hart Crane. Kaufman's spontaneous style incorporates several elements of Surrealism, drawing especially from the *négritude* of Caribbean Surrealist Aimé Césaire. Kaufman lived a precarious life like those chronicled in "Howl," battling drug addiction and suffering numerous arrests and beatings by the police. His poetry speaks of anger, revolution, and nuclear apocalypse, but it also celebrates Black art and culture and even Black patriotism, in the form of the iconic Crispus Attucks, martyr of the Boston Massacre. Kaufman's is an essentially oral poetry, addressed often to specific occasions, and he was reluctant to write it down or publish it.

One of his most renowned poems, "Bagel Shop Jazz," chronicles the social layers of the Beat scene in North Beach, making clear how each layer depends on its own relationship to jazz. The poem begins ominously, as do many of Kaufman's poems, with a reference to nuclear nightmare: he speaks of "Shadow people, projected on coffee-shop walls" from "a generation past," as though the coffee shop contained revenants from the atomic blast at Hiroshima. As the poem continues, it becomes clear that "shadow people" refers also to social misfits in the present who frequent the Coexistence Bagel Shop. Kaufman devotes a stanza each to three different groups of habitués: "Mulberry-eyed girls in black stockings," "Turtle-neck angel guys ... with synagogue eyes," and "Coffee-faced Ivy Leaguers." Kaufman sees that the girls will never fulfill their "coffee dreams" but will instead settle for becoming sexual partners, "Losing their doubts in the beat" – that is, losing their inhibitions to the jazz beat while taking a Beat lover. The Jewish guys dressed in turtlenecks and dungarees show their worldly sophistication by "Mixing jazz with paint talk." The Black hipsters, "Whose personal Harvard was a Fillmore district step," gained their education hanging out around jazz. They are the most essential denizens of the coffee house, advertising their hipness by talking about the jazz pantheon ("Bird and Diz and Miles") and at the same time concealing the "secret terrible hurts" of racial discrimination. For them, jazz and the life built around it define the limits of aspiration; they are "Hoping the beat is really the truth." Kaufman paints a picture of a coffee house filled with inquisitive young people for whom jazz supplies the "beats" that contour their time. Although he lovingly depicts these various groups of hipsters, the poet acknowledges the precarious and even illusory nature of their nighttime revels: at the end of the poem "The guilty police arrive," breaking up the conviviality and leaving behind the "beautiful shadows" burned on the wall with which the poem began.[20]

The subtle Black-White interplay in Kaufman's poetry finds a powerful locus in his repeated invocation of the Spanish poet Lorca, whose *Poet in New York* (1940), with its penetrating portrait of Harlem at the beginning of the Great Depression, haunted Kaufman. *Poet in New York* is Lorca's most Surrealist work, comprising poems, such as "The King of Harlem," "Standards and Paradise of the Blacks," and "Ode to Walt Whitman," that chronicle his devastating sojourn in the United States in 1929 and 1930. From the second of these poems Kaufman takes a phrase, "crackling blueness" ("el azul crujiente"), which he makes a touchstone of the Black experience: "crackling blueness" connotes the electrifying quality of African American sorrow as it is transmuted into art.[21] In fact, it could serve as an epithet for bebop jazz, in its rapid-fire, flickering rhythmic ascensions. Lorca and his crackling blueness appear in many of Kaufman's poems, such as "THE NIGHT THAT LORCA COMES," in which the poet's arrival signals a racial liberation. In this poem, "NEGROES LEAVE THE SOUTH / FOREVER" and ascend "INTO CRACKLING BLUENESS."[22] Near the end of his long apocalyptic prose poem, "The Ancient Rain," Kaufman quotes a number of lines from "The King of Harlem" and then repeats them with variations. He claims Lorca as his own, recalling that after he left the Merchant Marine, he followed Lorca's footsteps around Manhattan and "decided to move deeper into crackling blueness." As a Black man, Kaufman feels he understands Lorca better than others: "I observed those who read him who were not Negroes and listened to their misinterpretation of him." He finds that Lorca's surrealistic vision of the spiritual power of African Americans in a United States whose soul has died offers the fullest scope for his ambitions as a shaman-poet: "I remember the day I went into crackling blueness."[23]

*

Lorca, especially in his book *Poet in New York*, forms a vital link between the spontaneous and the hermetic strains in San Francisco poetry. Ginsberg found *Poet in New York* inspirational in the writing of "Howl"; in his annotated edition he reprints "Ode to Walt Whitman" among the explicit "precursor texts" for the poem.[24] On the hermetic side, Spicer and Duncan both saw Lorca's poetry, and *Poet in New York* in particular, as central to their aesthetic explorations during the 1940s and 1950s. For Ginsberg, Duncan, and Spicer, Lorca's example was not only that of a Surrealist in the New World but also that of a modernist gay poet. Duncan read *Poet in New York* in Spanish when it first appeared in 1940 and incorporated its incantatory rhythms into some of his earliest poems. Like Kaufman, he identified with the prophetic fire in the book, although as a member of a sexual rather than a racial minority: "The impact of Lorca's *Poeta en Nueva York* was ... immediate, a voice speaking for my own soul in its rage it seemed." Duncan recounts how in the late 1940s he and Spicer, "as young poets seeking the language and lore of our homosexual longings as the matter of a poetry, [sensed] that Lorca was one of us, that he spoke from his unanswered and – as he saw it – *unanswerable* need."[25] As Duncan discusses at length in a later preface to his 1955 *Caesar's Gate*, while writing the book, during 1949 and 1950, he was haunted by Lorca's poetry of war and of veiled homosexuality and by the seemingly unutterable pain associated with both conditions. In the title of one of his own poems, Duncan asks in bewilderment, "What Is It Have You Come to Tell Me, García Lorca?"[26]

In 1957, the year when *On the Road* appeared in print and *Howl and Other Poems* went on trial, Spicer published his own breakthrough book, *After Lorca*, which could be read as a response to Duncan's question. The book begins with an introduction, supposedly written by the dead poet, in which he declares himself "fundamentally unsympathetic" to the "difficult and unrewarding task" Spicer has undertaken – namely, to write a book in English that includes translations and transformations of poems by Lorca, original poems by Spicer posing as translations, and letters to Lorca.[27] In the introduction, Spicer ventriloquizes Lorca, even to the point of gloating, "I have further complicated the problem (with malice aforethought I must admit) by sending Mr. Spicer several poems written after my death which he has also translated and included here" (*MVD*, p. 107). Right at the outset of his first book, Spicer thus enacts the mysterious theory of dictation for which he would become famous. In the simplest sense, by presenting Lorca as a barely cooperative interlocutor, Spicer dramatizes the uneasy relationships between original poem and translation and between an earlier author and his epigone. In a more occult sense, Spicer becomes a kind of shaman when he makes the dead author speak, in the manner of Pound's Odysseus, who proffers sheep's blood so that Tiresias will speak from the Underworld in "Canto I." Like Pound, Spicer calls up the spirits of dead poets in an attempt to escape his own personality and gain a wider vantage point. To a certain extent, both poets believe they can receive instruction from dead poets or mythological beings and that this mediumship gives them entry into transpersonal states of being.

Setting forth his theory of dictation in lectures delivered just prior to his early death in 1965, Spicer claims that he heard the new poems he wrote in *After Lorca* through "a direct connection like on the telephone": it "was Mr. Lorca talkin' directly."[28] Another media metaphor Spicer uses more commonly to describe poetic dictation is the radio. He seizes on scenes in Jean Cocteau's film *Orphée*, in which Orpheus receives radio transmissions of new verse from a dead poet and publishes them as his own, as providing an image of the process of dictation: "Essentially you are something which is being transmitted into" (*HJB*, p. 7). Spicer contrasts his technique of dictation to T. S. Eliot's contention that the poet participates in the entirety of tradition and alters it slightly by his new contribution: "I think when you pay attention to a tradition like Eliot does, you get into all sorts of the most soupy static that you can possibly have, so that you don't know what is your reading of English literature and what is ghosts" (*HJB*, p. 138). Spicer insists that his poetry represents a static-free transmission from the "ghosts," whether dead poets or other beings outside the phenomenal world (sometimes he calls them "Martians"), who tell him things that can't be learned through literary interpretation. The content of such "communication," however, is not "spiritual" knowledge but a clearer view of reality. The practice of dictation purportedly enables the poet to slip beyond the grasp of the ego and to use language to disclose the real world without distortion, rather than revealing the poet's personality or his imaginative or interpretive prowess. In one of the letters to Lorca in *After Lorca*, Spicer avows:

> I would like to make poems out of real objects. The lemon to be a lemon that the reader could cut or squeeze or taste – a real lemon like a newspaper in a collage is a real newspaper. I would like the moon in my poems to be a real moon, one which could be suddenly covered with a cloud that has nothing to do with the poem – a moon utterly independent of images. The imagination pictures the real. I would like to point to the real, disclose it, to make a poem that has no sound in it but the pointing of a finger. (*MVD*, pp. 133–34)

By eschewing what he calls "the big lie of the personal," Spicer endeavors to perform a Zen disappearing act, in which the finger that points to the objects in the world can vanish – leaving only the quivering lemon (*MVD*, p. 150).

The reference to collage is also telling. Beginning with *After Lorca*, Spicer conceives of each book of poetry as a serial composition, as a collage of interrelated elements. If the two essential criteria for creating a collage are the importation of fragments of found material and the juxtaposition of these fragments in a nonlogical or nonhierarchical or paratactic composition, then in Spicer's books imported fragments (such as Lorca poems and pieces of poems in *After Lorca* and folk motifs, baseball plays, or Grail characters in others) are strewn among the poems and reflect back on one another within the structure of the book. He thinks of this found material as so much "furniture" that fills the rooms of the poet's mind; as such, it has no inherent poetic meaning until a force outside the mind orders it: "Given the cooperation between the host poet and the visitor – the thing from Outside – the more things you have in the room the better if you can handle them in such a way that you don't impose your will on what is coming through." Most poets, however, "can't resist, if they have all of these benches and chairs in the room, not to arrange them themselves instead of letting them be arranged by whatever is the source of the poem" (*HJB*, p. 9). This would be another way of stating Spicer's objection to Eliot, who for all his vaunted impersonalism orders the fragments of *The Waste Land* through an emotional logic rather than allowing them to be structured by "the thing from Outside." The outside force intervenes both at the level of the individual poem and at the level of the book. Just as a Spicer poem does not originate in a lyric voice but is a collage arranged by impersonal intervention, so entire books become serial compositions in which materials within the book "correspond" with one another and thus interact to create larger structures: "Poems should echo and re-echo against each other. They should create resonances. They cannot live alone any more than we can" (*MVD*, p. 163).

In addition to spiritualistic composition and a penchant for occult sources, such as the Grail myth or the tarot deck, there are two other strikingly hermetic qualities to Spicer's oeuvre. The first is social. Beginning in the mid-1940s, when he joined Duncan and Blaser in Berkeley and began studying medieval history with Ernst Kantorowicz (an original member of the German poet Stefan George's *kreis* – his eroticized "ring" of male aesthetic/religious seekers), Spicer adhered faithfully to the notion that art should be created and circulated within a coterie of like-minded initiates. Like his sometime rival, Bob Kaufman, Spicer held court in a few select bars in San Francisco, but he demanded a much tighter group allegiance than did Kaufman and actively policed the boundaries of his circle. In what would seem a bald contradiction to his insistence on impersonality, many of Spicer's poems are addressed to specific members of the clique. Although such poems can include personal or interpersonal details of a sexual or romantic nature, Spicer also manages to make the poems uncannily abstract by treating such intimate matters as "furniture" available to outside composition. He generates a powerful tension in the practice of dictated poetry by recounting excruciating moments of romantic rejection and offering biting criticism of other poets and their poetics, as well as by insisting that members of the coterie not stray beyond its confines. One of Spicer's serial books, *Admonitions* (written 1957), lays bare this tension in poems written for specific individuals. "Each one of them," he explains in a letter that opens the book, "is a mirror, dedicated to the person that I particularly want to look into it. But mirrors can be arranged. The frightening hall of mirrors in a fun house is universal beyond each personal reflection" (*MVD*, p. 157).

The other hermetic aspect of Spicer's poetry involves his relationship to language. Trained as a professional linguist, he lost his position as a graduate student at the University of California at Berkeley in 1950 when he refused to sign a loyalty oath during the postwar Red Scare. In the early 1950s he attended the national linguistics convention and published an article in *Language: Journal of the Linguistic Society of America* (1952). The cover of this issue of the journal, listing John L. Spicer as co-author of "Correlation Methods of Comparing Idiolects in a Transition Area," was reproduced in green as the cover of Spicer's book, *Language* (1965), with title, author, and press information scrawled across it in red crayon. Throughout his writing, he remains highly attuned to sophisticated linguistic issues and, like one of his models, the French symbolist poet Stéphane Mallarmé, revels in seeing language take on a life of its own in poetry. Spicer's linguistic concerns come to a head in the serial book *Language*, which is filled with propositional sentences calling attention to their own linguistic fabrication. In "Spicer's Language," Ron Silliman, one of the Bay Area poets who inaugurated Language poetry in the 1970s, acknowledges Spicer as a crucial forerunner. Silliman discusses in detail the first (untitled) poem in "Thing Language," the first section of the book. The poem begins, "This ocean, humiliating in its disguises / Tougher than anything. / No one listens to poetry. The ocean / Does not mean to be listened to" (*MVD*, p. 373). Silliman's microreading of this poem attends to the self-contradictory qualities of its language, which he sees as the most powerful feature of Spicer's writing.

According to Silliman, self-contradiction begins with the title, "Thing Language," which posits the two nouns as equivalent and impermeable entities while also seeming to turn "thing" into an adjective modifying "language." Spicer's linguistic knowledge of the arbitrary nature of signs makes him aware that words and things will never meet, and so he makes disjunction the subject of this section of *Language*. Silliman investigates how the passage cited previously stages the nonmeeting of two voluble entities – poetry (language) and the ocean (thing) – and he points out the logical nonalignment that takes place among the three sentences and across the four lines. He sees Spicer's skillful manipulation of such breaks within and between sentences as anticipating "the essential feature of the 'new sentence,'" which is the disjunctive, linguistically attuned form most closely associated with Language poetry.[29] Silliman reads *Language* as a book of metapoetry in carefully lineated sentences, in which the skillful use of enjambment often makes subtle points about the self-contradictory operations of language: "Through his line breaks, suppressed verbs and numerous insertions of sentences apparently taken from other discourses," Spicer upsets the sentence's ability to predicate and to offer propositions about reality. "It is precisely in these nooks and crannies, gaps and lacunae," Silliman notes, "that the 'outside' is permitted finally to speak."[30]

★

Although the Language poets rebelled against spontaneity, devaluing it along deconstructive lines as a naïve and necessarily failed attempt to place the self ahead of language, another form of hermeticism at work in the poetry of the San Francisco Renaissance led to a rapprochement between the hermetic and the spontaneous strains. The practice of meditation and the invocation of Buddhism and other Asian concepts of nothingness and emptiness took root forcefully in the poetry of San Francisco and have continued to exert an influence on American encounters with Asian culture as part of rapidly expanding Pacific Rim exchanges. For example, one of the Language poets, Leslie Scalapino, uses the Buddhist concept of the essential emptiness of all phenomena to guide her in a performative poetry that continually fractures concepts and social realities, leaving her fruitfully vulnerable to "how phenomena appear to unfold" (the title of one of her books).[31] The history of Asian cultural inroads into California, whether through immigration or appropriation, is too vast even to outline, but it would be fair to say that San Francisco poets, such as Rexroth, Snyder, Kaufman, Ginsberg, Kerouac, Whalen, and Welch, carried Asian aesthetic and religious ideas forward in their poetry of the 1950s and 1960s and became important midcentury conduits for transpacific interactions. In San Francisco poetry, the Asian influence has given support to both spontaneity and hermeticism: spontaneity is regarded highly, for instance, in Zen Buddhism and in the Japanese arts that rely on it, while meditation and the study of Asian philosophical treatises can be seen as hermetic practices that require initiation and isolation. Of course, immersion in Asian philosophies did not obliterate earlier religious training or cultural proclivities in these poets. For instance, the impact of Buddhism was quite distinct on Snyder, Ginsberg, and Kerouac. Taking Kerouac's novel *The Dharma Bums* as evidence for this impact, it could be argued that Snyder's Zen is a Protestant Buddhism, laced with a healthy disdain for authority; that Ginsberg's (which expands later with his instruction into Tibetan Buddhism) is a Jewish Buddhism, based on practice more than belief and evincing a deep-seated sense of compassion; and that Kerouac's is a Catholic Buddhism, concerned chiefly with salvation and with social equality.

During the 1950s and 1960s, the figure most fully associated with the many influences of Asia was Gary Snyder. Raised in the Pacific Northwest and majoring in anthropology at Reed College in Portland, Oregon, Snyder moved to the Bay Area to learn Chinese poetics at the University of California at Berkeley. Shortly after the Six Gallery reading, at which he performed "A Berry Feast," Snyder embarked for Japan and spent a decade mainly pursuing Zen study in monasteries. Like Spicer, he contends that the purpose of poetry is not to reveal personality or to show off stylistic acumen but rather to disclose the world. His practice of Zen and study of Asian poetry contribute to a didactic poetics, in which (contra Spicer) seeing is prior to language: "There are poets who claim that their poems are made to show the world through the prism of language. Their project is worthy. There is also the work of seeing the world without any prism of language, and to bring that seeing into language. The latter has been the direction of most Chinese and Japanese poetry."[32] From Snyder's Buddhist perspective, the poetry of pure seeing takes place not through dictation from outside but through heightened attention to the precise contours of the present moment. His lifelong enthusiasm for mountain climbing, fed by early jobs as a logger and mountain lookout, joined with his studies of Chinese and Japanese poetry and Zen to make Snyder a pioneer in the transmission of Asian aesthetic and philosophical concepts to a White American audience. He also combined his outdoorsman ethos and the elevation of nature he learned from Asian aesthetics with an appreciation for Native American investments in landscape, thus becoming one of the earliest and most passionate spokesmen for the Ecology Movement that began in the 1960s.

In addition to Asian aesthetics, Snyder's main stylistic influences are Pound, Williams, Rexroth, and Robinson Jeffers. "A Berry Feast" displays these influences especially in its laconic style, vernacular diction, and heavy consonance. The latter is particularly striking in lines such as "Bronze bells at the throat / Bronze balls on the horns, the bright Oxen," in which Snyder draws from a number of earlier poetic techniques for emphasizing consonants: Pound's attempts to imitate the troubadours' effect of separating individual words by beginning and ending them with consonants; the partial elision of articles to speed up the pace, to separate words, and to emphasize imagery – also borrowed from Pound and from other translators of Chinese and Japanese poetry; and the Anglo-Saxon-based practice of alliteration employed by Pound and Jeffers.[33] The key consonant in "A Berry Feast" is *b*, which continually evokes the huckleberries that appear in each of the four sections of the poem, as well as their foremost consumer, the bear, whose intimate encounters with humans form one of the major themes of the poem: "Blackbear / eating berries, married / To a woman whose breasts bleed / From nursing the half-human cubs."[34] Although nearly all of the poetry of the San Francisco Renaissance is urban, most of Snyder's poetry is not. His work embodies a powerful attraction to natural beauty and solitary pursuits. The prominence of Zen, Native American, and wilderness strands in Snyder's life and work made him an object of reverence for a number of poets and an object of near worship for Jack Kerouac, who enshrined him in *The Dharma Bums* as its hero, Japhy Ryder. The fictional portrait of Snyder as an ascetic, studious, free-loving, anarchist, ecstatic mountain climber was extremely seductive as a model not only for the Beats but also for the hippies who would arrive in San Francisco in the mid-1960s. Snyder willingly took on the mantle of spokesperson for the hippies, promoting a vision of communal anarchism, ecstatic eroticism, and ecological activism that he hoped would bring North America into alignment with the often-suppressed indigenous values of the entire Pacific Rim.

The social vision that developed out of Beat culture and the San Francisco Renaissance united the spontaneous, performative strain with the hermetic, initiatory strain. This is true not only for Gary Snyder but also for many in the arts in postwar San Francisco. One manifestation of this shared aesthetic and social project has been called *"Semina* culture."[35] A journal consisting of collages, poems, and photographs on loose-leaf cards, *Semina* (1955–1964), was printed, stuffed into decorated envelopes, and mailed to friends by the artist Wallace Berman. The poets who took part in *Semina*, among them Duncan, Meltzer, McClure, Wieners, Lamantia, di Prima, and Kaufman, joined a circle of Beat artists, including Bruce Conner, Jess, George Herms, Jay DeFeo, Joan Brown, Dennis Hopper, and Berman himself in creating an aesthetic culture that became a way of life. As Duncan puts it, "We began to see ourselves as fashioning unnamed contexts, contexts of a new life way in the making, a secret mission."[36] The aesthetic components that went into fashioning this context include the vernacular compositional form of collage or assemblage, shared among both poets and artists, and a healthy regard for Surrealism as provoking psychological breakthroughs. All of these figures were fascinated by various forms of esoteric thought, religious mysticism, or drug experimentation as offering alternative realities amid Cold War conformism. Sexual nonconformity was paramount as well, whether in the form of bodily display or of queer confession and performance. If there was a "secret mission," it was a broadly anarchist one of overthrowing the mundane reality of the 1950s and early 1960s, substituting a transgressive, ecstatic mode of life. The assemblage art of San Francisco during this period was known as funk or junk art; much of it involved drawing together discarded or unremarked fragments (whether visual or verbal) from daily life in order to reveal "secret" meanings, insisting on the regenerative potential of everyday experience.

Although critics have separated spontaneous poets like Ginsberg and Kaufman from hermetic poets like Spicer and Duncan, the separation is based on distinctions that tend to break down when we take a more encompassing view. Ginsberg, for instance, saw his opposite number Spicer as engaged in a similar compositional style to his own. First, he notes the stated distinctions between them: Spicer "held a different vision of poetry. I think he had a thing that has nothing to do with Ego, messages come through the radio stations of the mind, so to speak, whereas I was thinking of the spontaneous mind."[37] Ginsberg was also aware of Spicer's critique of his practice: "He thought that my own method was much too involved with personal statement and ego: it's a legitimate objection." Although he acknowledges the conflict in their stances toward the personal and generously admits the force of Spicer's critique, Ginsberg doesn't feel that their poetic practices are "actually very different in operation." Regardless of how inspiration arrives, "as a practical matter of composition" there is a basic similarity: they both bring fragments of obsessive interest into collage poems marked by unanticipated juxtapositions.[38] Whether Ginsberg, Spicer, and others in San Francisco create Surrealist-inspired collages via spontaneous improvisation, following the model of jazz, or via hermetic practices of dictation or meditation, all of the poets have designs on disrupting the status quo. They mean poetry as "the living water" to burst through what Rexroth calls the "dense crust of custom over American cultural life."[39] To a remarkable extent they have succeeded.

Notes

1. Brenda Knight, *Women of the Beat Generation: The Writers, Artists and Muses at the Heart of a Revolution* (San Francisco: Conari Press, 1996); Richard Peabody (ed.), *A Different Beat: Writings by Women of the Beat Generation* (London: Serpent's Tail, 1997).

2. Donald Allen (ed.), *The New American Poetry, 1945–1960* (New York: Grove, 1960), pp. xi–xiii.

3. Allen Ginsberg, *Howl: Original Draft Facsimile*, ed. Barry Miles (New York: Harper and Row, 1986), p. 156.

4. Robert Duncan, *Faust Foutu: A Comic Masque* (1960; Barrytown, N.Y.: Station Hill, 1985).

5. Lewis Ellingham and Kevin Killian, *Poet Be Like God: Jack Spicer and the San Francisco Renaissance* (Hanover, N.H.: Wesleyan University Press, 1988), p. 62.

6. Jack Kerouac, *The Dharma Bums* (1958; New York: Penguin, 2006), pp. 6–7, 9–11.

7. Ginsberg, *Howl*, p. 3.

8. John Suiter, *Poets on the Peaks: Gary Snyder, Philip Whalen and Jack Kerouac in the North Cascades* (Washington, D.C.: Counterpoint, 2002), pp. 153–54.

9. Ginsberg, *Howl*, p. xii.

10. Jonah Raskin, *American Scream: Allen Ginsberg's Howl and the Making of the Beat Generation* (Berkeley: University of California Press, 2004), pp. 153–54.

11. T. S. Eliot, *The Waste Land: A Facsimile and Transcript of the Original Drafts*, ed. Valerie Eliot (New York: Harcourt, 1971); Ginsberg, *Howl*.

12. *Evergreen Review* 1:2 (1957), table of contents.

13. Kenneth Rexroth, "San Francisco Letter," *Evergreen Review* 1:2 (1957), p. 5; reprinted in Kenneth Rexroth, *World Outside the Window: The Selected Essays of Kenneth Rexroth*, ed. Bradford Morrow (New York: New Directions, 1987), pp. 57–64, 57, 58, 63.

14. Rexroth, "San Francisco Letter," pp. 5–14.

15. Kenneth Rexroth, "Noretorp-Noretsyh," *Evergreen Review* 1:2 (1957), pp. 15–16.

16. Jack Kerouac, "Essentials of Spontaneous Prose," in Allen Ginsberg, *Deliberate Prose: Selected Essays 1952–1995*, ed. Bill Morgan (New York: HarperCollins, 2000), pp. 344–45.

17. Lawrence Ferlinghetti, *A Coney Island of the Mind* (New York: New Directions, 1958).

18. Michael McClure, *Ghost Tantras* (San Francisco: City Lights, 1967); Ray Manzarek and Michael McClure, *Piano Poems: Live in San Francisco*, audio CD (Oglio, 2012).

19. Gregory Corso, *Gasoline* (San Francisco: City Lights, 1958), p. 11.

20. Bob Kaufman, *Cranial Guitar: Selected Poems*, ed. Gerald Nicosia (Minneapolis: Coffee House, 1996), pp. 107–08.

21. Federico García Lorca, *Poet in New York*, trans. Greg Simon and Steven F. White, ed. Christopher Maurer, rev. ed. (New York: Farrar, Straus, Giroux, 1998), p. 20.

22. Kaufman, *Cranial Guitar*, p. 128.

23. Kaufman, *Cranial Guitar*, p. 139.

24. Ginsberg, *Howl*, pp. 185–86.

25. Robert Duncan, *Caesar's Gate: Poems 1949–50* (1955; Berkeley: Sand Dollar, 1972), pp. xv, xxii.

26. Duncan, *Caesar's Gate*, pp. 44–46.

27. Jack Spicer, *My Vocabulary Did This to Me: The Collected Poetry of Jack Spicer*, ed. Peter Gizzi and Kevin Killian (Middletown, Conn.: Wesleyan University Press, 2008), p. 107. This collection will be cited in the text as *MVD*.

28. Jack Spicer, *The House That Jack Built: The Collected Lectures of Jack Spicer*, ed. Peter Gizzi (Middletown, Conn.: Wesleyan University Press, 1998), p. 138. This collection will be cited in the text as *HJB*.

29. Ron Silliman, *The New Sentence* (New York: Roof, 1989), p. 151.

30. Silliman, *The New Sentence*, p. 165.

31. Leslie Scalapino, *How Phenomena Appear to Unfold* (Elmwood, Conn.: Potes and Poets, 1989).

32. Gary Snyder, *Riprap and Cold Mountain Poems* (San Francisco: Four Seasons, 1965), p. 67.

33. Gary Snyder, *No Nature: New and Selected Poems* (New York: Pantheon, 1992), p. 86.

34. Snyder, *No Nature*, p. 84.

35. Michael Duncan and Kristine McKenna (eds.), *Semina Culture: Wallace Berman and His Circle* (New York: D.A.P.; Santa Monica, Calif.: Santa Monica Museum, 2005), pp. 9–15.

36. Robert Duncan, *A Selected Prose*, ed. Robert Bertholf (New York: New Directions, 1995), p. 198.

37. Ellingham and Killian, *Poet Be Like God*, p. 58.

38. Ellingham and Killian, *Poet Be Like God*, p. 58.

39. Rexroth, "San Francisco Letter," p. 57.

Chapter 37

The New York School

BRIAN M. REED

Donald Allen's anthology *The New American Poetry: 1945–1960* (1960) first introduced a national audience to a "generation" of "younger poets," "long awaited but only slowly recognized," that he claimed represents the "true continuers of the modern movement in American poetry."[1] He labeled one subset of this new literary phenomenon "the New York Poets." The name was rough and ready; it simply designated where most of the relevant writers lived at the time the anthology saw print. Allen explained that John Ashbery (b. 1927), Kenneth Koch (1925–2002), and Frank O'Hara (1926–1966) "first met at Harvard where they were associated with the Poets' Theatre," but this core group "migrated to New York in the early fifties" and was gradually joined by other figures, most importantly Barbara Guest (1920–2006) and James Schuyler (1923–1991).[2]

Later critics have not shared Allen's understated approach to the topic. A year after the appearance of *The New American Poetry*, John Myers – whose Tibor de Nagy Gallery had already published books by Ashbery, Guest, Koch, O'Hara, and Schuyler – rechristened the circle the "New York School of Poets." He wanted to elevate a cluster of friends into a full-scale literary movement. As Ashbery recalls, "Myers ... thought that the prestige of New York School Painting" – by which he meant abstract expressionists such as Jackson Pollock, Willem de Kooning, Mark Rothko, and Franz Kline – "might rub off on 'his' poets; he coined the term in an article in the California magazine *Nomad* in 1961, and it has stuck."[3] Indeed, it has become one of the principal *points de repère* in the landscape of post–World War II American literary history. If critics declare that a particular poet is affiliated with or has been influenced by the New York School, their auditors are sure to nod knowingly. Moreover, one will frequently find mentions of multiple generations of the New York School, as if it were possible to draw a genealogical chart tracing the descendants of Ashbery and company down unto the third and fourth begats. Significantly, these New York School scions need not live in the five boroughs, nor even be

American by birth or residence. They are implicitly credited with inheriting a bundle of traits identified closely with one or more precursors.

These ways of talking are liable to mystify the uninitiated, not least because the term "New York School" itself can be confusing. The word "school" falsely suggests a well-defined shared agenda. No such slate of uniform goals existed. While some of the poets did write pieces that could conceivably be called manifestos, they tend, like O'Hara's "Personism" (1959) and Ashbery's "The Invisible Avant-Garde" (1968), to be idiosyncratic exercises that combine wicked satire and coy shenanigans with illuminating advice. The poets' careers also diverge too greatly to imagine them working consistently in concert. O'Hara died in a freak beach vehicle accident on Fire Island in 1966, whereas Schuyler's first major collection, *Freely Espousing*, dates to 1969. Guest arguably came into her own only in the 1980s, and Ashbery continues to write stellar work well into the twenty-first century.[4] The attribution "New York" can also be as misleading as "school." The poets only lived together in the city for a relatively brief time in the 1950s. Ashbery, for example, had left for Paris even before Allen's anthology came out, and Guest was ultimately to become more influential as a Californian than as a Manhattanite.

What can one, then, say about these poets as a group? Even if they lack the into-the-breach élan of the Italian Futurists, the Russian Constructivists, and other early twentieth-century avant-gardes, the members of Allen's and Myers's original short lists of writers were nonetheless good friends whose early work was shaped by the same milieu. As already stated, Koch, O'Hara, and Ashbery knew one another as undergraduates; they later met Guest via *Semi-Colon* (1953–1956), a poetry newsletter put out by the Tibor de Nagy Gallery. Schuyler was O'Hara's roommate for several stretches during the 1950s; Ashbery and Schuyler collaborated on a novel, *Nest of Ninnies* (1969); and Koch, Ashbery, and Schuyler each edited one or two issues of the little magazine *Locus Solus* (1961–1962). They all shared a proclivity for a distinctive but eccentric and cosmopolitan blend of literary models: Francophone poets such as Rimbaud, Apollinaire, and Pierre Reverdy; European Dadaists and Surrealists such as André Breton and Tristan Tzara; British modernist masters of dialogue such as Ivy Compton-Burnett, Ronald Firbank, and Henry Green; and three Anglophone authors whose poetics one might have thought wholly immiscible, W. H. Auden, William Carlos Williams, and Gertrude Stein. The New York School poets were all involved, too, in experimental theater, and they wrote a number of plays, among them O'Hara's *Try! Try!* (1951), Ashbery's *The Heroes* (1952), Koch's *George Washington Crossing the Delaware* (1962), and Guest's *The Office* (1963). And all five poets were passionate about the fine arts. In addition to acquiring a connoisseur's knowledge of classical music, opera, jazz, ballet, modern dance, and avant-garde cinema, they had contact with composers such as John Cage and Morton Feldman; filmmakers such as Rudy Burckhardt and Jack Smith; and dance-world luminaries such as George Balanchine, Edwin Denby, Lincoln Kirstein, and James Waring.

Then there is the connection to the visual arts. In addition to rubbing elbows with the marquee abstract expressionists in the Cedar Tavern, the Club, and elsewhere, the poets cultivated close relationships with, and even collaborated with, a younger cohort of New York painters that included Norman Bluhm, Jane Freilicher, Michael Goldberg, Grace Hartigan, Joan Mitchell, Fairfield Porter, and Larry Rivers. They continued to be au courant, too, in the years 1955 to 1965, as Jasper Johns, Robert Rauschenberg, and Andy Warhol wreaked havoc in the art world; each of the poets tested literary analogs to neo-Dada assemblage and pop appropriation in their own verse. Four of them – Ashbery, Guest, O'Hara, and Schuyler – contributed essays to *Art News*. Ashbery also wrote art reviews for the *New York Herald-Tribune*; Guest published in *Arts Magazine* and *Art in America*; O'Hara worked his way up to curating major shows for New York's Museum of Modern Art (MoMA); and Schuyler, too, spent six years as a curator at the MoMA. To learn more about the New York School's involvement with the art world, one should consult the collections of all four poets' prose about art, above all O'Hara's *Art Chronicles*.[5]

*

There is no such thing as a representative New York School poem. The New York School poets are too different, and they change too much over the course of their careers, for any one lyric to bear such a burden. This diversity, however, does not preclude family resemblances. Few good New York School poems would ever be confused with lyrics from the same years written in rival styles, such as Black Mountain projectivism, Beat oral athleticism, Black Arts populism, and confessional pyrotechnics.

The poets share a delight in the messy complexity of urban life, a desire to challenge norms governing sexuality and gender, a suspicion of grand schemes and totalizing systems, a faith in self-reinvention, and a belief that bliss can be found in the here and now. Unsurprisingly, given their biographies, they are also drawn to ekphrasis, the re-creation of a visual artwork by verbal means. They test every available means of achieving it, too, from learned commentary (Ashbery's verse essay "Self-Portrait in a Convex Mirror" [1975] even includes block quotations) to manipulations of a poem's layout (the two rectangular arrangements of text in O'Hara's "Joseph Cornell" [1955] echo Cornell's signature use of wooden boxes in his sculptures).

Their most frequently pursued ekphrastic strategy is probably *homology*, the attempt to coax language to approximate what visual artists can achieve in their own media of choice. Guest's "Poetess" (1973), for instance, strives to evoke a small Surrealist gouache of the same name by Joan Miró that is full of bold primary colors and biomorphic curved shapes: "A dollop is dolloping / her a scoop is pursuing / flee vain ignots."[6] The words "dollop" and "scoop" suggest how Miró applied paint, whereas "pursuing" and "flee" convey the dynamism of the composition. The phrase "dollop is dolloping" is more than a tautology; it captures one word morphing into another. Guest hints that Miró's painting did not copy something in the external world but rather was generated by riffing imaginatively on a few basic shapes and gestures. Finally, the neologism "ignots" is like one of Miró's parti-colored amoebas or flattened blobs. Although the term might call to mind more familiar things (for example, the words "ingots" and "ignorance" and the name "Ignaz"), it nonetheless remains stubbornly, uncannily an independent entity.

Ekphrastic verse of this variety might push at the accepted boundaries of reason and logic, but that, significantly, is also its attraction. One learns what happens when divergent means of communication are forced to find common ground. Collectively, the New York School is fascinated with the countless ways that language functions, and from poem to poem and even from line to line they will switch approaches, now tediously exploring documentary realism, now spouting glossolalia, now launching into passionate arias. Like the artists that they admire, these authors dramatize their inquiry into the very tools, conditions, concepts, limits, and processes that make self-expression possible. In doing so, they frequently concentrate on the local texture of verse, churning out only tenuously connected quotable quotes or proposing quaint, profound, bizarre, or incomprehensible juxtapositions. As far as they are concerned, a poem can begin anywhere, go anywhere at any time, and end anywhere. They do not hold that a poet has a responsibility to pursue an idea, a description, or a narrative in a sustained, rewarding manner, nor must he or she make sure that all details prove pertinent to the artwork's unfolding. Readers, in short, must set aside New Critical dicta concerning architectural structure and forget the Romantic ideal of an organic coherence in which parts and wholes align pleasingly and harmoniously. They must steel themselves for sudden, unpredictable vertiginous shifts. Even veteran poetry critics can suffer whiplash.

Why peruse such demanding verse when there are surely less head-spinning alternatives? One reason: It is surprisingly pleasurable. Readers can usually discern and appreciate patterns or trajectories operative if not throughout then within or across smaller segments (repetition and variation is especially common). More importantly, the New York School believes that a poet can be serious about exploring the outer boundaries of artistic possibility without necessarily producing dour, gloomy work. A hallmark of their poetry is its whimsical free association, outlandish puns, and other sorts of brash wordplay that one more readily associates with stand-up comedy than highfalutin' poesy. Kenneth Koch's "A Poem of the Forty-Eight States" (1969), for example, opens with a stanza ostensibly about Kentucky, but he appears to know nothing about the place beyond its nickname, "the Bluegrass State":

> O Kentucky! my parents were driving
> Near blue grass when you became
> For me the real contents of a glass
> Of water also the first nozzle of a horse
> The bakery truck floating down the street
> The young baboon woman walking without a brace
> Over a fiord [7]

Here "grass" suggests "glass" via rhyme, and "blue" plus "glass" leads Koch to think about water. He then forges gaily on, "water" becoming first spray from a "nozzle" and then flooding waters rushing "down the street" and finally a "fiord." He ornaments this chain of word association with other tropes ("nozzle" leads to "horse" via the double entendre "hose"); further rhymes ("glass" suggests the suppressed term "ass," which Koch replaces, ahem, by "baboon woman"); and plain old slapstick lunacy (a "bakery truck" floating away).

Such writing can seem pointless, the literary equivalent of doodling. When faced with a New York School poem, though, one should never prejudge what constitutes *making a point*. True, Koch might not be describing a real location, and he teaches no immediately obvious moral, ethical, or political message. He is, however, relying on his readers to have a rudimentary knowledge of American poetic history. He mocks the vatic swagger of would-be American bards from Walt Whitman to Allen Ginsberg who write as if they are speaking on behalf of a country that is, in fact, exceedingly large and diverse, well beyond the capacity of any one poet to comprehend as a whole. Such bards, Koch cheekily informs us, have to improvise and playact like mad if they are to live up to their implicit impossible claim to be all-knowing about all of America. At the same time – a twist that raises the work above a cheap shot – Koch is also poking fun at his own provincialism, his utter lack of experience with the goings-on outside Manhattan. What is Kentucky to him, or he to Kentucky? His comedy, in short, is fairly sophisticated. It depends on a reader's awareness of precursors and intertexts, and its tone is slippery, combining satire of others with self-deflationary gestures.

New York School humor can be hilarious, infuriating, vaudevillian, adolescent, ambivalent, un-PC, and groan-a-minute bad, but it generally serves ends beyond laughter, often ones that self-reflexively concern the nature and function of poetry. Readers have to be prepared to think not simply about a lyric's contents, that is, what it says denotatively and connotatively, but also about the exemplarity of a particular statement. That is, what kind of writing would one normally expect to encounter under these circumstances, and how does this particular gesture of refusal or dissidence or amateurism challenge business as usual? Why does this passage or line register as indecorous or purposeless? What do these prerational judgments reveal about a person's underlying values and assumptions?

Closely allied with the New York School's delight in whimsy is its fascination with games and game play. If Romantic poets stereotypically wait for nature, God, or other agents to inspire them to write, a New York School poet is more likely to begin composing by flipping coins, seizing on strange found texts, running through musical scales, or posing crossword-puzzle-like verbal challenges. For instance, Ashbery wrote "Into the Dusk-Charged Air" (1966) based on the rule that every line must name a river: "The Liffey is full of sewage, / Like the Seine, but unlike / The brownish-yellow Dordogne. / Mountains hem in the Colorado."[8] He manages to keep the poem going for 150 lines, a testament to his ingenuity. Moreover, he adds details (a movement through the seasons climaxing with winter, for example) that transform a brainstorming exercise into an engrossing read.

On occasion, New York School writers push to drastic extremes the sorts of wordplay to be found in "Poem of the Forty-Eight States" and "Into the Dusk-Charged Air." Partly, they do so to explore what happens, what principles still function, if a poet suspends referentiality, and sometimes grammar too, almost completely. What is left: Song? Flashes or fragments of imagery? The play of a sensuous imagination? In such cases, their writing approaches pure abstraction. Koch's *When the Sun Tries to Go On* (1969) is a virtuosic example, extending to more than sixty pages:

> Hats! hacks! heads! Is buzz. An
> Cow-oyster, dollars! alimony of disease-art-lemons, O
> Poo, the knack of name's plate's poodle, "Ends" is
> Sang, "House! mate of jim-jam controlling puce

Teak!" Out! Badder, yell-place and nick and socker-
Glow, each is and, joyous handlike knickers
Cuckoo. "How could you have gone, bitter
Roistering hint glove task phone 'ache' factory hoop device?"[9]

Although such gleeful babble cannot be paraphrased, one can trace different threads of sound or association that keep it from degenerating into total chaos. This passage begins with *h*'s and exclamations ("Hats! hacks! heads!"). The exclamations, though, do eventually give way to a rhetorical question, even as *h*'s recede and first plosive *p*'s ("Poo … plate's poodle … puce … place") and then hard *c*'s and *k*'s move to the fore ("Teak … nick and socker … handlike knickers / Cuckoo"). The last line in this passage tries out a march of heavy monosyllables ("hint glove task phone 'ache'"), a series of emphatic spondees that designedly contrast with a prior equally heavily accented string of trochees ("joyous handlike knickers / Cuckoo"). Koch aspires to give his readers an absorbing spectacle: the flashy, rapid, inventive deployment of verse's nonsemantic resources.

Ashbery's second book, *The Tennis Court Oath* (1962), is especially well known for its turn toward an antirealist agrammatical lyricism. Some poems of this type, such as "Rain," are highly evocative. Their verbal pointillism suggests story lines, landscapes, characters, and events that never quite hove fully into view:

> At night
> Curious – I'd seen this tall girl
>
> I urge the deep prune of the mirror
> That stick she carries
> The book – a trap
> The facts have hinged on my reply
> Calm
> Hat against the sky
> Eyes of forest[10]

One wants such moments to lead somewhere, to culminate in a love story, a mystery, or some other tried-and-true genre. Instead, as with *When the Sun Tries to Go On*, the words tend to slip away, leaving trails of sound instead of sense (*c*'s and *k*'s again – "Curious … stick … carries … book … facts … Calm … sky"). There is another kind of disappearing act, too, an Ashbery trademark: memorable but ultimately empty figures of speech ("the deep prune of the mirror"). Other, thornier poems in *The Tennis Court Oath* recall Stein at her most obdurate: "Neutral daylight sitting things / Like it. It woofed. It liked it.

// Ordeal a home and / My lake and sat down.”[11] For Ashbery – and for the members of the New York School of the 1950s and 1960s more generally – this rigorously antimimetic mode of writing represents an asymptote. They would repeat but not exceed its challenges to conventional English usage. For half a century, *The Tennis Court Oath* has served as a litmus test. For some readers, it strays too far in the direction of nonsense and hence represents a wrong turn in an otherwise glorious career. Other readers, more at home with unanchored wordplay, consider the book to be Ashbery's true contribution to literary history, a leap into new expressive territory akin to Arnold Schönberg's break with tonality in *Das Buch der Hängenden Gärten*, op. 15 (1908–1909).

★

After *The Tennis Court Oath*, Ashbery, like the other New York School poets, would continue to employ nonnormative syntax on occasion (especially dangling modifiers, ambiguous antecedents, run-on sentences, violations of the sequence of tenses, and anacoluthon). Although he did not cease to experiment with form, he did shift his focus. Like Guest, Koch, O'Hara, and Schuyler, he made tone central to his innovative poetics. "Tone" is notoriously difficult to define and describe, but it is shorthand for, among other things, the stance that writers adopt toward both their material and their audience. New York School poets will disregard decorum, alter perspective, provide contradictory evidence, mix stylistic levels, and otherwise write in such a way that it becomes difficult to say whether they are being sincere, arch, jokey, serious, frivolous, vacuous, wise, or all of the above at the same time. The consequent tonal instability – a reader's uncertainty regarding who is speaking and why – is one reason why the work of the New York School can still feel remarkably contemporary. Its self-awareness concerning the scene of writing translates into a theatrical poetry in which speech is never natural or unmediated. Poetic *voice*, they believe, is a construct that produces calculated effects; it is not a unique innate property would-be poets cultivate en route to becoming authentic writers.

The opening lines of Ashbery's "The Other Tradition" (1977) can illustrate his mature style and the role that tone plays in it:

> They all came, some wore sentiments
> Emblazoned on T-shirts, proclaiming the lateness
> Of the hour, and indeed the sun slanted its rays
> Through branches of Norfolk Island pine as though
> Politely clearing its throat, and all ideas settled
> In a fuzz of dust under trees when it's drizzling.[12]

The poem begins dramatically in medias res, but who "came" and why? We learn only that "some" were wearing "T-shirts." Yes, he does specify that the shirts have "sentiments / Emblazoned" on them, but we do not hear what those sentiments are, nor do we discover whether we are supposed to interpret "emblazoned" as referring to images, text, or some blend of the two. No matter; the shirts somehow inform us about "the lateness / Of the hour." At this point, the story line begins to feel curiously unmoored, a bit like an updated version of Tennyson's *Idylls of the King* (1885), with its glittering heraldry; its effusive, vague declarations of heartfelt passion; and its pervasive mood of belatedness. The bookish transition "indeed" prolongs the intimations of an old-fashioned, high-mannered style, and then Ashbery elegantly alludes to Emily Dickinson's "There's a certain Slant of light" (1862). His sun's "slanted" rays, however, do not cause "Despair" or deliver "Heavenly Hurt."[13] Weirdly, his afternoon light "[p]olitely [clears] its throat," acting like a functionary interrupting a meeting. Equally jarring is the next image, of "ideas" washed out of the air by drizzle and left lying in "a fuzz of dust." What ideas? Whose? The word "fuzz" is just slightly wrong as well, rendering a bit too concrete the cliché "bite the dust." The tenses go haywire as well. The clause "when it's drizzling" does not match up with "slanted its rays" and "all ideas settled." Has the speaker become careless or forgetful? While the setting of this passage is conventionally Romantic – a forest at dusk – within this single meandering sentence the language careens between apt and dodgy, imprecise ("all," "some") and exact ("Norfolk Island pines"). Ultimately, one has to say that Ashbery leaves readers uncertain whether he endorses or mocks the nineteenth-century rhetoric that he echoes.

The modulations of tone in New York School poetry tend to raise vexing dilemmas instead of offering resolutions. Audiences are encouraged to speculate how and whether a poem might obliquely address the relevant issues, but in the end there might be no answer, or only a provisional one. A preferred New York School target for this unsettling treatment is the boundary between high and low culture. Their lyrics higgledy-piggledy refer to topics such as Hollywood movies, modernist symphonies, musical theater, French highbrow fiction, tawdry pornography, Renaissance epics, and animated cartoons. Common are poems such as Koch's "En l'An Trentiesme de Mon Eage" (2000), which might have a professor-friendly allusive title (here quoting the first line of François Villon's *Le Testament* [1489]), and which might genuflect, as this poem does, to canonical poets such as Swinburne, but which nonetheless also spotlight less filling fare, in this case comic strips such as *Terry and the Pirates* (1934–1973). Adopting the same impassioned tone toward both elite and popular culture can leave a writer's taste level in doubt, as well as lead to reservations concerning his or her fundamental aesthetic values. When O'Hara gushes about James Dean, when Ashbery pens a sestina about Popeye, when Schuyler elegizes Janis Joplin, and when Guest names a poem "Jaffa Juice" (1960) after a British soft drink, one has to wonder whether these wear-their-erudition-on-the-sleeve poets can truly be all that enthusiastic about their subject matter. Are they temporarily slumming? Laughing at uptight snobs – or at bourgeois Middle America? How would one ever know for sure?

The word "postmodern" is regularly used to describe New York School poetry. The term has many meanings, of course, but critics often have in mind its poets' games with tone, in particular their disorienting traipsing back and forth across the high–low divide. Fredric Jameson, for example, singles out Ashbery as "one of the most significant postmodern artists" in part because his verse refuses to settle into a straightforwardly imitative or parodic mode.[14] Instead he reprocesses a myriad of other discourses in ways that are eerily unmarked. One cannot decide whether he is engaging in pastiche on autopilot, subtle satire, or incisive critique. Does he intentionally stud his verse with advertising clichés, sugary sentimentality, and empty ideological formulae? Why do his sentences often sound freestanding, as if written by different people at different times? Jameson contrasts such equivocal later twentieth-century work with earlier masterpieces such as Edvard Munch's *The Scream* (1893) that do not hesitate to take a definite, strong stand against the ills and horrors of modernization.[15]

Mutlu Konuk Blasing argues that New York School poetry restlessly declines to endorse any stance that implies direct or privileged access to "transcendent truth." Those poses, though, she goes on to state, are not so much discarded as made newly available for rhetorical play.[16] In other words, all speech acts are exposed as motivated artifice, and the poets permit themselves to scramble, invert, reinvent, and otherwise tinker with every available discourse without respecting any of them as sacred or outside the limits. New York School poets often exalt in this freedom by making artifice and artificiality a central theme in their work. The title of Schuyler's "Fabergé" (1969), for example, calls to mind the jeweled and enameled eggs made by the House of Fabergé from 1885 to 1917, especially the exquisite Russian imperial Easter eggs. The poem goes on, appropriately enough, to talk about gemstones, but each new mineral becomes an opportunity for a new flight of fancy: "I keep my diamond necklace in a sparkling pond for invisibility. / My rubies in Algae Pond are like an alligator's adenoids. / My opals – the evening cloud slipped in my pocket and I felt it and vice versa."[17] The first line here is a play on the idea of hiding in plain sight, and then the second elaborates on the idea of jewels in water by identifying another kind of pond (one covered with algae) that could conceivably hide not translucent diamonds but "rubies" as red and large (and ideally as well-protected) as an alligator's tonsils. Changing tacks, Schuyler then compares "opals" to being felt up by a cloud, a unique but, it appears, heavenly brand of seduction. The tone of "Fabergé" combines the ebullience of a collector and the arrogance of the writer who presumes readers can keep up with a swiftly leaping intellect. Schuyler is singing the praises of (and, of course, simultaneously poking fun at) his ability to generate images, ideas, and scenarios as glittering, seductive, and treasured as rare crystals. Losing confidence in transcendent truths can be a prelude to discovering the intoxicating power of one's own creative capacities.

The New York School writers each have their own shorthand for the thrill of losing oneself in the delights of artifice. Guest refers to far-off countries, Mediterranean or Eastern European, that exist for her more as fantasy lands than as actual historical states: Morocco, Illyria, Egypt, Tsarist Russia, Turkey, and above all Byzantium, whose rich silks she writes movingly about in her essay "Mysteriously Defining Mystery: Byzantine Proposals for Poetry" (1986). For Ashbery, pageants, masques, tapestries, and sculpture will do, although architecture is perhaps his favorite, as in "Vetiver" (1987), in which he makes his habitual equation between buildings and poems unusually overt: "The pen was cool to the touch. / The staircase swept upward / Through fragmented garlands, keeping the melancholy / Already distilled in letters of the alphabet."[18] O'Hara, a talented trained pianist, is drawn to music, both lushly Romantic (Rachmaninoff) and austerely modern (Schönberg), but painting is truly his idée fixe. Whenever paint, painters, or paintings show up in his writing, these images announce an increased attentiveness to the decisions, processes, and stakes that inform every effort at making art.

The emphasis on affectation and mannered artifice in New York School poetry, one must add, coexists with what can appear to be a countervailing tendency, namely, immersion in everyday particulars. While it might be hard to miss the self-reflexive dimension to a piece titled "On Seeing Larry Rivers' *Washington Crossing the Delaware* at the Museum of Modern Art" (1956), O'Hara is in fact better known for his so-called "I do this, I do that" poems, which recount in simple, direct fashion where he goes, what he sees, and what he purchases, often during a lunch hour:

> I walk up the muggy street beginning to sun
> and have a hamburger and a malted and buy

> an ugly NEW WORLD WRITING to see what the poets
> in Ghana are doing these days.[19]

Schuyler, too, builds numerous lyrics out of what can seem like straightforward observations:

> The dogs are barking. In
> the studio music plays
> and Bob and Darragh paint.
> I sit scribbling in a little
> notebook at a garden table,
> too hot in a heavy shirt[20]

Schuyler also names numerous poems after the date on which they were
written – "3/23/66," "Dec. 28, 1974," "October 5, 1981" – and otherwise uses
titles to indicate the setting where both watching and writing took place – "En
Route to Southampton," "4404 Stanford," and "Noon Office." In such diary-
like poetry, artistry can at first be notable chiefly in its absence.

This way of writing is not, however, offered as an escape from artifice –
quite the opposite. It teaches that mundane sights and events can provoke
aesthetic responses that, although different in kind and intensity from, say,
reading Ariosto's *Orlando Furioso* (1532) or viewing a painting by Ingres, are
nonetheless quite real. "I do this, I do that" poems demonstrate that intensified inspection of each moment as it passes causes speakers to pause over and
marvel at things that might otherwise escape their notice. And these feelings
of wonder can translate into bursts of joyful rhetoric, as in Guest's "On the
Way to Dumbarton Oaks" (1960):

> The air! The colonial air! The walls, the brick,
> this November thunder! The clouds Atlanticking,
> Canadianing, Alaska snowclouds,
> tunnel and sleigh, urban and mountain routes!   (*BGC*, p. 12)

As always with a New York School poem, the tone at such moments is trickier
than a quick read-through might suggest. The naïve pleasure here of watching clouds form and reform as they scud across the sky (all! those! exclamation! points!) is undermined by grace notes of sophisticated self-awareness.
Dumbarton Oaks, after all, is a center in Washington, D.C., dedicated to the
study of ancient and medieval Byzantium, and Guest's transposition of "colonial" from D.C.'s architecture to the heavens ("The colonial air!") prepares a
reader to think about empires, ancient and modern. She then draws not on
nature but on culture to provide metaphors to describe roiling clouds (Canada,

Alaska, sleighs, tunnels, roads). People constrain the world, she hints, by using political fictions and merely human creations as standards by which to measure, and to rein in, its boundlessness and its glories. Tracking how a New York School poet describes a scene or a series of actions, even when such scrutiny might appear to verge on overinterpretation, often deepens into a lesson about phenomenology, more specifically, about the kinds of prerational, prejudicial, and ideological factors that shape and filter one's perceptions of quotidian goings-on.

The desire to record the texture of ephemeral everyday life – and an accompanying puckish impulse to provoke readers to question the whole purpose of such an endeavor – reaches its deadpan extreme in lyrics such as Ashbery's "Grand Galop" (1976), which incorporates verbatim a school menu from a newspaper that the poet picked up during a tour of the Midwest: "Today's lunch is Spanish omelet, lettuce and tomato salad, / Jello, milk and cookies. Tomorrow's: sloppy joe on a bun, / Scalloped corn, stewed tomatoes, rice pudding, and milk."[21] A reader stumbles over passages of this kind because of their ordinariness. Why put such neutral language into a poem? Can the imagination redeem or transfigure it? Or are readers supposed to stop and think for a moment about routine existence, the welter of undistinguished things and happenings that one normally overlooks? The dilemma recalls the challenge that Pop Art posed during the early 1960s. Is a can of tomato soup or a box of scouring pads really truly a worthy subject for a contemporary visual artist? By framing and presenting an audience with subject matter generally considered too banal for artistic treatment, the New York School poets again draw attention to the problem of artifice, this time by probing its zero degree, the boundary between art and nonart. Somewhat paradoxically, they manage to elevate this investigation into a compelling species of lyricism.

*

How does one read a New York School poem? The process can be compared to looking at a still life by Paul Cézanne (1839–1906). Seeing an apple on the canvas is only a starting point. One must then ask how, specifically, that apple looks, as well as how the artist has played within and against conventions and expectations when rendering it in oil. A viewer should reflect carefully, too, on the experience of interacting with the artwork, noting the course, character, and outcome of that experience. Such an interpretive practice is not, it must be emphasized, dryly formalist. How, why, when, and what we see (and read) are among the most pressing political, moral, historical, and cultural questions anyone could pose.

When applied to New York School poems, labels such as "postmodern," "avant-garde," and "experimental" are, more often than not, ways of conveying the shock of encountering writing that treats mimesis – the imitation of reality – as only one tool, and certainly not a privileged one, within a poet's utility kit. The sophistication of this position, and its many dizzying literary, philosophical, and political ramifications, helps explain why a small circle of friends, first brought to national attention by a countercultural anthology, has over the last half century proved to be such a spectacular success among tweedy academics and other establishment gatekeepers. Ashbery and Koch have won Bollingen Prizes; Ashbery and Schuyler have won Pulitzers; Ashbery and O'Hara have won National Book Awards; and Ashbery and Schuyler have been Fellows of the American Academy of Poets. Rafts of scholarly books and articles have appeared since 1975, and the rate of their arrival seems to be increasing, not tapering off.[22] Over the last decade there has been a sustained effort, too, to make as much of the poets' writings as widely and easily available as possible.[23] Since the Berlin Wall came down in 1989, humanists have been reevaluating the Cold War era, and, at least among poetry critics and readers of poetry, the New York School has retrospectively taken on unexpected prominence.

One could argue that the group's reputation has also benefited to an unusual degree from the succession of trends in literary criticism over the last half century. During the 1950s and 1960s, the New York School's radical rethinking and loosening of poetic form appealed to readers constitutionally averse to the dumbed-down New Criticism prevalent at the time in schools and universities. The popularization of poststructuralism and deconstruction in the 1970s and 1980s similarly prepared a new generation to appreciate a highly performative poetics that takes nothing for granted about language or representation. The popularization of queer theory in the early 1990s again seems to have served the same ends. One can read Ashbery, O'Hara, and Schuyler as pursuing a deconstructive approach to sexuality in which assertions of gay identity are present but countered and complicated by wild, discursive mashups and other disconcerting rhetorical means of troubling received sociocultural categories.

Turning from the overall picture to individual cases, however, such a narrative of lucky convergence between New York School poetics and academic criticism is hard to sustain across the board. The poets' reception histories and their relative statuses over time vary greatly, and they include dramatic ups and downs. In comparison to his friends, for example, O'Hara had an almost immediate impact. Intimately friendly with a remarkable number of talented people, he inspired, provoked, and cajoled them into producing inventive, high-quality work. At the center of the New York art and poetry scenes, he was able to leave his mark through wit, banter, and scorn on an entire generation. After his premature death in 1966, he quickly became a legend, even a bit of a saint, in the circles in which he had traveled. Within a decade, his admirers had assembled and published most of his uncollected writings. The sheer amount of them was a revelation. O'Hara had always been laid-back about publication, and during his lifetime only three slim collections had appeared in print – *Meditations in an Emergency* (1957), *Lunch Poems* (1964), and *Love Poems (Tentative Title)* (1965) – plus a few limited-edition chapbooks and collaborative projects. Suddenly, it became possible to gauge the true extent of his accomplishments. One consequence, the presentation of the National Book Award for his *Collected Poems* (1971), gave him something he had never sought – credibility among university-based scholars – and the first monograph surveying the whole of his career, Marjorie Perloff's *Frank O'Hara: Poet Among Painters*, appeared in 1977.[24] A cult figure had become canonical.

O'Hara's best-known verse remains his "I do this, I do that" poems, such as "A Step Away from Them" (1956), "Personal Poem" (1959), and "Adieu to Norman, Bonjour to Joan and Jean-Paul" (1959). Nearly as celebrated are lyrics such as the Billie Holiday elegy "The Day Lady Died" (1959) and "Poem (Lana Turner has collapsed!)" (1962) that similarly depict the everyday pressing chaos of life in a modern metropolis. Opening lines such as "It is 12:20 in New York a Friday / three days after Bastille Day" (*FOC*, p. 325) and "It is 12:10 in New York and I am wondering / if I will finish this in time to meet Norman for lunch" (*FOC*, p. 328) have been imitated by so many ephebes that they have since become a cliché.

The winsome, gregarious speaker of the "I do this, I do that" poems is prepossessing, and his casualness and lightheartedness can be a welcome relief after reading such pomposity-prone contemporaries as Bly, Duncan, Olson, and Lowell. These particular poems, too, provide welcome historical insight into the urbane and cosmopolitan intellectual culture in New York during the early years of the Cold War. A lyric such as "Poem (Khrushchev is coming on the right day!)" (1959) illustrates how cheerful a person could be despite (or perhaps because of) the constant threat of atomic oblivion. In search of details about the thriving 1950s and 1960s pre-Stonewall queer subculture in Manhattan, one will find no more vivid and evocative sources than "At the Old Place" (1955) or "Poem (I live above a dyke bar and I'm happy)" (1957), and few homoerotic love poems in English surpass "Les Luths" (1959), "Poem (Light clarity avocado salad in the morning)" (1959), and "Having a Coke with You" (1960), all written for the dancer Vincent Warren.

The "I do this, I do that" poems, however, represent only one small part of O'Hara's oeuvre, and, if readers are not careful, they will fail to perceive their artfulness, that is, the precision with which he employs characteristically estranging New York School devices such as non sequitur, intense local sound patterning, repetition and variation, bizarre juxtapositions, obstructive enjambment, and, everywhere, rhetorical dodges. ("Why I Am Not a Painter" [1956], for instance, entirely fails to answer the question posed by the title in a straightforward manner.) To acquire an accurate sense of O'Hara's poetics, one should read widely in his nearly six-hundred-page *Collected Poems*. Particularly rewarding is the series of odes that he wrote in the later fifties, which includes "Ode to Joy" (1957), "Ode on Causality" (1958), and "Ode to Michael Goldberg('s Birth and Other Births)" (1958). Veering between sublimity, sappiness, and bathos, these lyrics ambivalently extend and subvert the high style of the Romantic ode:

> Buildings will go up into the dizzy air as love itself goes in
> and up the reeling life that it has chosen for once and all
> while in the sky a feeling of intemperate fondness will excite the birds
> to swoop and veer like flies crawling across absorbèd limbs
>
> (*FOC*, p. 281)

Other poems illustrate his love of French Surrealism: "The razzle dazzle maggots are summary / tattooing my simplicity on the pitiable / The perforated mountains of my saliva leave cities awash" (*FOC*, p. 96). The goal, though, is not to give access to either his or a collective unconscious. Like Richard Crashaw, Luis de Góngora y Argote, Jan Andrzej Morsztyn, and other baroque poets, he seeks to impress with a deluge of mad ornamentation: "Now! / in cuneiform, of umbrella satrap square-carts with hotdogs / and onions of red syrup blended, of sand bejeweling the prepuce / in tank suits" (*FOC*, p. 146). One should never confuse O'Hara's investment in what he calls the "personal" with the forthrightly autobiographical or the confessional. "I" in his poetry is an occasion to launch a performance, to try out new ways of combining words. Like Marcel Duchamp, Jasper Johns, and Robert Rauschenberg taking up ordinary objects and declaring them art – bottle racks, shovels, clothes hangers, flashlights, rubber tires – O'Hara often sorts through the jumble of daily experience and assembles a poem. He reserves the right, however, to draw on other materials and resources, and his poetry accordingly possesses an impressively wide range, from knee-slapping one-liners to grotesques, to touching aubades, and to majestic meditations on death's inevitability.

Ashbery's career trajectory bears little resemblance to O'Hara's. Although it started out brightly – Auden awarded his first full collection, *Some Trees* (1956), the Yale Younger Poets Prize – he failed to capitalize on that early success. Even before winning the prize, he had fled New York and its manic get-ahead whirl. In 1955 he traveled to France on a Fulbright Fellowship, where he taught American literature at the University of Rennes. Afterward he stayed on in Paris, earning his keep as an art reviewer and as a translator of detective fiction. His sophomore outing, *The Tennis Court Oath* (1962), especially its long poem "Europe," responded thoughtfully to living in a nation still grimly struggling under the long shadow of World War II. The book's frequent recourse to collage and its extreme syntactical breakdown have parallels in such contemporary French artworks as Jacques Villeglé's and Raymond Hains's torn, lacerated posters and Arman's accumulations of refuse. As he would soon discover, though, his writing was no longer in step with developments in America, where the sunny soullessness and deceptive legibility of Pop Art better captured the superpower's love affair with consumerism. (Warhol, significantly, had his first one-man show the same year *The Tennis Court Oath* came out.)

After returning to the United States in 1965, Ashbery's next two volumes, *Rivers and Mountains* (1966) and *Double Dream of Spring* (1970), put him on a different path. Grammatically better behaved and generally written in either meandering free verse or strict form, his verse now began to sound more like Auden's, sometimes even like Bishop's, and the pas de deux that he struck up with the ghost of Romanticism brought him nearer to another precursor, Wallace Stevens. He revealed a new versatility as a poet, too. Highlights include the oddball sestina "Farm Implements and Rutabagas in a Landscape," the introspective discursive lyrics "Clepsydra" and "Soonest Mended," and the eerily indeterminate "These Lacustrine Cities." Finally, these two collections established a pattern followed by most of his volumes over the next four decades: a clutch of short- to medium-length lyrics supplemented by a daringly original long poem. After two more abortive stabs at complete self-reinvention – *Three Poems* (1973), which consists of three very long, sinuous prose poems, and *The Vermont Notebook* (1975), a diaristic experiment – he returned to the meditative-lyrics-plus-a-long-poem format in *Self-Portrait in a Convex Mirror* (1975). It promptly won the Pulitzer, the National Book Award, and the National Critics Book Circle Award. Virtually overnight, he went from being a difficult pleasure to a critics' darling. Famously, Harold Bloom used his "considerable power as a cultural commentator" to tout him as the central postwar poet.[25]

For a while, it seemed Ashbery could do no wrong. One well-received book followed another, a series that includes *Houseboat Days* (1977), *As We Know* (1979), *A Wave* (1984), *April Galleons* (1987), and, finally, a free verse quasi-autobiographical epic, *Flow Chart* (1991). Throughout the 1980s, Ashbery's reputation was at its height. He managed to write beautifully, to touch on the sublime, to let demotic English run riot, and to reinvigorate literary tradition – all while, as if an enrolled member of the Yale School of Deconstruction, decentering the self, denaturalizing discourses, and unmasking claims of access to transcendent truth. (Here academic fashion did verifiably seem to play a role in New York School reception.) His influence seemed inescapable: young poets aped his shifting pronouns, his mix of the concrete and vague, his hollow metaphors, and his oscillation between grandeur and camp.

During the 1990s and 2000s, he continued publishing, in fact at an increased rate. Some critics began complaining that he was publishing too much. More accurately, one could say that scholars and readers have simply proved incapable of keeping up. His first twelve or so books, from *Some Trees* to *Flow Chart*, are far from thoroughly digested. How can anyone claim mastery, too, of the next ten plus? Collections such as *Hotel Lautréamont* (1992), *And the Stars Were Shining* (1994), and *Can You Hear, Bird?* (1995) are clearly as ambitious as the better-studied but similar successes of the 1980s, whereas more recent volumes such as *As Umbrellas Follow Rain* (2001), *A Worldly Country* (2007), and *Planisphere* (2009) shift toward a sparer, more epigrammatic style that is also bawdier than heretofore. There are other surprises, too, such as the book-length poem *Girls on the Run* (1999), which is ostensibly based on the work of the outsider artist Henry Darger but which reads like Victorian children's literature put through a food processor. Ashbery might be one of a small number of late twentieth- and early twenty-first-century American poets to enjoy an international reputation, but, as anyone who has read all of his books quickly discovers via an MLA bibliography search, appreciation of the diversity and depth of his achievements is still preliminary. Whole continents have yet to be explored.

Of course, one should keep such declarations in perspective. When turning from Ashbery to the remaining major New York School poets – Guest, Koch, and Schuyler – "preliminary" has another meaning altogether. They, too, might have won numerous awards, but they have yet to receive anything resembling the celebrity treatment accorded to O'Hara and Ashbery. The secondary literature on their work remains quite limited in size and scope, and instead of being treated as authors who develop and deepen over time, they are still usually approached via discrete close readings that provide scattered, isolated snapshots of their poetics. Alternatively, they receive praise for work in other genres entirely. Schuyler, for example, is noted as a diarist, Guest as a novelist, and Koch as a pedagogue. (Teachers still regularly consult his *Wishes, Lies, and Dreams: Teaching Children to Write Poetry* [1970].)[26]

At the present time, though, one of these three "other" New York School poets seems poised to start receiving star billing in her own right: Barbara Guest. A generation ago, such a claim would have sounded ludicrous. For many years she was the most neglected New York School poet. She was regularly omitted from anthologies, articles, and monographs devoted to the phenomenon, and if her name did come up, the impression left was that her verse was derivative, less skilled, or somehow just not worthy of being set alongside that of her male counterparts. This insinuation was wholly unwarranted. She followed up her early volumes *The Location of Things* (1960) and *The Open Skies* (1962), which admittedly do overlap in forms and themes with *Some Trees* (1956) and *Lunch Poems* (1964), by two much stronger books, *The Blue Stairs* (1968) and *Moscow Mansions* (1973), which should have firmly established her independence as a writer. "A Handbook of Surfing" (1968), for example, is a long poem that draws on a found text to expose connections between the idyllic golden-boy masculinity at the heart of the 1960s surfing craze and the bellicose posturing in the pro–Vietnam War rhetoric of the same period. Such a description can make the poem sound like propaganda. It is not. Guest is tempted by the myths and trappings of conventional maleness, and she writes with a mix of sympathy and repulsion that puts strain on the poem's language and renders its speculations and criticisms anything but cardboard thin. Other long poems of the time, such as "Knight of the Swan" (1973), go on to ponder whether a female artist might in fact selectively appropriate and redeem masculine heroic ideals. Guest's work of the late 1960s and early 1970s is only just beginning to receive the attention that it has long deserved.

Her later work has fared better. During the 1980s, her profile began to increase. Instrumental was the appearance of *Herself Defined: The Poet H.D. and Her World* (1984), a pathbreaking study of the modernist author that alerted academics to Guest's name.[27] Around the same time, a younger generation of experimental women poets rediscovered her, and the feminist newsletter *How(ever)* (1983–1992) both honored her and gave her a welcome new outlet for publication. Venues associated with the West Coast branch of Language poetry began adopting her as a respected elder. Los Angeles's Sun & Moon Press, for instance, published *Fair Realism* (1989), *Defensive Rapture* (1993), and her *Selected Poems* (1995); the Post-Apollo Press of Sausalito, California, put out *Quill, Solitary APPARITION* (1996); and *Poetics Journal*, edited by Lyn Hejinian and Barrett Watten, printed her essay "Shifting Personas" (1991). By century's end, she had attained a national reputation. In 1999 she won the Robert Frost Medal for Distinguished Lifetime Work, and soon thereafter she received another institutional imprimatur, when Wesleyan University Press became her chief publisher.

Guest's verse from the early 1980s onward is marked by a turn toward the ethereal and the fantastic. Her lineation and word placement becomes pronouncedly visual, and she starts to use white space in an almost sculptural manner. She seems to be intent on injecting silence into her statements, or perhaps she wishes readers to focus on each line individually and in isolation. At times, her poems sound like scrambled scraps lifted from medieval romances or pilfered from post-Tolkien heroic fantasy novels:

> tell us where light comes from
>
>   white curtains in its beak;
>
> closer closer to the splintered mountains
>
> O king endlessly
>
> scattering   (*BGC*, p. 300)

Her references are highly literate, ranging from Ovid to Mallarmé to Theodor Adorno, and the settings often seem medieval or classical, albeit at a peculiar remove, as if filtered through an intermediary pair of eyes, perhaps a rococo master such as Antoine Watteau:

> Beyond the roof tiles,
> lap of a hill, *fleur d'or*
> gold ass on the threshold
> Apuleius's other . . .
> Of many colors porcelain
>
>   with faerie glove   (*BGC*, p. 439)

While obviously revisiting the New York School fascination with artifice, Guest at times seems to commit to it almost wholly, allowing imaginary landscapes and scenarios to displace any direct treatment of the world around her. Naturally, one has to ask what she gains and loses thereby, and whether she, in roundabout ways, is challenging readers to think about how and whether poetry can any longer fulfill – whether it has ever fulfilled – expectations that it serve documentary or instrumental ends. Are imaginary voyages enough, if they are seductive, variegated, and well constructed, and if they run the gamut of emotions from grief to rapture?

Since the publication of Guest's *Collected Poems* in 2008, scholars at long last have an opportunity to view the whole arc of her career and to map its landmarks, ruptures, and high points. Ill served in the past by the few anthologies that included her verse – "Parachutes, My Love, Could Carry Us Higher" (1960) and "Red Lilies" (1973), for example, simply are not representative of her poetry at its best – her canon remains in flux. As scholars become more familiar with her work, its excellences should become more evident. Young poets are helping. The British poets Andrea Brady and John Wilkinson, for instance, have written invaluably about her poetics.[28] One can no longer talk about the mid-twentieth-century New York School as if it were a boys' club. We still do not know, however, what the circle's achievements and legacy will look like once we fully appreciate that Guest was in the tree house all along.

*

Critics still might not have a complete picture about the original core group of New York School poets, but that has not prevented them from talking confidently about second, third, and even fourth generations of the New York School. The second generation, for example, is usually taken to include such figures as Ted Berrigan, Joe Brainard, Joe Ceravolo, Clark Coolidge, Bernadette Mayer, Alice Notley, Ron Padgett, and Anne Waldman, all of whom were active in New York in the later 1960s or the early 1970s. After O'Hara's untimely death in 1966, he was especially revered, and much of Berrigan's work, as well as Notley's and Waldman's earliest verse, reads like pastiche of O'Hara's writings, especially his "I do this, I do that" poems:

> Time of, dress warmly, 3 A.M. walk
> Coat over sweater, shawl over
> Hair, boots over slippers, snow
> On & over all, I forgot
> To mention I'm drunk (martini
> & piece of toast)[29]

Other writers pushed further the radical linguistic experiments that characterize such works as Koch's *When the Sun Tries to Go On* and Ashbery's *The Tennis Court Oath*. Coolidge's *The Maintains* (1974) is a good example of this tendency: "at in as on ones / one soon at some as / book on coition lies / abrase snails."[30] Perhaps the most inventive figure in second-generation circles was Mayer, who was more deeply involved than the others in the New York art world of the period. (She co-edited the journal *o to 9* with the conceptual and body artist

Vito Acconci, for example.) Her work sometimes incorporates photography, and she is as liable to exhibit the results in a gallery as to publish them. Her project *Studying Hunger*, which still has yet to be published in full, is a prolonged inquiry into the most fundamental aspects of her existence, namely, how and what she thinks, feels, and perceives. The resulting prose poetry is self-interrupting, slow moving, and, as it accretes over page after page, extraordinary in its wholly focused unceasing act of introspection:

> A start. A stop. I am woman of beginning. You are all at the shore. You are a center, you design a week, the meek, a mile, the shore, endless beginnings of entropy, endless universe of design. New words. What can I speak of, what can I call? Can I call you, all of you, all, call you to me, can I embrace, can embrace all, all parade, all center & all (a picture) never, & ever the bird that speaks, that bird cannot speak, this call to all, eternal rhyme & time, she only knows the simplest words, the smallest prose closed of design. She opens, she is cool, she is call of all that wild, she is unerring, she is fall.[31]

In such writing, Mayer reprises the New York School fascination with everyday experience and pushes it in a dramatically new direction.

While a second generation of New York School writers is relatively easy to identify – one can discern a number of young poets who moved to New York and self-consciously styled themselves as the heirs of O'Hara and his friends – it becomes increasingly more difficult and tendentious to track further generations. A critic has to decide which institutions, which poets, and what kind of aesthetics should deserve priority. One could, for example, single out St. Mark's Poetry Project as the core of an ongoing New York School tradition, because many of the second-generation figures either helped found it or have served as its director. Putting too much emphasis on any one milieu, however, risks arbitrarily excluding contemporary writers such as, say, John Ash, Anne Lauterbach, Marjorie Welish, and John Yau whose poetry is manifestly in dialogue with Ashbery's yet who are not usually associated with St. Mark's. Alternatively, one could limit the label "third generation" to a circle of poets, including Eileen Myles and Tim Dlugos, who came into their own in the 1980s and whose verse, while drenched in O'Hara and Schuyler, is more in-your-face queer in both its themes and politics:

> Leonard wears a shark's tooth
> on a chain around his neck
> and long blond hair.
> These days he's the manager
> of Boots and Saddles ("Bras

and Girdles," my beloved
Bobby used to say) and
costumer for the Gay Cable
Network's *Dating Game*.[32]

Why, however, consider such poetry more worthy of the New York School label than its 1980s rival, the New York branch of Language writing? Both Charles Bernstein and Bruce Andrews, co-editors of the journal *L=A=N=G=U=A=G=E* (1977–1982), which gave the movement its name, could be read as poet-heirs of a lineage including *The Tennis Court Oath*, Coolidge, and Mayer, as these lines from Andrews's *Edge* (1973) illustrate: "stallpart / retro-bulb / spun-a-off / amethyst trunk."[33] This kind of asyntactical word string confronts readers with the bare, brute materiality of language. They are encouraged to contemplate sound play, indentation, and whatever else is left when referentiality is suspended. One does not have to grasp the complex theoretical and socioeconomic motives informing such verse to appreciate that it carries on, in rarefied form, the New York School proclivity to think of a poem as an abstract composition in which conveying information can be secondary to arranging letters and words on the page in a striking manner. In short, there are many contemporary candidates for the New York School label. After 1975 or so, it is perhaps best to stop tracing poetic Jesse Trees and to speak more specifically about which of the many aspects of the New York School legacy continue to be inspiring – and to whom.

One of the most oft-cited studies of the New York School, David Lehman's *The Last Avant-Garde* (1998), looks back nostalgically at the 1950s and 1960s, as if Ashbery, Koch, O'Hara, and Schuyler (he omits Guest) stood at the end of a fabulous but doomed enterprise.[34] If a person surveys subsequent American writing, however, that is not a defensible moral to the story. It makes even less sense if one looks at the school's international impact. In Britain, for example, a prominent line of poets, from Lee Harwood and Tom Raworth in the 1960s to Drew Milne and Mark Ford in the 2000s, have drawn on the New York School for inspiration. Moreover, the group's influence has not been limited to English-speaking countries. In postcommunist Poland, poets such as Marcin Świetlicki, Jacek Podsiadło, and Miłosz Biedrzycki have promoted "O'Harism" as a means of grappling with a swiftly changing society and culture. Around the world, numerous authors have carried on in sundry, provocative, and occasionally contradictory ways the pioneering, estranging, heady, giddy poetics of the New York School.

Notes

1. Donald Allen (ed.), *The New American Poetry: 1945–1960* (New York: Grove, 1960), p. xi.
2. Allen (ed.), *The New American Poetry*, p. xiii.
3. John Ashbery, *Selected Prose* (Ann Arbor: University of Michigan Press, 2005), p. 249.
4. John Ashbery, *Notes from the Air: Selected Later Poems* (New York: Ecco, 2007).
5. John Ashbery, *Reported Sightings: Art Chronicles 1957–1987* (New York: Knopf, 1989); Barbara Guest, *Dürer in the Window, Reflexions on Art* (New York: Roof, 2003); Frank O'Hara, *Art Chronicles, 1954–1966* (New York: Braziller, 1975); Frank O'Hara, *Jackson Pollock* (New York: Braziller, 1959); Frank O'Hara, *Nakian* (New York: Museum of Modern Art, 1966); Frank O'Hara, *Robert Motherwell* (New York: Museum of Modern Art, 1965); James Schuyler, *Selected Art Writings* (Santa Rosa, Calif.: Black Sparrow Press, 1998).
6. Barbara Guest, *Collected Poems* (Middletown, Conn.: Wesleyan University Press, 2008), p. 121. This collection will be cited in the text as *BGC*.
7. Kenneth Koch, *The Collected Poems* (New York: Knopf, 2005), p. 183.
8. John Ashbery, *Selected Poems* (New York: Penguin, 1985), p. 54.
9. Kenneth Koch, *On the Edge: The Collected Long Poems* (New York: Knopf, 2009), p. 10.
10. John Ashbery, *The Tennis Court Oath* (Middletown, Conn.: Wesleyan University Press, 1962), p. 31.
11. Ashbery, *The Tennis Court Oath*, p. 23.
12. Ashbery, *Selected Poems*, p. 208.
13. Emily Dickinson, *Selected Poems* (New York: Bloomsbury, 1992), p. 27.
14. Fredric Jameson, *Postmodernism, or the Cultural Logic of Late Capitalism* (Durham, N.C.: Duke University Press, 1991), p. 26.
15. Jameson, *Postmodernism*, pp. 11–15.
16. Mutlu Konuk Blasing, *Politics and Form in Postmodern Poetry: O'Hara, Bishop, Ashbery, and Merrill* (Cambridge: Cambridge University Press, 1995), p. 10.
17. James Schuyler, *Collected Poems* (New York: Farrar, Straus and Giroux, 1993), p. 12.
18. John Ashbery, *April Galleons* (New York: Farrar, Straus and Giroux, 1987), p. 1.
19. Frank O'Hara, *Collected Poems* (Berkeley: University of California Press, 1971), p. 325. This collection will be cited in the text as *FOC*.
20. Schuyler, *Collected Poems*, p. 231.
21. Ashbery, *Selected Poems*, p. 14.
22. Recent high-profile studies include Andrew Epstein, *Beautiful Enemies: Friendship and Postwar American Poetry* (New York: Oxford University Press,

2006); Maggie Nelson, *Women, the New York School, and Other Abstractions* (Iowa City: University of Iowa Press, 2007); Lytle Shaw, *Frank O'Hara: The Poetics of Coterie* (Iowa City: University of Iowa Press, 2006); John Emil Vincent, *John Ashbery: His Later Books* (Athens: University of Georgia Press, 2007).

23. Ashbery, *Selected Poems*; Ashbery, *Notes from the Air*; Guest, *Collected Poems*; O'Hara, *Collected Poems*; Frank O'Hara, *Selected Poems*, ed. Mark Ford (New York: Knopf, 2008); James Schuyler, *Selected Poems* (New York: Farrar, Straus and Giroux, 2007); James Schuyler, *Other Flowers: Uncollected Poems*, ed. James Meetze and Simon Pettet (New York: Farrar, Straus and Giroux, 2010).

24. Marjorie Perloff, *Frank O'Hara: Poet Among Painters* (1977; Chicago: University of Chicago Press, 1997).

25. David Fite, *Harold Bloom: The Rhetoric of Romantic Vision* (Amherst: University of Massachusetts Press, 1985), p. 128.

26. Kenneth Koch, *Wishes, Lies, and Dreams: Teaching Children to Write Poetry* (New York: Chelsea House, 1970).

27. Barbara Guest, *Herself Defined: The Poet HD and Her World* (Garden City, N.Y.: Doubleday, 1984).

28. Andrea Brady, "Shadowy Figures in *Quill, Solitary APPARITION*," *Chicago Review* 53/54:1–2 (2008), pp. 120–25; John Wilkinson, "'Couplings of Such Sonority': Reading a Poem by Barbara Guest," *Textual Practice* 23:3 (2009), pp. 481–502.

29. Alice Notley, *Grave of Light: New and Selected Poems 1970–2005* (Middletown, Conn.: Wesleyan University Press, 2006), p. 9.

30. Clark Coolidge, *The Maintains* (Oakland, Calif.: This Press, 1974), p. 88.

31. Bernadette Mayer, "From *Studying Hunger*," in Ron Silliman (ed.), *In the American Tree: Language, Realism, Poetry* (Orono, Maine: National Poetry Foundation, 1986), pp. 410–24, 416.

32. Tim Dlugos, *Powerless: Selected Poems 1973–1990* (London: High Risk, 1996), p. 74.

33. Bruce Andrews, *Edge* (Washington, D.C.: Some of Us Press, 1973), n.p.

34. David Lehman, *The Last Avant-Garde: The Making of the New York School of Poets* (New York: Doubleday, 1998).

Chapter 38

The Uses of Authenticity: Four Sixties Poets

NICK HALPERN

The 1960s was an explosive decade in America, in poetry as in every other aspect of culture. Adding to the atmosphere of challenge and risk was an extraordinary emphasis on "authenticity." What was meant by the word? Lionel Trilling in *Sincerity and Authenticity* (1972) wrote,

> The word "authenticity" comes so readily to the tongue these days and in so many connections that it may very well resist ... definition ... but I think that for the present I can rely on its suggesting a more strenuous moral experience than "sincerity" does ... and a less acceptant and genial view of the social circumstances of life. At the behest of the criterion of authenticity, much that was once thought to make up the very fabric of culture has come to seem of little account.[1]

Many cultural critics have doubted the success, even the authenticity, of the decade's efforts at achieving authenticity. Trilling himself wrote that "concerted effort ... to achieve authenticity generates its own conventions."[2] And although Paul Breslin writes that the poets of the 1960s "shared a conception of poetry as engaged in the liberation of human consciousness," he suggests that the same has been true many times before, most notably in the Romantic period. Some poetry "praised for its 'openness to experience,'" Breslin adds, "has been every bit as narrowly 'closed' in its own way, as the poetry it replaced."[3]

For many writers in the 1960s, authenticity was necessary only as a prerequisite for a life dedicated to radical change: to the civil rights movement, for example, or to the rise of feminism, or to work against the Vietnam War. To become truly authentic, a poet had to put herself into some relation with the enormous social and political changes around her. But what relation? Should one concentrate one's authentic energies on one's inner or private life or on the outer political and public world?

Adrienne Rich, James Wright, Robert Duncan, and Denise Levertov all did some of their best and most influential work in the 1960s, and in response to the changes that vexed decade brought. These four poets offer a range of versions of authenticity and at the same time show the variety of possibilities open to poets about the uses of authenticity. Each of the four poets tried to write about both the inner and outer worlds. Poets, of course, have always written about both, but these poets saw enormous pressure to choose one or the other. Everything seemed to hinge on the choice. These four poets – it's one of the most interesting things about their work – refused to choose. The poems they produced in attempting (for better or for worse) to do justice to *both* realms are a significant part of what we think of (with admiration and chagrin) when we remember the poetry of the 1960s.

*

Poets of the 1960s were divided into several camps. Poets were at times over-confident about the poetic voices coming from their own camp and impatient with those they heard from other camps. Behind this bravado there was for many poets a profound anxiety about finding an authentic voice. The sixties poets didn't think ahistorically: they understood that others had undergone this struggle earlier. If the Romantics had experienced the same anxieties, that didn't bother these poets, who welcomed whatever help they could get, especially because, as Devin Johnston writes, "the Romantic self-definition was, through the 1950s, heretical in New Critical terms."[4]

The belief that many of the poets of that time had in common was the notion that one's poetic voice was something to which one had to win access. (Having already published books of well-regarded verse was no guarantee of poetic authenticity.) Winning access, though, didn't have to be a slow or painful process. Allen Ginsberg's fearlessness in the face of social norms and legal obstacles and Robert Lowell's mildly anxious but mostly untroubled accounts of getting from the impersonal obscurities of *Lord Weary's Castle* to the autobiographical complexities of *Life Studies* could seem to suggest that access to an authentic voice might not be so difficult. And when Donald Allen's anthology, *The New American Poetry*, came out in 1960, with its division of poets into camps, many of the poets in its pages felt confident that the future belonged to their camp. By 1965 Allen's anthology had gone through eight printings, for a total of 40,000 copies. Whatever the writers in *The New American Poetry* thought of one another, many of them shared a sense of condescension toward the writers in *New Poets of England and America* (1957), edited by Donald Hall, Robert Pack, and Louis Simpson. They were representative, all of them, of the past – and not of the useful (Romantic) past.[5]

But powerful inhibitions were in play for some poets who wanted to escape the past. Some of the obstacles were external and seemed to be permanent. There were the New Critics, Cleanth Brooks, for example, and Robert Penn Warren – or Allen Tate, who proudly announced that he, on a trip to Europe, had thrown *The New American Poetry* into the mid-Atlantic.[6] The New Critics' prose emphasized craft; a poem was held together by means of tensions and ambiguities and paradox, its unity revealed through close reading. Many poets wrote such poems dutifully, some with a nagging sense that they were producing period pieces.

Authentic poets would have to declare their independence not only from the New Critics but also from the modernists. It made the situation worse that many of the modernists were still alive as the sixties began. Stanley Kunitz remembered that "immediately after Eliot and Pound, and Hart Crane and Stevens and William Carlos Williams, to mention only a handful, it was difficult to be taken seriously as a new American poet.... These [modernist] poets would never consent to die."[7] James E. B. Breslin refers to "a crowded and stultifying space, one filled with the most suffocating presences of all – canonized revolutionaries."[8] Ezra Pound, William Carlos Williams, or H.D. could be written to and visited, and they were ready to encourage younger poets. But the younger poets, returning to their desks, might ask, with Randall Jarrell, "How can poems be written that are more violent, more disorganized, more obscure, more – supply your own adjective – than those that have already been written?"[9] No wonder some poets (James Wright, Robert Duncan, and Elizabeth Bishop, for example) took to referring to themselves, defensively, as "minor." The challenge, for many poets, was daunting. They had to reject the New Critical rules regarding an acceptable poetic voice, then break away from all or most of the modernist versions of poetic voice, and then imagine new, more authentic versions for themselves – and also make the choice of *what* to write about, the outer or the inner world.

Meanwhile, there was a matter of initial inhibitions, and some of these inhibitions were internal. What if one felt a double loyalty to the new ways of writing and to the old ways of writing? James Wright, in his letters, shows how passionately some poets struggled with their divided loyalty. For some poets, no project could have been more exhilarating, but for Wright it was a series of occasions for blind panic. Wright had already published two well-received books, *The Green Wall* (1957), chosen by W. H. Auden for the Yale Younger Poets Award, and then *Saint Judas* (1959). Influenced by John Crowe

Ransom, Thomas Hardy, and E. A. Robinson, the books were more than simply attempts to do homage. They were full of memorable and moving poems about people in trouble – "A Note Left in Jimmy Leonard's Shack," "At the Executed Murderer's Grave," and "St. Judas," for example. Why couldn't he keep writing poems in their vein? Richard Wilbur and John Hollander were not disowning their poems. In addition, the iambs and trochees in his first two books had given him a badly needed sense of psychic stability and coherence. Why should he reject them? And what if a poet frightened by the turmoil of his emotions gave up meter, form, stanzas, ironies, and paradoxes, and in exchange got nothing but the old chaos without the means to organize it? Or, worse, what if all the new poems one wrote would seem to posterity merely "representative" of a new decade? What if all the forward-looking poets were creating nothing more than a new period style?

James Wright grew up in the middle of the Great Depression in the Ohio River valley. Neither his mother nor his father graduated from high school, and his father was repeatedly laid off by the Hazel-Atlas glass factory in Wheeling, West Virginia. Wright experienced his first breakdown at age sixteen and missed an entire year of high school. After serving in Japan with the U.S. Army's occupation force, he entered Kenyon College on the G.I. Bill, where he studied with John Crowe Ransom. He spent 1953 in Vienna on a Fulbright Scholarship. Receiving a Ph.D. from the University of Washington in Seattle (where his adviser was Theodore Roethke), he got a job in 1957 teaching literature at the University of Minnesota, where one of his colleagues was Allen Tate.

In 1958, Wright wrote the poet, translator, and editor Robert Bly a letter, sixteen single-spaced pages long, introducing himself, and Bly responded by inviting Wright to visit him at his farm in Rochester, Minnesota. Bly had the knack of making transformation look both urgent and easy. He encouraged poets to undertake a journey inward or downward to the so-called deep images of the unconscious. The useful modernists for Bly were the Surrealists, particularly those from continental Europe and South America. Bly advised Wright to translate Gottfried Benn, George Trakl, Paul Eluard, Rene Char, César Vallejo, Pablo Neruda, and Antonio Machado and to let their lines work their magic on his own poetry. Wright was already familiar with some of the poets Bly mentioned, especially the Germans. In one of his letters to Bly he wrote,

> So I used to get hideously drunk at parties of academic intellectuals, and after the point of no return I would stand and bellow Trakl, and Carossa, and Rilke, and Hölderlin, because nobody knew what the hell I was saying, and because I

only slightly *felt*, rather than *understood*, what I in the name of God was crying in the miracles of those images that were sane to the depths of their being and which yet followed no rules.[10]

Wright was eager to learn from Bly. Quickly, the closings of his letters changed from "Sincerely, James Wright," to "Love, Jim." In 1958 he wrote Bly, "Every rhythm must be new and original if it is to contain genuine *imagery*? Right? Or am I missing the point? But if this *is* the point about rhythm then I want to ask if you do or do not think it is possible to build a new and original rhythm *on the basis of* the iambic measure." In 1958 Wright wrote to Donald Hall, "I was divided – really divided, as on the blade of a sword – between my loyalty to those of my contemporaries who were trying to write with intellectual grace and to those, far more disturbing and ruthless, who were raising hell and demanding greatness" (*WP*, p. 131).

Who wouldn't want to raise hell and demand greatness? Grateful as he was for Bly's help as a mentor, Wright began to chafe under his authority. Flattering and attacking him in one sentence, he wrote to Bly: "Your mention of the possibilities available to us in other literatures is a great, a major statement – or it would be, if you offered it as a possibility (the opening of a door) rather than as what you still too often seem to make it: a despotic command" (*WP*, p. 235). Whatever his qualms, the work went on. In a letter to Roethke, Wright wrote, "I work like hell, chipping away perhaps one tiny pebble per day from the ten-mile-thick granite wall of formal and facile 'technique' which I myself erected, and which now stands ominously between me and whatever poetry may be in me" (*WP*, p. 139). All he could see now, sometimes, when he looked at his poems of the 1950s, was competence. "I have been depressed as hell," he told Theodore Roethke. "My stuff stinks, and you know it. It stinks because it is *competent*. . . . I am trapped by the very thing – the traditional technique – which I labored so hard to attain" (*WP*, pp. 138–39).

What could be harder to unlearn than technical mastery? Yet there were good reasons for trying. Some painters in the sixties had become interested in the idea of "deskilling"; Bly shared in that interest. "All the traditional applications of the word craft," he wrote, "have to be dropped."[11] There was something darker, richer, wilder than craft, and Wright asked Bly question after question about it. "Will you please explain, however generally," he asked him, "what you mean by 'the ocean world'? I don't know Jung at all," he added. "I know Freud too little" (*WP*, p. 146). Again, though, he would resist what he saw as Bly's dictatorial manner. "Bob, I'm trying to say that your insistence on the utter rejections of iambics is, I believe, an expression of fanatical absolutism" (*WP*, p. 182). He could be sly, writing to Hall that "we would have to write iambics without Bob's knowing it" (*WP*, p. 187).

His poet friends – Theodore Roethke, James Dickey, Donald Hall, and Anne Sexton – were sympathetic to his struggle, but not all poets were. Denise Levertov (whom Wright called "one of the best living poets in America") wrote to Robert Duncan in 1961,

> I wasn't surprised about J Wright. I heard him read a year or so ago and his Oxford Group-type confession of guilt & conversion in regard to the iambic pentameter & the poetry of the French & Spanish Surrealists, followed by a reading of his *old* poems (disavowed 5 minutes before) . . . struck me as a weak hypocrisy. He didn't have the courage of his convictions because he didn't really have any convictions.[12]

It was easy for poets from other camps, the Black Mountain School, for example, to see Wright's passionate ambivalence as an absence of convictions. It might have been truer to say that for Wright – as Wright said of himself – "every absolute command that my imagination hears is almost immediately turned into an insistence on its opposite – and this takes place not only as an assertion of the imagination's freedom; but also as a desire to subversively overthrow all the critical absolutes" (*WP*, p. 235). He was never able decisively to turn his back on his old poems, and, because of that divided loyalty, Wright's transformation into a new kind of poet was, as it turned out, not as radical as it was for other poets. He kept the tone of melancholy and discouragement from his first two books, as we will see, rather than adopting Bly's sometimes facile confidence. And he retained the people from his first two books. He was not going to journey inward to a space without bringing other people, the troubled people he had known back in Ohio.

Adrienne Rich, too, came to question the value of the poetry she had written in the 1950s. In "The Roofwalker," a poem in response to Levertov, Rich asks, "Was it worth while to lay – / with infinite exertion – a roof I can't live under?"[13] Born in 1929 in Baltimore, Rich grew up, unlike Wright, in a bookish household. If Wright had Bly as his problematic mentor, Rich's difficult mentor was her father, a doctor and pathology professor at Johns Hopkins University. Her memories of him suggest that the only presence more formidable than a father figure (such as Bly) may be an actual father. Rich would recall,

> My own luck was being born white and middle-class into a house full of books, with a father who encouraged me to read and write. So for about twenty years I wrote for a particular man, who criticized and praised me and made me feel I

was indeed "special." The obverse side of this, of course, was that I tried for a long time to please him, or rather, not to displease him (*ARP*, p. 170).

Writing to "not displease" was a habit that many poets of that time had to break free from if they were to find an authentic voice.

In the 1950s Rich wrote two books of well-received poetry. Her first book, *A Change of World* (1951), published while she was still an undergraduate at Radcliffe, was chosen by W. H. Auden for the Yale Younger Poets Award. Auden, in his foreword to *A Change of World*, was decidedly not displeased, praising Rich's poems in words that have become notorious: "I suggested at the beginning of this introduction that poems are analogous to persons; the poems a reader will encounter in this book are neatly and modestly dressed, speak quietly but do not mumble, respect their elders but are not cowed by them, and do not tell fibs."[14] Like Wright, Rich was influenced by Frost and Robinson, and also by Yeats, Stevens, Dickinson, and Auden. Living in Cambridge with her economist husband, who taught at Harvard; writing elder-respecting, father-pleasing poetry; and having three children in four years, her work and her life were full of examples of what Wright was worrying about: competence. But almost the only thing readers say today about the poems in *A Change of World* and *The Diamond Cutters* (1955) – almost the only thing she herself could say later – is that she seems memorably alert to various kinds of impending doom. In poems like "Storm Warnings" and "Aunt Jennifer's Tigers" she predicts calamities and writes about the need to prepare for them. Many of the poems are about the intuition that the world (which usually consists of everything the speaker understands by ordinary domesticity) will have to come to an end. The construction of these poems – and this must have been, in part, what frustrated Rich about them later – suggests that great changes *can* be prepared for and guarded against. Meter, stanzaic form, rhyme: formalism was useful against any eventuality. Looking back in 1971 at her earlier poems, Rich wrote, "In those years formalism was part of the strategy – like asbestos gloves, it allowed me to handle materials I couldn't pick up barehanded" (*ARP*, p. 171). It was not clear to her yet that it would ever be necessary to pick the materials up barehanded.

Robert Duncan seems to have been prepared for something resembling the 1960s, although it seems fair to say that he would have been prepared for an even freer, weirder decade. According to Michael Davidson, Duncan "wrote self-consciously as an outsider to the literary establishment, a gay writer in a homophobic society, an anarchist within the anti-Stalinist left, a bookish poet among bohemians, a bohemian among academics, a formalist among free versists, a field poet among closed formalists."[15] Duncan, too, had grown up in a house full of books, but the books were of a particular kind. Born in 1919, he was, at the age of six months, adopted by a Theosophist family. His grandmother was a member of a splinter group of Madame Blavatsky's Theosophical Society. His aunt, Fayetta Harris Phillip, wrote books with titles like *The New Hypothesis*, *Soul Psyche*, and *The Lady Alchemist*. It was an upbringing to which he returned again and again in his essays and poetry. He wrote to H.D, "For me as a child there was the beneficial sense of the cosmos, of *life* being shared with everything in the universe."[16] In another letter to H.D., he wrote, "You know I was surrounded in my childhood by the cast of a Hermetic Brotherhood ... we were told how we were adopted (my sister and I) by design of the stars; and we were told that we had past-lives."[17]

The fact that the Theosophical conversations went on endlessly (as another letter says) "over his head," and that, as he says, he was never "initiated," may have spared him the kind of parental pressure that Rich struggled to escape. In his notes to his book on H.D., Duncan remembered "that my worship belonged to no church, that my mysteries belonged to no cult, that my learning belonged to no institution, that my imagination of my self belonged to no philosophic system."[18] What he inherited instead of "the rites" was a sense (like Yeats had, while he was writing *A Vision*) of imminent possibility, a kind of perpetual spiritual suspense. Anything could happen at any moment (in the world or on the page) and with wonderfully unforeseeable consequences. Although he sought out mentors (Pound and H.D., among the modernists), he treated their doctrines with a determined lightness; he was cautious and exploratory in his relation to them. Their doctrines were true and untrue; one believed and did not. (James Merrill was similarly ambivalent in his attitude to the occult doctrines presented in *The Changing Light at Sandover*.) In the poem "Roots and Branches," he referred to "casual certainties," and he called one of his books of essays *Fictive Certainties*.[19] Not that the influences weren't important. Duncan wrote to H.D.,

> I remember most clearly the aura [of Pound's canto 1] "And then went down to the ships, set keel to the breakers, forth on the godly sea" had. I was seventeen, away at college then ... I went to the bookstore and read those opening lines, just the two, from which dreams of everything poetry could be to fulfill old promises seemd to flow.[20]

As Duncan tells her more than once in his letters, he was also deeply influenced by H.D. "Your presence had spoken so directly to me in your work, and freed in me some force, even *the* force, of my own work."[21] But presences were always speaking directly to him, and forces within him were frequently being freed – and somehow he was always himself, miraculously, free *of* those forces. He published essays toward an extended study of H.D. called *The H.D. Book*, but he never completed it. (It was published by the University of California Press in 2011.) At the same time he read Edith Sitwell, Saint-John Perse, Coleridge, Blake, Christopher Smart, Thomas Browne, Plotinus, Plato, and Heraclitus. And (as he says in "Night Songs," a poem in *Roots and Branches*) he dreamed about the earliest songs, the songs at the beginning of everything. "O to release the first music somewhere again / for a moment to touch the design of the first melody."[22] A lover of "the old lore," which he found every-where – in old books, in everyday life, and in his dreams – Duncan was a collapser of distinctions. What sets him apart in this quartet is that, from the beginning, the inner and private and the outer and public worlds (for better or worse) were one to him.

Duncan went to the University of California at Berkeley in 1936. In 1940, he was drafted and served at Fort Knox, and in 1941 he was discharged for homosexuality. After his 1943 essay "The Homosexual in Society" appeared in *politics*, a journal edited by Dwight MacDonald, his poem "An African Elegy," which had been accepted for the *Kenyon Review* by John Crowe Ransom, was rejected by Ransom. Ransom wrote that "I read the poem as an advertisement or a notice of overt homosexuality, and we are not in the market for literature of this type."[23]

In 1945 Duncan enrolled at Berkeley to study medieval history and began his friendship with Jack Spicer, Robin Blaser, and James Broughton. Duncan's first book, *Heavenly City, Earthly City*, was published in 1947. Meeting Charles Olson that year, Duncan was highly influenced by Olson's theory of projective verse and "composition by field." Like Wright, he thrived on assertions of the imagination's freedom from every critical absolute – including the insistence on total liberation from the past. In 1950 Duncan published *Medieval Scenes*. In 1951 he began his long relationship with his lover, Jess Collins, a painter and col-lagist with whom he collaborated. They lived in Mallorca for several years, as did Robert Creeley, who published Duncan in the magazines (*Origin* and *Black Mountain Review*) that Creeley edited or co-edited; in 1956 Duncan, like Creeley, came to teach at Black Mountain College in North Carolina, where Olson was the rector. Duncan's major works in the sixties included *The Opening of the Field* (1960), *Roots and Branches* (1964), and *Bending the Bow* (1968). All the while, he insisted that his work was not major and not even original. In his second letter to Denise Levertov, he wrote, "My titles now for volumes of poetry are: IMITATIONS, and DERIVATIONS. "originality" is NOT either interesting or available to me" (*DLL*, p. 5). He saw himself as bringing all his influences together into a sort of grand collage. Christopher Beach writes that

> Duncan is a poet so highly aware of his own use of poetic models that in his work the poem, book or entire corpus can be viewed as an open field for the interplay of poetic sources. Duncan is not confused by this complex relationship to past writers and texts; instead, he speaks forthrightly about the natural process of derivation, which is a central aspect of all poetry.[24]

Just as forthrightly, Duncan rejected the idea of achievement itself. In his essay "Pages from a Notebook," he asks, "Why should one's art then be an achievement? Why not, more an adventure?" He added,

> Poems are now, when they are "ours," fountains: as in Oz, of life or of forgetfulness of self-life. What we expected poetry to be when we were children. A world of our own marvels. Doors of language. Adoration. We dreamd not originally of publishing. What a paltry concern. No child of imagination would center there. But we dreamd of song and the reality of romance.[25]

After *Bending the Bow* (1968), Duncan vowed not to publish another book for fifteen years, and he kept his vow. Michael Davidson writes that Duncan preferred instead "to distribute typescript copies of his work in progress to friends.... Duncan felt that the demands of writing 'toward' a book (many of his previous books had been composed as unified texts rather than selections of poems) limited his ability to compose at random."[26] Publishing, for Duncan, was a distraction from the work, from the interplay of poetic sources, and from the world within and the world without.

Meanwhile he (cheerfully) called himself trendy and pretentious and fraudulent. Self-descriptions that would paralyze any other poet had the effect of spurring Duncan on. While Wright had been anxious about becoming a merely representative poet, a poetaster following fads, Duncan was blithely unconcerned. It wasn't arrogance but a kind of infinitely patient fascination with all the byways of his mysterious creative itinerary. (At the same time, he was generous in encouraging other poets to follow their own paths. After Duncan published Aram Saroyan's one-word poem "Lighght" in the *Chicago Review* in 1968, George Plimpton included the poem in the *American Literary Anthology*, which was published in 1969 with help from a National Endowment of the Arts grant. A controversy then erupted in Congress, with Senator Jesse Helms demanding to know how a poem could consist of one word, especially when that word was misspelled. Saroyan's career was made.)

Duncan continued on his own idiosyncratic path. He had organized his writing life so that nothing could ambush him, certainly no sense of having gone the wrong way. Alan Williamson writes, "Duncan would argue that at least in a certain kind of self-exploratory poetry there are, as in psychoanalysis, no wrong turnings. Every statement, and every misstatement, reveals the self."[27] And there were his precursors, constant presences, giving him encouragement, as did Denise Levertov, who wrote him that everything he did had "a crazy exalted validity, *no matter what*" (*DLL*, p. 17). Their relationship involved an intimate, ongoing exchange of permissions. His poem "Often I Am Permitted to Return to a Meadow" (the first poem in *The Opening of the Field*) begins,

> as if it were a scene made-up by the mind,
> that is not mine, but is a made place,
>
> that is mine, it is so near to the heart,
> an eternal pasture folded in all thought
> so that there is a hall therein
>
> that is a made place, created by light
> wherefrom the shadows that are forms fall.[28]

Levertov helped him believe (what he already knew) that the space he wrote about and the space he wrote from were both his and not his. The worlds of the collective unconscious and of his own imagination were (again, for better or worse) the same world to him. Collapsing all distinctions (or hoping to), Duncan wrote with a sly, childlike, sometimes ecstatic confidence. Davidson writes that in Duncan "the poet returns to 'a place of first permission' where suppressed meanings intrude onto the surface text. Those meanings include archaic survivals of cultic and atavistic relations whose doctrines propose a unity of spirit and form.... The ultimate meaning of this 'field' of origins is often a sexual mystery – an allegory of homosexual or bisexual love."[29] Levertov was instrumental throughout the 1950s and 1960s in helping him maintain his confidence in writing his poems, as he was in helping her to maintain hers.

Denise Levertov was born in 1923 in Ilford, a suburb of London, and was educated at home. Levertov's father, a Russian immigrant Jewish scholar, joined the Church of England as a student at Konigsberg in the 1890s; his lifelong hope was to unify Judaism and Christianity. Levertov was proud of her mystical lineage: among her father's ancestors was the nineteenth-century Hasidic mystic Schneur Zalman, and among her mother's visionary ancestors was the Welsh tailor and mystic Angel Jones.

Levertov published her first poem in 1940, when she was seventeen. During the Second World War she served as a civilian nurse in London. One of the New Romantics (along with Dylan Thomas, Kathleen Raine, and George

Barker), Levertov published her first book of poems, *The Double Image*, in 1945. After the war she met her future husband, Mitchell Goodman, in Switzerland. Moving to America with him in 1948, she broke with the New Romantics and began writing poems of "dailiness" influenced by William Carlos Williams's short lyrics and by Pound's Imagist poems. In 1953 she visited Williams at his home in Rutherford, New Jersey, and maintained a friendship with him until his death in 1963. If Williams opened up the world of the everyday for Levertov, Robert Duncan suggested ways to write poems responsive to the mysterious world of her spiritual inheritance. (His interests were not enormously different from those of Kathleen Raine.) In addition, Duncan and Creeley introduced her to the ideas of Black Mountain. Would it be possible to be both kinds of poet: a follower of Williams, writing about the ordinary world, and a student of Duncan's, writing about the magic worlds within and without? Duncan was sure it would be. So was Levertov. Not everyone believed her. Robert Bly wrote, "She wants to live as other people and then write as a mystic. That is impossible."[30] Levertov, undiscouraged in her ambitions, trusted in her American mentors. It does not seem to have been a struggle for her to adapt and alter her voice, and once she assumed it she kept it, for better or worse, until the end of her life. Over the years she had developed what Charles Altieri calls "an aesthetics of presence," a determination (in part derived from her spiritual background) to bear witness to the spiritual fullness of the passing moment.[31] (Hence her relationship to Duncan and Williams.) The poems to which readers most responded came out of that aesthetic, and she trusted it. Meanwhile, as the sixties continued, she began to take on a more public role. In 1961 and again from 1963 to 1965, she was poetry editor of the *Nation* (and in the 1970s for *Mother Jones*); her academic employment included Vassar, City College of New York, Berkeley, and MIT.

Duncan and Levertov's letters (seven hundred pages of them, published in 2004 by Stanford University Press) record a long series of acts of mutual encouragement: two poets on opposite coasts, almost never meeting, engaged in an intense, affectionate, wide-ranging conversation. The letters communicate a sense of almost unimpeded intimacy. *Almost*, because there were signs of tension in the 1950s, and in the 1960s the signs began to increase. In "Some Duncan Letters – A Memoir and a Critical Tribute (1975)," Levertov wrote,

> Throughout the correspondence there run certain threads of fundamental disagreement; but a mentor is not necessarily an absolute authority, and though Duncan's erudition, his being older than I, his often authoritative manner, and an element of awe in my affection for him combined to make

me take, much of the time, a pupil role, he was all the more a mentor when my own convictions were clarified for me by some conflict with his.[32]

When she had a conflict with Duncan, it usually had to do with her taking the side of day-to-day reality in an aesthetic debate. Sometimes their arguments had to do with their sense of what was and wasn't poetry. Levertov could not find a way to share Duncan's enthusiasm about Gertrude Stein's language games, nor was she interested in the kind of verbal ambiguities with which Duncan was enthralled.

But they always had Georges Ivanovitch Gurdjieff or Gershom Scholem to correspond about. What they shared, always, was a sense of gratitude for the "old lore" and a feeling of excitement about the ways it came alive in their poetry. Albert Gelpi writes that "what bonded them was the effort to invest the kinds of formal experimentation they learned from Pound and Williams with something of the metaphysical aura and mystique of the Romantic imagination" (*DLL*, p. xiii). Levertov was more securely in touch with the world of the everyday (as it included both ordinary objects and political events) than Duncan was, and again and again he told her that she gave him a sense of the concrete particular that he longed for – when he did long for it. "Is there something in our undertaking religion or magic that declines, has begun to decline, the open risk of life?"[33] Duncan had asked H.D. It was a question that preoccupied him, and Levertov was able (when called on) to answer it for him. "I don't think any poet," she wrote him, "however different in kind, can afford to forget the words 'No ideas but in things'" (*DLL*, p. 59). Had the 1960s turned out differently, she and Duncan would have been friends for life.

Eight years passed between Rich's second book, *The Diamond Cutters*, and her third book, *Snapshots of a Daughter-in-Law*, in 1963. Great changes were happening everywhere the poet looked. Nations were testing nuclear weapons and each other: in October 1962 there was the Cuban Missile Crisis, the brink of nuclear annihilation. In November, George Wallace was elected governor of Alabama, and in January he gave his "Segregation Forever" inauguration speech. In the summer of 1963 Martin Luther King, Jr., delivered his "I Have a Dream" speech in Washington, D.C. In the fall of 1963 President Kennedy was assassinated in Dallas.

This was the atmosphere in which Rich's new poems were written and the world her book faced. No longer organized around elegant intimations of disaster, Rich's poems now employ flat descriptions of fact and plain statements of feelings. The storm was in progress, and Rich needed an answerable style, one that could talk about events outside houses and inside them.

She wanted to be able to say not only what had happened in America and the world but also how it had been experienced by her and people like her, how the events had influenced their domestic and inner worlds. She recalled, in 1964,

> In the period in which my first two books were written I had a much more absolutist approach to the universe than I now have. I also felt as many people still feel – that a poem was an arrangement of ideas and feeling, predetermined.... Only gradually, within the last five or six years, did I begin to feel ... that in many cases I had suppressed, omitted, falsified even, certain disturbing elements, to gain that perfection of Order. (*ARP*, p. 165)

"Perfection of Order" was a difficult thing to surrender. A patient attention to craft was what she had been raised to value. At the same time there was the "extraordinary relief" (as she also remarked) of writing angry, impatient poems, of taking on the tremendous energy of the storm she had earlier dreaded.

But some of her strongest poems were about exhaustion. In "Snapshots of a Daughter-in-Law," she writes, "Banging the coffee-pot into the sink / she hears the angels chiding, and looks out / past the raked gardens to the sloppy sky. / Only a week since They said *Have no patience*" (*ARP*, p. 9). What's notable in these lines is the tone of grim reportage, of a stubborn commitment, no matter how tiring and destructive it might prove, to accuracy about her feelings. Everything makes ugly, unpleasant sounds. The coffee pot bangs, the angels chide. Work is never done. The garden is raked, but the sky is still sloppy. Whatever good may come will not arrive in an atmosphere of grandeur or grace. But something, some change will come. The lines are memorable in their insistence on fidelity to experience and their refusal to draw prematurely optimistic conclusions from that experience.

These changes became the subject of her most memorable poems of the 1960s. Rich moved with her family to New York in 1966. Her husband took a teaching position at City College, and she taught in a remedial program for minority students entering CUNY colleges. In 1967 Rich held positions at Swarthmore College and Columbia University and, from 1968, with City College of New York. In *Necessities of Life* (1966), *Leaflets* (1969), and *The Will to Change* (1971), she writes about contemporary topics, "Vietnam and the lover's bed" (*ARP*, p. 263). Again, Rich strove to write poems that showed how an individual's inner and private world could be, must be, radically affected and altered by outside events, hopeful and nightmarish, both at home and abroad. The rise of feminism was particularly important to her, although it didn't consume her attention until the 1970s.

Many poets were sympathetic to Rich's work, but some were not. When Levertov became an editorial adviser for the publisher W. W. Norton in the mid-1960s, she added Rich to its list. Robert Duncan's response was condescending about what he called the "genteel sensibilities" of the new poets Levertov favored (*DLL*, p. 543). Duncan believed in 1966 that Rich's sensibilities were still (would always be) genteel. Probably he meant that she had gone to Harvard. (Not every poet she added to the list was uncongenial to Duncan: for example, Ronald Johnson, a poet associated with the Black Mountain School's second generation and later with concrete poetry, whose mystical, difficult, 250-page poem *ARK* was, like Duncan's serial poem *Passages*, decades in the writing.)

No one's condescension could discourage Rich, though. She had broken away from unsupportive figures and was on her own now. There was always her father, but she was breaking away from him as well. In *Snapshots of a Daughter-in-Law* there is a powerful poem about her father, "After Dark." She writes, "That terrible record! how it played // down years, wherever I was / in foreign languages even." And she continues with repetition: "over and over, *I know you better / than you know yourself I know // you better than you know / yourself I know / you* until, self-maimed, / I limped off, torn at the roots" (*ARP*, pp. 24–25). I know you better / than you know yourself. Like James Wright, and Robert Duncan (in his way), Rich had to declare a kind of independence from her mentors, to say that she knew herself better than her mentors knew her. Rich had the sense after *Snapshots of a Daughter-in-Law* that she had left – with varying degrees of difficulty and regret – her father and the New Critics and the high modernists behind. In "In the Evening," from *Leaflets*, she writes, "The old masters, the old sources, / haven't a clue what we're about, / shivering here in the half-dark sixties."[34] And in "The Blue Ghazals," from *The Will to Change*, she addresses Wallace Stevens, one of the "old masters" who influenced her early work: "Would this have left you cold, our scene, its wild parades, / The costumes, banners, incense, flowers, the immense marches?"[35]

Poets who have had to break away from mentors will (sometimes) be for that reason more useful as examples. Adrienne Rich, as the 1960s continued, was concerned with making herself a model for others, and she wrote more and more about her life in the world. She insisted on writing poems about politics and about her personal life, arguing again and again that they were part of the same phenomenon. Let others choose the political or the personal. She chose both. Where Duncan collapsed distinctions between the inner and the outer, and Wright brought the memories of the outer world with him on his journey into his inner world, Rich was more alert to the tensions between the two worlds, writing poems that showed the constant and complicated tension between them.

   Another poet of that time might have chosen the confessional mode. But, although Rich wrote powerful poems about the end of relationships, the confessional mode didn't attract her. She was determined to tell her stories in a way that would prove useful to sympathetic readers. Like Wright, Duncan, and Levertov, Rich wanted to attach her poetry to something more capacious than her personal biography. She developed new tonalities appropriate to political rage and to subversive acts of tenderness. In order to avoid a tone of magisterial isolation, that of the leader moving ever ahead of her followers – a tone to which she was drawn – Rich fought to keep herself on the same level as the readers (women, more and more) to whom her poems were addressed. Prophetic isolation was a temptation, but Rich kept fighting it. David Kalstone wrote, "Rich's poems are bound to be restless, bound to be looking constantly for new beginnings, because they will never resign themselves to solitude."[36] Over and over, she imagined herself in conversation with her readers. "Our future depends on the sanity of each of us," Rich wrote in 1975, "and we have a profound stake, beyond the personal, in describing our reality as candidly and fully as we can to each other."[37] Kalstone writes that "her poems, however public in reference, proceed in a tone of intimate argument, as if understanding – political as well as private – is only manifest in the tones with which we explain ourselves to lovers, friends, our closest selves."[38]

   James Wright's *The Branch Will Not Break* (1963) showed the extent of his engagement with Deep Image poetics. Galway Kinnell, another Deep Image poet (others included W. S. Merwin, William Stafford, Donald Hall, David Ignatow, and John Haines), described the strategy of making a progress inward "until you're just a person. If you could keep going deeper and deeper, you'd finally not be a person either; you'd be an animal; and if you kept going deeper and deeper, you'd be a blade of grass or ultimately perhaps a stone. And if a stone could read, [Deep Image] poetry would speak for it."[39] David Perkins writes that Deep Image poetry "appealed as a way of evading the ego and making contact with a deeper self, sometimes identified as the unconscious. Or it allowed one, so the theory went, to get beyond the personal, social and historical and to reach a more essential reality."[40] Among the words the Deep Image poets used were "stone," "dark," "water," "blood," "tree," "night," "wind," "branch," "voice," "light," "face," "ashes," "moon," "dead," "snow," "birds," and "silence." Even for an unsympathetic reader guarded against them, these words instantly evoked a certain atmosphere. More was promised by the images, though, than simply a mysterious mood. The deep image carried with it a kind of promise of happiness, especially in Bly's account. For him, the deep image had power to heal.

But not every Deep Image reader or poet felt the healing effect. To Robert and Carol Bly, Wright wrote, "I am just alien, that's all. My relation to everyday life, in short, is incredibly tortured" (*WP*, p. 236). He was, unlike Rich, resigned to solitude. Writing, in 1972, to Helen McNeely Sheriff, his high school Latin teacher, Wright remembered that "for me personally, the years between 1962 and 1968 were riddled with a confusing and sometimes harrowing loneliness. I was teaching all the time … but even so, I did a good deal of rootless prowling all around the United States whenever I got the chance" (*WP*, p. 375). Along with a sense of despair, Wright's poems communicated a sense of compassion for the poor and homeless, the alcoholics, and the physically or mentally ill. "The suffering of other people," Robert Hass explained, "particularly the lost and the derelict, is actually a part of his own emotional life."[41] *Shall We Gather at the River* (1967), in particular, is a book notable for the sadness pervading it. Nothing breaks the hushed spell of the book unless it's the speaker's intermittent sense of panic. It reads as if it were a last book. Even the poems that feel theatrical take on the special power of occasions in which some small event or terrible feeling is being enacted or experienced for the last time. "The Life" ends with the words, "It is the old loneliness. / It is. / And it is / The last time."[42] A reader would be tempted to call it a final testament – but "testament" is too elevated a word for a book of poems that often have recourse to mumbling and muttering and silence.

The sense of a real person, of unaccommodated humanness, in the poems of Wright's two 1960s books kept his Deep Image poems from appearing to play simply the same trick over and over. His work remains compelling to so many readers in part because of the poems in which he brooded (sometimes in oblique ways) on his disappointment with the images, with their power to heal or even comfort. Here is the last stanza of one of the poems in *Shall We Gather at the River*:

> No!
> I kneel down, naked, and ask forgiveness.
> A cold drizzle blows into the room,
> And my shoulders flinch to the bone.
> You have nothing to do with us.
> Sleep on.[43]

Words emerge from the Deep Image lexicon – "cold," "bone," "sleep" – and they try to do what is expected of them, but the speaker is already beyond the reach of consolation. The deep images are not helping. At the same time, he doesn't depend entirely on them. He is looking outward as well.

Wright died in 1980 of cancer of the tongue. His widow, Anne Wright, choosing the poems to include in Wright's *Selected Poems*, wrote in the preface to that book, "It was natural to me to gravitate to the later books, especially those written after our first trip to Europe in 1970. It was then that the darkness in his poems became infused with the light of Italy and France."[44] Still, although Stephen Yenser calls *Moments of the Italian Summer* "a splendid little book," the Wright poems that most readers remember and value are mostly in the books of the 1950s and 1960s.[45]

As the decade moved into its second half, the Vietnam War increasingly took over the consciousness of Americans who were following it on the news. Poets made statements and wrote poetry against it. Paul Breslin writes, "From 1965 onward, the war in Vietnam was the central political issue in American life, whether one supported it or opposed it. Among intellectuals and writers, the opposition was, by the late 1960s, almost universal."[46] In addition, more and more Americans began to make connections between the civil rights movement and the Vietnam War. Levertov collected signatures from hundreds of artists and writers for an antiwar advertisement that appeared in the *New York Times* in April 1965. That month, 25,000 people attended the first antiwar march in Washington. In October 1965, there were 100,000 antiwar protesters in 80 cities. In his poem, "Wichita Vortex Sutra" (1966), Allen Ginsberg pronounced that the war – at least in his mind – was over.[47] (Ginsberg's particular place in the culture had, to a considerable extent, been taken over by Bob Dylan, whose lyrics were a constant inspiration and provocation to poets and protesters.) Meanwhile, Robert Bly began to organize a series of poetry readings in various colleges and universities across the United States. All the poems selected for recitation in some way reflected the feelings of opposition to the war on the part of the participants. In 1966, Bly and David Ray collected a number of these poems and published them at the Sixties Press under the title *A Poetry Reading against the Vietnam War*.[48] Among the members of Bly and Ray's organization, American Writers Against the Vietnam War, were James Wright, Robert Creeley, Lawrence Ferlinghetti, Donald Hall, Galway Kinnell, and Robert Lowell. Levertov gave talks and readings against the war all over the country, both as part of this group and on her own.

Martin Luther King, Jr., too, was beginning to give speeches against the Vietnam War. In March 1967 when Vice President Hubert H. Humphrey addressed the National Book Award ceremonies in Manhattan, Denise Levertov's husband, Mitchell Goodman, led fifty people in a walkout, shouting,

"Mr. Vice President, we are burning children in Vietnam, and you and we are responsible!"[49] In 1968 Goodman organized, along with Dr. Benjamin Spock and William Sloane Coffin, an antidraft protest, which involved gathering up draft cards from young war protesters in Boston and elsewhere and turning them in to the Justice Department in Washington. The three activists were sentenced to two years in prison (overturned on appeal). Paul Breslin objects that "the New Left ... could mount attention-getting events – demonstrations, draft card burnings, sit-ins at campuses and draft boards – but fared poorly with the unglamorous tasks of recruitment and organization."[50] But this is to underestimate the courage required to participate in many of these "theatrical" events. In August 1968 antiwar demonstrators were beaten by police outside the Democratic National Convention.

More and more poets wanted to write powerful antiwar poetry in support of the cause, and many poets were forced to adopt public voices for the first time in their careers. Those who weren't sure how to do it could learn from Robert Bly. He believed that because the authentic poet must address both worlds, the surreal world and the real world, the "deepest privacy" (luckily) would not have to be abandoned. In his essay "Leaping Up into Political Poetry," he claimed, "The political activists in the literary world are wrong – they try to force political poetry out of poets by pushing them more deeply into events, making them feel guilt if they don't abandon privacy. But the truth is that the political poem comes out of the deepest privacy."[51] Whether this version of the statement "the personal is political" was productive of good poetry can be seen by looking at Bly's antiwar poems of the period. It is clear, though, why antiwar poets were drawn to Deep Image poetics. David Perkins writes that "during the 1960s [Deep Image poetry] seemed to many poets the only literary language in which it was possible to write of the war in Vietnam."[52]

How could Deep Image poetry be useful as a language with which to protest the war? Paul Breslin tries to re-create the process by which a Deep Image politics was formulated. "White Americans and western Europeans, from whom I am descended," thinks Breslin's imagined composite Deep Image poet, "have imposed their will on other peoples in terrible ways. What they have done to others is analogous to what they have done to their own instincts, justifying such oppression and repression by appeals to reason and law. It is the ego that has done this; away with it, therefore, and with reason and law, which are its instruments."[53] The fact that news from overseas seemed increasingly horrific and unimaginable made Bly's strategy seem sensible.

Levertov began to write more and more antiwar poems – she was beginning to write hardly anything but antiwar poems – but she wanted to make them her own. In the early 1960s she had published *With Eyes at the Back of Our Heads* (1960), *The Jacob's Ladder* (1962), and *O Taste and See* (1964). Although she might at that time have said that the central tension in her poetry (if there was a tension) was between the everyday and the sacred or magical, the real tension turned out to be between the everyday, the sacred, the magical, and the Vietnam War, which was neither an everyday nor a sacred nor a magical event. For Bly, the war was surreal. Levertov didn't want to look at it that way: it seemed too easy. But her models – William Carlos Williams, Robert Duncan, and Charles Olson – were no help either, when she wanted to write poems that would express her horror at Vietnam War atrocities. Nevertheless, she pressed on. Her moral fervor would see her through.

Duncan made his own decisions about how to respond to the Vietnam War. Although he did write poems like "The Up-Rising," he made the decision to stop writing antiwar poems. As Gelpi writes, "Convinced that his own rage at the war, however morally justified, implicated him in the violence and betrayed his deepest responsibilities as a visionary artist, Duncan chose, after 1966, to maintain an anarchist detachment from the war zone for the sake of his life in poetry" (*DLL*, p. xviii). In his "Vancouver Lecture I," Duncan's friend, the poet Jack Spicer, said,

> So one day … suddenly there comes a poem which you just hate and would like to get rid of, that says just exactly the opposite of what you mean, of what you have to say. Like you want to say something about your beloved's eyebrows and the poem says the eyes should fall out, and you don't really want the eyes to fall out. Or you're trying to write a poem about Vietnam and you write a poem about skating in Vermont.[54]

If Duncan's poem about Vietnam turned out to be a poem about Vermont, so be it. In 1966 he accused Levertov of allowing her horror at the war to diminish her ability to experience visionary wonder:

> Denny, the last poem brings with it a sense of how the monstrosity of this nation's War is taking over your life, and I wish that I could advance some – not consolation, there is none – wisdom of how we are to at once bear constant (faithful and ever present) testimony to our grief … and at the same time continue as constantly in our work … to keep alive the immediacy of the idea and of the eternal. (*DLL*, p. 563)

One can imagine how irritating such a letter must have been for Levertov to receive. His manner had been "often authoritative" but never so patronizing. More condescending letters were to come.

Levertov responded to Duncan that she needed to write the poems she was writing, even if they were taking over her life. In "Life at War," from *To Stay*

Alive (1971), for example, she wrote of the pain and horror of knowing that human beings,

> delicate Man, whose flesh
> responds to a caress, whose eyes
> are flowers that perceive the stars
>
> whose music excels the music of birds . . .
>
> still turns without surprise, with mere regret
> to the scheduled breaking open of breasts whose milk
> runs out over the entrails of still-alive babies,
> transformation of witnessing eyes to pulp-fragments,
> implosion of skinned penises into carcass-gulleys.[55]

She had celebrated the numinous in the everyday and the divine in the human for decades, and she could not understand how human beings could commit such appalling acts on one another's bodies. But an aesthetic that had valued spontaneity and open-endedness now came to seem stiff and didactic. A way of writing (Williams with a touch of the spiritual) that had seemed adequate to any occasion, an aesthetic that found or made occasions for so many poems, now came to seem inadequate to any. A sense of desperation entered her anti-war poems when – to take an example from "Life at War" – words like "mercy" and "lovingkindness" showed their uselessness except in the service of a savage irony and when the divine in the human seemed impossible to believe in. At such crisis moments her voice became shrill: "burned human flesh / is smell-ing in Vietnam as I write." Sensing her own stridency and wanting to stabilize the poem, she often fell back on a tone of absolute certainty. By 1971, Duncan, offended by her tone of moral certainty, attacked her antiwar pronouncements as riddled with sentimental "Polonius pieties"; although he ultimately apolo-gized, Levertov wrote, "Your letter came *at least* 2 years too late. I don't find it in me to respond with the warmth & gladness you expected" (*DLL*, p. 717).

In 1970 Rich ended her marriage. Her collection *Diving into the Wreck* (1974) won the National Book Award. Rich refused the award individually but joined with Alice Walker and Audre Lorde to accept it on behalf of all women. In 1976 she came out in prose: "Heterosexuality as an institution has also drowned the erotic feelings between women," she wrote. "I myself lived half a life-time in the lie of that denial. That silence makes us all, to some degree, into liars" (*ARP*, p. 200). Her pamphlet "Twenty-One Love Poems," the first direct treatment of lesbian desire in her work, was included in *Dream of a Common Language* (1978). She has continued to write strong poetry that is both intro-spective and politically committed.

What happened to Deep Image poetry? Is there such a thing as post–Deep Image poetry? The excitement didn't last, although readers are still drawn to Wright's poems of the 1960s. But the poets themselves began to lose interest. The Vietnam War came to an end. Jacques Derrida came to deliver a talk at Johns Hopkins in 1966, and it became possible to question the idea of "depth" without seeming uninterestingly down-to-earth. (The "image," chastened, returned to its place in Pound's lexicon.) Some poets stopped descending to the depths only because they recognized that surfaces are just as productive of strangeness – certainly its strangeness can seem fresher. Language poets and minimalist poets took up the burden of writing the strangest possible poems: Robert Grenier's work *Sentences*, for example, consists simply of a box of cards, on each of which a few words or phrases are typewritten. On one card is the phrase "waiting it out"; on another, "tree is so hazy"; and on another, "absence of clutter." There are five hundred cards.

Duncan continued to keep all his influences in a state of suspense about him. As Devin Johnston writes, "In both his poetry and his critical writings on that poetry, Duncan exhibits the desire to maintain all possible interpretations."[56] As Duncan himself put it, "I have never been and never will be baptized, converted, psychoanalyzed, initiated, graduated, endowed, sacramented or insured."[57] Although Levertov was no longer there to tell him that everything he wrote had a "crazy exalted validity, *no matter what,*" he succeeded in remaining a strong poet in the 1970s and 1980s. Because, as he wrote in his notes to his book on H.D., "my worship belonged to no church … my imagination of my self belonged to no philosophic system," he continued to write idiosyncratic and distinctive poetry about both the inner and outer worlds, refusing to acknowledge that there was any tension between them. If his work suffered for this refusal, it gained a kind of eccentric grandeur at the same time. In 1984 he published *Ground Work: Before the War.* That same year he was diagnosed with kidney failure. In 1987 he published *Ground Work: In the Dark,* his final collection. He died in 1988 of heart and kidney complications.

In 1972 Levertov and Muriel Rukeyser visited Hanoi as representatives of the American peace movement. (One can imagine Duncan telling her again that the war was taking over her inner life.) Her book *A Door in the Hive* included an elegy to Duncan. The poem begins,

> You were my mentor. Without knowing it,
> I outgrew the need for a mentor.
> Without knowing it, you resented that,

and attacked me. I bitterly resented
the attack, and without knowing it
freed myself to move forward
without a mentor.[58]

Levertov had sailed through the 1950s and 1960s with a style possibly too easily achieved. The British New Romantics were, as a group, easily left behind. She found a new American style by mixing Williams and Duncan. It was possible that she hadn't had to work hard enough for her new hybrid style, or hadn't ever had to make it work harder in her poems. Whether she ever did free herself to move forward from her mentors – from Duncan or Williams – is doubtful. If David Perkins is right in saying that she "has the dubious merit of being a completely representative poet," her struggles show how difficult it was to achieve an independent, authentic voice in the 1960s.[59]

Notes

1. Lionel Trilling, *Sincerity and Authenticity* (Cambridge, Mass.: Harvard University Press, 1972), p. 11.
2. Trilling, *Sincerity and Authenticity*, p. 105.
3. Paul Breslin, *The Psycho-Political Muse: American Poetry Since the Fifties* (Chicago: University of Chicago Press, 1987), p. xiv.
4. Devin Johnston, *Precipitations: Contemporary American Poetry as Occult Practice* (Middletown, Conn.: Wesleyan University Press, 2002), p. 51.
5. Donald Allen (ed.), *The New American Poetry, 1945–1960* (New York: Grove, 1960); Donald Hall, Robert Pack, and Louis Simpson (eds.), *New Poets of England and America* (New York: Meridian, 1957).
6. James E. B. Breslin, *From Modern to Contemporary: American Poetry, 1945–1965* (Chicago: University of Chicago Press, 1984), p. 12.
7. Breslin, *From Modern to Contemporary*, p. 1.
8. Breslin, *From Modern to Contemporary*, p. 2.
9. Randall Jarrell, *Kipling, Auden and Company, Essays and Reviews, 1935–1964* (New York: Farrar, Straus and Giroux, 1981), p. 48.
10. James Wright, *A Wild Perfection: The Selected Letters of James Wright*, ed. A. Wright and S. R. Maley (New York: Farrar, Straus and Giroux, 2005), p. 113. This collection will be cited in the text as *WP*.
11. David Perkins, *A History of Modern Poetry*. Vol. 2, *Modernism and After* (Cambridge, Mass.: Harvard University Press, 1987), pp. 567–68.
12. Robert Duncan and Denise Levertov, *The Letters of Robert Duncan and Denise Levertov*, ed. Robert Bertholf and Albert Gelpi (Stanford, Calif.: Stanford University Press, 2004), p. 266. This collection will be cited in the text as *DLL*.

13. Adrienne Rich, *Adrienne Rich's Poetry and Prose*, ed. Barbara Charlesworth and Albert Gelpi (New York: W. W. Norton, 1993), pp. 15–16. This collection will be cited in the text as *ARP*.

14. Adrienne Rich, *A Change of World* (New Haven, Conn.: Yale University Press, 1951), p. 10.

15. Michael Davidson, *Ghostlier Demarcations: Modern Poetry and the Material World* (Berkeley: University of California Press, 1997), p. 174.

16. H.D. and Robert Duncan, *A Great Admiration: H.D. / Robert Duncan: Correspondence 1950–1961*, ed. Robert Bertholf (Venice, Calif.: The Lapis Press, 1992), p. 13.

17. H.D. and Duncan, *A Great Admiration*, p. 45.

18. Robert Duncan, *The H.D. Book*, ed. Michael Boughn and Victor Coleman (Berkeley: University of California Press, 2011), p. 69.

19. Robert Duncan, *Roots and Branches* (New York: New Directions, 1964), p. 3; Robert Duncan, *Fictive Certainties* (New York: New Directions, 1985).

20. H.D. and Duncan, *A Great Admiration*, p. 17.

21. H.D. and Duncan, *A Great Admiration*, p. 26.

22. Duncan, *Roots and Branches*, p. 6.

23. Ekbert Faas, *Young Robert Duncan: Portrait of the Poet as Homosexual in Society* (Santa Barbara, Calif.: Black Sparrow, 1983), p. 153.

24. Christopher Beach, *Ezra Pound and the Remaking of American Tradition* (Berkeley: University of California Press, 1992), p. 188.

25. Robert Duncan, *A Selected Prose*, ed. Robert Bertholf (New York: New Directions, 1995), p. 14.

26. Davidson, *Ghostlier Demarcations*, p. 177.

27. Alan Williamson, *Introspection and Contemporary Poetry* (Cambridge, Mass.: Harvard University Press, 1984), p. 10.

28. Robert Duncan, *The Opening of the Field* (New York: Grove Press, 1960), pp. 5–7.

29. Davidson, *Ghostlier Demarcations*, p. 175.

30. Robert Bly, *American Poetry: Wildness and Domesticity* (New York: Harper and Row, 1990), p. 119.

31. Charles Altieri, *Enlarging the Temple: New Directions in American Poetry During the 1960s* (Lewisburg, Pa.: Bucknell University Press, 1979), p. 24.

32. Denise Levertov, *New and Selected Essays* (New York: New Directions, 1992), pp. 205–06.

33. Robert Duncan, in H.D. and Duncan, *A Great Admiration*, p. 54.

34. Adrienne Rich, *Leaflets* (New York: W. W. Norton, 1969), p. 15.

35. Adrienne Rich, *The Will to Change* (New York: W. W. Norton, 1971), p. 21.

36. David Kalstone, *Five Temperaments* (New York: Oxford University Press, 1977), p. 162.

37. Adrienne Rich, *On Lies, Secrets and Silence* (New York: W. W. Norton, 1995), p. 190.
38. Kalstone, *Five Temperaments*, p. 142.
39. A. Poulin, Jr., and M. Waters (eds.), *Contemporary American Poetry*, 8th ed. (Boston: Houghton Mifflin, 2006), p. 628.
40. Perkins, *A History of Modern Poetry*, p. 559.
41. Robert Hass, *Twentieth Century Pleasures: Prose on Poetry* (Hopewell, N.J.: Ecco, 1984), pp. 31–32.
42. James Wright, *Shall We Gather at the River* (Middletown, Conn.: Wesleyan University Press, 1967), p. 38.
43. Wright, *Shall We Gather at the River*, p. 44.
44. James Wright, *Selected Poems*, ed. A. Wright and R. Bly (New York: Farrar, Straus and Giroux, 2005), p. xii.
45. Stephen Yenser, "Open Secrets," *Parnassus* 6:2 (1978), pp. 125–42, 142.
46. Breslin, *The Psycho-Political Muse*, p. 7.
47. Allen Ginsberg, *Planet News* (San Francisco: City Lights, 1968), p. 132.
48. Robert Bly and David Ray (eds.), *A Poetry Reading Against the Vietnam War* (Madison, Minn.: Sixties Press, 1966).
49. "Mitchell Goodman, Antiwar Protest Leader, Dies at 73," *New York Times*, February 6, 1997.
50. Breslin, *The Psycho-Political Muse*, p. 17.
51. Bly, *American Poetry: Wildness and Domesticity*, p. 247.
52. Perkins, *A History of Modern Poetry*, p. 559.
53. Breslin, *The Psycho-Political Muse*, p. 128.
54. Peter Gizzi (ed.), *The House that Jack Built: The Collected Lectures of Jack Spicer* (Middletown, Conn.: Wesleyan University Press, 1998), pp. 6–7.
55. Denise Levertov, *Poems 1968–1972* (New York: New Directions, 1987), p. 122.
56. Johnston, *Precipitations*, p. 98.
57. Duncan, *A Selected Prose*, p. 3.
58. Denise Levertov, *A Door in the Hive* (New York: New Directions, 1989), p. 4.
59. Perkins, *A History of Modern Poetry*, p. 509.

Chapter 39

James Merrill and His Circles

DAVID BERGMAN

Few triumphs would be odder than if James Merrill emerged as the premier American poet of his highly talented and various generation. And what a generation it is. The year Merrill was born, 1926, also saw the births of A. R. Ammons, Robert Creeley, Allen Ginsberg, and Frank O'Hara. The next year John Ashbery, W. S. Merwin, and James Wright were born. Merrill is far more conservative than most of his cohort, writing in rhyme and standard meter. In a period whose poetry is marked by self-revelation, emotional intensity, and extremity, he is decidedly cool, discreet, and even remote. He did not encourage disciples, although followers came. He did not seek to become a cult figure. Yet his ambitions outstripped those of his contemporaries. In sheer volume, even Ashbery's 200-page elegy *Flow Chart* seems puny next to the 550 pages of *The Changing Light at Sandover*. Only a few have dared to engage in a Virgil-like career in which short poems of technical virtuosity gave way to an epic on cosmological themes. He asked to be compared to the leading voices of continental modernism – Yeats, Proust, Cavafy, Rilke, and Montale – not as a modest follower but as an equal. W. H. Auden, who influenced so many poets, was Merrill's most important predecessor; Merrill made Auden a central character in *Sandover*, one whose lessons on poetry, life, and the cosmos they discuss as comrades.

In various ways Merrill's aspirations and ambitions are consistent with his privileged birth. He was the son of Charles Merrill, the founder of Merrill Lynch, at one time the largest stock brokerage firm in the world. He grew up surrounded by servants in a palatial home designed by Stanford White. He went to Amherst College, then an exclusive men's school. He could afford to devote himself to literature, never needing to earn money. He traveled the world and owned homes in Athens, Key West, and Stonington, Connecticut. Given such privilege, how could he aspire to anything less than greatness?

And, indeed, Merrill came to win the most important awards given to American poets. He began slowly enough. His first volume, *Jim's Book* (1942), financed by his father, was published when he was only sixteen. Another limited edition followed four years later, and it was not until his third commercially published volume, *Water Street* (1962), that his work became widely noticed. In the 1960s and 1970s he won the National Book Award twice (1966 and 1978), the Pulitzer Prize (1976), and the Bollingen Prize for Poetry (1974). Only John Ashbery could be said to be more celebrated.

Yet in many ways the work deflects the very greatness to which it so clearly aspires. The coolness of the work makes it hard to love. Its formality made it seem like a throwback to an earlier era. Its difficulty makes it hard to assimilate. Its vastness is not bridged by the manic energy of James Schuyler or A. R. Ammons. Its lyrics rarely float with the limpid musicality of W. S. Merwin. He does not charm like Frank O'Hara, exhort with the moral conviction of Adrienne Rich, bemuse like Ashbery, nor sound the deep humanistic chord of Richard Wilbur. The *donné* of his epic *The Changing Light at Sandover* is goofy – cosmic lessons learned through a Ouija board. How can one take that seriously? How could greatness arise from a source so tawdry, contemptible, even camp? These are questions the poem raises and in raising both deflects the terms it invites and invites the terms it deflects. And because Merrill always kept readers on their toes, he may well emerge as *the* major poet of his time, even as he seems unlikely to do so.

One sort of deflection started early – a deflection of the homosexual erotics that would become central to *Sandover*. As Merrill explains in his memoir, *A Different Person* (1993), "I never doubted that almost any poem I wrote owed some of its difficulty to the need to conceal my feelings, and their objects. Genderless as a figleaf, the pronoun 'you' served to protect the latter but one couldn't be too careful."[1] Sometimes such deflections have interesting consequences, as Merrill circumnavigates the issue by sailing into new waters. Sometimes they merely muffle the poem. "River Poem," from Merrill's earliest commercial publication, *First Poems* (1951), is one that gets muffled. Ostensibly, "River Poem" is about the inability of knowing the contents of another person's mind, a theme it enacts by withholding what is on Merrill's mind. But as Merrill, who underwent extensive psychoanalysis, would know all too well, the repressed always makes its return and becomes knowable (to other minds), albeit in coded and displaced form. The poem begins at the banks of a river where Charles – Merrill's alter ego (and the name of both his father and brother) – and his friends (all seemingly male) observe a well-dressed, older man watching a crew team practicing.[2] As if it were a Thomas Eakins painting of the Schuylkill, the entire poem is cast in shades of purple. Significantly, the older man has "lavender skin," and his handkerchief topples "from his breast pocket like an iris."[3] In short, the poem codes him by color and his dandyish apparel as an elderly homosexual, and the scene recalls that celebrated episode of Whitman's "Song of Myself" when "twenty-eight young men bathe by the river" ogled by the lonesome housewife.[4] And just as Whitman wonders "Which of the young men does she like the best?" so Charles muses whether the rowers mean to the older man "As much as I can imagine they mean to him" (*JMC*, p. 23). Charles is certain that the rowers mean *something* to the older man; he is uncertain only whether they hold *as much* significance as Charles imagines. The first question that is dodged is just how much Charles thinks they mean to the man. Or rather, how much does the older man share Charles's erotic excitement over the rowers? But the poem immediately deflects those questions with the vague assertion: "Charles was like that." The poem then obscures the question of desire still further by turning the elderly man into "a river flower, thinking of rivery things." The rowers, the true object of the nattily dressed older man, have become the generalized "rivery things," and then, as though that were still a bit too close for comfort, the poem ends:

> We would never
> Know, this we knew, how much it had meant to him –
> Oars, violet water, laughter on the stream.
> Though we knew, Charles said, just how much *he* meant to the river.
> For he moved away, leaving us there on the grass,
> But the river did not vanish, or not then at least.   (*JMC*, p. 23)

The issue now has changed. No longer is the poem about the contents of other people's minds; it is now about nature's indifference to the human. The river's indifference to the elderly man is hardly wisdom, even for the callow Charles. The poem seems to have reached a dead end. Yet what would happen if we replaced "river" with "rowers"? Would Charles be so certain if he asked how much the older man meant to the *rowers*? Are the rowers going to ignore the old man? Are beautiful young men always going to ignore their admirers? Or, to put it in Proustian terms: do we get what we want only after we no longer want it? "River Poem" on the surface muffles the very terms it sets up, but if we do not allow these evasions and work against the poem's deflections, it holds together reasonably well. Is "River Poem" "wholly successful," as Daniel Mark Epstein asserts?[5] I do not think so. But it is a far more interesting poem if we do not give into its suave deflections.

"The Lovers" is another poem in which the erotic situation is immediately swamped by metaphor. Stephen Yenser says that the "vehicle nudges the tenor aside," but it seems to me the nudge is more a crushing blow – a poetic hit and run.[6] Merrill explains that the poem is "one of a great number ... where the human situation *is* a metaphor or perhaps even a vision," and although he's "never altogether pleased to see this happen ... it does again and again."[7] Once again, readers are forced to stay on their toes. The lovers of the title appear, if they can be said to appear at all, only in the first line, when "They met in loving like the hands of one / Who having worked six days with creature and plant / Washes his hands" (*JMC*, p. 64). The rest of the thirty-line poem narrates the washing and drying of those Godlike hands. Loving as a Godlike force is a theme that Merrill will develop many times, but here the tenor gets sidetracked as he develops the farmer / God analogy. Indeed, by concentrating on the singular farmer, Merrill obscures the plural lovers. The conclusion obscures even the humanity of the lovers, from whose hands "issue ... harvest, flood, motherhood, mystery" (*JMC*, p. 64).

As Merrill grew stronger as a poet and as attitudes toward homosexuality changed, he found less need to deflect the subject and more interesting ways to deflect it. These deflections became ways of capturing the most elusive emotions and ideas. His was a personality that revealed itself most when kept partially out of view, and yet because his essential subject was love and because he lived in an age – unlike that of Proust – when the "thin gold mask" of literature could no longer be a fig leaf altering the sex of the beloved, he needed to devise ever more subtle means to reveal himself (*JMC*, pp. 139–40).

Among Merrill's most revealing poems is his nightmare / vision "Childlessness," which David Kalstone feels is the most important poem in *Water Street* (1962).[8] The poem grows out of a crisis described in his memoir in which Merrill accused himself of being "nearly thirty and not yet a father!" He felt that his childlessness was an attempt to put his parents "in their place" and that only by siring children could he "make peace" with them (*JMC*, p. 203). So anxious was he about having no children – and it is a theme that reappears throughout his work – that he consulted his psychoanalyst. It is, therefore, not surprising that the poem that emerged is a dream poem. It begins with Merrill harangued by a shrewish "dream-wife" for failing to plant a garden with "certain rare growths yielding guaranteed / Gold pollen, gender of suns, large, hardy, / Enviable blooms" (*JMC*, p. 148). Merrill's reluctance to plant seems connected to the fact that children constitute not a new beginning but rather a continuation of what is already "tainted," because the rain that feeds the garden is drawn "up from the impure ocean" and passed "through poisons visible at sunset"; he sees himself clothed by "slow colors" that burst on him "like buds, / Like bombs" (*JMC*, p. 148). Children are bombs (not balms), and children lead to an apocalypse.

> Later I am shown
> The erased metropolis reassembled
> On sampans, freighted each
> With toddlers, holy dolls, dead ancestors.   (*JMC*, p. 148)

The poem ends with a cloak – not unlike the one worn by the dream wife – thrown down for the earth to wear "in token of past servitude." The cloak falls "onto the shoulders of my parents / Whom it eats to the bone" (*JMC*, p. 148). The poem plays out a Malthusian drama that is central to *The Changing Light at Sandover*: reproduction leads not to greater fertility but rather to greater competition over scarce resources. Childlessness is not an act of disobedience to natural law but rather one way to curb the curse of overpopulation. The dream wife is an "enchantress, masked as friend," whose cape of what appears to be "voluminous pistachio, / Saffron and rose" is gemmed by bombs that will eat us to the bone (*JMC*, p. 148). There is no escape from the violence and corruption of the world; we can refuse only to play along with it. The dream poem is one way to deflect the homosexual subject and still keep it in play.

One of the ways Merrill developed to deflect his meanings is through riddles – refusing to utter key words. Take, for example, that late, light poem "b o d y," in which the "little kohl-rimmed moon" of an *o* appears on the proscenium, coursing between the uprights of the *b* and *d*, while *y* "unanswered, knocks at the stage door" (*JMC*, p. 646). To understand this little drama of the body, one needs to know "what the *b* and *d* stood for" (*JMC*, p. 646), yet Merrill keeps mum that in the sexual slang of the day, B and D (cousins to S and M) stand for bondage and discipline. The body oscillates between the various signs of abuse. The theatrical context may indicate that Merrill sees these various strictures as merely playacting or role-playing, but it does not alter the fact that at some level love requires – don't ask why – submission to punishing forces. The body binds us and asks for discipline.

A similar but far more elaborate riddling passage occurs in "Strato in Plaster." The poem takes place in Greece, where Merrill lived part of each year during the 1960s and early 1970s. Strato, a construction worker, was a friend of Merrill; how close a friend the poem leaves unsaid. Indeed, one of its central jobs is to deflect the depth of their relationship. Nevertheless, Merrill makes clear that Strato was so remarkably handsome in his day that people compared him to the Apollo at Olympia; now instead of having a body carved from marble, he has an arm cast in plaster. But that is hardly the only change

Strato has suffered. With "Those extra kilos, that mustache / Lies found out and letters left unanswered," Strato "Just won't do" (*JMC*, p. 336). The break in their friendship came when Merrill refused Strato's request for a loan. Still, Merrill is willing to have him visit, and as he leaves, Merrill takes Strato's "swollen hand in both of mine," uttering

> No syllable of certain grand tirades
> One spent the worse part of a fall composing,
> Merely that word in common use
> Which means both *foolishness* and *self-abuse*
> Coming to mind, I smile
> Was the break caused by too much malakía?
> Strato's answer is a final burst
> Of laughter: "No such luck!
> One day like this the scaffold gave beneath me.
> I felt no pain at first." (*JMC*, pp. 337–38)

What is "that word in common use / which means both *foolishness* and *self-abuse*"? In English it is "jerk off," and in Greek the slang term is *malakía*. Strato is a jerk-off, interested in his own pleasure and his own benefit. The "break" in their friendship was not caused, however, by too much *malakía* but happened when scaffolding gave way. The final line could be interpreted in many ways. Literally, of course, it means that the broken arm did not immediately hurt, yet it might signal that, after his break with Merrill, Strato felt no immediate pain but regretted it later. He also might be contrasting his absence of pain over their breakup with Merrill's apparent anguish, and finally he may be indicating that now he feels belatedly the sadness of their rupture. Yet for all the wordplay about masturbation, Strato's actual relationship to Merrill remains unspoken in "Strato in Plaster." In a later poem, "The House Fly," the relationship is made much more explicit, but even then it is depicted in chaste terms. Like John Donne's "The Flea," "The House Fly" uses an insect as the intermediary between people. But while Donne's flea draws blood from the two lovers, Merrill's housefly only alit "on the bare chest of Strato Mouflouzélis / Who stirred in the lamp-glow but did not wake" (*JMC*, p. 436). The poem ends years later with another house fly and Merrill partaking of the "mist-white wafer" of the sun, "making a rite / Distinct from both the blessing and the blight" (*JMC*, p. 436). Merrill and the housefly take communion, but with the sun, not with Strato, who is both blessing and blight. If in "The Lover" Merrill's vehicle overwhelmed his tenor, here he plays a subtle game of suggesting a variety of vehicles so that Strato's bare chest and the October sun might both be the "mist-white wafer." The point to keep in mind is that as Merrill developed as a poet, his reticence, his tendency to deflect information, served to open up depth of meaning and subtle possibilities of significance.

One more riddle poem, "Up and Down," is presented in two parts. The first part, "Snow King Chair Lift," recounts a journey to the top of Snow King Mountain in Wyoming, which Merrill undertook with David Jackson, "when we still thought we were each other's meat" (*JMC*, p. 340). The poem concerns the changes in their relationship, how "each summit is a cul-de-sac," and that their once sexually exciting relationship has flattened into domesticity. The section ends:

> Before I led you to the next chair back
>
> And made my crude but educated guess
> At why the wind was laying hands on you
> (Something I no longer think to do)
> We gazed our little fills at boundlessness.   (*JMC*, p. 340)

Once again we have a riddle. What is that "crude but educated guess / At why the wind was laying hands" on Jackson? The answer is erotic – the wind wants to blow him. But Merrill won't speak the word, nor does he indicate the sex of his companion, who is addressed by a genderless "you." Indeed, one of the themes of the poem is the value of reticence. Only the "very great or very fatuous" have a right to make speeches and "complicate the pinnacles they reach"; Merrill and Jackson do best by speaking a few words "in that chill / Lighthearted atmosphere" (*JMC*, p. 340). The ecstatic is most effectively addressed by near silence. Truly passionate moments need to be deflected to be discussed at all.

There is something sad in the fact that Merrill no longer thinks to lay hands on David Jackson, that the physical dimension of their relationship has ended. Yet this is a love poem, and part of the delicate dance that is typical of Merrill is the way he treats these painful episodes by producing a "chill / Lighthearted atmosphere." Many poems leave Merrill dangling by a thin cable over a seemingly boundless landscape and making the best of his dangerous and comic position. Merrill remains refined and cheery, even under the darkest and most painful conditions.

Passionate relations do not last for Merrill except in memory. They are translated – to use a metaphor that is central to Merrill – into the domestic if they last at all. One of the purposes of Merrill's deflections is to reduce the pain that comes from the dissolution of these relationships. Among the most painful of these dissolutions is the divorce of his parents, a trauma he rehearses repeatedly. The broken home is at once personal, historical, and mythic in nature. It is the need to render the event on all three levels that occupies him in two of his most celebrated poems: "The Broken Home" and "Lost in Translation."

"The Broken Home" begins with one of those deflections that contribute to the complexity of the poem. Crossing the street one twilight, Merrill sees parents and a child "At their window, gleaming like fruit / With evening's mild gold leaf": Merrill uses this domestic tableau to light "what's left of my life," but his belief in such a scene of domestic tranquility is almost immediately thrown into doubt. "Tell me, tongue of fire," he demands in the tercet that ends the first of the sonnet-like units from which the poem is constructed, "That you and I are as real / At least as the people upstairs" (*JMC*, p. 197). The family seems to be more real than he is, but if that is so, what reality do they have? He needs the icon of domestic ideality in order to make sense of the dysfunctional family he came from. Yet the Merrills are not an oddity; they are very much the product of their times. His father, a veteran flyer in World War I, returns home set on victory in the financial world as he was set on victory in the skies over Europe. His mother was raised in the time when suffragists demanded from men that they *"Give us the vote!"* Even the Depression does not stop them, and they proceed with the intensity of "metal poured at the close of a proletarian novel," molten into precast figures (*JMC*, p. 198). But the Merrills are not simply symptomatic of the interwar years; they are embodiments of an archetypal pattern – "Father Time and Mother Earth, / A marriage on the rocks" (*JMC*, p. 198). Even the Oedipal drama played out in the mother's boudoir, when she, startled awake, reaches out for her fleeing son, even this conflict is less about individual pathology than the eternal drama of the family romance. The poem ends not with a reinvocation of the family upstairs but with "the real home," which is the broken home. Real homes are not ones that you look into as much as look out from to "watch a red setter stretch and sink in cloud" (*JMC*, p. 200).

Tightly bound up by the interweaving strands of the personal, historic, and mythic is the procreative urge; it is the one imperative that Merrill "Obeyed, at least inversely." He will not reproduce as his parents had; in fact, Merrill does not even "try to keep a garden, only / An avocado in a glass of water – / Roots pallid, gemmed with air"; when the avocados get too large, he lets "them die, yes, yes, / And start another." His interest in the avocado is neither breeding nor food but the aesthetic pleasure of its "small gilt leaves ... Fleshy and green." Merrill concludes that he is "no less time's child" and "earth's no less"; in short, he is the product of both Father Time and Mother Earth (*JMC*, p. 199).

By translating his personal trauma into historic and biologic terms, he deflects the pain of the divorce, reenvisions it as a cosmic necessity.

The interweaving strands of the personal, historic, and mythic are even more tightly bound in "Lost in Translation." The scene is the library of Merrill's parents' estate, where he is watched by Mademoiselle, his nanny, while his parents are off attending to their marital difficulties and subsequent custody battle. But Merrill is not the only person with conflicted loyalties. Mademoiselle is French only by marriage; her mother was English, and her father Prussian. She represents a European marriage on the rocks. To occupy the time while others squabble, Mademoiselle and Merrill cooperatively assemble jigsaw puzzles, sent each month from "A New York / Puzzle-rental shop (*JMC*, p. 363). Instead of being anxious about his parents, young Jimmy is concerned about his puzzle. One eventually arrives, and as nanny and child assemble the pieces – border first – they discover that the puzzle appropriately depicts an Arabian allegorical scene in which Houri and Afreet both claim a young page as their own, the child torn between them. Yet another marriage is ending in divorce.

What is the resolution to this constant process of marriage and separation? The symbolic answer may reside in Mademoiselle's nephew, who is a translator for the United Nations. His job is to use language to bridge the divisions between nations. But his is only one kind of translation. Merrill's parents' battle over his custody can be said to be translated into the Houri/Afreet jigsaw puzzle, which is a translation of a French Romantic painting, which is itself a translation of some other tale. For Merrill, "all is translation / And every bit of us is lost in it" (*JMC*, p. 367). The poet gets lost in language to find himself in it. Art translates experience by finding equivalencies between life and languages.

Yet there are no perfect equivalents, just as there are no perfect marriages. The translations of art are filled with mismatches, odd pairings, and strange deflections. The Ouija board may be viewed as a great translation machine, and the spirit world seems fascinated by translations. We learn from Mirabell, one of Merrill's interlocutors, that everyone can be translated into a formula. For example, we are "told" that Merrill is equal to "268 / 1:1,000,00 / 5.5 / 741."[9] But because the numbers are so abstract (and even this string of numerals is "vastly simplified"), the only way to communicate the cosmic reality to human consciousness is through metaphor – the trope of translation. The truth worth telling – the lived experience – can never be reduced to language, numbers, or formulae, but we are forced to use language, numbers, or formulae to suggest or invoke that experience. But because translation is always a mismatch and a deflection, Merrill is constantly playing with and alerting readers to the gaps. Each poem asks us to "mind the gap," as the British say.

These gaps can have profoundly comic effects. Merrill is an inveterate punster, and puns can be said to be the accidental mismatch between sounds and ideas. In "Lost in Translation," for example, Merrill does not know who painted the scene reproduced on the jigsaw puzzle, but he assumes it was "A minor lion attending on Gérôme," in short, a less celebrated follower of the French painter Jean-Léon Gérôme, who specialized in oriental subjects (*JMC*, p. 365). But the line also punningly refers to St. Jerome, who is traditionally accompanied by a small lion; the saint translated the Bible into Latin. This punning allusion to painter and patriarch is one of the accidental mismatches of language that Merrill revels in.

But there are more profound mismatches. One of Merrill's finest poems is "Days of 1964," a title that relates the poem to a number of poems by Constantine Cavafy, the Greek poet, who wrote about homosexual love. "Days of 1964" concerns Merrill's maid Kyria Kleo, who "wore brown, was fat, past fifty / And looked like a Palmyra matron, / Copied in lard and horsehair" (*JMC*, p. 220). Yet despite her looks, her age, and her disabilities – she has bad legs – Merrill comes to believe that "she *was* love," that she was an embodiment of Eros or Aphrodite. He discovers her about to climb a hill where people meet for illicit sex. She is wearing a tight sweater, and her face is painted into "the erotic mask / Worn the world over by illusion / To wedding of itself and simple need." Kyria Kleo reminds Merrill that love is anarchic, sacred, and comic. It does not obey laws, or cling to decorum. It will not be limited to the domestic. It pops out where least expected. The dowdy, middle-aged housekeeper who otherwise attends to her aged mother and wastrel son can be transformed or translated into a goddess.

The Changing Light at Sandover is filled with such transformations. Indeed, the first book of the trilogy, "The Book of Ephraim," is mostly concerned with the process of reincarnation. According to Ephraim, souls are continually reborn until they achieve a certain level of spiritual development. But even in the spirit world there is possibility for transformation. No one and no thing is quite what it seems to be. The bat-like creature called 741 is transformed by his association with humans into the peacock that is given the name Mirabell. Maria Mitsotáki, who with W. H. Auden is the leading guide through the spirit world, turns out to have been in previous lives Plato and Beatrice and in her new life a boy in Bombay, "THE YOUNGEST / ORDAINED [BRAHMIN] PRIEST IN HISTORY! ALREADY / CREDITED WITH 8 MIRACLES" (*CLS*, p. 542).

Spirits are not always happy with their next reincarnation. They also can get lost in translation. Chester Kallman, Auden's lover, is to be reborn as a black male in Johannesburg, which he sees as "GETTING THE / ULTIMATE REJECTION SLIP" (*CLS*, p. 184). This note of playful seriousness and sublime tawdriness – a note that Merrill had been developing throughout his career – is constantly struck in *Sandover*. After all, the Ouija board is a kind of game, which Merrill and his partner David Jackson were given as a present in 1955, in their second year of living in the house in Stonington, Connecticut, where they had yet to develop friends. They figured if they could not make friends with the living, then they might as well try to get acquainted with the dead. And sure enough, on their first night of playing with the Ouija board, they encountered the voice of Ephraim, who told them that he was a Greek Jew (with a Christian father) born in 8 C.E. in Xanthos, a favorite of Tiberus, and a lover of Caligula (*CLS*, p. 8). From 1955 through 1974, Merrill and Jackson stayed in touch with Ephraim, and "The Book of Ephraim" narrates their often outrageously funny experiences. Merrill believed he had come to the end of his Ouija board narrative, but then in 1976 a new voice demanded, "WE MUST HAVE / POEMS OF SCIENCE THE WEORK FINISHT [*sic*] IS BUT PROLOGUE," and he began what eventually became "Mirabell's Books of Number," "Scripts for a Pageant," and "Coda" (*CLS*, p. 113). What had started out as a 100-page poem – hardly a minor undertaking – mushroomed into more than 550 pages. What had begun as a wonderfully comic encounter with the spirit world now took on a new seriousness. It was a strange marriage.

There is something jerry-built about the poem despite its obvious surface structure. "Ephraim" has twenty-six sections, one for each letter of the alphabet; "Mirabell" has a hundred sections; and "Scripts" is dived into three parts – "Yes," "&," "No." Yet despite this elaborate superstructure, the poem seems highly improvised, and it contains recurrent discussions about how to organize and present the revelations dictated by the Ouija board. The work, for all its formal expertness, is wonderfully spontaneous – and it is this spontaneity that makes it difficult to know how seriously to take the voices in the poem and how far our attention is being deflected from serious matters.

The two principal concerns of Mirabell and the angels who come to instruct Merrill and Jackson are serious enough. Mankind's continuation is threatened by two forces: atomic energy and overpopulation. (In his work of the 1980s and 1990s, the anxiety over a nuclear catastrophe is replaced by the fear of environmental apocalypse.) "THE ATOM MUST," they are told, "BE RETURNED TO THE LAB & THE USES OF PARADISE" (*CLS*, p. 247). The population must be seriously cut down to two million. Yet is the urgency of these problems heightened by coming through a Ouija board? Doesn't this mode of transmission trivialize the issue? How are we to take these revelations? Is something in this message lost in translation?

These questions are ones that Merrill himself asks, and part of "Ephraim" recounts a visit to his old psychoanalyst, Tom Detre, who tells Merrill that "what you and David do / We call folie à deux." According to Dr. Detre, it is a way that Jackson and Merrill can "sound each other's depths of spirit" and, by producing the poem together, compensate for being childless (*CLS*, p. 30). Merrill realizes that he had not so much accepted the truth of what Ephraim said as ignored the absence of proof. It was hard to pin Ephraim down because his "grasp of dates and places" was feeble, his Latin "Vestigial," and his memory "spotty." Moreover, Merrill and Jackson both understood that it was quite possible that "his lights and darks were a projection / Of what already burned, at some obscure / Level or another, in our skulls" (*CLS*, p. 31). Nevertheless they were quite willing to play along with him. Indeed, according to Mirabell, it is precisely because Merrill and Jackson have passively entertained the voices from the Ouija board that the voices have come. When he came to other writers, Mirabell was met by a series of demands: "HARDLY HAD WE / FOLDED OUR MANY WINGS THAN SMALL GREEDY HANDS PLUCKED AT US / SAYING: WHAT OF TOMORROW? WHAT OF AUNT MIN? WHERE IS THE / BURIED TREASURE? & O LEAVE BEHIND THE FEATHER OF PROOF?" (*CLS*, p. 258). Merrill and Jackson do not ask for future predictions; they do not ask the spirits to protect them. They welcome the voices as widening and deepening their experiences; they recognize "How banal / Our lives would be, how shrunken, but for" Mirabell (*CLS*, p. 258). In short, Merrill reads the transcripts of the Ouija board as he would read a poem and as he would ask us to read his *Sandover* – as an imaginative experience whose aesthetic pleasures are independent of what "truths" they might contain.

One of the central distinctions made in *Sandover* is between thought and ideas. Thought is the aggressive intellectual process that analyzes and evaluates ideas, trying to determine their logical consistency and empirical truth. It does not allow itself to be deflected, and as a result, thinking destroys ideas (*CLS*, p. 426). It is just this aggressive intellectual process that brought about nuclear war and threatens the survival of humans. At the end of "Scripts for the Pageant," Nature tells Merrill and Jackson that the paradise to come "WILL HOLD A CREATURE MUCH LIKE DARLING MEN, YET PHYSICALLY MORE ADAPTABLE" (*CLS*, p. 512). This new, improved humanlike creature will be "A SIMPLER, LESS WILLFUL BEING. DULLER TOO? / IF SO, IS THAT SHARP EDGE NOT WELL LOST / WHICH HAS SO VARIOUSLY

CUT AND COST?" (*CLS*, p. 512). This Alpha Man will be able to entertain ideas and enjoy poems like *Sandover* but will not pursue the kind of aggressive intellectual activity that leads to war and global destruction.

In many ways the good reader of *The Changing Light at Sandover* is learning the skills needed to be an Alpha Man. Readers demanding logic and consistency will be flummoxed again and again by *Sandover*. Things that Ephraim tells Merrill are corrected by Mirabell, and things said by Mirabell are corrected by the archangels. On one of the rare occasions that Merrill in frustration asks for clarification, "Won't *someone* please explain the Black?" he is told:

> IN AMONG EARTH'S TREASURES ARE
> THE INFRA-TREASURES OF THE MONITOR:
> NOT FORWARD TIME COMPRESSED (COMBUSTIBLE
> OILCAN OF "THINNER") BUT ATOMIC BLACK
> COMPRESSED FROM TIME'S REVERSIBILITY,
> THAT IDEA OF DESTRUCTION WHICH RESIDES
> BOTH IN MAN & IN THE ACTINIDES
> PART OF THE GREENHOUSE, FOR (THO MATTER HOLDS)
> THESE FORK TONGUES FLICKER FROM ITS OILS & GOLDS.
>
> (*CLS*, p. 453)

Judith Moffett calls these lines "the mad, plausible voice of a fever-dream," of which "there is little point in struggling to make sense."[10] The poem defeats attempts to create a coherent, rational structure of the thought. Thought would destroy the poem. But if we entertain the entire work as a cosmological masque filled with gods and goddesses, talking animals and creatures (a loveable unicorn is part of the large cast), angels and demons, and wizards and fairies, then we would be preparing ourselves for the next stage in human development, or at least moving away from the destructive attitudes that plague humankind.

The Changing Light at Sandover is a celebration of poetry and the poetic sensibility that delights in ideas, plays with them, but insists that fact is fable (*CLS*, p. 263). It is significant that W. H. Auden, who famously proclaimed that "poetry makes nothing happen," is one of Merrill's two guides to the Other Side. One of the great English poets of the twentieth century, Auden was born in 1907 and died in Austria in 1973. In 1939, he came to America and, in 1946, became a U.S. citizen. Not only Auden's poetry but his voluminous essays exerted a considerable force on a wide variety of American poets, including Allen Ginsberg, Randall Jarrell, Muriel Rukeyser, and John Ashbery. But on no one was the influence as decisive as it was on Merrill. In *Sandover*, Auden answers Merrill's doubts about the project of writing the epic by giving a sustained defense of being a poet:

IS NOT ARCADIA TO DWELL AMONG
GREENWOOD PERSPECTIVES OF THE MOTHER TONGUE
ROOTSYSTEMS UNDERFOOT WHILE OVERHEAD
THE SUN GOD SANG & SHADES OF MEANING SPREAD
& FAR SNOWCAPPED ABSTRACTIONS GLITTERED NEAR
OR FAIRLY MELTED INTO ATMOSPHERE?   (*CLS*, p. 262)

Piotr Gwiazda points out how the figure of Auden in *Sandover* is different from the historical Auden, but there is no doubt that Auden meant a good deal not only to Merrill but to the poets that surrounded Merrill.[11] Among the most significant virtues that Auden exemplified for these poets were his formal virtuosity, his linguistic variety, and his wit. Aidan Wasley enumerates seven lessons Merrill learns from Auden, the last two being that "poets inherit and employ the voices of their predecessors" and "construct their own voices out of those they receive from the tradition."[12] *Sandover* fittingly sees Auden as occupying not a main salon in the house of poetry but "A BARE LOWCEILINGED MAID'S ROOM AT THE TOP" (*CLS*, p. 262). He lives in the servants' quarters, cleaning up after the grander poets have gone to sleep. And one should not ignore the camp image of Auden in a maid's outfit, wearing a clean white apron and a little starched cap. If such an image puts the reader off balance, so much the better. It is a comic method that Merrill learned from Auden, a method adopted by Auden's followers.

Auden is the master of that "chill / Lighthearted atmosphere" that Merrill breathes into his poems. Take, for example, Auden's poem "The More Loving One," whose most famous lines are the couplet, "If equal affection cannot be, / Let the more loving one be me" – his stoic acceptance of the way relationships break down. But the poem ends with a more cosmic sense of loneliness and emptiness.

> Were all stars to disappear and die,
> I should learn to look at an empty sky
> And feel its total dark sublime,
> Though this might take me a little time.[13]

What gives the "rueful joke" – as Edward Mendelson calls the final line – its bite is the inability to decide whether it is an example of understatement or a grim acknowledgement of the speed with which Auden is habituated to isolation and abandonment.[14] The anapestic substitution gives it a kind of skipping, throwaway rhythm that deflects the seriousness of the apocalyptic vision. Those like Merrill, Richard Howard, and J. D. McClatchy, whom we will examine, are sometimes criticized, as was Auden, for their lack of emotion. To be sure, compared to contemporaries such as Allen Ginsberg, Anne Sexton, or James Wright, they keep their hearts up rather than wearing them on their sleeves. With such sleight of hand, Auden uses humor to deflect readers not from deep emotion but from an abyss of feeling into which they might fall. Auden's poetry, like Merrill's, Howard's, and McClatchy's, is all the more deeply felt because his emotions are not allowed free rein but are kept in check by formal conventions, literary tradition, and personal irony.

A near contemporary of Merrill, Richard Howard (b. 1929) grew up in comfortable circumstances in Cleveland, Ohio, and attended Columbia University. He was adopted as a child, and his mother went through several divorces, yet his poetry rarely engages in Merrill's theme of the broken home. A prolific translator from the French – he was named in 1982 a chevalier of l'Ordre National du Mérite by the French government – Howard won the Pulitzer Prize for Poetry in 1969.

In Howard's mythology, Auden is Hephaistos, the blacksmith of the gods. It is an association that emphasizes the poem as something made, a sweaty job requiring heavy lifting. Hephaistos is also ugly and lame; the beauty he produces is separate from his person, and yet Hephaistos's very presence is inspiring. In the first of Howard's two poems on Auden, "For Hephaistos, with Reference to the Deaths in a Dry Year of Cocteau, Roethke and MacNeice," Howard runs into Auden at the doorway of a New York bookshop, where Auden casts an "air / Of tweedy degeneration" and is saved from looking like a bum only by "A final harmlessness." This unexpected encounter with the great man leaves Howard speechless; Auden, however, appears unaware that he has run into anyone, and the two poets pass without exchanging a word. Instead of being crushed by the failure to be recognized, Howard takes it as a lesson:

> You taught me, taught us all a way
> To speak our minds, and only now, at last
> Free of you, my old ventriloquist,
> Have I suspected what I have to say
> Without hearing you say it for me first.[15]

Howard is hurt, perhaps, by Auden's failure to recognize him, but he sees it as one of the stages in his own liberation. "Like my old love, I have survived you best / By leaving you, and so you're here to stay." In this slightly campy paradox, Howard exhibits the "chill / Lightheartedness" that Merrill addresses.

Howard's second Hephaistos poem, "Again for Hephaistos, the Last Time" is an elegy written ten years later, and it is much campier. At that time, Howard was long past his poetic apprenticeship and was the winner of the Pulitzer Prize. The poem is a defense against the accusation in the *Times* that Auden "had failed to make, / or even make [his] way inside, 'a world of emotion,'"[16] But instead of directing the reader to poems in which Auden struck "the *lacrimae rerum* note," Howard points to two anecdotes. The first concerns college students who mistakenly ask Auden whether he is Carl Sandburg and get the response: "You've ruined mother's day." The second places Howard and Auden backstage at the Y, where Auden is about to give a reading "to the rustling thousands out front." To make conversation Auden asks Howard

> why it was I no longer endured a difficult mutual friend.
> "Because he calls everyone *else* either a kike or a cocksucker,
> and since, Wystan, both he and I are ... well, both of them ..."
>
> "My *dear*," you broke in, and I think you were genuinely excited,
> "I never knew you were Jewish!"[17]

For Howard, Auden's campy wit represents if "not a world of emotion" then "the emotion of a world." Curious, playful, and accepting, it successfully deflects the problems of anti-Semitism and homophobia. For Howard, Auden opened up a range of references; thus "Again for Hephaistos" mentions Ginifer, Tintagel, and Santa Maria sopra Minerva as well as Rod McKuen, cocksuckers, and kikes. The campiness that Howard learned to use from Auden is neither the failure to enter the world of emotion nor the evasion of emotion but the ability to invite emotions that might become too painful and sentimental and then deflect them through humor or paradox.

J. D. McClatchy is perhaps the most prominent poet of the next generation who falls squarely into the Auden tradition. Born in 1945, he attended Georgetown University and received a Ph.D. in English from Yale University in 1974. Like Merrill, he grew up in considerable comfort. It is quite fitting that he was a friend of Merrill, and with Stephen Yenser has edited Merrill's complete works. His poem "Auden's OED" develops a genealogy of transmission, for the copy of the *Oxford English Dictionary* now in his possession was first Auden's, on whose death it came to Auden's lover Chester Kallman, then to Merrill, and only then to McClatchy. The *OED* had a special place in Auden's literary arsenal. It was "a fixture / in the second-story Kirchstetten / room" where Auden worked.[18] According to Edward Mendelson, Auden read the *OED* daily and used it extensively in his later poems.[19] Indeed, Auden was always looking for opportunities to add new words to the *OED* and believed that he was the first to put in print the words "plain-sewing" for mutual masturbation and "Princeton-first-year" for intercrural sex.[20]

McClatchy feels a particular contact with Auden through possession of his *OED*, and although he will not go so far as Whitman, who proclaimed that those "Who touches this [book], touches a man,"[21] he does feel that Auden

> could be sitting beside one, chin in hand
> listening to a late quartet, a gaze
> on his face only the final chord will break.
> Here is the faraway something else,
> here between the crowded lines of scholarship.
> Here is the first rapture and final
> dread of being found out by words, terms, phrases
> for what is unknown, unfelt, unloved.
> Here in the end is the language of a life.[22]

Indeed, so imbued is the *OED* with Auden's spirit that when McClatchy's cat, named Wystan, claws a page, McClatchy for a second sees Auden's face in the wrinkled paper. Startled, McClatchy prays for protection from "St. Wiz."

At the center of "Auden's OED" is an account of McClatchy's first meeting with Auden, and it exemplifies the process of invitation and deflection that marks the poetry of these men. On his farewell tour of colleges, Auden came to McClatchy's university to give a reading. After the reading and reception, McClatchy accosted the elderly poet, who "wambled tipsily toward his guest suite" and asked him to autograph his book. "Turn around and bend over," Auden orders, and momentarily McClatchy imagines that Auden is about to initiate a sexual act. But no, Auden needed a surface to write on, and "My back would do as well as any / Tree trunk or cafeteria tabletop." Auden invites the erotic and then deflects it. The result is comic, but with a sexual frisson that will not completely dissipate. On reflection, McClatchy realizes that Auden had

> been writing
> on me ever since that encounter
> or that I'd unconsciously made of myself
> a desk so that he could continue –
> the common imagination's dogsbody
> and ringmaster – still to speak up,
> however halting or indirect the voice.[23]

The voice that Auden provides McClatchy – the language inscribed into his very body – is one of indirection, one that is deflected, that comes at queer angles and at odd moments and that puts one in compromising and comic positions and requires patience and poise as well as a certain vulgar fun. As Auden put it in "'The Truest Poetry Is the Most Feigning'":

Be subtle, various, ornamental, clever,
And do not listen to those critics ever
Whose crude provincial gullets crave in books
Plain cooking made still plainer by plain cooks.[24]

Following Auden's example, the works of Merrill, Howard, or McClatchy are not meant for stomachs that must be coddled. Sometimes basted with unusual savory spices, sometimes beaten to lofty heights, their poetic dishes lure us to eat without our paying attention to how hearty and filling a banquet they have set for us.

Notes

1. James Merrill, *A Different Person* (New York: Knopf, 1993), p. 141.
2. Ross Labrie, *James Merrill* (Boston: Twayne, 1982), p. 52.
3. James Merrill, *Collected Poems*, ed. J. D. McClatchy and Stephen Yenser (New York: Knopf, 2001), p. 23. This collection will be cited in the text as *JMC*.
4. Walt Whitman, *Complete Poetry and Collected Prose*, ed. Justin Kaplan (New York: Library of America, 1982), p. 36.
5. Daniel Mark Epstein, "Merrill's Progress," *The New Criterion* 20:7 (March 2002), pp. 24–32, 31.
6. Stephen Yenser, *The Consuming Myth: The Work of James Merrill* (Cambridge, Mass.: Harvard University Press, 1987), p. 60.
7. James Merrill, *Recitative*, ed. J. D. McClatchy (San Francisco: North Point Press, 1986), p. 44.
8. David Kalstone, *Five Temperaments* (New York: Oxford University Press, 1977), p. 90.
9. James Merrill, *The Changing Light at Sandover*, ed. J. D. McClatchy and Stephen Yenser (New York: Knopf, 2006), p. 143. This collection will be cited in the text as *CLS*.
10. Judith Moffett, *James Merrill: An Introduction to the Poetry* (New York: Columbia University Press, 1984), p. 221.
11. Piotr Gwiazda, *James Merrill and W.H. Auden: Homosexuality and Poetic Influence* (New York: Palgrave Macmillan, 2007), p. 131.
12. Aidan Wasley, *The Age of Auden: Postwar Poetry and the American Scene* (Princeton, N.J.: Princeton University Press, 2011), p. 99.
13. W. H. Auden, *Collected Poems*, ed. Edward Mendelson (New York: Random House, 2007), p. 582.
14. Edward Mendelson, *Later Auden* (New York: Farrar, Straus, and Giroux, 1999), p. 426.
15. Richard Howard, *The Damages* (Middletown, Conn.: Wesleyan University Press, 1967), p. 64.

16. Richard Howard, *Fellow Feelings* (New York: Atheneum, 1976), p. 12.
17. Howard, *Fellow Feelings*, p. 12.
18. J. D. McClatchy, *Ten Commandments* (New York: Knopf, 1998), p. 89.
19. Mendelson, *Later Auden*, pp. 485, 503.
20. Mendelson, *Later Auden*, p. 498.
21. Whitman, *Complete Poetry and Collected Prose*, p. 611.
22. McClatchy, *Ten Commandments*, p. 89; for McClatchy on Auden's *OED*, see also J. D. McClatchy, *Twenty Questions* (New York: Columbia University Press, 1998), pp. 47–48.
23. McClatchy, *Ten Commandments*, p. 90.
24. Auden, *Collected Poems*, p. 617.

Chapter 40

Science in Contemporary American Poetry: Ammons and Others

ROGER GILBERT

A common way to characterize the shift from modern to contemporary American poetry is as a turn from sweeping, impersonal myths and symbols to more locally grounded, experiential stories and images. Yet poetry's hunger for transcendent vision is not so easily renounced. Having lost faith in the religious, metaphysical, and national ideals that traditionally sustained their claims to vatic authority, where might late twentieth-century poets turn for modes of knowledge extending beyond private experience? One answer is to poetry's ancient rival, science. An important, if not a defining, tendency in American poetry since 1950 has been the incorporation of scientific concepts and vocabulary, not as mere ornamentation but as a way of enlarging the poem's thematic and visionary scope. The name most frequently associated with this tendency is A. R. Ammons, whose work from its beginnings displays an unprecedented openness to the language and insights of science. More than any other twentieth-century American poet, Ammons validated science as a source of inspiration, a kind of rationalist muse whose teachings have proved surprisingly compatible with the imaginative extravagances of poetry.

The poetic invocation of science needs to be distinguished from several related topics. These include that most venerable of all literary subjects, nature. Traditional nature poetry takes a predominantly aesthetic view of the nonhuman realm, one that may at times seem willfully naïve in its avoidance of scientific explanations for natural phenomena. Knowledge of photosynthesis or plate tectonics threatens to disrupt the unmediated, pastoral vision that most nature poetry seeks. One of the challenges for Ammons and other contemporary science poets is to let such knowledge into their poems while maintaining the sense of wonder that nature has always inspired in artists. By contrast, late twentieth-century nature poets like William Stafford, David Wagoner, Robert Bly, James Wright, and Mary Oliver often write a kind of stripped-down Wordsworthian landscape lyric whose affective power stems in large part from its cultivation of a prerational, animistic awareness of nature that resolutely excludes science. Although the results can be moving, they are not my focus in this chapter.

I'll briefly mention three other topics that intersect with but differ from mine. Science and technology are often grouped together, but their roles in contemporary poetry are quite distinct – particularly so now that technology has begun to change the ways in which poems are written, circulated, and read. Poets who engage with technology tend to do so either from a Luddite perspective that emphasizes its dehumanizing effects or with an excited sense of the possible affinities between poetic and technological innovations; neither mode has much in common with the kind of poetry that takes scientific knowledge as material for rumination. Like technology, medicine represents a meeting point between pure science and practical agency, but its emotional stakes are more immediate. Where poems about science generally seek to bracket human experience or to locate it within a vastly variegated cosmos, poems on medical themes must deal with specifically human issues of pain and mortality. Finally, there is a growing body of sci-fi or "speculative" poetry that draws on scientific and technological discoveries but subordinates them to narratives of imagined times and places distinct from our own; here again the governing impulse is quite different from that of science poetry, which seeks to assimilate facts and theories grounded in empirical observation.

Before I turn to contemporary poetry, it may be helpful to give a brief historical overview of poetry's engagement with science. Ever since Plato exiled poets from his ideal republic, poetry has been viewed as a flawed medium for truth, irredeemably contaminated by imagination and passion. Yet just as epic poetry often purports to give a factual account of human history, so certain classical genres have claimed to transmit accurate knowledge of the physical universe. The Latin poet Lucretius's long cosmological poem *De Rerum Natura* offers an early version of the atomistic theory of matter, drawn from the Greek philosophers Democritus and Epicurus; it thus provides the first known instance of a poet incorporating scientific teachings in his work. The *Georgics* of Virgil, Lucretius's contemporary, are more practical in their emphasis on agriculture and animal husbandry, but they too include a good deal of natural science. The georgic mode was revived in the eighteenth century by English poets like James Thomson, John Dyer, and John Philips, who produced long, didactic poems that mix scenic description with detailed instruction in the finer points of sheepshearing and cider making. The latent scientism of this mode culminates in the work of the poet-physician Erasmus Darwin, whose long poem *The Botanic Garden* (1791) presents versified speculation on a range of topics, from cosmology to the classification of plants, including ideas that anticipate his grandson Charles's theory of evolution. In Darwin's work, science and poetry achieve their closest convergence before the twentieth century (although not, it is generally thought, to the benefit of the poetry).

The Enlightenment rationalism that governs much eighteenth-century English poetry receded in the early nineteenth century, as Romanticism became the guiding aesthetic and intellectual movement. Mary Shelley's *Frankenstein* is the most enduring Romantic critique of the scientific mind, a critique expressed more concisely in Edgar Allan Poe's 1829 "Sonnet – to Science":

> Science! true daughter of Old Time thou art!
>   Who alterest all things with thy peering eyes.
> Why preyest thou thus upon the poet's heart,
>   Vulture, whose wings are dull realities?
> How should he love thee? or how deem thee wise,
>   Who wouldst not leave him in his wandering
> To seek for treasure in the jewelled skies,
>   Albeit he soared with an undaunted wing?
> Hast thou not dragged Diana from her car?
>   And driven the Hamadryad from the wood
> To seek a shelter in some happier star?
>   Hast thou not torn the Naiad from her flood,
> The Elfin from the green grass, and from me
> The summer dream beneath the tamarind tree?[1]

Poe's open hostility is an extreme manifestation of the widely held fear that science would rob nature of its beauty and enchantment, leaving the poet stranded amid "dull realities." In a similar mood, John Keats voiced his dread that Newtonian physics would "Conquer all mysteries with rule and line," and in so doing "unweave the rainbow."[2] Not all Romantic poets were so resistant to the allure of scientific discovery, as Richard Holmes has shown.[3] Still, most nineteenth-century poets only flirted tentatively with scientific language and ideas in their verse. In America, Walt Whitman offered a more nuanced appraisal of science's dangers than did his countryman Poe:

> When I heard the learn'd astronomer;
> When the proofs, the figures, were ranged in columns before me;
> When I was shown the charts and the diagrams, to add, divide, and
>   measure them;
> When I, sitting, heard the astronomer, where he lectured with much
>   applause in the lecture-room,
> How soon, unaccountable, I became tired and sick;
> Till rising and gliding out, I wander'd off by myself,

> In the mystical moist night-air, and from time to time,
> Look'd up in perfect silence at the stars.[4]

Whitman does not accuse the astronomer of destroying the beauty of the stars; he merely juxtaposes two modes of vision, the scientist's and the poet's. His confidence that the poetic eye will prevail in this contest reflects his belief that "Exact science and its practical movements are no checks on the greatest poet but always his encouragement and support.... In the beauty of poems are the tuft and final applause of science."[5] As he so often does, Whitman here echoes his mentor Ralph Waldo Emerson, who proclaimed, "The poet alone knows astronomy, chemistry, vegetation, and animation, for he does not stop at these facts, but employs them as signs."[6] Both Whitman and Emerson invest poetry with the power to absorb science while translating it to a symbolic plane. Yet as Whitman's vague reference to "proofs" and "figures" illustrates, neither poet goes deeply into the particulars of scientific thought in his work.

In the early twentieth century, poets began to embrace science more whole-heartedly, often drawing parallels between the work of major discoverers like Marie Curie and Albert Einstein and the literary innovations being carried out under the banner of modernism. Perhaps the most explicit version of this analogy appears in a short poem by Mina Loy entitled "Gertrude Stein":

> Curie
> of the laboratory
> of vocabulary
> she crushed
> the tonnage
> of consciousness
> congealed in phrases
> to extract
> a radium of the word[7]

Like her contemporary William Carlos Williams, Stein attended medical school (although, unlike him, she did not complete a degree). Both poets introduced a spirit of radical experimentation into American poetry that was modeled in many respects on pathbreaking work in the sciences. Williams's dictum that a poem is a "machine made out of words" reflects this new openness to science and technology, as does T. S. Eliot's use of terms like "catalyst" in his criticism.[8] But while words borrowed from physics and chemistry make occasional appearances in modernist poems, one still sees little sustained engagement with the actual substance of science in American poetry before 1950.

A partial exception may be found in the work of Robinson Jeffers (1887–1962). Although often viewed as a primitivist transposing Greek tragedy to the California coast in long, roughhewn verse narratives, Jeffers was in fact deeply conversant with the sciences, both as a medical student with special interests in forestry and bacteriology and through his brother's work as an astronomer at Lick Observatory, where Jeffers was a frequent visitor.[9] Jeffers typically invokes science to justify his doctrine of "inhumanism," a view that rejects human beings' narcissistic belief in their own centrality and instead affirms the beauty and nobility of nature in all its guises. In an early poem called "Science," Jeffers sardonically observes how the incremental expansion of human knowledge over the past century threatens to destroy anthropocentric illusions:

Man, introverted man, having crossed
In passage and but a little with the nature of things this latter century
Has begot giants; but being taken up
Like a maniac with self-love and inward conflicts cannot manage his hybrids.
Being used to deal with edgeless dreams,
Now he's bred knives on nature turns them also inward: they have
    thirsty points though.
His mind forebodes his own destruction;
Actaeon who saw the goddess naked among leaves and his hounds tore him.
A little knowledge, a pebble from the shingle,
A drop from the oceans: who would have dreamed this infinitely little too
    much?[10]

Although he sees the destructive power of science, Jeffers does not share the fear voiced by Keats and Poe that beauty will be among its victims. Instead he welcomes the disillusionment science breeds, precisely because it fosters a new, larger appreciation of the extrahuman universe in all its harsh elegance. While he shows a particular fondness for granite cliffs and birds of prey, Jeffers finds instances of the violent yet beautiful workings of the cosmos in phenomena ranging in scale from atoms to nebulae. The poem "Nova" describes the death of a star with astronomical precision and then ponders the similar fate awaiting the sun and the "probable death-passion / For the sun's planets," concluding that "the enormous invulnerable beauty of things / Is the face of God."[11] Perhaps Jeffers's most sustained exploration of scientific material comes in a late poem posthumously published under the title "The Beginning and the End," which offers a wide-ranging account of creation inspired by Lucretius yet replete with notions gleaned from modern physics, chemistry, and evolutionary biology.

Various factors might help explain why American poets began taking a more active interest in science after World War II, including such large historical developments as the atom bomb, the Cold War, and the space race; but the influence of individual innovators should not be discounted. Central among postwar poets who drew on science was A. R. Ammons (1926–2001). Born to a farming family in North Carolina, Ammons served in the navy during World War II and then attended Wake Forest College on the G.I. Bill, where he majored in general science. In later years he credited a professor of evolutionary botany, Budd Smith, as his most formative influence, telling Smith in a letter that "I have used everything you taught me in my poetry, over and over."[12] Ammons's first book, *Ommateum* (1955), is largely mythopoeic in style and contains only fleeting allusions to science, but even before finishing it, he had begun contemplating what he called a poetry of "synthesis":

> The poet, like the philosopher, does not have a subject matter, on the factual level, that will give him the authority the scientist enjoys – has never had. The early poet, like Lucretius, was scientist and poet; he found out his facts, through reading and observation, interpreted them into his own synthesis and converted the synthesis into poetry. Specialization has now made it impossible for the poet or anyone else to be on the frontier of discovery in many fields. Nevertheless, the poet must consider knowledge his province and gather as much as he can. For it is not necessary to be original in details – to use only what one personally discovers. Culture is cumulative, and the poet must strive to add a new dimension of meaning to what already exists. The proper place for the expression of originality is in the poet's own synthesis.[13]

These sentences come from an unpublished essay called "Defense of Poetry" that Ammons wrote in 1954. His assertion that poetry should take all of knowledge as its domain, and not just those areas that lend themselves to personal expression, betokens a new attitude toward science as a potential source of poetic material that would become increasingly common over the next half century.

The first poem in which Ammons can be said to approach this kind of synthesis is "Hymn," written in 1956. As its title suggests, the poem adopts the tone and rhetoric of religious devotion, yet its language is deeply informed by science. "I know if I find you I will have to leave the earth / and go on out," Ammons writes, "over the sea marshes and the brant in bays … and on up through the spheres of diminishing air / past the blackset noctilucent clouds," then continues:

> And I know if I find you I will have to stay with the earth
> inspecting with thin tools and ground eyes
> trusting the microvilli sporangia and simplest
>   coelenterates

and praying for a nerve cell
with all the soul of my chemical reactions
and going right on down where the eye sees only traces[14]

While it's possible to interpret the poem's dialectical structure in terms of such traditional religious categories as transcendence and immanence, it should be noted that the two paths charted in these lines also correspond to distinct vectors of scientific inquiry. The vast phenomena observed by astronomy and the microscopic organisms studied by biology are equally the domain of the "you" the speaker seeks, whether God or some other unifying principle. With their blend of precision and opacity, phrases like "light diffusions" and "microvilli sporangia" evoke the infinite complexity to be found at every level of existence. Such phrases define a verbal register that resonates powerfully even when it does not convey a specific meaning to untrained readers. Ammons deepens that resonance by modulating from the dense literality of "sporangia" and "coelenterates" to more metaphorical conjunctions of spirit and matter in "praying for a nerve cell / with all the soul of my chemical reactions," phrases whose incongruity never quite breaks into irony. Where earlier poets accused science of emptying out the spiritual realm, Ammons insists on the equal validity of prayer and cell, soul and chemistry.

Ammons's next major foray into the realm of science came in a poem called "Mechanism," which appeared, along with "Hymn," in his 1963 collection *Expressions of Sea Level*:

> Honor a going thing, goldfinch, corporation, tree,
>   morality: any working order,
>   animate or inanimate: it
>
> has managed directed balance,
>   the incoming and outgoing energies are working right,
>   some energy left to the mechanism,
>
> some ash, enough energy held
>   to maintain the order in repair,
>   assure further consumption of entropy,
>
> expending energy to strengthen order:
>
> (ARA, p. 77)

Where "Hymn" invokes an indeterminate "you," "Mechanism" posits the category of "going thing[s]" as its unifying principle. That principle informs a wide array of phenomena, as the list in the first stanza implies: "goldfinch, corporation, tree, / morality." All these things exemplify what Ammons calls a "working order," a dynamic system that takes in and puts out energy, organizes and repairs itself, and staves off entropy and chaos. Although in theory he might illustrate this concept in greater depth using any of his four examples, he settles on the goldfinch:

> honor the chemistries, platelets, hemoglobin kinetics,
>   the light-sensitive iris, the enzymic intricacies
> of control,
>
> the gastric transformations, seed
>   dissolved to acrid liquors, synthesized into
> chirp, vitreous humor, knowledge,
>
> blood compulsion, instinct: honor the
>   unique genes,
>   molecules that reproduce themselves   (*ARA*, p. 78)

The poem consists of one extremely long sentence, a result Ammons achieves through his highly unorthodox use of the colon as an all-purpose connective between clauses. As in much of his poetry, the colon works to establish a radical continuity among entities and processes. After showing us the goldfinch in its natural habitat, flitting through bushes and eluding a hawk, Ammons catalogues the many levels of activity taking place inside the bird – physiological, chemical, reproductive, genetic, molecular – while repeatedly asking us to "honor" the subtleties of its inner workings as we might admire the craftsmanship of a great work of art. Indeed the poem can be taken as an implicit rebuke to Yeats's paean to artifice in "Sailing to Byzantium"; for Ammons the mechanisms contained by this living creature far exceed any mechanical golden bird's in their intricate elegance.

"Mechanism" goes even further than "Hymn" in pushing the boundaries of poetic diction. The heavily Latinate lexicon that dominates much of the poem might seem hopelessly prosaic, yet Ammons unlocks a latent musicality in terms like "platelets," "hemoglobin," "enzymic," and "nucleic," playing them against more common words like "rising," "cloaking," and "staying." The phrase "synthesized into / chirp" nicely illustrates Ammons's penchant for such contrapuntal effects, a strong enjambment accentuating the abrupt leap from abstraction to onomatopoeia. In the poem's closing lines, the language of science gives way to a much simpler descriptive vocabulary as we return to the familiar appearance of the bird in its natural surroundings. The wry parenthetical comment "not a great songster" (*ARA*, p. 79) quietly suggests that the music embodied by this bird is not vocal but innate, that its beauty lies not in its singing but in the infinitely complex operations that allow it to exist at all.

In this respect it serves as a kind of mascot for Ammons's poetics of synthesis, which sacrifices conventional lyricism for cognitive density.

Ammons also writes poems whose scientific content does not depend on specialized words. One of the best known of these is "Cascadilla Falls," whose speaker

> picked up a
> handsized stone
> kidney-shaped, testicular, and
>
> thought all its motions into it,
> the 800 mph earth spin,
> the 190-million-mile yearly
> displacement around the sun,
> the overriding
> grand
> haul
>
> of the galaxy with the 30,000
> mph of where
> the sun's going:
> thought all the interweaving
> motions
> into myself: (*ARA*, pp. 206–07)

Numbers replace words as the primary vehicle for science in this poem, lending mathematical exactitude to the speaker's apprehension of the cosmos as a collection of "interweaving / motions." For Ammons, the "proofs" and "figures" that Whitman dismissively sets against silent contemplation deepen rather than deaden the feelings such contemplation arouses. In place of Whitman's serenity, Ammons projects a naked vulnerability limned by the stone's metaphorical descent from hand to kidney to testicle, and condensed in the poignant epithet "shelterless." Science here is internalized, "thought . . . into" the self so deeply that knowledge itself becomes unmoored: "Cascadilla Falls" ends, "Oh / I do / not know where I am going / that I can live my life / by this single creek" (*ARA*, p. 207). Where "Mechanism" extracts the minute operations that keep a goldfinch alive, "Cascadilla Falls" projects vast cosmic motions into a stone; yet although their vectors may differ, the results in both cases are an intensification and an expansion of awareness in the act of perceiving everyday phenomena. Ammons's route to the visionary entails not the cultivation of simplicity but the ennobling estrangement produced by the knowledge of complexity.

Like "Hymn," "Cascadilla Falls" leaps across extremes of scale, distilling sublimity from the disjunction between great things and small. Another phase of Ammons's poetry explores a middle region of measurable forces and events. Poems like "Expressions of Sea Level," "One:Many," "Corsons Inlet," and "Saliences" record the myriad transactions that shape each moment in a rich natural environment, while acknowledging that no human observer can account for all their particulars. In these poems Ammons enters the realm of what is now called ecopoetics, a mode he anticipates in his long poem *Tape for the Turn of the Year*:

> ecology is my word: tag
> me with that: come
> in there:
> you will find yourself
> in a firmless country:
> centers & peripheries
> in motion,
> organic,
> interrelations![15]

Ammons is especially drawn to complex ecosystems like estuaries and marshes, whose incessantly fluctuating conditions create countless "risks and possibilities." In the much-anthologized "Corsons Inlet," he traces one line of causality from space to earth:

> the moon was full last night: today, low tide was low:
> black shoals of mussels exposed to the risk
> of air
> and, earlier, of sun,
> waved in and out with the waterline, waterline inexact,
> caught always in the event of change . . .
> the small
> white blacklegged egret, how beautiful, quietly stalks and spears
> the shallows, darts to shore
> to stab – what? I couldn't
> see against the black mudflats – a frightened
> fiddler crab? (*ARA*, pp. 149–50)

Large astronomical and tidal motions help determine the fates of innumerable creatures, whose Darwinian competition Ammons evokes with a distinctive blend of delight ("how beautiful"), curiosity ("what? I couldn't / see"), and empathy ("frightened"). In "Saliences," a poem that seems explicitly intended as a sequel to "Corsons Inlet," Ammons focuses on a different aspect of the same landscape's internal dynamics:

> a variable of wind
> among the dunes,
> making variables
> of position and direction and sound
> of every reed leaf
> and bloom,
> running streams of sand   (*ARA*, p. 152)

Here Ammons uses the language of algebra and geometry to graph the fluid interplay of matter and motion, even as he concedes that the totality of forces and events occurring at any moment in this environment is incalculable: "wind alone as a variable / takes this neck of dunes / out of calculation's reach." These poems, written in the early 1960s, show a striking affinity with the then-emerging science of chaos theory, which considers how unpredictable, seemingly random patterns arise within dynamic systems.

When Ammons took up a position at Cornell University in 1964, he exchanged the coastal landscape of southern New Jersey for the lacustrine one of Ithaca, New York, and the scope of his ecological inquiries changed accordingly. The primary crucible for his thought experiments was now his own backyard, a simplified ecosystem consisting of a few trees and bushes, some birds and squirrels, and an endless supply of weather. At one point he even entertained the idea of devoting a whole book to one tree: "I was thinking last / June, so multiple and dense is the reality of a tree, that I / ought to do a booklength piece on the elm in the backyard here" (*ARA*, p. 303). These lines come from "Essay on Poetics," a long poem exploring the parallels between poetic and natural principles of organization. For Ammons, the elm tree exemplifies the synthesis of unity and multiplicity, one and many, that he strives to achieve in his poems. A stable, recognizable landmark that "enters / the ground at a fairly reliable point," the tree is nonetheless made up of "twelve quintillion cells," in each of which "more takes place by way / of event, disposition, and such ... than any computer / we now have could keep registration of" (*ARA*, pp. 303, 308). Ammons's poetic tour of the elm goes on to consider the mathematics of branches and foliage, the behavior of seedpods, and the complex role of elm worms in the tree's ecology. Although he never produced that book-length study, Ammons returned repeatedly to the elm tree in later poems. In "Extremes and Moderations," another verse essay, he ponders the significance of dead branches that break off and become lodged in the tree's lower boughs, finding in these a parable of the relationship between the living and the dead in human culture.

Another prominent backyard resident in Ammons's poems, a quince bush, enjoys a more volatile, even violent relation to its environment than the elm tree. A short poem called "The Quince Bush" begins, "The flowering quince bush / on the back hedge has been / run through by a morning / glory vine," and goes on to find in this image an emblem of hostility and struggle in the human sphere (*ARA*, p. 217). If the quince is vulnerable to the parasitic onslaught of the morning glory, however, it also harbors its own will to power, as a passage from Ammons's long poem *Sphere* suggests:

> ... even though the bush
> has put on the strain of blossoming and fruiting, it has
> at the same time shot out shoots all over, threatening the
>
> upcoming hollyhock and lemon lilies: a green rage to possess,
> make and take room: to dominate, shade out, whiten: I
> identify with the bush's rage, its quiet, ruthless, outward
>
> thrust: whatever nears me must shrink, wither up, or widen
> overlarge and thin with shade[16]

All the rapacity that Ammons beheld on the shore at Corsons Inlet can also be found within the seemingly pastoral enclave of the backyard, as rival plants compete for precious light and soil. Ammons clearly feels a special bond with the quince bush, whose rage to expand and possess resonates with his own ambition to unfold into as much space as he needs. But this expansive urge is threatened from within by a lurking enemy, the morning glory waiting to strike. Even the grass, Whitman's symbol of democratic community, proves on close inspection to be a scene of struggle. Ammons sums up the spectacle in a bitingly concise phrase whose grammar hovers between possessive and declarative modes: "being's terror."[17] This is hardly the lesson most people would derive from the sight of a peaceful suburban backyard, but Ammons refuses to sentimentalize nature in any form.

"Essay on Poetics" was the first of several densely discursive poems Ammons wrote in the late sixties and early seventies that draw on such conceptual languages as cybernetics, information theory, anthropology, and structural linguistics, all of which straddle the border between scientific thought and sociocultural analysis. These abstract discourses supplement the more empirical observation Ammons continued to practice, allowing him to develop ambitious analogies between natural and human forms and processes. In these longer works, the poetics of synthesis Ammons first proposed in his 1954 essay "Defense of Poetry" achieves its fullest realization:

> ... I am seeking the
> mechanisms physical, physiological, epistemological, electrical,
>
> chemical, esthetic, social, religious by which many, kept
> discrete as many, expresses itself into the
> manageable rafters of salience, lofts to comprehension, breaks
>
> out in hard, highly informed suasions, the "gathering
> in the sky" so to speak   (*ARA*, p. 300)

Ammons's singular innovation as a poetic thinker lies in his recognition of the affinity between the mind's generalizing faculty and its hunger for images of transcendence. In passages like this one, from "Essay on Poetics," he insists on the equal claims of intellectual and spiritual categories. Favorite terms like "salience" and "suasion" serve as switch points, effecting a smooth modulation from abstract exposition to hymnlike lyricism. This strain of totalizing vision reaches its pinnacle in Ammons's book-length *Sphere* (1974), a poem inspired by the image of the earth seen from space during the Apollo space missions. In *Sphere*, physics and metaphysics are continuously interwoven in a rambunctious cosmological divagation dedicated to the principle that "a single dot of light, traveling, will memorize the sphere."[18]

The diagrammatic tendency in Ammons's imagination is balanced by his fascination with matter, particularly in its lowest forms: excrement, waste, carrion, and garbage. "Scientific objectivity puts / radiance on / duckshit even," he writes in "Summer Session," characteristically triangulating science, beauty, and nature at its homeliest (*ARA*, p. 254). His best-known lyric, "The City Limits," offers a more sustained celebration of the radiance that bathes all things, including "the dumped / guts of a natural slaughter or the coil of shit" (*ARA*, p. 320). The excremental theme receives its fullest elaboration in a comic litany called "Shit List," which catalogues dozens of varieties of feces, pausing to observe their distinguishing features with a wryly clinical eye. Ammons's most extended exploration of the poetics of waste comes in his late masterpiece *Garbage* (1994), which takes a massive, smoldering landfill as a symbol of the eternal circuit between matter and spirit:

> this is just a poem with a job to do: and that
>
> is to declare, however roundabout, sideways,
> or meanderingly (or in those ways) the perfect
>
> scientific and materialistic notion of the

spindle of energy: when energy is gross,

rocklike, it resembles the gross, and when
fine it mists away into mystical refinements,

sometimes passes right out of material
recognizability and becomes, what?, motion,

spirit, all forms translated into energy, as at
the bottom of Dante's hell all motion is

translated into form: so, in value systems,
physical systems, artistic systems, always this

same disposition from the heavy to the light,
and then the returns from the light downward

to the staid gross: stone to wind, wind to
stone:[19]

Despite Ammons's characterization, the "spindle of energy" is not a concept found in any textbook, yet his impulse to claim a scientific provenance for his metaphor is consistent with his career-long desire to make all realms of knowledge the province of his art (even as his allusion to Dante's *Inferno* suggests a continuity with older traditions of poetic cosmology). After reading Ammons, American poets could never again be quite as complacent about the division between imaginative literature and the sciences. His work demonstrates, on a very broad scale, that poetry can assimilate the language and logic of science without surrendering its lyric and visionary capacities.

In 1967 Ammons served as poetry editor for a special issue of the literary magazine *Chelsea* devoted to science and technology. Among the poets whose work he included was his mentor Josephine Miles (1911–1985), who gave Ammons his first significant encouragement while he was a graduate student at Berkeley. In an unpublished interview with Alice Fulton, Ammons paid tribute to Miles as a "crisp rationalist who had a true mastery of her life," despite the disabling arthritis that confined her to a wheelchair for much of her adulthood. Miles's early poems were taut and epigrammatic, but over the course of her career they gradually grew more porous, taking in particulars from many areas: nature, politics, personal memory, and science. Her 1968 chapbook *Fields of Learning* dramatizes this opening to the diversity of knowledge, particularly as mapped in academia. The title poem collates bits of erudition from all over campus and then is followed by more subject-specific poems, entitled "Botany" and "Physics." The latter opens:

> The mean life of a free neutron, does it exist
> In its own moving frame a quarter-hour?
> In decibel, gram, ohm, slug, volt, watt, does it exist?
> Not objects answer us, not the hand or eye,
> But particles out of sight.[20]

Like her student Ammons, whose work she had by this time thoroughly assimilated, Miles savors the quirky, mythopoeic sound of scientific terms (many of them derived from proper names), while pondering the deeper mystery of how the world is made of invisible particles whose existence we can only infer, not observe. After stanzas that muse on the paradoxical behaviors of matter, energy, light, and sound, the poem ends with a return to the free neutron, whose brief life-span makes it a surrogate for all transient beings.

Subatomic particles of all kinds are a running preoccupation for Ruth Stone (1915–2011), a poet who only began to achieve wide recognition in her eighties. Her tone ranges from playful to plangent as she explores the nested realms of molecules, atoms, and their still-tinier kin, finding in them a powerful analogue for the hidden spaces of the self and the secret residues of loss. In "Moving Right Along," Stone jauntily declares, "At the molecular level, / in another dimension, / oy, are you different!"[21] "The Latest Hotel Guest Walks over Particles That Revolve in Seven Other Dimensions Controlling Latticed Space" stages an apocalyptic fantasy in which the "escaped molecules" of the previous residents of a hotel room reassemble into "an antihero composed of all the lost neutrinos," whose appearance heralds a coming Armageddon.[22] More poignantly, "At the Center" juxtaposes the confident assurance of science –

> They say at the Fermi accelerator,
> "Rejoice. A clear and clean
> explanation of matter is possible,"
> as they bombard subatomic particles
> at energies never before attained.

– with the wrenching knowledge of a particular loss:

> Your eyes, the eyes of a madman that I loved,
> far underground, fall apart,
> while their particles still shoot like meteors
> through space making their own isolated trajectories.[23]

Viewed by a physicist, the centrifugal motion of particles opens an exhilarating perspective on the material universe, but when seen in the light of grief for a dead lover, that knowledge brings an unbearable clarity to the facts of death.

Where Miles and Stone take atoms and molecules as instances of the alien element within and around us, May Swenson (1919–1989) inspects the intimate mechanics of matter with a tinkerer's curiosity. Swenson is best known for the ingeniously shaped visual texts she called "iconographs." Poems like "3 Models of the Universe," "How Everything Happens (Based on a Study of the Wave)," and "Of Rounds" both anatomize and illustrate dynamic forms from the oceanic to the planetary to the cosmic.[24] Perhaps her most remarkable exercise in verbal visualization is "The DNA Molecule," whose elaborately shaped format is meant to evoke the spiraling contours of its subject. The poem opens with a bold conflation of science and art, asserting that "THE DNA MOLECULE / is The Nude Descending a Staircase," and then draws out the analogy with reference both to Marcel Duchamp's famous Futurist painting and to the female body itself, which is, like the DNA molecule, a miraculous mechanism for self-reproduction (with some incidental aid from the male body). I quote from the version of the poem that appeared in *Poetry* magazine, without its iconographic format:

> As a woman ingests the demon sperm and with
>
> the same membrane regurgitates
> the mitotic double of herself
>
> upon the slide of time
> so The DNA Molecule produces with a little pop
>
> at the waistline of its viscous drop
> a new microsphere the same size as herself.[25]

While respecting the intricate topology that governs its workings, Swenson superimposes human lineaments on the DNA molecule, granting it a kind of primordial sexuality that precedes all bodily sex. Her graphic and syntactic evocation of the molecule's twining movements reflects a deeply aesthetic response, one by no means alien to scientists themselves. Eleven years after Swenson's poem appeared in *Poetry*, Andrew Weiman (b. 1956) published a poem called "Andy-Diana DNA Letter" in the same magazine. Although it makes no explicit mention of molecular biology, the poem represents an even more ambitious attempt to mimic the double helix structure, arraying parallel strands of rhyming syllables so they cross from one side of the page to the other at regular intervals. While this fiendishly complex form may seem at odds with the poem's chatty content, Weiman's point is that even a casual love letter ultimately grows from imperatives written into the very molecules that make us up.[26]

Along with the discovery of DNA, the emergence of quantum physics and its increasingly counterintuitive successors is the scientific development twentieth-century poets have found most alluring. Frederick Seidel (b. 1936) has ventured further into the complexities of modern physics than most of his peers, particularly in *The Cosmos Poems* (2000), commissioned by the Hayden Planetarium. The sequence explores some of the most difficult of recent scientific notions, from string theory to dark matter to eleven dimensionality, while drawing unexpected connections to the realm of human experience. At times Seidel's verse merely sketches and paraphrases: "The massless spin-2 particle whose / Couplings at long distances / Are those of general relativity."[27] But in some passages Seidel succeeds in evoking by metaphor the essential strangeness of these new conceptions of time and space:

> Think of the suckers on the tentacles
> Without the tentacles. A honeycomb
> Of space writhing in the dark.
> Time deforming it, time itself deformed.
>
> Fifteen billion light-years later a president
> Of the United States gives the Gettysburg Address.
> Two minutes. The solar system
> Star beams down on him.[28]

In its engagement with bafflingly esoteric ideas, *The Cosmos Poems* represents something of a limit case for contemporary science poetry. Where the intricacy of the DNA molecule can be visualized and refigured in ways that make it imaginatively accessible, the elusive concepts of quantum physics resist easy metaphorical appropriations. Yet Seidel's work begins to offer some poetic purchase on those concepts, and other poets will no doubt continue to bring them into focus for the untrained reader.

Although he is explicitly commanded by higher beings to produce "Poems of Science" in his epic trilogy *The Changing Light at Sandover*, James Merrill (1927–1995) does not grant science the same degree of authority that poets like Ammons, Swenson, and Seidel do. The occult premise of his long poem, composed largely at the Ouija board, gives spirit lore precedence over rational knowledge. Merrill is disarmingly candid in voicing his ambivalence toward scientific discourse:

> Opaque
> Words like "quarks" or "mitochondria"

Aren't *words* at all, in the Rilkean sense of
House, Dog, Tree – translucent, half effaced,
Monosyllabic bezoars already
Found in the gullet of a two-year-old.
Whereas through Wave, Ring, Bond, through Spectral Lines
And Resonances blows a breath of life,
Lifting the pleated garment.[29]

For Merrill, the assimilation of science to poetry is essentially a problem of diction; certain words are too rebarbatively opaque to be acceptable, while others partake of the archetypal translucency that poets prize. (Merrill slyly qualifies his polemic by using the arcane medical term "bezoar" to describe the simple words he favors.) Because his interest is less in the content of science than in its adaptability to mythmaking, Merrill is drawn to words whose metaphorical associations he can activate and exploit. This odd cooptation of science in the service of theology culminates in the discovery of a deity called "God Biology," who oversees the comings and goings of souls both on earth and in the higher spheres.

Perhaps the most concerted effort to wed the languages of science and religion in post-1950 poetry can be found in the work of Ronald Johnson (1935–1998). Like Ammons's *Sphere*, Merrill's *The Changing Light at Sandover*, and Seidel's *Cosmos Poems*, Johnson's *ARK* (begun in 1970 and published in 1996) is a postmodern cosmogony, a book-length poem drawing elements from Dante, Milton, and Blake while incorporating vocabularies from disciplines ranging from physics and optics to cell biology. Its most immediate source may be Ammons's "Hymn," whose devotional impulse *ARK* expands to epic proportions.[30] Throughout the work, Johnson deftly weaves scientific terms into his predominantly oracular style. In "Beam 31," after proclaiming physics "the music of our time," he offers a series of propositions that conflate realms and scales with nearly manic speed:

> *Proportions*, all things proportions. The solar system is a whoosh of some doubler bloom than the atom at snowflake's edge. Matter, which shakes an electron in the eye, is the pattern of slowed light. The ripple-counter-ripple of Space-Time-Light is, as an Ancient said of God, "an infinite circle whose center is everywhere and the circumference nowhere." ...
> ITEM: Physics = Psychics. Space is our "compass," and conflux with time, makes a tree (vein, river) form twixt trinities through opposed spirals: vortex to vortex: in with out: burning bush.[31]

This lapidary prose alternates with verse sections whose centered lines seem to insist on the centrality of each moment, particle, and organism:

> this is called spine of white cypress
> roughly cylindrical
> based
> on the principle
> of the intervals between cuckoos
> and molecules, and molecules
> reechoing:
> these are the carpets of
> protoplast, this
> the hall of crystcycling waltz
> down carbon atom[32]

Johnson forgoes Ammons's patient exposition in favor of a more incantatory synthesis of material and spiritual elements. This impulse toward compaction reaches its limit in the concrete poems he scatters throughout *ARK*, which serve to diagram the deep structures, at once verbal and metaphysical, he wishes to evoke. The most famous of these is "Beam 24":

> earthearthearth
> earthearthearth
> earthearthearth
> earthearthearth
> earthearthearth
> earthearthearth

"Earth" and "heart" become linked in an endless chain, reinforcing the anagrammatic proposition "Physics = Psychics." The following section, "Beam 25," features an actual diagram of cell mitosis, another instance of the splitting of a primordial substance into distinct entities. A work of ravishing lyricism and sweeping vision, *ARK* is finally less a poem of science than a radically heterodox ode to a cosmos in which cells and stars share space with angels and gods.

Although Ammons associated himself with the term "ecology" as early as 1964, he never embraced the politics of environmentalism with the fervor of some poets of his generation. Of these, Gary Snyder (b. 1931) has been both the most ardent and the most scientifically informed. In "What Happened Here Before" he gives an accelerated overview of geological and evolutionary history, leaping forward in hundred-million-year increments to place human activity in global perspective.[33] A similar vastness of temporal vision informs "Toward Climax," which draws on the concept of "climax communities," ecosystems that have attained maximum stability and diversity. The poem opens with a passage whose elliptical syntax evokes the fluid exchanges between environments and organisms:

teeth, all-purpose little early mammal molars.
primate flat-foot
front fore-mounted eyes –

watching at the forest-grassland (interface
richness) edge.
scavenge, gather, rise up on rear legs.
running – grasping – hand and eye;
hunting.
calling others to the stalk, the drive.[34]

"Science walks in beauty," Snyder writes later in the poem, as he contemplates the notion of "detritus pathways," the weblike relays that distribute food, energy, and information throughout a well-balanced system. Like Ammons, Snyder honors the principle of "working order," although he finds its human aspect better exemplified in tribal cultures than in corporations.

Although it would be inaccurate to claim that Ammons fostered anything resembling a school or movement, it should nevertheless be noted that several prominent poets who draw on science in their work have had strong personal and institutional associations with him. These include the Nobel Prize–winning chemist Roald Hoffmann (b. 1937), a close friend and colleague of Ammons at Cornell, whose books *The Metamict State* (1987) and *Gaps and Verges* (1990) trace wayward paths between science and feeling. Another Cornell colleague and fellow North Carolinian, Robert Morgan (b. 1944), named his recent volume of selected poems *The Strange Attractor*, a term borrowed from chaos theory. Ammons's students include the poet and naturalist Diane Ackerman (b. 1948), whose first book, *The Planets: A Cosmic Pastoral* (1976), is equally indebted to Ammons and to his Cornell colleague, the popular astronomer Carl Sagan. Another of Ammons's students, Alice Fulton (b. 1952), has emerged as his most thoughtful and inventive successor, bringing a distinctively feminist bearing to the poetic assimilation of science. Her poem "Shy One" seems a conscious revision of Ammons's "Hymn." Like that poem, it begins by addressing an indeterminate "you":

Because faith creates its verification
and reaching you will be no harder than believing
in a planet's caul of plasma,
or interacting with a comet
in its perihelion passage, no harder
than considering what sparking of the vacuum, cosmological
impromptu flung me here, a paraphrase, perhaps,
for some denser, more difficult being,

> a subsidiary instance, easier to grasp
> than the span I foreshadow, of which I am a variable,
> my stance is passional toward the universe and you.[35]

The poem goes on to cite particular instances of faith as a necessary component of knowledge: "the way electrons exist only when they're measured" and "thirteen species / of whiptail lizards consisting entirely of females" that remain undiscovered because of a "bias against such things existing." Concluding that "faith is a cascade," Fulton adds a further layer of epistemological subtlety to Ammons's synthesis of science and religion. Her restless curiosity has also led her to develop analogies between poetic form and the complex geometric shapes called fractals.[36]

Other contemporary poets known for incorporating science into their work include John Allman (b. 1935), Pattiann Rogers (b. 1940), Linda Bierds (b. 1945), and Albert Goldbarth (b. 1948). The last two decades have seen a veritable explosion of science poetry, much of which falls outside the historical scope of this volume. Books published since 1990 that engage with scientific themes include Alison Hawthorne Deming's *Science and Other Poems* (1994), Mei-mei Berssenbrugge's *Endocrinology* (1997), Forrest Gander's *Science and Steepleflower* (1998), Christian Bök's *Crystallography* (2003), A. Van Jordan's *Quantum Lyrics* (2007), Anna Leahy's *Constituents of Matter* (2007), Lyrae Van Clief-Stefanon's *]Open Interval[* (2009), Susan Somers-Willett's *Quiver* (2009), Karen Leona Anderson's *Punish Honey* (2009), Kimiko Hahn's *Toxic Flora* (2010), Deborah Poe's *Elements* (2010), and Katherine Larson's *Radial Symmetry* (2011). Ranging through theoretical and particle physics, astronomy, chemistry, and various strains of biology, these books show that poetry's appetite for science as material for thematic reflection, metaphorical transmutation, and visionary elaboration is healthier than ever. If Ammons opened the door to science for twentieth-century poets, twenty-first-century poets seem intent on breaking down the wall.

Writing in 1963, the great physicist and teacher Richard Feynman reflected on what he saw as the unhealthy antagonism between poetry and science:

> Poets say science takes away from the beauty of the stars – mere globs of gas atoms. Nothing is "mere." I too can see the stars on a desert night, and feel them. But do I see less or more? The vastness of the heavens stretches my imagination – stuck on this carousel my little eye can catch one-million-year-old light. A vast pattern – of which I am a part – perhaps my stuff was belched from some forgotten star, as one is belching there. ... It does not do harm to the mystery to know a little about it. For far more marvelous is the truth than any artists of the past imagined! Why do the poets of the present not speak of

it? What men are poets who can speak of Jupiter if he were like a man, but if he is an immense spinning sphere of methane and ammonia must be silent?[37]

While the antiscientific views ascribed to them by Feynman can indeed be found in the writings of nineteenth- and even some twentieth-century poets, these views have become vanishingly rare today. The same year those sentences were written, Ammons's *Expressions of Sea Level* appeared, containing "Hymn" and "Mechanism." In the decades since, poets have more than risen to the challenge voiced by Feynman. Whether looking out far or in deep, toward the distant reaches of time and space or the intricate workings of cells and atoms, contemporary poets have found in science an alternative to more traditional sources of word and image: myth, religion, history, visible nature. Major twentieth-century discoveries from relativity and quantum mechanics to black holes and the DNA molecule have taken root in poets' imaginations, furnishing powerful metaphors that often seem to reconcile opposed realms. At once mysterious, uncanny, and counterintuitive and verifiable, rational, and objective, these concepts have given twentieth-century poets the means with which to construct a new kind of visionary poetics, in which reason and imagination are no longer sworn enemies but uneasy collaborators. To some degree this development has been spurred by the mass migration of poets into the university, where they perennially find themselves competing for institutional recognition and support with scientists. In any case, more and more poets appear to be heeding Ammons's call for a poetry that considers all knowledge its province, that stakes its claim to the materials of science while insisting on its right to reimagine them. The enterprises of poet and scientist can never be identical, of course, but as we move into a new millennium, they seem increasingly to hold converse.

Notes

1. Allen Tate (ed.), *The Complete Poetry and Selected Criticism of Edgar Allan Poe* (New York: New American Library, 1968), p. 48.
2. John Keats, *Complete Poems*, ed. Jack Stillinger (Cambridge, Mass.: Harvard University Press), p. 357. For a seminal discussion of this and related passages, see M. H. Abrams, "Science and Poetry in Romantic Criticism," in *The Mirror and the Lamp: Romantic Theory and the Critical Tradition* (New York: Oxford University Press, 1953), pp. 303–12.
3. Richard Holmes, *The Age of Wonder: How the Romantic Generation Discovered the Beauty and Terror of Science* (New York: Pantheon, 2008).
4. Walt Whitman, "When I Heard the Learn'd Astronomer," in *Poetry and Prose*, ed. Justin Kaplan (New York: Library of America, 1982), pp. 409–10. For a

distinguished mathematician's response to Whitman's poem, see David Gale, "The Sun, the Moon, and Mathematics," in *Tracking the Automatic Ant and Other Mathematical Explorations* (New York: Springer-Verlag, 1998), p. 199.

5. Whitman, *Poetry and Prose*, p. 15.

6. Ralph Waldo Emerson, "The Poet," in *Essays and Lectures*, ed. Joel Porte (New York: Library of America, 1983), p. 456.

7. Mina Loy, "Gertrude Stein," in *The Lost Lunar Baedeker*, ed. Roger L. Conover (New York: Farrar, Straus and Giroux), p. 94.

8. William Carlos Williams, "Author's Introduction to *The Wedge*," in *The Collected Poems of William Carlos Williams*. Vol. II, *1939–1962*, ed. Christopher MacGowan (New York: New Directions, 1991), p. 54; T. S. Eliot, "Tradition and the Individual Talent," in *Selected Prose of T. S. Eliot*, ed. Frank Kermode (New York: Farrar, Straus and Giroux, 1975), p. 41. For extended discussions of modernist poets' engagements with science, see Lisa M. Steinman, *Made in America: Science, Technology, and American Modernist Poets* (New Haven, Conn.: Yale University Press, 1987), and Daniel Albright, *Quantum Poetics: Yeats, Pound, Eliot and the Science of Modernism* (Cambridge: Cambridge University Press, 1997).

9. For an early but still useful discussion of Jeffers's engagement with science, see Hyatt H. Waggoner, "Science and the Poetry of Robinson Jeffers," *American Literature* 10:3 (1938), pp. 275–88. A much more recent account of Jeffers as a poet of scientifically informed biophilia is Christopher Cokinos's essay "Nature's Oracle," *Los Angeles Times*, January 23, 2012, p. 13.

10. Robinson Jeffers, *The Selected Poetry of Robinson Jeffers* (New York: Random House, 1938), p. 173.

11. Jeffers, *The Selected Poetry*, pp. 597–98.

12. A. R. Ammons to Budd Smith, October 1, 1973, A. R. Ammons Papers, box 21, journal 56, Kroch Rare and Manuscripts Collections, Cornell University.

13. A. R. Ammons, "Defense of Poetry," *Epoch* 52:3 (2004), p. 462.

14. A. R. Ammons, *Collected Poems 1951–1971* (New York: W. W. Norton, 1972), p. 39. This collection will subsequently be cited in the text as *ARA*.

15. A. R. Ammons, *Tape for the Turn of the Year* (Ithaca, N.Y.: Cornell University Press, 1965), p. 112.

16. A. R. Ammons, *Sphere* (New York: W. W. Norton, 1974), p. 56.

17. Ammons, *Sphere*, p. 56.

18. Ammons, *Sphere*, p. 36.

19. A. R. Ammons, *Garbage* (New York: W. W. Norton, 1993), pp. 24–25.

20. Josephine Miles, *Collected Poems 1930–83* (Urbana: University of Illinois Press, 1983), pp. 183–84.

21. Ruth Stone, *Second-Hand Coat: Poems New and Selected* (Cambridge, Mass.: David R. Godine, 1987), p. 10.

22. Stone, *Second-Hand Coat: Poems New and Selected*, pp. 40–41.

23. Stone, *Second-Hand Coat: Poems New and Selected*, p. 3.

24. May Swenson, *Poems to Solve* (New York: Scribner, 1966), p. 32; May Swenson, *Iconographs* (New York: Scribner, 1970), p. 70; May Swenson, *More Poems to Solve* (New York: Scribner, 1971), p. 23.

25. May Swenson, "The DNA Molecule," *Poetry* (December 1968), pp. 176–77.

26. Andrew Weiman, "Andy-Diana DNA Letter," in John Frederick Nims (ed.), *The Harper Anthology of Poetry* (New York: Harper and Row, 1981), p. 760.

27. Frederick Seidel, *The Cosmos Trilogy* (New York: Farrar, Straus and Giroux, 2003), p. 15.

28. Seidel, *The Cosmos Trilogy*, p. 9.

29. James Merrill, *The Changing Light at Sandover* (New York: Alfred A. Knopf, 1982), p. 110.

30. Johnson and Ammons crossed paths briefly in 1960 through their shared connection with the poet and publisher Jonathan Williams. It seems safe to surmise that Johnson had read at least Ammons's early poetry, although his primary allegiances were to the Black Mountain and San Francisco Renaissance poets.

31. Ronald Johnson, *ARK* (Chicago: Flood Editions, 2013), pp. 88–89.

32. Johnson, *ARK*, p. 100.

33. Gary Snyder, *Turtle Island* (New York: New Directions, 1974), p. 78.

34. Snyder, *Turtle Island*, p. 82.

35. Alice Fulton, *Cascade Experiment: Selected Poems* (New York: W. W. Norton, 2004), p. 59.

36. Alice Fulton, "Fractal Amplifications: Writing in Three Dimensions," in *Feeling as a Foreign Language: The Good Strangeness of Poetry* (St. Paul, Minn.: Graywolf, 1999), p. 61.

37. Richard P. Feynman, *Six Easy Pieces: Essentials of Physics Explained by Its Most Brilliant Teacher*, ed. Robert B. Leighton and Matthew Sands (New York: Basic Books, 1996), pp. 59–60.

Chapter 41

The 1970s and the "Poetry of the Center"

EDWARD BRUNNER

No one, least of all American poets, was prepared for the "succession of upheavals" that, in Natasha Zaretsky's study of the 1970s, challenged whether the county possessed "the political, military, economic and moral resources to prevail in world affairs and provide for domestic prosperity."[1] An unpopular war divided the populace and questioned the nation's ability to protect its far-flung interests; an oil embargo exposed limited national resources and confirmed an economy going global; and a White House scandal exposed government corruption and demonstrated how a sensationalist media could shape public thinking. As the decade began, poets likened America to the Roman Empire, but their vision of a great civilization undermined by imperialist adventures was a dead-end model, a "warning" equivalent to confessing despair. The 1970s, then, have been described as a time of severe contraction. "Embarrassed by the failure of projected spiritual revolutions," Charles Altieri wrote, "all the arts withdrew into a defensive pluralism suspicious of all theoretical claims and anxious to align with mainstream cultural values."[2]

In the midst of such regrouping, some poets conceived a style of versifying in direct opposition to doom-saying gestures. Robert Pinsky, Philip Levine, and Robert Hass took from their teachers at Stanford, Yvor Winters and Donald Davie, examples of poetry and critical writings that envisioned poetry as a public art that blended responsiveness to large concerns with responsibility to the poetic tradition. Such a "poetry of the center," as Robert von Hallberg was first to show, was timely, upholding discursive virtues whose "Augustan" perspective (in Robert Archambeau's words) was "a matter of commentary, abstraction and moral statement."[3] Older poets in midcareer (W. S. Merwin, Gary Snyder, and Adrienne Rich) also responded to the demands of their time (ecology, loss of the wilderness, and injustice against women), but when they took up matters of common concern, they extended the linguistic and structural boundaries of the poem, modeling alternate styles of perception. They thought ecologically, not just historically; saw globally, not nationally; and worked across deep time. Of these poets, it is Hass who works the intersection between the two groups. He finds global significance in the natural life of a region; his sense of history confirms the need for ecological balance. He refines the urbanity of an Augustan perspective by testing its validity within a shifting series of frameworks, a restless set of viewpoints.

★

Robert Pinsky's *The Situation of Poetry* (1976) looked back and forward, a cross between an overview and a manifesto; it summarized the decade of poetry before it and influenced the decades to follow by championing a discursive, speech-oriented poetics that highlighted the intellect's capacity to describe, consider, and evaluate. These values had been heralded by Winters (acknowledged by Pinsky on his dedication page) since the 1940s in critical essays associating morality with discipline and were further developed by Davie (Winters's successor at Stanford) in studies in the 1950s that singled out diction and syntax as underappreciated features that, by displacing image and rhythm as centrally expressive, countered the influence in England of "Bohemian" poets of rhetorical excess such as Dylan Thomas and the early W. S. Graham.[4]

England in the 1950s could be pertinent to America in the 1970s because America's young poets had been experimenting with programmatic language that, though different from the excessive rhetoric of Thomas and Graham, had become in its own way similarly formulized. A sympathetic description of the Deep Image poetry of the late 1960s would consider it on the one hand as stylized to evoke the stress of its time while on the other hand designed to serve as a haven of stability. Such writing was a staple of *Poetry* magazine under Daryl Hine, who regularly printed free verse that portrayed a mythic or unconscious psychic state in language that was tonally sober, aurally portentous, and visually impoverished, as in these opening lines to poems by Josephine Saunders, Jon Anderson, and Mark Strand, respectively: "What is to be found / on the underside of words?" "The heart is a violent muscle; it opens & shuts. / The subject is death." "I have a key / so I open the door and walk in. / It is dark and I walk in. / It is darker and I walk in."[5]

Although such language might appear strange, unnerving, and dangerous, its wholesale usage had turned it into coterie talk. Pinsky identified a lexicon of key words by distributing them throughout a three-line parody that, he claimed, any "young poet" could have written on any "campus in America": "The silence of my / blood eats light like the / breath of future water."[6] By 1978, the poetics of this "new surrealism" was so compromised that Paul Breslin could dismiss it as a "shared set of rhetorical and ideological formulas ... rearranged to make any number of more or less interchange-able poems."[7] Although this poetry affiliated itself with activism, it pre-sented acts of withdrawal that it regarded as necessary self-protection in a bad time.

Breslin's dismissal downplayed, however, the stress that the ongoing Vietnam War placed on poets for whom language was an index of cultural health. The September 1972 issue of *Poetry,* scheduled for appearance on the eve of a national election, consisted entirely of poems that answered editor Hine's solicitations for new work "protesting the acceleration of the unde-clared Indo-Chinese War."[8] The issue's unprecedented all-black cover evoked an air of mourning, while its complete darkness augured a disruption of the senses, a blindness the poets verbally reproduced by insisting the working material of their language had been damaged. The issue confirms Subarno Chattarji's observation that poets against the war united in the belief that "the state manipulated language to wage and sustain the war."[9] Richard Hugo (now remembered for his rough-edged poems about working-class life in the Pacific Northwest) warned, in the poem that Hine offered readers first: "Beware certain words: Enemy, Liberty. Freedom." "Believe those sounds," Hugo concluded, "and you're aiming a bomb."[10]

Yet the deep images into which these poets descended could also reveal what had been lost and what might return. James Wright's "Eclogue at Nash's Grove," from his 1971 *Collected Poems*, features language under such stress that it veers between muttering and cursing. When moments of eloquence emerge, they are voiced by others, such as a colloquial translation of Virgil's *"optima dies primus fugit"* (sometimes rendered as "the best days are first to leave," from his *Bucolics*). The poem records a visit to a neglected nineteenth-century cem-etery in southwest Minnesota. Rare wildflowers can abound in isolated mid-western burial grounds like Nash's Grove, whose consecrated land remains unbroken by a plow. When Wright finds instead a site choked with weeds, its pioneers' gravestones crumbling, he collapses into despair, rage, and self-pity: "Virgin America, all right," he cries. "The whole place is a grave, a virgin / Whose belly is black stone."[11]

What dislodges Wright from despair is Virgil's Latin, whose compressed, incisive phrasing carries such wisdom that it not only survives but merits recy-cling as Americanized colloquial talk, as if it could emerge from not a book but a happenstance meeting: "A man whom I never saw told me / The best days are the first / To flee away." By recasting Virgil's words as a linguis-tic wildflower from a poetic ancestor who understood loss to be inevitable, Wright is able to recognize, encompass, and embrace the neglected. All the

Minnesotans relegated to an overgrown graveyard now can be placed tenderly in relation to one another and to Wright, allowing him to embrace his own injuries through acknowledging theirs. The poem we are reading becomes a new kind of eclogue, not a stylized exchange between "shepherds" whose rural upbringing purifies their thought but a chance for Wright to align himself with the forgotten people of whom he is sweepingly self-aware. He signs off in a final line: "This poem is a little / Darkness for them, where they do not have to weep. / Not for me, anyway."[12]

The Virgilian clarity that salvages Wright from emotional wreckage is scarcely evident in his own poetry, which ends with a sentence fragment. This effect of a downward spiral was surely intended, because the poem's Latin epigraph is an untranslated and unattributed quote from Catullus – *"cui dono lepidum novum libellum?"* – lines that resonate ironically for Wright (who is among the few with the knowledge to translate them): "To whom do I dedicate my elegant little book?" That is the kind of question Pinsky wants to rehabilitate, to strip of its irony, not just in his critical writing but in his own poetry. For him, the clarity and directness of ancient poets who concentrate thought into compelling phrases need not be taken as the neglected virtue of a remote past; rather, it can be seen as that which the present has available as its heritage from the medium of poetry that has been shaped over time. To illustrate Pinsky's embrace of such linguistic elements as "clarity, flexibility, efficiency," James Longenbach, two decades later, chose "Tennis," from Pinsky's inaugural volume *Sadness and Happiness* (1975), in which a description of the familiar game becomes the source of rules for upright living, as this passage from section V illustrates: "Call questionable balls his way, not yours; / You lose the point but have your concentration, / The grail of self-respect. Wear white. Mind losing."[13] "If Virgil could write poems about the skills of farming," Longenbach asks, "why not poems about the skills of tennis?"[14] Pinsky delivers one sentence after another, serving up a compressed, aphoristic wisdom, a vernacular ethics in which humility, grace, and endeavor operate in tandem. It is as if the game has become a poem and the poem a game (its precise blank verse nodding to an American Virgil, the Robert Frost who famously disparaged free verse as tennis without a net).

Pinsky establishes, in his volume's title, a vast polarity within which to work. "Sadness and Happiness" proclaims its fluency by stepping effortlessly across the divisions separating each of the thirteen sections (each one with five stanzas in four lines each): "Well, somewhere in the mind's mess / feelings are genuine," Pinsky begins, introducing a sentence in section III that continues with a list of such feelings:

                                    cool
             blue of Indian summer, happiness
                      IV
             like the sex-drowsy saxophones
             rolling flatted thirds of the blues
             over and over, rocking the dulcet
             rhythms of regret, Black music

             which tumbles loss over in the mouth
             like a moist bone full of marrow.[15]

The poet's form, its division into numbered sections, here exists as an obstacle that can be overtopped and played against, much as the flatted-third blue notes that are supposed to connote sadness can be rolled "over and over" until their tumbling makes loss palpable, physical, and bodily. Pinsky's rhapsodic meditations are an extravaganza of equivalences, networks of association that verge on the tumultuous. To float productively between sadness and happiness is to evoke jazz and the blues as allies in versifying.

Pinsky never writes for long without returning to the music he grew up with, which crosses racial lines, unites disparate groups, and mixes high and low culture. Extended sequences that consider an America both popular and elite are a signature of Pinsky's work. The tercets of "Essay on Psychiatrists," a sequence that floats in and out of blank verse, teasingly investigate psychiatrists ("It's crazy to think one could describe them," it begins) and then conclude, twenty-one sections later, by deciding "we are all psychiatrists," all professionals in one form or another.[16] Willard Spiegelman observes that the sequence moves "from a contemplation of *The Bacchae* (is Pentheus or Dionysus the true psychiatrist in the play?), through descriptions of the comic strip figure Rex Morgan, M.D., through Landor's Imaginary Conversation between Sidney and Fulke Greville, and to memories of Yvor Winters."[17] In Pinsky's fluency, moving laterally across a broad cultural terrain, poetry regains its authority to comment on the world beyond it.

How did Pinsky achieve such a breakthrough? Winters, for one, served as a guide beyond formulaic diction, because the words he had relied on in his modernist free verse of the 1920s – "cold," "stone," "silent," "alone" – formed the "rudiments of a personal code," as Robert von Hallberg observed, that would "constitute a generation's poetic diction forty years later." Winters's cure had been to employ a "deliberate, even willful, use of words ... to situate his own utterances in implicit relation to the utterances of older poets."[18] Winters, famous for the rigor with which he examined poetry in English, saw the poem supreme as an accurate, measured exchange between the poet and a subject in which the tradition of poetry provides resources that result in an artwork that both portrays and assesses.[19] Precision is so necessary to such a task that, in a sense, every writer who submits to such a standard is being tested ethically, while in another sense, the very idea at the heart of poetry – examining its given subject with the critical care afforded by such a deep and strong tradition – is inherently ethical. Thom Gunn, a Stanford arrival fresh from a 1950s-era Cambridge education dominated by F. R. Leavis, swiftly transitioned to Winters's view of poetry "as an art toward which you have to have responsibility ... a more *exact* and *precise* form of writing than any other."[20] Gunn developed tight rhymed iambics, as in "Misanthropos" from *Touch* (1967), in which he found the words of trust to be voiced by a "last man" looking for others in the days after nuclear disaster, a catastrophe whose unsparing devastation terribly anticipated his poetry on AIDS in the 1990s.[21]

Pinsky also found in Davie (who filled Winters's place at Stanford after his death, from 1968 to 1978) a model that bridged the worlds of objective scholarship and engaged reviewing. Davie's "Afterword for the American Reader," in his 1973 study *Thomas Hardy and British Poetry*, called for a poetry that presented civic sense and political responsibility, and Davie elsewhere defined his study as "making the case for the political Centre."[22] Davie's own poetry, as von Hallberg observed, demonstrated the many ways "that a poet who wishes to speak for the center of his culture can stake his claim."[23] Calvin Bedient has described Davie's style with an accuracy that accommodates Pinsky's work:

> The urbane mind scorns the folly and fears the vice of all private perspective; it trusts in the justice of the general. Accordingly, the ideal style, to it, is a style without style, as clear, unmarked, and compliant as water – and like water, wholesome, easy to assimilate, and used by everyone (for as the lines go, so goes the nation).[24]

Pinsky's acclaimed book-length sequence *An Explanation of America* (1979) features just such a "clear, unmarked, and compliant" style at its most endearing:

> In a way, every stranger must imagine
> The place where he finds himself – as shrewd Odysseus
> Was able to imagine, as he wandered,
> The ways and perils of a foreign place:
> Making his goal, not knowing the real place,
> But his survival, and his progress home.[25]

With this style, Pinsky introduces a charmed world of orderly proportion, thoughtful ritual, and attentive community: "I want our country like a common dream / To be between us in what we want to see" (*EA*, p. 10). Yet his readiness to select conventional paradigms for describing the country – its love of speed, its vast geography, and its openness to the future – also reveals a work anxiously testing the ability to locate national standards at a time of unsettling change. He finesses that project, moreover, by proposing to explain to his young daughter what America means, thus permitting himself to define his work space along vast polarities: on the one hand, he speaks of the nation in its past and future; on the other hand, he speaks to the child he is nurturing. Limiting himself to addressing the young restricts where his investigations might lead him. History approached in this manner is no longer a dark hole with an aura of criminality, as it seemed earlier in the decade. When he takes up "Rome," it is not the swollen-with-ambition late Rome of Lowell's Juvenal but a morning-in-Italia Rome of Virgil and Horace, whose perspective he embeds by translating one of Horace's epistolary-advice poems as if a suburbanite were writing to a cosmopolitan. History is not made subordinate to literature, but literature is the place where history is fully embodied, imaginatively sustained.

Pinsky's project tests the capacity of poetry to be epic and lyric, to be broadly descriptive and deeply intimate, yet what is most striking is its resemblance to romance. The tormented family of confessional verse is replaced by a nuclear family that is a model of hard work and achievement, and the poem begins and ends in classroom settings within which his daughter flourishes. When Pinsky takes up the most distressing moment in recent American history, he sharply sequesters that discussion. "Someday the War in Southeast Asia," he writes, addressing his daughter in stumbling words, "somewhere – / Perhaps for you and people younger than you – / Will be the kind of history and pain / Saguntum is for me" (*EA*, p. 50). ("Saguntum," mentioned in one of Ben Jonson's famous elegies, is remote indeed: it won its battleground status in the Second Punic War.) Pinsky banishes Vietnam through scare quotes and italics. He backs away from "The words – '*Vietnam*' – that I can't use in poems / Without the one word threatening to gape / And swallow and enclose the poem" (*EA*, p. 45). Alfred Corn thought Pinsky's title was a mistake: "Wouldn't 'Reflections on America' have been (though no more appetizing) more exact?"[26] But an explanation of America is not reflecting on America: "as all things have their explanations, / True or false, all can come to seem domestic" (*EA*, p. 18). His concluding section stresses art's importance but centers on Shakespeare's masque-like drama about artifice, *The Winter's Tale*, in which aristocrats play at being rustics. Yet that work also features a mad ruler who regains his sanity, and the uniting of a family long thought scattered. Pinsky presents a country in desperate need of healing, eager to find stability, and he frames his words to comfort and soothe.

Pinsky would proceed less cautiously in his later years: he came to describe *An Explanation of America* as a "weird experiment," not a didactic poem but an example of imagining a didactic poem.[27] Frank Bidart, introducing Pinsky at a 1990 reading, described his post-*Explanation* poems not as "discursive" but as "almost the mirror-reverse. Fragmentation, quicksilver transitions, delirium, dream, brokenness now create the characteristic verbal texture."[28] "The Figured Wheel" (in *The History of My Heart* [1984]) imagines the poem as an archival device that absorbs and preserves generational traces of humans through time and across space. For Pinsky, it is an instrument of humility that brutally and heedlessly engorges all there is, even as it is brilliantly, dazzlingly festooned with what others believed to be important: "It is Jesus oblivious to hurt turning to give words to the unrighteous, / And it is also Gogol's feeding pig that without knowing it eats a baby chick / / And goes on feeding."[29] Structures like this one – lyrics as epics and short poems that encapsulate multiple extended sequences – are signature texts of Pinsky's later work. "Shirt" (in *The Want Bone* [1990]) peels back the layers of significance from an everyday item, moving beyond its components (listed like an incantatory chant: "The back, the yoke, the yardage") into the actual labor behind its making, touching on the history of sweatshops and the origin of fabrics, and stressing the class divisions and racial differences that are both elided and preserved within an ordinary artifact. At the center of the poem, incidents from "the infamous blaze / / At the Triangle Factory in nineteen-eleven" stand in as re-creations of the lost histories that drive the poem.[30]

*

Pinsky's career unfolds from its sharply focused beginning. From celebrating the professionalism that served as an avenue of upward mobility for a nation settled by immigrants, he turns to celebrating the mongrel attributes of a country that too easily forgets its checkered past. He has moved closer to the position that Philip Levine, also a student of Winters, developed in the 1970s. Levine's "first and most powerful commitment," Edward Hirsch wrote, "has been to the failed and lost, the marginal, the unloved, the unwanted."[31] Levine may have transferred from Winters his proclivity for "discovering or gaining attention for unrecognized or neglected poets" – a "serious matter," von Hallberg writes, "to which Winters brought intelligence and taste – and perseverance."[32]

Yet if Levine admired Winters's propensity for the underdog, he bonded with Winters through a mutual interest in prizefighting. The pugnacious

Winters, who appears as the garrulous "Old Man" in Pinsky's "Essay on Psychiatrists," is recalled by Levine, in a memoir of his Stanford days, as a frustrated boxer.[33] Levine's turn away from the Anglo-American tradition championed by Winters and his embrace of the explosive and intuitive imagery of poetry in Spanish by Neruda, Vallejo, and others were a shift from one style of battle to another. Far from aristocratically colonizing these Spanish poets, Levine borrows their phrasing to disclose American practices; he anticipates an America viewed as "hemispheric" rather than transnational. If the words are awry and the phrasing bizarre, such distortions can be used, *pace* Breslin, not to register the inner world of the sensitized poet but to glimpse the strained sensibility of the laboring class neglected by an indifferent culture. In a series of interconnected volumes that represent conditions of the working poor in Detroit, Levine recast the poetic idioms of Deep Image surrealism to record the sentiments of the alienated, translating their struggle for dignity into language now meaningfully distraught.

Levine's workers are ground down by routine labor, pressured by invisible racism, their anger simmering. In one sense, these voices could not have been clearer: "Out of burlap sacks, out of bearing butter, / Out of black bean and wet slate bread, / Out of the acids of rage, the candor of tar, / Out of creosote, gasoline, drive shafts, wooden dollies, / They Lion grow."[34] This title poem from *They Feed They Lion* (1972) draws energy from the same sources as the Anglo-Saxon alliterative verse it strikingly resembles – the rhythms of repetitive labor, the burden of bodies moving within exhaustion. But there is nothing quaint about the poem: the poor will not be ground down – their very bodies are accustomed to absorbing brutalization. If this is an environment of detritus, of the leftover and discarded, then its fragments and floating phrases have been shaped by Levine into savagely clustered lists that sound both damaged and reconstituted, both destructive and creative, inhuman and human.

"They Feed They Lion" depicts a generalized voice that sounds harsh; we are unused to hearing hard labor articulated in verse. What some might dismiss as "surreal" by the standards of the Anglo-American poetic tradition becomes, when viewed through the street life of a damaged American city, an imagery that reflects the cobbled-together tactics that inhabitants need to survive. Levine's battle to express the loss of his father at the age of five is recorded in "Zaydee," a poem in which the grandfather is the stabilizing figure to whom the child turns in his drive to understand. But for Levine at five, the answer to the question "Where did my father go in my fifth autumn?" is always going to be elusive, enigmatic, mysterious: "In the blind night of Detroit / on the front porch, Grandfather points up / at a constellation shaped like a cock and balls."[35] The memories cannot be sorted from a baffling network of contradictory impressions, of images simultaneously elevated and demeaning, expansive and constricted, adult and childlike: "He carries a card table out under the moon / and plays gin rummy and cheats"; "He sings a song of freestone peaches / all in a box." The poem ends when the child steps in to shape an answer he might comprehend to the question he asked his grandfather:

> Where did he go when his autumn came?
> He sat before the steering wheel
> of the black Packard, he turned the key,
> pressed the starter, and he went.
>
> The maples blazed golden and red
> a moment and then were still,
> the long streets were still and the snow
> swirled where I lay down to rest.[36]

If this closure is final, it remains just as surely open, as though his father in time will return to the "long streets" that are still for the moment, just a time of resting. (He returns in spirit in all Levine's subsequent poems.) Even so, the son also knows that what he wants to dream to be temporary – that his father's voyage will end in his father's safe return – is all too permanent. The reality of death, there in the construction of "lay down to rest," is both admitted and refused.

Levine may have had his own bluntness confirmed in Winters's example, but he took away an additional lesson – the need to protect against hurting others. Winters was famous for his brusque dismissals, and his candid remarks must have stung. "There are a few poems that I should, in fact, have liked to omit," Winters wrote in his foreword to the 1937 anthology *Twelve Poets of the Pacific*, and he then went on to name the four authors whose work he disvalued.[37] Levine will not forget incidents in which violence intruded, but he is also eager to notice violence rebuffed by unexpected generosity. *The Names of the Lost* (1976) sets out not only to retrieve the forgotten and identify the nameless but also to honor the guardians, those who found their voice. While "New Season" appears as a chronicle poem, listing Levine's anxiety about his teenage son's male friends, who inhabit a culture of violence, and written on the occasion of his mother's seventieth birthday, at its center is an anecdote that carries transcendent weight; it slowly emerges from the anecdotal violence that surrounds his memory of the 1942 Belle Isle riots, when Levine was fifteen and Detroit found itself a city "at war for real," as angry gangs marauded the streets, enraged by the rumor that "a sailor had thrown a black baby / off the Belle Isle Bridge":

7 years passed
before Della Daubien told me
how three white girls from the shop
sat on her on the Woodward Streetcar
so the gangs couldn't find her
and pull her off like they did
the black janitor and beat
an eye blind. She would never
forget, she said, and her old face
glowed before me in shame
and terror.[38]

Levine's poetry remains close to violent incidents, an injured child devising compensations for his loss, shaping from vivid fragments of memory a narrative sensible and practical enough to allow him to move on. To remain close to the Detroit streets, even to find traces of those same streets in 1930s Spain, is crucial. He is the "poet of the night shift," writes Edward Hirsch, "a late ironic Whitman of our industrial heartland, a Romantic anarchist."[39] While Levine's Detroit waits for its resurrection, its citizenry endlessly demonstrates their ingenuity as survivors: the only trace of a solution lies in the exceptional acts of individuals. Levine's further poetry is adroit at amplifying such moments without diminishing their humanity.

*

The poetry of Levine and Pinsky is not affianced to Winters through commitment to any orthodoxy. Neither poet aspires to the mantle of the rigorous moralist whose aim is to forge a "truism" that the poem "then has to make real for the reader."[40] Instead, Winters's spirit endures in writing that, for Pinsky (he said in a 1984 talk), embodies a "resistance or transformation of communal values," or, for Levine (he said in a 1977 interview), aims "to effect some kind of moral change."[41] Their communally focused, ethically attentive poems willingly take on a burden of responsibility – a commitment associated with another group of poets who defined a crisis whose proportions intensified during the 1970s and reached beyond any nation.

April 1970 marked the first celebration of Earth Day, and as *Hudson Review* editor Frederick Morgan wrote in a 1970 issue featuring work by W. S. Merwin, Gary Snyder, William Stafford, A. R. Ammons, and others, "'Ecology' has become a key word of our time." A threatened environment offered itself as a metacrisis, a problem that drew on rhetoric that had earlier circulated around nuclear holocaust: "We are living on the brink of an enormous catastrophe, and ... probably the human race wiped out, or reduced to a suffering frag-ment, within the next half-century."[42] Unlike atomic war, though, this crisis was evolving, palpable, and susceptible to individual involvement. The crisis had sweep and grandeur – a disaster unfolding on a worldwide scale – yet its problems encouraged innovative approaches. Wendell Berry created "The Mad Farmer" to disrupt the bucolic observations ("The known / returns to be known again") in *Farming: A Handbook* (1970), calling for revolution, describing a "year of catastrophe," and offering "Prayers and Sayings" that placed "hands into the mire" to learn the "kinship ... of the living and the dead."[43]

The free verse in Merwin's *Writings to an Unfinished Accompaniment* (1973) (Morgan published four examples in his 1970 issue) exemplified a "deep ecol-ogy" that, historian Bruce J. Schulman explains, challenges "the anthropo-morphic outlook of most mainstream environmentalists with their stress on human welfare and aesthetic appreciation of natural beauty."[44] In the 1950s, Merwin had written of the coal-mining facilities in his Pennsylvania home-town, and he ended "Burning Mountain" (in *The Drunk in the Furnace* [1960]) by describing a smoldering coal seam that has become "normal / With farms on it, and wells of good water, / Still cold, that should last us, and our grand-children."[45] This denial of a deteriorating environment becomes a deliberate blindness Merwin imagines at the center of *The Lice* (1967), portraying the Vietnam War as the offshoot of a larger technocratic impulse to dominate the natural world. A nation that can eradicate species can fecklessly devastate a country, but with fearful consequences: "When the forests have been destroyed their darkness remains / The ash the great walker follows the possessors."[46]

Merwin's free verse in the 1960s offered grim, symptomatic sketches of a deeply distressed culture that were widely adapted by other poets (Paul Breslin targeted these poems in his 1978 article).[47] To turn from despair to hopefulness, as Merwin did, demanded repositioning. This free verse, structured as para-ble but using the riddle's gnomic language, discerns items from the natural world – mountains, clouds, stars, water, and sun – as reflecting a system that addresses us through acts we fail to grasp: "the same wind that tells you every-thing at once / unstitches your memory"; "everywhere / the vision has just passed out of sight / like the shadows sinking."[48] Poems sidle from one para-dox to another, embracing and inverting contradictions, sounding like legends or folklore or primitive tales: "nothing on earth / says it's ours"; "Every word / runs the hills at night."[49] Are these the last stories, the fragmentary narratives that a handful of survivors might recall after world's end? Or are they the first stories, sudden glimpses into truths that can sustain a future? We live in such a moment that we cannot tell; the natural environment that once helped guide our ancestors now sends scrambled messages: "the skies are looking for you / they've left everything / they want you to remember them," but they resemble "shadows of doors calling calling / sailing / the other way // so it sounds like good-bye."[50] What these poems offer, Evan Watkins wrote shortly after their appearance, is "the possibility of living one's life as a continual transformation through being observed, being touched, being judged even by what is around us, a recognition that at the very point of personal identity there is an otherness which presses continually upon us."[51]

The medium of poetry, as Merwin reconfigures it, should be capacious enough to reproduce concepts from other cultures. Solidarity is found in writings that are conspicuously transnational. The dangers are global, the planet is threatened, yet poets know the wisdom transmitted over generations. Merwin's translations in *Selected Translations 1968–1978* (1980) sound translation-like – disembodied, simplified, and without associational overtones – and he comes away with moments that are humble, respectful, and patient, as in "Pilgrim Songs," from an anonymous nineteenth-century Russian source ("Our life on earth / is like the grass growing"), or the thirteenth-century Persian of Rumi ("Teacher give me a name so that I'll know / what to call myself") or the twentieth-century Spanish of Vicente Huidobro ("I'm absent but deep in this absence / There is the waiting for myself").[52] These direct words convey a transnational alliance of poets operating as a communality that transmits across continents and centuries. Poets in an uncertain time become archivists of ancient knowledge. *The Rain in the Trees* (1988) centers on a Hawaiian landscape midway between continents with a double project: Merwin reclaims local vegetation damaged by industrial farming and records the indigenous language overridden by colonists from east and west. *The Folding Cliffs* (1998), a narrative poem of Hawaii set in the 1890s, dramatizes the clash between natives and colonists while lovingly portraying the exotic trees, flowers, and animals of a lost time. Hawaii's fragility, in Merwin's handling, represents the planet's besiegement, even as this distinctive geography offers a practical framework within which to accomplish productive work.

The ability to work across cultures and reconstruct fields of knowledge beyond the current time frame is crucial to the verbal networks that Gary Snyder weaves into loosely connected sequences. For Snyder, the medium of poetry is inseparable from deep time, equivalent to an artifact with an ancient design. Isomorphic correspondences that link Native American myth and Buddhist principles clarify the dynamic exchanges among creatures and vegetation. *Turtle Island* (1974) is the "new / old" name given to the continent by Native Americans, "based on many creation myths of the people who have been living here for millennia."[53] The work of a scholar-poet who studied anthropology at Reed, who read Chinese philosophy and the poetry of the T'ang dynasty (618–907 C.E.) at Berkeley, who hung out with Beat poets sojourning in San Francisco, who crewed on oil tankers and manned forest lookout towers, and who eventually resettled his family into a wilderness area of California, Snyder's *Turtle Island* is, depending on which passage we examine, environmentalist logbook, scholarly citation, fervent prayer to mythic deities, outraged tract, or amiable memoir. Snyder can write from the viewpoint of the log-truck driver who knows the wilderness as a work site – "In the high-seat, before-dawn dark, / Polished hubs gleam" – or he can launch into diatribes that target caricaturized enemies – "The robots argue how to parcel our Mother Earth / To last a little longer / like vultures flapping / Belching, gurgling, / near a dying Doe"– or just as easily describe creatures interacting with transcendent grace:

> A whoosh of birds
> sweeps up and round
> tilts back
> almost always flying all apart
> and yet hangs on!
> together[54]

Yet *Turtle Island* never lingers over pictorial grandeur. Its moments of grace are fleeting, and its territory is under siege. Snyder identifies with species under attack: "The insects side with the Viet Cong," he insists, as humans bomb and destroy, moving "across the planet / blinding sparrows / breaking the ear-drums of owls."[55] The natural environment within which Snyder locates himself, although embattled, contains within it resources for survival. Snyder's pages exercise freedoms both verbal and visual. Organizations of words cluster concepts or use line breaks for drama, and linguistic registers shift from the vernacular to the scientific or slip into non-English languages to represent alternate cultures.

By contrast, Adrienne Rich regards her cultural environment as profoundly hostile – as it indeed had become by the midpoint of the decade. With the failure of the Equal Rights Amendment to the U.S. Constitution, antifeminist campaigns "that had been in progress for some time," Philip Jenkins writes, were "winning victories that startled a liberal movement long used to victory."[56] "Both the victimization and the anger experienced by women are real, and have real sources," Rich wrote in a 1971 essay, "built into society, language, the structures of thought."[57] Her subject, then, exists within the very language she has inherited, which she must work with, yet somehow alter: "Our whole life a translation / the permissible fibs // and now a knot of lies / eating at itself to get undone."[58] To convey those damaged words, those half-present meanings, Rich sometimes offers a poetic line scarred with visible gaps:

> Death of the city   Her face
> sleeping   Her quick stride   Her
> running   Search for a private space   The city
> caving from within   The lessons badly
> learned   Or not at all[59]

Even when Rich's individual lines blur, grow agitated, or turn opaque, they affirm an alternate space that still dreams that language might become common. The Manhattan in "Twenty-One Love Poems" is, in its public façade, a toxic environment where "screens flicker / with pornography, with science-fiction vampires," and its violence is inescapable, even seeping into private spaces, where "wounds / break open further with tears."[60] Only in the interior of "(The Floating Poem, Unnumbered)" can Rich find an intimacy with another woman in which expression is more bodily than verbal, in which it is possible to claim "Whatever happens, this is."[61] One "irregular" text dominates the twenty-one others, flourishing apart from yet in relation to the series, in the first book of poetry in which Rich identified as a lesbian. To make a space that had not previously existed is to open possibility, to include others who have been excluded, and to envision an alternate future. Indeed, traditional forms such as the sestinas and sonnets that Marilyn Hacker demonstrated in a series of volumes beginning with *Presentation Piece* (1974) were also available (as, in a sense, they had always been) as vehicles for channeling love's power, no matter what public attitudes might be: "the skin wakes / up in humming networks, audibly whispers / over the dead wind."[62]

Rich was "breaking down language," Suzanne Juhasz declared in 1976, "in order to be able to recompose it."[63] Helen Vendler saw this process as evolving, with Rich's 1991 collection *An Atlas of the Difficult World* placing in its title "an adjective of bafflement and struggle rather than of revolt and revolution."[64] Rich has continued to develop an alternate orthography, with a backslash in mid-line that evokes prose transcription within a poetic discourse: "This woman/ the heart of the matter."[65] Sometimes she borrows from forebears such as Muriel Rukeyser, from whom she takes the colon – sometimes surrounded by space, and sometimes paired with another – as a mark that both interrupts and equates, that distinguishes among items while relating them. While such intrusions/insertions appear in a minority of Rich's later poems, their intransigence identifies with the poem's position as harshly delimited by the politics of persisting social customs and fiercely expressive of resistance to limits rigorously evoked.

Not unlike Rich's obduracy is the "ecofeminism" that David Harvey describes as an environmental justice movement, that poses "matters in terms of the defilement, violation, and even 'rape' of a sacred Mother Earth" to adopt a "nonnegotiable position of intense moral rectitude untouchable by legal, scientific or other rationalistic discourse."[66] To refuse negotiation is to establish a critical boundary; however, the strength of poetry can also bring the environmental crisis into manageable proportions. Mary Oliver's immensely popular writing substitutes intuitions and feeling for oppositional stances. Moving against what Patrick Curry calls an "inflated rationalism" through understanding the "embodied and embedded, situated and engaged, local and particular," Oliver speaks for the human community's need for contact with that which lies beyond them.[67] The social divisions, hierarchical distinctions, and entrenched customs that Merwin, Snyder, and Rich encounter in their work tend to dissolve in Oliver's handlings.

In *Twelve Moons* (1979), each month gives rise to its own poem, advancing the seasons beginning with April, a calendar originating when life returns, a matrix from which events emerge. When Oliver writes of "a woman's body," or calls one woman "round and full and milk-white / as a woman's breast," or populates a poem with her great aunt, her mother, and women who attend childbirth, as she does in the opening moon-poems, she summons a realm that is not only fecund but void of men.[68] Galway Kinnell's "The Bear" promotes the stalking of a creature into a quest that ends by killing the bear and then inhabiting its body in a symbolic possession that is the beginning of poetry.[69] Oliver's "Hunter's Moon – Eating the Bear" speaks to the bear with reverence as "Good friend," as if its spirit could hear. She carefully describes to its spirit how the bear will be consumed yet still live on. "The shadows of the pines" that, she explains, "are blue on the field" as the poem begins will become, at poem's end, "the pines you can no longer see" now "twisted and small / their shadows stretching out, still turning around."[70] The poem is a prayer, a request for forgiveness, and an act of humility.

Oliver's poetry takes no totem creature for its own, no coyote or gray wolf such as Snyder admires in his work; bears recur throughout her books, but so do black snakes, birds of all kinds (blue herons, vultures, egrets), as well as whales, dogfish, and mussels. The natural scene isn't defined by any limits or shouldn't be. In the final moon-poem, set in March, when "the earth remembers its own name," and when "once more the moon and the earth are eloping" to bring forth "fantastic children" "who will believe, for years, / that everything is possible," Oliver emphasizes that sense of a continuity that generates a future by closing her poem (and her book) with words of hope: "and probably / everything / is possible."[71] Among the poets who began in the 1970s, Oliver has consistently held the attention of a large, ever-growing public. She returns readers to a rich emotional site that is positively contained by detailed descriptions; in her work, the otherness of nature exists as a delicate counterpoint to the human.

★

Robert Hass "might be called a nature poet," George Bradley wrote, introducing work from his first book, *Field Guide* (1973), for "he writes lovingly plain descriptions of landscape, mostly Californian – but he is a politicized one, unsurprisingly so given his time and place."[72] Hass is the poet of his generation most energized by the uncertainties of the last decades. His poems and prose poems continually unsettle as they shift from one viewpoint to another, several times within a single work. His interests overlap with Pinsky and Levine in mapping the rituals and affects of a distinct community, even as his West Coast upbringing places him in a crossroads-like setting.

Hass offers a third career shaped by an early experience with Winters, although his studies in Stanford led to a doctoral dissertation on eighteenth- and nineteenth-century fiction. Recalling Winters's classroom lectures as "high drama," Hass regards him as neither ethicist nor pugilist but as victim to the youthful tuberculosis that sidelined him to "the loneliness of provincial places" in New Mexico, Colorado, and Idaho. For Hass, Winters valued poets of the sixteenth and seventeenth centuries because he appreciated "poems that looked directly and without flinching at the loneliness of human death." As a poet, however, Winters failed to solve "the problem of getting from image to discourse in the language of his time, and instead borrowed the solution of another age."[73] Hass's own poems capture not just a moment but that moment in all its fleeting associations, the ebb and flow of daydream, with its clutter of ill-matched but illuminating perceptions.

Hass's lyrics seem produced expediently, but their rag-tag quality belies the constellations of meaning they assemble. The poet who writes (and Hass is quick to make us aware that he is writing what we are reading, that he is setting down words that he wants us to hear) works under a kind of duress to patch together smart answers to large questions. The fourteen-section sequence "Songs to Survive the Summer" (from *Praise* [1979]), with its rapidly firing three-line stanzas, is close enough to the haiku form that Hass was assembling for an

953

anthology at this time that the poem accommodates an adaptation from Issa as an unspecified citation –"*What a strange thing! / To be alive / beneath plum blossoms*" – and then abruptly counterpoints it with a raucous California version: "The black-headed / Steller's jay is squawking / in the plum."[74] Hass works with clashes as unlike as the feathery delicacy of those "plum blossoms," which have been etched over centuries of Asian poetry, and the blunt actuality of the California plum, with its annoying jaybird, as he shapes one story after another in which loss or demise or violent dying figure in some way. While these stories may be, as he confesses to his daughter, "the frailest stay against / our fears," their placement alongside each other forges an ongoing continuity, or as Stephen Yenser observes: "The secret is that we share.... Death is the very warp of it all, the thing included in everything else."[75] Hass acknowledges the necessity of singing "a broken song": his poem's charge is to hold together the pieces.

In the collections that follow, a shift toward prose rhythms reveals "a new reliance on the discursive form of the sentence," Terence Doody has argued, opening Hass to "a greater range of feelings" with the sentence's capacity or "greater drama, higher rhetoric, and ideas that images cannot support."[76] It also reflects his collaborations with the Polish Nobel laureate Czeslaw Milosz in translating Milosz's works, a journey as described in the 1976 translation "On Pilgrimage" as "Searching, not finding, gathering rumors, / Always comforted by the brightness of day."[77] The environmental poem is reconceptualized in Hass's "Spring Rain," which takes rainwater falling this moment, "freshly, in the intervals between sunlight," and after tracing it back to a Pacific squall, anticipates its return through larkspur "sprouting along a creek above Sonora Pass next August." This leads to recalling that without the "gray jays of the mountains" ingesting these seeds, their propagation would require soaking seeds overnight in the acids of coffee and scoring each one "gently with a very sharp knife" that might be found among the coffee in a kitchen where orange poppies "on the table in a clear glass vase, stained" at its bottom "to the color of sunrise."[78] Rainfall finds its place within an intricate system that is also the poem's. Hass's works enact the regenerative systems found in nature whose borders are too elusive to define.

The sentence-based poetry of Hass's recent work has been described by von Hallberg as exemplifying "standard American English as an artistic medium"; it is important that "literary language" not be isolated "from the idioms of the administrative class," for such poems are able to alter the language "by combining with general terms the complicating, refining features of more specific language."[79] That his poetry might take effect on just that very public that has the capacity to craft "just legislation, judicious litigation, and progressive social policy" is surely central to Hass, who openly declared political views from his start.[80] Reagan was described by Hass, pausing in the middle of a book review, as "another California president with yet another set of plans," among them "the intensification of a civil war in Central America" and "the selling of unadulterated foodstuffs to the underdeveloped world."[81]

To chart a lineage from Pinsky's "Tennis" of 1973 to Hass's "Spring Rain" and his other works of the 1980s is to realize that poetry that encourages language's discursive aspects develops tools that provide access to, and describe with increasing acuity, "real-world" situations. It should be no surprise, then, to find these poets gravitating toward book-length verse, extended sequences, multipart texts, and lyrics as epics, for the discursive turn derives poetic form less from literary inheritances (sonnet, ode, or eclogue) than from subject matter (psychiatry, America's next generation, or Detroit's rust belt) or controversy (deep ecology's antianthropomorphism, cross-cultural isomorphic correspondences, or ecofeminism's epistemology of the local) or some mixture of the two (how to mourn or ecology as a system). Their work demonstrates how effectively poetry can be an art that gains energy by encountering problems, an art superbly equipped to describe, consider, and appraise the complications that surround us.

Notes

1. Natasha Zaretsky, *No Direction Home: The American Family and the Fear of National Decline, 1968–1980* (Chapel Hill: University of North Carolina Press), p. 1.
2. Charles Altieri, "Modernism and Postmodernism," in Alex Preminger and T. V. F. Brogan (eds.), *The New Princeton Encyclopedia of Poetry and Poetics* (Princeton, N.J.: Princeton University Press, 1993), pp. 792–96, 794.
3. Robert von Hallberg, "Yvor Winters 1900–1968," in A. Walton Litz (ed.), *American Writers: A Collection of Literary Biographies*, supplement 2, part 2, ed. A. Walton Litz (New York: Scribner, 1981), pp. 785–816, 806–07; Robert von Hallberg, "Donald Davie and 'the Moral Shape of Politics,'" *Critical Inquiry* 8:3 (1982), pp. 415–36, 419–20; Robert Archambeau, *Laureates and Heretics: Six Careers in American Poetry* (South Bend, Ind.: University of Notre Dame Press, 2010), p. 25.
4. Archambeau, *Laureates and Heretics*, pp. 190–93; Donald Davie, *Purity of Diction in English Verse* (1955; New York: Schocken, 1967), pp. 197–202.
5. Josephine Saunders, "The Underside of Words," *Poetry* 116:2 (1970), p. 97; Jon Anderson, "Creative Writing 307," *Poetry* 116:3 (1970), p. 143; Mark Strand, "Seven Poems (VII)," *Poetry* 116:3 (1970), p. 181.
6. Robert Pinsky, *The Situation of Poetry: Contemporary Poetry and Its Traditions* (Princeton, N.J.: Princeton University Press, 1976), p. 242.

7. Paul Breslin, "How to Read the New Contemporary Poem," *American Scholar* 47:3 (1979), pp. 357–70, 358.

8. Daryl Hine, [Editorial], *Poetry* 120:6 (1972), p. 361.

9. Subarno Chattarji, "Vietnam Poetry," *Irish Journal of American Studies* 6 (1997), pp. 139–69, 145; see also Subarno Chattarji, *Memories of a Lost War* (New York: Oxford University Press, 2001).

10. Richard Hugo, "On Hearing a New Escalation," *Poetry* 120:6 (1972), p. 319.

11. James Wright, *Collected Poems* (Middletown, Conn.: Wesleyan University Press, 1971), pp. 195–96; Paul Craigmire, private correspondence, June 7, 2010.

12. Wright, *Collected Poems*.

13. Robert Pinsky, *Sadness and Happiness* (Princeton, N.J.: Princeton University Press, 1975), p. 16; James Longenbach, *Modern Poetry After Modernism* (New York: Oxford University Press, 1997), p. 148.

14. Longenbach, *Modern Poetry After Modernism*, p. 148.

15. Pinsky, *Sadness and Happiness*, p. 21.

16. Pinsky, *Sadness and Happiness*, pp. 57, 74.

17. Willard Spiegelman, *The Didactic Muse: Scenes of Instruction in Contemporary Poetry* (Princeton, N.J.: Princeton University Press, 1989), p. 101.

18. Von Hallberg, "Yvor Winters," p. 806.

19. Robert von Hallberg, *American Poetry and Culture, 1945–1980* (Cambridge, Mass.: Harvard University Press, 1985), p. 233; Robert von Hallberg, "Poetry, Politics and Intellectuals," in Sacvan Bercovitch (gen. ed.), *The Cambridge History of American Literature* (Cambridge: Cambridge University Press, 1996), vol. 8, pp. 65–66; Longenbach, *Modern Poetry After Modernism*, pp. 143–44; Archambeau, *Laureates and Heretics*, pp. 35–54.

20. Thom Gunn, *The Occasions of Poetry* (San Francisco: North Point, 1982), p. 204.

21. Thom Gunn, *Touch* (Chicago: University of Chicago Press, 1968), pp. 29–49.

22. Donald Davie, *Thomas Hardy and British Poetry* (London: Routledge and Kegan Paul, 1973), p. 18; Donald Davie, "A Comment," *Poetry Nation* 1 (1973), pp. 56–57.

23. Von Hallberg, "Donald Davie," p. 420.

24. Calvin Bedient, *Eight Contemporary Poets* (New York: Oxford University Press, 1974), p. 25.

25. Robert Pinsky, *An Explanation of America* (Princeton, N.J.: Princeton University Press, 1979), p. 25. This collection will be cited in the text as *EA*.

26. Alfred Corn, *The Metamorphoses of Metaphor* (New York: Viking, 1987), p. 119.

27. Robert Pinsky, "The Art of Poetry: LXXVI," *Paris Review* 39 (1997), pp. 188–220, 198.

28. Frank Bidart, "Introduction to a Reading by Robert Pinsky," *Pequod* 31:1 (1990), pp. 159–60.

29. Robert Pinsky, *The History of My Heart* (Hopewell, N.J.: Ecco, 1984), pp. 3–4.

30. Robert Pinsky, *The Figured Wheel: New and Selected Poems* (New York: Farrar, Straus and Giroux, 1996), pp. 84–85.
31. Edward Hirsch, "The Visionary Poetic of Charles Wright and Philip Levine," in Jay Parini and Brett C. Millier (eds.), *The Columbia History of American Poetry* (New York: Columbia University Press, 1993), pp. 777–806, 778.
32. Von Hallberg, "Yvor Winters," p. 815.
33. Philip Levine, *The Bread of Time: Toward an Autobiography* (New York: Knopf, 1994), pp. 208–212.
34. Philip Levine, *They Feed They Lion* (New York: Athenaeum, 1972), p. 34.
35. Philip Levine, *1933* (New York: Athenaeum, 1974), pp. 3–4.
36. Levine, *1933*, pp. 3–4.
37. Yvor Winters (ed.), *Twelve Poets of the Pacific* (Norfolk, Conn.: New Directions, 1937), p. 10.
38. Philip Levine, *The Names of the Lost* (New York: Athenaeum, 1976), pp. 19–21.
39. Hirsch, "The Visionary Poetic of Charles Wright and Philip Levine," p. 779.
40. Dick Davis, *Wisdom and Wilderness: The Achievement of Yvor Winters* (Athens: University of Georgia Press, 1991), p. 166.
41. Robert Pinsky, *Poetry and the World* (Hopewell, N.J.: Ecco, 1988), p. 98; Philip Levine, *Don't Ask: Interviews* (Ann Arbor: University of Michigan Press, 1981), p. 99.
42. Frederick Morgan, "Poetry and Ecology: Editorial," *Hudson Review* 23:3 (1970), pp. 399–400.
43. Wendell Berry, *Farming: A Handbook* (New York: Harcourt Brace Jovanovich, 1970), pp. 7, 38, 57.
44. Bruce J. Schulman, *The Seventies: The Great Shift in American Culture, Society and Politics* (New York: Da Capo, 2001), p. 91.
45. W. S. Merwin, *The Drunk in the Furnace* (New York: Macmillan, 1960), p. 48.
46. W. S. Merwin, *The Lice* (New York: Athenaeum, 1967), p. 63.
47. Breslin, "How to Read the New Contemporary Poem," pp. 358–60.
48. W. S. Merwin, *Writings to an Unfinished Accompaniment* (New York: Athenaeum, 1973), pp. 53, 46.
49. Merwin, *Writings to an Unfinished Accompaniment*, pp. 51, 49.
50. Merwin, *Writings to an Unfinished Accompaniment*, pp. 29–30.
51. Evan Watkins, *The Critical Act: Criticism and Community* (New Haven, Conn.: Yale University Press, 1978), p. 228.
52. W. S. Merwin, *Selected Translations* (Port Townsend, Wash.: Copper Canyon, 2012), pp. 195, 249, 171.
53. Gary Snyder, *Turtle Island* (New York: New Directions, 1974), "Note" (n.p.).
54. Snyder, *Turtle Island*, pp. 63, 48, 53.
55. Snyder, *Turtle Island*, pp. 21–22.
56. Philip Jenkins, *Decade of Nightmares: The End of the Sixties and the Making of Eighties America* (Oxford: Oxford University Press, 2006), p. 109.

57. Adrienne Rich, *On Lies, Secrets and Silence: Selected Prose, 1966–1978* (New York: W. W. Norton, 1979), p. 28.

58. Adrienne Rich, *The Will to Change* (New York: W. W. Norton, 1971), p. 37.

59. Adrienne Rich, *The Dream of a Common Language* (New York: W. W. Norton, 1978), p. 39.

60. Rich, *The Dream of a Common Language*, p. 27.

61. Rich, *The Dream of a Common Language*, p. 30.

62. Marilyn Hacker, *Presentation Piece* (New York: Viking Press, 1974), p. 87.

63. Suzanne Juhasz, *Naked and Fiery Forms: Modern American Poetry by Women: A New Tradition* (New York: Harper, 1976), p. 198.

64. Helen Vendler, *Soul Says: On Recent Poetry* (Cambridge, Mass.: Harvard University Press, 1995), p. 218.

65. Adrienne Rich, *Dark Fields of the Republic* (New York: W. W. Norton, 1995), p. 21.

66. David Harvey, "What's Green and Makes the Environment Go Round?" in Fredric Jameson and Masao Miyoshi (eds.), *The Cultures of Globalization* (Durham, N.C.: Duke University Press, 1998), pp. 327–55, 348.

67. Patrick Curry, *Ecological Ethics: An Introduction* (Cambridge: Polity, 2005), p. 98.

68. Mary Oliver, *Twelve Moons* (Boston: Little, Brown, 1979), pp. 8, 11, 16–17.

69. Galway Kinnell, *Body Rags* (Boston: Houghton Mifflin, 1968), p. 60.

70. Oliver, *Twelve Moons*, pp. 50–51.

71. Oliver, *Twelve Moons*, p. 77.

72. George Bradley (ed.), *The Yale Younger Poets Anthology* (New Haven, Conn.: Yale University Press, 1998), p. 200.

73. Robert Hass, *Twentieth Century Pleasures* (Hopewell, N.J.: Ecco, 1984), pp. 146, 148.

74. Robert Hass (ed.), *The Essential Haiku: Versions of Basho, Buson and Issa* (Hopewell, N.J.: Ecco, 1994), p. 156; Robert Hass, *Praise* (Hopewell, N.J.: Ecco, 1979), p. 55.

75. Stephen Yenser, *A Boundless Field: American Poetry at Large* (Ann Arbor: University of Michigan Press, 2002), p. 46.

76. Terence Doody, "From Image to Sentence: The Spiritual Development of Robert Hass," *American Poetry Review* 26:2 (1997), pp. 47–56, 47.

77. Czeslaw Milosz, *The Collected Poems*, trans. Robert Hass, Czeslaw Milosz et al. (Hopewell, N.J.: Ecco, 1988), p. 344.

78. Robert Hass, *Human Wishes* (Hopewell, N.J.: Ecco, 1989), pp. 135–36.

79. Robert von Hallberg, *Lyric Powers* (Chicago: University of Chicago Press, 2008), pp. 90, 97, 98.

80. Von Hallberg, *Lyric Powers*, p. 90.

81. Hass, *Twentieth Century Pleasures*, p. 171.

Chapter 42

Latino Poetry and Poetics

RIGOBERTO GONZÁLEZ

The term "Latino" as an ethnic label used to refer to any citizen or resident of the United States who is of Latin American descent is the latest designation of choice in popular and academic culture. Although it is a convenient collective term, it also homogenizes disparate populations with roots in the twenty unique countries of Latin America, and it offers no knowledge of specific national identities, political struggles, or immigrant trajectories. In the general vocabulary of the media, "Latino" is used interchangeably with the label "Hispanic," which has been slowly falling out of favor since its adoption by the U.S. Census Bureau in 1970. Added to the list of labels and demonyms is the propensity of Latino communities to reclaim their distinct nationalities either by hyphenating their ethnic identities (Mexican-American, Dominican-American, Panamanian-American) or by constructing names of their own (e.g., Chicano and Nuyorican). And then there are those who reject labels entirely and who refer to themselves simply by their current citizenship: American.

According to recent census data, Latinos compose approximately 15.5 percent of the total U.S. population, or approximately 47 million people. Of this figure, approximately two-thirds are of Mexican descent. The two other ethnic groups with sizable numbers and long-standing relationships with the United States are the Puerto Rican community (about 10 percent of the total U.S. Latino population) and the Cuban American community (about 3 percent of the total U.S. Latino population). Not surprisingly, this also translates into three distinct, complex interactions with the cultural, political, and social fabric of the American landscape.

The proliferation of labels causes much confusion and anxiety among Latinos and non-Latinos alike, because declaring what one prefers to be called can also reveal such personal information as one's political affiliations, views on assimilation, immigration status, or even linguistic ability. Therefore, in the larger social arena, terms like "Latino" (and "Hispanic"), terms that are essentially apolitical and inert, are a safe starting point when interacting with a person of Latin American descent. Each Latino will then guide the conversation toward more specific avenues of inquiry.

The same process applies to an examination of Latino poetry and poetics. Within the collective term thrive dozens of literary histories, movements, and aesthetics – threads that this single entry cannot appropriately cover. But even exploring a few of these avenues will challenge certain misconceptions about Latino poetry. There is the belief, for example, that Latinos write in Spanish or that their works are in translation, that the dominant narrative is an immigrant narrative, that the dominant theme is identity politics, and that Latino literature is insularly influenced by Latin American letters. All of these facile assumptions only mischaracterize and dismiss an expansive, diverse, dynamic, and ever-growing body of writing that will eventually become one of the most important literary legacies of American culture, because it is estimated that by 2050, Latinos will compose nearly 30 percent of the entire U.S. population, making them the largest minority group in the country.[1]

In the meantime, what's worth examining is how the three main U.S. Latino populations have shaped their respective literatures in order to come to terms with their identity, language, and history. Although their immigrant trajectories and political leanings are distinct, the Chicano, Puerto Rican, and Cuban American poetry communities have followed parallel journeys from marginalized voices to visible presences in twentieth-century American letters.

Chicano Poetry

In the Chicano community there is no dividing line between a poet and an activist. The term "Chicano," which refers specifically to Latinos of Mexican descent, also designates a set of values that took shape during the Chicano Movement of the late 1960s, which was mostly concentrated in the American Southwest. During that activist movement, Mexican American youth adopted a political identity that was strongly antiwar, antiassimilationist, proeducation, and procommunity, bringing national attention to such pressing issues as exploitation of labor, housing discrimination, and other injustices committed against Mexicans, Mexican Americans, and Chicanos (referred to as *la raza*) in order to instigate social change. Forty years later, as members of this population have climbed the socioeconomic ladder, new groups of immigrants continue to cross the U.S.-Mexico border, confronting the same challenges and obstacles as earlier immigrants, thereby keeping the Chicano sensibility relevant and active.[2]

One of the most important points of pride of the Chicano community continues to be cultural production that expresses and celebrates the triumphs and struggles of *la raza*. Highly valued among these avenues of expression is poetry.

Setting its literary legacy apart from Mexican poetry, much of which was penned by the educated aristocracy, Chicano poetry from the sixties and seventies (although conscious of Latin American popular figures like Pablo Neruda and Ruben Darío) attempted to implement a working-class consciousness into the poems that were usually presented at political rallies, community centers, school events, and literary festivals (called *floricantos*). Much of this material carried a nationalistic tone, paid homage to a Mexican indigenous heritage, and reclaimed Spanish, Spanglish (also called code-switching, an intralingual wordplay), and caló (Chicano slang, the language of the barrio) as valid languages for verse. The opening stanza to the poem "La Huelga" by Lalo Delgado, for example, was also a call to action to support a workers' strike:

> Wash well your throat with tequila
> so your voice comes out tranquila
> and then softly whisper, huelga
> or shout huelga
> > with anger
> as if someone
> had killed your parents,
> someone has.[3]

The Chicano Movement period of poetry made a strong effort to document the everyday Chicano experience, particularly in praise of the family, cultural traditions, religious beliefs, and secular superstitions. Its purpose was educational and communicative and not primarily artistic; the majority of the poetry from this period vanished, because much of it was not published, collected, or preserved. There were other limitations with the early period of Chicano poetry: it was dominated by male voices, it overromanticized the female roles in the Chicano family, it expressed sentimental connections to pre-Columbian mythology, and it often lacked a fresh use of language and metaphor. (The role of nostalgia and sentimentality in Chicano poetry, however, cannot be easily dismissed, because these are important emotional pulls that help communities organize and identify common social and political goals.)

From this group of self-taught poets, a select few voices managed to survive because they found their way to publication and popularity, their poems serving more as testimonies and archives to the early literary endeavors of the

Chicano Movement. Among this small group is Rodolfo "Corky" Gonzales (*I Am Joaquín: An Epic Poem* [1967]), Ricardo Sánchez (*Canto y grito mi liberación* [1971]), raúlrsalinas (*Un Trip Through the Mind Jail y Otras Excursiones* [1980]), Luis Omar Salinas (*Crazy Gypsy* [1970]), José Montoya (*El Sol y Los De Abajo and Other Royal Chicano Air Force Poems* [1972]), Leroy V. Quintana (*Hijo del Pueblo: New Mexico Poems* [1976]), and Alurista (*Nationhood plumaroja, 1969–1972* [1972]). All except the latter two are deceased, and – with the exception of Quintana, Luis Omar Salinas, and Alurista – most of the subsequent works published by the authors were self-published projects or were published by small presses that could not keep them in print. These pioneers, however, kept the spirit of poetry vibrant and accessible for the next wave of Chicano poets, who would bring to the practice of verse an artistic discipline learned from the new degree program available to a new generation of Chicanos: the masters in fine arts.

Three of the more prominent contemporary Chicano poets were all enrolled in writing programs during the mid- to late 1970s: Gary Soto completed his M.F.A. at the University of California–Irvine in 1976, Alberto Ríos completed his M.F.A. at the University of Arizona in 1979, and Sandra Cisneros completed her M.F.A. at the Iowa Writers' Workshop in 1978. These writers also represent the three regions with sizable Mexican and Chicano populations: the West Coast, the Southwest, and the Midwest.

Soto, raised in the central California valley, infused his work with details of the agricultural landscape in his early books, *The Elements of San Joaquín* (1977) and *The Tale of Sunlight* (1978). He has since published countless picture books, young adult novels, and nonfiction titles, but his eleven books of poetry continue to influence a newer generation of California writers whose poetry captures the conflicted urban and rural narratives of the working people of Fresno and its surrounding areas. Among them are Blas Manuel de Luna (*Bent to the Earth* [2005]), David Domínguez (*Work Done Right* [2003]), and Andrés Montoya (*The Iceworker Sings and Other Poems* [1999]). The poetry of Soto and his followers has married a love and respect for an imperfect community to an intellectual engagement of craft to produce a type of central California ode, as in Soto's "Mission Tire Factory, 1969":

> The oven we would enter, squinting
> – because earlier in the day Manny fell
> From his machine, and when we carried him
> To the workshed (blood from
> Under his shirt, in his pants)
> All he could manage, in an ignorance
> Outdone only by pain, was to take three dollars

From his wallet, and say:
"Buy some sandwiches. You guys saved my life."[4]

The ode reaches back to an important Latin American influence, Pablo
Neruda, whose *Elemental Odes* (1954) was universally praised for its simplicity
of language, concrete imagery, and use of humor. These qualities appealed
to Chicano poets because they could also be found in other genres valued in
Mexican / Chicano culture, among them, song lyrics, folk stories, riddles, and
jokes. For Soto and other poets, the ode allowed them to find a muse in ordinary things. Soto's *Neighborhood Odes* (1992), for example, highlighted a number of Mexican objects that contained sentimental and cultural value, such as
odes to "La Tortilla," "La Piñata," and "El Molcajete."

Alberto Ríos's work taps into a landscape that is inescapable in the works by
writers living in the Southwest: the desert and the borderlands. The Chicano
Movement held on to the notion that the American Southwest, which was
Mexican territory before the Treaty of Guadalupe Hidalgo in 1848, was the birth-
right of the Chicano community. Referred to as Aztlán, meaning "homeland"
(which gestured back to the Aztec belief in an ancestral home far north of the
Aztec Empire), this claim to the American Southwest fueled anger against the
policing of the U.S.-Mexico border, and frustrations over the poverty of the barrios
and the overcrowded, crime-infested border towns. But it also gave permission to
la raza to feel at home, and to trust that the beauty and wonders of the desert
landscape were theirs to protect and appreciate. Ríos's poem "Rabbits on Fire"
captures the duality of the appalling and appealing qualities of the landscape:

> During brush fires in the Sonoran desert,
> Brush fires that happen before the monsoon and in the great,
> Deep, wide, and smothering heat of the hottest months, . . .
> Jackrabbits can get caught in the flames,
> No matter how fast and big and strong and sleek they are.
> And when they're caught,
> Cornered in and against the thick
> Trunks and thin spines of the cactus,
> When they can't back up any more,
> When they can't move, the flame –
> It touches them,
> And their fur catches fire.[5]

Ríos, who was born and raised in Nogales, Arizona, created a complex and magical portrait of the borderlands with an extensive body of work that included
story collections, a memoir, and his first full-length collection, *Whispering to
Fool the Wind* (1982). It must be noted that Ríos's work usually sidesteps any

direct social or political message, which is why his oeuvre has fallen out of favor with Chicano readers.

Instead, Chicanos turn to another borderlands territory, the Texas South Valley and El Paso, specifically. This city has produced more Chicano writers than any other in the United States, perhaps because it is the quintessential border town that has witnessed, along with its sister city across the international border, Juárez, a number of afflictions and conflicts, from the exploitation of sweatshop labor to the femicide epidemic. Poets who have been weaving into their work the bittersweet experience of life on the border include Pat Mora (*Chants* [1984]), Bejamin Alire Sáenz (*Calendar of Dust* [1991]), and Alicia Gaspar de Alba (*La Llorona on the Longfellow Bridge* [2003]).

Although Sandra Cisneros, who was raised in Chicago, focused on prose after the hugely successful *The House on Mango Street* (Arte Público Press, 1984), her first publications were in poetry. *Bad Boys* (1980) and *My Wicked Wicked Ways* (1987) helped usher in a feminist sensibility and bravado that had been present but largely ignored within the Chicano community because feminism challenged the sexist beliefs inherited from Mexican culture. "You Bring Out the Mexican in Me" has spawned numerous imitations, even outside of the Latino literary scene:

> You bring out the Uled-Nayl in me.
> The stand-back-white-bitch-in me.
> The switchblade in the boot in me.
> The Acapulco cliff diver in me.
> The *Flecha Roja* mountain disaster in me.
> The *dengue* fever in me.
> The *¡Alarma!* murderess in me.
> I could kill in the name of you and think
> it worth it. Brandish a fork and terrorize rivals,
> female and male, who loiter and look at you,
> languid in you light.[6]

Cisneros stylized the use of cultural references (in the preceding stanza, she not only inserts elements familiar to the Chicano community, such as the *Flecha Roja* economy bus line and the *¡Alarma!* tabloid newspaper, but she also makes a transcultural connection by mentioning an Arabic/Algerian dance, Uled-Nayl), but she also broke social taboos, in this case by calling attention to the capacity of females to become violent and by the declaration that gay men are also attracted to the object of her affection.

The wave of feminist expression gained momentum in the creative and scholarly fields, shaping the literary careers of such Chicana prose writers as

Ana Castillo, Denise Chávez, and Helena María Viramontes. And although Chicano poetry publications into the late 1990s continued to be written mostly by males – among those gaining attention were Luis J. Rodríguez (*The Concrete River* [1995]) and Jimmy Santiago Baca (*Immigrants in Our Own Land* [1990]) – the most critically acclaimed poet of that era was a woman: Lorna Dee Cervantes.

Cervantes made her debut with *Emplumada* (1981), a book containing a number of political poems that recalled the activist fervor of the Chicano Movement. Although she did not attend an M.F.A. program (she received her Ph.D. from the History of Consciousness Program at the University of California–Santa Cruz), she was part of a collective of writers that included the gay writer Francisco X. Alarcón and the spoken word poet Juan Felipe Herrera, which thrived in the artistic community of San Francisco in the 1970s and 1980s. They formed writing workshops that stressed a preoccupation with expanding their knowledge of world poetry and with linguistic experimentation and craft, while retaining their activist roots. With *From the Cables of Genocide: Poems of Love and Hunger* (1991) and *Drive* (2006), Cervantes engaged race relations, gender conflicts, and the dangers of globalization in a poetics of politics that had not quite been achieved with such success in the Chicano Movement. The following is an excerpt from her most anthologized poem, "Poem for the Young White Man Who Asked Me How I, an Intelligent, Well-Read Person, Could Believe in the War Between Races":

> I am a poet
> who yearns to dance on rooftops,
> to whisper delicate lines about joy
> and the blessings of human understanding.
> I try. I go to my land, my tower of words and
> bolt the door, but the typewriter doesn't fade out
> the sounds of blasting and muffled outrage.
> My own days bring me slaps on the face.
> Every day I am deluged with reminders
> that this is not
> my land
> and this is my land.
> I do not believe in the war between races
> but in this country
> there is war.[7]

The Stanford-educated Francisco X. Alarcón did not collect his work into a book until the publication of *Body in Flames/Cuerpo en llamas* (1990), and he had the distinction of being the only successful Chicano poet writing in Spanish. His poems, usually minimalist verse, were translated into English. He was also one of the few openly gay Chicano poets, writing numerous homoerotic (but subtle) poems that added a new dimension to the body of Chicano poetry. In reality, the "queering" of Chicano poetry has been slow, because Chicano letters has historically excluded homosexual voices, especially gay men.[8]

A watershed moment in Chicano letters occurred when the National Book Critics Circle awarded Juan Felipe Herrera the top prize in poetry in 2008 for his new and selected volume of poems *Half the World in Light* (2008). That volume marked a thirty-year career that began with small-press publications in the mid-1970s. A latecomer to the M.F.A. program, Herrera was admitted into the Iowa Writers' Workshop in 1988, although at the time he had already published four books of poetry. Before his two-year program at Iowa, Herrera was mostly known as a performance poet, but with the publication of *Night Train to Tuxtla* (1994), four years after his Iowa degree, Herrera demonstrated strengths that would sustain him through a lengthy career in poetry. His work engaged philosophical thought, pre-Columbian symbolism, Language poetry, political satire, social critique, and linguistic wordplay. In brief, he was the amalgamation of all the poetic directions discussed so far, and his literary recognition in 2008 validated for the Chicano community its place in American letters. The following is an excerpt from "Fuzzy Equations":

Humility + oppression + a Virgin − territory = Latin America
Democracy + annihilation by color × 12 = Education
Militarization of Brazil + Xingu extinction × deforestation = Money
Castro Street × Wall Street ÷ 7 straight boulevards = Here[9]

Before Juan Felipe Herrera, the only other notable Chicano poet working with avant-garde poetics was Alurista, who is still writing today, although mostly outside of the spotlight; his new and selected volume *Xicano Duende* was published in 2011. Nevertheless, it is Herrera who continues to gain a reputation as the primary literary forefather of a new generation of poets publishing in the new millennium who are looking to move away from the traditional narrative and to experiment with the postmodern form, even if the content remains unapologetically Chicano or ethnic identified. This hybrid poetics is the merging of two seemingly mutually exclusive schools of poetry (the narrative and the postmodern experimental).

As a literary movement, Chicano poetry has demonstrated that it can change with the times, expand to include groups that have been traditionally excluded (such as women and the LGBT community), and continue its mission to respond to social injustices by shaping emotion into artistic articulation, and to take personal responsibility as a writer and citizen. There is very little opportunity to remain static, because, of all the Latino ethnic groups in the United States, the group most antagonized by government legislation continues to be the Mexican population.

Puerto Rican Poetry

The relationship between the United States and its unincorporated territory, the Commonwealth of Puerto Rico, bears a long and conflicted history. A Spanish colony since the days of Columbus, the island of Borinquen (the Taino name of the island many Puerto Ricans still use; island-born Puerto Ricans refer to themselves as Boricua) became a U.S. colony in 1898 (along with Cuba), after the Spanish-American War. Two historical moments that continue to influence the way Puerto Ricans frame a cultural identity are the passage of the Jones Act of 1917 and the ratification by the U.S. Congress of the Constitution of Puerto Rico in 1952. The first granted all Puerto Ricans U.S. citizenship, thus beginning a heavy period of migration to the mainland, which was concentrated in New York City and which didn't slow down until the 1960s. The second initiated a political split that continues to create conflict among Puerto Ricans to this day: one side accepts the commonwealth status as a form of conditional independence that precedes complete autonomy, while the other sees it as an important first step toward U.S. statehood.[10]

New York City has the largest Puerto Rican population outside of the island, with enclaves in every borough, although the most notable in Manhattan took root in Spanish Harlem and in Loisada, an epithet for the Lower East Side, locations that continue to be celebrated as the birthplaces of the Nuyorican Movement. "Nuyorican" as an identity term was coined by poets and eventually adopted by the Puerto Rican community in New York City as the cultural presence of the Nuyorican Poets Café, founded in 1975, grew in popularity and significance. The founding of the Nuyorican Poets Café was a communal effort, and many of the key players went on to have literary careers. Among them are Miguel Piñero (a playwright), Miguel Algarín (*On Call* [1980]), Sandra María Estéves (*Yerba Buena* [1980]), Pedro Pietri (*Puerto Rican Obituary* [1974]), Piri Thomas (known for the memoir *Down These Mean Streets* [1967]), and Giannina Braschi (*Asalto al tiempo* [1980]). The Nuyorican Movement stressed a performance-based presentation of work that gave voice and visibility to a working-class urban experience, which was proudly bilingual and independent of an island Boricua identity. This cultural center eventually coalesced the Puerto Rican community in New York City, which led to important activist and political efforts that became documented and commemorated in the writings and stage performances by Nuyorican poets.[11] But this New York–centered identity also resulted in an embattled relationship with island-born populations, who perceived this new identity as a diluted and misguided expression of Puerto Rican nationalism. Take, for example, the following excerpt from Pietri's poem "Puerto Rican Obituary":

> Here lies Milagros
> Here lies Olga
> Here lies Manuel
> who died yesterday today
> and will die again tomorrow
> Always broke
> Always owing
> Never knowing
> that they are beautiful people
>
> Never knowing
> the geography of their complexion
>
> PUERTO RICO IS A BEAUTIFUL PLACE
> PUERTORRIQUENOS ARE A BEAUTIFUL RACE ...
>
> If only they
> had kept their eyes open
> at the funeral of their fellow employees
> who came to this country to make a fortune
> and were buried without underwears.[12]

Similar to the early literary efforts of the Chicano Movement, the early literary efforts of the Nuyorican Movement were delivered orally. Translated onto the page, the work demonstrated idiosyncratic punctuation and spelling. These performance pieces privileged voice, particularly when it captured neighborhood vernacular, such as the use of the word "underwears."

Additional poets who had set the groundwork for the Nuyorican Movement, and who are considered important literary pioneers, include Clemente Soto Vélez (*La tierra prometida* [1979]), Victor Hernández Cruz (*Papo Got His Gun* [1969]), Tato Laviera (*La Carreta Made a U-Turn* [1979]), and Jack Agüeros (*Correspondence between Stonehaulers* [1991]). Soto Vélez, who was also a journalist, was a key figure in the Puerto Rican Nationalist Party. He was imprisoned in 1936 for his participation in an uprising against U.S. rule and then emigrated to New York City after his release, becoming a mentor to a number of young poets. Hernández Cruz and Laviera flourished as practitioners of socially conscious verse in English, Spanish, and Spanglish. Agüeros was also a community activist who was a celebrated curator of another important Nuyorican cultural center, El Museo del Barrio, which was founded in 1969.

It is important to note the relationship between the Nuyorican Movement and what would eventually become known as the spoken word/poetry slam movement, which began in the mid-1980s in Chicago. By the time this urban, youth-oriented forum made its way to New York City, Nuyorican poets had eased into the competitive nature of this performance-driven presentation – a method of expression that was familiar to them. The popularity of spoken word has not waned as an empowering and confidence-building tool, even if critics within and outside of the community find that the stage-based verse does not always translate into original and endurable verse on the page. A few poets, however, have crossed over successfully and continue to excel in both poetry scenes, among them Urayoán Noel (*Kool Logic* [2005]), Elliot Torres (*Five Years of Solitary* [2002]), and Emanuel Xavier (*Pier Queen* [1997]). All three, incidentally, are openly gay. Xavier, in particular, is credited with establishing a space for LGBT performers in the poetry slam scene by creating the glam slam. There has been less resistance to the queering of the Nuyorican scene (unlike the queering of the Chicano scene) because one of its founders, Piñero, was a bisexual writer who gained fame and critical acclaim for his plays, particularly *Short Eyes*. The play's graphic depictions of violence and gay sex outed this complex dimension of Puerto Rican sexuality. Xavier and other gay Nuyorican poets acknowledge that representation but also address more positive components of queer identity such as same-sex romance and love.

Two dynamic female performers worth mentioning are Caridad de la Luz, also known as "La Bruja," and Teresa Fernández, also known as "Mariposa." Unapologetically feminist, they infuse their work with literary allusions and references to figures in pop culture. Both have yet to collect their work in print, although like many contemporary cutting-edge performers, their pieces are easily available in audio and video. Despite these new venues for Nuyorican poetics, what does not change is its affirmation of ethnic pride, particularly in conversation with island Boricuas, who continue to contest the validity of that claim to nationality. The following is an excerpt from Mariposa's poem "Ode to the DiaspoRican":

> What does it mean to live in between
> What does it take to realize
> that being Boricua
> is a state of mind
> a state of heart

a state of soul …

¡Mira!

No nací en Puerto Rico.
Puerto Rico nació en mi.

Mira a mi cara Puertorriqueña
Mi pelo vivo
Mis manos morenas
Mira a mi corazón que se llena de orgullo
Y di me que no soy Boricua.

[Translation of the Spanish:]

Look!

I wasn't born in Puerto Rico.
Puerto Rico was born in me.

Look at my Puerto Rican face
My living hair
My dark hands
Look at my heart that fills with pride
And tell me that I am not Boricua.[13]

Although the Nuyorican scene dominates the body of Puerto Rican literature in the continental United States, the three most recognized names in Puerto Rican poetry do not identify as members of the Nuyorican Movement: Martín Espada, Judith Ortiz Cofer, and Rane Arroyo.

Espada was born in Brooklyn in 1957, but unlike the rest of his contemporaries, he left New York City to pursue an education in law and a career as an attorney. He has spent most of his professional life in Massachusetts. Espada eventually found his way to the literary scene with the publication of *The Immigrant Iceboy's Bolero* (1982), inspired by his father's arrival in New York City at the age of nine and his family's struggles with the hostility against Puerto Rican immigrants in the 1930s and 1940s. This debut set the tone for the direction of Espada's subsequent collections: concrete imagery is set against a landscape of social injustice and political struggles across many cultures. One of the reasons he prefers the identity label "Latino" over "Puerto Rican" is that he argues that, within a white-dominant society, all Latinos are subject to the same oppressions and discriminations, and therefore each Chicano, Puerto Rican, or Cuban American should not isolate himself within his group but stand in solidarity with all others. Espada's sensibilities gesture toward the politics of Neruda, who also used his poetry to critique capitalist ventures in Third World countries and government institutions that abuse power. But so too is Espada a literary heir to Neruda's authoritative and healing voice, as illustrated in the following excerpt from "Alabanza: In Praise of the Local 100":

> *Alabanza.* When the war began, from Manhattan and Kabul
> two constellations of smoke rose and drifted to each other,
> mingling in icy air, and one said with an Afghan tongue:
> *Teach me to dance. We have no music here.*
> And the other said with a Spanish tongue:
> *I will teach you. Music is all we have.*[14]

In 1956, Ortiz Cofer's family settled in another hub of Caribbean migration, Paterson, New Jersey, when she was only four years old. A decade later, they relocated to the state of Georgia, where Ortiz Cofer has spent most of her adult life as a student and later as a professor at the University of Georgia. But it is the New Jersey landscape that continues to inhabit her fiction, nonfiction, and poetry, particularly the sense of disorientation she felt as a young girl flying back and forth between Paterson and Hormigueros, Puerto Rico; between English and Spanish; and between the rural and urban landscapes. A consummate optimist, Ortiz Cofer aims for the discovery of beauty and light, even in the most distressing or unpleasant situations.

Arroyo was born in 1954 and raised in Chicago, another important center of Puerto Rican migration, which began in the late 1940s. The Puerto Rican community settled among other working-class immigrant populations, like the Mexicans and the Polish, but each group maintained its separate cultural identity. And because of the poor educational opportunities available to the second- and third-generation Puerto Ricans in Chicago, it is estimated that 60 percent of the population continues to work in manufacturing and service industries. Unlike Nuyoricans, who had been developing a cultural identity independent of island Boricuas, Chicago Puerto Ricans maintained close political and economic ties to the homeland, but the cultural gap has since widened, with the youth adopting a distinctly "Chicago Rican" identity. (A similar phenomenon is taking place in the Puerto Rican communities in other urban cities like Philadelphia, where the young people call themselves "Philly Ricans.") Arroyo's poetry, although personal and informed by an earlier period in Chicago history, remains timeless because of the unchanging working-class reality of this community, as is evident in the poem "Write What You Know":

> I know Papi
> worked in factories reigned by melodrama
> (a sick day = the righteous anger of

waltzing bosses in Kmart suits). I know
the word "knowledge" has the words
"now" and "ledge." I know that
my parents dared to color the suburbs
with their shy children.[15]

Arroyo, who died in 2010, was also openly gay and a significant voice of
the queer experience, such as in the poem "That Flag," about an encounter with two boisterous white men whose truck waves the Confederate
symbol:

I sit there thinking the fuckers
are right, that they are big
handsome, that they are our
America's perfect heirs and
that I'm not – aging Puerto Rican
homosexual poet exiled
to a borrowed bed.[16]

Cuban American Poetry

Politically, the Chicano community has always expressed admiration for the
Cuban Revolution of 1959 but maintains a conflicted opinion about its leader,
Fidel Castro. In any case, Chicanos have historically positioned themselves on
the opposite side of the political spectrum to Cuban Americans, who, as mid-
dle- and upper-class exiles, flourished quite differently in the United States.
Although they share the same mother tongue and the same Spanish colonial past as Chicanos, Cuban Americans have been stereotyped as Spanish-
speaking whites with conservative views. And the fact that the Cuban
American population remains concentrated mainly in Florida, far removed
from the Southwest, has only sustained the psychic distance between the
two communities. Cuban exiles held on to the belief that Castro would be
overthrown by the American government and that those who had lost their
properties would return to reclaim them. Newer generations, assimilated
into American society, don't hold the same sentimental attachment to a place
they have never known and are not opposed to visiting the island, but only as
tourists, not exiles.

In reality, the Cuban American story is much more complex, and prose
writers have been giving depth to this identity through the novel and short
story. The most celebrated of these writers is Oscar Hijuelos, the first Latino

to be awarded the Pulitzer Prize, for *The Mambo Kings Play Songs of Love* (1990). The number of Cuban American poets, however, has yet to reach a level that will also illustrate the diversity of experience within the Cuban American community. In fact, the most visible and accomplished Cuban American poets are three males: Pablo Medina, Virgil Suárez, and Richard Blanco, all three the children of exiles.

Medina arrived in New York on the last freedom flight from Havana, in 1960, at the age of twelve, old enough to experience culture shock and to understand the trauma of his family's separation from Cuba. His family's struggle to regain their middle-class lifestyle is the subject of his memoir *Exiled Memories* (1990). And his critically acclaimed novel *The Return of Félix Nogara* (2000) is a thinly veiled critique of Cuba, forty years after the Revolution. Although there is much disdain for Castro expressed in his work, what more appropriately characterizes Medina's poetry is a longing for the beauty of the island of Cuba, now suspended in memory, what is referred to as *añoranza*. Medina's first two books, *Arching in the Afterlife* (1991) and *The Floating Island* (1999), attempt, among other concerns, to reclaim or reconstruct an Eden by weaving together the imagery of a new home and the faint memories of the old one:

> It snows because there is a widow hiding
> under her mother's bed,
> because the birds are resting their throats
> and three wise men are offering gifts.
> Because the clouds are singing
> and trees have a right to exist,
> because the horses of the past are returning.
> They are grey and trot gently into the barn
> never touching the ground.[17]

Virgil Suárez also published a childhood memoir (*Spared Angola* [1997]), which traces his family's journey from Cuba to Spain to Florida in the early 1970s, when he was only eight years old. Life in a cultural limbo and the painful hunger for a home that becomes increasingly romanticized with the passage of time take root in Suárez's eight books of poetry, particularly *In the Republic of Longing* (2000).

Unlike Medina and Suárez, Richard Blanco was born outside of Cuba, because his family left the island while his mother was seven months pregnant. With his first two books of poetry, *City of a Hundred Fires* (1998) and *Directions to the Beach of the Dead* (2005), Blanco takes Cuban Americans a step closer toward healing. His work addresses coming to terms with the knowledge of the political and historical weight that burdens his community and shaping metaphors for belonging instead of clinging to the imagery of loss and displacement:

> I am alone with the moon on its path, staring
> like a blank page, shear and white as the snow
> on the peaks echoing back its light. I am this
> solitude, never more beautiful, the arc of space
> I travel through for a few hours, touching
> nothing and keeping nothing, with nothing
> to deny the night, the dark pines pointing
> to the stars, this life, always moving and still.[18]

Unlike many Chicano poets, a number of Cuban American poets do not reject or feel disconnected from the literary lineage of their homeland. This legacy was shaped before the Cuban Revolution, and much of it was inspired by classical Spanish literature. Even if the language of choice is now English, descendants of exiles continue to build on a nineteenth-century aesthetic (with its preoccupation with beauty and the arts) and a formalist tradition. Such is the case with poets like Dionisio D. Martínez (*Bad Alchemy* [1995]), Rafael Campo (*What the Body Told* [1996]), Ricardo Pau-Llosa (*Bread and Imagined* [1991]), and Aleida Rodríguez (*Garden of Exile* [1999]). The territory of the work is expansive enough, however, that it does not always have to engage Cuban history or identity. Campo, especially, has moved into a whole different set of contemporary concerns – gay men's health and AIDS, in particular – influenced by his occupation as a medical doctor:

> Last night I watched it happen. It was death,
> As usual and present as the view
> Of downtown Boston from my patient's room.
> Before the bleed, he pointed out for me
> A wisp of smoke that rose like mystery.[19]

Males dominate the Cuban American poetry scene and the critical attention that it garners, although there are a few notable women poets in Florida. Among them are Sandra M. Castillo (*My Father Sings to My Embarrassment* [2002]), Mia Leonin (*Braid* [1999]), Silvia Curbelo (*The Secret History of Water* [1991]), and Emma Trelles (*Tropicalia* [2011]). These poets bring a feminist and feminine exploration to Cuban American letters.

Two other lesser-known Cuban American poets worth mentioning are Adrian Castro (*Cantos, Blood and Honey* [1997]) and Orlando Ricardo Menes (*Rumba Atop the Stones* [2001]), whose poetry pays homage to Cuba's Afro-Caribbean heritage by reinscribing a vocabulary that comes from African myth and religion. For example, consider the following excerpt from Menes's poem "Ironman's Song":

> These arrowheads
> covered in dross-mud once touched
> Oshún's anvil breasts, scarified face.
> When flesh dressed my bones,
>
> I wore Obatalá's white tunic
> and like him lived chastely, ate no meat.
> Derived joy from my work as blacksmith
> to the mountain's *orishas*.[20]

It is unfair to make broad assessments out of a small body of work; but in reality, the Cuban American poetry landscape is still very young and narrow, yet it is also the most promising, because poets like Medina and Menes have been expending extraordinary energy translating into English works of Cuban writers who are lesser known in the United States. There is an expectation that the two Cuban-identified literary communities (the one in exile and the one inside Cuba) will eventually cease their mutual exclusion and interact in the spirit of cultural and political exchange.

Conclusions

Despite this entry's initial objections against the label "Latino," there are some benefits to claiming a pan-Latino identity: it can be used to publicize, for example, a Latino poetry reading or to organize a Latino poetry discussion panel. Such events become opportunities to explore and unravel this multifaceted ethnic identity. It also allows poets from other Latino groups (especially those of Central American and South American descent) to belong to a larger artistic community while their own ethnic literary communities in the United States grow and become organized. One of the complaints by Latino poets who do not identify as Chicano, Puerto Rican, or Cuban American is that they are systematically excluded and alienated by the nationalistic tendencies of those three dominant groups. Indeed, poets such as the Dominican American Julia Alvarez (*The Other Side/El Otro Lado* [1996]), the Colombian American Maurice Kilwein Guevara (*Poems of the River Spirit* [1996]), and the Salvadoran Americans William Archila (*The Art of Exile* [2009]) and Marcos McPeek Villatoro (*On Tuesday, When the Homeless Disappeared* [2006]), whose works offer insights into entirely different cultures from the Latin American diaspora, should not be marginalized by a collective of already marginalized groups.

Additionally, even though all three groups are products of a cultural *mestizaje*, that is, of a mixed-race heritage and history, there is still a tendency to question the inclusion of mixed-race poets or to demand greater loyalty for the group allowing membership. This tendency places undue stress on poets who are already producing a Latino poetics of the future: that which explores multiracial and multiethnic identity. Among these exciting voices are the Afro-Latino poets Aracelis Girmay (*Teeth* [2007]) and John Murillo (*Up Jump the Boogie* [2010]), the Ecuadoran Puerto Rican poet Juan J. Morales (*Friday and the Year That Followed* [2006]), the Argentinian Latvian poet Julie Sophia Paegle (*Torch Song Tango Choir* [2010]), and the Puerto Rican Filipina poet Kristin Naca (*Bird Eating Bird* [2009]).

There is also the issue of the Chicano, Puerto Rican, and Cuban poetry communities thriving mostly in the American Southwest, New York City, and Florida, respectively, which locks each distinct identity into a specific geographic location. In the coming years it will be interesting to see how migration patterns shift and what new poetic sensibilities are practiced by Chicanos living in the Northeast or in the South, Puerto Ricans in the Southwest, and Cuban Americans on the West Coast.

Notes

1. Important anthologies of Latino poetry generally include Victor Hernández Cruz, Leroy Quintana, and Virgil Suárez (eds.), *Paper Dance: 55 Latino Poets* (New York: Persea, 2000); Ray Gonzalez (ed.), *After Aztlán: Latino Poets of the Nineties* (Boston: David R. Godine, 1993); Rigoberto González (ed.), *Camino del Sol: Fourteen Years of Latina and Latino Writing* (Tucson: University of Arizona Press, 2010); Bryce Milligan and Angela de Hoyos (eds.), *Floricanto Sí: A Collection of Latina Poetry* (New York: Penguin, 1998). For anthologies with more specific rubrics, see subsequent notes.
2. Two significant studies specific to Chicano and Chicana writing are Alfred Arteaga, *Chicano Poetics: Heterotexts and Hybridities* (Cambridge: Cambridge University Press, 1997) and Rafael Pérez-Torres, *Movements in Chicano Poetry: Against Myth, Against Margins* (Cambridge: Cambridge University Press, 1995).
3. Abelardo Delgado, *Here Lies Lalo: The Collected Poems of Abelardo Delgado* (Houston: Arte Público Press, 2011), p. 4.
4. Gary Soto, *New and Selected Poems* (San Francisco: Chronicle, 1995), p. 49.
5. Alberto Ríos, *The Smallest Muscle in the Human Body* (Port Townsend, Wash.: Copper Canyon, 2002), p. 74.
6. Sandra Cisneros, *Loose Woman* (New York: Knopf, 1994), p. 4.

7. Lorna Dee Cervantes, *Emplumada* (Pittsburgh, Pa.: University of Pittsburgh Press, 1981), p. 35.

8. On queer Latino poetics generally, see Emanuel Xavier (ed.), *Mariposas: A Modern Anthology of Queer Latino Poetry* (Mountain View, Calif.: Floricanto Press, 2008).

9. Juan Felipe Herrera, *Notebooks of a Chile Verde Smuggler* (Tucson: University of Arizona Press, 2002), p. 74.

10. On Puerto Rican poetry generally, see Robert Márquez (ed.), *Puerto Rican Poetry: An Anthology from Aboriginal to Contemporary Times* (Amherst: University of Massachusetts Press, 2007).

11. Miguel Algarín and Bob Holman (eds.), *Aloud: Voices from the Nuyorican Poets Café* (New York: Holt, 1994); Susan B. A. Somers-Willett, *The Cultural Politics of Slam Poetry: Race, Identity and the Performance of Popular Verse in America* (Ann Arbor: University of Michigan Press, 2009).

12. Pedro Pietri, *Puerto Rican Obituary* (New York: Monthly Review Press, 1974), p. 10.

13. Mariposa, *Born Bronxeña* (Bronx, N.Y.: Bronxeña, 2000), pp. 7–8; reprinted at http://www.virtualboricua.org/Docs/poem_mtf01.htm.

14. Martín Espada, *Alabanza: New and Selected Poems 1982–2002* (New York: W. W. Norton, 2003), p. 251.

15. Rane Arroyo, *Home Movies of Narcissus* (Tucson: University of Arizona Press, 2002), p. 68.

16. Arroyo, *Home Movies of Narcissus*, p. 27.

17. Pablo Medina, *The Floating Island* (Buffalo, N.Y.: White Pine, 1999), p. 76.

18. Richard Blanco, *Directions to the Beach of the Dead* (Tucson: University of Arizona Press, 2005), p. 8.

19. Rafael Campo, *Diva* (Durham, N.C.: Duke University Press, 1999), p. 79.

20. Orlando Ricardo Menes, *Rumba Atop the Stones* (Leeds: Peepal Tree Press, 2001), p. 71.

Chapter 43

Asian American Poetry

JOSEPH JONGHYUN JEON

In suggesting that the practice of history has much in common with the writing of fiction, Hayden White famously challenged the truth-value of historical writing. Whether imaginative or documentary, every narrative, White argues, "is constructed on the basis of a set of events that might have been included, but were left out."[1] This historiographic problem in the case of Asian American literary history is exacerbated by the fact that the term "Asian American" is itself a fairly recent construct – a coalition first built in the 1960s and 1970s – that takes part of its name from the largest and most populated continent but was originally defined more narrowly, emphasizing immigrants from China, Japan, and the Philippines. The category has morphed over the years, widening geographically and retroactively encompassing cultural production that predates the term; Susan Koshy has even suggested that the rubric "Asian American" is catachrestic, not reducible to any stable referent, and instead reflects the internal contradictions that produced it.[2] The task of organizing and tracking such a complex, multivalent set of elements thus becomes complicated.

One could narrate the history of Asian American poetry, for example, as a kind of political Bildungsroman, moving from early expressions of marginalized voices to agitated demands for inclusion to final mainstream acceptance, and foreground the political history of the post–civil rights era, as well as the gradually widening scope of the Asian American movement. Alternately, one could map Asian American poetry onto the trajectory followed by the artistic movements of the twentieth century, from, say, modernist abstraction to jazz-inspired beat cadences to postmodern pastiche. One could also think in regional terms and foreground the particular trajectories in places like New York, San Francisco, and Hawai'i, where institutions like the Basement Workshop, the Kearny Street Workshop, and Bamboo Ridge Press supported groups of writers. Finally, one could trace the appropriation of "Asianness" in Western, canonical, poetic forms and the way in which Asian American poets respond to this legacy, beginning with the exotic, orientalist visions of Asian aesthetics employed by Ernest Fenollosa and Ezra Pound and moving to the fetishization of Asian spiritualism by Beat poets like Gary Snyder and Allen Ginsberg before tracking how Asian American poets have resisted these stereotypical constructs. While all of these accounts are accurate in some ways, their insights come at the cost of inevitable blind spots. This chapter does not avoid this perhaps unavoidable condition. But, rather than choosing an option from those rehearsed previously, it emphasizes a series of historical pressures, tensions, and anxieties that contextualize poetic production in each period.

One overarching dialectic is the relationship between a civil rights–inspired political imperative, on one hand, and an experimental literary ethos, on the other. Part of the reason for this particular fault line is a pervasive anxiety in minority discourse about poetry as a sufficiently social form. In contrast to the novel and memoir, which are often considered to be more adept at representing the harsh realities of racial injustice, poetry is sometimes regarded by those invested in minority politics as overly private and idealized, failing to address the empirical realities of the lived world. This critique is further amplified in the case of the more avant-garde forms, whose characteristic difficulty often seems anathema to the inclusive, egalitarian ethos that frequently drives Asian American studies. In the most forceful account, aesthetic experimentation in poetry is not just ineffective at communicating historical realities but also socially irresponsible. But such critiques are too quick to read difficulty as categorically apolitical and aesthetic experimentalism as antisocial, just as it would be mistaken to read more overtly political poetry as unconcerned about form. Asian American poetry has always been interested in both polarities, but in varying proportions and to varying degrees of success.

Orient Reoriented

The earliest Asian American poetry predates the political movement and hence the term itself. These poets would have identified more with individual ethnic groups, and their ambiguous status as Americans was frequently a preoccupation in poetry that often described attempts to gain precarious footholds, be they social or aesthetic, in the United States. What complicates our understanding of this period is the way in which parts of it have been retroactively claimed or disowned as originary moments for later groups and figures in Asian American poetry. Most historical accounts of Asian American poetry begin in the 1890s with the poems of Sadakichi Hartmann and Yone Noguchi,[3] but these have become vexed figures because, although they are the earliest Asian American poets writing in English, their work does not explicitly address Asian American social concerns. As a result, one interesting aspect of this early poetry is the discursive function it plays for later Asian American writers and critics who either acknowledge or disavow these figures as literary antecedents.

Raised in Germany and the United States, Sadakichi Hartmann was a poet and art critic but dabbled as both a playwright and a screenwriter. At various points in his colorful, bohemian life, he was an associate of Walt Whitman, Stéphane Mallarmé, Emma Goldman, and John Barrymore. Ezra Pound mentions Hartmann with admiration in his *Cantos*,[4] and again in *Guide to Kulchur*.[5] As a poet, he was among the first to write in English tanka and haiku, Japanese poetic forms, which he tried to reconcile with symbolist aesthetics. This synthetic effort is visible in his "Tanka I" (1920):

> Winter? Spring! Who knows!
> White buds from the plumtrees wing
> And mingle with the snows.
> No blue sky these flowers bring.
> Yet their fragrance augurs Spring.[6]

Here, Hartmann uses indeterminate images of flowers to evoke without explicitly describing inchoate internal states in a manner suggestive of symbolism (complete with synesthesia), modulating the elegant expressiveness that characterizes what is traditionally a Japanese courtly form into an appreciation of ambiguity that is more suitable for modern times. He further blends the tanka, a thirty-one-syllable poem broken down in lines of five, seven, five, seven, and seven syllables (although Hartmann inserts an extra syllable in the third line), with the rhyme scheme of the English quintain (*ababb*), as in Robert Browning's dramatic monologue "Porphyria's Lover."

A contemporary of Hartmann, Yone Noguchi, father of the well-known sculptor Isamu Noguchi, also experimented in English with Japanese forms. His critical publication, *The Spirit of Japanese Poetry* (1914) – part of which he delivered as a lecture at Oxford University – established him in the West as an authority on the subject, and it has even been speculated that Noguchi was an important source for Pound regarding Japanese aesthetic forms.[7] Noguchi's poetry was also well received and recognized by some of the literary elite of the period. As in his criticism, Noguchi's poetry worked to present Japanese forms to Western audiences, particularly the haiku, or hokku, but he also wrote about his time in the United States, as in "Song of Day in Yosemite Valley" (1898), in which Noguchi, unmoored from traditional Japanese form, embraces Whitmanian free verse and apostrophe: "I, a muse from the Orient, where is revealed the light of dawn, / Harken to the welcome strains of genii from the heart of the Sierras –."[8] Juxtaposing his own Asian subjectivity against this sublime American backdrop, the poem goes on to narrate the way in which the latter seems to overwhelm the former: "Behold! Yosemite, sermoning Truth and Liberty, battles in spirit with the Pacific Ocean afar! / O unfading wonder, eternal glory! I pray a redemption from the majesty that chains me – / (Lo, Hell offers a great edifice unto Heaven!) O, I bid my envy and praise reset against thee."[9] Here the overwhelmed Asian subject seems to submit to not only the physical grandeur of Yosemite but also the values that it seems to proffer. The enthusiastic tone of the passage, however, seems to reflect less the ultimate virtue of these values, and more their persuasive power. Perhaps not surprisingly in this context, Noguchi, unlike Hartmann, did not settle permanently in the United States, returning to Japan in 1904, just more than a decade after his arrival in 1893 in San Francisco at the age of eighteen.

Neither Hartmann's nor Noguchi's poems seem to engage Asian American political issues overtly, and both were later criticized as "Americanized Asians" in the preface to *Aiiieeeee!* (1974), an important anthology of Asian American literature that articulated a cultural nationalist Asian American ethos.[10] Poets that abided by this activist ethos, particularly those with Japanese ancestry like Janice Mirikitani and Lawson Fusao Inada, tended to avoid writing in traditional Japanese poetic forms because they felt it important to reject orientalist expectations and to distinguish their poetry as Asian American. Although Hartmann and Noguchi may indeed be read as complicit with orientalizing appropriations of Asian aesthetics, their attempts to adapt Japanese forms to English, however, are not *replications* of Japanese forms in English but rather *adaptations*, in which, as Edward Marx describes in botanical terms, "a subgenre is simply grafted onto an equivalent genre within the new culture, to wither or flourish under the prevailing local conditions."[11] In this regard, the efforts of Hartmann and Noguchi are also legible, not simply as translations of an Asian form into a new idiom but as attempts to invent synthetically an entirely new American form. Here, formal inclusion may function subtly as a mode of social inclusion.

Such inklings of a proto–Asian American poetics, however, were massively overshadowed by Western modernism's appropriation of Asian forms, most influentially by Pound and Fenollosa. Pound in particular made his understanding of classical Asian artistic forms and philosophy central to his sense of modernist aesthetics. Although he treated classical Asian culture with great intellectual appreciation, in doing so he also exoticized it. With Pound (as Eric Hayot and Josephine Park suggest), Asia came to function as central to the West's conception of itself, which relied on an imaginary idealization of the East in orientalizing terms.[12] This highly influential image of Asia was so dominant in the Western imagination throughout the twentieth century, according to these critics, that even Asian American poets could not approach their subject matter without confronting this legacy. It is this conception of Asia that the editors of *Aiiieeeee!* reacted against.

Written and published primarily in the 1940s and 1950s, the poetry of José Garcia Villa (also devalued in *Aiiieeeee!*) follows in the tradition of Hartmann and Noguchi in their encounters with modernism. Garcia Villa's case offers an example of the double bind that often characterizes this early period of Asian American formal experimentation. In his heyday, Garcia Villa, an early transnational figure, was regarded as an important figure in Filipino literature and as a promising up-and-comer in American letters. Living most of his adult life in the United States, although Garcia Villa wrote at a turbulent time in the history of the Philippines and in the legacy of U.S. colonial aggression, he remained relatively apolitical, focusing instead on poetic innovation. In his first book of poetry, *Have Come, Am Here* (1942), he introduced an idiosyncratic rhyme scheme, which he described as "reversed consonance," in which the last-sounded consonants of a word are reversed in the corresponding line, as in the following:

> It is what I never *said*, (a)
> What I'll always *sing* – (b)
> It's not found in *days*, (a)
> It's what always *begins* (b)[13]

Volume Two (1949) unveiled a genre that Garcia Villa called "comma poems," which used commas after nearly every word and was meant to invoke the pointillism of the French impressionist painter Georges Seurat.

Focusing on the reception of his work, which was reviewed by major publications and attracted the attention of important literary figures of the period (Marianne Moore, Edith Sitwell, E. E. Cummings), Timothy Yu describes Garcia Villa's conundrum as his work became increasingly experimental: "Readers, unable to reconcile this device with the covert orientalism through which they read Garcia Villa, lambasted his attempt to behave like any other American modernist."[14] Yu's account here describes the larger problematic of positioning these proto–Asian American poets in relation to current Asian American discourse. For writers like Garcia Villa, formal experimentation and associations with prominent Western literary figures and ideas seem to promise a kind of literary inclusion that opposes orientalism and allows the poet to transcend the limited racial category, but the promise is never realized, because the refashioning of the Asian writer as American negates the original exotic appeal. Formal experimentation becomes a mode of denying orientalizing assumptions, but it also negates the very mode through which the non-Western subject becomes legible to the Western audience. Furthermore, as in the denouncement of these writers by the editors of *Aiiieeeee!*, formal experimentalism becomes read retroactively as assimilationist and complicit with the very orientalist ideals that these poets sought, in varying degrees, to complicate.

If these poets were rejected as authentic origins for Asian American poetry, the poetry inscribed on the walls of the Angel Island Immigration Station detention building (active between 1910 and 1940) often takes their place, not least because it manifests a central trope in Asian American history, that of the perpetual foreigner. The institutional embodiment of the Yellow Peril discourse of the period, Angel Island detained primarily Chinese immigrants, and although it was sometimes called the Ellis Island of the West, its ultimate purpose was not to facilitate immigration, like its eastern counterpart, but to enforce the highly restrictive Chinese exclusion laws that governed Chinese immigration to the United States from 1882 to 1943. Written in Chinese, the poetry inscribed on the walls of the detention building by anonymous detainees, and thus physically marked on the very institution that repressed them, collectively serves as a historical record of marginalized Asians. Translated and anthologized in *Island: Poetry and History of Chinese Immigrants on Angel Island, 1910–1940* (1980), the poems have been read primarily as historical records, more in documentary rather than literary terms.[15] But these poems are also interesting, as Steven Yao has argued, for their formal characteristics, which Yao reads transnationally in relation to both classical Chinese models and American jazz aesthetics.[16]

The Social Poetics of Labor and Internment

Although the Asian American movement of the 1960s and 1970s was certainly the first to codify ideological fault lines, define political imperatives, and group different Asian ethnicities under a single unified rubric, it did follow in the footsteps of a nascent activist tradition that arose midcentury, initially to confront labor issues. Many of the earliest Asian immigrants to the United States were manual laborers, and much of the legislation restricting Asian immigration to the United States was motivated in part by anxieties within the U.S. labor movement that Asian workers were taking the jobs from their constituents. But, as Colleen Lye has suggested, Asian exclusion did not exactly succeed in keeping Asian workers out of the United States but rather "merely guaranteed a disempowered class of laborers."[17] These workers thus found themselves working difficult, low-paying jobs for employers who were ambivalent to their well-being, while remaining unprotected by the often nativist labor unions, who viewed them as threatening. The earliest Asian American poems relating to labor are the various oral forms, such as the *hole-hole bushi* sung on Hawaiian sugarcane plantations in Japanese. In addition, the Chinatown Cantonese rhymes that Marlon K. Hom has translated and collected in *Songs of Gold Mountain* (1987), from a pair of original manuscripts that date from 1911 and 1915, depict the struggles of Chinese immigrants. And though their concerns vary widely, they exemplify a certain realist sensibility that calls attention to economic hardship.

In the 1920s and 1930s, Hsi-Tseng (H. T.) Tsiang published proletarian poems that expressed his dedication to global class revolution, which he believed should cut across national and racial lines. According to Floyd Cheung, Tsiang followed the principle of *nalai zhuyi* (or "grabbism"), which was an aesthetic theory formulated by the prominent modern Chinese writer Lu Xun that advocated strategic appropriation of often foreign ideas and forms. In this mode, Cheung suggests, "Tsiang created a new hybridized literature by reworking formal and thematic elements from classical and contemporary Chinese literature, the proletarian works of 1920s and 1930s America, and western classics like the plays of William Shakespeare."[18] Although he often also included poetic interludes in his prose, his main poetic contribution was his one volume of published poetry, *Poems of the Chinese Revolution* (1929), which is introduced by a short note by Upton Sinclair, who recommends not the poems themselves (he describes them as "not perfect") but rather "the movement which he voices."[19] Tsiang's leftist politics drew the ire of state officials in both China, which he fled in fear of persecution, and the United States, which attempted unsuccessfully to deport him. In the poems of this volume – such as "Rickshaw Boy," "Chinaman, Laundryman," "Sacco-Vanzetti," and "Canton Soviet" – Tsiang attempts to inscribe marginalized Chinese/American laborers into Western socialism, particularly in the context of the United States, where Chinese people were excluded from labor politics ("Don't call me 'Chinaman' / I am the Worldman / 'The International Soviet / Shall be his human race'!").[20]

Although he is best known for his novel *America Is in the Heart* (1946), Carlos Bulosan began his literary career primarily as a poet who, like Tsiang, called attention to the plight of alienated workers of Asian descent. After arriving in the United States in 1930, at the beginning of the Great Depression, Bulosan worked a series of jobs that were typical for Filipino immigrants of the day, in canneries and agricultural fields. Disgusted by the poor conditions and racist treatment that characterized such labor, which was made worse by the reclassification of Filipinos in the United States as "aliens" by the Tydings-McDuffie Act in 1934, he eventually became active in organizing unions for fellow Filipino migrant laborers, who were unprotected at the time by existing labor unions. His experiences during these years inform his poetry, including his first volume, *Letter from America* (1942). Although these poems do not all employ the epistolary mode alluded to by the volume's title, they do follow letters in fashion, according to Oscar V. Campomanes, by bridging "the gaping distance between Bulosan and his imaginary reader" in order to conquer "the historical alienation that becomes the lot of the exiled."[21] Although the title of the volume nominally imagines a non-American reader, the poems invite a general audience to witness harsh social realities in a kind of empathic, journalistic tone.

> The streets scream for life, where men are hunting
> Each other with burning eyes, mountains are made of sand,
> Glass, paper from factories where death is calling
> For peace; hills are made of clothes, and trees
> Are nothing but candies.[22]

Like Tsiang, Bulosan depicted a fractured and unjust world, recognizing the way in which racial politics collided with the nativist interests of American labor politics. This bleak vision of "America bleeding," as he describes it following the quoted passage, speaks not only to the difficulty of the labor endured by these workers but also to their marginal social status.

The most extreme example of marginal status in Asian American history came in 1942, when Franklin Delano Roosevelt issued Executive Order 9066, which effectively called for the removal of approximately 110,000 people of Japanese descent from the West Coast of the United States to camps located in desolate inland areas. As did anti-Asian immigration legislation, Japanese American internment clearly demonstrated the extent to which Asians in the United States were regarded as perpetual foreigners, despite legitimate claims to citizenship. Although the memoir fiction about this history is more well known – for example, John Okada's *No-No Boy* (1957) and Jeanne Wakatsuki Houston's *Farewell to Manzanar* (1973) – the poetry on the subject is equally important. There have been a number of poetic manuscripts in both Japanese and English associated with various camps, some anonymous and some attributed to authors. Recently, critics have called attention to the highly censored newspapers and journals run by internees at the camps, which sometimes published subtly resistant poetry.[23] At the Topaz camp, Toyo Suyemoto and Taro Katayama published poems that quietly attempted to make sense of the traumatic experience and to register dissent, in camp publications like *Trek* and *All Aboard*.[24] In many cases, poetry from the camps was rediscovered and appreciated much later, as was the case for Violet Kazue De Cristoforo's *May Sky: There Is Always Tomorrow: An Anthology of Japanese American Concentration Camp Haiku* (1997). Because it was such a traumatizing event, a common reaction among the imprisoned population, once released, was silence, and internment literature initially failed to gain a broad audience.[25] Consequently, most of the poetic treatments of internment – such as Mitsuye Yamada's *Camp Notes and Other Poems* (1976), Janice Mirikitani's *Shedding Silence* (1987), and Lawson Fusao Inada's *Legends from Camp* (1993) – do so retroactively as historical memory, although Yamada's text stands out as one that was written during and immediately following her family's internment.

Dialectics of Asian American Activism and Antiessentialism

From the late 1960s to the mid-1990s, Asian American poetry developed and diversified rapidly and, for the first time, embraced the term "Asian American" as an organizing rubric. The legacies of the labor and internment experiences of the first half of the twentieth century were invisibility and silence for Asian Americans, who were marked as perpetually foreign and marginalized from representational politics. The Asian American movement of the 1960s and 1970s redressed this legacy by privileging visibility and voice as political values: it imagined a pan-Asian coalition based on a history of similar experiences. Central to this politics was the construction of a sense of Asian American identity that rejected both orientalist stereotypes on one hand and assimilation into white American culture on the other. The editors of *Aiiieeeee!* make this bifurcated claim on behalf of Asian American literature as anthologized in its collection (although it did not include poetry until later editions), which reflects "the existence of Asian American sensibilities and cultures that might be related to but are distinct from Asia and white America."[26] Numerous poetry anthologies have taken up this task of delineating Asian American literary aesthetics, such as David Hsin-fu Wand's *Asian American Heritage* (1974), Joseph Bruchac's *Breaking Silence* (1983), Garrett Hongo's *The Open Boat* (1993), and Walter K. Lew's *Premonitions* (1995). This interest in circumscribing a field of Asian American poetry also gave impetus to the recovery and reconsideration of the antecedents that I have discussed in previous sections as well as to the desire to claim origins and formulate historical narratives for this newly emergent category of writing.

Critics have generally narrated this period from the late 1960s to mid-1990s as a progression from early activist poetry (Mirikitani, Inada, and Merle Woo) to a more mainstream antiessentialist lyric poetry by poets trained in American M.F.A. programs (Cathy Song, Li-Young Lee, and David Mura) and, finally, to an avant-garde period (Theresa Hak Kyung Cha and John Yau) that challenges the legacy of identity politics and the coherency of the lyric "I" with poststructuralist and postmodern experimental modes.[27] Although they are useful as general accounts, such narratives purchase narrative cleanliness at the cost of historical accuracy. Sunn Shelley Wong, for example, has pointed out that the Asian American poetic production of the 1970s is characterized not only by activist modes but also by "a range of poetic styles and themes that resist conflation."[28] In addition, John Yau's first collection, *Crossing Canal Street*, was published in 1976, and Cha's *DICTEE*, which is arguably the most significant Asian American avant-garde text, was published in 1982 (although not widely read until the early 1990s); hence, both were published before what are regarded as the landmark antiessentialist texts, like Cathy Song's *Picture Bride* (1983), David Mura's *After We Lost Our Way* (1989), and Li-Young Lee's *The City in Which I Love You* (1990). Furthermore, the periodization of these poets tends to ignore their development in careers that outlast the small window of time with which they are associated, as is the case for Mirikitani and Inada, both still active today.

Although these genealogies can be schematically useful, they tend also to elide their own erasures when exceptions threaten the sanctity of the scheme. So rather than treating this crucial time in the development of Asian American poetry as a series of quick epistemic changes in which values radically shift (activist, antiessentialist, avant-garde), I want to think of the first two stages instead as polarities or modes implicated in a dialectical relationship, in which one value might outweigh another in prominence at a given moment but never vanquishes the other entirely. The third term, "avant-garde," becomes one recurring and prominent mode of negotiating and synthesizing the first two. In practical terms, this means not only that different kinds of poets coexist at various moments but also that both polarities also coexist within the work of individual poets.

Mirikitani's "Breaking Silence" (1981), which Joseph Bruchac took as a title for his 1983 anthology, might exemplify the activist polarity.[29] Mirikitani participated in the student strike in 1968–1969 at San Francisco State, an important moment for the Asian American movement, and, with the poet Francis Naohiko Oka, founded *Aion* in 1970, which, although short-lived, was the first Asian American literary magazine. Occasioned by her mother's testimony to the Commission on Wartime Relocation and Internment of Japanese American Civilians in 1981, "Breaking Silence" alternates back and forth between a private lyrical introspection about the experience of internment that is gleaned from her mother's comments over the years ("We were told / that silence was better") and the mother's public speech before the commission. The private mode recounts a history of silence and resigned compliance to historical injustice that contrasts with the mother's brave testimony of anger and resistance:

> Mr. Commissioner . . .
> So when you tell me I must limit
> testimony,
> when you tell me my time is up,
> I tell you this:
> pride has kept my lips
> pinned by nails
> my rage confined.
> But I exhume my past
> to claim this time.[30]

Inspired then by the mother's decision to "kill this silence," the poem resolves into a rallying cry for a collective identity that emerges from history – citing "war-dead sons / red ashes of Hiroshima / jagged wounds from barbed wire" – with a sense of self-recognition and pride that accumulates with every repetition of the first person plural that closes the poem. In so doing, the poem claims a Japanese American history and links it to a collective political identity, transforming inward introspection, associated with quiescence, into a public, performative declaration of unity and strength:

> We must recognize ourselves at last.
> We are a rainforest of color
> and noise.
> We hear everything.
> We are unafraid.[31]

Suggested by the prominent positioning of "and noise," voice is only effective when it becomes openly resistant in a public forum, clamoring for political representation, and when it comes to encapsulate a collective (rather than individual) subject position. In claiming a political identity in relation to history, the poem demonstrates what has been critiqued as a kind of *tribalism*, which calls attention to shared experiences of subjugation and uses these commonalities in order to build a coalition.[32]

The antiessentialist polarity finds fault in what it regards as an overly reductive form of tribalism and favors instead a broader appreciation of difference. Garrett Hongo and David Mura have made forceful claims on behalf of these values. In his introduction to his anthology *The Open Boat*, Hongo articulates the antiessentialist polarity in polemical terms, particularly in his comments about a 1991 Asian American writers' conference at the University of California at Berkeley, by enumerating what he thought to be a set of nefarious assumptions that he felt pervaded the conference: a sociopolitical understanding of an *essential* Asian American experience, the expectation of a writer's compulsory loyalty to his or her ethnic community, and a dismissal of *assimilationist* or *commercial* writing. Hongo proceeds to sum up these assumptions harshly, as "nothing more than fascism, intellectual bigotry, and ethnic fundamentalism of the worst kind."[33] Mura extends this critique into a valuation of fluid, multiple identities: "In our postmodern, multicultural, global world, our identities are multiple, are conditioned by our historical circumstances, are something we have been given and something we choose, are always changing, are subject to political and cultural forces beyond our control, are a continuous creation."[34] Far from discarding the interest of identity in the activist poetics, writers committed to the antiessentialist line of thought make self-knowledge about identity more central and pressing, by making it more inchoate and ephemeral, something that is highly desired and sought, "a continuous creation," but slippery and elusive.

Perhaps because of the difficult multiplicity of identity, a central poetic mode for this line of poetry is the lyric. As Charles Altieri has suggested, in a world that increasingly values empirically derived, impersonally verifiable forms of clarity, poetic lyricism in the Romantic tradition is increasingly aware of its own marginality and thus can only produce "an exhilarating yet problematic amalgam of intense modes of self-consciousness, riddled with continual worry that one's basic values may be only anachronistic escapes from the reality of a much-diminished world."[35] Altieri's description here of lyric values, although focused specifically on modernist aesthetics, might also serve to gloss Li-Young Lee's "Persimmons" (1986).[36] On the surface, Lee's poem seems to have much in common with Mirikitani's "Breaking Silence." Both consider cultural inheritance through the relationship to one's parents and compare this heritage to other forms of authority that regulate racial difference. Mirikitani's poem juxtaposes the mother's voice and the power of the commissioner who arbitrates her public speech; Lee's poem invokes the memory of his father in relation to Mrs. Walker, the speaker's sixth-grade teacher, who punishes the speaker's otherness, slapping the back of his head for not knowing the difference between the words "persimmon" and "precision."

But whereas Mirikitani moves from private memory to public performance as a way to dramatize political mobility, Lee, who in interviews has rejected the moniker "Asian American poet," moves inward toward lyrical introspection and sensual memory. The poem culminates with the speaker's account of rummaging through his parents' cellar, searching for something he has lost, while his now-blind father sits with him. This search for the lost object doubles the father's eyesight, which he describes as *"All gone."* In the final lines of the poem, the speaker locates what he has been looking for, a still-life painting by his father of two persimmons.

> *This is persimmons, Father.*
>
> *Oh, the feel of the wolftail on the silk,*
> *the strength, the tense*
> *precision in the wrist.*
> *I painted them hundreds of times*
> *eyes closed. These I painted blind.*
> *Some things never leave a person:*
> *scent of the hair of one you love,*
> *the texture of persimmons,*
> *in your palm, the ripe weight.*[37]

Although the poem ends with quoted speech, signaled by italicization, the father's speech in the final stanza is far from public. The location, the cellar of the house, suggests remoteness. More importantly, the speaking "I" of the father in these lines seems to blend into the lyric "I" of the poem that responds to Mrs. Walker's enforcement of racial difference through the figure of the persimmon (which she had earlier described as a *"Chinese apple"*[38]) by collapsing the difference between "persimmon" and "precision." The elision of linguistic difference thus implies a rejection of the racialization implicit in Mrs. Walker's semiviolent reproach. Instead, identity in these final lines comes with a sensual identification with the father's precise rendering of persimmons. What the speaker shares with the father is not so much a shared set of historical experiences that authorizes coalition building but rather a more radically individualized sense of subjective experience that contests the imposition of crude, reductive categories like race. And because identity is such a private, individualized entity – a highly contingent amalgam of personal and familial history and experience – identity becomes a fluid, continuous creation.

The critique of the activist polarity is implicit in the antiessentialist line, which regards the former as overly reductive, but some of what has been filed under the rubric of activist poetry, however, seems already to anticipate this criticism. From his first volume of poems, *Before the War: Poems as They Happened* (1971), Inada's jazz aesthetics have privileged syncopated variation and performative play. So while his invocations of historical trauma link him firmly to the activist tradition, a link that is bolstered by his editorial participation in *Aiiieeeee!*, his use of African American jazz aesthetics imports a slipperier ethos under the rubric of performative politics. Juliana Chang has suggested that Inada's cross racial identification with these musical forms does not imply an essential, ontological connection between minority subject positions but rather "is articulated through practices of knowledge formation and code reading."[39] Chang's analysis suggests that, while Inada is indeed specific and explicit about the racial history of the Japanese American subject, this history does not summarily determine identity, which has more to do with variable modes of engagement than essential modes of being. In a poem entitled "On Being Asian American" from his volume *Legends from Camp* (1993), Inada seems to reply implicitly to the antiessentialist critique:

> Take me as I am, you cry,
> I, I, am an individual.
> *Which is certainly true.*
> *Which generates an echo.*[40]

In the broader context of the poem as a whole – which consists of a series of quatrains in which the second couplet is italicized – the lines read not as an outright admonishment on the insistence on individuality but as a pair of gentle qualifications that suggest that the fact of individuality does not negate the larger echoes or reverberations that connect the individual to a political identity. But as in his more directly jazz-inspired poetics, these echoes influence without determining individual identity.

The antiessentialist polarity has also had its critics, who regard this poetics as ultimately authorizing only the most uncritical and anesthetic forms of liberal humanist multiculturalism, which David Palumbo-Liu has contrasted with what he terms *critical* multiculturalism. The former functions to contain the dangerous energy of the civil rights movement by ignoring the "complex material specificities" of minority discourse, which might "occasion the critique of the ideological apparatuses that distribute power and resources unevenly among the different constituencies of a multicultural society."[41] Instead, liberal multiculturalism institutionalizes a watered-down sense of pluralism that simply respects cultural difference as such, without engaging in any ideological investigation. A similar charge has been leveled against poets associated with the antiessentialist line, like Li-Young Lee, David Mura, Cathy Song, and Marilyn Chin. Although these poets have been the most visible, mainstream successes in Asian American poetic history, their success, according to this critique, has much to do with the compatibility of their poetics to the kind of multicultural, and ultimately apolitical, ethos that Palumbo-Liu critiques.[42]

This account, however, is also somewhat reductive. First, this poetry is not so much categorically apolitical as it is arguably politically limited, because of the way in which it channels its political energies into easily containable forms. Despite the attention often paid to Asian American history in these poems, political content here tends to get sublimated into an identity poetics that projects social content inward onto the subjective terrain of the individual and, in so doing, transforms racial difference into individual difference. Second, the antiessentialist ethos is not without its virtues. The sentiment behind the central metaphor of Hongo's anthology, that of the open boat, is certainly vulnerable to the critique of liberal multiculturalism, but it also allows for a broader vision of what constitutes Asian American poetry. Hongo's anthology, for example, participates in the gradual inclusion of writers with ancestry from other parts of Asia, including Indran Amirthanayagam, Chitra Banerjee Divakaruni, and the Kashmiri American Agha Shahid Ali (1949–2001), who found himself influential in America at the very end of his life, both for his evocations of Kashmir in *The Country without a Post Office* (1997) and for his work to promote the Persian and Urdu form called the ghazal.

Finally, this categorical critique undervalues the individual differences among poets that fall under this rubric. Although she is sometimes called an activist poet, Marilyn Chin, for example, is often categorized with the antiessentialist polarity because of the tendency of her poetry to demonstrate the complexity of identity constructs. Her oft-cited poem "How I Got That Name: An Essay on Assimilation," from her 1994 volume *The Phoenix Gone, the Terrace Empty*, explores individual identity by narrating how her birth name, Mei Ling, was transliterated into English as "Marilyn" by her father, who was obsessed with Marilyn Monroe.[43] The speaker's meditation on her name thus becomes a way of thinking through questions of assimilation, or more specifically about how Asian Americans register in American culture and history. The poem contextualizes individual identity in relation to a field of signifiers: historical events (e.g., Angel Island and the paper son phenomenon, through which some Chinese immigrants skirted exclusion legislation by falsely claiming that they were the sons of U.S. citizens), historical constructs (the Asian American model minority myth), literary allusions to iconic poems by William Carlos Williams and John Berryman, and pop-culture references to the soap opera *Santa Barbara*. The poem ends with a mock epitaph ("So here lies Marilyn Mei Ling Chin . . .") that calls attention to the impossibility of encapsulating identity in stone:

> She was neither black nor white,
> neither cherished nor vanquished,
> just another squatter in her own bamboo grove
> minding her poetry –
> when one day heaven was unmerciful,
> and a chasm opened where she stood.
> Like the jowls of a mighty white whale,
> or the jaws of a metaphysical Godzilla,
> it swallowed her whole.[44]

This excerpt encapsulates the poem's attempt to render identity not as entirely unintelligible but rather as relationally intelligible in historical and cultural contexts. After a pair of negations that narrow the field of identity without specifying it, the poem turns to a stereotype of an Asian exotic minding poetry in a bamboo grove, and then to a fantastical account of the poet's death, which characterizes the blankness of her subject position, an opening chasm, in relation to an American literary antecedent and an Asian pop-culture reference that registers in the United States as well. Chin's antiessentialism does not involve an apolitical withdrawal into private sensuality but rather depends on the constantly shifting relationship between the individual and the world in which she gains definition.

Avant-Garde Syntheses and Transnational Reconfigurations

As already suggested, avant-garde Asian American poetry is not a discrete period in a larger historical trajectory of formal and ideological development but rather one prominent mode of negotiating a central dialectic of Asian American poetry. Debate about what constitutes an avant-garde is as old as avant-garde movements themselves. For the purpose of this chapter, I highlight three characteristics as constitutive of avant-garde art. First, avant-garde art often mobilizes a fundamental defamiliarizing gesture that can be disorienting, jarring, or even offensive and that thus functions to signal to the reader or viewer that he or she must alter familiar interpretive practices in order to engage the piece at all. Second, the avant-garde artwork typically engages in some kind of theoretical work, which is frequently staged by the formal and stylistic properties of the work and is thus often accompanied by an explicit, sometimes polemic critical discourse (manifestos, statements of poetics, etc.). Third, avant-garde artworks usually mobilize some kind of community, whether we understand community in strictly sociological terms (coteries, movements, and even institutions) or in looser value terms (an interpretive community). Like many avant-garde works, Asian American avant-garde poetry generally attempts to imbricate formal/aesthetic experimentation with sociopolitical investigation, and, in particular, to reconstitute an Asian American poetics that picks up on the activist concern for history and ideological investigation without relying on an essentialized vision of identity overly determined by social positionality, on one hand, while rejecting the mainstream lyrical modes that characterize the antiessentialist polarity, on the other, aspiring ultimately to relocate Asian American studies on new conceptual grounds.

Among the earliest to experiment in this poetic mode, Jessica Hagedorn and Theresa Hak Kyung Cha both have worked in a number of different artistic media, paying specific attention to the intersections of feminist and racial issues. Hagedorn has published both poetry and fiction, sometimes in the same volumes; written and produced plays; performed with a musical act (West Coast Gangster Choir); and worked as a performance artist. Her poetry was first published in a collection edited by Kenneth Rexroth entitled *Four Young Women: Poems* (1973), which was followed by a pair of monographs that mixed poetry and prose: *Dangerous Music* (1975) and *Pet Food and Tropical Apparitions* (1981). Imbued with a decidedly performative ethos, Hagedorn's poetry is frantically paced, often incantatory, and driven by rock, jazz, and Latin musical rhythms and is full of references to American pop culture, with a heavy dose from the 1940s and 1950s (Rita Hayworth, Desi Arnaz, Tito Puente). In "Sorcery," a poem from *Dangerous Music*, the speaker issues what is ultimately a disingenuous warning:

> stay away
> from crazy music.
> they most likely
> be creating it

cuz
when you're that beautiful
you can't help
putting it out there.
everyone knows
how dangerous
that can get.[45]

Hagedorn is drawn to precisely this type of music, which is dangerous because it rails against conformity or, as George Uba has described it, against "the exercise of reason over the less reducible, holistic rhythms of experience."[46] Like her fiction, which has garnered more critical attention, Hagedorn's poetry investigates the postcolonial Philippines in relation to American political and cultural intrusions, hybrid identities, immigration, and assimilation and eschews easy forms of coherency, jumping from image to image, figure to figure, at such a rapid clip that what is ultimately delivered is not a coherent narrative but an idiosyncratic composite of snapshots as well as an ethos that is equally as suspicious of stasis as it is of authority.

Best known for her experimental text *DICTEE* (1982), which mixes fiction, photography, poetry, and found documents, Theresa Hak Kyung Cha's oeuvre encompasses various forms of language art (which often straddles genres and media), film, book art, sculpture, photography, and performance. Although she is more a conceptual artist than a poet, Cha's experiments with language in her visual art often dovetail with the various experimental poetics of her day. Of all the sections of the text, the ELITERE/LYRIC POETRY section is most committed to poetic forms. The section ends with a meditation on the life and death of words:

> Dead words. Dead tongue. From disuse. Buried in
> Time's memory. Unemployed. Unspoken. History.
> Past. Let the one who is diseuse, one who is mother
> who waits nine days and nine nights be found.
> Restore memory. Let the one who is diseuse, one
> who is daughter restore spring with her each ap-
> pearance from beneath the earth.
> The ink spills thickest before it runs dry before it
> stops writing at all.[47]

The verse paragraph here begins clipped and paratactic before resolving into dramatic incantation. Alluding to the mythic story of Demeter and her daughter Persephone, which explains the changing of the seasons, the passage here turns on the pun between "disuse" and "diseuse," a French-derived term that refers to a specifically female performer of monologues. Associated with the diseuse, Persephone is a figure of traversal, and one that resonates with the immigrants and exiles on which Cha dilates in *DICTEE*. According to myth, Persephone returns every year from Hades and restores spring to the earth. Speech, the medium of the diseuse, and writing, figured by the spilling ink in the final lines, are thus associated with vitality, but also transience, capable of interrupting only temporarily the death of language, time, and perhaps history with which the section begins and that is echoed in its conclusion. The passage as a whole thus calls attention to the kind of boundaries and limits (national, linguistic, political) with which *DICTEE* as a whole is obsessed, even as they are breached. In addition to *DICTEE*, Cha's most well-known text, a wealth of material is archived at the Berkeley Art Museum, which has only recently begun to receive critical attention. Much of this work was displayed in a 2001 exhibit, entitled *The Dream of the Audience: Theresa Hak Kyung Cha (1951–1982)*; more recently, a collection of her language art, entitled *Exilée and Temps Morts: Selected Works* (2009), was published. In her introduction to the volume, Constance Lewallen points out that "there was no firm distinction between Cha's visual and linguistic practices."[48] This blurring of boundaries is a characteristic ethos in Cha's work. In her *Commentaire*, the pages of the book invoke a film screen, as if to call attention to words as images. In her film / video installations, on the other hand, words are projected onto the screen, as if the screen was now to be understood as a book page. Crucially, these sorts of aesthetic ambiguities – of genre, medium, and form – parallel cultural and nationalistic indeterminacies. For Cha, language itself becomes a strange material object that reflects the complex and uncertain material histories of immigration, diaspora, and race. Her work is extremely theoretically engaged, particularly with film theory, a collected volume of which, entitled *Apparatus*, she published in 1980. Cha's life was violently cut short in 1982, just as she was beginning to do her most important work.

Although he worked as a critic and curator rather than a practitioner, the poet John Yau, like Cha, is firmly rooted in the world of visual arts. Among his numerous publications of art criticism, two books, both on Jasper Johns, stand out: *The United States of Jasper Johns* (1997) and *A Thing Among Things: The Art of Jasper Johns* (2008). What Yau seems to admire most about Johns's work is the way in which its repetitions of form and pattern play out the inevitable failures of stasis and the ultimate triumph of entropy and flux. Yau's volume *Corpse and Mirror* (1983) takes its title from Johns's iconic painting. Here and elsewhere, Yau plays with Johns's formal notion of repetition and variation: one witnesses this logic in, for example, "Variations of a Sentence by

Laura (Riding) Jackson"; in his Hollywood poems, which often focus on white actors that played stereotypical Asian characters in films (Peter Lorre, Boris Karloff); and, perhaps most famously, in his Genghis Chan: Private Eye series, whose name is a hybrid between the legendary Mongol ruler and the stereotypical Asian detective. Yau's poems explore an iconology of race, performing a historically informed inquiry into the ways in which race, and specifically Asianness, has been constructed over the course of time.

Like Cha's language art, the poetry of Mei-mei Berssenbrugge is steeped in theoretical and philosophic thought. And like both Cha and Yau, she is deeply invested in visual art. In fact, her mode of composition – in which she writes out words on strips of paper, cuts them up, and reassembles them – operates as much according to a visual logic as it does a linguistic one. She was active in the early Asian American political movements; was included in Bruchac's 1983 anthology *Breaking Silence*; and even had a play, *One, Two Cups* (1974), which was directed by Frank Chin. As her work became more philosophical and abstract, it was regarded as moving away from the terrain occupied by Asian American literature. Increasingly influenced by contemporary avant-garde visual art and music in addition to theoretical writing, Berssenbrugge's later work does not so much abandon the concerns of Asian American literature as much as it attempts to reimagine the various idioms through which these concerns are addressed. Her volumes *Empathy* (1989) and *Endocrinology* (1997), for example, investigate the phenomenological body and its perceptive capacities. Although race is not named as an explicit context, the mode of philosophic investigation resonates with the more explicit racial phenomenology of Frantz Fanon, which considers the possibilities of perception when the perceiver is the object of so much surveillance and derision. *Nest* (2003) considers questions of home and belonging, interrogating what it means to be inside or outside, native or foreign.

As is the case for Berssenbrugge, a prevailing characteristic in much contemporary Asian American poetry in this avant-garde mode is a highly self-conscious concern for language and rhetoric as a point of entry for other Asian American social issues. Influenced no doubt by language poetics and poststructuralist theory, this metacritical attention to language, in fact, seems to have surpassed and subsumed the interest in identity as a primary organizing matrix for Asian American poetics in recent years. One prominent strain within this emergent tradition is concerned with the interrelation between English and Asian language along with related issues of translation and transnationalism. This poetry is thus particularly attuned to the recent imperative in "Asian/American" studies in which the solidus in the middle of the term implies an imperative to track the increasingly complex ways in which "'Asia' and 'America' have merged and continue to merge."[49]

Myung Mi Kim, for example, approaches the English language as a poet who has clearly mastered its intricacies and cadences, but from the point of view of someone for whom it is a second language. So although she is deft in her presentations of words and keenly aware of their sound and musicality, she also treats them as strange objects that must always be viewed from a defamiliarized distance. As demonstrated in *Under Flag* (1991), *The Bounty* (1996), and *Commons* (2002), one abiding concern in her poetics is an interest in the Romanization of Korean into English, which is a concern less for semantic translation than for the perhaps more primal and affective way in which sound, and implicitly voice, gets transliterated and reproduced in other languages. By framing issues of historical violence, immigration, and diaspora through linguistic rather than social lenses, Kim dramatizes mutually transformative exchanges between languages that might model broader social reconfigurations. Not unlike Kim's poetry, Meena Alexander's work is informed by a lifetime of migration (from India to Sudan, to England, and to the United States) and thus by a heteroglossic relationship to language. Although she writes in English, her usage is informed by Arabic, French, Malayalam, and Hindi, and this complex relationship to language allows Alexander in her poetry to negotiate her complicated relationship to the colonial history of India. The title poem of *Raw Silk* (2004), for example, dilates on one of the fetishized commodities of European colonialism in India, the image of which evokes both fond family memories and ugly reminiscences of brutal violence. Similarly, the speaker recalls her fondness for the poetry of Rimbaud and Verlaine in the face of her mother's disapproval: "why mutter poems in a language I can't understand?"[50] Like French poetry, silk is ultimately a deeply vexed object: beautiful and delicate, on one hand, but inconceivable outside of the violent history of its acquisition. Like Alexander, Kimiko Hahn attempts in her poetry to integrate Asian languages and literary forms into an inventive English-language poetics that embeds personal experience, in specifically gendered terms, within a broader ideological network of global power. *The Unbearable Heart* (1996), for example, moves from fairly conventional lyrics occasioned by the sudden death of the poet's mother to more experimental forms, including an adaptation of a *zuihitsu* (a Japanese literary genre in which the writer offers a loose series of personal insights and fragment miscellany) and then two poems that respond to quotations from Roland Barthes's *The Pleasure of the Text* and from Gustave Flaubert's orientalist account of his intimate relationship with an Egyptian courtesan named Kuchuk Hamen. Hahn's text as a whole thus connects personal trauma to a colonialist history in which sexual conquest of the oriental woman subtends imperialist aggression. As in *Mosquito and Ant* (1999) – in which she appropriates the archaic Chinese writing system *nu shu*, which was used exclusively and surreptitiously by women who were otherwise denied access to literacy – Hahn interrogates the ideological foundations of gender and race in *The Unbearable Heart* as relationships to various forms of linguistic heritage.

What It Means to Be a Postidentity Poet

It is perhaps too early to chart out the contemporary landscape of Asian American poetry. More work than ever is currently being published and is supported by institutions like Kaya Press, the Asian American Writers' Workshop, Kundiman, and the Association for Asian American Studies. One prominent value, which might serve as a guiding coordinate, might be a postidentity ethos, which is accompanied by a robust sense of adventurousness, both formal and ideological. Authorized by the tradition of avant-garde and transnational poetry described in the previous section, this movement away from poetic models that foreground identity as an anchoring concept leaves the future of Asian American poetry wide open for work as varied as, for example, Kazim Ali's measured, minimalist, often spiritual contemplations; Young-Hae Chang's transnational, transcultural, digital poetics; Linh Dinh's irreverent, sardonic humor; Sesshu Foster's innovative, genre-bending prose poems; Tan Lin's endlessly concatenated oddball musings; Timothy Liu's impassioned, feverish hauntings; and Cathy Park Hong's wonderfully bizarre sci-fi romps. But although the brave new world for Asian American poetry is indeed one of radical possibility, within the scope of this widening gyre, the devaluation of identity as a foundational concept seems also to threaten the coherence of Asian American poetry itself; one wonders if and how the center will hold when not just the circumference of identity itself but also the question of whether or not identity is at stake is always expanding and exfoliating. After all, how does one circumscribe the category of Asian American poetry when what has been a defining concern is ready to be abandoned? The answer to this question is uncertain at present. Indeed, the task of much of this new poetry is to search for provocative answers. Whatever these answers might entail, the best of them will hopefully formulate futurity in relationship to the past and not count history, however complicated it might be, as a casualty of innovation.

Notes

1. Hayden White, *The Content of the Form: Narrative Discourse and Historical Representation* (Baltimore, Md.: Johns Hopkins University Press, 1987), p. 10.

2. Susan Koshy, "The Fiction of Asian American Literature," *Yale Journal of Criticism* 9 (1996), p. 342.

3. See Juliana Chang (ed.), *Quiet Fire: A Historical Anthology of Asian American Poetry, 1892–1970* (New York: Asian American Writers' Workshop, 1996).

4. Ezra Pound, *The Cantos of Ezra Pound* (New York: New Directions, 1970), p. 515.

5. Ezra Pound, *Guide to Kulchur* (New York: New Directions, 1970), pp. 309–10.

6. Sadakichi Hartmann, "Tanka I," in Chang (ed.), *Quiet Fire*, p. 7.

7. See Yoshinobu Hakutani, "Ezra Pound, Yone Noguchi, and Imagism," *Modern Philology* 90:1 (1992), pp. 46–69, and Edward Marx, "A Slightly Open Door: Yone Noguchi and the Invention of English Haiku," *Genre* 3 (2006), pp. 107–26.

8. Yone Noguchi, *Selected Poems* (Boston: Four Seas, 1921), p. 21.

9. Noguchi, *Selected Poems*, p. 22.

10. Frank Chin, Jeffrey Paul Chan, Lawson Fusao Inada, and Shawn Hsu Wong (eds.), *Aiiieeeee!: An Anthology of Asian American Writers* (Washington, D.C.: Howard University Press, 1974), p. xv.

11. Marx, "A Slightly Open Door," p. 121.

12. See Eric Hayot, *Chinese Dreams: Pound, Brecht, Tel quel* (Ann Arbor: University of Michigan Press, 2004), pp. 1–53, and Josephine Nock-Hee Park, *Apparitions of Asia: Modernist Form and Asian American Poetics* (New York: Oxford University Press, 2008), pp. 23–56.

13. José Garcia Villa, "A Note on 'Reversed Consonance,'" in Eileen Tabios (ed.), *The Anchored Angel: Selected Writings* (New York: Kaya, 1999), p. 31.

14. Timothy Yu, "'The Hand of a Chinese Master': José Garcia Villa and Modernist Orientalism," *MELUS* 29:1 (2004), p. 51.

15. Him Mark Lai, Genny Lim, and Judy Yung (eds.), *Island: Poetry and History of Chinese Immigrants on Angel Island, 1910–1940* (1980; Seattle: University of Washington Press, 1991).

16. See Steven Yao, *Foreign Accents: Chinese American Verse from Exclusion to Postethnicity* (New York: Oxford University Press, 2010), p. 70.

17. Colleen Lye, *America's Asia: Racial Form and American Literature, 1893–1945* (Princeton, N.J.: Princeton University Press, 2005), p. 20.

18. Floyd Cheung, "Introduction," in *Works of H.T. Tsiang* (unpublished manuscript).

19. Hsi-Tseng Tsiang, *Poems of the Chinese Revolution* (New York: Liberal Press, 1929), p. 3.

20. Tsiang, *Poems of the Chinese Revolution*, p. 8.

21. Oscar V. Campomanes, "Two Letters from America: Carlos Bulosan and the Act of Writing," *MELUS* 15:3 (1998), p. 29.
22. Carlos Bulosan, *Letter from America* (Prairie City, Ill.: Decker, 1942), p. 20.
23. See Susan Schweik, "The 'Pre-Poetics' of Internment: The Example of Toyo Suyemoto," *American Literary History* 1:1 (1989), pp. 91–92.
24. Schweik, "The 'Pre-Poetics' of Internment," p. 104.
25. King-Kok Cheung, *Articulate Silences: Hisaye Yamamoto, Maxine Hong Kingston, Joy Kogawa* (Ithaca, N.Y.: Cornell University Press, 1993), p. 72.
26. Chin et al. (eds.), *Aiiieeeee!*, p. vii.
27. See George Uba, "Versions of Identity in Post-Activist Asian American Poetry," in Shirley Geok-lin Lim and Amy Ling (eds.), *Reading the Literatures of Asian America* (Philadelphia: Temple University Press, 1992), pp. 33–48, and Timothy Yu, *Race and the Avant-Garde: Experimental and Asian American Poetry Since 1965* (Stanford, Calif.: Stanford University Press, 2009). Yu's account complicates this account by claiming the early activist poetry as avant-garde.
28. Sunn Shelley Wong, "Sizing Up Asian American Poetry," in Sau-ling Cynthia Wong and Stephen H. Sumida (eds.), *A Resource Guide to Asian American Literature* (New York: Modern Language Association, 2001), p. 291.
29. "Breaking Silence" was first published in *Amerasia Journal* 8:2 (1981), pp. 107–10.
30. Janice Mirikitani, *We, the Dangerous: New and Selected Poems* (Berkeley, CA: Celestial Arts, 1995), p. 58.
31. Mirikitani, *We, the Dangerous*, p. 59.
32. See Uba, "Versions of Identity," p. 35.
33. Garrett Hongo (ed.), *The Open Boat: Poems from Asian America* (New York: Doubleday, 1993), pp. xxxv–xxxvi.
34. David Mura, "No-No Boys: Re-X-Amining Japanese-Americans," *New England Review* 15:3 (1993), p. 157.
35. Charles Altieri, *Painterly Abstraction in Modernist American Poetry: The Contemporaneity of Modernism* (New York: Cambridge University Press, 1989), pp. 62–64.
36. Li-Young Lee, *Rose* (Rochester, N.Y.: BOA, 1986), pp. 17–19.
37. Lee, *Rose*, p. 19.
38. Lee, *Rose*, p. 18.
39. Juliana Chang, "Time, Jazz, and the Racial Subject: Lawson Inada's Jazz Poetics," in Ellen J. Goldener and Safiya Henderson-Holmes (eds.), *Racing and (E)Racing Languages: Living with the Color of Our Words* (Syracuse, N.Y.: Syracuse University Press, 2001), pp. 154.
40. Lawson Fusao Inada, *Legends from Camp* (Minneapolis: Coffee House Press, 1993), p. 169.
41. David Palumbo-Liu (ed.), *The Ethnic Canon: Histories, Institutions, and Interventions* (Minneapolis: University of Minnesota Press, 1995), p. 2.

42. See Yu, *Race and the Avant-Garde*, pp. 73–74, 98–99.

43. Marilyn Chin, *The Phoenix Gone, the Terrace Empty* (Minneapolis: Milkweed Editions, 1994), pp. 16–18.

44. Chin, *The Phoenix Gone, the Terrace Empty*, p. 18.

45. Jessica Hagedorn, *Dangerous Music* (San Francisco: Momo's Press, 1975), p. 2.

46. George Uba, "Jessica Hagedorn," in Guiyou Huang (ed.), *Asian American Poets: A Bio-Bibliographical Critical Sourcebook* (Westport, Conn.: Greenwood, 2002), pp. 104–05.

47. Theresa Hak Kyung Cha, *DICTEE* (New York: Tanam, 1982), p. 133.

48. Theresa Hak Kyung Cha, *Exilée and Temps Morts: Selected Works*, ed. Constance M. Lewallen (Berkeley: University of California Press, 2009), p. 2.

49. David Palumbo-Liu, *Asian/American: Historical Crossings of a Racial Frontier* (Stanford, Calif.: Stanford University Press, 1999), p. 3.

50. Meena Alexander, *Raw Silk* (Evanston, Ill.: TriQuarterly Books, 2004), p. 35.

Chapter 44

Psychoanalytic Poetics

REENA SASTRI

In his 1939 elegy for Sigmund Freud, W. H. Auden described the groundbreaking work of "this doctor" in everyday terms:

> He wasn't clever at all: he merely told
> the unhappy Present to recite the Past
>   like a poetry lesson till sooner
> or later it faltered at the line where
>
> long ago the accusations had begun.[1]

Bringing compassion and "enlightenment" to the accusing past, Freud's work would enable his patients to replace judgment and "excuses" with "forgive[ness]" and "change," and thus "to approach the Future as a friend."[2] This work is accomplished through language: in Adam Phillips's suggestive phrasing, "One goes to psychoanalysis, as one might go to poetry, for better words."[3] Auden's scenario implies that psychoanalysis will produce a new poem.

Poets writing in the United States after Auden developed that implication. An interest in intimate, seemingly autobiographical material, and an approach to childhood, memory, and family that made knowing use of psychoanalytic accounts of gendered identity formation, the impact of early traumas on later emotional life, and how unconscious wishes shape conscious actions, characterized the poetry of the late fifties and beyond that attracted the label "confessional." This term first appeared in M. L. Rosenthal's review of Robert Lowell's *Life Studies* (1959), often considered a watershed: in Philip Rahv's reported phrase, "the one real advance since Eliot."[4] Suggesting the Catholic ritual of confession whereby penitents are absolved of their sins, and implicitly the psychoanalytic dialogue that Freud in 1895 described by analogy (the patient "giv[es] utterance" to what has been repressed; the analyst works "as a father confessor who gives absolution [... and] sympathy"), the term "confessional," Rosenthal later said, "seemed appropriate" to describe "the way

Lowell brought his private humiliations, sufferings, and psychological problems" into poems usually "in the first person and intended without question to point to the author himself."[5] It came to be applied not only to Lowell's *Life Studies* but also to W. D. Snodgrass's *Heart's Needle* (1959), to John Berryman's *77 Dream Songs* (1964) and later volumes, and to the work of Anne Sexton and Sylvia Plath. In 1970, Marjorie Perloff argued that *Life Studies*'s real innovation was the way it transformed the "greater Romantic lyric" (M. H. Abrams's term) through metonymic, novelistic detail.[6] However, criticism has largely emphasized this poetry's subject matter – marriage and divorce, childhood trauma, and mental illness – linking it to the looser stanzaic and metrical forms and more colloquial diction adopted. The "breakthrough narrative's" account of a decisive shift in poetic careers from formally adept but emotionally restrained verse to more personal subject matter and freer – hence supposedly more psychologically authentic – forms oversimplifies; however, shifts to more personal-sounding poetry appear in the careers of not only Lowell, Berryman, and Plath but also younger contemporaries including James Merrill and Adrienne Rich.[7]

Whether or not the events recounted matched the poet's biography, poems about family life's pathologies and mental breakdown seemed to defy T. S. Eliot's influential view that the poet need not be "in any way remarkable or interesting" in "his personal emotions" and that poetry should represent an "escape from personality."[8] Eliot insisted on impersonality in order to advance aesthetically oriented criticism: he wanted critics to attend not to the poet's biography or his emotions but to the "new art emotion," that is, to the poem's shapes and sounds, its cognitive and affective valences.[9] Although it does not strictly follow, his position was taken to imply that poetry that sounded personal lacked aesthetic value.

Poets were at times guilty of promoting the same misleading opposition, as when Lowell called the style of *Life Studies* a "breakthrough back into life."[10] More consistently, however, they insisted that their poetry's directness, intimacy, and authenticity were aesthetic effects: Lowell wanted his poems to have the feel of historical truth, to "make the reader believe he was getting the real Robert Lowell," even though he had "tinker[ed] with fact" and "invented" much.[11] Anne Sexton, who began writing poetry in therapy, insisted on the difference between the two processes: "I've heard psychiatrists say, 'See, you've forgiven your father. There it is in your poem.' But I haven't forgiven my father. I just wrote I did."[12] Poets protested that the term "confessional" ignored meticulous craftsmanship and knowing self-dramatization. Their resistance has been echoed by critics who argue that the term implies authorial passivity, encourages moral arrogance on the part of readers implicitly positioned as priest or doctor, and slights the poetry's complexity and artistry.[13] Above all, it encourages category errors, leading critics to mistake poetic fiction for biographical fact; to confuse aesthetic with moral judgment; and to see the poem as an unmediated cry, degrading the poet's status as maker.[14]

Alternatives proposed include "personal poetry" (Alan Williamson) and "Freudian lyric" (Helen Vendler).[15] Yet the term "confessional" remains valuable because it rightly suggests (even, or especially, when distanced by scare quotes) that the questions of poetry's relation to personality, of the status of poetic fictions as fictions, and of the peculiarly intimate scenario of reading remain open, complex, and compelling. The effects of intimacy and vulnerability created in (for example) Lowell's "Home After Three Months Away," with its parenthetical address to his baby daughter and closing diminuendo, "Cured, I am frizzled, stale, and small," or Ginsberg's *Kaddish*, with its compassionate evocation of the harrowing details of his mother Naomi's mental and physical illness, depend on particular strategies of crafting a speaking "I": colloquial diction, contemporary references, and enjambment that disguises rhyme patterns (in Lowell) or extended accumulative syntax (in Ginsberg), among others.[16] They also depend on specific ways of understanding the "I" and its relation to the reader.

Psychoanalysis helps to illuminate the kind of "I," and the kind of poem, these poets created. Its implications include diagnostic patterns for making sense of familial relationships and their impact on later life, patterns experienced as intensely private, but understood as widely shared; the concept of the unconscious, and therefore of a divided and only partially knowable self; a questioning of freedom or agency (if our desires and actions are unconsciously scripted, in what sense are they ours?); and, lastly, an emphasis on dialogue: in the talking cure, after all, "nothing takes place between" analyst and patient "except that they talk to each other."[17] These elements are apparent when Lowell recounts his childish return from college to his mother's plate of milk and Triskets; when Berryman's *Dream Songs* mix vaudeville staging, slang, baby talk, and self-consciously literary locutions to suggest how unconscious energies both breach decorum and motivate grandiose poeticizing; when Plath's daughter figures act an "old tragedy" Freud made new; or when Jarrell's speakers address themselves to others and seek affirming response.[18]

Because psychoanalysis is centrally concerned with understanding the effects of the past on the present and aims through that understanding to enable an orientation of both pleasure and agency toward the future, it implicitly offered a paradigm for the creative transformation not only of personal but also of poetic inheritance. (This need not imply Harold Bloom's repressed struggle, described in *The Anxiety of Influence*, between father-son pairs; in practice more open, and more collaborative, relations may obtain.) While New Criticism drew from Eliot's essays doctrines of impersonality and aesthetic reserve, poets including Jarrell and Berryman read Eliot's poetry against his prose. Jarrell wrote:

> Won't the future say to us in helpless astonishment: "But did you actually believe that all those things about objective correlatives, classicism, the tradition, applied to *his* poetry? Surely you must have seen that he was one of the most subjective and daemonic poets who ever lived? . . . From a psychoanalytical point of view he was far and away the most interesting poet of your century."[19]

To read Eliot as "daemonic" and psychoanalytically interesting was both an astute observation and a way of discovering within modernism elements that the next generation could develop on new terms. Both *The Waste Land*'s collage of textual fragments, musical refrains, and pub speech and *Four Quartets*'s shifts from symbolic to discursive, prosy to oracular, radically severed voice from a single speaker. The midcentury poets did not return unproblematically to a model of Wordsworthian poetic speech or the "spontaneous overflow of powerful emotion . . . recollected in tranquility"; instead, many used psychoanalytic paradigms to interrogate poetic voice in new ways, ways that placed the psychic fragmentation of the first person center stage.[20]

At its inception, psychoanalysis concerned a move "from body to speech," replacing the hysterical symptom with the patient's and analyst's verbal work: voice is as central to psychoanalysis as it is to lyric poetry.[21] Poets from midcentury on have explored psychoanalytic models of personhood, voice, and dialogue to complicate models of lyric expressivity without rejecting self and speech. After the first confessional generation, poets including Frank Bidart and Louise Glück deploy psychoanalysis's connection with myth and its orientation toward a scientific impartiality to mediate the personal and to reengage with modernist poetics. Their experiments within (rather than dismissal of) the first-person lyric challenge narratives of the poetry divides from the seventies on, an era of social atomization and, later, of politicized identities and suspicion of Enlightenment ideals, shifts that posed fundamental challenges to the genre of lyric.

★

Sylvia Plath (1932–1963) has been a test case for the term "confessional." She can occupy a polar position: as an exemplar of Al Alvarez's "extremist" poetry, of feminist voice, of authentic selfhood, or of sociological analysis of Cold War femininity and domesticity, Plath's poetic voice has seemed "scandalously" gendered and embodied.[22] Yet the impossibility of tracing voice's origin to a singular, historical, embodied self is one of her greatest themes, and the varied, uncomfortable, and unforgettable ways in which she stages the uncanniness of voice – as Gothic haunting or as theatrical scenario – are her truest legacy. A critical industry has met her expanding archive: work she published, including *The Colossus* (1960) and the novel *The Bell Jar* (1963); the poems in *Ariel* (1965) following her death, and in *Crossing the Water* (1971) and *Collected Poems* (1981), which won a posthumous Pulitzer; stories, collected in *Johnny Panic and the Bible of Dreams* (2001); *Letters Home* (1975); and selections from her journals. Necessary attention to the issues of ownership and control raised by the troubled archival history should not overshadow the arresting urgency with which the poems interrogate poetic voice, an interrogation central both to confessional poetry and (differently) to later experimental poetics.

Plath's suicide at the age of thirty has impacted her work's reception, beginning with *Ariel*, a version of the manuscript she had been preparing, edited by her estranged husband, poet Ted Hughes. Plath had attended Robert Lowell's poetry workshop at Boston University (alongside Anne Sexton), and Lowell wrote an influential foreword to the 1965 edition of *Ariel*, emphasizing "control": "Everything in these poems is personal, confessional, felt, but the manner of feeling is controlled hallucination.... What is most heroic in her ... is not her force, but the desperate practicality of her control."[23] But in Lowell's account, control of poetic effects involves forfeiting control over a suicidal drive; the poetry's daring is inseparable from risks to mental health: "These poems are playing Russian roulette with six cartridges in the cylinder."[24] Although Lowell is a sensitive reader of Plath's poems, his account nonetheless implies that the inevitable outcome of *Ariel*'s poetic achievement was its author's death.

While much criticism has pivoted both consciously and unwittingly on agency, Plath's work itself thematizes agency and control, often in explicitly psychoanalytic terms.[25] Father-daughter relations follow Freudian patterns in "Electra on Azalea Path," "The Colossus," and "Daddy." Accepting these patterns is no different, Plath sometimes suggests, than calling one's birth "ill-starred," or believing that "fixed stars / Govern a life" (*SPC*, pp. 118, 270). That conviction, at the close of "Words," one of Plath's last poems, concluded *Ariel* as edited by Hughes. But the 1965 *Ariel* tells a different story than Plath's manuscript (published in 2004 as *Ariel: The Restored Edition*). The manuscript concluded with an image of hibernation leading to rebirth and renewal; according to Frieda Hughes, the volume was to have opened with the word "Love" and closed with the word "spring."[26] In addition to removing several poems Plath had included, Ted Hughes added eleven poems written later. The trajectory toward death seems fixed by these poems, particularly "Words" and "Edge," which describes a "woman ... perfected" in death: "The illusion of a Greek necessity // Flows in the scrolls of her toga" (*SPC*, p. 272).

What has drawn Plath's most subtle inheritors repeatedly back to her work, however, is not its teleological trajectory toward death or rebirth but its varied, complex, and poetically daring evocations of the otherness of self and of poetic voice. This otherness – fundamentally psychoanalytic – appears in socially, historically scripted performances, particularly of gender – "A living doll ... It can sew, it can cook ... Will you marry it, marry it, marry it" (*SPC*, pp. 221–22) – and in Plath's arresting evocations of physical, psychic, and linguistic boundaries. Cuts, wounds, bruises, blood, and skin abound. Bodies are distressingly vulnerable, from the "museum-cased lady" with gnawed ankle bone in "All the Dead Dears" to the willing patient in "Face Lift" – "Skin ... peels away easy as paper"; the victim of "Cut," her thumb "a hinge // Of skin" bleeding "red plush"; and the wife in "The Jailer," "drugged and raped, ... Hung, starved, burned, hooked" (*SPC*, pp. 70, 156, 235, 227). Bodies turn to stone or to works of art, while bodily processes infect the inanimate realm; both scenarios unsettlingly sever animation and agency from human selfhood. In the early "Poem for a Birthday," images of physical and psychic permeability, eating and being eaten (*SPC*, p. 131), and digestion and dissolution suggest the pre-Oedipal emergence of selfhood as described by theorists including Melanie Klein and Julia Kristeva.[27]

Mouths recur throughout Plath's poetry, mediating between the realm of bodies, blood, and wounds and the potentially more ethereal realm of voice. In "The Moon and the Yew Tree," the moon's face wears an "O-gape of complete despair"; in "Poppies in October," the flowers are "late mouths" that "cry open," prompting the speaker's own cry, "O my God, what am I"; in "Poppies in July," they are "wrinkly and clear red, like the skin of a mouth. // A mouth just bloodied"; in "Tulips," they "are opening like the mouth of some great African cat" (*SPC*, pp. 173, 240, 203, 162). Most notoriously, in "Daddy," the mouth is where the body, the psyche, language, and history tangle in an impossible "snare." The speaker addresses her father, imagined as a Nazi speaking "the German tongue":

> I never could talk to you.
> The tongue stuck in my jaw.

It stuck in a barb wire snare.
Ich, ich, ich, ich,
I could hardly speak.
I thought every German was you.
And the language obscene

An engine, an engine
Chuffing me off like a Jew.   (*SPC*, p. 223)

The stuttering repetition of the pronoun "I" in a foreign language, one fraught (in the context the poem evokes) with murderous implications, starkly confronts the linguistic, interpersonal, and political bases of subjectivity. While Plath's reference to the Holocaust in this poem has seemed to many a distasteful appropriation of historical trauma for the expression of a much lesser, personal, private suffering, for others, it powerfully evokes the inextricability of the psychoanalytic and political-historical spheres.[28]

Here and elsewhere words can have the agency, the animation, usually attributed to selves.[29] Language cuts across and into selfhood. In "Daddy," the relation of "I" to "you" is violently mediated by a physicalized and estranging language. Yet the barb wire snare is not Plath's only paradigm for the production of speech. In "Morning Song," language – both the infant's "handful of notes," the "clear vowels" that "rise like balloons," and, implicitly, the mother's speech, including the poem itself, addressed to the child – crosses the space that separates the pair after birth, forging a new relation (*SPC*, p. 157).[30]

The sequence of poems about beekeeping that closes Plath's *Ariel* manuscript links poetic creation with organic production and reproduction. The box containing the bees suggests a coffin or the unconscious. A struggle for power ensues: "I ordered this, this clean wood box"; "The box is locked, it is dangerous / I have to live with it overnight"; "They can be sent back ... I am the owner"; "I am in control"; "it is they who own me" (*SPC*, pp. 212–18). The hive is a smooth-running factory, a "honey-machine, / [that] will work without thinking" but also "a box of maniacs" speaking "unintelligible syllables" (*SPC*, pp. 213–15). Plath's images link poetic production with pregnancy and maternity, evoking both in terms, on the one hand, of Gothic scenarios of invasion and "Possession" and, on the other, of redemptive narratives of organic renewal (*SPC*, p. 218).[31] Plath does not simply undermine the long-standing metaphor of literary production as the creation of children; she extends it to suggest how both types of creation depend on a generative strangeness of body and mind.

In "Elm," a speaking tree meditates on voice as an otherness within the self that escapes to prey on a world of others:

> I am inhabited by a cry.
> Nightly it flaps out
> Looking, with its hooks, for something to love.
>
> I am terrified by this dark thing
> That sleeps in me;
> All day I feel its soft, feather turnings, its malignity.
>
> (*SPC*, p. 193)

The tree addresses the reader: "Is it the sea you hear in me ... Or the voice of nothing, that was your madness?" (*SPC*, p. 193). To hear this question is to have our own sanity called into question: we as readers, as much as the tree, are invaded by a voice.

Such performative effects are among the most difficult elements of Plath's poetry to describe. Plath's gloss on "Daddy" in a script for a BBC broadcast, written in 1962, obliquely addresses this performativity via the notion of "acting out": the poem is "spoken by a girl with an Electra complex" whose father was "a Nazi" and mother "part Jewish. In the daughter the two strains marry and paralyze each other – she has to act out the awful little allegory once over before she is free of it."[32] In psychoanalytic terms, "acting out" describes a compulsive repetition of psychic patterns: the patient "does not remember ... what he has forgotten and repressed, but *acts* it out."[33] In "Daddy," analysis takes place only (implicitly) outside the poem, which itself stages an unresolved acting out.

In "Lady Lazarus," the speaker stages herself; this text does not represent repetition compulsion but enacts the performativity of the first-person poem (*SPC*, pp. 244–47). Awareness of audience is this poem's most striking feature, yet critics have frequently insisted that Plath did not intend its unsettling effects.[34] "Lady Lazarus" is essentially not a narrative (the story of two suicide attempts takes up only a small fraction of the poem) but rather "a theatrical // Comeback in broad day," a conjuring trick that hides in plain sight. Commands, vocatives, invitations, warnings, deictic terms, and gestural phrases emphasize performativity:

> Gentlemen, ladies
>
> These are my hands
> My knees....
> Beware
> Beware. (*SPC*, pp. 245–46)

The poem's "miracle" is precisely the audience's belief that someone is speaking. The speaker warns,

> There is a charge
>
> For the eyeing of my scars ...
> a very large charge
> For a word or a touch
> Or a bit of blood
>
> Or a piece of my hair or my clothes.   (*SPC*, p. 246)

For critics who take this self-display as Plath's own and castigate it as morbid and tasteless, the charge is high: their moral and aesthetic condemnation forfeits recognition of art's fictionality. For the reader who can at once believe in this speaker and recognize that she is an illusion, however, the charge is instead a frisson, a pleasurable astonishment in the ability of the trick to work.

*

Since Plath's death, American culture has privileged personal testimony and contrition, suggesting that we continue to view the self as something to disclose, and the therapeutic language of healing and closure has been widely, and sometimes inappropriately, applied.[35] Psychoanalysis proper, by contrast, has become a much more specialized interest. Movements for racial and gender equality have claimed political voice for groups previously excluded; simultaneously, intellectual trends have radically undermined Enlightenment ideals of sovereign selfhood and – particularly after 1968 – political agency. These cultural trends underlie the dominant divide in American poetry since the seventies, between late Romantic sincere lyric – the mode of "scenically grounded personal emotions" and minor epiphany – and a poststructuralist- and Marxist-inflected experimentalism – in particular that of the Language writers – that would sever poetry from expressivity, and whose practitioners associate the sincere lyric both with a false illusion of a coherent self and with a commodification of the poem that can only be combated by radical disruptions to surface intelligibility.[36] Seen as outpourings of personal emotion, confessional poems seemed to exemplify ideals of lyric and the autonomous self that Language writing would reject. Yet as Plath's work demonstrates, this was far from the case.

The following generation has drawn variously on the confessional legacy. Sharon Olds (b. 1942) vividly renders embodiment, sexuality, and maternity, in poems like "The Moment the Two Worlds Meet"; criticism of her work as merely candid repeats the simplifying gesture applied to earlier poets.[37] Robert

Hass (b. 1941) invokes Lacanian theory in poems like "Meditation at Lagunitas," "Picking Blackberries with a Friend Who Has Been Reading Jacques Lacan," and "My Mother's Nipples," at best balancing reflexivity with pathos.[38] C. K. Williams (b. 1936) questions whether sexual and political selfhood, and confession itself, is merely mechanistic – "Freud, Marx, Fathers, tell me, what am I, doing this, telling this, ... but a machine ... ?" – but also memorably evokes how, psychoanalytically and poetically, learning to speak for oneself means learning to speak with others.[39]

Frank Bidart (b. 1939) and Louise Glück (b. 1943) have steadily and self-consciously drawn on, and inventively modified, both confessional and modernist poetics. Both are much acclaimed: Glück's honors include positions as U.S. poet laureate (2003–2004) and two-term judge of the Yale Series of Younger Poets. Both teach: Bidart at Wellesley, Glück at universities including Williams College, Yale, and Boston University. Bidart counted Bishop and Lowell among his close friends and worked closely with the latter on revisions of his poems; Glück studied with Stanley Kunitz and Léonie Adams. In these ways they are part of the, or a, poetic mainstream. More importantly, their writing positions itself in relation to an inheritance central to modern American poetry, opening up fresh ways to see that heritage. Inventing new ways to join the impersonal with the personal, these poets interrogate lyric voice from within, rather than in combative opposition to, a voice-based poetics.

While the Lowell-Plath-Berryman generation harnessed psychoanalysis to return the "I," and its multiple, unruly energies, to the center of the poem, Glück and Bidart, adopting the centrality of that "I," use psychoanalysis as a tool of impartial analysis; drawing out its associations with myth, they triangulate psychoanalysis with the modernism of Eliot, Yeats, Pound, and Joyce. Myth further enables access to structures of meaning larger than the individual, but not susceptible to the demand for directly topical public speech in response to historical crises. At a time when poetry's "I," when not replaced by the text's materiality, became increasingly allied with social representation and the forging of ethnically separate poetic identities, the legacy of the confessional and psychoanalysis has enabled Bidart and Glück to explore an "I" that is lyric, not sociological. For Glück, lyric tradition is inclusive: reading Shakespeare, Blake, Yeats, Keats, and Eliot, she writes, "I did not feel exiled, marginal [due to gender. I felt that this] was *my* tradition. My inheritance. My wealth."[40] Bidart's refrain "We fill existing forms and when we fill them we change them and are changed," referring to literary creativity in "Borges and I" and family dynamics in "The Second Hour of the Night," captures how psychoanalysis offers a paradigm both of the Freudian subject's struggle with his psychic, familial inheritance and of the poet's struggle with literary tradition.[41]

Bidart's discursiveness can seem unpoetic; he risks a loss of lyric intensity in order to capture the mutual imbrication of thinking and feeling. His haunted conscience understands the "relational and psychological," in Vendler's words, as "instances of the metaphysical, and even of the theological."[42] The intensity of psychic violence in his work – as when the mother hangs her child's cat in "Confessional" – is matched by the energy of "making," which carries a Yeatsian value. Yeatsian, too, is Bidart's insistence on the proximity of spiritual and physical: "First, I was there where unheard / harmonies create the harmonies / / we hear – / / then I was a dog, sniffing / your crotch" (*FBC*, p. 7).

In a recent interview, Bidart calls the desire to make "a species of the will to power" whose "enactment . . . always must confront metaphysical and epistemological limits."[43] At the stylistic level, seeking these limits creates a tense, taut surface, characterized by chiasm, paradox, and outright contradiction. Evoking "nonmastery" as they rework tropes of authenticity and vulnerability, yet harnessing the language of "thought, abstraction, discussion," his poems strive to embody, not record, articulate, passionate thought.[44] Bidart explained in 1983:

> If a poem is "the mind in action," I had to learn how to use the materials of a poem to *think*. I said to myself that my poems must seem to embody not merely "thought," but necessary thought. And *necessary* thought (rather than mere rumination, ratiocination) expresses or acknowledges what has resisted thought, what has forced or irritated it into being.[45]

Bidart's poems of "necessary thought" answer Eliot's "dissociation of sensibility" in modes quite different from the compression and wit of the metaphysical poets Eliot praises. To dramatize poetic thinking as a strenuous, self-resistant process, at once cognitive and emotional, Bidart employs an unusual and striking variety of typographical effects: frequent italics, block capitals, varied line lengths and indentations, and idiosyncratic combinations of punctuation marks. The poems' appearance conveys intense struggle and the extreme psychic states his speakers often inhabit; their prominent use of white space suggests a dynamic interplay of opposed forces, an intensified Yeatsian quarrel with oneself. This self-resisting dialogue is implicitly psychoanalytic: what resists conscious thought demands and enables the psychoanalytic dialogue, in which "each fresh resistance of the patient drives the process forward"; resistance "drives the engine of change."[46]

The "silently-occurring internal dialogue / of the soul with itself" that one poem names "thought" is also a dialogue with earlier poets.[47] Bidart stages openly his confrontation with Western philosophy, religion, and art, perhaps most notably in his three long poems, each naming an "Hour of the Night." Often such confrontations arise within psychological narratives: in "The First Hour of the Night" (1990), the speaker's "'DREAM OF THE HISTORY OF PHILOSOPHY'" – in which the cast of Raphael's *School of Athens* expands to include modern figures who debate freedom and necessity, knowledge and illusion – occurs while he is visiting the son of his friend who has died, a son struggling with his material and emotional inheritance.[48] Bidart reflected in 2008 on his response to the generation that included Lowell, Ginsberg, and Plath: "They were part of a moment that, to my mind, was not Post-Modernist but Neo-Modernist, ... not a repudiation of Modernism's seriousness and ambition, but a reinvention – a continuing attempt to discover what Modernism left out."[49] In combining Yeatsian oppositional making and Eliotic innovation within tradition with contemporary idiomatic dissection of psychic wounds and familial trauma, Bidart continues this reinvention.

Distinguishing his poetics from those of his mentor and friend Robert Lowell, Bidart says that the poems of *Life Studies* seemed

> to communicate an overwhelmingly grim, helpless sense that the dragons in [Lowell's] life were simply *like that.* ... [They evoke] a world that refuses knowledge of the *causes* beneath it, without chance for change or escape. But ... *my* poems had to be about trying to figure out why the past was as it was, what patterns and powers kept me at its mercy (so I could change, and escape). (*FBC*, p. 299)

In "California Plush," from Bidart's first book, *Golden State* (1973), the speaker's father "does not want to change"; for him, "the debris of the past // is just debris ... useless, irretrievable" (*FBC*, p. 142). The speaker's own "need for the past" reflects his understanding that because "the past in maiming us, / makes us" (*FBC*, p. 141), the future depends on its creative revision. In the later "Borges and I," "Frank" had "never had a self that wished to continue in its own being, survival meant ceasing to be what its being was" (*FBC*, p. 232).

Golden State opens with Herbert White's brutally direct, casual recounting of his murder of a young girl and rape of her body. "Herbert White" is followed by "Self-Portrait, 1969," inviting comparison. The former deliberately shocks, offending decency; the third-person subject of "Self-Portrait," "Sick of being decent," nonetheless uses a respected form, the sonnet. Its closing couplet's off rhyme of "another" with "disaster" leaves the portrait's subject precariously poised emotionally, but by affirming the sonnet's devastating power, it positions its author solidly within tradition.

"Herbert White" was the first of Bidart's distinctive dramatic monologues. His most famous may be "Ellen West," from *The Book of the Body* (1977). The poem juxtaposes Ellen's voice with commentary by Ludwig Binswanger, the doctor treating her for anorexia, quoting from Binswanger's case study. But it does not contrast the rational voice of the doctor with the irrational, emotive voice of madness; Ellen takes an analytic stance toward her own dilemma. Like Yeats in "Sailing to Byzantium" – like all artists – Ellen would like to *"defeat 'Nature'"* (*FBC*, p. 112); she attempts to do this through the literal rejection of her own natural being, a starvation that expresses indignation at the body's hold over the soul. Ellen admires opera singer Maria Callas, whose dramatic weight loss seemed to reduce her to expressive voice. As Ellen recounts,

> – The gossip in Milan was that Callas
> had swallowed a tapeworm.
>
> But of course she hadn't.
>
> > The *tapeworm*
> was her *soul* ...   (*FBC*, p. 114)

The bathetic juxtaposition of digestive parasite and soul makes the point; to Ellen, the soul's dependence on the body is just this grotesque. The risk Bidart runs here compares to those Plath takes with tone, but the mimesis of impassioned thought, the reflective, analytic clarity of the suffering persona, are his own.

Ellen's reflections unfold in a series of self-contradictions:

> > Only by
> acting; choosing; rejecting; have I
> made myself –
> > > discovered who and what *Ellen* can be ...
>
> – But then again I think, *NO*. This *I* is anterior
> to name; gender; action;
> fashion;
> > MATTER ITSELF, –   (*FBC*, p. 118)

The semantic, spatial, and aural relentlessness of the series that ends here, which includes "know," "not," "no," "No," "not," "NOT," "No," "*know*," "I," "myself," "*Ellen*," "*NO*," and "*I*," conveys the agon and entanglements, the nots and knots, of self-knowledge.

In "Ellen West," Bidart approaches the tropes of nonmastery and vulnerability via Callas's operatic artistry; in "Confessional," from *The Sacrifice* (1983), he confronts his inheritance of the poetry thus labeled. In his "Afterword: On 'Confessional' Poetry" in Lowell's *Collected Poems* (2003), Bidart distances the poetry he admires (and implicitly his own) from this term, which "implies helpless outpouring, secrets whispered with an artlessness that is their badge of authenticity, the uncontrolled admission of guilt that attempts to wash away guilt. Or worse: confession of others' guilt; litanies of victimization." However, Bidart goes on, "there is an honorific meaning to the word *confession*, at least as old as Augustine's *Confessions*: the most earnest, serious recital of the events of one's life crucial in the making of the soul."[50] "Confessional" distinguishes its poetic project from any simple echo of "the Saturday confession box or the rituals of talk therapy"; yet it engages in complex ways with both religious and psychoanalytic paradigms, in part through its dialogue form, in which the speaker's narration alternates with questions, indented and printed in italics, from a real or imagined interlocutor.[51] The speaker calls this interlocutor "Confessor / incapable of granting 'rest' or 'absolution,'" yet nonetheless demands, "LISTEN" (*FBC*, p. 58). The interlocutor neither judges nor forgives. Instead, by probing at what has resisted thought – "*Did you forgive her?*"; "*Why are you so angry?*"; "*How do you explain it?*" – he offers the speaker a space for the making of the soul and of the poem (*FBC*, p. 58).

"Confessional" cannot be reduced to the two statements that close its two parts: "*Forgiveness doesn't exist*"; "*Man needs a metaphysics; he cannot have one*" (*FBC*, pp. 57, 74). It enacts a struggle to build a structure that "contains" – both includes and limits – their harsh truths. This structure also contains an ideal of forgiveness and redemption that the speaker finds emotionally compelling, if not ultimately credible: an ideal located in Augustine's account, in Book IX of the *Confessions*, of his reconciliation with his mother, Monica, on his conversion to Christianity. Bidart situates his retelling of a foundational Western text within a psychological narrative in which the speaker and his mother implicitly encounter idealized versions of themselves in Augustine's book; the layering of "confessional" texts and paradigms destabilizes a sense that the personal narrative is the poem's origin.

Forgiveness is resisted in part because

> "forgiveness" seems to say: –
> *Everything is forgotten, obliterated,* –
> > *the past*
> *is as nothing, erased …*   (*FBC*, p. 65)

The poem itself creates a transformative space in which the past is not erased but refigured. The speaker despairs that "THERE WAS NO PLACE IN NATURE WE COULD MEET," but the poem creates a Yeatsian space "out of nature" (*FBC*, p. 58). A Keatsian "MAKING OF [A] SOUL" and a Yeatsian aesthetic "ENTERPRISE," the poem is both a rewriting and an original making, both an investigation of forgiveness – with that word's associations with debt, claim, and what is owed – and itself a giving, a free and gratuitous bestowal (*FBC*, p. 63). After his retelling of Augustine, the speaker steps back:

> In words like these, but not
> exactly these, (Augustine then says,)
>
> they talked together that day –
>
> (just as the words I have given you are
> not, of course, exactly Augustine's).   (*FBC*, p. 72)

The poem's givens – the mother's violence and breakdown, the son's feelings of guilt and complicity, and the ideal in Augustine – have been transformed into "the words I have given you." The poem's words have made of the past something given *by* the poet.

*

Like Bidart's, Glück's prose establishes the modernist elements of her poetics. Her introduction to *Best American Poetry* (1993) echoes surprisingly closely Eliot's advocacy of impersonality: "Poems *are* autobiography," she concedes, "but divested," not only of "chronology" and "anecdote" but also of "personal conviction": in the work the poet "strives to be free of the imprisoning self" (*PT*, p. 92). Her polemically titled "Against Sincerity" would distinguish art's "truth" from "honesty or sincerity": these "refer back to the already known," achieving only "relief and not ... discovery" (*PT*, pp. 33, 35). Art requires openness to the unknown, a "scientist's absence of bias" – poems are "like experiments" – or Keats's negative capability; "the only illuminations are like Psyche's, who did not know what she'd find" (*PT*, p. 45). Psyche is a telling figure for the artist. While admiring poets like Plath and Berryman whose "poems seemed blazingly personal," Glück stresses that their "materials are subjective, but the methods are not" (*PT*, pp. 35, 45). Psychoanalysis, for Glück, is such a method: a technique of insight and of analysis and distance, of illuminating discovery but also of humorous or deflating perspectives on the self. She writes of the seven years she spent in psychoanalysis – a response to her struggle with anorexia in adolescence – as her "education": "Analysis taught me to think ... to use my tendencies to object to articulated ideas on my own ideas ... to examine my own speech for its evasions and excisions ... to use native detachment to make contact with myself" (*PT*, p. 12).

Drawing from myth, psychoanalysis can point not only toward the personal but equally away, toward what Glück has called "myth's helpless encounter with the elemental" (*PT*, p. 95). While Bidart does as much through exposition and inventive forms, Glück combines lyric intensity with plainness of diction and minimalist brevity with a mining of the possibilities of syntax. Overtly psychoanalytic in its concern with family and childhood and its preoccupation with gender as a fall, a division felt as loss, Glück's work is no less psychoanalytic in its orientation toward interlocution, address, and performance. For her, this preoccupation is also a tie with modernism: her commentary on Eliot (which draws on Berryman) emphasizes Eliot's poetry's urgent desire for a listener and implicitly reminds us that Eliot's later prose advocates poetry's tie to conversation and everyday language (*PT*, p. 21). Glück rewrites *The Waste Land* twice, in *The Wild Iris* (1992) and *Averno* (2006), both concerned with earthly barrenness and fertility and with the origins of poetic voice. Her combined modernist and confessional inheritance has to do with both the strangeness of lyric voice and the ordinariness of poetic language, with both the urgent necessity for communication and the precedence of the communicative situation over any commitment to the coherence of the selves who might be communicating. Her eleven volumes pursue an ambitious lyric project that is also a questioning of lyric.

Published in 1968 – not long after *Ariel* and *77 Dream Songs* – Glück's debut volume, *Firstborn*, is strongly inflected with disgust, often Plathian in its assault on the reader. (Her deeper Plathian inheritance will emerge later.) Subsequent volumes, beginning with *The House on Marshland* (1975), establish Glück's signature tone of "spiritual prophecy."[52] Greek myth, biblical stories, and fairy tales (as in "Gretel in Darkness") share space with poems of private experience, embodied and gendered. Anticipating later strategies of combining the domestic, the psychoanalytic, and the mythic, "Lamentations" retells the biblical fall, the birth of a child yielding a recognition of God's irrelevance – "they were the mother and father, / there was no authority above them" – but also imagines God's "lea[p] into heaven": "How beautiful it must have been, / the earth, that first time / seen from the air," the psychological perspective not wholly displacing the transcendent.[53]

In Glück's earlier poems, psychoanalytic insights often appear as tragic: "Eros," from *Descending Figure* (1980), evokes an orthodox Freudian paradigm that distances the girl child from her own desire, requiring her to transfer her love from mother to father.[54] Published in *Threepenny Review* and not collected, "Psychiatrist's Sestina" (1984) aligns the sestina's work with that of psychoanalysis, questioning whether the form's reiteration of six end words represents "paralysis," or whether their rearrangement points, on the contrary, to growth and change.[55] While Bishop's "Sestina," with its "child," "grandmother," and unexplained "tears," kept the psychoanalytic notions of trauma and mourning implicit in the form, Glück's end words "death," "live," "pleasure," "time," "dream," and "patient" point directly to Freud.

In later poems, needed distance from the past emerges via humor. In *Meadowlands* (1997) the amused detachment of an adolescent son provides a freeing perspective on the dissolution of his parents' marriage. In "Telemachus's Detachment," the now-adult son remembers how he once thought his "parents' lives ... heartbreaking"; "Now I think / heartbreaking, but also / insane. Also / very funny."[56] Syntax, the grammatical rearrangement of a few words, suggests how Telemachus rearranges the elements of his childhood. His new perspective relies equally on the healing power of time and the comic power of timing.

The first of Glück's volumes to consist, as her subsequent volumes would regularly do, of a single poetic sequence, *Ararat* (1990) opens with a psychoanalytic, and a confessional, donnée: "Long ago, I was wounded."[57] Glück's speaker – a woman who, in the wake of her father's recent death, diagnoses her own and her family's dysfunctions – seems to anticipate psychoanalytic readings of this wound as Freud's castration, Lacan's gap between coherent self-representation and an inchoate self that constitutes a formative self-alienation, or birth as the original wound. Her confident self-diagnoses present one version of a psychoanalytic perspective. But the volume's poetics both incorporate and interrogate that perspective. "In Confession," Freud wrote, "the sinner tells what he knows; in analysis the neurotic has to tell more."[58] The speaker of *Ararat* tells more, paradoxically, mainly through insisting on what she knows; "I know" is her stylistic signature. Certain about the past's continuity with the present, she is determined to protect herself from future fulfillment, because "all happiness / attracts the Fates' anger" (*LGA*, p. 25). For a speaker who has forsworn happiness, who believes "you never heal" (*LGA*, p. 55), what good is psychoanalytic understanding?

"The Untrustworthy Speaker" illuminates the volume's complex relation to its speaker's knowingness:

> Don't listen to me; my heart's been broken.
> I don't see anything objectively.

> I know myself; I've learned to hear like a psychiatrist.
> When I speak passionately,
> that's when I'm least to be trusted. (*LGA*, p. 34)

While insisting she is not objective, the speaker claims the knowledge and authority of the expert. Declaring, "I never see myself" and "In my own mind, I'm invisible," she nonetheless ends the poem with a confident self-diagnosis: "That's why I'm not to be trusted. / Because a wound to the heart is also a wound to the mind" (*LGA*, p. 35). Glück lets us see this central character as an "untrustworthy speaker" precisely in her certainty.

By exposing the speaker's limits, the volume suggests a perspective outside of, and more generous than, hers. As important as what the speaker tells is the fact, and the style, of telling. Glück has spoken of her delight in discovering a greater tonal range in writing *Ararat*, with greater scope for "comic elements"; she found a way to "sound on the page the way I spoke."[59] There is pleasure in finding the right language, a no-nonsense, darkly funny way to talk about the past. Moreover, with its frequent address to the reader – "I'll tell you something"; "I'll tell you what I meant" – *Ararat* makes interlocutors of its readers.[60] We become the poems' "you," answering the speaker's confidence that she will be heard and understood. In *Ararat*'s speaker Glück has contributed a new psychoanalytically inflected voice, building on the examples of Berryman's manic *Dream Songs*, Lowell's chastened "Waking in the Blue," and Sexton's vulnerable "Music Swims Back to Me."[61]

Ararat's single speaker gives way to a multiplicity of voices in *The Wild Iris* (1992). Spoken by a gardener, her flowers, and something resembling a god, the poems of the Pulitzer Prize–winning volume are implicitly psychoanalytic in being structured by direct address. The volume, especially the flower poems, might be said to unfold both from the opening lines of Eliot's *Waste Land*, in which speech seems to emerge from underground, and from Plath's "Elm." Just as the elm could say, "I know the bottom," "I do not fear it: I have been there" (*SPC*, p. 192), Glück's wild iris has experienced "that which you fear, being a soul and unable to speak," and says: "I tell you I could speak again: whatever / returns from oblivion returns / to find a voice."[62]

Plath's and Glück's nonhuman speakers dramatize the complex relationships between poet and poetic speaker, self and language, interiority and expression or confession, and feeling and poetry. "The Red Poppy," ruled by "Feelings" rather than "mind," addresses us, her "brothers and sisters":

> were you like me once, long ago,
> before you were human? Did you

permit yourselves
to open once, who would never
open again? Because in truth
I am speaking now
the way you do. I speak
because I am shattered.   (*WI*, p. 29)

To speak because one is "shattered" might be to utter a cry of emotional devastation. But it might equally be to recognize that to speak is to be open to, and broken open by, the conditions of speech: psychoanalytic, linguistic, social, and historical. The guileless poppy shows her heart, suggesting the quintessential Romantic and post-Romantic lyric speaker overflowing with emotion. But by asking, "What could such glory be / if not a heart?," the poem throws into doubt the idea that poetic display expresses psychological depths.

The red poppy claims kinship with human speakers; the white rose asserts difference. Protesting, "I am not like you, I have only / my body for a voice: I can't / disappear into silence," the rose speaks as a patient signaling psychic distress through bodily symptoms (*WI*, p. 47). But the rose's words equally describe a poem, a textual body that may or may not be read, but that, once printed, cannot withdraw the simulated speech that constitutes it. Across the page from "The Red Poppy," "Field Flowers" disdains confessional speakers, lyric poets, or both as infants:

I'm talking
to you, you staring through
bars of high grass shaking
your little rattle – O
the soul! the soul!   (*WI*, p. 28)

But ultimately, Glück's work lays claim both to the "shattered" speakers of psychoanalysis and to the "soul" of lyric poetry and works to show their mutual imbrication.

*

In the new century, the divide between "sincere lyric" and "experimental" poetry has been perceived to have broken down. However, articulations of the new hybridity, such as Cole Swensen's introduction to the 2009 anthology *American Hybrid*, retain experimental poetry's suspicion of the easily assimilable surface: Swensen's representative "hybrid poem" might combine "a stable first person" with disrupted temporal sequence or scrambled syntax, or traditional form with "illogicality or fragmentation"; both combinations resist intelligibility.[63]

This resistance (borne out by the anthology's selection) implies a suspicion of language's communicative character. Affirming that character, Glück and Bidart fall outside such models of lyric-language rapprochement. In contrast with a skeptical poetics emphasizing the materiality or opacity of words, their distinctive versions of plain speech suggest a commitment to language as a shared medium, a "good faith in intelligibility," in poet and critic Susan Stewart's words, by means of which "we recognize each other as speaking persons."[64] Adam Phillips writes that, for psychoanalysis – a discipline wholly reliant on words – poetry, because it makes "words [seem] self-evidently compelling," provides reassurance that "language works."[65] In Glück and Bidart, language works toward both unsparing analysis and faith in words and persons.

In the next generation, the work of Lucie Brock-Broido (b. 1956), author of *A Hunger* (1988) and *The Master Letters* (1995), while much further from everyday speech, revolves consistently around interpersonal dynamics and strategies of address. Her psychic dynamics of power and pain and contemporary stories of pathology and violence resemble Bidart's, but her playful, and elaborately embroidered, surfaces do not. Her artifice suggests less the high polish of the opera house than the mildly disturbing delight of a child with a dress-up box (that suggestion of the precocious being part of the artifice). Her anachronistic capitalizations and ampersands, flaunting sound play and lushness of diction, recall Berryman; but the import of variousness for Berryman's Henry depends on this character's continuity *as* Henry: Brock-Broido's variable, volatile "I" draws attention to its self-creation, and in particular its relation to a speech that both reveals and conceals. "Domestic Mysticism," the opening poem of her first book, describes a kingdom "peopled by Wizards, the Forlorn, / The Awkward, the Blinkers, the Spoon-Fingered, Agnostic Lispers, / Stutterers of Prayer, the Flatulent, the Closet Weepers, / The Charlatans," its speaker declaring, "I am one of those"; the list invokes the poet as conjurer, as penitent, as full of hot air.[66] "Autobiography" plays with J. S. Mill's famous definition of poetry as overheard, self-addressed, and unconscious of a listener. Here the noisy next-door neighbors are unconscious of listeners as they "make love without apology," while the poet is an eavesdropper, "alone" with the "autoerotic sounds of my American voice / Getting it all down."[67]

Emily Dickinson's drafted letters to an unknown "Master" inspire the preoccupation of *The Master Letters* with twinned distance and intimacy. Scholars have attempted to identify a biographical "Master," but, as Brock-Broido's "Preamble" suggests, Dickinson's letters may be fictions. Brock-Broido's volume relishes the dynamics (erotic and otherwise) of role-playing through language, referring to "My voice thrown, my Other littler self on my own knee ... the tongue of the Inventor wagging the tongue of the Invented."[68] Ventriloquy does not displace confessional and Freudian paradigms of hidden interiority: "each self keeps a secret self which cannot speak when spoken to."[69] Brock-Broido later writes: "I was looking to become inscrutable. / I was longing to be seen through."[70] Such paradoxical longing might characterize both a poetic speaker, lifelike yet transparently fictional, and a human speaker, both desiring and fearing to be known. This invented, inventive "I" sustains and makes new confessional poetry's interrogation of what it means to speak, in a poem and as a self.

Notes

1. W. H. Auden, *Collected Poems*, ed. Edward Mendelson (London: Faber and Faber, 1991), p. 274.
2. Auden, *Collected Poems*, p. 274.
3. Adam Phillips, *Promises, Promises: Essays on Literature and Psychoanalysis* (London: Faber and Faber, 2005), p. 5.
4. Robert Lowell, *The Letters of Robert Lowell*, ed. Saskia Hamilton (London: Faber and Faber, 2004), p. 306.
5. Sigmund Freud and Joseph Breuer, *Studies in Hysteria*, in Sigmund Freud, *The Standard Edition of the Complete Psychological Works of Sigmund Freud*, trans. and ed. A. Freud, A. Strachey, J. Strachey, and A. Tyson (London: Vintage, 2001), vol. 2, pp. 282–83; M. L. Rosenthal, *The New Poets: American and British Poetry Since World War II* (New York: Oxford University Press, 1967), p. 26.
6. Marjorie Perloff, "Realism and the Confessional Mode of Robert Lowell," *Contemporary Literature* 11:4 (1970), pp. 470–87.
7. On the "breakthrough narrative" and its failings as literary history, see James Longenbach, *Modern Poetry After Modernism* (New York: Oxford University Press, 1997).
8. T. S. Eliot, *Selected Prose*, ed. Frank Kermode (New York: Farrar, Straus and Giroux, 1975), p. 43.
9. Eliot, *Selected Prose*, p. 43.
10. Robert Lowell, *Collected Prose*, ed. Robert Giroux (New York: Farrar, Straus and Giroux, 1990), p. 244.
11. Lowell, *Collected Prose*, pp. 246–47.
12. J. D. McClatchy, *Anne Sexton: The Artist and Her Critics* (Bloomington: Indiana University Press, 1978), p. 46.
13. Thomas Travisano, *Mid-Century Quartet* (Charlottesville: University Press of Virginia, 1999), pp. 44–66.
14. Lawrence Lerner, "What Is Confessional Poetry?" *Critical Quarterly* 29:1 (1987), pp. 46–66, 59.

15. Alan Williamson, *Introspection and Contemporary Poetry* (Cambridge, Mass.: Harvard University Press, 1984); Helen Vendler, *The Given and the Made* (Cambridge, Mass.: Harvard University Press, 1995).

16. Robert Lowell, *Collected Poems*, ed. Frank Bidart and David Gewanter (New York: Farrar, Straus and Giroux, 2003), p. 186; Allen Ginsberg, *Kaddish and Other Poems* (San Francisco: City Lights, 1961), pp. 7–36.

17. Sigmund Freud, "The Question of Lay Analysis," in *The Standard Edition of the Complete Psychological Works of Sigmund Freud*, trans. and ed. A. Freud, A. Strachey, J. Strachey, and A. Tyson (London: Vintage, 2001), vol. 20, pp. 179–258, 187.

18. Lowell, *Collected Poems*, p. 181; Sylvia Plath, *Collected Poems*, ed. Ted Hughes (London: Faber and Faber, 1981), p. 117. Plath's collection will be cited in the text as *SPC*.

19. Randall Jarrell, *The Third Book of Criticism* (New York: Farrar, Straus and Giroux, 1969), pp. 314–15.

20. William Wordsworth and Samuel Taylor Coleridge, *Lyrical Ballads*, ed. R. L. Brett and A. R. Jones, 2nd ed. (London: Routledge, 1991), p. 246.

21. Jessica Benjamin, *The Shadow of the Other: Intersubjectivity and Gender in Psychoanalysis* (New York: Routledge, 1998), p. 1.

22. A. Alvarez, *The New Poetry: An Anthology*, rev. ed. (Harmondsworth: Penguin, 1968); Christina Britzolakis, "*Ariel* and Other Poems," in Jo Gill (ed.), *The Cambridge Companion to Sylvia Plath* (Cambridge: Cambridge University Press, 2006), p. 107.

23. Sylvia Plath, *Ariel* (New York: Harper and Row, 1965), p. vii.

24. Plath, *Ariel*, p. vii.

25. On Plath and agency, see especially DeSales Harrison, *The End of the Mind: The Edge of the Intelligible in Hardy, Stevens, Larkin, Plath and Glück* (New York and London: Routledge, 2005).

26. Sylvia Plath, *Ariel: The Restored Edition* (New York: HarperCollins, 2004), p. xiv.

27. Jacqueline Rose, *The Haunting of Sylvia Plath* (London: Virago, 1991), pp. 29–64.

28. Rose, *The Haunting of Sylvia Plath*; Harrison, *The End of the Mind*.

29. Steven Gould Axelrod, *Sylvia Plath: The Wound and the Cure of Words* (Baltimore, Md.: Johns Hopkins University Press, 1990), p. 9.

30. Diane Ward Middlebrook, "What Was Confessional Poetry?" in Jay Parini and Brett Millier (eds.), *The Columbia History of American Poetry* (New York: Columbia University Press, 1993), p. 645.

31. Susan Van Dyne, *Revising Life: Sylvia Plath's Ariel Poems* (Chapel Hill: University of North Carolina Press, 1994), pp. 106–15.

32. Plath, *Ariel: The Restored Edition*, p. 196.

33. Sigmund Freud, "Remembering, Repeating, and Working-Through," in *The Standard Edition of the Complete Psychological Works of Sigmund Freud*, trans. and ed. A. Freud, A. Strachey, J. Strachey, and A. Tyson (London: Vintage, 2001), vol. 12, pp. 147–56, 150.

34. Deborah Forbes, *Sincerity's Shadow: Self-Consciousness in British Romantic and Mid-Twentieth-Century American Poetry* (Cambridge, Mass.: Harvard University Press, 2004), pp. 112–14.

35. Frank Furedi, *Therapy Culture: Creating Vulnerability in an Uncertain Age* (New York: Routledge, 2003), pp. 1–2.

36. Charles Altieri, *Self and Sensibility in Contemporary American Poetry* (Cambridge: Cambridge University Press, 1984), p. 25.

37. Sharon Olds, *Strike Sparks: Selected Poems 1980–2002* (New York: Knopf, 2004), p. 52.

38. Robert Hass, *Praise* (Hopewell, N.J.: Ecco, 1979), pp. 4, 36; Robert Hass, *Sun Under Wood* (Hopewell, N.J.: Ecco, 1996), p. 12.

39. C. K. Williams, *Selected Poems* (New York: Farrar, Straus and Giroux, 1994), p. 112.

40. Louise Glück, *Proofs and Theories: Essays on Poetry* (Hopewell, N.J.: Ecco, 1994), p. 7. This collection will be cited in the text as *PT*.

41. Frank Bidart, *Desire: Collected Poems 1965–1997* (Manchester: Carcanet, 1998), p. 231. This collection will be cited in the text as *FBC*. The much shorter U.S. book, also entitled *Desire* (New York: Farrar, Straus and Giroux, 1998), is not a book of collected poems.

42. Liam Rector and Tree Swenson (eds.), *On Frank Bidart: Fastening the Voice to the Page* (Ann Arbor: University of Michigan Press, 2007), p. 139.

43. Rector and Swenson (eds.), *On Frank Bidart*, p. 91.

44. Jeffrey Gray, "'Necessary Thought': Frank Bidart and the Postconfessional," *Contemporary Literature* 34:4 (1993), pp. 714–39, 716, 718.

45. Frank Bidart, *In the Western Night: Collected Poems 1965–1990* (New York: Farrar, Straus and Giroux, 1991), p. 294.

46. Benjamin, *The Shadow of the Other*, p. 10.

47. Bidart, *In the Western Night*, p. 204.

48. Bidart, *In the Western Night*, p. 193.

49. Frank Bidart, *Watching the Spring Festival* (New York: Farrar, Straus and Giroux, 2009), p. 61.

50. Frank Bidart, "Afterword: On 'Confessional' Poetry," in Lowell, *Collected Poems*, p. 997.

51. Bidart, "Afterword," p. 997.

52. Helen Vendler, *Soul Says: On Recent Poetry* (Cambridge, Mass.: Harvard University Press, 1995), p. 16.

53. Louise Glück, *The First Four Books of Poems* (Hopewell, N.J.: Ecco, 1995), pp. 149–50.

54. Glück, *The First Four Books of Poems*, p. 132.

55. Louise Glück, "Psychiatrist's Sestina," *Threepenny Review* (Autumn 1984), p. 15.

56. Louise Glück, *Meadowlands* (Hopewell, N.J.: Ecco, 1997), p. 13.

57. Louise Glück, *Ararat* (Hopewell, N.J.: Ecco, 1990), p. 15. This collection will be cited in the text as *LGA*.

58. Freud, "The Question of Lay Analysis," p. 189.

59. Joanne Feit Diehl (ed.), *On Louise Glück: Change What You See* (Ann Arbor: University of Michigan Press, 2005), p. 184.

60. Jane Hedley, "'I'll Tell You Something': Reader-Address in Louise Glück's *Ararat* Sequence," *Literature Compass* 2 (2005), pp. 5–6.

61. John Berryman, *The Dream Songs* (New York: Farrar, Straus and Giroux, 1968); Lowell, *Collected Poems*, pp. 183–84; Anne Sexton, *The Complete Poems* (New York: Houghton Mifflin, 1981), p. 6.

62. Louise Glück, *The Wild Iris* (Hopewell, N.J.: Ecco, 1992), p. 1. This collection will be cited in the text as *WI*.

63. David St. John and Cole Swensen (eds.), *American Hybrid* (New York: Norton, 2009), p. xxi.

64. Susan Stewart, *Poetry and the Fate of the Senses* (Chicago: University of Chicago Press, 2002), p. 105.

65. Phillips, *Promises, Promises*, p. 31.

66. Lucie Brock-Broido, *A Hunger* (New York: Knopf, 1988), p. 3.

67. Brock-Broido, *A Hunger*, p. 13.

68. Lucie Brock-Broido, *The Master Letters* (New York: Knopf, 1995), p. 6.

69. Brock-Broido, *The Master Letters*, p. 6.

70. Lucie Brock-Broido, *Trouble in Mind* (New York: Knopf, 2004), p. 64.

Chapter 45

American Poetry of the 1980s: The Pressures of Reality

LISA M. STEINMAN

Oppositionally defined schools of poetry are certainly not unprecedented among twentieth-century American poets. Nonetheless, there was a distinctive rhetoric used to describe poetic practices that were defined against one another in the 1980s, a rhetoric that persisted, if in changed form, in the decades that followed. Much was made of the effects and theoretical significance of poetic style, with style defined as encompassing not only diction, syntax, and imagery but also the formal features that cause poems to be heard as accessible or opaque, coherent or fragmented, representing spokenness or rhetorical artifice. Debates about the meaning and effects of poetic style from the 1980s – and American poets of the time were self-conscious and articulate about the styles in which they wrote – suggest how the ways in which style was understood positioned readers and writers and may to some degree have masked commonalities between what seemed to be opposed poetic practices.

This chapter ultimately focuses on the work of two apparently quite different American poets who came of age as poets in the 1980s, in order to consider how poets responded to, resisted, and participated in exchanges about the significance of style as those assumptions unfolded and changed between 1980 and 1990. Throughout, this study hopes to consider the ways in which larger cultural dialogues informed and were affected by poetic theories and practices. I want to start, however, by sketching in broad strokes the two primary poetic styles – often called "mainstream" and "experimental" – that were invoked and defended in the 1980s.

Many poets by 1980 wrote so-called mainstream or lyric poetry; that is, they wrote personal lyrics or – to use Charles Altieri's term – "scenic lyrics," in which the situation and feelings of a sensitive, often first-person, speaker were dramatized.[1] The language was usually characterized as accessible, although

This chapter was written with the support of the National Endowment for the Humanities.

those who defined themselves in opposition to the mainstream often argued that the poets who wrote such lyrics had exclusive access to elitist institutions (such as publishing firms, universities, or journals) that distributed and authorized their work. Those who wrote lyric poetry, however, defended their practices in other terms. In 1982, the University of Michigan Press, itself one of those authorizing institutions, published a volume called *Claims for Poetry* edited by Donald Hall that included and circulated such defenses. Although first written in 1966, Richard Wilbur's "Poetry and Happiness," included in Hall's collection, crisply encapsulates assumptions informing what was celebrated or deplored as mainstream poetry through at least the 1980s. Wilbur remarks on poetry's origin in the need for "deliberate human meaning" and sees in poetry "a longing to possess the whole world, and ... to feel it," "to produce models of inclusive reaction," and, at the same time, to offer a "discovery and projection of the self," linking all of these impulses centrally to description, and further linking descriptive power to a quest for "conversancy or congruence between self and world."[2] In short, for Wilbur, feeling, meaning, and self-knowledge – in particular, the relationship between selves and the physical or social world – are all central. Finally, for Wilbur, poetry both arises from and nourishes in its readers "a vital sense of community" and a "model of felt experience" (*CFP*, pp. 484, 486). Wilbur typically wrote formally careful, often rhyming, poems in a style usually associated with the 1950s. Still, between the mid-1960s and the late 1980s, his poetics would hardly have surprised readers attuned to expressive theories of poetry in confessional verse, American versions of Surrealism, or so-called Deep Image poetry, represented along with Wilbur's ideas about poetry in *Claims for Poetry*'s essays by writers such as Sandra Gilbert, Richard Hugo, and Charles Simic.

I will return to say more about such theories of the lyric and about one of Wilbur's poems, but first let me characterize the other prominent poetic camp at the time, innovative or experimental or avant-garde poetry, which was characterized less by what the poetry was about – indeed, "aboutness" was used as a negative term – than by the use and valorization of innovative forms, fractured syntax, and mixed tones and dictions, without an obvious speaking self of any sort. Experimental poetry was often also called elitist by opponents, being seen as difficult, overly intellectual or theory driven, and inaccessible to common readers. Again, defenses of experimental poetry, and in particular of what is now called Language (then called L=A=N=G=U=A=G=E) poetry, had more nuanced theories of the purposes served by such stylistic experiments. Charles Bernstein, along with Ron Silliman and others, practiced, theorized, and promoted Language poetry in journals such as *L=A=N=G=U=A=G=E*, published from 1978 to 1981, and in *The L=A=N=G=U=A=G=E Book* (1984), edited by Bruce Andrews and Charles Bernstein, as well as in the anthology *In the American Tree* (1986), edited by Ron Silliman. Coterie presses such as Segue Distributing, Sun & Moon Press, and Chax Press promoted and grew out of the sense of a movement or common project generated by L=A=N=G=U=A=G=E poetry; the movement was also linked to other small communities that had earlier gathered around journals featuring experimental poetry, journals like the 1971 *This* or the 1964 *Joglars*.[3] Although these groups reasonably positioned themselves as marginal, not mainstream, most professional poets with trade or university press publishers were well aware of Language poetry, as is evident from the fact that an abbreviated version of Ron Silliman's seminal 1979 piece, "The New Sentence," was included in Hall's widely circulated and more mainstream collection by 1982.

Despite the poetic genealogy traced in his essay, which invokes the writings of William Carlos Williams and Gertrude Stein among others, Silliman's work and theories did sound new. At first blush, "The New Sentence" seems simply to dismiss poetics like Wilbur's, questioning the idea of selves, of reference, and of ordinary procedures for constructing human meaning, arguing for the "limiting of syllogistic movement [and for writing that] keeps the reader's attention at or very close to the level of language, that is, most often at the sentence level or below"; Silliman thus promotes the ways in which Language poetry resists – even as it calls attention to – more typical or less self-conscious forms of reading (*CFP*, p. 397). Yet Silliman also insists on the ways Language poetry can "suggest the internal [i.e., syntactical] presence of once exteriorized poetic forms" and "incorporate [while defamiliarizing; Silliman might add "rematerializing by recontextualizing"] ordinary sentences of the material world" (*CFP*, pp. 394, 396). In other words, Language poetry is said to affect the material world with its refashioning of how language is used. There are also implicit truth claims made about Language poetry's representational power, however stylistically unconventional; of Gertrude Stein's "Custard," for example, Silliman writes: "The portrait of custard is marvelously accurate" (*CFP*, p. 391). This is in part a joke, because custard is a perfect emblem of instability, in line with Silliman's skepticism about language as stable or referential, and it is in part an act of defamiliarization, because the literary style of Stein's portraits is not what most readers would think of as representational; Stein's portrait begins: "Custard is this. It has aches, aches when. Not to be. Not to be narrowly" (*CFP*, p. 390). Yet Silliman nonetheless claims that "accuracy" characterizes Stein's portrait. Finally, too, Silliman's essay focuses on "the collective work and interinfluence" of his poetic community's endeavor, which, he thus implies, connects writers with one another, while the community's "new sentences" are meant to refashion readers' awareness not so much of the languages of the everyday world but of how the act of reading normally moves from language (or away from language) to integrative meaning (*CFP*, p. 398).

As detailed by Vernon Shetley, there were also other positions staked out in the 1980s about what poetry should do, and about how it should sound, by schools that saw themselves as opposed to both Language poetry and at least some scenic lyric.[4] For example, one could point to the so-called New Narrative poetry featured in Mark Jarman and Robert McDowell's journal *The Reaper* (published from 1981 to 1989), which resisted what was seen as the "solipsistic meditation" of free verse scenic lyrics and which promoted images used in service of what Jarman at the time thought of as more accessible or populist poetry, poetry that could memorably tell stories, paying more attention to plot and character than to the poets' states of mind or to figurative language that called attention to itself as such.[5]

The exchanges between proponents of these different schools tended to be acrimonious. Still, looking at the ways in which Jarman, Wilbur, and Silliman locate poetic power actually underlines how all claim not only that poetry concerns "what is" (aiming at some form of "accuracy" or truth telling) but also that "what is" finally involves the meeting of what might be called an agent with a world (social, linguistic, or material), a meeting arrived at – or described – in terms of feeling or seeing, even if Silliman most often emphasizes sight as seeing through the usual ways in which language represents or constructs inner and outer realities.

Despite these shared assumptions and despite the quarrels that tended to caricature opposing positions, in practice none of the poetic schools just described were monolithic, and poetry from the 1980s may not so tidily divide into two or three camps. One can nevertheless pick out poems and poets that would clearly have been seen as falling on one or the other side of the main perceived divide. In the remainder of this chapter, I want to focus on two such poets, Thylias Moss and Charles Bernstein, whose work and practice can be used to characterize the substance and the effects of debates about poetic style in the period. They would have seemed on opposite sides of the literary universe in the mid-1980s, when the various manifestos I have just characterized were issued, defending and defining opposing poetic camps from L=A=N=G=U=A=G=E poetry to various kinds of lyricism, especially where defenses of lyricism intersected with calls for previously underrepresented voices to be published, anthologized, and taught. The latter phenomenon in particular helped frame Moss's first three books, *Hosiery Seams on a Bowlegged Woman* (1983), *Pyramid of Bone* (1989), and *At Redbones* (1990), which first seem and at the time were received as postconfessional or testimonial works informed by identity politics.[6]

Moss's early poems are in some ways exemplary scenic lyrics, in that they are most easily read as dramatizing an apparently autobiographical and, in Moss's case, ethnically identified self. Moss's biography and her early statements about her poetry – like the literary circles that embraced and publicized her work – also made her appear as a representative of African American identity and poetry. Although she received numerous awards and a significant amount of praise, Moss's work was and is not as widely known or anthologized as that of some other African American women poets of her generation, perhaps at first because of her subject matter, which a few early reviews found "strident" or "full of anger [and] self-loathing."[7] As more books by Moss appeared, many critics seemed most taken aback by Moss's range of reference and allusion, as well as her use of a style that was not quite what was expected of African American poetry – not, in other words, what the rather different African American poet Harryette Mullen, writing in 1996, called "representative blackness" in "speakerly" poems.[8] From one perspective, it seems Moss was expected to write ethnically inflected scenic lyrics, and various readers found it difficult to follow what she wrote when her poems did not sound, to some, sufficiently like mainstream scenic lyrics or, to others, sufficiently African American.

Certainly many reviews of the volumes that followed her first book judged Moss's work to be either too difficult or simply unclear. For example, Mark Jarman reviewed Moss's fourth book, the 1991 *Rainbow Remnants in Rock Bottom Ghetto Sky*, voicing a mistrust of Moss's discursiveness and syntax and suggesting that the "distant connections" sought in the poems often seemed to him undisciplined "exercises in association," full of what Jarman deemed "errors."[9] It is useful to ask why or by what standard Jarman judged Moss's poetry to be flawed. He insists, for instance, that Moss's line about a Bible held by an elderly reverend (the Bible is "a dialysis, transfusion that keeps him alive") uses the comma to define what Jarman finds an unconvincing appositive.[10] Yet it might be more to the point to see Moss's lists as consistently redefining terms – similar to the same poem's lines about an onion as "a globe, a honeymoon, a cook's bible," in which we are asked not to imagine the globe as a honeymoon, but to witness a speaker refining or redefining the image.[11] Jarman reads the poems thematically – in light of his well-publicized commitment to narrative poetry and his participation in the heated polemics of the period – rather than attending to the shifting poetic focus and to what the shifts per se might signify; he thus does not hear how the images replacing one another might form neither careless writing nor Language poetry's new sentences but something closer to an image anthology, a traditional trope related to the Latin use of the nonexclusive "or" (familiar in the English tradition from, among other places, Milton's "Il Penseroso") used to call attention to the creativity, and interiorized perspective, of a speaker. Instead, for Jarman, Moss's poems seem badly written and therefore difficult to read.

As Michael Warner has noted in a somewhat different context, difficulty is not necessarily synonymous with lack of clarity, and charges of a lack of clarity beg the obvious question: "Clarity for whom?"[12] Still, Jarman's judgment was not unique; many critical assessments of Moss's work seem to rest on a sense that Moss's use of mixed registers – what she herself later and arguably in response to her critics called "multiple actualizations of self and mergers of what is believed disparate" – were either opaque or a betrayal of the African American heritage she was expected to represent.[13] My point here is not to propose a rereading of Moss's poems so much as to point out that clarity rests in part on readers' expectations, and readers' expectations are in turn informed by cultural and literary politics, as well as coming from what is on the page or what is brought to poems from past reading experiences.

Moss was born in 1954; her parents, originally from the American South, moved to Ohio, where her father worked as a recapper for Cardinal Tire Company and her mother worked as a maid. Raised in Cleveland, after graduating from high school Moss enrolled in Syracuse University for two reportedly unhappy years, from 1971 to 1973, before she withdrew from college. After working at clerical jobs, she entered and won a poetry competition sponsored by the Cleveland Public Library, after which she returned to college, to Oberlin, from which she graduated in 1981, having won an Academy of American Poets Prize. She completed her master of fine arts degree at the University of New Hampshire in 1983 just as her first book, *Hosiery Seams on a Bowlegged Woman*, was published by the Cleveland State University Poetry Center, the editors having seen and admired the poem ("Coming of Age in Sandusky") that earlier received the Cleveland Public Library's prize.

Given how and where Moss's early poetry circulated and was recognized, her work would have been read when it first appeared as scenic lyric or mainstream and at the same time as giving voice to a marginalized social identity – whence the expectation of speakerly poems. *Hosiery Seams on a Bowlegged Woman* features photographs of Moss reading her poems publicly; the pictures reinforce the invitation to read the poems as part of identity politics in that they clearly register Moss as African American and suggest the speakerly quality of her work.

Hosiery Seams does contain mostly short-lined, first-person dramatic monologues, a style influenced by the poet Ai, whose subject matter and mixed ethnic background appealed to Moss. Moss has looked back on her discovery of Ai's first book, *Cruelty*, saying: "Ai herself was me, of fragmented identity.... Ai was dark epiphany and ... for ten years my writing exclusively erected bleak monuments, recognizing authenticity nowhere but in the brutal" (*TSB*, pp. 207, 235). Indeed, the poems in *Hosiery Seams* are spoken by narrators who most often testify to traumatic lives or events. Moreover, most of the voices are identifiably African American or Native American, although in retrospect the range of voices might have suggested to readers that the poem's voices are dramatized character studies. Alvin Aubert did say of Moss's voice in *Hosiery Seams* that "it allows for the representation of diverse personae," but even Aubert's early, and positive, review takes the poetic voice less as polyvocal performance than as reaffirming the artistic worth of African American, folk, and popular cultural voices.[14]

In her next book, *Pyramid of Bone*, Moss drew on yet more disparate voices, Anglo-American as well as African American, exploring how cultural icons and languages are understood differently from different cultural positions, as in "A Reconsideration of the Blackbird," a poem in dialogue not only with popular culture (film, educational pieties, nursery rhymes) but also with Wallace Stevens (including but not limited to his "Thirteen Ways of Looking at a Blackbird"). The poem opens, "Let's call him *Jim Crow*" (*PB*, p. 10). At the same time that she argues with Stevens, however, Moss's poems display a Stevensian sense of language – in particular, his linguistic playfulness and, thematically, his turn to poetry for comforts comparable to those offered by religion. And there is also a less obviously Stevensian religious resonance increasingly present in Moss's work. Although several of the poems in the first book do draw on biblical stories, the very title of *Pyramid of Bone* echoes the image of a valley of bones in Ezekiel 37:1. Moreover, the book not only opens with a poem about treating God badly but ends with a stark refusal of obedience and a challenge: "Being in God's hand doesn't mean being in a full house"; the same poem, "Doubts During Catastrophe," includes the quotation from Ezekiel as an epigraph: "The hand of the Lord was upon me, and set me down in the midst of the valley; it was full of bones" (*PB*, p. 41).

Both this increasing focus on spirituality and Moss's continued interwoven uses of African American and Anglo-American cultural and literary predecessors can be seen throughout the volume, as in "Fisher Street," the title and first line of which place us in an urban, African American neighborhood ("I like to walk down Fisher Street"), but which also operates in a biblical register (reminding readers of the "fisher of men") (*PB*, pp. 37–38). In the poem, "song rises like vapor ... white and bleached / like all that laundry waving on the line ... struggling like all of us to be free." Moss continues, "I don't expect to see / any other angels" (*PB*, p. 38).

Anticipating what Roger Gilbert calls "a plague of angels" in poetry of the 1990s, at the same time that Moss's poem places its speaker in a neighborhood scene, it engages other voices, perhaps Stevens's "Evening Without Angels," but most explicitly "Love Calls Us to the Things of This World"(1956), by Richard Wilbur: "The morning air is all awash with angels."[15] She thus invokes even as she repudiates, or at least resituates, Wilbur's well-known trope. What we might call Moss's signifying – or dialectical doubled visions – becomes increasingly characteristic of her poetry. Some of this double voicing is reminiscent of what Charles Bernstein, albeit in the context of defending L=A=N=G=U=A=G=E poetry, also claimed for his early poetry in a 1981 interview, namely "polyentendres."[16] But Moss's early poems are at least as clearly in conversation with Wilbur's or Stevens's lyricism and with social realities – settings in which white sheets would call to mind the violent history of lynchings, not angels – as with Language poetry.

Stylistically, most of the poetry in Moss's third volume, *At Redbones*, works even more insistently with shifting subject positions and mental landscapes (and longer lines), even as a quotation from Marilyn Hacker on the back cover continues to contextualize the work as a representative poetry of witness, naming "black truths behind white lies" but still "informed with a sense of the sacred ... [making music out of] bitterness."[17] The images in *At Redbones* once again are of the sacred, frequently framed in terms of nourishment, from the opening poem, "Fullness," through images of lunch counters, provolone, baking, sugar, potatoes, biscuits, and bread. Typically, the images do double duty. The bread is consistently Eucharistic; a lunch counter menu is described by a woman involved in an antisegregation sit-in. As Moss emphasized in a later comment, "hunger" for her is both physical and spiritual: "What makes us human ... keeps us hungry. ... But since hunger demands feeding and what we want to be are gluttons, I have every faith that we will seek answers to eat." She has also described poetic sight (which in context is both physical sight and insight) as "a kind of a hunger to see as much as I can."[18] In other words, Moss marks the work of poetry as involving sight – and the process of seeing. While she also describes how she reevaluated the early influence of Ai, whose "bleakness" she says she replaced with a "sense of joy," there is nonetheless a consistency to Moss's poetic project throughout her first three books, linking poetry not only with the social project of representing multiple voices and perspectives from different cultural communities but (as insistently) with less worldly forms of desire or hunger, with both sight and insight.[19]

I have been trying to sketch how Moss's style and her individual thematic concerns developed while also attending to the contexts in which her poetry circulated. Continuing this, I want quickly to glance at *Rainbow Remnants in Rock Bottom Ghetto Sky*, which appeared in 1991, and even more quickly at the 1993 *Small Congregations*. The first was selected by Charles Simic for the National Poetry Series. Also in 1991, Moss won a Whiting Writers' Award and a Witter Bynner Prize, suggesting her growing reputation, at least in poetry circles; the winners of such competitions were advertised and prominently featured in journals such as *Poets & Writers* or *The Writer's Chronicle*, that is, in trade publications that would have been considered mainstream.

Not surprisingly, *Rainbow Remnants* was more widely reviewed than Moss's earlier books; most critics agreed that Moss's poems embodied contradictory motions and were increasingly complex, even if evaluations differed sharply, with divergent judgments identifying complexity with meaningful difficulty (Aubert distinguished Moss's "abstraction" from Language poetry's "non-referentiality"), with error or incompetence (as in Jarman's review, discussed earlier), and even with an abdication on the part of a poet whose work was expected to represent African American experience.[20] Critical expectations and the rhetorics available to describe the significance of poetic styles more generally were equally in flux. And Moss's work was not only read in light of shifting cultural and poetic frameworks but also written in part in response to both her critics and her own ear for changes in the larger poetic culture. Among other things, by 1993, the arrangement of even previously published poems in her fifth book, *Small Congregations*, seems designed to address her critics' questions about what it meant to assume multiple subject positions or voices.

In 1998 Stephen Burt was asked to introduce recent American poets to British readers and challenged "to coin a term for a school"; half tongue in cheek, he introduced the term "Elliptical poets" to characterize younger American poets, primarily those who came of age as writers in the mid-1980s.[21] On Burt's account, Elliptical poets are those centrally concerned with questions of epistemology and language, who avoid straightforward narratives or confessional lyrics, and yet who use an experimentalist style – or at least "a 'Stein tradition' of dissolve and fracture" – as a resource, rather than to bolster or embody a theoretical position.[22] When Burt's essay titled "The Elliptical Poets" appeared in *American Letters & Commentary* in 1999, it circulated widely, not so much because it announced a new school but because it seemed to many to affirm what most readers of journals featuring American poetry in the 1990s already heard, namely a shift in younger poets' practices. Moss is included among Burt's Ellipticists. And Moss herself would have been hearing the same changes as Burt.

Yet the very title of *Small Congregations* is not so Elliptical, returning as it does to the sense of small social and linguistic communities figured in the earlier books. The title also is almost an insider's joke, given that the title poem appeared first in *Rainbow Remnants* under the title "Congregations": as reprinted, it is quite literally a "small" version of "Congregations," with only half of the first section of the earlier poem retained.[23] Apparently responding to her critics, Moss refashioned many of the poems, using more regularized stanzaic forms, more conventional punctuation, and in places changing both typeface and titles in order to emphasize her shifting poetic speakers. In other words, many of the revisions in *Small Congregations* appear to respond to critical puzzlement over the voices and mixed cultural references in Moss's earlier volumes. The volume does also contain some poems with more fractured syntax – what Burt was hearing as an increasingly common practice – although these poems may suggest a turn to what theorists like Kimberly W. Benston found particular to the work of younger contemporary African American poets. As Benston puts it, we "need to see Afro-American poetry not as a static alignment of proclamations ... but rather as a performative activity that sees itself in struggle with other practices. ... More specifically, we need to investigate further the nature of 'textuality' in black poetry."[24] While not about syntax per se, Benson's reference to textuality suggests among other things that the style (including the use of vernacular imagery and idiom) typically taken to represent spoken, first-person testimony was being rethought by younger African American poets; Moss's use of nonstandard syntax, like her range of intertextual references, can thus be read at times as giving voice to African American speakers, but also as performative in its rewriting of standard modes of representing spokenness. Benston's formulation, then, offers a theory of the self-consciousness that increasingly characterized Moss's work, suggesting another shifting cultural expectation, in effect a questioning of the assumption that African American writing should be – and of how as well as whether black poetry might be marked as – speakerly.

By the late 1980s, Moss was writing prose pieces that also responded both to early reviews of her work and to what those around her were writing. She defended what others saw as flaws in her poetry, saying she was trying for, among other things, a "poetry of struggle in which [she sought] to discover meaning – perhaps by creating it," and she defined desire (including the hunger for revelation) not only as the motive for art but as that which art reveals; as Moss put it: "The products of struggle and striving are made of the grace sought" (*TSB*, p. 251). In particular, Moss explicitly aligned her associative leaps and sudden shifts of direction or diction with acts of the mind, specifically with spiritual questing. From one perspective, Moss's work moved from a poetics representative of the accessible scenic lyric to an insistence on difficulty, but for her, difficulty was associated with the spiritual and, more tacitly, with ethnic identity or, more precisely, with changing ideas about the representation of ethnic identity. Throughout, however, Moss characterizes poetry as a way to connect (and an examination of the connection between) individual selves and something larger – a social world, a smaller community within a mass cultural society, or a numinous sense of grace.

I hope this examination of Moss's poetry and poetics helps to underline some of the problems with characterizing poetry as either mainstream lyric, meaning broadly accessible, or, alternatively, experimental, meaning theory driven and difficult. Moreover, revisiting what has already been said, how Moss's work circulated further complicates the question of how to characterize her poetic project, highlighting the multiple ways her poems could be heard. As mentioned, the presses that published Moss's work and reviews of her work were prestigious or at least highly visible in poetry writing communities; she worked with known older poets from her student days through her appointment to the faculty at the University of Michigan in 1993. Moss has expressed skepticism about the cultural institutions that mark and market literary success, but her work has nonetheless gathered support and publicity from the literary and larger cultural institutions that in 1983 Charles Bernstein dubbed "official verse culture" (*CD*, pp. 246–48). At the same time, Moss's subject matter and biography identified her as growing up in a working-class, African American family, while mainstream poetry was usually seen as describing privileged white speakers, as well as addressing privileged white audiences. Moreover, some readers continued to fault her for not being as accessible as they thought a speaker for minority culture should be, meaning by "accessible" writing that was both scenic lyric and speakerly. Moss's own descriptions of her work, on the other hand, suggest that her move to more demanding and process-oriented poems was fueled by her quest for "grace," and for accuracy – specifically for accurate seeing. As she would write in 1998, "I'm nothing but language," and "I am a namer, assigning words, and therefore also value, to what is beheld; my real work is taxonomy ... acknowledging the complexity"(*TSB*, pp. 243, 246). I have been arguing that the claim to be "nothing but language" does not make Moss a Language poet. Her not-fully-articulated link between "what is beheld" and "complexity" underlines her view of how poetry negotiates the fluid boundary between selves and worlds and also reveals the difficulty of characterizing "difficulty," which is finally a matter of contemporary public rhetoric, of readers' expectations, of context and text. Yet for all the differences between Moss and Bernstein, they can seem oddly similar in some respects.

In 1983, the same year that Moss's first chapbook appeared, Bernstein – four years older than Moss – published his fifth chapbook, *Resistance*, as well as his seventh full-length book, *Islets/Irritations*. It is harder to chart the critical response to Bernstein's first volumes than to Moss's. His 1975 *Asylums* appeared from Asylums Press (a press Bernstein helped launch) in an edition so limited there appears to be no record of how many were printed; the same press issued the 1976 *Parsing*, which was set on a manual typewriter, xeroxed, and staple-bound. When reprinted in the year 2000 by Sun & Moon Press in a volume called *Republics of Reality*, *Parsing* – by then listed and often referred to as Bernstein's first book – did receive more critical notice. But by 2000 *Parsing* was, in effect, a different book, seen in hindsight after seventeen more chapbooks and full-length books by Bernstein had appeared.[25]

More to the point, not only had Language poetry been widely publicized and heatedly debated for almost two decades by 2000, but electronic exchanges between readers in places such as the Electronic Poetry Center were circulating responses to Bernstein's poetry in new ways. That is, the context in which the texts were read had shifted. As Susan Schultz has nicely detailed, Bernstein helped to orchestrate how his work was received.[26] By 1995, Bernstein noted: "One day I woke up and found myself metamorphosed into a tiny businessman.... For poetry, after all, is the ultimate small business.... I have wanted to bring poetry into the 'petty, commercial,' indeed material and social world of everyday life" (MW, p. 234). The comment insists on poetry's embeddedness in the "material and social" world, but it also half-ironically addresses the fact that Bernstein's anti-institutional writing had become something else – having formed its own institutions – by the turn of the century. Indeed, ten years earlier Bernstein had been appointed to his first named chair at SUNY, Buffalo, and had become director of the Poetics Program there, although he continued to reaffirm his interest in "experimental" poetry (MW, p. 29).

One should add that, by 2000, the contexts in which Bernstein's work was received were not all of his own making, nor all from the self-consciously formed, often personalized communities of readers and writers forming what twenty years earlier had been a newly constituted avant-garde associated with

L=A=N=G=U=A=G=E poetry. Part of why it is difficult to trace the reception of Bernstein's earliest work is that the responses that have circulated most widely tend to be later responses, often responses to reissued editions of his early work. Yet one can at least say that if Moss's first poetry prizes and publications were from better-known, more visible literary institutions even as her background and subject matter were not those of the dominant culture in America, almost the opposite was true of Bernstein.

Bernstein was born in Manhattan, of Russian Jewish immigrant background; he describes his father as a dress manufacturer who worked for and eventually became co-owner of Smartcraft Corporation, which sold imitations of designer dresses. While the family experienced financial difficulties in the early 1960s, his father recovered, going to work as the American consultant to Teijin, Ltd, Japan's largest textile manufacturer, and moving the family to Central Park West, which is to say to a fashionable neighborhood (*MW*, pp. 229–52). From there, Bernstein went on to earn an undergraduate degree from Harvard but did not attend graduate school aside from a one-year fellowship at Simon Fraser University in Canada. Moss, given her midwestern, mixed-race, nonaffluent family background, might be called upwardly mobile, while Bernstein persuasively describes how his "choice, at least initially, [was] toward downward social mobility" (*MW*, p. 234). In short, Moss's literary career was shaped by and in literary communities associated for the most part with academic institutions, and with what might be called public or even mainstream cultural entities, while the circles in which Bernstein began shaping himself as a writer were not specifically literary (he graduated from Harvard with a concentration in philosophy) and not initially associated with any long-standing literary institutions (although he did receive a fellowship from the National Endowment for the Arts as early as 1980). But Moss's family background and subject matter were hardly socially mainstream, while Bernstein's family background was more privileged; more importantly, to draw on Pierre Bourdieu's account of cutting-edge artistic practices, so was Bernstein's early avant-gardist stance.[27]

In 1995, Bernstein gave a paper called "Warning – Poetry Area: Publics under Construction," in which he looked at the academy's definition and adoption of multiculturalism, a phenomenon that framed and probably helped promote some of Moss's earlier work; Bernstein proposed that "the trend toward a representative poetry is as much market or consumer-driven, not to say demographic, in origin as it is ideological," qualifying this statement by adding that "contemporary poetry remains an indispensable site for the exploration of the multiplicities, and multiplicitousness, of identities" (*MW*, p. 305).

A focus on the fluidity of identity has been a constant in Bernstein's writings, as in Moss's, and, indeed, in Wilbur's description of what poetry offers readers. Admittedly, when Wilbur writes that poems try "to produce models of inclusive reaction," the claim is not quite Bernstein's. Wilbur, that is, proposes that poems (and poets) can respond to or include apparently unpoetic images and language; his example is having found a way to use "the words 'reinforced concrete'" in a poem (*CFP*, p. 476). Bernstein, on the other hand, talks about poems as part or even constitutive of, not references to, the material world, and he mistrusts descriptive language. Still, when Bernstein speaks in the passage just quoted of the "multiplicitousness of . . . identities," or mentions elsewhere his own engagement with "exploring and realizing alternative identity formations," we find something close to Wilbur's claim that poetry is related to self-discovery and even closer to Moss's statement that she enjoys adopting "aliases" or "multiple actualizations of self and mergers of what is believed disparate" (*MW*, p. 233; *TSB*, pp. 123, 9).

Moss's and Bernstein's poems, as well as their careers, nonetheless seem, and certainly in the 1980s seemed, at first reading to set them at odds. The first piece in Bernstein's 1976 *Parsing*, called "Sentences," in fact seems to mock poetry like Moss's, certainly as her early work was first received, although the voices and diction in "Sentences" are multiple, and the tone difficult to parse (to use Bernstein's image). Take, for example, the following passage:

> I find it very discouraging.
>
> I get no word from her.
>
> I don't like all this waiting.
>
> I feel she's not very considerate of me.
>
> I feel left out.[28]

The passage can be read as a catalogue of examples of the rhetoric of anxiety. Early reviews suggest that "Sentences" also allowed readers to imagine a narrative (of some failed relationship). It may even thereby have moved readers, although it also underlines the impoverished therapeutic vocabulary used to present or dramatize the self. As Paul Quinn – a sympathetic reader of Bernstein's work – concluded, noting the title's pun on prison sentences, such poetry may "suggest a subject, or a number of subjects, coming to awareness of their own subjection, yet unable to express this in anything other than the language that enchains them."[29]

Bernstein himself said in an early interview, "I think of some of my poems as a series of remarks, either in the aphoristic sense or in the sense of observations, constructed items, etc., occurring at the level of phrases or sentences. These can be interpreted in multiple ways: they are each, perhaps to say, polyenten-dres ... suggest[ing] the continuous choices of interpretation that confronting the world involves" (*CD*, p. 396). It is worth pausing to note three features of Bernstein's remarks (written roughly five years after "Sentences"). First, he seems to authorize almost any interpretation; indeed, he explicitly says his polyentendres might be read multiply as "true, ironic, false, didactic, satiric, fantastical, inscrutable, sad, funny, my view, someone else's view" (*CD*, p. 396). Second, he characterizes the style of his poems as particularly open to readerly interventions, which has led to criticism like that voiced by Vernon Shetley, who argues that in poems like Bernstein's there "is no meaning hiding behind any other, all are equally available," so that reading or writing such poems is "too easy."[30] Third, however, Bernstein's claims for his poetry ultimately emphasize the way his poems do not invite simple or singular interpretations but rather call attention to how acts of interpretation are always involved in "confronting the world." He seems, then, most interested in how higher-order readings of his work underline the way selves encounter worlds.

Moss's view of the work poetry does is not all that different, but Bernstein privileges higher-order readings over interpretations that might, for example, hear – or even be moved by hearing – in poems like "Sentences" the language or speech of ordinary people (the kind of speech with which Moss's early work was first associated). While Bernstein does insist that he wants multiple interpretations of his poetry, many of his poems are difficult to read without hearing them primarily as parodies that invite a reexamination of ordinary language, that is, without hearing them as poems that aim for what I have called higher-order readings. For instance, the title of Bernstein's 1989 chap-book, *The Nude Formalism*, obviously parodies and so undermines the New Formalists' calls for traditional forms.[31] Similarly, the later (2001) "Thank You for Saying Thank You" includes the lines, "This is a totally / accessible poem. / There is nothing / in this poem / that is in any / way difficult / to under-stand," which cannot easily be read except as a parody of calls for authentic voices – and thus as unmasking the accepted rhetoric of sincerity or the con-ventions of self-representation – in accessible lyric poems.[32]

At the same time, Bernstein does not deny there are representations of voices even in poems like "Sentences." In 1983, he wrote approvingly of a poetry "that takes as its task finding and inhabiting origins and voices," and as early as 1976 he noted that voice "is a possibility for poetry [just] not an essence" (*CD*, pp. 250, 45). The "voices" speaking in poems like "Sentences" are not all middle class, however. Bernstein's earlier-mentioned suspicion of calls for "representative poetry" – by which he means both poems using conventional descriptive language and poems that are seen to represent ethnic and cultural diversity (like Mullen's "representative blackness") – suggests that his project is to debunk both kinds of representation. The issues potentially attending this punning conflation of the linguistic and the political can be seen by looking at a second passage from "Sentences": "I came up the hard way. We was treated pretty rough / We come up at the hind and get what we can to live on. / We was just children."[33] The passage marks the beginning of a short piece that has the look of a prose poem, and, like much of "Sentences," it appears without narrative setting or characterization of a speaker or speakers; it is, as the title suggests, a series of sentences. The question is whether readers are authorized to take this as a parody of literary conventions or more specifically a parody of the language of poets like Moss. Apparently, they are, at least in theory. Certainly, from the early books through the more recent, Bernstein consistently uses fractured idioms to (as he said when asked about his early poetic project) debunk usual "notions of voice, self, expression, sincerity, and representation" (MW, p. 249). Yet ethical and interpretive difficulties arise when the voices Bernstein targets are like Moss's, something Bernstein's later essays acknowledge.

Even in his 1990 "State of the Art" one can see Bernstein trying to distinguish between a laudable "idealized multi-culturalism: the image of poets from different communities reading each other's work" and the "superficial" idea of diversity; he adds that he is all in favor of "radical alternatives to parochial and racist reading habits."[34] There seems to be a growing recognition in his essays that polyvocality and polyentendres are not quite the same, and that the latter might be particularly problematic when poetic style is claimed as a form of resistance (Bernstein's word), at least insofar as it is implied that resistance is possible only for those to whom meta- or higher-order readings are available. The distinction between superficial diversity and actual social difference seems to revisit just this question. My primary point is that Bernstein's early description of his polyentendres calls for an open-ended poetry (to model our interactions with the world), but he also not so open-endedly, if tacitly, privileges higher-order readings and insists on the intrinsic value of disrupting "normal" reading habits or ordinary speech, even for those whose speech or norms are not culturally mainstream.

If Moss came to seem less recognizably a poet of the personal lyric, Bernstein's poems increasingly emphasize moments reviewers have variously called "lyrical," "Romantic," or (a bit more precisely) "utopian" (as in R. D. Pohl's, Ethan Paquin's, and Paul Quinn's reviews of *Republics of Reality*).[35] As early as 1981, Bernstein spoke of "how reading and writing can partake of non-instrumental values and thus be utopian formations," which is to say (following Theodor Adorno, not to mention William Carlos Williams) that the use of poetry may be its uselessness, which Bernstein insists serves a social purpose – nothing less than the "transformation of society" (*CD*, p. 386). Such statements again suggest that poetry's function is to model the self's possible engagement with the world – described by Bernstein in terms of sight in poems such as "Artifice of Absorption," in which he speaks of how "envisionment" and offering "a vision-in-sound" involve redirecting "the gaze of consciousness" – whereby poetry might change the individual self's relationship with the actual world.[36] Bernstein more or less explicitly says that his poetry models the self's engagement with both real and possible worlds (enacting or requiring recognition of "the continuous choices of interpretation that confronting the world involves" [*CD*, p. 396]). It seems the self's or individual's connections with the world, posed in terms of sight, are as central to Bernstein's project for poetry as to Moss's. As Christopher Beach has put it: "If the individual is no longer seen as [an] active historical force . . . or as [a] 'self' in the process of relating to his or her immediate environment . . . the concept of a clearly demarcated and particularized 'individual' is still in evidence in Bernstein's writing."[37]

Moreover, it seems that affect is also central to Bernstein's poetics. Admittedly, this is not a straightforward matter. Although a sympathetic critic like Paul Quinn reads the last line of the 1981 "The Occurrence of Tune" – "desire projected & recast, to unmake the borders of logic" – as a recurring, even obsessive, figure for Bernstein of language as desire, it is not always easy to talk about the tone of such lines.[38] To take another example, in the 1984 poem "The Only Utopia Is in a Now," Bernstein addresses the question of emotion, saying that "people here who talk about emotion don't really want to experience it, they only want simulations of it in patterns of words they've already heard," and he goes on to discuss the need for a new language for "the syntax of the heart."[39] This appears to be a straightforward, even late Romantic, defense of feeling or affect, but the voice represented in this passage is clearly marked as someone else's voice, enclosed in quotation marks and said to emerge from "amidst" – and to some degree out of – "the blue," a voice we are told "almost seemed to sing." The suspicion of emotion (as opposed to a new "syntax of the heart") does sound like a defense of poetry like Bernstein's. Yet by redefining affect, he is in effect also reclaiming the centrality of feeling in poems. Not allowing readers to hear the disembodied voice in "The Only Utopia" as personal may not so much disclaim the self as gesture toward a desired utopian "oneness," described as the unity of "our communal body, [which is] language."[40] Even so, the diction (words like "amidst" and the word "voice" itself) makes it more difficult to read this as an earnest claim rather than a parody, despite the resonance with Bernstein's later, more straight-forward claims for poetry, as when in 1995 he says that poetry "sings of values not measurable as commercial sums," or when, even later, he proposes "that the thirst for knowledge can only be quenched if one learns how to remain hungry," a trope of desire very much like Moss's (*CD*, p. 240).[41]

I am not arguing that the experience of reading Bernstein's work is or was or should be similar to that of reading Moss's; among other things, Bernstein's style – his emphasis on discontinuity at the level of the sentence and his studied avoidance of dramatized speakers – distinguishes his poems from Moss's. Still, stylistic differences notwithstanding, Moss's and Bernstein's claims for poetry – that poems explore, model, or negotiate the connection between individuals and worlds; that they involve feeling; and that poetry is connected and connects readers to something that might be called the "real" – are remarkably similar.

I want to conclude by underlining two or three points. First, I am sug-gesting (to borrow a term from the anthropologists) that we need a "thick" description of literary history and that statements of poetics from apparently opposed camps reveal similar descriptions of poetry's project. In particu-lar, I have suggested that the apparently opposed poetry camps of the 1980s reveal in effect a continuing late Romantic understanding of poetry's purpose, namely that, however the self and the world are defined, poetry expands or recasts the borders between self and world, a process seen to require accuracy of seeing and feeling.

My final point may seem almost contradictory, although I do not think it is a contradiction so much as a suggestion that we may have misidentified where differences and similarities lie. I have been suggesting that the rhetoric used to define and defend poetry, like poetic practices, shifted over time in relation to larger cultural changes (including the slippery dynamics of interactions between literary and other communities and the marketing or visibility of literary communities) as well as to individual poetic projects. Specifically, in the 1980s the rhetorics used to defend different poetic styles drew on larger cul-tural debates involving identity politics or political and social representation, as well as more theoretical analyses of identity formation under late capital-ism and sometimes less theorized responses to the growth of consumer cul-ture and new media. A self-consciousness about the effects and implications of how language was used – that is, about poetic style – thus inflected Language poetry and lyric poetry written by poets from a range of socioeconomic backgrounds differently. At the same time, the debates heard in and between various poetry circles helped to sharpen writers' articulations of their poetics *and* led to what might be called cross-fertilization, so that the way poetry was being written and read did not long remain all one thing or another. Thus, one might read Moss's stylistic development as a post-Bernstein strategy, an Elliptical poet's uses of disjunction as a resource and not a theorized choice, as well as in light of redefinitions of African American literary practices. One might equally hear Bernstein's qualifications of his early and defiant difficulty as an awareness brought to light by work like Moss's of how cultural practices inform readers' and writers' ears as well as in light of what one might call the mainstreaming of the stylistic features of Language poetry. That is, we may read the styles of poems written in the 1980s as contextualized by conversations between writers as well as by the often internalized, if shifting, responses of larger reading communities. What matters is both text and context. In other words, defining poetic camps per se may not be all that easy or useful a project for critics. Camps are by definition temporary places.

Notes

1. Charles Altieri, *Self and Sensibility in Contemporary American Poetry* (Cambridge: Cambridge University Press, 1984), pp. 10–15.
2. Donald Hall (ed.), *Claims for Poetry* (Ann Arbor: University of Michigan Press, 1982), pp. 470–71, 476, 480. This collection will be cited in the text as *CFP*.
3. Charles Bernstein, *My Way: Speeches and Poems* (Chicago: University of Chicago Press, 1999), p. 250; Christopher Beach, *ABC of Influence: Ezra Pound and the Remaking of American Poetic Tradition* (Berkeley: University of California Press, 1992), p. 241. *My Way* will be cited in the text as *MW*.
4. Vernon Shetley, *After the Death of Poetry: Poet and Audience in Contemporary America* (Durham, N.C.: Duke University Press, 1993).
5. Mark Jarman and Robert McDowell, *The Reaper Essays* (Brownsville, Ore.: Story Line, 1996), p. 2.
6. Thylias Moss, *Hosiery Seams on a Bowlegged Woman* (Cleveland, Ohio: Cleveland State University Poetry Center, 1983); Thylias Moss, *Pyramid of Bone* (Charlottesville: University Press of Virginia, 1989); Thylias Moss, *At Redbones* (Cleveland, Ohio: Cleveland State University Poetry Center, 1990). *Pyramid of Bone* will be cited in the text as *PB*.
7. Review of *Pyramid of Bone* by Thylias Moss, *Publishers Weekly*, January 20, 1989, p. 143; review of *Pyramid of Bone* by Thylias Moss, *Virginia Quarterly Review* 65 (1989), p. 100.
8. Harryette Mullen, "Poetry and Identity," in Mark Wallace and Steven Marks (eds.), *Avant-Garde Poetics of the 1990s: Telling It Slant* (Tuscaloosa: University of Alabama Press, 2002), pp. 27–31, 28–29.

9. Mark Jarman, "The Curse of Discursiveness," *Hudson Review* 45 (1992), pp. 158–66, 163–65.

10. Thylias Moss, *Rainbow Remnants in Rock Bottom Ghetto Sky* (New York: Persea, 1991), p. 63; Jarman, "The Curse of Discursiveness," pp. 164–65.

11. Moss, *Rainbow Remnants in Rock Bottom Ghetto Sky*, p. 64.

12. Michael Warner, *Publics and Counterpublics* (New York: Zone, 2005), p. 138.

13. Thylias Moss, *Tale of a Sky-Blue Dress* (New York: Avon, 1998), p. 9. This collection will be cited in the text as *TSB*.

14. Alvin Aubert, review of *Hosiery Seams on a Bowlegged Woman* by Thylias Moss, *Epoch* 36 (1987), pp. 91–94, 92.

15. Roger Gilbert, "Awash with Angels: The Religious Turn in Nineties Poetry," *Contemporary Literature* 42 (2001), pp. 238–69, 238; Richard Wilbur, *The Poems of Richard Wilbur* (New York: Harcourt, Brace & World, 1963), p. 65.

16. Charles Bernstein, *Content's Dream: Essays 1975–1984* (1986; Evanston: Northwestern University Press, 2001), p. 396. This collection will be cited in the text as *CD*.

17. Moss, *At Redbones*, back cover.

18. Jorie Graham (ed.), *The Best American Poetry 1990* (New York: Collier, 1990), p. 261; Sean Thomas Dougherty, "Interview: Thylias Moss," *Onthebus* 4–5 (1992), pp. 296–301, 297.

19. Daugherty, "Interview," p. 299.

20. Alvin Aubert, "Bountiful Tension," *American Book Review* 13 (1992), p. 29.

21. Stephen Burt, "The Elliptical Poets," *American Letters & Commentary* 11 (1999), pp. 45–55, 46.

22. Burt, "The Elliptical Poets," p. 46.

23. Moss, *Rainbow Remnants in Rock Bottom Ghetto Sky*, pp. 63–67; Thylias Moss, *Small Congregations* (Hopewell, N.J.: Ecco, 1993), pp. 43–44.

24. Kimberly W. Benston, "Performing Blackness: Re/Placing Afro-American Poetry," in Houston A. Baker, Jr., and Patricia Redmond (eds.), *Afro-American Literary Study in the 1990s* (Chicago: University of Chicago Press, 1989), pp. 164–93, 182–83.

25. Charles Bernstein, *Republics of Reality: 1975–1995* (Los Angeles: Sun & Moon, 2000).

26. Susan M. Schultz, *A Poetics of Impasse in Modern and Contemporary American Poetry* (Tuscaloosa: University of Alabama Press, 2005), pp. 199–200.

27. Pierre Bourdieu, *Distinction: A Social Critique of the Judgement of Taste*, trans. Richard Nice (Cambridge, Mass.: Harvard University Press, 1984).

28. Bernstein, *Republics of Reality*, p. 17.

29. Paul Quinn, "Bernstein's Republics: The Horizon of Language" (2000), http://epc.buffalo.edu/authors/bernstein/reviews/pn-quinn.html.

30. Shetley, *After the Death of Poetry*, p. 151.

31. Charles Bernstein, *The Nude Formalism* (Los Angeles: Sun & Moon, 1989).

32. Charles Bernstein, *Girly Man* (Chicago: University of Chicago Press, 2006), p. 7.
33. Bernstein, *Republics of Reality*, p. 21.
34. Charles Bernstein, *A Poetics* (Cambridge, Mass.: Harvard University Press, 1992), p. 4.
35. Ethan Paquin, review of *Republics of Reality* by Charles Bernstein, *Boston Review* 26:2 (2001), http://epc.buffalo.edu/authors/bernstein/reviews/bostonreview.html; R. D. Pohl, "A Strong Focus on the Language," http://epc.buffalo.edu/authors/bernstein/books/republics.html; Quinn, "Bernstein's Republics."
36. Bernstein, *A Poetics*, pp. 75, 77.
37. Beach, *ABC of Influence*, p. 248.
38. Bernstein, *Republics of Reality*, p. 232; Quinn, "Bernstein's Republics."
39. Charles Bernstein, *The Sophist* (Los Angeles: Sun & Moon, 1987), pp. 35–36.
40. Bernstein, *The Sophist*, p. 36.
41. Bernstein, *Girly Man*, p. 10.

Chapter 46

Black and Blues Configurations: Contemporary African American Poetics

WALTON MUYUMBA

For much of the twentieth century, critics, scholars, writers, and readers often set American literature's parameters to exclude African American literary artists. For much of that century, African American writers produced art designed to represent and affirm black humanity as part of a larger, unscripted, multilateral effort to win citizenship and political, sociocultural, and economic equality for all black Americans. Along the way, African American writers, critics, and scholars began theorizing and defining the aesthetic practices and critical techniques used in generating black literary art. A large portion of the theorizing and defining was drawn from the body of African American expressive practices. Whether considering Zora Neale Hurston's anthropologically driven essay, "Characteristics of Negro Expression," or Hortense Spillers's dynamic deconstruction of American English's gendered grammatical structures, "Mama's Baby, Papa's Maybe," one finds African American artists and critics demonstrating how black aesthetics reinvent forms and genres while expressing America's sociopolitical realities.[1]

The tradition's wide array of poetic voices and approaches has forced poetry critics and scholars to develop various interpretive modes. Although the African American literary tradition has its impetus in earlier poets such as Phillis Wheatley, Jupiter Hammon, George Boyer Vashon, and Benjamin Banneker, not until the mid-twentieth century did critics begin reading black poets as, say, literary modernists, rather than walling them within racialized or sociological categories. Gwendolyn Brooks's and Robert Hayden's poems widened the possible formal and intellectual lanes African American poets could traverse. Space emerged for Bob Kaufman and Ted Joans, urban and urbane Surrealists; Sonia Sanchez and Haki Madhubuti, political poets and Black Arts theorists; Jay Wright, Audre Lorde, and Carl Phillips, modernist antiessentialists; and Sherley Anne Williams and Yusef Komunyakaa, blues-idiom experimentalists. During the twentieth century's second half, poets as diverse as Melvin Tolson, Etheridge Knight, June Jordan, Al Young, Ai, Toi

Derricotte, Thylias Moss, Cornelius Eady, Elizabeth Alexander, and Thomas Sayers Ellis defined an improvisational modernist poetics that emphasized African American aesthetics while redescribing America's literary history.

The story of contemporary African American poetics begins with Gwendolyn Brooks and her collection *A Street in Bronzeville*, published in 1945. Brooks's clearly envisioned poems detail African American lives on Chicago's South Side while calling attention to structural racism.[2] Brooks is the "queen of the poetic tableau"; her poems interweave black life in public with the intimate interior lives of black folks.[3] Raised in Chicago, Brooks (1917–2000) began writing poems as a middle schooler, publishing her earliest efforts in the *Chicago Defender*. Although she was a student in integrated educational environs, Brooks's literary efforts exhibited her exclusive, close attention to the specific practices of African American life. Brooks is a central figure in the story of "the Indignant Generation." Made up of black writers who were part of the massive black population shift from America's rural south to its urban north and west, known as the Great Migration (1915–1970), these artists came of age during the period between 1934 and 1960.

Brooks documented both the Great Depression and the Great Migration as they flowed on Chicago's South Side in the final years of World War II. Early on, Brooks polished her modernist aesthetic in the house magazines for the NAACP and the Urban League, the *Crisis* and *Opportunity*. Her style evolved in part from her personality – she was naturally curious and sensitive. Brooks's participation in an artist/intellectual group that included writers like Theodore Ward, Fern Gayden, Frank Marshall Davis, and Edward Bland also enhanced her poetry. Bland, a student of dialectical materialism, helped Brooks evade racially idealizing the black voices in her poems. Rather than connecting her characters according to ephemeral self-conscious race values, Brooks devoted closer attention to the way that the material experience affected her characters psychologically and emotionally.[4]

Brooks focuses on lives in kitchenettes, among the street hustlers and ruined youths, among poor mothers, and in blighted tenement buildings. In finely tuned poems like "a song in the front yard," "The Sundays of Satin Legs Smith," and "mentors," Brooks yokes her social observations to her modernist formal arrangements. In "a song in the front yard" Brooks offers the voice of a young girl who wants to explore the backyard, alleyway dangers of the "bad woman" lifestyle: "And wear the brave stockings of night-black lace / And strut down the streets with paint on my face."[5] "The Sundays of Satin Legs Smith" is a rambling ballad about a South Side playboy whose "ancestors lean against / Him. Crowd him. Fog out his identity," interrupting his hedonist foray through life. Brooks can also turn macabre, as in "mentors," a sonnet spoken by a young man whose "best allegiances are to the dead."[6]

Among Brooks's influences are Emily Dickinson, John Crowe Ransom, James Joyce, Ezra Pound, T. S. Eliot, Merrill Moore, Robert Frost, and Langston Hughes. With all these artists Brooks shares the ability to control structure tightly, present detail precisely, and highlight the pleasures of the English language.[7] Although these literary ancestors all offered Brooks models for using older forms in new ways, it's Hughes who presents a model for Brooks's desire to express black experience through the absorption of blues-idiom music and African American vernacular speech into modern lyrical forms. In fact, Brooks's sense of the blues is pervasive throughout this collection. The collection even boasts a blues poem dressed as a ballad, "Queen of the Blues," Brooks's homage to the spirits of Ma Rainey and Bessie Smith. Although Hughes's blues lyrics did not influence Brooks's poems formally, she did want *A Street in Bronzeville* to illustrate the poetics of Chicago's ordinary black working people, as Hughes had done for Harlemites, Washingtonians, and Kansans.

One of Robert Hayden's strongest early poems, "Middle Passage," was first published in the journal *Phylon* in 1945. "Middle Passage" is a poetic dramatization of the traumatic journey of African slaves across the Atlantic. The poem's formal movement and multivocal sound evokes a narrative of African victory: it tells the story of Joseph Cinque's seaborne slave revolt. Drawing on biblical narratives, looping funereal black wailing throughout, and riffing on historical evidence, Hayden formed an antiphonal exchange between the voices of the Christian slavers and the rebellious Africans. The poem's speaker shepherds readers through the narrative, pointing out significant historical details with the refrain "to flower stubbornly." Stubborn flowering was the new fate of the descendants of the stolen tribe, a new anchor for black identity. Hayden's masterpiece also marks his awareness of black artists and intellectuals' precarious cultural position at midcentury; they, too, were trying to flower stubbornly in a place without mentoring or succor.[8]

Brooks and Hayden did not receive extensive literary mentoring from established poets. Both poets believed that African American history and culture were inextinguishable artistic founts able to instruct and advance their literary works. During the 1940s, those reservoirs fed a new revolutionary African American music: bebop. Bebop is special within the context of American arts and, specifically, African American aesthetics because the black musicians who developed it presented ways of taking up various modernist traditions (visual art, dance, literary arts, and music), revising and reorienting their elements improvisationally. While Brooks and Hayden had crafted their poetics with their ears attuned to the innovations of Bessie Smith, Ma Rainey, Louis Armstrong, Nat King Cole, and Duke Ellington, the black poets coming of age in postwar America created a new poetics that corresponded with Thelonious Monk's, Dizzy Gillespie's, and Charlie Parker's inventions.

Parker, Gillespie, and Monk, along with Coleman Hawkins and Max Roach, theorized progressive musical concepts that emerged both from inherited American and European musical traditions and from the conditions of urban African American life during the 1940s. Developed in a range of locations from Kansas City dance halls to Harlem jam session parlors like Minton's Playhouse, bebop accentuated solo improvisation during group performance. Jam sessions featured house rhythm sections (piano, bass, and drums) that created improvisational space by layering generous chord sequences over angular, second-line bomb beats and pedal point or strutting bass lines.

The music's accelerated pace made the "cutting sessions" – battles that anchored the jamming by pitting soloists against each other – seem primal. Emulating its mother tongue, the blues, bebop is a matrix, adapting other styles (New Orleans syncopation, Ellingtonia, southwestern swing, rags, gospel, Broadway show tunes, popular songs, and classical music) through melodic quotation or technical integration. Although not a racially exclusive music, bebop's politically engaged avant-garde responded to the terrible realities of America's racial history by producing an aesthetic practice meant to stave off efforts by the mainstream, white-controlled music industry to co-opt and contain revolutionary black music.[9]

The most significant poets bridging New Negro / Harlem Renaissance modernist poetics and midcentury high modernism, Langston Hughes and Melvin Tolson, are also the key connectors between the high modernists and the experimental poets. Tolson is especially important because his late collections, *Libretto for the Republic of Liberia* (1953) and *Harlem Gallery* (1965), demonstrate his modernist revision of the canto and the epic poetic forms; allusive, improvisational sensibility; and scholarly renderings of African diasporic history.[10] The African American poets who emerged in the 1950s and 1960s as the literary avant-garde not only referenced black music in their works but also shaped their poems through bebop.[11] For example, the poet Bob Kaufman followed Hughes's and Tolson's concepts, adopting blues-idiom music as an inspiration and bebop as an aesthetic and poetic model for his own New American poetics.

Bebop's revolutionary impulse informed Bob Kaufman's lineation and phrasing, and, like Lester Young or Charlie Parker, he grouped images or linked them as if arranging an improvised solo around a set of sonic licks or riffs. In the middle of "Walking Parker Home," for example, Kaufman works a lyrical groove as he writes to join his opening ("Sweet beats of jazz impaled on slivers of wind") and closing (that fierce dying of humans consumed / In raging fires of Love) sound images together:

> New York altar city/ black tears / secret disciples
> Culture gods / mob sounds / visions of spikes
> Panic excursions to tribal Jazz wombs and transfusions
> Heroin nights of birth / and soaring / over boppy new ground.
> Smothered rage covering pyramids of notes spontaneously exploding[12]

Kaufman's poem expands on Hughes's imagist inclination, but it veers sharply from the solid modernist elements of Hayden's or Brooks's poetry. Kaufman's images compound, edging his bebop-inflected poetics into avant-garde experimentation.

European, Latin American, and Caribbean Popular Front–associated artistic radicals such as Aimé Césaire, Pablo Neruda, Rafael Alberti, Nicolas Guillén, Federico García Lorca, and Tristan Tzara inspired Kaufman to create a cosmopolitan, lyrical poetics that emerged from black American experiences but wasn't bound by racial categorization. Although he was too young to have participated in the Popular Front, Kaufman was attracted politically and aesthetically to the movement's continual, simultaneous address of American culture's "high / low" products – "popular / literary" genres, folk idioms/ mass consumed forms, and cross-pollinated media and genres.[13] Kaufman was also attentive to the Popular Front's concerted focus on racial and ethnic identities.

Although the poet and jazz critic Amiri Baraka was born nine years after Kaufman, he shares with the older poet similar influences (William Carlos Williams, Kenneth Rexroth, and Langston Hughes) and literary communities (Beats and Black Mountain poets). In his musicological works *Blues People* and *Black Music*, Baraka argues that bebop and avant-garde jazz are rooted in the African American experiential continuum but still offer listeners and other artists routes toward surreal, experimental, modern, and revolutionary practices. Additionally, Baraka's and Kaufman's lyrical innovations helped initiate the Black Arts Movement (BAM). Baraka's diverse literary skill set – he was also a top-shelf essayist and playwright – made him, arguably, the most significant BAM artist/theorist and an essential figure in twentieth-century American literature.

Across his first three collections, *Preface to a Twenty Volume Suicide Note* (1961), *The Dead Lecturer* (1964), and *Black Magic* (1969), Baraka grapples with the problems of identity, identity-in-transition, and blackness. In early poems such as "In Memory of Radio" and "Look for You Yesterday, Here You Come Today," Baraka turns to the representative heroes of his youth for guidance, the radio and literary heroes who might save him from falling prey to postwar, middlebrow / middle-class American life. Baraka's lineation in these poems shifts between long and short phrases, with some ideas broken and drifting down and across the page. In "Look for You," for example, Baraka shoves some stanzas hard against the right margin in order to create internal asides to the ongoing work:

> Descriptions of celibate parties
> Torn trousers: Great Poets dying
> with their strophes on. & me
> incapable of a simple straightforward
> anger.[14]

In the same poem, Baraka breaks an image-idea mid-phrase – "old envious blues feeling / ticking like a big cobblestone clock" – emphasizing the ticking measurements of the clock while referencing a surreality similar to Kaufman's. Baraka eventually sheds this questioning pose and the desire for straightforward anger in favor of presenting his "self" as lyrical invention – the poet becomes the heroic interrogator of American ideals. He learns finally "what a poem is) / A / turning away" (*BT*, p. 41).

As Baraka turned away from his associations with white American poets and their literary movements, he turned toward jazz's improvisational practices and soul music's radical spirituality in order to narrate his changes. *The Dead Lecturer* is a dramatic testament to these transitions. While he does not eschew the technical influence of his Beat and Black Mountain contemporaries, Baraka does begin offering poetic resolutions for his philosophical changes. In "The Liar," Baraka ponders these transitions and the possibility of identification through self-naming. Although calling attention to his own fears about change and self-realization, the speaker relinquishes his "flesh" in search of his spiritual self. As the speaker changes, so does the poem. This transition plays out publicly and on the page, the poem disintegrating down the page toward the speaker's re-collected final thoughts: "When they say, 'It is Roi / who is dead?' I wonder / who will they mean?"[15] The "Roi" mentioned here is some version of Le Roi Jones – the name the poet relinquished when he transitioned away from liberalism toward the leftist / radical black nationalism and the moniker Imamu Amiri Baraka. Rather than essentializing Le Roi, Baraka announces that flesh or skin cannot count outside of its contextualization, that the improvisations of the soul begin a process of continuously *othering* the self.

Baraka's poetic concept of othering the self makes improvisation a metaphor for both intellectual work and African American identity. Baraka's "continual alteration," his changing sameness, is what has made his theory of literary improvisation an influential element of contemporary criticism of African American culture from avant-garde jazz to hip-hop. For Baraka, black music is held together by long-standing African sensibilities that survived the middle passage, slavery, Reconstruction, and Jim Crow to form gospel, blues, ragtime, jazz, bebop, free jazz, rhythm and blues, and soul. Even as we parse black music into separate styles with differing performance ideals, Baraka argues that the music's improvisational imperative connects these styles while maintaining the core of African American aesthetics. Thus, at the core of African American identity – blackness – is a need to change and shift while remaining wedded to foundational African sensibilities.[16] As the titles of his collections suggest, Baraka's transitions are attempts to kill off the old selves in favor of newer, improvised selves. It is a progression, if you will, that moves toward a "blacker" American sensibility.

Baraka's poems offered initial ideas for the founding principles of the BAM. In the mid-1960s, when "black power" became the rallying cry among some young, radical intellectual participants in the civil rights movement, they had begun constructing a nationalist ideology. By developing a unified, conscious black proletariat – a black nation – the argument went, American apartheid could be ended forcefully. The artists among the intellectuals in the Black Power Movement argued that the best route for creating this collective black pride was through the arts, most notably music and poetry.

In the early 1950s, like Toni Morrison and Lucille Clifton, Baraka was an undergraduate at Howard University. While there, Baraka studied with Sterling Brown, the author of the powerful poetry collection *Southern Road* (1932). Brown influenced Baraka to think seriously about mining the blues and jazz for both aesthetic and political concepts. The riches of these explorations are present in Baraka's sociomusicological study *Blues People* (1963) and his essay collection on avant-garde jazz, *Black Music* (1968). Baraka explains African American musical tradition as the expression of African American experience. Blues-idiom music communicates African Americans' history of oppression and marginality in the West; that music alters the way Western history is narrated, once it's invoked as a frame of reference.[17] Embedded in the various blues-idiom styles, especially in bebop, are constituent elements of African American nonconformist social protest.[18] The best jazz criticism, Baraka maintains, will illustrate that the music is as much the emotional expression of a culture as it is a technical style of music making. Baraka's objective is to bring black cultural tools to bear on the criticism of black art – if white critics are to continue writing about jazz or any other black art, they must know African American history and culture and incorporate black cultural theories into their critical vernaculars and practices.[19]

Baraka's arguments about black music are useful for understanding the objectives of Black Arts poetry. Critics ought to read the poems in relation to the cultural systems that Black Arts poets negotiate. But Black Arts theorists like Larry Neal, Addison Gayle, Sarah Fabio, Hoyt Fuller, and Don L. Lee (Haki Madhubuti) wanted even more: they wanted to define a black aesthetic that was separate, exclusive from mainstream American culture, and unique to the African American condition and political agenda. Although the aforementioned writers used critical essays to crystallize and disseminate the principles of the black aesthetic, it was Baraka's poem "Black Art" that initially proffered the tenets. Beginning with images – "Poems are bullshit unless they are / teeth or trees or lemons piled / on a step" – Baraka launches a poetic assault against both the political and the literary status quo (*BT*, p. 142). Constructed from long thoughts enjambed so as to create a chant-like effect when recited, Baraka's poem layers combative, violent, surreal scenes, like Charlie Parker's twittering blues quotations in the midst of an improvised solo, or like John Coltrane's "sheets of sound" improvisational technique. At the poem's end, Baraka calls for a "Black World" created lyrically and spoken by all black people "Silently / or LOUD" (*BT*, p. 143). While the ideological desire and ethic meet the demands of the black aesthetic, Baraka's formal choices illustrate his collaboration with modernist and Black Mountain techniques rather than an alienation from them.[20]

One of the most compelling and pervasive innovations of the BAM is the "Coltrane poem."[21] As more poets came to view poetry and jazz combined as a powerful artistic weapon, they searched for heroic voices and figures to design their armaments around. If poets were to lead the assembly of black consciousness, they believed that formal and typographical evocations of Coltrane's sound and ethos were crucial to this community building. Baraka was one of Coltrane's most ardent and significant critics. His close listening led him to argue that Coltrane embodied both the emergence of new black expressive possibilities and the complete eradication of white thinking, white art. Coltrane's music communicated the nonverbal, musical theses of Black

Arts ideology. One urgent, strident example of this kind of writing is Sonia Sanchez's "a/coltrane/poem."

Born in 1934 in Birmingham, Alabama, Sonia Sanchez was reared in Harlem. Her cultural and political instruction began there, watching African American activists and cultural workers such as Jean Hudson, a curator at the Schomburg Center for Research in Black Culture; Lewis Micheaux, owner and operator of the National Memorial African Bookstore (1933–1975); and John Henrik Clarke, the renowned historian and pioneer of black studies. These Harlem luminaries provided Sanchez with models for merging aesthetic practices with collective community action.

Across her earliest collections, *Homecoming* (1969), *We a BaddDDD People* (1970), *Love Poems* (1973), and *A Blues Book for Blue Black Magical Women* (1973), Sanchez displays a dexterous use of both free verse inventions and the strictures of haiku. Writing about love and politics, these poems are infused with blues thinking and blues-idiom musicality. As a young reader, Sanchez took in Paul Laurence Dunbar, Langston Hughes, Countee Cullen, Margaret Walker, and Gwendolyn Brooks. A student of Louise Bogan's at New York University, Sanchez absorbed modernist formal ideals. Among those styles, E. E. Cummings's lineation, lowercase typography, and meandering formal arrangements asserted the most influence on Sanchez's early poems like "homecoming" and "for our lady." At the end of *We a BaddDDD People* she urges these technical elements into her crafting of "a/coltrane/poem."

For Sanchez, Coltrane's sound and musical approach is best represented by lines that power down the page as if they are musical sounds descending a notational scale. The speaker hears in the saxophonist's music the murder and massacre of "all blk/musicians. planned / in advance." Coltrane clears space for the New Thing – both experimental black music and Sanchez as an avant-garde, revolutionary black female poet represent the new here. Sanchez contracts words to single letters or expands words by several letters throughout the poem, attempting simultaneous representation of the black vernacular voice, the voice of the political consciousness, and Coltrane's multivocal soloing:

> ... u blew away our passsst
> and showed us our futureeeeee
> screech screech screeeeech screech
> a/love/supreme, alovesupreme a lovesupreme.
> A LOVE SUPREME
> scrEEEccCHHHHH screeeeEEECHHHHHHH[22]

Late in the poem Sanchez links Coltrane's "SOLO / SOUND OF YO / FIGHT IS MY FIGHT / SAXOPHONE" to African American freedom. Coltrane's screeching and screaming meant to communicate African Americans' righteous indignation and demands for full citizenship.[23] Sanchez's poem converses with and references poetic connections to other Black Arts Coltrane poems, like A. B. Spellman's "Did John's Music Kill Him?" and Haki Madhubuti's "Don't Cry, Scream."

While Black Arts poets used the Coltrane poem to demonstrate their bona fides, many African American poets who were not strict adherents to the Black Arts ideology still turned to Coltrane for his modernist artistic profile. Take Michael Harper's poems "Dear John, Dear Coltrane" (a poem also inspired by Coltrane's composition "A Love Supreme") and "Brother John," both from the collection *Dear John, Dear Coltrane* (1970). Born in Brooklyn in 1938, Harper spent his teenage years in Los Angeles; his poems draw together New York bebop heat and Los Angeles' cool modernism. Harper's conception of Coltrane's import turns away from sonic homage in favor of an elegant, formalized rendering of the musician's art. In the final stanza of "Brother John," Harper catalogues a set of interpretive angles on the line "I'm a black man":

> I'm a black man; I am;
> Black; I am; I'm a black
> Man; I am; I am;
> I'm a black man;
> I'm a black man;
> I am; I'm a black man;
> I am:[24]

Using semicolons to delineate the series of ideas he finds within the opening statement of identification, Harper plays through the concept in a fashion similar to Coltrane's style of stating a musical theme at the beginning of a solo, chopping the riff into bits, examining each claim thoroughly, and rebuilding the idea as an open, ever-evolving notion. Harper works this vein again in the penultimate stanza of "Dear John, Dear Coltrane" by mimicking Coltrane's habit of building call and response into his solos, one riff responding to another lick's call: *why you so sweet? / cause I am / why you so black? / cause I am / a love supreme, a love supreme.*[25]

Harper's controlled, brief, sharp lineation and sculpted free verse forms in *Dear John, Dear Coltrane* display his extension of the Brooks-Hayden-Tolson poetic lineage. By the early 1970s however, after the historic Black Arts writers' conferences at Fisk University (1966 and 1967), Brooks had reshaped her aesthetic to align with Black Arts criteria; Melvin Tolson had died sympathizing with some elements of the younger poets' agenda, but without adjusting his literary subjects or personal poetics in alignment with the BAM; and Robert Hayden – recognized as a significant black poet but chastised for his lack of sympathy with Black Power / Black Arts theories – held fast to his personal modernism, refusing to politicize it explicitly. And yet it is important to acknowledge that Hayden's interpretations of African American experiences were politically oriented, even though his formal arrangements were not.

Take, for example, Hayden's participation in Dudley Randall's collection *For Malcolm: Poems on the Life and Death of Malcolm X* (1969), which arose from those Fisk conferences. Hayden's contribution, the poem "El-Hajj Malik El-Shabazz," is a four-section, elegiac poem about Malcolm X. Each movement has five parts, some parts as short as one line. In the third movement, for instance, Hayden exclaims Malcolm's rise in the Nation of Islam and as a national figure with the opening greeting *"Asalam alaikum!"* followed by two stanzas; an individual line; and an ending, unrhymed couplet.[26] Although the lines and stanzas are not governed by any specific metrics or rhyme scheme, Hayden is still able to plot Malcolm's character development through each instance, across the four movements.

While the poet illustrates awareness of both Malcolm X's cultural significance and African America's political reality, he refuses hagiography. Instead, Hayden argues that when Malcolm became "his people's anger," his iconic status ushered in faulty intelligence and faith, both. Hayden explains that, "Rejecting Ahab, he was of Ahab's tribe"[27]; rejecting white racist constructs for black racist ones made Malcolm (and his tribe) into the kind of racist he battled to defeat.[28] Ahab, here, is both the biblical king and Herman Melville's questing captain. But Hayden also sees some semblance between Malcolm X and the protagonist of Richard Wright's *Native Son*, Bigger Thomas. All three literary characters resound in the poem's epigraph, *"O masks and metamorphoses of Ahab, Native Son."*[29] At the third section's ending, when Hayden exhorts, "Strike through the mask!" he's commanding his Black Arts contemporaries to "look beyond a dogma that only transposed racial terms within an inherently oppressive ideological formulation."[30] In fact, the poem's final movement might best be read as Malcolm's unmasking. Those final stanzas describe Malcolm on the hajj, the holy pilgrimage to Mecca, on the road to his final conversion to Sunni Islam, en route to becoming the pilgrim Malik. Hayden envisions not an icon but rather a man bowing before a raceless Allah, in the process of self-revision and self-renewal, who, in that moment, became "much more than there was time for him to be."[31]

And yet, on the surface, it may be difficult to distinguish between Hayden's personal poetics and Black Arts aesthetics. In his mission statement, "The Black Arts Movement," Larry Neal exclaims that the movement "eschews 'protest' literature" in order to speak "directly to Black people."[32] Although this argument seems to include most African American poets, Neal clarifies his directive, stating that this black aesthetic emerges from both the African American cultural tradition and the "useable elements of Third World culture"; charging through Third World culture and black American/diasporic experiences, the Black Arts poet finds herself addressing the demand "for a more spiritual world."[33] Once she's entered this realm of awareness, the poet will be creating and extending the movement's ethical tenets. Neal explains, finally, that "the Black Arts Movement believes that your ethics and your aesthetics are one."[34]

Stephen Henderson's anthology, *Understanding the New Black Poetry* (1972), illustrates in its long introduction how postwar black poetics is the merger of African American musical traditions and oral expressive practices such as naming, interpolating blues-idiom rhythms, freestyle rhyme schemes, evoking experience through surreal image making, developing metaphysical ideas, signifying, coupling blues feelings with references to black musical figures, name checking or implying song titles, adapting song forms to lyrical forms, and invoking black vernacular tonalities in lyric forms to create Black Arts poetry.[35] Both Neal's manifesto and Henderson's critique were developed to guide poets (and other artists) toward defining the essence of black identity/ experience. Once the Black Arts establishment had grounded blackness aesthetically and metaphysically, then they could describe a specific black audience whose members could identify themselves through poems emerging from their cultural traditions and, thus, could identify themselves as a conscious collective, spiritually and politically.

One of the places readers can see the aesthetic at work is in Gwendolyn Brooks's collection *In the Mecca* (1967). The collection announced Brooks's turn to Black Arts poetics and her departure from the Harper and Row publishing house. Subsequently, Brooks began producing books solely through African American publishers, including Dudley Randall's Broadside Press. Brooks's style changed, but her clearest goals never did: "Brooks never wrote directly or explicitly for a white audience. She was always concerned to represent, to speak to, and to sanctify Black life as she knew it."[36] "In the Mecca," the collection's eponymous, epic poem, is about African American families living in the apartment complex called the Mecca, at 34th and State Streets on

Chicago's South Side. Brooks uses the poem to demystify sociological and cultural claims made against African Americans. In so doing, the poet also "issues a prophetic call for radical reader-response and responsibility – even across the very lines of race and culture, time and place."[37] Brooks's blues-idiom speaker delineates these lines, illustrating how oppressive systems operate on inhabitants while naming routes to liberation. The speaker signals modernist techniques while developing a specific African American referential network.

With "In the Mecca" Brooks modeled a lyric mode that younger poets like Audre Lorde, Clarence Major, Ishmael Reed, Jayne Cortez, Jay Wright, and Lucille Clifton could retrofit for their own personal poetics. This group of poets illustrate that the BAM has at least two main waterways. One branch, the Baraka-Sanchez-Madhubuti stream, offers the strictest articulation of Black Arts poetics, while the other branch, the Reed-Cortez-Wright-Clifton rivulet, extends Brooks's combination into various aesthetics tributaries rather than adhering to Neal's and Henderson's shorelines.[38]

Although most often read as a postmodern novelist and passionate cultural critic, Ishmael Reed became prominent when his novel *Mumbo Jumbo* and his poetry collection *Conjure* were both finalists for 1973 National Book Awards. Like Baraka and Kaufman before him, Reed's early poems are drawn from American popular culture, African American cultural particulars, and various mythological systems. Reed's experimentation developed in part through his time in the Umbra Poets Collective, which included writers and musicians such as Steve Cannon, Tom Dent, David Henderson, Archie Shepp, Lorenzo Thomas, and Askia Touré. In those workshops, Reed shaped poems that arose from what Aldon Nielsen calls the "Africanity of international modernism."[39]

In "I am a Cowboy in the Boat of Ra," Reed retells an ancient Egyptian myth of divine conflict as a wild West showdown. Invoking Osiris, Horus, Set, and Isis, Reed plots his narrative of chaos and cultural regeneration as an exile's return. Reed's poetics are born of Western poetic traditions and textual representations of African American countercultural aesthetics. For instance, when Sonny Rollins appears in "I am a Cowboy in the Boat of Ra," he's an avatar of Egyptian/West African spiritual practices, vodun, gnosticism, and Western mythology simultaneously. Here, "Ra" references both the Egyptian sun god and the time- and space-traveling, avant-garde composer Sun Ra.[40] However, for all his polytheistic invocations, the base elements of Reed's blues-idiom aesthetic are specifically American.

Reed's prose poems "Neo-HooDoo Manifesto" and "Neo-HooDoo Aesthetic" detail this American amalgam as well as counterclaims to the Baraka-Sanchez aesthetic and Larry Neal's definition of the BAM. Rather

than forwarding the Black Arts determination of a politically conscious, col-
lected black public, Reed translates African spiritual life into specific African
American practices such as dance – "the Juba the Congo and the VooDoo."⁴¹
"Neo-HooDoo believes that every man is an artist and every artist a priest.
You can bring your own creative ideas to Neo-HooDoo. Charlie 'Yardbird
(Thoth)' Parker is an example of the Neo-HooDoo artist as an innovator and
improviser" (*IRC*, p. 27). For Reed, the ibis-faced Egyptian god has a cognate
in Parker and his trilling bebop progressions – "Neo-HooDoo is a Church
finding its lyrics" (*IRC*, p. 32). If the incantatory "I am a Cowboy in the Boat
of Ra" announces the spirit's return, then "Neo-HooDoo Manifesto" states
the agenda: "Almost 100 years ago HooDoo was forced to say / Goodbye
to America. Now HooDoo is / back as Neo-HooDoo / *You can't keep a good
church down!*" (*IRC*, p. 33).

Reed's poetic practice allows African Americans to position themselves
as "cowboys" and "priests" in the tradition. As "Neo-HooDoo Aesthetic"
instructs, *"The proportions of ingredients used depend upon the cook!"* (*IRC*, p. 34).
Reed amplifies this notion at the beginning of "The Reactionary Poet," from
A Secretary to the Spirits (1978). Exclaiming, "If you are a revolutionary / Then
I must be a reactionary," Reed's speaker pushes against the strictures of a so-
called revolutionary art:

> Enchantment will be found
> Expendable, charm, a
> Luxury
> Love and kisses
> A crime against the state
> Duke Ellington will be
> Ordered to write more marches
> "For the people," naturally.   (*IRC*, pp. 197–98)

For the speaker, the Black Arts revolution is unappealing: "If you are what's
coming / I must be what's going"; his departure, his turn to hoodoo lyric, will
happen on a sauntering steamboat because, he tells us, "I likes to take it real
slow" (*IRC*, pp. 197–98). Sardonic and humorous, Reed eschews punctuation,
allowing the chain of thoughts to become a long chant, pulsing in the final
couplets, stalled by the end (near) rhymes. Reed's mocking code switch into
southern dialect ("likes") dramatizes his desire for the past's pleasures rather
than the regulations of the revolutionary future.

Like Reed, Jay Wright challenges essentialist conceptions of African
American literary expression by rereading African American intellectual and

spiritual traditions as a complex mixture of sources without foundation. One version of this antiessentialist vision appears in Wright's second collection, *The Homecoming Singer* (1971), in "The End of an Ethnic Dream." After taking in a musical performance, the jazz bassist at the poem's center notes that his fingers were too soft "to rattle / rafters in second-rate halls. / The harmonies I could never learn / stick in Ayler's screams. / An African chant chokes us. My image shot."[42] Here the saxophonist and composer Albert Ayler is a sign for revolutionary Black Arts. After John Coltrane's death in 1967, Ayler became the torchbearer for the free / avant-garde jazz sometimes called the New Thing. The apogee of black improvisational music, Ayler's angular sound recalled Coltrane's honking, screeching multitonality (think of Sanchez's earlier typographical representation of the Coltrane sound) and was said to bring forth African ancestral spirits. The speaker's soft sound and his inability to rise into Ayler's screaming ruins his reputation as a participant on the avant-garde music scene: "My image shot." But just as significant is the claim that the music's Africanity chokes the listeners.

Unable to perform, the bassist takes an imaginative flight over New York City's Hudson River. The poem takes its shape from the flight – shifting from the opening eight-line stanza to three consecutive three- and two-line stanzas, each one darting away from a specific meter or lineation. It is possible to read this opening musically, as a kind of eight-measure statement, deconstructed improvisationally in the next eight bars. Interestingly, this attempt at musicality ends the speaker's "ethnic dream." Here, blackness, Africanness, and African Americanness do not merge into a seamless ethnic identity. Rather, the speaker's turn away from performing such completion allows him to "shoot off / every day to new horizons." At the poem's opening, the speaker calls his bass a "fine piece of furniture" and attempts to "puncture the blisters"[43] in his brain by smoking cigarettes. When the poem ends, the bass still has not become a musical instrument, and the speaker's brain is riddled with sores. Wright's poem marks both the failure to accomplish a black / ethnic whole and the failure to make the mind whole through performance or accomplishment of the African / avant-garde sound.

We might say that Wright's subsequent poetry is an attempt to rectify or redescribe this blistered failure. Part of this effort has included an encompassing knowledge of West African linguistic / cultural systems, specifically Dogon and Bambara. In the mid-1970s Wright began describing the arc of his ongoing exchange between West African, Western, and African American cultural traditions; he achieved this transformative mixture by "developing and articulating a new kind of spiritual vision."[44] For instance, in *The Double Invention of Komo* (1980), Wright lines out a complex Afro-Western poetic interaction that anticipates wholeness but avoids solidity, instead intricately shifting shape into more and more expression. Wright claims that his definition of spirituality arrives from attention to and reconciliation with what he calls the African American's "double / exile."[45] Feeling alienated from both African and American traditions, Wright's poetry attempts to announce and affirm his tenuous relation to both. Having no culture to call his own, Michael Manson explains, Wright turns to the Komo ritual in order to heal his "battered body with a care for belonging." So, in Wright's case, one way of healing the blistered brain and battered body is by producing an improvisational poetry that is steeped in and that embraces African, Western, and African American traditions at once.[46]

Wright's encompassing poetics, Reed's neo-hoodooism, and Nielsen's conception of international modernism's Africanity help give contexts to Jayne Cortez's poetics in performance. Cortez was a major participant in what Daniel Widener calls "Black Arts West."[47] During the 1960s, performing with various Los Angeles–based BAM groups, Cortez developed her poetics in theater, dance, and experimental jazz settings. Cortez merged text and music as "interdictions within American musical and political discourse, as 'gifts' designed to prevent America from hearing what it had intended and desired of black people."[48] A strong example of Cortez's gift giving is the blues poem for John Coltrane, "How Long Has Trane Been Gone." Cortez's speaker charts Coltrane's rise from black music's deep well, tracing the saxophonist's route to becoming a representative figure for black manhood. Sharing poetic traits with Sanchez and Kaufman, Cortez's one-hundred-line poem draws together a Surrealist vision of the black experience with what Tony Bolden calls Cortez's revolutionary blues. For instance, when Cortez calls for black people to hear their experiences and histories in Coltrane's music, she implores her audience:

> Rip those dead white people off
> your walls Black people
> black people whose walls
> should be a hall
> A Black Hall Of Fame
> so our children will know
> will know & be proud
> Proud to say I'm from Parker City – Coltrane City – Ornette City
> Pharoah City living on Holiday street next to
> James Brown park in the State of Malcolm[49]

Building a momentum through internal rhyme and repetitions that cross the enjambed clauses, Cortez approximates Coltrane's style of repeating riffs and creating dialogical runs within his improvised solos. Cortez describes a future time and place where "our children will know" representative Americans as black heroes, not Anglo-American ones. Coltrane announces that imminent tense, participating in both a jazz saxophonist genealogy – Charlie Parker, Ornette Coleman, and Pharoah Sanders – and the gamut of African American musical tradition from "[Billie] Holiday street" through "James Brown park," out toward a black nation, a separate (physical or psychological) "State of Malcolm [X]." A secular blues priestess, Cortez blends the Coltrane poem and the Malcolm X poem into a dynamic whole.[50]

Just as jazz artists extend blues-idiom concepts by improvising on them, we can better appreciate Cortez's achievement, as Tony Bolden explains, by "comparing the poet's artistic method to common practices in blues culture," from the black preacher to the blues singer.[51] With *Scarifications* (1973) and *Mouth on Paper* (1977), Cortez began producing simultaneously poetry collections and long-play recordings with her improvisational musical group, the Firesplitters. In her role as blues priestess, Cortez performs on the bridge between African American and Afro-diasporic poetics.

Writing about Cortez's recording *There It Is* (1982) and her poem "I See Chano Pozo," from *Coagulations* (1984), Aldon Nielsen finds the poet expressing a sonic history of black Atlantic aesthetic practices. Chano Pozo was a bongo and conga master who, working with Dizzy Gillespie, helped develop cu-bop. In Cortez's poem, Pozo's figure and sound embody the return of an African/Caribbean anterior already echoed in the structures of jazz. When Cortez and her band chant "olé okay / Oye I say / I see Chano Pozo," they return to a repeated, percussive internal rhyming similar to the kind in "How Long Has Trane Been Gone." However, here, Cortez has grafted Spanish, English, and African-derived words into an onomatopoetic line that carries the rhythm of Pozo's drumming. Additionally, this New World linguistic chain becomes a "technology of newness" that links "Nicolás Guillén to Langston Hughes and William Carlos Williams, that brings Chano Pozo together with Dizzy Gillespie, that Charlie Haden hears in Gonzalo Rubalcaba."[52] These priestly expansions express African American poetics' atomic nucleus: cosmopolitanism.

Malin Pereira suggests that readers think of African American poetic cosmopolitanism as a "revisionist universalism" that values the "racial and cultural particulars" of African American–invented forms as expressive of human experience.[53] By the late 1970s, even Baraka, whose poems often chafed against

Black Arts essentializing even as they promoted it, had recalibrated his literary and political positions. Practicing his own brand of Third World Marxism, Baraka produced two demanding, large-scale blues-idiom poems: his Coltrane biography "Am/Trak" (1979) and his history poem (inspired by the Arthur Blythe tune of the same title) "In the Tradition" (1980). Baraka's poems (as well as those of Cortez, Reed, and Wright) articulate New World black history as international history and African American aesthetics – specifically blues-idiom improvisational practices – as the ultimate systems of modern, international experience.

Although her early collections, *Good Times* (1969) and *Good News about the Earth* (1972), fit loosely within the Black Arts intellectual vision, Lucille Clifton's poems offered alternatives to long forms, clearing more routes away from essentialist thinking and poetics. Clifton captured the spirit and attitude of the late 1960s and early 1970s using short lyrics presented in fragmented, epigrammatic style, such as "malcolm" (about Malcolm X), "after kent state," and "the meeting after the savior gone: 4/4/68" (about Martin Luther King):

> we was going to try and save you but
> now i guess you got to save yourselves
> (even if you don't know
>   who you are
>   where you been
>   where you headed[54]

Her formal idiosyncrasy – sparse punctuation and no capitalization – demonstrates a willingness to draw from referential systems both within and without African American literary reservoirs. On one hand, Clifton presents a careful distillation of Black Arts poetry: the political subject; the direct address of a black audience; and dropping the copula or using irregular conjugation, thus producing the black vernacular voice. On the other hand, Clifton's invocation of modernist, free verse forms suggests some aesthetic indebtedness to poets like E. E. Cummings, H.D., and William Carlos Williams. Clifton could be read productively and provocatively as a cosmopolitan, epic miniaturist.

Clifton has used her family's specific story to initiate her cosmopolitan project. She claims that "all of our stories become The Story.... I am a black human being, and that is part of The Story."[55] Clifton places this family narrative in and on her body. Clifton's genealogical poems invoke the blues idiom, aiding her illuminating black life as human and diverse.[56] Clifton's corporeal concentration is an argument for "the special properties of the female spirit and body," placing her body and poems in "the long tradition of poets mythologizing womanhood."⁵⁷ In the untitled poem that begins, "I was born with twelve fingers," Clifton explains that she; her mother, Thelma Sayles; and her firstborn daughter, Sidney, were all "born wearing strange black gloves."⁵⁸ However, fears of witchcraft and spell casting led consecutive parental genera-tions to have the extra digits, these "wonders," amputated. Yet those "invisible fingers," powerful with the "memory of ghosts," connect, Clifton explains, "my dead mother my live daughter and me / through our terrible shadowy hands."⁵⁹ The spatial gaps on the page between the three linked subjects are the invisible fingers.

In another poem about absence and death, "speaking of loss," Clifton returns to her finger narrative, extending the myth as an explanation of her poiesis: "someone has stolen / my parents and hidden my brother. / my extra fingers are cut away. / i am left with plain hands and / nothing to give you but poems."⁶⁰ Clifton's terrible shadowy hands are made plain but still deliver spells through her poetry. During the 1980s, in praise poems such as "poem in praise of menstruation," "poem to my uterus," and "to my last period," Clifton's bodily focus becomes singing for her "body electric" and its aging, while reaching for the cosmopolitan female ethos, those "animals / beauti-ful and faithful and ancient / and female and brave."⁶¹ Using the solidity of her personal and familial narratives, Clifton's poetics turn away from BAM notions of a large, amorphous black consciousness/collective.

Whether considering Clifton's bodily concerns, Brooks's intimate tour of Chicago's black South Side, Hayden's Malcolm X, or Reed's avenging cowboy, the nomadic blues subject speaks the poetic vision and triggers the "cosmo-politan interplay" among the various cultural streams black poets draw from in developing their poetic narratives.⁶² These connected concepts – cosmopol-itanism and blues subjectivity – are especially useful when taking up African American poetry at the end of the twentieth century.

When the 1980s opened, African American poets who'd been practicing as apprentice artists adjacent to but not within the BAM aesthetic rubric began advancing various black aesthetics. That is, rather than hewing to the BAM ideologies, poets born during the 1940s and 1950s, like Toi Derricotte, Rita Dove, Yusef Komunyakaa, and Nathaniel Mackey, began forwarding per-sonal aesthetics to correspond to their varied experiences of blackness and American life. A second wave of post–Black Arts poets, including Harryette Mullen, Cornelius Eady, Carl Phillips, and Elizabeth Alexander, were born in the 1950s and early 1960s and emerged on the heels of the first shift. Rather than advance a totalizing black aesthetic, these poets developed "a multifari-ous, contingent, non-delimited complex of strategies [for negotiating] gaps or conflicts between their artistic goals and the operation of race in the production, dissemination, and reception of their writing."[63] Their negotiations of the gaps and conflicts still relied on their abilities to integrate the blues idiom into their aesthetic processes.

Dove is a quintessential post-BAM poet: her aesthetic leans on an array of European influences and classical references far away from what she's called the BAM's essentialist ideologies and "poetics of rage." Her open rejection is best described in "Upon Meeting Don L. Lee, in a Dream." Dove contextualizes her rebuke with sly references to the BAM's masculinist, Afrocentric, and Surrealist tendencies. Approaching the speaker with "lashless eyes" and "fists clenched," Lee (Haki Madhubuti) embodies black poetic rage.[64] With robed and beaded women stretching their arms to him and chanting "in wooden cadences," Lee begins to declaim within the poem – "'Seven years ago . . .'" – but the speaker cuts him off: "'Those years are gone – / What is there now?'" The speaker's questioning ignites fury: "He starts to cry; his eyeballs / Burst into flame" (*RDS*, p. 12). Dove's poem is also a deft critique: rather than accepting Lee's exhortation or inheriting the BAM's free-form, free verse, free-improvisational styles, Dove guides the speaker's irregularly metered lines into five quatrains, wresting aesthetic control from one of the BAM's leading figures while formalizing her rejection.

But Dove is a learned student of African American poetics, including blues-idiom poetics. For example, see Dove's poem "Lightnin' Blues" from her Pulitzer Prize–winning collection, *Thomas and Beulah* (1986). The poem recalls one of Thomas and Beulah's family trips, a Friday jaunt to the country for fishing and relaxation. Dove, like an apt student of the tradition, can distill the blues in a simple line: "On the radio a canary bewailed her luck" (*RDS*, p. 157). The poet doesn't need to conjure like Reed or name-check a black pantheon like Cortez in order to establish her blues context. The bird calling out her bad luck announces and initiates the blues. At the poem's ending, however, the idiomatic voices coming from the car's radio have turned "trickster," as if devilish blues gods had made sport with their experience: "Turned around, the car started / meek as a lamb" (*RDS*, p. 157). Malin Pereira argues that "Lightnin' Blues" is an instance of Dove's negotiating "the racial particular and the unraced universal."[65]

"Lightnin' Blues" has a cousin in "Canary," from *Grace Notes* (1989), a poem dedicated to Michael S. Harper. Dove displays a BAM revisionist sensibility: instead of a Coltrane poem, Dove builds a Billie Holiday poem, and she wants to debunk Holiday mythologies rather than reify them.[66] Although listeners are conditioned to think of Holiday's "burned voice" and "ruined face" as descriptions of the blues, Dove argues that the blues arrive with as "many shadows as lights."[67] Rather than dwelling in those shadows, angling toward an ideological definition of blackness or feminine weakness, Dove faces the lights in order to speak a cosmopolitan truth about art and freedom: "Fact is, the invention of women under siege / has been to sharpen love in the service of myth. / If you can't be free, be a mystery."[68] Holiday turned blues and bad luck into art; she played the trickster, feigning fragility as style in order to communicate her human complexity. In blues-idiom musical expression and African American history Dove hears classical tonalities; we can find her chiming these tonalities in collections like *Mother Love* (1995), in which she riffs on the myth of Demeter and Persephone, and *On the Bus with Rosa Parks* (2000), in which she works through the civil rights movement.

Yusef Komunyakaa has concocted his own cosmopolitan blues-idiom blendings. Like Dove's sensibility, Komunyakaa's aesthetic emerges from his mixture of African American history, Greek mythology, European modernism, postmodern linguistics, and jazz and blues music, and of his memories of the Vietnam War. Komunyakaa is indebted to the tradition: three of his earliest poems are entitled "Mississippi John Hurt," "Langston Hughes," and "Blues Tonality." Derricotte argues that his layered lyrics interrogate "the most complex moral issues, the most harrowing ugly subjects of our American life" in order to illustrate in "deeper ways what it is to be human."[69]

Komunyakaa's aesthetic turns away from the BAM but refutes the suggestion "that the primary ideal of the artist is to articulate some putative 'universal' that transcends the limits of race into models of cultural homogeneity."[70] In post-BAM poetry, as Komunyakaa demonstrates, blues-idiom markers don't need to be represented with the names of musicians or with lexical or formal arrangements that mimic the blues or improvisation. Komunyakaa's innovation has been to describe blackness as improvisational rather than as political loyalty or a pure cultural lineage. Komunyakaa's poetic improvisations express the individual mind's psychological, emotional, and cultural churnings.

Born in Bogalusa, Louisiana, in 1947, Komunyakaa was coming of age when exclaiming black beauty and chanting "black power" was in vogue. When he began his army service in 1968, the decade-long sociopolitical revolutions had forced many young Americans to reevaluate their definitions of Americanness. In poems like "Tu Do Street" and "Facing It," both from *Dien Cai Dau* (1988), Komunyakaa shifts between racial and national identities, writing as a Vietnam War veteran, an American, and an African American. From these tense, contingent subject positions, Komunyakaa's poetic vision arises. He can improvise on these oppositions, eschewing hierarchical arrangements in favor of palimpsests. "Tu Do Street," for instance, is a poem about black soldiers entering a Vietnamese bar that white soldiers have claimed as their turf. In keeping with southern American ways, the white soldiers want to maintain racial segregation even at the Far East Asian front. Toggling between his memories of his southern childhood – "I am a small boy / again in Bogalusa. *White Only* / signs & Hank Snow" – and his attempt to order a beer in this "segregated" bar – "the mama-san / behind the counter acts as if she / can't understand, while her eyes / skirt each white face, as Hank Williams / calls from the psychedelic jukebox" – the speaker layers these moments against each other, using the two Hanks and country music to improvise a statement about the ironies of American blackness. Snow and Williams are blues-idiom white country musicians – they're both sonic signifiers of segregation and American music's biracial (at the least) roots.[71]

Komunyakaa amplifies the claim at the poem's end when the speaker notes how the music and the Vietnamese prostitutes connect these soldiers intimately and mythologically:

> There's more than a nation
> inside us, as black & white
> soldiers touch the same lovers
> minutes apart, tasting
> each other's breath,
> without knowing these rooms
> run into each other like tunnels
> leading to the underworld.[72]

Komunyakaa's earlier palimpsest plays out logically as the black and white soldiers touch and taste each other through shared lovers. Noting the soldiers' "tunneling" among the bar's back rooms, their merger into "more than a nation," the speaker offers a subtle, deft improvisation on Derek Walcott's supposition in "The Schooner *Flight*": "either I'm nobody or I'm a nation."[73] For Komunyakaa, the Americans soldiers and Vietnamese sex workers represent more than nation-states. His idea silences the notion that racial essences identify these participants clearly. There is an orphic quality to the poem's last image, drawing our ears to the sound of music, as the poet-speaker searches for beauty and entertainment in war's hellish underworld. In "Facing It," an equally intense and beautiful poem, Komunyakaa generates a nuanced, ambivalent response to Maya Lin's Vietnam War Memorial in Washington, D.C. The polished, black granite walls, engraved with the names of fallen warriors, offer Komunyakaa's speaker the possibility to "watch himself look," as he reflects and as his reflection blends with the white visitors around him.[74]

In "February in Sydney," Komunyakaa's looking, reflecting, and imagining blends Bob Kaufman's Surrealist bebop poetics with metaphysical modernist statement. Set in Sydney, Australia, the speaker rides a city bus home after watching Dexter Gordon's lead performance in the film 'Round Midnight (1981). The speaker hears in bebop humiliation and pain distilled to jubilant art: "Bud, Prez, Webster, & the Hawk, / their names run together riffs. / Painful gods jive talk through / bloodstained reeds & shiny brass / where music is anesthetic."[75] Naming Bud Powell, Lester Young, Ben Webster, and Coleman Hawkins, the speaker generates a musicological pantheon and a sonic history. Thinking through bebop triggers an "old anger" as the musical memories merge with the speaker's recollection of an incident that occurred on his exit from the movie theater: "Another scene keeps repeating itself: / I emerge from a dark theater, / passing a woman who grabs her red purse / & hugs it to her like a heart attack." No simple emotion rises from this scene; instead the speaker feels "a loneliness" lingering "like a silver needle" beneath his black skin as he tries to "feel how it is / to scream for help through a horn."[76] The speaker's desire to "scream for help" "is important not for its sound or greater authenticity but for its model of improvisational self-constitution."[77]

Komunyakaa's "tonal logic" is produced through his alternating accents, three or four per line, thus lengthening and shortening lines "to mirror the process of consciousness."[78] Ultimately, Komunyakaa's musical or poetic representation of self-reflection holds the possibility of unifying the self in the process of becoming and the self's various communities into a useful whole: "Jazz discovers the emotional mystery behind things; it provides a spiritual connection to the land, reconnecting us to places where its forms originated."[79] In later poems like "Changes; or Reveries at a Window Overlooking a Country Road, with Two Women Talking Blues in the Kitchen," "Palimpsest," "Testimony," and "No Good Blues," Komunyakaa has designed an array of original formal structures for presenting blues-idiom improvisation as the spiritual link between individual consciousness and group reconnection.

Nathaniel Mackey has explained that post-bebop jazz has inspired his poetics.[80] Mackey has developed an improvisational literary aesthetic that even he admits could be called "experimental, avant-garde, vanguard or difficult."[81] It derives from the "intersection of the African American vernacular and Euro-American 'open form' poetics," making him the inheritor of Baraka, Robert Creeley, Robert Duncan, Clarence Major, Charles Olson, Wilson Harris, and Jay Wright. Like Wright, Mackey has been exploring Dogon culture, in works such as his serial poem Song of the Andoumboulou. Mackey also has been delineating the confluence of cultures in his second ongoing poem, "Mu."[82] Of these two extended poetic works, Mackey explains, "the two now understood as two and the same, each the other's understudy. Each is the other, each is both, announcedly so."[83] Both works are generated from Mackey's listening to the Dogon funeral dirge "Song of the Andoumboulou" and Don Cherry's *"Mu"*– the intersection of West African song and African American experimental jazz.

Since *Four for Trane* (1977) – the title of which references Archie Shepp's vanguard recording honoring Coltrane – and *Eroding Witness* (1985), in which *Song of the Andoumboulou* debuted, Mackey has been improvising, insistently and radically, a poetic/musical system. In Mackey's poetics, black music doesn't cohere as a singular individual voice. Rather, the music is "a figure for a pursuit of voice that questions, and is questioned by, the very limits of its expressive capacity."[84] Mackey's serial art presents poetry as an "irresolvable process of 'root-work'" – each series session offers a further excavation of language and origin.[85] "Song of the Andoumboulou: 13" opens, for example, with the speaker's bottom lip against his teeth "like a rock but unsteady," stuttering, "'Fa . . .' / as in fox, as in Fon, as in fate."[86] As these lines skitter down the page, readers might imagine the speaker's stuttering as an aftereffect of his attempt to play a "Song so black it / burnt" his lip, in "Song of the Andoumboulou: 12."[87]

In songs 12 and 13, Mackey invokes Eshu Elegba or Legba, the West African and voodoo deity standing at the crossroads between the heavens and earth, issuing passage and determining destinies. Importantly, Eshu also speaks all human languages. In the speaker's "fa" we hear the root sound for a perforated line of contingent connections: the fox in several Native American tribal mythologies is a cognate for Eshu Elegba; Fon, the Niger-Congo language, people, and religion, is a founding cultural system for voodoo and the black Atlantic diaspora; fate, in this human cycle described in Mackey's work, is yet to be announced. In fact, Mackey's admixture of Native American, Dogon, and African American cosmologies is a hoodoo healing concoction for the speaker, who tore his throat raw in his "green / attempt to sing the blues."[88] Mackey, too, has made a jazz record, *Strick* (1995), with the avant-garde musicians Royal Hartigan and Hafez Modirzadeh. Reciting sessions 16–25 from *Song of Andoumboulou* in conference with the musicians, Mackey's singing plunges toward Federico García Lorca's deep songs, *duende*, cante jondo, and cante moro. For Mackey, deep singing is the poet's calling: "World hollowed out, the Andoumboulou / beckoned. Echoed aboriginal / cut, / chthonic spur."[89]

Harryette Mullen is also a deep blues singer. Her underground, aboriginal poetics offer ways of thinking through gender and racial concerns that acknowledge the BAM aesthetic while holding BAM ideologies at bay. As a poet and critic, Mullen has forged an oeuvre dedicated to innovating dexterous claims about African American womanhood and identity. Mullen's earliest collections – *Tree Tall Woman* (1981) and *Baby Blues: Early Poems* (2002) – display BAM traits and are spoken by somewhat coherent black voices. In *Trimmings* (1991) and *S*PeRM**K*T* (1992), Mullen worked through her interests in Language poetry, critical theory, and poststructuralist linguistics.

By the mid-1990s, with the publication of *Muse & Drudge* (1995), Mullen was working from the premise that "to be black *is* to be innovative."[90] Written in a terse, pun-driven style, *Muse & Drudge* is a long, epic poem measured in quatrains, printed four to a page and rhymed irregularly. In these 320 stanzas, Mullen plays across languages and styles, mixing African American vernacular, urban slang, colloquial sayings, standard English diction, and Spanish phrases. Mullen's blues-idiom knowledge aids her seamless merging of her black lyrical voices and her formal innovations. Her ability to invent arrangements that work "black cultural material into an investigation of the particular question of black women's identity" sets her work in lively discourse with Cortez's, Clifton's, and Mackey's poems.[91] Each stanza could stand alone as short, weird epigrams. But in sequence, the collection builds momentum as if Mullen were a soloist, riffing new ideas into her in-progress improvisation.

Early in *Muse & Drudge* Mullen's speaker names herself: "random diva nation of bedlam / headman hoodlum doodling / then I wouldn't be long gone / I'd be Dogon."[92] Mullen's Dogon Sapphire, whose "lyre styles / pluck eyebrows," refers playfully and caustically to the ancient poetess Sappho and the negative American stereotype of black femininity. "Sapphire" signifies Mullen's literary history – Western literature, women's writing, and African American poetics – and initiates her recycling of those traditions. Mullen's quatrains are exploded and redescribed blues stanzas, and Sapphire is a "random [blues] diva," improvising on her lyre. As with Mackey's *Song of the Andoumboulou*, Mullen's drawing the Western/Greek reference into the blues context positions her as part of the Dogon practice, rather than as "long gone" down the road, blues hellhounds on her trail. Rejecting a single-voiced, linear narrative in *Muse & Drudge*, Mullen's Sapphire becomes many women's voices throughout the poem. As Evie Shockley argues, "Mullen . . . presents us with a collective hero, the great 'tribe' of black women who lived in the U. S."[93]

Mullen thinks diasporically through these traditions. When Mullen's speaker suggests restoring "lost nature / with hoodoo paraphernalia," it's the charming Cuban "shaman in an urban turban" who offers "seven / powers of Africa la mano / ponderosa ayudame numeros sueños."[94] The Spanish

Black and Blues Configurations

invocation calls on the mighty hand of the seven African powers to fuel the speaker's dreams with the key numbers. Those numbers "help souls in misery / get to the square root / of evil and render it moot."[95] Allison Cummings suggests that Mullen's improvising is linguistic play literally: her "text rephrases black orality as aurality. The wordplay takes place not in a conceptual realm of denotation and connotation, but over airwaves" between the page and the mind's ear.[96]

Many of the strongest voices of the post-BAM third wave participated in the Dark Room Collective during the late 1980s and 1990s. Thomas Sayers Ellis and Sharan Strange founded the Dark Room reading series in 1987, while still Harvard undergraduates. When Ellis and Strange began inviting established writers to read in their Cambridge, Massachusetts, meeting space, they wanted to develop a black literary community that could include exchange and mentorship without being bound or determined by specific political ideologies or aesthetic agendas. As undergraduates or graduate students, Natasha Trethewey, Kevin Young, John Keene, and Major Jackson all participated in the collective.[97] By 2001 Dark Room poets had begun achieving national recognition. In Young's renewal of elegiac and blues poetry, Trethewey's lyrical explorations of southern history and African American culture, and Jackson's urbane, formal sophistication, blues-idiom poetics are extended, and readers can see the African American poetic tradition's influence on contemporary American poetry.

Over the past several decades, African American literary artists have introduced an array of new techniques and styles to Anglophone poetics. While some poets hew closely to modernist poetry, they have also innovated practices that allow them to balance African American expressive modes and blues-idiom tropes with formalist desires. Others' palettes are multicultural, multilingual, and postmodern, allowing them free improvisational range in length, versification, lineation, form, voice, and musicality. It's possible to read this lineage without thinking about groupings – modernists versus postmodernists, the BAM versus the post-BAM – because these artists all use the blues idiom as a touchstone. And when a poet invokes that idiom, she's also explaining that her aesthetic approach necessitates invention, improvisation, and innovation.

Notes

1. Angelyn Mitchell (ed.), *Within the Circle: An Anthology of African American Literary Criticism, from the Harlem Renaissance to the Present* (Durham, N.C.: Duke University Press, 1994), pp. 79, 254.

2. Lawrence P. Jackson, *The Indignant Generation* (Princeton, N.J.: Princeton University Press, 2011), p. 205.
3. Elizabeth Alexander, *The Black Interior* (St. Paul, Minn.: Graywolf, 2004), p. 15.
4. Jackson, *The Indignant Generation*, pp. 205–06.
5. Gwendolyn Brooks, *Blacks* (Chicago: Third World Press, 1987), p. 28.
6. Brooks, *Blacks*, pp. 42, 69.
7. D. H. Melham, *Gwendolyn Brooks: Poetry and the Heroic Voice* (Lexington: University Press of Kentucky, 1987), pp. 20–21.
8. Jackson, *The Indignant Generation*, p. 212.
9. Walton Muyumba, *The Shadow and the Act: Black Intellectual Practice, Jazz Improvisation, and Philosophical Pragmatism* (Chicago: University of Chicago Press, 2009), pp. 25–27.
10. As David Moore explains in the present volume, it's useful to read Hughes's poetry as one exemplary consequence of the African American literary lineage hatched before him – Phillis Wheatley to Paul Laurence Dunbar – and of his awareness of his immediate African American contemporaries – Jean Toomer, Claude McKay, and Countee Cullen. Tolson's poetry might be read as one wellspring for future works by Jay Wright and Rita Dove. See Diane V. Cruz's astute comparison of Tolson and Dove in Cruz, "Refuting Exile: Rita Dove Reading Melvin Tolson," *Callaloo* 31:3 (2008), pp. 789–802.
11. Meta DuEwa Jones, "Listening to What the Ear Demands: Langston Hughes and His Critics," *Callaloo* 25:4 (2002), pp. 1145–75. Although literary historians often attribute the combination of jazz and poetry to the poets of the Beat Movement, Hughes was most likely the first writer to develop a new American poetics from bebop aesthetics, as in his composite poem *Montage of a Dream Deferred* (1951) and in *Ask Your Mama* (1961).
12. Bob Kaufman, *Solitudes Crowded with Loneliness* (New York: New Directions, 1965), p. 5.
13. James Smethurst, "Remembering When Indians Were Red: Bob Kaufman, the Popular Front, and the Black Arts Movement," *Callaloo* 25:1 (2002), pp. 146–64, 148–49.
14. Amiri Baraka, *Transbluesency: Selected Poems 1961–1995* (New York: Marsilio, 1995), p. 17. This collection will be cited in the text as *BT*.
15. Amiri Baraka, *The LeRoi Jones/Amiri Baraka Reader* (New York: Basic, 1999), p. 75.
16. Muyumba, *The Shadow and the Act*; see also Nathaniel Mackey, *Discrepant Engagement: Dissonance, Cross-Culturality, and Experimental Writing* (Cambridge: Cambridge University Press, 1993).
17. Le Roi Jones (Amiri Baraka), *Blues People: Negro Music in White America* (New York: Morrow, 1963), p. 70.
18. Jones, *Blues People*, p. 23.
19. Amiri Baraka, *Black Music* (1968; New York: Da Capo, 1998), p. 20.

20. James Smethurst, *The Black Arts Movement* (Chapel Hill: University of North Carolina Press, 2005); Meta DuEwa Jones, *The Muse Is Music: Jazz Poetry from the Harlem Renaissance to Spoken Word* (Urbana: University of Illinois Press, 2011).

21. On John Coltrane and the Coltrane poem, see Kimberley Benston, *Performing Blackness* (New York: Routledge, 2001), throughout but in particular pp. 145–86, 313–30, and Jones, *The Muse Is Music*, pp. 85–128.

22. Sonia Sanchez, *We a BaddDDD People* (Detroit: Broadside Press, 1970), pp. 70–71; reprinted in Stephen Henderson (ed.), *Understanding the New Black Poetry* (New York: Morrow, 1973), p. 275.

23. Henderson (ed.), *Understanding the New Black Poetry*, p. 276.

24. Michael S. Harper, *Dear John, Dear Coltrane* (Pittsburgh: University of Pittsburgh Press, 1970), p. 4.

25. Harper, *Dear John, Dear Coltrane*, p. 75.

26. Robert Hayden, *Collected Poems*, ed. Frederick Glaysher, rev. ed. (New York: Liveright, 1996), p. 88.

27. Hayden, *Collected Poems*, p. 88.

28. Derik Smith, "Quarreling in the Movement: Robert Hayden's Black Arts Era," *Callaloo* 33:2 (2010), pp. 449–66, 461–62.

29. Hayden, *Collected Poems*, p. 86.

30. Smith, "Quarreling in the Movement," p. 462.

31. Hayden, *Collected Poems*, p. 89.

32. Mitchell (ed.), *Within the Circle*, p. 185.

33. Mitchell (ed.), *Within the Circle*, p. 186.

34. Mitchell (ed.), *Within the Circle*, p. 186.

35. See Stephen Henderson, "Introduction: The Forms of Things Unknown," in Henderson (ed.), *Understanding the New Black Poetry*, pp. 1–70.

36. Sheila Hassell Hughes, "A Prophet Overheard: A Juxtapositional Reading of Gwendolyn Brooks's 'In the Mecca,'" *African American Review* 38:2 (2004), pp. 257–80, 257.

37. Hughes, "A Prophet Overheard," p. 258.

38. Charles Rowell, "The Editor's Note," *Callaloo* 27:4 (2004), pp. vii–ix.

39. Aldon Lynn Nielsen, *Black Chant: Languages of Afro-American Postmodernism* (Urbana: University of Illinois Press, 1997), p. 7.

40. See Zamir Shamoon, "The Artist as Prophet, Priest and Gunslinger: Ishmael Reed's Cowboy in the Boat of Ra," *Callaloo* 17:4 (1994), pp. 1205–35.

41. Ishmael Reed, *New and Collected Poems 1964–2007* (New York: Thunder's Mouth, 2007), p. 25. This collection will be cited in the text as *IRC*.

42. Jay Wright, *The Homecoming Singer* (New York: Corinth, 1971), p. 22.

43. Wright, *The Homecoming Singer*, p. 22.

44. Michael Tomasek Manson, "The Clarity of Being Strange: Jay Wright's *The Double Invention of Komo*," *Black American Literature Forum* 24:3 (1990), p. 474.

45. Charles Rowell, "The Unraveling of the Egg: An Interview with Jay Wright," *Callaloo* 6:3 (1983), pp. 3–15; Jay Wright, *The Double Invention of Komo* (Austin: University of Texas Press, 1980), p. 22.

46. Manson, "The Clarity of Being Strange"; Wright, *The Double Invention of Komo*, p. 23.

47. Daniel Widener, *Black Arts West: Culture and Struggle in Postwar Los Angeles* (Durham, N.C.: Duke University Press, 2010).

48. Nielsen, *Black Chant*, p. 7.

49. Jayne Cortez, *Pisstained Stairs and the Monkey Man's Wares* (New York: Phrase Text, 1969), p. 42.

50. Tony Bolden, *Afro-Blue: Improvisations in African American Poetry and Culture* (Urbana: University of Illinois Press, 2004), pp. 121–22.

51. Bolden, *Afro-Blue*, pp. 62–63.

52. Aldon Lynn Nielsen, *Integral Music: Languages of Afro-American Innovation* (Tuscaloosa: University of Alabama Press, 2004), p. 184.

53. Malin Pereira, *Rita Dove's Cosmopolitanism* (Urbana: University of Illinois Press, 2003), p. 11.

54. Lucille Clifton, *Two-Headed Woman* (Amherst: University of Massachusetts Press, 1980), p. 31.

55. Charles Rowell, "An Interview with Lucille Clifton," *Callaloo* 22:1 (1999), pp. 55–72, 58.

56. Sherley Anne Williams, "The Blues Roots of Contemporary Afro-American Poetry," *Massachusetts Review* 18:3 (1977), p. 552.

57. Hilary Holladay, *Wild Blessings: The Poetry of Lucille Clifton* (Baton Rouge: Louisiana State University Press, 2004), p. 65.

58. Lucille Clifton, *Good Woman: Poems and a Memoir, 1969–1980* (Brockport, N.Y.: BOA, 1987), p. 166.

59. Clifton, *Good Woman*, p. 166.

60. Clifton, *Two-Headed Woman*, p. 174.

61. Lucille Clifton, *Blessing the Boats: New and Selected Poems 1988–2000* (Brockport, N.Y.: BOA, 2000), p. 64.

62. Pereira, *Rita Dove's Cosmopolitanism*, p. 94.

63. Evie Shockley, *Renegade Poetics: Black Aesthetics and Formal Innovation in African American Poetry* (Iowa City: University of Iowa Press, 2011), p. 9.

64. Rita Dove, *Selected Poems* (New York: Vintage, 1993), p. 12. This collection will be cited in the text as *RDS*.

65. Pereira, *Rita Dove's Cosmopolitanism*, p. 105.

66. Rita Dove, *Grace Notes* (New York: W. W. Norton, 1989), p. 64.

67. Dove, *Grace Notes*.

68. Dove, *Grace Notes*.

69. Toi Derricotte, "The Tension Between Memory and Forgetting in the Poetry of Yusef Komunyakaa," *Kenyon Review* 15:4 (1993), p. 222.

70. Keith Leonard, "Yusef Komunyakaa's Blues: The Postmodern Music of *Neon Vernacular*," *Callaloo* 28:3 (2005), p. 826.

71. Yusef Komunyakaa, *Pleasure Dome: New and Collected Poems* (Middletown, Conn.: Wesleyan University Press, 2001), pp. 209–10.

72. Komunyakaa, *Pleasure Dome.*

73. Derek Walcott, *Collected Poems: 1948–1984* (New York: Farrar, Straus and Giroux, 1986) p. 345.

74. Sally Minogue and Andrew Palmer, "Memorial Poems and the Poetics of Memorializing," *Journal of Modern Literature* 34:1 (2010), pp. 162–81, 176.

75. Komunyakaa, *Pleasure Dome*, p. 254.

76. Komunyakaa, *Pleasure Dome*, p. 254.

77. Leonard, "Yusef Komunyakaa's Blues," p. 832.

78. Leonard, "Yusef Komunyakaa's Blues," p. 832.

79. Yusef Komunyakaa, *Blue Notes: Essays, Interviews, and Commentaries*, ed. Radiciani Clytus (Ann Arbor: University of Michigan Press, 2000), p. 4.

80. Robert L. Zamsky, "A Poetics of Radical Musicality: Nathaniel Mackey's '-mu' Series," *Arizona Quarterly* 62:1 (2006), pp. 113–40.

81. Craig Morgan Teicher, "A Conversation with Nathaniel Mackey," *PW Daily*, November 22, 2006, www.publishersweekly.com/pw/by-topic/authors/interviews/article/725-a-conversation-with-nathaniel-mackey-.html.

82. Mackey is also the author of an ongoing, serialized fiction project, *From a Broken Bottle Traces of Perfume Still Emanate*, which includes the novels *Atet A. D.* (2001), *Djbot Baghostus's Run* (1993), and *Bedouin Hornbook* (1986).

83. Nathaniel Mackey, *Splay Anthem* (San Francisco: New Directions, 2006), p. ix.

84. Brent Hayes Edwards, "Notes on Poetics Regarding Mackey's 'Song,'" *Callaloo* 23:2 (2000), p. 575.

85. Zamsky, "A Poetics of Radical Musicality," p. 113.

86. Nathaniel Mackey, *School of Udhra* (San Francisco: City Lights, 1993), p. 11.

87. Mackey, *School of Udhra*, p. 10.

88. Mackey, *School of Udhra*, p. 10.

89. Nathaniel Mackey, *Whatsaid Serif* (San Francisco: City Lights, 1998), p. 13.

90. Farah Griffin, Michael Magee, and Kristen Gallagher, "A Conversation with Harryette Mullen" (1997), http://epc.buffalo.edu/authors/mullen/interview-new.html.

91. Shockley, *Renegade Poetics*, p. 85.

92. Harryette Mullen, *Recyclopedia: Trimmings, S*PeRM**K*T, and Muse & Drudge* (St. Paul, Minn.: Graywolf, 2006), p. 109.

93. Shockley, *Renegade Poetics*, p. 93.

94. Mullen, *Recyclopedia*, p. 126.
95. Mullen, *Recyclopedia*, p. 126.
96. Allison Cummings, "Public Subjects: Race and the Critical Reception of Gwendolyn Brooks, Erica Hunt, and Harryette Mullen," *Frontiers* 26:2 (2005), p. 28.
97. Walton Muyumba, "The Dark Room Collective," in Stephen Cushman and Roland Greene (eds.), *The Princeton Encyclopedia of Poetry and Poetics*, 4th ed. (Princeton, N.J.: Princeton University Press, 2012).

Chapter 47

Amy Clampitt, Culture Poetry, and the Neobaroque

WILLARD SPIEGELMAN

Amy Clampitt (1920–1994) holds a unique position in American poetry of the late twentieth century. Although technically a member of the generation that goes from Elizabeth Bishop and Robert Lowell (born in 1911 and 1917, respectively) to Howard Nemerov (1920), Richard Wilbur (1921), Anthony Hecht (1923), and, slightly later, James Merrill (1926) and John Ashbery (1927), she did not appear on the literary scene until the late 1970s, when Howard Moss, poetry editor at the *New Yorker*, began accepting her poems. Her first volume, *The Kingfisher* (1983), brought her to national prominence. In the next decade, four more books appeared – filled with poems of complex syntax and ornate diction, and on themes of travel, history, natural science, contemporary politics, and "high" culture – before her death from ovarian cancer. In many ways, her work bridges the divide between the poetry of her actual contemporaries, who came of age during the Depression and World War II, and that of her fellow "young" poets in the 1970s and 1980s. Many poets of her generation shared her aesthetic, while the poets who got their publishing start when she did shared her political and social concerns. Like the younger ones, she relished the hopeful confidence of the early civil rights movement, and she then shared with them the disillusionment of the Carter and Reagan eras. The assassination of President Kennedy on November 22, 1963, marked the start of a new era and a new, more anxious national spirit. Clampitt had just turned forty-three. For the next decade and a half she became enmeshed in political activism. Poetry, at least the publication of poetry, had to wait.

Because of Clampitt's odd position – she was born in one era but flourished in another – reading her work is not only a pleasure in itself but also a means of surveying the landscape from 1945 to the present. Her intense style, her inclination to decorative embellishment, and, above all, her elaborate syntactic structures might be termed baroque (or neobaroque), in the sense of "irregularly shaped" or "odd." We might also call it rococo, suggesting a spun,

1079

fanciful filigree quality rather than the fiercely melodramatic hardness we associate with the baroque. In either case, "ornate" certainly applies, as does, perhaps, "indispensable." She provides a link between 1950 and 1990. (The label "neobaroque," or "neobarroco," also refers to ways of writing, and ways of reading, crucial to twentieth-century Latin American fiction, poetry, and literary theory, and to some present-day U.S. and Canadian writers influenced by it, although those authors and their approach to the term do not seem to affect the U.S. poetry discussed here.[1])

Clampitt's subjects were in many ways out of fashion when she came to prominence in the 1980s. Her devotion to the dead white males (and females) of both Europe and America, in fact to the entire Western canon from Homer through the nineteenth century, seemed quaint or antique. The nineteenth century especially (the English Romantic poets, Emily Dickinson, George Eliot, Margaret Fuller, and Gerard Manley Hopkins) came alive, almost vicariously, in her. The combination of style and subject matter did not please all of her readers, especially those who harbored a suspicion of ornament, and a preference for the plain over the fancy. They found Clampitt's style overburdening, turning her poems into "a parody of the Victorian silk that Pound sought to unravel."[2] Or they mocked the "bathetic enthusiasm" that emerges from the "forced accumulation of her details."[3] But in her subjects, if not entirely her style, Clampitt resembled her (mostly male) well-educated contemporaries, who knew, often firsthand, the deprivations of the 1930s and the horrors of warfare. These were people as hungry for Europe as she was.

Any cultural history of American poetry must consider the importance of the closing of the European continent for almost two decades. Following the expatriate years of the Roaring Twenties, when Hemingway, the Steins, and other American artists lived well and cheaply in France, in the 1930s few Americans except the wealthy could even afford passage. And from 1939 until several years after the war had ended, tourism was never a real possibility. Even people with some money, Lowell and Merrill most prominently, did not visit the Continent until 1950. By the early 1950s, Europe had opened up. Artists and writers and recent college graduates – many of them veterans who had gone to college courtesy of the G.I. Bill of Rights – were able to see sites they had known about only through books or as servicemen in battle. In 1952 James Wright won a Fulbright to Vienna. Richard Howard studied at the Sorbonne. In 1955 John Ashbery arrived in Paris and stayed for a decade, writing poetry and journalism. The advantages of peacetime and postwar plenty were bolstered by fellowships, government-sponsored programs, and clear, easy passage across an Atlantic free of peril.

The poet Karl Shapiro, another World War II veteran, coined the phrase "culture poetry" more than a half century ago to describe the work of many of these poets, always refined and didactic, which "dives back into the historical situation, into culture, instead of flowering from it."[4] A quarter century later, the scholar Robert von Hallberg picked up the phrase and looked from a farther distance at the tourist poems of "taste, sophistication, intelligence, and inventiveness" like those of the young Adrienne Rich, and Mona Van Duyn, W. S. Merwin, Richard Howard, John Hollander, and especially James Merrill.

Although much of the European terrain – urban and rural – still lay in ruins, and although living conditions in the great cities were far from lavish (the British had rationing through the mid-1950s), Americans flocked abroad. Aesthetic pleasure, and the glories of art and architecture, superseded personal discomforts. The writers were young. Their eyes and ears were hungry. Here is the opening of Richard Wilbur's early poem "A Baroque Wall-Fountain in the Villa Sciarra":

> Under the bronze-crown
> Too big for the head of the stone cherub whose feet
>   A serpent has begun to eat,
> Sweet water brims a cockle and braids down
>
>   Past spattered mosses, breaks
> On the tipped edge of a second shell, and fills
>   The massive third below. It spills
> In threads then from the scalloped rim, and makes
>
>   A scrim or summery tent
> For a faun-ménage and their familiar goose.
>   Happy in all that ragged, loose
> Collapse of water, its effortless descent
>
>   And flatteries of spray,
> The stocky god upholds the shell with ease,
>   Watching, about his shaggy knees,
> The goatish innocence of his babes at play.[5]

The quatrains, fifteen in all, continue. The poem's middle section contemplates another, different fountain – Carlo Maderno's upward-spouting masterpiece in front of St. Peter's Cathedral – and ends with an elegant application to our human lives of the measure of water, rising or falling, which Wilbur says is "a shade of bliss ... the dreamt land / Toward which all hungers leap, all pleasures pass."[6]

From the start Wilbur had mastered the art of finding an appropriate form for his subjects. Other poets of the 1950s imitated, but few ever exceeded, his gracefulness.[7] Everything above is coolly spoken, although the fountain Wilbur describes has properties both voluptuous and grotesque. Phrases like "effortless descent" and "flatteries of spray" possess a disarmingly sweet appeal. The "effortless" Renaissance quality known as *sprezzatura* (we might call it "cool") applies equally to the fountain and to Wilbur himself. His *abba* quatrains, with their un-twentieth-century metric (trimeter and tetrameter odd lines, alternating with pentameter even ones) affirm the poet's mastery of an intricate craft and match the complex fluidity of the baroque fountain. So does Wilbur's use of enjambment: notice that none of the preceding stanzas is end-stopped.

From a similar poetic sensibility comes the early work of Anthony Hecht. Here is the opening of "The Gardens of the Villa d'Este":

> This is Italian. Here
> Is cause for the undiminished bounce
> Of sex, cause for the lark, the animal spirit
> To rise, aerated, but not beyond our reach, to spread
> Friction upon the air, cause to sing loud for the bed
> Of jonquils, the linen bed, and established merit
> Of love, and grandly to pronounce
> Pleasure without peer.
>
> Goddess, be with me now;
> Commend my music to the woods.
> There is no garden to the practiced gaze
> Half so erotic: here the sixteenth century thew
> Rose to its last perfection, this being chiefly due
> To the provocative role the water plays.
> Tumble and jump, the fountains' moods
> Teach the world how.[8]

Wilbur's poem seems positively chaste, even plain, set beside Hecht's bravura performance, with its echoes of Yeats's "Sailing to Byzantium" and its quasi-Renaissance formalities ("commend") and diction ("thew") mixed in with contemporary lingo ("bounce / Of sex"), as well as its even more elaborate expanding and diminishing lines, an homage to Donne or Herbert.

It was not surprising that war veterans like Hecht, Nemerov, and Wilbur should seek their poetic subjects, as well as some spiritual respite, from among "aesthetic" monuments, objects, and occasions. But even a younger poet like Adrienne Rich (b. 1929), with her freshly minted Radcliffe College diploma,

W. H. Auden's choice for the prestigious Yale Younger Poets Award of 1951, could share their predisposition. Aestheticism was a form of politeness and precocity, homage to Rich's academic background and the decision to devote her life to "art." Auden, citing Eliot, praises the precocious poet in his introduction to *A Change of World*, for her "craftsmanship" that gives "evidence of a capacity for detachment from the self."[9]

A withdrawal from turbulent emotions, a reluctance to display merely personal concerns, and a "detachment from," rather than an unfolding of, "the self" represent one legacy of Eliot's own hold over much Anglo-American poetry until his death in 1965, or at least until Allen Ginsberg and the other Beat poets began to shake the doors from their jambs in the mid-1950s. Until then, however, restraint rather than explosiveness characterized the tones, forms, and subjects of the young poets. In her second book, *The Diamond Cutters* (1955), composed largely in Europe thanks to a Guggenheim Fellowship in 1952–1953, Rich – still in her early twenties – performs the same meticulous maneuvers of homage, maneuvers that she would gradually but completely abandon within the following decade, as she "came out" (in many senses) from the delicacies of her juvenilia. Von Hallberg has correctly observed that, for the most part, the poets of the 1950s, with the exception of Elizabeth Bishop and Robert Lowell, wrote with little "sense of imperial doom ... there was mainly earnest optimism among intellectuals about the expansion of American industry and the obvious accomplishment of the military."[10] Rich, who became increasingly more political in the following decades, was as earnest as the others.

Clampitt's poems of the 1980s are more politically and historically alert than those of her contemporaries written in the Eisenhower or even the Kennedy years. Although some of her hostile critics have found her work self-indulgent, inattentive to the cultural realities of her day, she proved herself one of the finest political poets of that decade. Her earlier involvement in Vietnam era–protests, as well as a lifelong Quaker commitment to principles of social justice and pacifism, resulted in strong socially conscious work: "A Procession at Candlemas," "Amaranth and Moly," "Beethoven, Opus III," "Or Consider Prometheus," "Letters from Jerusalem," "The Dahlia Gardens," "A Hedge of Rubber Trees," "Nothing Stays Put," "Mataoka," and her masterpiece and longest poem, "The Prairie," which tackles problems of history, migration, and invasion, all the patterns of American life that depend on the vastness of our geography.[11] Art, she would agree with André Malraux and Max Weber, is the real history of nations.

Consider "A Procession at Candlemas," which is both ornate *and* politically engaged. In two sections, each composed of twenty-four tercets, the poem tackles American history and geography; the nature of nomadism and "transhumance" (a term from the historian Fernand Braudel); protests against the Vietnam War; the presentation of the Virgin Mary at the temple on the holiday now known as Candlemas; Mary's associations with Pallas Athena, another "virgin" goddess; childbirth and motherhood; and, the subject with which the poem begins and ends, a trip across America on Interstate 80 to visit the poet's dying mother in Iowa.

It is a remarkable tour de force; I call attention here to only two of its features. The first is its circular construction. This is a poem about many sorts of journeys. Its opening sounds like an updating of Frost's "Directive":

> Moving on or going back to where you came from,
> bad news is what you mainly travel with:
> a breakup or a breakdown, someone running off
>
> or walking out, called up or called home:
> death in the family. . . .
>
> . . . Sooner or later
> every trek becomes a funeral procession.
> The mother curtained in Intensive Care –
>
> a scene the mind leaves blank, fleeing instead
> toward scenes of transhumance.   (*ACP*, p. 21)

One thing leads naturally to another, and Clampitt is off and running. At the end, she circles back to where she had begun:

> . . . the mother
> curtained in Intensive Care: a Candlemas
>
> of moving lights along Route 80, at nightfall,
> in falling snow, the stillness and the sorrow
> of things moving back to where they came from.
>   (*ACP*, p. 25)

The language is easy; the pace is slow. But in between come the other 100 lines of historical, political, social, and geographical meandering; thoughts about the condition of women giving birth, women dying; and religious ceremonies and political vigils. Clampitt casts a wide net.

Another, far from gratuitous, aspect of the poem is something an unfriendly critic would object to: a sumptuous description of the contents of a cafeteria and a vending machine at a "nowhere oasis" called "Indian Meadows." Clampitt asks a question and proceeds to answer it:

> ... What is real except
>
> what is fabricated? The jellies glitter
> cream-capped in the cafeteria showcase;
> gumball globes, Life Savers cinctured
>
> in parcel gilt, plop from their housings
> perfect, like miracles. Comb, nail clipper,
> lip rouge, mirrors and emollients embody,
>
> niched into the washroom wall case,
> the pristine seductiveness of money.   (*ACP*, p. 22)

Like the painter Wayne Thiebaud, Clampitt lavishes loving care on mundane things. From high to low, nothing is beneath attention. Her poem tries to answer the important question about reality and fabrication, the given and the made in our lives as individuals and cultures. This is a poem by a mature poet, not a novice but someone who understands that "reality" depends on what we make of it.

*

Clampitt found her vocational reality – or, if not her vocation, her genre – late. She always knew she was a writer. Bookish and eccentric, the eldest of five children of Quaker farmers in Iowa, she made a beeline to Manhattan following graduation from Grinnell College in 1941. After a very brief graduate career at Columbia, she worked in a series of editorial jobs for Oxford University Press, and in 1949 she won a Press-sponsored essay contest, for which the first prize was a trip to England. It quite literally changed her life. On her return from seeing places she had only read and dreamed about, she quit her job to write a novel. No publisher accepted it, nor two subsequent novels. She went back to work as a reference librarian for the National Audubon Society. Engaged in antiwar activity, and soliciting votes for Eugene McCarthy in 1968, she met Harold Korn, a law professor, who remained her partner for the next quarter century. They married several months before her death.

Clampitt had been toying with poems since the 1950s, but twenty years later, she rose like a comet. In the 1970s she began taking poetry-writing classes at the New School in Manhattan and developed enough self-confidence to read at open mic evenings in Greenwich Village bars and coffee houses. Her first important poems – sent to Howard Moss at the *New Yorker* without her knowledge by her editorial boss at Dutton – were accepted and began to appear in the late 1970s. *The Kingfisher*, her first book, appeared when she was sixty-three. Submitting poems to literary journals, Clampitt found a soul mate in Mary Jo Salter, a recent Harvard graduate who was reading the slush pile for Peter Davison at the *Atlantic Monthly*. Salter incorrectly assumed that Clampitt was, like her, a young, unknown, aspiring poet. They began a close friendship, exchanging letters and manuscripts for the next fifteen years. Other young friends and acolytes surrounded her: Salter's husband, Brad Leithauser; Alfred Corn; Dana Gioia; William Logan and Debora Greger (another poet couple); and J. D. McClatchy. Some of these people, along with Moss, Marilyn Hacker, Mark Jarman, and X. J. Kennedy, have been gathered under the heading of the "New Formalists," often derided in avant-garde circles for their commitment to strict poetic strategies, to rhyme and conventional meter, and even to – of all things! – sonnets. Hilton Kramer's neoconservative journal *New Criterion* has prominently displayed the work of these poets, which represents a kind of right-wing populism. Clampitt, however, always aligned her complex aware-ness of political, cultural, and literary history with the left-of-center.

She was nothing like the New Formalists. Her poems – rich in assonance, alliteration, and metric "effects" – for the most part do without conventional metrical forms and end rhyme. But they are loaded with musical and syntactic complexities, which complement the subject matter that remains more or less constant through her five individual volumes. Clampitt resists the cool per-fection of Wilbur, Hecht, and early Rich, but she also refrains from imitating the "confessional" poets, who flourished between the 1950s and the 1970s. She makes a place for her own voice not by focusing solely on her self, especially her inner self, but by weaving with fervor as well as ingenuity references to her life into her experiences as a tourist, reader of books, and looker at paint-ings. Her poems exhibit the same energy and capacity to be pleased evident in her letters, and the same blend of Quaker severity, or austerity, and Keatsian lushness. She combined her old-fashioned commitment to high culture with the patience and attentiveness necessary for deep reading, looking, and lis-tening. Clampitt's subjects and diction were out of step with the zeitgeist of the 1980s and its insistence, especially within university circles, on what were called "political correctness" and "identity politics." Now that the so-called culture wars of the 1980s have faded, it is easier to take the measure of her achievement.

Clampitt writes about other writers, intellectuals, paintings, music, travel sites, politics, and history. Her second book, *What the Light Was Like* (1985), contains her longest poem about a predecessor, the sequence "Voyages: A Homage to John Keats," a poetic biography in the form of a reimagining of Keats's inner and external life based on a full absorption of his poems and letters. Clampitt had been moved by Keats's poems ever since her girlhood on her Iowa farm. She once said that only a person who knew in her bones what coldness really was could fully appreciate "The Eve of Saint Agnes." (See her early poem "On the Disadvantages of Central Heating" [*ACP*, p. 17].) "On Seeing the Elgin Marbles" nimbly interweaves Keats's responses to the newly acquired sculpture in the British Museum – which he called "A sun – a shadow of a magnitude" – with facts of his life in 1818, when he made his fateful walking tour through Scotland, during which he came down with the first signs of the tuberculosis that would eventually kill him. Clampitt could identify with Keats in many ways. Hunger for a place in the poetic pantheon was the most important, coupled with a fear that vocational ambition might never be satisfied. "I think I shall be among the English poets after my death," wrote Keats in one letter, but, in another, "If I should die … I have left no immortal work behind me."[12] Likewise, Clampitt, at the age of thirty-five, well before she had published a single poem, wrote to her youngest brother, Philip: "I feel as if I could write a whole history of English literature, and know just where to place everybody in it, with hardly any trouble at all. The reason being, apparently, that I feel *I am in it*."[13] But twenty years later, to Salter, she admits to her own vocational loneliness: "I've yearned secretly for a poet I could write to."[14]

Unlike Hecht, Lowell, Merrill, Nemerov, and Wilbur – and even Elizabeth Bishop, who in spite of her early orphancy had sufficient income to go to college and live afterward on a modest inheritance – Clampitt was born neither to privilege nor on the East Coast. Like Keats, but for different reasons, she felt herself an outsider. Although she lived as a New Yorker for more than half a century, she remained attached to her Iowa farm roots. Her interest in high culture did not come from a sense of entitlement or belonging. Exile, loneliness, and deracination figure as much in her poems as the worship of, and the sense of attachment to, what Yeats called "monuments of unaging intellect."[15] She is a poet of places and of displacement; she is equally a poet of the book.

Clampitt loved botanical and zoological nomenclature. She was attentive to landscape wherever she happened to be. She learned such attention both in life – looking at things on the farm – and from her reading. Marianne Moore, another poet deeply versed in science, was as great an influence as Hopkins and the Romantics. "The Cove," the first poem in *The Kingfisher*, begins with an offhand reference to Moore *and* Mozart (*ACP*, p. 5). This is not poetic showing off. Clampitt lived with music and literature; they became part of her. "The Reedbeds of the Hackensack" uses the sestina, that difficult form, as the basis for a contemplation of urban detritus and garbage in northern New Jersey (*ACP*, p. 165). It makes its ecological points via allusions to Virgil, Dante, Shakespeare, and Milton, proving that we can understand the contemporary natural scene best by folding it into a larger literary landscape. Similarly, "John Donne in California" imagines a landscape through a triple remove: one poet looking through the eyes of another, from a different age and from a different place. Donne, who never crossed the Atlantic to the newfound land, asked famously, in his "Hymn to God, My God, in My Sickness," "Is the Pacifique Sea my home?"[16] With that line, Clampitt begins a contemplation of place that includes other adroitly planted echoes. Although Donne never saw California's richness and strangeness, she allows in her conclusion that he

> ... would have been more at home
> than the frail wick of metaphor I've brought
> to see by, and cannot, for the conflagration
> of this nightfall's utter strangeness.   (*ACP*, p. 279)

Seeing through another poet's eyes and language affords the twentieth-century poet access to a truth different from what her own naked vision might allow.

One exemplary poem among many that dramatize how the intersection of life and culture can inspire a full range of reportorial and emotional responses is "Losing Track of Language" (*ACP*, pp. 182–83). Clampitt was – as I have noted – a poet of both journeys and stasis, aware of loss and dislocation in her own life and that of others.[17] She wrote a whole series of poems detailing her travel, by ship, by train, and by – her favorite conveyance in the States – bus. This poem recounts a train trip from the south of France into Italy and uses the resources of culture, history, and language to make deeper, more personal points about human communication and understanding.

Clampitt's energetic enthusiasm for human encounters finds apposite expression in her signature style. Her subtle puns, literary echoes, and long, sinuous sentences maintain a speed comparable to that of the train on which she and her companion sit, wedged among strangers as they hurtle from the Vaucluse in Provence into northern Italy. The poem adopts one of literature's oldest similes, Homer's image of the generations of men as "fallen leaves," and plays with the words "falls," "falling," "fallen," "descended," "fleeing," and "losing," and with Homer's "leaves": "leaf," "bloom," "laurel," and "left" (i.e., "leaves" as a verb as well as a noun). The rush of the train inspires an equally eager and rapid conversation of its polyglot passengers. The babble of language creates solidarity as well as confusion, communication rather than the lack of it. (See "Babel Aboard the Hellas International Express" for another version of the same trope [*ACP*, p. 255].)

Clampitt expects the reader to catch her literary references: to Petrarch, himself an exile in the Vaucluse, where he loved and immortalized his Laura, at the same time virtually inventing the tradition of the sonnet, and to Sappho, the early Greek lyric poet whose work exists almost entirely in fragments. All that is left of *her* leaves is frustratingly incomplete. We must always fill in the blanks. "What are words?" the traveling poet asks, as she contemplates Petrarch's beloved:

> What is left of her is language;
> and what is language but breath, leaves,
> petals fallen or in the act of falling, pollen
> of turmoil that sifts through the fingers?　　(*ACP*, p. 182)

As the conversation with her Italian cabin mate extends to the subject of Sappho, whose work he also knows, she admits: "Though I don't understand a word, what are words?" And she concludes that, with language, as with travel in T. S. Elliot's aphorism, the journey rather than the arrival matters. Everything moves; words are air; we are all in transit:

> The train leaps toward Italy; words fall away
> through the dark into the dark bedroom
> of everything left behind, the unendingness
> of things lost track of – of who, of where –
> where I'm losing track of language.　　(*ACP*, p. 183)

The poem finally and paradoxically commemorates and solidifies an experience all about loss, remembrance, and the effort to recollect (regather and remember) what has been left behind.

The richness of Clampitt's signature diction and syntax – along with her commitment to European culture – appealed to some of her younger contemporaries in the 1980s and 1990s precisely because it went against the prevailing grain. Much American poetry in the wake of William Carlos Williams, especially in the creative writing programs that have proliferated over the past half century, hews to the virtues of simplicity, syntactic straightforwardness, and a turning away from ornament. Poetry like Clampitt's that prefers florid diction and expansive phrasing might seem like a hothouse flower, suspect to some, welcome to others.

Our default mode from the 1960s onward is the plain *koine* of ordinary speech and straightforward sentence structure. Clampitt never wrote this way. She had the singular distinction of writing more one-sentence poems, and indeed very long sentences of all sorts, than any other contemporary poet except, perhaps, those whom we label radically experimental, like Allen

Ginsberg and Jorie Graham (discussed subsequently). Complex syntax, and a reliance on hypotaxis rather than parataxis (on subordination rather than simple lists or compound sentences), is a staple of earlier poetry in English, especially after Milton reimagined his native tongue within a tighter Greco-Latin frame. To readers with no Latin, or no Milton, and especially to those who prefer plainness of articulation, Clampitt's long and often reticulated sentences can seem like syntactic thickets, or a return to an antiquated preference for the baroque.

Take, for instance, the opening of "Thermopylae":

> Where the bay flashed, and an unrecorded number
> of the Persian troops, whip-flicked into the spear-
> clogged hourglass of the pass, were impaled and fell
> screaming from the precipice to drown, the mirror
>
> clogs: geography too gathers dust, though busloads
> of us (sandaled Germans mostly), hankering for
> an attar or a foothold, a principle that still
> applies, a cruse of oil, a watershed no rain erodes,
>
> find small inkling of what was staved off here,
> or saved.   (*ACP*, p. 205)

This is history, tourism, high culture, and ecology mixed together in a style that imitates a tourist's breathless pace. It imitates, too, the poet's engagement with a real landscape as well as the heroic sacrifice of Leonidas and his noble Spartans in 480 B.C.E. We notice that the sentence falls into two parts, divided by a colon, and that each half has its own subordinate divisions. The onrush is contained by a sense of balance and repetition. "Clogs" matches "clogged," and the press of the Persian troops prepares us for the stampede of the modern tourists. Antithesis and division also exist. The first part of the sentence contains many phrases dividing the subject and verb: "Where the bay flashed ... the mirror clogs." Everywhere obscurity threatens to interfere with revelation. You can't be sure what is happening, just as in warfare no certainty exists, because you can't be everywhere at once.

Style conveys meaning; it is not merely something added. Clampitt's diction, her references, and her syntax, which owes a great deal to Hart Crane as well as to Milton, bear the weight of her thought. Clampitt was not alone. Her kind of style, and of learning, reflects the bookish and cultural heritage she shared with Wilbur and Hecht. Hecht, especially, grew as a poet, taking on increasingly darker themes and tones, but he never abandoned the glittering surfaces and formal properties of his earliest poems. He never felt a tension between human tragedy, what he witnessed as a foot soldier in World War II, or the horrors of civilization, and the elegant – one might call them "civilizing" – stanzas and rhymes he used to present them. His style both conveyed and also countered the bleakness of his subjects. "The Feast of Stephen," a scene of locker room romping, in which "Boys for the first time frankly eye each other, / Inspect each other's bodies at close range," even includes a witty pun, *"Mens sana* in men's sauna," before launching into a scene of sadomasochistic terror redolent of Nazi storm troopers. That scene then merges into the torture "of a young man whose name is Saul" (the Jew who became St. Paul); all of this is handled in four exquisitely patterned, unrhymed sonnets.[18]

In *The Venetian Vespers* (1979) we find another poem of exquisite cruelty in an exquisitely subtle style. "The Deodand" (a technical term for a forfeiture to expiate a crime) opens artfully as a description of Renoir's painting *Parisians Dressed in Algerian Costume* and then investigates George Santayana's famous aphorism: those who ignore the lessons of history are doomed to repeat them. Hecht wonders about the "crude imperial pride" within the "exploitation of the primitive / Homages of romantic self-deception, / Mimes of submission glamorized as lust."[19] His poem's final stanzas describe a French Legionnaire who, in the final months of the French-Algerian War, is captured and dressed grotesquely as a woman. His captors cut off his fingers, and he must take his food literally from their hands. They lead him from town to town on a leash. The lesson is simple: cruelty begets cruelty, and the innocent suffer. The poem's meter is a kind of loose pentameter, clear within bounds but never rigid. Its diction is crisp, sometimes learned. The deliberate rhythmic fluctuations within conventional forms, the way the poem begins with what appears to be innocent description, the reminder of art's social contexts and consequences, and the pairing of scenes and uncertain time schemes: all of these reflect Hecht's fascination with the moral ambiguities that lie beneath apparent simplicities.

Hecht's great theme throughout his distinguished career was, in fact, a religious one: the question of *unde malum*. Where does evil come from? The fact that his verse forms always conveyed an aesthetic conservatism in no way means that his moral, political, and religious stances are equally conservative. One chilling later poem is "The Book of Yolek." It is a sestina, that most difficult of conventional forms, but its subject is the death of a small boy at the hands of the Nazis in 1942. The pleasures of repetition, in the end words of the sestina, are surpassed by the reader's gradual realization of the poem's true subject.[20]

One other major poet of the second half of the century shared with Hecht a deep learning, a fondness for formal experimentation, and a commitment to the entire range of Western civilization and art. John Hollander (b. 1929) had a distinguished career as both poet and scholar at (for the most part) Yale University. The epithet "academic" is often used derogatorily, but poetry has always had an attachment to the academy, from the early Greek lyric poets connected to the library in Alexandria during the third century B.C.E. to contemporary poets who find a haven in the "creative writing" sections of American university English departments. Hollander is one of the rare ones who wrote major books of scholarship and criticism, including *Rhyme's Reason* (1981), the best introduction to poetic forms, done in a performative show-and-tell way that not only describes iambic pentameter or Petrarchan sonnets but also handles the description and analysis *through* and *within* the forms themselves.

For Hollander, elaborate verse forms, syntactical arrangements, and a commitment to the library and high culture were never in rivalry with investigations of private life. (He wrote movingly about the breakup of his first marriage in the 1978 *In Time and Place*.) Hollander's poetry has ranged from the difficult subject matter of Jewish Gnosticism to the sheer fun of "shaped" poems (see the new and expanded edition of *Types of Shape* [1991]). *Tales Told of the Fathers* (1975) and *Spectral Emanations* (1978) demonstrated the deepening as well as the expanding of his themes, repertoire, and techniques. But the poems of *In Time* are written in the simple *abba* stanzas favored by Tennyson in *In Memoriam*. In other words, Hollander has been able to accommodate many styles, many subjects.

To prove my point that wit and high seriousness can go hand in hand, as can the inner life and the literary one, consider "To Elizabeth Bishop" (from the 1988 *Harp Lake*). Written in easy rhyming tercets (*aaa*, *bbb*, *ccc*), the poem records Hollander's 1977 efforts to track down the French word for "moose."[21] Finding out that the word was "original" ushers in a riff on the nature of poetic originality. But then, after Bishop's death two years later, Hollander looks again and discovers his earlier misreading: the French word for "moose" is not "original" but "orignal," and he's off on another riff, this time on the subject of the missing, or added, *i* and the relationship of human subjectivity to acts of reading and misreading, repeating, and revising, and to the whole literary and linguistic debt that one poet owes to another, the lineage that keeps literary history in some kind of order.

Hollander's playfulness, as well as his baroque sensibility, was evident from the start. In the title poem of *Movie-Going* (1962), he writes an elegiac ode to the movies and the movie theaters of his Manhattan boyhood. What amazes in the poem, and what keeps it fresh well after all the Broadway theaters of Hollander's youth have been destroyed or replaced, is the combination of wit and wonder with which the poet treats his subject. As he would go on to prove in *Rhyme's Reason*, "poetry" is made of tropes, or figures of speech, while "verse" consists of "schemes" and patterns, all of the nonlinguistic or nonsemantic musical, rhythmic, and syntactic units that make up an utterance. And these two aspects of a single poem need never be at odds. Notice how the poem's opening lines end:

> One needs to feel
> That the two empty, huddled, dark stage-boxes keep
> Empty for kings. And having frequently to cope
> With the abominable goodies, overflow
> Bulk and (finally) exploring hands of flushed
> Close neighbors gazing beadily out across the glum
> Distances is, after all, to keep the gleam
> Alive of something rather serious, to keep
> Faith, perhaps, with the City.[22]

The rhyme is prodigious and unexpected: the long vowel of "feel" is repeated in "keep" and then in "frequently," while "keep" links up to "cope," "cope" lends its vowel twice to "overflow," "neighbors" to "gazing," "glum" and "keep" combine in "gleam," and so forth. Everything matches, but nothing is predictable. We move through the experience with surprise and gratitude. And on it goes for more than four pages. The end, a nine-line stanza followed by a single line, asks us to "honor" the stars, the films, and moviegoing itself, that quintessentially American experience. The poem turns out to be a cultural as well as a personal reminiscence. America is always moving westward, waiting for a revelation

> Of something different from Everything Here, Now, shine
> Out from the local Bijou, truest gem, the most bright
> Because the most believed in, staving off the night
> Perhaps, for a while longer with its flickering light.
> These fade. All fade, Let us honor them with our own fading sight.[23]

From part rhymes, interlocking and onward moving, to a static conclusion with a final purely rhymed quatrain ("bright," "night," "light," "sight"), "Movie-Going" pays homage to, among other things, a relationship between vision and music, between what we see at the cinema and what we hear rising from the poem's sounds. This is a "talkie" in the best tradition.

Rhymes can exist in full sight (or at full volume) or as partially hidden. Both kinds exist in "Movie-Going." Hollander's *Powers of Thirteen* (1984) is an ingenious stylistic experiment: 169 poems, each composed of thirteen lines with thirteen syllables. Thirteen: the eccentric, unlucky number, the number of Wallace Stevens's "Thirteen Ways of Looking at a Blackbird." And 169 is also, of course, 13 squared. Hollander's poems are more than ingenious web spinning. They experiment with both form and fable. One fine example is number 9, "Hidden Rhymes," a variation on the Parable of the Talents (Matthew 25 and Luke 19) and a homage, as well, to Milton's sonnet on his blindness ("When I consider how my light is spent"). Because the parable of the talents concerns hiding, using, investing, and earning, it makes sense for the poet to make his own contribution to a tradition by hiding his rhymes, his echoes of his talents and those of his forerunners. The first line announces a legacy: "One evening in the early spring Father gave us dimes." There follow one long Miltonic sentence and a shorter conclusion: in the poet's pocket, "my dime could rhyme with its own echoes, / Down inside a buried sound it was no death to hide."[24] The whole poem alludes to the New Testament, to Milton, and to Wordsworth, in Hollander's internal rhyme: groupings of "hard," "yard," and "card"; "kind" and "blind"; and "dime" and "rhyme" itself.

Salter (b. 1954) became Clampitt's literary executor as well as her friend. Although not as stylistically dense as Clampitt's work, her poems exhibit a genteel sense of learning and a dedication to high art and domesticity. J. D. McClatchy (b. 1945), a poet in the tradition of Auden and Merrill, earlier gay mentors, maintains a similar aestheticism without the syntactic tangles and the emotional exuberance of Clampitt's tones. Kay Ryan (b. 1945) was, like Clampitt, a relative late starter, or at least someone who came to public notice only in middle age. Her first widely reviewed volume, *Flamingo Watching*, was published in 1994; there followed three others, and the Pulitzer Prize–winning *The Best of It: New and Selected Poems* (2010). Ryan is not a culture poet, although plenty of the epigraphs to individual poems give evidence of her wide and deep reading. Nor is she a poet of heavily subordinated sentences. Unlike Clampitt, Ryan writes with simple diction and an often Emily Dickinson–like syncopated meter. All of her poems are short, often less than a page long, with plenty of surrounding white space. And unlike Clampitt, but like Hecht, Hollander, Wilbur, and most of the so-called New Formalists, she enjoys rhyming. But she rhymes in an offbeat, off-kilter way; the rhymes are often jagged, unexpected, or "hidden," that is, internalized (again, see Hollander). Take, for example, "Dew":

> As neatly as peas
> in their green canoe,
> as discretely as beads

> strung in a row,
> sit drops of dew
> along a blade of grass.
> But unattached and
> subject to their weight,
> they slip if they accumulate.
> Down the green tongue
> out of the morning sun
> into the general damp,
> They're gone.[25]

These are three prim little sentences, which open with an easy simile (dew is like peas). The novelty is the fact that Ryan's genius allows her to make her comparisons through sound as well as trope: the off rhymes of "peas" and "beads"; the full rhyme of "canoe" and "dew" surrounding the semirhyming "row"; the full rhyme of "weight" and "accumulate" (the poem's longest word, and therefore its weightiest); and then the disappearing triple rhyme in "tongue," "sun," and "gone." As in the cliché "Now you see it, now you don't," we have found that Ryan has virtually told us, "Now you hear it, now you don't."

The wit inherent in rhyme generates poetic revelation. Ryan is a poet who never writes about her "lived" life; we learn almost nothing about it, or her, through these objective lyrics, part Marianne Moore, part Ogden Nash. An even more rococo poet is Heather McHugh (b. 1948), who reveals more of herself than Ryan does, but whose style and rhythms are more distinctly jazz and pun inflected. See, for example, "The Trouble With 'In,'" whose first eleven lines follow:

> In English we're in trouble.
> Love's a place
> we fall into, so
> sooner or later they ask
>
> How deep? Time's a measure
> of extent, so sooner or later
> they ask How long? We keep
> some comforters inside a box,
> the heart inside a chest,
>
> but still it's there the trouble with the dark
> accumulates the most.[26]

Hollander wrote an essay titled "Of 'Of': The Romance of a Preposition," and McHugh is clearly bound to the same fascination with the peculiarities of English speech, its duplicities and the oddness of its easiest colloquialisms. Why are we *in* trouble? Why fall *in* love, rather than rise to it? "In" is where we find our innermost thoughts, recesses, fears, and selves. Darkness resides always within, never without.

Gjertrud Schnackenberg (b. 1953) and Jorie Graham (b. 1950) now live in Cambridge, Massachusetts. Their work often gives off a whiff of the library, the concert hall, the museum, and the university. Both are poets of high culture, although Graham has increasingly turned away from an earlier interest in ekphrasis (most prominently displayed in *Erosion*, her second volume [1983]), toward more speculative, philosophical, political, and scientific concerns. Schnackenberg's chiseled spiritual poems mingle autobiographical reminiscences with historical and literary references. Each volume contains pages of notes, as do many other volumes of culture poetry written during the past four decades. T. S. Eliot's disingenuous notes for *The Waste Land* spawned an entire progeny of annotations and poetic annotators since 1922. Schnackenberg's third volume, *A Gilded Lapse of Time* (1992), intricately sets the creation of art against the catastrophes of world history. Like Clampitt, Schnackenberg has no problem with incorporating learning, from the book or the museum, into her work, and she coolly mixes formal dexterity with strong feeling. Adam Kirsch has called her verse "dense and musical, anchored in the pentameter even when it veers into irregularity; behind it are formidable masters, Robert Lowell most notably, but also Yeats and Auden."[27]

Schnackenberg is prone to economic tightness, to repetition – even conservation – of materials. As in Clampitt, art and history are mediums of thought, not easy deflections from meditation or self-analysis. "Supernatural Love" appears in *The Lamplit Answer* (1982). The volume's title comes from a phrase in this poem, and the poem's title reappears later as the title for a 2000 selection of poems from her first three volumes.[28] In tightly rhymed tercets (*aaa, bbb, ccc*) that flow delicately into one another with little end-stopping (sentences tend to end in the middle of lines), Schnackenberg tenderly recalls a moment from her childhood during which her professor father scans the dictionary for the meaning and etymology of the word "carnation."

The poem looks at the world through several lenses: the dictionary; the actual "magnifying glass" with which the father is scanning it; the young girl's sewing needle, through which *she* scans her father's looking; and, at least implicitly, William Blake's aphorism from *Auguries of Innocence*: "To see a World in a Grain of Sand, / And a Heaven in a Wild Flower, / Hold Infinity in the palm of your hand, / And Eternity in an hour."[29] The poem opens up: the carnation is identified as "Christ's flowers" because, in part, of etymology (from the Latin word for "flesh"). One pink variety of the flower is called the clove. So the father turns the dictionary's page to "clove" (related to the word for nail): "The incarnation blossoms, flesh and nail." Here is the poem's last sentence, in which many tropes are woven back together:

> I lift my hand, it is myself I've sewn,
> The flesh laid bare, the threads of blood my own,
>
> I lift my hand in startled agony
> And call upon his name, "Daddy daddy" –
> My father's hand touches the injury
>
> As lightly as he touched the page before,
> Where incarnation bloomed from roots that bore
> The flowers I called Christ's when I was four.[30]

The snaking sentence uses literary and cultural echoes as well as repeated sounds. Christ calls on God the Father when he is dying on the cross ("Why hast thou forsaken me?"). "Roots" are those of the earth and of the Latin language through which carnations come to embody, or "incarnate," many meanings and associations. And if a Christian is to embark on an *imitatio Christi*, then the young Trudie has already, at four, taken on herself a religious vocation by shedding her blood.

All good poets are concerned with sentence structure. Louise Glück has always used clear-cut syntax that complements her equally straightforward diction. The subject-verb-object paradigm of the simple English sentence has become one pole of contemporary poetic usage. The other, exemplified in the work of the high culture poets in this chapter, is the densely compacted or sinuous sentence of which I have cited examples. Style constitutes, as well as represents, meaning; a craving for expressive syntax matches any poet's search for the *mot juste* and the right tropes. Roland Barthes used the term "layered-ness" (*feuilleté*), as in the image of an onion, for certain styles: "A construction of layers (or levels, or systems) whose body contains, finally, no heart, no kernel, no secret, no irreducible principle, nothing except the infinity of its own envelopes – which envelop nothing other than the unity of its own surfaces."[31] Such an idea was more popular during the heyday of "deconstructive" literary criticism, which tried to undermine old-fashioned notions of purposefulness and meaning in literary texts; it is still useful for understanding what I call the content of style on which all poems depend.

I have called the long sentences of Schnackenberg, Clampitt, and their predecessors "baroque." These complex articulations demand a mental journey on the part of both writer and reader. A century ago, the critic Morris Croll, whose work Clampitt read in college, outlined some varieties of seventeenth-century baroque prose, attending to matters of symmetry and asymmetry, grammar, parallelism and its absence, and punctuation. He concludes: "[The] purpose [of his baroque writers] was to portray, not a thought, but a mind thinking, or, in Pascal's words, *la peinture de la pensée*."[32] "A mind thinking" echoes Emerson's 1837 essay "The American Scholar" as well as Pascal.[33]

Clampitt loved the English Romantic poets. In her last decade, she worked on an ill-conceived play about the intersecting lives of the Wordsworths and Coleridge. More important, she learned how to write what the critic M. H. Abrams labeled the "greater Romantic lyric," a long poem – like "A Procession at Candlemas" – with a circular structure.[34] She also learned her syntax from her Romantic predecessors. Of long, hypotactic sentences, Coleridge said it best, in a letter to his friend Thomas Poole:

> Of parentheses I may be too fond, and will be on my guard against them.
> But I am certain that no work of impassioned and eloquent reasoning
> ever did or could subsist without them. They are the *drama* of
> reason, and present the thought growing, instead of a mere
> *Hortus siccus*.[35]

A thought can grow through sentence structure as well as diction. "Baroque," "rococo," or even "ramifying," when applied to syntax, means the opposite of "simple," "balanced," or "straightforward." Still, a long sentence in the manner of Allen Ginsberg's *Howl* is not quite the same as the sentences favored by the neobaroque poets I have mentioned. Ginsberg, like Whitman, works by principles of breath and association and pays less attention to syntax per se than to the onward rolling, rather than reticulating, of his sentences.

Jorie Graham, on the other hand, has moved from the artful, reasonably condensed lyrics of her first two volumes to a Whitmanian swirling energy in her later work. She has also moved from being an art and culture poet to a political and philosophical one. In *Materialism* (1993), she sounds like Coleridge in his description of "the drama of reason," and of the relationship of nature to sentence structure:

> ... Reader,
> wind blowing through these lines I wish were branches,
> searchlight in daylight, trying as I
> am trying
> to find a filament of the real like some twist of
> handwriting glowing in the middle
> distance – somewhere up here, in the air – .[36]

At the start, Graham had a simpler style, but then her sentences began branching out in order to reflect both her subjects and her mind contemplating them. This may have had something to do with her own transatlantic moves. Born in New York, she was raised by American parents in France and Italy. When she returned to the United States for university, English was the weakest of her three languages; she grew into it slowly, and her poems became more forceful and original, as well as odd, as she settled paradoxically into her native language and country. In some of her poems from the 1990s and later, she seems to forgo conventional grammar altogether. Her metaphysical "filaments" become more "twisted" as her poems become longer.

Her "art" book, *Erosion* (1983), has poems about the Renaissance Italian painters Piero della Francesca, Masaccio, and Luca Signorelli; the Viennese expressionist painter Gustav Klimt; and the unicorn tapestries in Paris's Cluny Museum, in addition to other poems centering on Keats and Plato. Graham carved out a niche for herself as a culture poet, a poet of dense syntax. Here, for example, is an earnest of the richer, *more* difficult poems that followed, the opening sentence of "Masaccio's Expulsion," about the painter's frescoes in Florence's Brancacci Chapel:

> Is this really the failure
> of silence,
> or eternity, where these two
> suffer entrance
> into the picture
> plane,
>
> a man and woman
> so hollowed
> by grief they cover
> their eyes
> in order not to see
> the inexhaustible grammar
>
> before them – labor, judgement,
> saints and peddlers –
> the daylight hopelessly even
> upon them,
> and our eyes.[37]

Although it lacks Clampitt's enthusiasm and Schnackenberg's sparkle, many kinds of ambiguity fill this sentence. Graham takes a long look at Masaccio's picture of Adam and Eve leaving Eden in tears. The opening question, posing as a declarative sentence, deals with the fresco, its placement on a wall, its relation to the ongoing human activity outside the church, and our own position as viewers. It engages us at the level of abstraction ("the failure / of silence" and "eternity" in the opening lines), and it also explicitly compares human activity and modes of speech ("inexhaustible grammar"). As she does throughout her work, Graham starts with a specific visual provocation and moves outward, or inward, from it. Looking and wondering become synonymous.

For Clampitt, Hecht, Merrill, Nemerov, Rich, Wilbur, and other poets who came of age during and immediately after World War II, "culture" had something of what hostile critics might label "elitism." Hungry for high art and the assurances of continuity and endurance that it offered to young people weary of war, these poets – who were of largely secular temperaments – adapted the aestheticism of Oscar Wilde and devoted themselves to the study, even the worship, of art objects. Poets of the following generation, even Jorie Graham (who in 1966 as a teenager helped to save Italian artifacts during the raging floods in Florence), have tended to look at art, indeed to define "art," somewhat differently. It is anything that meets the eye, is well made, or offers an opportunity for contemplation. And while the earlier poets often thought of art as an escape from history, the younger ones have embedded the art objects they write about into history, and also into contemporary events.

Notes

1. On the Latin American neobaroque, see, for example (in English), Lois Parkinson Zamora, *The Inordinate Eye: New World Baroque and Latin American Fiction* (Chicago: University of Chicago Press, 2006); Rolando Perez, *Severo Sarduy and the Neo-Baroque Image of Thought in the Visual Arts* (West Lafayette, Ind.: Purdue University Press, 2011); Severo Sarduy, "The Baroque and the Neo-Baroque," *Descant* 17:4 (1986), pp. 133–60. For another way of seeing the neobaroque in late twentieth-century culture, especially film, see Angela Ndalianis, *Neo-Baroque Aesthetics and 20th Century Entertainment* (Cambridge, Mass.: MIT Press, 2004).

2. Mary Karr, "Against Decoration," *Parnassus* 16:2 (1991), pp. 277–300, 277.

3. Robert McDowell, "The Wilderness Surrounds the Word," *Hudson Review* 43 (1991), pp. 669–78, 672.

4. Karl Shapiro, *In Defense of Ignorance* (New York: Random House, 1960), p. 22.

5. Richard Wilbur, *Collected Poems 1943–2004* (New York: Harcourt, 2004), p. 344.

6. Wilbur, *Collected Poems*, p. 346.

7. See John Hollander, *The Gazer's Spirit: Poems Speaking to Silent Works of Art* (Chicago: University of Chicago Press, 1995), pp. 267–75, for a brief analysis of this poem.

8. Anthony Hecht, *Collected Earlier Poems* (New York: Knopf, 1990), p. 92.

9. Adrienne Cecile Rich, *A Change of World* (New Haven, Conn.: Yale University Press, 1951), p. 10.

10. Robert von Hallberg, *American Poetry and Culture, 1945–1980* (Cambridge, Mass.: Harvard University Press, 1985), p. 83.

11. Amy Clampitt, *The Collected Poems* (New York: Knopf, 1997), pp. 21, 34, 50, 89, 93, 96, 334, 339, 369, 343. This collection will subsequently be cited in the text as *ACP*.

12. John Keats, *Selected Letters of John Keats*, ed. Grant F. Scott, rev. ed. (Cambridge, Mass.: Harvard University Press, 2002), pp. 199, 422.

13. Amy Clampitt, *Love, Amy: The Selected Letters of Amy Clampitt*, ed. Willard Spiegelman (New York: Columbia University Press, 2005), p. 53.

14. Clampitt, *Love, Amy*, p. 199.

15. William Butler Yeats, *Poems*, ed. Richard J. Finneran (New York: Macmillan, 1989), p. 193.

16. John Donne, *Divine Poems*, ed. Helen Gardner (Oxford: Oxford University Press, 1978), p. 50.

17. For further discussion, see Willard Spiegelman, *How Poets See the World: The Art of Description on Contemporary Poetry* (New York: Oxford University Press, 2005), pp. 57–81.

18. Hecht, *Collected Earlier Poems*, p. 150.

19. Hecht, *Collected Earlier Poems*, p. 188.

20. Anthony Hecht, *The Transparent Man* (New York: Knopf, 1990), p. 73.

21. John Hollander, *Harp Lake* (New York: Knopf, 1988), pp. 75–77.

22. John Hollander, *Movie-Going and Other Poems* (New York: Atheneum, 1962), p. 2.

23. Hollander, *Movie-Going*, p. 6.

24. John Hollander, *Selected Poetry* (New York: Knopf, 1993), p. 10.

25. Kay Ryan, *Elephant Rocks* (New York: Grove, 1996), p. 93.

26. Heather McHugh, *Hinge and Sign: Poems 1968–1993* (Middletown, Conn.: Wesleyan University Press, 1994), p. 159.

27. Adam Kirsch, "All Eyes on the Snow Globe," *New York Times Book Review*, October 29, 2000, http://www.nytimes.com/books/00/10/29/reviews/001029.29kirscht.html.

28. Gjertrud Schnackenberg, *Supernatural Love: Poems 1976–1992* (New York: Farrar, Straus and Giroux, 2000), pp. 129–31.

29. William Blake, *Complete Poetry and Prose*, ed. David V. Erdman, rev. ed. (Berkeley: University of California Press, 1982), p. 490.

30. Schnackenberg, *Supernatural Love*, p. 131.

31. Roland Barthes, "Style and Its Image," in Seymour Chatman (ed.), *Literary Style: A Symposium* (New York: Oxford University Press, 1971), pp. 3–15, 10.

32. Morris Croll, *Style Rhetoric and Rhythm: Essays by Morris W. Croll*, ed. J. Max Patrick and Robert O. Evans, with John M. Wallace and R. J. Schoeck (Princeton, N.J.: Princeton University Press, 1966), p. 210.

33. Ralph Waldo Emerson, *Essays and Lectures*, ed. Joel Porte (New York: Library of America, 1983), p. 54.

34. M. H. Abrams, "Structure and Style in the Greater Romantic Lyric," in Frederick W. Hilles and Harold Bloom (eds.), *From Sensibility to Romanticism* (New York: Oxford University Press, 1965), pp. 527–60.

35. Samuel Taylor Coleridge, *The Letters of Samuel Taylor Coleridge*, ed. Ernest Hartley Coleridge (Boston: Houghton Mifflin, 1895), vol. 2, pp. 558–59.

36. Jorie Graham, *Materialism* (Hopewell, N.J.: Ecco, 1993), p. 137.

37. Jorie Graham, *Erosion* (Princeton, N.J.: Princeton University Press, 1983), p. 66.

Chapter 48

Modern and Contemporary Children's Poetry

JOSEPH T. THOMAS, JR.

Angela Sorby begins her contribution to this collection with a claim as seemingly radical as it is true: "Children's poetry is ... a marginal subfield within the already-somewhat-marginal field of poetry. It is barely studied and barely taught.... And yet, ironically, nineteenth-century verses for children ... are among the best-known and most culturally influential texts in American literary history." With but one change ("nineteenth-century" to "twentieth-century") these words could – and I suppose shall – work as an introduction to the topic of *this* chapter. Children's poetry is the popular poetry of the twentieth and twenty-first centuries. David Russell suggests, and rightly so, "that few American children ever move far beyond the joyous nonsense of Shel Silverstein or Jack Prelutsky in their elementary classroom experiences," and yet poems for children (to echo Sorby) number among the most culturally influential texts in American literary history, and the most readily recognizable poets in our nation are those who have made a career writing for children.[1] Add Dr. Seuss to the pair of poets Russell mentions, and you have a triad equally if not more well known than Robert Frost, and Frost owes much of his broader fame to his secret second life as a children's poet. Furthermore, the best-selling collections of poetry today are invariably those marketed and sold to children (or, more precisely, to their gift-giving caretakers), and our shared tradition of folk poetry – "Miss Suzy Had a Steamboat" and "Miss Mary Mack, Mack, Mack," to cite two obvious examples – is firmly centered in the domain of childhood.

However, to note that children's poetry is a marginal area within the already marginal field of poetry is only half the story. Yes, those who study poetry for adults largely ignore children's poetry as an academic subject. Frost's reputation as a children's poet may not really be a secret, but it does seem an embarrassment, and Theodore Roethke's rigorous study of nursery rhymes and his own collections of children's poetry (*I Am! Says the Lamb* [1961], *Party at the Zoo* [1963], and the posthumous *Dirty Dinky and Other Creatures* [1973]) are largely ignored by the ample scholarship surrounding his life and work. Likewise, John Ciardi's still-declining reputation lies solely on the perceived inadequacies of his adult poetry, although he is one of the most successful and talented of late century children's poets. And Randall Jarrell's reputation still rests – despite the work of Richard Flynn and Stephen Burt – on his extraordinary criticism rather than his poetry for children or for adults.[2] Russell insists, "American poetry for children has long suffered from neglect, and occasional abuse, from scholars, teachers, and, indeed, from poets themselves."[3] His claim is born out by even a cursory survey of American poetry anthologies and syllabi, in which children's poetry is woefully underrepresented – if there at all. Yet this neglect comes not only from scholars and teachers and writers of adult poetry (and here is the other half of the story) but also from colleagues within the fairly marginalized study of children's literature itself.

This anxiety informs even the writing of this chapter: to treat in a single essay the subject of twentieth-century American children's poetry is a daunting task, for the endeavor suggests the subject is more homogenous than it is. As Flynn writes, U.S. children's poetry is, "like poetry for adults[,] ... a clouded battleground for competing camps."[4] And yet, as I suggested previously, children's poetry today is not limited to *literary* poetry – that is, poetry printed up in books and sold in stores – but extends to playground poetry, a fluid body of traditional folk rhymes shared by children (and later by adults) of nearly all social classes and racial and ethnic backgrounds. For these reasons, the subject of children's poetry can be more vexing than its adult counterpart, for we cannot be sure even what a children's poem *is*. Limiting ourselves momentarily to the literary variety, a systematic look at the kinds of poetry offered up to children in our most celebrated children's poetry anthologies (including *The Golden Treasure of Poetry* [1959], *Reflections on a Gift of a Watermelon Pickle* [1966], *Knock at a Star* [1982], *The Random House Book of Poetry for Children* [1983], and *A Child's Anthology of Poetry* [1995]) demonstrates immediately the problem: the poets most commonly featured in these collections are known chiefly for their adult work, and the poems that represent these poets are only tentatively children's poems: E. E. Cummings, Robert Frost, Theodore Roethke, Carl Sandburg, Langston Hughes, and William Carlos Williams top the list of the most commonly anthologized poets, and their poems, for example, "In Just –" (Cummings), "The Road Not Taken" (Frost), "My Papa's Waltz" (Roethke), "Fog" (Sandburg), "Dreams" (Hughes), and "The Red Wheelbarrow" (Williams), are poems written for an adult audience and published first in collections and poetry magazines marketed to adults.[5]

In *Poetry's Playground* I argue that the history of contemporary American children's poetry is the history of poetry for adults.[6] However, as Sorby (and Donald Hall, if less thoroughly) demonstrates, the history of these two genres has been interwoven since the beginnings of our nation.[7] Poetry for children and adults branched away from each other significantly in the early twentieth century, only after the wild success and popularization of what Sorby calls "schoolroom poetry," but even then there was overlap. Schoolroom poetry was a fundamental part of middle-class life from the nineteenth to the early twentieth century, in competition with "comic strips or silent films," not the developing avant-garde.[8] But as we began to draw the line between adult and child more starkly, the "tremendous popularity" of children's poetry began to suggest "(and perpetuate) a 'natural' connection between children and poetry," especially narrative poetry and "verse" that employs self-consciously regular rhyme and meter.[9] This connection between form and childhood is doubtlessly one of the reasons so much "adult" twentieth-century poetry deemed appropriate for children displays traditional form. (The work of Robert Frost is a salient example.) If there was a conflict between modernism and schoolroom poetry, it existed primarily in the minds of poets like Ezra Pound, who, even as a champion of Frost, sought to distance himself from the kind of verse found in primers like the McGuffey or Appleton readers (the latter of which, as Jarrell's Uncle Wadsworth reminds us in "The Schools of Yesteryear," contained not only poems by the usual schoolroom poets but also work by John Milton, William Wordsworth, "Addison, Bishop, Berkeley, Bunyan, Byron, Coleridge, Carlyle, Cervantes, Coleridge," and a host of others besides).[10] Therefore, when Ezra Pound urged poets "To break the pentameter," he was really breaking away from a tradition of schoolroom poetry (and prosody) that effectively infantilized meter and, Sorby might add, that infantilized popular poetry in general.[11] (I should note that the vast number of books of poetry published for children, even in these early years of the twenty-first century, regularly feature rhymed, anapestic meter, a meter still shunned by even the most conservative of formalist adult poets.[12]) Of course, more than a few U.S. modernists tried their hand at children's poetry: T. S. Eliot (*Old Possum's Book of Practical Cats* [1939]), Langston Hughes (*The Dream Keeper* [1932]), Carl Sandburg (*Early Moon* [1930]), and even Gertrude Stein (*The World is Round* [1939]), among others.

However, most children's poets writing during the first quarter of the twentieth century shared the aesthetic sensibilities of those in the previous century. Although their reputations have since declined, Elizabeth Coatsworth, David

McCord, Elizabeth Madox Roberts, and Sara Teasdale are just a handful of the popular poets enjoyed by literate Americans in the first half of the twentieth century. Their poems joined what Sorby calls the "hit singles" of nineteenth-century giants of schoolroom poetry like Elizabeth Akers ("Rock Me to Sleep"), Sarah Josepha Hale ("Mary's Lamb"), Joyce Kilmer ("Trees"), and Walt Whitman ("O Captain! My Captain!"). These poems functioned as "an archive of popular memory" sustained by schools, "museums, lyceums, theaters, newspapers, and children's magazines and clubs."[13] Among these poets, the most popular – remaining so until Frost unseated him in the 1960s – was Carl Sandburg, famous for his long, Whitmanesque lines. Unlike his major poetic competitors, Sandburg eschews meter and rhyme, as we see in his most enduring contribution to children's literature, *Early Moon* (1930). One of the collection's typical celebrations of the working class, "Fish Crier," is composed of three sentences, each a single, long line. It begins, "I know a Jew fish crier on Maxwell Street with a voice like a north wind blowing over stubble in January."[14] In "Street Window," another of his city poems, we find an unusually tender example of Sandburg's tendency to depict unflinchingly social ills: "The pawn-shop man knows hunger, / And how far hunger has eaten the heart / Of one who comes with an old keepsake."[15] *Early Moon* is also remarkable for its "Short Talk on Poetry," which opens the collection:

> We have heard much in our time about free verse being modern, as though it is a new-found style for men to use in speaking and writing, rising out of the machine age, skyscrapers, high speed and jazz. Now, if free verse is a form of writing poetry without rime, without regular meters, without established and formal rules governing it, we can easily go back to the earliest styles of poetry known to the human family – and the style is strictly free verse.[16]

This dedication to addressing pertinent debates in twentieth-century poetry is typical: Sandburg addresses his child readers as an intellectually curious and capable audience.

Langston Hughes's *The Dream Keeper* (1932) similarly resists the commonplaces of popular poetry, in terms of both content and form. While Hughes does use rhyme and meter, he is freer in their application, writing in traditional poetic forms, free verse, and the blues, all to great effect. The final stanza of "Wide River" illustrates his command of the blues form and his fearlessness in employing an African American dialect uncommon to the print culture of his time: "Got to cross that river / An' git to ma baby somehow. / Cross that river, / Git to ma baby somehow – / Cause if I don't see ma baby / I'll lay down an' die right now."[17] In *The Dream Keeper* Hughes engages topics traditional to lyric poetry – youth, old age, death, poverty, and love – but manages them with more nuance than most twenty-first-century children's poetry. Consider, for instance, these lines, which describe how the speaker's lover, a "beauty [in] red / Burns in my heart a love-fire sharp like pain."[18] Or note the striking candor evident in the final pair of couplets (an apt formal choice) in "Passing Love." Addressed to the speaker's paramour, it is a moving meditation on a love affair, all the sweeter for its clandestine evanescence:

> Because you are to me a prayer
> I cannot say you everywhere.
>
> Because you are to me a rose –
> You will not stay when summer goes.[19]

The darker poems ("Parisian Beggar Woman," for example, a cruel meditation on old age and that which it leaves behind) are tempered by the light (the title poem, for instance). In addition to its formal inventiveness and range of subject, *The Dream Keeper*'s diverse speakers (some men and some women, some children and some adults) and linguistic diversity (Hughes writes in several dialects, including standard English) make for a fresh and arresting book.

The populist politics shared by Hughes and Sandburg lent itself to the project of writing for youngsters. However, many of the high modernists had a more troubled relationship with children's literature. Stein demonstrates this discomfort when she insists, on the one hand, that "children themselves are poetry.... My poetry was children's poetry," while, on the other, banning William Carlos Williams from her home for saying in essence the very same thing: "I hope it pleases you, but the things that children write have seemed to me so Gertrude Steinish in their repetitions. Your quality is that of being slowly and innocently first recognizing sensations and experience."[20] This modernist ambivalence about children's poetry, however, was short lived. A more integrated understanding of children's poetry returned in the 1950s, although the modernist (and New Critical) discomfort with seemingly easy, popular poetry lingered, especially in the academic world.

By midcentury, many U.S. poets who previously wrote exclusively for adults – including Gwendolyn Brooks, Sylvia Plath, William Jay Smith, May Swenson, Richard Wilbur, and the aforementioned Ciardi, Frost, Jarrell, and Roethke – began writing for children as well. This turn to children's poetry – and, importantly, the fact that these writers saw their work in this area as both artistically and professionally acceptable – signals a broader interest in childhood and its literature in the United States (an interest academics have been slow to cultivate). Stephanie Coontz notes that the years immediately following the war brought with them the "youth market" and a concomitant "institutionaliz[ation]" of "youth culture."[21] After World War II, the United States saw a precipitous rise in birthrates, and as these children grew, so did the market for children's texts.[22] Frost exemplifies American poetry's return to the child audience, for although he got his start in children's poetry (three of his early poems were first published in *The Youth's Companion*: "Ghost House" [1906], "October" [1912], and "Reluctance" [1912]), Frost did not publish a collection marketed for children until 1959, when his well-known *You Come Too: Favorite Poems for Young People* was released.[23]

In the years between 1959 and his death in 1963, Frost became "*the* American school poet," unseating Carl Sandburg, Frost's "popular rival."[24] Frost's poems are regularly collected in children's poetry anthologies and commented on in education textbooks, "Stopping by Woods on a Snowy Evening," for example, remaining the most anthologized poem in the English language; according to Donald Hall, "Stopping by Woods" has "*become* a poem for children," one of the most commonly taught poems in U.S. schools.[25] The 1978 picture book version of the poem, illustrated by Susan Jeffers, remains a winter favorite, but it is far from the only edition of his children's work regularly trotted out by publishers looking to court buyers with a recognizable name on the cover. Frost's turn to children's poetry paved the way for adult poets closely associated with him to do the same. For instance, around the time *You Come Too* was published, Hall, one of the three co-editors of the rather traditional anthology *New Poets of England and America* (1957) – for which Frost wrote an introduction – also tried his hand at children's literature, although his contributions over the years have been mostly prose (such as *Andrew the Lion Farmer* [1959] and *The Ox-Cart Man* [1979], a prose revision of an adult poem by the same name). Hall also edited the impressive *Oxford Book of Children's Verse in America* (1985), a work he later refashioned into a collection marketed to young children: *The Oxford Illustrated Book of American Children's Poems* (1999). X. J. Kennedy, whose work was featured in the "second selection" of Hall and Pack's *New Poets of England and America* (1962) also became (and continues to be) a strong advocate for and writer of children's literature; however, unlike Hall, he has focused his talents on children's poetry specifically (his most recent collection, *City Poems*, was released in 2010). Additionally, Kennedy has commented on children's poetry in essays and has edited with his wife, Dorothy Kennedy, two successful anthologies of children's poetry.[26] Again, the worlds of adult poetry and its children's counterpart overlap far more than most realize.

This overlap is not limited, however, to the more traditional poetic community. Since the 1960s, poets associated with Donald Allen's controversial anthology *The New American Poetry, 1945–1960* (1960) also have grown increasingly interested in writing for children and teaching them to write. New York School poets Kenneth Koch and Ron Padgett, for example, were active in the Teachers and Writers Collaborative, a landmark poets-in-the-schools program. Koch, Padgett's teacher at Columbia, wrote a pair of seminal works about teaching children poetry: *Wishes, Lies, and Dreams* (1970) and its companion anthology of poetry by children, *Rose, Where Did You Get That Red?* (1973). Over the next several decades, these books sparked a great deal of debate on the issue of creative writing pedagogy – particularly concerning how (and whether) to teach young people to write poetry. Poet-critic Myra Cohn Livingston critiqued Koch's double thesis that children are "natural poets" and have a natural connection to poetry in her two-part essay "But Is It Poetry?" (1975, 1976), the arguments therein developed in Livingston's contentious but undeniably important book *The Child as Poet: Myth or Reality?*[27] Koch did not limit himself to teaching, however, and in 1985 he and his regular collaborator Kate Farrell, founding member of the New York Art Theater Institute, would put together the beautiful *Talking to the Sun* (1985), a collection notable not only for its superb reproductions of visual art from the Metropolitan Museum but also for including poems by often-ignored twentieth-century avant-garde poets like Stein, Tristan Tzara, and Guillaume Apollinaire, poems the editors believed perfect for a child audience.[28]

The perceived connection Koch and Farrell found among the historical avant-garde, children's literature, and childhood is not as unusual or as radical as one might think. Kennedy, a poet not known for his experimental tendencies, includes in *Knock at a Star* some strikingly unusual selections. For instance, in addition to poems by concrete / visual poet Ian Hamilton Finlay (work originally published for adults), he includes his own visual poem "Concrete Cat," poetry by Koch, Myra Cohn Livingston's visual / found poem "Four Way Stop," and poems by Charles Reznikoff, Sandburg, and Stein. This interest in avant-garde and experimental literature has continued into the twenty-first century: Robin Hirsch's grotesquely beautiful 2002 collection *FEG: ~~Stupid~~ Ridiculous Poems for Intelligent Children* (strikethrough in original) alludes to New York School poet Frank O'Hara, Stein (again), and even Oulipian Georges Perec, turning his child readers on to both Perec's "5,000 letter palindrome" and his lipogrammatic novel *La Disparition* ("an entire novel," Hirsch tantalizingly explains, composed "without using the letter e").[29] The Oulipians are also summoned by JonArno Lawson, a dual citizen of the United States and Canada: in his 2008 book *A Voweller's Bestiary, from Aardvark to Guineafowl (and H)*, Lawson makes explicit his debt to the avant-garde by choosing the lipogram as a formal constraint (the poems use only the vowels found in their title, and no others). For instance, the poem "Turtle" charts the "luckless" yet persevering reptile of its title, ending with the lipogrammatic lines

Turtle gurgles, unnerved.
Blunders rudderless,

suffers, unsure.
Fumbles, tumbles,

returns,
endures.[30]

(Note that each word uses *both* the *e* and the *u* of the title.) *Voweller's* is a virtuoso performance. Lawson isn't, however, some soulless technician, as the understated "Deer" demonstrates, with this concluding observation: "Whenever we freeze, / then flee – / Whenever we're tender, / then severe – / / we resemble deer."[31] Lawson links himself to the historical and contemporary avant-garde in his extraordinary afterword, in which he acknowledges "the direct inspiration" of Christian Bök's experimental tour de force *Eunoia* (2001), Richard Wilbur's *The Disappearing Alphabet* (1998), and Dr. Seuss's *On Beyond Zebra* (1955). Additionally, on the back cover we find a blurb authored by none other than the Language writer Charles Bernstein.

But the historical avant-garde has had a less obvious influence on American children's poetry. Lawson is not the first writer to suggest the avant-garde pedigree of the ever-popular Dr. Seuss (the pen name of Theodor Geisel). Philip Nel argues convincingly that as "a painter and cartoonist living in New York from 1928 through 1942, Seuss felt the influence" of Dada and Surrealism.[32] Noting the visual echoes of Cubism, Surrealism, and Dada in Seuss's adult paintings reproduced in *The Secret Art of Doctor Seuss* (1998), Nel also points out their Dada-inflected titles, particularly *The Rather Odd Myopic Woman Riding Piggyback on One of Helen's Many Cats* and *The Joyous Leaping of Uncanned Salmon*.[33] The avant-garde spirit also informs Seuss's writing, most obviously the naked, eponymous black cat of his Cat in the Hat books. The Cat, Seuss's most popular creation, debuted in *The Cat in the Hat* (1957), which shares the sensibility of Oulipian writers like Perec and Harry Mathews – namely, the crafting of art while shackled by difficult and seemingly arbitrary procedural constraint (in this case, limiting his vocabulary to a 348-word list). "I can hold up the cup," the Cat says, "And the milk and the cake! / I can hold up these books! / And the fish on a rake!"[34] These verses exude an anarchic, aleatory energy, Seuss's formal constraint encouraging their surreal juxtapositions. Nel makes much of the collage-like effect of these juxtapositions. Seuss's love of chance – *fish* and *rake* just happening to appear on his vocabulary list and thus engendering the fine, nonsensical line I cited above – was one he shared with André Breton (chance, of course, is a key element in both Surrealism and Dada). In *The Annotated Cat*, Nel takes great pains to trace the recurrence of the cat image – especially one that wears clothes, gloves in particular – in the visual and literary art important to Seuss, and in Seuss's own oeuvre, besides. Yet the rhyming pair *cat* and *hat*'s chance appearance on his vocabulary list may very well have crystalized Seuss's influences and artistic habits into the cat we know and love.[35] And there are certainly other less speculative cases of a surreal serendipity: *Horton Hears a Who* (1954) was inspired when (in Seuss's words) a "sketch of an elephant … happened to fall on top of a sketch of a tree…. An elephant in a tree! What's he doing here?"[36]

Of course, Seuss's cartoony, lively art plays a central role in his success as a children's author, while his poetry, with its inventive nonsense, infectious rhythms, and gripping narrative, has largely been discounted by academics. Nel works to recuperate Seuss's reputation as a poet, placing him alongside titans of nonsense and light verse like Walt Kelly and Spike Milligan, Ogden Nash and James Thurber, part of the "newer generation of nonsense-writers who popularized and developed the form for twentieth-century readers."[37] Nel notes that Seuss's nearly exclusive use of the anapest, forever associated with the limerick, has much to do with "why Seuss is rarely studied as a poet."[38] The limerick, he acknowledges, is "the punch line of poetic forms," and as such, even a line as memorable as "And to think that I saw it on Mulberry Street" is often thoughtlessly dismissed as doggerel, despite its being at least as important to the history of American verse as "'Twas the night before Christmas and all through the house." Yet unlike so many of his imitators, Seuss uses meter to do more than propel his narratives forward. For instance, Nel notes that "although the Cat in the Hat will later speak in anapestic dimeter, his first line ['Why do you sit there like that?'] reverses that meter – dactylic dimeter" – concluding with a single, Manx tail of a syllable: "Since he will soon reverse the order of the house, his first line very aptly reverses the rhythm of the verse."[39] This sort of rhythmic nuance is not uncommon in Seuss's poetry, as Nel demonstrates through the metrical analysis of poems like *The Cat in the Hat* and *Yertle the Turtle* (1958). As Nel puts it, "to examine the poetics [of Dr. Seuss] is to understand that meter matters."[40]

The Cat in the Hat and Ciardi's first children's book, *The Reason for the Pelican* (1959), signaled a crucial change in both the market for and perspective on U.S. children's poetry. Along with poet and illustrator Maurice Sendak, these poets added some much-needed heat to the rather bland midcentury nature poem. Their poetry began in the United States what John Rowe Townsend has dubbed the school of "urchin verse."[41] This poetic mode eschews "social or literary pretension" while focusing on "family life in the raw, with its back-chat, fury and muddle." It is a poetry more apt to treat "disused railway lines, building sites and junkheaps" than the "woods and meadows" so common to the midcentury nature lyric.[42] Characterizing the midcentury nature poem – of the kind written by David McCord and Elizabeth Coatsworth – as a "garden," Myra Cohn Livingston laments its "invasion" by poets who "glori[fy] the unconscious ... with a sort of 'garbage delight' that assaults literature itself"; she warns that these poets (including the Canadian Dennis Lee) produce a poetry akin to "werewolfs [sic] and ghouls ... creeping into the garden where children play."[43] Seuss, Ciardi, and Sendak anticipated by ten to fifteen years the British poet Michael Rosen's supposed invention of urchin verse, as well as his irreverent, disobedient, and back-talking kids (a perfect example of the latter is Max, the naughty young hero of Sendak's *Where the Wild Things Are* [1963], and his infamous, iambic yawp: "I'll eat you up!").[44]

Like Seuss, Sendak is praised primarily for his inimitable visual art, but his liltingly rhythmic free verse is as memorable as it is popular, challenging dominant notions of childhood *and* children's poetry. Aimed at a very young readership, the poetry in *Wild Things* is as overlooked as it is remarkable. Consider, for example, this single sentence describing the beginning of Max's adventure:

> That very night in Max's room a forest grew
> and grew –
> and grew until his ceiling hung with vines
> and the walls became the world all around
> and an ocean tumbled by with a private boat for Max
> and he sailed off through night and day
> and in and out of weeks
> and almost over a year
> to where the wild things are.[45]

The long, wending sentence's paratactic litany of *ands* suggests the language of childhood (*and I did this and I did that and I did this and I did that*) while formally echoing our hero's epic journey (the subtle quirkiness of *almost* over a year is characteristically delightful). Although the odyssey's exact perils are left to the illustrations, once Max arrives at his titular destination, the poetry becomes horrifyingly vivid, Sendak's description of Max's initial encounter with the wild things directly contradicting the art, the illustrated beasts less terrifying than cuddly. Note how the meter in the first line rocks along sweetly – this is a bedtime story, after all – two iambs, two anapests, and a concluding spondee ("where the *wild things are*"):

> And when he came to the place where the wild things are
> they roared their terrible roars and gnashed their terrible teeth
> and rolled their terrible eyes and showed their terrible claws
> till Max said "BE STILL!"
> and tamed them with the magic trick
> of staring into all their yellow eyes without blinking once
> and they were frightened and called him the most wild thing of all
> and made him the king of all wild things.[46]

The verses of *In the Night Kitchen* (1970) also demonstrate Sendak's signature, paratactic syntax, while recalling the nursery rhyme with their loose, accentual rhythms and irregular rhyme:

> Did you ever hear of Mickey,
> How he heard a racket in the night
> And shouted "Quiet down there!"
> And fell through the dark, out of his clothes
> Past the moon & his mama & papa sleeping tight
> Into the light of the night kitchen?[47]

The rhythmic music of the chant, "Milk in the batter! Milk in the batter! Stir it! Scrape it! Make it! Bake it!" (to which Mickey replies, "I'm not the milk and the milk's not me! / I'm Mickey!"), is unmistakably poetry. Its neglect in the academic treatment of children's poetry is an embarrassing oversight.

While Sendak and Seuss are best known for their visual art, Ciardi's poetic bona fides are unquestioned. Known primarily as a poet and critic, Ciardi was popular on the lecture circuit, his audience swelled by readers of his regular column in the *Saturday Review* and fans of *Accent*, "a weekly cultural magazine show" that he hosted for CBS television.[48] Ciardi's fame as a public intellectual during the 1950s and 1960s cannot be overstated. As X. J. Kennedy writes in his afterword to Ciardi's *The Reason for the Pelican*, the well-respected Ciardi was "responsible to a large extent for [the] change in climate" that allowed "a poet to publish a collection of children's verse without being exiled from the literary republic."[49] (Ciardi's fame has long since cooled, however, and outside the world of children's poetry, he is largely neglected these days.)

Kennedy celebrates the vigor with which Ciardi "threw open the musty old parlor of American children's poetry, with its smell of rose petals and camphor, and ... let in a blast of fresh air."[50] In *The Monster Den* (1963), for instance, Ciardi caricatures the elevated, mannered diction so common to midcentury children's poetry. In lines like these, spoken by a father to his children, Ciardi playfully satirizes the myth of the happy middle-class family: "your Mummy [and I] thought we were / Living happily ever after, sir, / As the stories say. We didn't know then / We were only starting a MONSTER DEN. / But that's what we did."[51] His poetry's tone is similar to that which Edward Gorey (his former student) made famous in collections like *The Wuggly Ump* and *The Vinegar Works*, both also published in 1963.[52] Many of Ciardi's books are illustrated by Gorey, whose connection to the world of children's poetry extends to a masterfully illustrated and regularly republished 1982 edition of Eliot's *Old Possum's Book of Practical Cats*. (Nota bene: this edition played no small role in resuscitating *Old Possum*'s reputation; couple it with Andrew Lloyd Webber's immensely popular adaptation, *Cats*, which ran for eleven years in London and eight in New York, and one realizes that Eliot, alongside more obvious choices like Seuss and Silverstein, may have written one of the most profitable and influential single books of children's poetry in American history.)

Ciardi grew up poor, in a working-class neighborhood noted for its Old World Italian values, and his hardscrabble childhood may be at the root of his children's poetry's dark humor. Ciardi began writing for children when first his nephews and then his own children began reading, publishing, between 1959 and 1966, nine books for children, among them the aforementioned *The Reason for the Pelican*, *The Man Who Sang the Sillies* (1961), and *You Know Who* (1964). Like Seuss, Ciardi tried his hand at poetry constrained by an early reader vocabulary list. In Ciardi's case, this experiment was prompted by his daughter's difficulty with reading. The result was *I Met a Man* (1961), an easy reader based on a first-grade vocabulary. Urged on by the success of Seuss – and perhaps Ciardi too, as they regularly corresponded throughout the fifties – Roethke also wrote a book using this constraint: *Party at the Zoo*, which contained a vocabulary of only 268 basic words. Similarly, in *You Read to Me, I'll Read to You* (1962), Ciardi alternates poems written with a basic vocabulary with those using a more advanced vocabulary, his aim being to encourage parents and children to read poetry together.

Ciardi was outspoken about his frustration with midcentury poetry – for children and adults – condemning a great deal of it for what he characterized as an unfortunate Victorian overseriousness. Several years before turning to children's poetry, Ciardi would write, "The nineteenth century was a great literary achievement, but it began with one dreadful flaw: it tended to take itself much too seriously."[53] Much of his children's poetry, coupled as it was with Gorey's oddly anachronistic illustrations, undercuts that seriousness while summoning it with anapestic meters and intricate form. Consider, for instance, the easy flow of iamb to anapest in the opening stanza of *The Man Who Sang the Sillies*, a master class in the music of poetry:

> I met a man with a triple-chin.
> Whenever he smiled, his chins would grin.
> The strangest sight that ever I saw
> Was a smile with three grins in its jaw.[54]

The result of this blend of irreverence and technical virtuosity is a body of poetry that, while sometimes criticized for its obscurity and dark humor, reminds readers that kids are complexly motivated people who can delight in intricately formed, accomplished poetry, especially when it's cut with more than a little sly, subversive humor.

Humor, or, as Flynn puts it, "comedy," is one of the major categories of contemporary children's poetry, along with the other Cs he enumerates in "Consolation Prize": cute, classic, and consoling.[55] Nel points to Seuss's words about the political import of humor: "Nonsense wakes up the brain cells. And it helps develop a sense of humor, which is awfully important in this day and age. Humor has a tremendous place in this sordid world. It's more than just a matter of laughing. If you can see things out of whack, then you can see how things can be in whack."[56] Although Seuss and Ciardi and even Roethke (the first half of his wonderful book *I Am! Says the Lamb* is labeled, rather directly, "The Nonsense Poems") set the commercial and aesthetic stage for nonsense and light verse, from the early 1970s that stage has been dominated by the comedic poetry of Prelutsky and Silverstein.[57] Borrowing from the gross-out traditions of playground rhyme (which we'll get to in a moment), these poets have developed the more gentle irreverence of Seuss and Ciardi into a fine art, although they temper their irreverence with just enough didacticism to appeal to the adults who so often do the book buying. Nevertheless, Silverstein, who first made his name drawing cartoons for *Playboy*, is often challenged for developing inappropriate themes in his work, despite such ostensibly didactic verses as "Jimmy Jet and His TV Set," which tells us "the story of Jimmy Jet" who "watched all day, he watched all night / Till he grew pale and lean ... And his bottom grew into his chair. / And his chin turned into a tuning dial, / And antennae grew out of his hair."[58] This poem's success lies less in its warnings about excessive television viewing and more in the delight with which the narrator describes Jimmy's uncanny transformation.

Likewise, "Sarah Cynthia Sylvia Stout Would Not Take the Garbage Out," which ends with the didactic message, "always take the garbage out!" wins the hearts of its child readers through the narrator's lavish and extended descriptions of Sarah's funky pile of garbage: "Greasy napkins, cookie crumbs, / Globs of gooey bubble gum, / Cellophane from green baloney, / Rubbery blubbery macaroni, / Peanut butter, caked and dry, / Curdled milk and crusts of pie," and so forth and so on.[59] One can detect in both of these pieces Silverstein's history as a songwriter (in fact, "Sarah Cynthia Sylvia Stout" appears on Silverstein's album, *Freakin' at the Freakers Ball* [1969] – on which he was backed by Dr. Hook and the Medicine Show). Indeed, in some circles Silverstein is better known for his hundreds of songs ("A Boy Named Sue," "On the Cover of *The Rolling Stone*," and "Queen of the Silver Dollar," just to name a few). Ruth K. MacDonald suggests "that a poet who comes to written verse from writing rock and roll or blues lyrics is more used to composing and revising out loud than drafting and redrafting on paper," and the immediate, draft-like effect of Silverstein's accentual folk meter is as infectious as the steadier Seussian anapest, if more roughly hewn.[60] Silverstein died in 1999, at the close of a century whose final quarter was dominated by his handful of children's poetry collections. Unlike Prelutsky (as we'll see), Silverstein's success as a poet rests on the broad shoulders of a mere three books: *Where the Sidewalk Ends* (1974), *A Light in the Attic* (1981), and *Falling Up* (1996), which were joined by two posthumous (and ultimately weaker) books: *Runny Babbit* (2005), a collection of spoonerisms, and *Every Thing on It* (2011), a miscellany of previously unpublished poems and drawings.

Silverstein is joined by (as Flynn calls him in "Consolation Prize") "his evil twin Prelutsky," the two poets who "occupy most of the small area allotted to children's poetry" in bookstores.[61] Prelutsky has published a great deal more poetry than Silverstein – some fifty collections – and has edited a slew of anthologies, including *Poems of A. Nonny Mouse* (1989), *For Laughing Out Loud* (1991), and *The Random House Book of Poetry for Children* (1983), his most popular anthology. Prelutsky's best-known book of original poetry is *The New Kid on the Block* (1984), notable for its winking, naughty-but-not-scandalous humor – typified by "You Need to Have an Iron Rear" ("to sit upon a cactus," we discover) – as well as its participation in the gross-out traditions of playground rhymes, as in "Drumpp the Grump" (who informs his audience: "I never wash, and like to squash / my fingers into worms, / I'm full of fleas and smelly cheese / and fifty million germs").[62]

Prelutsky is also a musician, and, as he reports to Karin Snelson, "I knew [Silverstein] before either of us had ever written any children's poems, when we were both in Greenwich Village in the late '50s and early '60s.... We were both involved with the folk music scene."[63] Their familiarity with folk traditions explains their debt to the folklore of childhood, specifically playground rhyme. Silverstein and Prelutsky offer children a kind of "defanged" play-ground rhyme, cleaning up the much dirtier playground poetry for parents and guardians.[64] Playground poetry is a received oral tradition flexible enough to allow for modification and revision by the children who perform it daily on playgrounds and street corners, its verses – sometimes chanted, sometimes sung – often engaging literary poetry (children's and adult) through parody and appropriation. Playground poetry refers to many forms of childhood folk poetry, each playing a variety of aesthetic and social roles. Some rhymes are sung while skipping rope ("Cinderella dressed in yellow / Went upstairs to kiss her fellow"), and others chanted when choosing players in games ("Eeny meeny miney-moe / Catch a tiger by the toe"); other pieces serve as the basis of hand-clapping games (Miss Mary Mack, Mack, Mack, / All dressed in black, black, black), and still others ridicule ("Hate to talk about your mama. / She's a good old soul. / She's got a ten-ton pussy and a rubber asshole") or defend against ridicule ("Sticks and stones may break my bones / But words will never hurt me"). Children also employ them to condemn peers who violate the cultural mores of childhood ("No cuts, no butts, no coconuts") and to mock authority ("We have tortured every teacher, / And we broke the golden rule. / We have torn up all the math books, / And the principal's a fool").[65]

Playground poetry is also remarkable for its engagement with social and linguistic taboos (as some of the preceding examples suggest). For instance, this poem, a riff on Jane Taylor's "The Star" (from her 1806 collection *Rhymes for the Nursery*) ends with language stronger than any even Silverstein would dare employ in his children's poetry:

> Twinkle, Twinkle, little star,
> Who the hell do you think you are?
> Up in heaven you think you're it;
> Down on earth you're full of shit.[66]

Playground poetry's tendency to engage taboo can be troubling, as in these racist but well-known rhymes: "Me Chinese, me play joke, / Me go pee-pee in your Coke" and "Eeny meeny miney-moe / Catch a nigger by the toe." Other poems are homophobic ("You don't go out with boys anymore, / You don't like Elvis Presley. / You sit in the corner and play with yourself. / Oops, you're a lesie"), describe rape ("He pushed me to the floor. / He lifted up my skirt. / He said it wouldn't hurt"), attack racism ("Two, four, six, eight, we don't want to integrate. / Eight, six, four, two, bet you sons a bitches do!"), and, on the whole, unsettle adults while reminding them that children have a rich and var-ied – if sometimes troubling – poetic tradition of their own. Common to this tradition is a glossolaliac exuberance and irrepressible catchiness: playground poetry is the most popular and present poetry in the United States, and also the most readily dismissed and underappreciated.

Although the most popular literary poetry of the contemporary scene is predominantly of the nonsense and light verse variety, a sort of domesticated playground poetry, other poets look back to the socially conscious poetry of Sandburg and Hughes for their inspiration. For instance, Arnold Adoff's visually and aurally arresting poetry is marked by an interest in identity politics as well as formal experiment. His *Black Is Brown Is Tan* (1973), for instance, is the first picture book to feature an interracial couple, while his collection of poems *Slow Dance Heart Break Blues* (1995) develops his earlier visual experiments, typographic puns, and other visual cues into resonant poetry. A capable poet and outspoken advocate for poetry and childhood, Adoff is best known for his anthologies, among them *I Am the Darker Brother* (1968).

Like Adoff, Naomi Shihab Nye is a poet and anthologist with her feet in the worlds of children's and adult poetry. Preoccupied with cultural difference and ethnic identity, Nye endorses the need for cross-cultural and intergenerational empathy. Nye's single-author collection *A Maze Me: Poems for Girls* (2005), especially, speaks powerfully from a young girl's perspective. Adoff and Nye's insistence on social relevance in children's poetry is by no means rare in contemporary children's poetry, although their high aesthetic standards are, recalling the children's poetry of June Jordan and Nikki Giovanni. Jordan's *Who Look at Me* (1969) is a touchstone of a book. Its speaker returns the gaze of the adult – perhaps white – reader, and it ends with a direct challenge: "Who see the roof and corners of my pride / to be (as you are) free? / WHO LOOK AT ME?"[67]

Another trend in contemporary children's poetry is the novel in verse. Unlike traditional long-form narrative poetry given to children (such as Alfred Noyes's *The Highwayman* and Henry Wadsworth Longfellow's *The Song of Hiawatha* and *Paul Revere's Ride*), the verse novel's narrative emerges over the course of many, fairly short poems, often lyrics. As teachers look for effective ways to entice youngsters into reading, poetry (cynically, one thinks, because of all the white space) appeals to both teachers and publishers. Yet when it comes to "serious" (that is, not comic) poetry, slapping the word "novel" on the cover appears to make books instantly more marketable. Regardless of the reasons behind their publication, many in this new form have been quite good, and the turn of the century has seen a proliferation of these largely free verse "novels." Karen Hesse's *Out of the Dust* (1997) and *Witness* (2001) are among the most successful, artistically and poetically. Marilyn Nelson's *Carver: A Life in Poems* (2001) – perhaps better characterized as a biography in verse – stands out as one of the finest collections of its kind, setting a new standard for well-crafted narrative poetry.

The editors of *Poetry and Childhood* insist that children's poetry is "the Cinderella of children's literature."[68] They may be right, just as Sorby is right to remind us that it remains marginalized within the study of poetry itself. But whether chanted on playgrounds when teachers aren't around or read from books provided by well-meaning relatives or librarians, children's poetry remains the most popular poetry in the United States. Indeed, it is a kind of holdout from the nineteenth century, a time when poetry was read widely by citizens who were neither poets nor academics. Why children seem so prone to growing out of poetry – leaving it behind with other childish things, only to take it up again when they or their loved ones have children – is a question for others to address. But as one of the last truly popular poetries left to us, children's poetry warrants more attention than it receives. Those of us invested in the future of poetry should take children's poetry and its rich traditions seriously.

Notes

1. David Russell, "Review: *Poetry's Playground*, by Joseph T. Thomas, Jr.," *The Lion and the Unicorn: A Critical Journal of Children's Literature* 33:3 (2009), pp. 401–05, 401–02.
2. See Richard Flynn, *Randall Jarrell and the Lost World of Childhood* (Athens: University of Georgia Press, 1990); Stephen Burt, *Randall Jarrell and His Age* (New York: Columbia University Press, 2002); and Joseph T. Thomas, Jr., *Poetry's Playground: The Culture of Contemporary American Children's Poetry* (Detroit: Wayne State University Press, 2007), particularly chapters 1, 2, and 4, on Frost, Jarrell, and Roethke and Ciardi, respectively.
3. Thomas, *Poetry's Playground*, p. 401.
4. Richard Flynn, "Can Children's Poetry Matter?" *The Lion and the Unicorn: A Critical Journal of Children's Literature* 17:1 (1993), pp. 37–44, 40.
5. See Thomas, *Poetry's Playground*, pp. 105–32.
6. Thomas, *Poetry's Playground*, p. xv.
7. Angela Sorby, *Schoolroom Poets: Childhood, Performance, and the Place of American Poetry, 1865–1917* (Durham: University of New Hampshire Press, 2005); Donald Hall (ed.), *The Oxford Book of Children's Poetry in America* (New York: Oxford University Press, 1985).
8. Sorby, *Schoolroom Poets*, p. 187.
9. Sorby, *Schoolroom Poets*, p. 189.
10. Randall Jarrell, *A Sad Heart at the Supermarket* (New York: Atheneum, 1962), pp. 50–52.

11. Ezra Pound, *The Cantos* (London: Faber and Faber, 1986), p. 532.
12. For recent examples of this anapestic tendency, see Laura Purdie Salas, *BookSpeak: Poems about Books* (New York: Clarion, 2011); C. M. Millen, *The Ink Garden of Brother Theophane* (Watertown, Mass.: Charlesbridge, 2010); Diane Z. Shore and Jessica Alexander, *This Is the Dream* (New York: Amistad, 2005); and the lamentable *The Legend of Messy M'Cheany* (New York: Running Press, 2011), by none other than Kathie Lee Gifford.
13. Sorby, *Schoolroom Poets*, p. xiii.
14. Carl Sandburg, *Early Moon* (New York: Harcourt, Brace, 1930), p. 84.
15. Sandburg, *Early Moon*, p. 90.
16. Sandburg, *Early Moon*, p. 24.
17. Langston Hughes, *The Dream Keeper and Other Poems* (New York: Knopf, 1996), p. 41.
18. Hughes, *The Dream Keeper*, p. 38.
19. Hughes, *The Dream Keeper*, p. 42.
20. Gertrude Stein, *A Primer for the Gradual Understanding of Gertrude Stein*, ed. Robert Bartlett Haas (Los Angeles: Black Sparrow Press, 1974), pp. 11–34, 18; John Malcolm Brinnin, *The Third Rose: Gertrude Stein and Her World* (Reading, Mass.: Addison-Wesley, 1987), p. 274.
21. Stephanie Coontz, *The Way We Never Were: American Families and the Nostalgia Trap* (New York: Basic, 1992), p. 38.
22. Thomas, *Poetry's Playground*, p. xiv.
23. Robert Frost, *You Come Too: Favorite Poems for Young Readers* (New York: Holt, 1959).
24. Thomas, *Poetry's Playground*, p. 2; Jeffrey Meyers, *Robert Frost: A Biography* (Boston: Houghton Mifflin, 1996), p. 81.
25. Thomas, *Poetry's Playground*, p. 3; Hall (ed.), *The Oxford Book of Children's Poetry in America*, p. xxvi.
26. X. J. Kennedy and Dorothy Kennedy, *Knock at a Star: A Child's Introduction to Poetry* (New York: Little, Brown, 1982); X. J. Kennedy, *Talking Like the Rain: A Read-to-Me Book of Poems* (New York: Little, Brown, 1992).
27. Myra Cohn Livingston, *The Child as Poet: Myth or Reality?* (Boston: Horn Book, 1984).
28. Kenneth Koch and Kate Farrell (eds.), *Talking to the Sun: An Illustrated Anthology of Poems for Young People* (New York: Henry Holt, 1985).
29. Robin Hirsch, *FEG: Stupid Ridiculous Poems for Intelligent Children* (Boston: Little, Brown, 2002), pp. 10, 20, 22–23.
30. JonArno Lawson, *A Voweller's Bestiary* (Erin Village, Ontario: Porcupine's Quill, 2008), p. 32.
31. Lawson, *A Voweller's Bestiary*, p. 10.
32. Philip Nel, "Dada Knows Best: Growing Up 'Surreal' with Dr. Seuss," *Children's Literature* 27 (1999), pp. 150–84, 152.

33. Nel, "Dada Knows Best," p. 154.

34. Dr. Seuss, *The Cat in the Hat* (New York: Houghton Mifflin, 1957), p. 18.

35. Philip Nel, *The Annotated Cat: Under the Hats of Seuss and His Cats* (New York: Random House, 2007), pp. 34–37.

36. Philip Nel, *The Avant-Garde and American Postmodernity: Small Incisive Shocks* (Jackson: University Press of Mississippi, 2002), p. 47.

37. Philip Nel, *Dr. Seuss: American Icon* (New York: Continuum, 2004), p. 22.

38. Nel, *Dr. Seuss*, p. 20.

39. Nel, *Dr. Seuss*, p. 37.

40. Nel, *The Annotated Cat*, p. 31.

41. John Rowe Townsend, *Written for Children*, 3rd rev. ed. (New York: Lippincott, 1987), p. 300.

42. Townsend, *Written for Children*, p. 300.

43. Myra Cohn Livingston, "David McCord's Poems: Something Behind the Door," in Perry Nodelman (ed.), *Touchstones: Reflections on the Best in Children's Literature* (West Lafayette, Ind.: Children's Literature Association, 1987), vol. 2, pp. 157–72, 157–58.

44. Morag Styles, *From the Garden to the Street* (London: Cassell, 1998), pp. 262–63; Maurice Sendak, *Where the Wild Things Are* (New York: Harper & Row, 1963), n.p.

45. Sendak, *Where the Wild Things Are*, n.p.

46. Sendak, *Where the Wild Things Are*, n.p.

47. Maurice Sendak, *In the Night Kitchen* (New York: HarperCollins, 1970), n.p.

48. Edward M. Cifelli, *John Ciardi: A Biography* (Fayetteville: University of Arkansas Press, 1997), p. 263.

49. John Ciardi, *The Reason for the Pelican* (Honesdale, Pa.: Boyds Mill Press, 1994), p. 61.

50. Ciardi, *The Reason for the Pelican*, p. 63.

51. John Ciardi, *The Monster Den: Or Look What Happened at My House – and to It* (Honesdale, Pa.: Wordsong, 1991), p. 15.

52. Kevin Shortsleeve convincingly argues that both of these works – as well as other unfortunately mischaracterized Gorey collections – ought to be considered children's poetry: see Kevin Shortsleeve, "Edward Gorey, Children's Literature, and Nonsense Verse," *Children's Literature Association Quarterly* 27:1 (2002), pp. 27–39.

53. John Ciardi (ed.), *Mid-Century American Poets* (New York: Twayne, 1950), p. xviii.

54. John Ciardi, *The Man Who Sang the Sillies* (New York: Lippincott, 1961), p. 9.

55. Richard Flynn, "Consolation Prize," *Signal: Approaches to Children's Books* 100 (2003), pp. 66–83, 66.

56. Nel, *Dr. Seuss*, p. 68.

57. Theodore Roethke, *I Am! Says the Lamb* (Garden City, N.Y.: Doubleday, 1961).

58. Shel Silverstein, *Where the Sidewalk Ends* (New York: HarperCollins, 1974), p. 28.
59. Silverstein, *Where the Sidewalk Ends*, p. 71.
60. Ruth MacDonald, *Shel Silverstein* (New York: Twayne, 1997), p. 66.
61. Flynn, "Consolation Prize," p. 66.
62. Jack Prelutsky, *The New Kid on the Block* (New York: Greenwillow, 1984), pp. 15, 12.
63. Karin Snelson, "Pure Poetry: A Talk with Jack Prelutsky," Amazon.com, http://www.amazon.com/gp/feature.html?ie=UTF8&docId=6200.
64. Thomas, *Poetry's Playground*, p. 18.
65. As an understudied form of folk poetry, these rhymes are collected in only a few works, largely by folklorists. See Josepha Sherman and T. K. F. Weisskopf, *Greasy Grimy Gopher Guts: The Subversive Folklore of Childhood* (Atlanta, Ga.: August House, 1995); Roger D. Abrahams, *Jump-Rope Rhymes: A Dictionary* (Austin: University of Texas Press, 1969); Roger D. Abrahams, *Positively Black* (Englewood Cliffs, N.J.: Prentice Hall, 1970); and Francelia Butler, *Skipping Around the World* (Hamden, Conn.: Library Professional Publications, 1989).
66. Sherman and Weisskopf, *Greasy Grimy Gopher Guts*, p. 177.
67. June Jordan, *Who Look at Me: Illustrated with Twenty-Seven Paintings* (New York: Thomas Y. Crowell, 1969), p. 91.
68. Morag Styles, Louise Joy, and David Whitley (eds.), *Poetry and Childhood* (Stoke on Trent: Trentham, 2010), p. xv.

Chapter 49

Multilingualism in Contemporary American Poetry

JULIANA SPAHR

"What *is* English now, in the face of mass global migrations, ecological degradations, shifts and upheavals in identifications of gender and labor? ... What are the implications of writing at this moment, in precisely this 'America'?"[1] These questions are asked by Myung Mi Kim, a poet of the disquieting linguistic disorientation brought on by immigration, in her book *Commons*. They are questions that haunt much contemporary U.S. poetry. And many of the poets who have taken these questions and embraced them in the late twentieth and early twenty-first century have written a poetry in English that includes other languages and/or is written mainly in the pidgins and creoles that resulted from English-language colonialism.

I use the unwieldy phrase "literature in English that includes other languages" because I am not in this chapter talking about the U.S. literature written in other languages that Werner Sollors and Marc Shell have collected.[2] What I am talking about is poetry written in English for English-speaking readers who may or may not have fluency in the languages of the poem. I am talking about the "bilingual," also known as the "multilingual," and also known as the "intralingual" traditions that so define the literature of the U.S.-Mexico border, such as that written by Juan Felipe Herrera and Alurista. And I am also at the same time talking about a poet such as Kim, who brings into her work, as do many writers associated with multiculturalism and/or identity poetries, her heritage language (a language that is not the speaker's dominant language but that is learned because of a cultural connection) of Korean, and about Craig Santos Perez, who includes Chamorro, and about Anne Tardos, who includes Hungarian, German, and French. And I am also talking about writers who include through appropriation and quotation languages that are unrelated to them in terms of heritage or location, or perhaps even fluency, such as Guillermo Gómez-Peña, who includes not only Spanish but also Nahuatl, and Theresa Hak Kyung Cha, who includes Greek and French. Like Doris Sommer and many other scholars of the bi-, the multi-, and the inter-,

I am interested in how this work is often full of "invitations to engage, to delay and possibly redirect our hermeneutical impulse to cross barriers and fuse horizons."[3] But at the same time, I argue against the idea that poetry is best served by seeing the sociocultural specificity of these various poetries as constitutive differences. And I refuse to define this literature in English as marginal. It is, I argue, central to U.S. poetry. If we categorize the use of polyglot elements in poetry as a similarity (rather than assuming that poetry's distinctive sociocultural traditions are constitutive differences), it is easy to recognize a long and broad history of literature in English that includes other languages.

For the significant number of U.S. poets who use languages other than English in their work, whether their motives are a form of realism or a pointed resistance to globalizing English varies from poet to poet. But these writers are inevitably writing out of an awareness of the changing role of English as it becomes a global language. By the 1990s, English was the dominant or official language in more than sixty countries and is represented on every continent and on three major oceans. Because of English's ties with colonialism and globalization, as Alastair Pennycock writes, it

> poses a direct threat to the very existence of other languages. More generally, however, it poses the less dramatic but far more widespread danger of what we might call linguistic curtailment. When English becomes the first choice as a second language, when it is the language in which so much is written and in which so much of the visual media occur, it is constantly pushing other languages out of the way, curtailing their usage in both qualitative and quantitative terms.[4]

And yet, at the same time, it is wrong to represent English as monolithic or simplistically dominant. Even within the United States, where English has an unchallenged dominance, and where the consistent underfunding of language-acquisition programs in schools makes this unlikely to change anytime soon, the story is complicated. Around 162 languages are now spoken in the United States. The U.S. government does not have an "official" language. And in some parts of the United States, English's dominance is maintained by institutional fiat, such as in Hawai'i, where if it were not for the insistence of the Department of Education, Pidgin might dominate. ("Pidgin" is the word commonly used for what linguists call Hawai'i Creole English, a language that was created by linguistically separated plantation workers in Hawai'i so they could communicate with one another; it includes vocabulary and syntaxes from English, Korean, Hawaiian, Chinese, and a few other languages.) Similar to how globalization provokes localism, the growth in English and the economic rise of the United States meant that in the 1990s, as more and more words were spoken in English in places new to English, more and more words that were not a part of English were being spoken within the United States. The number of U.S. residents who declare that they speak a language other than English at home has increased dramatically, from 32 million in 1990 to 47 million in 2000.

As an example of how these two oppositional yet related tendencies – the expansion of English globally and the expansion of languages other than English within the United States – shape U.S. poetry, I want to start by discussing two oddly similar works written in English that include Narragansett: James Thomas Stevens's *Tokinish* (1994) and Rosmarie Waldrop's *A Key into the Language of America* (1994). These two works – both written in English but pointedly including the indigenous language Narragansett, both suggesting that the lyric's intimacy is inflected and even enriched by global histories – function like indicator species in that they define something distinctive about the ecosystem of contemporary poetry and also announce a mutation in the part of this ecosystem in which "multilingual" or "macaronic" forms turn from an almost relentless exploration of a heritage language to a questioning investigation of what it means to be a writer in English when English is a global and imperial language. Both books were published in the early 1990s; both poets have lived in Providence, Rhode Island; and both poets are aligned with the lyric's more innovative moments. That two writers of such disparate cultural identities – Stevens is a member of the Akwesasne Mohawk Nation; Waldrop is a German immigrant – wrote such similar books should be read not as a lack of imagination but rather as one of the interesting ways poetry takes up questions and investigates them in dialogue. (Although Stevens and Waldrop know each other, each claims not to have known that the other was working with Narragansett material.)

Both poets take their Narragansett from Roger Williams's 1643 book *A Key into the Language of America*, a work that is very much a sort of primer on how to negotiate the beginnings of the globalization of the continent that is now America, a book very much aware that English is not the "natural" language of the continent.[5] Stevens's *Tokinish* is a series of page-long sections spread out over forty-two pages. It begins with four epigraphs: two quotes from John Donne and two definitions of Narragansett words quoted from Williams. In the first set of paired epigraphs, Stevens contrasts a translation of the Narragansett *tokinish* – "wake him" – with a passage about sleep from Donne's *Devotions upon Emergent Occasions* (1624). In the second, he juxtaposes

Donne – "But yet the body is his booke" (from "The Extasie") – with two more translations:

| Awaunkeesitteoúwincohòck? | Who made you? |
| Wússuckwheke. | The book[6] |

These epigraphs obviously literalize the doubled view that is *Tokinish*'s concern. And they also point to how this is a work that is, despite its lyric interiority, somewhat about globalization. Donne's *Devotions* was written at the beginning of this current wave of colonial expansion. Among other things, it is a work about connection, about the idea that no man is an island. This is the global Donne, poet of empire, advocate of connective intimacy. This is the Donne who, in "To His Mistress Going to Bed," calls his beloved "my America, my new found land."[7]

Although it might be easy to argue that beside the global Donne Stevens places the local Narragansett, I think it is otherwise, as he takes his Narragansett from Williams's *Key*, a work that should be required reading in any globalization studies class. Williams is, like Donne, constitutive of seventeenth-century globalization. Along with some nine thousand others, he immigrated to Boston in 1631. He was expelled from Massachusetts in 1635 for nonconformism. He bought land from the Narragansett and established Providence Plantation in what is now called Rhode Island. He was an outspoken advocate of Native American rights (as the Rhode Island tourist bureau likes to remind visitors), and yet in 1672 he also sold a number of Native Americans into involuntary servitude (a fact overlooked by that same Rhode Island tourist bureau). And his *A Key into the Language of America* is both a unique work and a product of its time. For its contemporary readers, it served as a how-to manual for contact and trade. And for many years it was considered a key anthropological work, providing an unusually detailed record of Narragansett culture in the mid-seventeenth century. The book has played a crucial role even among the Narragansett. Although there is some debate about the continued use of the language among those who identify as Narragansett (some say the Narragansett language has been extinct since 1810), *Narragansett Dawn*, a journal started in the 1930s, has a lesson in Narragansett in each issue that draws extensively from Williams. The editor, Princess Red Wing, argues that she includes the lessons "because it is generally believed that nothing remains of the Narragansett tongue."[8]

Stevens frequently engages with colonialism, with indigenousness, and with queerness in his poetry. So the complicated uses of Williams's *Key* would not have been lost on him. But unlike Williams, he is not writing something with a dictionary's desire for fluency or an immigrant's desire for cataloguing explanation. And although Narragansett is not a heritage language for him, his interest in Narragansett culture is not entirely arbitrary; in 1992 Stevens worked as a data collector at the Narragansett Community House, working with inner-city children on a program called Whateanuonk that was designed to counter Providence gang and drug culture.

Stevens, though, is, like Donne, writing a lyric poem. And one productive way to read the English that is interrupted by Narragansett in *Tokinish* is as suggestively refiguring lyric intimacy as necessarily always in dialogue with global exchanges. Édouard Glissant, in *Poetics of Relation*, says that a decolonized Caliban might reply to Prospero "through the individual ardor of lyricism and the collective practice of politics."⁹ While there is no suggestion of the Narragansett being decolonized anytime soon in this poem, there is no better way of describing the negotiations between the individual and the collective that motivate a work such as *Tokinish*. The bulk of the poem uses lyric's possible metaphors of contact – both cultural and sexual – to discuss how often-conflicting frames and traditions meet. Even the most intimate of moments, *Tokinish* suggests, are riddled with global histories. Sexuality is figured as contiguous with other relations. "To walk the periphery of islands," reads the first line, "as if knowing the border of body" (*CSH*, p. 107). In this poem, the genders of both lover and beloved are indeterminate, and while the beloved is marked as white, the lover is not directly marked. Stevens uses the age-old Petrarchan tradition of listing the beloved's body parts, but none of them are gender specific. At only one point is there an indication that the beloved might be male: "*In him I have found a House, a Bed, / A Table, Company …*" (*CSH*, p. 140). The contiguity and ambiguity Stevens enacts works to trouble Donne's language of desire and, by extension, the tropes of European imperialism and its accompanying racial and sexual categorical tendencies. *Tokinish* critiques Donne's erotics not directly but by dismantling the Petrarchan tradition – by, for instance, dividing its body parts into a multilingual duality:

Néepuck.	The blood.
Wunnícheke.	The hand.
Wunnáks.	The bellie.
Mapànnog.	The breast.
Apòme.	The thigh.
Sítchipuck.	The necke.
Wuttòne.	The mouth.
Wuskeésuckquash.	The eyes.
Mscáttuck.	The fore-head.	(*CSH*, p. 142)

This list is not in Williams's *Key*. Stevens has instead cobbled it together from various parts of the *Key* to create an erotic subtext, an exploration of desire's separated conjunctions, multiplicities, and variable points of view.

On the surface, Waldrop's *A Key into the Language of America* is structured very much like Williams's *A Key into the Language of America* (and less like Stevens's *Tokinish*). She collages a great deal of text from Williams. Yet Waldrop is, as Susan Vanderborg notes, an unreliable and tricky collager; she will do things like substitute "**white men**" for Williams's "*Englishman.*" Still, in her *Key*, Waldrop uses Williams's chapter titles, beginning with "Salutations" and ending with "Of Death and Buriall." Each chapter is divided into four sections, a form that is indebted to Williams, although Waldrop adapts it to her own ends. The chapters begin with lyrical prose blocks that are mainly about Narragansett traditions and tend to contain most of the collaged language from Williams. The first section of the first chapter begins with words from Williams (in bold) and immediately alludes to the frame of language, to the inclusion of two languages with very different histories. The title, or word printed as a title, is "Salutations"; the following text begins "**Are of two sorts** and come immediately before the body. The pronunciation varies according to the point where the tongue makes contact with pumice found in great quantity."[10] After the prose block comes a loose, associational list of words. In most chapters, these words are in English, but in this first chapter Waldrop starts off with Narragansett:

> **Asco Wequassunnúmmis. Good morrow.**
> sing
> salubrious
> imitation
> intimate   (*KLA*, p. 3)

The lists are followed by first-person monologues. The one in the first chapter begins: "*I was born in a town on the other side which didn't want me in so many*" (*KLA*, p. 4). Throughout the book, these sections involve an unspecified narrational "I." Finally, each chapter ends with a passage that most closely adheres to the conventions of a free verse poem (with its ragged right margin and lines halfway across the page), but these poems are not syntactically conventional. The first chapter's reads:

> **the Courteous Pagan**
> barefoot and yes
> **his name laid down**
> **as dead**
> one openness
> one woman door
> so slow in otherwise
> so close   (*KLA*, p. 4)

As with the word lists, these poems are associational and offer themselves to varied and unconventional readings.

Waldrop was born in Germany in 1935 and moved to the United States after World War II "as a white, educated European who did not find it difficult to get jobs, an advanced degree, a university position" (*KLA*, p. xix). Her introduction to *Key* begins with the story of her arrival from Germany, how she came "expecting strangeness, expecting to be disorientated" but experienced little culture shock – except for the Narragansett place names (*KLA*, p. xiii). It was these that brought her to Williams's *Key*.

Waldrop's work is frequently lyrical, quietly elliptical, and full of collaged language, and the tendency has been to read her work as feminist and/or experimental, as loosely associated with Language poetry. Although Waldrop's work is important to these discussions, what is distinctive about *A Key into the Language of America* is the way it remains both an immigrant and an experimental work and yet also addresses continuing colonialism within the United States and immigrant complicity with that colonialism. Her *Key* interests me because, rather than relying, as many North American "experimental" works do, on modernist forms such as repetition or fragmentation or parataxis to disrupt the conventional syntaxes of English, she includes an indigenous and local language.

It would be easy to say something dismissive here about Waldrop as yet another Native American–obsessed German. It would also be easy to continue to insist that Waldrop's work is immigrant and/or experimental and avoid noticing the linguistic recognitions within her work, to take them as only incidental not constitutive. And it is not that Waldrop completely avoids some of the endless difficulties of cross-cultural contact. Waldrop's *Key* only touches on the political and economic issues that are more directly engaged by explicitly anticolonial poets who see poetry as having a part to play in struggles to regain land or cultural uplift. And yet she does not take Native American knowledge and present herself as a guide for a mainly Anglo audience. She doesn't present a nostalgic view of the Native past as a time of innocence before a current fall from grace. And her work is not a tale of ethnopoetic mastery. It is crucial here instead to notice that Waldrop's turn to Narragansett is through Williams. Her narrative is, like his, rooted in the shared history of contact, of globalization. And her *Key* is an attempt to recover place names rather than true, pure cultures.

Both Stevens and Waldrop in their works dwell with the peculiar and contradictory relationship that writers have to their medium of language. These are works that explore how languages have geographies and how they can layer on top of one another; how one can be invasive and another can be at risk or disappear as a result; how they can feel personal and intimate and yet are clearly cultural, created by groups of individuals over time, requiring consensus; how they are full of political uses and valences, often carrying nationalisms; and how they are somewhat permeable for those who want to do the work and learn them.

This emerging formation of a poetry in English that includes other languages includes not only Stevens and Waldrop but also Kim. The title of *Dura*, her third book, is one of the more resonant examples of this.[11] "Dura" can be the dense, tough, outermost membranous envelope of the brain and spinal cord, literally "hard mother" in the Arabic, *al-ʿumm al-jalīda* or *al-jāfiya*. It can be derived from *durare*, "to last, endure" in Italian; *durer*, "to last, to run, to go on" in French; or *durar*, "to last" or, in its feminine form, "hard, stale, tough, stiff," in Spanish. It can be "a door" in Faroese; it can be "to spit" in Filipino; it can be "to build" in Romanian; it can be the name of an ancient city in Syria; it can be the Romanized transcription of the phrase "listen up" in Korean; it can be the name of the group of people who in live in the hills of Dura Danda, Turlungkot, Kunchha Am Danda of Lamjung District, and some adjacent villages of Tanahun District in Nepal; it can be the language of the Dura; it can be *duras*, a variety of sorghum in southern Asia and northern Africa; and so on ... Whether or not (and my guess is not) Kim intended all of these meanings, the word is interestingly meaningful in a variety of languages.

Furthermore, throughout her work, rather than suggesting that Korean (Kim was born in Seoul and came to the United States when she was nine) or English is constitutive of any sort of identity, Kim returns again and again to question the naturalness of English. Language lessons and bureaucratic questions about language repeatedly show in her work. In *Under Flag*, for instance, she asks, "Can you read and write English? Yes _____. No _____."[12] In *The Bounty*, the poem "Primer" announces, "This is the study book" as an epigraph and charts comparisons between Korean and English:

mostly translations of		
the Scriptures into Chinese		to learn
which educated Koreans	inculcate its shame	the English
could read		of a Midwest town[13]

In "Thirty and Five Books" in *Dura* she writes: "9.8 One of the first words understood in English: stupid."[14] Also in *Dura*, "Cosmography" includes a section that looks like the short answer part of a language quiz; the definitions are in English and the answers that fill in the blank are in Hangul (the script used for Korean). "Hummingbird" also begins with what looks like a quiz: a somewhat difficult and impossible-to-imagine quiz, but still one that begins with the request for a name.

I will briefly continue listing works in English that include other languages just to give a hint of the linguistic and geographic diversity of what I am talking about, for among these writers are not only Stevens, Waldrop, and Kim, but also Joe Balaz, a poet whose work uses many different forms – from performance poetry to lyric poetry to spoken word poetry to rap and to wordplay – for anticolonial intent. In *Ola* he writes a series of teasing visual poems that pun in Hawaiian and English at the same time.[15] The poem "'Elua Pololia" shows two jellyfish (or *'elua pololia*), one labeled "maoli" (or "native") and the other "haole" (or "white person"). They are linked by tentacles that spell out "hapa" (or "mixed blood"). And one cannot read this poem without moving between languages. However, his poems are not like those optical illusions in which one looks at the black space and sees two faces, and one looks at the white space and sees a vase, but one can never see both at the same time. Rather, one must be open to seeing both the Hawaiian and the English meanings unmixed yet side by side for the poem to make any sense.

Francisco X. Alarcón, in *Snake Poems* (1992) – in a move that is eerily similarly to that of Stevens and Waldrop – writes a personal, lyric history in dialogue with a seventeenth-century colonial text: Hernando Ruiz de Alarcón's *Tratado de las supersticiones y costumbres gentílicas que oy viven entre los indios naturales desta Nueva España* (*Treatise on the Superstitions and Heathen Customes That Today Live Among the Indians Native to This New Spain*).[16] Ruiz de Alarcón wrote his treatise as a denunciation of Native religious and medical beliefs and in the process transcribed a number of spells and invocations in Nahuatl. The introduction and the back cover present Alarcón's decision to use Ruiz de Alarcón's treatise as a personal one (the back cover states that Alarcón was "intrigued by the manuscript and by the disquieting possibility that Ruiz de Alarcón might be a distant relation"), and the poems are short, quiet lyrics, often elliptical in their personal reference. The poems are in English and include both Spanish and Nahuatl. The poem "Songs," for instance, reads in its entirety, "*xochitl* / flower / *flor.*"[17] What seems telling about *Snake Poems* is that it is yet another example of a contemporary U.S. poet who makes a pointed gesture to include an indigenous language in a book written in English and who does so, very similarly to Waldrop, in order to place himself as part of a global history, perhaps a history that is less than heroic.

Mark Nowak's *Revenants* (2000) is an exploration of the Polish American communities of his childhood around Buffalo, New York. In a reversal of universalism's tendency to speak the dominant language, Nowak uses Polish as a point of complicated specificity to explore what are often abstract concepts. The poems are built around concepts such as *zwyczaj* (custom), *zakorzenić się* (get roots in, take root), *rozum* (reason, wisdom), and *Grzech Pierworodny* (original sin). The poem "Zwyczaj" literalizes this by having the Polish interrupt a quote from a scholarly article in the book *Writing Ethnographic Fieldnotes*:

> "With immersion the field
> researcher sees
> > from inside
> how people lead their lives
> [*zakorzenić się*]
>
> how they carry out their
> daily rounds of activities
> [*zakorzenić się*]
>
> what they find
> meaningful [*zakorzenić się*]
>
> and how they do ... "[18]

As might be obvious, I am performatively grouping together writers that might not be recognized as having anything to do with one another.

I want to suggest that these writers – and I have discussed merely six here of a long possible list – might be part of not minority traditions but rather a significant political-aesthetic formation of U.S. literature, if considered together as the emergence of a literature in English that includes other languages. It would be easy to place these somewhat messy, big, book-length projects in the tradition of modernism. But to consider them only as modernist risks overlooking the complicated relation of this poetry to U.S. identity categories and to specific sociopolitical histories. This literature in English that includes other languages that I am talking about here is under the influence of the hothouse of the poetry of the late 1960s and early 1970s that is associated with minority cultural activist movements. Many of these movements see poetry as one genre among many that can be used for cultural representation, cultural uplift, and preservation of the culturally disenfranchised. The creation of the Black Arts Repertory Theatre / School in 1965 by Amiri Baraka is often seen as a foundational moment here. But that is just one moment among many. Bamboo Ridge, a workshop and press that publishes mainly literature written by Asian Americans in Hawai'i and that has preserved and cultivated a literature in Pidgin, was founded in 1978. Arte Público, with its claim to "providing a national forum for Hispanic literature," was founded in 1979.[19]

But this hothouse is not just limited to small arts institutions. Cultural movements in the 1970s often saw poetry as a part of their activism. The Hawaiian Renaissance, the Native American movement, the Chicano/a movement, and the various activisms around feminist and queer issues – all consider poetry as one possible genre in which to propose, examine, and cultivate cultural change. Hawaiian sovereignty activist and poet Haunani-Kay Trask, for instance, succinctly explains that poetry is one arena in which she explores Hawaiian struggles to regain land, when she writes of poetry as "both decolonization and re-creation. It is creativity in the Hawaiian grain and, therefore, against the American grain. Part of an encompassing Hawaiian cultural expression, my writing is exposé and celebration at one and the same time; it is a furious, but nurturing *aloha* for Hawai'i."[20] This interest in poetry as a possible arena for change by cultural activist movements, combined with a lack of interest in publishing poetry on the part of increasingly profit-driven multinational publishing conglomerates, dramatically changes the social formations around poetry and the institutions that preserved and promoted it in the United States in the last half of the twentieth century. The members of these cultural activist movements develop community-based patronage systems in which they create distribution networks for poetry such as publishing houses, journals, anthologies, and reading series that support themselves and others in the group.

At the beginning, these activist poetries were often written in English only or English mainly. (There are, of course, exceptions, such as the work of Alurista.) But eventually many came to see language usage as part of their cultural politics. This is not surprising, because, as Walter Mignolo notes, numerous language-preservation movements came to activist prominence in the last third of the century, along with a "clear and forceful articulation of a politics and philosophy of language that supplants the (al)location to which minor languages had been attributed by the philosophy of language underlying the civilizing mission and the politics of language enacted by the state both within the nation and the colonies."[21] English-language activist poetries began to develop a series of somewhat distinctive – even as there are formal areas of overlap – language practices in which the language other than English that is included in the work is the author's heritage language. Gloria Anzaldúa sums up this position in 1987 in *Borderlands*: "Ethnic identity is twin skin to linguistic identity – I am my language."[22] Hawai'i Pidgin writer Darrell H. Y. Lum notes similarly: "The persistence of Pidgin in the islands ... suggests that it is less a matter of Pidgin speakers being *unable* to speak standard English but their *choosing* it as a symbol of local identity."[23]

As a result of its colonial occupation by the United States and the migration patterns that fed its plantation system during the sugar boom, Hawai'i has extraordinarily complex linguistic, political, and cultural situations. It is a place of many languages and many arguments about languages. Three languages – English, Pidgin, and Hawaiian – have their own, often warring but just as often amicable, literary traditions. Writers of Hawai'i thus make decisions about whether to write in any or all or some of three languages, one with a precontact history, one colonially imposed, and one a mixture of many languages that comes out of the labor history of the plantation system. As long as there has been the Hawaiian language, there has been a literature composed (and later written) in Hawaiian. But the development of what one might call, perhaps problematically to some, Hawaiian American literature – or literature written by those who identify as Hawaiian but write mainly in English using the formal conventions of a U.S. poetry of identity (free verse, approximate lineation that goes two-thirds of the way across the page, a first-person point of view, etc.) – did not really develop until about 1980. Much of this literature is provocatively anticolonial, calling for Hawaiian sovereignty. When this literature began, it featured work that was mainly in English with at most a sprinkling of Hawaiian words. By the end of the century, however, a very different picture of Hawaiian literature developed. And a glance at anthologies from the 1980s such as *Seaweeds and Constructions: Anthology Hawaii* (1979), *Mālama: Hawaiian Land and Water* (1985), and *Hoʻomānoa: An Anthology of Contemporary Hawaiian Literature* (1989) next to the Native Hawaiian journal *'Ōiwi* (which began publication in 1999) shows an intensification in the use of Hawaiian language within the literature. While the earlier anthologies feature work that is mainly in English with the occasional Hawaiian word often marked as "foreign" by italics, in *'Ōiwi* English-only poems are the rare exception.

At the same time that Hawaiian literature turned more and more to the Hawaiian language, there was a parallel move in the literature in Pidgin written by Asian Americans in Hawai'i. The first literary book in Pidgin might be 1972's *Chalookyu Eensai* by Bradajo (Jozuf Hadley), but literature in Pidgin did not really gather much momentum until closer to the end of the century.[24] At the beginning, if Pidgin showed up, it showed up as accent or local color in works with a standard English omniscient voice. For instance, the first issue of *Bamboo Ridge*, the journal and press that has done the most to argue for Pidgin as an important literary language, has only one work that obviously includes Pidgin (Philip K. Ige's "The Forgotten Flea Powder," a short story with a Pidgin voice embedded in a standard English omniscient narrative).[25] And although 1978's *Talk Story: An Anthology of Hawaii's Local Writers* is often mentioned as the beginning of the local and Pidgin literary renaissance, most of the Pidgin in this anthology, and there is not a whole lot of it, is also embedded in a standard English narrative frame.[26] But in the 1990s, Bamboo Ridge Press published a number of books in which Pidgin is a compositional language for entire poems, and sometimes even for the entire book, such as Eric Chock's *Last Days Here* and Lois-Ann Yamanaka's *Saturday Night at the Pahala Theatre*.[27] And a quick look through back issues of the journal *Bamboo Ridge* shows more and more work in Pidgin (and in Hawaiian, although less so, and this has been a constant point of contention) as time goes by.

Because the literary scene in Hawai'i is vibrant, community supported, and fairly isolated, one would expect a lot of cross talk and coalition building among its various poets, no matter their identity affiliation. But there is remarkably little overlap between the writers published in *'Ōiwi* and those published in *Bamboo Ridge*. Rodney Morales portrays "a contentious community, a community divided by degree of familiarity with place; a community as divided as it is united by ethnicity, gender, and race, a community that has historically privileged the colonizer spirit."[28] Among the distinct and thoughtful differences are ones as to whether Pidgin can be a language of resistance or whether it is limited to being a language of accommodation; whether the category of "local" is colonial or neocolonial or possibly resistant; whether Pidgin literature, as exemplified by *Bamboo Ridge*, erases Native Hawaiian concerns and questions of sovereignty with its attention to "local identity" and its lyric poems that celebrate local childhood; and about who "owns" Pidgin.

The conflicts between Pidgin and Hawaiian literature (and also, although I have not discussed it much here, the English-only literature written in Hawai'i) are a sort of microexample of what Charles Bernstein is talking about when he calls his book *A Poetics* ("a," as in one among many) and writes in it that "the state of American poetry can be characterized by the sharp ideological disagreements that lacerate our communal field of action."[29] Although there is still a claim to dominance for lyric free verse in standard English made by both higher education and many of poetry's institutions, such as the Poetry Society of America, the Academy of American Poets, and the Poetry Foundation, the genre of poetry as it is practiced in the whole of U.S. culture is defined by a series of "schools" or linguistic practices, in which it is presumed that these various poetries have more in common with the various communities that support them than with one another. For both scholars and writers themselves, when they consider the literature of the late twentieth century, it has made more sense to talk about Chicano/a literature and the connections between a poet like Alarcón and other Chicano/a writers such as Anzaldúa than it does to talk about Alarcón with Stevens and Waldrop under the frame of "American poetry."

No major anthology has yet grouped all of these writers together. (The only place in which I think such connections are recognized and explored are within the pages of Nowak's journal *XCP*.) And it would be unusual for their work to appear together in the sort of course called "U.S. poetry." The tendency is to keep the identity categories separate, to read Stevens as exemplary of Native American literature, Waldrop as experimental (presuming that "experimental" is mainly white Euro-American), Kim as Asian American, Balaz as Pacific Islander, and Alarcón as Chicano. And in the process, scholars tend to present these literatures as marginal or counter to not only some imagined dominant U.S. tradition but also one another. This is not only true of how literature functions in the academy – which it did in the late twentieth century through a series of ethnic/racial formations such as African American, Asian American, Native American, and Chicano/a literature – but it is also true of how poets group themselves. As Steve Evans notes,

> Anyone acquainted with contemporary American poetry, for example, is aware that certain basic *positions* organize the field, that these draw in their wake specific kinds of *position-takings*, and that what constitutes a viable *possibility* from the standpoint of one position may well be strictly ruled out with respect to another. If Bob Perelman and Maya Angelou switched curricula vitae and a month's worth of reading engagements, publication venues, and institutional functions, no one would *not* notice.[30]

Both Bernstein's "ideological disagreements" and Evans's "position-takings" are observations that are very much local and very much of the moment. But what they notice in the moment is very much related to what Pascale Casanova notices in her more historically and geographically wide-ranging *The World Republic of Letters*. In this work she charts out with impressive international scope how various national literatures attempt to gather resources through the "inescapably political instrument" of language.[31] And as she points out, one of the stories that is often told about poetry again and again is of poets freeing their work from ossified national traditions by either using a vernacular or misusing the national language. This story can be told with many examples. It is the story of Dante, and the story of the English Romantics, and the story, as Casanova tells with great detail, of the Euro-American modernists. And then the story that comes after is usually one in which these literatures, written in resistance, become the new national tradition. It is, as she notes, this very constant process of resistance and recuperation that defines the written word as literature:

> Literature is invented through a gradual separation from political obligations: forced at first to place their art in the service of the national purposes of the state, writers little by little achieved artistic freedom through the invention of specifically literary languages. The uniqueness and originality of individual writers became apparent, indeed possible, only as a result of a very long process of gathering and concentrating literary resources.[32]

Casanova ends her study with a claim that she has wanted to write "a sort of critical weapon in the service of all deprived and dominated writers on the periphery of the literary world."[33] And although it would be easy to dismiss this as naïve, the claim embedded here – that literature criticism upholds or dismisses certain literary formations while pretending to be neutral – is worth remembering. The tendency to particularize the various literatures that ferment in the various hothouses of identity politics (Casanova's "periphery of the literary world") is almost a cliché at this point. Long dismissed by detractors for being overly specific, particular, and self-involved, even defenders of this type of literature tend to argue using an assumption of its marginality and to place it in resistance to that imagined dominant national literary formation that had itself also collapsed by the end of the twentieth century. Mark McGurl, for instance, in his book about U.S. literary institutions, does not spend much time on the heyday of cultural activist movement literature that I have just described. But he does discuss it when it enters the academy. And what he describes are literatures of institutional individualisms. In his discussion of Chicano/a literature, for instance, McGurl ends up suggesting that Chicano/a literature might have been created for "the increasingly paramount value of cultural diversity in U.S. educational institutions" and might be yet another example of something that is more "a new way of accumulating symbolic capital in the fervently globalizing U.S. academy, pointing scholars toward valuable bodies of expertise they might claim as their own and offering a rationale for the inclusion of certain creative writers in an emergent canon of world literature."[34]

Whether one buys Auden's line that "poetry makes nothing happen" or Vladimir Mayakovsky's that one must "smash to smithereens the myth of an apolitical art," it is worth noting that there is a moment when literary cultures in the United States decentralize, and as they do, they refuse the more universalist content of American literary nationalism and align themselves with various specific forms of resistant activism.[35] While McGurl is using Chicano/a literature as exemplary of institutional individualisms, it is worth remembering that this was not always so. One of the foundational poems of Chicano/a literature is "Yo Soy Joaquín/I am Joaquín" by Rodolfo "Corky" Gonzales. It was originally published with Spanish (translated by Juanita Domínquez) and English versions in parallel columns. "Yo Soy Joaquín/I am Joaquín" could be read as a literal statement of individualism, with its "I am ..." refrain, but it is also written, as Rafael Pérez-Torres notes, as "an organizing tool": it was "written in 1967 for the Crusade for Justice, distributed by mimeographed copy, recited at rallies and strikes."[36] It is also a poem that uses the singular and heroic identity of its subject, "Joaquín," for Whitman-influenced multitudes. Joaquín is many things. He rides with Don Benito Juarez; he is "the black-shawled / Faithful women"; he is "Aztec prince and Christian Christ."[37] It is a poem that echoes and one-ups in homage Langston Hughes's "Negro," a poem that begins, "I am a Negro" and then goes through a series of different qualifying identities such as slave, worker, singer, and victim; it is a poem that perhaps also draws from Carl Sandburg's poem that begins "I am the people – the mob – the crowd – the mass."[38] All of these are poems of a collective, permeable identity with activist desires.

"Yo Soy Joaquín/I am Joaquín" is just one example among many possible examples. Kaplan Page Harris, for instance, in "Causes, Movements, Poets," discusses another larger example of poetry's one-time cultural activism – the "benefit" readings that were advertised in the 1970s in the Bay Area journal *Poetry Flash*.[39] Harris's list contains around twenty-two benefit readings that he noted between 1973 and 1980 in the Bay Area alone. It is a telling list. There were readings for farm workers, for women, for the People's Community School, for the Greek resistance, for stricter regulation of nuclear power plants, for the prisoners of San Quentin, and so on. However, as Harris notes, benefit readings more or less faded away from the listings in the 1980s. Similarly, I keep thinking here of how the "I am ..." poem has mutated from the inclusive and activist drive of "I am Joaquín" in the early days to something like Marilyn Chin's "How I Got that Name," which begins, "I am Marilyn Mei Ling Chin" and is all about Chin, not all about "the people" or a specific group of people within "the people."[40]

But my desire here is to suggest that it would be insistently ahistorical to read a poem like "I am Joaquín" as merely individualist and that, at the same time, to read a poem such as Marilyn Chin's as an organizing tool would probably also be just as ahistorical. The "I am ..." differences here are yet another example of the closeness between poetry and cultural activism that was so present in the 1970s and that was no longer so by the end of the century. And yet to give adequate attention to the histories of connection between the community formations that supported the activist language politics of various literatures of the 1970s and the more contemporary poetry in English that includes other languages feels especially important, as this literature keeps returning to this issue of individualism again and again, but in really complicated ways. Let us take as an example the long, established tradition of literature in English that includes Spanish: while Anzaldúa writes, "I am my language," Edwin Torres, even as he, like Anzaldúa, moves between Spanish and English in his writings, questions the untroubled representation of Spanish – an imposed and colonial language – as marginal and as a crucial marker of anyone's identity in the Americas. Torres can claim Spanish as a heritage language, as his parents were Puerto Rican. And like Anzaldúa and Gonzales, Torres wrote a manifesto that is in part about language and identity. But his is called "A Nuyo Futurist Manifestiny," and it is full of a poking, joking "I" and a critique of "knowing" this "I" through languages: "I yo NEO-why KNOW who say NO you say ME I see WHY Know NUYO know YOU ..."[41] In a perhaps less jokey but no less interesting moment, Alarcón's *Snake Poems* keeps returning to the phrase "nomatca nehuatl," which Alarcón translates as "I myself" (a provocatively doubled singularity). Every time this phrase appears, it shows up as complicated by two languages. One poem, called "Nomatca Nehuatl," begins with "*I myself:*" as its first line; the rest of the poem is a list that begins "the mountain / the ocean / the breeze / the flame."[42]

To return to Kim's work, Zhou Xiaojing quotes Kim at a reading in Buffalo in 1998 talking about *Dura* as "a kind of strange autobiography."[43] The phrase "a kind of strange autobiography" sums up what makes Kim's work so resonant. Her work is notably sprawling and insistently places the self next to various histories. Kim's work, for instance, returns again and again to how the legacies of colonialism are connected. In *Dura*, she again and again orders her readers to "Translate"; "Translate: 38th parallel. Translate: the first shipload of African slaves was landed at Jamestown."[44] The 38th parallel, the line that separates North and South Korea, is also the line that crosses the San Francisco Bay (the line on which Kim was living in California when she wrote *Dura*) and the line that crosses the continent, including the Chesapeake Bay and Jamestown. In "Lamenta," in the book *Commons*, she includes notes on vivisection from Vesalius, passages from Da Vinci's notebooks, retellings of conditions in war-torn regions, locust plagues, and environmental crises. In one especially moving passage, the poem juxtaposes a first-person account of the 1980 Kwangju uprising in South Korea with the 1992 bombing of Sarajevo.

The piece is clearly attempting to put disparate moments in dialogue with one another, to suggest something about the difficulties of understanding the events of the contemporary. Much of Kim's work avoids the "I." Here it is, buried toward the end of *Dura*, tellingly meta-deleted: "[the first deleted *me* written over."[45]

I keep thinking here of the attention to linguistic recognition called for by Judith Butler's most recent work. In *Giving an Account of Oneself*, Butler's interest is in how our complicity in the violence done to others, even when we are not the doer of the violence, defines us; how we have an obligation to give an account of this; and how this accounting – if it is to be something like ethical – has to be disorienting, full of the languages of others. She puts it this way: "We are not mere dyads on our own, since our exchange is conditioned and mediated by language, by conventions, by a sedimentation of norms that are social in character and that exceed the perspective of those involved in the exchange."[46] In *Frames of War*, Butler extends these concerns with how we define ourselves into how we define others into and out of the category of the human. Among the things to be recognized are claims of language and social belonging: "If we are to make broader social and political claims about rights of protection and entitlements to persistence and flourishing, we will first have to be supported by a new bodily ontology, one that implies the rethinking of precariousness, vulnerability, injurability, interdependency, exposure, bodily persistence, desire, work and the claims of language and social belonging."[47] Butler asks, "What might be done to produce a more egalitarian set of conditions for recognizability? What might be done, in other words, to shift the very terms of recognizability in order to produce more radically democratic results?"[48] It is with an interest in the claims of recognizability, in recognition, that I began this discussion with two books that include Narragansett by writers who do not claim Narragansett as part of their identity. Both these books take up the question of the implications of writing in English; both acknowledge the presence of other languages and the complicated histories that language use carries. Both these works suggest that literary representations of the self in their most intimate moments benefit from including relations to others, even those not present in the room; and both argue for recognition of interrelations, and of interdependency.

Notes

1. Myung Mi Kim, *Commons* (Berkeley: University of California Press, 2002), p. 108.

2. Werner Herzog and Marc Shell (eds.), *The Multilingual Anthology of American Literature: A Reader of Original Texts with English Translations* (New York: New York University Press, 2000).

3. Doris Sommer, *Proceed with Caution, When Engaged by Minority Writing in the Americas* (Cambridge, Mass.: Harvard University Press, 1999), p. xv.

4. Alastair Pennycock, *The Cultural Politics of English as an International Language* (New York: Addison-Wesley, 1995), p. 14.

5. Roger Williams, *A Key into the Language of America* (1643; Bedford, Mass.: Applewood, 1997).

6. John Donne, *The Complete English Poems*, ed. A. J. Smith (New York: Penguin, 1996), p. 53; James Thomas Stevens, *Combing the Snakes from His Hair* (Lansing: Michigan State University Press, 2002), p. 107. Stevens's collection will be cited in the text as *CSH*.

7. Donne, *Complete English Poems*, p. 125.

8. Princess Red Wing, "Lesson in Our Native Tongue," *The Narragansett Dawn* 1:1 (1935), p. 18.

9. Édouard Glissant, *Poetics of Relation*, trans. Betsy Wing (Ann Arbor: University of Michigan Press, 1997), p. 54.

10. Rosmarie Waldrop, *A Key into the Language of America* (New York: New Directions, 1997), p. 3. This collection will be cited in the text as *KLA*.

11. Myung Mi Kim, *Dura* (Los Angeles: Sun & Moon Press, 1999).

12. Myung Mi Kim, *Under Flag* (Berkeley, Calif.: Kelsey Street, 1991), p. 29.

13. Myung Mi Kim, *The Bounty* (Minneapolis: Chax, 1996), p. 23.

14. Kim, *Dura*, p. 79.

15. Joseph P. Balaz, *Ola* (Honolulu: Tinfish Network, 1997).

16. Francisco X. Alarcón, *Snake Poems* (San Francisco: Chronicle Books, 1992); Hernando Ruiz de Alarcón, *Tratado de las supersticiones y costumbres gentílicas que oy viven entre los indios naturales desta Nueva España* (1629; Mexico City: Secretária de Educación Pública, 1988), and in English translation, *Treatise on the Heathen Superstitions That Today Live Among the Indians Native to This New Spain*, trans. J. Richard Andrews and Ross Hassig (Norman: University of Oklahoma Press, 1983).

17. Alarcón, *Snake Poems*, p. 19.

18. Mark Nowak, *Revenants* (Minneapolis: Coffee House, 2000), p. 83.

19. "About Arte Público Press," http://artepublicopress.uh.edu/arte-publico-wp/about-arte-publico-press/.

20. Haunani-Kay Trask, "Writing in Captivity: Poetry in a Time of Decolonization," in Cynthia Franklin, Ruth Hsu, and Suzanne Kosanke (eds.), *Navigating Islands and Continents: Conversations and Contestations in and around the Pacific* (Honolulu: University of Hawai'i Press, 2000), pp. 51–55, 55.

21. Walter Mignolo, *Local Histories/Global Designs: Coloniality, Subaltern Knowledges, and Border Thinking* (Princeton, N.J.: Princeton University Press, 2000), p. 296.

22. Gloria Anzaldúa, *Borderlands/La Frontera: The New Mestiza* (San Francisco: Spinsters/Aunt Lute, 1987), p. 81.

23. Darrell H. Y. Lum, "Local Genealogy: What School You Went?" in Eric Chock et al. (eds.), *Growing Up Local: An Anthology of Prose and Poetry from Hawai'i* (Honolulu: Bamboo Ridge, 1998), p. 13.

24. Bradajo (Jozuf Hadley), *Chalookyu Eensai: Three Poems in Pidgin English* (Honolulu: Sandwich Islands, 1972).

25. Philip K. Ige, "The Forgotten Flea Powder," *Bamboo Ridge: The Hawaii Writer's Quarterly* 1 (1978), pp. 56–59.

26. Eric Chock et al. (eds.), *Talk Story: An Anthology of Hawaii's Local Writers* (Honolulu: Petronium Press/Talk Story, 1978).

27. Eric Chock, *Last Days Here* (Honolulu: Bamboo Ridge, 1990); Lois-Ann Yamanaka, *Saturday Night at the Pahala Theatre* (Honolulu: Bamboo Ridge Press, 1993).

28. Rodney Morales, "Literature," in Michael Haas (ed.), *Multicultural Hawai'i: The Fabric of a Multiethnic Society* (New York: Garland, 1998), pp. 107–29, 108.

29. Charles Bernstein, *A Poetics* (Cambridge, Mass.: Harvard University Press, 1992), p. 1.

30. Steve Evans, "The Dynamics of Literary Change," *The Impercipient Lecture Series* 1:1 (1997), p. 23.

31. Pascale Casanova, *The World Republic of Letters*, trans. M. B. DeBevoise (Cambridge, Mass.: Harvard University Press, 2007), p. 115.

32. Casanova, *The World Republic of Letters*, pp. 45–46.

33. Casanova, *The World Republic of Letters*, pp. 354–55.

34. Mark McGurl, *The Program Era: Postwar Fiction and the Rise of Creative Writing* (Cambridge, Mass.: Harvard University Press, 2011), pp. 332, 333.

35. W. H. Auden, *Collected Poems*, ed. Edward Mendelson (New York: Modern Library, 2007), p. 246; Vladimir Mayakovsky, *How Are Verses Made? with A Cloud in Trousers and To Sergey Esenin*, trans. G. M. Hyde (Bedminster: Bristol Press, 1990), p. 88.

36. Rodolfo "Corky" Gonzales, *Message to Aztlan: Selected Writings* (Houston: Arte Público Press, 2001), p. 12; Rafael Pérez-Torres, *Movements in Chicano Poetry: Against Myths, Against Margins* (Cambridge: Cambridge University Press, 1995), p. 47.

37. Gonzales, *Message to Aztlan*, pp. 21, 29.

38. Langston Hughes, *Collected Poems*, ed. Arnold Rampersad (New York: Vintage, 1995), p. 24; Carl Sandburg, *The Complete Poems of Carl Sandburg*, ed. Archibald MacLeish (New York: Harcourt Brace, 1970), p. 71.

39. Kaplan Page Harris, "Causes, Movements, Poets" (unpublished manuscript).

40. Marilyn Chin, *The Phoenix Gone, the Terrace Empty* (Minneapolis: Milkweed Editions, 1994), p. 16.

41. Edwin Torres, *The All-Union Day of the Shock Worker* (New York: Roof, 2001), p. 109.

42. Alarcón, *Snake Poems*, p. 27.

43. Zhou Xiaojing, "'What Story What Story What Sound': The Nomadic Poetics of Myung Mi Kim's *Dura*," *College Literature* 33:4 (2007), pp. 63–91, 64.

44. Kim, *Dura*, pp. 97, 68.

45. Kim, *Dura*, p. 98.

46. Judith Butler, *Giving an Account of Oneself* (New York: Fordham University Press, 2005), p. 28.

47. Judith Butler, *Frames of War: When Is Life Grievable* (Brooklyn, N.Y.: Verso, 2009), p. 2.

48. Butler, *Frames of War*, p. 6.

Chapter 50

American Poetry at the End of the Millennium

STEPHEN BURT

Writing literary history for one's own time "is like overlaying a constellation on a bunch of stars in the heavens; a good opportunity to inscribe one's own mythology on the sky but also ideology-bound and hegemonic, arrogant and inaccurate."[1] So the poet and critic Joshua Clover warned in the first issue of the magazine *Fence* in 1998. If that sky represents American poetry, by that year it held more stars than ever before. One thousand to three thousand books of new poetry (depending on how one counts chapbooks and the publications of small presses) came out per year over that decade; the number of U.S. graduate programs in creative writing nearly doubled between 1985 and 2005.[2] A more crowded landscape for American poetry brought increased dissensus about its landmarks. The editors – eminent poets all – for the annual *Best American Poetry* often remarked on the field's extent. John Ashbery praised in 1988 "the exciting diversity of American poetry *right now*" and then apologized for "using this hoary phrase"; Charles Simic decided, after compiling the 1992 volume, "Poetry proves again and again that any single overall theory of anything doesn't work."[3] By 2006 Craig Dworkin could claim that "surveys, broad synoptic claims, arguments based on norms," and "strong accounts of large-scale historical change ... can no longer be maintained."[4]

There is something dispiritingly uninformative about attempts to characterize anything by its resistance to characterization, or by its diversity; there is, on the other hand, something peculiarly contemporary about our insistence on our diversity, our resistance to sweeping characterizations, conclusive arguments, and large-scale claims. Such resistance itself says something about recent times; it is the same resistance to closure, to authoritative tones and statements, and to simulations of a unified argument or a confident, consistent voice that we can see within the developed styles of so many late-in-the-century poems. What the poet Lyn Hejinian calls, in the title of her most influential essay, "the rejection of closure" marks some of the most characteristic – and most imitated – achievements in American poetry at the end of the twentieth century; skepticism as to whether we can say anything clearly or firmly might also mark an attempt to write the history of that poetry in those years, and to connect that history to previous verse.[5]

We might connect that rejection to what other critics have taught us to call the postmodern, which, if it meant anything by the late 1990s, connoted a coy resistance to master narratives and truth claims beyond its own. Yet the poet and scholar James Longenbach, in *Modern Poetry After Modernism* (1997), mounted convincing attacks on accounts of "postmodern American poetry," especially on "'breakthrough' narratives," about heroic works (such as Robert Lowell's *Life Studies* or Donald Allen's *New American Poetry*) that supposedly left older paradigms behind.[6] Instead, Longenbach argued, the best poets of the late century – from Richard Wilbur to Ashbery and Jorie Graham – continued the projects of modernism, itself a dialectical development from Wordsworthian Romanticism. The prominent critic Marjorie Perloff also concluded, in *21st-Century Modernism* (2002), that "ours may well be the moment when the lessons of early modernism are finally being learned."[7] Perloff and Longenbach differ as to what those lessons are, as they differ in their tastes among present-day writers. Both, however, admire Ashbery; and both valorize varieties of skepticism, modes of canny or overt resistance to certainties about society, emotion, and truth. Thus Longenbach regards Wilbur's "undogmatic openness," Graham's "repeated condemnations of narrative closure," and Ashbery's "healthy distrust of what seems natural," while Perloff lauds Ashbery's "refusal to spell out what sort of 'received vision' [he] might produce" along with Hejinian's "room for contingency."[8] Their shared validation of styles that leave room for doubt, their distrust of clear speakers and clean endings, makes one robust story about American poetry just before the year 2000, a story with Ashbery at its ever-receding center, and a few midcareer poets at the fore.

Another story inextricable from the first (with Ashbery, once again, near its center) involves the dialectic common to many accounts of change in the arts. In it, supposedly opposing tastes, styles, and institutions come together after a generational divide, generating syntheses in the work of younger poets, who themselves provoke new forms for dissent. The stories turn out to reinforce each other, and to leave room for a third story about the poet as inspired seer rather than self-conscious maker, about Romantic, intuitive, vatic survivals in a skeptical, self-analytical, and disillusioned age. The first two stories describe the 1990s, or at least an important part of those years; the third will conclude the present chapter by looking back almost a century, at one poet whose significance seemed to change even as this book was being created, and another who seemed almost as anomalous – and as brilliant – to his peers as he seems now.

All three stories might begin with an ending: the last issue of the journal *Antaeus*, in 1994. Started in Morocco in 1970 by Paul Bowles and Daniel Halpern, relocated to New York and New Jersey, and shepherded through the 1980s by Halpern, who also ran Ecco Press, *Antaeus* was never as prominent as the *New Yorker*, but its heft and consistency made it an incomparable guide to a so-called mainstream, associated with New York City and with trade presses, at the last moment when its participants could regard it as the single important literary domain.

The final *Antaeus* included poetry by Ashbery, Frank Bidart, Lucie Brock-Broido, Allen Ginsberg, Louise Glück, Jorie Graham, Robert Hass ("Dragonflies Mating"), Brenda Hillman, Richard Howard, Galway Kinnell, James Merrill, W. S. Merwin, Sharon Olds, Robert Pinsky (his magnificent elegy on his mother, "Poem with Refrains"), and Gary Snyder; it also offered such non-American poets as Joseph Brodsky, Seamus Heaney, Ted Hughes, and Czeslaw Milosz. Among the prose writers were then-president Bill Clinton, with notebook entries from 1987 ("We have put off progress in favor of survival"); Helen Vendler, known for her studies of Keats and Stevens and for reviews in the *New Yorker*, with a rare autobiographical reflection, "One Reviewer's Beginnings"; and fiction by Margaret Atwood, Joyce Carol Oates, and Stephen King.[9]

Wordsworthian models of meditative and elegiac lyric govern a plurality of the *Antaeus* poems; at least ten mourn named individuals, beginning with Bidart's concise memorial to the New York School writer Joe Brainard, "A Coin for Joe in the Image of a Horse." Deborah Digges contributes an anguished, long-lined elegy for her past self: "Such were the serial exhaustions of my beliefs." Chase Twichell's poem "Recorded Birds" applies its nostalgia instead to literary history, asking whether the poetry of the past can surmount the audiovisual present: "watching the suffering on TV," Twichell wishes she could hear, instead, "Keats, Jesus ... Whitman, Dickinson." Wordsworthian models of introspective sincerity also guide Stephen Dunn's "The Living," which takes place during an ice storm: "Will the mail get through? What is uppermost / and most deep down? / I'd like to feel, once again, what I know."[10]

Pulitzer Prizes for poetry during the 1990s went to Glück, Graham, Yusef Komunyakaa, Philip Levine, Liesl Mueller, Charles Simic, Mark Strand, James Tate, Mona Van Duyn, and Charles Wright. All but Komunyakaa, Mueller, and Tate had already published with New York trade houses (Tate moved to Ecco afterward); all but Komunyakaa, Mueller, and Van Duyn appeared in

Antaeus. Returning to all ten in 2001, Willard Spiegelman noted that almost all relied on "autobiographical reminiscence," on "transformations of nostalgia," and on "Romantic nature lyric," in which the poet's psychological history seeks correspondence in the spirit of a place (the same structure Charles Altieri, in 1982, decried as a cliché).[11] Spiegelman also complained about the plain or conversational diction that most poets chose: such *Antaeus* poems as Dunn's and Wright's point back to the clearest, simplest goals of the personal lyric in the 1970s.

Graham's poem in the last *Antaeus* points forward instead. Using the fast, accretive, lengthy sentences and irregular lines that had become one of Graham's trademarks, "Flood" produced a vision of apocalypse, the end of "the private life" and of cities and "schools," a vision that resonated throughout Graham's next book, *The Errancy* (1997). In it the unpredictability and instability of perception become almost as salient as the ruin of visible things:

> (It is an honor) (this carrying what is being said)
>
> Sun fingers down, weakening, to the city-park
> > below;
> row-houses; fencing; schools turning abruptly, catching
> > the light –
> the private life, what is the private life, what is it
> > that is *nobody's*
> > *business*
> through this glassless display-case,
>
> through this length of hallway holding corridors of water?[12]

Graham's turn to long lines, long sentences, and elaborate, sometimes unfinished syntax helped her new poems fit a millennial zeitgeist. "Confused rather than weary, screen-mobile rather than painting-static, jump-cut rather than continuous, interrogative rather than declarative, and ambiguous rather than conclusive," as Vendler put it, Graham's poems could now show how "the events of history are mentally and textually constructed into acts and scenes rather than 'objectively' recorded."[13] Graham's irregular, often very long lines represent self-revision and inconclusiveness in thought, and Heraclitean flux in nature:

> *The war is over* says the river, *the stars are all in me.*
> I peer from the bank, forgotten things seem to fly by.
> *There is novelty, feel its blades*, says the river, rippling,
> *push into perdition, your fault is eternal, exciting, exciting with seeming* –
> > (*TE*, p. 96)

Although Graham's poems can take in the largest possible subjects – God, for example, or genocide – they tend to begin from fleeting perceptions: for example, "one bloodshot / cardinal call" or a glimpse across a shopping mall parking lot (*TE*, p. 59). Only those percepts, at times, seem clearly real; everything larger or longer lasting might be mere epiphenomenon, or illusion. Graham's lines (as Fiona Green put it) "wear themselves out and hold themselves in check by perpetual commentary on their own meanings."[14] "The Guardian Angel of the Swarm," also from *The Errancy*, decides that "the soul is what has folds and is full of folds," going on to ask, "does what is folded exist only / in something that envelops it? – / it is not exactly point of view that includes?" (*TE*, p. 83).

Such language draws on Continental philosophy from Blaise Pascal to Gilles Deleuze and Félix Guattari: it also echoes, in substance although not in tone, Ashbery's earlier images for the paradoxical, hard-to-grasp self, "built out of the meshing of life and space / At the point where we are wholly revealed / In the lozenge-shaped openings."[15] If the self is a fold, a garment, a negative space ("openings"), an effect created by the concealments of garment-like phenomena (biology, society, intellection), then ideas about the self are like clothes, like a frame, like the hat in the rapturous invitations of Graham's "Manteau," with its

> theory emerging like a flowery hat,
> there, above the head,
> descending,
>
> while outside, outside, this coat –
> which I desire, which I, in the tale,
> desire – as it touches the dream of reason,
> which I carry inevitably in my very shoulders, my very carriage, forgive me,
> begins to shred like this, as you see it do, now ... (*TE*, p. 73)

If Graham wants a valid starting point for her passionate epistemological inquiry, she also wants to find out whether she can be guilty, whether almost everyone capable of reading her poems can be guilty, of a masculinist and Euro-American "Imperialism" (a title from her 1987 volume *The End of Beauty*) that appropriates objects for interpretation just as it appropriates land and water, plants and animals, for destructive and nonrenewable use. In a pun that links philosophy to real estate, *The Errancy* speaks against "the nationstate of my premises," premises she may have no right to hold; and if Graham shows the self attempting to hang together, she also depicts it as it dissolves, revising Psalm 22 by inserting quotation marks: "'I' am poured out like water" (*TE*, pp. 62–63).

The Errancy (like The End of Beauty) can indict literary traditions, habits of thoughts, or the history of "the West," but it cannot escape them: it can even present itself (like the last Antaeus) as the end of a cultural line. The poet Forrest Gander called The Errancy "a kind of echo chamber of Western literary culture."[16] In "Sea-Blue Aubade," the sea is "an icy thing, even in its fluency," offering only "more days, more nights, more roads, shouts, flowers, / all making towards what pebbled shore, / each changing place with that which went before," in a long echo of Shakespeare's sonnet 60 (TE, pp. 42, 29); "Untitled Two" takes phrases and plot points from E. A. Robinson's "George Crabbe," "The Mill," and "Reuben Bright," while "Flood" itself adapts Ashbery's "Parergon": "We are so happy in our way of life."[17]

Graham's work in turn would echo through many younger poets' work in the 1990s, not least because they encountered her at the Iowa Writers' Workshop, where Graham taught from 1983 to 1999. With her unpredictably extensive sentences ending in unanswered guilty inquiries, her ways of stretching out perceptual time, Graham by The Errancy had found ways to fit what Hejinian called "the incapacity of language to match the world," "the gap between what one wants to say (or what one perceives there is to say) and what one can (what is sayable)."[18] Those qualities made her seem like a poacher, or an invader, for readers committed to antiestablishment solidarity, and a puzzle or a betrayer for readers (such as the formally conservative young critic Adam Kirsch) committed to Frostian notions of explicit coherence and metrical contract.[19] For still other readers, those qualities made her work central. "If anyone can unify the disjointed fields of contemporary discourse," the poet David Baker mused when reviewing Materialism (1993), "it might well be Jorie Graham."[20] "Like the Language poets, she resists paraphrase," Spiegelman decided, "but unlike them she is – however unconventionally – autobiographical, lyrical and descriptive ... sometimes simultaneously."[21]

During the 1990s, that simultaneity became a frequent goal. We can find it regularly in Fence: the magazine started in New York in 1998, edited by the poet Rebecca Wolff (who holds an M.F.A. from Iowa) along with other fiction writers and poets with links to Iowa and to Columbia University. "These writers are fence-sitters," Wolff explained in the first issue; "each of them occupies a distinguished grey area in the literary field." Fence promised both to cross and to describe a boundary, to facilitate traffic among competing schools, especially between the difficult poetry represented by Language writers such as Hejinian and the trade publisher–oriented "mainstream."[22]

Poets in Fence 1:1 included Rae Armantrout, Anne Carson, Fanny Howe, Heather McHugh, Mark Levine, Thylias Moss, Paul Muldoon, Twichell, John

Yau, and the Slovenian émigré Tomaz Salamun, along with younger writers who had yet to publish a book (myself among them). Their poems often sought immediacy and shock, along with fragmentation and open-endedness: some poets pursued both the puzzling and the risqué. Catherine Wagner in "Three Love Poems" portrayed herself as a conundrum, a minx and a man-trap: "I am in my lucky phase, am solvent, / i.e. where can you hit me? / Not getting out of bed I lime my edges ... Mind everything, missy."[23] Yau flirted with signs of "bad" taste, as well as with nonsense verse, in "Lucubration": "I'm the fan leaning on the spongy / red ledge of the Egyptian motel."[24] Such evasions of prose sense looked back to Surrealism, to the vivid juxtaposition of dreamlike images, rather than to the drier interrogations of a U.S. avant-garde.

Nonetheless, *Fence* remained conscious of that avant-garde: Clover, for example, tried to provide "a lineage of Language poetry, and its essence," although "any lineage is flawed, and essence more so."[25] Clover drew all his quotations from Michael Palmer (discussed subsequently). The only member of the Language group who contributed new poems to the first *Fence* was Armantrout, with "Falling: 1" and "Falling: 2." The former warns against the routinization of the new and shocking, "the new / old / binary // exhibitionism," while the latter appears to criticize a confessional poet, or an attention-seeking acquaintance, whose life and work wrongly assume that true selves and real lives exist and can be revealed: "it is exactly / your relation to exposure / which comprises your act," "a familiarity that threatens / to melt // into uniform poignance."[26]

Armantrout grew up in San Diego, amid the stultifying suburbia described in her pithy memoir *True*: she began to write and publish poetry in Berkeley during the late 1960s, where she encountered Ron Silliman and other Language writers, although her first book did not come out until 1978. Soon afterward she moved back to San Diego, where she remained, publishing more frequently, and gathering more attention, each decade. Sometimes her poems begin from "a few particulars of the San Diego landscape," as Bob Perelman put it; sometimes they begin from degraded commercial phrases, or from the poet's dreams.[27]

Armantrout's intellectual goals, her unstable takes on perception and cognition, resemble Graham's – together they might present a zeitgeist. And yet the experiences of reading the two poets remain far apart. With their clipped lines and compact stanzas, Armantrout's poems stop short over and over, whereas Graham's try not to stop at all. The title in Armantrout's "Retraction" (from *Made to Seem* [1995]) refers both to the impossible taking back of language already used (a quip uttered, a memo sent) and to the back-and-forth motion of branches and leaves:

Interest disguises hope.

Out the window
two junipers are twitching
back and forth in sync
behind the palm which,
I now see,
is also moving.[28]

Made to Seem, like most of Armantrout's volumes, includes a parade of bitterly comic miniatures:

The extra-terrestrial
is made to appear
as a ballerina,

a flamenco dancer
and a disco stud
in succession.   (*MTS*, p. 25)

What, or who, is she "really"? Who knows?

Armantrout's poems remind her, and her readers, that Wordsworthian, or confessional, ideals of sincerity, truth to feeling, consistency, and experience seem (to her) compromised by their dependence on received – and commercially useful – ideas (the same ideas that Graham's works apologize for having used, for having shared). The two lovers in Armantrout's "Covers," for example, realize that their sex life owes its stories to a pornographic film: "If only either one of them believed in the spontaneity of the original actors and could identify with one" (*MTS*, p. 11). Because meaning depends on use, use on learning, and learning on habit and acculturation, the poems, like their characters, realize that they can say nothing meaningful if they try to assert something new: "*Die Mommy scum!* // To come true, / a thing must come second" (*MTS*, p. 14). Armantrout wrote about this poem, "The Creation," in her essay "Cheshire Poetics," the closest she has ever come to a statement of principles: its "declarative statements have a 'truth-effect,' like a false bottom, which gives way on second thought. There is, in fact, no voice which can be trusted in this poem."[29] Nor is there such a voice in many other poems by Armantrout; their lines seem to see through us as we see through them.

Armantrout's poems can undermine not only notions of time and memory, notions of self, and notions of accuracy but also notions of artistic quality, which may consist only of adherence to norms:

Not just light
at the end of the tunnel,

but hearts, bows, rainbows –

all the stickers
teachers award if pleased.

Her poems also confound her own relations to memory: they make, as she put it, "a quick trip back / to mark the spot / where things stop / looking familiar" (*MTS*, p. 24). For Wordsworth and his successors, up to the present day of Pinsky or Dunn, memory teaches us who we are and have been by connecting present to past, thus shaping experiences that imagined persons then share. Armantrout's jagged shapes, too short for their speakers – as Graham's shapes in *The Errancy* seem too fast, or too long – prevent and undermine those stories; "'When names perform a function,'" warns a "stubborn old woman" in *Made to Seem*, "'that's fiction'" (*MTS*, p. 42).

Graham and Armantrout, read side by side in the 1990s, demonstrate the erased and reconstituted, dispelled and reassembled value of such contested terms as "lyric," "voice," and "self." The two poets – and their reception – also testify in the domain of poetry to the process that Mark McGurl describes in recent American fiction, a "struggle between a dominant 'conventional realism' and a minority 'radical experimentalism' mediated in part by the academy ... in which opposing sides begin, despite themselves, to interpenetrate."[30] Such struggles generate, from the "conventional" side, defenses of old techniques and, from the "radical" side, accusations of selling out, or of stealing (thus "fence"). Steve Evans duly attacked *Fence* in 2001 as a kind of third way in poetry, akin to Bill Clinton's or Tony Blair's third way in politics. Inspired and promoted (Evans alleged) by Graham, Hass, and Hillman, with their "top-down taste," *Fence* was "by tendency eclectic and apolitical, allergic to commitment and against principles on principle," because it severed interest in anticlosural rhetoric, post-Surrealist imagery, and epistemological skepticism from "radical social projects and values."[31]

David Kellogg – whose essay appeared in *Fence* 3:2 – also noted the recent emergence of "lyric poets ... fond of innovative technique"; he noted, too, "new literary journals" that emerged around them: "*Chain, COMBO, Explosive, Rhizome, Samizdat*."[32] Because the Language writers proved so adept at theorizing themselves, and because their stated objectives could mesh with the goals of advanced literary academics, discussions of poetic hybridity, synthesis, or "new lyric" in the 1990s and afterward sometimes treated that synthesis as a collision or merger of one Wordsworthian, descriptive, or lyrical "mainstream" with one discrete body of Language writing: *Where Lyric Tradition Meets Language*, as one conference (later an anthology) put it. Yet the New American, post-Stein, and post-Williams traditions that became broadly available to younger writers during those years had many sources, not only the writers who published in $L=A=N=G=U=A=G=E$, *Hills*, or *This* but also the countercultural, sometimes visionary writers associated with the Poetry Project at St. Mark's Church in the Bowery, such as Bernadette Mayer, Alice Notley, and Ted Berrigan; the aggressive, sometimes theatrical styles of Amiri Baraka and other poets of the Black Arts Movement; and the legacies of Continental Surrealism.

Critics saw these changes as they took place. "The bifurcation of the poetry world into square versus hip, official versus renegade, metropolitan versus provincial, was rapidly eroding," Jed Rasula claimed in 2004.[33] Christopher Beach asked whether the supposed split "between an academic mainstream of 'workshop' orientation … and an experimental, oppositional, or countercultural poetry" no longer fit the facts. Roger Gilbert agreed: "The nineties saw a decided softening of the boundaries between competing poetic modes."[34]

The end of *Antaeus* and the founding of *Fence* might be two points (forming one line) where the boundaries softened. Other such points, where old binaries fail, schools mingle, and ascendant ideas about present-day poems become clear, might be the first annual National Poetry Slam, held in San Francisco in 1990; the founding of the Buffalo-based magazine *Apex of the M* (1994), with its "ecstatic … millennial utopian program," presented as a successor to Language writing; the start of the annual West Chester conference, devoted primarily to rhymed or metered verse, in 1995; the first annual Cave Canem retreat, a week-long workshop for African American poets, held in 1996; or the first online-only poetry magazine (there are several candidates).[35] Beach himself picks "the publication of Paul Hoover's Norton anthology *Postmodern American Poetry* and the production and broadcast of Bob Holman's television series *The United States of Poetry*." The first, in 1994, made Language writers and their allies widely available in the academy; the second, in 1996, made spoken word and performance poetry widely visible outside it.[36]

Graham and Armantrout both found whole styles, and kinds of poetic line, appropriate for an end-of-the-century skepticism. Other poets founded not styles but subgenres and modes. One such mode was the unstable or canceled epistolary poem, which uses the rhetoric of a personal letter (salutations, for example, and reference to prior letters and to envelopes) but does not maintain the consistent fiction that it *is* a letter to another human being. That lack of consistency is, in Hejinian's terms, another rejection of closure: we cannot decide who the poet pretends to be, nor to whom she speaks, in salutations such as "Dear You: Accuser" (Geoff Nutter), "Dear Evasive Precaution" (Amy Catanzano), or "Dear Errant Kid ... Dear Dying Town" (C. D. Wright).[37]

This new mode governed entire collections. Joe Wenderoth's *Letters to Wendy's* (2000) collects prose poems purportedly written on customer-comment cards from Wendy's fast-food restaurants ("Wendy is not a girl; she is a sign"); the book attracted improbably widespread notice, including a review in *Rolling Stone*.[38] The poems in Lucie Brock-Broido's *The Master Letters* (1995), derived very loosely from Emily Dickinson, address a mysterious "master" in elaborate couplets and prose poems distinguished by salutations ("*Revd Sir*," "My Most Courteous Lord") or sign-offs ("*Your Gnome*," "*Your Lodestar, Your – / Andromeda*").[39] Here, as Ann Keniston suggests, "the prose letter ... functions both as an alternative to and an extreme version of lyric." These canceled fictions of presence and of speaking persons repeat at the level of subgenre the insistence on skepticism and on broken-up, constantly interrogated, or split-up selves and voices that we have seen in Armantrout, and in Graham, as matters of line-by-line style.

The popularity of this new, self-undermining epistolary subgenre might also reflect the influence of Palmer, whose quasi- or semiepistolary pages play with the idea of personal address while deleting the signals that say who speaks to whom, as if "to unlearn them."[40] Such poetry asks (to quote Palmer himself) "how the pronouns, how the *I* and the *we*, the *you* and the *they*, the *he* and *she* are spoken, invoked and meant."[41] *Sun* (1990) includes epistles to aspects of language:

> Dear Lexicon, I died in you.
> as a dragonfly might
> or a dragon in a bottle might
>
> Dear Lexia, There is no mind[42]

In Palmer's 1997 "Letters to Zanzotto," Andrea Zanzotto (a real contemporary Italian poet) becomes another of Palmer's impersonal presences: "Dear Z," he writes, in "Letter 6," "So we accused mimesis, accused // anemone / and the plasma of mud."[43] Such merging of alphabetical with epistolary letters, unsettling fictions of address and person, also turns up in other late-century poets: Juan Felipe Herrera, for example, writes in "explode this letter w/ this" (1999):

> X is for fancy tacos sold w/ Mayan Rebellion
> J is for the first White God initially meant for burial in Juarez....
> J is for never enter the Nirvana Joke Tree.
> T is simple. Ten glove will mark your dishes, in eternal
> service boy, jackal. This bean dish is familiar isn't it?[44]

Future readers may look for a self-skeptical, anticlosural zeitgeist in Graham, in Armantrout, in Brock-Broido or Palmer, and in the journals to which they contributed and the lines or subgenres that they invented. They may look as well to major writers whose long careers ended during the 1990s, such as James Merrill; they may focus on first and second books by poets whose nationwide influence on other writers became apparent only after 2000, such as Herrera, Terrance Hayes, Laura Kasischke, or D. A. Powell. Future readers should also cherish such unfashionable singletons as the persistent miniaturist Samuel Menashe, a Jewish veteran of World War II, whose careful stanzas meditate on mortality and eternity:

> Keep your ear to the ground
> I was told without fear
> Now I am hollowed for sound
> And it is my heart I hear[45]

This poet once tried to listen to the ground (to his contemporaries, to his time); now (perhaps older and lonelier, or wiser) he hears instead the *Abgrund*, the subject of mortality, the void that stands below and beyond the merely historical questions that other poets – and literary critics – ask.

Yet the questions remain. The poetry of the American 1990s, taken en masse, might leave us suspicious of any story we can tell about it, not just because there's so much of it (who read it all?) but because so many of the poets, and so many of its arbiters (excluding those invested in "conservative" narratives about decline) seemed to argue for diversity, for democracy, or (as in Armantrout's quip about "stickers") for self-conscious resistance to judgments of value. Skeptical poets tried to register these arguments, that resistance, as matters of style.

Attempting to make sense of "the conflicting principles by which poetry is currently valued," Kellogg came up with four: "self, community, tradition and innovation." John Ashbery's poetry, as Kellogg explained, had such prominence (as of 2001) because it could be very plausibly "claimed by powerful critics for all four poles: Helen Vendler views him as a poet of the self, Harold Bloom as a reviser of [Romantic and Stevensian] tradition, Marjorie Perloff as a formal innovator, and John Shoptaw [among others] as a writer of 'encrypted' gay poems."[46] To contemplate Ashbery's work, with its "extraordinarily wide range of precursors" as well as its range of inheritors, is to contemplate the insufficiency of any single narrative about the historical line of American verse.[47] Ashbery's poem in the final *Antaeus*, "Dangerous Moonlight," made fun of the idea that poems could support claims about the zeitgeist, or about anything else:

> Well that's
> poetic argument for you. It stands on its own ("the cheese stands alone")
> but can at the drop of a speculation be seen again as a part,
> a vital one, of the mucus cloud that is generalized human thought aimed at
> a quarrel or a rebus in the lining. And that's the way
> we get old with poetry.[48]

Not all poets resigned themselves as readily as Ashbery to "the way / we get old," to "failed," incomplete, or inevitably cloudy representation. While many sought ways to represent a prevailing skepticism within, or among, prevailing styles, others put forward alternatives to that skepticism, and to the versions of literary history that it entailed. The magisterial poet and critic Allen Grossman imagined in poems and in philosophical prose how the trope of a person, the fiction of consistent utterance, might overcome modern doubts; indeed, his signature poem "The Piano Player Explains Himself" depicts a kind of orphic resurrection, in which traditional goals and models for lyric come back triumphant – yet irreparably damaged, and dissonant – from the dead:

> When the corpse revived at the funeral
> The outraged mourners killed it; and the soul
> Of the revenant passed into the body
> Of the poet because it had more to say.
> He sat down at the piano no one could play
> Called Messiah, or The Regulator of the World,
> Which had stood for fifty years . . . The musician was
> Skillful but the Messiah was out of tune
> And bent the time and the tone.[49]

Grossman revives not only clear line and clear argument, not only visionary and consistent scene setting, but also the tradition of blank verse, which, according to his own theorizing, could represent "the fate of social man."[50] Not by coincidence, Graham in her typical very long line and Armantrout in her short one both find an almost unprecedented distance, not just from accentual-syllabic English meter (other patterns propel them instead), but from the mere count of a decasyllabic norm.

Still other poets of the 1990s allowed skepticism to inform their syntax and their external form, while seeking confidence, ecstasy, and authenticity in topic and tone. C. D. Wright, as Lynn Keller put it, "combines . . . language-centered skepticism with faith in what she sees with her own eyes and experiences in her own female body."[51] Wright's *Tremble* (1997) was widely believed to be the last book of poetry published by Ecco as an independent press (Ecco survives as an imprint of HarperCollins). *Tremble* begins with "Floating Trees," a poem of married love:

> a bed is left open to a mirror
> a mirror gazes long and hard at a bed
>
> light fingers the house with its own acoustics
>
> one of them writes this down
> one has paper
>
> bed of swollen creeks and theories and coils
> bed of eyes and leaky pens[52]

Such evocative lines may unsettle our sense of who speaks, of what we know about who is speaking (the poem includes no pronominal "we" nor "I"), but they do not hold back in their strongly embodied emotion. Wright's lines thus join a tradition of ambiguity less postmodern than Pindaric, both self-abasing and self-exalting: her work at the limits of sense is also work toward ecstasy.

Wright grew up, and started publishing her poems, in Arkansas, part of a 1970s circle that also included the prolific and self-mythologizing Frank Stanford, commemorated in Wright's first full-length book, *Translation of the Gospel Back into Tongues* (1983). She evolved her recognizable styles after her move to San Francisco in 1979, where she encountered Language writers such as Ron Silliman (who has also collaborated with Armantrout); there Wright also met her husband, the poet, critic, and translator Forrest Gander (both now teach at Brown University in Rhode Island). Although Wright learned much from the Language writers, she remained more Romantic than skeptic, more realist than nominalist. Indeed, Wright tries to become at once Romantic, realist in the philosophers' sense (ideas are to her real things), and realist in the journalistic and novelistic sense – her other works include a book-length poetic travelogue in rural Georgia (*Deepstep Come Shining* [1998]), sequences about her native Ozarks (*String Light* [1991]), and hybrid verse-and-photography about prisons in Louisiana (*One Big Self* [2001]).

This unusual, ambitious merger of realist and Romantic goals with techniques drawn from antirealist writers helped to make Wright's poems suddenly and broadly influential as the century closed. And if we look for precursors when we look at Wright, if we look in earlier literary history for poets who aspired at once to Romantic heights, to American chronicle, and to open, broken forms, we might return to Gertrude Stein, an influence on all the Language writers and on Ashbery, with her "difficulty ... at once intellectual and affective," as Emily Setina writes. A minority taste for most of the twentieth century, Stein may be a wider influence in the twenty-first, as poets try to find rationales for poetry that do not depend on older ideas about purpose and about audience: her most demanding prose and verse show "how it is that it does not make any difference / To please them or not or not," with an orneriness, a determined idiosyncrasy, akin to what Wright would praise in her later prose.[53]

To read American poetry with Stein, rather than (say) Williams, Moore, Hughes, Eliot, or Stevens, as the center of an enduring modernism is to make it hard or impossible to segregate poetry from other things called experimental writing, or prose. (For most of the twentieth century, Stein's effect on modern American fiction, through Ernest Hemingway and others, remained more widely known than her poems.) Indeed the most widely influential work of Stein's poetry at this point might be her first book of prose poems (or experimental, narrative prose), *Tender Buttons* (1913). That book, with its short, supposedly descriptive passages about "objects," "food," and "rooms," presents a Stein whose language seems opaque, material, and proudly distant from the semantic functions of language in other hands. It is that Stein of materiality and opacity – the Stein whose "genius" declares its independence both from the semantic functions of prose and from older verse forms – who appealed first to the Language writers, to Ashbery (who has cited "Stanzas in Meditation" as a particular influence), and to the Harryette Mullen of *Trimmings* (1991) and *S*PeRM**K*T* (1992).

Yet Stein's demanding poetry of the 1910s through the 1930s – from *Tender Buttons* to *Lifting Belly* (1915–17) or "As a Wife Has a Cow" (1926) – can also (to quote Elisabeth Frost) "create a private language of lesbian experience," whose "sound play ... suggest[s] Stein's intimate erotic life."[54] This version of Stein for decades eluded readers who had not sought it out, but it now seems inescapable in such passages (from *Tender Buttons*) as "A cool red rose and a pink cut pink, a collapse and a sold hole, a little less hot ... Please could, please could, jam it not plus more sit in when," as "Feeling or for it, as feeling or for it, came in or come in, or come out of there ... As a wife has a cow."[55] And that Stein seemed newly available, and newly imitated, during the 1980s and 1990s, not in place of but alongside the Stein of materiality and resistance.

This dual Stein of queer sexual permission and reinvented cognition, a Stein through whose polyvalent language "Patriarchal poetry might be withstood," informed Mullen and C. D. Wright and Juliana Spahr, among many others, in the 1990s.[56] *Tender Buttons* itself became widely available, in Spahr's own words, as "an optimistic demonstration of how possible it is to read, of how, luckily, our imaginations are impossible to regulate."[57] And the same powerful, dual Stein, not so much newly discovered as finally widely visible, increasingly informed non-"mainstream" institutions of poetry as they developed toward the end of the century, from marathon readings of Stein's books to newly founded independent publishers (such as Lee Ann Brown's press Tender Buttons), new poetry written and circulated *by* those publishers, and new editions of Stein's individual works (*Lifting Belly* among them).[58]

It may be that Stein will emerge as *the* modernist writer who became more important to a twenty-first-century future than to much of the twentieth-century past. And yet if we want to find *a* modernist writer whose work anticipates the 1990s, containing within himself both the line of Romantic lyric and the desire to be fractured, without a single voice, we can no longer overlook Hart Crane (1899–1932). Crane, Grossman wrote, "lived in and through the logic of the poetic principle" and "wrote poems that told stories about the impossibility of its imperatives."[59] The final *Antaeus* concluded with ten texts by Crane never published in his lifetime. One fragment aspired to "altitudes, / Abstractions ... Pure heights – Infinity resides below"; another announced, "I have seen my ghost broken / My body blessed / And Eden / Scraped from my mother's breast."[60]

Along with Langston Hughes, Crane was the first significant American poet to begin writing after American modernism (or "the New Poetry," as it was sometimes called) had established itself in the 1910s. Raised in Ohio by a candy-company entrepreneur, his soon-estranged wife, and her mother, Crane moved to New York in 1916 to establish himself as a writer; for the next decade he migrated among Cleveland, New York City, and upstate New York, taking and leaving clerical and advertising jobs, as he wrote the poems that entered his two completed books. Crane's many friends and correspondents included the cultural critics Gorham Munson and Waldo Frank, the modernist writer Jean Toomer, and the poets and critics Allen Tate and Yvor Winters, both of whom would turn against his extravagant poems. Crane pursued and fell in love with men, including the sailor Emil Oppfer; his writings can exalt their romance. By the time he finished his signature long poem, *The Bridge* (published in 1929), Crane had become a trial to some of his friends, as well as an alcoholic: months in southern California, in France, and in Mexico produced the rest of the poems gathered posthumously as *Key West: An Island Sheaf.* Crane died by leaping, or falling, from a passenger ship off the coast of Florida in 1932.

In the first poem in his first book, *White Buildings* (1926), "tremorous ... Kisses are, – / The only worth all granting" (*HCLA*, p. 3). *White Buildings* also granted access to elevated, concentrated diction, along with attempts to renew the heroic quatrain:

> New thresholds, new anatomies! Wine talons
> Build freedom up about me and distill
> This competence – to travel in a tear
> Sparkling alone, within another's will.   (*HCLA*, p. 17)

Crane here praises drinking wine, or becoming drunk ("when wine redeems the sight"), in service to an ecstatic, sense-defying ideal. His essay "General Aims and Theories" (1925), possibly written for the playwright Eugene O'Neill, now looks like a program for *The Bridge*: Crane declared that he "was really building a bridge between our so-called classic experience and … our seething, confused cosmos of today, which has no formulated mythology yet" (*HCLA*, p. 160). In its nine parts, *The Bridge* presents an idiosyncratic survey of American geography and history, encompassing Virginia, Indiana, Louisiana, the Mississippi River, "Connecticut farms, abandoned pastures," the whole of the East and West Coasts, the global reach of American nautical power ("round the Horn / to Frisco, Melbourne"), the early colonial past (Columbus, "Powhatan's Daughter"), and technology: the Wright brothers' flights inspire delight and yearning and the New York City subway, despair (*HCLA*, p. 55). He planned but could not complete another section, "Calgary Express," attentive to African American life, and to the career of John Brown.

The Bridge is also a poem for New York, finding in the Brooklyn Bridge a symbol for unions political, spiritual, and erotic. Its "bound cable strands" and "arching path / upward" bring to America both the Homeric lyre and the Romantic Aeolian harp (*HCLA*, pp. 72–74). They also uphold the promise of union that Whitman saw in Lincoln. "Cape Hatteras," which praises the Wright brothers' flight, ends with the famous hope "never to let go / My hand / in yours, / Walt Whitman – / so – " (*HCLA*, p. 60). Like T. S. Eliot's *The Waste Land*, to which it attempts an optimistic answer, *The Bridge* becomes a cyclopedia of verse forms, among them cut-up conversational free verse, Dickinsonian ballad stanzas, blues, sheet-music-era popular song, quasi-Homeric unrhymed hexameters, and variations on the heroic quatrain, as in the proem "To Brooklyn Bridge":

> How many dawns, chill from his rippling rest
> The seagull's wings shall dip and pivot him,
> Shedding white rings of tumult, building high
> Over the chained bay waters Liberty –
>
> Then with inviolate curve, forsake our eyes
> As apparitional as sails that cross
> Some page of figures to be filed away;
> – Till elevators drop us from our day. . . .   (*HCLA*, p. 33)

"Crane endeavored to find a way to combine ... self-conscious modernity of technique ... with ... the exuberant expression of a particularly [American] continental heritage," writes Robert K. Martin, who adds that Whitman "helped Crane understand the sexual origin of his own art."[61] Yet Crane never emulated Whitman's technique; instead, his "near childlike delight in the full battery of traditional poetic artifice" (as Brian Reed put it) drew staunchly on the European past.[62] If other, more widely influential modernists – Stein most of all – invite contemporary readers to start again, as if from scratch, to do something that looks as little as possible like the poetry of the past, *The Bridge* invites readers to claim the whole of poetry (not only American poetry) for ourselves. "What Emerson proposed the poet should do," wrote Grossman, "Crane really does."[63] He is at the least *a* bridge, if not indeed *the* bridge, between Emerson and C. D. Wright, Whitman and J. F. Herrera, and Emily Dickinson and D. A. Powell.

Not coincidentally, Crane's poetry includes – by name and by implication and allusion – the nineteenth-century canon, centered on Whitman, Dickinson, and Melville, that was just coalescing in Crane's day. He wrote an exultant sonnet "To Emily Dickinson" and a monody set "At Melville's Tomb" (*HCLA*, pp. 87, 24).[64] Crane aspired to unite in his own voice, or in a cable of transfigured voices, American social and literary history. Later readers such as Winters and Tate believed Crane's "failure" inseparable from the "failure" of something else – of his life, because it ended in apparent suicide; of Emersonian, Romantic optimism and individualism; of modernism; or of same-sex desire and love. Langdon Hammer explains that Crane's "pursuit of a major, culturally central poetry" has remained "anomalous, hard to place," and "always outside the paradigms that govern the field."[65]

If Stein often stands for a radical discontinuity, for modernism as a way of starting again, Crane stands for the modern and the contemporary as continuations-with-a-difference of what came before. Crane has for some later poets thus come to stand for the American poet generally: poets have tended to put their own words in his mouth. Robert Lowell's "Words for Hart Crane" denounces American inattention to poetic vocation: "Who asks for me, the Shelley of my age, / must lay his heart out for my bed and board."[66] Melvin Tolson paid homage to Crane through choice of forms, modeling *Libretto for the Republic of Liberia* (1953) to some extent on *The Bridge*; Tate, who had written a preface for *White Buildings*, did the same for Tolson, dubbing him "in the direct succession of Crane."[67] The former U.S. poet laureate Philip Levine opened his collection *The Simple Truth* (1992) with a tormented, self-undermining poem called "On the Meeting of García Lorca and Hart Crane":

the "two ... poetic geniuses'" homosexual desires, and their foreshortened lives, seem to Levine inseparable from "the visionary powers of the human, / the only animal that's got it."[68]

Other poets find in Crane more hopeful models. Clayton Eshleman's "several poems about Hart Crane" and "imagined conversations with him" make Crane a kind of martyr for the ecstatic self of poems, resurrected and multiplied "to wander under Dionysus and to suffer Dionysus in the flesh."[69] Powell pays homage to Crane in *Tea* (1997), quoting him twice, and making him a pivot point in the countercanon of gay men's writing and music that *Tea* constructs.[70] Charles Wright's "Portrait of the Artist with Hart Crane" imagines poetry in general, and Crane's brand of American poetry in particular, as an unfinishable, inexplicable vocation: "I've been writing this poem for weeks now," Wright admits, "With a pencil made of rail, smudging my face / And my friend's face, making a language where nothing stays."[71] Adrienne Rich in 1999 gave pride of place to Crane in a poem about artists who remade themselves in New York: with "deadweight trophies borne / through *interboro fissures of the mind* ... Hart Miles Muriel Julia Paul / you will meet the eyes you were searching for."[72]

To contemplate Crane's afterlife is also to contemplate how we narrate – or fail to narrate – the procession of poets that leads up to our own day: *The Bridge* remains a monument and an argument (in John Irwin's words) for "the possibility that every American poet, no matter how late he [*sic*] comes in the tradition, can enjoy an original relationship with the muse."[73] Harold Bloom's neo-Romantic model of poetic succession, by which each strong poet "misreads" and therefore surpasses a poetic father, provided from the 1970s into the 1990s a standing alternative to versions of literary history (such as Perloff's) that highlight modernism as innovation, as well as to the pluralist version put forward by the book you are reading right now. Behind Bloom's model, as Bloom has said, stands Crane, "a religious poet without even a faithless faith," whose "gifts for vision and rhetoric ... surpassed all his American forerunners and those who have come after in the Age of Ashbery."[74] Where Graham and Armantrout, and Ashbery, and (at least) the early Hejinian would emphasize the slipperiness, the resistances and doubts, intrinsic to even the most intuitively musical circuits of supposed communication, Crane flaunts instead – like Keats and like Dickinson – "the poet's power to speak to readers from beyond the grave."[75]

To conclude with Crane – with Crane's voices, and with Crane's would-be heirs – at the end of the century is to see how hard it might be, even in a time (like Crane's) when many fewer books of poems were published, to fit everything important about a period into any one story about it – to see both the necessity (built into *The Bridge*) and the inadequacy of literary history as such. Crane's projects and his reputation may even have become a synecdoche for literary inheritance in general – unpredictable, ramifying, unfinished if not forever unfinishable, and often unsettling too. He is at once a bearer of orphic modes and a cause for continued skepticism, hard to pin down as to where he stands, what he can mean: his verse seems both to summarize and to surpass American literary history, and hence to call for ways of reading that only the future can know.

Notes

1. Joshua Clover, "The Rose of the Name," *Fence* 1:1 (1998), pp. 35–41, 37.
2. Christopher Beach, *Poetic Culture: Contemporary American Poetry Between Community and Institution* (Evanston, Ill.: Northwestern University Press, 1999), p. 22; Mark McGurl, *The Program Era: Postwar Fiction and the Rise of Creative Writing* (Cambridge, Mass.: Harvard University Press, 2009), p. 25. McGurl's bar graph counts fewer than 150 programs in 1985, about 225 in 1995, and 300 in 2005.
3. Harold Bloom (ed.), *The Best of the Best American Poetry, 1988–1997* (New York: Scribner, 1998), pp. 349, 351.
4. Craig Dworkin, "Seja Marginal," in Craig Dworkin (ed.), *The Consequences of Innovation: 21st Century Poetics* (New York: Roof, 2008), pp. 7–24, 13.
5. Lyn Hejinian, *The Language of Inquiry* (Berkeley: University of California Press, 2000), p. 40.
6. James Longenbach, *Modern Poetry After Modernism* (New York: Oxford University Press, 1997), p. 5.
7. Marjorie Perloff, *21st-Century Modernism: The "New" Poetics* (Oxford: Blackwell, 2002), p. 200.
8. Longenbach, *Modern Poetry After Modernism*, pp. 83, 166, 100; Perloff, *21st-Century Modernism*, pp. 8, 189.
9. Bill Clinton, "Notebook," *Antaeus* 75–76 (1994), p. 345; *Antaeus* 75–76 (1994), passim.
10. Deborah Digges, "Rune for the Parable of Despair," *Antaeus* 75–76 (1994), p. 250; Chase Twichell, "Recorded Birds," *Antaeus* 75–76 (1994), pp. 325–26; Stephen Dunn, "The Living," *Antaeus* 75–76 (1994), p. 255.
11. Willard Spiegelman, "The Nineties Revisited," *Contemporary Literature* 42:2 (2001), pp. 206–37, 210, 213; Charles Altieri, "Sensibility, Rhetoric and Will: Some Tensions in Contemporary Poetry," *Contemporary Literature* 23:4 (1982), pp. 451–79.
12. Jorie Graham, *The Errancy* (Hopewell, N.J.: Ecco, 1997), p. 32. This collection will be cited in the text as *TE*.

13. Helen Vendler, "Fin-de-Siècle Lyric," in Elaine Scarry (ed.), *Fins de Siècle* (Baltimore, Md.: Johns Hopkins University Press, 1995), pp. 123–40, 130, 131.

14. Fiona Green, "Reading Lyric in Jorie Graham's Aubades," *Genre* 45:1 (2010), pp. 121–42, 129.

15. John Ashbery, *Selected Poems* (New York: Penguin, 1985), p. 237.

16. Forrest Gander, "Listening for a Divine Word," in Thomas Gardner (ed.), *Jorie Graham: Essays on the Poetry* (Madison: University of Wisconsin Press, 2005), pp. 75–81, 75–76.

17. Ashbery, *Selected Poems*, p. 107.

18. Hejinian, *The Language of Inquiry*, p. 56.

19. Adam Kirsch, *The Modern Element* (New York: W. W. Norton, 2008), pp. 25–40.

20. David Baker, *Heresy and the Ideal: On Contemporary Poetry* (Fayetteville: University of Arkansas Press, 2000), p. 83.

21. Spiegelman, "The Nineties Revisited," p. 233.

22. Rebecca Wolff, "Editor's Note," *Fence* 1:1 (1998), p. 1.

23. Catherine Wagner, "Three Love Poems," *Fence* 1:1 (1998), p. 95.

24. John Yau, "Lucubration," *Fence* 1:1 (1998), p. 97.

25. Clover, "The Rose of the Name," p. 37.

26. Rae Armantrout, *Veil: New and Selected Poems* (Middletown, Conn.: Wesleyan University Press, 2001), pp. 115, 116.

27. Bob Perelman, *The Marginalization of Poetry: Language Writing and Literary History* (Princeton, N.J.: Princeton University Press, 1996), p. 136.

28. Rae Armantrout, *Made to Seem* (Los Angeles: Sun & Moon, 1995), p. 8. This collection will be cited in the text as *MTS*.

29. Rae Armantrout, *Collected Prose* (San Diego, Calif.: Singing Horse, 2007), p. 58.

30. McGurl, *The Program Era*, p. 33.

31. Steve Evans, "The Resistible Rise of Fence Enterprises," Third Factory (2004), http://www.thirdfactory.net/resistible.html.

32. David Kellogg, "The Self in the Poetic Field," *Fence* 3:2 (2001), pp. 97–108, 106–07.

33. Jed Rasula, *Syncopations: The Stress of Innovation in Contemporary American Poetry* (Tuscaloosa: University of Alabama Press, 2004), p. 6.

34. Beach, *Poetic Culture*, p. 8; Roger Gilbert, "Awash with Angels: The Religious Turn in Nineties Poetry," *Contemporary Literature* 42:2 (2001), pp. 238–69, 245.

35. Rasula, *Syncopations*, p. 36. For the history of Cave Canem, see especially Meta DuEwa Jones, *The Muse Is Music: Jazz Poetry from the Harlem Renaissance to Spoken Word* (Urbana: University of Illinois Press, 2011), pp. 168–208.

36. Beach, *Poetic Culture*, p. 18.

37. Geoff Nutter, *A Summer Evening* (Fort Collins: Colorado State University Center for Literary Publishing, 2001), p. 17; Amy Catanzano, "Anti-Guardian

6:7:9," *American Letters & Commentary* 13 (2001), pp. 8–10; C. D. Wright, *Steal Away: Selected and New Poems* (Port Townsend, Wash.: Copper Canyon, 2002), pp. 222–23.

38. Joe Wenderoth, *Letters to Wendy's* (Northampton, Mass.: Verse Press, 2000).

39. Lucie Brock-Broido, *The Master Letters* (New York: Knopf, 1995), pp. 37, 38, 4, 62, 10, 53.

40. Michael Palmer, *The Lion Bridge: Selected Poems 1972–95* (New York: New Directions, 1998), p. 87.

41. Michael Palmer, *Active Boundaries: Selected Essays and Talks* (New York: New Directions, 2008), p. 105.

42. Palmer, *The Lion Bridge*, p. 151.

43. Palmer, *The Lion Bridge*, p. 204.

44. Juan Felipe Herrera, *Border-Crosser with a Lamborghini Dream* (Tucson: University of Arizona Press, 1999), p. 43.

45. Samuel Menashe, *New and Selected Poems*, ed. Christopher Ricks (New York: Library of America, 2005), p. 153.

46. Kellogg, "The Self in the Poetic Field," p. 99.

47. Longenbach, *Modern Poetry After Modernism*, p. 88.

48. John Ashbery, "Dangerous Moonlight," *Antaeus* 75–76 (1994), p. 235.

49. Allen Grossman, *The Ether Dome and Other Poems: New and Selected 1979–1991* (New York: New Directions, 1991), p. 3.

50. Allen Grossman, *The Sighted Singer* (Baltimore, Md.: Johns Hopkins University Press, 1992), p. 279.

51. Lynn Keller, *Thinking Poetry: Readings in Contemporary Women's Exploratory Poetics* (Iowa City: University of Iowa Press, 2010), p. 42.

52. Wright, *Steal Away*, p. 148. Kirsch rejects this style of writing, too, for its "surface confusion"; see Kirsch, *The Modern Element*, pp. 113–24.

53. Emily Setina, "From 'Impossible' Writing to a Poetics of Intimacy: John Ashbery's Readings of Gertrude Stein," *Genre* 45:1 (2012), pp. 143–66, 144; Gertrude Stein, *Stanzas in Meditation*, ed. Susannah Hollister and Emily Setina (New Haven, Conn.: Yale University Press, 2010), p. 172; C. D. Wright, *Cooling Time: An American Poetry Vigil* (Port Townsend, Wash.: Copper Canyon, 2005).

54. Elisabeth Frost, "Signifying on Stein: The Revisionist Poetics of Harryette Mullen and Leslie Scalapino," *Postmodern Culture* 5:3 (1995).

55. Gertrude Stein, *Selections*, ed. Joan Retallack (Berkeley: University of California Press, 2008), pp. 138–39; Gertrude Stein, *Selected Writings*, ed. Carl Van Vechten (New York: Vintage, 1990), p. 544.

56. Stein, *Selected Writings*, p. 226.

57. Juliana Spahr, "Afterword," in Gertrude Stein, *Tender Buttons: The Corrected Centennial Edition*, ed. Seth Perlow (San Francisco, Calif.: City Lights, 2014), pp. 107–29, 113.

58. For example, M. H. Jensen, "Gertrude Stein All the Time, Time, Time, and Time," *Hyperallergic*, February 1, 2014, http://hyperallergic.com/106247 /gertrude-stein-all-the-time-time-time-and-time/; Gertrude Stein, *Lifting Belly*, ed. Rebecca Mark (Tallahasee, Fla.: Naiad Press, 1989); Gertrude Stein, *The Making of Americans* (Normal, Ill.: Dalkey Archive, 1995); Bernadette Mayer, *Sonnets* (New York: Tender Buttons, 1989); Lee Ann Brown, *Polyverse* (Los Angeles: Sun & Moon, 1999).

59. Allen Grossman, *The Long Schoolroom* (Ann Arbor: University of Michigan Press, 1997), p. 85.

60. Hart Crane, "Ten Poems," *Antaeus* 75–76 (1994), pp. 352–55; Hart Crane, *Complete Poems and Selected Letters*, ed. Langdon Hammer (New York: Library of America, 2006), pp. 137, 144. This collection will be cited in the text as *HCLA*.

61. Robert K. Martin, *The Homosexual Tradition in American Poetry*, rev. ed. (Iowa City: University of Iowa Press, 1998), pp. 138, 148. The first edition of Martin's book appeared in 1979.

62. Brian Reed, *Hart Crane: After His Lights* (Tuscaloosa: University of Alabama Press, 2006), p. 26.

63. Grossman, *The Long Schoolroom*, p. 110.

64. Edward Brunner, *Splendid Failure: Hart Crane and the Making of* The Bridge (Urbana: University of Illinois Press, 1985), p. 96.

65. Langdon Hammer, *Hart Crane and Allen Tate: Janus-Faced Modernism* (Princeton, N.J.: Princeton University Press, 1993), pp. xiv, 124, 127.

66. Robert Lowell, *Collected Poems*, ed. Frank Bidart and David Gewanter (New York: Farrar, Straus and Giroux, 2003), p. 157.

67. Allen Tate, "Preface to *Libretto for the Republic of Liberia*," *Poetry* 76:4 (1950), pp. 216–18, 216.

68. Philip Levine, *The Simple Truth* (New York: Knopf, 1992), p. 3.

69. Clayton Eshleman, "Stanza by Stanza Gloss of Hart Crane's 'Lachrymae Christi,'" *Fascicle* 2 (2007), http://voltagepoetry.com/2014/02/20/1355/.

70. D. A. Powell, *Tea* (Middletown, Conn.: Wesleyan University Press, 1998), pp. 47, 67, 71.

71. Charles Wright, *The Southern Cross* (New York: Random House, 1981), p. 38.

72. Adrienne Rich, *Midnight Salvage* (New York: W. W. Norton, 1999), p. 50. The first names refer to Crane, to the jazz musician Miles Davis, to the poets Muriel Rukeyser and Julia de Burgos, and to the cultural critic and poet Paul Goodman.

73. John T. Irwin, *Hart Crane's Poetry: "Appollinaire Lived in Paris, I Live in Cleveland, Ohio"* (Baltimore, Md.: Johns Hopkins University Press, 2011), p. 53.

74. Harold Bloom, *The Anatomy of Influence: Literature as a Way of Life* (New Haven, Conn.: Yale University Press, 2011), pp. 266, 279.

75. Bloom, *The Anatomy of Influence*, p. 163.

Selected Bibliographies

Introduction and General Literary History

Ashton, Jennifer (ed.). *The Cambridge Companion to American Poetry Since 1945* (Cambridge: Cambridge University Press, 2013).

Bauer, Dale (ed.). *The Cambridge History of American Women's Literature* (Cambridge: Cambridge University Press, 2012).

Bercovitch, Sacvan (general ed.). *The Cambridge History of American Literature*. 8 vols. (Cambridge: Cambridge University Press, 1995–2006).

Fletcher, Angus. *A New Theory for American Poetry: Democracy, the Environment, and the Future of Imagination* (Cambridge, Mass.: Harvard University Press, 2006).

Fredman, Stephen (ed.). *A Concise Companion to Twentieth-Century American Poetry* (Oxford: Blackwell, 2005).

Gelpi, Albert. *The Tenth Muse: The Psyche of the American Poet* (Cambridge: Cambridge University Press, 1991).

Graham, Maryemma, and Jerry W. Ward (eds.). *The Cambridge History of African American Literature* (Cambridge: Cambridge University Press, 2011).

Haralson, Eric (ed.). *Encyclopedia of American Poetry*. 2 vols. (Chicago: Fitzroy Dearborn, 1998–2001).

Kreymborg, Alfred. *Our Singing Strength: An Outline of American Poetry* (New York: Coward McCann, 1929).

Larson, Kerry (ed.). *The Cambridge Companion to Nineteenth-Century American Poetry* (Cambridge: Cambridge University Press, 2011).

Nelson, Cary (ed.). *The Oxford Handbook of Modern and Contemporary Poetry* (New York: Oxford University Press, 2012).

Ostriker, Alicia Suskin. *Stealing the Language: The Emergence of Women's Poetry in America* (Boston: Beacon Press, 1986).

Parini, Jay, and Brett Millier (eds.). *The Columbia History of American Poetry* (New York: Columbia University Press, 1998).

Pearce, Roy Harvey. *The Continuity of American Poetry* (Princeton, N.J.: Princeton University Press, 1961).

Perkins, David. *A History of Modern Poetry*. 2 vols. (Cambridge, Mass.: Harvard University Press, 1976, 1987).

Roberts, Neil (ed.). *A Companion to Twentieth-Century Poetry* (Oxford: Blackwell, 2001).

Rubin, Joan Shelley. *Songs of Ourselves: The Uses of Poetry in America* (Cambridge, Mass.: Harvard University Press, 2007).

Stauffer, Donald. *A Short History of American Poetry* (New York: Dutton, 1974).

Waggoner, Hyatt. *American Poets from the Puritans to the Present* (Baton Rouge: Louisiana State University Press, 1984).

Wolosky, Shira. *Poetry and Public Discourse in Nineteenth-Century America* (New York: Palgrave, 2010).

1 Remembering Muskrat: Native Poetics and the American Indian Oral Tradition

Astrov, Margot (ed.). *The Winged Serpent: American Indian Prose and Poetry* (Boston: Beacon, 1947).

Bahr, Donald, Lloyd Paul, and Vincent Joseph. *Ants and Orioles: Showing the Art of Pima Poetry* (Salt Lake City: University of Utah Press, 1997).

Brandon, William (ed.). *The Magic World: American Indian Songs and Poems* (Athens: Ohio University Press, 1971).

Castro, Michael. *Interpreting the Indian: Twentieth-Century Poets and the Native American* (Norman: University of Oklahoma Press, 1991).

Day, A. Grove (ed.). *The Sky Clears: Poetry of the American Indians* (Lincoln: University of Nebraska Press, 1951).

Donohue, Betty Booth. *Bradford's Indian Book: Being the True Roote & Rise of American Letters as Revealed by the Native Text Embedded in* Of Plimoth Plantation (Gainesville: University Press of Florida, 2011).

Harjo, Joy, and Gloria Bird (eds.). *Reinventing the Enemy's Language: Contemporary Native Women's Writings of North America* (New York: W. W. Norton, 1997).

León-Portilla, Miguel. *Pre-Columbian Literatures of Mexico*, trans. Grace Lobanov and Miguel León-Portilla (Norman: University of Oklahoma Press, 1969).

Lerner, Andrea (ed.). *Dancing on the Rim of the World: An Anthology of Contemporary Northwest Native American Writing* (Tucson, Ariz.: Sun Tracks, 1990).

Lincoln, Kenneth. *Sing with the Heart of a Bear: Fusions of Native and American Poetry* (Berkeley: University of California Press, 2000).

Parker, Robert Dale. *Changing Is Not Vanishing: A Collection of Early American Indian Poetry to 1930* (Philadelphia: University of Pennsylvania Press, 2011).

Rothenberg, Jerome (ed.). *Shaking the Pumpkin: Traditional Poetry of the Indian North Americas* (Garden City, N.Y.: Doubleday, 1972).

Womack, Craig S. *Red on Red: Native American Literary Separatism* (Minneapolis: University of Minnesota Press, 1999).

2 Rhyming Empires: Early American Poetry in Languages Other Than English

Bauer, Ralph. *The Cultural Geography of Colonial American Literatures: Empire, Travel, Modernity* (Cambridge: Cambridge University Press, 2003).

Bauer, Ralph, and José Antonio Mazzotti (eds.). *Creole Subjects in the Colonial Americas: Empire, Texts, Identities* (Chapel Hill: University of North Carolina Press, 2009).

Castillo, Susan. *Colonial Encounters in New World Writing: Performing America, 1500–1786* (London: Routledge, 2006).

Castillo, Susan, and Ivy Schweitzer (eds.). *A Companion to the Literatures of Colonial America* (Oxford: Blackwell, 2005).

———. *The Literatures of Colonial America: An Anthology* (Oxford: Blackwell, 2001).

Dawdy, Shannon Lee. *Building the Devil's Empire: French Colonial New Orleans* (Chicago: University of Chicago Press, 2008).

3 The World, the Flesh, and God in Puritan Poetry

Colacurcio, Michael J. *Godly Letters: The Literature of the American Puritans* (Notre Dame: University of Notre Dame Press, 2006).

Daly, Robert. *God's Altar: The World and the Flesh in Puritan Poetry* (Berkeley: University of California Press, 1978).

Davis, Thomas M. *A Reading of Edward Taylor* (Newark: University of Delaware Press, 1992).

Gatta, John. *Gracious Laughter: The Meditative Wit of Edward Taylor* (Columbia: University of Missouri Press, 1989).

Hammond, Jeffrey A. *Sinful Self, Saintly Self: The Puritan Experience of Poetry* (Athens: University of Georgia Press, 1993).

Martin, Wendy. *An American Triptych: Anne Bradstreet, Emily Dickinson, Adrienne Rich* (Chapel Hill: University of North Carolina Press, 1984).

Rosenmeier, Rosamond. *Anne Bradstreet Revisited* (Boston: Twayne, 1991).

Rowe, Karen E. *Saint and Singer: Edward Taylor's Typology and the Poetics of Meditation* (Cambridge: Cambridge University Press, 1986).

Schweitzer, Ivy. *The Work of Self-Representation: Lyric Poetry in Colonial New England* (Chapel Hill: University of North Carolina Press, 1991).

White, Peter (ed.). *Puritan Poets and Poetics: Seventeenth-Century American Poetry in Theory and Practice* (University Park: Pennsylvania State University Press, 1985).

4 Confronting Death: The New England Puritan Elegy

Cavitch, Max. *American Elegy: The Poetry of Mourning from the Puritans to Whitman* (Minneapolis: University of Minnesota Press, 2007).

Elliott, Emory. "The Development of the Puritan Funeral Sermon and Elegy: 1660–1750," *Early American Literature* 15 (1980): 151–64.

Hall, David D. *Worlds of Wonder, Days of Judgment: Popular Religious Belief in Early New England* (New York: Knopf, 1989).

Hambrick-Stowe, Charles E. *The Practice of Piety: Puritan Devotional Disciplines in Seventeenth-Century New England* (Chapel Hill: University of North Carolina Press, 1982).

Hammond, Jeffrey A. *The American Puritan Elegy: A Literary and Cultural Study* (Cambridge: Cambridge University Press, 2000).

———. *Sinful Self, Saintly Self: The Puritan Experience of Poetry* (Athens: University of Georgia Press, 1993).

Leverenz, David. *The Language of Puritan Feeling: An Exploration in Literature, Psychology, and Social History* (New Brunswick, N.J.: Rutgers University Press, 1980).

Meserole, Harrison T. (ed.). *American Poetry of the Seventeenth Century* (1968; University Park: Pennsylvania State University Press, 1985).

Pettit, Norman. *The Heart Prepared: Grace and Conversion in Puritan Spiritual Life* (New Haven, Conn.: Yale University Press, 1966).

Piercy, Josephine K. *Studies in Literary Types in Seventeenth Century America (1607–1710)* (1939; Hamden, Conn.: Archon, 1969).

Silverman, Kenneth (ed.). *Colonial American Poetry* (New York: Hafner, 1968).

Stannard, David E. *The Puritan Way of Death: A Study in Religion, Culture, and Social Change* (New York: Oxford University Press, 1977).

White, Peter (ed.). *Puritan Poets and Poetics: Seventeenth-Century American Poetry in Theory and Practice* (University Park: Pennsylvania State University Press, 1985).

5 The Emergence of a Southern Tradition

Davis, Richard Beale. *Intellectual Life in the Colonial South 1585–1763*. 3 vols. (Knoxville: University of Tennessee Press, 1978).

Egan, Jim. *Oriental Shadows: The Presence of the East in Early American Literature* (Columbus: Ohio State University Press, 2011).

Hubbell, Jay B. *The South in American Literature, 1607–1900* (Durham, N.C.: Duke University Press, 1954).

Lemay, J. A. Leo. *A Calendar of American Poetry in the Colonial Newspapers and Magazines and in the Major English Magazines through 1765* (Worcester, Mass.: American Antiquarian Society, 1970).

———. *Men of Letters in Colonial Maryland* (Knoxville: University of Tennessee Press, 1972).

Shields, David S. *Civil Tongues and Polite Letters in British America* (Chapel Hill: University of North Carolina Press, 1997).

———. *Oracles of Empire: Poetry, Politics, and Commerce in British America, 1690–1750* (Chicago: University of Chicago Press, 1990).

Spengemann, William C. *A Mirror for Americanists* (Hanover, N.H.: University Press of New England, 1989).

———. *A New World of Words: Redefining Early American Literature* (New Haven, Conn.: Yale University Press, 1994).

Warner, Michael. *Letters of the Republic: Publication and the Public Sphere in Eighteenth-Century America* (Cambridge, Mass.: Harvard University Press, 1990).

Wroth, Lawrence C. *The Colonial Printer* (New York: Dover, 1965).

6 Poetry in the Time of Revolution

Brooks, Joanna. *American Lazarus: Religion and the Rise of African-American and Native American Literatures* (New York: Oxford University Press, 2003).

Carretta, Vincent. *Phillis Wheatley: Biography of a Genius in Bondage* (Athens: University of Georgia Press, 2011).

Hayes, Kevin J. *A Colonial Woman's Bookshelf* (Knoxville: University of Tennessee Press, 1996).

———. *The Mind of a Patriot: Patrick Henry and the World of Ideas* (Charlottesville: University of Virginia Press, 2008).

———(ed.). *The Oxford Handbook of Early American Literature* (New York: Oxford University Press, 2008).

———. *The Road to Monticello: The Life and Mind of Thomas Jefferson* (New York: Oxford University Press, 2008).

Howard, Leon. *The Connecticut Wits* (Chicago: University of Chicago Press, 1943).

Leary, Lewis. *The Literary Career of Nathaniel Tucker, 1750–1807* (Durham, N.C.: Duke University Press, 1951).

Shields, David S. (ed.). *American Poetry: The Seventeenth and Eighteenth Centuries* (New York: Library of America, 2007).

Walser, Richard. "Alexander Martin, Poet," *Early American Literature* 6 (1971): 55–61.

7 Asserting a National Voice

Brown, Charles H. *William Cullen Bryant* (New York: Scribner, 1971).

Gado, Frank. *William Cullen Bryant: An American Voice* (Hartford, Vt.: Antoca Press, 2006).

Hallock, John W. *The American Byron: Homosexuality and the Fall of Fitz-Greene Halleck* (Madison: University of Wisconsin Press, 2000).

Howard, Leon. *The Connecticut Wits* (Chicago: University of Chicago Press, 1943).

Hunter, Doreen M. *Richard Henry Dana, Sr.* (Boston: Twayne, 1987).

McWilliams, John P., Jr. *The American Epic: Transforming a Genre 1770–1860* (Cambridge: Cambridge University Press, 1989).

Muller, Gilbert H. *William Cullen Bryant: Author of America* (Albany: State University of New York Press, 2008).

Overmyer, Grace. *America's First Hamlet* (New York: New York University Press, 1957).

Widmer, Ted. *Young America: The Flowering of Democracy in New York City* (New York: Oxford University Press, 1999).

Woodress, James L. *A Yankee's Odyssey: The Life of Joel Barlow* (Philadelphia: Lippincott, 1958).

8 The Emergence of Romantic Traditions

Baym, Nina. *Feminism and American Literary History* (New Brunswick, N.J.: Rutgers University Press, 1992).

Bennett, Paula Bernat (ed.). *Nineteenth-Century American Women Poets: An Anthology* (Malden, Mass.: Blackwell, 1998).

———. *Poets in the Public Sphere: The Emancipatory Project of American Women's Poetry, 1800–1900* (Princeton, N.J.: Princeton University Press, 2003).

Bennett, Paula Bernat, Karen L. Kilcup, and Philipp Schweighauser (eds.). *Teaching Nineteenth-Century American Poetry* (New York: Modern Language Association, 2007).

Brennan, Matthew C. *The Poet's Holy Craft: William Gilmore Simms and Romantic Verse Traditions* (Columbia: University of South Carolina Press, 2010).

Chai, Leon. *The Romantic Foundations of the American Renaissance* (Ithaca, N.Y.: Cornell University Press, 1987).

Larson, Kerry C. *Imagining Equality in Nineteenth-Century American Literature* (Cambridge: Cambridge University Press, 2008).

Richards, Eliza. *Gender and the Poetics of Reception in Poe's Circle* (Cambridge: Cambridge University Press, 2004).

Rubin, Louis D., Jr., Blyden Jackson, Rayburn S. Moore, Lewis P. Simpson, and Thomas Daniel Young (eds.). *The History of Southern Literature* (Baton Rouge: Louisiana State University Press, 1990).

Walker, Cheryl (ed.). *American Women Poets of the Nineteenth Century: An Anthology* (New Brunswick, N.J.: Rutgers University Press, 1992).

———. *The Nightingale's Burden: Women Poets and American Culture before 1900* (Bloomington: Indiana University Press, 1982).

Watt, Emily Stipes. *The Poetry of American Women from 1632 to 1945* (Austin: University of Texas Press, 1977).

9 Linen Shreds and Melons in a Field: Emerson and His Contemporaries

Bloom, Harold. *Figures of Capable Imagination* (New York: Seabury Press, 1976).

Buell, Lawrence. *Emerson* (Cambridge, Mass.: Harvard University Press, 2005).

———. "The Transcendentalist Poets," in Jay Parini (ed.), *The Columbia History of American Poetry* (New York: Columbia University Press, 1993), pp. 97–119.

Clayton, Sarah T. *The Angelic Sins of Jones Very* (New York: Peter Lang, 1999).

Folsom, Ed. "Transcendental Poetics: Emerson, Higginson, and the Rise of Whitman and Dickinson," in Joel Myerson, Sandra Harbert Petrulionis, and Laura Dassow Walls (eds.), *The Oxford Handbook of Transcendentalism* (Oxford: Oxford University Press, 2010), pp. 263–90.

Gittleman, Edwin. *Jones Very: The Effective Years, 1833–1840* (New York: Columbia University Press, 1967).

Gura, Philip F. *American Transcendentalism: A History* (New York: Hill and Wang, 2007).

Harding, Walter. *The Days of Henry Thoreau: A Biography.* New ed. (1970; Princeton, N.J.: Princeton University Press, 1992).

Marshall, Meghan. *Margaret Fuller: A New American Life* (Boston: Houghton Mifflin Harcourt, 2013).

Morris, Saundra. "'Metre-Making' Arguments: Emerson's Poems," in Joel Porte and Saundra Morris (eds.), *The Cambridge Companion to Ralph Waldo Emerson* (Cambridge: Cambridge University Press, 1999), pp. 218–42.

New, Elisa. *The Regenerate Lyric: Theology and Innovation in American Poetry* (Cambridge: Cambridge University Press, 1993).

Richardson, Robert. *Emerson: The Mind on Fire* (Berkeley: University of California Press, 1995).

Stula, Nancy, Barbara Novak, and David M. Robinson. *At Home and Abroad: The Transcendental Landscapes of Christopher Pearse Cranch* (New London, Conn.: Lyman Allyn Art Museum, 2007).

Sullivan, Robert. *The Thoreau You Don't Know* (New York: HarperCollins, 2009).

Waggoner, Hyatt H. *Emerson as Poet* (Princeton, N.J.: Princeton University Press, 1974).

Witherell, Elizabeth. "Thoreau as Poet," in Joel Myerson (ed.), *The Cambridge Companion to Henry David Thoreau* (Cambridge: Cambridge University Press, 1995), pp. 57–70.

10 Edgar Allan Poe's Lost Worlds

Carlson, Eric W. *The Recognition of Edgar Allan Poe: Selected Criticism since 1829* (Ann Arbor: University of Michigan Press, 1966).

Felman, Shoshana. "On Reading Poetry: Reflections on the Limits and Possibilities of Psychoanalytical Approaches," in John P. Muller and William J. Richardson (eds.), *The Purloined Poe: Lacan, Derrida, and Psychoanalytic Reading* (Baltimore, Md.: Johns Hopkins University Press, 1988), pp. 133–56.

Fried, Debra. "Repetition, Refrain, and Epitaph," *ELH* 53:3 (1986): 615–32.

Frye, Stephen (ed.). *The Poetry of Edgar Allan Poe* (Pasadena, Calif.: Salem Press, 2011).

Hoffman, Daniel. *Poe Poe Poe Poe Poe Poe Poe* (1972; Baton Rouge: Louisiana State University Press, 1998).

Johnson, Barbara. *A World of Difference* (Baltimore, Md.: Johns Hopkins University Press, 1987).

McGill, Meredith. *American Literature and the Culture of Reprinting, 1834–1853* (Philadelphia: University of Pennsylvania Press, 2003).

Miller, John Carl (ed.). *Poe's Helen Remembers* (Charlottesville: University Press of Virginia, 1979).

Quinn, Arthur Hobson. *Edgar Allan Poe: A Critical Biography* (1941; Baltimore, Md.: Johns Hopkins University Press, 1998).

Richards, Eliza. *Gender and the Poetics of Reception in Poe's Circle* (Cambridge: Cambridge University Press, 2004).

———. "Outsourcing 'The Raven': Retroactive Origins," *Victorian Poetry* 43:2 (2005): 205–21.

Thomas, Dwight. *The Poe Log: A Documentary Life of Edgar Allan Poe, 1809–1849*, ed. David Kelly Jackson (Boston: G. K. Hall, 1987).

Whitman, Sarah Helen. *Edgar Poe and His Critics*, ed. Oral Sumner Coad (1860; New Brunswick, N.J.: Rutgers University Press, 1949).

11 Longfellow in His Time

Buell, Lawrence. "Introduction," in *Henry Wadsworth Longfellow: Selected Poems* (New York: Penguin, 1988).

Calhoun, Charles C. *Longfellow: A Rediscovered Life* (Boston: Beacon Press, 2004).

Fletcher, Angus. "Whitman and Longfellow: Two Types of the American Poet," *Raritan* 10:4 (1991): 131–45.

Gale, Robert A. *A Henry Wadsworth Longfellow Companion* (Westport, Conn.: Greenwood, 2003).

Gioia, Dana. "Longfellow and the Aftermath of Modernism," in Jay Parini (ed.), *The Columbia History of American Poetry* (New York: Columbia University Press, 1993).

Irmscher, Christoph. *Longfellow Redux* (Urbana: University of Illinois Press, 2006).

———. *Public Poet, Private Man: Henry Wadsworth Longfellow at 200* (Amherst: University of Massachusetts Press, 2009).

Rubin, Joan Shelley. *Songs of Ourselves: The Uses of Poetry in America* (Cambridge, Mass.: Harvard University Press, 2007).

12 Whittier, Holmes, Lowell, and the New England Tradition

Baym, Nina. "Early Histories of American Literature: A Chapter in the Institution of New England," *American Literary History* 1:1 (1989): 459–88.

Bennett, Whitman. *Whittier: Bard of Freedom* (Chapel Hill: University of North Carolina Press, 1941).

Cohen, Michael. "Whittier, Ballad Reading, and the Culture of Nineteenth-Century Poetry," *Arizona Quarterly* 64:3 (2008): 1–29.

Dowling, William C. *Oliver Wendell Holmes in Paris: Medicine, Theology, and the Autocrat of the Breakfast Table* (Hanover, N.H.: University Press of New England, 2006).

Gibian, Peter. *Oliver Wendell Holmes and the Culture of Conversation* (Cambridge: Cambridge University Press, 2001).

Hoyt, Edwin P. *The Improper Bostonian: Dr. Oliver Wendell Holmes* (New York: Morrow, 1979).

Mordell, Albert. *Quaker Militant: John Greenleaf Whittier* (Boston: Houghton, 1933).

Rodríguez, J. Javier. "The U.S.-Mexican War in James Russell Lowell's *The Biglow Papers*," *Arizona Quarterly* 63:3 (2007): 1–33.

Smith, Henry N. "That Hideous Mistake of Poor Clemens's." *Harvard Library Bulletin* 9 (1955): 145–80.

Sorby, Angela. *Schoolroom Poets: Childhood, Performance, and the Place of American Poetry, 1865–1917* (Durham: University of New Hampshire Press, 2005).

Stokes, Claudia. *Writers in Retrospect: The Rise of American Literary History, 1875–1910* (Chapel Hill: University of North Carolina Press, 2006).

Tilton, Eleanor M. *Amiable Autocrat: A Biography of Dr. Oliver Wendell Holmes* (New York: Schuman, 1947).

Wagenknecht, Edward. *John Greenleaf Whittier: A Portrait in Paradox* (New York: Oxford University Press, 1967).

13 Other Voices, Other Verses: Cultures of American Poetry at Midcentury

Bennett, Paula Bernat (ed.). *Nineteenth-Century American Women Poets: An Anthology* (Oxford: Blackwell, 1998).

———. *Poets in the Public Sphere: The Emancipatory Project of American Women's Poetry, 1800–1900* (Princeton, N.J.: Princeton University Press, 2003).

Cavitch, Max. "Emma Lazarus and the Golem of Liberty," in Meredith L. McGill (ed.), *The Traffic in Poems: Nineteenth-Century Poetry and Transatlantic Exchange* (New Brunswick, N.J.: Rutgers University Press, 2008), pp. 97–122.

Diehl, Joanne Feit. *Dickinson and the Romantic Imagination* (Princeton, N.J.: Princeton University Press, 1981).

Jackson, Virginia. *Dickinson's Misery: A Theory of Lyric Reading* (Princeton, N.J.: Princeton University Press, 2005).

———. "Thinking Dickinson Thinking Poetry," in Martha Nell Smith and Mary Loeffelholz (eds.), *A Companion to Emily Dickinson* (Malden, Mass.: Blackwell, 2008), pp. 205–21.

Lauter, Paul. *Canons and Contexts* (Oxford: Oxford University Press, 1991).

Morris, Timothy. *Becoming Canonical in American Poetry* (Urbana: University of Illinois Press, 1995).

Sherman, Joan R. (ed.). *African American Poetry of the Nineteenth Century: An Anthology* (Urbana: University of Illinois Press, 1992).

Williams, Gary. *Hungry Heart: The Literary Emergence of Julia Ward Howe* (Amherst: University of Massachusetts Press, 1999).

Wilson, Edmund. *Patriotic Gore* (1962; New York: W. W. Norton, 1994).

Winters, Yvor. "A Discovery," *Hudson Review* 3 (1950): 453–58.

———. *Maule's Curse: Seven Studies in the History of American Obscurantism* (Norfolk, Conn.: New Directions, 1938).

14 American Poetry Fights the Civil War

Barrett, Faith. *To Fight Aloud Is Very Brave: American Poetry and the Civil War* (Amherst: University of Massachusetts Press, 2012).

Fahs, Alice. *The Imagined Civil War: Popular Literature of the North and South, 1861–1865* (Chapel Hill: University of North Carolina Press, 2001).

Garner, Stanton. *The Civil War World of Herman Melville* (Lawrence: University Press of Kansas, 1993).

Hutchison, Coleman. *Apples and Ashes: Literature, Nationalism, and the Confederate States of America* (Athens: University of Georgia, 2012).

Maslan, Mark. *Whitman Possessed: Poetry, Sexuality, and Popular Authority* (Baltimore, Md.: Johns Hopkins University Press, 2001).

Miller, Cristanne. *Reading in Time: Emily Dickinson in the Nineteenth Century* (Amherst: University of Massachusetts Press, 2012).

Morris, Roy, Jr. *The Better Angel: Walt Whitman in the Civil War* (New York: Oxford University Press, 2000).

Richards, Eliza. "Weathering the News in US Civil War Poetry," in Kerry Larson (ed.), *The Cambridge Companion to Nineteenth Century American Poetry* (Cambridge: Cambridge University Press, 2011), pp. 113–34.

St. Armand, Barton Levi. *Emily Dickinson and Her Culture: The Soul's Society* (Cambridge: Cambridge University Press, 1984).

Sweet, Timothy. *Traces of War: Poetry, Photography, and the Crisis of the Union* (Baltimore, Md.: Johns Hopkins University Press, 1990).

Wolosky, Shira. *Emily Dickinson: A Voice of War* (New Haven, Conn.: Yale University Press, 1984).

15 Walt Whitman's Invention of a Democratic Poetry

Allen, Gay Wilson, and Ed Folsom (eds.). *Walt Whitman and the World* (Iowa City: University of Iowa Press, 1995).

Aspiz, Harold. *So Long! Walt Whitman's Poetry of Death* (Tuscaloosa: University of Alabama Press, 2004).

Bauerlein, Mark. *Whitman and the American Idiom* (Baton Rouge: Louisiana State University Press, 1991).

Beach, Christopher. *The Politics of Distinction: Whitman and the Discourses of Nineteenth-Century America* (Athens: University of Georgia Press, 1996).

Ceniza, Sherry. *Walt Whitman and Nineteenth-Century Women Reformers* (Tuscaloosa: University of Alabama Press, 1998).

Erkkila, Betsy. *Whitman the Political Poet* (New York: Oxford University Press, 1989).

Folsom, Ed. *Walt Whitman's Native Representations* (Cambridge: Cambridge University Press, 1994).

Folsom, Ed, and Kenneth M. Price (eds.). The Walt Whitman Archive (1995–present). http://www.whitmanarchive.org.

Genoways, Ted. *Walt Whitman and the Civil War* (Berkeley: University of California Press, 2009).

Greenspan, Ezra. *Walt Whitman and the American Reader* (Cambridge: Cambridge University Press, 1990).

Hollis, C. Carroll. *Language and Style in Leaves of Grass* (Baton Rouge: Louisiana State University Press, 1983).

Killingsworth, M. Jimmie. *Whitman's Poetry of the Body: Sexuality, Politics, and the Text* (Chapel Hill: University of North Carolina Press, 1989).

Klammer, Martin. *Whitman, Slavery, and the Emergence of Leaves of Grass* (University Park: Pennsylvania State University Press, 1995).

LeMaster, J. R., and Donald D. Kummings (eds.). *Walt Whitman: An Encyclopedia* (New York: Routledge, 1998).

Loving, Jerome. *Walt Whitman: The Song of Himself* (Berkeley: University of California Press, 1999).

Miller, Matt. *Collage of Myself: Walt Whitman and the Making of Leaves of Grass* (Lincoln: University of Nebraska Press, 2010).

Moon, Michael. *Disseminating Whitman: Revision and Corporeality in Leaves of Grass* (Cambridge, Mass.: Harvard University Press, 1991).

Perlman, Jim, Ed Folsom, and Dan Campion (eds.). *Walt Whitman: The Measure of His Song* (Duluth, Minn.: Holy Cow!, 1998).

Pollak, Vivian. *The Erotic Whitman* (Berkeley: University of California Press, 2000).

Price, Kenneth M. *Whitman and Tradition: The Poet in His Century* (New Haven, Conn.: Yale University Press, 1990).

Reynolds, David S. *Walt Whitman's America: A Cultural Biography* (New York: Knopf, 1995).

Robertson, Michael. *Worshipping Walt: The Whitman Disciples* (Princeton, N.J.: Princeton University Press, 2008).

Thomas, M. Wynn. *The Lunar Light of Whitman's Poetry* (Cambridge, Mass.: Harvard University Press, 1987).

16 Emily Dickinson: The Poetics and Practice of Autonomy

Cody, John. *After Great Pain: The Inner Life of Emily Dickinson* (New York: Belknap, 1971).

Franklin, Ralph W. *The Editing of Emily Dickinson: A Reconsideration* (Madison: University of Wisconsin Press, 1967).

Fuss, Diana. *The Sense of an Interior: Four Writers and the Rooms that Shaped Them* (New York: Routledge, 2004).

Habegger, Alfred. *My Wars Are Laid Away in Books: The Life of Emily Dickinson* (New York: Modern Library, 2002).

Heginbotham, Eleanor Elson. *Reading the Fascicles of Emily Dickinson: Dwelling in Possibilities* (Columbus: Ohio State University Press, 2003).

Johnson, Thomas H. (ed.). *The Complete Poems of Emily Dickinson* (New York: Little, Brown, 1960).

——. *Emily Dickinson: An Interpretive Biography* (Cambridge, Mass.: Harvard University Press, 1955).

——. *The Letters of Emily Dickinson* (Cambridge, Mass.: Harvard University Press, 1986).

Juhasz, Suzanne (ed.). *Feminist Critics Read Emily Dickinson* (Bloomington: Indiana University Press, 1983).

Keller, Karl. *The Only Kangaroo Among the Beauty: Emily Dickinson and America* (Baltimore, Md.: Johns Hopkins University Press, 1979).

Martin, Wendy. *An American Triptych: Anne Bradstreet, Emily Dickinson, Adrienne Rich* (Chapel Hill: University of North Carolina Press, 1984).

——. *The Cambridge Introduction to Emily Dickinson* (Cambridge: Cambridge University Press, 2007).

Messmer, Marietta. *A Vice for Voices: Reading Emily Dickinson's Correspondence* (Amherst: University of Massachusetts Press, 2001).

Miller, Cristanne. *Emily Dickinson: A Poet's Grammar* (Cambridge, Mass.: Harvard University Press, 1987).

——. *Reading in Time: Emily Dickinson in the Nineteenth Century* (Amherst: University of Massachusetts Press, 2012).

Rich, Adrienne. "Vesuvius at Home: The Power of Emily Dickinson," *Parnassus: Poetry in Review* 5:1 (1976): 49–74. Reprinted in *Adrienne Rich, Selected Prose, 1966–1978* (New York: W. W. Norton, 1979).

Wolosky, Shira. *Emily Dickinson: A Voice of War* (New Haven, Conn.: Yale University Press, 1984).

17 The South in Reconstruction: White and Black Voices

Bain, Robert, and Joseph M. Flora (eds.). *Fifty Southern Writers Before 1900: A Bio-Bibliographical Sourcebook* (New York: Greenwood, 1987).

Boyd, Melba Joyce. *Discarded Legacy: Politics and Poetics in the Life of Frances E. W. Harper, 1825–1911* (Detroit, Mich.: Wayne State University Press, 1994).

Cisco, Walter Brian. *Henry Timrod: A Biography* (Madison, N.J.: Farleigh Dickinson University Press, 2004).

Fishkin, Shelly Fisher, Gavin Jones, Meta DuEwa Jones, Arnold Rampersad, and Richard Yarborough (eds.), "Paul Laurence Dunbar." Special issue, *African American Review* 41:2 (2007).

Foner, Eric. *Reconstruction: America's Unfinished Revolution, 1863–1877* (New York: Harper & Row, 1988).

Gabin, Jane S. *A Living Minstrelsy: The Poetry and Music of Sidney Lanier* (Macon, Ga.: Mercer University Press, 1985).

Griffin, Martin. *Ashes of the Mind: War and Memory in Northern Literature, 1865–1900* (Amherst: University of Massachusetts Press, 2009).

Harris, Trudier, and Thadious M. Davis. *Afro-American Writers Before the Harlem Renaissance* (Detroit, Mich.: Gale, 1986).

Kerkering, John D. *The Poetics of National and Racial Identity in Nineteenth-Century American Literature* (New York: Cambridge University Press, 2003).

Moore, Rayburn S. *Paul Hamilton Hayne* (New York: Twayne, 1972).

———. "Poetry of the Late Nineteenth Century," in Louis D. Rubin, Jr., Blyden Jackson, Rayburn S. Moore, Lewis P. Simpson, and Thomas Daniel Young (eds.), *The History of Southern Literature* (Baton Rouge: Louisiana State University Press, 1985), pp. 188–98.

18   The "Genteel Tradition" and Its Discontents

Barrineau, Nancy Warner (ed.). *Theodore Dreiser's Ev'ry Month* (Athens: University of Georgia Press, 1996).

Beatty, Richmond Croom. "Bayard Taylor and George H. Boker," *American Literature* 6:3 (1934): 316–27.

Bennett, Paula Bernat (ed.). *Nineteenth-Century American Women Poets: An Anthology* (Oxford: Blackwell, 1998).

———. *Poets in the Public Sphere: The Emancipatory Project of American Women's Poetry, 1800–1900* (Princeton, N.J.: Princeton University Press, 2003).

Cary, Edwin H. "Introduction," in William Dean Howells, *Pebbles, Monochromes, and Other Modern Poems, 1891–1916*, ed. Edwin H. Cary (Athens: Ohio University Press, 2000), pp. xi–xlvi.

Cary, Richard. *The Genteel Circle: Bayard Taylor and His New York Friends* (Ithaca, N.Y.: Cornell University Press, 1952).

Cohen, Michael. "E.C. Stedman and the Invention of Victorian Poetry," *Victorian Poetry* 43:2 (2005): 165–88.

DeMille, G. E. "Stedman, Arbiter of the Eighties," *PMLA* 41:3 (1926): 756–66.

Fenn, William Purviance. "Richard Henry Stoddard's Chinese Poems," *American Literature* 11:4 (1940): 417–38.

Haralson, Eric L. (ed.). *Encyclopedia of American Poetry: The Nineteenth Century* (Chicago: Fitzroy Dearborn, 1998).

Hollander, John (ed.). *American Poetry: The Nineteenth Century*. 2 vols. (New York: Library of America, 1993).

McGill, Meredith (ed.). *The Traffic in Poems: Nineteenth-Century Poetry and Transatlantic Exchange* (New Brunswick, N.J.: Rutgers University Press, 2008).

Newcomb, John Timberman. *Would Poetry Disappear? American Verse and the Crisis of Modernity* (Columbus: Ohio State University Press, 2004).

Piatt, Sarah Morgan Bryan, *Palace-Burner: The Selected Poetry of Sarah Piatt*, ed. Paula Bernat Bennett (Urbana: University of Illinois Press, 2001).

Renker, Elizabeth. "The 'Twilight of the Poets' in the Era of American Realism, 1875–1900," in Kerry Larson (ed.), *The Cambridge Companion to Nineteenth-Century American Poetry* (Cambridge: Cambridge University Press, 2011), pp. 135–53.

Spengemann, William, with Jessica Roberts (eds.). *Nineteenth-Century American Poetry* (New York: Penguin, 1996).

Walker, Cheryl (ed.). *American Women Poets of the Nineteenth Century: An Anthology* (New Brunswick, N.J.: Rutgers University Press, 1992).

19 Disciplined Play: American Children's Poetry to 1920

Crain, Patricia. *The Story of A: The Alphabetization of America from the New England Primer to the Scarlet Letter* (Stanford, Calif.: Stanford University Press, 2003).

Flynn, Richard. "Can Children's Poetry Matter?" *The Lion and the Unicorn: A Critical Journal of Children's Literature* 17:1 (June 1993): 37–44.

Gray, Janet. *Race and Time: American Women's Poetics from Antislavery to Racial Modernity* (Iowa City: University of Iowa Press, 2004).

Hall, Donald (ed.). *Oxford Book of Children's Verse in America* (New York: Oxford University Press, 1990).

Kelley, Mary. *Private Woman, Public Stage: Literary Domesticity in Nineteenth-Century America* (1984; Chapel Hill: University of North Carolina Press, 2002).

Mintz, Stephen. *Huck's Raft: A History of American Childhood* (Cambridge, Mass.: Harvard University Press, 2006).

Philips, Elizabeth. *Emily Dickinson: Personae and Performance* (State College: Pennsylvania State University Press, 2004).

Smith, Kate Capshaw. *Children's Literature of the Harlem Renaissance* (Bloomington: Indiana University Press, 2006).

Sorby, Angela. *Schoolroom Poets: Childhood, Performance, and the Place of American Poetry, 1865–1917* (Durham: University of New Hampshire Press, 2005).

20 Dialect, Doggerel, and Local Color: Comic Traditions and the Rise of Realism in Popular Poetry

Harrell, Willie J., Jr. (ed.). *We Wear the Mask: Paul Lawrence Dunbar and the Politics of Representative Reality* (Kent, Ohio: Kent State University Press, 2010).

Jones, Gavin. *Strange Talk: The Politics of Dialect Literature in Gilded Age America* (Berkeley: University of California Press, 1999).

Redding, J. Saunders. *To Make a Poet Black* (1939; Ithaca, N.Y.: Cornell University Press, 1988).

Sorby, Angela. *Schoolroom Poets: Childhood, Performance, and the Place of American Poetry, 1865–1917* (Durham: University of New Hampshire Press, 2005).

Stanley, David, and Elaine Thatcher (eds.). *Cowboy Poets and Cowboy Poetry* (Urbana: University of Illinois Press, 2000).

Sloane, David E. E. "In Search of a Realist Poetic Tradition," *American Literary Realism, 1870–1910* 5 (Fall 1972): 489–91.

———. *The Literary Humor of the Urban Northeast, 1830–1890* (Baton Rouge: Louisiana State University Press, 1983).

———. "Will Carleton as Realist Poet," *Markham Review* 4 (October 1975): 81–85.

Van Allen, Elizabeth J. *James Whitcomb Riley: A Life* (Bloomington: Indiana University Press, 1999).

21 Political Poets and Naturalism

Bendixen, Alfred. "Charlotte Perkins Gilman's 'Toolbox': The Value of Satiric Poetry and Social Reform," in Paula Bernat Bennett, Karen Kilcup, and Phillipp Schweighauser (eds.), *Teaching Nineteenth-Century American Poetry* (New York: MLA, 2007), pp. 161–71.

Blair, John. "The Posture of a Bohemian in the Poetry of Stephen Crane," *American Literature* 61 (1989): 215–29.

Cavitch, Max. "Stephen Crane's Refrain," *ESQ: A Journal of the American Renaissance* 54:1–4 (2008): 33–53.

Dooley, Patrick K. *The Pluralistic Philosophy of Stephen Crane* (Urbana: University of Illinois Press, 1993).

Goldstein, Jesse Sidney. "Edwin Markham, Ambrose Bierce, and 'The Man with the Hoe,'" *Modern Language Notes* 58:3 (1943): 165–75.

Halliburton, David. *The Color of the Sky: A Study of Stephen Crane* (Cambridge: Cambridge University Press, 1989).

Hoffman, Daniel. *The Poetry of Stephen Crane* (New York: Columbia University Press, 1957).

Kessler, Carol Farley. "Brittle Jars and Bitter Jangles: Light Verse by Charlotte Perkins Gilman," in Sheryl L. Meyering (ed.), *Charlotte Perkins Gilman: The Woman and Her Work* (Ann Arbor, Mich.: UMI Research Press, 1989), pp. 133–43.

Nelson, Cary. *Revolutionary Memory: Recovering the Poetry of the American Left* (New York: Routledge, 2001).

O'Donnell, Thomas F. "A Note on the Reception of Stephen Crane's *The Black Riders*," *American Literature* 24 (1952): 233–35.

Pizer, Donald. *Realism and Naturalism in Nineteenth-Century American Literature* (1966; Carbondale: Southern Illinois University Press, 1984).

Rudd, Jill, and Val Gough (eds.). *Charlotte Perkins Gilman: Optimist Reformer* (Iowa City: University of Iowa Press, 1999).

Scharnhorst, Gary. "Reconstructing *Here Also*: On the Later Poetry of Charlotte Perkins Gilman," in Joanne B. Karpinski (ed.), *Critical Essays on Charlotte Perkins Gilman* (New York: G. K. Hall, 1992), pp. 249–68.

22 The Twentieth Century Begins

Beach, Christopher. *The Politics of Distinction: Whitman and the Discourses of Nineteenth-Century America* (Athens: University of Georgia Press, 1996).

Brown, Bill. *The Material Unconscious: American Amusement, Stephen Crane, and the Economies of Play* (Cambridge, Mass.: Harvard University Press, 1997).

Churchill, Suzanne W., and Adam McKible (eds.). *Little Magazines and Modernism* (Aldershot: Ashgate, 2007).

Clark, Suzanne. *Sentimental Modernism: Women Writers and the Revolution of the Word* (Bloomington: Indiana University Press, 1991).

Douglas, Ann. *Terrible Honesty: Mongrel Manhattan in the 1920s* (New York: Farrar, Straus and Giroux, 1995).

DuPlessis, Rachel Blau. *Genders, Races, and Religious Cultures in Modern American Poetry, 1908–1934* (Cambridge: Cambridge University Press, 2001).

Harrington, Joseph. *Poetry and the Public: The Social Form of Modern U.S. Poetics* (Middletown, Conn.: Wesleyan University Press, 2002).

Kalaidjian, Walter. *American Culture Between the Wars: Revisionary Modernism and Postmodern Critique* (New York: Columbia University Press, 1993).

Marek, Jayne. *Women Editing Modernism: "Little" Magazines and Literary History* (Lexington: University of Kentucky Press, 1995).

Morrisson, Mark S. *The Public Face of Modernism: Little Magazines, Audiences, and Reception, 1905–1920* (Madison: University of Wisconsin Press, 2001).

Newcomb, John Timberman. *How Did Poetry Survive? The Making of Modern American Verse* (Urbana: University of Illinois Press, 2012).

———. *Would Poetry Disappear? American Verse and the Crisis of Modernity* (Columbus: Ohio State University Press, 2004).

Thurston, Michael. *Making Something Happen: American Political Poetry Between the Wars* (Chapel Hill: University of North Carolina Press, 2001).

Van Wienen, Mark W. *Partisans and Poets: The Political Work of American Poetry in the Great War* (Cambridge: Cambridge University Press, 1997).

Wilson, Christopher P. *The Labor of Words: Literary Professionalism in the Progressive Era* (Athens: University of Georgia Press, 1985).

23 Robert Frost and Tradition

Brodsky, Joseph, Seamus Heaney, and Derek Walcott. *Homage to Robert Frost* (New York: Farrar, Straus, and Giroux, 1996).

Costello, Bonnie. *Shifting Ground: Reinventing Landscape in Modern American Poetry* (Cambridge, Mass.: Harvard University Press, 2003).

Faggen, Robert (ed.). *The Cambridge Companion to Robert Frost* (Cambridge: Cambridge University Press, 2001).

———. *Robert Frost and the Challenge of Darwin* (Ann Arbor: University of Michigan Press, 1997).

Hass, Robert Bernard. *Going by Contraries: Robert Frost's Conflict with Science* (Charlottesville: University Press of Virginia, 2002).

Hoffman, Tyler. *Robert Frost and the Politics of Poetry* (Hanover, N.H.: Middlebury College Press, 2001).

Jarrell, Randall. *Poetry and the Age* (1953; Gainesville: University Press of Florida, 2001).

Kearns, Katherine. *Robert Frost and a Poetics of Appetite* (Cambridge: Cambridge University Press, 1994).

Lentricchia, Frank. *Modernist Quartet* (Cambridge: Cambridge University Press, 1994).

———. *Robert Frost: Modern Poetics and the Landscapes of Self* (Durham, N.C.: Duke University Press, 1975).

New, Elisa. *The Line's Eye: Poetic Experience, American Sight* (Cambridge, Mass.: Harvard University Press, 1998).

Parini, Jay. *Robert Frost: A Life* (New York: Henry Holt, 1991).

Poirier, Richard. *Robert Frost: The Work of Knowing* (Stanford, Calif.: Stanford University Press, 1990).

Pritchard, William H. *Frost: A Literary Life Reconsidered* (New York: Oxford University Press, 1984).

Richardson, Mark. *The Ordeal of Robert Frost: The Poet and His Poetics* (Urbana: University of Illinois Press, 1997).

Wilcox, Earl J., and Jonathan N. Barron (eds.). *Roads Not Taken: Rereading Robert Frost* (Columbia: University of Missouri Press, 2000).

24 T. S. Eliot

Bush, Ronald (ed.). *T. S. Eliot: The Modernist in History* (Cambridge: Cambridge University Press, 1991).

Chinitz, David E. *T. S. Eliot and the Cultural Divide* (Chicago: University of Chicago Press, 2003).

Gordon, Lyndall. *T. S. Eliot: An Imperfect Life* (New York: W. W. Norton, 2000).

Habib, M. A. R. *The Early T. S. Eliot and Western Philosophy* (Cambridge: Cambridge University Press, 1999).

Moody, A. David (ed.). *The Cambridge Companion to T. S. Eliot* (Cambridge: Cambridge University Press, 1994).

Rainey, Lawrence. *Institutions of Modernism: Literary Elites and Public Culture* (New Haven, Conn.: Yale University Press, 1998).

Ricks, Christopher. *True Friendship: Geoffrey Hill, Anthony Hecht and Robert Lowell Under the Sign of Eliot and Pound* (New Haven, Conn.: Yale University Press, 2010).

———. *T. S. Eliot and Prejudice* (London: Faber and Faber, 1988).

25 William Carlos Williams: The Shock of the Familiar

Altieri, Charles. *The Art of Twentieth Century American Poetry* (Oxford: Blackwell, 2006).

Copestake, Ian (ed.). *The Legacy of William Carlos Williams* (Newcastle-upon-Tyne: Cambridge Scholars Press, 2007).

Corn, Wanda, and Tirza True Latimer. *Seeing Gertrude Stein: Five Stories* (Berkeley: University of California Press, 2011).

Crawford, T. Hugh. *Modernism, Medicine and William Carlos Williams* (Norman: University of Oklahoma Press, 1993).

Cushman, Stephen. *William Carlos Williams and the Meaning of Measure* (New Haven, Conn.: Yale University Press, 1985).

DeKoven, Marianne. *A Different Language: Gertrude Stein's Experimental Writing* (Madison: University of Wisconsin Press, 1983).

Dydo, Ulla P. *Gertrude Stein: The Language That Rises* (Evanston, Ill.: Northwestern University Press, 2003).

Halter, Peter. *William Carlos Williams and the Revolution in the Visual Arts*. Rev. ed. (Cambridge: Cambridge University Press, 2009).

Hejinian, Lyn. *The Language of Inquiry* (Berkeley: University of California Press, 2000).

Mariani, Paul. *William Carlos Williams: A New World Naked* (New York: McGraw-Hill, 1981).

Meyer, Steven. *Irresistible Dictation: Gertrude Stein and the Correlations of Writing and Science* (Stanford, Calif.: Stanford University Press, 2001).

Newcomb, John Timberman. *How Did Poetry Survive? The Making of Modern American Verse* (Urbana: University of Illinois Press, 2012).

Perelman, Bob. *The Trouble with Genius: Reading Pound, Joyce, Stein and Zukofsky* (Berkeley: University of California Press, 1994).

Perloff, Marjorie. *The Poetics of Indeterminacy: Rimbaud to Cage* (Evanston, Ill.: Northwestern University Press, 1983).

Sayre, Henry. *The Visual Text of William Carlos Williams* (Urbana: University of Illinois Press, 1983).

Tichi, Cecilia. *Shifting Gears: Technology, Literature, Culture in Modernist America* (Chapel Hill: University of North Carolina Press, 1987).

Weaver, Mike. *William Carlos Williams: The American Background* (Cambridge: Cambridge University Press, 1977).

26 Finding "Only Words" Mysterious: Reading Mina Loy (and H.D.) in America

Burke, Carolyn. *Becoming Modern: The Life of Mina Loy* (New York: Farrar, Straus and Giroux, 1996).

Churchill, Suzanne. *The Little Magazine* Others *and the Renovation of American Poetry* (London: Ashgate, 2006).

Collecott, Diana. *H.D. and Sapphic Modernism* (Cambridge: Cambridge University Press, 1999).

DuPlessis, Rachel Blau. *Genders, Races, and Religious Cultures in Modern American Poetry, 1908–1934* (Cambridge: Cambridge University Press, 2001).

———. *The Pink Guitar: Writing as Feminist Practice* (New York: Routledge, 1990).

Friedman, Susan Stanford, and Rachel Blau DuPlessis (eds.). *Signets: Reading H.D.* (Madison: University of Wisconsin Press, 1990).

Goody, Alex. *Modernist Articulations: A Cultural Study of Djuna Barnes, Mina Loy, and Gertrude Stein* (Hampshire: Palgrave / Macmillan, 2007).

Kinnahan, Linda. *Poetics of the Feminine: Authority and Literary Tradition in William Carlos Williams, Mina Loy, Denise Levertov, and Kathleen Fraser* (Cambridge: Cambridge University Press, 1994).

Kuenzli, Rudolf E. (ed.). *New York Dada* (New York: Willis Locker & Owens, 1986).

Miller, Cristanne. *Cultures of Modernism: Marianne Moore, Mina Loy, Else Lasker-Schüler: Gender and Literary Community in New York and Berlin* (Ann Arbor: University of Michigan Press, 2005).

———. "Tongues 'Loosened in the Melting Pot': The Poets of *Others* and the Lower East Side," *Modernism / Modernity* 14:3 (2007): 455–76.

Potter, Rachel, and Suzanne Hobson (eds.). *The Salt Companion to Mina Loy* (Cambridge: Salt, 2010).

Shreiber, Maeera, and Keith Tuma (eds.). *Mina Loy: Woman and Poet* (Orono, Maine: National Poetry Foundation, 1998).

Vetter, Lara. *Modernist Writings and Religio-Scientific Discourse: H.D., Loy, and Toomer* (New York: Palgrave / Macmillan, 2010).

27 Marianne Moore and the Printed Page

Bornstein, George. *Material Modernism: The Politics of the Page* (Cambridge: Cambridge University Press, 2001).

Costello, Bonnie. *Marianne Moore: Imaginary Possessions* (Cambridge, Mass.: Harvard University Press, 1981).

Holley, Margaret. *The Poetry of Marianne Moore* (Cambridge: Cambridge University Press, 1987).

Kineke, Sheila. "T. S. Eliot, Marianne Moore, and the Gendered Operations of Literary Sponsorship," *Journal of Modern Literature* 21:1 (1997): 121–36.

Miller, Cristanne. *Marianne Moore: Questions of Authority* (Cambridge, Mass.: Harvard University Press, 1995).

Rainey, Lawrence. *Institutions of Modernism: Literary Elites and Public Culture* (New Haven, Conn.: Yale University Press, 1998).

Rotella, Guy. *Reading and Writing Nature: The Poetry of Robert Frost, Wallace Stevens, Marianne Moore, and Elizabeth Bishop* (Boston: Northeastern University Press, 1991).

Turner, Catherine. *Marketing Modernism Between the Two World Wars* (Amherst: University of Massachusetts Press, 2003).

28 The Formalist Modernism of Edna St. Vincent Millay, Helene Johnson, and Louise Bogan

Bowles, Gloria. *Louise Bogan's Aesthetic of Limitation* (Bloomington: Indiana University Press, 1987).

Clark, Suzanne. *Sentimental Modernism: Women Writers and the Revolution of the Word* (Bloomington: Indiana University Press, 1991).

Collins, Martha (ed.). *Critical Essays on Louise Bogan* (Boston: G. K. Hall, 1984).

DuPlessis, Rachel Blau. *Genders, Races, and Religious Cultures in Modern American Poetry, 1908–1934* (Cambridge: Cambridge University Press, 2001).

Freedman, Diane P. (ed.). *Millay at 100: A Critical Reappraisal* (Carbondale: Southern Illinois University Press, 1995).

Gilbert, Sandra M., and Susan Gubar. *No Man's Land: The Place of the Woman Writer in the Twentieth Century.* 3 vols. (New Haven, Conn.: Yale University Press, 1988, 1989, 1994).

Harrington, Joseph. *Poetry and the Public: The Social Form of Modern U.S. Poetics* (Middletown, Conn.: Wesleyan University Press, 2002).

Hull, Gloria T. *Color, Sex, and Poetry: Three Women Writers of the Harlem Renaissance* (Bloomington: Indiana University Press, 1987).

Milford, Nancy. *Savage Beauty: The Life of Edna St. Vincent Millay* (New York: Random House, 2001).

Nelson, Cary. "The Fate of Gender in Modern American Poetry," in Kevin J. H. Dettmar and Stephen Watt (eds.), *Marketing Modernisms: Self-Promotion, Canonization, Rereading* (Ann Arbor: University of Michigan Press, 1996), pp. 321–60.

———. *Repression and Recovery: Modern American Poetry and the Politics of Cultural Memory, 1910–1945* (Madison: University of Wisconsin Press, 1989).

Schweik, Susan. *A Gulf So Deeply Cut: American Women Poets and the Second World War* (Madison: University of Wisconsin Press, 1991).

Walker, Cheryl. *Masks Outrageous and Austere: Culture, Psyche, and Persona in Modern Women Poets* (Bloomington: Indiana University Press, 1991).

Wheeler, Lesley. *Voicing American Poetry: Sound and Performance from the 1920s to the Present* (Ithaca, N.Y.: Cornell University Press, 2008).

29 The Romantic and Anti-Romantic in the Poetry of Wallace Stevens

Bloom, Harold. *The Poems of Our Climate* (Ithaca, N.Y.: Cornell University Press, 1977).

Brazeau, Peter. *Parts of a World: Wallace Stevens Remembered* (New York: Random House, 1977).

Critchley, Simon. *Things Merely Are: Philosophy in the Poetry of Wallace Stevens* (London: Routledge, 2005).

Filreis, Alan. *Wallace Stevens and the Actual World* (Princeton, N.J.: Princeton University Press, 1991).

Fisher, Barbara. *Wallace Stevens: The Intensest Rendezvous* (Charlottesville: University Press of Virginia, 1990).

Leggett, B. J. *Early Stevens: The Nietzschean Intertext* (Durham, N.C.: Duke University Press, 1992).

Leighton, Angela. *On Form: Poetry, Aestheticism, and the Legacy of a Word* (Oxford: Oxford University Press, 2007).

Lensing, George. *Wallace Stevens: A Poet's Growth* (Baton Rouge: Louisiana State University Press, 1986).

———. *Wallace Stevens and the Seasons* (Baton Rouge: Louisiana State University Press, 2001).

Longenbach, James. *Wallace Stevens: The Plain Sense of Things* (New York: Oxford University Press, 1991).

Miller, J. Hillis. *The Linguistic Moment: From Wordsworth to Stevens* (Princeton, N.J.: Princeton University Press, 1985).

Richardson, Joan. *Wallace Stevens* (New York: Beech Tree, 1988).

Serio, John (ed.). *The Cambridge Companion to Wallace Stevens* (Cambridge: Cambridge University Press, 2007).

Vendler, Helen. *On Extended Wings: The Longer Poems of Wallace Stevens* (Cambridge, Mass.: Harvard University Press, 1969).

———. *Wallace Stevens: Words Chosen out of Desire* (Knoxville: University of Tennessee Press, 1984).

30 Ezra Pound, William Carlos Williams, and the East Coast Projectivists

Armand, Louis (ed.). *Contemporary Poetics* (Evanston, Ill.: Northwestern University Press, 2007).

Beach, Christopher. *Ezra Pound and the Remaking of American Tradition* (Berkeley: University of California Press, 1992).

Butterick, George F. *A Guide to the Maximus Poems of Charles Olson* (Berkeley: University of California Press, 1980).

Davie, Donald. *Studies in Ezra Pound* (Manchester: Carcanet, 1991).

Kenner, Hugh. *The Pound Era* (Berkeley: University of California Press, 1971).

Makin, Peter. *Pound's Cantos* (London: Allen & Unwin, 1985).

Maud, Ralph. *Charles Olson at the Harbor: A Biography* (Vancouver, B.C.: Talon, 2008).

Moody, A. David. *Ezra Pound: Poet* (New York: Oxford University Press, 2009).

Nadel, Ira (ed.). *Ezra Pound in Context* (Cambridge: Cambridge University Press, 2010).

Perelman, Bob. *The Trouble with Genius: Reading Pound, Joyce, Stein and Zukofsky* (Berkeley: University of California Press, 1994).

Terrell, Carroll F. *A Companion to the Cantos of Ezra Pound* (Berkeley: University of California Press, 1993).

Von Hallberg, Robert. *Charles Olson: The Scholar's Art* (Cambridge, Mass.: Harvard University Press, 1978).

31 Langston Hughes and His World

Dace, Tish (ed.). *Langston Hughes: The Contemporary Reviews* (Cambridge: Cambridge University Press, 1997).

De Santis, Christopher (ed.). *Dictionary of Literary Biography*. Vol. 315, *Langston Hughes: A Documentary Volume* (Detroit, Mich.: Thomson Gale, 2005).

Huggins, Nathan. *Harlem Renaissance* (1971; New York: Oxford University Press, 1997).

Jones, Meta DuEwa. "Listening to What the Ear Demands: Langston Hughes and His Critics," *Callaloo* 25:4 (2002): 1145–75.

Lewis, David Levering. *When Harlem Was in Vogue* (New York: Alfred A. Knopf, 1981).

Rampersad, Arnold. *The Life of Langston Hughes*. 2 vols. (New York: Oxford University Press, 1986, 1988).

Santos, Irene Ramalho. "Langston Hughes: The Color of Modernism," in Sacvan Bercovitch (ed.), *The Cambridge History of American Literature*. Vol. 5, *Poetry and Criticism 1900–1950* (Cambridge: Cambridge University Press, 2003), pp. 311–42.

Saul, Scott. *Freedom Is, Freedom Ain't: Jazz and the Making of the Sixties* (Cambridge, Mass.: Harvard University Press, 2003).

Tracy, Steven. *Langston Hughes and the Blues* (Urbana: University of Illinois Press, 2011).

Young, Kevin. "'If You Can't Read, Run Anyhow!': Langston Hughes and the Poetics of Refusal," in *The Grey Album* (Minneapolis: Graywolf, 2012), pp. 169–88.

32 The Objectivists and the Left

DuPlessis, Rachel Blau, and Peter Quartermain (eds.). *The Objectivist Nexus: Essays in Cultural Poetics* (Tuscaloosa: University of Alabama Press, 1999).

Filreis, Alan. *Modernism from Right to Left: Wallace Stevens, the Thirties, and Literary Radicalism* (Cambridge: Cambridge University Press, 1994).

Heller, Michael. *Conviction's Net of Branches: Essays on the Objectivist Poets and Poetry* (Carbondale: Southern Illinois University Press, 1985).

Kenner, Hugh. *A Homemade World: The American Modernist Writers* (New York: Knopf, 1975).

Nelson, Cary. *Repression and Recovery: Modern American Poetry and the Politics of Cultural Memory, 1910–1945* (Madison: University of Wisconsin Press, 1989).

———. *Revolutionary Memory: Recovering the Poetry of the American Left* (New York: Routledge, 2001).

Nicholls, Peter. *George Oppen and the Fate of Modernism* (Oxford: Oxford University Press, 2007).

Penberthy, Jenny (ed.). *Lorine Niedecker: Woman and Poet* (Orono, Maine: National Poetry Foundation, 1996).

Scroggins, Mark. *The Poem of a Life: A Biography of Louis Zukofsky* (Emeryville, Calif.: Shoemaker and Hoard, 1997).

Stanley, Sandra Kumamoto. *Louis Zukofsky and the Transformation of a Modern American Poetics* (Berkeley: University of California Press, 1994).

Teres, Harvey. *Renewing the Left: Politics, Imagination, and the New York Intellectuals* (New York: Oxford University Press, 1996).

Zukofsky, Louis (ed.). "Objectivists." Special issue, *Poetry* 37:5 (1931). http://www .poetryfoundation.org/poetrymagazine/toc/221.

33 "All the Blessings of This Consuming Chance": Robert Lowell, John Berryman, Theodore Roethke, and the Middle-Generation Poets

Axelrod, Steven Gould. *Robert Lowell: Life and Art* (Princeton, N.J.: Princeton University Press, 1978).

Bell, Vereen. *Robert Lowell: Nihilist as Hero* (Cambridge, Mass.: Harvard University Press, 1983).

Blake, David Haven. "Public Dreams: John Berryman, Celebrity and the Culture of Confession," *American Literary History* 13:4 (2001): 716–36.

Haffenden, John. *The Life of John Berryman* (Boston: Routledge and Kegan Paul, 1982).

Hamilton, Ian. *Robert Lowell: A Biography* (New York: Random House, 1982).

Haralson, Eric (ed.). *Reading the Middle Generation Anew* (Iowa City: University of Iowa Press, 2006).

Kirsch, Adam. *The Modern Element: Essays on Contemporary Poetry* (New York: W. W. Norton, 2008).

London, Michael, and Robert Boyers (eds.). *Robert Lowell: A Portrait of the Artist in His Time* (New York: David Lewis, 1970).

Mariani, Paul. *Dream Song: The Life of John Berryman* (New York: William Morrow, 1990).

Rudman, Mark. *Robert Lowell: An Introduction to the Poetry* (New York: Columbia University Press, 1983).

Tillinghast, Richard. *Robert Lowell's Life and Work: Damaged Grandeur* (Ann Arbor: University of Michigan Press, 1995).

Vendler, Helen. *The Given and the Made* (Cambridge, Mass.: Harvard University Press, 1995).

———. *Last Books, Last Looks: Stevens, Plath, Lowell, Bishop, Merrill* (Princeton, N.J.: Princeton University Press, 2010).

34 Elizabeth Bishop, Randall Jarrell, and the Lost World of Real Feeling

Burt, Stephen. *Randall Jarrell and His Age* (New York: Columbia University Press, 2002).

Cleghorn, Angus, Bethany Hicok, and Thomas Travisano (eds.). *Elizabeth Bishop in the 21st Century* (Charlottesville: University of Virginia Press, 2012).

Costello, Bonnie. *Elizabeth Bishop: Questions of Mastery* (Cambridge, Mass.: Harvard University Press, 1993).

———. "Elizabeth Bishop's Impersonal Personal," *American Literary History* 15:2 (2003): 334–66.

Ferguson, Suzanne (ed.). *Jarrell, Bishop, Lowell, and Co.* (Knoxville: University of Tennessee Press, 2003).

Flynn, Richard. *Randall Jarrell and the Lost World of Childhood* (Athens: University of Georgia Press, 1990).

Harrison, Victoria. *Elizabeth Bishop's Poetics of Intimacy* (Cambridge: Cambridge University Press, 1993).

Kinzie, Mary. *The Cure of Poetry in an Age of Prose: Moral Essays on the Poet's Calling* (Chicago: University of Chicago Press, 1993).

Longenbach, James. *Modern Poetry After Modernism* (New York: Oxford University Press, 1997).

Millier, Brett C. *Elizabeth Bishop: Life and the Memory of It* (Berkeley: University of California Press, 1993).

Pickard, Zachariah. *Elizabeth Bishop's Poetics of Description* (Montreal: McGill University Press, 2009).

Pritchard, William. *Randall Jarrell: A Literary Life* (New York: Farrar, Straus and Giroux, 1990).

Travisano, Thomas. *Midcentury Quartet* (Charlottesville: University of Virginia Press, 1999).

35 Writing the South

Blotner, Joseph. *Robert Penn Warren: A Biography* (New York: Random House, 1997).

Brinkmeyer, Robert H., Jr. *The Fourth Ghost: White Southern Writers and European Fascism, 1930–1950* (Baton Rouge: Louisiana State University Press, 2009).

Burt, John. *Robert Penn Warren and American Idealism* (New Haven, Conn.: Yale University Press, 1989).

Gioia, Dana, and William Logan (eds.). *Certain Solitudes: On the Poetry of Donald Justice* (Fayetteville: University of Arkansas Press, 1997).

Gray, Richard. *Writing the South: Ideas of an American Region* (Cambridge: Cambridge University Press, 1986).

Hart, Henry. *James Dickey: The World as a Lie* (New York: Picador, 2000).

Moffett, Joe. *Understanding Charles Wright* (Columbia: University of South Carolina Press, 2008).

Suarez, Ernest. *Southbound: Interviews with Southern Poets* (Columbia: University of Missouri Press, 1999).

Young, Thomas Daniel. *Gentleman in a Dustcoat: A Biography of John Crowe Ransom* (Baton Rouge: Louisiana State University Press, 1976).

36 San Francisco and the Beats

Allen, Donald (ed.). *The New American Poetry: 1945–1960* (1960; Berkeley: University of California Press, 1999).

Duncan, Michael, and Kristine McKenna (eds.). *Seminal Culture: Wallace Berman and His Circle* (Santa Monica, Calif.: Santa Monica Museum, 2005).

Ellingham, Lewis, and Kevin Killian. *Poet Be Like God: Jack Spicer and the San Francisco Renaissance* (Hanover, N.H.: Wesleyan University Press, 1988).

Fredman, Stephen. *Contextual Practice: Assemblage and the Erotic in Postwar Poetry and Art* (Stanford, Calif.: Stanford University Press, 2010).

Knight, Brenda. *Women of the Beat Generation: The Writers, Artists and Muses at the Heart of a Revolution* (San Francisco: Conari Press, 1996).

Raskin, Jonah. *American Scream: Allen Ginsberg's Howl and the Making of the Beat Generation* (Berkeley: University of California Press, 2004).

Suiter, John. *Poets on the Peaks: Gary Snyder, Philip Whalen and Jack Kerouac in the North Cascades* (Washington, D.C.: Counterpoint, 2002).

Vincent, John Emil (ed.). *After Spicer: Critical Essays* (Middletown, Conn.: Wesleyan University Press, 2011).

37 The New York School

Altieri, Charles. *Painterly Abstraction in Modernist American Poetry: The Contemporaneity of Modernism* (Cambridge: Cambridge University Press, 1989).

Dubois, Andrew. *Ashbery's Forms of Attention* (Tuscaloosa: University of Alabama Press, 2006).

Epstein, Andrew. *Beautiful Enemies: Friendship and Postwar American Poetry* (New York: Oxford University Press, 2006).

Herd, David. *John Ashbery and American Poetry* (Manchester: Manchester University Press, 2001).

Lehman, David. *The Last Avant-Garde: The Making of the New York School of Poets* (New York: Doubleday, 1998).

Nelson, Maggie. *Women, the New York School, and Other Abstractions* (Iowa City: University of Iowa Press, 2007).

Perloff, Marjorie. *Frank O'Hara: Poet Among Painters* (1977; Chicago: University of Chicago Press, 1997).

Shaw, Lytle. *Frank O'Hara: The Poetics of Coterie* (Iowa City: University of Iowa Press, 2006).

Vincent, John Emil. *John Ashbery: His Later Books* (Athens: University of Georgia Press, 2007).

Ward, Geoff. *Statutes of Liberty: The New York School of Poets*. Rev. ed. (New York: Palgrave/Macmillan, 2001).

Wilkinson, John. "'Couplings of Such Sonority': Reading a Poem by Barbara Guest," *Textual Practice* 23:3 (June 2009): 481–502.

38 The Uses of Authenticity: Four Sixties Poets

Altieri, Charles. *Enlarging the Temple: New Directions in American Poetry During the 1960s* (Lewisburg, Pa.: Bucknell University Press, 1979).

Bly, Robert. *American Poetry: Wildness and Domesticity* (New York: Harper and Row, 1990).

Breslin, James E. B. *From Modern to Contemporary: American Poetry, 1945–1965* (Chicago: University of Chicago Press, 1984).

Breslin, Paul. *The Psycho-Political Muse: American Poetry since the Fifties* (Chicago: University of Chicago Press, 1987).

Davidson, Michael. *Ghostlier Demarcations: Modern Poetry and the Material World* (Berkeley: University of California Press, 1997).

Hedley, Jane. *I Made You to Find Me: The Coming of Age of the Woman Poet and the Politics of Poetic Address* (Columbus: Ohio State University Press, 2009).

Jarnot, Lisa, and Michael Davidson. *Robert Duncan, the Ambassador from Venus: A Biography* (Berkeley: University of California Press, 2012).

Johnston, Devin. *Precipitations: Contemporary American Poetry as Occult Practice* (Middletown, Conn.: Wesleyan University Press, 2002).

Smith, Dave (ed.). *The Pure Clear Word: Essays on the Poetry of James Wright* (Urbana: University of Illinois Press, 1982).

Williamson, Alan. *Introspection and Contemporary Poetry* (Cambridge, Mass.: Harvard University Press, 1984).

39 James Merrill and His Circles

Berger, Charles, and David Lehman (eds.). *James Merrill: Essays in Criticism* (Ithaca, N.Y.: Cornell University Press, 1983).

Blasing, Mutlu Konuk. *Politics and Form in Postmodern Poetry* (Cambridge: Cambridge University Press, 1995).

Gwiazda, Piotr. *James Merrill and W.H. Auden: Homosexuality and Poetic Influence* (New York: Palgrave Macmillan, 2007).

Howard, Richard. *Alone with America* (New York: Atheneum, 1980).

Kalstone, David. *Five Temperaments* (New York: Oxford University Press, 1977).

Labrie, Ross. *James Merrill* (Boston: Twayne, 1982).

McClatchy, J. D. *Twenty Questions* (New York: Columbia University Press, 1998).

Moffett, Judith. *James Merrill: An Introduction to the Poetry* (New York: Columbia University Press, 1984).

Phillips, Siobhan. *The Poetics of the Everyday* (New York: Columbia University Press, 2011).

Polito, Robert. *A Reader's Guide to* The Changing Light at Sandover (Ann Arbor: University of Michigan Press, 1994).

Sastri, Reena. *James Merrill: Knowing Innocence* (New York: Routledge, 2007).

Wasley, Aidan. *The Age of Auden: Postwar Poetry and the American Scene* (Princeton, N.J.: Princeton University Press, 2011).

Yenser, Stephen. *The Consuming Myth: The Work of James Merrill* (Cambridge, Mass.: Harvard University Press, 1987).

40 Science in Contemporary American Poetry: Ammons and Others

Brown, Kurt (ed.). *The Measured Word: On Poetry and Science* (Athens: University of Georgia Press, 2001).

Crawford, Robert (ed.). *Contemporary Poetry and Contemporary Science* (Oxford: Oxford University Press, 2006).

Halpern, Nick. *Everyday and Prophetic: The Poetry of Lowell, Ammons, Merrill, and Rich* (Madison: University of Wisconsin Press, 2003).

Holmes, John (ed.). *Science in Modern Poetry: New Directions* (Liverpool: Liverpool University Press, 2012).

Schneider, Steven P. *A. R. Ammons and the Poetics of Widening Scope* (Madison, N.J.: Fairleigh Dickinson University Press, 1994).

——— (ed.). *Complexities of Motion: New Essays on A. R. Ammons's Long Poems* (Madison, N.J.: Fairleigh Dickinson University Press, 1999).

Scigaj, Leonard. *Sustainable Poetry: Four American Ecopoets* (Lexington: University Press of Kentucky, 1999).

Steinman, Lisa M. *Made in America: Science, Technology, and American Modernist Poets* (New Haven, Conn.: Yale University Press, 1987).

Tiffany, Daniel. *Toy Medium: Materialism and Modern Lyric* (Berkeley: University of California Press, 2000).

Walpert, Bryan. *Resistance to Science in Contemporary American Poetry* (London: Routledge, 2011).

41 The 1970s and the "Poetry of the Center"

Archambeau, Robert. *Laureates and Heretics: Six Careers in American Poetry* (South Bend, Ind.: University of Notre Dame Press, 2010).

Davis, Dick. *Wisdom and Wilderness: The Achievement of Yvor Winters* (Athens: University of Georgia Press, 1991).

Juhasz, Suzanne. *Naked and Fiery Forms: Modern American Poetry by Women: A New Tradition* (New York: Harper, 1976).

Longenbach, James. *Modern Poetry after Modernism* (New York: Oxford University Press, 1997).

Pinsky, Robert. *The Situation of Poetry: Contemporary Poetry and Its Traditions* (Princeton, N.J.: Princeton University Press, 1976).

Rich, Adrienne. *On Lies, Secrets and Silence: Selected Prose 1966–1978* (New York: W. W. Norton, 1979).

Spiegelman, Willard. *The Didactic Muse: Scenes of Instruction in Contemporary Poetry* (Princeton, N.J.: Princeton University Press, 1989).

Von Hallberg, Robert. *American Poetry and Culture, 1945–1980* (Cambridge, Mass.: Harvard University Press, 1985).

Yenser, Stephen. *A Boundless Field: American Poetry at Large* (Ann Arbor: University of Michigan Press, 2002).

42 Latino Poetry and Poetics

Algarín, Miguel, and Bob Holman (eds.). *Aloud: Voices from the Nuyorican Poets Café* (New York: Holt, 1994).

Arteaga, Alfred. *Chicano Poetics: Heterotexts and Hybridities* (Cambridge: Cambridge University Press, 1997).

Cruz, Victor Hernández, Leroy Quintana, and Virgil Suárez (eds.). *Paper Dance: 55 Latino Poets* (New York: Persea, 2000).

Falconer, Blas, and Lorraine López (eds.). *The Other Latin@: Writing Against a Singular Identity* (Tucson: University of Arizona Press, 2011).

Pérez-Torres, Rafael. *Movements in Chicano Poetry: Against Myth, Against Margins* (Cambridge: Cambridge University Press, 1995).

Somers-Willett, Susan B. A. *The Cultural Politics of Slam Poetry: Race, Identity and the Performance of Popular Verse in America* (Ann Arbor: University of Michigan Press, 2009).

43 Asian American Poetry

Chang, Juliana (ed.). *Quiet Fire: A Historical Anthology of Asian American Poetry, 1892–1970* (New York: Asian American Writers' Workshop, 1996).

Hongo, Garrett (ed.). *The Open Boat: Poems from Asian America* (New York: Doubleday, 1993).

Jeon, Joseph. *Racial Things, Racial Forms: Objecthood in Avant-Garde Asian American Poetry* (Iowa City: University of Iowa Press, 2012).

Lai, Him Mark, Genny Lim, and Judy Yung (eds.). *Island: Poetry and History of Chinese Immigrants on Angel Island, 1910–1940* (1980; Seattle: University of Washington Press, 1991).

Marx, Edward. "A Slightly Open Door: Yone Noguchi and the Invention of English Haiku," *Genre* 3 (2006): 107–26.

Park, Josephine Nock-Hee. *Apparitions of Asia: Modernist Form and Asian American Poetics* (New York: Oxford University Press, 2008).

Uba, George. "Versions of Identity in Post-Activist Asian American Poetry," in Shirley Geok-lin Lim and Amy Ling (eds.), *Reading the Literatures of Asian America* (Philadelphia: Temple University Press, 1992), pp. 33–48.

Yao, Steven. *Foreign Accents: Chinese American Verse from Exclusion to Postethnicity* (New York: Oxford University Press, 2010).

Yu, Timothy. "'The Hand of a Chinese Master': José Garcia Villa and Modernist Orientalism," *MELUS* 29:1 (2004): 41–59.

———. *Race and the Avant-Garde: Experimental and Asian American Poetry Since 1965* (Stanford, Calif.: Stanford University Press, 2009).

44 Psychoanalytic Poetics

Altieri, Charles. *Self and Sensibility in Contemporary American Poetry* (Cambridge: Cambridge University Press, 1984).

Axelrod, Steven Gould. *Sylvia Plath: The Wound and the Cure of Words* (Baltimore, Md.: Johns Hopkins University Press, 1990).

Diehl, Joanne Feit (ed.). *On Louise Glück: Change What You See* (Ann Arbor: University of Michigan Press, 2005).

Forbes, Deborah. *Sincerity's Shadow: Self-Consciousness in British Romantic and Mid-Twentieth-Century American Poetry* (Cambridge, Mass.: Harvard University Press, 2004).

Gill, Jo (ed.). *The Cambridge Companion to Sylvia Plath* (Cambridge: Cambridge University Press, 2006).

Gray, Jeffrey. "'Necessary Thought': Frank Bidart and the Postconfessional," *Contemporary Literature* 34:4 (1993): 714–39.

Harrison, DeSales. *The End of the Mind: The Edge of the Intelligible in Hardy, Stevens, Larkin, Plath and Glück* (New York and London: Routledge, 2005).

Kendall, Tim. *Sylvia Plath: A Critical Study* (London: Faber and Faber, 2001).

Keniston, Anne. *Overheard Voices: Address and Subjectivity in Postmodern American Poetry* (New York: Routledge, 2006).

Lerner, Lawrence. "What Is Confessional Poetry?" *Critical Quarterly* 29:1 (1987): 46–66.

Rector, Liam, and Tree Swenson (eds.). *On Frank Bidart: Fastening the Voice to the Page* (Ann Arbor: University of Michigan Press, 2007).

Rose, Jacqueline. *The Haunting of Sylvia Plath* (London: Virago, 1991).

Sewell, Lisa. "'In the End, the One Who Has Nothing Wins': Louise Glück and the Poetics of Anorexia," *Literature Interpretation Theory* 17 (2006): 49–76.

Vendler, Helen. *Soul Says: On Recent Poetry* (Cambridge, Mass.: Harvard University Press, 1995).

Williamson, Alan. *Introspection and Contemporary Poetry* (Cambridge, Mass.: Harvard University Press, 1984).

45 American Poetry of the 1980s: The Pressures of Reality

Benston, Kimberly W. "Performing Blackness: Re/Placing Afro-American Poetry," in Houston A. Baker, Jr., and Patricia Redmond (eds.), *Afro-American Literary Study in the 1990s* (Chicago: University of Chicago Press, 1989), pp. 164–93.

Bernstein, Charles. *Content's Dream: Essays 1975–1984* (1986; Evanston, Ill.: Northwestern University Press, 2001).

Burt, Stephen. *Close Calls with Nonsense* (St. Paul, Minn.: Graywolf Press, 2009).

Caplan, David. *Questions of Possibility: Contemporary Poetry and Poetic Form* (New York: Oxford University Press, 2005).

Hall, Donald (ed.). *Claims for Poetry* (Ann Arbor: University of Michigan Press, 1982).

Jarman, Mark, and Robert McDowell (eds.). *The Reaper Essays* (Brownsville, Ore.: Story Line Press, 1996).

Perloff, Marjorie. *Radical Artifice: Writing Poetry in the Age of Media* (Chicago: University of Chicago Press, 1991).

Schultz, Susan M. *A Poetics of Impasse in Modern and Contemporary American Poetry* (Tuscaloosa: University of Alabama Press, 2005).

Shetley, Vernon. *After the Death of Poetry: Poet and Audience in Contemporary America* (Durham, N.C.: Duke University Press, 1993).

Silliman, Ron. *The New Sentence* (New York: Roof, 1995).

46 Black and Blues Configurations: Contemporary African American Poetry

Alexander, Elizabeth. *The Black Interior* (St. Paul, Minn.: Graywolf, 2004).

Anderson, T. J. *Notes to Make the Sound Come Right: Four Innovators of Jazz Poetry* (Fayetteville: University of Arkansas Press, 2004).

Bentson, Kimberly. *Performing Blackness: Enactments of Afro-American Modernism* (London: Routledge, 2000).

Cummings, Allison. "Public Subjects: Race and the Critical Reception of Gwendolyn Brooks, Erica Hunt, and Harryette Mullen," *Frontiers* 26:2 (2005): 3–36.

Gabbin, Joanne V. (ed.). *The Furious Flowering of African American Poetry* (Charlottesville: University Press of Virginia, 1999).

Henderson, Stephen (ed.). *Understanding the New Black Poetry* (New York: William Morrow, 1973).

Holladay, Hilary. *Wild Blessings: The Poetry of Lucille Clifton* (Baton Rouge: Louisiana State University Press, 2004).

Jackson, Lawrence P. *The Indignant Generation* (Princeton, N.J.: Princeton University Press, 2011).

Jones, Meta DuEwa. *The Muse Is Music: Jazz Poetry from the Harlem Renaissance to Spoken Word* (Urbana: University of Illinois Press, 2011).

Mackey, Nathaniel. *Discrepant Engagement: Dissonance, Cross-Culturality, and Experimental Writing* (Cambridge: Cambridge University Press, 1993).

Melham, D. H. *Gwendolyn Brooks: Poetry and the Heroic Voice* (Lexington: University Press of Kentucky, 1987).

Naylor, Paul (ed.). "Nathaniel Mackey: A Special Issue." Special issue, *Callaloo* 23:2 (2000).

Nielsen, Aldon Lynn. *Black Chant: Languages of Afro-American Postmodernism* (Urbana: University of Illinois Press, 1997).

———. *Integral Music: Languages of Afro-American Innovation* (Tuscaloosa: University of Alabama Press, 2004).

Pereira, Malin. *Rita Dove's Cosmopolitanism* (Urbana: University of Illinois Press, 2003).

Shockley, Evie. *Renegade Poetics: Black Aesthetics and Formal Innovation in African American Poetry* (Iowa City: University of Iowa Press, 2011).

Smethurst, James. "Remembering When Indians Were Red: Bob Kaufman, the Popular Front, and the Black Arts Movement," *Callaloo* 25:1 (2002): 146–64.

Smith, Derik. "Quarreling in the Movement: Robert Hayden's Black Arts Era," *Callaloo* 33:2 (2010): 449–66.

Thomas, Lorenzo. *Extraordinary Measures: Afrocentric Modernism and Twentieth Century American Poetry* (Tuscaloosa: University of Alabama Press, 2000).

Widener, Daniel. *Black Arts West: Culture and Struggle in Postwar Los Angeles* (Durham, N.C.: Duke University Press, 2010).

Williams, Sherley Anne. "The Blues Roots of Contemporary Afro-American Poetry," *Massachusetts Review* 18:3 (1977): 542–54.

47 Amy Clampitt, Culture Poetry, and the Neobaroque

Brunner, Edward. *Cold War Poetry* (Urbana: University of Illinois Press, 2000).

Costello, Bonnie. *Shifting Ground: Reinventing Landscape in Modern American Poetry* (Cambridge, Mass.: Harvard University Press, 2003).

Hollander, John. *The Gazer's Spirit: Poems Speaking to Silent Works of Art* (Chicago: University of Chicago Press, 1995).

Karr, Mary. "Against Decoration," *Parnassus* 16:2 (1991): 277–300.

Longenbach, James. *Modern Poetry After Modernism* (New York: Oxford University Press, 1997).

McDowell, Robert. "The Wilderness Surrounds the Word," *Hudson Review* 43 (1991): 669–78.

Quinn, Justin. *American Errancy: Empire, Sublimity and Modern Poetry* (Dublin: University College Dublin Press, 2005).

Spiegelman, Willard. *How Poets See the World: The Art of Description on Contemporary Poetry* (New York: Oxford University Press, 2005).

Vendler, Helen. *The Music of What Happens* (Cambridge, Mass.: Harvard University Press, 1988).

Von Hallberg, Robert. *American Poetry and Culture, 1945–1980* (Cambridge, Mass.: Harvard University Press, 1985).

48 Modern and Contemporary Children's Poetry

Cifelli, Edward M. *John Ciardi: A Biography* (Fayetteville: University of Arkansas Press, 1997).

Flynn, Richard. "Can Children's Poetry Matter?" *The Lion and the Unicorn: A Critical Journal of Children's Literature* 17:1 (June 1993): 37–44.

———. "Consolation Prize," *Signal: Approaches to Children's Books* 100 (2003): 66–83.

Hall, Donald (ed.). *The Oxford Book of Children's Poetry in America* (New York: Oxford University Press, 1985).

Livingston, Myra Cohn. *The Child as Poet: Myth or Reality?* (Boston: Horn Book, 1984).

———. "David McCord's Poems: Something Behind the Door," in Perry Nodelman (ed.), *Touchstones: Reflections on the Best in Children's Literature.* Vol. 2 (West Lafayette, Ind.: Children's Literature Association, 1987), pp. 157–72.

MacDonald, Ruth. *Shel Silverstein* (New York: Twayne, 1997).

Nel, Philip. *Dr. Seuss: American Icon* (New York: Continuum, 2004).

Sorby, Angela. *Schoolroom Poets: Childhood, Performance, and the Place of American Poetry, 1865–1917* (Durham: University of New Hampshire Press, 2005).

Styles, Morag. *From the Garden to the Street* (London: Cassell, 1998).

Styles, Morag, Louise Joy, and David Whitley (eds.). *Poetry and Childhood* (Stoke on Trent: Trentham Books, 2010).

Thomas, Joseph T., Jr. *Poetry's Playground: The Culture of Contemporary American Children's Poetry* (Detroit, Mich.: Wayne State University Press, 2007).

49 Multilingualism in Contemporary American Poetry

Balaz, Joseph P. (ed.). *Hoʻomānoa: An Anthology of Contemporary Hawaiian Literature* (Honolulu: Ku Paʻa Incorporated, 1989).

Franklin, Cynthia, Ruth Hsu, and Suzanne Kosanke (eds.). *Navigating Islands and Continents: Conversations and Contestations in and around the Pacific* (Honolulu: University of Hawaiʻi Press, 2000).

Morales, Rodney. "Literature," in Michael Haas (ed.), *Multicultural Hawaiʻi: The Fabric of a Multiethnic Society* (New York: Garland, 1998), pp. 107–29.

Pennycock, Alastair. *The Cultural Politics of English as an International Language* (New York: Addison-Wesley, 1995).

Sommer, Doris. *Proceed with Caution, When Engaged by Minority Writing in the Americas* (Cambridge, Mass.: Harvard University Press, 1999).

Spahr, Juliana. *Everybody's Autonomy: Connective Reading and Collective Identity* (Tuscaloosa: University of Alabama Press, 2001).

Stein, Gertrude. *Selections*, ed. Joan Retallack (Berkeley: University of California Press, 2008).

Xiaojing, Zhou. "'What Story What Story What Sound': The Nomadic Poetics of Myung Mi Kim's *Dura*," *College Literature* 33:4 (2007): 63–91.

50 American Poetry at the End of the Millennium

Altieri, Charles. *Postmodernisms Now: Essays on Contemporaneity in the Arts* (State College: Pennsylvania State University Press, 1998).

Beach, Christopher. *Poetic Culture: Contemporary American Poetry Between Community and Institution* (Evanston, Ill.: Northwestern University Press, 1999).

Gardner, Thomas (ed.). *Jorie Graham: Essays on the Poetry* (Madison: University of Wisconsin Press, 2005).

———. *Regions of Unlikeness: Explaining Contemporary Poetry* (Lincoln: University of Nebraska Press, 1999).

Grossman, Allen. *The Long Schoolroom* (Ann Arbor: University of Michigan Press, 1997).

Irwin, John T. *Hart Crane's Poetry: "Appollinaire Lived in Paris, I Live in Cleveland, Ohio"* (Baltimore, Md.: Johns Hopkins University Press, 2011).

Keller, Lynn. *Thinking Poetry: Readings in Contemporary Women's Exploratory Poetics* (Iowa City: University of Iowa Press, 2010).

Kellogg, David. "The Self in the Poetic Field," *Fence* 3:2 (2001): 97–108.

Keniston, Anne. *Overheard Voices: Address and Subjectivity in Postmodern American Poetry* (New York: Routledge, 2006).

Martin, Robert K. *The Homosexual Tradition in American Poetry* (1979; Iowa City: University of Iowa Press, 1998).

Nealon, Christopher. *Foundlings: Lesbian and Gay Historical Emotion Before Stonewall* (Durham, N.C.: Duke University Press, 2001).

Perelman, Bob. *The Marginalization of Poetry: Language Writing and Literary History* (Princeton, N.J.: Princeton University Press, 1996).

Perloff, Marjorie. *21st-Century Modernism: The "New" Poetics* (Oxford: Blackwell, 2002).

Rasula, Jed. *Syncopations: The Stress of Innovation in Contemporary American Poetry* (Tuscaloosa: University of Alabama Press, 2004).

Reed, Brian. *Hart Crane: After His Lights* (Tuscaloosa: University of Alabama Press, 2006).

Vendler, Helen. *Soul Says: On Recent Poetry* (Cambridge, Mass.: Harvard University Press, 1995).

Wallace, Mark, and Steven Marks (eds.). *Avant-Garde Poetics of the 1990s: Telling It Slant* (Tuscaloosa: University of Alabama Press, 2002).

Index